NATIONS IN
TRANSIT 2006

NATIONS IN
TRANSIT 2006

Democratization from
Central Europe to Eurasia

Edited by Jeannette Goehring

FREEDOM HOUSE

NEW YORK ■ WASHINGTON, D.C. ■ BUDAPEST

Published by:
AQUINCUM Publishing
a division of T-MART PRESS Publishing and Printing Solution Provider Ltd.
H-1036 Budapest
Pacsirtamezo u. 41
Hungary
E-mail: aquincum@tmart.hu
www.tmart.hu

ISBN 963 86615 8 5

Printed in Hungary

www.freedomhouse.org
www.freedomhouse.hu

Contents

Country Reports

Acknowledgements

N*ations in Transit 2006* could not have been completed without the contributions of numerous Freedom House staff and consultants. This study was also made possible by the generous support of the U.S. Agency for International Development.

Freedom House is grateful to the country report authors for their painstaking efforts to provide clear, concise, and informed analysis of the dramatic changes occurring in the countries under study. They are: Florian Bieber, Annette Bohr, Zhidas Daskalovski, Rashko Dorosiev, Bhavna Dave, Juris Dreifelds, Jeremy Druker, George Dura, Kate Fearon, Payam Foroughi, Robert Freedman, Georgy Ganev, Paul Goble, Miroslav Kollar, Roland Kovats, Ivan Krastev, Andrzej Krajewski, Lisa McLean, Grigorij Meseznikov, Alina Mungiu-Pippidi, Mirsada Muzur, Kaan Nazli, Ghia Nodia, Robert Orttung, Bruce Pannier, Aneta Piasecka, Barbara Peranic, Nicu Popescu, Olena Prystayko, Bashkim Rrahmani, Vitali Silitski, Oleksandr Sushko, Eno Trimcev, Michal Vasecka, Viktoria Villanyi, Anna Walker, and Ali Zerdin.

A number of distinguished scholars and regional experts served on this year's academic oversight committees and ratings board. They are: Audrey Altstadt of the University of Massachusetts, Amherst (United States), Zamira Eshanova of Radio Free Europe/Radio Liberty, Prague (Czech Republic), Charles Gati of Johns Hopkins University, Washington, D.C. (United States), Olga Kryshtanovskaya of the Institute for Applied Politics, Moscow (Russia), Rajan Menon of Lehigh University (United States), Sergiu Miscoiu of Babes Bolyai University, Cluj-Napoca (Romania), Alexander Motyl of Rutgers University, Newark (United States), and Susan Woodward of the Graduate Center, City University of New York (United States).

Freedom House also thanks: Alexander Baturo of Trinity College, Dublin (Ireland), Anton Bebler of the University of Ljubljana (Slovenia), Artan Hoxha of the Institute for Contemporary Studies, Tirana (Albania), Abdiraim Jorokulov of United Nations Development Programme, Bishkek (Kyrgyzstan), Valts Kalins of the Centre for Public Policy Providus, Riga (Latvia), Charles Kovacs of Hir Radio, Budapest (Hungary), Jelica Minic of European Movement, Belgrade (Serbia and Montenegro), Elena Parfenova of the EastWest Institute, Prague (Czech Republic),

Jiri Pehe of the New York University, Prague (Czech Republic), David J. Smith of the University of Glasgow, (United Kingdom), and Lenka Surotchak of Pontis Foundation, Bratislava (Slovakia) for their comments on specific reports.

Several members of the Freedom House staff took time out of their schedules to read and provide valuable feedback on the country reports. They are: Sanja Pesek, Mike Staresinic, and Lloyd Tudyk of the Belgrade office; Cristina Guseth of the Bucharest office; Kristie D. Evenson, Roland Kovats, and Alexander Kourylev of the Europe/Budapest office; Svetlana Franchuk, Juhani Grossmann, Orysia Lutsevych, and Vitaly Moroz of the Kyiv office; John Kubiniec and Krzysztof Filcek of the Warsaw office; Antonio Stango of the Almaty office; Stuart Kahn, Mike Stone, and Ruslan Yakhtanigov of the Bishkek office; Lisa Davis and Alexander Gupman of the Washington, D.C. office.

Jeannette Goehring of Freedom House managed and edited the 2006 study. Jennifer L. Windsor, Thomas O. Melia, Kristie D. Evenson, Christopher Walker, and Amanda Schnetzer of Freedom House provided overall guidance and support for the project. Fraser Allan was responsible for the design and layout of the book. Sona Vogel served as copy editor; John Ewing, Eileen G. P. Brown, and Jeremy Druker as line editors. Lisa Mootz of Freedom House provided editorial, research, and administrative assistance, aided by Annamaria Preisz, Astrid Larson, and Thomas Webb.

Methodology

*N*ations in Transit 2006 measures progress and setbacks in democratization in 29 countries and administrative areas from Central Europe to the Eurasian region of the former Soviet Union. A section on Kosovo appears in the Serbia and Montenegro report. This volume, which covers events from January 1 through December 31, 2005, is an updated edition of surveys published in 2005, 2004, 2003, 2002, 2001, 2000 (covering years 1999-2000 and noted as 1999 in ratings tables), 1998, 1997, and 1995.

Country Reports

The country reports in *Nations in Transit 2006* follow an essay format that allowed the report authors to provide a broad analysis of the progress of democratic change in their country of expertise. Freedom House provided them with guidelines for ratings and a checklist of questions covering seven categories: electoral process; civil society; independent media; national democratic governance; local democratic governance; judicial framework and independence; and corruption. Starting with the 2005 edition, Freedom House introduced separate analysis and ratings for national democratic governance and local democratic governance to provide our readers with more detailed and nuanced analyses of these two important subjects. Previous editions included only one governance category. The ratings for all categories reflect the consensus of Freedom House, the *Nations in Transit* advisers, and the report authors. Each country report is organized according to the following outline:

- **National Democratic Governance.** Considers the democratic character and stability of the governmental system; the independence, effectiveness, and accountability of legislative and executive branches; and the democratic oversight of military and security services.

- **Electoral Process.** Examines national executive and legislative elections; electoral processes; the development of multiparty systems; and popular participation in the political process.

▮ **Civil Society.** Assesses the growth of nongovernmental organizations (NGOs), their organizational capacity and financial sustainability, and the legal and political environment in which they function; the development of free trade unions; and interest group participation in the policy process.

▮ **Independent Media.** Addresses the current state of press freedom, including libel laws, harassment of journalists, editorial independence, the emergence of a financially viable private press, and Internet access for private citizens.

▮ **Local Democratic Governance.** Considers the decentralization of power; the responsibilities, election, and capacity of local governmental bodies; and the transparency and accountability of local authorities.

▮ **Judicial Framework and Independence.** Highlights constitutional reform, human rights protections, criminal code reform, judicial independence, the status of ethnic minority rights, guarantees of equality before the law, treatment of suspects and prisoners, and compliance with judicial decisions.

▮ **Corruption.** Looks at public perceptions of corruption; the business interests of top policy makers; laws on financial disclosure and conflict of interest; and the efficacy of anticorruption initiatives.

Ratings and Scores

For all 29 countries and administrative areas in *Nations in Transit 2006*, Freedom House, in consultation with the report authors and a panel of academic advisers, has provided numerical ratings in the seven categories previously listed. The ratings are based on a scale of 1 to 7, with 1 representing the highest and 7 the lowest level of democratic progress.

The ratings follow a quarter-point scale. Minor to moderate developments typically warrant a positive or negative change of a quarter (0.25) to a half (0.50) point. Significant developments typically warrant a positive or negative change of three-quarters (0.75) to a full (1.00) point. It is rare that the rating in any category will fluctuate by more than a full point (1.00) in a single year.

As with *Freedom in the World*, Freedom House's global annual survey of political rights and civil liberties, *Nations in Transit* does not rate governments per se. Nor does it rate countries based on governmental intentions or legislation alone. Rather, a country's ratings are determined by considering the practical effect of the state and nongovernmental actors on an individual's rights and freedoms.

The *Nations in Transit* ratings, which should not be taken as absolute indicators of the situation in a given country, are valuable for making general assessments of how democratic or authoritarian a country is. They also allow for comparative analysis of reforms among the countries surveyed and for analysis of long-term developments in a particular country.

The ratings process for *Nations in Transit 2006* involved four steps:

1. Authors of individual country reports suggested preliminary ratings in all seven categories covered by the study.
2. The U.S. and Central Europe/Eurasia academic advisers evaluated the ratings and made revisions.
3. Report authors were given the opportunity to dispute any revised rating that differed from the original by more than .50 point.
4. Freedom House refereed any disputed ratings and, if the evidence warranted, considered further adjustments. Final editorial authority for the ratings rested with Freedom House.

Nations in Transit 2006 Checklist of Questions

Items appearing in italics reflect changes or additions to the methodology since the last edition. Governance categories include subquestions.

National Democratic Governance

1. Is the country's governmental system democratic? Does the Constitution or other national legislation enshrine the principles of democratic government?
   - Is the government open to meaningful citizen participation in political processes and decision making in practice?
   - Is there an effective system of checks and balances among legislative, executive, and judicial authority?
   - Does a freedom of information act or similar legislation ensure access to government information by citizens and the media?
   - Is the economy free of government domination?

2. Is the country's governmental system stable?
   - Is there consensus among political groups and citizens on democracy as the basis of the country's political system?
   - Is stability of the governmental system achieved without coercion, violence, or other abuses of basic rights and civil liberties by state or nonstate actors?
   - Do citizens recognize the legitimacy of national authorities and the laws and policies that govern them?
   - Does the government's authority extend over the full territory of the country?
   - Is the governmental system free of threats to stability such as war, insurgencies, and domination by the military, foreign powers, or other such groups?

3. Is the legislature independent, effective, and accountable to the public?
   - Does the legislature have autonomy from the executive branch?
   - Does the legislature have the resources and capacity it needs to fulfill its lawmaking and investigative responsibilities? (Consider financial resources, professional staffs, democratic management structures, and so on.)

- Do citizens and the media have regular access to legislators and the legislative process through public hearings, town meetings, published congressional records, and the like?
- Do legislative bodies operate under effective audit and investigative rules that are free of political influence?
- Does the legislature provide leadership and reflect societal preferences by providing a forum for the peaceful and democratic resolution of differences?

4. Is the executive branch independent, effective, and accountable to the public?
- Is the executive branch's role in policy making clearly defined vis-?-vis other branches of government?
- Does the executive branch have the resources and capacity it needs to formulate and implement policies?
- Do citizens and the media have regular access to the executive branch to comment on the formulation and implementation of policies?
- Does a competent and professional civil service function according to democratic standards and practices?
- Do executive bodies operate under effective audit and investigative rules that are free of political influence?
- Does the executive branch provide leadership and reflect societal preferences in resolving conflicts and supporting democratic development?

5. Are the military and security services subject to democratic oversight?
- Does the Constitution or other legislation provide for democratic oversight of and civilian authority over the military and security services?
- Is there sufficient judicial oversight of the military and security services to prevent impunity?
- Does the legislature have transparent oversight of military and security budgets and spending?
- Do legislators, media, civil society have sufficient information on military and security matters to provide oversight of the military and security services?
- Does the government provide the public with accurate and timely information about the military, the security services, and their roles?

Electoral Process

1. Is the authority of government based upon universal and equal suffrage and the will of the people as expressed by regular, free, and fair elections conducted by secret ballot?
2. Are there fair electoral laws, equal campaigning opportunities, fair polling, and honest tabulation of ballots?
3. Is the electoral system free of significant barriers to organization and registration?
4. Is the electoral system multiparty based, with viable political parties, includ-

ing an opposition party, functioning at all levels of government?

5. Is the public engaged in the political life of the country, as evidenced by membership in political parties, voter turnout for elections, or other factors?

6. Do ethnic and other minority groups have sufficient openings to participate in the political process?

7. Is there opportunity for the effective rotation of power among a range of different political parties representing competing interests and policy options?

8. Are the people's choices free from domination by the specific interests of power groups (the military, foreign powers, totalitarian parties, regional hierarchies, and/or economic oligarchies)?

9. Were the most recent national legislative elections judged free and fair by domestic and international election-monitoring organizations?

10. Were the most recent presidential elections judged free and fair by domestic and international election-monitoring organizations?

Civil Society

1. Does the state protect the rights of the independent civic sector?

2. Is the civil society vibrant? (Consider growth in the number of charitable, nonprofit, and nongovernmental organizations; improvements in the quality of performance of civil society groups; locally led efforts to increase philanthropy and volunteerism; the public's active participation in private voluntary activity; the presence of effective civic and cultural organizations for women and ethnic groups; the participation of religious groups in charitable activity; or other factors.)

3. Is society free of excessive influence from extremist and intolerant nongovernmental institutions and organizations? (Consider racists, groups advocating violence or terrorism, xenophobes, private militias and vigilante groups, or other groups whose actions threaten political and social stability and the transition to democracy.)

4. Is the legal and regulatory environment for civil society groups free of excessive state pressures and bureaucracy? (Consider ease of registration, legal rights, government regulation, fund-raising, taxation, procurement, and access-to-information issues.)

5. Do civil society groups have sufficient organizational capacity to sustain their work? (Consider management structures with clearly delineated authority and responsibility; a core of experienced practitioners, trainers, and the like; access to information on NGO management issues in the native language; and so forth.)

6. Are civil society groups financially viable, with adequate conditions and opportunities for raising funds that sustain their work? (Consider sufficient organizational capacity to raise funds; option of nonprofit tax status; freedom to raise funds from domestic or foreign sources; legal or tax environment that encourages private sector support; ability to compete for government procurement opportunities; ability to earn income or collect cost recovery fees.)

7. Is the government receptive to policy advocacy by interest groups, public policy research groups, and other nonprofit organizations? Do government officials engage civil society groups by inviting them to testify, comment on, and influence pending policies or legislation?
8. Are the media receptive to civil society groups as independent and reliable sources of information and commentary? Are they positive contributors to the country's civic life?
9. Does the state respect the right to form and join free trade unions?
10. Is the education system free of political influence and propaganda?

Independent Media

1. Are there legal protections for press freedom?
2. Are journalists, especially investigative reporters, protected from victimization by powerful state or nonstate actors?
3. Does the state oppose onerous libel laws and other excessive legal penalties for "irresponsible" journalism?
4. Are the media's editorial independence and news-gathering functions free of interference from the government or private owners?
5. Does the public enjoy a diverse selection of print and electronic sources of information, at both national and local levels, that represent a range of political viewpoints?
6. Are the majority of print and electronic media privately owned and free of excessive ownership concentration?
7. Is the private media's financial viability subject only to market forces (that is, is it free of political or other influences)?
8. Is the distribution of newspapers privately controlled?
9. Are journalists and media outlets able to form their own viable professional associations?
10. *Does society enjoy free access to and use of the Internet, is diversity of opinion available through online sources, and does government make no attempt to control the Internet?*

Local Democratic Governance

1. Are the principles of local democratic government enshrined in law and respected in practice?
   * Does the Constitution or other national legislation provide a framework for democratic local self-government?
   * Have substantial government powers and responsibilities been decentralized in practice?
   * Are local authorities free to design and adopt institutions and processes of governance that reflect local needs and conditions?
   * Do central authorities consult local governments in planning and decision-making processes that directly affect the local level?
2. Are citizens able to choose their local leaders in free and fair elections?

- Does the Constitution or other national legislation provide for local elections held on the basis of universal, equal, and direct suffrage by secret ballot?
- Do local governments derive their power on the basis of regular, free, and fair local elections (either through direct election or through election by local assemblies or councils)?
- Are free and fair local elections held at regular intervals and subject to independent monitoring and oversight?
- Do multiple candidates representing a range of views participate in local elections and in local government bodies?
- Are voters' choices in local elections free from domination by power groups such as national political parties, central authorities, economic oligarchies, and the like?
- Are citizens engaged in local electoral processes, as evidenced by party membership, voter turnout, or other factors?

3. Are citizens ensured meaningful participation in local government decision making?
- Do local governments invite input from civil society, business, trade unions, and other groups on important policy issues before decisions are made and implemented?
- Do local governments initiate committees, focus groups, or other partnerships with civil society to address common concerns and needs?
- Are individuals and civil society groups free to submit petitions, organize demonstrations or initiate other activities that influence local decision making?
- Do women, ethnic groups, and other minorities participate in local government?
- Do the media regularly report the views of local civic groups, the private business sector, and other nongovernmental entities about local government policy and performance?

4. Do democratically elected local authorities exercise their powers freely and autonomously?
- Do central authorities respect local decision-making authority and independence?
- Are local governments free to pass and enforce laws needed to fulfill their responsibilities?
- Do local authorities have the right to judicial remedy to protect their powers?
- Do local governments have the right to form associations at domestic and international levels for protecting and promoting their interests?
5. Do democratically elected local authorities have the resources and capacity needed to fulfill their responsibilities?

- Are local governments free to collect taxes, fees, and other revenues commensurate with their responsibilities?
- Do local governments automatically and regularly receive resources that are due from central authorities?
- Do local governments set budgets and allocate resources free of excessive political influences and central controls?
- Are local authorities empowered to set staff salaries, staff size, and staffing patterns, and is recruitment based on merit and experience?
- Do local governments have the resources (material, financial, and human) to provide quality services, ensure a safe local environment, and implement sound policies in practice?

6. Do democratically elected local authorities operate with transparency and accountability to citizens?
- Are local authorities subject to clear and consistent standards of disclosure, oversight, and accountability?
- Are local authorities free from domination by power groups (economic oligarchies, organized crime, and so forth) that prevent them from representing the views and needs of the citizens who elected them?
- Are public meetings mandated by law and held at regular intervals?
- Do citizens and the media have regular access to public records and information?
- Are media free to investigate and report on local politics and government without fear of victimization?

Judicial Framework and Independence

1. Does the constitutional or other national legislation provide protections for fundamental political, civil, and human rights? (Includes freedom of expression, freedom of conscience and religion, freedom of association, and business and property rights.)
2. Do the state and nongovernmental actors respect fundamental political, civil, and human rights in practice?
3. Is there independence and impartiality in the interpretation and enforcement of the Constitution?
4. Is there equality before the law?
5. Has there been effective reform of the criminal code/criminal law? (Consider presumption of innocence until proven guilty, access to a fair and public hearing, introduction of jury trials, access to independent counsel/public defender, independence of prosecutors, and so forth.)
6. Are suspects and prisoners protected in practice against arbitrary arrest, detention without trial, searches without warrants, torture, and abuse, and excessive delays in the criminal justice system?
7. Are judges appointed in a fair and unbiased manner, and do they have adequate legal training before assuming the bench?

8. Do judges rule fairly and impartially, and are courts free of political control and influence?
9. Do legislative, executive, and other governmental authorities comply with judicial decisions, and are judicial decisions enforced effectively?

Corruption

1. Has the government implemented effective anticorruption initiatives?
2. Is the country's economy free of excessive state involvement?
3. Is the government free from excessive bureaucratic regulations, registration requirements, and other controls that increase opportunities for corruption?
4. Are there significant limitations on the participation of government officials in economic life?
5. Are there adequate laws requiring financial disclosure and disallowing conflict of interest?
6. Does the government advertise jobs and contracts?
7. Does the state enforce an effective legislative or administrative process–particularly one that is free of prejudice against one's political opponents–to prevent, investigate, and prosecute the corruption of government officials and civil servants?
8. Do whistle-blowers, anticorruption activists, investigators, and journalists enjoy legal protections that make them feel secure about reporting cases of bribery and corruption?
9. Are allegations of corruption given wide and extensive airing in the media?
10. Does the public display a high intolerance for official corruption?

Democracy Score

With the 2004 edition of *Nations in Transit*, Freedom House introduced a Democracy Score, a straight average of the ratings for all categories covered by *Nations in Transit*. Freedom House provided this aggregate for comparative and interpretive purposes of evaluating progress and setbacks in the countries under study.

> *Background Note:* In the years before the 2004 edition, Freedom House used two aggregate scores to assist in the analysis of reform in the 27 countries covered by *Nations in Transit*. These were Democratization (average of electoral process, civil society, independent media, and governance) and Rule of Law (average of corruption and constitutional, legislative, and judicial framework). Analysis showed a high level of correlation between the previous scoring categories and the Democracy Score.

For *Nations in Transit 2006,* Freedom House once again uses the Democracy Score. Based on the Democracy Score and its scale of 1 to 7, Freedom House defined the following regime types:

Democracy Score	Regime Type
1-2	Consolidated Democracy
3	Semiconsolidated Democracy
4	Transitional Government or Hybrid Regime
5	Semiconsolidated Authoritarian Regime
6-7	Consolidated Authoritarian Regime

Ratings and Democracy Score Guidelines

Starting with this 2006 edition, the following new guidelines were used to assist Freedom House staff and consultants in determining the ratings for electoral process; civil society; independent media; governance; constitutional, legislative, and judicial framework; and corruption. Based on the aggregate Democracy Scores, the descriptions are intended to explain generally the conditions of democratic institutions in the different regime classifications.

1.00-2.99 Consolidated Democracies

1.00-1.99 Countries receiving a Democracy Score of 1.00-1.99 closely embody the best policies and practices of liberal democracy.

- The authority of government is based on universal and equal suffrage as expressed in regular, free, and fair elections conducted by secret ballot. Elections are competitive, and power rotates among a range of different political parties.
- Civil society is independent, vibrant, and sustainable. Rights of assembly and association are protected and free of excessive state pressures and bureaucracy.
- Media are independent, diverse, and sustainable. Freedom of expression is protected, and journalists are free from excessive interference by powerful political and economic interests.
- National and local governmental systems are stable, democratic, and accountable to the public. Central branches of government are independent, and an effective system of checks and balances exists. Local authorities exercise their powers freely and autonomously of the central government.
- The judiciary is independent, impartial, timely, and able to defend fundamental political, civil, and human rights. There is equality before the law, and judicial decisions are enforced.
- Government, the economy, and society are free of excessive corruption.
- Legislative framework, including strong conflict-of-interest protection, is in place so that journalists and other citizens feel secure to investigate, provide media coverage of, and prosecute allegations of corruption.

2.00-2.99 Countries receiving a Democracy Score of 2.00-2.99 closely embody the best policies and practices of liberal democracy. However, challenges largely associated with corruption contribute to a slightly lower score.

- The authority of government is based on universal and equal suffrage as expressed in regular, free, and fair elections conducted by secret ballot. Elections are competitive, and power rotates among a range of different political parties.
- Civil society is independent, vibrant, and sustainable. Rights of assembly and association are protected and free of excessive state pressures and bureaucracy.
- Media are independent, diverse, and sustainable. Freedom of expression is protected, and journalists are free from excessive interference by powerful political or economic interests.
- National and local governmental systems are stable, democratic, and accountable to the public. Central branches of government are independent, and an effective system of checks and balances exists. Local authorities exercise their powers freely and autonomously of the central government.
- The judiciary is independent, impartial, and able to defend fundamental political, civil, and human rights. There is equality before the law, and judicial decisions are enforced, though timeliness remains an area of concern.
- While government, the economy, and society are increasingly free of corruption, implementation of effective anticorruption programs may be slow, and revelations of high-level corruption may be frequent.

3.00-3.99 Semiconsolidated Democracies

Countries receiving a Democracy Score of 3.00-3.99 are electoral democracies that meet relatively high standards for the selection of national leaders but exhibit some weaknesses in their defense of political rights and civil liberties.

- The authority of government is based on universal and equal suffrage as expressed in regular elections conducted by secret ballot. While elections are typically free, fair, and competitive, irregularities may occur. Power rotates among a range of different political parties.
- Civil society is independent and active. Rights of assembly and association are protected. However, the organizational capacity of groups remains limited, and dependence on foreign funding is a barrier to long-term sustainability. Groups may be susceptible to political or economic pressure. Media are generally independent and diverse, and freedom of expression is largely protected in legislative framework and in practice. However, special interests–both political and economic–do exert influence on reporting and editorial independence and may lead to self-censorship. While print media are largely free of government influence and control, electronic media are not.

▌ National and local systems of government are stable and democratic. Although laws and structures are in place to promote government transparency and accountability, implementation is lacking. The system of checks and balances may be weak and decentralization of powers and resources to local self-governments incomplete.

▌ The framework for an independent judiciary is in place. However, judicial independence and the protection of basic rights, especially those of ethnic and religious minorities, are weak. Judicial processes are slow, inconsistent, and open to abuse.

▌ Corruption is widespread, and state capacities to investigate and prosecute corruption are weak. Efforts to combat the problem produce limited results.

4.00-4.99 Transitional Governments or Hybrid Regimes

Countries receiving a Democracy Score of 4.00-4.99 are typically electoral democracies that meet only minimum standards for the selection of national leaders. Democratic institutions are fragile, and substantial challenges to the protection of political rights and civil liberties exist. The potential for sustainable, liberal democracy is unclear.

▌ National elections are regular and competitive, but substantial irregularities may prevent them from being free and fair. Government pressure on opposition parties and candidates may be common.

▌ Civil society is independent and growing, and rights of assembly and association are generally protected. However, philanthropy and volunteerism are weak, and dependence on foreign funding is a barrier to long-term sustainability. Democratically oriented NGOs are the most visible and active groups, especially during election seasons, and may be subject to government pressure.

▌ Media are generally independent and diverse. Legislative framework to protect media may be in place but is not matched by practice. Special interests – both political and economic – exert influence on reporting and editorial independence and may lead to self-censorship. Harassment of and pressure on journalists may occur.

▌ National and local systems of government are weak and lacking in transparency. While the balance of power is fragile, a vocal yet fractionalized opposition may be present in the Parliament. Governance may remain highly centralized. Local self-government is not fully in place, with some local or regional authorities owing allegiance to the central authorities who appointed them.

▌ The judiciary struggles to maintain its independence from the government. Respect for basic political, civil, and human rights is selective, and equality before the law is not guaranteed. In addition to the judiciary

being slow, abuses occur. Use of torture in prisons may be a problem.
- Corruption is widespread and presents a major impediment to political and economic development. Anticorruption efforts are inconsistent.

5.00-5.99 Semiconsolidated Authoritarian Regimes

Countries receiving a Democracy Score of 5.00-5.99 attempt to mask authoritarianism with limited respect for the institutions and practices of democracy. They typically fail to meet even the minimum standards of electoral democracy.
- Although national elections may be held at regular intervals and contested by opposition parties and candidates, they are marred by irregularities and deemed undemocratic by international observers. Public resources and state employees are used to guarantee incumbent victories. Political power may change hands, yet turnovers in the executive are well orchestrated and may fail to reflect voter preferences.
- Power is highly centralized, and national and local levels of government are neither democratic nor accountable to citizens. Meaningful checks on executive power do not exist, and stability is achieved by undemocratic means.
- Space for independent civil society is narrow. While governments encourage NGOs that perform important social functions, they are hostile to groups that challenge state policy. Institutional weaknesses and insufficient funding, save for international support, also contribute to the limited impact of politically oriented groups.
- Although independent media exist, they operate under government pressure and risk harassment for reporting that is critical of the regime. Investigative reporting on corruption and organized crime is especially risky. Harsh libel laws sustain a culture of self-censorship. Most media, particularly radio and television, are controlled or co-opted by the state.
- The judiciary is restrained in its ability to act independently of the executive, and equality before the law is not guaranteed. The judiciary is frequently co-opted as a tool to silence opposition figures and has limited ability to protect the basic rights and liberties of citizens.
- State involvement in the economic sector is sizable, and corruption is widespread. Efforts to combat corruption are usually politically motivated.

6.00-7.00 Consolidated Authoritarian Regimes

Countries receiving a Democracy Score of 6.00-7.00 are closed societies in which dictators prevent political competition and pluralism and are responsible for widespread violations of basic political, civil, and human rights.
- Elections serve to reinforce the rule of dictators who enjoy unlimited authority for prolonged periods of time. Pro-governmental parties and

candidates dominate elections, while an independent opposition is typically barred from seeking office. Rotations of executive power are unlikely absent death or revolution.

▌ Power is highly centralized, and the country's national and local governmental systems are neither democratic nor accountable to the public.

▌ Civil society faces excessive government restrictions and repression. A formal state ideology, or cult of personality, may dominate society and serve to justify the regime.

▌ Freedom of expression is stifled, and independent media are virtually nonexistent. Media are typically state owned or controlled by individuals connected to the regime. Censorship is pervasive, and repression for independent reporting or criticism of the government is severe.

▌ The rule of law is subordinate to the regime, and violations of basic political, civil, and human rights are widespread. Courts are used to harass members of the opposition.

▌ Corruption and state involvement in the economy are excessive. Allegations of corruption are usually intended to silence political opponents of the regime.

Research Team and Data Sources

Freedom House developed the initial survey and subsequent editions after consultations with the U.S. Agency for International Development. Freedom House staff members and consultants researched and wrote the country reports. Consultants are regional or country specialists, who are either from, based in, or travel frequently to the country of study. The research team used a wide variety of sources in writing the reports, including information from international and local NGOs, NIT country governments, intergovernmental organizations, and a variety of media outlets.

The economic and social data contained in the country header pages of the 2006 edition were taken from the following sources:

GNI/Capita, Population: *World Development Indicators 2006* (Washington, D.C.: World Bank, 2006).

Ethnic Groups: *CIA World Factbook 2006* (Washington, D.C.: Central Intelligence Agency, 2006).

Nations in Transit 2006:
Shifting Influences and Challenges

Jeannette Goehring and Kristie D. Evenson

*N*ations in Transit 2006 marks the 10th edition of Freedom House's comprehensive, comparative study of post-Communist transitions from Central Europe to Eurasia. Focused on 29 countries and administrative areas, Nations in Transit 2006 covers a 12-month period, from January 1 to December 31, 2005, and provides comparative ratings and in-depth analysis of electoral process, civil society, independent media, national and local governance, judicial framework and independence, and corruption.

The report evaluates democratic performance in a wide range of states, encompassing the democracies of the new European Union (EU) member states to Central Asian authoritarian regimes. The 2006 report comes at a time when efforts to support democratization efforts in some of these regions are particularly challenging. Optimism over the color revolutions in Eurasia has been partially tempered by other Eurasia states' increasingly coordinated and energy-financed attempts at consolidating authoritarian rule. Closer to Europe, efforts to consolidate democratic gains in the Balkan region made progress but continued to be offset by uncertainties over the status of Kosovo and state-building challenges for most of the Balkan countries to attain membership in an increasingly reluctant EU. And even in the new member states of the EU, democratic consolidation throughout the past year has been hampered by persistent corruption concerns.

Sobering Year for Democracy Advances

Unlike the last two years, which saw clear examples of significant democratic advancement in the *Nations in Transit* (*NIT*) region, 2005 experienced few dramatic gains in democratic standards in Central Europe and Eurasia; overall, in fact, improvements only slightly outpaced setbacks in ratings in Nations in Transit 2006. This year's study shows 13 progressions, 12 regressions, and 4 countries in which no net change was registered from the previous year. Where progress was noted, it was modest and found mostly in middle performers. Two notable positive exceptions were Albania and Bulgaria. Albania improved in six out of seven *NIT* ratings categories, while Bulgaria improved in five out of seven. On the opposite side of the index, Uzbekistan showed the most dramatic decrease in democratic standards, declining in six out of seven *NIT* ratings categories.

While non-Baltic former Soviet states demonstrated overall decline and EU countries demonstrated general constancy, the countries of the Balkans on average continued their upward trend. This modest progress was encouraging despite the difficult transition challenges that continue to confront the region. This is particularly true for those of the former Yugoslavia, where the legacies of conflict and fundamental state-building processes that are under way remain partially dependent on the EU's willingness to continue aggressive preaccession and accession processes.

No dramatic democratic breakthroughs occurred in 2005, and although still early, the immediate exuberance associated with recent significant transitions has waned considerably as the enormity of the reform challenge has set in. Ukraine showed the greatest overall democracy score progress in 2005, most notably in independent media, yet throughout 2005 the reform agenda showed signs of losing consensus. Despite significant steps in Ukraine and smaller steps in Georgia, the reform implementation is still in its early stages. For example, the government in Georgia two years after the Rose Revolution is still struggling to find a proper democratic balance of power. In Bishkek, massive political upheaval occurred in March, resulting in a change of presidential leadership. Yet by the end of 2005, Kyrgyzstan lacked notable concrete reforms. Civil society and media experienced relative freedom after March, yet few institutional guarantees for this freedom were put in place during the year. Consequently, Kyrgyzstan remains a fragile state whose capacity to advance meaningful reforms is an open question.

In established autocracies such as Belarus and Azerbaijan, regimes took even more vigorous steps to tighten their grip. This repressive trend was particularly prevalent in the Eurasia region as authoritarian countries took comprehensive steps to ensure regime security. One year after the government's violent crackdown at Andijan, the opportunities for democratic progress in Uzbekistan appear increasingly remote. This trend of consolidating power has been heightened by the growing nondemocratic influence of other major states like Russia, creating a spillover effect in the region.

This spillover was felt most directly in the civil society sector during 2005. Almost all of the countries with a downturn in the civil society indicator in 2005 were from the Eurasia region. Although the most widely publicized restrictions on civil society were in Russia, this edition notes serious setbacks also in Azerbaijan, Kazakhstan, Tajikistan, and Uzbekistan. Authorities in these states reacted to the color revolutions of the past two years by placing new restrictions on civil society, with particular scrutiny on those organizations receiving international funding in the democracy and governance field.

For example, weeks after the March events in Kyrgyzstan, as *Nations in Transit* analyst Payam Foroughi puts it: "Tajikistan's Ministry of the Interior...ordered financial audits of various domestic groups and called for all international organizations and foreign embassies to inform the ministry in advance of meetings and topics of discussion with domestic NGOs, political parties, and local journalists." In Kazakhstan, the Nazarbaev regime tightened governmental control over civil society through laws, formal and informal pressure, and increased funding by the state or agencies controlled by the state, which *NIT* analyst Bhavna Dave identifies as "efforts to shape the civil sector through financial aid and support to NGOs engaged in social and infrastructure development, as well as to those loyal to the government."

The Influence of Energy Resources

The historically high energy revenues many of the Eurasian states are receiving facilitate the movement toward authoritarianism. Highlighting the phenomenon of energy rich and democracy poor, the study documented a marked decline in the overall democracy scores in the key energy supplier states of Azerbaijan, Kazakhstan, Russia, and Turkmenistan. The 2005 drop falls in line with a multi-year trend of worsening democracy scores in these countries.

At least in the short term, the high energy revenues have been a disincentive for governments to create the long-term independent and accountable institutions normally associated with economic development. The revenues also have allowed governments to generally improve basic social expenditures at the expense of democratic institution building and basic civil and political rights. Noting the oil revenue effect on Azerbaijan, *NIT* analyst Kaan Nazli remarked: "President Aliyev continued to enjoy overwhelming authority in Azerbaijan's government system in 2005 and was able to maintain political and economic stability thanks to a high level of continued economic growth."

As energy resources in these states prove increasingly important strategically for Europe and the United States, the accompanying decline in democratic performance suggests uncertainty ahead for both energy providers and consumers. All four of the previously mentioned countries witnessed a downturn in democracy standards owing to weak institutions, deteriorating governance standards, worsening media and judicial freedom, and rising corruption.

At the same time, opportunities for corruption have increased with the state elite's steady reestablishment of control over the energy industries. And despite the establishment of special fund mechanisms to save and allocate energy revenues for long-term economic development, oil nationalism has diminished most oversight mechanisms that could provide a check on rent-seeking activities. For example, advancing his already entrenched authoritarian powers, Turkmen president Saparmurat Niyazov assumed direct control over the country's oil and gas resources by the end of 2005; in the same year, he closed most hospitals across the country, claiming financial constraints while international investigations pointed to significant funds present in major European banks.

Corruption as an Enduring Challenge

Issues of corruption remain a common challenge throughout the *NIT* region. Even in the best-performing states in the study, the corruption indicator lags behind other areas of performance. In fact, the collective democracy score for new EU members has dropped slightly owing to decreasing performance on the corruption indicator. The eight countries that joined the EU on May 1, 2004, remain the highest-ranking in the study but consistently score lower on the corruption indicator than in any of the other six ratings indicator categories.

Of the nine consolidated democracies listed in the 2006 edition, the corruption rating improved for only two (Bulgaria, Latvia), whereas it worsened for four (Hungary, Lithuania, Poland, and Slovenia). Whether these low scores indicate an enduring characteristic of political and economic transition or reflect the struggles that most consolidating and consolidated democracies face is an area of research that merits more careful examination. In Lithuania, the corruption indicator continued its multiyear trend of being at least a full point (or more) worse than all other indicators and decreased even more in 2005. Even as other high-level scandals became known and dealt with during 2005 in Lithuania, there was an increase in unofficial payments related to business regulations. Similarly, in Poland the corruption indicator has worsened since 2002; in 2005, more cases became known in new spheres, and effective countermeasures are lacking. And at the top of the *NIT* index, Slovenia's corruption indicator edged downward, owing in part to the country's decision to place the competences of the (previously independent) Slovene Commission for the Prevention of Corruption under parliamentary oversight.

State Building and Democratization

Another challenge that should be highlighted is the dual difficulty of "state building" and democratization. Whether it is through violent conflict or peaceful means, almost half of the *NIT* countries covered continue to grapple with building basic structures and consensus about belonging together in a state. A state must be able to have in place and control basic institutions in order to engage in processes of democratization. Across the *NIT* region, reform processes remain dependent on the ability of the state and its people to agree on and build up basic functions. During 2005, this challenge was especially apparent in the Balkans and the Caucasus region.

As this edition goes to print, citizens of the State Union of Serbia and Montenegro have decided on their Balkan version of a "velvet divorce" toward building separate states. This is good news for the reformers in the two republics who have been repeatedly blocked by the larger issues of the dysfunctional State Union; or, as *NIT* analyst Florian Bieber explains, in 2005 Serbia was still unable to put together a new (republic-level) Constitution to update the 1990 Serbian Constitution created under Milosevic. This was due partly to the disinterest of either republic to sort through State Union competences. Overall in 2005, democratic performance in both Serbia and Montenegro demonstrated only one rating improvement: Serbia made progress in designing a legal framework to better fight corruption. Yet independence does not necessarily suggest an easy road for either republic to enact necessary democratic reforms. *NIT*'s assessment on both republics noted decreasing media and civil society space to support government reforms.

Kosovo illustrates the competing challenges of building the institutions of a state while being under international administration and having an unresolved status. Unclear levels of responsibility, competency, and accountability have taken their toll on the population's willingness to support acceptance of a step-by-step reform process. This is due partly to competency, for example, as described by *NIT* analyst Bashkim Rrahmani: "Seventy laws were approved by the Parliament in 2005, though the body is (still) not effective in implementing legislation." As well, basic monitoring mechanisms remained weak, with the third sector demonstrating less willingness to criticize government performance owing to status talk considerations. Resolution of Kosovo's status does not imply dramatic gains in democracy. The institutional weakness described in *NIT* will require substantial technical improvements and political will on the domestic level to reach EU reform standards.

In the Caucasus, the frozen conflicts of the region continue to cast a shadow over other reform efforts. For example, in states like Georgia where the apparent goodwill of the government for the reform process is in place, the government still becomes distracted by periodic upsurges in tension with Abkhazia and South Ossetia, where wars for secession from 1991 to 1993 brought some 15 percent of the country's territory under the control of unrecognized governments. This has affected the government's ability to implement its ambitious yet fragile reform strategy in such areas as minority integration and larger judicial reform. As described by *NIT* analyst Ghia Nodia: "...these zones of so-called frozen conflict have been major impediments to Georgia's development: They contain threats of renewed violence and undermine Georgia's chances for political and economic stabilization." The frozen conflicts also have provided a convenient method of constricting the transparency of the security-related functions of the government, including civilian oversight of the military and security services.

Encouraging and Expecting Reform

The *NIT* region remains a zone of contrasting democracy trends: EU states, although still grappling with enduring legacies like corruption, are generally on course; the Balkan region continues its slow progress toward institutionalized democracies and Euro-Atlantic integration; and several states on the edge of Europe like Moldova and Georgia struggle to put in place the basic foundations for democratic development even while other former Soviet republics continue their consolidation of authoritarian rather than democratic practices.

If we apply the study findings to policy considerations, the expectations of new EU member states are clear as they focus on reaching the next hurdle of EU integration, through being accepted into the Schengen zone and adopting use of the euro as currency. However, expectations for the rest of the region require clear, consistent, and coordinated efforts by the international community. Any engagement with these countries must continue to expect reform and emphasize human rights and democracy standards as outlined in already existing agreements and relationships (the Organization for Security and Cooperation in Europe, UN Charter, Council of Europe, EU Neighborhood partnership agreements, Millennium Challenge Corporation, and so forth). And any new agreements, like a European Country Action Plan or a strategic European or U.S. bilateral treaty, should prioritize and include strong conditionality clauses for fulfillment of key human rights and democracy governance criteria.

Carrots and sticks still work, but they must be consistent and targeted in a way that support the ideas of the democracy advocates within these states as well as hold state powers to the democratic principles to which they formally ascribe.

Nations in Transit 2006: Ratings and Scores

Produced annually, *Nations in Transit* provides ratings that serve as signposts of democratic advancements and setbacks in the 29 countries and administrative areas under study. Although the ratings for electoral process, civil society, independent media, national democratic governance, local democratic governance, judicial framework and independence, and corruption are not absolute indicators of conditions in a given country, they provide valuable assistance in making general assessments of the levels of democracy or authoritarianism within a country or administrative area. They also facilitate comparative analysis of post-Communist change from Central Europe to Eurasia. Furthermore, the 2006 edition, in addition to continuing to provide a separate section on Kosovo in the Serbia and Montenegro country report, introduced separate authorship of the Montenegro and Serbia sections to provide a more detailed analysis of each administrative area.

The 2006 edition retained the expanded ratings categories from 2005 (local democratic governance and so on) and has expanded thematic coverage this year. For example, country analysts were asked to provide information about the Internet – including diversity of information available; access to, registry, and use; and level of state control – in an attempt to assess the growing influence of Internet-based media within the independent media category.

The *Nations in Transit* ratings are based on a scale of 1 to 7, with 1 representing the highest level of democratic development and 7 the lowest. Each country's Democracy Score is the average of ratings for all categories covered by the study. These scores follow a 1-to-7 scale as well. Changes in ratings and scores reflect events that occurred during the period under study: January 1 through December 31, 2005.

Changes by Category

Electoral Process

↑ Five countries experienced ratings improvements in electoral process: Albania, Bosnia-Herzegovina, Kyrgyzstan, Moldova, and Ukraine.

↓ Six countries or administrative areas experienced declines in electoral process: Azerbaijan, Croatia, Macedonia, Montenegro, Russia, and Tajikistan.

Civil Society

↑ Three countries or territories showed gains in civil society: Albania, Croatia, and Ukraine.

↓ Seven countries or territories experienced setbacks in civil society: Azerbaijan, Kazakhstan, Kosovo, Montenegro, Russia, Tajikistan, and Uzbekistan.

Independent Media

↑ Three countries experienced improvements in independent media: Albania, Bulgaria, and Ukraine.

↓ Five countries or administrative areas showed declines in independent media: Poland, Kazakhstan, Slovenia, Tajikistan, and Uzbekistan.

National Democratic Governance

↑ Five countries experienced improvements in national democratic governance: Albania, Bulgaria, Latvia, Macedonia, and Ukraine.

↓ Six countries showed declines in national democratic governance: Belarus, Kazakhstan, Poland, Russia, Tajikistan, and Uzbekistan.

Local Democratic Governance

↑ Five countries experienced improvements in local democratic governance: Albania, Bulgaria, Macedonia, Georgia, and Slovakia.

↓ Two countries showed declines in local democratic governance: Kyrgyzstan and Uzbekistan.

Governance Compared

▮ Eight countries or territories showed better national democratic governance than local democratic governance: Armenia, Croatia, Estonia, Georgia, Hungary, Kyrgyzstan, Latvia, and Ukraine.

▮ Thirteen countries or administrative areas showed better local democratic governance than national democratic governance: Albania, Belarus, Czech Republic, Kazakhstan, Kosovo, Montenegro, Poland, Romania, Russia, Serbia, Slovenia, Tajikistan, and Uzbekistan.

▮ Eight countries received the same ratings for national and local democratic governance: Azerbaijan, Bosnia-Herzegovina, Bulgaria, Lithuania, Macedonia, Moldova, Slovakia, and Turkmenistan.

Judicial Framework and Independence

↑ Nine countries or territories had ratings improvements in this category: Albania, Armenia, Bosnia-Herzegovina, Bulgaria, Croatia, Czech Republic, Georgia, Lithuania, and Moldova.

↓ Two countries experienced setbacks in their ratings for this category: Poland and Uzbekistan.

Corruption

↑ Eight countries or administrative areas showed improvements in their ratings for corruption: Bosnia-Herzegovina, Bulgaria, Croatia, Georgia, Latvia, Macedonia, Moldova, and Serbia.

↓ Eight countries showed regression in their ratings in corruption: Belarus, Hungary, Lithuania, Poland, Russia, Slovenia, Turkmenistan, and Uzbekistan.

Two years ago Freedom House introduced a Democracy Score – a straight average of all seven subcategories – to enhance its ability to compare and interpret change in the countries under study. The Democracy Score determines the classification of regime type. In 2005, no countries moved downward from one category to another, but three countries improved their regime classification:

▌ Bulgaria moved upward from Semiconsolidated Democracy for the first time to Consolidated Democracy;

▌ Albania moved upward from Transitional Government/Hybrid Regime for the first time to Semiconsolidated Democracy;

▌ Moldova moved upward from Semiconsolidated Authoritarian Regime to Transitional Government/Hybrid Regime.

Jeannette Goehring is editor of Nations in Transit. Kristie D. Evenson is the director of Freedom House Europe. Both are based in Budapest.

Nations in Transit 2006
Country Summaries*

6.96↓ **Turkmenistan.** Turkmenistan's democracy score continues to edge ever downwards as the country retains its position as the most authoritarian on the NIT index. The year 2005 may well be called the "Year of the Ruhnama," as promotion of the two-volume national code of conduct written by President Saparmurat Niyazov dominated both political and social life and fed into Niyazov's cult-authoritarian rule. At the same time, the continued practice of purging senior government officials, staging elections, use of the judiciary as an instrument of repression, and refusal to address human rights concerns plague Turkmenistan's democratic development. While some potential for improvement exists, such as nominal changes in the electoral process stating that regional, district, and city council members shall be elected by simple majority vote and decriminalizing unregistered NGO activity, the government continues to interfere with appointments and harasses civil society groups, including religious communities. The government banned importing and circulating foreign print media, ensuring its control over information regarding other post-Soviet states. Allegedly acting against corruption, Niyazov took direct control of the country's energy resources, allowing him the potential to further increase his presidential funds, leading to a deterioration in the country's corruption rating.

6.82↓ **Uzbekistan.** Perhaps best marked by the events in the city of Andijan on May 13, 2005, ratings fell across nearly every aspect of Uzbekistan's democratic measures and resulted in the most reduced democracy score of all the countries for 2005. The government's tightening of power to the point of executive domination continues to weaken local democratic governance and the judiciary, as appointed officials accede to executive demands for

*The 2006 Democracy Scores are sorted within regions from worst to best performers. The regions are: Central Asia, Western Commonwealth of Independent States, The Caucasus, The Balkans, and New European Union Members. The Democracy Score represents an average of subcategory ratings for electoral process, civil society, independent media, national democratic governance, local democratic governance, judicial framework and independence, and corruption. Nations in Transit ratings and scores are based on a scale of 1 to 7, with 1 representing the highest level of democratic development and 7 the lowest. Arrows indicate if the Democracy Score has improved (↑), worsened (↓), or had no change (→) from the previous year.

fear of losing their positions. Furthermore, corruption continues to run riot among civil servants and members of the president's family and senior government officials. Most notably, following the events in Andijan in 2005, the government began a campaign to rid Uzbekistan of "alien ideologies" via repression of civil society and international media. As a result, human rights defenders and journalists were arrested or placed under house arrest and the security of their families was threatened. Several international NGOs and media groups were suspended, evicted, or harassed.

6.39↓ **Kazakhstan.** The reelection of President Nursultan Nazarbaev in 2005 ensures that control over national and local governance as well as the judiciary will remain within the financial, business, political, and even civil interest groups close to and/or loyal to the president and will greatly limit the possibility for democratic development. The government's quest for social and financial "stability" has led to greater restrictions on opposition parties as well as the independent media and reduced transparency and democratic accountability, leading to a worsening national democratic rating, while electoral process, local democratic governance, and judicial framework remain stagnant. Civil society and independent media ratings also worsened this year as a result of government favoritism toward explicitly loyal organizations involved in social development and infrastructure and following the passage of new restrictions on the right to assemble. Furthermore, in addition to the campaign of abuse, disinformation, confiscation, and criminalization that accompanied the last election, a new law allows for an even greater media bias, as the government now has the power to easily close those media outlets critical of the regime.

6.39↓ **Tajikistan.** The ousting of Kyrgyzstan president Askar Akayev provided such a great shock to the seemingly stable government of Tajikistan that much of 2005 can be seen as attempts to ensure the reelection of President Imamali Rahmonov and, hence, the continued privileges of those in the government's regional- and clan-affiliated patronage network. The government's systematic oppression of the opposition, despite their lack of popular support, including harassment and arrest of oppositional figures, closing major oppositional papers, and tightening overall control of information sources, has led to ratings decline in both national democratic governance and independent media ratings. Election procedures improved slightly with the 2005 parliamentary elections, yet opposition participation was hindered, and elections once again failed to meet international standards. Furthermore, following what seemed to be a trend in 2005 for countries neighboring the so-called color revolutions, the government placed heavy restrictions on the activities of civil society organizations, especially those receiving foreign assistance. Corruption remained widespread.

5.68↓ **Kyrgyzstan.** Despite massive political upheaval wherein former president Askar Akayev was replaced by Kurmanbek Bakiyev, by the end of 2005 Kyrgyzstan lacked any concrete reforms. Electoral developments sparked by political changes in March have raised hopes for future electoral proceedings. Civil society and independent media continue to await the government support necessary for further development. Corruption, a priority issue for the new government, plagued inept local government officials to the point of serious breakdowns in law and order in the southern part of the country. Government links to criminal organizations were reported soon after the July election of Bakiyev when three deputies with such alleged connections were murdered, and tensions were heightened again in October following a series of prison riots.

Western Commonwealth of Independent States (CIS)

6.71↓ **Belarus.** The year 2005 was marked by government restrictions and preemptive strikes against the opposition, civil society, and the independent press in anticipation of early elections for the presidential seat and the Belarusian House of Representatives. Totalitarian measures to eliminate all possibility of a "colored revolution" included increased punishment for publicly expressing independent opinions and amending the law to allow shooting protesters as a last resort. The government criminalized most civil society activities involving international cooperation, human rights protection, independent analytical work, and membership in unregistered nongovernmental organizations (NGOs). It continued to harass independent media and failed to investigate the deaths of two independent reporters. Corruption continued to worsen in 2005, with high-profile arrests, criminal cases, bribery, and abuse of authority despite countercorruption measures. Hence, ratings for both national democratic governance and corruption deteriorated in 2005 as a result of continued abuse and centralization of power.

5.75↓ **Russia.** In 2005, President Vladimir Putin continued to centralize control over political life, enhancing his own power and countering previous democratic developments in Russia, thus leading to falling ratings in electoral process, civil society, national democratic governance, and corruption. The government's failure to adopt effective policies in the North Caucasus, as well as its inability to reform the military and police, has exacerbated the situation and fed into extremism. Corruption marked by increased state control over the energy sector, attacks on oversight bodies, and ongoing troubles in the North Caucasus contributed to continuing destabilization of the political system. Furthermore, with its onslaught against media freedoms, harassment of oppositionists, amendment of electoral laws making it more difficult for independent observers to monitor elections, and near obliteration of NGOs, the state demonstrated an isolationist attitude from the West, despite its pending chairmanship of the G8.

4.96↑ **Moldova.** Progress in 2005 was shaped by Moldova's attempts to strengthen its partnership with both the United States and the European Union and as a result of reform promises given in exchange for oppositional support in the March 6 elections, allowing the Party of Moldovan Communists to keep its leader, Vladimir Voronin, in power. To this end, improvements were made in the areas of electoral process, judicial framework and independence, and corruption. Specifically, the government made efforts to reform the electoral code, granted the Central Electoral Commission independence, privatized two national newspapers, began reform of the judicial system, and initiated the National Anticorruption Strategy and Action Plan. Serious problems remain, however, including promoting democracy in Transnistria, strengthening local democratic governance, decreasing the backlog of judicial decisions awaiting implementation, developing a sustainable civil society, and carrying out remaining reforms.

4.21↑ **Ukraine.** In 2005, Ukraine continued to experience the positive effects of its 2004 Orange Revolution, especially in the areas of media independence and national democratic governance. Independent media displayed drastic improvements, including removal of government censorship, increased media pluralism, and more balanced coverage. The amendment of the Law on the Elections of Peoples Deputies demonstrated the government's willingness to heed not only international recommendations, but media and civil society demands in improving election processes. Furthermore, the new government made great efforts to increase transparency and accountability in all sectors of national democratic governance. In September, the government chaired by Yulia Tymoshenko was replaced by Yury Yechanurov's government, demonstrating that along with positive developments and intentions, the need for systematic reform and structuring to ensure further developments and stability remains.

The Caucasus

5.93↓ **Azerbaijan.** President Ilham Aliyev continued to consolidate his authority in 2005. Azerbaijan's democratic performance showed signs of deterioration, especially in the categories of electoral process and civil society. The rating for electoral process worsened this year as, despite improvements in electoral legislation, the November 6 parliamentary elections were marked with irregularities and failed to meet international standards. Civil society also worsened owing to continued government harassment (detainment, fines, physical abuse, university expulsion), especially of youth groups linked with the opposition. Furthermore, while continued economic growth has produced a degree of political and economic stability, it comes at the cost of ongoing governmental pressure on civil society, media, local governance, and the judiciary. As a result, corruption, especially among government officials, remains one of the greatest hurdles to democratic progress.

5.14↑ **Armenia.** Democratic developments in Armenia remain, for the most part, stagnant owing to weak governance, tensions between the government and opposition, and ongoing corruption. In November 2005, a national referendum that occurred by a flawed and much criticized process nevertheless ushered in constitutional amendments that should provide a more even balance of power between the president, the Parliament, and the judiciary. Although slight improvements were noted in the judicial framework and independence rating, the government's failure to ensure democratic elections and slow decentralization of authority and the popular perception that most Armenians have not benefited from macroeconomic growth have led to disillusionment in Armenia's political and economic transition.

4.86↑ **Georgia.** In 2005, Georgia made modest yet promising steps in its fight against corruption, in ensuring the protection of human rights and the independence of the judiciary, and in strengthening local democratic governance. Ratings in these areas have risen, while those in electoral process, civil society, media independence, and national governance have remained unchanged, owing in part to tensions between the government and opposition as well as slackened activities of civil society following the Rose Revolution. In May 2005, Georgia reached an agreement with Russia on the withdrawal of its military bases from Georgian territory within three years. In June, the government adopted the National Anticorruption Strategy and Action Plan, which focuses on, among many things, increased efficiency and transparency in civil service, strengthening the offices of general inspectorates within public agencies, and instituting reforms in law enforcement bodies.

The Balkans

5.36↓ **Kosovo.*** In early 2005, the international community initiated talks to determine Kosovo's status, beginning with UN envoy Kai Eide's report to the Security Council, which set the stage for a year of critical analysis of Kosovo's governing institutions. Despite increased international scrutiny, few if any steps were taken toward reform. Voter turnout in 2005 once again proved poor. Elections brought the opposition to the Parliament, from which they frequently walked out over power struggles. Activities of the civil society, especially those related to anticorruption and transparency, have decreased. Courts remained overloaded owing in part to the confusion caused by three sets of laws and a lack of implementation. While the necessary long haul of local governance reforms has been put on hold, a general consolidation of services took place. Corruption remains a high concern, especially with widespread reports in 2005 of national- and local-level corruption.

4.07↑ **Bosnia-Herzegovina.** In late 2005, a deal on police reform paved the way for opening Stabilization and Association Agreement negotiations with the EU, demonstrating the efforts taking place throughout the year to integrate Bosnia-Herzegovina into Euro-Atlantic structures. Ratings improvements were noted in electoral process, judicial framework and independence, and corruption. Public broadcast reform, a secondary issue for entering negotiations, proved problematic throughout the year. Governance remained surprisingly stable despite the January resignation of the Republika Sprska government and strained relationships among cabinet members. The Election Commission initiated several projects, including an evaluation of the Law on Elections and implementation of the Law on Conflict of Interest. The Law on Local Self-Governance, passed early in the year, awaits implementation. The War Crimes Chamber became fully functional in March, and a number of reforms addressing efficiency, backlogs, independence, and capacity continued throughout 2005. Corruption remains widespread.

3.89↓ **Montenegro.*** Debates over the 2006 referendum on independence dominated much of 2005. Media independence came under fire in relation to the referendum, leading to the dismissal of the public TV program director and the resignation of the entire editorial team. Despite a number of positive steps in the fight against corruption, the development of a stable system of governmental checks and balances, and the adoption of several long-awaited laws in the Parliament, implementation is either lacking or just under way, leaving most ratings unchanged in 2005. Both electoral process and civil society ratings worsened this year as a result of blurring of political, state, and civil functions as well as political antagonisms hindering the electoral procedure.

3.82↑ **Macedonia.** In the run-up to gaining EU candidacy status, Macedonia made positive reforms in the areas of national and local democratic governance and corruption, leading to improved ratings in each. At the same time, the first round of postponed local government elections was severely flawed. The government focused on reforming the judiciary, ensuring its independence and tackling long-standing backlogs; however, these efforts await implementation. Likewise, while decentralization processes led to a transfer of central competences to local governments in July, many municipalities must overcome low staff capacity in taking on new responsibilities. Attacks on journalists decreased in 2005, yet a number of editors and journalists from A1 Television resigned, claiming lack of independence. Libel remains a criminal offense, and in 2005 several journalists were given probationary prison sentences.

3.79↑ **Albania.** In 2005, Albania made the greatest progress among Balkan countries and territories. Ratings improved in every area except corruption, as recent government efforts to combat corruption, including adoption of the Law on the Prevention of Conflicts of Interest, have yet to yield results. While considerable obstacles remain for Albania's continued growth, including organized crime, partially free and fair elections, weak civil society, low freedom of the media, and uneven enforcement of the law, 2005 showed positive trends to counter these concerns. Efforts to enhance the efficiency of local democratic governance were especially striking, displaying increased managerial and administrative capacities, receptiveness to citizens' needs, and willingness to tackle decentralization.

3.71↑ **Serbia.*** The voluntary surrender of more than a dozen indicted war criminals to the International Criminal Tribunal for the Former Yugoslavia (ICTY) was perhaps the most notable event for Serbia in 2005, followed by the European Commission's invitation to begin negotiations for a Stabilization and Association Agreement in October. Problems related to lack of political will and ongoing power struggles have severely limited Serbia's democratic progress. The Parliament met on only seven occasions in 2005. Power struggles resulting from elections in 2004 have locked local governance into a stalemate. Civil society continued to face hostile government, media, and society. And despite some legal reforms and positive initiatives, including increased cooperation with the ICTY, the judiciary, prone to corruption and political interference, remains the weakest point in Serbia's transformation. Corruption formally improved slightly owing to changes in the legal framework, while visible efforts on behalf of the government are blatantly lacking.

3.71↑ **Croatia.** With EU accession negotiations beginning late in 2005, following greater cooperation with The Hague tribunal, the development and initiation of major reforms are expected for Croatia only in the next few years. In 2005, Croatia carried out much needed reform in the judicial system by tackling serious backlogs in the Land Registry Office and adopting a new Law on the Courts. Limited progress was made in public administration reform by adopting the Law on Civil Service. Deficits in the electoral procedure became evident in presidential and local government elections held in 2005, raising concerns over misuse of voter lists. The outcome of local elections led to a number of attempts at power brokerage, stymieing local governance functions for some months and strengthening the proposed draft bill on direct elections of mayors and county prefects put forth in September. Government responses to worsening public perception included the resignation of Foreign Minister Miomir Zuzul and preparation of the National Program for the Fight Against Corruption, to be presented in 2006. Ratings improved for judicial framework and independence and civil society, but worsened for electoral process.

3.39→ **Romania.** Romania signed the Treaty of Accession to the European Union in April 2005. Yet policy making, cooperation, and civil service reform took a backseat to ongoing power struggles such as the question of early elections, which locked the Parliament in debate and led to dismissals and replacements within the coalition government in late August. Civil society continued to play an important role in EU accession and democratization efforts by cooperating as an advocate for policy reform and was especially successful in the transparency field, where NGOs brought decisive input to new legislation on procurement and to the regulation of state advertising in the media. In the first half of the year, the government adopted the Strategy and Action Plan 2005-2007 for judicial reform, which focuses directly on judicial processes, and a revision of a 2004 package for judicial reform, with results anticipated in 2006. Corruption remains a major concern.

2.96↑ **Bulgaria.** In 2005, Bulgaria signed the Treaty of Accession to the European Union and continued ongoing processes of stabilizing governance structures. In this regard, Bulgaria's ratings for 2005 have improved in the areas of independent media, national and local democratic governance, judicial framework and independence, and corruption. National and local democratic governance improved markedly this year as parliamentary elections in June led to a trilateral coalition focused on reforms needed for EU accession and as new laws enhanced the structure of local governance and allowed the right to issue debt. Judicial reforms, the most serious problem facing Bulgaria, are progressing slowly; however, a national ombudsman was appointed in 2005. Despite advancements in fighting corruption, criminal activity persists.

---

*In *Nations in Transit 2006*, Freedom House provides separate ratings for Serbia, Montenegro, and Kosovo in order to provide a clearer picture of processes and conditions in the three different administrative areas. Doing so does not indicate a position on the part of Freedom House regarding the territorial integrity of the State Union of Serbia and Montenegro; neither does it indicate a position on Kosovo's future status. As this edition goes to print, the population of Montenegro voted in a referendum in support of independence from the State Union of Serbia and Montenegro; international authorities accepted the referendum results as legitimate and binding. Negotiations will take place over the course of 2006 for the separation of Serbia and Montenegro into independent states. The decision to keep Serbia and Montenegro together in this edition was based on country status as of the end of 2005, the year in study.

New European Union Members

2.25↓ **Czech Republic.** One year following the Czech Republic's entry into the EU, Czech citizens remain optimistic regarding their standard of living but disillusioned with the intentions of politicians and their will to tackle corruption. Indeed, following the reforms that marked 2004, the lack of reform in 2005, numerous corruption cases, and the scandal that led to the replacement of Prime Minister Stanislaw Gross suggest that politicians have lost their inspiration. As a result, with the exception of the judiciary, the performance of democratic institutions has stagnated in the Czech Republic. Judicial framework and independence saw a slight improvement as, while awaiting necessary reforms, judicial appointments and pay raises were made, strengtheningthe independence of the judiciary from other branches.

2.21→ **Lithuania.** In 2005, rampant political corruption became clearly visible when a chain of scandals broke among top politicians. Numerous ad hoc commissions investigating conflict-of-interest allegations frequently interrupted the legislative work of the new Parliament and coalition government. Yet parliamentary oversight was strengthened through a new audit committee whose work quickly led to a number of assessments and reforms of local and national governance. Electoral and public campaign laws were amended to ban the use of gifts, concerts, and events as campaign tools. Civil society continued to grow despite low public awareness and support. At the same time, public confidence in the media continued to drop following consolidation trends in the media market. Courts remain the least trusted institutions in public opinion polls, most likely as a result of unsatisfactory prison conditions and police abuse, despite improvements made in 2005 in both the bailiff system and the expansion of the equal opportunity ombudsman's mandate.

2.14↓ **Poland.** Among new EU members, Poland's democracy score reflects the most significant decline and worsening trends in national democratic governance, independent media, judicial framework and independence, and corruption. Within the judicial system, considered the weakest aspect of governance, cases of judges and prosecutors engaging in illegal activities arose, while problems such as delays, political influence over prosecutors, and prison crowding went unaddressed. Corruption remained a serious problem in 2005, notably in the areas of health care, military, and sports. Following elections in September, a new right-wing government led by the Law and Justice Party gained power and took on old and new problems of addressing the past and balancing power. At the same time, media independence suffered at the hands of the new government, which took over public media, applied pressure to journalists, and displayed a particular bias for a Catholic media conglomerate.

2.07↑ **Latvia.** Although Latvia continues to experience post-Communist economic growth and development, problems surrounding economic disparity, corruption, and minority dissonance continue to prevent further growth and enhanced satisfaction with quality of life. Economic disparity is especially visible in the widening and debilitating gulf among 500 units of local governance. Media, civil society, and national government provide ample information to engage citizens in processes of governance, yet voter participation, as witnessed in municipal elections in March, has dropped significantly from 2001. The four-party coalition government demonstrated openness, stability, and focus in 2005. Although problems of prolonged pretrial detention and limited access to legal aid persist, positive developments have been made in fighting corruption, mostly through strengthening Latvia's anticorruption organization, the KNAB.

2.00↓ **Hungary.** Hungary's democratic institutions remained stable in 2005 despite the Parliament's continued noncompliance with a number of Constitutional Court adjudications aimed at improving its operations. In November, an updated procedural Law on Administration entered into force, responding to Internet-based service provision and the need for increased efficiency. Fiscal viability continued to present a concern, especially among institutions of local democratic governance that have otherwise served as a model in the region. Civil society gained victories by embedding nonviolent civic participation in political processes that were otherwise focused on early campaigning for the 2006 national elections. Continued debates over legal regulation and the financing of public service broadcasting as well as a high number of libel lawsuits stymied independent media. Nontransparent business activities among political parties and public officials also continued in 2005 as a result of ineffective implementation of anticorruption legislation, worsening Hungary's 2005 rating for corruption.

1.96↑ **Slovakia.** Slovakia's democratic institutions remained stable and effective throughout 2005. Although the ruling coalition underwent formal changes in its composition, these changes did not alter the operations and focus of the national government, resulting in an improved local democratic governance rating. Regional elections were held and deemed free and democratic. The Parliament passed a number of laws and reforms to increase transparency and accountability and combat overall corruption. These reforms especially strengthened local governance and allowed local and regional self-governments to take on those duties transferred to them by the central government. The new penal code was enacted in 2005, increasing efficiency of the judiciary, while at the same time the Parliament's inability to nominate a judge limited the competency of the Constitutional Court.

1.96→ **Estonia.** Estonia's ratings remain unchanged this year despite increased public confidence in the presidency, intensified efforts to integrate its non-citizens, and progress towards meeting European Union requirements for adoption of the euro and inclusion in the Schengen Zone. However, Estonia continues to face problems linked to uneven economic growth, lack of public trust in authorities, low electoral turnout, poor prison conditions, and public perception of widespread corruption. Discussions on the noncitizen issue, direct presidential elections, and the transfer of taxation power, while a positive indicator of civil interest, did not lead to any specific actions or reforms.

1.75↓ **Slovenia.** The new ruling coalition, composed mostly of right-wing parties, spent most of 2005 involved in takeover procedures, reflecting the general political atmosphere of talk without action. Political elites and state actors continued to influence the economy and – as demonstrated in passing the Law on Radio Television Slovenia in 2005 – threaten the independence of media as well as the representation of civil society in public broadcast services. The government's receptiveness toward civil society initiatives appears to be waning and warrants concern. The corruption rating slipped as an amendment transferring the competences of the Slovene Commission for the Prevention of Corruption to the Parliament also raised concerns over its independence.

Tables

Table 1. Nations In Transit 2006

Rating and Democracy Score Summary

Country/Territory	EP	CS	IM	NGOV	LGOV	JFI	CO	DS
Albania	3.50	3.00	3.75	4.00	2.75	4.25	5.25	3.79
Armenia	5.75	3.50	5.50	5.00	5.50	5.00	5.75	5.14
Azerbaijan	6.50	5.00	6.00	6.00	6.00	5.75	6.25	5.93
Belarus	7.00	6.75	6.75	7.00	6.50	6.75	6.25	6.71
Bosnia	3.00	3.75	4.00	4.75	4.75	4.00	4.25	4.07
Bulgaria	1.75	2.75	3.25	3.00	3.00	3.00	3.75	2.93
Croatia	3.25	2.75	3.75	3.50	3.75	4.25	4.75	3.71
Czech Rep.	2.00	1.50	2.00	2.50	2.00	2.25	3.50	2.25
Estonia	1.50	2.00	1.50	2.25	2.50	1.50	2.50	1.96
Georgia	4.75	3.50	4.25	5.50	5.75	4.75	5.50	4.86
Hungary	1.25	1.25	2.50	2.00	2.25	1.75	3.00	2.00
Kazakhstan	6.50	5.75	6.75	6.75	6.25	6.25	6.50	6.39
Kosovo	4.75	4.25	5.50	5.75	5.50	5.75	6.00	5.36
Kyrgyzstan	5.75	4.50	5.75	6.00	6.25	5.50	6.00	5.68
Latvia	1.75	1.75	1.50	2.00	2.50	1.75	3.25	2.07
Lithuania	1.75	1.50	1.75	2.50	2.50	1.50	4.00	2.21
Macedonia	3.25	3.25	4.25	3.75	3.75	3.75	4.75	3.82
Moldova	3.75	4.00	5.00	5.75	5.75	4.50	6.00	4.96
Montenegro	3.50	3.00	3.25	4.50	3.50	4.25	5.25	3.89
Poland	1.75	1.25	1.75	2.75	2.00	2.25	3.25	2.14
Romania	2.75	2.25	4.00	3.50	3.00	4.00	4.25	3.39
Russia	6.25	5.00	6.00	6.00	5.75	5.25	6.00	5.75
Serbia	3.25	2.75	3.25	4.00	3.75	4.25	4.75	3.71
Slovakia	1.25	1.25	2.25	2.00	2.00	2.00	3.00	1.96
Slovenia	1.50	1.75	1.75	2.00	1.50	1.50	2.25	1.75
Tajikistan	6.25	5.00	6.25	6.25	5.75	5.75	6.25	5.93
Turkmenistan	7.00	7.00	7.00	7.00	7.00	7.00	6.75	6.96
Ukraine	3.25	2.75	3.75	4.50	5.25	4.25	5.75	4.21
Uzbekistan	6.75	7.00	7.00	7.00	6.75	6.75	6.50	6.82
Average	3.84	3.44	4.14	4.40	4.26	4.12	4.87	4.15
Median	3.25	3.00	4.00	4.50	3.75	4.25	5.25	3.89

The ratings are based on a scale of 1 to 7, with 1 representing the highest level of democratic progress and 7 the lowest. The 2006 ratings reflect the period January 1 through December 31, 2005.

The Democracy Score (DS) is an average of ratings for Electoral Process (EP); Civil Society (CS); Independent Media (IM); National Democratic Governance (NGOV); Local Democratic Governance (LGOV); Judicial Framework and Independence (JFI); and Corruption (CO).

In *Nations in Transit 2006*, Freedom House provides separate ratings for Serbia, Montenegro, and Kosovo in order to provide a clearer picture of processes and conditions in the three different administrative areas. Doing so does not indicate a position on the part of Freedom House regarding the territorial integrity of the State Union of Serbia and Montenegro; neither does it indicate a position on Kosovo's future status.

Table 2. Electoral Process

Ratings History and Regional Breakdown

	1997	1998	1999	2001	2002	2003	2004	2005	2006
New EU Members									
Czech Rep.	1.25	1.25	1.75	1.75	2.00	2.00	2.00	2.00	2.00
Estonia	2.00	1.75	1.75	1.75	1.75	1.75	1.50	1.50	1.50
Hungary	1.25	1.25	1.25	1.25	1.25	1.25	1.25	1.25	1.25
Latvia	2.00	2.00	1.75	1.75	1.75	1.75	1.75	1.75	1.75
Lithuania	2.00	1.75	1.75	1.75	1.75	1.75	1.75	1.75	1.75
Poland	1.50	1.25	1.25	1.25	1.25	1.50	1.50	1.75	1.75
Slovakia	3.75	3.50	2.50	2.25	1.75	1.50	1.50	1.25	1.25
Slovenia	2.00	2.00	2.00	1.75	1.75	1.50	1.50	1.50	1.50
Average	1.97	1.84	1.75	1.69	1.66	1.63	1.59	1.59	1.59
Median	2.00	1.75	1.75	1.75	1.75	1.63	1.50	1.63	1.63
The Balkans									
Albania	4.25	4.50	4.25	4.00	3.75	3.75	3.75	3.75	3.50
Bosnia	n/a	5.00	5.00	4.75	4.25	3.75	3.50	3.25	3.00
Bulgaria	3.25	2.75	2.25	2.00	2.00	2.00	1.75	1.75	1.75
Croatia	4.00	4.25	4.25	3.25	3.25	3.25	3.25	3.00	3.25
Macedonia	3.50	3.50	3.50	3.75	4.50	3.50	3.50	3.00	3.25
Romania	3.25	3.25	2.75	3.00	3.00	2.75	2.75	2.75	2.75
Yugoslavia	n/a	5.00	5.50	4.75	3.75	3.75	n/a	n/a	n/a
Serbia	n/a	n/a	n/a	n/a	n/a	n/a	3.50	3.25	3.25
Montenegro	n/a	n/a	n/a	n/a	n/a	n/a	3.50	3.25	3.50
Kosovo	n/a	n/a	n/a	n/a	n/a	n/a	5.25	4.75	4.75
Average	3.65	4.06	3.93	3.64	3.50	3.25	3.42	3.19	3.22
Median	3.50	4.25	4.25	3.75	3.75	3.50	3.50	3.25	3.25
Non-Baltic Former Soviet States									
Armenia	5.50	5.75	5.25	5.50	5.50	5.50	5.75	5.75	5.75
Azerbaijan	5.75	5.50	5.50	5.75	5.75	5.75	6.00	6.25	6.50
Belarus	6.00	6.25	6.75	6.75	6.75	6.75	6.75	7.00	7.00
Georgia	5.00	4.50	4.00	4.50	5.00	5.25	5.25	4.75	4.75
Kazakhstan	5.50	5.50	6.00	6.25	6.25	6.50	6.50	6.50	6.50
Kyrgyzstan	5.00	5.00	5.00	5.75	5.75	6.00	6.00	6.00	5.75
Moldova	3.25	3.50	3.25	3.25	3.50	3.75	4.00	4.00	3.75
Russia	3.50	3.50	4.00	4.25	4.50	4.75	5.50	6.00	6.25
Tajikistan	6.00	5.75	5.50	5.25	5.25	5.25	5.75	6.00	6.25
Turkmenistan	7.00	7.00	7.00	7.00	7.00	7.00	7.00	7.00	7.00
Ukraine	3.25	3.50	3.50	4.00	4.50	4.00	4.25	3.50	3.25
Uzbekistan	6.25	6.50	6.50	6.75	6.75	6.75	6.75	6.75	6.75
Average	5.17	5.19	5.19	5.42	5.54	5.60	5.79	5.79	5.79
Median	5.50	5.50	5.38	5.63	5.63	5.63	5.88	6.00	6.25

The ratings are based on a scale of 1 to 7, with 1 representing the highest level of democratic progress and 7 the lowest. The 2006 ratings reflect the period January 1 through December 31, 2005.

Table 3. Civil Society

Ratings History and Regional Breakdown

	1997	1998	1999	2001	2002	2003	2004	2005	2006
New EU Members									
Czech Rep.	1.50	1.50	1.50	1.50	1.75	1.50	1.50	1.50	1.50
Estonia	2.25	2.25	2.50	2.25	2.00	2.00	2.00	2.00	2.00
Hungary	1.25	1.25	1.25	1.25	1.25	1.25	1.25	1.25	1.25
Latvia	2.25	2.25	2.25	2.00	2.00	2.00	2.00	1.75	1.75
Lithuania	2.25	2.00	2.00	1.75	1.50	1.50	1.50	1.50	1.50
Poland	1.25	1.25	1.25	1.25	1.25	1.25	1.25	1.25	1.25
Slovakia	3.25	3.00	2.25	2.00	1.75	1.50	1.25	1.25	1.25
Slovenia	2.00	2.00	1.75	1.75	1.50	1.50	1.50	1.75	1.75
Average	2.00	1.94	1.84	1.72	1.63	1.56	1.53	1.53	1.53
Median	2.13	2.00	1.88	1.75	1.63	1.50	1.50	1.50	1.50
The Balkans									
Albania	4.25	4.25	4.00	4.00	3.75	3.75	3.50	3.25	3.00
Bosnia	n/a	5.00	4.50	4.50	4.25	4.00	3.75	3.75	3.75
Bulgaria	4.00	3.75	3.75	3.50	3.25	3.25	3.00	2.75	2.75
Croatia	3.50	3.50	3.50	2.75	2.75	3.00	3.00	3.00	2.75
Macedonia	3.75	3.75	3.50	3.75	4.00	3.75	3.25	3.25	3.25
Romania	3.75	3.75	3.00	3.00	3.00	2.75	2.50	2.25	2.25
Yugoslavia	n/a	5.00	5.25	4.00	3.00	2.75	n/a	n/a	n/a
Serbia	n/a	n/a	n/a	n/a	n/a	n/a	2.75	2.75	2.75
Montenegro	n/a	n/a	n/a	n/a	n/a	n/a	2.75	2.50	3.00
Kosovo	n/a	n/a	n/a	n/a	n/a	n/a	4.25	4.00	4.25
Average	3.85	4.14	3.93	3.64	3.43	3.32	3.19	3.06	3.08
Median	3.75	3.75	3.75	3.75	3.25	3.25	3.00	3.00	3.00
Non-Baltic Former Soviet States									
Armenia	3.50	3.50	3.50	3.50	3.50	3.50	3.50	3.50	3.50
Azerbaijan	5.00	5.00	4.75	4.50	4.50	4.25	4.50	4.75	5.00
Belarus	5.25	5.75	6.00	6.50	6.25	6.50	6.75	6.75	6.75
Georgia	4.50	4.25	3.75	4.00	4.00	4.00	3.50	3.50	3.50
Kazakhstan	5.25	5.00	5.00	5.00	5.50	5.50	5.50	5.50	5.75
Kyrgyzstan	4.50	4.50	4.50	4.50	4.50	4.50	4.50	4.50	4.50
Moldova	3.75	3.75	3.75	3.75	4.00	3.75	4.00	4.00	4.00
Russia	3.75	4.00	3.75	4.00	4.00	4.25	4.50	4.75	5.00
Tajikistan	5.50	5.25	5.25	5.00	5.00	5.00	5.00	4.75	5.00
Turkmenistan	7.00	7.00	7.00	7.00	7.00	7.00	7.00	7.00	7.00
Ukraine	4.00	4.25	4.00	3.75	3.75	3.50	3.75	3.00	2.75
Uzbekistan	6.50	6.50	6.50	6.50	6.75	6.50	6.50	6.50	7.00
Average	4.88	4.90	4.81	4.83	4.90	4.85	4.92	4.88	4.98
Median	4.75	4.75	4.63	4.50	4.50	4.38	4.50	4.75	5.00

The ratings are based on a scale of 1 to 7, with 1 representing the highest level of democratic progress and 7 the lowest. The 2006 ratings reflect the period January 1 through December 31, 2005.

Table 4. Independent Media

Ratings History and Regional Breakdown

	1997	1998	1999	2001	2002	2003	2004	2005	2006
New EU Members									
Czech Rep.	1.25	1.25	1.75	2.00	2.50	2.25	2.25	2.00	2.00
Estonia	1.75	1.75	1.75	1.75	1.75	1.75	1.50	1.50	1.50
Hungary	1.50	1.50	2.00	2.25	2.25	2.25	2.25	2.50	2.50
Latvia	1.75	1.75	1.75	1.75	1.75	1.75	1.50	1.50	1.50
Lithuania	1.75	1.50	1.75	1.75	1.75	1.75	1.75	1.75	1.75
Poland	1.50	1.50	1.50	1.50	1.50	1.75	1.75	1.50	1.75
Slovakia	4.25	4.00	2.25	2.00	2.00	2.00	2.25	2.25	2.25
Slovenia	1.75	1.75	1.75	1.75	1.75	1.75	1.75	1.50	1.75
Average	1.94	1.88	1.81	1.84	1.91	1.91	1.88	1.81	1.88
Median	1.75	1.63	1.75	1.75	1.75	1.75	1.75	1.63	1.75
The Balkans									
Albania	4.75	4.75	4.50	4.25	4.00	4.00	3.75	4.00	3.75
Bosnia	n/a	4.75	5.00	4.50	4.25	4.25	4.25	4.00	4.00
Bulgaria	3.75	3.50	3.50	3.25	3.25	3.50	3.50	3.50	3.25
Croatia	4.75	4.75	5.00	3.50	3.50	3.75	3.75	3.75	3.75
Macedonia	4.00	4.00	3.75	3.75	3.75	4.00	4.25	4.25	4.25
Romania	4.25	4.00	3.50	3.50	3.50	3.75	3.75	4.00	4.00
Yugoslavia	n/a	4.50	5.75	4.50	3.50	3.25	n/a	n/a	n/a
Serbia	n/a	n/a	n/a	n/a	n/a	n/a	3.50	3.25	3.25
Montenegro	n/a	n/a	n/a	n/a	n/a	n/a	3.25	3.25	3.25
Kosovo	n/a	n/a	n/a	n/a	n/a	n/a	5.50	5.50	5.50
Average	4.30	4.32	4.58	3.96	3.71	3.79	3.94	3.94	3.89
Median	4.25	4.50	4.50	3.75	3.50	3.75	3.75	4.00	3.75
Non-Baltic Former Soviet States									
Armenia	5.25	5.25	4.75	4.75	4.75	5.00	5.25	5.50	5.50
Azerbaijan	5.50	5.50	5.50	5.75	5.50	5.50	5.75	6.00	6.00
Belarus	6.25	6.50	6.75	6.75	6.75	6.75	6.75	6.75	6.75
Georgia	4.50	4.25	3.75	3.50	3.75	4.00	4.00	4.25	4.25
Kazakhstan	5.25	5.50	5.50	6.00	6.00	6.25	6.50	6.50	6.75
Kyrgyzstan	5.00	5.00	5.00	5.00	5.75	6.00	6.00	5.75	5.75
Moldova	4.00	4.25	4.00	4.25	4.50	4.75	5.00	5.00	5.00
Russia	3.75	4.25	4.75	5.25	5.50	5.50	5.75	6.00	6.00
Tajikistan	6.25	6.00	5.75	5.50	5.75	5.75	5.75	6.00	6.25
Turkmenistan	7.00	7.00	7.00	7.00	7.00	7.00	7.00	7.00	7.00
Ukraine	4.50	4.75	5.00	5.25	5.50	5.50	5.50	4.75	3.75
Uzbekistan	6.50	6.50	6.50	6.75	6.75	6.75	6.75	6.75	7.00
Average	5.31	5.40	5.35	5.48	5.63	5.73	5.83	5.85	5.83
Median	5.25	5.38	5.25	5.38	5.63	5.63	5.75	6.00	6.00

The ratings are based on a scale of 1 to 7, with 1 representing the highest level of democratic progress and 7 the lowest. The 2006 ratings reflect the period January 1 through December 31, 2005.

Table 5. Governance*

Ratings History and Regional Breakdown

	1997 GOV	1998 GOV	1999 GOV	2001 GOV	2002 GOV	2003 GOV	2004 GOV	2005 NGOV	2005 LGOV	2006 NGOV	2006 LGOV
New EU Members											
Czech Rep.	2.00	2.00	2.00	2.00	2.25	2.25	2.25	2.50	2.00	2.50	2.00
Estonia	2.25	2.25	2.25	2.25	2.25	2.25	2.25	2.25	2.50	2.25	2.50
Hungary	1.75	1.75	2.50	3.00	3.00	2.50	2.50	2.00	2.25	2.00	2.25
Latvia	2.50	2.50	2.50	2.25	2.25	2.25	2.25	2.25	2.50	2.00	2.50
Lithuania	2.50	2.50	2.50	2.50	2.50	2.50	2.50	2.50	2.50	2.50	2.50
Poland	1.75	1.75	1.75	1.75	2.00	2.00	2.00	2.50	2.00	2.75	2.00
Slovakia	3.75	3.75	3.00	2.75	2.25	2.25	2.25	2.00	2.25	2.00	2.00
Slovenia	2.50	2.50	2.25	2.50	2.25	2.25	2.00	2.00	1.50	2.00	1.50
Average	2.38	2.38	2.34	2.38	2.34	2.28	2.25	2.25	2.19	2.25	2.16
Median	2.38	2.38	2.38	2.38	2.25	2.25	2.25	2.25	2.25	2.13	2.13
The Balkans											
Albania	4.75	5.00	4.75	4.25	4.25	4.25	4.25	4.25	3.25	4.00	2.75
Bosnia	n/a	6.00	6.00	6.00	5.50	5.25	5.00	4.75	4.75	4.75	4.75
Bulgaria	4.25	4.00	3.75	3.50	3.50	3.75	3.75	3.50	3.50	3.00	3.00
Croatia	4.00	4.00	4.00	3.50	3.50	3.75	3.75	3.50	3.75	3.50	3.75
Macedonia	4.00	4.00	3.00	3.75	4.25	4.50	4.00	4.00	4.00	3.75	3.75
Romania	4.25	4.00	3.50	3.75	3.75	3.75	3.75	3.50	3.00	3.50	3.00
Yugoslavia	n/a	5.00	5.50	5.25	4.25	4.25	n/a	n/a	n/a	n/a	n/a
Serbia	n/a	n/a	n/a	n/a	n/a	n/a	4.00	4.00	3.75	4.00	3.75
Montenegro	n/a	n/a	n/a	n/a	n/a	n/a	4.00	4.50	3.50	4.50	3.50
Kosovo	n/a	n/a	n/a	n/a	n/a	n/a	6.00	5.75	5.50	5.75	5.50
Average	4.25	4.57	4.36	4.29	4.14	4.21	4.28	4.19	3.89	4.08	3.75
Median	4.25	4.00	4.00	3.75	4.25	4.25	4.00	4.00	3.75	4.00	3.75
Non-Baltic Former Soviet States											
Armenia	4.50	4.50	4.50	4.50	4.50	4.75	4.75	5.00	5.50	5.00	5.50
Azerbaijan	6.25	6.25	6.25	6.25	6.00	5.75	5.75	6.00	6.00	6.00	6.00
Belarus	6.00	6.25	6.25	6.25	6.50	6.50	6.50	6.75	6.50	7.00	6.50
Georgia	4.50	5.00	4.50	4.75	5.00	5.50	5.75	5.50	6.00	5.50	5.75
Kazakhstan	5.50	5.50	5.00	5.00	5.75	6.25	6.25	6.50	6.25	6.75	6.25
Kyrgyzstan	4.25	4.50	5.00	5.25	5.50	6.00	6.00	6.00	5.75	6.00	6.25
Moldova	4.25	4.50	4.50	4.50	4.75	5.25	5.50	5.75	5.75	5.75	5.75
Russia	4.00	4.50	4.50	5.00	5.25	5.00	5.25	5.75	5.75	6.00	5.75
Tajikistan	7.00	6.75	6.25	6.00	6.00	6.00	5.75	6.00	5.75	6.25	5.75
Turkmenistan	6.75	6.75	6.75	6.75	6.75	6.75	7.00	7.00	7.00	7.00	7.00
Ukraine	4.50	4.75	4.75	4.75	5.00	5.00	5.25	5.00	5.25	4.50	5.25
Uzbekistan	6.00	6.25	6.25	6.00	6.00	6.25	6.25	6.50	6.25	7.00	6.75
Average	5.29	5.46	5.38	5.42	5.58	5.75	5.83	5.98	5.98	6.06	6.04
Median	5.00	5.25	5.00	5.13	5.63	5.88	5.75	6.00	5.88	6.00	5.88

The ratings are based on a scale of 1 to 7, with 1 representing the highest level of democratic progress and 7 the lowest. The 2006 ratings reflect the period January 1 through December 31, 2005.

*Starting with the 2005 edition, Freedom House introduced separate ratings for national democratic governance and local democratic governance.

Table 6. Judicial Framework and Independence*

Ratings History and Regional Breakdown

	1997	1998	1999	2001	2002	2003	2004	2005	2006
New EU Members									
Czech Rep.	1.50	1.50	2.25	2.50	2.50	2.50	2.50	2.50	2.25
Estonia	2.25	2.25	2.00	2.00	1.75	1.75	1.75	1.50	1.50
Hungary	1.75	1.75	1.75	2.00	2.00	1.75	1.75	1.75	1.75
Latvia	2.25	2.25	2.00	2.00	2.00	2.25	2.00	1.75	1.75
Lithuania	2.25	2.00	2.00	1.75	2.00	1.75	1.75	1.75	1.50
Poland	1.50	1.50	1.50	1.50	1.50	1.50	1.50	2.00	2.25
Slovakia	4.00	4.00	2.50	2.25	2.00	2.00	2.00	2.00	2.00
Slovenia	1.75	1.50	1.50	1.50	1.75	1.75	1.75	1.50	1.50
Average	2.16	2.09	1.94	1.94	1.94	1.91	1.88	1.84	1.81
Median	2.00	1.88	2.00	2.00	2.00	1.75	1.75	1.75	1.75
The Balkans									
Albania	4.75	5.25	5.00	4.50	4.50	4.25	4.25	4.50	4.25
Bosnia	n/a	6.00	6.00	5.50	5.25	5.00	4.50	4.25	4.00
Bulgaria	4.25	3.75	3.50	3.50	3.50	3.50	3.25	3.25	3.00
Croatia	4.75	4.75	4.75	3.75	3.75	4.25	4.50	4.50	4.25
Macedonia	4.25	4.50	4.25	4.25	4.75	4.50	4.00	3.75	3.75
Romania	4.25	4.25	4.25	4.25	4.25	4.25	4.25	4.00	4.00
Yugoslavia	n/a	5.00	5.75	5.50	4.25	4.25	n/a	n/a	n/a
Serbia	n/a	n/a	n/a	n/a	n/a	n/a	4.25	4.25	4.25
Montenegro	n/a	n/a	n/a	n/a	n/a	n/a	4.25	4.25	4.25
Kosovo	n/a	n/a	n/a	n/a	n/a	n/a	6.00	5.75	5.75
Average	4.45	4.79	4.79	4.46	4.32	4.29	4.36	4.28	4.17
Median	4.25	4.75	4.75	4.25	4.25	4.25	4.25	4.25	4.25
Non-Baltic Former Soviet States									
Armenia	4.75	5.00	5.00	5.00	5.00	5.00	5.00	5.25	5.00
Azerbaijan	5.50	5.50	5.50	5.25	5.25	5.25	5.50	5.75	5.75
Belarus	6.00	6.25	6.50	6.75	6.75	6.75	6.75	6.75	6.75
Georgia	5.00	4.75	4.00	4.00	4.25	4.50	4.50	5.00	4.75
Kazakhstan	5.00	5.25	5.50	5.75	6.00	6.25	6.25	6.25	6.25
Kyrgyzstan	4.50	4.50	5.00	5.25	5.25	5.50	5.50	5.50	5.50
Moldova	4.25	4.00	4.00	4.00	4.00	4.50	4.50	4.75	4.50
Russia	4.00	4.25	4.25	4.50	4.75	4.50	4.75	5.25	5.25
Tajikistan	6.25	6.00	5.75	5.75	5.75	5.75	5.75	5.75	5.75
Turkmenistan	6.75	6.75	6.75	7.00	7.00	7.00	7.00	7.00	7.00
Ukraine	3.75	4.00	4.50	4.50	4.75	4.50	4.75	4.25	4.25
Uzbekistan	6.50	6.50	6.50	6.50	6.50	6.50	6.50	6.25	6.75
Average	5.19	5.23	5.27	5.35	5.44	5.50	5.56	5.65	5.63
Median	5.00	5.13	5.25	5.25	5.25	5.38	5.50	5.63	5.63

*This category was called Constitutional, Legislative and Judicial Framework in editions before 2005.

The ratings are based on a scale of 1 to 7, with 1 representing the highest level of democratic progress and 7 the lowest. The 2006 ratings reflect the period January 1 through December 31, 2005.

Table 7. Corruption

Ratings History and Regional Breakdown

	1999	2001	2002	2003	2004	2005	2006
New EU Members							
Czech Rep.	3.25	3.75	3.75	3.50	3.50	3.50	3.50
Estonia	3.25	2.75	2.50	2.50	2.50	2.50	2.50
Hungary	2.50	3.00	3.00	2.75	2.75	2.75	3.00
Latvia	3.50	3.50	3.75	3.50	3.50	3.50	3.25
Lithuania	3.75	3.75	3.75	3.50	3.50	3.75	4.00
Poland	2.25	2.25	2.25	2.50	2.50	3.00	3.25
Slovakia	3.75	3.75	3.25	3.25	3.25	3.00	3.00
Slovenia	2.00	2.00	2.00	2.00	2.00	2.00	2.25
Average	**3.03**	**3.09**	**3.03**	**2.94**	**2.94**	**3.00**	**3.09**
Median	**3.25**	**3.25**	**3.13**	**3.00**	**3.00**	**3.00**	**3.13**
The Balkans							
Albania	6.00	5.50	5.25	5.00	5.25	5.25	5.25
Bosnia	6.00	5.75	5.50	5.00	4.75	4.50	4.25
Bulgaria	4.75	4.75	4.50	4.25	4.25	4.00	3.75
Croatia	5.25	4.50	4.50	4.75	4.75	4.75	4.75
Macedonia	5.00	5.00	5.50	5.50	5.00	5.00	4.75
Romania	4.25	4.50	4.75	4.50	4.50	4.25	4.25
Yugoslavia	6.25	6.25	5.25	5.00	n/a	n/a	n/a
Serbia	n/a	n/a	n/a	n/a	5.00	5.00	4.75
Montenegro	n/a	n/a	n/a	n/a	5.25	5.25	5.25
Kosovo	n/a	n/a	n/a	n/a	6.00	6.00	6.00
Average	**5.36**	**5.18**	**5.04**	**4.86**	**4.97**	**4.89**	**4.75**
Median	**5.25**	**5.00**	**5.25**	**5.00**	**5.00**	**5.00**	**4.75**
Non-Baltic Former Soviet States							
Armenia	5.75	5.75	5.75	5.75	5.75	5.75	5.75
Azerbaijan	6.00	6.25	6.25	6.25	6.25	6.25	6.25
Belarus	5.25	5.25	5.25	5.50	5.75	6.00	6.25
Georgia	5.00	5.25	5.50	5.75	6.00	5.75	5.50
Kazakhstan	6.00	6.25	6.25	6.25	6.50	6.50	6.50
Kyrgyzstan	6.00	6.00	6.00	6.00	6.00	6.00	6.00
Moldova	6.00	6.00	6.25	6.25	6.25	6.25	6.00
Russia	6.25	6.25	6.00	5.75	5.75	5.75	6.00
Tajikistan	6.00	6.00	6.00	6.00	6.25	6.25	6.25
Turkmenistan	6.00	6.25	6.25	6.25	6.25	6.50	6.75
Ukraine	6.00	6.00	6.00	5.75	5.75	5.75	5.75
Uzbekistan	6.00	6.00	6.00	6.00	6.00	6.00	6.50
Average	**5.85**	**5.94**	**5.96**	**5.96**	**6.04**	**6.06**	**6.13**
Median	**6.00**	**6.00**	**6.00**	**6.00**	**6.00**	**6.00**	**6.13**

The ratings are based on a scale of 1 to 7, with 1 representing the highest level of democratic progress and 7 the lowest. The 2006 ratings reflect the period January 1 through December 31, 2005.

Table 8. Democracy Score

Year to Year Summaries by Region

	1999	2001	2002	2003	2004	2005	2006
New EU Members							
Czech Rep.	2.08	2.25	2.46	2.33	2.33	2.29	2.25
Estonia	2.25	2.13	2.00	2.00	1.92	1.96	1.96
Hungary	1.88	2.13	2.13	1.96	1.96	1.96	2.00
Latvia	2.29	2.21	2.25	2.25	2.17	2.14	2.07
Lithuania	2.29	2.21	2.21	2.13	2.13	2.21	2.21
Poland	1.58	1.58	1.63	1.75	1.75	2.00	2.14
Slovakia	2.71	2.50	2.17	2.08	2.08	2.00	1.96
Slovenia	1.88	1.88	1.83	1.79	1.75	1.68	1.75
Average	**2.12**	**2.11**	**2.08**	**2.04**	**2.01**	**2.03**	**2.04**
Median	**2.17**	**2.17**	**2.15**	**2.04**	**2.02**	**2.00**	**2.04**
The Balkans							
Albania	4.75	4.42	4.25	4.17	4.13	4.04	3.79
Bosnia	5.42	5.17	4.83	4.54	4.29	4.18	4.07
Bulgaria	3.58	3.42	3.33	3.38	3.25	3.18	2.93
Croatia	4.46	3.54	3.54	3.79	3.83	3.75	3.71
Macedonia	3.83	4.04	4.46	4.29	4.00	3.89	3.82
Romania	3.54	3.67	3.71	3.63	3.58	3.39	3.39
Yugoslavia	5.67	5.04	4.00	3.88	n/a	n/a	n/a
Serbia	n/a	n/a	n/a	n/a	3.83	3.75	3.71
Montenegro	n/a	n/a	n/a	n/a	3.83	3.79	3.89
Kosovo	n/a	n/a	n/a	n/a	5.50	5.32	5.36
Average	**4.46**	**4.18**	**4.02**	**3.95**	**4.03**	**3.92**	**3.85**
Median	**4.46**	**4.04**	**4.00**	**3.88**	**3.83**	**3.79**	**3.79**
Non-Baltic Former Soviet States							
Armenia	4.79	4.83	4.83	4.92	5.00	5.18	5.14
Azerbaijan	5.58	5.63	5.54	5.46	5.63	5.86	5.93
Belarus	6.25	6.38	6.38	6.46	6.54	6.64	6.71
Georgia	4.17	4.33	4.58	4.83	4.83	4.96	4.86
Kazakhstan	5.50	5.71	5.96	6.17	6.25	6.29	6.39
Kyrgyzstan	5.08	5.29	5.46	5.67	5.67	5.64	5.64
Moldova	4.25	4.29	4.50	4.71	4.88	5.07	4.96
Russia	4.58	4.88	5.00	4.96	5.25	5.61	5.75
Tajikistan	5.75	5.58	5.63	5.63	5.71	5.79	5.93
Turkmenistan	6.75	6.83	6.83	6.83	6.88	6.93	6.96
Ukraine	4.63	4.71	4.92	4.71	4.88	4.50	4.21
Uzbekistan	6.38	6.42	6.46	6.46	6.46	6.43	6.82
Average	**5.31**	**5.41**	**5.51**	**5.57**	**5.66**	**5.74**	**5.78**
Median	**5.29**	**5.44**	**5.50**	**5.54**	**5.65**	**5.72**	**5.84**

The ratings are based on a scale of 1 to 7, with 1 representing the highest level of democratic progress and 7 the lowest. The 2006 ratings reflect the period January 1 through December 31, 2005.

Table 9. Democracy Score Rankings 2006

Consolidated Democracies

Slovenia	1.75
Estonia	1.96
Slovakia	1.96
Hungary	2.00
Latvia	2.07
Poland	2.14
Lithuania	2.21
Czech Rep.	2.25
Bulgaria	2.93

Semi-Consolidated Democracies

Romania	3.39
Croatia	3.71
Serbia	3.71
Albania	3.79
Macedonia	3.82
Montenegro	3.89

Transitional Governments or Hybrid Regimes

Bosnia	4.07
Ukraine	4.21
Georgia	4.86
Moldova	4.96

Semi-Consolidated Authoritarian Regimes

Armenia	5.14
Kosovo	5.36
Kyrgyzstan	5.64
Russia	5.75
Tajikistan	5.93
Azerbaijan	5.93

Consolidated Authoritarian Regimes

Kazakhstan	6.39
Belarus	6.71
Uzbekistan	6.82
Turkmenistan	6.96

The Democracy Score follows the 1-to-7 ratings scale, with 1 representing the highest level of democratic progress and 7 the lowest. For more information about regime classifications, see the Ratings and Democracy Score Guidelines in the Methodology.

Albania

Capital: Tirana
Population: 3.1 million
GNI/capita: $2,120
Ethnic Groups: Albanian (95%), Greek (3%),
other (2%)

Nations in Transit Ratings and Averaged Scores

	1997	1998	1999	2001	2002	2003	2004	2005	2006
Electoral Process	4.25	4.50	4.25	4.00	3.75	3.75	3.75	3.75	3.50
Civil Society	4.25	4.25	4.00	4.00	3.75	3.75	3.50	3.25	3.00
Independent Media	4.75	4.75	4.50	4.25	4.00	4.00	3.75	4.00	3.75
Governance *	4.75	5.00	4.75	4.25	4.25	4.25	4.25	n/a	n/a
National Democratic Governance	n/a	n/a	n/a	n/a	n/a	n/a	n/a	4.25	4.00
Local Democratic Governance	n/a	n/a	n/a	n/a	n/a	n/a	n/a	3.25	2.75
Judicial Framework and Independence	4.75	5.25	5.00	4.50	4.50	4.25	4.25	4.50	4.25
Corruption	n/a	n/a	6.00	5.50	5.25	5.00	5.25	5.25	5.25
Democracy Score	4.55	4.75	4.75	4.42	4.25	4.17	4.13	4.04	3.79

* With the 2005 edition, Freedom House introduced seperate analysis and ratings for national democratic governance and local democratic governance to provide readers with more detailed and nuanced analysis of these two important subjects.

NOTE: The ratings reflect the consensus of Freedom House, its academic advisers, and the author of this report. The opinions expressed in this report are those of the author. The ratings are based on a scale of 1 to 7, with 1 representing the highest level of democratic progress and 7 the lowest. The Democracy Score is an average of ratings for the categories tracked in a given year.

The economic and social data on this page were taken from the following sources:
GNI/capita, Population: *World Development Indicators 2006* (Washington, D.C.: World Bank, 2006).
Ethnic Groups: *CIA World Factbook 2006* (Washington, D.C.: Central Intelligence Agency, 2006).

EXECUTIVE SUMMARY

Albania has made remarkable political, economic, and social progress in the 15 years since the country first began its tortuous transition to democracy. Yet its achievements remain tenuous and the consolidation of democracy far from certain. Putting recent developments in perspective, Albania started its post-Communist transition under the burden of the most vicious Communist regime in Eastern Europe, economic development that resembled sub-Saharan Africa, and disintegrating state institutions. Since then, the country has established the institutions of a parliamentary democracy and has made impressive strides in the establishment of a functioning market economy.[1] Perhaps most important, the elites as well as the people have shown a striking consensus on the issues of democratization and Euro-Atlantic integration.[2] However, the fraudulent parliamentary elections of 1996 and the meltdown of state institutions following the bankruptcy of the pyramid schemes in 1997 wiped out Albania's democratic gains as well as more than US$1 billion in savings of Albanian families.[3] While the Socialist Party (SP) succeeded in rebuilding state institutions and reestablishing the rule of law and economic growth, considerable obstacles remain today: organized crime, corruption, a tradition of only partially free and fair elections, weak administrative and technical capacities of state institutions, low rates of foreign direct investment, political interference in the judiciary, uneven enforcement of the law, a weak civil society, and a patchy record on freedom of the media. Although it remains to be seen how the new administration of the center-right Democratic Party (DP) will perform on each indicator, the parliamentary elections of July 3, 2005, offered the country a new chance to move toward a more pluralistic, consolidated democracy. Moreover, the green light by the European Commission for the country to complete the Stabilization and Association Agreement in 2006 should give fresh impetus to the reforms necessary for the country's integration into the European Union.

Two years ago, Freedom House's *Nations in Transit* report on Albania noted that "Albanian democratization brings to mind the legend of Sisyphus: It is marked by periods of progress followed by serious setbacks that bring it repeatedly to the starting point."[4] During 2005, Sisyphus was climbing up the hill again. The year was marked by free although not fair elections,[5] which were followed by a peaceful rotation of power, the resignation of SP chairman Fatos Nano following the SP electoral defeat, and renewed optimism on the country's progress toward EU integration.[6] The new administration has come to power on an overarching campaign promise of fighting organized crime and corruption, the major obstacles on the country's road to European integration. The administration has moved energetically to fulfill its promise by introducing an initiative on the voluntary renouncement of parliamentary immunity, putting a three-year moratorium on small motor vessels on Albanian waters in order to fight trafficking, impounding the goods of firms that have failed to pay customs duties, and cutting operational costs and the privileges of top political and bureaucratic staff. The latter move especially helped restore the idea that winning elections does not mean a *carte blanche* to unlimited privilege and ostensible arrogance. Although it is too early to give a clear verdict on the effectiveness of these measures – the new government took over only at the beginning of September – there are fears that these initiatives have been introduced through sheer willpower and have not been backed up by the necessary legislative packages that would give the required long-term effectiveness.

National Democratic Governance. As 2005 was an election year, the political dynamics generated by the elections highlighted the improvements as well as the problems in democratic governance. On the positive side, compared with other years, 2005 witnessed two relatively stable governments, although the overly protracted election process and the severe energy crisis that hit the country in November absorbed most of the attention of the executive. The adoption of new rules of procedure has strengthened the legislature's capacity to oversee the work of the executive and improve the quality of legislative work. Furthermore, consensual amendments to the electoral code with mediation from the Organization for Security and Cooperation in Europe (OSCE), less partisan rhetoric during the electoral campaign, the peaceful rotation of power, and a greater opening by both main political parties to civil society made Albanian politics more consensual in 2005. Nevertheless, the short boycott of the Parliament by the new SP opposition over perceived bullying by the DP governing majority demonstrated the fragility of consensual politics in Albania. The use of parts of the public administration to score points for the ruling party during the election campaign showed that despite organizational improvements, the public administration remains deeply vulnerable to political control. *The rating for national democratic governance improves from 4.25 to 4.00 owing to advances in government stability and efficiency.*

Electoral Process. The July parliamentary elections signaled considerable improvement over past electoral processes. Political parties worked together to amend the electoral code, generally respected the code of conduct initiated by the country's president during the electoral campaign, and managed a peaceful rotation of power. Yet the elections also demonstrated that Albania has a long way to go before it fulfills internationally accepted standards for democratic elections. The two main political parties distorted the constitutional principle of proportionality by encouraging voters to cast the proportional vote for their political allies in order to maximize the number of seats they could earn together. The outcome was a legislature that does not reflect popular will where the smaller parties are concerned. Moreover, a protracted election process and administrative problems, as well as allegations of political violence, sullied the progress made. *Nevertheless, the electoral process showed significant improvements, meriting an improvement in rating from 3.75 to 3.50.*

Civil Society. Civil society organizations displayed an improved capacity to monitor the election process. Moreover, they have increased their effectiveness by cooperating better with one another as well as with state institutions, although there is still much room for improvement. As a result, 2005 witnessed an increase in civil society input in policy making and improved watchdog capacities. However, the structural problems inhibiting civil society growth and effectiveness in the past have continued in 2005. Most nongovernmental organizations (NGOs) remain donor-dependent, while locally sustainable civil society organizations have not shown any progress. *Albania's civil society rating improves from 3.25 to 3.00 owing to enhanced influence on policy making and more effective cooperation among NGOs.*

Independent Media. Albanian media continued to grow quantitatively in 2005. An increasingly crowded market dictated improvements in technology and professionalism, especially in the case of electronic media. Moreover, the decision to decriminalize insult and defamation decreased the amount of political pressure. Yet the lack of financial, audience/circulation, and ownership transparency continued to characterize the media market. A concentrated ownership structure of powerful business groups and a deregulated labor market have made the media subservient to the particular business interests of its owners. Editorial freedom, professionalism, and a market distorted by below cost pricing still plague the Albanian media. *In 2005, the rating for independent media improves from 4.00 to 3.75 owing to decreasing political interference and slight advances in professionalism.*

Local Democratic Governance. Decentralization continued at a brisk pace in 2005. Local governments showed that they are more responsive to citizens' demands and have increased their managerial and administrative capacities. The legal framework and policies of decentralization have been completed, and the main challenges exist on the technical side of the transfer of competences to local governments. On the whole, local governments managed to discharge their duties well during the parliamentary elections, while continued problems in voter lists tended to reflect national rather than local weaknesses. *Since governance at the local level has improved public services delivery and demonstrated increased capacities, this rating improves from 3.25 to 2.75.*

Judicial Framework and Independence. Although Albania has made some progress in improving the organization and transparency of the judicial system, this sector continues to be plagued by low efficiency, political interference, and a sporadically implemented legislative framework. The quality of judges has improved, but a great deal remains to be done. The right of full access by all citizens to the courts is not fully respected in practice. The new government has been very active in judicial reform, but positive results have yet to materialize. In addition, before being forced to retreat, the government applied intense pressure on the prosecutor general to resign, raising fears of political meddling with an independent office. *The rating for judicial framework and independence improves from 4.50 to 4.25 owing to improved transparency and reform initiatives by the new government.*

Corruption. There were two positive developments in anticorruption efforts. First, the victory of the DP-led coalition on an anticorruption platform injected much-needed energy into the efforts of the executive to combat corruption. Second, the adoption of the Law on the Prevention of Conflicts of Interest and a detailed schedule for its implementation and civil society monitoring have increased expectations that the war on corruption will soon show results. Nevertheless, Albania's perceived corruption rating worsened, an increasing number of cases of corruption in the public administration were reported during the protracted period of elections and appeals, and the measures of the new government have yet to bear fruit. *Albania's corruption rating remains at 5.25 owing to the lack of results in the fight against corruption.*

Outlook for 2006. The most important event in 2006 will be the local government elections. They present an excellent opportunity for the new governing coalition to show its commitment to the consolidation of democracy in Albania. The stakes will be high since the ruling DP will see these elections as a referendum on its first year in office, while the opposition SP will need to test the electoral performance of its new chairman, Edi Rama, and its revamped leadership structures. The election outcome may also have important repercussions on the outcome of the decentralization process, since the history of the last 15 years has shown that central governments tend to devolve power more willingly when the political party in power controls both levels of government. Moreover, the government will need to demonstrate the political will to forge ahead with the reforms necessary for the process of European integration. The conclusion, or lack thereof, of the Stabilization and Association Agreement with the EU in 2006 may also act as a verdict of the international community on the first year of DP governance. Thus the DP will need to prove that it can govern effectively without undermining the basic principles of democracy or the institutions that sustain it.

MAIN REPORT

National Democratic Governance

1997	1998	1999	2001	2002	2003	2004	2005	2006
n/a	n/a	n/a	n/a	n/a	n/a	n/a	4.25	4.00

Albania is a parliamentary republic. Elected by the Parliament through a qualified majority of three-fifths, the president is invested with limited and largely symbolic powers. The Assembly of Albania is a unicameral Parliament with 140 seats: 100 are elected directly by a simple majority system, and 40 are allotted through a proportional system.[7] The intent of the proportional allocation is to balance any distortions in political representation that might result from the majority system. Nevertheless, in the last two parliamentary elections political parties have used legal loopholes in the electoral code to gain overrepresentation in the Parliament, thus increasing the distortions of the majority system. Parliamentary elections occur every four years. Political parties need to pass a threshold of 2.5 percent in order to gain representation in the Parliament, while party coalitions need to pass a threshold of 4 percent. The president nominates the prime minister at the suggestion of the coalition of parties controlling the majority of seats in the Parliament. The Constitution provides for a system of checks and balances among the legislative, executive, and judicial branches. In practice, the executive's hold over the other branches, as well as over state institutions in general, is greater than foreseen in the Constitution, but continuous efforts have reduced it over time.

Followers of Albania's post-Communist developments all viewed the July elections as critical for the country's European integration and democratic stabilization. The country lived up to the challenge, managing a peaceful transfer of power for only the second time since March 1992 – out of six parliamentary elections since the establishment of multiparty politics.[8] Despite the OSCE/Office for Democratic Institutions and Human Rights (ODIHR) conclusion that the elections "complied only in part with OSCE commitments and other international standards for democratic elections,"[9] the European Commission deemed the poll democratic enough to signal a green light for the completion of a Stabilization and Association Agreement in 2006.[10] Nevertheless, the repercussions of an election year – which witnessed the involvement of parts of the public administration in the election effort of the governing Socialist Party, a two-month period of postelection complaints that left Albania with little political leadership, and an intense energy crisis that demanded the full attention of the new Democratic Party administration – negatively impacted the efficiency of governing institutions. The challenges of the new government include quickly resolving the energy crisis, showing tangible results in the fight against organized crime and corruption (its priority as well as the EU's), furthering the achievements of the previous government in institution building, and stimulating the fragile politics of consensus that is tentatively taking hold of the Albanian political scene.

Although the election process showed that Albania still has a long way to go to fulfill international democratic standards, the electoral campaign, the conduct of the elections, and the postelection climate opened the way to more consensual politics in Albania. Both main political parties showed a new openness and less combative tendency throughout the process. The successful efforts of the DP to create the Policy Orientation Committee – a technocratic policy-making structure staffed with highly qualified personnel from the nongovernmental and business sectors – and integrate some of its members in the party leadership structures did much to undermine the claim that the party suffered from internal authoritarianism and hence was not ready to lead the democratic consolidation of the country. With respect to the SP, the resignation of Fatos Nano from the chairmanship after the party lost the elections and the televised democratic election of his replacement, Edi Rama, demonstrated that the SP could handle defeat in a mature and democratic manner. Finally, the interaction between both major parties was a great deal more pragmatic than in past years, as demonstrated by the bipartisan amendments to the electoral code and the signing of the code of conduct for the electoral campaign initiated by the country's president.

Although it remains to be seen whether the new government will be able to stimulate this atmosphere further, this new approach constitutes an encouraging trend in national democratic governance. To date, there are contradictory indications in this regard. On the one hand, the enhanced role of the Parliament and especially the standing committees and the skillful use of the changed rules of procedure by the opposition[11] show that the executive may be decreasing its hold on other state institutions and nourishing a less partisan political atmosphere. Government officials have also pledged to preserve the monitoring role of international institutions such as the OSCE as a check on the government's behavior toward the opposition.[12] On the other hand, the decision of the SP to boycott two meetings of the Parliament in November over the tense atmosphere of parliamentary debate during a motion on corruption[13] demonstrated how easily Albania could relapse into past experiences of extra-institutional politics when the opposition often took the political struggle outside of Parliament and into the streets.

The public administration's internal rules of human resource management and procedure improved during 2005, continuing a trend that started with the 1999 Law on Civil Service, which protects civil servants from arbitrary dismissal and mandated the establishment of the Department of Public Administration (DPA).[14] The publication of job vacancies has become a standard procedure, bringing about an increase in the number of applicants per position. The results of open competitions are published on the Web site of the DPA, which has also drafted a manual on recruitment in order to reduce political interference.[15] Detailed career advancement rules of procedure that include a division of civil service career levels are also being prepared.[16] The Civil Service Commission mandated by the 1999 Law on Civil Service to oversee the proper application of laws relating to the civil service is beginning to work more effectively. Finally, the Training Institute of Public Administration (TIPA) trained more civil servants than in 2004, and in a new initiative with the Ministry of European Integration and the DPA, the TIPA has begun to provide training related to the EU.[17] Nevertheless, the civil service remains hindered by a lack of real separation of the political and administrative levels. Political appointments, down to director level in most ministries, are still the norm. Crucially, the role of secretaries general to formulate personnel management policies and ensure effective policy implementation and service delivery is compromised by the fact that these positions are staffed through political appointments.[18] The involvement of political appointees in the internal operations of the ministries continues to hinder the career prospects of civil servants and diminish the performance of the civil service.

The elections revealed that the progress of recent years is highly vulnerable to political whims. Several directors of high-profile state institutions, such as the Albanian Electricity Corporation and the Customs Directorate, earned nominations on the SP list of candidates. The use of public administration employees, mostly but not exclusively from customs and tax offices, to campaign for their political bosses not only wasted resources and decreased efficiency,[19] but proved that when push comes to shove, the governing party can still use state institutions for political purposes. Moreover, from an intra-institutional perspective, weak methods of performance measurement and lack of performance-related financial bonuses, very weak human resources departments, and career-making rules that are enforced irregularly and subjectively lower the attractiveness of civil service positions and the performance of the public administration.[20] Although the new DP administration has dismissed a number of top civil servants, the courts have generally ruled in favor of the dismissed employees.

The Parliament has increased its role as the main forum for political debates. The adoption of new rules of procedure in January 2005 through a multiparty effort enhanced the transparency of the work of the Parliament, restricted the powers of the Speaker, and strengthened the Parliament's oversight capacities.[21] The creation of the Conference of Chairpersons and Bureau established a structure of secretariats on the Italian model while restricting the power of the speaker. Transparency has been enhanced through the publication of the minutes of plenary meetings within a day. The number of standing committees was cut from 13 to 8 to increase the workload of each committee while enhancing its technical capacities. The creation of the new Standing Committee on European Integration as separate from the Foreign Affairs Committee was another positive development. Furthermore, the new rules share the burden among members of Parliament more effectively – each committee member is responsible for a particular piece of legislation. Thus, while the quantitative output of 2005 has been lower than in 2004 owing to parliamentary elections and the slow constitution of the new government, the Parliament's capacities to exercise its functions more effectively have been enhanced.[22]

A changed mood in the Parliament has also contributed to increased performance. The election of a young, politically powerful female speaker in September 2005 has raised the profile of the Parliament on the political scene. The energetic speaker has demanded increased openness in the daily work of the Parliament, the formulation of new strategies of communication with the public, and a reduction of benefits for parliamentary deputies (although these last measures have yet to pass). Despite a minor boycott in November, the new SP opposition seems determined to use the Parliament as its main platform of communication with the public – as long as the DP majority does not hinder its rights. The opposition has shown a strong capacity to use the new rules of procedure in its interest, thus enhancing the profiles of the standing committees, bringing ministers in front of these committees, and increasing the involvement of business groups and civil society in legislative work. The DP caucus in the new legislature has also benefited from the election of members that have higher professional and technical capacities than in the past.

Electoral Process

1997	1998	1999	2001	2002	2003	2004	2005	2006
4.25	4.50	4.25	4.00	3.75	3.75	3.75	3.75	3.50

Albania held its sixth parliamentary elections since the beginning of political pluralism on July 3, 2005. The elections were conducted under a new electoral code adopted in June 2003. The frantic amendments to the code in October 2004, January 2005, and April 2005 – with OSCE mediation – showed the intensity of political jockeying by both major political parties prior to the elections for the best possible starting position. The bipartisan amendments brought about changes in the criteria for drawing electoral zone boundaries, compiling voter lists, organizing the vote-counting process, and handling complaints and appeals.[23] One hundred deputies were elected through a direct simple majority system in 100 electoral zones, while 40 mandates were distributed according to party lists in accordance with the proportional results of the vote.

These elections proved to be a significant improvement on Albania's poor electoral track record, although the country has still a ways to go to fulfill the standards of free and fair elections. Since the manipulated elections of May 1996, the international community has deemed local and national elections "acceptable," although they were never free and fair. The losing party has always contested the results, while international monitoring organizations have uncovered politically motivated fraud, irregular voting lists, and other administrative shortcomings. There are strong indications that the international community accepted these low standards because of fears of the security implications of political instability in Albania.[24] That had a negative impact on the process of democratic consolidation – in fact, public opinion is becoming increasingly skeptical of the possibility of holding completely free and fair elections in Albania.[25] This time around, the EU made it clear that the signing of the Stabilisation and Association Agreement depended upon the holding of free and fair elections.[26] Moreover, the main political parties realized the high stakes of failing this test, since the then opposition DP had made it clear that it would use protests to attempt to overthrow the government if the SP manipulated the elections.[27]

In order to maximize the number of seats in the Parliament, the two main political parties encouraged voters to cast their majority vote for them and the proportional vote for their allies, which would thus maximize the number of seats they would take through their allies from the 40 seats of the proportional vote. Called the "Dushk phenomenon," this tactic was named after the electoral district where the parties first employed the strategy during the 2001 parliamentary elections. As a result, the Republican Party (RP), for example, took 22 percent of the vote, although its electoral base is 10 times smaller.[28] Most of the seats won by small parties in the proportional vote came from the electorate of the two main parties. The Dushk phenomenon most penalized the Socialist Movement for Integration (SMI), led by former prime minister Ilir Meta, which received 8.5 percent of the vote nationwide and only 5 mandates in the Parliament.[29] Whether the SMI will be able to maintain its popular support and eventually become the third pole in Albanian politics is an open question.

The DP agreements with other right-wing parties resulted in the formation of the Alliance for Freedom, Justice, and Welfare (AFJW). The DP fielded 100 candidates, 15 nominated by its allies on the common list. For the party list contest, AFJW members registered separate lists, but the RP list contained about 30 DP members, including DP parliamentary deputies from the outgoing Parliament. On the other side of the political spectrum, the SP registered 100 candidates, but in many districts SP allies had their own single-seat candidates as well. Also, the left-wing parties had separate party lists contending for the 40 mandates of the proportional system.[30] Although the leader of the DP, Sali Berisha, had offered a deal to amend the electoral code in order not to repeat the Dushk phenomenon, the SP rejected the offer. Yet it was the DP and its allies that, through better organization, profited most from this strategy, ensuring that the SP lost the proportional distribution of mandates. The split of the SMI from the SP may have been key to the SP's loss in the single-seat section of the vote – especially considering that in absolute terms the SP managed actually to increase its votes in comparison with its returns in the 2001 elections, which it won.

The DP-led coalition gained 57 percent of seats followed by SP and its allies with 39 percent and the SMI with 4 percent. Despite fears of unrest, the elections brought about a peaceful rotation of power that culminated in the swearing in of a new government formed by the DP and its allies on September 3, but only after a lengthy process of mostly unsubstantiated appeals by losing SP candidates.

These elections marked several improvements from previous ones. First, the bipartisan commission's work on the new electoral code improved the legal framework by taking into account the recommendations of the OSCE/ODIHR on the local elections of October 2003. In this regard, a notable advance was the obligation of local governments to administer the voter lists, thus decreasing the capacity of political parties to manipulate the lists – one of the main problems of previous elections when voter lists were prepared by the Ministry of Decentralization and Local Government with no oversight from the opposition.[31] Political representation in the seven-seat Central Election Commission (CEC) was also improved, especially in October 2004 when the SP surrendered one of its five seats to the opposition.[32] Second, the code of conduct initiated by the country's president and signed by 16 political parties obliged the signatories to abide by the law and exercise restraint during the campaign. Although the code did not have any formal monitoring mechanisms, the parties conducted the least partisan electoral campaign to date. Third, the media generally followed the guidelines of the electoral code on campaign coverage quite closely,[33] though some complained that the guidelines were too restrictive.[34] Fourth, the CEC administered the election process in line with the electoral code and without political bias despite facing enormous political pressure and logistical and administrative challenges.[35]

Although the elections cleared the main roadblock to concluding the Stabilization and Association Agreement with the EU, the ODIHR still qualified them as "[complying] only in part with OSCE commitments and other international standards."[36] The Citizens Advocacy Office (CAO), a watchdog anti-corruption organization, evaluated them as "free but not fair and equal."[37] The problems manifested in these elections may be classified as administrative and political. In spite of improvements in the voter lists, insufficient political will on the part of local government structures and basic shortcomings, such as missing personal identification documents and the lack of a uniform system of building addresses, meant that irregularities continued in these elections as well. Also, voting center commissions did not sufficiently respect procedures, particularly regarding the use of ink to prevent multiple voting, the secrecy of the vote, and the checking of voters' identity. The counting of votes was often contentious and took considerably longer to complete than was foreseen in the law, mainly because of obstruction of process.[38]

However, it was the political problems that created the most controversy. First, there were sporadic allegations of politically motivated violence, negligence, or pressure on public employees to perform political tasks. Two people lost their lives during the elections; one of them was an election observer killed in an election center, and the other was head of the DP for the Kukes region.[39] Still, compared with incidents in other elections, these were random in nature and had a marginal effect on the electoral atmosphere. The main political problem was the use of electoral strategies by both major political camps that distorted the constitutional objective of proportionality "to the closest possible extent"[40] through formal (DP) or informal (SP) use of the previously mentioned Dushk phenomenon.

Since the elections, a vigorous debate has sprung up on how to reform the electoral system in order to avoid such distortions of popular will in parliamentary representation. For example, the citizens movement MJAFT! has organized debates with politicians on how to reform the system. All political actors have formally agreed that the electoral system should be reformed in line with ODIHR recommendations in order to avoid distortions of the objective of proportionality, improve voter lists by issuing new identity documents, and ensure consistency in campaign finance provisions. The great loser of the Dushk phenomenon, the SMI, has taken the lead in proposing electoral reform. The SMI proposal recommends establishing a unicameral Parliament elected through a proportional system with a 5 percent threshold. Understandably, the two main political parties have supported the threshold segment of the SMI proposal, but their stand on a unicameral Parliament is unclear.

Although attempts to amend the electoral code in order to nullify the Dushk phenomenon have yet to make headway, the parties have moved more aggressively toward solving some of the administrative problems that marred the July 3 vote. The elections demonstrated that the accuracy of voter lists, transparency of campaign finance, and an election administration controlled by the two main parties continued to present problems. The new center-right administration has acknowledged these deficiencies and has made their solution a priority.[41] A bipartisan parliamentary committee was set up on October 20 to reexamine the application of electoral laws in the last elections, with both major parties emphasizing the need to deal with administrative drawbacks. Furthermore, the Albanian president called a roundtable of all parlia-

mentary political parties on December 7 in order to build up the political will necessary for reform.[42] Everything points toward eventual amendments of Albania's electoral code – another common feature of all Albanian parliamentary elections since the
beginning of political pluralism.

Civil Society

1997	1998	1999	2001	2002	2003	2004	2005	2006
4.25	4.25	4.00	4.00	3.75	3.75	3.50	3.25	3.00

No civil society organizations existed in Communist Albania, and the country's pre-
Communist history reflected very low levels of civic participation in collective action.
That may partially explain the structural weaknesses of the civil society sector in
Albania – a cluster of donor-dependent and thus donor-driven local NGOs and very
few genuine local interest groups. This is a regional problem in Southeastern Europe
that has led some academics to term local civil society as "ersatz civil society."[43]

In Albania, the Constitution and relevant legislation protect civil liberties.
Creation of business associations and Chambers of Commerce are not only allowed
but encouraged. The same is true for nonprofits, NGOs, and trade unions. The
2001 Albanian Law on NGOs is considered one of the most liberal such laws in
the region, allowing NGOs considerable latitude in their activities, rights, and
responsibilities. NGOs generally operate without government restriction. Over the
last 15 years, Albanian NGOs have demonstrated an increasing capacity to impact
policy making while they have lagged behind in their watchdog and monitoring
roles. Nonetheless, the lack of local sustainability capacities has stunted the growth
of the civil society sector.

In the course of 2005, NGOs gained influence and took on a growing role in
virtually all aspects of public life,[44] making important gains even in watchdog and
monitoring roles. The main field of activity in which local NGOs made their presence felt was the monitoring of the parliamentary elections, which saw the most
massive mobilization of such groups for an election in the country's history. The
electoral code provides for observation of the elections by domestic NGOs, which
have to be accredited by the CEC within five days of a request's submission. The
CEC adopted an open and flexible approach to accrediting observers, rejecting very
few requests, all on reasonable grounds.[45] The biggest organizations accredited by
the CEC were the Domestic Observer Forum, led by the Albanian Coalition Against
Corruption (ACAC), and the Albanian Youth Council, which mobilized around
2,500 and 1,000 observers, respectively.[46] However, other NGOs launched smaller
campaigns as well.[47]

The ACAC mounted the largest campaign and covered about half of the voting centers. This monitoring had a positive impact by changing voting procedures
to decrease the possibility of rolling vote fraud, voting with birth certificates (of
which thousands went missing prior to the elections, constituting a fraud threat),

and cell phone vote fraud.[48] Moreover, the ACAC closely monitored media coverage of the electoral campaign and published its findings, which were mainly positive, in detailed public reports.[49] Overall, civil society monitoring and reports helped the democratic legitimacy of these elections in the face of political challenges from the losing parties. In the postelection period, civil society organizations initiated debates on the need to reform the electoral system in order to prevent legalized distortions of popular representation (as in the Dushk phenomenon). For example, the MJAFT! movement organized several such debates in its Speaker's Corner program.

Albanian civil society counted several highly visible successes in its policy-making input and watchdog roles as well. For example, the CAO acted to outlaw the conflict of interest inherent in having judges sit on the High Council of Justice (HCJ), a body taxed with overseeing the behavior of judges. The CAO then drafted a proposal for HCJ reform that would make the mandate of HCJ members incompatible with any other private or public positions except for teaching.[50] Also, the ACAC lobbied for and eventually participated in drafting the Law on the Prevention of Conflicts of Interest, which was approved by the Parliament in April 2005.[51] Although the role of civil society organizations as actual drafters of bills caused some controversy in the media, it is noteworthy that civil society initiatives have rarely, if ever, had such an impact on policy making in Albania.

Another major initiative was MJAFT!'s sustained campaign against the opening of a casino in downtown Tirana by Hyatt Regency Hotel and Tourism Hellas S.A. MJAFT! mobilized citizens and representatives of religious communities in order to present the casino issue as a fight between community welfare and vice.[52] Although the campaign ultimately failed, MJAFT! did demonstrate that policy decisions without extensive consultations with interested groups may be costly for the government. In its watchdog role, civil society's most noteworthy success came in November 2005 when Prime Minister Berisha agreed to have the ACAC closely monitor the implementation of the Law on the Prevention of Conflicts of Interest. However, it remains to be seen how the agreement will be implemented in practice.

Despite these success stories, the structural shortcomings of Albanian civil society have not changed. As foreign donors signal their intent to slowly withdraw funding from Albania as the country progresses toward EU integration, there are concerns among the NGO community about local sustainability capacities. The lack of funding by government and private businesses remains the greatest handicap in this regard. The Open Society Foundation – Albania which has been one of the main pillars of civil society support in the country, announced in 2005 that it would shift its emphasis toward providing support for a network of local NGOs judged to have the best capacity to adapt to changes in the long run, with the goal of eventual self-sustainability.

In the field of labor rights and trade unions, the Albanian Constitution guarantees the right to earn a living by choosing or accepting lawful work. The legal minimum wage for all workers over the age of 16 is approximately US$106.95 per month, which is insufficient to provide a decent standard of living for a worker and his or her household.[53] There was no change in the legislative framework that regulates trade unions and guarantees the right of workers to exercise this right in practice through the labor code of 1995. A minimum of 20 people can form a trade union. Albania has two "umbrella" unions: the Confederation of Albanian Trade Unions (KSSH) and the Union of Independent Albanian Trade Unions (BSPSH). According to their own sources, BSPSH membership has grown from 84,000 in 2004 to 90,000 in 2005,[54] while the number of KSSH members is 98,908 and reportedly growing.[55] Both unions are politically affiliated: the BSPSH with the governing DP and the KSSH with the opposition SP. However, trade unions continue to remain very weak actors in labor relations. The decline of the manufacturing sector in Albania, high unemployment, organizational weaknesses, and a general distrust of collectivist forms of political action have left trade unions on the margins of Albanian economic life.

Although several journalists associations exist, they remained relatively inactive in 2005. The two principal associations, the League of Albanian Journalists and the Association of Albanian Journalists, have not made any notable attempts to raise journalists' awareness of their rights and organize them for their common good. There are also other journalists associations, established on the basis of shared interests, such as environmental reporting, or on a regional basis, such as the League of Northern Journalists, or by gender, but they have not contributed to the plight of journalists in the unregulated Albanian media labor market, either. The International Research & Exchanges Board has supported the idea of establishing a trade union for journalists, but all attempts to set up an effective organization have failed so far, owing to lack of cooperation within the media community or lack of interest in changing the situation.[56]

Cooperation among NGOs remains inefficient and takes place primarily because of donor funding conditionality. Nevertheless, 15 years of working experience has created a shared culture among NGOs that facilitates cooperation. Given the increasingly more challenging environment faced by local civil society groups, a number of informal initiatives have been launched to facilitate cooperation – although they have yet to bear fruit. The most sustained and institutionalized effort so far has been the Network for Open Society in Albania, which the Open Society Foundation–Albania launched to create a core self-sustainable network of organizations that will hopefully provide the basis of homegrown civil society in Albania in the future. After a rocky start, the ACAC, sponsored by the U.S. Agency for International Development (USAID), took a key role in election monitoring and in November concluded an agreement with the Berisha administration to monitor the transparency of procurements and financing of Albanian government ministries.

Independent Media

1997	1998	1999	2001	2002	2003	2004	2005	2006
4.75	4.75	4.50	4.25	4.00	4.00	3.75	4.00	3.75

The Albanian media have come a long way from the total control exercised by the Communist Albanian Labor Party to relatively free, sophisticated, professional, and diverse print and electronic offerings that exercise important informative and over-sight functions in society. Although the continued proliferation of media outlets and market forces brought about increased professionalism by journalists and editors, the basic structural problems that have hindered the qualitative growth of Albanian media remained unchanged. The lack of financial, circulation, and ownership trans-parency has distorted the market and hampered professional growth as well as thor-ough assessments of media market characteristics. Although there was less political interference in the media, media outlets continued to be subordinated to the busi-ness interests of their owners. The precarious position of the media in Albanian soci-ety was also reflected in the country's fall by 12 places in the annual ranking con-ducted by Reporters Without Borders, the international media-monitoring group. That decline occurred mainly because of a physical attack by the mayor of Korca municipality on a broadcast journalist, poor professional ethics due to an irregular labor market, financial unsustainability, and the stranglehold of business concerns on the media. Despite the challenges previously listed, 2005 marked no changes in the legislative framework regulating the Albanian media market.

In 2004, Freedom House reported that Albania had the largest number of print media per capita in Europe but the lowest circulation per capita. Yet the prolifera-tion of media outlets continued unabated in 2005. The number of daily papers increased from 19 in 2004 to 26 in 2005, but the circulation of all of them com-bined does not exceed that of the first opposition newspaper in 1991.[57] Very few (if any) of these papers make a profit – though the continued lack of reliable circula-tion data makes the situation unclear.[58] In the electronic media market, Albania now has 66 television stations and 45 radio stations – a far cry from the situation in 1995, when state radio and television had a complete monopoly.[59]

The proliferation of media outlets has injected dynamism, information diversi-ty, and professionalism in Albanian media. Moreover, political interference has decreased, as noted by the objective and professional performance of the media dur-ing the election campaign coverage of July 2005.[60] On October 13, 2005, Prime Minister Berisha announced that he had ordered his officials to use only the right of public response, rather than legal proceedings, to seek redress for defamatory state-ments made by the media. That decision signaled the intent of the new administra-tion to dispatch with one of the few legislative tools at its disposal to influence the media.[61] Nevertheless, the lack of legal provisions regarding the allocation of state advertising leaves it up to the government to decide whether to use that financial "carrot" to encourage favorable press coverage. The Law on Public Procurement stipulates that government advertisements should be allocated to the three papers with the highest circulation, but without a transparent circulation-tracking system, that mechanism remains insufficient to prevent potential politicization.

The decline of political interference in the media has made editorial control of the media by a few powerful business groups, unfair pricing practices, and an unregulated labor market the greatest challenges faced by the media. A concentrated ownership structure characterizes both the broadcast and print media markets, a problem exacerbated by the lack of legislation regulating cross-ownership of print and electronic outlets. Owners of electronic outlets are simply required to state their ownership when applying for a broadcast license from the National Council of Radio and Television (NCRT). As a result, all major media groups – Klan, Spekter, Koha, and Edisud – own at least one publication as well as a radio and/or television station. The owners use their other businesses to finance their media holdings, which in return act as public relations tools to further their owners' business interests. Even the most popular commercial television outlets, which have benefited from considerable investment, have not managed to become self-sustaining. Only half of their total annual income comes from advertising revenues.[63] The price for this dependency is strong control over editorial policy, which is worsened by a lack of employment contracts and labor instability. Although there are no reliable figures, according to the Institute of Media as much as 90 percent of journalists may be working without contracts.[64] The end result is financially unviable media that respond feebly to market demands and suffer from weak public credibility.

Although media legislation is considered to fulfill basic requirements for a free and independent media, revisions are still needed to protect journalists from libel suits and ensure ownership and financial transparency. Already amended four times since its adoption in 1998, the Law on Radio and Television still fails to fully regulate the activity of the electronic media – a reality confirmed by the recent launch of two digital operators which broadcast without licenses because the NCRT does not yet have the authority to license them.[65] Even with these legal deficiencies, after a timid start in 2000, the NCRT, which also regulates the electronic media market, has gradually improved its performance and forced Albanian broadcasters to comply with property rights by not broadcasting bootlegged programs. The NCRT has also drafted a strategy for how it may achieve financial independence from the state budget and become self-sustainable. At present, Articles 119 and 120 of the criminal code make insult and defamation criminal offenses punishable by a fine and up to six months' imprisonment.[66] However, a series of amendments are being prepared to make defamation punishable only under the civil code. In addition, the prime minister's directive alluded to previously has already de facto decriminalized defamatory statements in the media – though some have raised concerns over a blanket ban on government officials' ability to invoke their basic rights to seek redress through the courts.

In 1991, the Soros Foundation became the first to introduce the Internet to Albania. Although Internet connection services have improved in the larger cities, the number of users remains very low at 75,000, or 2.4 percent of the population,[67] since monthly tariffs vary between US$16 and US$35, or 15 to 45 percent of an average monthly income.[68] However, Albania has about 130 Internet cafes that are very popular with young people, who have no other means of access. Moreover, the government has adopted a master plan that aims to ensure free Internet access in all schools by 2008. By the end of 2006, the plan calls for establishing Internet connections in 65 to 75 percent of the country's high schools and 8 to 10 percent of elementary schools.

Local Democratic Governance

1997	1998	1999	2001	2002	2003	2004	2005	2006
n/a	n/a	n/a	n/a	n/a	n/a	n/a	3.25	2.75

The decentralization of power from central to local government structures has been one of the success stories of governance in Albania. The legal framework for the creation of accountable and decentralized government was already in place prior to 2005. This year, however, witnessed better implementation of existing laws as the central government began to transfer the management of water utility companies to local government structures and to provide unconditional grants to local entities for education and health care. Overall, despite growing resistance from central government institutions such as the Water Regulatory Entity on further decentralization,[69] a clear political will exists to complete the reform of decentralization.

Albania's decentralization reform is based on the Law on Organization and Functioning of Local Governments, adopted in 2000. This law outlines the duties and responsibilities of local governments and is the legal cornerstone of the decentralization process. In order to strengthen the administrative and technical capacities of local governments, the Council of Ministers approved in March 2005 a package of amendments to the Law on Civil Service to ensure that local government structures would come under its jurisdiction. The amendments aim to improve the recruitment and retention of civil servants in the public administration. However, the new legislature has yet to adopt them.[70]

With the specific policies on how to complete decentralization already adopted, it is now a matter of solving the technical issues to allow for full functional decentralization.[71] Local governments earned the right to spend local taxes in 2001, and they started taking advantage of these new opportunities in 2002. With the help of USAID, the central government adopted a formula to determine the amount of unconditional transfers to local governments – the first Balkan country to implement such a formula. From 8 percent of local expenditures in 1998, local governments now control about 50 percent of their expenditures.[72]

Although the new center-right administration folded the Ministry of Decentralization and Local Government into the new Ministry of the Interior in September 2005, the government has indicated that it will forge ahead with the decentralization of power. Particular emphasis has been placed on the devolution of fiscal powers and enlargement of the fiscal autonomy of local governments. For the period 2006-2009 government officials envisage a three- to four-fold increase in state budget grants to local entities.[73] Although it is still too early to measure the effects of this move on the progress of decentralization reform, the government is preparing to remove conditional transfers for local government structures, determine capital investments with a specific formula, and decentralize water utility companies and the power to collect small-business taxes.[74]

In 2003, local governments earned the right to maintain and operate all pre-university education facilities in their communities through grants allocated to them by the state budget.[75] In 2005, the responsibility for the allocation of capital expenditures in the areas of primary education and health care was transferred to regional councils. Currently, they are responsible for the allocation of investments for communes and municipalities (with the exception of the 12 capitals of the regions/counties, to which these funds were transferred directly). Despite some initial confusion due to a lack of preparation, the quality of service has improved. The government is also in the process of eliminating conditional grants, which were often allocated according to political preferences, in favor of unconditional grants, which are allocated according to an objective formula and allow local governments to have more realistic expectations about the financial inflows from the central government.

Another area where decentralization reform has progressed relatively well in 2005 is the decentralization of water utility companies. It is expected that by the end of 2005, about 20 percent of customers will be served by decentralized water utility companies, while in 2006 the process should be complete.[76] However, some of these companies remain in poor financial shape, as they have yet to receive promised funds from the Ministry of Public Works, Transportation, and Telecommunications. Nevertheless, on the whole, water provision services have improved as local governments have proved to be more customer-oriented and have demonstrated a constant increase in their administrative capacity. Neighboring local government units have cooperated in managing water utility companies together in order to earn economies of scale and cover costs,[77] showing that fears that smaller companies would lose such financial advantages were exaggerated.

In 2005, the major test for local governments was the administration of voter lists for the July parliamentary elections. Between October 2004 and January 2005, the central government transferred the responsibility for handling voter registration, as well as compiling and maintaining voter lists, to local entities. It was presumed that since local governments maintained the civil registers, the political manipulation of voter lists that had occurred in previous elections would be avoided.[78] Voter lists were updated by door-to-door verification between November 2004 and February 2005. However, problems with inconsistent methodology, multiple entries, and 470,000 incomplete entries – especially in urban areas, owing to mass migration and the existence of informal residential areas or slums – marred the process, opening the way to allegations of political manipulation of voter lists.[79] Despite these problems, the new voter lists were a great deal more accurate than previous ones. Yet the challenge of reforming the civil registration process by introducing a uniform system of building addresses and issuing personal identification documents remains to be met in the future. In this sense, the 2006 local government elections will be not only politically important, but also a litmus test for the capability of local governments to properly discharge their duties.

The conflict between the new center-right administration and the municipality of Tirana in November-December 2005 showed that the gains made by local governments in the last few years are susceptible to rollback by an antagonistic central government. Given that the mayor of Tirana, Edi Rama, is also chairman of the SP, the political struggle between the governing Democrats and the opposition Socialists spilled over onto the local government level. The decision of the Council for Regulation of the Territory of the Republic of Albania – the country's highest urban planning body – to demolish the Zogu i Zi overpass sparked the row, since the municipality of Tirana had approved the contract for building the overpass. Soon developing into the hottest political news at the end of the year, the dispute brought relations between the municipality and the central government to a deadlock. The mayor of Tirana filed a civil court case against Prime Minister Berisha for defamation and other charges. The European Commission agreed to send a delegation to monitor the situation, since the gridlock was "endanger[ing] the normal functioning of local autonomy in Tirana."[80] Despite the fact that the Office of the Ombudsman issued a report in favor of the municipality of Tirana, by the end of the year neither side seemed willing to back down.

Judicial Framework and Independence

1997	1998	1999	2001	2002	2003	2004	2005	2006
4.75	5.25	5.00	4.50	4.50	4.25	4.25	4.50	4.25

Albania has a three-layered court system: 29 district courts, 6 civilian appeals courts, and the Constitutional Court and the High Court.[81] The president proposes the names of Constitutional and High Court judges, while the Parliament has to approve the appointments. Judges then serve nine-year court terms. The Constitutional Court interprets the Constitution following a request from state institutions. On the other hand, the High Court is the last instance of appeal after the appeals courts.[82] The High Council of Justice, the regulatory body of the judiciary, appoints, transfers, disciplines, and dismisses judges of the courts of first instance and the courts of appeal.[83] The HCJ comprises 15 members, including 9 judges. A judge sitting on the HCJ faces an obvious conflict of interest between his or her daily work as a judge and the HCJ mandate of overseeing the behavior of judges. The new center-right administration pushed through new legislation, the Law on Organization and Functions of HCJ, which requires judges to resign their judicial posts once they have accepted an HCJ nomination.[84] Adopted in November 2005, the law made it illegal for anyone to hold on to a judgeship or any position other than teaching for as long as he or she is a member of the HCJ. A major obstacle to the proper functioning of the HCJ was thus removed.

Although in 2005 Albania made progress in several vital areas – organizational capabilities, transparency, the functioning of the HCJ, criminal and juvenile justice, and training – the proper implementation of the legislative framework and the overall effectiveness of the justice system remain problematic. It was an ironic but truthful evaluation of the state of Albanian justice when the new justice minister, Aldo Bumci, reported that although the Tirana Office of the Bailiff declared that it had closed 51 percent of court cases, a Ministry of Justice checkup showed that only 38 percent had been executed.[85] Although the rate of execution of judicial rulings has constantly improved – 3,704 files were closed in 2002, 4,856 in 2003, and 6,050 in 2004 [86] – the scandal shed light on the distance left to travel. In a speech to the Parliament on November 7, Bumci declared that 12,933 rulings were awaiting execution in September 2005, of which proceedings had been initiated on 5,594 while work on the remaining 7,339 had not yet started.[87]

On the positive side, the new Legal Reform Commission, an advisory body, has already prepared a study on the reorganization of district courts. Second, an "anti-Mafia" package contains new legal tools to facilitate the seizure of criminal proceeds and to focus the priorities of the serious crimes court solely on organized crime. Third, a new memorandum of cooperation among the prosecutors general of the western Balkans has improved regional judicial cooperation. Fourth, the quality of judges has been improving, as the Albanian School of Magistrates has enhanced its capacity to plan and deliver both initial and ongoing training of judges and prosecutors following the adoption of amendments governing the school's operation.[88] These amendments have made continuous, on-the-job training mandatory for judges and prosecutors, and a long-term strategy has been adopted to ensure future sustainability. Finally, together with the Ministry of the Interior, the Ministry of Justice is the largest recipient of additional funding in the new draft budget that the government has sent to Parliament. The extra funds should prove especially useful in providing bailiffs with the basic requirements for discharging their duties properly.

However, the effectiveness of the judicial system is still a matter of concern. The right of full access by all citizens to the courts has yet to be fully respected in practice. Poor cooperation between prosecutors and the police and the lethargic prosecution of court cases need to be addressed. The existence of two parallel inspection services from the HCJ and the Ministry of Justice should be resolved by divesting the ministry of an investigatory role – beyond purely administrative measures – in order to safeguard the independence of the judiciary.[89] Finally, the institutional relationship between the minister of justice and the HCJ may need to be revised. The minister sits on the HCJ, and although he has no voting rights in disciplinary proceedings against judges, he has the power to initiate such proceedings. This arrangement has raised concerns over judicial independence. Finally, the justice system has been plagued by low staff morale because of the relatively low status and salary of judicial staff, such as court and judicial administrators. Except for judges, judicial employees do not have civil servant status, and their salaries are as a rule lower than those of their equivalents in other ministries.

The judiciary is one of the areas in which the new center-right administration has been the most active. Besides the planned increase in the budget for the Ministry of Justice, the government plans to improve the juvenile justice system and the efficiency of the Prosecutor General. On the former, preparatory work is being carried out in order to amend the legislative framework in consultation with UNICEF and the European Commission.[90] On the latter, by noting that the Prosecutor General had failed to open a single case against a high official or politician – despite damning reports from the High State Audit, the media, and the international community on the scale of corruption in state institutions – the governing party has publicly placed pressure on the Prosecutor General. The DP, however, lacked a constitutional basis on which to act against the Office of the Prosecutor, an independent body, and faced suspicions that such a move would represent the first step toward political control of the judicial system. In the end, the DP prudently decided not to act even though a simple majority in the Parliament and presidential approval would have sufficed to remove the Prosecutor General.[91] It remains to be seen whether the political storm caused by this issue will improve the performance of the Office of the Prosecutor.

In the area of torture and ill-treatment, the Center for Rehabilitation of Trauma and Torture Survivors (CRTTS) issued a damning report on the police's use of torture.[92] The CRTTS report noted that ill-treatment of minors in pretrial detention centers continued despite improvements in the overall conditions of these centers. Also, the process of transferring the management of predetention centers from the Ministry of Public Order to the Ministry of Justice lags far behind the original target of March 2004. Lengthy pretrial detentions as a result of delayed investigations remain a serious problem.

A number of measures have been taken to improve the legislative, institutional, organizational, and infrastructural shortcomings of the penitentiary system, but overcrowding and poor living conditions remain problematic. A number of laws in compliance with European standards, such as a code of ethics for the prison system and a law on prison police were introduced.[93] New prisons were opened in the towns of Peqin and Lezha, and other establishments had their capacities expanded. Yet these improvements were funded almost exclusively by foreign donors, and the government lacks a long-term strategy on bettering the conditions in the penitentiary system.

Corruption

1997	1998	1999	2001	2002	2003	2004	2005	2006
n/a	n/a	6.00	5.50	5.25	5.00	5.25	5.25	5.25

The victory of the DP-led coalition in the July elections on an anticorruption platform has brought renewed vigor to the struggle against corruption in Albania. Although it is too soon to evaluate the results of these efforts, the government has taken a variety of organizational, legislative, political, and financial measures to live up to its electoral promises.

The new administration inherited one of the most comprehensive anticorruption legislative frameworks in the region, while poor implementation had turned Albania into one of the most corrupt countries in Europe. Designed by the Anticorruption Monitoring Group – an interministerial body – the government's 2005 Action Plan on the Prevention of and Fight Against Corruption[94] failed to be put adequately into practice, a victim of a lack of sufficient political will.[95] According to Transparency International's Corruption Perceptions Index, the rating for Albania in 2005 fell to 2.4 from 2.5 in the previous two years, where 10 indicates the lowest level of perceived corruption. The annual report of the High State Audit for 2004, released on October 21, 2005, stated that 24.4 billion lek (more than US$ 200 million) had been wasted.[96]

Nevertheless, it is by no means clear whether actual corruption levels had actually increased over the past year.[97] A poll conducted by the World Bank and the European Bank for Reconstruction and Development suggested that corruption was declining in all Balkan countries except Serbia and Macedonia.[98] The high profile that this issue has taken in public debates, the media, and the electoral campaign – as well as the statements of international community representatives – may have heightened popular perceptions of corruption levels. Although this awareness is a precondition for the political will necessary to combat corruption, it seems that in Albania anticorruption discourse envisions this fight as an end in itself rather than as a means to improve governance.[99]

Moving quickly to define the war against corruption as its primary goal, the new government created an Anticorruption Task Force headed by Prime Minister Berisha. The adoption of the Law on the Prevention of Conflicts of Interest and the expansion of the mandate of the High Inspectorate of Declaration and Control of Assets (HIDCA) both strengthened the legal framework. The detailed asset declarations of the ministers of the new DP-led government and ongoing efforts to verify these declarations established a positive precedent, though some concerns remain that the law failed to cover some potential conflicts of interest.[100] An agreement between the HIDCA and the Ministry of Foreign Affairs for the provision of help by the latter to verify the asset declarations of public officials abroad may yield results in the future. The new administration amended the Law on the Prevention of Conflicts of Interest in order to increase its scope beyond the central public administration. And on November 2, the prime minister issued a detailed order outlining specific deadlines for the implementation of the law and the setup of working groups in each ministry to oversee the implementation process.[101]

Furthermore, on November 11 the prime minister agreed to allow the ACAC to monitor the implementation of the Law on the Prevention of Conflicts of Interest. He also ordered the full publication of financial transactions of government institutions in order to further public transparency.[102] After an initially shaky start, the ACAC – a coalition of 25 civil society organizations – has taken a primary role from the civil society perspective in the fight against corruption. Finally, after a heated debate in which the opposition accused the government of using the excuse of corruption to put political pressure on state institutions, the Parliament adopted a resolution on November 15 on the increased role of the legislature in handling corruption-related issues.[103] It seems quite probable that the success of the government's anticorruption initiatives will be one of the key issues on which Albanians will judge the performance of the new government.

Eno Trimcev is executive director of the Albanian Institute for International Studies.

[1] U.S. Embassy in Tirana, "Albania Today: Looking Toward the Future," remarks by Ambassador Marcie B. Ries, Institute of Balkan Studies, Thessaloniki, October 17, 2005, www.usemb-tirana.rpo.at.

[2] Eno Trimcev, Democracy, Intellectuals and the State: The Case of Albania, Albanian Institute for International Studies, Tirana, 2005.

[3] Elez Biberaj, Albania in Transition: The Rocky Road to Democracy (Boulder: Westview Press, 1998).

[4] Freedom House, Nations in Transit 2004: Albania, www.freedomhouse.org.

[5] Citizens Advocacy Office (CAO), Dritare per Transparencen, (Window on Transparency) Tirana, November 8, 2005.

[6] Albanian Institute for International Studies, Albania and EU: Perceptions and Realities 2005, Tirana, 2005.

[7] European Commission, Albania: 2005 Progress Report, Brussels, November 9, 2005, p. 9.

[8] The second multiparty elections of March 1992 also resulted in an orderly transfer of power. However, at the time, the governing SP did not have the will to continue governing anymore since it had lost almost all internal social control. Thus its campaign was lukewarm and self-defeatist-the governing party could not shoulder the responsibility of governance anymore. Elez Biberaj, Albania in Transition: The Rocky Road to Democracy (Boulder: Westview Press, 1998), pp. 35-38.

[9] OSCE/ODIHR Election Observation Mission Report, Republic of Albania: Parliamentary Elections 3 July 2005, Warsaw, November 2005, p. 1.

[10] Olli Rehn, Address to the Albanian Parliament, November 11, 2005.

[11] Interview with Eric Roman Filipink, political officer, OSCE presence in Albania, November 3, 2005.

[12] H. E. Besnik Mustafaj, The Foreign Policy Vision of the New Albanian Government, Albanian Institute for International Studies, Tirana, October 10, 2005.

[13] Shekulli, November 7, 2005.

[14] Law 8549, Status of the Civil Servant, November 11, 1999, www.pad.gov.al.

[15] European Commission, p. 12.

[16] Interview with Artan Hoxha, executive director of the Institute for Contemporary Studies, November 8, 2005.

[17] European Commission, p. 12.

[18] Ibid.

[19] Interview with Artan Hoxha, executive director of the Institute for Contemporary Studies, November 8, 2005.

[20] Ibid.

[21] OSCE report, Modernising the Capacity of the Assembly of the Republic of Albania, OSCE presence in Albania, October 13, 2005.

[22] Interview with Eric Roman Filipink, political officer, OSCE presence in Albania, November 3, 2005.

[23] OSCE/ODIHR Election Observation Mission Report, Republic of Albania: Parliamentary Elections 3 July 2005, Warsaw, November 7, 2005, pp. 3-4.

[24] Albert Rakipi, Aldo Bumci, and Blendi Kajsiu, "Albania – A Weak Democracy, a Weak State," in The Inflexibility Trap: Frustrated Societies, Weak States and Democracy (Sofia, Bulgaria: Center for Liberal Strategies, January 2003), pp. 115-168.

[25] An October 2005 survey by the Albanian Institute for International Studies found that only one-third of respondents believed that Albania will have free and fair elections in the future. See Albanian Democratization: In Search of Accountability, Albanian Institute for International Studies, Tirana, 2005.

[26] Ambassador Osmo Lipponen, head of the OSCE presence in Albania, declared that these elections were "the ticket to [Albania's] integration, be it in the security structures or in the European Union." Interview with Ambassador Osmo Lipponen by Eva Simoni, TeleArberia (TVA), May 5, 2004.

[27] Freedom House, Nations in Transit 2005: Albania, www.freedomhouse.org, p. 1.

[28] OSCE/ODHIR Election Observation Mission Report, "Annex I: Summary of Official Results," in Republic of Albania: Parliamentary Elections 3 July 2005, Warsaw, November 7, 2005, p. 30.

[29] OSCE/ODIHR Election Observation Mission Report, Republic of Albania: Parliamentary Elections 3 July 2005, Warsaw, November 7, 2005.

[30] OSCE/ODIHR Election Observation Mission Report, Republic of Albania: Parliamentary Elections 3 July 2005, Warsaw, November 7, 2005, pp. 9-10.

[31] Koalicioni i Vezhguesve Vendor, Raporti Perfundimtar.

[32] OSCE/ODIHR, p. 7.

[33] Albanian Coalition Against Corruption, Monitorimi i Mediave Per Zgjedhjet Parlamentare 2005 (Media Monitor for the Parliamentary Elections 2005) Raporti III, Tirana: 1 Korrik, 2005.

[34] Interview with Remzi Lani, executive director of the Albanian Media Institute, November 1, 2005.

[35] OSCE/ODIHR, p. 8.

[36] Ibid., p. 1.

[37] Zyra per Mbrojtjen e Qytetareve, Dritare per Transparencen, Tirana, November 8, 2005.

[38] OSCE/ODIHR, p. 2.

[39] Albanian Institute for International Studies, Albanian Democratization: In Search of Accountability, Tirana, 2005.

[40] Ibid., p. 1.

[41] Interview with Selami Xhepa, councilor to the Minister of Economics, December 12, 2005.

[42] Office of the President, Presidenti Moisiu mblodhi tryezen e partive politike parlamentare (President Moisiu calls the table of parliamentary political parties), December 7, 2005, www.president.al.

[43] Jacques Rupnik, "On Two Models of Exit from Communism: Central Europe and the Balkans," in Sorin Antohi and Vladimir Tismaneanu, eds., Between Past and Future: The Revolutions of 1989 and Their Aftermath (Budapest: CEU Press, 2000), pp. 19-20.

[44] European Commission, p. 20.

[45] ODIHR, p. 18.

[46] Ibid.

[47] For example, the Albanian Human Rights Group (AHRG) mobilized 92 volunteers to monitor the election process in several prisons and pretrial detention centers as well as regular polling stations. For the AHRG's election report, see AHRG, Raporti Paraprak i Zgjedhjeve Parlaemntare 3 Korrik 2005, Tirana, 2005.

[48] In this case, the "voter" photographs his marked ballot and then presents the picture to a fixer, who then pays the "voter" for voting for the given party. Interview with Pjerin Marku, executive director of the Albanian Coalition Against Corruption, November 15, 2005.

[49] Albanian Coalition Against Corruption, Monitorimi i Mediave Per Zgjedhjet Parlamentare 2005, Raporti III (Tirana, July 1, 2005).

[50] Interview with Citizens Advocacy Office members, December 2005.

[51] Interview with Bardhi Kadilli, adviser on corruption issues to the Office of the Prime Minister, February 27, 2006.

[52] Shekulli, "MJAFT!: Te Minimizohet Klientela Shqiptare e Kazinose," December 5, 2005.

[53] European Commission, p. 21.

[54] Interview with BSPSH official.

[55] Interview with KSSH official.

[56] Albanian Media Institute, Television Across Europe: Regulation, Policy and Independence, Albania, Open Society Institute, Tirana, 2005, p. 30.

[57] Ilda Londo, Albania, Institute of Media, p. 49.

[58] Interview with Remzi Lani.

[59] Keshilli Kombetar i Radio Televizionit (KKRT) list of licensees in the Institute of Media, Television Across Europe: Regulation, Policy, and Independence, Albania, Open Society Institute, Tirana, 2005, p. 2.

[60] OSCE/ODIHR, p. 14; Albanian Coalition Against Corruption, Monitorimi i Mediave, p. 3.

[61] Article 19, Concerns over the Retention of Criminal Defamation in South-East Europe, London, November 2005, www.article19.org.

[62] Institute of Media, Television Across Europe, pp. 61-62.

[63] Ibid., p. 7.

[64] Ibid., p. 71.

[65] Ibid., p. 56.

[66] Article 19, Concerns over the Retention of Criminal Defamation in South-East Europe, London, November 2005.

[67] As of September 2005. See www.internetworldstats.com.

[68] A. Nune, Sudosteureopaissches Mediezentrum, soemz.euv-frankfurt-o.de/media-see/newmedia/main/articles.

[69] Co-Plan, UN Development Program and World Bank, Decentralization and Water Sector Privatization in Albania, Tirana, December 2004, p. 2.

[70] European Commission, p. 12.

[71] Ministry of the Interior, Ministry of Public Works, Transportation, and Telecommunications, and Ministry of Finance, Roundtable on the 2006 Budget: The Reform of Decentralization and Local Autonomy, November 4, 2005.

[72] USAID, www.usaidalbania.org.

[73] USAID Mission Report, Albanian Regional Development: Opportunities and Challenges, September 12-26, 2005, p. 5.

[74] Interview with Sabina Ymeri, USAID expert on local government, November 7, 2005.

[75] Zana Vokopola, Improving Service Quality at Education – A Process That Started in Albania, Urban Research Institute, July 2005, p. 7.

[76] Interview with Artan Hoxha, executive director of the Institute for Contemporary Studies, November 8, 2005.

[77] One example is the agreement between the municipality of Pogradec and the Bucima commune to manage the water utilities together. Interview with Artan Hoxha, executive director of the Institute for Contemporary Studies, November 8, 2005.

[78] OSCE/ODIHR, p. 11.

[79] Ibid., pp. 11-12.

[80] Giovanni di Stassi, representative of the Congress of Local Governments, quoted in "KE-ja ne Tirane per te hetuar ngercin Bashki-Qeveri," (CE in Tirana to investigate Municipality-Government Deadlock) Gazeta Shqiptare, December 20, 2005.

[81] European Commission, p. 13.

[82] Freedom House, Nations in Transit 2005: Albania, www.freedomhouse.org.

[83] Mbaresa Veleshnja Gentry, "A Guide to Researching the Albanian Legal System," http://www.nyulawglobal.org/globalex/Albania.htm, July 2005.

[84] Shekulli, October 19, 2005.

[85] Rilindja Demokratike, Vetem 38% e dosjeve te ekzekutuara ne Tirane (Only 38% of judicial rulings executed in Tirana), October 26, 2005.

[86] Tedi Malaveci, "Veprimtaria e Sherbimit Permbarimor Gjyqesor dhe Aktiviteti i tij ne Nivel Qendror dhe Lokal per vitin 2004," (The Activity of Bailiff's Office in Central and Local Areas for the Year 2004) Ministry of Justice of the Republic of Albania, Tirana.

[87] Shekulli, November 8, 2005.

[88] European Commission, pp. 13-15.

[89] Ibid., p. 13.

[90] Ibid.

[91] Balkanweb, October 26, 2005, www.balkanweb.com

[92] Center for Rehabilitation of Trauma and Torture Survivors, Raport Alternativ Vjetor mbi Situaten e Tortures ne Shqiperi (Yearly Alternative Report on the Situation of Torture in Albania) CRTTS: Tirana, 2005.

[93] European Commission, p. 17.

[94] Council of Ministers, Action Plan on the Prevention of and Fight Against Corruption, 2005, Anticorruption Monitoring Group and Anticorruption Unit, Tirana, 2005.

[95] Interview with Pjerin Marku, executive director, Albanian Coalition Against Corruption.

[96] Shekulli, October 21, 2005.

[97] Interview with Pjerin Marku

[98] South East European Times, "Poll Shows Mixed Picture of Corruption in Balkans," November 15, 2005, www.setimes.com.

[99] Albanian Institute for International Studies, Albanian Democratization: In Search of Accountability (AIIS: Tirana, 2005).

[101] European Commission, Albania, p. 16.

[101] Interview with Artan Hoxha, executive director of the Institute for Contemporary Studies, November 8, 2005.

[102] Shekulli, "Berisha: Kontroll Buxhetit te Ministrave," November 12, 2005.

[103] South East European Times, "Albanian Parliament Adopts Resolution on Combating Corruption," November 16, 2005.

Armenia

Capital: Yerevan
Population: 3 million
GNI/capita: $1,060
Ethnic Groups: Armenian (93%), Azeri (1%), Russian (2%), Kurd and others (4%)

Nations in Transit Ratings and Averaged Scores

	1997	1998	1999	2001	2002	2003	2004	2005	2006
Electoral Process	5.50	5.75	5.25	5.50	5.50	5.50	5.75	5.75	5.75
Civil Society	3.50	3.50	3.50	3.50	3.50	3.50	3.50	3.50	3.50
Independent Media	5.25	5.25	4.75	4.75	4.75	5.00	5.25	5.50	5.50
Governance *	4.50	4.50	4.50	4.50	4.50	4.75	4.75	n/a	n/a
National Democratic Governance	n/a	n/a	n/a	n/a	n/a	n/a	n/a	5.00	5.00
Local Democratic Governance	n/a	n/a	n/a	n/a	n/a	n/a	n/a	5.50	5.50
Judicial Framework and Independence	4.75	5.00	5.00	5.00	5.00	5.00	5.00	5.25	5.00
Corruption	n/a	n/a	5.75	5.75	5.75	5.75	5.75	5.75	5.75
Democracy Score	4.70	4.80	4.79	4.83	4.83	4.92	5.00	5.18	5.14

* With the 2005 edition, Freedom House introduced seperate analysis and ratings for national democratic governance and local democratic governance to provide readers with more detailed and nuanced analysis of these two important subjects.

NOTE: The ratings reflect the consensus of Freedom House, its academic advisers, and the author of this report. The opinions expressed in this report are those of the author. The ratings are based on a scale of 1 to 7, with 1 representing the highest level of democratic progress and 7 the lowest. The Democracy Score is an average of ratings for the categories tracked in a given year.

The economic and social data on this page were taken from the following sources:
GNI/capita, Population: World Development Indicators 2006 (Washington, D.C.: World Bank, 2006).
Ethnic Groups: CIA World Factbook 2006 (Washington, D.C.: Central Intelligence Agency, 2006).

EXECUTIVE SUMMARY

A rmenia's democratic development has proceeded unevenly in the 14 years since independence. Although Armenia was one of the first Soviet republics to end Communist rule, the absence of an effective system of checks and balances, the concentration of power in the presidency, the centralized system of government, and the lack of an independent civil service have fostered weak governance and widespread corruption. This has been exacerbated by the close links between the country's political and business elites, which have impeded the development of a more transparent political system. Elections have generally failed to meet international standards, contributing to public cynicism toward the authorities and skepticism about the value of participating in political and civic activities. The unresolved conflict with Azerbaijan over the disputed territory of Nagorno-Karabakh remains a potential source of instability in the region and has deterred foreign investors and hampered trade diversification. However, the country's progress in macroeconomic stabilization has been relatively successful. Successive governments have generally adhered to the economic reform measures prescribed by international financial institutions, ensuring continuity in macroeconomic policies and a steady improvement in economic and financial indicators. Nevertheless, though poverty rates are declining, the popular perception is that most Armenians have yet to benefit from these macroeconomic successes. This has contributed to disillusionment in Armenia's political and economic transition.

Tension between the government and the opposition remained a defining feature of Armenia's political scene in 2005, when the opposition continued to question the legitimacy of the current authorities, elected in flawed elections in 2003. Debate over amendments to the Constitution, aimed at balancing the distribution of power more evenly, dominated political discussion throughout the year. The amendments were approved in a nationwide referendum in November 2005, although local observers and the opposition questioned official data reporting high turnout. The prosecution of officials for corruption remained rare. Fewer assaults on journalists were reported, but independent media were dissatisfied that constitutional changes relating to the composition of the industry's regulatory body were insufficient to ensure the body's independence from the executive.

National Democratic Governance. Weak governance and ongoing disputes between the authorities and the opposition continued to test Armenia's political stability in 2005. A long-awaited constitutional referendum was held in November 2005, with the aim of ensuring a more even distribution of the balance of power between the president, Parliament, and judiciary. Official results showed that turnout was sufficient to render the vote valid and that a majority of participants had approved the proposed amendments, which the Council of Europe had assessed as generally favorable. However, the opposition parties had urged their supporters to boycott the referendum and consequently asserted that the official turnout figures were grossly inflated – a stance backed by local observers. Armenia's rating for national democratic governance remains at 5.00. *Although the changes to the Constitution endorsed by a nationwide referendum will usher in a more even distribution of powers, the conduct of the referendum, in particular doubts over the official turnout figures, prevents an improvement in the rating.*

Electoral Process. The failure of authorities to ensure democratic elections has contributed to a lack of public confidence in the electoral process and Armenia's progress toward a functioning democracy. The Parliament approved revisions to the electoral code in May 2005, with the aim of addressing some of the flaws that have characterized Armenia's elections. These include a reduction in the number of presidential appointees on election commissions and an increase in the number of parliamentary seats allocated by proportional representation at the expense of those contested under the single-mandate system, with a view to reducing opportunities for vote buying. A new national voters' register has also been compiled. *Armenia's rating for electoral process remains unchanged at 5.75. Although the revised electoral code improves the legal framework for elections, its success will depend on its implementation, particularly with regard to the authorities' commitment to identify and take measures against those guilty of electoral violations.*

Civil Society. Civil society groups are becoming more active in public life but remain hampered by financial constraints and a reliance on external funding, mainly from diasporic groups. Under discussion in 2005 was a new Law on Lobbying, which aims to regulate lobbying of state institutions by organizations and private individuals; unofficial lobbying practices have in the past tended to benefit those with privileged access to state institutions. A change to the structure of university governing boards, half of whose members are now appointed by the government, and pressure on teachers to promote the government's constitutional amendments raised concerns about growing political influence in the education system. *Armenia's rating for civil society remains at 3.50 owing to evidence of increased politicization of the education system, which offsets the positive steps toward regulating lobbying activities.*

Independent Media. Coverage of the constitutional referendum campaign in late 2005 confirmed the bias by the broadcast media (Armenia's most influential news source) in favor of the authorities that has characterized earlier election campaigns. Newspapers continued to offer more diverse opinions, but total circulation remains low, at just 60,000 in 2005. A1+, Armenia's main independent television station until it lost its broadcasting license in 2002, has been ordered to leave its state-owned premises in Yerevan in what it believes is a further attempt by the authorities to curtail its activities. Fewer attacks on journalists were reported in 2005, but self-censorship from fear of prosecution remains widespread. Local media associations pressed unsuccessfully for the revised Constitution to exclude the president entirely from the process of appointing the industry's regulatory body. *Armenia's rating for independent media remains at 5.50 owing to the absence of reform efforts.*

Local Democratic Governance. Although the Constitution and national legislation provide a framework for local self-government, there has been little real decentralization of authority. The autonomy of local governments is limited by their weak financial resources, and they remain reliant on the national budget for much of their funding. A local nongovernmental organization (NGO), Choice Is Yours, gave the conduct of the local elections in September–October 2005 a negative assessment, reporting that candidates had been hindered in their campaign, that the voter lists remained inaccurate, and that the campaign was marred by bribery. Council of Europe observers, by contrast, judged that the elections were an improvement on previous years. A survey carried out by a local think tank in September 2005 found that 60 percent of the 1,000 respondents questioned were unfamiliar with the activities of their local self-governing bodies. With the passage of the constitutional amendments, responsibility for choosing the mayor of Yerevan passes from the president to an as yet unformed municipal council. *Armenia's rating for local democratic governance remains unchanged at 5.50. The positive assessment by international observers of the 2005 local elections and a provision for an indirectly elected mayor of Yerevan notwithstanding, the accountability and effectiveness of local government bodies remains weak.*

Judicial Framework and Independence. Despite constitutional provisions guaranteeing a full range of basic human rights, in practice there remain substantial barriers to effective protection of said rights. The judiciary enjoys little independence and has been unable to fulfill its role as a guarantor of law and justice. The constitutional amendments go some way toward increasing the impartiality of the judiciary, as the right to appoint the Council of Justice (which oversees the judicial system) passes from the president to the General Assembly of Judges. Similarly, the Office of the Human Rights Ombudsman becomes a parliamentary rather than a presidential appointment. However, the executive has reduced the legal powers of the ombudsman to request documents from the courts. *Armenia's rating for judicial framework and independence improves to 5.00. The lessening of presidential influence over judicial appointments has, on balance, outweighed the negative implications of the attempts by the executive to reduce the ombudsman's authority.*

Corruption. Corruption remains a substantial obstacle to Armenia's political and economic development. The close links between the political and economic elite and the lack of effective law enforcement procedures have fostered official corruption. Government efforts to address the issue are focused on an anticorruption strategy adopted in late 2003. However, although the number of corruption crimes solved by law enforcement structures increased in 2005, prosecutions remained rare. Doubts remain whether the authorities have sufficient political will to make genuine inroads into reducing corruption. *Armenia's rating for corruption remains unchanged at 5.75.*

Outlook for 2006. Tension between the government and the opposition will remain high in 2006, particularly toward the end of the year as the next general election, due in mid-2007, approaches. Vested interests in the political hierarchy are likely to prevent substantive improvements in governance, but ongoing reforms should result in an increase in tax revenue. This will enable increased spending in sectors such as health care and education, which will go some way toward ensuring that the benefits of Armenia's strong economic growth of recent years are spread more widely – essential if public belief in the country's progress toward democracy is to be restored.

MAIN REPORT

National Democratic Governance

1997	1998	1999	2001	2002	2003	2004	2005	2006
n/a	n/a	n/a	n/a	n/a	n/a	n/a	5.00	5.00

The Constitution enshrines the principle that Armenia "is a sovereign, democratic state, based on social justice and the rule of law"[1] and provides for the separation of powers. However, it has so far failed to ensure an effective system of checks and balances among the branches of government, owing to the extensive powers vested in the presidency.

Following pressure from the Council of Europe, a nationwide referendum on constitutional amendments to rectify the imbalance of power was held in November 2005. (An earlier referendum, held in May 2003, was deemed invalid owing to insufficient turnout.) In July 2005, the Council of Europe's Venice Commission gave the draft amendments a generally favorable assessment, regarding them as a positive step toward Armenia's integration into European structures. Most notably, they include the removal of the president's right to dismiss the prime minister virtually at will; the election of the mayor of the capital, Yerevan, by an elected council rather than the president; and the election of the Council of Justice by members of the judiciary (rather than its appointment by the president).

Official turnout in the 2005 referendum was 64 percent, according to the Central Election Commission, with just over 93 percent of voters approving the amendments. The official referendum results have exacerbated the tension between the opposition and the authorities that has tested Armenia's political stability over the past two years. This stems from the flawed parliamentary and presidential elections in 2003 – whose results the opposition have continued to dispute – and the subsequent constitutional debate. Since the 2003 elections, the opposition has kept up a parliamentary boycott and has also attempted to force the authorities to hold a vote of confidence in the president, staging a series of street demonstrations in 2004. Rejecting the government's draft constitutional changes as insufficiently far-reaching, the opposition parties urged their supporters to boycott the referendum, leading the opposition – along with local referendum observers and the few international observers monitoring the process – to question the apparently high official turnout. Some members of the government also expressed concern at the official turnout figures. Artur Baghdasarian, leader of the Country of Law Party and parliamentary chairman, reported examples of ballot box stuffing and other fraudulent practices to the prosecutor general. However, the prosecutor's office took no action, citing the absence of specific evidence. Another issue of concern surrounding the conduct of the referendum was the bias of the broadcast media in favor of the authorities in the run-up to the ballot.

Legislative authority is vested in the Parliament, which is empowered by the Constitution to dismiss the government by majority vote and to remove the president from office with a two-thirds majority if the Constitutional Court judges him guilty of serious offenses. In actuality, however, the Parliament has little power to hold the executive to account and enjoys substantially less authority than the presidency, even after the constitutional referendum. The government has substantial influence over the Parliament's legislative agenda, which is a major constraint on its lawmaking capacity, and most government-sponsored initiatives tend to be approved. Although the process of drafting and amending laws is comparatively straightforward, implementation and enforcement are weak.

The effectiveness of both the government and Parliament is impeded by their weak financial resources. Armenia has a poor tax collection record, owing in part to the scale of the shadow economy (estimates range from 33 percent to 53 percent of the official gross domestic product [GDP] in 2004, depending on the methodology used).[2] Central government tax revenue was equivalent to just 13.2 percent of GDP in 2004, according to data from the National Statistical Service, but is estimated to have risen to 13.7 percent in 2005, thanks in part to the implementation of measures to reduce tax evasion.

A parliamentary Oversight Chamber audits government budget performance, assesses its compliance with budget targets, and evaluates its borrowing and privatization policies. The chamber submits annual reports to the Parliament and has frequently criticized the executive's handling of public finances. However, its role as a watchdog over the government is limited owing to the legislature's weakness relative to the executive branch. In addition, the existence of other audit and investigative bodies within ministries creates a duplication of functions and the absence of clearly separated roles, further reducing the effectiveness of the chamber as an oversight body.

Citizen participation in decision making is limited, although civil society groups are becoming increasingly involved in political processes (for example, in the monitoring of elections). The Parliament has a Web site, debates are usually open to the public and are widely reported in the media, draft legislation is generally made available to the public, and all legislation approved by the Parliament is published in an official bulletin. In December 2005, the Ministry of Justice launched a new Web site containing a database of legislation, government decisions, and Constitutional Court rulings.

The Law on Freedom of Information, adopted in September 2003, aims to improve public access by obliging government bodies and public service providers to release within 30 days official information relating to their activities.[3] They are permitted to refuse the release of information in only a few cases, and failure to comply with the law is a criminal offense. However, imperfect enforcement of the legislation has hampered its effectiveness.

Reform of the civil service and public administration is under way. The civil service is a professional body, in theory independent of the executive and legislative branches of power, and is not subject to change after general elections. A seven-member Civil Service Council is charged with selecting staff for government agencies on a competitive basis and monitoring the performance of government officials. Critics of the council argue that because it is appointed by the president, it lacks independence and is vulnerable to political influence.

Moreover, although adoption of the Law on Civil Service in 2001 was a first step toward improving the quality of state institutions, enforcement of the legislation has been problematic.[4] Issues such as low wages have prevented the civil service from attracting and retaining skilled staff, although periodic wage increases are addressing this concern.

The National Police and National Security Service are responsible for Armenia's domestic security, intelligence activities, border control, and police force. Several parliamentary committees are responsible for defense and security policy, but the legislature's weakness relative to the presidency and government results in its having little control over the country's military and security services. The president is the supreme commander of the armed forces and is entitled to deploy the army without seeking parliamentary approval. The defense minister, the head of the police, and the head of the National Security Service are all presidential appointees. Armenia's security and military doctrines are classified documents and therefore unavailable for public scrutiny.

Nevertheless, issues such as corruption in the police force and poor conditions in the armed forces, including mistreatment of conscripts, are frequently covered in the media. A two-year reform of the armed services is due to start in 2007, with the assistance of NATO, as part of which a new national security strategy will be devised.

The ongoing territorial dispute with Azerbaijan over Nagorno-Karabakh remained a potential source of instability in 2005, although peace negotiations continued at both presidential and foreign ministerial levels. The unresolved conflict has had wide-ranging economic repercussions on the region as a whole, and for Armenia specifically it has proved a deterrent to foreign investors. In addition, the dispute has led to substantial expenditures for defense (the military is set to receive the largest share of budgetary spending in 2006, at 15 percent)[5] to the detriment of other sectors such as health care and education.

One legacy of the 1988-1994 war with Azerbaijan over the area of Nagorno-Karabakh has been that the armed forces and security services have played a large role in the country's political development. Military leaders, through the Yerkrapah parliamentary faction of Nagorno-Karabakh veterans, were instrumental in forcing the resignation of President Levon Ter-Petrossian in 1998, having rejected his apparent willingness to negotiate a stage-by-stage resolution of the conflict with Azerbaijan. The influence of military leaders has lessened since then, and in 2005 Yerkrapah lost members to a new organization, Test of Spirit, whose founders were dissatisfied at Yerkrapah's support of Robert Kocharian's administration.

Electoral Process

1997	1998	1999	2001	2002	2003	2004	2005	2006
5.50	5.75	5.25	5.50	5.50	5.50	5.75	5.75	5.75

Armenia's constitutional and electoral framework enshrines the principle of universal and equal suffrage by secret ballot and provides for regular, free, and fair elections. Since independence, however, the authorities have failed to ensure free and fair elections, as vested interests within the political and business elites have sought to preserve their privileges. This has contributed to a lack of public confidence in the electoral process and Armenia's progress toward a functioning democracy.

Political parties are regulated by the Law on Political Parties and must be registered with the Ministry of Justice. The electorate has a wide range of parties to choose from, although political parties are generally driven more by personality than policy. Of the more than 110 parties registered at the time of the May 2003 parliamentary election, only 6 exceeded the 5 percent vote threshold required to win parliamentary representation. The number of registered parties has dropped sharply since the introduction in July 2002 of new registration requirements that stipulate political parties must have at least 200 members and maintain branches in at least one-third of Armenia's regions. According to the Ministry of Justice, there were 49 parties in December 2003.

The Republican Party of Armenia (RPA) is the dominant party at both national and local levels. Headed by Prime Minister Andranik Markarian, the RPA is the leading party in the coalition government, controlling several ministries and the majority of subministerial posts. Under a power-sharing agreement concluded after the May 2003 parliamentary election, the nationalist Armenian Revolutionary Federation and the center-right Country of Law Party make up the other two parties in the coalition. Each of these has two cabinet-level positions and several subministerial posts. The Ministries of Defense, the Interior, and National Security are headed by presidential loyalists. Together with leading businesspeople, often termed oligarchs, these parties and ministers form the so-called power class.

As in other former Soviet republics, political and economic circles are closely linked in Armenia. This stems partly from inadequate party funding legislation, which leaves parties heavily reliant on private financial sources and therefore susceptible to donor influence. The immunity from prosecution enjoyed by parliamentary deputies has also encouraged business monopolists to seek election.

Direct presidential elections are held every five years; elections to the 131-member Parliament are currently held every four years, but the legislature will move to a five-year term on the expiry of its current mandate in 2007. The most recent presidential election was won by the incumbent, Kocharian, who beat Stepan Demirchian in a second-round runoff on March 5, 2003, winning 67.5 percent of the vote, according to the Central Election Commission. A total of nine opposition parties formed the Justice Alliance bloc, headed by Demirchian, to contest the parliamentary election held on May 25, 2003. However, the RPA and other pro-presidential parties retained their majority in the Parliament, with the Justice Alliance and the opposition National Unity Party of Artashes Geghamian (who secured third place in the first round of the presidential election) winning just 24 seats.

Both elections were monitored by the Organization for Security and Cooperation in Europe/Office for Democratic Institutions and Human Rights (OSCE/ODIHR) and were found to be below international standards for democratic elections, although international monitors judged the flaws insufficient to negate the results. Turnout for the 2003 parliamentary election was 52.2 percent, according to the Central Election Commission, down from 68.4 percent in the second round of the presidential election, indicating declining public confidence in the electoral process.

According to the OSCE, women accounted for just 15 percent of the candidates on the proportional lists in the 2003 election and only 4 percent of the majoritarian candidates. Seven women won seats in the new Parliament, up from four in the outgoing assembly. Ethnic minorities make up only about 3 percent of Armenia's population, and their participation in the political process is correspondingly low. No ethnic minorities are represented in the Parliament.

With the aim of addressing some of the flaws in the electoral process, revisions to Armenia's electoral code were enacted in May 2005.[6] The Council of Europe's Venice Commission gave these revisions a generally positive assessment. Under the revised code, the number of parliamentary deputies elected by proportional representation on the basis of party lists rises from 75 to 90, while 41 deputies will be elected from single-mandate constituencies, down from 56. This could help reduce electoral fraud by lessening the potential for bribery.

Other changes include increased rights for candidate proxies and stricter rules for the summarization and publication of voting results – delays in publicizing results in previous elections increased the scope for fraud. Areas of concern remain, including insufficient safeguards for the filing of election complaints and appeals, although in a positive move, in September 2005 a Yerevan court upheld an appeal by an independent candidate against the decision by a local election commission to annul his election result. This suggests that the appeals procedure is improving. Nevertheless, government critics remain skeptical that the new code will improve the electoral process, arguing that in the past the shortcomings in Armenia's electoral process stemmed from the implementation of the electoral framework rather than the framework itself.

The revised electoral code also alters the composition of election commissions, aimed at reducing presidential influence over the electoral process. The number of presidential appointees on the central commission and each of the 56 territorial election commissions has been reduced from three to one: Each party faction in the Parliament will nominate a commission member, and two members of the judiciary will now be included. The judicial members will not be permitted to preside over any case involving electoral irregularities. Given the dependence of the judiciary on the executive, however, concerns remain over the impartiality of the new commissions.

The revised code aims to address flaws in the voter registration procedure. This is now the responsibility of the police rather than local governments. New passports have been issued, replacing Soviet-era identity documents, and the data have been used to compile a national voters register. Observers of the September–October 2005 local elections noted that old identity papers were still being used in some constituencies, but the authorities asserted that the new register marked an improvement over the old system.

Civil Society

1997	1998	1999	2001	2002	2003	2004	2005	2006
3.50	3.50	3.50	3.50	3.50	3.50	3.50	3.50	3.50

The number of civil society groups in Armenia grew rapidly following the breakup of the Soviet Union. However, their effectiveness was hampered by deteriorating socioeconomic conditions due to the war with Azerbaijan over Nagorno-Karabakh and the collapse of the country's economic base. The result is that public participation in civil society activities has not been as high as the number of groups would suggest, although improving macroeconomic conditions in recent years have enabled public involvement to increase.

As of September 2005, 4,350 NGOs were registered with the Ministry of Justice, of which over 1,000 were registered during the previous year. Over the past decade, the focus of NGO activities has moved from humanitarian assistance to democracy building and broader development programs in sectors such as education, public policy, and health care, as well as ethnic minorities and the disabled. Issues such as domestic violence and the trafficking of women, as well as campaigns to promote more active participation of women in politics, are gaining greater recognition, and domestic groups such as Choice Is Yours actively monitor the country's elections.

NGOs are well established throughout Armenia, with some participating in regionwide networks across the South Caucasus and Commonwealth of Independent States. Most civil society groups remain dependent on international funding, as the income level of most Armenians is insufficient to permit charitable donations. According to a survey of 347 NGOs and 61 experts carried out in 2004 by the U.S. organization World Learning, 87 percent of the NGOs surveyed relied entirely on foreign donors.[7] Domestic charities, such as the Hayastan All-Armenian Fund, and the U.S.-based Lincy Foundation successfully raise funds from the Armenian diaspora. The dependence of most NGOs on foreign donations has led to concerns that this practice weakens the civic sector's incentive to establish strong links with Armenian society. Nevertheless, the financial viability of NGOs is strengthening, owing partly to legislative improvements and more effective preparation of requests for funding by NGOs.

Media coverage of civil society activity is generally positive, although it tends to be limited to isolated initiatives and is often dependent on personal contacts. Popular perception of NGOs is similarly favorable, although public knowledge of most NGO activities is still limited: 45.8 percent of adults questioned in the 2003 Citizens' Awareness and Participation in Armenia survey could not name a single NGO. Nonetheless, NGOs reported a growing level of public participation in private voluntary activity. Religious organizations attract the largest number of participants, reflecting the strong position of the Armenian Apostolic Church in society. The Apostolic Church itself engages in charitable work, financed largely through diasporic donations, as do other domestic and foreign religious charities.

The state protects the rights of the independent civic sector, and civil society groups are generally able to carry out their work without interference either from the government or from extremist organizations. The Law on Charity (October 2002) and the Law on Foundations (December 2002)[8] regulate the establishment and activities of charities and NGOs and have been judged by the International Center for Not-for-Profit Law to be in compliance with international good practices of NGO regulation, although implementation of the legislation is at times patchy. The Ministry of Justice's registration process for NGOs is relatively straightforward.

Nonprofit organizations are subject to taxation on property, vehicles, and employee wages, and NGOs must disclose their revenue sources in order to establish their tax liability. The Law on Public Organizations (different from the Law on Foundations mentioned above) prohibits direct income generation, and public organizations are not permitted to participate in government tenders. This has serious implications for the financial sustainability of nonprofit organizations. The establishment of limited liability companies is one way in which NGOs are able to generate income, but these are subject to taxation in the same way as businesses. Armenia's tax legislation does not contain provisions for charitable donations, which inhibits private sector philanthropy.

Officials rarely canvass public opinion in meetings or through surveys, but government engagement with civil society and policy research groups has increased in recent years. This is partly attributable to an improvement in the organizational capacity and advocacy skills of civil society groups, which have benefited from expanded training programs. NGOs are increasingly lobbying the government, with some success. In 2005, environmentalists succeeded in persuading the government to reroute part of a new road linking Armenia with Iran to protect a nature reserve. Debate was under way in 2005 on a draft Law on Lobbying that would regulate lobbying of state institutions by organizations and private individuals. Unofficial lobbying practices have hitherto tended to benefit those with privileged access to state institutions. NGO members are also participating increasingly in the drafting and monitoring of government initiatives (for instance, the Poverty Reduction Strategy Paper), and the establishment of a Civil Society Monitoring Board in 2004 has opened up the prison service to public scrutiny.

Several private policy think tanks are active in Armenia, but their influence on government policy is limited. They include the International Center for Human Development, which focuses on projects such as poverty reduction, regional integration, and good governance; and the Armenian Center for National and International Studies and the Armenia International Policy Research Group, which concentrate on foreign and domestic public policy issues.

Armenia's Constitution guarantees the right to establish and join trade unions, although this right can be restricted for those serving in the armed forces and law enforcement agencies. The Confederation of Labor Unions unites about 30 individual unions, but most of these are relatively inactive and have limited power to guarantee workers' rights. Private sector employees enjoy little protection against dismissal – this combined with the high rate of unemployment has meant that strikes in private enterprises are rare. Strikes in the public sector are more common, generally over issues such as wage increases or payment of back wages. The Union of Industrialists and Entrepreneurs represents the interests of Armenia's largest businesses.

The low level of budget revenue has weakened the education system. Access to education in rural areas remains poor, and students report that bribery is frequently needed to secure a university place and to obtain good marks. In November 2005, students protested against structural reforms to university governing boards, half of whose members will now be appointed by the government, in effect strengthening government control over universities. Moreover, in the run-up to the November 2005 constitutional referendum, the government urged teachers to promote the proposed amendments among their students and staff, which raises concerns about the politicization of the education system.

Independent Media

1997	1998	1999	2001	2002	2003	2004	2005	2006
5.25	5.25	4.75	4.75	4.75	5.0	5.25	5.50	5.50

Armenia's press freedoms are guaranteed in Article 27 of the Constitution. However, in practice, press freedom has come under threat in recent years, prompting Freedom House to downgrade Armenia's press rating in its annual survey of press freedom from "Partly Free" in 2002 to "Not Free" in 2003. This rating was unchanged in 2004, a year in which several assaults on journalists highlighted the dangerous working conditions faced by the independent media, and in 2005. In that year, independent journalists continued to come under attack, although there were fewer incidents than in earlier years. For example, in April 2005 a car belonging to the editor of a regional newspaper was vandalized, an incident he attributed to the paper's critical coverage of local government issues.

Armenia's libel laws have created a difficult legal environment for investigative journalists and have contributed to widespread self-censorship, particularly where corruption or national security is concerned. Libel is classified as a criminal offense punishable by a fine, while insulting a government official in the mass media is also deemed a criminal offense. This seems to contradict the provisions of the Council of Europe's February 2004 Declaration on Freedom of Political Debate in the Media – to which Armenia is a signatory – which recognizes the media's right to "disseminate negative information and critical opinions concerning political figures and public officials."[9]

Other media-related legislation is more favorable. This includes the Law on Freedom of Information, which was passed in 2003,[10] and an amendment to the Code of Administrative Offenses that states that government officials who obstruct the gathering of news can be fined. Since December 2003, when the Law on Mass Media was approved,[11] media outlets have no longer been required to register with the Ministry of Justice. The law also rescinded the need for journalists to disclose their sources of information and funding, except in cases where judges are hearing related criminal offenses.

According to the Yerevan Press Club, as of November 2005 there were just over 60 private television stations in Armenia, of which 28 were based in Yerevan. As well as the state-owned public radio broadcaster, there were about 12 private radio stations, which focus on entertainment and brief news reports. The programs of Radio Free Europe/Radio Liberty and the Voice of America are broadcast on state radio, while international news channels such as CNN are also available.

The state-run Armenian Public Television is the country's most influential media outlet. Its output, along with that of the leading private stations – for example, Armenia, ALM, and Shant – is biased in favor of the authorities. In the run-up to the November 2005 constitutional referendum, the majority of coverage in the broadcast media, including on public television, promoted the authorities' "yes" campaign, with the opposition largely unable to gain media access. A new television channel, Yerkir Media, was established in 2004, the first to be associated with a political party. Despite Orinats Yerkir's position in the government (as one of the junior coalition parties), however, the channel does offer critical coverage of the authorities.

Armenia's main independent television station, A1+, lost its broadcasting license in a controversial tender in April 2002 and failed to regain a broadcasting frequency in many subsequent tenders. The National Commission on Television and Radio (NCTR), whose members are currently appointed by Kocharian and hence have faced criticism from international observers at their lack of impartiality, cited financial and technical reasons for its decision not to award new frequencies to

A1+ and another leading broadcasting organization, Noyan Tapan. However, A1+ believed that the decision was politically motivated owing to the investigative nature of its reporting. Although the company has continued to make programs for regional television and operates an online news service, it has been unable to resume broadcasting. In early 2005, it failed to win a license for a radio frequency and in July was ordered to leave its premises (which are state-owned) in central Yerevan and to move to smaller offices.

In 2005, local press associations lobbied unsuccessfully for constitutional amendments to change the way the NCTR is appointed. The final version, as endorsed by the Council of Europe and approved in a referendum in November, envisages that the Parliament and the president will each appoint half of the members, once the term of the current members expires. Local media associations had wanted to exclude the president entirely from the appointment process, effective immediately.

Armenia's 70 or so newspapers (data from the Yerevan Press Club) offer more diverse opinions than the broadcast media. Total circulation is extremely low, however, at about 60,000 in 2005, although this was up by about 20,000 compared with 2003. The state-owned national daily is *Hayastani Hanrapetutyun*, and there are 5 privately owned national dailies. Pro-Kocharian papers include the daily *Hayots Ashkhar*, the biweekly *Golos Armenii*, and the weekly *Yerkir*. Offering a more liberal, pro-Western perspective are *Aravot* and *Haykakan Zhamanak*.

Most broadcast and print media organizations in Armenia are privately owned and funded. Although the country's newspapers offer a plurality of views, including in their coverage of the 2005 referendum campaign, their low circulation presents them with serious financial constraints. They are dependent on private sponsors, often with significant vested political or economic interests, and this affects their objectivity. More than half of Armenia's newspapers are distributed by the Haymamul agency, which is run by a government-appointed director. The government declared its intention to privatize the agency in 2001 but since then has sold off only the sales kiosks, leaving Haymamul with control over distribution (and hence able to influence circulation).

Access to the Internet is not formally restricted, but high connection costs render it unaffordable for most households; about 5 percent of the population had access to the Internet in September 2005, according to the company World Internet Stats. There are about 30 Internet service providers (ISPs) in Armenia, although only about one-third are actually functioning. Development of and access to Internet services have been hampered by a lack of competition in the sector. Compared with print and broadcast media, however, a greater diversity of opinions is available on the Internet, with companies such as A1+ able to use this medium. Although as of mid-2005 competing providers have offered mobile telephone services, all ISPs are still reliant on a monopoly provider, Armentel, for connection to outside services. The government does not attempt to control the Internet directly, although the fact that there is still only one company providing connection to outside services is an impediment to both Internet users and other service providers.

Local Democratic Governance

1997	1998	1999	2001	2002	2003	2004	2005	2006
n/a	n/a	n/a	n/a	n/a	n/a	n/a	5.50	5.50

Armenia's Constitution and national legislation provide a framework for local self-government, but in practice the authority and activities of the local administrations are circumscribed by the presidency and the central government, which wield extensive control over local issues.

Chapter 7 of the Constitution covers issues relating to territorial local self-government. Armenia has a two-tiered administrative structure. It is divided into 10 regions, which are subdivided into more than 900 communities. The country's 10 regions are administered by governors appointed by the central government, who in turn appoint their own staff. Regional governors are responsible for administering policy in a wide range of fields (including finances, public utilities, and urban development), coordinating the activities of regional agencies of state administration, mediating between the central and local governments, and regulating intercommunity issues. A Ministry of Local Government, created in 2005 following the merger of several government agencies, exercises control over the regional governors.

The mayor of Yerevan, which has the status of a community under the revised Constitution, is currently appointed by the president, but the constitutional amendments approved in November 2005 provide for the election of the mayor by a new municipal council. Opposition parties had pushed for direct election of the mayor by the city's residents; according to a survey carried out by the Armenian Center for National and International Studies (ACNIS), a local think tank, in September 2005, 62 percent of respondents would have preferred to elect the mayor directly, with a view to increasing accountability.

Community heads (equivalent to a mayor) and Councils of Elders, made up of 5 to 15 members, are chosen for three-year terms on the basis of universal, equal, and direct suffrage by secret ballot. The community head is accountable to the Council of Elders but can be dismissed by the central government on the recommendation of the regional governor (under the revised Constitution, the Constitutional Court has to approve any such dismissal). The community head also sits on a regional council with the regional governor to coordinate regional policy.

Political parties do not play a major role in local elections, although they are entitled to nominate candidates. More commonly, citizens are nominated as independent candidates through civil initiatives, but they can state their party affiliation on the ballot. The most recent local elections were held in September-October 2005. As in previous years, the opposition largely boycotted the elections, regarding the process as deeply flawed. Although the elections were to a certain extent competitive, in that multiple candidates took part, these tended to be rival pro-government figures vying for influence over local resources. Reports of vote buying and indirect bribery of voters by candidates – for example, promises of repairs to local infrastructure – remained a defining feature of the 2005 local elections.

Assessments of the elections varied. A local election-monitoring group, Choice Is Yours, reported that candidates had been hindered during the campaign and that voter lists remained inaccurate. A small observation mission sent by the Council of Europe judged that the electoral process and voter lists had improved compared with previous elections and stated, "The local elections were generally in keeping with the Council of Europe's electoral standards. The electoral process was generally satisfactory."[12]

Local governments are regulated by the 2002 Law on Local Self-Government. Their autonomy is limited by their weak financial resources. The Council of Elders (which acts as the representative body for communities) is responsible for approving community budgets and supervising their implementation. However, the central government has authority over budgetary loans, credits, and guarantees and establishes procedures for the collection and distribution of local taxes.

Land and property taxes are the only form of community tax revenue, but even these must be collected by regional branches of the state treasury. Communities also receive revenue from state duties. They are therefore heavily dependent on financial transfers from the state budget, but disbursement delays are common, limiting the capacity of local governments to meet their spending requirements or ensure the timely payment of staff salaries. Moreover, the distribution of financial resources from central to local government is uneven and poorly targeted.

The autonomy of local governments is further circumscribed by the powers of regional governors, who often use administrative resources as a means to influence local authorities. In theory, local authorities have the courts to protect their powers and defend the rights of the local community, but because of the judiciary's dependence on the executive, its impartiality in such cases is questionable. Local governments have the right to form associations to protect and promote their interests. As of 2005, there were three main local government associations: the Community Union of Armenia, the Union of Yerevan Elders, and the Community Finance Officers Association. International organizations are working with local government associations to strengthen the capacity of local government (for example, through more effective budget mechanisms and increased decentralization).

Citizens are entitled to submit draft resolutions to local governments, and most meetings of the Council of Elders are open to the media and the public. The public is entitled to full access to information concerning the activities and decisions of regional and local governments, but a lack of funds restricts the capacity of these governments to publicize the information.

In practice, citizen participation in local government decision making is low, owing in part to the limited authority of local administrations. This has contributed to a correspondingly low awareness of the activities of local bodies. According to a survey of 1,000 citizens, carried out nationwide (excluding Yerevan) by ACNIS in September 2005, 60 percent of respondents were unfamiliar with the activities of their local self-governing bodies, while 44.8 percent believed that their local council played no role. Just 22.8 percent expressed satisfaction with their community leaders' work, while 63.5 percent said that they would like to elect their regional governor and 36.7 percent expressed the opinion that this would make the governor more accountable to the people.

Judicial Framework and Independence

1997	1998	1999	2001	2002	2003	2004	2005	2006
4.75	5.00	5.00	5.00	5.00	5.00	5.00	5.25	5.00

Chapter 2 of Armenia's Constitution provides for fundamental political, civil, and human rights, but there are substantial barriers to protecting them effectively. These stem largely from the weak judiciary, which enjoys little independence and inadequate funding. This has led to low public confidence in the capacity of the judicial system to protect the population from unjust treatment by the state. Nevertheless, the passage of constitutional amendments in November 2005 goes some way toward enhancing the independence of the judiciary.

Under the revised document, responsibility for appointing the Council of Justice, which has a supervisory and disciplinary role within the judiciary, passes to the General Assembly of Judges. The president and the Parliament will each appoint two legal scholars to the Council of Justice; previously, the president appointed the entire council. Critics of the changes have argued that even though the president has lost the right to appoint the Council of Justice, he retains some control over judicial appointments. Another important reform is that access to the Constitutional Court (which interprets and enforces basic law and ensures the constitutionality of legislation) has been broadened to enable ordinary citizens to appeal. Access to the Constitutional Court had previously been restricted to the president, one-third of members of Parliament, election candidates, and, in limited cases, the government.

Reform of the legal and judicial system is being carried out with assistance from, among others, the American Bar Association and the World Bank. A Chamber of Advocates was inaugurated in January 2005 as part of measures to improve judicial independence, although the election of its chair was marred by allegations of fraud. However, the continued bias in the legal system toward prosecutors has hampered the chamber's ability to protect the independence of the judiciary. Some World Bank funding has been used to renovate court infrastructure, with a view to increasing the efficiency of judicial services.

Armenia's judicial system guarantees the presumption of innocence, the right of persons not to incriminate themselves, and access to a public hearing by a fair and impartial court. Police officials are permitted to keep suspects in custody for up to 72 hours before filing criminal charges, and a court decision is required to turn detention into an arrest. Prosecutors' requests for arrests are rarely refused. However, in April 2005 the Office of the Prosecutor General experienced a rare setback when the Court of Appeals overturned its decision not to prosecute a businessman accused of fraud.

About 20 percent of some 1,450 human rights violations reported to the Office of the Human Rights Ombudsman in the first half of 2005 related to the courts, police, and prosecutors' offices, in particular to court bias in favor of the prosecution. A lack of training for judges in commercial issues has left many investors disillusioned with the court system as a viable legal recourse. However, a positive trend is apparent in the Economics Court, which reported that of 274 lawsuits lodged by businesses against the tax authorities in 2004, 178 were successful. The State Tax Service nevertheless prevailed when bringing tax evasion cases to court, winning about 650 out of 800 such cases in 2004.

In 2005, witnesses continued to have no right to legal counsel while being questioned in police custody. The legal requirement stating that only the courts are permitted to authorize searches is often violated. Although Armenia's procedural justice code sets a one-year maximum for criminal inquiries, delays in the criminal justice system are common, owing in part to a shortage of qualified judges. A Civil Society Monitoring Board was established in 2004 to increase civil supervision over the prison service. In June 2005, the board reported that conditions in prisons remain overcrowded and unsanitary, problems attributable in part to a shortage of funding, according to the Ministry of Justice, which assumed control of the prison service from the police in 2002.

The police system is reported to use force and psychological pressure to secure confessions. According to the annual report of the human rights ombudsman, presented in April 2005, citizens had reported the use of torture to extract testimonies that were later used in court. Victims of abuse are often reluctant to press charges for fear of the consequences. Human Rights Watch has also criticized the Code of Administrative Offenses, whose Soviet-era provisions permit courts to detain people without legal counsel for 15 days and to sentence defendants in closed hearings. This was used to arrest up to several hundred opposition demonstrators in 2004, but there were fewer reports of its use in 2005, probably because there were no such large-scale public protests.

The Armenian Constitution and laws guarantee freedom of religion but also provide for the legal authority of the Armenian Apostolic Church, which enjoys a privileged status. As such, the church uses its influence over the government to press for restrictions on nontraditional religious groups. Under the terms of its membership in the Council of Europe, Armenia is committed to ensuring freedom from discrimination for nontraditional religious groups, of which 56 were officially registered as of November 2005. This is generally observed, although some incidents of anti-Semitism were reported in 2005, including the defacing of a Holocaust memorial in January.

Jehovah's Witnesses were finally permitted to register in October 2004, having previously been denied registration because of their opposition to compulsory military service. The July 2004 Law on Alternative Military Service provides for civilian service, but those choosing this option must serve for 42 months – almost twice as long as those carrying out military service. As of June 2005, 14 Jehovah's Witnesses remained in prison for refusing to carry out the alternative service on the grounds that it was overseen by the military.[13] The legislation permits every male to opt for alternative service, not just those objecting on religious grounds.

The right to own and inherit property is guaranteed in the Constitution, which also states that no one can arbitrarily deprive a citizen of his property. In 2005, the eviction of some residents from central Yerevan to make way for the development of new housing and streets prompted criticism from local lawyers and NGOs that people's property rights were not being respected. Chapter 2 of the Constitution guarantees intellectual property rights. Amendments approved in October 2005 to the Law on Copyright and Associated Rights increase the penalties for infringement of intellectual property rights. Noncitizens are prohibited from owning land, except under special circumstances.

The Constitution enshrines the freedom of assembly, but this has not been fully observed. The Law on Demonstrations, approved in April 2004 shortly after the opposition had staged a series of demonstrations in protest of the 2003 elections, was criticized by the OSCE for leaving no room for spontaneous mass events, thereby in practice restricting freedom of movement. The legislation did remove an earlier requirement that demonstration organizers secure permission, replacing it with a need simply to notify the authorities; however, most large public places in Yerevan were placed off limits to protesters.

The OSCE's criticism of the legislation resulted in some changes to the document in May 2005. These included an amendment limiting the right of law enforcement bodies to disperse a demonstration only if it poses a threat to public and state security, rather than simply for violations of the law, as in the original document. The authorities retain discretionary powers to restrict demonstrations, however.

Larisa Alaverdian, formerly a member of the presidential human rights commission, was appointed Armenia's first ombudsman by the president in February 2004. In 2005, she criticized the government for its decision to evict residents from central Yerevan to make way for new residential developments, on the grounds that this violated their property rights. She also reported in May that people who had lodged complaints against government officials were being harassed by the security services, following the confiscation of a computer from her office. Alaverdian's critical stance was regarded by local observers as one factor behind a government decision to remove the ombudsman's right to request documents from judges. The Parliament enacted amendments to the Law on the Ombudsman to this effect in late 2005.

Under the revised Constitution, the Parliament assumed the right to appoint the ombudsman, as recommended by the Council of Europe. While this in theory is a positive step, the way in which the election was organized – with Alaverdian expected to step down from office in January 2006, one month before the election of her successor – raises questions as to the Parliament's commitment to the independence of the Office of the Human Rights Ombudsman.

A new criminal code, adopted by the Parliament in April 2003, came into effect in August 2003. Most prison sentences were shortened under the new code, which also formally abolished the death penalty, providing instead for life imprisonment. Prisoners receiving the life sentence are entitled to apply for parole after 20 years, compared with the maximum prison sentence under the previous criminal code of 15 years. In 2005, the maximum prison sentence (other than life) was 15 years.

Corruption

1997	1998	1999	2001	2002	2003	2004	2005	2006
n/a	n/a	5.75	5.75	5.75	5.75	5.75	5.75	5.75

Armenia ranks well in international corruption surveys, but corruption at all levels of government continues to impede the country's political and economic development. Not only has this fostered public cynicism toward the authorities, it has impeded the development of a competitive business environment.

Armenia has signed on to several international anticorruption initiatives, including the Council of Europe's Group of States Against Corruption, which it joined in 2004. An evaluation of its progress will be carried out in mid-2006. The focus of the government's anticorruption policy is a strategy adopted in late 2003 that sets out measures to combat corruption in the political sphere, the state bureaucracy, law enforcement agencies, and the judiciary. A Council for Combating Corruption was inaugurated in June 2004, headed by the prime minister and other high-ranking officials; a coordinating committee oversees implementation of the strategy.

Armenia's score in the Transparency International 2005 Corruption Perceptions Index deteriorated to 2.9 from 3.1 in 2004 (with 10 being the least corrupt), although it was still the best scoring of the former Soviet republics. The worsening score adds some justification to the skepticism among local and international observers that the government's anticorruption strategy will be effective. This stems from doubts over the government's political will to tackle corruption and the lack of independence of the strategy's implementation bodies.

The Center for Regional Development (CRD), an affiliate of Transparency International, operates a National Anticorruption Resource Center, with offices in Yerevan and five provinces, that aims to raise public awareness about corruption. The CRD published an assessment of Armenia's anticorruption institutions in October 2004, based on 2003 analyses, and concluded that none of the institutions evaluated is functioning effectively. Factors influencing this finding included the absence of political will, the lack of institutional autonomy, poor law enforcement, and the low level of public participation in policy making.

Public officials encounter few limitations to economic participation. The state's formal involvement in the economy is low in comparison with that of other transition countries: The European Bank for Reconstruction and Development (EBRD) estimates that the public sector contributed 25 percent to GDP in 2005.[14] However, public officials at all levels, including parliamentary deputies, have extensive business interests. This has adversely affected government attempts to reduce economic corruption: In March 2005, the Parliament rejected proposals to increase the prison sentence for tax evasion from two years to a maximum of seven years. The revised Constitution explicitly bans parliamentary deputies and government members from engaging in business interests; however, as of late 2005 it was too early to judge whether this prohibition was being observed.

Armenia's financial disclosure laws are insufficient to combat corruption. The 2001 Law on Declaration of Incomes and Assets requires senior government officials, including the president and government ministers, to annually declare revenue and property belonging to them and their families. The law came into effect in 2002, but many observers dismissed the income declarations made by officials as unrepresentative and far too low. Although amendments to the law in 2003 broadened the number of officials covered by the declaration requirement, they removed the provision that declarations be published. The law does not require tax authorities to verify the financial statements and imposes only relatively lenient fines for reporting false information. Moreover, gaps in the legislation enable officials to register property in the names of relatives. Few officials have been punished for corrupt practices, and the lack of legal protection for whistle-blowers acts as a strong disincentive to report corruption.

A focus on inspections and audits as the main tools of legislation enforcement has increased the opportunity for bribe taking in the civil service. Despite progressive salary raises since mid-2003, average monthly civil service wages, at 60,000 dram (US$130) in 2005, are still insufficient to attract and retain high-caliber staff or deter them from seeking bribes. Bribery is also commonplace when dealing with traffic police, universities, and other areas where official salaries are low, such as health care.

In 2005, there was an increase in the number of identified corruption crimes, although prosecutions remained rare. Law enforcement structures solved 227 corruption crimes (mainly embezzlement and misuse of government funds) in the first half of 2005, according to the president's anticorruption aide, up from 198 in the same period of 2004. However, just seven people were prosecuted for taking bribes. In February, a former head of the Ministry of Finance oversight department was arrested on fraud charges.

Armenia's business-related legislation is relatively sound. The country performed well in the Heritage Foundation/*Wall Street Journal* 2005 Index of Economic Freedom, scoring 2.58 (the only member of the Commonwealth of Independent States to be rated "Mostly Free"), which places it 42nd out of 155 countries. However, weak implementation of the legislation has increased the opportunities for official corruption. There is a perception that it is difficult to run a successful business legally or without personal connections to public officials. The situation is exacerbated by the absence of an independent judiciary, and judges are reported to be susceptible to bribery in exchange for a favorable ruling in disputes. Kocharian singled out the State Customs Committee for particular criticism in 2005 for its preferential treatment of some importers in return for kickbacks. Conflicts of interest also exist in the State Tax Service, whose head admitted in 2005 that about 200 employees had business interests.

Nevertheless, some positive steps to reduce corruption have been implemented, including the streamlining of property registration procedures in 2004. In its 2005 Business Environment and Enterprise Performance Survey,[15] the EBRD found that although the share of businesses' annual sales paid in bribes had increased from 0.92 percent in 2002 to 1.17 percent in 2005, the frequency of bribery had decreased from 14.28 percent of respondents in 2002 to 10.1 percent in 2005.

The lack of independent media has precluded unbiased press coverage of official corruption. As long as most print media are sponsored by wealthy business individuals, they have little incentive to draw attention to the scale of corruption in a system where they play a part. Moreover, attempts to expose official corruption carry risks for the media. The effective closure of A1+ as a broadcasting outlet is attributed to the investigative nature of its reporting, contend observers.

Public perceptions of official corruption are highly negative. According to the International Foundation for Election Systems, 71 percent of those questioned in its 2003 survey considered corruption to be a serious problem (up from 68 percent in 2002), although the number believing it to be very serious had fallen from 20 percent to 16 percent. There is a widespread perception that corruption is too deeply entrenched to be eradicated: 81 percent of those questioned in the survey believed that Armenians accept corruption as a way of life. Another survey, conducted in September 2004 by ACNIS, revealed that 62 percent of respondents believed that corruption exists at all levels and that health care institutions, followed by the courts, were the most corrupt structures. Corruption within the political sphere is also widespread: 63 percent of those surveyed were offered a bribe in the 2003 presidential or parliamentary elections, while evidence of vote buying, in the form of promises to upgrade local infrastructure, was reported in the 2005 local elections.

Anna Walker is an analyst specializing in the Commonwealth of Independent States at the Economist Intelligence Unit in London.

---

[1] Constitution of the Republic of Armenia.

[2] Bagrat Tunyan, The Shadow Economy of Armenia: Size, Causes and Consequences, Armenia International Policy Research Group, Paper No. 05/02, Washington, DC, January 2005, p. 19.

[3] Law on Freedom of Information, National Assembly, September 23, 2003.

[4] Law on Civil Service, National Assembly, December 12, 2001.

[5] Astghik Bedevian, "Parliament Approves Armenian Budget for 2006," Armenialiberty.org, www.armenialiberty.org/armeniareport/report/en/2005/11/CC5B43E1-DD16-4C74-947A-28A3837DAF5D.asp, November 11, 2005.

[6] Law on the Amendments and Additions to the Electoral Code of the Republic of Armenia, National Assembly, May 17, 2005.

[7] World Learning Armenia, Armenia NGO Sector Assessment: A Comparative Study, Yerevan:, 2004.

[8] Law on Charity, National Assembly, October 8, 2002; Law on Foundations, National Assembly, December 24, 2002.

[9] Council of Europe Committee of Ministers, Declaration on Freedom of Political Debate in the

Media, February 12, 2004, wcm.coe.int/ViewDoc.jsp?id=118995&Lang=en.
[10] Law on Freedom of Information, National Assembly, September 23, 2003.
[11] Law on Mass Media, National Assembly, December 2003.
[12] "Congress Delegation Declares Local Elections in Armenia Generally Satisfactory and Calm," Council of Europe Information Office in Armenia, Strasbourg, October 17, 2005, www.coe.am/en/?go=pressreleases&id=78
[13] U.S. Department of State, Bureau of Democracy, Human Rights, and Labor, Armenia International Religious Freedom Report, www.state.gov/g/drl/rls/irf/2005/51538.htm, November 8, 2005.
[14] European Bank for Reconstruction and Development, Transition Report 2005, November 2005, p.100.
[15] European Bank for Reconstruction and Development, Transition Report 2005, November 2005, p.13

Azerbaijan

Capital:	Baku
Population:	8.3 million
GNI/capita:	$940
Ethnic Groups:	Azeri (90.6%), Dagestani (2.2%), Russian (1.8%), Armenian (1.5%), other (1.8%)

Nations in Transit Ratings and Averaged Scores

	1997	1998	1999	2001	2002	2003	2004	2005	2006
Electoral Process	5.75	5.50	5.50	5.75	5.75	5.75	6.00	6.25	6.50
Civil Society	5.00	5.00	4.75	4.50	4.50	4.25	4.50	4.75	5.00
Independent Media	5.50	5.50	5.50	5.75	5.50	5.50	5.75	6.00	6.00
Governance *	6.25	6.25	6.25	6.25	6.00	5.75	5.75	n/a	n/a
National Democratic Governance	n/a	n/a	n/a	n/a	n/a	n/a	n/a	6.00	6.00
Local Democratic Governance	n/a	n/a	n/a	n/a	n/a	n/a	n/a	6.00	6.00
Judicial Framework and Independence	5.50	5.50	5.50	5.25	5.25	5.25	5.50	5.75	5.75
Corruption	n/a	n/a	6.00	6.25	6.25	6.25	6.25	6.25	6.25
Democracy Score	5.60	5.55	5.58	5.63	5.54	5.46	5.63	5.86	5.93

* With the 2005 edition, Freedom House introduced seperate analysis and ratings for national democratic governance and local democratic governance to provide readers with more detailed and nuanced analysis of these two important subjects.

NOTE: The ratings reflect the consensus of Freedom House, its academic advisers, and the author of this report. The opinions expressed in this report are those of the author. The ratings are based on a scale of 1 to 7, with 1 representing the highest level of democratic progress and 7 the lowest. The Democracy Score is an average of ratings for the categories tracked in a given year.

The economic and social data on this page were taken from the following sources:
GNI/capita, Population: *World Development Indicators 2006* (Washington, D.C.: World Bank, 2006).
Ethnic Groups: *CIA World Factbook 2006* (Washington, D.C.: Central Intelligence Agency, 2006).

EXECUTIVE SUMMARY

Azerbaijan, which had a brief period of independence between 1918 and 1920, regained its independence when the Soviet Union collapsed in 1991 in the midst of a war with Armenia over Nagorno-Karabakh that began as a low-level conflict between 1988 and 1990 and resulted in massive social problems and more than 1 million refugees. The sides signed a cease-fire agreement in 1993 under President Heydar Aliyev, former first secretary of the Azerbaijan Communist Party who came to power after a coup ousted the country's first democratically elected president, Abulfaz Elchibey. The country achieved a period of relative political and economic stability under Aliyev, who continued to strengthen his hold on the country through an enormous concentration of power in the presidency. During his 10-year term in office, Aliyev pursued a balanced foreign policy aimed at maintaining close ties with the United States, Russia, Iran, and Turkey and struck oil and gas deals with Western energy companies. A peace agreement with Armenia is yet to be signed.

Current president Ilham Aliyev, Heydar's son, came to power through a carefully orchestrated succession strategy, winning the controversial presidential elections in October 2003 after his father withdrew for health reasons two months before the polls. The president has so far maintained political and economic stability in the country, while failing to push forward a genuine democratization program (hopes for which were weakened even further by the serious irregularities observed in the November 2005 polls) or a credible anticorruption drive. The country's economic prospects remain positive, while chances for a Nagorno-Karabakh agreement remain low.

National Democratic Governance. President Aliyev continued to enjoy overwhelming authority in Azerbaijan's governmental system in 2005 and was able to maintain political and economic stability thanks to a high level of continued economic growth. The series of dismissals following an alleged coup attempt to bring opposition Azerbaijan Democratic Party leader Rasul Guliyev to power and the tragic murder of a high-profile opposition journalist raised questions about the cohesiveness of the ruling administration. The National Assembly, Azerbaijan's legislative branch, maintained a low profile in 2005, effectively serving as a rubber-stamp authority for the president. The administration also continued to exert substantial pressure on its political opposition. *Azerbaijan's rating for national democratic governance remains at 6.00, which reflects the government's continued reliance on an authoritarian regime and use of force rather than democratic institutions and the rule of law.*

Electoral Process. The November 6 parliamentary elections, in which Aliyev's New Azerbaijan Party won the highest number of seats, once again failed to meet international standards. A number of changes to election legislation and improved campaigning rights for the opposition have heightened hopes for a free and fair election, although serious irregularities persisted on the day of the election. International and local observers deemed the election fraudulent and below international standards. Although there were a number of improvements to increase the transparency of the election, such as the eleventh-hour acceptance of ink-marking the fingers of voters, these were approved by the regime late enough in the process that at least some changes did not make a difference. Continued intimidation of political opposition and irregularities in vote tabulation favored ruling party candidates. *Azerbaijan's rating for electoral process declines from 6.25 to 6.50 as improvements in the campaigning period were offset by significant election irregularities and continued postelection pressure on the opposition despite the president's June decision to allow rallies.*

Civil Society. Little progress was made in 2005 in Azerbaijan's civil society sector, with nongovernmental organizations (NGOs) still facing registration, tax, and funding problems. The government imposed increased pressure on NGOs that are affiliated with the opposition, particularly the Yeni Fikir (New Thinking) youth organization. The National Assembly's decision to allow foreign-funded NGOs to monitor polling stations on the day of the election was positive but came too late in the process to make a difference. *Azerbaijan's rating for civil society declines from 4.75 to 5.00 as the government continued to refuse registration to some NGOs, imposed substantial pressure on Yeni Fikir, and announced its decision to allow foreign-funded NGOs to monitor the election too late for its implementation to make an impact.*

Independent Media. The media continued to operate under governmental and legal pressure, with most opposition outlets facing substantial financial hardship in the face of unreasonably high libel penalties and limited resources. Print media remained divided into either pro-government or pro-opposition camps, while the code of conduct signed by government and media representatives in May 2005 failed to resolve problems with the government and to improve professional and ethical standards among journalists. An important development was the formation of a new public broadcaster, albeit with higher governmental authority over it than advised by international observers. *Azerbaijan's rating for independent media remains at 6.00 owing to the government's continued mistreatment of opposition journalists and press and strong government influence on the public broadcaster.*

Local Democratic Governance. Local governance in Azerbaijan is not democratic, as the government continues its practice of directly appointing local administrators. The influence of municipal councils, which are formed through elections, remains limited. *Azerbaijan's rating for local democratic governance remains at 6.00, reflecting the ruling party's continued dominance in local governance and local executives' unwillingness to liberalize the political environment. president; and the election of the Council of Justice by members of the judiciary (rather than its appointment by the president).*

Judicial Framework and Independence. The government maintained substantial authority over the judiciary in 2005, particularly with the seemingly engineered trials of Ruslan Bashirli and other members of the Yeni Fikir and Maqam! (Enough!) youth organizations as well as former government ministers Farhad Aliyev and Ali Insanov for planning to overthrow the constitutional order. Although the former ministers had some access to due process, albeit with delays, the youth activists suffered even further constraints and were reported to have faced torture. Despite the president's June decision to allow opposition rallies, the right to assemble publicly continued to be considered a privilege by the authorities, as local executive committees saw fit to hinder, prohibit, or break up opposition rallies. *Azerbaijan's rating for judicial framework and independence remains at 5.75 owing to the judiciary's continued lack of independence and the increase in politically engineered trials in violation of political rights and civil liberties.*

Corruption. Corruption remained one of the most problematic issues in 2005, permeating society from top to bottom and creating a major impediment to economic development. There remains a culture of intolerance toward any discussion of government corruption. The auditing capacity of the legislative branch is weak, and government investigations of civil servants are usually politically driven. Legal and other forms of harassment are commonplace for persons who publicly allege corruption on the part of government officials. *Azerbaijan's rating for corruption remains unchanged at 6.25, as the government still does far too little to combat corruption despite new corruption legislation and continued government influence on the newly established anticorruption commission.*

Outlook for 2006. President Ilham Aliyev is expected to maintain his position thanks to the impressive level of economic growth based on substantial oil revenues, which will increase further as the Baku-Tbilisi-Ceyhan pipeline starts exports in the second quarter of 2006. The president, however, more than two years into his term, will encounter increased domestic and international pressure to promote younger and more reform-oriented faces to his cabinet and demonstrate genuine efforts against corruption. The opposition parties will remain weak until the 2008 presidential elections loom closer, but individual opposition National Assembly members may strengthen their profiles. There appears limited chance of progress toward resolving the Nagorno-Karabakh conflict in 2006, although the possibility of a military standoff between Azerbaijan and Armenia is also remote.

MAIN REPORT

National Democratic Governance

1997	1998	1999	2001	2002	2003	2004	2005	2006
n/a	n/a	n/a	n/a	n/a	n/a	n/a	6.00	6.00

Azerbaijan has a highly centralized presidential system, with an executive branch made up of the president, the Office of the President, the prime minister, and the cabinet of ministers. The president enjoys overwhelming authority over the executive, legislative, and judicial branches. President Ilham Aliyev remained strong in 2005, but a series of cabinet dismissals alongside coup speculations in October and scandals in the Ministry of Internal Affairs indicated that his regime continues to rely upon undemocratic means lacking transparency and the rule of law.

President Aliyev continued to consolidate his position through 2005. He convened on March 26 the third congress of the ruling New Azerbaijan Party (YAP), where he was elected as party chairman. His election violates the 1992 Law on Political Parties, which stipulates that the president cannot lead a political party, although the YAP later announced that the law will be amended to enable the president to maintain his position.[1] An International Republican Institute survey found in June 2005 that 56 percent of the 1,200 participants were satisfied with the status quo, in contrast with the 31 percent that were dissatisfied. Full government coffers due to high economic growth above 20 percent and high oil prices enabled the Aliyev government to push forward a series of generous social spending measures while also boosting public employment. A December 2004 survey announced on March 1, 2005, by local polling organization PULS-R found that 64 percent of respondents trusted the president (remaining at the same level with the group's 2003 and 2004 surveys), whereas the share of respondents who considered that their families live in acute financial hardship declined to 14.4 percent from 19.2 percent in 2003.[2] Rasim Musabekov, who conducted the poll with a representative of Germany's Friedrich-Ebert-Stiftung, noted when announcing the poll that Azerbaijanis are not used to responding to such polls and that the findings could therefore not be trusted wholly as an accurate reflection of popular perceptions.[3] A poll by InterMedia found a 60 percent approval rating for the president.[4]

Despite continued cabinet reshuffle speculations throughout the year, there were no ministerial changes until October, when President Aliyev dismissed two cabinet ministers alongside several officials within a week following self-exiled Azerbaijan Democratic Party (ADP) chairman Rasul Guliyev's failed October 17 return to Baku. The president removed Economic Development Minister Farhad Aliyev (no relation to the president) and Health Minister Ali Insanov. Both men were subsequently arrested for charges of embezzlement of state funds and financing Guliyev's supporters, leading to a coup upon his return. Akif Muradverdiyev, a presidential administration official responsible for financial issues; Fikrat Sadikov, a parliamentarian and director of the state-owned Azerkimya petrochemical company; and Eldar Salayev, former president of the National Academy of Sciences, were also arrested on charges of financing the alleged plot.

The ongoing conflicts between the detained ministers and other powerful figures in the administration, the questionable evidence used for the detentions – an alleged confession by former finance minister Fikret Yusifov – and the manner in which the authorities proceeded with the dismissals (with widely televised police raids into the former ministers' residences) raised questions on whether the dismissals were politically motivated. The fact that the authorities charged neither Guliyev nor any of his close associates in the opposition – and there appears to be no indication that they will be in the future – contributed to the speculations.

Tensions between Farhad Aliyev and former State Customs Committee (DGK) chairman Kemaleddin Heydarov (appointed as minister of emergency situations in January 2006) had been high. An Economic Development Ministry investigation blamed consumer price increases on import monopolies and called for close monitoring of DGK-imposed tariffs on imported goods, urging former minister Aliyev to announce in August that his life could be in danger for his actions threatening powerful monopolies.[5] In a move that reduced Aliyev's powers, the president transferred the responsibility of overseeing privatization from his ministry to a reestablished State Property Committee in September. The pro-government press had accused Aliyev of harboring political ambitions.[6] His brother, Rafig Aliyev, who was also arrested on October 19 (and remained in custody until the end of the year), was a top business leader as president of the petrol giant Azpetrol, Azerbaijan's first private oil company. There were also reported tensions between Ramiz Mekhtiyev, head of the Office of the President, and Ali Insanov, who was widely alleged to have used state health services for personal gain.[7]

The president serves as commander in chief of the Azerbaijani armed forces. In this capacity, he oversees defense and security efforts undertaken by the prime minister and the ministers of defense, internal affairs, and security. The Defense Council, created in 1993 by former president Heydar Aliyev, reports to and advises the president in supervising the activities of the armed forces. A series of events regarding the Ministry of Internal Affairs in 2005 has also triggered controversy about the extent to which President Aliyev is able to control this part of his administration. First, opposition journalist Elmar Huseinov was murdered in March 2 in an operation that seemed to be well organized enough to suggest the involvement of state organs, or at the very least people closely connected to the state. Second, it was revealed in March that several high- and middle-level officials of the Ministry of Internal Affairs were involved in a kidnapping ring. While an investigation of Huseinov's murder has yet to be concluded, the president moved swiftly in the second case by sacking the probed officials. In an address on March 10, Aliyev condemned the series of abductions perpetrated over the past decade and acknowledged that the groups were also involved in several high-profile murders.[8]

The legislative branch consists of the 125-member National Assembly (Milli Mejlis). Members are elected for five-year terms from single-mandate constituencies

– a rule that was established by constitutional referendum in August 2002. The third National Assembly since independence was elected in the November 6 parliamentary elections, which gave the YAP the largest number of seats – 58 out of 125. The opposition parties won 13, with the Azadliq (Freedom) bloc getting the highest share (7 seats) and mostly pro-government independents winning 42 seats. All main opposition parties other than former parliamentary Speaker Isa Gambar's Musavat Party have decided to boycott the current National Assembly in order to protest election irregularities and to not participate in the May 13, 2006, reruns in 10 districts. The Nakhichevani Autonomous Republic, an exclave of Azerbaijan bordering Armenia, Iran, and Turkey, has a 45-seat regional legislature, which was also renewed on November 6. The YAP won 37 seats, while nonpartisan candidates won 6 and the Azadliq 2.

The parliamentary sessions are generally open to the media, but there were instances in which journalists from opposition newspapers were denied entry. There is limited public or expert input in the legislative process, as many NGOs and the general public are not invited to committee hearings. It is also difficult for the public or NGOs to obtain copies of draft laws and deputies' voting records, since these are not published in a consistent and timely fashion. The National Assembly has not conducted any investigations of the government so far, although amendments were made in 2002 requiring the prime minister and the cabinet of ministers to present an annual report to the National Assembly.

The National Assembly's Chamber of Commerce has not been effective in auditing governmental functions, and the Ministry of Finance has initiated only a few investigations into the financial dealings of several oil industry enterprises and Azerbaijani embassies abroad; these have revealed some irregularities in financial accounts. The Ministry of Economic Development's investigation into customs practices has indeed disclosed serious discrepancies on tariffs imposed on imports of food products, yet no sanctions have been imposed on the DGK. Overall, the public and media have little direct access to the financial operations of the government.

Electoral Process

1997	1998	1999	2001	2002	2003	2004	2005	2006
5.75	5.50	5.50	5.75	5.75	5.75	6.00	6.25	6.50

Elections in Azerbaijan have been characterized by significant irregularities and government interference in the voting process since independence, except for the June 2002 election in which Abulfaz Elchibey, leader of the nationalist opposition Popular Front of Azerbaijan (AXCP), was elected president. The 1993 presidential elections (in which then president Heydar Aliyev, who had replaced Elchibey following a coup the same year, won 99 percent of the vote), 1995 parliamentary elections, 1998 presidential elections in which Aliyev received more than 70 percent of the vote), and 2000 parliamentary elections were marred by serious fraud. The

October 2003 elections that brought Ilham Aliyev (appointed prime minister after his father's health suddenly declined in August 2003) to power with 77 percent of the vote were also deemed fraudulent by monitors. The first parliamentary elections under his rule were held in November 6, 2005.

On May 11, Aliyev issued a sweeping decree that mandated full media access for all parties, freedom of assembly during the electoral campaign, and the right of independent organizations to conduct exit polls without interference. Most significant, the decree stated that local government and election officials would be held "legally responsible" for any interference with a free and fair electoral process. Aliyev also instructed local officials not to obstruct preelection meetings by opposition parties, affirming that equal conditions must be created for pro-government and opposition political forces. The government also decided in June to authorize opposition rallies in a change from what has been its policy since the presidential elections in October 2003.

The government also revised the unified election code in June, but the changes omitted several recommendations issued by the Council of Europe's Venice Commission and the Organization for Security and Cooperation in Europe/Office for Democratic Institutions and Human Rights (OSCE/ODIHR) relating to the composition of the election commission, venues for election rallies, the right to campaign, complaints and appeals, and intimidation of election staff. The Venice Commission had recommended that the Central Election Commission (MSK) and local election commissions be restructured so that the opposition representatives have parity with government appointees. The YAP instead maintained the current system, where the government and opposition each appoint six commissioners, but the appointment of the remaining six commissioners by the National Assembly tips the balance in the government's favor.

Aliyev issued a second decree on October 25, which ordered the MSK to make immediate arrangements for the marking of voters' fingers with indelible ink to preclude multiple voting and recommended that the National Assembly consider abolishing the restrictions on allowing local NGOs to monitor the ballot.[9] Although positive, the measure came too late in the process to make a significant difference. The Office of the Prosecutor General reported on October 31 that it investigated 35 alleged electoral law violations, among which it confirmed 4 instances of violence against the opposition and 2 cases in which candidates attempted to buy votes.

The registration process went smoothly in comparison with previous elections. The MSK registered more than 2,000 candidates representing some 48 parties and blocs, with no significant violations reported by OSCE/ODIHR preliminary reports. The authorities registered two opposition leaders in exile, Rasul Guliyev and former president Ayaz Mutallibov, but on August 27 the Office of the Prosecutor General stripped Guliyev of his immunity from prosecution as a parliamentary candidate. Azerbaijan's three major opposition parties, Musavat, AXCP, and ADP, established a common election platform named Azadliq and entered the November elections with a single list of candidates. Yeni Siyaset (YeS; New Politics), a less confrontational bloc, united the Azerbaijan National Independence Party (AMIP), the Social-Democratic

Party of Azerbaijan, and a few individual politicians. By the day of the election, over 500 candidates had withdrawn.

The government's attitude toward the political opposition was extremely hostile throughout the year, with the election campaign marred by widespread arrests and intimidation of opposition party members and supporters. The YAP and opposition parties met officially in May, but the talks reached a deadlock when the government refused the opposition's demand that the president or Mekhtiyev participate in the talks directly. AXCP member Mansum Bayramov was assaulted and beaten in Baku late on February 24 by men who followed and then halted his car.[10] The authorities also continued to break up regional election campaign meetings such as those in Zakatala and Lenkoran in August and use force to disperse unauthorized opposition rallies. AXCP's current chairman Ali Kerimli's adviser Ramiz Tagiev said on August 22 that the Ministry of National Security sought in July to co-opt him in a bid to replace Kerimli with a figure who would cooperate with the authorities.[11] Unidentified individuals systematically combed two Baku shopping centers on August 10 and confiscated all items of orange-colored clothing and accessories in a move to intimidate opposition parties that had made references to the 2004 Orange Revolution in Ukraine.

October witnessed a dramatic standoff between the government and the opposition when ADP chairman Rasul Guliyev – who has been in self-imposed exile since 1996 owing to criminal charges of large-scale embezzlement dating from 1990 to 1995, when he was director of Azerbaijan's largest oil refinery – announced that he would return to Baku. The authorities had insisted that they would arrest Guliyev on his stated date of return of October 17, when Baku reached a state of frenzy over an alleged coup. Internal Affairs Minister Ramil Usubov called on citizens, foreign diplomats, and journalists to stay away from the airport, stating that Guliyev's supporters planned to arouse public unrest. The road to Baku's airport was blocked while the riot police detained hundreds of opposition supporters deemed to be potential protesters. Guliyev's plane, which was refused landing permission, flew back to Ukraine, where he was detained briefly before leaving for London.

The OSCE Election Observation Mission in Baku on October 4 expressed concern over disproportionate restrictions on freedom of assembly, intervention by local government officials in support of the YAP, attempts to pressure or bribe voters, lack of objectivity on the part of local election commissions in addressing complaints by opposition or independent candidates, the inaccuracy and incompleteness of some voter lists, and the haphazard distribution of voter identification cards. Similarly, U.S. NGO Human Rights Watch concluded on October 31 that the authorities had "extinguished" the possibility that the ballot would be free and fair.[12] The report detailed arrests of and reprisals against opposition candidates and activists during the election campaign and the authorities' overt support for candidates from the ruling YAP. United States ambassador Reno Harnish also expressed concern regarding continued reports that local government officials are intervening openly in the election process.[13]

The preliminary results announced by the MSK indicated that the YAP won 63 of the 125 mandates, while independent candidates garnered 41 seats, with Azadliq winning 6 seats in total. Only 47 percent of the electorate turned out, in contrast with 69 percent in the previous legislative elections in 2000, suggesting serious public apathy with a system that has repeatedly produced fraudulent elections. Exit polls funded by the U.S. Agency for International Development and conducted in 65 constituencies by the U.S. firm PA Consulting showed the YAP to be the victor in 18 and members of Azadliq in 12, with independents winning the rest. A second exit poll conducted jointly by Mitofsky International and Edison Media Research gave the YAP 56 seats countrywide compared with 13 for Azadliq.

The OSCE announced on November 7 that the elections failed to meet international standards, while U.S. and EU representatives also expressed disappointment in the process. The OSCE noted that "continued restrictions on the freedom of assembly during the election campaign" and "interference from executive authorities and media bias favoring incumbents resulted in a failure to provide equitable conditions for all candidates during the campaign period." U.S. State Department spokesman Adam Ereli said on November 7 that the vote was accompanied by "major irregularities and fraud that are of immediate concern" and that the United States would urge investigations into those irregularities.

In the week after the November 6 elections, the opposition united under a new banner, the Democratic Popular Front – including Azadliq, YeS, AMIP, and the Liberal Party – and announced a boycott of the National Assembly, stating that it did not recognize the assembly's legitimacy. It claimed that Azadliq had been robbed of some 38 to 40 seats and the opposition as a whole of some 50. The Democratic Popular Front organized rallies to protest election results on November 9, 13, 19, and 26 and vowed not to participate in the runoffs unless they were held in 100 districts and the composition of election commissions was amended.[14] The AXCP office in the Nakhichevani Autonomous Republic had also announced even before the ballot that it would not recognize the outcome as fair and valid, stating that the republic's election commission was formed exclusively from YAP members and that opposition parties were not allowed to stage preelection rallies.

In a move to reduce domestic and international criticism, the MSK immediately annulled results in four districts and ordered two recounts, enabling Kerimli and Musavat deputy chair Arzu Samedov to win seats initially (police had expelled observers from the polling station in a Baku constituency where votes cast for Kerimli were being counted and tallied after the initial count showed him in the lead).[15] Aliyev dismissed on November 9 the regional administrators of the Surakhan and Sabirabad districts, Natik Mekhtiyev and Ashraf Mamedov, for failing to prevent election irregularities in their respective districts.

The Constitutional Court announced the final results of the election on December 1, confirming the outcome of the November 6 elections in 115 of the 125 constituencies while annulling the results in 6 additional constituencies, including 2 in which preliminary returns gave victory to prominent opposition candidates Kerimli and Gulamhuseyn Alibeyli of the AXCP. The YAP retained 58 deputies, while the opposition gained 13, with Azadliq winning 8. The revotes are scheduled for May 13, 2006. The opposition demonstrations following the election were generally peaceful, but the police resorted to violence – injuring dozens of people – to end a protest in Gelebe Square in Baku on November 26, the last opposition demonstration before the Constitutional Court announced final results. Since then, municipal authorities have withheld permission for opposition rallies on Gelebe Square.

Civil Society

1997	1998	1999	2001	2002	2003	2004	2005	2006
5.00	5.00	4.75	4.50	4.50	4.25	4.50	4.75	5.00

Both Article 58 of the Azerbaijani Constitution and the European Convention on Human Rights that came into force in Azerbaijan in 2002 recognize and protect freedom of association. Yet the state appears to be more hostile toward youth organizations that are funded by foreign organizations or affiliated with the opposition. The Aliyev administration continues to exert a dominating influence over grassroots activity, and the National Assembly has shown little willingness to engage NGOs in the legislative process or invite their input on draft legislation.

There are approximately 2,100 NGOs in Azerbaijan. The strongest and most active (approximately 50-60) are concerned with Nagorno-Karabakh refugees, health and children's issues, human rights and women's rights, and environmental and ecology issues. Azerbaijani authorities impose difficult registration procedures upon NGOs, and applications are often rejected. Local financial support to NGOs is limited, as the tax code does not allow tax-deductible contributions. The code does provide tax exemption to charitable organizations, unless they engage in entrepreneurial activities. Therefore, most NGOs rely primarily on foreign grants to continue their activities. In a positive move, the National Assembly amended the Law on Elections on October 28 to lift the prohibition on election monitoring by NGOs that receive more than one-third of their funding from abroad, but this was offset by the fact that it occurred too late in the election process to make a difference.[16] The Law on NGOs prohibits civil society organizations from providing political parties with financial and other kinds of assistance, although they can carry out advocacy activities to improve law and regulation. International NGOs are typically blamed for providing financial assistance to the opposition.

Government pressure on youth groups that are affiliated with the opposition parties and receiving foreign assistance increased in 2005. Ruslan Bashirli, leader of the Yeni Fikir youth group, was arrested on August 9 after he allegedly conspired with and received money from Armenian secret service agents to overthrow the constitutional order in Azerbaijan. Bashirli was arrested after Azerbaijan's security agencies released footage of a secretly videotaped meeting in which he stated he was acting on the instructions of the U.S.-based National Democratic Institute and was seen receiving US$2,000 from two alleged Armenian agents. Osman Alimuradov, a former bodyguard for the Caucasus Muslim Board chairman

Allahshukur Pashazade who was present at the videotaped meeting, relinquished the tape to the Office of the Prosecutor General, which has based the investigation on his testimony.

Although it is difficult to confirm whether Bashirli was detained in a carefully orchestrated operation by intelligence services, the government's swift leakage of the tape to the state media, which ran it frequently, indicated that the government had no qualms about using the episode to discredit its rivals. Investigators impounded on August 17 two computers from Yeni Fikir's headquarters, whereas the authorities reportedly pressured Yeni Fikir member Sarvan Sarkhanov to incriminate AXCP chairman Ali Kerimli.[17] Sarkhanov was beaten and threatened with arrest when he refused to comply with that demand but was subsequently released.

Pressure on youth activists sympathizing with the opposition continued through the end of the year. Five activists from the Yeni Fikir and Maqam! youth movements had been arrested by the end of the year, and two of their number were expelled from Baku State University and the Azerbaijan State Pedagogical Institute, respectively. While the authorities contended that the students were expelled for poor academic performance that had nothing to do with their personal political activities, the students claimed to have been expelled for attending opposition demonstrations. The activists started a hunger strike on December 28 to protest the expulsions, and the situation had not been resolved by the end of the year.

The government founded the State Committee for Work with Religious Associations (SCWRA) in 2001 to reregister religious groups, giving SCWRA chairman Rafig Aliyev (not to be confused with former Azpetrol chairman Rafig Aliyev) sweeping powers over these groups, including control over religious literature. Muslim religious groups must receive a letter of approval from the state-dominated Caucasus Muslim Board (DUMK), a body that appoints Muslim clerics to mosques and monitors sermons before they can be registered. The DUMK also has a monopoly over the selection of pilgrims and the organization of the Hajj, the annual Muslim pilgrimage to Mecca. There are 1,300 officially certified mosques in Azerbaijan, although no more than 500 offer regular religious services.

A public opinion poll by the ADAM Social Research Center conducted in September-October 2004 and announced in February found that 93.2 percent of the respondents identified themselves as Muslims, while those who worshipped regularly constituted less than 20 percent, and only 13.5 percent recognized the authority of any Islamic religious authority. But 23.2 percent of respondents said they supported the introduction of Islamic laws in Azerbaijan – given the low rates of worship and deference to Islamic religious authorities, this likely means laws reflecting higher morality and religious freedom rather than those based on a rigid interpretation of Islam – whereas nearly 70 percent said that they were ill disposed to people who practiced another religion.

Azerbaijan's educational system includes approximately 4,600 primary and secondary schools, 180 technical high schools, 90 colleges, and 27 institutions of higher education (including 8 universities and 5 academies). Education is compulsory for at least eight years according to the Constitution and is guaranteed by the state. The Ministry of Education is the central body that develops state education policy and manages the educational system. Since independence, the Azerbaijani educational system has not undergone major structural changes. Those changes that have occurred include the reestablishment of religious education, banned during the Soviet Union's hegemony. Changes to the curriculum emphasize the use of the Azerbaijani language and eliminate Marxist-Leninist content.

Although appointments to government-controlled academic positions depend heavily on political connections, several senior professors are also active in opposition parties, and academic freedom is generally respected. In October, the authorities arrested Eldar Salayev, the 72-year-old head of the National Academy of Sciences and an Azadliq candidate for the parliament, for alleged involvement in a coup attempt by Rasul Guliyev, to whom he is related through marriage. He was released from pretrial custody on November 17, but the charges against him have yet to be dropped.

Independent Media

1997	1998	1999	2001	2002	2003	2004	2005	2006
5.50	5.50	5.50	5.75	5.50	5.50	5.75	6.00	6.00

The National Assembly adopted Azerbaijan's Law on Mass Media in 2000. It guarantees freedom of speech, support for media, access to information, and protection of journalists' rights. In practice, though, Azerbaijan's media sector encounters numerous obstacles to conducting its work and maintaining independence.

In order to meet Azerbaijan's Council of Europe membership commitments, the administration established a public service broadcast, transforming the second state television channel (AzTV2) while retaining the first channel under state control. The new public television channel (ITV), which began broadcasting 12 hours a day on August 29, is meant to provide objective and unbiased coverage, although the nine members on its board are considered too close to the leadership, with only one having media expertise.[18] Opposition journalists and NGOs criticized General Director Ismail Omarov, a former senior administrator of AzTV1, as a strongly pro-government parliamentarian. Meanwhile, President Aliyev signed a decree on March 23 that transforms AzTV, the state-run radio and television company, into a joint-stock company that will initially be 100 percent state owned, with a 49 percent stake to be sold at a later date – the Council of Europe had demanded the abolishment of the state radio and television after the opening of the new public broadcaster. The ITV's coverage of the election campaign was indistinguishable from other pro-government channels; an OSCE monitoring report suggested that the ITV devoted 68 percent of prime-time news coverage to Aliyev, the government, and the ruling party, while Azadliq received 23 percent of the airtime, of which 53 percent was assessed as negative and 1 percent positive.

The Law on Elections entitles the four parties and blocs that have nominated at least 60 candidates in the parliamentary elections to 90 minutes of free airtime each on state television. The Azadliq bloc complained to AzTV over the channel's refusal to permit a live campaign broadcast by the bloc on October 17. Two leading Azadliq members, including Musavat chairman Isa Gambar, were denied access to television studios, and four minutes were cut from a prerecorded Azadliq campaign broadcast. The OSCE Election Observation Mission noted in October that the free airtime on television was being distributed in accordance with legal requirements, including the staging of debates among candidates, but the remaining coverage of political events by both AzTV and the newly launched public television channel devoted disproportionate coverage to the president, the government, and the YAP. The mission added that the coverage of the government is almost always positive or neutral in tone compared with generally negative coverage of the main Azadliq opposition election bloc.

Antigovernment journalist Elmar Huseinov was shot dead in front of his residence on March 2. Huseinov was founder and editor of *Monitor* magazine, which had been very outspoken in attacking the government, most of all on the issue of corruption. The murder appeared to be well enough organized to suggest that it could not have been committed without the active cooperation of state organs, or at the very least people closely connected to the state. Huseinov's BakCell mobile phone had been blocked for no reason earlier in the day, and just before the shooting, the electricity supply to his building was cut off. Although it is unlikely that President Aliyev himself had any role in or knowledge of Huseinov's assassination, it was certain to have been precipitated by some forces within the current administration. Akper Hasanov, another journalist for *Monitor*, was reportedly taken against his will to Defense Ministry headquarters, where he was held for five hours and forced to write a rebuttal of a January 29 article in which he highlighted the appalling conditions in a military unit in the Geranboy region.

While Aliyev denounced the murder on March 3 as an attempt to tarnish Azerbaijan's international image and called for the police to find those responsible,[19] Musavat, AXCP, and other opposition parties termed it a political killing and asked for mass demonstrations.[20] The Office of the Prosecutor General and Ministries of Internal Affairs and National Security rebuffed the call with a joint statement on March 3 against attempts to use the murder for political purposes. Police blocked access on March 9 to Huseinov's grave to prevent his relatives and friends from congregating to celebrate the traditional repast seven days after his death, while on March 8 Baku city officials refused permission for a mass meeting of journalists scheduled for that day to protest Huseinov's killing. The perpetrators have yet to be apprehended, contributing to the perception of a climate of impunity for violence against journalists.

Television is the dominant media source, with many Azerbaijanis reportedly using various TV channels much more than radio or newspapers, according to data from the International Foundation for Election Systems (IFES) 2004 survey *Public Opinion* in Azerbaijan. In addition to the two state-funded channels, there are five major national stations and nine regional stations. The major national channels are Lider TV (84 percent of viewers surveyed), AzTV1 (79 percent), Space (77 percent), ANS (75 percent), and ATV (25 percent).

On July 12, the Council of Europe, the Office of the President, and the Independent Press Council jointly signed a code of conduct to promote impartiality and balanced reporting of the parliamentary elections. Zeynal Mamedli, head of the monitoring group, published a report on November 18 covering an 11-week period up to the elections. The report found that most mainstream media gave little space to the opinions of citizens and national and religious minorities, while opinions of officials, party leaders, and the candidates dominated. Television channels except for ANS did not issue any airtime to discuss important questions regarding voter participation, while Lider TV was the biggest violator, with 29.2 percent of the violations. Space registered 27.9 percent of the violations, AzTV1 17.7 percent, ITV 10.9 percent, and ATV 10.6 percent. The private stations Space, Lider TV, and ATV are reportedly controlled either by family members of President Aliyev or by people close to the Aliyev family. ANS is owned independently and has given increased coverage to the opposition in its programming in 2005. The most popular radio stations are Lider (20 percent), ANS (19 percent), and Space (15 percent).

Since the formal abolition of censorship in 1998, the print media in Azerbaijan have remained freer than television and radio outlets, although they too are generally biased in their coverage. The overall quality of journalism and reporting remains unprofessional in Azerbaijan. Most newspapers cover scandal-oriented political news as opposed to social or economic developments. Of the 200 newspapers published in Azerbaijan, the most popular are *Yeni Musavat* (7 percent of readers surveyed), Zerkalo (7 percent), Azerbaycan (5 percent), *Xalg Gazeti* (5 percent), *Azadlig* (4 percent), *Ekho* (4 percent), and *Azerbaijan Maullimi* (4 percent). The Russian dailies *Ekho* and *Zerkalo* are generally considered to be neutral and bipartisan, but less so now because of rising government pressure since the 2003 election. Other popular newspapers such as *Yeni Musavat* and *Azadlig* serve as the political mouthpieces of certain opposition parties and are increasingly inclined toward unprofessional reporting. The pro-government, state-funded newspapers *Xalg Gazeti* and *Azerbaycan* cover only the ruling party's position on issues. The greatest violators of the code of conduct among the newspapers in the July-November period were *Rating, Ses, Yeni Musavat, Olaylar, Iki Sahil, Parity, Azadlig, 525ci qazet, Caspian* (different from the Russian-language newspaper *Caspian*), and *Adalet*. The newspapers that adhered best to the code of conduct were *Zerkalo* (15.9 percent), *Ayna* (15.1 percent), *New Time* (9.7 percent), *Express* (9.1 percent), and *Gun Seher* (4.1 percent).

Government pressure on independent journalists continued through 2005. The police beat an unidentified *Zerkalo/Ayna* journalist during an unauthorized Azadliq rally on May 21. ANS journalist Aytekhin Alkhasli was deported from the Nakhichevani Autonomous Republic, and there was an attempt to run down a regional correspondent for the *Azadlig* paper. *Azadlig* editor Ganimat Zahidov and technical director Azer Ahmedov were forcibly abducted on February 24 and taken to a Baku restaurant, where they were stripped naked and photographed with two naked women, then beaten and threatened for printing materials criticizing President Aliyev. The two journalists were released on February 26 after being robbed of nearly US$840 and their cell phones.

Yeni Musavat resumed publication on January 9 after a brief publication suspension due to hefty fines levied after a series of libel suits, six of which imposed nearly US$165,500 on the paper, which was already facing grave financial problems. Although the daily enjoys the largest circulation among opposition newspapers, it is widely held to be an unreliable news source. Meanwhile, a media club named Friends of the Army was founded by reservists in February to deter journalists from negative coverage of defense-related issues.[21] Friends of the Army announced it would monitor the media on a monthly basis and publicly condemn journalists whose articles show the military in a negative light.

Internet access remains free of governmental control and influence, but a mere 5 percent of the country is actually connected to the Internet, according to the International Telecommunications Union. There are currently 15 to 18 computers per 1,000 people in the country. The number of Internet cafés around the country has increased rapidly, but there were a few instances in which owners were harassed by the authorities.

Local Democratic Governance

1997	1998	1999	2001	2002	2003	2004	2005	2006
n/a	n/a	n/a	n/a	n/a	n/a	n/a	6.00	6.00

Local executive committees (excoms) and municipal councils share power at the local governmental level. The president appoints the members and heads of the excoms, as required by the constitution, whereas seats on municipal councils are filled through municipal elections, which are held every five years. The government set up municipal councils for the first time in 1999, but the municipal elections held that same year and in December 2004 were characterized by the OSCE as falling short of international standards. The MSK announced on January 6 the final results of the December 2004 municipal election, in which the YAP won 64.5 percent of the vote. The results of the ballot were invalidated in 409 precincts owing to violations of election legislation. Voter turnout was 49 percent and in some municipalities as low as 20 percent. Although the constitution defines municipalities as bodies for local self-government, the municipal councils lack a complete legal framework and proper funding and are subordinate to the excoms.

President Aliyev's May 11 decree, in which he warned local executives of harsh penalties if they interfered in election processes, and his removal of two local executives following the November election appeared to be a positive step. But pre- and postelection monitoring reports suggest that irregularities persisted particularly in regions outside Baku. Addressing a Baku conference on February 11 to mark the first anniversary of the launch of his five-year program to promote the socioeconomic development of Azerbaijan's rural regions, Aliyev called on local administrators to assist local businesspeople rather than create problems for them through repeated needless inspections and warned that local administrators who harass business owners would lose their jobs.[22] Aliyev said that over the past year, 90,000 new permanent jobs were created in rural areas, and 200 billion manats (US$40.8 million) will be made available in grants for local businessmen in 2005, double the amount allocated in 2004.

The Azerbaijani government continued to have no administrative control over the self-proclaimed Nagorno-Karabakh Republic (NKR) and the seven surrounding regions (Kelbajar, Gubatli, Djabrail, Fizuli, Zengilan, Lachin, and Agdam) that are occupied by Armenia. This area constitutes about 17 percent of the territory of Azerbaijan. The NKR rejected an August 12 statement addressed by the MSK to the Nagorno-Karabakh population, informing them of their right to vote in the parliamentary election.[23] The NKR held elections for the 33-seat legislature on June 19, 2005, in which the ruling Democratic Party of Artsakh won 12 seats, while Free Motherland won 10.

Continued meetings between Azerbaijan and Armenia appear to have improved prospects for progress toward a resolution of the Nagorno-Karabakh conflict. Armenian officials announced in July that the two countries had reached agreement on the key points of a formal peace accord, while Azerbaijani deputy foreign minister Araz Azimov, President Aliyev's special envoy for Nagorno-Karabakh, stated on July 18 that the sides were closer to a final agreement than ever before.[24]

The sides seem to have agreed upon a gradual approach, with the probable first step being the withdrawal of Armenian troops from some of the seven Azerbaijani districts surrounding the Nagorno-Karabakh enclave in return for Azerbaijan's loosening of trade sanctions on Armenia. Although agreement over a possible timeline for troop withdrawal should certainly be considered a breakthrough, the issue of a referendum in Nagorno-Karabakh will remain a key obstacle for the foreseeable future. Armenia insists on a referendum in which the predominantly Armenian population of Nagorno-Karabakh would determine the status of the region. Complicating matters is the fact that a referendum in Nagorno-Karabakh would require an amendment to Azerbaijan's constitution, which currently prohibits the holding of referendums in some parts of Azerbaijani territory and on issues relating to the country's territorial integrity.

Judicial Framework and Independence

1997	1998	1999	2001	2002	2003	2004	2005	2006
5.50	5.50	5.50	5.25	5.25	5.25	5.50	5.75	5.75

The Azerbaijani constitution, adopted in 1995, provides a wide range of human rights protections, yet these rights are often violated in practice. Judicial power is implemented through the Constitutional Court, Supreme Court, Economic Court, and the ordinary and specialized law courts. The judges of the high courts are appointed by the National Assembly on the recommendation of the president and remain heavily dependent on the executive branch. The president appoints and dismisses the prosecutor general of the Azerbaijan Republic. The influence of the government on the judiciary remained substantial in 2005 as youth organizations affiliated with the opposition as well as political rivals were detained through seemingly politically engineered trials.

The Law on the Judicial Legal Council, as well as the law amending and completing the 1997 Law on Courts and Judges, entered into force in January 2005. In a positive move that was offset by the politically motivated trials, the National Assembly made changes to the Law on Advocacy that went into effect in August 2005, simplifying requirements for over 200 formerly licensed lawyers to join the Collegiums of Advocates (the bar) and thereby to practice whether or not they have passed a separate bar exam. Other legislation established a new selection process for judges, assessed as more professional by international observers.

The judiciary remains corrupt, inefficient, and open to executive influence, generally failing to observe constitutional prohibitions on arbitrary arrest and detention. Detainees are presumed innocent until found guilty, but harassment, intimidation, and evidence gathered under physical pressure are not uncommon. Access to lawyers for defendants is generally respected, but there have been cases where detained individuals were not allowed to speak to their lawyers and were held longer than is allowed or required. This was particularly true among the arrests in connection with the alleged coup attempt involving Rasul Guliyev and a number of prominent government ministers and officials, including Economic Development Minister Farhad Aliyev, his brother and Azpetrol chairman Rafig Aliyev, and Health Minister Ali Insanov. Youth activists affiliated with Maqam! and Yeni Fikir faced even higher constraints, limited access to attorneys, and reportedly torture.

The authorities based the charges of involvement of the former government ministers in an attempt to overthrow the constitutional order primarily on confessions by former finance minister Fikret Yusifov, who was detained on October 16-17 and, under interrogation, is believed to have said that Farhad Aliyev provided funds to the political opposition. The Office of the Prosecutor General and Ministries of Internal Affairs and National Security issued a statement on November 1 that Insanov had confessed to unspecified unconstitutional acts and to providing financing to Guliyev's election campaign, while Farhad Aliyev continued to reject the charges until the end of the year.

Hussein Yusifov, father of former finance minister Fikret Yusifov, who reportedly informed the authorities of the planned coup attempt in which he implicated Insanov, Aliyev, and Guliyev, wrote to President Aliyev to register concern that his son was reportedly kept in solitary confinement and had not yet been permitted to meet with his lawyers.[25] A number of former ministers also reported health problems stemming from being kept in the National Security Ministry's pretrial investigation prison. Insanov's lawyer, Togrul Babaev, said on December 31 that his client suffered severe back pain and risked losing the use of his legs in the absence of expert medical attention, while Presidential Administration-official Akif Muradverdiyev's lawyer said on December 29 that his client suffered from high blood pressure.[26] Farhad Aliyev was taken on December 22 to a Baku hospital, where he was diagnosed as suffering from low arterial blood pressure.

The reputation of the Ministry of Internal Affairs was undermined after it was revealed in March that a number of high- and middle-level officials were involved in a kidnapping ring. The Ministry of National Security launched an operation on March 10 to secure the release of Zamira Hajieva, wife of the president of the International Bank of Azerbaijan, who was abducted a month earlier by a group that demanded US$20 million for her release. She was found in a concrete bunker belonging to a senior police official, who was apprehended together with some 20 other people, 7 of them Internal Affairs Ministry officials. On March 23, Minister Ramil Usubov dismissed his first deputy, Zakhid Dunyamaliev, Criminal Investigations Department head Zakir Nasibov, and two of Nasibov's deputies. The National Security Ministry and the Office of the Prosecutor General released a joint statement the same day on additional crimes allegedly committed in recent years by a criminal gang headed by former Ministry of Internal Affairs official Haji Mamedov.[27] The U.S. State Department's annual report noted that Azerbaijani police failed to investigate four deaths in police custody and numerous complaints of torture and ill-treatment in detention.

In its annual overview of human rights observance worldwide, released on January 13, Human Rights Watch noted that ongoing pressure by the Azerbaijani government on the political opposition reached a new intensity in the wake of the 2003 presidential election, with 46 opposition activists receiving prison terms ranging from two to six years, but also noted as a positive step that 32 political prisoners have been released. The government initially resisted Council of Europe, OSCE, and other Western calls for a fresh amnesty for the 40 political prisoners associated with the postpresidential election events, but later it opened the way for the Supreme Court to consider appeals by 7 high-profile defendants, including ADP deputy chairman Sardar Jalaloglu and *Yeni Musavat* editor and *Musavat* deputy chairman Rauf Arifoglu. Some of those 40 had petitioned for pardon, but the 7 defendants had not done so, arguing that they were innocent of the charges against them. The OSCE released a February 2005 report detailing procedural violations during the trials of some of the 40 political prisoners since the 2003 election and affirmed that in some cases the charges against them were unfounded.

President Aliyev finally issued a decree on March 20, 2005, pardoning 115 prisoners, including 53 who are considered by the Council of Europe to be political prisoners, among them the 7 high-profile oppositionists. Similarly pardoned was former defense minister Rahim Gaziyev, regarded by the Council of Europe as a political prisoner. The government and local human rights NGOs set up a task force on June 11 to settle the remaining political prisoner cases, some 45 of whom were estimated to remain in detention in October 2005, including 4 with serious health problems.Apparently as a result of pressure from the Czech government, Saday Nazarov, a close associate of former prime minister Suret Huseinov, has been released from detention but forbidden to leave Azerbaijan. Nazarov, who left Azerbaijan 10 years ago and was granted political asylum in the Czech Republic, was detained in January 2005 shortly after he arrived in Azerbaijan to visit his elderly father. Czech foreign minister Cyril Svoboda wrote to Azerbaijan's deputy foreign minister Araz Azimov to request his immediate release from detention. Huseinov was sentenced in 1999 to life imprisonment but pardoned in 2004 by President Aliyev.

Azerbaijan's prison conditions remained harsh in 2005. Even after a number of renovations and the construction of five new prisons in 2004, the majority of prisoners depend on their families for basic needs, such as food and medicine, with tuberculosis the primary cause of death in prisons. Some pretrial detainees are kept in solitary confinement, where interrogators reportedly deprive them of food and sleep to secure confessions without physical evidence of abuse. Elchin Gambarov, an attorney representing Yeni Fikir leader Ruslan Bashirli, said on August 17, 2005, that Bashirli was systematically beaten after being taken into custody on August 3, 2005.[28] Gambarov said interrogators tried without success to coerce Bashirli into giving testimony incriminating AXCP chairman Ali Kerimli.

The situation inside prisons had reached a critical point in February 2005, when Internal Affairs Ministry troops violently repressed several riots. Some 100 of the total 842 inmates at high-security prison no. 11 near Baku escaped from their cells and congregated on the roof of the three-story building on February 15 to demand the resignation of prison governor Oktai Gasymov, whom they accused of brutality. Having initially ruled out the use of force against the protesters, the Azerbaijani authorities deployed some 100 Ministry of Internal Affairs troops and riot police to the prison. Journalists reported gunfire and explosions on February 16, after which fire hoses were trained on the protesters, who finally capitulated several hours later. The Office of the Prosecutor General has opened a criminal case in connection with the protest, which triggered similar demands at prisons no. 12 and no. 13. An unknown number of prisoners who took part in the February 15 protest at no. 11 were transferred to other prisons. President Aliyev issued a decree on March 3 expressing "horror" over the conditions in Azerbaijan's prisons and firing three prison directors, including Gasymov.[29] Alqayit Maharramov, a 20-year-old demonstrator jailed for his participation in the post-election protests in October 2003 was found dead in his cell on February 17. His official cause of death was reported as "suffocation."[30]

Aydin Gasymov, deputy minister of justice in charge of the penitentiary system, was dismissed alongside two lower-level Justice Ministry officials in February in connection with widespread abuses and corruption within the prison system. Among the abuses being investigated are the misappropriation of funds, including money allocated to purchase food for prisoners; forgery of official documents to release prisoners before they have served their full terms; and authorization to prisoners of privileges to which they were not entitled. A joint statement by the Ministry of Internal Affairs and the Office of the Prosecutor General alleged that criminal gang leader Nadir Salifov, who was sentenced in 1996 for unspecified serious crimes, committed further criminal offenses between 2001 and 2004 while serving his sentence in the Gobustan jail.[31] Specifically, Salifov allegedly managed with the help of the prison administration to procure eight women, who alleged after visiting him in jail that they had been raped. Salifov also allegedly used four cell phones to extort money from wealthy businessmen.

After a closed trial, Azerbaijan's Court for Serious Crimes passed sentence on February 8, 2005, on 6 men convicted of preparing a terrorist act. Amiraslan Iskenderov and Alirza Babaev were sentenced to 14 years in prison, Abdullah Magamedov and Zaur Aliyev to 7□ years, Khidayat Piriev to 5 years, and Rizvan Abdurezegov to 3 years. They had reportedly photographed buildings in Baku. The six men, all of whom pleaded not guilty, were also suspected of links with the al-Qaeda terrorist network, but it is unclear whether any hard evidence was produced at the trial to substantiate those suspicions.

Corruption

1997	1998	1999	2001	2002	2003	2004	2005	2006
n/a	n/a	6.00	6.25	6.25	6.25	6.25	6.25	6.25

Corruption remains one of the most problematic issues in Azerbaijan. Bribery and nepotism have intervened at all levels of society – from the education system to the workplace to the government – and continue to hinder the development of the country and the eradication of poverty. A legacy of former president Heydar Aliyev's regime, corrupt patronage networks drive both politics and the economy, while the growing oil wealth appears to reinforce the position of deeply entrenched, corrupt elites, hindering hopes that Azerbaijan might change into a transparent society from its current state as an opaque economy.

Most people prefer to pay small bribes instead of the much higher fees imposed by the state. Thirty-three percent of Azerbaijanis report that they have paid bribes in the past; 20 percent say that they have been asked for bribes but have not paid; and 33 percent say that they have not been asked for bribes in the past. Among Azerbaijanis who have paid bribes, the most common occasions are for medical care (12 percent) and higher grades for their school-age children (6 percent), states the IFES 2004 survey Public Opinion in Azerbaijan. A different survey, undertaken in March by PULS-R, found that 16.2 percent of the respondents identify corruption and incompetence within the government bureaucracy as the biggest problem facing Azerbaijan, after the unresolved Karabakh conflict identified by 61.9 percent of the respondents.

The criminal code does not define penalties for most corrupt activities other than bribery, although it forbids a government official from receiving gifts valued at more than US$55, holding other jobs (other than in teaching or the arts), and "being engaged in business activity directly, indirectly or through proxies." A soft measure against low-level corruption was the increase of monthly salaries in

September 2005 for regular traffic police to US$350 and for officers to between US$500 and US$700.

A new Law on Combating Corruption, which defines corruption and outlines official responsibilities, and the State Program on Fighting Corruption came into force in January 2005. The statute for an anticorruption commission set up in April 2004 was approved on May 3, 2005. It is led by Ramiz Mekhtiyev and is composed equally of presidential, parliamentary, and Constitutional Court appointees but lacks the participation of civil society and media representatives. The commission created an ad hoc Anticorruption Legislative Working Group, which has met four times in 18 months without direct effect on any cases.[32] The Legislative Working Group is staffed with 13 government officials, 3 NGO representatives, and 2 foreign experts from the American Bar Association's Central and East European Law Initiative and the OSCE. The NGO and international organization representatives do not have voting rights.

The National Assembly's Audit Chamber remains weak and inefficient, and NGOs and media lack access to information about its activities or statistics regarding government revenues and expenditures. So far, the state has failed to enforce an effective legislative or administrative process to investigate the corruption of government officials and civil servants, a process that would at the same time be free of prejudice against political opponents. The law bans anonymous complaints of corrupt activities while there is no effective legal protection for witnesses.[33]

A U.S. State Department report noted that corruption remains a significant deterrent to foreign investment, especially in the nonenergy sector, and identified the State Customs Committee and Ministry of Taxation as the institutions of greatest concern to foreign business.[34] Azerbaijan's rating in the Transparency International Corruption Perceptions Index 2005 stands at 2.2 (a slight improvement from 1.9 in 2004) and 137th among 159 countries (that is, near the end of the scale that signifies the highest level of corruption perception).

Kaan Nazli is an analyst at Eurasia Group, focusing on emerging Europe and the Caspian region. He is a regular commentator on the region on CNN and CNBC and has written for the Financial Times, *the* National Interest, Turkish Policy Quarterly, Investor Turkey, Insight Turkey, *and* EurasiaNet.

---

[1] BBC Monitoring, "Azeri president to be elected ruling party's chairman - party official," March 24, 2005.

[2] Radio Free Europe/Radio Liberty Newsline - Transcaucasus & Central Asia, "Poll suggests 'velvet revolution' unlikely in Azerbaijan," March 2, 2005.

[3] Radio Free Europe/Radio Liberty Newsline - Transcaucasus & Central Asia, March 2, 2005.

[4] www.intermedia.org/news_and_publications/publications/ Azerbaijan%20News%20Release%203.pdf.

[5] AzerPress News, "The minister of economic development of Azerbaijan does not exclude possible threat to his life," September 2, 2005.

[6] BBC Monitoring, "Azeri government infighting resuming again - paper," August 20, 2005.

[7] International Crisis Group, Azerbaijan's 2005 Elections: Lost Opportunity, November 21, 2005.

[8] BBC Monitoring, "Azeri leader says capture of criminal gang 'biggest success'," March 11, 2005.

[9] Radio Free Europe/Radio Liberty Newsline - Transcaucasus & Central Asia, "Azerbaijani president advocates measures to preclude election falsification," October 26, 2005

[10] Radio Free Europe/Radio Liberty Newsline - Transcaucasus & Central Asia, "Azerbaijani oppositionist, editor harassed," February 28, 2005.

[11] Radio Free Europe/Radio Liberty Newsline - Transcaucasus & Central Asia, "Azerbaijani opposition party accuses security ministry of smear campaign," August 22, 2005.

[12] hrw.org/backgrounder/eca/azerbaijan1005.

[13] BBC Monitoring, "US envoy urges Azeri town officials not to back pro-government candidates", October 25, 2005.

[14] International Crisis Group, Azerbaijan's 2005 Elections: Lost Opportunity, November 21, 2005.

[15] New York Times, "Azerbaijan Votes, Amid Accusations of Fraud and Abuse," November 7, 2005.

[16] Radio Free Europe/Radio Liberty Newsline - Transcaucasus & Central Asia, "Azerbaijani parliament gives green light to NGOs," October 31, 2005.

[17] Radio Free Europe/Radio Liberty Newsline - Transcaucasus & Central Asia, "Azerbaijani youth activist beaten, threatened," August 10, 2005.

[18] Radio Free Europe/Radio Liberty Reports - Media Matters, "New media outlets debut in run-up to Azerbaijani parliamentary elections," March 8, 2005.

[19] Radio Free Europe/Radio Liberty Newsline - Transcaucasus & Central Asia, "Journalist gunned down in Azerbaijan, March 3, 2005.

[20] Info Prod - Strategic Business Information, "Azerbaijani opposition terms political killing," March 6, 2005.

[21] AzerPress News, "A press club 'Friends of Army' is set up in Azerbaijan," February 10, 2005.

[22] Radio Free Europe/Radio Liberty Newsline - Transcaucasus & Central Asia, "Azerbaijani president cautions regional administrators not to pressure businessmen," February 12, 2005.

[23] Radio Free Europe/Radio Liberty Newsline - Transcaucasus & Central Asia, "Karabakh rejects invitation to participate in Azerbaijani ballot," August 24, 2005.

[24] Khachatrian, Haroutiun, "Nagorno-Karabakh: peace on the horizon?", EurasiaNet, August 17, 2005.

[25] Radio Free Europe/Radio Liberty Newsline - Transcaucasus & Central Asia, "As father of a second appeals to Azerbaijani president," October 27, 2005.

[26] Radio Free Europe/Radio Liberty Newsline - Transcaucasus & Central Asia, "More Azerbaijani coup suspects experience health problems," January 5, 2006.

[27] AzerPress News, "Murders of a number of Azeri luminaries are cracked," March 23, 2005.

v Radio Free Europe/Radio Liberty Newsline - Transcaucasus & Central Asia, "Lawyer says arrested Azerbaijani youth leader subjected to 'torture'," August 20, 2005.

[29] BBC Monitoring, "Azeri leader 'appalled' by situation in prisons," March 3, 2005.

[30] BBC Monitoring, "Azeri convicted over post-election riots dies in prison," February 17, 2005.

[31] BBC Monitoring, "Azeri warders face charges for encouraging crime in prisons," February 9, 2005.

[32] International Crisis Group, Azerbaijan's 2005 Elections: Lost Opportunity, November 21, 2005.

[33] International Crisis Group, Azerbaijan's 2005 Elections: Lost Opportunity, November 21, 2005.

[34] U.S. Department of State, 2005 Investment Climate Statement - Azerbaijan, http://www.state.gov/e/eb/ifd/2005/41980.htm

Belarus

Capital:	Minsk	
Population:	9.8 million	
GNI/capita:	$2,140	
Ethnic Groups:	Belarusian (81.2%), Russian (11.4%),	
	Polish, Ukrainian, and other (7.4%)	

Nations in Transit Ratings and Averaged Scores

	1997	1998	1999	2001	2002	2003	2004	2005	2006
Electoral Process	6.00	6.25	6.75	6.75	6.75	6.75	6.75	7.00	7.00
Civil Society	5.25	5.75	6.00	6.50	6.25	6.50	6.75	6.75	6.75
Independent Media	6.25	6.50	6.75	6.75	6.75	6.75	6.75	6.75	6.75
Governance *	6.00	6.25	6.25	6.25	6.50	6.50	6.50	n/a	n/a
National Democratic Governance	n/a	n/a	n/a	n/a	n/a	n/a	n/a	6.75	7.00
Local Democratic Governance	n/a	n/a	n/a	n/a	n/a	n/a	n/a	6.50	6.50
Judicial Framework and Independence	6.00	6.25	6.50	6.75	6.75	6.75	6.75	6.75	6.75
Corruption	n/a	n/a	5.25	5.25	5.25	5.50	5.75	6.00	6.25
Democracy Score	5.90	6.20	6.25	6.38	6.38	6.46	6.54	6.64	6.71

* *With the 2005 edition, Freedom House introduced seperate analysis and ratings for national democratic governance and local democratic governance to provide readers with more detailed and nuanced analysis of these two important subjects.*

NOTE: The ratings reflect the consensus of Freedom House, its academic advisers, and the author of this report. The opinions expressed in this report are those of the author. The ratings are based on a scale of 1 to 7, with 1 representing the highest level of democratic progress and 7 the lowest. The Democracy Score is an average of ratings for the categories tracked in a given year.

The economic and social data on this page were taken from the following sources:
GNI/capita, Population: *World Development Indicators 2006* (Washington, D.C.: World Bank, 2006).
Ethnic Groups: *CIA World Factbook 2006* (Washington, D.C.: Central Intelligence Agency, 2006).

EXECUTIVE SUMMARY

Belarus's prospects for democratization have faded over the decade of authoritarian rule by President Alexander Lukashenka, first elected in 1994. The country's constitution, amended in a highly controversial referendum in 1996, fully institutionalized a system of unlimited presidential authority. Another controversial constitutional referendum conducted in 2004 removed term limits for the presidency and opened an opportunity for Lukashenka's "infinite rule." His regime ignores international criticism and continues to harden its grip on power. The Belarusian economy, although unreformed and extensively bureaucratized, recently recorded sound growth owing to the economic upturn in neighboring countries, particularly Russia. This allows the government to preserve social stability through welfare and industrial policies that provide acceptable standards of living and almost full employment for the population.

In 2005, the policies of the Lukashenka regime reflected efforts to resist the democratic "colored revolutions" that swept through post-Communist Eurasia starting in 2004. Although the October 2004 constitutional referendum, carried out with little organized resistance, proved the regime's high degree of immunity from electoral changes, Lukashenka took no chances and ordered mobilization of the entire state apparatus to combat democracy in Belarus.

A new series of preemptive strikes against the opposition, civil society, and the independent press marked 2005, even though the opposition community had already been emasculated by repression in previous years. The legitimate space for independent political and social activity was severely curtailed and paralleled a speedy increase in punishment for political opponents and ordinary citizens. The regime's most outspoken and active opponents were put in jail, while independent press and civil society were pushed to the brink of extinction. New laws introduced in November–December 2005 criminalize almost any opposition activity considered by the authorities as pursuing regime change. The Belarusian House of Representatives, the lower chamber of the Parliament, scheduled presidential elections for March 19, 2006, four months ahead of the date mandated by the Constitution. This move, although considered by the opposition to be a sign of panic in the regime, was undertaken to hamper the efforts of opponents to connect to the electorate and turn public opinion against the regime.

National Democratic Governance. Although the Constitution of the Republic of Belarus proclaims the country to be "a unitary, democratic, social state based on the rule of law," in reality the government is based on unlimited presidential authority. The president is in full control of the cabinet, the legislature, and all defense and security structures. The centralized Belarusian economy remains unreformed and is considered among the most repressive in the world. The government thoroughly cleansed the political field in 2005, introduced Soviet-era regulations punishing the public expression of independent opinion and unauthorized political activity, and amended laws to legitimize the shooting of protesters as a last resort. *Belarus's rating for national democratic governance worsens from 6.75 to 7.00. Whereas major democratic institutions or practices have been in place in Belarus for almost a decade, the government has fully resorted to totalitarian methods of repression and has openly declared its commitment to defending the status quo by all means necessary.*

Electoral Process. The March 2005 by-elections to the House of Representatives in the only constituency where a deputy was not elected in 2004 ended with a resounding victory by a pro-regime candidate and were marred by gross violations. The opposition united in the run-up to the 2006 presidential elections, but this is unlikely to be a factor in the campaign given the overall climate of fear and repression in the country. *Belarus's rating for electoral process remains at 7.00 owing to the executive branch's control over the process, which has ultimately ceased to play a role in allowing citizens to elect and change the government.*

Civil Society. The campaign to squeeze the independent civic sector out of existence continued in 2005 with the adoption of highly restrictive laws and decrees that culminated in the November amendments to the criminal code. The government delegalized almost all forms of international cooperation, independent analytical work, academic exchange, and human rights protection with the introduction of severe criminal punishment for membership in unregistered nongovernmental organizations (NGOs) or "discrediting" Belarus in the international arena. *Belarus's rating for civil society remains unchanged at 6.75. In spite of the sharp and paralyzing increase in punishments for unauthorized social activities, independent civil society remains active and committed to promoting democracy in Belarus.*

Independent Media. The government continued its routine campaign of attacking independent newspapers with libel suits, suspensions, and denials of distribution in 2005 and continued to deport and arrest foreign journalists. Failure to investigate the 2004 murder of leading independent journalist Veranika Charkasava and the mysterious death of *Narodnaja Volja* journalist Vasil Hrodnikau in October 2005 highlighted the dangers faced by independent reporters in Belarus. *Belarus's rating for independent media remains unchanged at 6.75. Although the condition of independent media worsened substantially in 2005, a small network of printed press uncontrolled by the government continues to provide alternative information for a limited segment of Belarusian society.*

Local Democratic Governance. Local self-government is nonexistent in Belarus, as municipal authorities continue to be fully subordinated to the central government. Heads of regional administration are appointed by the president, and local councils have limited responsibilities. The president's total disregard of protests in

Minsk over the renaming of central avenues in the capital city confirmed the powerlessness of local authorities. *Belarus's rating for local democratic governance remains at 6.50 owing to the country's overcentralized, top-down administrative structure, which provides little room for pluralism and responsibility at the grassroots level.*

Judicial Framework and Independence. The political pressure on the Constitutional Court to revisit the 2002 decision lifting restrictions on foreign travel, as well as the inhumane treatment of political prisoner Mikhail Marynich, highlighted the role of the judiciary as subordinate to the government. Opposition activists, civil society leaders, and independent journalists rarely prevail in appeals to the authorities' arbitrary decisions. Protesters at mass events have been severely beaten without investigation by the authorities. *Belarus's rating for judicial framework and independence remains at 6.75.*

Corruption. Belarus's downward slide in corruption ratings by independent surveys continued in 2005. A series of high-profile arrests and criminal cases destroyed the official propaganda claiming Belarus to be a corruption-free state. A highly etatized economy creates ubiquitous opportunities for bribery and abuse by authorities, whereas the countercorruption measures considered by the government are inherently flawed with opportunities for their selective application. *Belarus's rating for corruption is lowered from 6.00 to 6.25 owing to the increasing evidence of serious problems related to corruption in the country and the creation of a favorable environment for corruption by the bureaucratization of the economy.*

Outlook for 2006. A systematic campaign to emasculate the political opposition and civil society leaves the opponents of President Lukashenka with little hope for the March 2006 presidential elections. Although the opposition had a modest success in nominating a single candidate and running a vigorous campaign, delegalization of any activities unapproved by the government and increasing political repression will be a paralyzing factor. As it is highly unlikely that the currently favorable economic conditions will change in the short run, Lukashenka will continue to enjoy his implicit social contract with the population, guaranteeing him acquiescence with repressive policies in exchange for the country's economic security.

MAIN REPORT

National Democratic Governance

1997	1998	1999	2001	2002	2003	2004	2005	2006
n/a	n/a	n/a	n/a	n/a	n/a	n/a	6.75	7.00

The Constitution of the Republic of Belarus proclaims the country to be "a unitary, democratic, social state based on the rule of law." In reality, the government is based on the unlimited authority of the president, who is in full control of the cabinet and dominates the legislative process. Presidential decrees have priority over laws adopted by the Parliament, whose bicameral composition enforces its subordination to the president. While the lower House of Representatives is elected on a single-member constituency basis, the upper Council of the Republic is appointed by regional assemblies of local councils, with the president appointing 8 of its 64 members.

The Parliament has extremely limited powers and virtually no control over the state budget, which can be amended by presidential decree. The Presidential Department of Affairs (PDA) is responsible for the financial and material resources of the Parliament, which lacks control even over its own internal finances and wages. Only a small part of lawmaking is carried out in the Parliament. The National Center for Legislative Activities – an agency responsible for the preparation of bills – is also subordinate to the president.

Major legislation is available to the public in printed and free Internet versions. However, no rules exist for disclosing the budgets of the central and local governments. Data on international treaties, military and defense spending, and state-sponsored research and development programs are designated top secret. There is no specific regulation authorizing the Parliament to make its records public. Likewise, citizens have no opportunity to view their representatives' voting records.

The constitutional referendum on lifting presidential term limits conducted on October 17, 2004, opened the possibility for a lifelong presidency for Lukashenka. There were violations of electoral law at every stage of the referendum, and the smallest sign of protest resulted in fines, imprisonment, arbitrary searches, break-ins, and hit-and-run attacks. Allegations of vote fraud were widespread and well documented. According to the Central Election Commission (CEC), 90 percent of eligible voters took part in the referendum and elections; 79 percent voted in favor of lifting the term limits. However, exit polls conducted by the Gallup Organization/Baltic Surveys Center and postelection polling conducted by the Independent Institute for Socio-Economic and Political Studies (IISEPS) showed that only 49 percent of respondents declared a vote in favor.[1] Nevertheless, the public was not informed about the real results of the referendum, and the overall perception that Lukashenka could win any ballot remained unchallenged. The IISEPS was closed down by court order in April 2005, apparently for its role in unmasking vote fraud during the referendum.

The Orange Revolution in Ukraine, which unfolded only five weeks after the constitutional referendum in Belarus, was a wake-up call for the Lukashenka regime. Although the possibility of an electoral revolution in Belarus is minimal, Lukashenka responded actively to the events just south of the border in order to preempt the development of a potential opposition. He immediately warned those in his inner circle that "modern political techniques and a weakly managed country are pregnant with serious consequences," and he vowed resistance against "acts of banditry"[2] (his own definition of electoral revolution) in Belarus.

The legal space in which opposition parties can operate in Belarus is steadily shrinking. Opposition and civil society groups are no longer allowed to rent state-owned property, so many party conferences and NGO meetings take place in restaurants, Western embassies, private apartments, and even forests. The use of new police tactics to disperse a few small demonstrations in early 2005 made it clear that the country's security forces have been specifically trained to stop street protests.

The political field has been cleansed in the run-up to the July 2006 presidential election. Mikalaj Statkievich, former chairman of the Belarusian Social Democratic Party, and Paval Seviarynec, leader of the unregistered organization Young Front movement, were both sentenced to two years of forced labor for organizing antireferendum protests in October 2004. Since both had a long record of mobilizing street rallies, their indictments may have been a disguised attempt to forestall street protests following the 2006 election. Another veteran politician, former member of Parliament (MP) and political prisoner Andrej Klimau, was sentenced to two years of forced labor in May 2005 for staging unsanctioned rallies two months earlier that he had advertised as the beginning of the democratic revolution in Belarus.

Several politicians who could be potential challengers in the forthcoming presidential elections have been kept behind bars. Siarhej Skrabets, leader of Respublika – the only opposition faction in the House of Representatives from the previous convocation – was arrested in May 2005 on charges of bribery and illegal soliciting of a loan. Skrabets held a 40-day hunger strike in protest of his imprisonment but was not released. He was eventually sentenced to two and a half years in jail. Before the launch of criminal proceedings against them, Statkievich and Skrabets had to pay heavy fines for participating in opposition protests in 2005.[3] Another potential challenger, Mikhail Marynich, former minister of foreign trade and ambassador to Latvia, who was sentenced to five years in jail in December 2004 for allegedly stealing computers from the NGO he heads, had his sentence reduced to three and a half years in 2005. The authorities refused to pardon Marynich despite his poor health.

Belarus's defense and security structures are controlled by the president. Law enforcement agencies – such as the State Security Committee (KGB), Ministry of the Interior, Office of the Prosecutor, State Control Committee, and Security Council – have grown in size and influence over the last decade and enhanced their role in virtually all spheres of public life. In the past year, Lukashenka has also boosted the law enforcement agencies and purged their ranks of potential dissenters. Viktar Sheiman, the former prosecutor general who was appointed head of the presidential administration in December 2004, has stated that his goal is to "consolidate the power systems, unify the command structure, and avoid situations such as those that had occurred south of the border."[4] The security forces have received an implicit order to fight the opposition, and the rules for opening fire in peacetime have been amended to allow the use of firearms not only in cases enumerated in the law, but also "in other cases determined by the president."[5] The amendment may thus be used to justify a crackdown on any protest, violent or peaceful.

The Heritage Foundation rates the Belarusian economy among the most repressive in the world. Although the government does pursue relatively prudent macroeconomic policies, the private sector and domestic competition are systematically stifled in favor of outdated and largely unprofitable Soviet-style industries. Bureaucratization of the economy is an important tool of political control. Since the government controls approximately 80 percent of all assets, it employs the vast majority of Belarusians. Labor regulations provide a wide range of pretexts for firing anyone at any time from a public job, including for poorly concealed political reasons.

Several factors contribute to the stability of the Lukashenka regime. First, all power is concentrated in the hands of the president, and there is little immediate threat to his position. Second, there are no significant inter-ethnic or inter-religious tensions inside the country; neither are there territorial disputes with neighboring states. Third, the government enjoys continuous support from elderly and rural constituencies who favor state paternalism and Soviet-style security and stability. Fourth, the Belarusian economy allows for the maintenance of acceptable living standards. According to a September 2005 poll by the IISEPS, about 47 percent of the population would support Lukashenka if he chooses to run for presidential elections. Meanwhile, about 40 percent believe that free and fair elections are impossible in Belarus.[6]

Electoral Process

1997	1998	1999	2001	2002	2003	2004	2005	2006
6.00	6.25	6.75	6.75	6.75	6.75	6.75	7.00	7.00

Since the consolidation of presidential authority in a 1996 referendum, representative institutions in Belarus have become largely ceremonial bodies that rubber-stamp policies made at the top of the vertical power structure. Likewise, elections have turned into exercises that validate Lukashenka's political dominance.

The current electoral code was adopted in February 2000 and "fails to provide for democratic elections," according to the Organization for Security and Cooperation in Europe (OSCE). The code does not provide election commissions with multiparty representation and independence. Moreover, it fails to provide sufficient transparency, guarantees against vote rigging during early voting, or uniform appeals for the decisions of election commissions. The code's regulations also stifle campaigning and freedom of speech.

The last presidential elections, held in September 2001, resulted in a resounding victory for Lukashenka. According to official results, he won 75 percent of the vote against 15 percent cast for the opposition candidate, Uladzimir Hancharyk, and 2 percent for the leader of the Liberal Democratic Party (LDP), Siarhej Hajdukevich. Official turnout was 83 percent. The opposition refused to accept the official results, complaining about the absence of opposition representation on election commissions, biased coverage of the campaign in the official media, imbalanced conditions for campaigning, harassment of opposition activists, and gross tabulation violations. The OSCE's International Election Observation Mission in Belarus declared that the "2001 presidential election process failed to meet OSCE commitment for democratic elections."

The most recent parliamentary elections took place on October 17, 2004. According to the CEC, the elections were valid in 109 constituencies out of 110, with 1 election invalidated. Of the 108 deputies elected to constituencies in the first round, not a single opposition candidate won a place in the House of Representatives. All of the declared winners, which included 8 from the Communist Party of Byelorussia, 3 from the Agrarian Party, and 1 from the LDP (an analogue of Vladimir Zhirinovsky's party in Russia), were pro-government and supported the president. The election result data were questioned by the opposition and condemned by international organizations. Elections to the upper house of the Parliament, the Council of the Republic, took place on November 2004, with the assemblies of local councils voting to fill 56 seats, or 8 per region. Several local councilpersons representing the opposition were not included in the list of electors.

Four opposition coalitions announced their intentions to run – the Popular Coalition Five Plus, the European Coalition Free Belarus, the Young Belarus Coalition, and the Respublika group of parliamentary opposition deputies – but the opposition was blocked at all stages of the campaign. Only 28 out of 328 opposition representatives were granted membership on election commissions. More than half of the leading opposition party candidates were denied registration. Several candidates lost their jobs or were forced to abandon their university studies after deciding to run. Others were subjected to raids on their homes, undercover police surveillance, or hit-and-run attacks. Opposition candidates were also denied legally guaranteed access to the media, and their campaign rallies were routinely banned.

Early voting, a procedure that begins five days before the elections for those who cannot vote on election day, turned into a compulsory exercise for students and public sector employees in the countryside, presumably because the process is almost impossible to observe. Almost 20 percent of voters cast their ballots early in 2004, and observers reported massive fraud, such as multiple voting and ballot stuffing. Most electoral observers were not allowed to directly watch the vote count, as complaints of irregularities were met with the expulsion of around 400 observers nationwide. According to the OSCE observation mission, irregularities marred vote counts at 60 percent of the polling stations observed.

By-elections to the House of Representatives were conducted in March 2005 in the one constituency where the election was invalidated in October 2004. The pro-government candidate staged an easy victory against two opposition challengers, including former MP Valery Fralou, who according to official data received only 12 percent of the votes. Independent and international observers recorded more than 200 electoral violations and denounced the results as fraudulent.[7]

With the adoption of a sharply amended Constitution in 1996, party development came to a standstill in Belarus. Pro-presidential parties continued as puppet groups whose only mission was to provide a pluralistic facade for the regime. Opposition parties were completely marginalized. The president does not have his own political party, and his insistence on staying aloof from party politics may be explained by his populist claim to represent "the people, not the parties." Party membership is low (rarely exceeding 2,000 to 3,000 members), and affiliation with an opposition party can result in various problems for individuals working in government, education, or private business.

Opposition party politics are notorious for personal rivalries among party leaders, the near absence of leadership rotation, and the inability of parties to unite behind common candidates. In 2005, the internal feud inside the Belarusian Social Democratic Party (BSDP) ended with the ouster of the veteran party chairman Mikalaj Statkievich, who refused to recognize his expulsion from the party and claimed leadership of a splinter group of his loyalists. The party elected as its chairman Alexander Kazulin, former rector of the Belarusian State University (fired by Lukashenka in 2003). The Ministry of Justice recognized the legitimacy of the pro-Kazulin group. However, its attempts to carry out a party congress were routinely disrupted in 2005. All local chapters of political parties had to reregister by February 1, 2005, to confirm their compliance with rules that forbid having offices at residential addresses.[8] As opposition parties have almost no chance to rent state-owned office space, this rule caused the near complete elimination of local party branches for many parties. As a result, more than 300 local branches of the opposition parties were deregistered[9] by September 2005.[10]

The ability of opposition parties to communicate is severely restricted by repressive government regulations regarding rallies, as well as attacks on independent media and civil society groups that are sympathetic to pro-democracy politicians. Rallies in Minsk are officially authorized in just one location on the outskirts of the city center, whereas participation in unsanctioned protest incurs heavy fines (up to US$2,500, slightly less than an average annual income for an entire family), dismissal from state jobs, and prison terms. As a result, attendance at opposition protests sank to just several hundred in 2005.

Dozens of protesters were arrested during the celebrations of the anniversary of the Belarusian Democratic Republic on March 25 and during the traditional Chernobyl memorial rally on April 26.[11] During the April 26 protests, several Russian and Ukrainian activists who joined the Belarusian opposition in solidarity were arrested, beaten, and briefly jailed.[12] The Russian ambassador failed to defend his compatriots, having issued instead a statement declaring his "disapproval" of their decision to join protests, apparently signaling solidarity with Lukashenka's authoritarianism following the Orange Revolution.[13]

The only sizable protest that took place in 2005 was the strike of small-business entrepreneurs who protested the introduction of a new value-added tax (VAT) in March 2005. At least 100,000 people participated nationwide, and several thousand rallied on the central square of Minsk. Unlike opposition protests, the strike was not violently disrupted, and the government negotiated with the protesters (even though the strike leader was jailed for 10 days). This relative lenience confirmed that Lukashenka's government is "really afraid of large-scale social unrest."[14] The strike, however, did not put forward any political demands, and its leaders refused to cooperate with the opposition, which indicates a general sense of hopelessness in Belarusian society about political opposition and electoral politics.

The government stepped up pressure on election observer organizations, most of which have already been denied registration or refused to be registered. On October 29 in Minsk, the authorities disrupted the inaugural congress of the civic initiative Partnership, one of the largest NGOs in Belarus specializing in election monitoring. Several leaders of the group were sentenced to 15 days in jail for staging an unsanctioned rally, even though the law requires no official permission for conducting indoor meetings. Head of the CEC Lidzia Yarmoshina summarized her attitude toward independent election monitors at the OSCE conference in Moscow in November by claiming that they "paralyze" the work of election commissions.[15]

Following six months of primaries in which delegates were invited to vote for one of four candidates, the Congress of Democratic Forces (CDF) held in Minsk on October 1–2 nominated Alyaksandr Milinkevich, leader of a provincial NGO, as a single candidate from the opposition to contest the presidential election, then scheduled for July 2006. The primaries took place in secrecy, as organizers had failed to receive official permits for most of the meetings. In September, Lukashenka publicly invited the opposition to hold the CDF in Minsk. The authorities presumably hoped that, unable to agree on a single candidate, the opposition would collapse, turning the meeting into a public relations disaster. The congress witnessed a tight race between Milinkevich and the leader of the United Civil Party, Anatol Liabedzka. Contrary to some expectations, Liabedzka accepted the result and pledged to work with Milinkevich.

The opposition coalition did not include the BSDP, whose leader, Alexander Kazulin, expressed his intention to run independently. In a surprise move, the House of Representatives convened on December 16 and set the date of presidential elections for March 19, 2006, four months before the date the election had to be carried out according to the Constitution. The authorities declared that this decision was "discriminatory" against the sitting president but was made in response to the "wishes of the citizens," who argued that summer elections would make it impossible for many agricultural workers and vacationers to vote. The opposition quickly declared that shifting the date represented a sign of panic inside the ruling circles.

However, the most important reason was arguably the shortening of a vigorous campaign by Milinkevich, the main opposition challenger, who started actively traveling across Belarus after his nomination by the CDF. On December 27, the CEC registered initiative groups of eight potential contesters, who were allowed to collect signatures to be nominated as candidates. Aside from Lukashenka and Milinkevich, the list included the BSDP's Alexander Kazulin, leader of the pro-presidential LDP Siarhej Hajdukevich, leader of the Conservative Christian Party – BPF Zianon Pazniak, political prisoner Siarhej Skrabets, former Speaker of the Council of the Republic Alyaksandr Vajtovich, and former member of the House of Representatives Valery Fralou. Only Lukashenka, Milinkevich, Kazulin, and Hajdukevich were expected to collect the 100,000 signatures necessary for nomination.

The authorities' first steps in organizing the elections in March 2006 demonstrated that a free and fair vote would be unlikely. Secretary of the CEC Mikalaj Lazavik declared that the main criterion in selecting members of local election commissions would be previous experience in the commissions' work.[16] All previous elections were organized with almost no presence of the opposition in the commissions.

Civil Society

1997	1998	1999	2001	2002	2003	2004	2005	2006
5.25	5.75	6.00	6.50	6.25	6.50	6.75	6.75	6.75

The Lukashenka government views the independent civil society sector as a source of political and social opposition to the regime and pursues a consistent policy to eliminate it. As a result, the authentic NGO sector in Belarus has turned into an underground network of individuals and banned groups opposed to the government. A modest space for legitimate existence is allowed for nonpoliticized NGOs loyal to the regime.

More than 2,200 NGOs were officially registered with the Ministry of Justice as of January 1, 2004, including 52 national trade unions and 2,214 public associations. Half of these are located in Minsk. Overall, volunteerism is low owing to the lack of a tradition of public participation, an extremely low level of awareness about NGO work, and fear of problems that might accompany membership in an "opposition" NGO.

For most NGOs, foreign grants remain the only source of financial support. Donations are not tax-exempt, and NGOs must pay heavy taxes if they choose to operate legally. This puts NGOs under intense scrutiny from tax authorities and, recently, the KGB. Domestic sponsorship is almost nonexistent since the private sector is small and businesses tend to avoid an association with the opposition. Government-controlled organizations attract financial aid from domestic and foreign-owned businesses that want to confirm their positive stance toward the authorities.

The existing Law on Public Associations does not provide adequate protection for civil society rights. Rules for NGO registration are complicated, and a variety of pretexts can be used to issue official warnings. Two warnings can result in the closure of an organization. The State Commission for Registration and Reregistration of Public Organizations and Political Parties was established in 2001 to give advice to the Ministry of Justice on the desirability of registering certain NGOs or parties. The commission is stocked with the president's close associates, all known for their hard-line views.

NGOs can be liquidated at the whim of the government. In 2003–2004, more than 100 NGOs were closed down by the authorities or forced to self-liquidate, mostly for technical reasons, such as incorrectly designed official forms used by organizations or failure to locate premises at the official legal address. Aimed at neutralizing political and social opposition to the regime in the run-up to the constitutional referendum of October 2004, this campaign targeted the strongest and most internationally connected NGOs, such as human rights organizations, regional resource centers providing assistance to smaller NGOs, and independent research institutions. The campaign continued in 2005: More than 10 NGOs were closed down by the Ministry of Justice in the first quarter of 2005, including the Women's Movement Renewal of the Motherland, and the Union of Belarusian Scouts.[17] Five NGOs were forced to self-liquidate by September 2005, and more than 30 were in the process of "self-liquidation," according to the Ministry of Justice.[18]

New amendments to the Law on Public Associations adopted by the House of Representatives in 2005 introduced further obstacles to NGO work. Civil society groups have been banned from conducting business activities. All audits will be conducted by state agencies, which will likely increase the possibilities for closing down NGOs at the whim of the authorities. Further restrictions have been introduced by the presidential Decree on Some Measures to Combat Human Trafficking, which has nearly delegalized educational exchanges and studies abroad, and by amendments to the presidential decree of 1999 regulating foreign assistance, promulgated by Lukashenka on August 16, 2005. The new rules of foreign assistance forbid using foreign aid for activities that advocate violent subversion of the government (a deed broadly understood by the authorities to include advocacy of any political change) and "meddling into the internal affairs of Belarus" (a definition that can include any analytical work, human rights advocacy, and educational and scientific cooperation unapproved by the government and any information exchange). The decree also mandated that any foreign assistance to NGOs must be registered with the government.

Liquidation of NGOs seriously disorganized the civil society sector but did not end its existence. According to some estimates, about 2,000 NGOs functioned in Belarus in 2005 without registration, either underground or on the premises of registered groups. Avoiding strict rules that heavily punish anyone working on behalf of or reporting about unregistered organizations, many groups advertised themselves not as NGOs, but as "civic initiatives." In September, the Ministry of Justice issued an order forbidding the activities of any unregistered group, including civic initiatives, which some groups have heeded out of fear of repression.

Amendments to the criminal code adopted by the House of Representatives in November 2005 criminalized activities of any group whose agenda does not correspond to the government policy or ideology. The amendments provoked sharp criticism in both Belarus and abroad. The International Helsinki Federation declared that the Belarusian authorities "equated human rights defense to crime,"[19] whereas Tadeusz Iwinski, deputy chairman of the Parliamentary Assembly of the Council of Europe, noted that the amendments "block those sources of free information in Belarus and from Belarus that still exist."[20]

International contacts with Belarusian NGOs are curtailed through visa denial and the deportation of Western NGO representatives. Most contacts are carried out in neighboring countries, primarily Poland, Lithuania, and Ukraine. Those who make it to Belarus face harassment and even imprisonment. On August 24, Giorgi Kandelaki and Luka Tsuladze, two activists of the Georgian organization Khmara, were detained by the authorities for "improper data in the passport." The official TV announced that they would be deported from Belarus; however, Kandelaki and Tseladze were sentenced to 15 days in jail for "petty hooliganism."

One of the largest NGOs functioning in Belarus, the Belarusian Union of Poles, was taken over by the government in 2005 after the union's congress elected a new chairperson, Anzelika Borys, whose loyalty was questioned by the authorities. Although neither the union nor its leadership could be considered opposition minded before the takeover, the crackdown was presumably carried out to reduce Poland's influence in Belarus through its educational, cultural, and academic projects. The government continued to attack the Belarusian Helsinki Committee (BHC), the last legally operating human rights NGO, in 2005. On December 20, the Supreme Economic Court mandated that the organization pay taxes for grants received under state-approved, tax-free assistance programs. The authorities have tried to extort tax payments from the BHC for several years, but three previous suits have been rejected by the courts, including the Supreme Economic Court.[21]

The government continues to persecute Protestant Christians based on the highly repressive religion law adopted in 2002. The Belarusian Gospel Church and the Calvinists were liquidated in 2005.[22] Church "New Life" in Minsk came under attack for improper use of property. The church is a reconstructed pig farm, and the authorities claimed that the community had no right to use it for ecclesiastical purposes, even though the law bans the continued use of the building as a farm since it is located within city limits.[23] The authorities also refused to extend the visa for Father Robert Krzywicki, a Roman Catholic priest and Polish citizen, and expelled him from the country in December.

The government systematically attacks think tanks and research-oriented NGOs, as these groups provide information and expert analysis to the West and give refuge to high-profile intellectuals who fall out of favor with the authorities. In April 2005, the court closed the IISEPS, the only think tank providing independent sociological information to the public.[24] The consolidation of political control over the education system continued in 2005. The government closed down three branches of the Institute of Modern Knowledge (a Minsk-based humanitarian college with branches around the country) after inspections found that its courses did not correspond to official regulations.[25] The government actively promotes and sponsors loyal organizations that help to transmit its propaganda, such as the Belarusian Republican Youth Union.

Independent Media

1997	1998	1999	2001	2002	2003	2004	2005	2006
6.25	6.50	6.75	6.75	6.75	6.75	6.75	6.75	6.75

In 2005, Freedom House ranked Belarus among countries with the lowest respect for freedom of speech (185th out of 194 countries and territories).[26] Only Turkmenistan received a lower ranking among the former USSR countries. Although Article 33 of the Constitution guarantees freedom of speech, this civil right hardly exists in practice, as the independent press is close to extinction.

The Ministry of Information controls the licensing of media and effectively acts as a tool of repression against criticism of the government in the press. Licenses can be withheld or revoked at the whim of the committee or on direct orders from the president. Two warnings received from the ministry within a year are sufficient to close down a newspaper. The ministry suspended 25 newspapers and issued 160 warnings to 61 periodicals in 2004 alone.[27]

In 2005, the list of closed independent periodicals included *Molodezhnyi Prospekt*, *Navinki*, and *Kur'yer iz Borisova*.[28] The content of publications is officially censored; for example, newspapers cannot inform about the activities of or even refer to unregistered organizations or inform about an unauthorized rally. Several leading independent newspapers, such as *Narodnaja Volja*, Barysau-based *Borisovskiye Novosti*, and Hlybokaje-based *Vol'naje Hlybokaje*, received warnings in April 2005 for reporting about the initiative Will of the People, headed by former rector of the Belarusian State University Alexander Kazulin, and the group Defenders of the Fatherland, led by the opposition veteran Aleh Vouchak.[29]

President Lukashenka issued a decree on May 31, 2005, banning nonstate newspapers and civic associations from using the words Belarusian and National in their titles. The minister of information, commenting on the decree, declared that these adjectives will be reserved only for groups and papers that "deserve it." The decree destroyed the brands of three leading independent newspapers, *Belorusskaya Delovaya Gazeta*, *Belorusskaya Gazeta*, and *Belorusskiy Rynok*, which were forced to rename themselves, correspondingly, *BDG-Delovaya Gazeta*, *Belgazeta*, and *Belorusy I Rynok*. The presidential Decree on Some Measures to Combat Human Trafficking, signed on March 9, created new pretexts for harassing independent media. Some publishers have been pressed throughout the year by the authorities to prove that models featured in advertisements are Belarusians, even when only a part of the body was displayed in the ad.[30]

State companies heavily dominate the publication and distribution of newspapers. State-run presses routinely refuse to publish materials critical of the authorities, and Belsajuzdruk, the state press distribution network, regularly refuses distribution of the independent press. The majority of leading independent nationwide and regional newspapers, including *Nasha Niva*, *Narodnaja Volja*, *BDG-Delovaya Gazeta*, *Salidarnasc'*, *Rehijanalnaja Hazeta*, *Intex-Press*, *Gazeta Slonimskaya*, *Vitebskiy Kur'jer*, and *Brestskij Kur'jer*, were denied distribution by Belsajuzdruk in November.[31] Most of them were also denied distribution by Belposhta, the national postal service. The International Federation of Journalists considered refusal to distribute "a part of a cynical and merciless campaign to stifle independent media before the presidential elections."[32] Alternative sources of distribution, such as supermarkets or bookstores, hardly exist owing to increasing pressure by authorities to stop the sale of nonstate press. Private distributors may be mandated to report the periodicals they sell to regional and district ideology departments.[33] Independent distributors of nonstate press are subject to arbitrary arrests and searches.[34]

State-owned media are extensively subsidized, and mandatory subscription to leading official outlets, such as the daily *Sovetskaya Belorussiya*, is commonplace at many institutions and state-run companies. Meanwhile, independent media are forced to shoulder high taxes and fees on printing and distribution. The independent press depends heavily on foreign assistance because of discriminatory pricing at state printing houses, difficulties in attracting advertisements from state-owned companies, and prohibitively high fines from libel suits or other punishments. Regional governments openly issue bans on advertisements by state companies in the independent media.[35]

The authorities failed in 2005 to effectively investigate the death of Veranika Charkasava, a veteran independent journalist who was brutally murdered on October 20, 2004, in unknown circumstances. Charkasava also investigated politically sensitive topics, such as KGB activities and arms trading with Arab states. The police were slow to accept other criminal scenarios beyond the domestic violence explanation and tried to frame her teenage son, Anton Filimonau, as a murderer. The boy was forced to go through psychiatric examinations before he was taken by his relatives to Moscow; Belarusian police tried unsuccessfully to extradite him back to Belarus. Filimonau was finally arrested in Belarus in December after returning home.[36] Also, Vasil Hrodnikau, a veteran journalist and longtime reporter of *Narodnaja Volja*, was found dead on October 18, 2005, in his house in Zaslauje. The police refused to start criminal proceedings, as it doubted that the death could have been violent.[37]

Independent journalists are subject to official harassment and have become victims of arbitrary lawsuits under Article 367 (slander against the president), Article 368 (insulting the president), and Article 369 (insulting government officials) of the criminal code. These stipulate large fines and prison sentences for journalists who are found guilty. Leading independent newspapers and their journalists faced prohibitively high fines for libel throughout 2005. Iryna Khalip, journalist of *Belorusskaya*

Delovaya Gazeta, was fined more than US$4,000 in a libel suit brought by the U.S. citizen Arkady Mar, who claimed to be editor in chief of the U.S.-based newspaper *Russkaya America*. Khalip claimed *Russkaya America* was a faux newspaper.[38] In the same libel suit, the publisher of *Belorusskaya Delovaya Gazeta* was fined US$20,000. *Belorusskaya Delovaya Gazeta* (now *BDG-Delovaya Gazeta*) was slapped with a US$23,000 fine again in September 2005 in a libel suit by an officer of the riot police, who claimed that the newspapers misinformed on the investigation of a crime pursued by his department.[39]

The libel suit against the largest independent daily, *Narodnaja Volja*, by the pro-regime MP Siarhej Hajdukevich resulted in a verdict awarding more than US$50,000 in June. Hajdukevich sued *Narodnaja Volja* for its reporting of his dealings with the Saddam Hussein regime in Iraq as leader of the Liberal Democratic Party (a clone of Vladimir Zhirinovsky's party in Russia). *Narodnaja Volja* claimed that Hajdukevich received generous sums of money from Hussein in 2001–2002 as loans and payments for facilitating business transactions in Minsk and failed to pay the debts in anticipation of the U.S. invasion into Iraq. The claims made by *Narodnaja Volja* were confirmed by Hajdukevich's former deputy Alexander Rabataj, but the court failed to take into account his testimony. Financial difficulties all but stopped publication of *Naronaja Volja* in September, but the newspaper was saved by donations, mostly from readers. Aliaksiej Karol, editor in chief of the newspaper *Zhoda*, was fined more than US$1,000 in September for publishing cartoons satirizing President Lukashenka. Zhoda was subject to searches and confiscation of its equipment in February 2005.

Foreign journalists critical of the government are not welcomed in Belarus. Mikhail Romanov, journalist of the Russian newspaper *Moskovskiy Komsomolets*, was arrested during the Chernobyl anniversary rally on April 26 and sentenced to eight days in jail.[40] Polish journalists covering the conflict around the Belarusian Union of Poles were routinely detained, searched, intimidated, and extradited from Belarus throughout the year.[41]

At the local level, state-controlled regional newspapers remain the most important source of printed information on regional events. Regional independent newspapers do exist, and some hold a significant share of the information market. However, the regional independent press was particularly hard hit by the closures and liquidations enforced by the Ministry of Information in the run-up to the October 2004 referendum. Repression of regional press continued throughout 2005. Anatol Bukas, editor in chief of the Barysau-based newspaper *Borisovskiye Novosti*, was sentenced to a fine and forced to pay a US$2,000 award in a libel suit pursued by the editor in chief of Barysau's official newspaper, *Edinstvo*, for defamation and insults (the court, however, refused to consider insults and slander published by *Edinstvo* against Bukas).[42] Another Barysau-based independent newspaper, *Kur'yer iz Borisova*, was closed down. Smaller publications with a circulation of up to 300 copies exist in many provincial towns, as they do not require registration.

Electronic media in Belarus are completely dominated by the state. Belarus currently has four national television channels. All-National Television (ONT),

Capital TV, and Lad fill the bulk of their airtime with rebroadcasts from Russian TV networks. None of the state channels offers alternative views on political issues, and all channels report on domestic and international affairs in a manner acceptable to the government. The First National Channel (BT-1) is the undisputed leader in pro-regime propaganda and is distinguished by uninhibited bias and slander in its reporting. Media attacks on the opposition, NGOs, foreign diplomats, and Western leaders are common on all TV channels. In 2005, Belarus launched its first satellite TV channel, which is essentially a rebroadcast of BT-1.

Russian TV networks have gradually lost their influence as they have been replaced by Belarusian outlets. Moreover, owing to tightening state control and censorship of the media in Russia, Russian TV networks are no longer a substantial source of alternative opinion for Belarusians. For example, both countries' state-controlled propaganda tirelessly attack the governments of the post-Soviet states that recently underwent democratic revolutions (such as Georgia and Ukraine) rather than actually report on social and political problems in these countries.

External sources of information are limited to the shortwave broadcasts of the Radio Free Europe/Radio Liberty Belarusian Service. Deutsche Welle began its broadcast in Belarus in September 2005 with two daily 15-minute programs in Russian provided by its Russian service and dedicated to Belarusian affairs. The Deutsche Welle broadcast caused a fierce discussion inside Belarus owing to the broadcast's short length and language (Russian only), which was regarded by some as an endorsement of the Russification policy pursued by the Lukashenka regime.

The Ministry of Information maintains tight control over FM radio broadcasting. Belarusian-language rock and folk groups that took part in the opposition rally on July 21, 2004, have been banned from the airwaves. The ministry has enforced its directive issued in November 2004 requiring that 75 percent of broadcasts be filled with music produced in Belarus or by Belarusian performers. This rule, together with the bans, destroyed the formats of many stations, as all of them had to broadcast the same, mostly Russian-language, pop music.

Internet sites within the country are under the control of the government's State Center on Information Security, which is part of the Security Council of Belarus. Less than 10 percent of the population has some access to the Internet, while other estimates suggest that only 2 percent of the population enjoy regular Internet access. Nevertheless, the impact of the Internet is gradually expanding, which prompts censorship and restriction of access at universities and government offices. In August 2005, the security services attacked producers of the independent site Third Way (www.3dway.org), which published political cartoons criticizing Lukashenka, confiscated their equipment and passports, and launched criminal proceedings for defaming the president. Internet controls in student dormitories and state institutions are particularly strict to prevent unauthorized visits to opposition Web sites.

Local Democratic Governance

1997	1998	1999	2001	2002	2003	2004	2005	2006
n/a	n/a	n/a	n/a	n/a	n/a	n/a	6.25	6.25

Belarus has three levels of local government: regional, district, and village or (in urban areas) township. Upper-level administrations direct and coordinate the work of lower levels. The total number of local governments is approximately 1,700. The Constitution does not separate local government from state authority. Heads of regional administrations are appointed by the president and are directly subordinated to him by law. Local councils are popularly elected but have no control over the executive bodies and are generally window dressing.

Subnational governments have extensive responsibilities, including housing, social services, public security, and education. The Constitution establishes that local councils have exclusive decision-making rights in adopting regional programs of social and economic development, establishing local taxes and adopting budgets, managing communal property within limits established by law, and calling local referendums. Notwithstanding these prerogatives, local governments have little control over their finances. Village and township governments are particularly impotent since the territory they cover is generally small, usually a collective farm whose head serves as the territory's de facto administrator.

The last local elections, held in 2003, were largely alternative-free. For 24,000 seats on local councils, only 26,500 candidates were nominated. Up to two-thirds of the opposition's initial nominees were denied registration, and it managed to secure only a minuscule representation in the election commissions. According to official sources, 73.4 percent of voters took part in the first round of the elections and early voting combined. One-fifth of the electorate voted early.

Altogether, out of 23,275 deputies elected to councils on all levels, only 107 were representatives of opposition parties, and the rest represented pro-government parties, noted the Belarusian Association of Resource Centers in its *Choice Through Elections* analysis. The opposition-dominated Assembly of the Deputies of Local Councils created in October 2003 unites just 50 deputies.

Local authorities usually avoid cooperation with most local civil society groups. Their participation at nonpoliticized events organized by entrepreneurial associations, women's groups, and so forth is often merely ceremonial. Local authorities must be responsive to independent groups in emergency situations such as strikes and organized protests. In 2005, the strike by private entrepreneurs protesting the new VAT led to negotiations between the strikers and the Minsk mayor, which failed, however, as local authorities had no prerogative to decide on the tax.

Protests emerged in 2005 in Minsk after President Lukashenka renamed two central avenues in the city previously named after celebrated figures in Belarusian history: 15th-century Bible scholar Francishak Skaryna and popular Soviet-era leader of the republic Piotr Masherau. The authorities, however, rejected a popular initiative to carry out a referendum on returning the previous names, citing that the local population has no right to overrule presidential decrees, even though the law stipulates that local authorities have the exclusive right to designate street names.[43]

The local press covers the activities of local authorities extensively. The state press, however, enjoys privileged access to information and officials and internal regulations in some districts, and regional committees and councils allow only the official press to have access to meetings and sessions. Local opposition deputies have problems organizing meetings with their voters and are often attacked by local government press and the executive authorities. Independent local media face attacks from the executive authorities whenever they voice criticism of official decisions.

The rules of disclosure, oversight, and accountability at the local level do not differ from those that apply to the central government. In theory, state bodies are obliged to present nonclassified information, but the local authorities may deny access to information to independent journalists, NGOs, or local deputies.

Judicial Framework and Independence

1997	1998	1999	2001	2002	2003	2004	2005	2006
6.00	6.25	6.50	6.75	6.75	6.75	6.75	6.75	6.75

Article 109 of the Constitution confers judicial power to the courts, and Article 110 stipulates that all judges shall be independent and any interference in the administration of justice is unlawful. However, the procedures for appointing judges give the president the upper hand. The president appoints 6 out of 12 members of the Constitutional Court; the remaining 6 are appointed by the Council of the Republic on his recommendation. The president also appoints the entire Supreme Court and Supreme Economic Court, as well as all military and district judges. The Constitution does not protect judges from summary removal during their tenure. No parliamentary approval is needed to remove judges from the Supreme Court and Constitutional Court; the president must simply "notify" the Council of the Republic. The institutional dependence of judges on the president is matched by their reliance on the executive branch for bonuses, promotion, and housing, which makes them vulnerable to coercion.

Although the Constitution provides for basic human rights, including freedom of expression, association, religion, and business and property rights, they are not adequately protected in practice. Moreover, many existing laws – including the Law on Public Associations, the Law on Freedom of Religion, and the Law on Meetings, Rallies, Street Processions, and Pickets – significantly restrict the constitutional rights of citizens.

The Constitutional Court issued a ruling in 2002 outlawing permission stamps for traveling abroad, a procedure used by the security forces to impede foreign travel of citizens suspected of committing crimes, those having debts or unpaid taxes, and politically active opposition figures. Although the Court authorized a three-year period to phase out the stamp practice, the authorities did nothing to end it. Instead, the Ministry of the Interior pressured the Constitutional Court to revise its decision. As a result, the Constitutional Court issued a new ruling on October 4 allowing the stamp issuing to continue indefinitely, "recommending" that the ministry cancel it and duly inform citizens about the change of practice.[44] The authorities routinely used the prerogative to deny or postpone the issue of the stamp to prevent foreign travel of opposition and civil society activists in 2005. Those affected included activists of the Union of Poles of Belarus prosecuted during the government's takeover of the organization[45] and activists of the unregistered Zubr (Bison) youth movement.[46]

The courts routinely refuse libel suits filed by the opposition and civil society activists who were slandered by the official media. Civil society activists and independent newspapers do manage occasionally to annul the unlawful decisions of courts or tax authorities, but new retributive charges and recriminations may follow. The Minsk City Court annulled on November 9 the decision of the Pershamajski City Court authorizing Belarusian TV and Radio to publicly apologize for slandering the regional organization Will to Development from the city of Slonim. BT-1 accused the NGO of financing the opposition and engaging in other illegal activities, such as tax evasion. The Pershamajski City Court found no evidence supporting the claims, whereas the Minsk City Court decided that the information distributed by BT-1 "just expresses opinions" of the authors.[47] On a positive note, the Minsk Economic Court issued a ruling on November 17 declaring it illegal for state printing houses to cancel publishing agreements with the largest independent newspaper, *Narodnaja Volja*.[48]

It is possible to receive a fair trial in Belarus. However, legal procedures can be violated in politically sensitive cases. Arrests and prosecution of opposition activists are conducted with gross violations of the law. Political prisoners are often denied their rights by the prison administration. Mikalaj Statkevich, who was sentenced to two years of forced labor for staging antireferendum protests in October 2004 and is serving his term in the provincial town of Baranavichy, was denied approval to vacation at home with the vague explanation "Complicated situation in the capital" from the police. Anatol Shumchanka, leader of the strike of private entrepreneurs, was sentenced to 10 days in jail in March 2005 for staging an unauthorized rally but was detained for several additional days after serving his time.[49] Valery Levaneuski, sentenced to two years in jail for insulting the president in 2004, was denied permission to travel to his father's funeral in December 2005.[50] Several activists of the youth movement Zubr, arrested in December on drug possession charges, claimed they had been framed by the police.[51] Opposition activist Alaxej Darafeeu was detained in Viciebsk in December on suspicion of organizing explosions in the city in September, even though the authorities initially declared that the incidents had no signs of terrorism or political violence.[52]

Independent law practice is restricted in Belarus, as all attorneys must register with state-controlled bar chambers. New regulations adopted in 2005 mandate the introduction of ideology commissioners in every bar chamber, whereas attorneys have been forbidden from speaking at international human rights conferences without the approval of authorities.[53]

The Constitution prohibits torture and cruel, inhuman, or degrading treatment. In practice, however, the rights of the convicted may be violated; suspects and convicts have reported being beaten by police and prison guards.[54] Mikhail Marynich, the opposition leader sentenced in 2004 to five years in jail on highly dubious charges (the term was subsequently reduced by pardon and amnesty), was routinely denied treatment while in jail.[55] Marynich suffered a brain hemorrhage in prison and was treated only after his wife used the right of visitation to pass him medicine. "Prosecution of Mikhail Marynich is the new evidence of the absence of judiciary independence in Belarus, which reflects the common absence of respect to the rule of law and the general atmosphere of political repression," declared the Parliamentary Assembly of the Council of Europe.[56]

Opposition activists are routinely arrested and beaten for staging rallies and distributing literature. Dozens of participants were severely beaten and arrested during the unauthorized opposition rallies on March 25 and April 26 and during actions to commemorate opposition leaders who disappeared in 1999.[57,58] The riot police beat Sviatlana Zavadskaja, wife of independent journalist Dzmitry Zavadski (abducted by former riot police and presumably assassinated in 2000) during the rally commemorating the fifth anniversary of her husband's disappearance.[59] State prosecution refused to carry out a criminal investigation of the beating.[60]

The courts confiscate property, freeze assets, and issue heavy tax punishments in cases that have obvious political underpinnings or involve the interests of the bureaucracy. The government implemented *de facto* nationalization of several private clinics in Minsk, having deprived them of licenses. The doctors were offered positions at high-profit state hospitals.

Corruption

1997	1998	1999	2001	2002	2003	2004	2005	2006
n/a	n/a	5.25	5.25	5.25	5.50	5.75	6.00	6.25

Belarus continued its precipitous decline in Transparency International's Corruption Perceptions Index in 2005; its rating deteriorated to 107th place, down from 36th place in 2002.[61] The reason for such a decline is the continuous spread of low- and high-level corruption. A series of high-profile corruption cases involving high-ranking government officials further put in doubt the claim of Lukashenka's regime that it remains corruption-free. Also, deepening bureaucratization and etatization of the economy has created a nourishing environment for bribery and the abuse of power.

Excessive and unstable regulation of business have created pervasive opportunities for corruption at all levels. Likewise, the tax system is complicated and cumbersome. According to a World Bank survey, businesses make 113 tax payments per year, which account on average for 121 percent of their gross profits.[62] The World Bank regards Belarus as the worst country in the world to pay taxes (with regard to complication, regulations, etc.) Moreover, opening a private business in Belarus is an arduous undertaking that requires passing 16 legal procedures (which can take 79 days on average) and costs an equivalent of 25 percent of the annual gross domestic product per capita. These nearly unenforceable regulations create opportunities for tax evasion and bribery. Additionally, the government is selective in punishing noncompliant businesses and persons either for political reasons or to eliminate competition for those companies placed under the patronage of bureaucracies.

Allegations of wrongdoing in the highest echelons of power are abundant, even though such allegations are often politically motivated. The 2004 arrest and imprisonment of Halina Zhuraukova, head of the PDA, and Yahor Rybakou, head of Belarusian TV and Radio, confirmed many of the opposition's claims. The PDA is a state-owned business empire directly accountable to the president. At one time, it was involved in the nation's most lucrative businesses, such as the cigarette trade and exploitation of national parks, and enjoyed a monopolistic status conferred by the president. Since 1994, there have been charges that these revenues are channeled into a "shadow" presidential budget. Officials do not deny the existence of a shadow budget but refuse to comment on its size.

Although the reason for Zhuraukova's arrest could have been revenge from law enforcement officers who competed with the PDA for access to administrative rents, the investigation unmasked huge legal violations and revealed that Zhuraukova was responsible for stealing several million dollars from the state. She was sentenced in 2005 to four years in jail but was eventually pardoned by the president. Critics of the government compare the fate of Zhuraukova with that of Mikhail Marynich, the opposition leader sentenced to five years (subsequently reduced to three and a half years) in jail for allegedly stealing several computers from his own NGO.[63] Additionally, the PDA's principal business, Belaya Rus, was forced to file for bankruptcy after it lost its "untouchable" status following Zhuraukova's arrest.[64]

Yahor Rybakou, another former high-profile official found guilty of corruption in 2005, was sentenced to 11 years in jail and is serving his term in a high-security prison.[65] Former managers of another institution that enjoyed business privileges from the Presidential Programs Fund were sentenced to long jail terms in March 2005 after being found guilty of pocketing profits from the fund's business operations.[66] Although this trial had no political implications, it reflects deficiencies in the system of privileges and administrative rents that is thriving in Belarus.

Corruption charges in Belarus are a useful tool for settling political scores with regime opponents; many cases involve representatives of the establishment who switched to the opposition. In 2005, Siarhej Skrabets, leader of the opposition faction in the previous convocation in the House of Representatives, was charged with illegal solicitation of a bank loan, and his arrest was preceded by a campaign of harassment, intimidation, and defamation in the official media. At the same time, several high-profile arrests in 2005 – including the former head of the State Aviation Committee, managers of the Brest liquor plant and the country's largest oil refinery Naftan, and the head of the Ministry of Sports – were not politically motivated.[67]

The Law on Public Service, signed on June 14, 2003, establishes conflict-of-interest rules. Civil servants (including MPs) are barred from entrepreneurial activities, either direct or indirect, or from taking part in the management of a commercial organization. The recently proposed new anticorruption legislation foresees strengthening the conflict-of-interest rules and expands the application of anticorruption legislation to a broader circle of government agencies and officials.

Owing to comprehensive state control over the economy in Belarus, the most lucrative private companies are either being destroyed by tax penalties and the revocation of licenses or being forced to renationalize under the patronage of the state. A series of high-profile cases in 2005 involved attacks on private health care establishments and the monopolization of the car insurance business, which was ordered in October 2005 by Lukashenka. Experts believe that such monopolization will create ubiquitous corruption opportunities for both the insurers and bureaucrats, who would decide which company would be allowed to remain in the market.[68]

Whereas top state officials, including the president, regularly declare fighting corruption as the top priority of the state, the opposite occurs in practice. The draft anticorruption legislation introduced in the House of Representatives in 2005 demands that all civil servants declare their incomes. Declarations by higher-ranking officials must be submitted to the president, thus bypassing tax authorities. The bill does not require declarations to be publicized and foresees only selective review of the correctness of the declarations.[69] If adopted, the law will create ubiquitous opportunities for its selective enforcement at the discretion of state officials.

Vitali Silitski is a Minsk-based independent analyst. In 2006, he will be a fellow at the Center for Democracy, Development, and Rule of Law at Stanford University.

---

[1] IISEPS information, http://www.iiseps.org/bullet04-4.html

[2] Jan Maksymiuk, "Lukashenka Plans 'No Democratic Change' for Belarus," Radio Free Europe/Radio Liberty Belarus and Ukraine Report, April 25, 2005, www.rferl.org/reports/pbureport/2005/04/15-250405.asp.

[3] Charter-97 News Service, "Leader of the Respublika Group Sentenced," www.charter97.org/bel/news/2005/02/28/lider;
Andrei Sannikau, "Political Reprisal in the Most Cynical Form," Charter-97 News Service, www.charter97.org/bel/news/2005/05/31/sannikov.

[4] David Marples, "Belarus: The Return of Sheiman," Eurasia Daily Monitor, December 8, 2004.

[5] Charter-97 News Service, "Interior Troops Will Fulfill Any Tyrant's Order," February 1, 2005, www.charter97.org/bel/news/2005/02/01/prikaz.

[6] See www.iiseps.org/comment1.html.

[7] Charter-97 News Service, "Independent Observers: Elections in Hrodna Did Not Correspond to International Standards," www.charter97.org/bel/news/2005/03/21/nez.

[8] Charter-97 News Service, "Parties Under the Threat of Liquidation,"

www.charter97.org/bel/news/2005/02/01/likvid.

[9] Deregistration of a party branch means that a party has no legal right to operate in the locality in question.

[10] Charter-97 News Service, "Almost 300 Party Structures Have Been Liquidated in Belarus in 2005," www.charter97.org/bel/news/2005/09/15/likvid.

[11] Charter-97 News Service, "Participants of Protest Actions Have Been Sentenced in Minsk," www.charter97.org/bel/news/2005/03/28/20.

[12] Charter-97 News Service, "Belarusians and Ukrainians on Trial in Minsk," www.charter97.org/bel/news/2005/04/27/sudy.

[13] Charter-97 News Service, "Russian Ambassador 'Does Not Approve' His Compatriots," www.charter97.org/bel/news/2005/04/27/posol.

[14] Radio Free Europe/Radio Liberty Belarusian Service, "Will Market Vendors Turn to Politics?" in Radio Free Europe/Radio Liberty Belarus, Ukraine, and Moldova Report, March 23, 2005, www.rferl.org/reports/pbureport/2005/03/12-230305.asp.

[15] See www.charter97.org/bel/news/2005/11/28/zik.

[16] Charter-97 News Service, "Only Skilled Ones Will Be Admitted to Electoral Commissions," http://www.charter97.org/bel/news/2005/12/23

[17] Charter-97 News Service, "Almost 10 Parties and Civic Associations Have Already Been Closed Down in Belarus," www.charter97.org/bel/news/2005/04/21/2005.

[18] Charter-97 News Service, "Almost 300 Party Structures Have Been Liquidated in Belarus in 2005," www.charter97.org/bel/news/2005/09/15/likvid.

[19] Charter-97 News Service, IHF: Human Rights Activism Equated with Crime in Belarus," http://www.charter97.org/bel/news/2005/12/01/mhf.

[20] Charter-97 News Service, "PACE Deputy Chairman Criticises Amendments to the Crimila Code," http://www.charter97.org/bel/news/2005/12/09.

[21] Charter-97 News Service, "Court Compels BHC to Pay Taxes From Grant," 10:26, December 21, 2005.

[22] Radio Free Europe/Radio Liberty Belarusian Service, "One More Protestant Community Under Threat of Liquidation," www.svaboda.org/articlesfeatures/society/2005/11/F274B16D-2C18-4F24-B115-A19E582B6B66.html.

[23] Radio Free Europe/Radio Liberty Belarusian Service, "Protestant Church 'New Life' Got a Respite," www.svaboda.org/articlesfeatures/society/2005/11/458C0A33-34DD-417D-BA81-BB79B082CE11.html.

[24] Charter-97 News Service, "Supreme Court of Belarus Liquidated the Largest Sociological Institute," www.charter97.org/bel/news/2005/04/15/zamana.

[25] Charter-97 News Service, "Institute of Modern Knowledge Closes Down the Law Department and Three Branches," www.charter97.org/bel/news/2005/07/04/institut.

[26] See www.freedomhouse.org/research/pressurvey/allscore2005.pdf.

[27] Information provided by the Ministry of Information; see the Belarusian Association of Journalists, www.baj.ru/2005/Jan/3101nav2.asp.

[28] Belarusian Association of Journalists News Service, "No More Newspaper Kur'yer iz Borisova?" www.baj.ru/2005/Aug/2408nav2.asp; "Newspaper Molodezhnyi Prospekt Denied Registration," www.baj.ru/2005/Nov/1711nav5.asp; "Navinki Will Sue Ministry of Information," www.baj.ru/2005/Nov/1811nav5.asp.

[29] Belarusian Association of Journalists News Service, "New Wave of Warnings to Non-State Newspapers," www.baj.ru/2005/Apr/2504nav.asp.

[30] Belarusian Association of Journalists News Service, "Belarusian Publishers Have Been Accused of Violating the Presidential Decree 'On Some Measures to Combat Human Trafficking,'" www.baj.ru/2005/Oct/1410nav.asp.

[31] Belarusian Association of Journalists News Service, "2006 Subscription: More Questions than Answers," www.baj.ru/2005/Nov/1711nav4.asp.

[32] Belarusian Association of Journalists News Service, "International Federation of Journalists Draws Attention to the Merciless Campaign of Elimination of the Independent Press in Belarus in the Year of Presidential Elections," www.baj.ru/2005/Nov/1811nav4.asp.

[33] Belarusian Association of Journalists News Service, "Ideologists Inspect the Assortment of Periodicals in the Retail Trade," www.baj.ru/2005/Feb/1402nav2.asp.

[34] Belarusian Association of Journalists News Service, "Activist of UCP Detained for Distributing

Newspaper Vremya in Viciebsk," www.baj.ru/2005/Jan/1801nav2.asp; "Arrests Began for Distributing Narodnaja Volja," www.baj.ru/2005/Oct/1010nav2.asp.

[35] Belarusian Association of Journalists News Service, "Hrodna Companies 'Not Recommended' to Publish Advertisement in Independent Media," www.baj.ru/2005/Jan/1901nav.asp; "Belarusian Association of Journalists Demands Explanations from the Minister of Trade," www.baj.ru/2005/Feb/1702nav.asp.

[36] Charter-97 News Service, "Son of journalist Veranika Charkasava arrested in Minsk," http://www.charter97.org/bel/news/2005/12/30

[37] Charter-97 News Service, "Prosecutor's Office Refused to Investigate the Murder of the Journalist," www.charter97.org/bel/news/2005/12/02/zapret?

[38] Belarusian Association of Journalists News Service, "Iryna Khalip Fined for 4.5 and BDG Published by 25 Thousand USD," www.baj.ru/2005/Apr/1104nav2.asp.

[39] Belarusian Association of Journalists News Service, "Court Slapped BDG with 23 Thousand Dollars fine," www.baj.ru/2005/Sep/3009nav5.asp.

[40] Belarusian Association of Journalists News Service, "Journalist of Moskovskiy Komsomolets Got 8 Days of Administrative Arrest," www.baj.ru/2005/Apr/2704nav5.asp.

[41] Belarusian Association of Journalists News Service, "Polish Journalists Detained in Hrodna," www.baj.ru/2005/Jul/2707nav3.asp; "Polish Journalist Detained in Shchuchyn," www.baj.ru/2005/Jul/2707nav4.asp.

[42] Belarusian Association of Journalists News Service, "Editor of Borisovskiye Novosti Found Guilty," www.baj.ru/2005/Jun/1606nav3.asp.

[43] Charter-97 News Service, "Orders of the Bosses Not Discussed," www.charter97.org/bel/news/2005/09/16/prikaz; "Law Is Not an Order," www.charter97.org/bel/news/2005/07/12/neukaz.

[44] Charter-97 News Service, "Permissive Stamp Not Abolished," www.charter97.org/bel/news/2005/10/04/pas.

[45] Charter-97 News Service, "Activist of the Union of Poles Denied Foreign Travel," www.charter97.org/bel/news/2005/11/15/graniza.

[46] Charter-97 News Service, "Zubr Coordinator Denied the Right to Travel Abroad," www.charter97.org/bel/news/2005/10/28/pravo.

[47] Belarusian Association of Journalists News Service, "BT Cannot Be Held Responsible," www.baj.ru/2005/Nov/1011nav.asp.

[48] Belarusian Association of Journalists News Service, "The Court Ruled the Decision of the Printing House to Cancel Agreement with Narodnaja Volja Illegal," www.baj.ru/2005/Nov/1711nav2.asp.

[49] Charter-97 News Service, "Entrepreneurs Demand End of Persecution of the Activists of the Entrepreneurial Movement," www.charter97.org/bel/news/2005/03/14/ruch.

[50] Charter-97 News Service, "Political Prisoner Valery Levaneuski Not Allowed to Attend His Father's Funeral," http://www.charter97.org/bel/news/2005/12/15/lev

[51] Charter-97 News Service, "Provocations aganist Zubr Activists in Homel," http://www.charter97.org/bel/news/2005/12/24/zubr

[52] Charter-97 News Service, "Opposition Members Alleged in Viciebsk Explosions," http://www.charter97.org/bel/news/2005/12/26/vzryv

[53] Charter-97 News Service, "Attornies Banned from Speaking at Human Rights Conferences," http://www.charter97.org/bel/news/2005/12/02/zapret

[54] Charter-97 News Service, "Torture Is Constant in the Belarusian Prisons," www.charter97.org/bel/news/2005/06/23/turma.

[55] See www.charter97.org/bel/news/2005/03/14/marinich.

[56] Charter-97 News Service, "PACE Committee Called for Immediate Release of Marynich," www.charter97.org/bel/news/2005/03/04/pace.

[57] Charter-97 News Service, "Sasim in the Hospital: Kuleshov Justifies SWAT," www.charter97.org/bel/news/2005/09/19/sasim

[58] Charter-97 News Service, "Three Days of Arrest for Nikita Sasim," www.charter97.org/bel/news/2005/10/10/prigova

[59] Charter-97 News Service, "Minsk Riot Police Dispersed the Action in Memory of Zavadski," www.charter97.org/bel/news/2005/07/08/omon.

[60] Charter-97 News Service, "Sviatlana Zavadskaja appealed the decision of the prosecutor's office"

www.charter97.org/bel/news/2005/08/15/zav.

[61] See www.transparency.org/cpi/2005/cpi2005.sources.en.html.

[62] World Bank, Doing Business Report,
www.doingbusiness.org/ExploreEconomies/Default.aspx?economyid=19.

[63] See www.charter97.org/bel/news/2005/03/03/galina.

[64] Charter-97 News Service, "The Decline of Belaya Rus: Bankruptcy Procedures Launched Against the Presidential Structure," www.charter97.org/bel/news/2005/07/01/delo.

[65] Charter-97 News Service, "Jahor Rybakou Sentenced to 11 Years in Jail," www.charter97.org/bel/news/2005/02/11/egor.

[66] Belorusskaya Delovaya Gazeta, "Shameful End of the Presidential Fund," March 11, 2005, www.charter97.org/bel/news/2005/03/11/fond.

[67] Charter-97 News Service, "Director of Naftan Under House Arrest," www.charter97.org/bel/news/2005/11/11/naftan; "Criminal Case Launched Against the Brest Liquor Store," www.charter97.org/bel/news/2005/02/22/liker; "Former Head of the State Aviation Committee Charged on Four Counts," www.charter97.org/bel/news/2005/10/25/glava; Radio Free Europe/Radio Liberty Belarusian Service, "Did Krot Pay for Tender Activities?" www.svaboda.org/articlesfeatures/economics/2005/11/F408E3A4-2B2F-45DB-B211-0C39C6D6BBE5.html.

[68] Charter-97 News Service, "State Monopolizes the Market of Mandatory Car Insurance," www.charter97.org/bel/news/2003/10/10/auto.

[69] See www.charter97.org/bel/news/2005/08/23/dohod.

Bosnia-Herzegovina

Capital: Sarajevo
Population: 3.9 million
GNI/capita: $2,040
Ethnic Groups: Serb (37.1%), Bosniak (48%), Croat (14.3%), other (0.6%)

Nations in Transit Ratings and Averaged Scores

	1997	1998	1999	2001	2002	2003	2004	2005	2006
Electoral Process	n/a	5.00	5.00	4.75	4.25	3.75	3.50	3.25	3.00
Civil Society	n/a	5.00	4.50	4.50	4.25	4.00	3.75	3.75	3.75
Independent Media	n/a	4.75	5.00	4.50	4.25	4.25	4.25	4.00	4.00
Governance *	n/a	6.00	6.00	6.00	5.50	5.25	5.00	n/a	n/a
National Democratic Governance	n/a	n/a	n/a	n/a	n/a	n/a	n/a	4.75	4.75
Local Democratic Governance	n/a	n/a	n/a	n/a	n/a	n/a	n/a	4.75	4.75
Judicial Framework and Independence	n/a	6.00	6.00	5.50	5.25	5.00	4.50	4.25	4.00
Corruption	n/a	n/a	6.00	5.75	5.50	5.00	4.75	4.50	4.25
Democracy Score	n/a	5.35	5.42	5.17	4.83	4.54	4.29	4.18	4.07

* With the 2005 edition, Freedom House introduced seperate analysis and ratings for national democratic governance and local democratic governance to provide readers with more detailed and nuanced analysis of these two important subjects.

NOTE: The ratings reflect the consensus of Freedom House, its academic advisers, and the author of this report. The opinions expressed in this report are those of the author. The ratings are based on a scale of 1 to 7, with 1 representing the highest level of democratic progress and 7 the lowest. The Democracy Score is an average of ratings for the categories tracked in a given year.

The economic and social data on this page were taken from the following sources:
GNI/capita, Population: World Development Indicators 2006 (Washington, D.C.: World Bank, 2006).
Ethnic Groups: CIA World Factbook 2006 (Washington, D.C.: Central Intelligence Agency, 2006).

EXECUTIVE SUMMARY

During 2005, 10 years after the war's end following the dissolution of Yugoslavia, Bosnia-Herzegovina made marked progress toward closer integration into Euro-Atlantic structures even as democratic governance and the reform agenda continued to be designed and driven by international actors. The two entities – the Croat-Bosniak-dominated Federation of Bosnia-Herzegovina (FBiH) and the almost exclusively Serb Republika Srpska (RS) – have been progressively weakened as central state structures have been put in place. The Office of the High Representative (OHR), the primary civilian authority established at Dayton, continues to be the main engine driving reform, though the use of the so-called Bonn Powers continues to decline as competences are transferred to local institutions to encourage local ownership.

The key development of 2005 was the announcement in November of negotiations opening on a Stabilization and Association Agreement (SAA) with the European Union (EU). Though Bosnia-Herzegovina now has a contractual relationship with the EU, it does not yet enjoy the same status with NATO. However, there has been progress on many of the NATO Partnership for Peace benchmarks, particularly on defense reform and cooperation with the International Criminal Tribunal for the Former Yugoslavia (ICTY), even though NATO has not formally considered an application from Bosnia-Herzegovina since the last rejection in December 2004.

During 2005, central state strengthening structures were consolidated and embedded in a number of key areas, most notably on police and defense reform. This was also the year that many reforms reached the legislative phase, after having been discussed in commission and working-group formats for several years. However, lower-level state strengthening reforms had less international engagement and fell victim to more obstruction by both entities. The FBiH and the RS resisted various components of competency and material transfer to the state level; only with key international interventions were a number of reforms pushed through. Yet incidents during 2005, such as the oath swearing of army recruits at Manjaca in the RS, the attempt to rename the airport in Sarajevo, and the aggressive pursuit of the policy known as "two curricula under one roof," demonstrate that political representatives of all three constituent peoples continue to seize opportunities to make political gain from interethnic fear.

Bosnia-Herzegovina also made fiscal centralization progress, though the impact will not be felt until 2006, when the implementation of a value-added tax (VAT) occurs. In 2005, a single (state-level) account was operable from the beginning of the year in preparation for the move from sales tax to VAT.

National Democratic Governance. Despite a challenging start to the year with the resignation in January 2005 of the RS government, the state was stable overall. The functionality and productivity of the executive branch were markedly greater in the latter half of 2005 than in the first. By early March, the crisis appeared to have passed and a new government took office in the RS. However, the prime minister's attempt in June to remove the minister of foreign affairs proved unsuccessful and led to a worsening of relations at the cabinet level. By summer's end, the Council of Ministers (CoM: the government) was functioning again, although the OHR had to intervene to make key appointments to two state security agencies. In the fall, the CoM met frequently and regularly, and the prime minister can be credited with brokering a deal on police reform that ultimately proved sufficient for the European Commission to approve opening negotiations toward an SAA.

The path to Euro-Atlantic structures had been well signposted through the EU's feasibility study, the standard post-Council of Europe EU accession requirements, and the NATO Partnership for Peace benchmarks. The key areas of reform related to defense, intelligence services, public broadcasting, state government, and cooperation with the ICTY. In 2005, after the EU clarified the security components of the feasibility study requirements, police restructuring dovetailed with the question of entry into SAA negotiations, and it consumed major energy on behalf of local and international actors throughout the year. The OHR kicked off the process of introducing the tenets of the Police Restructuring Commission Report in the domestic theater. Unexpectedly, toward the end of September the prime minister and the president of the RS brokered a deal that was subsequently passed in October at a stormy session of the RS National Assembly, thus paving the way for the start of SAA negotiations. Though government activity was underscored by trenchant nationalism and petty personality rows, it remained stable and, moreover, achieved a major goal in securing a contractual relationship with the EU. *But none of this would have been achieved without the direct and sustained assistance of the international community, so the national democratic governance rating remains at 4.75.*

Electoral Process. No countrywide elections took place in 2005, but several mayoral by-elections were conducted, owing to either the death of the incumbent or, in one case, the recall of the incumbent via a referendum. These all passed peacefully and were conducted properly by the Election Commission. The international members withdrew from the Election Commission in June, though they did stay on as observers. The Election Commission also made a substantial start on or completed several big projects, not least of which was the implementation of the Law on Conflict of Interest, with the production of several party audits for the first time. It also conducted a review of the Law on Elections and liaised and contributed to a Parliamentary Working Group on the same topic. The work started in late 2005 and was performed largely by domestic actors, with only light intervention from the international community. The political scene continued to be dominated mainly by ethnic parties as all began gearing up for the 2006 elections. *The electoral process rating improves from 3.25 to 3.00 because the Election Commission demonstrated that it had the capacity to apply the laws for which it is responsible and to plan for improvement of the election process in the long term.*

Civil Society. The legal framework and overall state of civil society remained generally unchanged in 2005 compared with the situation the previous year. Civil society action took the form primarily of strikes in reaction to nonpayment or late payment of salaries; and teachers, other public sector workers, and private sector workers were all on strike in 2005. However, their actions were generally ignored by decision makers. Nongovernmental organizations (NGOs) are still perceived largely as service providers, and it is rare that they are included in any kind of policy formulation. The Farmers Association was the only significant body engaged in any kind of direct action during the year, staging a protest outside the Parliament for approximately six months (from July to December), but the government refused to meet their demands. *The rating for civil society remains unchanged at 3.75.*

Independent Media. There is a growing awareness in Bosnia-Herzegovina that pressure on the media and individual journalists is unacceptable. Yet politics continues to have a hand in the world of Bosnian media – many titles and broadcasters unabashedly take editorial and reportage positions that reflect both ethnicity and political parties. In 2005, all Croatian, Bosnian, and Serbian press outlets were generally available across the country. In addition, the Journalists Union formed a single association in 2005, whereas previously there had been entity bodies. Alongside police reform, reform of the public broadcasting system and service was the second touchstone issue for SAA negotiations, and although it began the year in the drafting stage, its parliamentary adoption was extremely difficult. The Communications Regulatory Agency (CRA) was active throughout the year, though it was criticized by the minister of communications and transport, and the CoM attempted to reallocate funds belonging to the CRA. A more serious development occurred at the very end of the year, when on December 29 the State Investigative and Protection Agency raided CRA premises on a warrant from the Bosnia-Herzegovina prosecutor, who demanded statements and evidence related to the CRA audit report of 2004. This was surprising given that the Bosnia-Herzegovina auditor's report for 2004 had rated the CRA among the top 10 most transparent state agencies in Bosnia-Herzegovina. The Press Council, a self-regulatory body formed in summer 2000, remains an institution without teeth. *The CRA vulnerability to both government and judicial threats, requiring continued protection of the international community, offsets the achievement of the passage of public broadcasting system legislation; thus the rating for independent media remains at 4.00.*

Local Democratic Governance. Among the manifold layers of government in Bosnia and Herzegovina, municipal government is where citizens have the most interaction and is generally the level of governance for which citizens have the most regard. However, municipalities in the FBiH still struggle with competences that overlap with those of the cantons, and although the RS did pass a Law on Local

Self-Governance in 2005, it remains to be implemented. Similarly, a Law on Local Self-Governance was drafted in the FBiH, but by the end of 2005 neither it nor an associated Law on Revenue Allocation had been passed by the FBiH Parliament. *As the legal framework remains largely the same, with foot-dragging from the FBiH on introducing clarity between municipalities and cantons, the local democratic governance rating remains at 4.75.*

Judicial Framework and Independence. In 2005, international community actors continued to disengage from this sector at policy and infrastructure levels, although a number of international judges and prosecutors remain. Domestic and international movement on war crimes cooperation and prosecution showed an increase in 2005. The War Crimes Chamber became fully functional by March, although by year's end it had not concluded any trials. Other judicial reform projects continued. The Law on Courts in both entities has now been passed. The reappointment of judges and prosecutors continued through 2005, through the High Judicial and Prosecutorial Council, which contributed to the independence and ethnic balance (to better reflect the population at large) of the judiciary. A number of important trials took place during the year, with perhaps the most significant verdict delivered in the Ante Jelavic case. In many other trials, prosecutors report that the judiciary began to use the criminal procedures code much more vigorously than before, so that plea bargaining began to take root as part of the judicial culture. While the judiciary continued to make gains in terms of independence, efficiency remains a challenge: There are huge case backlogs. And despite a few new donor-supported courtrooms, the majority of the buildings and infrastructure are in disrepair. *The judicial framework and independence rating improves from 4.25 to 4.00 because, although requiring some assistance from the international community, the organs of the judiciary functioned independently and the local judiciary began to use the criminal procedures code more vigorously.*

Corruption. Corruption remains endemic as a way of life in Bosnia. It is normal to expect to pay bribes for basic services like health care or to offer police officers small bribes for minor traffic offenses. This culture extends and expands upward through business and politics. In 2005, several prominent politicians were indicted or put on trial. The international community intervened on several occasions, most notably to remove one of the central government presidents, Dragan Covic, after his indictment. In another important development, the chief auditor of the RS examined several public companies for lack of transparency. When the companies complained, the state apparatus supported the auditor. *The rating for corruption improved slightly from 4.50 to 4.25 because the checks and balances established have been allowed to conduct their work and point to the exposure and prosecution of corruption.*

Outlook for 2006. Politics in Bosnia-Herzegovina in 2006 will be dominated by four issues: continuing SAA negotiations and the associated reform agenda; the general elections; the future role of the international community; and constitutional reform. While the actual SAA negotiations are largely technical, the explicit conditionality of their success on police restructuring and completed reform of the public broadcasting sector will continue to be politically problematic. Public participation in elections in Bosnia-Herzegovina continues to decline, with an expected low turnout of around 40-45 percent. Most polling data indicate that there will be a change of government in the RS. However, there is little evidence to suggest that there will be any significant changes in the FBiH. While this will be the background context, the international community – principally the OHR, but also other international agencies that depend on the OHR for political advice and muscle – will have to determine its future course. Christian Schwarz-Schilling, who will replace Paddy Ashdown as high representative in January 2006, has already signaled his intent to reduce the use of the Bonn Powers. By the end of 2006, the OHR should have a transition plan, with a timetable detailing when it will shift exclusively to the Office of the EU Special Representative. In tandem, this should involve a prescription for the future use (if any) of the Bonn Powers.

MAIN REPORT

National Democratic Governance

1997	1998	1999	2001	2002	2003	2004	2005	2006
n/a	n/a	n/a	n/a	n/a	n/a	n/a	4.75	4.75

Despite a challenging start to the year with the resignation in January of the Republika Srpska government subsequent to sanctions issued by the Office of the High Representative in December 2004, the state was stable overall. In the RS, the Serb Democratic Party (SDS) nominated a government that did not include any card-carrying SDS members, so in February Pero Bukejlovic took over as RS prime minister. His inaugural address was a relatively robust policy speech focused on the need to adhere to the Dayton peace accords in order to secure its protections – that is, the guaranteed existence of the RS as an entity. Specifically, he noted the need for cooperation with the International Criminal Tribunal for the Former Yugoslavia and stressed his dedication to preserving RS institutions. He also stated his government's commitment to economic and social issues. His speech further recognized that his is the first government in the RS to have two female ministers. However, the functionality and productivity of the executive branch were markedly greater in the latter half of 2005 than in the first.

In February, it looked as if the RS crisis would escalate to the state level owing to resignations submitted by two Serb state-level ministers: Mladen Ivanic, foreign affairs minister, and Branko Dokic, who briefly held the position of minister of communications and transport. The resignation of these two ministers from the

Progressive Democratic Party (PDP) brought enormous pressure on the remaining two Serb ministers to also resign. If only one of the remaining two had done so, the government could not have maintained a quorum and thus would have fallen. Though it asked for resignations, the SDS did not force its ministers to resign, thus averting the crisis. The prime minister adopted an ostrich-like attitude and did not convene any cabinet meetings.

By June when the crisis appeared to have passed, the state prime minister Adnan Terzic, motivated by personal animosity, dusted off the (earlier tendered, never accepted) resignation of the minister of foreign affairs and attempted to remove him. The prime minister explained that he had to make such a move: The foreign minister's obstruction of the Council of Ministers' appointment of the director of the State Investigation and Protection Agency had forced him to ask for the intervention of the high representative (HR).

Prime Minister Terzic went before the Parliament to explain his plans, but Minister Ivanic simply continued to come to work. This humiliated the prime minister somewhat and led to a worsening of relations at the cabinet level. It also came to the attention of EU High Representative Javier Solana and Commissioner for Enlargement Oli Rehn, who met with Terzic to discuss the deadlock in the implementation of reforms and pending requirements for the EU feasibility study, especially in the context of the CoM situation.

Between April and June, the CoM met only three times and adopted two pieces of legislation (the Law Establishing the Information Society Agency of Bosnia and Herzegovina (BiH) and amendments to the criminal procedures code of BiH). However, on a more positive note, the CoM for the first time adopted a constitutional amendment that would ensure the fiscal sustainability of state building by securing wage flexibility for state employees. While the amendments ultimately did not pass through the Parliament in 2005, the very fact that the CoM passed them demonstrated that indigenous actors could contemplate change to the BiH Constitution (Annex 4 of the Dayton accords).

The OHR characterized the artificial crisis as "summer madness" but did not intervene further except to make the senior appointment of the State Border Service director owing to the inability of the CoM to do so. But in the fall, as focus turned to the announcement of Stabilization and Association Agreement negotiations, the CoM became much more cohesive and productive, and Minister Ivanic did not instigate any further turbulence at the state level. He announced his withdrawal from the RS government in December 2005.

Despite the entity- and state-level resignations, business in the BiH Parliament continued apace. In early January 2005, it passed laws enacting a state-level, single-rate value-added tax system scheduled to be in force by January 2006. Throughout the year, the Parliament proved keen to pass other supplementary legislation necessary for the successful introduction of the VAT, even as opposition parties put forward amendments against the notion of a single rate. This basket of laws marked a major step toward the creation of a true single economic space. Additionally, the 2005 state budget proposed by Finance and Treasury Minister

Ljerka Maric in late December 2004 was passed by the Parliament in January 2005. This was the quickest that the government and the Parliament had ever passed a state budget.

The number of decisions[1] issued by the HR continued to decline. Indeed, the HR introduced a program that sought to arrest and reverse many prior decisions. In part a response to a report of the Venice Commission published in March, this "rehabilitation" process began in the same month, when it was announced that there would be a review of some cases where people had previously been removed from political or public life by HR decisions. The legal basis for all removals was that they were never intended to be permanent but would be kept under review and, when the HR decided, could be rescinded. The HR declared that he believed the BiH's present state of development compelled him to make this principle a reality.

After careful internal review and several investigations of the individuals concerned, the HR decided to lift the ban on participating in public life for three individuals in May. This was followed by another decision concerning two more individuals in June. Altogether, five persons were "rehabilitated" in this first phase, none of whom were assessed to be a continuing threat to peace implementation. In November, a further extension to this process was announced: All those who had been removed by the HR for obstructing peace implementation (not those who were removed for protecting persons indicted for war crimes) would henceforth be able to apply for nonmanagerial positions in public companies through open competition. This was a matter of recognizing the Venice Commission's opinion and the development of the country over time. Individuals removed for obstructing returns in a municipality in 1996, even if under political pressure from their own ethnic group to do so, could not at that time take a job as a teacher or in a public company such as the postal service. This new decision meant that these individuals could now at least apply for public sector jobs.

Taking account of increased cooperation with the ICTY, the HR in November lifted the ban on 23 individuals prohibited from participating in public and political life. Thirteen of those individuals had been removed in June and December 2004 for obstructing RS fulfillment of ICTY obligations. In line with passing accountability to domestic authorities, the OHR prepared amendments to existing legislation that would effectively move the process of vetting, currently undertaken by the OHR, to a special committee of the Parliament, somewhat akin to U.S. confirmation hearings. The Parliament will consider these cases in early 2006.

Thus, many of the HR interventions in 2005 were taken to stop and reverse previous decisions – made by the incumbent and his predecessors – taking into account the improved political context and acknowledging the impermanence of HR removal decisions and the transience of the HR office.

With negotiations on police reform taking center stage for most of the year, other areas of reform received less attention and, accordingly, greater chances for obstruction. For example, the RS government put forward opposition to a European Commission (EC)-supported agreement to improve the work of the single statistics structure in the BiH, was uncooperative in finalizing the transfer agreement on defense, blocked an agreement on guidelines for writing history and geography textbooks, and resisted proposals for a state-level Law on Higher Education.

And at the BiH level, the RS authorities intervened directly or through instructions to state-level officials from the RS to obstruct or delay progress on reforms, including the BiH Law on Obligations (to ensure equity in business contracts across the country and thus contributing to the EU feasibility study requirement of creating a single economic space), the BiH Pharmacy Law, amendments to the Law on the High Judicial and Prosecutorial Council, the Law on the Prevention and Suspension of Abuse of Narcotics, the Consumer Protection Law, and the State Debt Settlement Law.

The RS government was also found wanting in leadership after the Manjaca oath incidents (when new army recruits refused to take an oath to the BiH, instead taking one to the RS) and on revealing all the information they could about the Srebrenica massacre. On Manjaca, the recruits did eventually retake the oath, but only after sustained international community pressure and the removal of the chief of staff of the army of the RS by NATO and the EU Force in Bosnia and Herzegovina (EUFOR). EUFOR closed the training camp until they were satisfied that the correct professional and constitutional procedures were respected.

This systemic obstructionism from the RS government on finalizing passage of many reform-related laws was the subject of an OHR d□marche in November, followed by a press conference in December. In the latter half of the month, the RS government did start to move positively on many of these issues, but only because the OHR continued to exert pressure on the RS authorities.

FBiH authorities continued to meet regularly, adopting key legislation in July concerning budgets and linked to the EU feasibility study. In the same month, the ruling coalition saw off a Social Democratic Party (SDP)-initiated no-confidence vote without any difficulty. However, the government was brought to the brink of crisis in August and September owing to disagreements concerning the appointment of two replacement ministers.

Privatization of entity assets was problematic, and government-brokered deals on key companies like Aluminijum Mostar and Energopetrol were stymied by the failure, respectively, to pass privatization legislation and to get the Parliament's endorsement.

Europe – as a broad and amorphous concept – is generally viewed by both citizens and politicians as a positive thing, if not a panacea for BiH's problems. There is public consensus that joining the EU is the most important policy goal for BiH, though there remain political questions over the acceptability of some of the changes BiH is required to make in order to "join the club."

The path to Euro-Atlantic structures had been well signposted through the EU feasibility study, the standard post-Council of Europe accession requirements, and the NATO Partnership for Peace benchmarks. The key areas of reform related to defense, intelligence, public broadcasting, state government, and cooperation with the ICTY. In 2005, after the EU clarified the security components of the feasibility study requirements, police restructuring dovetailed with the question of entry to SAA negotiations, and it consumed major energy on behalf of local and international actors throughout the year.

However, when the Consultative Task Force (CTF), a body of the European Commission established to assess BiH's compliance with feasibility study requirements, met in Sarajevo in May, the prospects were less than bright, and Bosnia-Herzegovina did not receive an invitation to begin SAA negotiations. As well as those areas listed earlier, the CTF noted that legislation on the ombudsman, auditing and accounting, and the Information Society Agency still needed to be passed by the Parliament.

In addition, laws ensuring that the legal infrastructure of the Indirect Tax Authority, the independent agency charged with tax administration and revenue collection, is appropriately completed prior to VAT implementation were still pending adoption by the CoM (including the Law on Customs Violations, Law on Procedures of Indirect Taxation, Law on Procedures of Forced Payment, and Law Establishing the Data Protection Commission of BiH). Small wonder no invitation was issued.

By the time the CTF came in May, though, much energy had been devoted to the thorny issue of police reform. The OHR had kicked off the process of introducing the tenets of the Police Restructuring Commission Report in the domestic theater. The commission finished its work in December 2004 but did not present its findings publicly until January 2005 at a press conference attended by the report's author, Chairman Wilfried Martens, Prime Minister Terzic, and the HR.

The commission's report emphasized three firm tenets that the European Commission stated also represented its minimal requirement for successful police restructuring in Bosnia and Herzegovina. First, the institutions of the BiH must be invested with all competences for police matters in Bosnia and Bosnia-Herzegovina. Second, this includes legislation and budgeting for police matters exclusively at the state level. Third, political oversight should be exercised by the Ministry of Security at the state level, and the size and shape of local policing regions should be determined according to the criteria of effective policing rather than by political considerations.

Initially, action to implement these principles took the form of a grassroots campaign; this effort extolled the benefits of police restructuring, deployed various international community actors, and lasted from February until April, when the first serious round of political negotiations took place at Mount Vlasic. This multiparty event, held over three days, produced a partial political agreement by all parties that the state should be exclusively competent for legislative and budgetary issues in all matters related to policing. Although maps were discussed on Vlasic, nothing was decided – a Maps Commission was established to attempt to reach consensus on that issue. This was a crunch issue: Establishing police regions that crossed the Inter-Entity Boundary Line (IEBL) would automatically decouple political control from policing.

Despite these positive events, the SDS began to renege on the spirit of accommodation commented on by many at Vlasic. The RS delegation at the Maps Commission refused to negotiate on the maps, relying instead on their proposal, which strictly followed the IEBL. In brief, instead of preparing the population for an EU-endorsed reform, the SDS and other parties preached another apocalyptic vision that would allegedly abolish the RS. Preparations continued nonetheless for a second round of negotiations held in Sarajevo. It soon became clear, however, that the Serbs were not willing – or not able – to negotiate the IEBL. They asked that talks be suspended while they sought a mandate from the RS National Assembly (RSNA) to negotiate further.

At the RSNA session, which took place in May, President Dragan Cavic failed to request from the assembly an open mandate for negotiators; consequently, the RSNA unanimously adopted a resolution that called for police reform along the lines of the three EU principles but adhering to the administrative structures delineated by the IEBL. The international community held a firm line on not diluting the principles and publicly assigned blame – but no sanctions – to the SDS. However, it reiterated its willingness to start SAA negotiations with the need to restructure police along the three EU principles.

A series of meetings then took place throughout the summer at various locations across the BiH, under the auspices of the local authorities and not attended by high-level international community officials. Despite a commitment from domestic authorities to focus all political energy on this process, the talks did not start in Banja Luka until July 28 and ended in the same city on September 12 – with meetings in Mrakovica, Hutovo Blato, Bjelasnica, and Sarajevo in between – but ultimately these did not produce anything by mid-September. This was the date by which the international community said agreement had to be reached in order for preparatory work to be done to allow SAA negotiations to be announced on the 10th anniversary of the Dayton accords. Unexpectedly, toward the end of September the prime minister Terzic and the RS president Cavic brokered a deal that was subsequently passed at a stormy session of the RSNA in October. After being passed by the other two legislatures – the FBiH Parliament and the BiH Parliamentary Assembly – the CoM passed a decision in November establishing the implementation organs contained therein, to the satisfaction of the EU.

The Agreement on Policing called for the establishment of a Directorate for Police Restructuring Implementation by December 31, 2005; the preparation of an implementation plan by September 30, 2006; entity and state government approval of the plan by December 31, 2006; and entity and state parliamentary adoption of the plan by end of February 2007. The Policing Directorate was established within the deadline on December 28, 2005.

In 2005, the mandate of the Defense Reform Commission (DRC) was adjusted to take into account the accelerated timetable for defense reform announced by the HR in December 2004. In early 2005, the defense minister (as one co-chair of the DRC) initiated a defense review. By midyear, a general consensus appeared to have been achieved that encompassed the elimination of entity competences, a transfer to the state of all defense responsibilities and personnel, the abolition of conscription, and a restructured, smaller reserve force.

However, at the last DRC meeting in June, Bosniaks showed signs of shying away from the general package; they tabled proposals to retain conscription and a reserve force. The RS, on the other hand, and particularly the SDS, showed signs that they were ready to cooperate and support defense reform. This was most likely because President Cavic was personally interested and knowledgeable about it. He had an understanding that command and control of defense forces had to be located at the state level, assessing that the army of the RS had already been reduced to a symbolic level and, further, that if he conceded on defense, he could hold a firmer line on police reform. Croats seemed to support the DRC general recommendations but continued to push for stock items, especially those that guaranteed them their own parts of the structures, in particular retaining the then current brigade or brigadelike characteristics of the armed forces.

Bosniak members of the DRC did ultimately sign the final document despite opposition from the party president, and the summer months were spent adapting the political agreement into legislative drafts and, in the fall, parliamentary adoption. Even after the state Parliament adopted the laws – in record time for such a complex package of legislation – and after the entities had adopted constitutional amendments to reflect the concomitant changes required, the RS prime minister dug in his heels over the signing of an explicit transfer agreement, as stated in the BiH Constitution. After much lobbying by the OHR, NATO, and the minister of defense, Bukejlovic finally agreed to sign the agreement on New Year's Eve 2005. All defense reform legislation was scheduled to enter into force on January 1, 2006. This was no small achievement, especially as it meant that the entities lost not only their ministers of defense (who became obsolete on December 31, 2005), but also much of their property previously in military use by the respective entity armies.

State functionality continues to be seriously impeded by the lack of basic premises and an independent and merit-based civil service. In the "Joint Action Plan-Staff and Premises for the Council of Ministers," which was presented by Prime Minister Terzic to the Peace Implementation Council in September 2004, the CoM was asked to create a body that would find long-term solutions to the state's premises problems. It would also be charged to look into issues of ownership at all levels of government, as well as the state's rights to acquire/expropriate property pursuant to its needs, not least of which would be those stemming from the SAA process. To this end, the State Property Commission was tasked with drafting a Law on State Property for the BiH and its entities and to identify state property that could house state institutions.

However, as nothing had materialized from the domestic authorities by March 2005, the HR issued a decision whereby the State Property Commission was given a deadline of the end of November 2005 to come up with a report of its work and/or draft state and entity laws. Unfortunately, the RS failed to appoint its members to the State Property Commission for months, and even with much negotiation and lobbying on the part of the OHR, the commission did not commence its work until November. Separate negotiations with FBiH prime minister Ahmet Hadzipasic fared little better, with the collapse of a deal midyear that would have resulted in the FBiH government vacating significant space it occupied in the presidency building, thus making space available for several state ministries.

As part of the March decision, and aimed particularly at the FBiH, the HR also imposed a law that froze the sale of any state assets for which usage and occupation rights were held by the entities. The RS had sold off a large number of assets that the state could have potentially laid claim to, but significant property portfolios still existed in the FBiH. Indeed, if the OHR had not intervened, the State Property Commission's work would have been much simpler: There would have been no property left to determine ownership over, never mind allocating anything to state use or ownership.

The situation with the civil service fared somewhat better. The first package of amendments to the BiH Law on the Civil Service were adopted by the CoM in February and sent to the Parliament. But several ministers had added to the amendments that had been recommended by the Civil Service Agency (CSA), the independent body for recruiting, training and administering all civil servants, rejecting two particular clauses. These spoke to the principles of merit and independence in the selection process by reducing ministerial powers to stymie appointments (by simply failing to sign off on them) and to make the recruitment exercise itself more open, transparent, and efficient. In a welcome move, the CSA itself agreed to spearhead the lobbying strategy, supported by the OHR. Happily, parliamentarians disagreed with the CoM on this occasion, and the CSA amendments were adopted unanimously by the Parliamentary Assembly in April.

Electoral Process

1997	1998	1999	2001	2002	2003	2004	2005	2006
n/a	5.00	5.00	4.75	4.25	3.75	3.50	3.25	3.00

No countrywide elections took place in 2005, but several mayoral by-elections were conducted, owing to either the death of the incumbent or, in one case, the recall of the incumbent via a referendum. These all passed off peacefully and were conducted properly by the Election Commission. The international members withdrew from the Election Commission in June, following an HR announcement in March, though they did stay on as observers.

The Election Commission also made a substantial start on or completed several large projects. These included the implementation of the Law on Conflict of Interest, which featured (for the first time) the production of several party audits. The Election Commission was able to conduct these audits primarily because of funds sequestered by the HR from the SDS because of its continued failure to arrest persons indicted for war crimes – namely, Radovan Karadzic and Ratko Mladic. Thus in March, the Law on Conflict of Interest transformed its Audit Department into an Audit Office and belatedly began implementation of the Law on Political

Party Financing. The Audit Office started off by auditing two medium-size political parties, finished with that in September, and moved on to audit four larger parties [Party for Democratic Action (SDA), SDS, Croatian Democratic Community (HDZ), and SDP] by the end of the year.

It also conducted a review of the Law on Elections and liaised and contributed to a Parliamentary Working Group on the same topic. The Working Group on Election Law Amendments (WGELA) began its work in May. The WGELA consisted of representatives from the BiH House of Representatives (HoR) House of Peoples (HoP), CoM, and Law on Conflict of Interest national members. The Organization for Security and Cooperation in Europe (OSCE), OHR, and Council of Europe participated as observers. And though it aimed to finish its work in the fall of 2005, by the end of the year the final report was not yet complete.

However, enough work had been completed by December to lead the international community (primarily the OHR and OSCE) to write to the WGELA expressing concern about suggested amendments. These proposed to abolish the system of "compensatory mandates," or at least to reduce the number of seats determined by compensatory mandate; to increase the threshold from 3 to 4 percent; to move to a closed-list system from the current open-list system; and to lower the requirement of minority gender representation on candidate lists. The latter two points particularly exercised the international community: Both represented rollbacks of international community reform efforts, effectively putting more power into the central party boards on the selection of candidates and further weakening the link between citizens and their elected representatives. Even though the Election Commission no longer had internationals as members, their presence as observers ensured that these proposals were dropped; but it is instructive that as soon as there was opportunity to reverse international community-introduced reform, political parties seized the chance.

The political scene was relatively stable, although nationalism remained barely suppressed in much of the political discourse during the year. Two parties in particular – the SDS and the HDZ – experienced ongoing internal turbulence amid strong signals all around that the general election campaign for 2006 had kicked off around September 2005.

On May 26, 2005, the SDA held its congress and reelected Sulejman Tihic as president despite speculation to the contrary. The SDA presented a new profile at the congress, focusing on Europe and the Bosnian identity and expressing commitment to reforms, the EU, the OHR, and an overall strong international community presence in Bosnia-Herzegovina. There were no extremist chants, no religious flag-waving, no representatives of the Islamic community, and no hate speeches at the event. Subsequent election of multiethnic representatives to its main board and a commitment to multiethnic candidate lists at the next general elections were also seen as indicators of a more moderate SDA.

However, the actions of President Tihic later in the year, particularly his attempt to change the name of Sarajevo International Airport to Alija Izetbegovic (the wartime leader of Bosnia, much loved by Bosniaks as a "father of the nation" figure but not held in the same esteem by either Serbs or Croats), would suggest that although the SDA was assertively trying to be modernist, it had not yet addressed its own nationalism.

Among the other Bosniak and multiethnic parties, the Party for BiH (SBiH) continued to threaten to bring down the FBiH government by withdrawing, but all proved to be empty threats. The SDP did not lose any more elected members and enjoyed some public success by leading the charge against the introduction of a single-rate VAT, with its opinion poll position buoyed a little as a result. But there were no significant personnel changes at the leadership level, which might have warranted renewed public appeal for the SDP.

In June, the HDZ held its party congress, which (in contrast with the SDA congress) took place in a hostile and tense atmosphere, pointing to division in the party. In a disputed (and close) election, Dragan Covic was elected party president. Covic immediately began the process of consolidating his win, but though he made some personal appointments to the party main board, expected replacements at the ministerial level did not materialize.

The bad blood generated at the congress underscored all party activities until the end of the year. Covic found himself having to quash general dissent and specific doubt over his election as party president by eventually having the chief internal opponents – Martin Raguz, Josip Merdo, and Bozo Ljubic – expelled from the party. These circumstances were so dubious that the European People's Party, in which the HDZ enjoyed associate membership until the end of the year, threatened to suspend the HDZ's associate status with the body. However, the HDZ continued to be well positioned in most polls – no Croat prefix party poses any serious alternative to it.

The SDS did not hold its party congress until November, and here President Cavic seemed to assert and consolidate his control of the party. Many new main board members were known Cavic supporters, so the event seemed more to demonstrate to the RS and the international community that Cavic is in control of a unified SDS than to present a new party reform platform. Cavic does have the support of the majority of SDS leaders at present; however, it is likely that this support hinges on continued international community backing.

In December, the PDP announced its "withdrawal" from the RS government – that is to say, the government could no longer rely on its support. This did not have a great impact in terms of the stability of the state-level government, but it did make the SDS government more vulnerable to no-confidence motions and certainly rendered inoperable its capacity to pass a 2006 budget for the RS. However, in terms of the PDP, this is nothing new – its party leader is a maestro at deflecting attention from the party's own difficulties by exposing the weaknesses of others.

While the leader of the Independent Party of Social Democrats (SNSD), Milorad Dodik, continued to enjoy high popularity ratings in opinion polls, his party did not win the mayoral by-election in Bijeljina in October as expected. His widely forecast victory in next year's general elections is therefore not a foregone conclusion.

Civil Society

1997	1998	1999	2001	2002	2003	2004	2005	2006
n/a	5.00	4.50	4.50	4.25	4.00	3.75	3.75	3.75

The legal framework and overall state of civil society remain generally unchanged relative to 2004. Nongovernmental organizations are still perceived largely as service providers, and it is rare that they are included in any kind of policy formulation. In 2005, the main development in the NGO sector was a lobby to implement the goals of To Work and Succeed Together, an NGO coalition of 200 member groups that presented a program to the CoM in December 2004. The key document of this program proposed an agreement on how the state and the NGO sector will interact. Discussions have been ongoing throughout the year, mainly refining the criteria of who represents the NGO (and informally organized coalitions) and how its representatives interact with the key state ministries of justice and civil affairs. Other programs related to how the NGO sector regulates itself in terms of transparency.

However, the sector as a whole is still finding its way and role in the maze of complicated state and local governmental structures. Individual parts of the sector did raise their profile unilaterally during the year, most notably the Farmers Association. This was the only significant body engaged in any kind of direct action during the year, staging a protest outside the Parliament for approximately six months; but the government refused to meet their demands. There were also instances of direct action protests from individual social groupings not normally classified as NGOs, such as pensioners protesting outside government offices over not having received their pensions. Additionally, teachers went on strike because they had not received their salaries; prisoners went on hunger strikes over prison conditions; and even schoolchildren (though manipulated by both parental and political parties) went on strike over the "two curricula under one roof" issue. This actually delayed the start of the school year for many children until October.

Independent Media

1997	1998	1999	2001	2002	2003	2004	2005	2006
n/a	4.75	5.00	4.50	4.25	4.25	4.25	4.00	4.00

In terms of press freedom, the 2005 Reporters Without Borders annual report on world media freedom places Bosnia-Herzegovina 33rd in the world and second to Slovenia among countries of the former Yugoslavia. The Free Media Helpline, originally established by the OHR and the OSCE but now independently run and funded, reported very low numbers of calls about threats or other violations of media freedom from journalists, and there was only one reported physical attack in 2005.

This is not to say that there are no politics in the world of Bosnian media. Many titles unabashedly take editorial and reportage positions that reflect both ethnicity and political parties. For example, *Avaz* switched its allegiance from the SDP in 2002 to the SDA and the SBiH at various times since. And in the latter half of 2005, it was supportive of the policies of SBiH founder Haris Silajdic, particularly his views on constitutional reform. *Oslobejdenje*, reflecting its Communist roots and Socialist outlook, still tends to support the SDP, giving it much more space than other parties. *Vecerniji List* is associated with the HDZ, and its editorial policy promotes Croat national interests. While *Nesavisne Novine* is generally supportive of the SNSD, it does tend to be truly independent where matters of corruption or criminality are involved. *Glas Sprske* remains the voice of the RS government. All these titles are daily newspapers.

There are also relationships between broadcasters and political parties. Federal Television (FTV) is perceived as having some SDP bias, and Radio Television Republika Sprska (RTRS) is seen as having some sympathy for the SNSD. These perceptions provide a platform for other parties to put pressure on the Public Broadcasting Service (PBS) governing boards, and this will intensify when the time comes to appoint new governing boards under the newly adopted PBS legislation.

While there is a dearth of investigative reporting and quality comment columns, the Sarajevo weeklies *Slobodna Bosna* and *BH Dani* generally publish corruption-based stories that have resulted in prosecutions. In 2005, all Croatian, Bosnian, and Serbian press outlets were available across the country. In addition, the Journalists Union formed a single association in 2005, where previously there had been only entity-based associations.

Alongside police reform, reform of the public broadcasting system and the PBS was the second touchstone issue for SAA negotiations, and although legislation began the year in the drafting stage, its parliamentary adoption was extremely difficult. The international community, principally the European Commission and the OHR, engaged heavily in the lobby for this reform, exerting pressure publicly from both Sarajevo and Brussels. But the HDZ resisted it every step of the way, using substantive arguments against the reform. And when those failed, it took advantage of procedural rules to delay the law further. Throughout, the HDZ maintained its position in demanding three ethnic channels, and ultimately the law was the subject of a rare invocation of vital national interest (VNI) by the Croat delegates (HDZ) in the BiH House of Peoples in June. The case was sent to the Constitutional Court of the BiH, which ruled in July that there were no grounds for invoking VNI. The Croat caucus drew out further consideration of the law when it returned to the Parliament, but it was eventually passed in October.

The Communications Regulatory Agency was active throughout the year, though it sustained criticism from a group of U.S. congressmen for its investigation of BNTV, a private station from Bijeljina. On this occasion, SDA president Tihic wrote in the CRA's defense. However, politicians did not always act in support of the CRA. The minister of communications and transport, Branko Dokic, publicly criticized the CRA and its director for being "biased" and overly "independent" in its regulation of state resources. In addition, the CoM attempted to reallocate funds that belonged to the CRA (collected through the licensing process) without the

CRA's consent. The CRA had to lobby the CoM to reverse its decision, which it did, albeit reluctantly. A more serious development occurred at the end of the year, when on December 29 the State Investigation and Protection Agency raided CRA premises on a warrant from the BiH prosecutor, who demanded receipt of statements and evidence related to the CRA audit report of 2004. This was surprising given that the BiH auditor's report for 2004 had ranked the CRA among the top 10 most transparent state agencies in Bosnia-Herzegovina. The Press Council, a self-regulatory body, remains an institution without teeth.

Local Democratic Governance

1997	1998	1999	2001	2002	2003	2004	2005	2006
n/a	n/a	n/a	n/a	n/a	n/a	n/a	4.75	4.75

There is a legislative framework for regular local elections and government at the municipal level, but functions remain problematic owing to dual competences with other administrative levels and insufficient resources. Public utilities, communal services, tourism, concessions, culture, sport, local financing , local land use, housing policy, urbanism, and property relations are just some of the areas in which there is overlap and confusion, especially in the FBiH. New laws on local self-government, not yet adopted in the FBiH, seek to clarify the order and interrelationship of responsibilities. The RS did pass a Law on Local Self-Governance in December 2005, but it remains to be implemented. Although a Law on Local Self-Governance was drafted in the FBiH, by the end of 2005 neither it nor an associated Law on Revenue Allocation had been passed by the FBiH Parliament.

Yet despite the confusion, this is the level at which citizens are most likely to interact with government. There are examples of municipalities that do deliver services to citizens in an effective and efficient manner, but the formula for revenue allocation in the FBiH means that many municipalities are starved of cash by the cantonal layer of government. In the RS, municipalities are also dependent on funding from a higher level, in this case the entity.

Examples of effective municipal governance would include Zenica and Ljubinje. Zenica has successfully obtained an International Standards Organization (ISO) 9001 certificate, meaning that it has set in place the structures to deliver efficient services. It is also widely recognized as working with other levels of government and investors to attract new capital and create jobs. Ljubinje, in east Herzegovina, faces practical challenges related to its relative remoteness and paucity of economic assets. The municipality has introduced modest financial incentives, including a "baby bonus," to persuade residents not to move away and has taken steps to make it easier and cheaper to build in the municipality. The mayor has also introduced performance-related salaries in the administration.

An issue with municipalities is that service delivery is often tied to political party patronage. But even this has apparently done little to improve efficiency and delivery. For example, Ilidza is run by the same party that runs Zenica, yet poor urban planning and use of the budget means infrastructure has not been improved, nor has one of the greatest assets of the municipality – Vrelo Bosna Park – been developed: It remains badly managed and does not serve the community to its full potential.

In Bijeljina, run by the same party as Ljubinje, bureaucracy has expanded. The budget for cabinet salaries has tripled since the new mayor was elected in October. The municipal assembly also increased its members' monthly allowance to higher than the average salary in the RS. In both entities, public meetings are rare, as is the promotion of active citizen participation. In 2005, there was no political change at the local level, such as in party representation, that would be significant in comparison with the situation at the canton or federation level.

Judicial Framework and Independence

1997	1998	1999	2001	2002	2003	2004	2005	2006
n/a	6.00	6.00	5.50	5.25	5.00	4.50	4.25	4.00

International community actors continued to disengage from this sector at policy and infrastructure levels in 2005, though a number of international judges and prosecutors remain out of necessity. The War Crimes Chamber became fully functional in March, with the appointment of the first group of judges and prosecutors. But by the end of the year, it had not yet concluded any trials.

In 2003, the BiH Human Rights Chamber ordered the RS to conduct an in-depth investigation into the fates of those persons still counted as missing following the massacres in and around Srebrenica in July 1995. The Srebrenica commission finally began work in January 2004 and produced a report, adopted by the RS government, that for the first time acknowledged the magnitude and nature of the atrocities committed following the fall of the Srebrenica "safe area." The report provided new details on mass grave sites.

However, the OHR was not satisfied that the RS authorities had processed and provided all the data actually in their possession and thus extended the deadline for the Srebrenica Working Group to March 2005. The foot-dragging displayed in other areas was also in evidence with this issue. In the run-up to the 10th-anniversary commemoration of the massacre (and burials) at Srebrenica in July, the HR extended the deadline again to June and, when that still did not prove adequate, to September.

Finally, the RS Defense Ministry and Ministry of the Interior complied and provided further information, but only after the OHR established a subgroup that had full access and authority to conduct spot checks of ministry archives. The information was then passed to the BiH chief prosecutor in October. The ceremonies commemorating the Srebrenica massacre of July 1995 passed peacefully, although tensions had been raised by the much televised amateur video of the Scorpions special military unit executing bound Bosniak soldiers – footage that had been submitted as evidence in the Milosevic trial.

In terms of international cooperation in 2005, there was a flood of arrests of persons indicted for war crimes for whom the RS is responsible. The flow began in January when RS Ministry of Internal Affairs authorities transferred ICTY indictee Savo Todorovic to The Hague in January, after his surrender. The RS minister of internal affairs, Darko Matijasevic, who accompanied Todorovic personally to The Hague, proclaimed that there would be more voluntary surrenders and extraditions but said little about operations and involuntary arrests, and indeed this proved to be the template for further transfers during the rest of the year.

The international community welcomed this as a significant step forward but highlighted that this was part of a process it believed could be accelerated through greater international community engagement, based on active monitoring. In this context, the OHR and Prime Minister Terzic discussed and established an ICTY Cooperation Monitoring Group whose mandate stemmed from the 12 tasks set for the BiH authorities by the ICTY.

The Cooperation Monitoring Group did have some success. It met from January through April and focused on correcting the obvious structural deficiencies in the BiH's approach to ICTY cooperation. Its results were seen not only in the numbers of indictees being handed over or surrendering, but also in terms of attitudinal change, connoted by the RS government-fronted public campaign. This was a hard-hitting TV and billboard campaign based on a "them or us" theme. The campaign helped raise awareness among RS citizens of the economic and political damage done by indictees at large. Furthermore, assets connected to the various networks of persons indicted for war crimes, including bank accounts, insurance policies, and properties, were frozen in line with decisions by the EU council.

Ten persons indicted for war crimes were arrested by or surrendered to Bosnian authorities in 2005. Of those who were still at large at the end of 2005, only four are held to be the responsibility jointly or singly of Banja Luka or Belgrade.

Other judicial reform projects continued. The Law on Courts in both entities was passed and provides (more or less) for the court structure, which was proposed by the Independent Judicial Council, which acted as secretariat to the body responsible for the appointment and discipline of judges. However, the FBiH provided for the opening of an additional four court branches. In the RS, seven additional court branches were opened in late 2005 by way of amendments to the Law on Courts. Opening additional branches is problematic because of the precarious financial position of the courts; their debt was 16 million KM (US$10.2 million) at the end of 2004. In addition, the restructuring of the basic and municipal courts was hampered by entity-level parliaments dragging their feet on the amalgamation of minor offense courts. This was for fear that they would lose certain facilities in their own constituencies.

The process of reappointing judges and prosecutors continued through 2005. As the candidates were subject to a rigorous vetting procedure and extensive scrutiny, this contributed not only to the independence of the judiciary, but also to a reflection of the population at large in the ethnicity of the judiciary. Amendments in December to the Law on the High Judicial and Prosecutorial Council will make it possible to appoint judges in 2006 to deal with minor offenses.

A number of important trials took place during the year, with perhaps the most significant verdict delivered in the Ante Jelavic case. Jelavic was successfully convicted and sentenced to 10 years in prison for office abuse related to the illegal redistribution/redirection of Croatia-donated funds while he was FBiH defense minister. In many other trials, prosecutors reported that the judiciary began to use the criminal procedures code much more vigorously than before, so that plea bargaining began to take root as part of the judicial culture.

There was little international community intervention in this area, with the notable exception of the HR imposing a law in December that acted as a one-off corrective for judicial salaries that were hugely out of line with those of the average citizen. Additionally, the judicial salary legislation provided for uniformity of compensation across the judicial sector, so that there is now equal pay for work of equal value, regardless of which entity judges and prosecutors reside or work in. While the judiciary continued to gain more independence, there remains a real question of efficiency: There are huge backlogs, and despite one or two new donor-supported courtrooms, the majority of the buildings are in disrepair.

Corruption

1997	1998	1999	2001	2002	2003	2004	2005	2006
n/a	n/a	6.00	5.75	5.50	5.00	4.75	4.50	4.25

Corruption remains endemic as a way of life in Bosnia. It is normal to expect to pay bribes for basic services like health care or to offer police officers small bribes for minor traffic offenses. And this culture of corruption extends and expands upward through business and politics.

There were indictments and trials of several prominent politicians in 2005. To insert and strengthen the principle of standards in public life, the international community intervened on several occasions, most notably in the Covic case. While acknowledging Covic's right of presumption of innocence, the HR, flanked by the steering board ambassadors of the Peace Implementation Council, directed that he be removed from public office, though he could continue to hold leadership positions in his party. Covic was indicted in March for abuse of office or official authority in his capacity as former FBiH minister of finance in relation to the issuance of decisions in June 2000. That indictment was confirmed by the state court, and the hearing of his testimony began in September.

In a case that was more than tangentially connected with the Covic trial, proceedings began on the trial for tax evasion of Mladen Ivankovic Ljianovici, another party leader. The leader of the SNSD, Milorad Dodik, also went to trial in the fall following an indictment on charges of abuse of office delivered in late 2004. As Dodik did not at the time of the indictment hold high executive office, the international community did not intervene, and he was acquitted. In the case of Minister Branko Dokic, also indicted, the OHR negotiated his voluntary resignation for the period of his trial, at which he was convicted. But the sentence was under the threshold for running as a candidate or holding office, so Dokic returned to office.

The notion of endemic corruption and special favors for the political elite, their families, and their friends came to light again in September. In November 2004, the BiH Parliament removed one of its members who had been pardoned by the FBiH president, and the HR intervened to curtail the powers of entity presidents in this regard. Despite this, in September 2005 the HR was again forced to intervene in response to another case, that of Miroslav Prce, a former FBiH Minister of Defence whom the FBiH pardoned, a clear abuse of the pardon system. Both the FBiH and the RS routinely granted pardons. The FBiH granted them virtually on a monthly basis. In fact, the statistics were such that one was more likely to be granted a pardon than to pass a driving test. The HR thus suspended the right to give pardons. The BiH Parliament subsequently received for consideration a state-level Law on Pardons designed to prevent such abuses and ensure that any future pardons will be made in a transparent manner.

The RS chief auditor delivered several damning reports on the running of RS public companies, citing political interference and bad management. In retaliation, Elektroprivreda RS filed a lawsuit against the chief auditor in September for "damaging the reputation and honor" of the company. However, shortly thereafter the RS Law on Audits was adopted to extend the mandate of the chief auditor for an additional seven years. The RS government threatened to dismiss the management of Elektroprivreda if it did not drop the lawsuit. The next day, the suit was dropped.

Kate Fearon is a political analyst who has lived and worked in Bosnia and Herzegovina since 2001. Mirsada Muzur is the managing director of the Center for Policy Studies and Prism Research in Sarajevo.

---

[1] Decisions are taken by what is popularly termed the "Bonn Powers," whereby the HR can intervene directly in the body politic, filling lacunae left by domestic authorities either by removing politicians from office, imposing laws, or making appointments that domestic authorities have proved politically unable to make because of ethnonational reasons.

Bulgaria

Capital:	Sofia
Population:	7.8 million
GNI/capita:	$2,750
Ethnic Groups:	Bulgarian (83.9%), Turk (9.4%), Roma (4.7%), other (2%)

Nations in Transit Ratings and Averaged Scores

	1997	1998	1999	2001	2002	2003	2004	2005	2006
Electoral Process	3.25	2.75	2.25	2.00	2.00	2.00	1.75	1.75	1.75
Civil Society	4.00	3.75	3.75	3.50	3.25	3.25	3.00	2.75	2.75
Independent Media	3.75	3.50	3.50	3.25	3.25	3.50	3.50	3.50	3.25
Governance *	4.25	4.00	3.75	3.50	3.50	3.75	3.75	n/a	n/a
National Democratic Governance	n/a	n/a	n/a	n/a	n/a	n/a	n/a	3.50	3.00
Local Democratic Governance	n/a	n/a	n/a	n/a	n/a	n/a	n/a	3.50	3.00
Judicial Framework and Independence	4.25	3.75	3.50	3.50	3.50	3.50	3.25	3.25	3.00
Corruption	n/a	n/a	4.75	4.75	4.50	4.25	4.25	4.00	3.75
Democracy Score	3.90	3.55	3.58	3.42	3.33	3.38	3.25	3.18	2.93

* With the 2005 edition, Freedom House introduced seperate analysis and ratings for national democratic governance and local democratic governance to provide readers with more detailed and nuanced analysis of these two important subjects.

NOTE: The ratings reflect the consensus of Freedom House, its academic advisers, and the author of this report. The opinions expressed in this report are those of the author. The ratings are based on a scale of 1 to 7, with 1 representing the highest level of democratic progress and 7 the lowest. The Democracy Score is an average of ratings for the categories tracked in a given year.

The economic and social data on this page were taken from the following sources:
GNI/capita, Population: *World Development Indicators 2006* (Washington, D.C.: World Bank, 2006).
Ethnic Groups: *CIA World Factbook 2006* (Washington, D.C.: Central Intelligence Agency, 2006).

EXECUTIVE SUMMARY

In the 15 years since the collapse of Communism, Bulgaria has managed to consolidate its democratic governance system with a stable Parliament, sound government structures, an active civil society, and free media. Over this period, a number of general, presidential, and local elections have been held freely, fairly, and without disturbance. Power has changed hands peacefully. Bulgaria has made significant progress in establishing the rule of law, yet further efforts are needed. After a period of poor performance, the economy has recorded eight years of robust growth. Economic reforms have advanced considerably, with more work needed to improve the business environment. In 2004, the country officially became a NATO member and in 2005 signed the Treaty of Accession to the European Union (EU), with a target date for membership in 2007. Despite these positive achievements, more attention must be paid to reforming the judiciary and to fighting corruption and organized crime. Better efforts are also needed to bring the public back to politics, to reestablish its trust in democratic institutions, and to relegitimize politics as a tool for engendering social change.

National Democratic Governance. The Bulgarian system of democratic governance is established and progressing steadily despite various problems. At the June 2005 parliamentary elections, the leftist Bulgarian Socialist Party (BSP) won the most votes but not enough to form a government on its own. After failing to form a minority government in coalition with the ethnic Turkish party Movement for Rights and Freedoms (MRF), the BSP reached a coalition agreement with the previously ruling National Movement Simeon II (NMSS) in August 2005. As a result, a trilateral governmental coalition was established between the BSP, NMSS, and MRF. The new government and the Parliament concentrated on intensifying progress in the reforms needed for Bulgaria's integration into the EU, especially judicial reform. However, the European Commission gave the country's judicial reform and fight against organized crime and corruption an unsatisfactory assessment. *Owing to the demonstrated ability of major Bulgarian parties to overcome considerable political fragmentation after the elections and to form a government that enjoys a substantial majority and preserves the pace of EU-related reforms, the national democratic governance rating is improved from 3.50 to 3.00.*

Electoral Process. Regular national parliamentary elections were held in Bulgaria in June 2005. Additionally, mayoral by-elections were held in October in several municipalities to replace two mayors elected to the Parliament. Voter turnout in the parliamentary elections was around 55 percent. The leftist BSP won the most votes, followed by the previously ruling centrist NMSS, the MRF, and several smaller center-right political formations. Surprisingly, the extremist Attack coalition managed to pass the 4 percent threshold for the Parliament. This development indicates antidemocratic sentiments in Bulgarian society, which under certain circumstances might threaten the functioning of the democratic system of governance. The 40th National Assembly, with seven separate political parties and coalitions, is the most fragmented in Bulgaria's postindependence history. *There are no considerable changes that may lead to an improvement or decline in the electoral process rating, and it remains unchanged at 1.75.*

Civil Society. For more than a decade, Bulgaria has managed to develop a vibrant civil society. However, the nongovernmental organization (NGO) sector has still not developed sustainable fund-raising mechanisms. The Bulgarian civil society sector was formed with a top-down approach, led by donor demands and visions and not by Bulgarian citizens. This is the major reason most NGOs are still heavily dependent on foreign donors and do not enjoy public support. In 2005, more than 80 percent of funding for NGOs came from foreign sources. Given the intentions of many foreign donors to withdraw from the country, this could cause problems for the financial stability of the NGO sector. Governmental structures, the National Assembly, and the media have all gradually learned to call upon NGO expertise. However, partnerships between civil society and the government are primarily project-based to take advantage of international or state funds. *Bulgaria's civil society rating remains unchanged at 2.75.*

Independent Media. The structures for media freedom in Bulgaria remained unchanged during 2005, but progress was seen in practice. Print media are independent from state interference but still not fully independent from economic and political special interests. Recently, the electronic media market has further developed and has also managed to avoid significant state influence and interference. However, the state-owned National Radio and National Television are influenced by the government and the state despite being nominally governed by the Council for Electronic Media. Although libel is still a criminal offense in the penal code, several libel cases were brought to court, and in most of them the courts interpreted the law in a manner that favored journalistic expression. In 2005, the court found not guilty a Romanian reporter charged in 2004 with illegal use of special surveillance devices for collecting information. *Despite libel remaining a criminal offense in the penal code, in actual practice the legal system protects journalists; therefore the independent media rating for Bulgaria improves from 3.50 to 3.25.*

Local Democratic Governance. Local self-government in Bulgaria is exercised at the municipal level, with councils and mayors being elected directly by secret ballot in universal and equal elections. Several cycles of such elections have taken place under the current Constitution, all free and fair, producing a multiplicity of local actors and coalitions. Local governments are empowered to resolve problems and make policies at the local level. They are responsible to the local public, and mechanisms for public control exist. Under a 2005 law – a major new development – municipalities have the right to issue debt to finance infrastructure and capital projects, yet they still have no right to set local tax rates, and their revenues are dominated by central government subsidies. The administrative capacity of municipalities remains limited. Although more reforms are needed, the process of actual decentralization is advancing slowly. *The structures for local governance have been improving steadily, and the landscape was additionally enhanced in 2005 by the municipalities' legal right to issue debt. Thus, Bulgaria's local democratic governance rating improves from 3.50 to 3.00.*

Judicial Framework and Independence. Judicial reform is the most serious and pressing problem for Bulgarian society. While the basic framework for an independent judiciary and political, human, and civil rights is in place, the way that judicial power is constituted and functions creates problems in its enforcement. Courts are slow, and the prosecution is ineffective, while the Supreme Judicial Council, the body of power in the judiciary, does not have the legal capacity to control and demand better performance from judges and prosecutors. In 2005, the most important development was the appointment of a national ombudsman. Social and political consensus on other needed changes has progressed significantly. *Owing to gradual improvement in the institutional environment, specifically the appointment of the national ombudsman, Bulgaria's rating for judicial framework and independence improves from 3.25 to 3.00.*

Corruption. In 2005, the regulatory and administrative framework for fighting corruption in Bulgaria continued to develop. A major development in this respect was the factual appointment of a national ombudsman. Economic freedom from excessive government taxes, bureaucratic regulations, and state involvement in the economy reduced opportunities for corruption. However, actual results in prosecuting and sentencing corrupt individuals, especially those at high levels of power, are modest. *Bulgaria's corruption rating improves from 4.00 to 3.75 owing to improvement in the institutional environment and in the measurements of economic freedom and government pressure on economic activity.*

Outlook for 2006. One major event will be of crucial significance for Bulgaria in 2006. In the middle of the year, the European Commission will decide whether to recommend a postponement of Bulgaria's membership in the EU until 2008. The decision will have an impact on the stability of the government and affect the overall development of political and economic processes within the country.

MAIN REPORT

National Democratic Governance

1997	1998	1999	2001	2002	2003	2004	2005	2006
n/a	n/a	n/a	n/a	n/a	n/a	n/a	3.50	3.00

Since the collapse of Communism in 1989, Bulgaria has succeeded in establishing a stable democratic system of governance. According to the Constitution adopted in 1991, Bulgaria is a parliamentary republic with a system of checks and balances guaranteed by the legislative, executive, and judicial branches.

However, the 1991 Constitution granted the judicial branch significant independence without sufficient accountability to the other branches and society as a whole. Over the last few years, the government has attempted to reform the judicial system, but with little success. In 2003, the Constitutional Court struck down a new law to reorganize the judicial system, declaring that only a Grand National Assembly[1] has the right to change the structure of state power. Over the last several years, judicial reform has been a key condition for Bulgaria's integration into the European Union, and some positive steps were made as a result. In September 2003, the Constitution was changed to reduce the immunity of magistrates. In October 2005, the Parliament adopted a new penal procedures code that reorganized the investigation service and moved most of its duties from the judiciary to the executive branch. These positive steps aside, there is still much to do to make the judicial branch more accountable and effective.

The Law on Access to Public Information, in force since 2000, provides Bulgarian citizens with the rights and instruments to obtain information about government activities. It includes a mechanism to initiate proceedings when these rights are violated. On the other hand, the Law on the Protection of Classified Information, in force since 2002 as a condition for Bulgaria to join NATO, is still often used by the government to refuse access to information. There were many cases where the court adjudicated access but the government used legal or administrative instruments to block it. According to the nonprofit Access to Information Program Association, many institutions, nongovernmental organizations (NGOs), and citizens have initiated cases charging violations of the law in 2004 and 2005, which indicates that Bulgarian civil society has recognized the right of access to public information as an important instrument to control the government.

Economic liberalization in Bulgaria has been a slow, difficult process. Most of the largest companies remained state owned until 1997 and maintained their monopoly market positions. After 1998, privatization efforts were intensified, and by 2005 state influence over the economy was much less significant relative to the private sector. As a whole, there are no significant government barriers to economic activity. Since 1998, Bulgaria's score in the annual Index of Economic Freedom produced by the Heritage Foundation has improved from 3.60 to 2.74 in 2005 (covering data up to 2004). The country is classified as "Mostly Free," with 1 representing the freest.

During Bulgaria's largely peaceful transition, no important political players have questioned democracy as the desired basis for the country's political system. Bulgarian citizens recognize the legitimacy of state institutions, and government authority extends over the full territory of the country. A considerable Turkish minority (about 8 percent of the population) lives predominantly separated from the majority but at the same time is well represented politically. However, in recent years public opinion polls have registered a growing discontent over the government's failure to raise Bulgaria's standard of living. In addition, the public's assessment of the political elite, mainstream political parties, and key democratic institutions has been mostly negative. Various 2004 and 2005 surveys suggested that public disaffection, combined with the growing political importance of crime prevention, might provoke the appearance of a possible "strong-arm" party representing nondemocratic ideas and sentiments.

In fact, shortly before the June 2005 general elections, an extremist political formation called the Attack coalition appeared and managed to pass the 4 percent parliamentary threshold. The Attack coalition is a typical antiestablishment voice relying on the traditional protest vote in Bulgaria and a negative anti-Turk and anti-Roma campaign. Although the Attack coalition does not question the current democratic system of Bulgaria, the ease with which its message won public popularity and a position in the Parliament is disturbing. This development has indicated to the mainstream political elite the pressing need to deepen the integration of some minority groups into Bulgarian society and address other social issues that have been ignored for the past decade.

Bulgaria has a unicameral National Assembly, the 240-member legislature, which is directly elected for a four-year term. Until 2001, the Bulgarian political system was dominated by two parties: on the left, the Bulgarian Socialist Party (BSP), successor to the former Communist Party; and on the right, the Union of Democratic Forces (UDF). Between 1995 and 2001, one of these parties had a majority in the Parliament, and the center of actual decision making was shifted from the National Assembly to the government and political party leadership. This bipolar episode ended with the victory of the National Movement Simeon II (NMSS) in the 2001 general elections, increasing the political importance of the National Assembly. This trend was reinforced after the June 2005 general elections when none of the major political parties won a majority.

The Bulgarian National Assembly receives sufficient resources to meet its constitutional responsibilities and has established strong committees and subcommittees. It also consults with a considerable number of experts and NGOs in the legislative process. Over the last 16 years, the National Assembly has established a tradition of transparency and accountability. Committee hearings and legislative sessions are open to the public and the media, and most bills are posted on the Parliament's Web site. All sessions are broadcast live on the parliamentary radio channel, and some are broadcast on television. Information about the government's decisions and activities can be found on its Web site and through the ministries' public relations offices. The work of the Council of Ministers is observable only through regular press conferences and through a daily bulletin published on the government's Web site.

None of the major political parties succeeded in winning enough votes in the June 2005 elections to form an independent government, resulting in the longest and most complicated negotiations since 1989. On August 16, the Parliament approved a government comprising the BSP, NMSS and Movement for Rights and Freedoms (MRF) after more than 50 days of intensive discussions and after the BSP and the MRF failed to elect a minority government in July. The current government is marked by a high level of distrust among the coalition members.

The BSP and the NMSS were fervent political opponents in the preelection campaign, exchanging allegations of corruption, lack of government experience, and so forth. In July, when the Socialists attempted to pass a minority government, they introduced a bill to restitute the estates of Simeon Saxe-Coburg-Gotha (then prime minister and leader of the NMSS), which had been taken by the Communist regime 50 years ago. This was done to force the NMSS parliamentary group to support the BSP/MRF government. However, there are serious differences in the governance programs of both parties, and it is still not clear how they will be harmonized. In terms of ideology, the NMSS supports a more liberal economic plan, while the BSP agenda is socially oriented. In terms of policy, the most obvious contradictions concern the BSP's preelection promises to investigate returning the Saxe-Coburg-Gotha property and deal with private companies to construct the Trakia motorway.

Many BSP members and followers do not trust the MRF because of the party's expedient political shifts and flexible commitments over the last 16 years. This was well illustrated in the second half of August when it appeared that the MRF would receive the right to appoint governors in six districts (in which Bulgarian Turks have no significant presence). Several BSP and NMSS local party structures officially protested, and some even took part in public protests against the government. Political tensions were calmed after the MRF decided to appoint ethnic Bulgarians as district governors. However, according to data from public opinion polls, negative perceptions of the MRF still dominate and are likely to create similar problems for the ruling coalition in the future.

Bulgaria's civil service is regulated by the Administration Law of 1998 and the Civil Service Law of 2000. These introduce competition for civil servant appointments, with selection based on the professional qualifications of candidates. The Civil Service Law has been amended several times since its adoption (most recently in August 2004) to improve the recruitment and performance of civil servants. Yet there is still room for improvement in the selection of candidates and the efficiency and quality of administrative services available to citizens. One of the official motives for the adoption of the Civil Service Law was its potential to curb corruption. Public surveys have indicated that civil servants are still perceived as one of the most corrupt professional groups in Bulgarian society.

The executive is subject to supervision by the legislature. Every Friday, ministers are obligated to answer questions raised by members of Parliament (MPs). In addition, governmental structures are obligated to provide information upon request on behalf of parliamentary committees or MPs. The executive is also supervised by the National Audit Office (NAO) through regular financial or performance audits of all governmental structures and agencies. The NAO has 11 members, elected and dismissed by the Parliament, to which it reports annually. For example, an NAO report in April 2004 resulted in the creation of an ad hoc parliamentary committee to investigate the spending of moneys received under various EU programs in the Ministry of Regional Development and Public Works.

Since military and security services are under the jurisdiction of the executive branch, they are also subject to parliamentary control. The Parliament discusses and approves their budgets as part of the total state budget. MPs also monitor the performance of different military and security structures operating under the Ministries of Defense and the Interior. At the same time, to avoid centralizing power in this key area, the government proposes, and the president approves, candidates for directors of the security services and the chief of staff of the Bulgarian armed forces. There is also judicial oversight of the military and security sector – a special prosecutorial body investigates military and security officials in Bulgaria.

The Bulgarian military and security services have gone through reforms during Bulgaria's NATO candidacy. The government established a modern system of democratic control over the armed forces and security services, based on clear organizational and functional structures, responsibility, and accountability. As a result, more information is currently available to the public and NGOs, especially about the activities of the Ministry of Defense. Several NGOs are working on problems in the security sector and civil control over the armed forces. Still, some problems exist regarding access to information. Often, military or security officials take advantage of the new Law on the Protection of Classified Information, adopted as part of the reform package required for membership in NATO. With a similar justification, some lawsuits against members of the military and security sector have been classified and closed to the public.

Electoral Process

1997	1998	1999	2001	2002	2003	2004	2005	2006
3.25	2.75	2.25	2.00	2.00	2.00	1.75	1.75	1.75

The Bulgarian Constitution provides all citizens over 18 with the right to vote by secret ballot in municipal, legislative, and presidential elections. Small glitches aside, elections since 1991 have been free, fair, and compliant with the law. The parliamentary elections in 2005 were also generally assessed as free by all political parties and observers. However, the government's decision to introduce a controversial elections lottery to increase voter turnout worsened the overall assessment of the elections. Several smaller opposition parties accused the ruling NMSS of abusing administrative power for narrow party benefits. According to some experts, the ruling party had direct political interest in higher voter turnout, and international observers defined this practice as unusual, emphasizing that it was unacceptable to publicly fund the lottery.

There is a strong history of different parties coming to power consecutively and peacefully in Bulgaria. None of the Bulgarian governments since 1990 has been reelected, suggesting that democratic procedures in Bulgaria are effective and no party has attempted or been successful in using its position in power to win elections. The last presidential election held in 2001 registered the first victory of a left-wing candidate, representing the BSP. The last local elections in October 2003 were the first in recent Bulgarian history to take place without international observers, an acknowledgment that Bulgaria has managed to establish a tradition of free and fair elections. Partial mayoral elections took place in October 2005 in the capital of Sofia and 10 other Bulgarian municipalities whose mayors had been elected to the Parliament in June.

The June 2005 general elections were won by the left-wing BSP, successor to the Bulgarian Communist Party, with 33.98 percent of the votes and 82 seats. After failing to elect a minority government in coalition with the ethnic Turkish party MRF in July, the BSP agreed to a government coalition with the previously ruling NMSS in August 2005. Since 1990, the party has been trying to move away from its Communist legacy and build a modern leftist organization. Following the 1997 crisis, when protesters took to the streets to force the BSP government's resignation, the BSP adopted Atlanticist ideas in its platforms. In 2003, it was accepted for full membership in the Socialist International, indicating international recognition of the party's reformation. Sergey Stanishev, a former BSP international affairs secretary, is the current party leader and was appointed prime minister after the June elections.

The previously ruling centrist NMSS won 21.83 percent of the votes and 53 parliamentary seats. Although declaring prior to the election that it would not enter into a coalition with the BSP, the NMSS had finally to agree on such an arrangement. This inconsistency was motivated largely by the need to maintain political stability for the sake of Bulgaria's forthcoming accession to the EU. The NMSS was created only three months before the 2001 general elections by Simeon Saxe-Coburg-Gotha, Bulgaria's former king, but succeeded in winning most of the votes and forming a government. Though lacking a clear political and ideological identity, the NMSS managed to complete its full four-year term in office. In 2003, the NMSS was admitted to the Liberal International, the world federation of liberal political parties, as an associate member.

The MRF achieved the best election results in its 15-year history, winning 14.07 percent of the votes and 34 seats. The party was established in 1990 as an organization representing the Turkish minority in Bulgaria and has been represented in the Parliament ever since. The MRF gained representation in the government for the first time in the 2001 elections and since then has continued to broaden its base of power. The party supports centrist political positions and is a member of the Liberal International. Ahmed Dogan has led the party since its establishment.

Though the June elections reflected the ongoing disintegration of the center-right political space, the major electoral surprise was the appearance of the extremist Attack coalition. It achieved unexpectedly good results and succeeded in entering the Parliament, leaving behind all major center-right political formations. The coalition won 8.93 percent of the votes and 21 parliamentary seats. The Attack coalition is a typical antiestablishment political formation benefiting from the traditional protest vote in Bulgaria. It was formed by Volen Siderov, a journalist who was editor in chief of *Democracia*, the official newspaper of the UDF in the 1990s. Siderov has produced the TV program *Ataka* for the last few years, and this launched his current political career as the Attack coalition's leader.

The Attack coalition's message is predominantly anti-Turk and anti-Roma, suggesting that the Bulgarian majority is threatened by the growing influence of Turkish and Roma minorities. The coalition accuses the entire political elite of corruption and betraying Bulgarian national interests. It also opposes Bulgarian membership in NATO and insists that European integration should strictly observe Bulgarian national interests. The new parliamentarians from the coalition include persons connected by their prior political failures, such as Petar Beron, deputy leader of the party, who left the UDF after it became known that he had worked for the Special Services during the Communist regime.

Bulgaria has a proportional electoral system, except in presidential and mayoral elections. The electoral system ensures fair polling and honest tabulation of ballots. Up to 2005, legislation for parliamentary elections provided all political parties, coalitions, and candidates with equal campaigning opportunities. However, amendments made to the electoral law in 2005 now require deposits to register MP candidates: 40,000 BGN (approximately US$25,500) for coalition candidates, 20,000 BGN (approximately US$12,750) for individual party candidates, and 5,000 BGN (approximately US$3,200) for individual candidates nominated by citizen committees. The rationale behind these amendments was to reduce the number of parties participating in the elections, since many do not represent actual social interests and only contribute to voter confusion. As a result, the number of registered parties and coalitions decreased from 65 in 2001 to 22 in 2005. Additionally, an integrated white ballot replaced the system of separate colored ballots. This is also considered a positive step, as the colored ballots were confusing to some of the voters and prompted endless quarrels among the parties over color choices.

The Bulgarian Constitution guarantees all citizens the right of free organization in political parties, movements, or other political entities. It bans the establishment of political organizations that act against national integrity and state sovereignty; that call for ethnic, national, or religious hostility; or that create secret military structures. Additionally, the Constitution prohibits the establishment of organizations that achieve their goals through violence. Until 2005, no substantial organizations used the ethnic card in their political rhetoric or practice. The Attack coalition was the first to use anti-minority statements in a campaign, and this became a reason for a broad alliance of NGOs to initiate a court case against the formation of the coalition and its leader in December 2005.

The political party registration process in Bulgaria is liberal and uncomplicated, and parties can appeal rejected applications. In October 2004, the Parliament passed on first reading a bill raising the number of members required for new party registration from 500 to 5,000. Although somewhat positive, the new law fell short of expected party funding reforms, including more transparent fund-raising and a reduction in the range of funding sources allowed by law. The Bulgarian electoral system is multiparty based, with mechanisms for the opposition to influence decision making. Twenty-two political parties and coalitions were registered to participate in the 2005 parliamentary elections, and 146 were registered for the 2003 local elections. The large number of parties participating in local elections reflects that local interests usually work through independent participation, a strategy that is less likely to succeed at the national level. According to data from the Alpha Research polling agency, 30 percent of participants in the 1999 local elections and 41 percent in the 2003 local elections voted for small or locally represented political entities.

In spite of the government's controversial efforts to increase participation in elections, voter turnout in June was 55 percent. During the last presidential elections, voter turnout was 42 percent in the first round and 55 percent in the second. Voter turnout in the 2003 local elections was around 50 percent in both rounds. In all cases, the numbers are lower than in previous elections. According to the Alpha Research agency,[2] approximately 6 percent of the population is currently affiliated with political parties. These data reflect a growing distance between voters and politicians, based on public disappointment with government reforms from both the Left and the Right. As a result, people are less confident that they can solve problems through political and collective instruments and turn instead to individual strategies. This also resulted in growing public support for extremist or nondemocratic political ideas represented by formations like the Attack coalition. Further, a rise in populism has been observed in the last several years. Boiko Borissov, a former chief secretary of the Home Ministry, was elected Sofia mayor in October 2005 on a campaign of antipolitical and populist sentiments; he enjoys wide support as a nonpolitical alternative to the mainstream Bulgarian political elite. In spite of the change in government, public opinion polls like Gallup BBSS Bulgaria[3] continued to measure worryingly low levels of trust in state institutions over 2005. About 18 percent of respondents stated they trusted the Parliament, and about 24 percent trusted the government.

The general legislative framework in Bulgaria provides all minority groups with essential political rights and participation in the political process. Although MRF bylaws state that members are welcome regardless of their ethnicity or religion, the party essentially represents the interests of Bulgarian Turks. As part of the current governing coalition, this Turkish minority party is well represented at all levels of government. In contrast, the Roma minority is still poorly represented in government structures, with some exceptions at the municipal level. The general hypothesis is that the political system discriminates against the Roma minority and impedes its political expression. Equally important, however, is the fact that a political party consolidating Roma interests and representing them at the national level still does not exist, even though there have been attempts to create one.

No particular businesses or other interests interfere directly in electoral procedures. However, there are suspicions that powerful economic interests influence the decision-making process by lobbying political parties or providing illicit party financing. A scandal exploded at the start of 2004 when it became clear that some Bulgarian companies close to the BSP had received oil gifts from the former Iraqi regime of Saddam Hussein. There are suspicions that in fact the oil gifts were destined for the BSP in return for political support of the Iraqi regime. In October 2005, the BSP was mentioned in the UN's Independent Inquiry Committee final report[4] on the oil-for-food investigation. BSP leadership denied the allegations and claimed the party never profited from oil deals with the former Iraqi regime.

Civil Society

1997	1998	1999	2001	2002	2003	2004	2005	2006
4.00	3.75	3.75	3.50	3.25	3.25	3.00	2.75	2.75

The Bulgarian Constitution guarantees citizens the right to organize freely in associations, movements, societies, or other nonprofit organizations. There have been no administrative or other barriers to NGOs over the last 16 years, nor do they experience significant state or other influence on their activities, which are regulated by the Noneconomic Purpose Legal Entities Law.

The 2005 Bulgarian Statistical Register indicates that there are 22,336 registered nonprofit organizations in the country. Of these, 4,010 are foundations, 18,305 are societies, and 51 are local branches of international nonprofits. The number of groups actually active is not known, but according to the Central Register for Nonprofit Legal Entities for 2005, there are 4,145 registered nonprofit organizations acting for public benefit. Both private and public benefit NGOs are focused on crucial areas of Bulgarian society, including human rights, minority issues, health care, education, women's issues, charity work, public policy, the environment, culture, science, social services, information technology, religion, sports, and business development. There are no clear statistics on volunteerism in Bulgaria.

The growth of civil society in Bulgaria after 1989 goes hand in hand with the emergence of programs and grants for NGO development. The sector was formed with a top-down approach led by donors, not the Bulgarian citizens. According to a 2005 *Civil Society Without the Citizens* report by Balkan Assist, a Bulgarian nonprofit association, this is the main reason Bulgarian NGOs have low levels of citizen involvement and are financially dependent on foreign donors. On the other hand, a positive result of the donor-driven emergence of Bulgarian NGOs is their well-developed instructional framework, human capital, and networking capacity. One of the major shortcomings of Bulgarian NGOs is their inability to involve the community in their decision making. NGOs expect resources from the central and local governments, but they are doing little to empower their own target groups within the community. Thus, citizen participation in civil society boils down mainly to the role of passive beneficiary.

All ethnic groups, including Turks, Roma, Muslims, Armenians, and Jews, have their own NGOs engaged in a variety of civic activities. Although the Roma ethnic minority is not represented in government, some Roma NGOs function as political discussion clubs and proto-parties. There are around 150 functioning Roma NGOs throughout the country, and the number of registered Roma groups is at least three times greater. Churches engage in charitable activities by distributing aid and creating local networks that assist the elderly and children. Organizations of Muslim, Catholic, and Protestant communities are among the most dynamic in the country. Although the Orthodox Church remains the most influential in Bulgaria, only a small percentage of the population attends services regularly. Anti-liberal nonprofit institutions are constitutionally banned, and no anti-liberal NGOs are officially registered. Several informal organizations could be considered anti-liberal, but they have a weak public influence.

NGO registration is inexpensive and takes approximately one month to complete. By law, all NGOs that work for public benefit are listed in a transparent public document known as the Central Register for Nonprofit Legal Entities. Groups are allowed to engage in for-profit activities under certain conditions, and all groups are required to conduct annual audits. The law distinguishes between NGOs acting for public benefit and those that act for private benefit. Public NGOs are not obliged to pay taxes on their funding resources, but they must be listed and report their activities annually in the Central Register. According to existing legislation, NGOs are allowed to carry out for-profit activities, provided the work does not clash with their stated organizational aims and is registered separately. Groups must pay normal taxes on all such for-profit work, and they must invest all net profits in their main activities.

Unfortunately, even though the Corporate Taxation Law of 1997 instituted various tax incentives, these have not induced businesses to give money to NGOs. The state usually funds some specific NGOs in the area of social services, but most NGOs rely on funding from foreign sources. Regrettably, a significant number of large foreign NGOs and their donors intend to withdraw from Bulgaria in the next few years, which could cause funding problems for some organizations. According to Balkan Assist, more than 80 percent of funding for local NGOs comes from abroad.

In 2001, a permanent parliamentary Committee on the Problems of Civil Society was created to serve as a bridge between civil society and the Parliament. This reflects the government's changing attitudes toward the NGO sector. The committee's public council includes 21 members representing 28 NGOs. Other parliamentary committees recruit NGO experts as advisers for public hearings on issues of national importance. In spite of this positive practice, no formal mechanism exists for civil society to consult in the development of legislation. The partnership between the media and NGOs has become reliable and stable. The government also included NGOs in preparing projects and monitoring the spending of financial assistance received through EU preaccession and accession programs. However, partnerships between civil society and the government continue to work primarily on a project-based approach. As noted by Balkan Assist, interaction between the government and civil society is most often built on the "opportunistic" goal of using financial resources from international or domestic government funders.

The activities of interest groups are largely unregulated. Bulgarian think tanks have advocated for increased transparency and decreased clientelism and repeatedly urge the Parliament to legalize and regulate lobbying. As a result, the Committee on the Problems of Civil Society launched a bill in the middle of 2002 calling for the registration of lobbyists and the publicizing of lobbying activities. The bill is still under consideration.

Bulgaria has three major independent trade unions. Participation is free, and the state respects the right of workers to form their own organizations. Trade unions take part along with the government and employers in the Tripartite Commission for Negotiations on various issues. The rights of workers to engage in collective bargaining and to strike are protected by law. There is also a growing number of farmers' groups and small-business associations. Balkan Assist's *Civil Society Without the Citizens* report concluded that Bulgarian civil society has a limited impact on the behavior of large businesses. People are often afraid to hold companies responsible for violations of their rights or failures to meet obligations. The activity of trade unions is focused mostly on bargaining with the government for common social policies rather than protecting the labor rights of employees in private companies.

Bulgaria's education system is largely free of political influence and propaganda. The most serious problems facing Bulgarian students are the continuous revisions in educational requirements imposed by the Ministry of Education, such as changes in the required number of years of schooling and mandatory comprehensive examinations. Education reform has proved to be fairly difficult and unpopular. According to data from the National Statistical Institute, there are 6,511 educational institutions in Bulgaria, including 3,301 child care centers, 3,157 primary and secondary schools, and 53 colleges and universities. Of these, 128 are privately owned, including 26 child care centers, 99 primary and secondary schools, and 16 colleges and universities.

Independent Media

1997	1998	1999	2001	2002	2003	2004	2005	2006
3.75	3.50	3.50	3.25	3.25	3.50	3.50	3.50	3.25

The Bulgarian Constitution proclaims that media are free and shall not be subject to censorship. An injunction on or confiscation of printed matter or other media formats is allowed only after a court decision. Legal provisions concerning media freedom are further developed in legislation. The right of citizens to seek, obtain, and disseminate information is also guaranteed by the Constitution and the Law on Access to Public Information.

There is still no specific legislation protecting journalists from victimization by state or nonstate actors. Libel, which can include criticizing government officials, is a criminal offense in the penal code. Both prosecutors and individual citizens can bring libel charges, with penalties running as high as US$6,400. Since the penal code was amended in 2000, a number of cases have been brought, but in most of them the courts have interpreted the law in a manner that has favored journalistic expression, with only a few convictions. However, this creates an atmosphere that might lead to self-censorship. In November 2004, the Office of the Prosecutor filed charges of illegal use of surveillance devices against a Romanian reporter investigating customs bribery on the Danube border; in 2005, the court found the Romanian reporter not guilty. Another similar case was the Sofia prosecutor's preliminary investigation of the BBC journalists who created the scandalous film *Buying the Games*. The film accused former Bulgarian International Olympic Committee member Ivan Slavkov of corruption.

In general, Bulgarian media are independent of the state, and there is free competition among different outlets and viewpoints. But it is not certain whether the media are independent of special interests, either political or economic. Print media have successfully emancipated themselves from governmental control; electronic media also manage to avoid significant state influence and interference. However, the state-owned National Radio and National Television are still heavily controlled by the state, although they are directly governed by the Council for Electronic Media (CEM). The CEM is responsible for selecting directors of the National Radio and National Television as well as overseeing their performance. The council's nine members are appointed by the National Assembly and the president. Although the CEM is not under government orders, the parliamentary majority approves its budget. Throughout its existence, the council has not managed to establish a reputation of political independence.

With the exception of a few local newspapers and the official *State Gazette*, all print media in Bulgaria are privately owned. Overall, there are more than 500 newspapers and magazines. At the end of 2005, the nation's largest newspapers with the highest levels of circulation were *Troud*, *24 Hours*, *Standard*, *Monitor*, *Sega*, *Novinar*, *Douma*, *Dnevnik*, and *Capital* (weekly). Their circulation numbers are a trade secret. *Troud* and *24 Hours*, which enjoy the highest circulation,[5] are owned by the German publishing group Westdeutsche Allgemeine Zeitung (WAZ). The newspaper market includes many other dailies, guaranteeing that readers have a broad selection of information sources and points of view.

The radio business as a whole has experienced radical change over the last six to seven years. In 2003, there were 89 radio stations; of these, 11 provide national coverage, and only 1 is state owned. There are also 77 local radio stations. As for television, there are 98 stations in the country; 3 reach national audiences through wireless broadcasting, only 1 is state owned, and the rest are cable networks.

The public's interest in politics has declined over the last few years, and this has resulted in a decrease in circulation of the main newspapers, especially those with ties to a party. Only the BSP-affiliated *Douma* maintains any public significance. Low public interest in newspapers has led to their increased commercialization. It is often suspected that newspapers are used by different economic players to pursue financial or political interests. The largest private newspapers are printed by IPK Rodina, the state-owned print house. In some cases, this permits a degree of government interference. However, during the last few years this has not resulted in any direct political pressure. There are a number of private distribution networks as well.

Among Bulgaria's most important journalistic associations are the Media Coalition and the Free Speech Civil Forum Association. The Journalists Union, a holdover from the Communist period, is trying to reform its image. More than half of the journalists in Bulgaria are women. The publishers of the biggest newspapers are united in their own organizations, such as the Union of Newspaper Publishers. Of the few NGOs that work on media problems, the most important is the Media Development Center, which provides journalists with training and legal advice.

In November 2004, journalists from 160 national and regional press and electronic/online media outlets signed the Bulgarian media code of ethics. The code includes standards regarding the use of information by unidentified sources, the preliminary nondisclosure of a source's identity, respect of personal information, and nonpublication of children's personal pictures (unless of public interest). Adopting the code of ethics demonstrated that Bulgarian media have matured enough to assume self-regulation of their activities.

The Internet in Bulgaria is free of regulation and restrictions for Web sites and private citizens, and access is easy and inexpensive. Over the last few years, the number of Bulgarian Web sites has grown significantly, with a subsequent enhancement of quality and the availability of a broader range of opinions. According to data reported by the Alpha Research polling agency in February 2005, the percentage of adult Bulgarians who have access to the Internet has increased over the last year to 22 percent.

Local Democratic Governance

1997	1998	1999	2001	2002	2003	2004	2005	2006
n/a	n/a	n/a	n/a	n/a	n/a	n/a	3.50	3.00

The basic framework for democratic local self-government is provided in Chapter 7 of the Bulgarian Constitution. It envisages the municipality as the basic unit of local self-government, the election of municipal councils and mayors, and the right of municipalities to own property and maintain budgets. Municipalities are defined as legal entities in which local democracy can work directly, through referendums or general assemblies of citizens. Local democratic governance in Bulgaria is elaborated in more detail in numerous normative laws, the more important being the Local Self-Government and Local Administration Law of 2002 (substituting the law of 1991), the Local Elections Law of 1995, the Local Taxes and Fees Law of 1997, and the Municipal Debt Law of 2005.

In Bulgaria, the process of decentralizing powers and responsibilities to local governments is ongoing. The above-mentioned legislation generally allows municipalities to have competences in designing, institutionalizing, and implementing solutions to problems affecting their citizens. A major new development is the April 2005 Municipal Debt Law, which regulates the opportunity of municipalities to issue debt for financing infrastructure and other capital projects. This instrument will increase the municipalities' access to resources.

Dialogue between the local and national levels of governance is well structured in the legislative branch (a specific standing parliamentary Committee on Local Governance Matters), in the executive branch (the National Association of Municipalities in the Republic of Bulgaria, NAMRB), and through numerous non-profit organizations devoted to local government issues and advocacy. In practice, the NAMRB is consulted regularly by the central government on various issues, proposals, and policies related to local governance.

At present, almost no municipality in Bulgaria has a council with a single party majority, and in most cases even the two largest party groups cannot form a majority in the municipal councils, leading to a multiplicity of strictly locally defined and focused coalitions throughout the country. In this setting, it is difficult for any single agenda – be it that of a national party, the central authorities, or a national or local economic group – to dominate voters' choices and sentiments or the actions of the local government.

Local government bodies in Bulgaria are open to citizens regardless of their gender or ethnic (or other) status, and there are many examples of women mayors (at the 2003 local elections, 19 women were elected as municipal mayors out of 263 municipalities) and different ethnic groups holding or being part of majorities in municipal councils. Citizens and civic society organizations are fully entitled to address the local authorities, and such practices have developed to some extent throughout the country. Also, there is a lively set of local and regional press and electronic media (mostly radio) focusing on local governance and the local public. A prime example of the accessibility of local power to civil society representatives is the newly elected mayor of Sofia, who was put on the ballot by a committee of citizens, did not represent any party, and explicitly avoided party endorsements. The new mayor campaigned against four strong party candidates and spent significantly less campaign money than any other candidate.

Municipal governments have four sources of revenue: central budget subsidies, local taxes and fees, municipal property, and issuance of debt. The Constitution requires the Parliament to approve all taxes and tax rates, including at the local level. Data from the NAMRB indicate that between 7 and 10 percent of all tax revenues are devoted strictly to local governments. Once the municipalities receive their subsidies from the central government, they have complete control over their own budgets. The only exception applies to money received for targeted national programs. Implementation of the government's medium-term fiscal decentralization program continued in 2005, and already texts amending the Constitution regarding the ability of municipalities to define local tax rates are being discussed in a parliamentary working group. However, any actual changes are still pending. The Municipal Debt Law has increased the access of municipalities to resources, but there is still a lack of sufficient resources to address local problems and provide quality public services. This situation makes some local governments dependent on a few strategic local economic actors. Additionally, local governments feel more pressure to be on good terms with the central government rather than accountable to the local public. Even though there are mechanisms for transparency, as well as public and media control over local authorities, these measures are not particularly effective at this stage of Bulgarian local government reform.

Judicial Framework and Independence

1997	1998	1999	2001	2002	2003	2004	2005	2006
4.25	3.75	3.50	3.50	3.50	3.50	3.25	3.25	3.00

The Bulgarian Constitution has provisions for protecting political, civil, and human rights. These include explicit texts securing freedom of expression, of association, and of religious beliefs, as well as the rights to privacy, property and inheritance, and economic initiative and enterprise. The abuse of monopoly power is also banned. In practice, the protection of these rights by the state is generally effective, but there is discrimination against the Roma minority and certain religious beliefs. An example of the latter was the banning of a prominent international religious leader[6] from entering the country under the pretext of "national security" in the fall of 2005.

The legislature adopts the country's supreme laws, but implementing them falls to the executive branch. The judiciary, whose main body of power is the Supreme Judicial Council (SJC), provides a check on both the legislature and the executive. The Bulgarian Constitution is applied directly by the Constitutional Court, which has established itself as a legitimate, independent, and impartial body.

However, the Bulgarian public does not perceive the law as applying equally for all. Public opinion polls indicate a low level of trust in the judiciary and the belief that some groups, such as politicians and the wealthy, get better treatment and are in a position to abuse the law, which is allowed by existing imbalances in the judiciary's power structure. Adjudication in Bulgaria is slow and inconsistent.

There were no major changes in the Bulgarian penal code in 2005, with the only notable development being the introduction of more severe treatment for a long list of public officials accused of felony. Bulgarian criminal law ensures a presumption of innocence until proven guilty and provides for fair and public trials. The defense receives a full opportunity to examine evidence, develop a case, and appeal decisions. Bulgaria has sufficient guarantees against search without warrant and arbitrary arrest. However, once persons are arrested, their rights are not sufficiently secure. In late 2005, there was a controversial case involving a prominent drug dealer who died during arrest. The police officers are under investigation for the use of excessive force, and the case is still pending.

Judges in Bulgaria are appointed by the SJC. Amendments in the Judicial System Law, in force since April 2004, regulate the appointment of judges. The newly created Attestations and Proposals Committees under the SJC are empowered to appoint and dismiss administrative positions within the judiciary. The amended Judicial System Law details rules for appointing administrators. However, dubious practices in appointing judges continue. A prominent example is the policy of the SJC to use a loophole in the legislation to appoint junior judges without the legally required concourse. It is publicly known that children and relatives of prominent members of the judiciary have been appointed in this manner.

In general, Bulgarian court decisions are inconsistently fair and impartial. There are reports about attempts to influence courts, as well as actual corruption. Members of the judiciary are immune from prosecution except for serious crimes and only then with the permission of the SJC, less than half of whose members are appointed by the Parliament. The judiciary reviews laws of the executive and legislative branches on a regular basis.

The authority of the courts is recognized, and judicial decisions are enforced effectively. However, the enforcement process is slow. New legislation adopted in the spring of 2005 allows private firms, along with court clerks, to enforce court decisions, and so far there is a consensus among all parties that this will speed up the process and make it more reliable and transparent.

A notable change in 2005 is the appointment of a national ombudsman under the 2004 Ombudsman Law, which affects Bulgarian citizens' access to the justice system. With this development, citizens have one more major tool to influence public decision making, effectively report corruption, and obtain information from the government.

Corruption

1997	1998	1999	2001	2002	2003	2004	2005	2006
n/a	n/a	4.75	4.75	4.50	4.25	4.25	4.00	3.75

The regulatory and administrative framework for fighting corruption in Bulgaria has reached a point where further institutional change seems less expedient than actual implementation and enforcement. As of March 2005, the National Strategy for Combating Corruption now includes the preparation of an ethical code of conduct for ministers and political appointees at the highest level, as well as the creation of a joint council of the executive and the private business sector. The goal is to establish a public-private partnership to curb corrupt practices. As of the end of

2005, however, the actual adoption of the ethical code and establishment of the joint public-private council are still pending. Also important is the institutionalization of the national ombudsman to hear complaints and initiate investigations of corruption.

The Bulgarian economy remains generally free from excessive state involvement. Bulgaria is recognized as a functioning market economy, with the private sector producing close to 80 percent of the gross value added and providing about 75 percent of the country's employment. About 90 percent of all state assets subject to privatization have been privatized. While the state redistributes a relatively high 40 to 42 percent of national income, its budget is balanced and has actually generated surpluses in 2004 and 2005 (projected). The structure of state revenues relies mostly on nondistortionary indirect taxes, and the most distorting direct tax – social security contributions – is expected to decrease significantly in 2006. In 2005, the Bulgarian economy moved from the "Mostly Unfree" into the "Mostly Free" category in the Heritage Foundation's Index of Economic Freedom,[7] with the scores on fiscal burden and government intervention ranking better than its overall score. In the Fraser Institute's Economic Freedom in the World index,[8] Bulgaria has improved its 2005 score (based on 2003 data) to 6.3 on a scale where 10 represents maximum freedom.

The Bulgarian branch of Transparency International indicates[9] that after a period of marked improvement between 1998 and 2002, corruption perceptions seem to have stagnated at a relatively moderate level over the last five years. Bulgaria's 2005 score on the index was 4.0, on a scale ranging between 10 (highly clean) and 0 (highly corrupt). Administrative pressure on economic activity in Bulgaria has continued to decrease slowly over 2005, owing mainly to the introduction of private entrepreneurship and the Private Judicial Enforcement Law, which came into force September 2005. The goal of the law is to speed up the enforcement of judicial decisions and limit incentives for corruption in the system. The law is expected to improve the contract enforcement environment. However, many other opportunities for corruption remain, especially in tax collection, licensing regimes, registration of firms, and safety and other regulations, as well as in public procurement tenders. Measures to introduce arbitrary checks by tax authorities and improve the speed and transparency of business registration are coming but have yet to become law.

Some clouding remains. The NMSS carried a negative legacy from its coalition governance with the MRF. The Turkish party has often used political blackmail over the last four years, most recently in the previous government's last attempt to privatize the state-owned tobacco monopoly Bulgartabac Holding. Most producers of raw tobacco are ethnic Turks and political supporters of the MRF. Therefore, the movement has direct political interest in Bulgartabac to remain state owned in order to retain political control over its voters. As a partner in the ruling coalition over the last four years, the MRF has been able to exercise control over Bulgarian ethnic Turks mainly through guaranteeing higher minimum raw tobacco prices, which are set by the government. In January 2005, Deputy Prime Minister and

Minister of the Economy Lidia Shuleva announced a deal to sell Bulgartabac to British American Tobacco (BAT). The MRF withdrew its support, claiming that the deal harmed national interests, and threatened to support a no-confidence vote in the Parliament if the deal was completed. BAT promptly withdrew from the negotiations, and days later Shuleva lost her government post.

The Civil Service Law of 2000 limits the ability of civil servants to engage in private economic activities. At higher levels of government, there is no such legal requirement, but limitations are imposed by the public solely through elections and the media and are also expected to be a part of the forthcoming ethical code for high-level government figures. The actual involvement of government officials in private economic activities is difficult to assess. There have been no major public or media exposures of illicit activities, suggesting these are limited.

All state bodies are obliged under the Administration Law, the Public Servants Law, and the Public Procurement Law to publicize job openings and procurement contracts and to use concourses for selection. Despite relatively adequate regulatory texts, the public seems convinced that selections are based on personal connections and clientele/business relations rather than merit.

Financial disclosure by state officials in Bulgaria is conducted via the Public Register within the National Audit Office under the Publicity of Personal Property of High Government Officials in the Republic of Bulgaria Law. The Public Register is accessible to the public through guaranteed media access. In most cases, public officials submit the required declarations on time, but the practice of non-submission by some MPs, who cannot be prosecuted, continues.

The Bulgarian state still has a limited capacity to effectively prevent, investigate, and prosecute corruption. Deficiencies in the legal system, rather than a lack of political will, are largely to blame. However, in the course of 2005 the judicial system has acted to prosecute corruption and check the executive branch for non-transparent actions. A prime example is the prosecution of the acting mayor of Sofia – who was later elected to the Parliament – for several deals involving municipal property. Another example is the Supreme Administrative Court's intervention into the concession for the construction and exploitation of the Trakia motorway.

Bulgarian media feel free to report corruption, and hundreds of stories alleging corruption appear every month. The media's heavy spin and lack of consistent investigation casts doubts on the seriousness of most of these allegations. As a result, while media are indeed instrumental in exposing cases of corruption, they may also be nurturing public perception of the widespread nature of the problem. In general, the Bulgarian public is highly sensitive to the issue of corruption, and there is a significant level of intolerance for it. Corruption is regularly among the top concerns in national polls and was an important aspect of the campaigns for both the Parliament and several mayorships in 2005. A prime example of civil society activism against corruption was the reaction to the previously mentioned Trakia concession deal. Civil society groups did cost-benefit analyses and undertook legal actions that ultimately put the deal under the supervision of the Supreme Administrative Court, where a decision is still pending.

Ivan Krastev is chairman of the Center for Liberal Strategies (CLS), a nonprofit think tank based in Sofia, Bulgaria. Rashko Dorosiev is project director and political analyst at CLS. Georgy Ganev is program director for economic research at CLS.

---

[1] Under the 1991 Constitution in Bulgaria there are two types of National Assemblies: Ordinary and Grand. A Grand National Assembly is elected in separate elections, has more deputies than an Ordinary one, and is entitled to change the constitution, where the texts concerning the form of government can be changed only by a Grand Assembly and not by an Ordinary one.

[2] Average data from the regular surveys of Alpha Research agency during 2005. Source: http://www.aresearch.org/

3 Source: http://www.gallup-bbss.com

[4] Independent Inquiry Committee into the United Nations Oil-for-Food Programme, Report on the Manipulation of the Oil-for-Food Programme (27 October 2005), Committee Tables, Table III, p. 16-17. Available at http://www.iic-offp.org/story27oct05.htm

[5] According to private communication between authors and headquarters of the major newspapers.

[6] The Reverend Sun Myung Moon of the Unification Church.

[7] Marc Miles, Kim Holmes, and Mary Anastasia O'Grady, 2006 Index of Economic Freedom(The Heritage Foundation and The Wall Street Journal, 2006), 121.

[8] James Gwartney, and Robert Lawson, Economic Freedom of the World 2005 Annual Report (The Fraser Institute, 2005), 61.

[9] Data can be found at http://www.transparency-bg.org.

Croatia

Capital:	Zagreb
Population:	4.4 million
GNI/capita:	$6,820
Ethnic Groups:	Croat (89.6%), Serb (4.5%), Bosniak (0.5%), Hungarian (0.4%), Slovene (0.3%), Czech (0.2%), Roma (0.2%), Albanian (0.1%), Montenegrin (0.1%), others (4.1%)

Nations in Transit Ratings and Averaged Scores

	1997	1998	1999	2001	2002	2003	2004	2005	2006
Electoral Process	4.00	4.25	4.25	3.25	3.25	3.25	3.25	3.00	3.25
Civil Society	3.50	3.50	3.50	2.75	2.75	3.00	3.00	3.00	2.75
Independent Media	4.75	4.75	5.00	3.50	3.50	3.75	3.75	3.75	3.75
Governance *	4.00	4.00	4.00	3.50	3.50	3.75	3.75	n/a	n/a
National Democratic Governance	n/a	n/a	n/a	n/a	n/a	n/a	n/a	3.50	3.50
Local Democratic Governance	n/a	n/a	n/a	n/a	n/a	n/a	n/a	3.75	3.75
Judicial Framework and Independence	4.75	4.75	4.75	3.75	3.75	4.25	4.50	4.50	4.25
Corruption	n/a	n/a	5.25	4.50	4.50	4.75	4.75	4.75	4.75
Democracy Score	4.20	4.25	4.46	3.54	3.54	3.79	3.83	3.75	3.64

* With the 2005 edition, Freedom House introduced seperate analysis and ratings for national democratic governance and local democratic governance to provide readers with more detailed and nuanced analysis of these two important subjects.

NOTE: The ratings reflect the consensus of Freedom House, its academic advisers, and the author of this report. The opinions expressed in this report are those of the author. The ratings are based on a scale of 1 to 7, with 1 representing the highest level of democratic progress and 7 the lowest. The Democracy Score is an average of ratings for the categories tracked in a given year.

The economic and social data on this page were taken from the following sources:
GNI/capita, Population: *World Development Indicators 2006* (Washington, D.C.: World Bank, 2006).
Ethnic Groups: *CIA World Factbook 2006* (Washington, D.C.: Central Intelligence Agency, 2006).

EXECUTIVE SUMMARY

Croatia's movement toward a democratic society with stable and independent state institutions is an ongoing transformation unfolding under specific conditions. Along with a change of regime and typical transitional problems – such as highly bureaucratized state institutions, an inefficient legal system, a lack of social security, and high unemployment; these have been heightened by Croatia's wartime legacies. Throughout the 1990s, political power was centralized in the hands of former president Franjo Tudjman and his party, the Croatian Democratic Union (HDZ). Despite a declarative multiparty system and regular elections that the Organization for Security and Cooperation in Europe (OSCE) deemed "free but not fair," political and social life was charged with a strong current of nationalism. Tudjman ruled by extra-constitutional methods and institutions throughout the decade. Numerous accusations of a lack of respect for human liberties and rights during his rule saw Croatia isolated and outside the scope of European integration processes.

The turnaround year was 2000, when, following Tudjman's death, the doors were opened to political change. In January 2000, Croatia got its first coalition government, led by the center-left Social Democratic Party (SDP), which resolutely announced it would deal with the failings of the HDZ regime that preceded it. A month later, Stjepan Mesic took office as president, and his powers were significantly reduced by subsequent constitutional amendments. The semipresidential system of government was replaced by the parliamentary system. Just a few months later, in the spring of 2001, the House of Counties was dissolved, making the Croatian Parliament a unicameral body. The new Croatian leadership immediately showed determination to entrench democratic values and made progress on the main outstanding political questions, particularly minority rights and securing an adequate legal and organizational framework for independent media. Membership in the European Union (EU) has been declared a strategic goal, with Brussels rewarding implemented reforms by signing a Stabilization and Association Agreement with Croatia's government in the capital city of Zagreb in 2001.

The HDZ government, which after a close contest in the 2003 parliamentary elections defeated the SDP ruling coalition, has continued to follow the European agenda. In regaining power, the HDZ won the support of the Croatian Social-Liberal Party, the Democratic Center, the Croatian Pensioners Party (HSU), and national minority representatives (including Serbs, for the first time since 1990). Prime Minister Ivo Sanader made it clear that the HDZ has embraced a new political profile and transformed itself into a modern European conservative party. Sanader also declared that the government was determined to cooperate fully with

The Hague-based International Criminal Tribunal for the Former Yugoslavia (ICTY), thus clearly distancing himself from the right-wing nationalist discourse and breaking away from the HDZ's past image as a war crimes instigator and primary protector of war criminals.

Meeting all obligations in cooperation with the ICTY was a prerequisite to starting negotiations for Croatia's EU membership. The government's failure to locate and arrest General Ante Gotovina – who had been declared one of The Hague's most wanted fugitives, along with Ratko Mladic and Radovan Karadzic – prompted the EU to delay membership talks with Croatia in March 2005. A green light for the start of talks came finally in October 2005, after The Hague's chief prosecutor Carla del Ponte informed European ministers she was satisfied with the cooperation from Croatia. Negotiations were launched just hours after those with Turkey began, in an apparent quid pro quo deal after Austria agreed to back off from its opposition to full membership for a large Muslim country (Turkey) in exchange for progress for neighboring Croatia. In December 2005, Gotovina was finally located and arrested in the Canary Islands.

Early reports from the negotiations show that Croatia's government is well prepared and will probably be able to complete accession talks in a relatively short period, in order to meet economic and political criteria by 2009. However, whether Croatia will indeed be invited to join the EU by that time remains uncertain owing to developments in the EU, especially the failure to adopt the European Constitution and enlargement fatigue.

National Democratic Governance. Croatia has a parliamentary system of government and stable democratic institutions that function properly, respecting the limits of their competences and cooperating with one another. Owing to progress achieved in cooperating with The Hague tribunal, the only critical issue in relations with the EU, accession negotiations with the EU were at last started in October 2005. A seven-month postponement was caused by an assessment that the government was not doing enough to locate and extradite one of the most wanted war crimes indictees, General Ante Gotovina. Gotovina was ultimately arrested in December in the Canary Islands. The HDZ government believes it is possible to finish the negotiations in two and a half to three years. Judiciary reform, the return of refugees, and respect of minority rights are some of the main challenges in Croatia's process to join the European bloc. Also among expectations from Brussels is public administration reform, but it appears that the incumbent government does not have a clear strategy to reduce the state apparatus and create an efficient administration. Limited progress has been made by adopting the Law on the Civil Service in July 2005. Since most of its provisions enter into force in January 2006, it remains to be seen to what degree its implementation will lead to a professional and transparent public administration. *Croatia's rating for national democratic governance remains at 3.50. Though accession talks have begun, confirming the maturity and stability of Croatia's political system, real progress is expected next year, when the process of meeting the acquis communautaire will show concrete results.*

Electoral Process. Two elections held in 2005, the presidential in January and local government in May, revealed certain deficits of the electoral procedure – namely, shortcomings in the management of voter lists. Incumbent president Stjepan Mesic won in a runoff (round two) by a high margin against HDZ ruling party candidate and Deputy Prime Minister Jadranka Kosor (66 to 34 percent). Before and even after the local elections, there was a serious lack of clarity regarding the allocation of reserved seats for minority representatives. Instead of taking into account updated voter lists, the government used the 2001 census list, thus neglecting changes registered in certain local units, particularly in return areas. Since parties won the necessary absolute majority in only a few places, the formation of local governments depended primarily on postelection negotiations between the HDZ (on one side), the SDP (on the other), and smaller parties such as the Croatian Party of Rights and the HSU. To prevent drawn-out manipulation of future election results, in September 2005 the government sent the Parliament a draft law to establish the direct election of mayors and county prefects. *Croatia's electoral process rating worsens from 3.00 to 3.25 owing to shortcomings in the management of voter lists.*

Civil Society. Nongovernmental organizations (NGOs) continue to grow and diversify, and the current number stands at 27,955. There is still work to be done to consolidate the legislative framework for civil society, and NGO influence on government policy remains limited. Nevertheless, there are positive examples, the most notable in response to the Druzba-Adria pipeline project that would transport Russian oil to the Adriatic Sea and from there to global markets. The project was abandoned through the continuous efforts of environmental NGOs to focus attention on the existence of environmental hazards. Many NGOs criticized the functioning of the National Foundation for Civil Society Development, accusing it of biased and nontransparent procedures in distributing funds to civil associations. *The rating for civil society improves from 3.00 to 2.75 owing to its continued growth and greater public impact.*

Independent Media. Media in Croatia are subject to free market rules. There are 19 television stations, 143 radio stations, 11 dailies, and several hundred magazines, some of which have substantial circulation while others struggle to survive in an uncertain market. The state remains the biggest media owner. Given that most local broadcasters are at least partially owned by or depend on the financial support of local authorities, they remain vulnerable to political pressure. The legal regulation of libel is still not satisfactory. Although changes to the criminal code eased the threat of prosecution, they fell short of full decriminalization. Three journalists received suspended prison sentences for libel in 2005. Although the law provides for freedom of the press, politicians frequently attempted to influence HTV public television. *Croatia's independent media rating remains at 3.75.*

Local Democratic Governance. Croatia has about 550 local (cities and municipalities) and 20 regional units (counties). The capital, Zagreb, has both city and county status. Decentralization planned in the government 2000–2004 program has been slower than originally foreseen. Though local self-government units gained greater competences, financial resources remained scarce, leaving authorities dependent on support from the central state budget. Following the May 2005 local elections, many local councils and assemblies faced crises following attempts by different parties and coalitions to shift the balance of power through postelectoral deal making. In some places, it took months to form workable councils. The proposed draft bill on direct elections of mayors and county prefects might create more democratic mechanisms by assigning executive responsibilities to the local and regional levels. The center-right Croatian Party of Rights did well at local elections, and the HSU – one of the surprise winners in the 2003 parliamentary elections – strengthened its position. The major drop in the number of council seats was recorded by the Croatian Peasant Party. The ruling HDZ lost more than 20 seats in county assemblies, and the opposition SDP lost 6 seats. Independent slates did well across the country. *Croatia's local democratic governance rating remains at 3.75.*

Judicial Framework and Independence. Many international reports and domestic analyses emphasize that improving the operation of Croatia's judiciary is a major challenge and that a reliable and efficient judicial system has yet to be achieved. The main problems are widespread inefficiency and the excessive amount of time needed to hand down and enforce rulings. There is a disturbing backlog of around 1.6 million unresolved court cases, most connected with the enforcement of civil judgments. Noteworthy progress has been made in tackling the serious backlogs affecting the Land Registry, the second largest problem area. In December 2005, the Parliament adopted a new Law on the Courts to rationalize the network of courts. Among European countries, Croatia has the largest number of courts, but the current distribution of caseloads is uneven; the largest courts are extremely overloaded, whereas smaller ones are not always used to their full capacity. With respect to the impartiality of the judicial system, according to the European Commission further steps need to be taken to eliminate any suggestion of ethnic bias against Serb defendants in war crimes trials. However, the OSCE mission to Croatia noted that Serb indictees in 2005 had a better chance of receiving a fair trial than in the past. *Croatia's judicial framework and independence rating improves from 4.50 to 4.25 owing to further reforms toward more efficient functioning of the courts and Land Registry.*

Corruption. Numerous surveys highlight a public perception that corruption has actually gotten worse over the past year. Citizens feel that corruption is especially widespread among political parties, in the judiciary, with representative bodies, and in land registration. The Ministry of Justice, with help from the international community, made progress in the latter area, introducing a digitalized Land Registry in May 2005 to increase public access to records and thereby remove a source of potential corruption. The government has prepared a National Program for the Fight Against Corruption, to be presented in 2006. Croatian foreign minister Miomir Zuzul stepped down from his office in January following public pressure related to charges of conflict of interest; he was the first Croatian minister ever to resign for this reason. *Croatia's corruption rating remains at 4.75; new anticorruption policies, though they have not yet yielded visible results, offset public perceptions.*

Outlook for 2006. The main priorities relate to the successful conduct of ongoing accession negotiations and to Croatia's capacity to meet EU criteria and conditions. These include implementing additional judiciary reforms, taking measures to reduce the backlog of cases in all courts, and ensuring proper and full execution of court rulings. Also, the government is expected to enhance the fight against corruption and to speed up the decentralization process.

MAIN REPORT

National Democratic Governance

1997	1998	1999	2001	2002	2003	2004	2005	2006
n/a	n/a	n/a	n/a	n/a	n/a	n/a	3.50	3.50

Croatia has a parliamentary system of government, with stable democratic institutions that function properly and cooperatively. The present system of government was established through a series of amendments to the Constitution: Those in 2000 and 2001 strengthened the role of the Parliament, transforming it from a bicameral to a unicameral body. The reduction of presidential powers secured a greater balance of power between the head of state, the prime minister and his cabinet, and the parliamentary majority.

This does not mean, however, that the office of the president – who is elected for a renewable five-year term by direct universal suffrage – has been reduced to a symbolic role. The head of state remains a significant factor in creating and implementing foreign policy, and Stjepan Mesic, who in January 2005 won his second term in power, frequently appears in public as a critic of the government.[1] In accordance with the Constitution, the president is the supreme commander of the armed forces, calls referendums, and gives the mandate to form the government to whoever is chosen by the parliamentary majority.

The Parliament (Hrvatski Sabor) is made up of a single chamber, and according to the Constitution, it exercises legislative power and shares the right of legislative initiative with the government. Laws typically undergo a lengthy parliamentary procedure of three consecutive readings. However, the Constitution allows for an emergency procedure. Using that option to continue work on harmonizing Croatian legislation with the European Union's acquis communautaire, the government in 2005 introduced into parliamentary procedure numerous emergency bills, such as the Law on Telecommunications, amendments to the Law on Chemicals, amendments to the Law on Public Gathering and the Law on Health Insurance, and so forth.

Accession negotiations between Croatia and the European Union (EU) were launched in October 2005 after a seven-month postponement resulting from Croatia's failure to meet all of its obligations in cooperation with The Hague's International Criminal Tribunal for the Former Yugoslavia – specifically, that it was doing nothing to locate and extradite one of the most wanted war crimes indictees, General Ante Gotovina. After the delay, the government initiated an action plan to locate and transfer Gotovina to The Hague. Eventually, Gotovina was arrested in the Canary Islands on December 7. Gotovina has been on the run since he was indicted in 2001 for alleged atrocities in August 1995 against rebel Serbs in an army offensive to retake rebel areas of Croatia.

After the launch of membership talks, Croatia underwent "screening" – an in-depth analysis to conform its legislation to that of the EU – before concrete negotiations on each chapter. According to the plans of Croatia's negotiating delegation, the country could open talks for 8 of the 35 chapters of the European acquis by mid-2006, during Austria's presidency of the EU. The HDZ government believes it is possible to finish accession negotiations in two and a half to three years. The launch of EU accession talks confirmed the maturity and stability of the political system, but as European officials pointed out, there is still much work ahead for Croatia.

Judiciary reform, the return of refugees, and respect of minority rights are some of the main challenges in the process of joining the EU.[2] Brussels also expects public administration reform, but it appears that the incumbent government does not have a clear strategy to reduce the state apparatus in order to create an efficient administration. Therefore, it remains politicized with an ambiguous system of promotion and mobility. The rules of recruitment and selection of candidates could also be improved.[3] Limited progress was made in July 2005 with the adoption of the Law on the Civil Service. Its amendments address a number of critical deficiencies in the legal status of civil servants and other public employees. These include the politicization of the administration, recruitment, selection, promotion, and training policies, and the regulation of possible conflicts of interest. Most provisions of the new law enter into force in January 2006, so it remains to be seen to what degree its implementation will lead toward establishing a professional, efficient, accountable, and transparent public administration.

There was no new movement to reform the secret services in 2005, despite the fact that the HDZ announced their reorganization immediately after assuming power in 2003. The intelligence community remains organized through three agencies: the Civil Intelligence Agency, the Counterintelligence Agency, and the Military Security Agency.[4] Work of the intelligence community is supervised by the parliament through its Committee for Internal Policy and National Security and, since 2003, by the Council for Civilian Supervision. As of early November 2005, the government had circulated for comment a working draft of a new law on the intelligence service, according to which two existing services, the Civil Intelligence Agency and the Counterintelligence Agency, would merge into one and intelligence would be provided with more sweeping investigative authority as well as additional oversight mechanisms.

Overall, the activities of the secret service have been subject to much public scrutiny, mainly in connection with possible violations of the human rights and freedoms of five journalists who were put under surveillance in 2003 and 2004. They filed a petition requesting authorities to investigate allegations that the Counterintelligence Agency tried to discredit them as being involved in operations that undermined national security after they reported on sensitive war crimes and criminal issues. The affair ended with a probe of the parliamentary Committee for Internal Policy and National Security, which in March 2005 concluded that there were grounds to suspect the agency had breached the journalists' fundamental freedoms without cause. There has been no specific follow-up on the case.

Croatian law guarantees the right to access information, but its provisions are unevenly applied in practice.[5] In August 2005, a court ruled in favor of a journalist who had been denied access to timely information by the government. The ruling revealed the extent to which state institutions in Croatia are closed to the public. Since the 2003 adoption of the Law on the Right to Access Information, citizens have filed 60 suits against state institutions that have denied this right.[6] Transparency International Croatia has also reported that almost half of the public institutions in the country are not in compliance with the Law on the Right to Access Information.[7]

Electoral Process

1997	1998	1999	2001	2002	2003	2004	2005	2006
4.00	4.25	4.25	3.25	3.25	3.25	3.25	3.00	3.25

On January 16, 2005, voters were called to the polls for a runoff to elect Croatia's president for the next five years. The State Electoral Commission confirmed 13 official candidates. For the first time, there were as many as 3 female candidates and 5 independent contestants. In the second round, victory went to incumbent president Mesic, who won 65.93 percent of the votes, while the ruling HDZ candidate, Deputy Prime Minister Jadranka Kosor, won 34 percent. Turnout in rounds one and two was 50.6 percent and 51 percent, respectively.[8]

According to the leading election monitoring and support NGO – Citizens Organized to Monitor Elections (GONG) – the campaign was conducted in an atmosphere of peace and tolerance. The observed irregularities mainly concerned out-of-country voting, particularly in neighboring Bosnia and Herzegovina. These irregularities included voting under names of deceased persons and double voting, where the same person voted both in Croatia and in Bosnia and Herzegovina. Both problems appear to have resulted from the inadequate management of voter lists. GONG concluded that the outdated 1992 Law on Voter Lists was one of the main obstacles to conducting fair elections and recommended amendments to the law, such as creating a central electoral register and increasing the responsibility of the central state administration office for updating voter lists.

In May 2005, outdated lists were also a problem in the poll for representatives to 246 municipal and 123 city councils, along with 20 county assemblies and the Zagreb City Assembly. The May local elections were the first in which those who broke the election silence (no campaigning ahead of the polling day) faced possible fines, which ranged from 3,000 kunas (US$500) for individuals to 100,000 – 500,000 kunas (US$16,700–$83,350) for legal entities.[9] Overall turnout was very low, around 30 percent, continuing a trend in recent years. Political analysts stressed that according to voter perceptions, local elections were less important than those for the parliament.

The HDZ lost more than 20 seats in county assemblies, and the opposition SDP lost 6 seats. The far right Croatian Party of Rights (HSP) more than tripled its number of seats in county assemblies, and the party was particularly successful within war-affected areas. Political analysts have assessed the decline of popular support for the HDZ as being directly related to difficult economic conditions and the failure of the government to initiate EU entry talks in March as scheduled. The main loser was the Croatian Peasant Party (HSS), which gave up about half of its county governors and mayors.[10] The decline of the HSS is a continuing trend that began with the 2003 parliamentary elections. The party's image was marred by accusations of horse trading and conflicts of interest. After 11 years with Zlatko Tomcic at its helm, the HSS got a new leader in December 2005, Josip Friscic, who promised to consolidate the party. Independent lists won a significant number of seats across the country, especially in Zagreb, Osijek, and Dalmatian cities and counties, indicating an important degree of popular disenchantment with national political parties. The shift was attributed to the fact that parties are increasingly losing their traditional ideological colors and that voters are pragmatically opting for candidates with the most name recognition.

The number of votes needed to win a representative seat differed radically among units. Winning a seat in the capital city assembly took 4,100 votes, while in sparsely populated Lika-Senj County, only 508 votes were needed. Since parties won the necessary absolute majority in only a few places, the formation of local governments depended primarily on postelection negotiations between the HDZ on one side, the SDP on the other, and various smaller parties, such as the HSP, the Independent Democratic Serb Party, and the HSU.

Before and even after the local elections, there was a serious lack of clarity on how to implement provisions of the constitutional Law on National Minorities concerning the allocation of reserved seats for minority representatives. The law requires that ethnic minorities be represented in local government bodies if the census shows that a minority group constitutes a specified percentage of the local population (above 5 percent in the case of counties or 15 percent in the case of municipalities and cities). As noted by GONG, the government did not consider updated voter lists when calculating the number of minority seats. Instead, the 2001 census list was used without taking into account the subsequent population changes in certain local units.

With regard to the Serb minority, the difference between the 2001 census and the 2005 voter list is considerable, particularly in return areas. Observers estimated that additional minority councillors would be seated in over 12 towns if voter lists were taken into consideration.[11] Hence, the old voter list impeded minority voters not only from fully taking part in the local government election process, but from successfully attaining representation at the local level as well. GONG filed a complaint before the Constitutional Court to clarify the issue.

Amid dissatisfaction over the intense bargaining during the long coalition formation process, the government announced changes to the electoral laws that would enable direct election of county prefects, mayors, and heads of municipalities. A draft law was approved in the first reading by the Parliament in September 2005. However, the relationship between the directly elected prefect or mayor and representative body remained to be defined before the second reading of the draft, scheduled for March 2006. The government further sent to the parliament a draft law on the establishment of a permanent State Electoral Commission, which is also a recommendation by the OSCE.

Given the lack of a precise legal framework, GONG called upon the Croatian parliament, the ministries, and other national institutions to launch a comprehensive reform of electoral legislation that would include the adoption of a single law to regulate all elections and rules to regulate all electoral campaign financing.

Civil Society

1997	1998	1999	2001	2002	2003	2004	2005	2006
3.50	3.50	3.50	2.75	2.75	3.00	3.00	3.00	2.75

Civil society in Croatia continues to grow and diversify. The number of registered NGOs has increased from 23,740 in August 2003 to 27,955 in 2005,[12] and a legislative framework is being prepared to help consolidate and support the work of civil society. Although official financial support is readily given to cultural, social, and humanitarian associations, public funding is less forthcoming for human rights and civic NGOs, which nonetheless play an important role in the democratic evolution of the society.[13]

The relationship between major NGOs and the government deteriorated in 2004 with the lifting of the value-added tax (VAT) exemption on foreign donations for associations and nonprofit organizations. The unresolved VAT issue and lack of a legal NGO framework continue to impede particularly those groups concerned with human rights and civil society. This is still a matter of dispute between some leading NGOs and the government, and it "highlights the limited role NGOs continue to play in influencing government policy."[14] Nevertheless, there are positive examples. One in particular has to do with those groups that responded to the

Druzba-Adria project, which envisaged an integration of oil pipelines that would transport Russian oil from Samara to the tanker terminal in Croatia's Omisalj and from there to global markets. In 2002, the project was given a green light by the governments of six countries: Russia, Belarus, Ukraine, Slovakia, Hungary, and Croatia. Environmental groups and the green movement spoke out against the project, saying that its risks were too great and its benefits doubtful. By warning of the danger of tanker accidents in the Adriatic Sea, raising the issue of ballast water discharges, and pointing to omissions in the project's environmental impact study, these groups succeeded in persuading the government to abandon the project.

However, civil society in Croatia was still burdened by inadequacies in the institutional framework established to allocate funds. Many NGOs criticized the functioning of the National Foundation for Civil Society Development, accusing it of biased and nontransparent procedures in distributing funds to civil associations.[15] In addition, the Government Office for Associations was condemned for displaying a bias toward associations stemming from the homeland war (1991–1995).[16]

According to a survey carried out by the Ivo Pilar Institute, citizens have a generally positive perception of NGOs and consider them "very or somewhat useful for society."[17] Most of those surveyed feel that associations make a pronounced contribution to raising awareness about citizen rights and the development of democracy in Croatia, but at the same time they feel that associations do not contribute much to solving concrete existential issues. They believe that social services and humanitarian work are the areas where associations can have the most impact. Following these in public esteem are groups that work in environmental protection (32.5 percent), health care (31.2 percent), legal affairs and politics (jointly 28 percent).

The survey showed that the most widely recognized NGOs are veterans associations and several environmental groups (Zelena Akcija, Osjecki Zeleni), followed by the consumer rights group Potrosac, the human rights group Croatian Helsinki Committee for Human Rights (HHO), and the women's rights group Be Active, Be Emancipated (B.a.b.e.), indicating that in most cases NGOs advocating for specific changes in society enjoy the highest visibility. The research also showed that there is a significant lack of understanding as to what NGOs actually are: Although four-fifths of those surveyed have heard the terms NGO and association, only half state they are familiar with their real meaning. This confirms that NGO activity has yet to become a proper and appreciated element of Croatian democracy. A disparity in civil society development still exists between urban and rural areas, particularly in war-affected areas.

Regarding education, some progress was made in 2005. A commission of historians has concluded work on a textbook covering the period of time from the homeland war to the present; This achievement follows two years of discussions after the expiry of a moratorium on teaching recent history in Serb-language classes in eastern Slavonia.[18] In August 2005, the Ministry of Education and representatives of the Serb minority agreed on the use of standardized history textbooks for all children regardless of their ethnicity, starting in 2006.

Independent Media

1997	1998	1999	2001	2002	2003	2004	2005	2006
4.75	4.75	5.00	3.50	3.50	3.75	3.75	3.75	3.75

The media in Croatia are subject to free market rules. There are 19 television stations, 143 radio stations, 11 daily newspapers, and several hundred magazines; some have substantial circulation, while some are struggling to survive in an uncertain market.[19] Three television stations have national coverage: HRT, Nova TV, and RTL. The state-owned HRT (Croatian Radio-Television), which broadcasts on three channels, is the largest and most influential. It earns around 40 to 50 percent of its revenues from the mandatory monthly subscription fee. Nova TV was the first commercial television with national coverage. The Croatian outlet of the German TV channel RTL was launched in April 2004.

The state is the biggest media owner. Along with the heavily subsidized daily newspaper *Vjesnik*, the state owns the HRT national broadcaster, the Hina news agency, and dozens of other media outlets. Local broadcast media are vulnerable to political pressure since most stations are at least partially owned by local governments or depend on the financial support of local authorities. According to the European Journalism Centre, the government controls approximately 40 percent of Croatian radio stations through local authorities. Local politicians and strongmen often sue journalists for mental anguish and libel.

The Internet in Croatia has begun to play an increasingly significant role as a source of information, with an estimated fourfold increase in users since 2000. According to a survey conducted by the GfK research agency in mid-July 2005, 35 percent of Croats (more than 1.2 million people) go online at least once a month. The Internet is becoming increasingly important in political campaigns, and political parties are paying more attention to online activities such as forum discussions, surveys, and so forth. The top 10 Croatian Web sites feature entertainment, sports, and lifestyle stories. The state imposes no obstacles or barriers to Internet service providers.

At the end of August 2005, the Council of Electronic Media allocated 18 million kunas (US$3 million) from the Fund for Pluralism (set up by the Law on Media) to 93 local radio and 17 local TV stations for the production of programs focusing on issues such as minorities and culture, among others. The council has been criticized by several media outlets, which claim that the criteria used for distributing funds lack transparency.[20]

International media corporations are new but powerful players in the media arena.[21] The two dailies with the highest circulation (*Jutarnji List* and *Vecernji List*) are owned by international companies. EuropaPress Holding (EPH), publisher of *Jutarnji List*, is owned by WAZ of Germany, while Styria of Austria is the majority owner of *Vecernji List*. In March 2005, Styria launched a tabloid-style daily newspaper, *24 Sata*.

The process of privatizing the Split-based *Slobodna Dalmacija*, one of the major Croatian dailies, was completed in August 2005 when EPH gained a 70 percent share. Thus, EPH's share of Croatia's print market has risen above the 40 percent limit stipulated in the Law on Media. EPH was therefore obliged to take measures to reduce its total stake to below 40 percent within six months.

Changes to the criminal code in effect since October 2004 eased the threat of prosecution for libel but fell short of full decriminalization.[22] Since October 2004, four journalists have received suspended prison sentences for libel. Though the law provides for freedom of the press, politicians have occasionally attempted to influence national television. In December 2005, members of Parliament debated a television talk show on the legacy of former president Franjo Tudjman. Members of the ruling party attacked the program as anti-Croatian, and the HTV program council subsequently suspended the program's editor and host.

The debate prompted the Croatian Helsinki Committee on Human Rights and the Croatian Journalists Association to express concern that the ruling party was using political pressure to establish program control over HTV. Both the editor and one of the guests of the talk show received death threats. During the course of the year, an editor at the independent weekly *Feral Tribune* who reported on war crimes also received death threats, as did his colleague, the editor of the Zagreb-based Radio 101, in connection with the talk show concerning the legacy of President Tudjman.

In late April, the ICTY indicted five print journalists and the former head of the secret service for contempt of the tribunal for revealing the identity and publishing the testimony of a protected witness. All six have pleaded not guilty at the ICTY, five appearing voluntarily and the sixth, the former editor of the daily *Slobodna Dalmacija*, appearing only after being arrested in Croatia for his initial failure to comply with the ICTY summons. The issue sparked debates and divided the public. The journalists concerned are known for their strong nationalist views, so it was widely believed that their reasons for revealing the protected witness's name were more political than anything having to do with press freedom. Even the president of the Croatian Journalists Association stressed that they had acted unprofessionally.

However, many in the journalistic community felt the indictments were a violation of press rights and freedoms. Vesna Alaburic, who lectures in media law at the Faculty of Political Sciences, Department of Journalism, at Zagreb University, said that because of the circumstances in the case (where the identity of the witness was "a public fact") and because "the witness himself talked in public in general terms about his own statements to the tribunal," there was no longer a reason for the tribunal to proceed with contempt charges.[23] On October 2005, the OSCE Representative on Freedom of the Media, supported by the International Press Institute and the South East Europe Media Organisation, appealed to the ICTY to change its rules dealing with contempt of court (rule 77 of the ICTY's Rules of Procedure) so that it would apply only to officials who have actually leaked confidential information. Inside the country, the Croatian Journalists Association is the dominant professional alliance; it drafts media laws and lobbies for media-related legislation.

Local Democratic Governance

1997	1998	1999	2001	2002	2003	2004	2005	2006
n/a	n/a	n/a	n/a	n/a	n/a	n/a	3.75	3.75

Croatia has about 550 local (cities and municipalities) and 20 regional (counties) units. The capital, Zagreb, has both city and county status. Local government responsibilities are defined by the Law on Local Government of 2001 and include water supply and sewerage, primary health care, preschool and primary education, and so forth. Decentralization, as planned in the government 2000-2004 program, has been slower than originally foreseen. Though local self-government units gained greater competences, financial resources have remained scarce, leaving authorities dependent on support from the central state budget. Overall, it seems that the issue of decentralization has not been an urgent priority for the current government.

Following the May 2005 local elections, many local councils and assemblies faced crises following attempts by parties and coalitions to shift the balance of power through postelectoral deal making. In some places, it took months to form workable councils. The election was held for 8,377 representatives; on average, 8 candidates ran for each seat on local councils, municipal bodies, and county assemblies. Political relations after the elections were so complex that in most units it was impossible to say who might form the local government. For most of the slates that managed to secure a leading position, that was only the beginning of lengthy negotiations with potential coalition partners. The HSP did well in the elections, while the HSU, one of the surprise winners of the 2003 parliamentary elections, continued to strengthen its position. In many places, these two parties would tip the scales when forming a governing majority.

A drop in the number of council seats was recorded by the HSS (45 fewer seats in county assemblies than in the 2001 elections) and by the HDZ (26 fewer seats). The SDP won 6 fewer seats overall in county assemblies.[24] The HDZ lost ground in big cities, defeated by the SDP-led opposition in Zagreb and Split, and at the same time performed below standard in Slavonia and Dalmatia, which were considered HDZ strongholds. There is a widespread public perception that the HDZ-led government has failed to deliver on its promises in the economic and social spheres. Moreover, many of the party's right-wing supporters, alienated by Ivo Sanader's moderate course, appear to have turned to the more stridently nationalist HSP, which managed to occupy some of the political ground on the Right that the HDZ had vacated.

The HSP is now strongly placed in a number of areas and has a good starting position for the next parliamentary elections, due in 2007. Various opinion polls show the continued decrease of HDZ popularity and an increase in the popularity of the opposition. In September 2005, the SDP was more popular than the HDZ, with a difference of 2 percent in favor of the SDP according to research agency PULS's survey.

An exceptionally long period of political bargaining was marked by numerous accusations of councillor "buying" leveled back and forth among the parties. The media were packed with reports of alleged "immoral offers" of financial and other types of compensation made by parties to councillors, with the hope of luring them to their camp to form a governing majority. *Večernji List* ran an article in May 2005 entitled "Millions for Council Seats," describing how two SDP members on the slate for the Sisak-Moslavina County Assembly were allegedly offered from 1.5 million to 2.5 million kunas (US$250,000 to $416,700) by the HDZ to cast votes needed to form a governing majority.

To prevent drawn-out manipulations of future election results, the government sent the parliament a draft law in September 2005 to establish the direct election of mayors and county prefects. The law included provisions on minority representation in executive and administrative bodies at the local level. Direct election is supported by all parties. In their arguments for such a move, they stress that direct election would give local leaders greater responsibility toward voters. The Association of Alliance of Cities and Alliance of Counties also backed the move, warning that a new model should also address the financing of local government. Members of the association claimed that income tax moneys should be channeled to local and regional self-government units so that larger cities would receive 60 percent of collected income tax. They point out that since finances need to be brought in line with responsibilities, consideration should be given to the economic strength of individual local units in choosing a model. The European Commission is providing Croatia with €1.3 million (US$1.58 million) for a fiscal decentralization project and a further €1.35 million (US$1.64 million) for administrative decentralization.[25]

Numerous public opinion polls – including a survey carried out by the Prizma Research Agency in May 2004, a year ahead of the local elections – have confirmed that citizens are in favor of direct elections.[26] In a sample of 619 Croatian adults, 76 percent support direct elections, saying they would rather vote for an individual than for a party or coalition that would then install a mayor. The fact that only 7 percent of citizens feel they are fully informed of the work of their local government is astonishing. Half feel that they are only partially informed, while as much as 38 percent say they are not at all informed about the work of their local government. Expressing their (dis)satisfaction, those polled gave evaluations from 1 to 5, with 5 indicating complete satisfaction. An average score of 2.7 indicated that most citizens were not satisfied with the work of the local government. According to the Prizma survey, "It appears that Croatian citizens are after all weary of political games at the local level and the trading of shots over party lines and feel that candidates not burdened by party-political discipline and directives might better address local issues and problems."

Indicative of this general public opinion is the good showing and upswing recorded by independent slates in the May 2005 local elections. In Zagreb, for example, an independent slate led by Tatjana Holjevac won about 6 percent of the vote and three council seats. Independent slates also did well in Osijek and Split.

Judicial Framework and Independence

1997	1998	1999	2001	2002	2003	2004	2005	2006
4.75	4.75	4.75	3.75	3.75	4.25	4.50	4.50	4.25

Many international reports and domestic analyses emphasize that improving the functioning of the Croatian judiciary is a major challenge and that a reliable and efficient judicial system has yet to be achieved. The main problems are widespread inefficiency and the excessive amount of time needed to hand down and enforce rulings. There is a disturbing backlog of around 1.6 million unresolved court cases,[27] most involving civil judgments.

The Constitutional Court has increasingly awarded damages to individuals complaining of delayed proceedings in lower courts. In the first nine months of 2005, the Constitutional Court received more than 1,000 complaints alleging unreasonable judicial delays in lower courts and the Supreme Court, finding violations and awarding damages in over 60 percent of the more than 400 complaints ruled on in that period. In 2005 alone, the Court awarded nearly 3 million kunas (€411,000/US$500,000) in damages. The European Court of Human Rights called the delays "excessive" and a violation of citizens' right to trial in a reasonable time.[28] Noteworthy progress has been made in tackling the serious backlogs affecting the Land Registry, which forms part of the municipal court system and constitutes the second main area of the overall case backlog. The digitalization of the Land Registry is under way, with the aim of making the system accessible online.

According to numerous pubic opinion polls, the judiciary in Croatia is perceived as corrupt. This problematic status is partly a legacy of the 1990s and partly the result of attempts by the ruling party to influence the appointment of judges and the functioning of the courts. In September 2005, the government adopted a comprehensive judicial reform strategy that specifies a number of short-, medium- and long-term measures to reduce delays.

In December 2005, the parliament adopted a new Law on the Courts that creates the framework for rationalizing the network of courts. The Ministry of Justice has announced a pilot project that would see the merger of 15 misdemeanor and municipal courts. Croatia has 110 misdemeanor, 106 municipal, 21 county, and 12 commercial courts, placing it among European states with the largest number of courts. Understaffing is not a concern within the judiciary. In relation to the total population, compared with the EU, Croatia has a relatively high number of judges (1,907 currently).[29]

The distribution of caseloads, however, is uneven; the largest courts are extremely overloaded, whereas smaller ones are not always used to their full capacity. In an effort to address this problem, a 2004 ruling of the president of the Supreme Court transferred almost 26,000 cases from backlogged courts to those less burdened by unresolved cases. The Law on the Courts introduces a new method to guarantee the right of citizens to court action of reasonable duration, which will entail a greater commitment on the part of county courts – namely, if a higher court establishes that an unreasonable judicial delay appeal is justified it will impose a deadline for a ruling on the court that "violated" the right to court action of reasonable duration. The law also foresees the establishment of a Justice Inspectorate and a stipulation that judges pursue continuing professional education.

In 2004, a Justice Academy was opened to increase professional education for judges. The project is financed through the EU's CARDS program. The European Commission noted that particular attention needed to be paid to providing specialized training to judges and prosecutors on white-collar crime, money laundering, the fight against corruption, and other issues.

There is no legal aid organized by the state in civil cases, and currently only the Croatian Bar Association provides free aid with no state control over eligibility criteria. The Ministry of Justice is drafting a new Law on Legal Aid with input from the Bar Association, NGO representatives, and experts from the Council of Europe.

With respect to the impartiality of the judicial system, further steps need to be taken to eliminate any suggestion of ethnic bias against Serb defendants in war crimes trials, according to the European Commission. However, the OSCE mission to Croatia noted that Serb indictees in 2005 had a better chance of receiving a fair trial than in the past. As part of its completion strategy, the ICTY approved the transfer to Croatia of the case against Generals Mirko Norac and Rahim Ademi. The ICTY indicted Norac and Ademi for war crimes allegedly committed against Serb civilians during a 1993 army operation in the so-called Medak Pocket action, in southwestern Croatia. Ademi surrendered voluntarily to The Hague in 2001 and was granted a provisional release until the beginning of the trial, while Norac is currently serving a 12-year prison sentence handed down by the Rijeka County Court for war crimes committed in the Gospic area.

There have been positive steps in processing crimes related to the 1990s war of independence; for example, an investigation has been reopened into the murder of Serb civilians in wartime Osijek. Also, in September 2005 five former members of the Croatian Interior Ministry's security forces were convicted and sentenced by the Zagreb County Court to a total of 30 years in prison for crimes, including the murder of Serbs in late 1991 at the Pakracka Poljana prison camp in western Slavonia. Charges were first filed in 1992, and the 2005 retrial took place after a Supreme Court reversal of a previous acquittal.

The other important test for Croatia's justice system is a new trial at the Lora military prison in Split for crimes allegedly committed in 1992 by eight military policemen accused of torturing and murdering ethnic Serb civilians. When the retrial began in September, only four of the defendants appeared before the court. The others went into hiding after the Supreme Court overturned their acquittal from the first trial in late 2002. The first "Lora prison trial" was a highly politicized affair. The authorities failed to provide protection for witnesses and released false information claiming some witnesses were themselves war crimes suspects. The result was that most witnesses were too intimidated to come to court. The first trial quickly became notorious as a miscarriage of justice. The behavior of the presiding judge, Slavko Lozina, was never officially questioned, although he has been removed from the retrial proceedings. The ongoing trial is being conducted in a professional manner, according to observers.

Corruption

1997	1998	1999	2001	2002	2003	2004	2005	2006
n/a	n/a	5.25	4.50	4.50	4.75	4.75	4.75	4.75

Numerous surveys highlight the public perception that corruption has actually gotten worse over the past year. According to the European Bank for Reconstruction and Development's 2005 Transition Report: "Croatia was among the few transition countries (Hungary, Azerbaijan, Armenia) in which corruption in 2005 was higher than in 2002."

Transparency International indicates in its Corruption Perceptions Index for 2005 that Croatia has dropped three places from the previous year, which places it in the company of Burkina Faso, Egypt, and Syria. Citizens feel that corruption is especially widespread among political parties, in the judiciary, and in representative bodies. On a scale of 1 to 5, with 5 representing total corruption, political parties scored a grade of 4, followed closely by representative bodies with 3.9 and the judiciary with 3.8. Citizens evaluated NGOs, the military, and the church as being the least corrupt.

Hospitals were among the institutions with the worst reputations. Agence France-Presse reports that 90 percent of Croatians feel that bribing doctors is not out of the ordinary.[30] Bribery, nepotism, and political patronage are a legacy of the former regime and the nation's past. Numerous surveys also highlight that corruption is perceived to be widespread in land registration. The Ministry of Justice, with help from the international community, made progress in this area by introducing a digitized Land Registry in May 2005. This will increase public access to records and thereby remove a source of potential corruption.

To deal effectively with the problem of corruption, which the European Commission's November 2005 Progress Report on Croatia called a serious threat to the functioning of society, the government has prepared a National Program for the Fight Against Corruption, which will be presented during negotiations with the EU on the justice chapter in 2006.

The European Commission has advised Croatia to set up internal controls in every area of the public administration to investigate corruption based on accountable and transparent rules. A more proactive approach also includes a coordinated awareness campaign involving media and NGOs to inform the public about the dangers of corruption and the institutions and measures involved in fighting it.[31]

In March 2006, amendments to the Law on the Office for the Suppression of Corruption and Organized Crime will strengthen the role and jurisdiction of the office and more clearly define its activities. It remains to be seen whether these amendments will be implemented effectively. Croatia still lacks legislation on political parties' financing to make their assets and financial supporters more transparent. The effectiveness of the parliamentary Commission for the Prevention of Conflict of Interest, which required officials to publicly declare their assets, was limited by infighting and an overly broad mandate.

In a governmental first for Croatia, Minister of Foreign Affairs Miomir Zuzul stepped down in January 2005 following public pressure related to charges of conflict of interest. He allegedly took a bribe in return for securing the government's intervention on behalf of a local company in a privatization deal. The press also accused him of other misdeeds, and opposition parties claimed that the scandal had damaged Zuzul's credibility to such a degree that he should resign, which he eventually did.

Without legal security and transparency, Croatia cannot expect the influx of foreign investment it earnestly counted on after the October 2005 decision to launch negotiations with the EU. Therefore, the HDZ government will have to make a more determined effort in the struggle against corruption. Based on the experience of the past 10 years, an improvement of one point on Transparency International's Corruption Perceptions Index purportedly attracts as much as a 15 percent increase in foreign investment. Clearly, improving the fight against corruption, as measured by moving up Transparency International's index, will pay off for Croatia's economy.

Barbara Peranic is a journalist for Croatia National Radio.

---

[1] President's speech at the December 22, 2005, government session: "Croatia lacks a long-term strategy of economic development. There are some working versions, but they are incomplete. Sometimes it appears to me that government compensates for this deficiency by accepting and implementing the instructions and even the dictates of international monetary – that is to say, financial institutions. If the impression I have is founded, then it is not good, indeed – then it is bad."
President's speech, November 28, 2005, commenting on an agreement prepared by the government on return of property to Austrians who left the former Yugoslavia after World War II:
"Based on my constitutional right and obligation to care for the functioning of the system, I must in this issue say…that I do not approve of the agreement and that I consider it a dangerous precedent that will affect more than just Croatia. If Croatia begins – all under the guise of correcting the injustices of Communism – to return this and that, outside of the scope of international agreements that have addressed the issue, then I have many reasons to assert that the functioning not only of the system but also of the state as a system will be brought into question. We, namely, cannot endure it. As president of the republic, the Constitution requires that I intervene in a situation like this, and that is precisely what I am now doing."
[2] Statement of the EU enlargement commissioner, Olli Rehn, on his October 9, 2005, visit to Zagreb.
[3] European Commission, Progress Report, Croatia, November 2005.
[4] Law on Security Services, 2002.
[5] Law on the Right to Access Information, 2003.
[6] See www.danas.org, September 7, 3005, author Ankica Barbir Mladinovic.
[7] Transparency International Croatia, on the occasion of International Right to Access to Information Day, September 28, 2005.

[8] State Electoral Commission, January 31, 2005.

[9] State Electoral Commission, May 15, 2005.

[10] OSCE, Spot Report: 15 May Local Elections in Croatia, May 20, 2005.

[11] U.S. Department of State: Country Reports on Human Rights Practices 2005 – Croatia, released by the Bureau of Democracy, Human Rights, and Labor, March 8, 2006.

[12] European Commission, Progress Report, Croatia, November 2005.

[13] OSCE, Croatia – Progress Report, November 2005.

[14] Ibid.

[15] The National Foundation for Civil Society Development was founded in 2003 with the aim of further activating the civil society scene.

[16] The Government Office for Associations was founded in 1998 with the aim of establishing a national program of transparent financial support for civil society organizations from the state budget fund.

[17] Ivo Pilar Institute – a comprehensive survey of public attitudes, perception, and understanding of NGOs for the Academy for Educational Development, July 2005.

[18] During the peaceful reintegration of the eastern Slavonia region (1996-1998), Croatia agreed on a five-year suspension of classroom teaching about the homeland war.

[19] Stjepan Malovic, "The Real Game Has Only Started," April 2005, www.mediaonline.ba.

[20] OSCE, Croatia – Progress Report, November 2005.

[21] Stjepan Malovic, "The Real Game Has Only Started," April 2005, www.mediaonline.ba.

[22] The liability of editors in chief for acts of libel has been removed. Also, the burden of proof of defamation has been shifted from the defendant to the plaintiff.

[23] Janet Anderson, "Contempt Charges Baffle Croatian Media," September 30, 2005, www.iwpr.net.

[24] Vecernji List, May 16, 2005, local elections.

[25] See www.urban-institute.hr.

[26] Prizma Research Agency, Public Opinion Poll on Local Elections and Local Government, May 31, 2004.

[27] European Commission, Progress Report, Croatia, November 2005.

[28] OSCE, Croatia – Progress Report, November 2005.

[29] European Commission, Progress Report, Croatia, November 2005

[30] Agence France-Press, November 28, 2005

[31] European Commission, Progress Report, Croatia, November 2005.

Czech Republic

Capital: Prague
Population: 10.2 million
GNI/capita: $9,130
Ethnic Groups: Czech (90.4%), Moravian (3.7%),
Slovak (1.9%), other (4%)

Nations in Transit Ratings and Averaged Scores

	1997	1998	1999	2001	2002	2003	2004	2005	2006
Electoral Process	1.25	1.25	1.75	1.75	2.00	2.00	2.00	2.00	2.00
Civil Society	1.50	1.50	1.50	1.50	1.75	1.50	1.50	1.50	1.50
Independent Media	1.25	1.25	1.75	2.00	2.50	2.25	2.25	2.00	2.00
Governance *	2.00	2.00	2.00	2.00	2.25	2.25	2.25	n/a	n/a
National Democratic Governance	n/a	n/a	n/a	n/a	n/a	n/a	n/a	2.50	2.50
Local Democratic Governance	n/a	n/a	n/a	n/a	n/a	n/a	n/a	2.00	2.00
Judicial Framework and Independence	1.50	1.50	2.25	2.50	2.50	2.50	2.50	2.50	2.25
Corruption	n/a	n/a	3.25	3.75	3.75	3.50	3.50	3.50	3.50
Democracy Score	1.50	1.50	2.08	2.25	2.46	2.33	2.33	2.29	2.25

* With the 2005 edition, Freedom House introduced seperate analysis and ratings for national democratic governance and local democratic governance to provide readers with more detailed and nuanced analysis of these two important subjects.

NOTE: The ratings reflect the consensus of Freedom House, its academic advisers, and the author of this report. The opinions expressed in this report are those of the author. The ratings are based on a scale of 1 to 7, with 1 representing the highest level of democratic progress and 7 the lowest. The Democracy Score is an average of ratings for the categories tracked in a given year.

The economic and social data on this page were taken from the following sources:
GNI/capita, Population: World Development Indicators 2006 (Washington, D.C.: World Bank, 2006).
Ethnic Groups: CIA World Factbook 2006 (Washington, D.C.: Central Intelligence Agency, 2006).

EXECUTIVE SUMMARY

An October 2005 survey of young people expressed the Czech Republic's current situation. A majority of the country's youth – for whom communism is nothing more than a distant memory – look to the future with optimism, believing in economic growth and higher living standards over the next five years. They consider unemployment a problem but do not fear poverty. Two-thirds believe the European Union (EU), which the country joined in May 2004, has a positive influence. On the other hand, in their view corruption and politicians are shaming their country. And despite economic development, they believe corruption will only worsen.[1]

Many older Czechs would also agree with this assessment. The country's first year in the EU proved successful. The economy surged, with one of the highest growths in exports in the world, and the agricultural sector made an astonishing comeback. The warnings of Euro-skeptics that unemployment and inflation would skyrocket were not fulfilled. Economic prosperity continued to spread, and a growing number of people were satisfied with their personal lives and ability to pursue a decent livelihood. One poll, conducted by the Median agency, showed that nearly 74 percent of Czechs agreed that in 2005 their personal lives finally began to change for the better.[2] By now, the vast majority have no doubt that their fundamental freedoms are guaranteed and democracy is assured.

Yet the country and its leaders appear to lack any grand strategy to advance the Czech Republic to the next stage of development. Few politicians inspire the electorate, and in the Median poll, more than two-thirds of respondents said political life was as bad as, if not worse than, previous years. Too many reforms remain unfinished in key areas, such as the fight against corruption, pension and education systems, transfer of authority to regional administrations, speed of the judicial system, and integration of the Roma minority. Success appears to be measured by scoring political points rather than passing effective legislation.

Unfortunately, the major events of 2005 indicated little to no progress in most of these areas, and the fall of Prime Minister Stanislav Gross over allegations of financial impropriety in his personal life highlighted issues of poor governance, corruption, and stunted political party development. Parliamentary elections in June 2006 will indicate whether widespread disappointment with the political elite will translate into apathy or high turnout at the ballot box.

National Democratic Governance. The first quarter of 2005 was mired in political crisis as Gross refused to step down, disorienting and disgusting much of the Czech population. The scandal confirmed many citizens' assumptions about overlapping political and business interests, the pervasiveness of corruption, and clientelism.

While Gross's replacement, Jiri Paroubek, dramatically improved the government's perceived effectiveness, an approaching election year, a fragile coalition, and political infighting combined to prevent the radical reform necessary in areas such as health, education, and social security. *The Czech Republic often resembles a fully functioning democracy – stable and secure, with checks and balances in place – but the inability to solve the political crisis highlighted the distance the elite must travel to improve efficiency and accountability. As a result, the national democratic governance rating stays at 2.50.*

Electoral Process. The Gross scandal created the very real possibility that the ruling Social Democratic Party (CSSD) – the only party aside from the outcast Communists offering a leftist political alternative – might fade forever from view. But Paroubek resurrected the party's chances for the 2006 parliamentary elections, ensuring a strong alternative to the right-wing Civic Democrats, who dominated the Senate and local elections in 2004. However, the Czech system allows little room for new faces or parties, and civic participation remains stunted. *With little to no progress in political party development and inclusion of the Roma minority, the country's rating for electoral process remains unchanged at 2.00.*

Civil Society. The reputation of nongovernmental organizations (NGOs) has continued to grow, with roughly half the population characterizing NGOs as influential in helping to solve society's problems. On the other hand, many politicians consider the more advocacy-oriented organizations, especially those attempting to change public policy, as unnecessarily interfering in and complicating their work. *Continued growth in the reputation and activities of NGOs are offset by disparaging comments from the president and little happening on the legislative side; the rating for civil society remains at 1.50.*

Independent Media. Czech media are independent and diverse, but critics continue to speculate about behind-the-scenes political and financial interference. Parliamentary deputies finally approved increased license fees to support public television but widely banned advertising, raising questions about its financial future. The cancellation of a popular political program on public television and press partisanship raised serious questions about the effect of the upcoming elections on the hard-earned independence of recent years. *Unfortunately, an apparent backsliding in independence offset gains in quality and plurality, leading to an unchanged rating of 2.00 for independent media.*

Local Democratic Governance. Over the past few years, the system of local government has improved considerably, especially at the regional level. Regionally, considerable progress has been made in tackling problems neglected by the central government, including education and health care. However, the flow of funds from the center has failed to keep pace with these newly added responsibilities, leaving local administrations short of funds and frustrated with the little control they have over their budgets. *With a solid system of local democratic governance proving its worth, but needing to secure resources and combat corruption, the rating for local democratic governance remains at 2.00.*

Judicial Framework and Independence. Reforms that would speed up judicial process-es remained under development, legislation to combat discrimination languished in the Parliament, and provisions to improve gender equality were ignored. Yet the year did mark some improvements, especially with a long-awaited wave of judicial appointments and pay raises. Political meddling in court cases declined relative to previous years, and landmark rulings in cases involving discrimination against Roma were made. *No real judicial reform took place, but incremental progress in addressing some of the courts' ills warrants a slight improvement in the country's ranking for judicial framework from 2.50 to 2.25.*

Corruption. The level of everyday corruption is slowly being reduced, but much of Czech society believes that graft is still widespread at both national and local levels of public administration. Faced with numerous cases of corruption throughout the year, the lower house of Parliament finally passed a conflict-of-interest law in January 2006. *The Czech Republic's corruption rating remains at 3.50, though the pas-sage of conflict-of-interest legislation may yield positive results in 2006.*

Outlook for 2006. After Prime Minister Paroubek rescued the CSSD from potential oblivion, opinion polls at the end of the year showed that the CSSD and the Communist Party would acquire a majority in the next parliamentary elections. Paroubek's refusal to reject unambiguously the notion of a minority government backed by the Communists led some to worry that such a partnership would negate the possibility of reform in key areas and might force the CSSD to curb its enthusi-asm for European integration. However, by early 2006, the two parties had lost their majority in opinion polls, as the Green Party rapidly gained support – enough to possibly play the role of kingmaker in a close election. Never before represented in Parliament and with a new chairman, the Greens would represent an unknown wildcard in any attempt to form a stable coalition, a real challenge in the current embittered political climate.

MAIN REPORT

National Democratic Governance

1997	1998	1999	2001	2002	2003	2004	2005	2006
n/a	n/a	n/a	n/a	n/a	n/a	n/a	2.50	2.50

The institutions of governance in the Czech Republic are stable and democratic. No single party dominates the political scene, and regular rotations of power occur at national and local levels. Political parties generally agree on the nature and direction of democratic change, with one major exception – the largely unreformed Communist Party (KSCM), which has not served in a post-1989 government. The party continues to attract those nostalgic for the old regime and frighten away those who worry that the KSCM will one day sit in power and backtrack on reforms. The Communists hold 41 of the 200 seats in the powerful lower house of Parliament, but other political parties' refusal to include the KSCM in coalitions has greatly complicated the process of forming stable governments among the remaining, often conflicting parties.

Although other parties may agree on the general direction of the country's development, they clash over many details and show a remarkable tendency to avoid compromise, preferring inflammatory attacks that keep the general political discourse at a comparatively low level. In 2005, the opposition Civic Democrats (ODS) adopted a policy of "zero tolerance," contesting every major piece of legislation proposed by the ruling CSSD. The party modified this approach as the year progressed, and the CSSD increased its popularity. With elections approaching in June 2006, the animosity and mudslinging will likely worsen, as exemplified by the ODS's November presentation of the "Black Book of CSSD Sins," which summarized the alleged scandals under CSSD reign.

In the ODS's defense, political scandals involving top CSSD figures were not hard to come by in 2005, especially with the stunning fall of Prime Minister Stanislav Gross. Early in his rule, which began in August 2004, events indicated that the CSSD had made a grave mistake selecting Gross to replace former prime minister Vladimir Spidla as head of the party and the government. At 34, Gross, who had long been one of the country's most popular figures, soon revealed a profound immaturity for the position, highlighted by his clumsy attempts to deal with inquiries into his suspect personal life. A series of evasive answers concerning the financing of a luxury apartment purchased in 1999 doomed him, as did revelations that his wife's business partner owned a building housing a brothel and had been indicted for insurance fraud.

As calls for his resignation grew, Gross refused to admit any wrongdoing, apparently confident that the scandal would blow over, like the many others involving top political figures in years past. Finally, under immense pressure from the public, the media, and his coalition partners, Gross consented to step down.

Throughout the crisis, the public was largely at a loss to interpret the moves and countermoves of various actors: In one poll, 71 percent of the population said they could not get their bearings in politics.[3]

Commentators hailed the prime minister's resignation as a step forward for the country's political culture. The momentum to pass effective conflict-of-interest legislation increased, and the conviction spread that hiding skeletons in the closet might be more difficult in the future with the downfall of a prominent politician.

On the downside, the Gross affair further boosted the public's suspicion of politicians' business dealings, and other scandals throughout the year highlighted what many saw as the unethical intersection of political and economic interests in the country. Lobbying the executive and the Parliament remains largely unrestricted, and the public continues to believe that special interests play a major role in determining the political agenda (one poll placed special interests and lobbying behind only corruption in that regard).[4] A lack of transparency in major business deals involving the state at both national and local levels remains a serious problem. While the country's highest control body, the Supreme Audit Office (NKU), has uncovered massive irregularities and overspending on various government contracts, politicians generally ignore its findings, calling the agency incompetent and toothless. Current law does not even allow the NKU to impose sanctions, reports the independent weekly *Respekt*. After the head of the NKU died in 2003, the Parliament was incapable of or unwilling to elect a new president until October 2005. While a Law on Freedom of Information is on the books, journalists often do not invoke their rights, and officials continue to be overly secretive.

Critics also point to political parties' widespread practice of nominating individuals to serve throughout the public administration, even at lower levels, and on the supervisory boards of companies partially owned by the state. This has increased both instability and clientelism, while interfering in the maturation of the civil service, already hampered by low wages, a poor reputation, and a corresponding turnover in qualified experts, according to the UN's *Human Development Report*. Implementation of the Law on Civil Service, which was to enter into force in 2005, was postponed to 2007. The government claimed that salary increases and the notion of secure positions would burden the budget.

Although the legislature is independent from the executive branch, critics charge that such autonomy has not prevented the Parliament from passing an excessive number of its own poorly prepared laws. There is also a chronic lack of skilled experts to assist in writing and editing legislation, as well as poor communication and insufficient cooperation among ministries and other bodies of the public administration. The Ministry of Justice, for example, has depended on judges to write legislation, which is problematic from a separation of powers point of view, as the branch charged with implementation should not play a leading role in the creation of laws. As a result of these deficiencies, the Parliament sometimes passes error-filled laws requiring repeated revision.

The legislative process is further complicated by the ability of parliamentary deputies to make an unrestricted number of proposed amendments during the second reading of bills. (Although most parliamentary democracies allow such additions, strict rules often apply, such as the need for a minimum number of deputies to make a joint amendment.) As the weekly *Respekt* has pointed out, this tradition often disorients even the most attentive parliamentarians and serves as a calculated strategy to derail long-needed legislation. In one case, the sponsors of a bill designed to protect victims of domestic violence pulled their proposal after several populistic comments during the second reading threatened the bill's integrity. While some deputies agree that this process is open to abuse and should be changed, others doubt that their colleagues will give up the power to influence legislation that this privilege grants each deputy.[5]

It does not help matters that the executive and the legislature rarely consult civil society for input on proposed legislation. This points partially to the lack of independent public policy actors but also reflects the unwillingness of most politicians to consider civil society a potentially important contributor to policy discussions. Legislators remain much more likely to meet with lobbyists behind closed doors than attend NGO-organized events with ordinary citizens debating key issues. Since various forms of "direct democracy" (plebiscites, petition drives, demonstrations, and so forth) are also underdeveloped and underused, public pressure remains minimal. Thus policy making is almost exclusively the domain of government officials, with little outside input.

Although the legislative and the judiciary are generally thought to exercise sufficient supervision with respect to military and security services, the Gross affair raised questions over the independence of the police. Some commentators accused investigators of moving particularly slowly in investigating the prime minister's dealings, especially when compared with a high-profile, alleged bribery case involving the ODS in 2004.

Some analysts believe that the Constitution creates an overlap of executive power between the government and the president. Actual confrontations depend largely on the personality of the president, since the position is chiefly ceremonial yet retains some important powers, such as forming a government.

In key areas such as foreign policy, President Vaclav Klaus has attempted to expand his real influence on the policy-making process – surpassing steps taken by his predecessor, Vaclav Havel, and clouding, in some cases, the division of power. Despite government criticism of his activities, he has espoused his Euro-skepticism at various international forums, clashing with the official government line on issues such as the European Constitution and the introduction of the euro. In 2005, Klaus also sought out candidates closely tied to his political philosophy in appointing new governors to the Central Bank and new justices to the Constitutional Court.

During the Gross government crisis, Klaus said he would take an active role in solving the deadlock by assuming that moves not explicitly forbidden by the Constitution are permissible. He then refused to accept the resignations of several ministers, essentially preventing Gross from reshuffling his cabinet. Critics accused Klaus of not respecting the unwritten rules of the presidency – namely, not interfering in the political process. Klaus's supporters countered that the president was only stopping Gross from forming a minority government without asking the Parliament for support.[6]

Electoral Process

1997	1998	1999	2001	2002	2003	2004	2005	2006
1.25	1.25	1.75	1.75	2.00	2.00	2.00	2.00	2.00

The Czech Republic is far beyond the fundamental electoral challenges facing parts of Eastern Europe and the former Soviet Union. No one doubts the fairness of the electoral process or reports on intimidation, fraud, or any other type of manipulation on the part of the authorities. Political organizations have no problems either registering or campaigning. Although a shaky coalition government has been in power for the last few years, the system itself is solidly multiparty, with a strong opposition and diversity at all levels of government.

The Czech Republic uses a parliamentary system with two houses. Real political power resides in the Chamber of Deputies, the 200-seat lower house, with deputies elected by proportional vote on party ballots. The 81-seat Senate is elected on the basis of single-mandate districts. Though serving as a check on the Chamber of Deputies, the upper house is weaker and continues to suffer low regard among the general public and some political parties. The Senate can return approved bills to the lower house, but the Chamber of Deputies can override the Senate by a simple majority. In a joint session, both houses elect the president for a five-year term by a simple majority.

In 2005, the Czech Republic did not conduct parliamentary, presidential, or local elections, nor did it carry out elections to the European Parliament. Although virtually unclear at the time, the CSSD's decision in April to support Jiri Paroubek, then minister of local development, as Gross's replacement as prime minister proved the most important vote of the year.

When Paroubek came to power, the CSSD seemed in free fall, a party left for dead after the failures of two past prime ministers – Vladimir Spidla and Gross. With plummeting support and the potential of a split between a leftist core and a younger, more progressive wing, CSSD's collapse could have altered the Czech political system for years to come, leaving a dominant right in control of all levels of power and the Communists inadequately representing the Left. This would have also left the ODS and the KSCM (both Euro-skeptic and against greater European integration) the two most powerful parties in the country.

Instead, Paroubek almost immediately reversed the CSSD's fortunes, uniting the party and quelling left-wing dissent to such an extent that he later received 130 of 132 votes in favor of his leading the CSSD in the 2006 parliamentary elections. He quickly gained the image of a man of action and looked likely to preserve the shaky coalition until the end of its term. That Paroubek had ordered a brutal police breakup of a techno music festival, that he followed coldhearted pragmatism rather than lofty convictions, and that he considered closer cooperation with the KSCM failed to affect his popularity. By the end of 2005, he narrowed the gap between the ODS and the CSSD in opinion polls to only a few percentage points.

The elections in June 2006 will clarify whether the electorate's indifference in several past polls was less a continuation of a long-term trend and more a reflection of the dislike of the Senate and ignorance of the European Parliament. Apathy has certainly played a key role in the stunted development of direct or participatory forms of democracy, such as petitions, demonstrations, and referendum drives, notes the UN's *Human Development Report*. Although starting from a low point in the 1990s, use of these tactics has increased in the past few years with some success.

Current legislation on communal referendums has also impeded increased public engagement in political life. According to the law, a referendum is valid only if 50 percent of the electorate participates. Even seemingly important issues in smaller towns and villages – such as closing a nursery school or founding a hospice – have attracted minuscule turnouts. Such examples have discouraged local activists and politicians who believed that issues closer to home would reverse voter apathy, reports the newsweekly *Tyden*.

Continued low membership in political parties does not help the situation. The KSCM remains the largest party (around 90,000 members), followed by the Christian Democrats (50,000), the ODS (around 20,000), the CSSD (17,000), and the Freedom Party (1,100). Several new parties formed in time to compete in elections to the European Parliament, but these have very small membership bases. Low figures persist despite generous state funding – to qualify, parties have to receive only 1.5 percent of the vote (well under the 5 percent threshold in the Parliament).

The parties' low membership base has clear repercussions for the political elite: With relatively few members to choose from, parties often recycle the same personalities, leading to a feeling that talented new faces rarely surface. Parties also often reward loyalty rather than expertise, handing out ministries to individuals whose only qualification is their long service to the party. Add to these deficiencies the continued poor management and insufficient democracy within parties, mediocre policy teams, and – still too often – arrogance of power, and it becomes clear why many analysts believe the current political class does not possess the capacity to push the country forward at a dynamic pace. Leading elite members are unable to seek, let alone achieve, consensus on issues of national interest and major reforms.

In addition to these problems, the country's largest minority, the Roma, are effectively shut out of participation in national politics. Although the number of Roma is estimated at between 200,000 and 250,000, there are currently no Roma parliamentarians. Prospective Roma politicians find themselves caught in a catch-22 situation: Mainstream parties believe that Roma candidates on their lists may do them more harm than good among average voters, while Czech Roma are not organized politically to compete actively for votes. There are, however, a handful of Roma who are active at the local level.

Civil Society

1997	1998	1999	2001	2002	2003	2004	2005	2006
1.50	1.50	1.50	1.50	1.75	1.50	1.50	1.50	1.50

The reputation of nonprofit organizations has continued to grow and recover from several scandals that tarnished their early post-Communist existence. Most Czechs now see NGOs as not only legitimate, but valuable instruments for creating and preserving social cohesion. Roughly half the population characterizes NGOs as influential organizations essential to a well-functioning democracy that help solve social problems. In a 2005 survey commissioned by the Donors Forum, almost 81 percent of respondents felt foundations were important and performed work the state did not; 83 percent found that foundations highlighted neglected issues in society. Consequently, there has been an increase in donations to nonprofits from both companies and individuals. In an April 2004 survey on civil society issues conducted by STEM, a Czech polling agency, 47 percent of respondents said they had made a donation to a nonprofit organization, up 4 percent from 2000.

Four kinds of NGOs exist in the Czech Republic: civic associations, public benefit organizations, foundations, and foundation funds. The most common form is the civic association – a legal entity comprising groups of individuals in pursuit of a common interest. By September 2005, the Ministry of the Interior had registered 54,373 civic associations, ranging from political think tanks to hobby groups and sports clubs – a growth of around 2,000 over the past year – and 368 foundations. According to the Czech Statistical Office, there were 4,600 church charities, 918 foundation funds (similar to foundations but not operating any of their funded assets), and 1,125 public benefit organizations (entities providing general services to recipients under the same conditions).

The relationship of the political elite to the nonprofit sector varies. The state provides extensive financial support to NGOs through grants and coordinates policies through the Council for NGOs. NGOs have the ability to influence decision making in the council and through various advisory bodies at ministries. In the country's most recent *UN Human Development Report*, Pavol Fric, one of the country's leading experts on the nonprofit sector, described the relationship between public administration and NGOs as positive, even though most NGOs still feel more like supplicants than true partners.

On the other hand, many politicians consider more active organizations, especially those that attempt to influence public policy, as unnecessarily interfering in and complicating their work. The political elite is particularly wary of what it considers more "aggressive" forms of action, such as demonstrations and petition drives, and is quick to label the initiators as politically motivated, although they usually are not. Many officials would prefer that NGOs serve strictly as service providers, filling in where the state cannot or will not, according to the UN report. This overall attitude may explain the remarkably small number of truly independent public policy organizations or think tanks in the Czech Republic.

Since the 1990s, when he served as prime minister, Czech President Vaclav Klaus has exemplified the political establishment's leery attitude toward the NGO sector. This reached new levels in 2005, when at a Council of Europe meeting Klaus called for a fight against so-called postdemocracy, whereby various NGOs supposedly attempt to influence public life without an electoral mandate – which he called a risky and dangerous phenomenon of the past few decades. Almost 90 Czech NGOs united to request an apology. Klaus refused, claiming he never spoke against the sector as a whole but only against those groups that misuse their standing for political purposes. Later in the year, at another conference, Klaus said that disappointed people expecting miracles from democracy turned to the "evangelists" of civil society and NGOs, losing trust in the parliamentary system. He then claimed that "NGOism" was almost on the same level as Communism.[7]

The legal environment – already disobliging to NGO fund-raising through taxpayer incentives – has improved slightly in recent years. However, these legal deficiencies appear to be the result of the state's insensitivity to the plight of NGOs rather than a concerted effort to apply financial pressure on their activities and limit their impact. Following the country's entrance into the EU, in 2004 the Parliament passed a new Law on Value-Added Tax, which lowered the limit above which organizations must pay a value-added tax to 1 million crowns (US$43,000). For NGOs gaining funds through their own activities, the change was significant, as no distinction is made between for-profit and nonprofit organizations. Additionally, the Donors Forum coalition has been unsuccessful in attempts to change tax laws to allow individuals to give 1 percent of declared taxes to socially beneficial projects. On the positive side, amendments to the Law on Value-Added Tax in early 2006 removed that tax from donations made through mobile phone text messages, a popular form of giving in the Czech Republic. According to the Donors Forum, since April 2004, 90 foundations and charities have benefited from over 4.2 million text messages valued at around US$5 million.

Local donations from individuals and companies are increasingly critical as foreign funding becomes more difficult to obtain. A decline in international funding may make some NGOs more dependent on the government for financial support, especially at the local level. Corporate philanthropy has increased in the past few years, with research conducted in 2004 by the Donors Forum showing 67 percent of companies engaged in sponsorship activities and/or donations. Yet companies complain about limited tax benefits and a lack of appreciation among the public and media. Current trends also show corporate philanthropy supporting recreational activities and young people more than issues such as human rights or ethnic minorities.[8] While international companies have increased their grant programs, Czech firms lag in the area of corporate responsibility, rarely initiating their own projects.[9]

Although Czech civil society is certainly more vibrant than a few years ago, grassroots initiatives are still not commonplace. The STEM research found that 14 percent of respondents had participated in a protest demonstration over the past five years; 43 percent had signed a petition; and 12 percent had written at least one letter to a newspaper. But motivation is often limited to a core group of activists. Several referendums have not had sufficient participation, and at the same time, a survey by the Center for Research of Public Opinion showed that only one-tenth of the respondents were satisfied with the level of citizens' participation in public life, a decrease from earlier surveys.[10]

Regarding the "negative" side of civil society growth – that is, the emergence of extremist organizations – the situation in the Czech Republic appears to have settled down. Violent attacks on foreigners and the Roma minority occur less frequently than in the 1990s and remain out of the headlines. However, in 2005 Jewish groups, among others, criticized the police for taking a passive approach to several neo-Nazi meetings and concerts where participants allegedly violated hate speech measures. Finally changing tactics in the fall, law enforcement agencies broke up a skinhead concert, prevented another from taking place, and charged several people with incitement to racial hatred after searching concert organizers' homes and finding explosives and Fascist/anti-Semitic materials.

Some continue to see the KSCM as an extremist group. Unlike its counterparts in other Central European countries, the KSCM remains largely unreformed, having failed to renounce its past. Prime Minister Paroubek has sent mixed signals about future cooperation with the Communists. During the 16th anniversary of the fall of Communism, he said that the party did not represent a threat to democracy. He also proposed the cancellation of the 1991 lustration law forbidding former secret police agents from holding positions in the state administration. On the other hand, the prime minister vowed not to form a government with the KSCM, regardless of the election results. Additionally, the official CSSD party line explicitly prohibits a coalition with the Communists, and the ODS, critical of supposed CSSD-KSCM cooperation, governs along with the KSCM in 31 cities across the country.[11]

Independent Media

1997	1998	1999	2001	2002	2003	2004	2005	2006
1.25	1.25	1.75	2.00	2.50	2.25	2.25	2.00	2.00

For the most part, the Czech media display sufficient independence and practice a decent, if unremarkable, level of journalism. Press freedom has long been secure in the Czech Republic, and no major media are state owned. Media are generally free of political or economic bias, though allegations still surface of pressure from both business and political interests. Rarely do newspapers publish comprehensive analyses getting to the heart of policy issues. Instead they prefer shorter, sensational articles. Still, they do provide the population with an adequate overview of the main events and issues facing society.

Anecdotal evidence suggests that media interference still takes place – especially in public broadcasting, with timid responses from management – but hard proof of direct pressure from politicians or financial groups rarely surfaces. Such was the case in December 2005, when Czech TV, the public television station, canceled its top-rated journalism program after Prime Minister Paroubek repeatedly complained about its objectivity. Management claimed to have canceled the program because it was expensive and an independent analysis had shown it to be unbalanced, rather than as a result of pressure. Many doubted this explanation, given the approaching elections.

The national print media offer a diverse selection of daily newspapers, weeklies, and magazines. Foreign corporations own many of these publications, including nearly all the dailies. (Media-related legislation includes minimal ownership restrictions and none on foreign ownership.) In contrast with the situation a mere six or seven years ago, the "serious" press has now matured to a point where it offers more balanced political coverage and opinions. However, some analysts believe that upcoming elections have prompted a relapse, with the press returning to the political polarization of the 1990s. Sacrificing impartiality and fairness in favor of waging thinly veiled wars against political enemies, some papers periodically publish attacks on the government based on hearsay and rumor.

According to ABC Czech Republic, the Audit Bureau of Circulations, *Mlada Fronta Dnes*, the most popular serious daily, sold an average of 290,424 copies in December 2005, as compared with the tabloid *Blesk* at 507,220, *Pravo* at 167,228, *Hospodarske Noviny* at 68,174, and *Lidove Noviny* at 66,473. *Respekt*, a well-regarded independent weekly, suffers from low sales (15,426 copies). More popular are *Tyden* (62,556 copies) and *Reflex* (52,091 copies), both respected weeklies concerning culture, society, and politics, and *Nedelni Svet* (26,773), the country's first quality Sunday newspaper. Many Czechs also receive their news from Web sites run by major dailies, though overall Internet usage continues to lag behind that of the West owing largely to very high dial-up costs. Estimates vary, with some figures quoting "Internet penetration" at nearly half of the population and others offering considerably lower numbers. However, the market has grown for high-speed mobile phone and wireless access, which should boost these numbers significantly.

Even with the wide range of publications available, true investigative journalism remains at a premium, appearing occasionally in some daily newspapers and on some television stations, but regularly only in *Respekt*. Some media analysts worry about the impact on investigative journalism of amending the criminal code to ban the use of hidden cameras (making it an offense punishable with up to five years in prison). Supporters of the bill – approved by the lower house – have insisted that the change was made to protect people from unscrupulous private security services, extorters, and aggressive tabloid newspapers and point out that the civil code allows exceptions for journalists who act in the public interest.[12]

In September, the Constitutional Court set a precedent by ruling that journalists do not have to disclose their sources, a landmark decision that could in fact bolster investigative journalism. The ruling effectively strengthened the 2000 Law on the Press – which provides the right to hide a source for publishers rather than individual journalists – and formalized an exception to the penal code, which mandates full cooperation with the police.[13] Changes to the Law on the Press may be on the horizon, however. Disgusted by the media coverage of his party, Prime Minister Paroubek has repeatedly threatened to change the law if he remains in power after the 2006 elections. In contrast, the Czech Syndicate of Journalists puts the fault not with the law's inability to deal with libel, but with the slow consideration of complaints by relevant courts.[14]

Some media critics have charged that certain publications practice a form of self-censorship by shying away from stories that capture top advertisers in a poor light. Others surmise that commercial TV stations occasionally ignore stories that might harm their parent companies' financial interests. In 2005, the editor in chief of an English-language publication, the *Czech Business Weekly*, resigned, saying that the owner of the paper, a powerful Czech businessman, had attempted to interfere in an article about one of the businessman's companies.

Journalists are loath to complain about ethical violations; they fear dismissal and know all too well the small size of the media market, where a huge number of applicants compete for each newly available position. (Along those lines, true media criticism hardly exists in the mainstream press because journalists refrain from antagonizing potential employers.) Furthermore, some foreign media owners have been denounced for not adhering to the same employment standards followed in their home countries. The lack of a collective bargaining agreement at the national level between publishers and the Czech Syndicate of Journalists means employers are bound only by normal labor law. The syndicate, which counts few influential members, has played a largely insignificant role post-Communism. It does, however, work in the field of media ethics, which includes setting standards.

Unfortunately, the public television station, Czech TV, is unable to fill the market's gaps in terms of independence and high-quality news programming. Czech TV's news programs have improved in recent years, but the station's financial difficulties make it particularly vulnerable to political and business interests. The Chamber of Deputies appoints Czech TV's supervisory board and controls viewer fees – the station's lifeblood. In 2005, parliamentarians decided to phase in higher fees and ban advertising except during key cultural or sporting events. Some called the decision a gift to commercial stations a year before a tight election battle. It has long been assumed that the private stations' powerful lobbying has had an undue influence on parliamentary deputies, resulting in laws favoring commercial stations over public broadcasters.

Digital television should eventually help level the market and provide more plurality in broadcasting – if additional stations receive licenses. Up to now, the debate on digitalization has fallen victim to a heated dispute over license regulation, and progress has been slow. The Parliament finally approved the necessary legislation in February 2005, but politicians have reportedly applied pressure to stagnate the licensing process to increase their control – despite attempts by the Radio and Television Broadcasting Council, the industry regulator, to accelerate the process of granting digital licenses.[15]

In the meantime, the past year has seen growing competition in the traditional television market. Prima TV's success has been reflected in a record share of the market, up to 28 percent, and declining numbers for TV Nova, now at around 38 percent, according to *Czech Business Weekly*.[16] Czech TV's two channels garner together almost 29 percent. These stations are more politically balanced than several years ago, when the most powerful station, TV Nova, was often accused of supporting the ODS.

Adding to the growing competition, the year saw the appearance of several new sources of quality information. Despite its continued financial troubles, Czech TV launched the country's first all-news channel, CT 24. Although the station is available only to a small percentage of the population through the Internet or satellite, the majority will have access with the introduction of digital broadcasting. In addition, Centrum, the Czech Republic's second largest Web portal, unveiled Aktualne.cz, the country's first exclusively online daily. The site has a staff of 60 editorial employees, including talented investigative journalists, and plans to compete by offering a serious alternative to the sensationalism of much of the print media. On the downside, the Czech service of the BBC will be closing in 2006 as a cost-cutting measure. The station's hard-hitting interviews and commentary will be missed.

Local Democratic Governance

1997	1998	1999	2001	2002	2003	2004	2005	2006
n/a	n/a	n/a	n/a	n/a	n/a	n/a	2.00	2.00

After long delays, the development of local government structures and authority has become one of the country's bright spots in recent years. Landmark legislation passed in 1997 led to the creation of 14 regions, which began functioning in 2001. The central government handed over significant powers to these regions in fields such as education, health care, and road maintenance. Additionally, 205 newly created municipalities replaced 73 district offices, which ceased all their activities by the end of 2002. Self-governed regions and municipalities own property and manage separate budgets. Voters directly elect regional assemblies, which then choose regional councils and regional governors. The regional councils may pass legal resolutions and levy fines. Directly elected municipal assemblies elect municipal councils and mayors. Municipalities wield considerable power over areas such as welfare, building permits, forest and waste management, and motor vehicle registration.

Some analysts consider the creation of the regions as one of the most important steps in the country's recent history. The regions have made considerable progress in tackling problems neglected by the central government. The education system is a prime example. Although the birth rate dropped rapidly from the end of Communism and reduced the number of pupils, the state failed to take the unpopular steps of closing schools and firing teachers. Since acquiring power, some regions have moved much more forcefully, shuttering schools and tying funding more strictly to the number of students. Such savings will go toward better equipment and higher salaries for teachers, reports *Respekt*. These improvements have emboldened regional administrations to seek more power and money from the state for education, and some regional leaders have even called for funds connected to high schools to go directly to the regions instead of the Ministry of Education, according to *Lidove Noviny*.

Overall, the success in regional management and greater autonomy has made a strong case for allowing regional governments to manage more of their money. They currently control only a small percent of their budgets, a fact that causes consternation among local leaders. For the large bulk of their budgets, regions essentially act as middlemen for the state, sending money to predetermined recipients, reports *Tyden*.

The failure of funds flowing from the center to keep pace with these newly added responsibilities has proven just as vexing for local politicians, with respect both to new laws and to EU commitments. For example, municipalities must now finance the last year of kindergarten but have not received any funds from the central government to do so.[17] Local politicians complain regularly that the central government has transferred major tasks without the money necessary to do their jobs well. The funds they do receive, they say, should be based on their communities' relative wealth rather than sheer size. The regions are allowed to keep only a fraction of the tax money they help collect, although that is an improvement from earlier amounts. The government has assisted occasionally – approving, for example, a transfer of billions of crowns to help impoverished hospitals – but that support has been insufficient. Municipalities, in turn, believe regions do not have the competences, money, or experience necessary to effectively influence local development.

Adding to the aggravation of local authorities, the law allocates a broad range of responsibilities to regional governments, but in practice the transfer has been gradual and the regions have not yet assumed full control over promised areas. Competences have sometimes been transferred, but legislation that would force change with "ownership" has lagged. For instance, the regions now receive funds to care for socially vulnerable citizens, yet no specific law exists to bind local authorities to certain minimum standards (only guidelines). Not surprisingly, some regions have taken the initiative and improved the system, while others have done little, claiming they don't have the money for major changes.

At this stage, insufficiencies at the local level can best be explained as a combination of limited resources and inexperience in areas long neglected even at the national level, such as implementing gender equality provisions, improving civic participation, and addressing the needs of marginal groups. For instance, a Ministry of Labor report in 2005 concluded that the performance of local authorities in integrating foreigners remains very uneven, with some municipalities and regions doing virtually nothing to further integration. Saying the situation had not improved much since 2003, the report called for changes in legislation that would better define the division of powers between the state administration and local governments and encourage the creation of local strategies for integrating foreigners.[18]

Greater transparency and corruption-fighting instruments have not kept up with the transfer of responsibilities and finances to local governments, and endemic cronyism remains a critical problem. A Transparency International-Czech Republic (TIC) study released in November indicated a widespread lack of transparency in awarding public contracts for construction projects in the country's eight largest cities. After reviewing contracts over the past five years for projects in which town halls had awarded more than 10 million crowns (US$413,000), TIC researchers cited possible favoritism and links between these companies and local officials. Among other problems, the lack of effective control mechanisms, frequent lapses in announcing open competitive biddings, and the failure to publicly announce decisions and provide other information about the tenders annually leads to enormous losses, TIC concluded.[19]

The NKU currently has no legal right to examine the financial management of regional governments or municipalities. Although Transparency International and some parliamentary deputies favor changing the law, others argue either that local governments should implement their own controls – in the spirit of self-government – or that sufficient controls already exist.[20] With local politicians immune from any conflict-of-interest regulations,[21] it is no wonder that numerous cases of unethical behavior continue to occur.

Public knowledge about regional authorities has improved considerably but still leaves much to be desired. Before the last elections, in 2004, a poll conducted by the Factum Invenio agency showed that an unusually high number of people held no opinion about their regional administration, with 40 percent claiming ignorance about the services these bodies provide. Despite these challenges, some regional politicians have already made names for themselves, indicating that the development of local governance has also had a positive effect on the political elite, enhancing its breadth and variety. Increasingly, success at local and regional levels is seen as a conduit to greater power on the national stage.

Judicial Framework and Independence

1997	1998	1999	2001	2002	2003	2004	2005	2006
1.50	1.50	2.25	2.50	2.50	2.50	2.50	2.50	2.25

The four-tier judicial system consists of district courts (86), regional courts (8), high courts (2), and the Supreme Court. The Czech Constitutional Court is a well-respected institution that may be addressed directly by citizens who believe their fundamental rights have been infringed. In 2005, President Klaus completed the process of appointing new Constitutional Court justices (following a drawn-out dispute with the Senate), appointing individuals reportedly close to his political philosophy. The independence of the Constitutional Court has, according to some respected constitutional experts, seriously declined.

Although the Czech judiciary is constitutionally independent, the minister of justice appoints, transfers, and terminates the tenure of the presidents and vice presidents of the courts. Recent reform attempts preserved the Ministry of Justice's central role in overseeing the judiciary and drew criticism that the executive continued to compromise the true independence of the courts, as noted in a report issued by EUROPEUM Institute for European Policy. However, there is more talk about the potential for abuse and systematic pressure on judges to follow the ministry line than about cases of overt meddling, which remain rare.

The critical financial situation in the judicial branch eased in 2005, and the year saw the first significant batch of new judicial appointments in recent years. In the process, however, President Klaus clashed with the Union of Judges when he refused to appoint several dozen judicial trainees under 30 years of age. (Although stipulating this age minimum, current legislation makes an exception for the current trainees because they joined the profession before the stipulation took effect.) Critics of Klaus's move complained that youth and lack of experience have not prevented many younger judges from outperforming their older peers.

The situation also improved with respect to salaries. Over the course of the year, the average pay of judges and state attorneys rose by around 18 percent.[22] Judges also applauded the Constitutional Court decision that the state pay them the bonus salaries from 2003 and 2004 that were abolished through the passage of an austerity law. The Court ruled that the cost-cutting measure clashed with the principle of judicial independence, placing judges' compensation at the whim of the cabinet and the Parliament.[23]

The Czech Republic continues to pay a monetary price for its slow judicial system, losing numerous cases in 2005 at the European Court of Human Rights in Strasbourg over the length of court proceedings. Some individuals have waited over a decade for decisions in business disputes; others have been illegally held in detention for extensive periods of time. In general, while some areas continue to have considerable problems – such as the settling of commercial cases – the backlog seems to be shrinking and the overall situation improving slowly. Laggards now face a greater likelihood of disciplinary action or even dismissal.

Although the public and much of the media continue to see the inefficiency of the judicial system as a direct result of too few judges, experts say this is an oversimplification. In fact, a Ministry of Justice report from 2004 concluded that the country actually has the highest per capita number of judges in the EU. The problem, says the ministry, lies in the departure of many compromised Communist-era judges in the 1990s and the subsequent abundance of unresolved cases from those years, including many complicated business and civil disputes. In addition, as the weekly Respekt has pointed out, the courts move slowly because the lack of reform has meant that judges continue to perform many chores, including administrative work. As a result, statistics have shown that raising the number of judges has not dramatically shortened the length of court proceedings.[24] Once reform does arrive and judges manage to clear the backlog of old cases, there may very well be too many judges.[25]

In October, the Ministry of Justice and the chairmen of the country's highest courts closed a series of agreements designed to ease some of these problems. The ministry pledged to enshrine in law the position of court assistant, who would handle much of the court's administrative work, freeing up judges, and also pledged to hire new judges and concentrate on sending them to understaffed regions. The deal also included a provision to quickly identify long-delayed cases. However, legal analysts have doubted whether these reforms will actually be implemented in the near future as a result of Justice Minister Pavel Nemec's lame duck position – his Freedom Party will almost certainly not gather enough votes to remain in the Parliament after the 2006 elections.

With some exceptions, fundamental freedoms – enshrined in the Charter of Rights and Freedoms section of the Constitution – are generally thought to be well protected in the Czech Republic. However, the country has dragged on passing antidiscrimination legislation in line with the UN Convention and European standards. The government finally approved the bill in December 2004, but it has since languished in the Parliament. Although an amendment to the labor code in 2001 mandated equal treatment for all employees, implementation lags as women remain underrepresented in senior positions and are paid materially less than men for similar jobs. No significant government measures have been undertaken to remedy these problems, and the bodies that do exist to combat discrimination remain powerless to do more than simply report it, according to a recent Open Society Institute report on equal opportunity. The report found lack of political will as a serious obstacle toward promoting gender equality.[26]

The government is planning a major campaign to promote gender equality, but as the daily *Mlada Fronta Dnes* pointed out, increased activity comes at a time when political parties have recently made clear that few women will appear at the top of candidate lists for the 2006 parliamentary elections. Overall, few women hold seats in the Parliament or attain other positions of leadership. Only 2 of 18 ministers are women, and there are no women regional governors. The country's first women's party – Equality – was officially registered in 2005, with the party's leaders describing as their main goal to increase the number of women in politics.

Discrimination against the Roma in employment and housing is also a serious problem, and a government report released in January 2005 showed that the situation worsened over the past few years. The report, which compared the current state of Roma affairs with that of the second half of the 1990s, found 75 percent of Roma out of work for over a year and at least 18,000 Roma living in growing ghettos. There were some bright spots, however. Fewer Roma children are being automatically sent to schools for the mentally handicapped, and many more are entering higher education, according to *Mlada Fronta Dnes*.

Several landmark cases involving the Roma were decided in 2005. A regional court in Ostrava ruled, for the first time anywhere in Central or Eastern Europe, that a Roma woman's rights had been violated when she was sterilized without her qualified consent in 2001. Courts also found in two cases that businesses had discriminated against Roma in their hiring practices and awarded thousands of crowns in damages. The NGO Poradna sparked both lawsuits by sending Roma and white Czech women with similar qualifications to pose as job seekers. Employees at the targeted businesses told the Roma women that they had no chance for the positions but encouraged their white counterparts to apply.[27]

Activist groups have previously complained about police brutality in detention, but the year's biggest outcry against law enforcement agencies took place after Czech police broke up a techno music festival in late July. According to media reports and complaints from many individuals who attended the CzechTek festival, police used brutal force and beat festival attendees as they lay on the ground. More than 100 people suffered injuries. The authorities claimed that such uses of force were limited to "individual excesses" as officers attempted to protect private plots from trespassers. An investigation by the Czech ombudsman deemed the police's behavior excessive, yet as of late November, 13 individuals had been accused of assaulting police officers or other crimes but no policemen had been charged.

Corruption

1997	1998	1999	2001	2002	2003	2004	2005	2006
n/a	n/a	3.25	3.75	3.75	3.50	3.50	3.50	3.50

Corruption is another area where gradual improvements are more a testament to the country's overall maturation than the result of concrete actions taken by the governing elite or the population at large. Ordinary people still complain about paying bribes or "giving gifts" in exchange for expediting services, as excessive regulation continues to plague parts of the public administration. Yet these are exceptions rather than the rule, and most people are able to conduct their daily lives without engaging in corrupt behavior.

Although few people encounter corruption directly, the perception of illegal activity, especially among the political elite, is widespread and escalating. That may be partly due to media and political exaggeration, but in 2005 the public did face countless examples of official wrongdoing – at national and local levels. Many view existing anticorruption measures as insufficient to dismantle the intricate web of connections between political and business elites. A September poll conducted by the Center for Research of Public Opinion showed that respondents believed bribes and corruption have the greatest influence over politicians' decision making, followed by interest groups and lobbying, and then voters and the media.[28] Another poll by the same organization indicated that respondents were most dissatisfied with the level of corruption (83 percent, a figure growing since 2003) and economic crime (80 percent).[29]

Expert surveys carry similarly pessimistic views, such as the Transparency International Corruption Perceptions Index, which measures the perceived level of corruption among politicians and public officials. In the 2005 survey, the Czech Republic tied with Greece, Slovakia, and Namibia for 47th to 50th places (out of 159 countries), with a rating of 4.3 (10 indicates a country without corruption). Although a slight improvement over 2004, when the country was 54th with a rating of 4.2, it was still bad enough to rate the Czech Republic with the third worst level of perceived corruption in the EU. While the situation has improved in other new member states, the rating for the Czech Republic continues to stagnate. In a press release announcing the new survey, the TIC said it viewed the situation as gravest in the areas of public contracts, conflict of interest, controls over public spending, nontransparency of the state administration, an overabundant bureaucracy, and lack of thorough and professional investigations when laws are broken.[30] A TIC report earlier in the year estimated that in 2004, ineffective and opaque methods of awarding public contracts cost taxpayers 32.4 billion crowns: 15 billion crowns (US$625 million) at the municipal level and 17.4 billon crowns (US$725 million) at the central government level. The organization placed the greatest responsibility on politicians at all levels of the state administration who continue to influence the course of public tenders and refuse to create an effective framework for awarding public contracts or appropriate control mechanisms.[31]

Among the most pressing control mechanisms – especially in light of the scandals that brought down former prime minister Stanislav Gross earlier in 2005 – is effective conflict-of-interest legislation. Despite widespread criticism that current regulations are insufficient and allow loopholes, it took two years of preparation for the government to finally approve a much more powerful bill in August. In January 2006, the lower house of Parliament passed the bill, which immediately faced criticism for not requiring asset declarations from the spouses of public officials covered by the law (members of the government and the Parliament, local government representatives, and others). Still, even most critics admitted the proposal was a step forward.[32] If passed by the Senate and signed by the president, the law would become valid in 2007. A new traffic law, which will introduce a point system and stricter penalties mid-2006, should also lessen corruption among traffic police, who often accept bribes instead of applying fines.

In 2005, parliamentary chairman Lubomir Zaoralek introduced a voluntary code of ethics, which would regulate, for example, the relationship between politicians and lobbyists, the acceptance of gifts, and the employment of family members. Complaints from his colleagues forced Zaoralek to remove provisions banning meetings with unregistered lobbyists and the obligatory publication of all forms of income. Prime Minister Paroubek vowed to have each CSSD candidate in the next election sign the code beforehand, but that requirement soon turned into a voluntary measure. By year's end, according to Mlada Fronta Dnes, only 9 deputies of 200 had signed the code of ethics.[33]

The Gross scandal set the stage for a year filled with corruption-related cases. Toward the end of the year, the press made almost daily revelations about wrongdoings. Prominent cases in 2005 included the resignation of Agricultural Minister Petr Zgarba, who, like his predecessors, presided over a string of suspicious activities at the Land Fund, which has long faced accusations of cronyism, conflict of interest, and sales of cheap land to the politically connected. The final straw came when an acquaintance of Zgarba's earned billions of crowns in another suspect deal. Also making headlines were allegations that privatization of the Czech chemical giant

Unipetrol involved high-level shenanigans in both the Czech Republic and Poland. In November, eight people, including a deputy minister in the Ministry of Local Development, were accused of stealing 229 million crowns (US$9.5 million) in EU funds, and in December the Parliament was set to withdraw the immunity of an ODS parliamentary deputy accused by police of mediating a bribe.

Jeremy Druker is executive director and editor in chief of Transitions Online, *an Internet newsmagazine covering Central and Eastern Europe, the Balkans, and the former Soviet Union. Alice Drukerova, a freelance journalist, and Samuel Murphey, a student at Truman State University in the United States, assisted in the research for this report.*

---

[1] Czech News Agency (CTK), "Young People Are Embarrassed About Their Politicians and Corruption," October 25, 2005.

[2] Radek Bartonicek, "For Three-Quarters of Czechs This Year Life Changed for the Better," Mlada Fronta Dnes, December 31, 2005-January 2006.

[3] Karel Hvizdala, "The Czech Elite Doesn't Think European," interview with Jacques Rupnik, Respekt, March 6, 2005. Poll cited in article was conducted by Center for Empirical Research.

[4] Czech News Agency (CTK), "CVVM: People Believe Bribes and Lobbying Most Influence Politicians," September 9, 2005.

[5] Hana Capova, "Anarchy in Parliament," Respekt, September 19-25, 2005.

[6] Silvie Blechova, "His Majesty Klaus," Respekt, April 25-May 1, 2005.

[7] Czech News Agency (CTK), "Klaus Compared Nongovernmental Organizations to the Communists," October 9, 2005.

[8] Results of Research About Corporate Philanthropy, Donors Forum in cooperation with the AGNES NGO, www.donorsforum.cz/index.php?id=1054&kat=4&lang=.

[9] Jaroslav Pasmik, "Report of a New Civilization," Respekt, March 14-20, 2005.

[10] Nadezda Horakova, "Satisfaction with the Situation in Several Areas," Center for Research of Public Opinion, September 5, 2005, www.cvvm.cas.cz/index.php?disp=zpravy&lang=0&r=1&s=&offset=&shw=100509.

[11] Ivan Motyl, "Red-Blue Chance," Tyden, November 28, 2005.

[12] Czech News Agency (CTK), "Planned Bill Does Not Threaten Media's Use of Hidden Camera-MP," November 14, 2005.

[13] Czech News Agency (CTK), "Journalist Does Not Have to Disclose Information Source-Court," September 27, 2005.

[14] Czech Syndicate of Journalists, "Czech Syndicate of Journalists' Statement About the Law on the Press," September 9, 2005, www.sncr.cz/index.phtml?id=173.

[15] Marius Dragomir, "Politicians Start to Get into the Picture over Allocation of Digital Television Licenses," Czech Business Weekly, February 21, 2005.

[16] Marius Dragomir, "Prima's Rescue?" Czech Business Weekly, October 10, 2005.

[17] Czech News Agency (CTK), "Towns, Government Agree on Better Cooperation," July 22, 2005.

[18] Czech News Agency (CTK), "Some Regions Do Nothing for Integration of Foreigners," January 3, 2005.

[19] "Public Contracting in Construction Industry Greatly Suffers from Nontransparent Procedures; at the Municipal Level, Clientelism Prevails," Transparency International–Czech Republic, November 1, 2005, www.transparency.cz/index.php?id=2796.

[20] Pravo, "Politicians Resist Giving NKU Control over Town Halls," November 2, 2005.

[21] "Politician and Academic Agree: Law on Conflict of Interest for All Representatives," statement of Bez Korupce alliance of NGOs working for a conflict-of-interest law, November 21, 2005, www.bezkorupce.cz/vypis_zpravy.php?id=2005112101.

Czech News Agency (CTK), "Government Releases Hundreds of Millions for Judges' Salaries," October 19, 2005.

[23] Czech News Agency (CTK), "State Must Pay 13th, 14th Salaries to Judges-Const. Court," August 12, 2005.

[24] Vaclav Moravec, interview with Jaromir Jirsa, BBC, December 1, 2005.

[25] Jaroslav Spurny, "2700 Angry Judges," Respekt, March 21-27, 2005.

[26] "Executive Summary for the Czech Republic," pp. 61-66. Equal Opportunities for Women and Men, Open Society Institute Network Women's Program, 2005. http://www.soros.org/initiatives/women/articles_publications/publications/equal_20050502/a_equal_20050502.pdf

[27] Brian Kenety, "'Wired' Czech Romani Women Win Racial Discrimination Cases," Radio Prague, March 23, 2005.

[28] Czech News Agency (CTK), "CVVM: People Believe Bribes and Lobbying Most Influence Politicians," September 9, 2005

[29] Nadezda Horakova, "Satisfaction with the Situation in Several Areas," Center for Research of Public Opinion, September 5, 2005, www.cvvm.cas.cz/index.php?disp=zpravy&lang=0&r=1&s=&offset=&shw=100509.

30 "Index CPI 2005: Czech Republic Has the Third Worst Rating in the EU," Transparency International – Czech Republic press statement, September 18, 2005.

[31] "Nontransparent Public Contracts Cost the Czech Republic 32 Million Crowns Last Year," Transparency International – Czech Republic press statement, June 28, 2005.

[32] Sabina Slonkova, "Confict of Interests Passes Lower House Pruned," aktualne.cz, January 25, 2006.

[33] Vaclav Dolejsi, "Promises Which Politicians Again This Year Didn't Fulfill," Mlada Fronta Dnes, December 30, 2005.

Estonia

Capital:	Tallinn
Population:	1.3 million
GNI/capita:	$7,080
Ethnic Groups:	Estonian (67.9%), Russian (25.6%), other (6.5%)

Nations in Transit Ratings and Averaged Scores

	1997	1998	1999	2001	2002	2003	2004	2005	2006
Electoral Process	2.00	1.75	1.75	1.75	1.75	1.75	1.50	1.50	1.50
Civil Society	2.25	2.25	2.50	2.25	2.00	2.00	2.00	2.00	2.00
Independent Media	1.75	1.75	1.75	1.75	1.75	1.75	1.50	1.50	1.50
Governance *	2.25	2.25	2.25	2.25	2.25	2.25	2.25	n/a	n/a
National Democratic Governance	n/a	n/a	n/a	n/a	n/a	n/a	n/a	2.25	2.25
Local Democratic Governance	n/a	n/a	n/a	n/a	n/a	n/a	n/a	2.50	2.50
Judicial Framework and Independence	2.25	2.25	2.00	2.00	1.75	1.75	1.75	1.50	1.50
Corruption	n/a	n/a	3.25	2.75	2.50	2.50	2.50	2.50	2.50
Democracy Score	2.10	2.05	2.25	2.13	2.00	2.00	1.92	1.96	1.96

* With the 2005 edition, Freedom House introduced seperate analysis and ratings for national democratic governance and local democratic governance to provide readers with more detailed and nuanced analysis of these two important subjects.

NOTE: The ratings reflect the consensus of Freedom House, its academic advisers, and the author of this report. The opinions expressed in this report are those of the author. The ratings are based on a scale of 1 to 7, with 1 representing the highest level of democratic progress and 7 the lowest. The Democracy Score is an average of ratings for the categories tracked in a given year.

The economic and social data on this page were taken from the following sources:
GNI/capita, Population: *World Development Indicators 2006* (Washington, D.C.: World Bank, 2006).
Ethnic Groups: *CIA World Factbook 2006* (Washington, D.C.: Central Intelligence Agency, 2006).

EXECUTIVE SUMMARY

Estonia recovered its independence in August 1991, and in the 15 years since, it has impressed both its own citizens and the international community by its commitment to move quickly toward a market economy, to organize and carry out competitive elections that all international observers have found free and fair, and to develop a system that includes those who did not qualify for citizenship in the Republic of Estonia because either they or their parents or grandparents were not citizens of Estonia before the Soviet occupation. Because of this and an effective international public relations effort, Estonia enjoys a remarkable reputation. In virtually all spheres of public life, Estonia has made so much progress since the collapse of Communism that it now begs comparison with states that have long had established free market economies, vibrant civil societies, and well-institutionalized democratic governance. Nevertheless, the country faces serious problems in the economic, social, and political spheres.

Although Estonia's economy continues to grow vigorously, maintaining the epithet "the little country that could," the benefits of this growth have not touched many groups. There are serious problems about providing transfer payments to the increasing number of elderly people, particularly given the flat tax structure. The country has a lively civil society, but one that has not yet solved either the problem of integrating noncitizens or the challenges arising from its small size. Its economic success may be limited by Russian plans to build a pipeline under the Baltic from the Russian Federation to Germany that will bypass Estonia. And it has established democratic institutions, but it has not developed effective political parties, which has generated widespread public mistrust of political institutions and kept political participation rates relatively low.

After an impressive start in the early 1990s, the pace of reform seemed to lose momentum and for the last six years Estonia has been facing largely the same set of problems. For many of its citizens, 2004 – the year in which Estonia became a member of both the European Union (EU) and NATO – represented the country's own version of "the end of history," with a number of Estonians concluding that their real problems were behind them and the future would be, as Johns Hopkins University Professor Francis Fukuyama predicted, boring. The year 2005 disabused Estonians on that score. Although there were no national elections in 2005, local elections in the fall were marked by declining public participation and concerns about the role of money and illicit power in the political process. A scandal involving the loss of classified documents at the Foreign Ministry – coming on the heels of a similar incident at the Defense Ministry at the end of 2004 and another in which the government appears to have assigned regional quotas for the arrest of people to be charged with corruption – did little to enhance public trust in the authorities.

But 2005 also brought three important advancements regarding Estonia's evolution as a civil society. First, by his decision to consult with the nation about whether he should attend the May 9 commemoration of the 60th anniversary of the end of World War II in Europe, President Arnold Ruutel increased public confidence in the presidency, especially when the Russian government backed out of an accord defining the borders between the two countries. That new popular support helped to increase the number of Estonians in favor of amending the Constitution to allow for a directly elected president. Second, Estonia intensified its efforts to integrate its noncitizens and passed an important milestone in November 2005: In that month, for the first time ever, there were more people who had been naturalized since the recovery of independence in 1991 than there were noncitizens. That prompted the country's leaders to suggest that the noncitizen issue, which has attracted so much international discussion, would be resolved completely within the next 10 years. Poll results about interethnic attitudes and the setting up of new Russian-language editions of some Estonian publications help to explain their confidence. Third, despite the presence of a great deal of Euro-skepticism among Estonians, leaders in Tallinn, the capital, have not only played an important role in key EU-wide institutions, but have more or less completed Estonia's adaptation of the country's legislation and regulatory schemes to EU standards, setting the stage for Estonia's likely integration into the euro and Schengen zones in the near term. Estonia has done this even as it continues to pioneer in the use of e-governance and other Internet-based technologies.

National Democratic Governance. Estonia remains a parliamentary democracy, but it was unable to get through the year without the fall of one government and continued ministerial shuffling – events that reflected shortcomings in the development of effective and disciplined parties and the highly personal nature of politics in such a small country. Because of this turbulence, the Parliament was unable to reach agreement on many key issues, and that in turn jeopardized public trust in political institutions. At the same time, however, the government was able to keep its finances in order thanks to strong economic growth, and Estonia's pioneering efforts in e-governance advanced. *Estonia's national democratic governance remains unchanged at 2.25.*

Electoral Process. There were no national elections in 2005, but voting for local governments in October sparked much debate about the country's political system, the level of corruption of its political leaders, and the balance of power between national and local government bodies. Participation remained low, although it did not fall as far as some had expected. Efforts fell short to revise the Constitution to allow for the direct election of the president in place of the current arrangement (in which the president is chosen either by the Parliament or, failing that, a special electoral college including parliamentarians and regional officials). *Estonia's electoral process rating remains unchanged at 1.50.*

Civil Society. Despite continuing government efforts to expand the nongovernmental organization (NGO) sector, Estonia's small population (just over 1.3 million people) continues to make it difficult for NGOs to attract the kind of domestic support necessary to achieve that goal. And the dependence of many groups in this sector on foreign funding has generated suspicions among some about their activities. But over the last year, several NGOs have begun to work more directly with both political parties and the government bureaucracy and have achieved some success in areas like alcoholism, drug abuse, and family violence. *Estonia's civil society score remains at 2.00.*

Independent Media. Estonia's media scene in 2005 showed mixed success. On the positive side, the media operate free of direct government regulation, and the press is vigorous in reporting on a wide range of problems. Moreover, Estonia is one of the most Internet-connected countries on earth. On the negative side, however, Estonia is a very small media market. As a result, newspapers are financed not by bundled advertising, but either by subscriptions and direct sales to readers, which drives up prices, or by owners, which in such a tiny media market leads inevitably to speculation about the politics behind certain reports. The most important development in 2005 was the appearance of a Russian-language edition of the country's largest daily, a step that may help promote a common public space for the two language communities. But the positive impact of that step was limited by a conflict over the future of Russian channels on Estonia's cable networks, one ultimately resolved in favor of continuing most but not all Russian-language broadcasts. *Estonia's independent media rating remains at 1.50.*

Local Democratic Governance. Local elections in October 2005 sparked new discussion about the transfer of power, especially taxation power, to local governments but did not lead to a resolution of that long-contentious issue. But more important, the run-up to the voting generated heightened attention to the continuing high level of corruption in many parts of the political system. *Reflecting the combination of those two trends, Estonia's rating for local democratic governance remains at 2.50.*

Judicial Framework and Independence. Following the country's accession to the EU in 2004, Estonia's judges continued to receive training in judicial activity. But efforts to provide training for prosecutors, a key part of the judicial system, have been stymied by officials who see prosecutors rather than judges as central to the control of the courts. Prison conditions remain troubling, especially since Estonia has one of the highest rates of incarceration in the EU. *Estonia's rating for judicial framework and independence remains at 1.50.*

Corruption. Estonians continue to view their government as more corrupt than monitoring organizations believe it to be. Most obvious forms of corruption have declined; indeed, by eliminating many regulations, leaders in Tallinn effectively diminished such corruption. But the country's small size means that people generally know one another, which breeds suspicions that some of these contacts will be used illegitimately. In addition, there is another kind of corruption – one that is powered either by domestic politicians seeking power or by foreign governments seeking influence – that many Estonians believe is widespread, even though it is seldom tracked effectively by monitors. *Estonia's corruption rating remains at 2.50.*

Outlook for 2006. The next year appears likely to be marked by greater political instability within the Parliament as various political figures and parties position themselves for parliamentary and especially presidential elections in 2006. In that environment, there seem certain to be more exposures about corruption real and imagined. At the same time, the integration of noncitizens is likely to continue to accelerate as ethnic Russians conclude that being a citizen of Estonia within the EU is their best choice. But virtually all other problems that Estonia faces today are likely to continue, their resolution blocked either by the country's small size or by the absence of the political will to address them.

MAIN REPORT

National Democratic Governance

1997	1998	1999	2001	2002	2003	2004	2005	2006
n/a	n/a	n/a	n/a	n/a	n/a	n/a	2.25	2.25

Estonia is a vibrant parliamentary democracy, but in 2005, as has been the case in many of the past years since the restoration of independence, it was unable to get through the year without the fall of one government and continued ministerial shuffling – developments that reflected shortcomings in the evolution of effective and disciplined parties and the highly personal nature of politics in a country this small. The government of Prime Minister Juhan Parts fell just short of its second anniversary, barely increasing the average tenure of post-Soviet Estonian governments. And ministerial reshufflings and resignations, including that of the foreign minister for mishandling classified information, continued as well, again doing little to alter the post-Soviet average of one new minister every 23.1 days.[1]

Because of this turbulence, the Parliament failed to reach agreement on many issues, and some ministers lacked the time needed to master their jobs, a pattern that led to a deterioration of public trust in the legislature and the government. According to Eurobarometer surveys in 2005, as was the case in the last five years, Estonians tended to have the lowest assessments of life overall among the titular nationalities of EU countries, which may help explain their attitudes toward the government[2] – and, at the same time, may explain the relatively high percentages of Estonians who say they would like to have the president elected by popular vote rather than (as now) by the Parliament or a larger electoral college.[3] Despite the level of popular support for changing the Constitution on this point, the Parliament did not do so in the course of 2005.

But if there was continuing turmoil at the level of personalities within the governing coalitions, a development that many might have expected to lead to either radical departures or gridlock, the Estonian government continued in the same basic directions in social, economic, and political life that have won it praise from a variety of international monitoring organizations. It was able to keep its finances in good order thanks to strong economic growth. It was able to cope with the challenges of applying nationally and locally the new requirements of EU membership. And it was able to continue its pioneering work with e-governance.[4]

The courts have remained strongly independent, although efforts to improve the training of prosecutors have run into some resistance from the government, according to the Estonian Law Center, largely because some officials still view political access to that part of the legal system critical to their ability to run the country.

Three other developments in this sphere during the course of 2005 were especially noteworthy. First, in November 2005 Estonia passed an important milestone in its continued efforts to integrate its noncitizens. In widely reported comments, the government announced that the number of people naturalized as Estonians since 1992 now exceeds at 137,000 the number of remaining noncitizens. Moreover, officials projected that Estonia is on target to integrate fully all of the latter within the next decade, as it has promised the EU and other international institutions it will do. (At the same time, however, it is worth noting that the number of Russian speakers in Estonia who have taken Russian Federation citizenship also increased in the past year by 1,500, according to the Estonian Foreign Ministry's Web site. Some Russian Federation officials have given slightly higher numbers.) Although it seems unlikely that all of those without citizenship on Estonian territory will gain citizenship before the decade is out, as some Estonian political leaders have suggested, it is clearly the case that Estonia in 2005 made signal progress in this regard.

Second, and parallel to this development, given the failure of parties appealing strictly to ethnic Russian groups to achieve representation in the national Parliament, ever more Russian politicians have shifted their allegiance to Estonian parties. A major reason for this, as developments in Latvia at the end of 2004 showed, is that about two years ago, Moscow shifted its policies in this regard, calculating not only in Estonia, but also in Latvia that working via parties dominated by the titular nationality may be more effective than maintaining "Russian" parties that will have little chance to come to power. While some international observers have complained that this shift shows Estonia's unwillingness to integrate the Russians, in fact it highlights the progress Estonia has made in fully integrating into the broader political system the members of one ethnic community.

Third, the past remained very much with Estonians in the political sphere. In what was a stocktaking year in the wake of gaining membership in the EU and NATO – some commentators had referred to 2004 as having ushered in a kind of "end of history" mentality in that Baltic republic – Estonians paid more attention than they have in recent years to the continued presence in Estonian political life of former Communist Party members and also of those with ties to Soviet-era security agencies. In 1992, 29 of the 101 members of the Parliament were former Communist

Party of the Soviet Union (CPSU) members; now that number has risen to 39. Moreover, half of the ministers and the president of the country are also former Communists.[5]

At the same time, articles accusing one or another member of the government or political establishment of having been in the KGB continued to surface. Some newspapers played up reports by the security police that some Estonians – and even some active Estonian political figures – continue to maintain ties to Russian secret services. After the country's security police published a new list of Estonians with a KGB or GRU past, both the Res Publica and Center parties promised to expel anyone in their ranks with that background. Other Estonian parties have done so over the past 15 years.

But such charges as well as suggestions that some of these people retain their connections to the government of a foreign country have also served to undermine public confidence in the government among some strata of the population. One example of this phenomenon is provided by a poll taken in April 2005 that found that 77 percent of Estonians believe democracy is the best form of government, but only 29 percent of the country's population believes that their government reflects the will of the people.[6]

Electoral Process

1997	1998	1999	2001	2002	2003	2004	2005	2006
2.00	1.75	1.75	1.75	1.75	1.75	1.50	1.50	1.50

There were no national elections in 2005, but voting for local governments on October 16 led to an intense debate about the country's political system at all levels, about the level of corruption in the political process and among its political leaders, and about the proper balance of power between national and local governments. Participation remained low, with some observers suggesting that at below 40 percent in most venues it was "too small" to legitimate democracy.[7]

At the national level, as noted earlier, the Parliament did not approve a measure allowing for direct election of the president. That sets the stage for yet another cliffhanger of an election in 2006, in which the Parliament may not be able to select a president and the country will again have its leader chosen by an electoral college consisting of less well-known regional officials. Nor did the deputies address Estonia's dauntingly complicated electoral system involving multimember electoral districts, multiple rounds of voting and redistribution of results, and a 5 percent threshold for the representation of parties in the Parliament – arrangements that limit transparency, accountability, and ultimately the legitimacy of the democratic process.

The October 2005 elections generated significant criticism from some quarters. Two days after they were concluded, parliamentarian Igor Gryazin called for the elections to be annulled. He pointed to the fact that the country's Supreme Court had ruled only two days before the vote that members of the Parliament could not serve in local government posts, effectively changing the electoral lists in Tallinn and other major cities where some national politicians sought to run. He also complained, as had many others, that the Center Party had gotten around the ban on public advertising in the last days of the campaign in Tallinn by having one of its business allies post a sign with the party's colors and "K" displayed prominently.[8]

Observers from the Russian Federation were equally critical. They argued that Internet reporting of the results limited the ability of candidates and others to challenge those results in court, that election materials in the Russian language were insufficiently available, that the security police had sought to pressure ethnic Russians not to vote, and that there had been abuses because of the use of electronic voting.[9]

Few other observers were as critical. Indeed, most celebrated the fact that Estonia permits noncitizens to vote in local elections, something they did in about equal share to Estonian levels of participation. But at the same time, many of the Estonian media writing on this issue pointed to some more fundamental problems. First, most "local governments" are not elected at all: There are no elections for the 15 county governments, which serve as Tallinn's representatives around the country.

Second, even where there are local elections in the nearly 2,000 towns and townships, the mayors and councils, which are now elected to five-year terms (up from four years previously), have little independent power. Although by law they can adopt policies in many areas, they lack the kind of independent taxation power that would allow them genuine freedom of action: At present, they raise less than 5 percent of the money they spend from local levies; the remainder comes from the central government. Consequently, while Tallinn routinely points to how important it is that noncitizens take part in the formation of such governments, many ethnic Russian noncitizens continue to complain that this is a sham, especially outside of areas like the northeast, where ethnic Russian noncitizens predominate.

Third, given demographic declines and the move of ever more Estonians to the cities, especially to Tallinn, rural Estonia and even some of the other cities, none of which are as much as one-quarter the size of the capital, are hollowing out. On the one hand, that means many of the electoral districts are now small and getting smaller in terms of the number of voters. On the other hand, the authorities at this level are forced to deal with two difficult problems: managing the reduction in the number of schools and developing the infrastructure to support the increasing share of the population of pension age, and to do so without much in the way of new resources.

In many respects, these problems should be understood as those of a maturing democracy rather than its birth pangs. Many of them are familiar to residents of long-established democracies. And the fact that Estonia is now facing them and not other kinds of problems is a reflection of its relative success rather than its failure. But focusing only on the country's positive achievements and ignoring these current challenges does no one any favors, certainly not Estonia.

Civil Society

1997	1998	1999	2001	2002	2003	2004	2005	2006
2.25	2.25	2.50	2.25	2.00	2.00	2.00	2.00	2.00

Despite continuing government efforts to expand the NGO sector, Estonia's small size – just over 1.3 million people – continues to make it difficult for NGOs to attract the kind of domestic support necessary to achieve that goal. And the dependence of many groups in this sector on foreign funding has generated suspicions among some about their activities. But over the last year, several NGOs have begun to work more directly with both political parties and the government bureaucracy and have achieved some success in areas like health (particularly the combating of sexually transmitted diseases), alcoholism, drug abuse, and family violence.

As in the past two years, the Estonian government has met or exceeded the goals it set for itself in 2002 with the adoption of its Civil Society Development Concept and as reaffirmed by the February 2003 memorandum between the government and 39 such groups. At present, there are three distinct kinds of NGOs: nonprofits, foundations, and nonprofit partnerships. Only the first two must register, and there are approximately 600 of them, although many are very small and relatively inactive or even dormant.

Despite their limitations, NGOs are increasingly recognized by Estonian officials and Estonian citizens as important and necessary players in their country. Some Estonians are suspicious of some of them because of their foreign funding – indeed, Estonians often refer to the NGOs the West subsidizes as DONGOs ("donor-organized NGOs") – but most recognize that given Estonia's small size and only recently reestablished capitalist system, the domestic funding of such groups is problematic, at least in the short term. Consequently, they accept the current situation as something they can live with. And comments posted online in newspapers frequently refer to NGOs as organizations to which this or that problem should be referred.

But it is extremely important to remember that the number of NGOs is not, as is sometimes assumed in the West, the best barometer of the existence of civil society. On the one hand, there is the question of a common public space, recognized as such and attended to by all members of society. That space includes churches and other communal bodies that are sometimes not included in a measurement of the strength of civil society. In Estonia, these bodies are increasingly important, with churches and fraternal organizations playing an ever larger role. Indeed, the enthronement of a new Catholic bishop in Tallinn in the fall was one of the major social and political events of the year.

On the other hand, there is the question of the cohesion of residents. On that score, too, Estonia has made significant progress over the last 15 years and continued to do so in 2005. Estonian society is increasingly consolidated across ethnic lines, with more than 8,000 predominantly ethnic Russians becoming Estonian citizens during the year. Moreover, cooperation between Tallinn and Moscow in the cultural sphere expanded, with an accord in March that helped reduce ethnic tensions still further. But new problems arose in October 2005 when Georgiy Boos, governor of Russia's Kaliningrad *oblast*, called on ethnic Russians in Estonia and Latvia to come to his region to live and work. That threatened to reethnicize politics, but most ethnic Russians in Estonia and Latvia as well had no interest in Boos's proposal, having concluded that they are much better off in the Baltic countries than they would be in his *oblast*.[10]

Perhaps the most important development in this sphere was the appearance in November of a Russian-language edition of the country's most widely distributed newspaper, *Postimees*, something the editors of Russian-language papers welcomed[11] and that will help promote a common information space. That positive contribution to bridging the linguistic divide was undercut somewhat at the end of the year, when there were fears that the country's cable television networks would drop almost all Russian-language programming emanating from the Russian Federation. This did not happen, but the discussion about it highlighted the continuing sensitivities on both sides.

One other development that affects this sphere concerns a language shift among young people. Both young ethnic Estonians and young ethnic Russians are learning English at an extremely rapid rate. Among young people in particular, English is rapidly becoming the language of interethnic communication in Estonia. This trend has sparked occasional but not entirely unserious suggestions that the country ought to make English an official language and comments that young ethnic Russians, who are learning Estonian, are now better positioned for employment than are young ethnic Estonians, who are not learning Russian. This trend also helps to explain various polls showing that many ethnic Russians in Estonia are now more upbeat about the consequences of Estonia's membership in the EU than are some Estonians.

The country's Russian-language schools continued to prepare for shifting over to ever greater amounts of Estonian-language instruction by 2007. That sparked many critical articles and comments in the Russian media, but both school directors and teachers overwhelmingly have supported the move, and it appears set to go through without the kinds of protests that have marked similar shifts in Latvia.

Independent Media

1997	1998	1999	2001	2002	2003	2004	2005	2006
1.75	1.75	1.75	1.75	1.75	1.75	1.50	1.50	1.50

Estonia's media scene is mixed. On the positive side, the media operate free of direct government regulation, and the press is vigorous in reporting on a wide range of problems. Indeed, in its annual report, the international media watchdog group Reporters Without Borders rated Estonia as the 11th freest media environment in the world. Other observers agree, impressed by the enormous size of its media space given the size of the country.[12] Moreover, Estonia is one of the most Internet-connected countries on earth, with schools, government offices, and businesses almost totally online and most people having access to the Internet at home as well.

On the negative side, however, Estonia is a microscopically small media market. As a result, despite the impressive number of publications, newspapers and journals are seldom financed by bundled advertising – the basis of the diverse funding that supports media freedom in many countries – but are supported either by readers, who must pay high prices for them and thus often do not, or by owners, whose involvement frequently invites speculation about the politics behind certain reports. The most important development in 2005 was the appearance of a Russian-language edition of country's largest daily, as noted earlier.

If the press is almost always vigorous, it is also often sensationalist. Indeed, former Estonian president Lennart Meri frequently observed that the road from a Soviet-style controlled press to a genuinely free press passes through a yellow press. Although much of Estonian journalism is outstanding and corresponds to international standards, some of it is still at the level of tabloid sensationalism, where gaining an audience seems more important than sticking to the facts. Indeed, both Estonian readers and some Estonian journalists speak of the increasing tabloidization of the Estonian press.

In addition to questions of the economic viability of various outlets given market size and the quality of reporting, there were new concerns about the role of the country's security police in monitoring the Internet; the expansion of libel and defamation laws, which some fear might limit criticism; and a plan to promote Estonia via government-financed films. Exactly how much officers of the security police have gotten involved in the media scene remains unclear. There have been accusations that they have taken steps to chill criticism,[13] but much of this criticism seems politically motivated itself and may be overstated.

In this situation, the Internet plays a special role, but one that is also not without problems. Estonia is one of the most Internet-savvy countries on earth. Most people have computers at home, and nearly all have access to them at work. And the government not only invented the public Internet sign now used around the world – an ampersand on a blue background – for public Internet access points, but has worked to open such offices across the country, especially in rural areas. Moreover, Estonia is a leader in e-governance, and over the course of 2005, the authorities made it easier than ever before to make use of a single plastic card to interact with all government functions.

That connectivity is impressive, but there is one downside: There is a major Internet divide between urban educated Estonians and the many ethnic Russians who often form lower-socioeconomic groups. This digital divide means that when Estonian authorities decide to do something like eliminate print versions of particular pieces of information, this ostensibly ethnically equal arrangement in fact hits one group far harder than the other, something Russian media in Estonia are increasingly concerned about.

Local Democratic Governance

1997	1998	1999	2001	2002	2003	2004	2005	2006
n/a	n/a	n/a	n/a	n/a	n/a	n/a	2.50	2.50

Local elections in October 2005 sparked new discussion about the transfer of power, especially taxation power, to local governments but did not lead to a resolution of that long-contentious issue. More important, the run-up to the voting generated heightened attention to the problematic interrelationship between local and central governments and to the complex sets of often hidden personal ties within political parties, jeopardizing the transparency that should be the basis of an open democratic society.

Because Estonia is so small, many politicians have been involved simultaneously in local and national politics, especially in the capital city of Tallinn. That is not by itself a problem, but it has three consequences for the future of the country that may prove serious. First, because national politicians sometimes run for local offices but then decide to remain in their national offices (rather than assume the ones they have been elected to locally), many voters – especially those who have voted for a local winner who then does not take office – become alienated from the political process.

Second, this only exacerbates the problems that local governments face in building authority and solving local problems. They are so interconnected with Tallinn and national politics that they cannot act in the ways their constituents might expect, again something that has the effect of undermining public confidence in this level of political activity.

Third, the lack of a clear distinction means that Estonian local government is not in the position that it could and should be to help select and provide training for the next generation of Estonian political leaders. One example of this is the fact that only six regional leaders now serve in the Parliament, a remarkably small percentage of the total but one that Estonia's leaders tout as a significant improvement in comparison with the 1990s. Another example is the fact that Estonia's national political elite has not been revitalized in the ways it might be; most of the candidates mentioned for the presidency and the Parliament in 2006 remained members of the generation of 1991 (rather than including a variety of new candidates), which tarnishes Estonia's reputation as a politically dynamic democracy.

As has been true since the restoration of Estonian independence, local and regional governments remained underfunded and understaffed except in Tallinn and other major cities. As a result, local government is often seen by the Estonian population as a plaything of the central authorities. One example of this is that the same authority that controls the Tallinn airport controls the airport at the university city of Tartu – and does not allow any regularly scheduled flights to land or take off from there. This is a major issue for the city, and many people there blame Tallinn, despite the airport authority's insistence that it is working on the problem.

Another problem, about which EU officials have complained but which is difficult to measure, concerns the introduction of EU standards at the local level. Brussels has complained of delays and distortions, but it is difficult to gauge just how much progress appears to have been made over the last 18 months.

Judicial Framework and Independence

1997	1998	1999	2001	2002	2003	2004	2005	2006
2.25	2.25	2.00	2.00	1.75	1.75	1.75	1.50	1.50

Estonia's court system is independent and plays a key role in ensuring that the Parliament follows the law, with the Supreme Court routinely ruling on the constitutionality of the legislature's actions. Moreover, the courts have continued to play an active role in promoting and protecting the civil rights of all groups. Following the country's accession to the EU in 2004, Estonia's judges continued to receive training in judicial activity. But efforts to provide training for prosecutors, a key part of the judicial system, continued to be restricted by some officials who view prosecutors rather than judges as central to the control of the courts. By the end of 2005, that had begun to change, but the success of judicial training has not yet been equaled by a similar success in the training of prosecutors. Prison conditions remain troubling, especially since Estonia has one of the highest rates of incarceration in the EU.

All international organizations agree that Estonia protects the fundamental rights of its citizens, that the courts are generally effective, and that legal aid works well. At the same time, there are in Estonia, as in all countries, problems involving the abuse of women and children and the treatment of those incarcerated in prisons.

The latter is an especially large problem. Estonia has one of the highest incarceration rates in Europe, 339 prisoners per 100,000 residents – more than four times the rate of neighboring Finland, to give but one obvious comparison. There are a total of 3,500 people in prisons and another 1,000 in detention, awaiting trial or other dispositions of their cases. Conditions in prisons are frequently well below EU and international standards, although the EU is providing Estonia with assistance to upgrade them.

One of the reasons Estonia's incarceration rate is so high is that although it has eliminated many of the regulations that lead to corruption, its people and government have decided that some offenses warrant punishments far more draconian than are typical of other EU countries. For example, if an individual is convicted a second time for drunk driving, he or she is judged guilty of a felony and is subject to incarceration. That risk leads many people in Estonia to be extremely careful about drinking and driving, but it highlights another problem that Estonia, like many other countries undergoing transition, has yet to face.

In the 15 years since Estonian independence was achieved, there have been only the rarest of consultations between lawmakers, executive officials, and criminologists about the best criminal procedures; such conversations might help guide the country in ways that would allow it to maintain law and order without the rate of incarceration it now has. Legal specialists interviewed in the media frequently complained about this lack during 2005, but there is little evidence that the government is ready to respond in a positive way.

The conditions in Estonian prisons remained difficult in 2005, according to many human rights activists and observers. Inadequate food, housing, and medical attention were only three of the problems they pointed to in reports to the Estonian Parliament, the media, and international groups, including the EU. As is the case in many other countries, there is little popular support among Estonians for spending more money on prisons, yet this is something the country will almost certainly have to do if it is to overcome its less than sterling reputation in this area.

Corruption

1997	1998	1999	2001	2002	2003	2004	2005	2006
n/a	n/a	3.25	2.75	2.50	2.50	2.50	2.50	2.50

Estonians continue to view their government as more corrupt than monitoring organizations like Transparency International, the Fraser Institute of Canada, the Heritage Foundation, and the Milken Institute all believe it to be. Most obvious forms of corruption directly involving citizens have declined, largely as a result of Estonia's decision to end the regulation of many activities and thereby reduce the number of points at which a citizen might be extorted by officials. And Estonia's decision, almost alone among transition countries, to make corruption a "distinct crime" has drawn praise. Indeed, most of the evaluations carried out by international groups focus on those positive developments.

But the country's small size and specific history mean that there are problems in this area that these organizations seldom track. On the one hand, the relatively small population of Estonia means that people generally know one another, which ultimately breeds suspicions that some of these contacts will be used illegitimately. And on the other hand, there are other kinds of corruption, including those used by domestic politicians seeking power or foreign governments seeking influence, that many Estonians believe are not only widespread, but may even be larger than they were earlier.

Three developments during 2005 only intensified Estonian concerns that corruption in these other forms was on the rise, even if the kind of corruption measured by international monitors was in fact continuing to decline. First, in March a Viljandi newspaper reported that the country's Justice Ministry had assigned each of the regions a "quota" for corruption arrests; this sparked a media firestorm, which together with the government's somewhat clumsy handling of the report helped bring down the Parts administration[14] – and sent a clear message that corruption revealed will not be tolerated. But the incident had the effect of leading more Estonians to focus on corruption as an issue and to worry that one way or another,

officials were getting funds and other goods in illegal ways. How accurate such perceptions are is difficult to gauge, but the existence of such concerns is real and not
trivial for the future of the country.

Second, in June several Tallinn newspapers reported that the number of state
employees being investigated for corruption was nearly three times as great in 2005
as it had been in 2004. On the one hand, these reports may simply have been fallout from the earlier Viljandi newspaper report noted previously. On the other hand,
some of them appear to reflect the adversarial scuffling that marks the beginning of
an election season, with various officials and candidates making charges to advance
their own interests; and some of it may reflect the fact that the security police in
2005 became more actively involved in investigating corruption at the local level.
But whatever its causes, many Estonians also viewed these statistics as an indication
that corruption was growing even if it was not the old visible kind.

Third, many Estonians during 2005, media reports suggested, were increasingly concerned about political corruption, the illegitimate use of power either by
domestic political figures or by the Russian government. The first of these concerns
was heightened by the apparent use by the Center Party of its business ties to skirt
the legislation on political advertising (see earlier) and the second by continued
charges from the former Estonian ambassador to Moscow that the Russian intelligence agencies have corrupted the Estonian political system – charges the security
police supported rather than denied.[15]

Such activities again may not be technically part of corruption as normally
understood, but they are often combined in the minds of Estonians and at the very
least help to explain why their judgments about corruption in their country are so
different from those of international observers.

*Paul A. Goble, who earlier served as an expert on ethnic issues in the Soviet and post-Soviet
states at the U.S. Department of State, is currently vice dean of social sciences and humanities at Audentes University in Tallinn and a senior research associate of the EuroCollege
of the University of Tartu.*

---

[1] Eesti Paevaleht, March 15, 2005.
[2] Delovoyye vedomosti, February 23, 2005.
[3] BNS, December 12, 2005. The findings of other polls reported by Regnum.ru, April 28, 2005.
[4] Some questions were raised about e-governance both in the course of local elections and over the
Estonian decision to discontinue hard-copy publication of the Russian-language editions of the country's new laws, given the continued existence of a digital divide between ethnic Estonians and ethnic
Russians.
[5] Ohtuleht, April 27, 2005.
[6] Regnum news agency summary on Estonia This Week, April 28, 2005.
[7] Andrus Saar of the Saar Poll, quoted by Regnum news agency, March 21, 2005.
[8] BNS, October 18, 2005.
[9] Regnum news agency, October 19, 2005.
[10] See the comment of Eleonora Mitrofanova in Moscow's Nezavisimaya Gazeta, October 24, 2005.

[11] Regnum news agency survey of Russian editorial opinion, November 21, 2005.

[12] In addition to the print media, Estonia has three national television networks, more than a dozen cable companies, five public service radio stations, and two dozen private radio stations serving a population of approximately 1.3 million.

[13] See Eesti Ekspress, February 11, 2005.

[14] Viljandi Sakala, cited by Regnum, March 10, 2005.

[15] Ohtuleht, March 1, 2005.

Georgia

Capital:	Tbilisi
Population:	4.5 million
GNI/capita:	$1,060
Ethnic Groups:	Georgian (70%), Armenian (8%), Russian (6%), Azeri (6%), Ossetian (3%), Abkhaz (2%), other (5%)

Nations in Transit Ratings and Averaged Scores

	1997	1998	1999	2001	2002	2003	2004	2005	2006
Electoral Process	5.00	4.50	4.00	4.50	5.00	5.25	5.25	4.75	4.75
Civil Society	4.50	4.25	3.75	4.00	4.00	4.00	3.50	3.50	3.50
Independent Media	4.50	4.25	3.75	3.50	3.75	4.00	4.00	4.25	4.25
Governance *	4.50	5.00	4.50	4.75	5.00	5.50	5.75	n/a	n/a
National Democratic Governance	n/a	n/a	n/a	n/a	n/a	n/a	n/a	5.50	5.50
Local Democratic Governance	n/a	n/a	n/a	n/a	n/a	n/a	n/a	6.00	5.75
Judicial Framework and Independence	5.00	4.75	4.00	4.00	4.25	4.50	4.50	5.00	4.75
Corruption	n/a	n/a	5.00	5.25	5.50	5.75	6.00	5.75	5.50
Democracy Score	4.70	4.55	4.17	4.33	4.58	4.83	4.83	4.96	4.86

* With the 2005 edition, Freedom House introduced seperate analysis and ratings for national democratic governance and local democratic governance to provide readers with more detailed and nuanced analysis of these two important subjects.

NOTE: The ratings reflect the consensus of Freedom House, its academic advisers, and the author of this report. The opinions expressed in this report are those of the author. The ratings are based on a scale of 1 to 7, with 1 representing the highest level of democratic progress and 7 the lowest. The Democracy Score is an average of ratings for the categories tracked in a given year.

The economic and social data on this page were taken from the following sources:
GNI/capita, Population: *World Development Indicators 2006* (Washington, D.C.: World Bank, 2006).
Ethnic Groups: *CIA World Factbook 2006* (Washington, D.C.: Central Intelligence Agency, 2006).

EXECUTIVE SUMMARY

Since independence, Georgia has created a hybrid regime haunted by instability. There were no constitutional transitions of power after 1990, while in 1992 and 2003 elected presidents were forced out of office following public protests. In the latter case, however, the change was peaceful and did not lead to a major disruption of the constitutional process. Wars for secession from 1991 to 1993 brought some 15 percent of the country's territory under the control of unrecognized governments in Abkhazia and South Ossetia. Since then, these zones of so-called frozen conflict have been major impediments to Georgia's development: They contain threats of renewed violence and undermine Georgia's chances for political and economic stabilization. The 1995 Constitution conformed to primary democratic criteria–this, along with the liberal policies of the government, allowed political parties to compete freely for the most part, independent media and civil society to grow, and the Parliament to develop into a fairly independent institution. However, under President Eduard Shevardnadze, the executive power was ineffective and corrupt, and elections were increasingly rigged. The political system was overcentralized, with almost no democratic institutions at the subnational level. Owing to incomplete territorial control, extremely low public revenues, and an inability to provide public goods, Georgia was often referred to as a "failing state."

In November 2003, fraudulent parliamentary elections triggered wide public protests that ended in the resignation of President Shevardnadze and brought to power a new generation of Georgian politicians led by the charismatic Mikheil Saakashvili. The new government declared joining NATO and the European Union (EU) as its strategic goals and embarked on an ambitious reform program. It focused its activities on rooting out corruption and developing effective state institutions. A strategic success was achieved in May 2004 in the Autonomous Republic of Achara, where the local autocratic regime was removed as the result of a democratic revolution supported from Tbilisi, the capital. The collection of public revenue was stepped up considerably, and institutionalized "pyramids" of corruption in state agencies such as the police were disrupted. The government started to provide visible public goods, such as repaired roads and other infrastructure and increased, timely paid salaries and pensions.

However, these rapid achievements were accompanied by certain setbacks in the democratic balance of power. Two years after the revolution, there is still no credible opposition to the United National Movement, the party that came to power after the Rose Revolution. Changes to the Georgian Constitution in February 2004 weakened the Parliament and moved Georgia in the direction of superpresidentialism. The judiciary rarely makes decisions that run counter to the will of the executive. The government's policy-making process lacks transparent, orderly, and predictable procedures. Independent media and civil society, though often openly critical of the government, have become less influential. Still, there have been important steps forward in democratic development: Elections have been much fairer and better organized (even if less competitive), there are fewer human rights abuses by the police, and in 2005 the first steps were made toward decentralizing the government.

National Democratic Governance. Georgia has a mixed political system that secures major civil and political rights and provides for political pluralism and meaningful expression of the citizens' will. However, the government's numerous imbalances, most notably the domination of the executive branch over all other state agencies, leads to authoritarian tendencies in different spheres of public life and prevents Georgia from becoming a consolidated democracy. Civil society has influence over some aspects of state policies, but the level of political participation–save for elections or public protests–is concentrated within a small elite. There is insufficient civilian oversight of the military. About 15 percent of Georgian territory is controlled by the secessionist regimes of Abkhazia and South Ossetia, which are backed by Russia. The effectiveness of the executive government has increased considerably in the last two years, especially in attracting public revenue and providing public goods. *As Georgia is a hybrid system with considerable democratic freedoms but still lacking fully consolidated state institutions and sufficient governmental checks and balances, and the government's authority does not extend over the entire territory, the rating for national democratic governance is unchanged at 5.50.*

Electoral Process. Snap presidential and parliamentary elections in 2004, as well as by-elections to the Georgian Parliament in the fall of 2004 and fall of 2005, were considered generally free and fair and constituted significant progress over the fraudulent and chaotic parliamentary elections in November 2003. Some problems persist, such as incomplete voter lists and the use of state administrative resources by the party in government. The inherent weakness of the opposition significantly reduces political pluralism. Opposition parties are engaged in building their base for future elections but are still unable to compete with the party in power and its popular leader. In 2005, there was a rising trend of incivility between the government and the opposition. *The rating for electoral process is unchanged at 4.75.*

Civil Society. Legislation regulating the activities of nongovernmental organizations (NGOs) is quite liberal. Nonprofit organizations are easy to register, their number is growing, and they can operate freely. A majority of the public appreciates its role in advancing democratic causes. However, after the Rose Revolution the sector's visibility diminished somewhat as many important civil society leaders moved to the government or–in some cases–to the opposition. NGO cooperation with the government is productive in some areas, but there is no stable mechanism for interaction between the government and civil society. There are organizations with illiberal, extreme right agendas, but their influence has diminished in the last two years. The social base for NGOs is rather narrow, and organizations in most regions outside the capital are less developed. They are dependent primarily on foreign funding. The new tax code that came into effect in 2005 instituted tax breaks for charitable activities, though these legal provisions are rarely used. Trade unions exist but have little influence. *The rating for civil society remains unchanged at 3.50.*

Independent Media. The Georgian Constitution and legislation ensure a liberal environment for the development of independent media. The 2004 Law on Freedom of Speech and Expression took libel off the criminal code and relieved journalists of legal criminal responsibility for revealing state secrets. However, after the Rose Revolution the media proved vulnerable to behind-the-scenes pressure from the government. The media are rather critical of the government but may be avoiding some sensitive topics. This is explained in part by the weakness of the media's economic base: Independent TV companies are usually unprofitable, serve to promote the agendas of their owners, and display a low level of editorial independence. The professional quality of journalists is insufficient, and there are no strong formal associations to set professional and ethical standards for the industry. *The rating for independent media remains unchanged at 4.25.*

Local Democratic Governance. Democratic institutions are least developed at the local level in Georgia. The Constitution does not define the territorial arrangement of the country or the competences of subnational institutions of state power. Legislation adopted in 2004 regarding the Autonomous Republic of Achara left very little power to the regional council. In December 2005, the Georgian Parliament adopted new legislation laying the groundwork to create new local government institutions after the local elections, which are expected in 2006. This legislation provides for elected government institutions at the district level, Georgia's six largest towns, and the capital, Tbilisi, which will be governed by locally elected councils with their own budgets and property. The law was criticized, however, for creating overly large local government units with insufficient authorities and resources. *Since important legislative steps were made in the direction of developing local government, the rating for local democratic governance improves from 6.00 to 5.75.*

Judicial Framework and Independence. The Georgian Constitution provides important safeguards for the protection of human rights and the independence of the judiciary. However, in 2005 the judiciary was still not able to withstand political pressure, and courts rarely disagreed with the prosecution's demands. There was a notable decrease in torture at preliminary detention facilities, at least in the capital. Further, important progress was made in curbing violence against religious minorities, with some perpetrators of past violence sentenced to prison, and new registration provisions improved the legal standing of religious organizations. *Owing to improvements on the issues of torture and religious freedoms, the rating for judicial framework and independence improves from 5.00 to 4.75.*

Corruption. Although a high rate of corruption has been typical for Georgia, the new government undertook resolute anticorruption measures. Several corrupt officials were arrested, including some appointed by the new government. The salaries of a large number of public servants and law enforcement officers were dramatically increased as an incentive against corruption. Certain official procedures have been simplified, and the government adopted a new National Anticorruption Strategy and Action Plan. There is evidence of improved public confidence in state institutions. *Owing to the persistent anticorruption measures of the new government, the rating in this category improves from 5.75 to 5.50.*

Outlook for 2006. In 2006, the Georgian government is expected to take important steps in several areas. Local elections scheduled for the fall are expected to be the most important political event of the year. They will test the ability of the opposition to compete with the ruling United National Movement. Most important, they are supposed to lay the foundation for a new system of local government. Education reforms are intended to produce a new system of self-government in Georgian universities, and a number of self-government bodies will be created in Georgian schools. The government will be under pressure to demonstrate at least some success toward an independent judiciary. It is expected that jury trials may be instituted, at least in some areas. Steps aimed at resolving the "frozen conflicts" in Abkhazia and South Ossetia will be high on the agenda. There are fears, however, that demanding the withdrawal of Russian peacekeeping forces will lead to mounting tensions in these areas as well as in relations between Georgia and Russia.

MAIN REPORT

National Democratic Governance

1997	1998	1999	2001	2002	2003	2004	2005	2006
n/a	n/a	n/a	n/a	n/a	n/a	n/a	5.50	5.50

The Rose Revolution, which followed the massively fraudulent elections in November 2003, was widely considered a significant step forward for Georgian democracy. It demonstrated a high level of intolerance in the society for infringements on political rights and the capacity to organize peaceful protest actions (in contrast with the 1992 violent coup), and it brought to power a political group that had long advocated democratic reforms modeled on Western countries. However, two years later the record of the new government is rather mixed. It has achieved a considerably higher level of effectiveness in state institutions, but so far the government is not based on a proper democratic balance of power.

The government's greatest defect is its inability to ensure territorial control.

There are two self-proclaimed territories in Georgia, Abkhazia and South Ossetia, which do not recognize national authority. Cease-fire agreements brokered and enforced by Russia have been in effect in these regions since 1994 and 1992, respectively, but there is no progress toward a final settlement. Moreover, during the last two years tensions in both conflict regions, especially South Ossetia, have increased. In January 2005, the government unveiled its peace plan for South Ossetia based on wide autonomy for the region. The plan gained the support of the international community but did not lead to any progress on the ground. The Georgian government has declared its commitment to using exclusively peaceful means to resolve the issue, but militaristic innuendo in the public statements of some leaders in 2004 and 2005 raised concerns that the military option is not off the table indefinitely.

The conflicts are complicated by poor relations with Russia, which the Georgian government accuses of supporting the separatists. In October 2005, the Georgian Parliament adopted a resolution calling for the withdrawal of Russian peacekeepers from South Ossetia and Abkhazia after February and July 2006, respectively, in the event Russia does not change its policy toward these conflicts. This may lead to either a more reliable security regime or a new round of instability in the conflict zones. In May 2005, Georgia secured an important success by reaching an agreement with Russia on the withdrawal of its military bases from Georgian territory within three years.

There is broad consensus in the country that strengthening democratic institutions is the only option for Georgia's development. The public and the political elite, including major opposition parties, are also solidly behind Georgia's bid to join NATO and the EU, goals that are central to the political aspirations of the new government. No political group of any influence contests these ambitions. The sovereignty of the national government is not disputed in other regions besides Abkhazia and South Ossetia, though some groups in the region of Javakheti, populated mainly by ethnic Armenians, call for special autonomous status for the region.

The 1995 Constitution defines Georgia's political system as a democratic republic. It stipulates that the people are the source of the state's authority, which shall be exercised through the separation of powers. Chapter 2 of the Constitution asserts all basic rights and freedoms of the individual.

Until 2004, the design of the central government generally followed the model of the U.S. Constitution. The president could not dissolve the Parliament and needed to secure parliamentary approval when appointing ministers and adopting the budget. On February 6, 2004, the Parliament introduced changes into the Constitution that unraveled the republican balance of power in favor of the president. The positions of prime minister and the Cabinet of Ministers were established. The president must secure approval from the Parliament to appoint the prime minister but can dismiss him at will. Most important, the president has acquired powers to dismiss the Parliament in specific circumstances, such as in the event of three consecutive no-confidence votes delivered to the cabinet by the Parliament. In practice, parliamentary independence has decreased in the last two years. The assembly passes an enormous amount of new legislation without sufficient deliberation, though it offers resistance to some draft legislation coming from the executive branch.

The public's right to join and create political parties, take part in elections, and create and engage in public associations or demonstrations is generally respected. There are occasional meetings between the government and civil society representatives at the highest levels. Government agencies have public boards/councils and other formats for dialogue with civil society, and in some instances state agencies take its advice. However, the trend is not increasing: In 2004, the president had several meetings with civil society representatives, but no such meetings occurred in 2005.

The 1999 administrative code includes the equivalent of the U.S. Freedom of Information Act, which makes all public information accessible. In practice, however, public agencies create serious obstacles to obtaining public information, and civil society organizations and the media complain that getting public information has become more difficult in the last two years. Despite introducing a more liberal tax code since 2005, there are complaints from the business community that frequent interventions by the financial police disrupt business activities and scare away investors.

Georgian legislation provides for democratic oversight of the military and security services. However, the actual level of civilian oversight is insufficient. During 2004-2005, a significant amount of financing for the Georgian army was channeled through the nonbudgetary Defense Fund and Law Enforcement Fund, which are not subject to normal public control procedures. The state has never disclosed a list of fund donors, describing them instead as "real friends of this country, true patriots, mostly people who are not currently in Georgia."[1] In response to internal and international criticism, these funds were closed down in 2005. On the other hand, the adoption of a National Security Concept in 2005 and public discussion around it constituted a step forward in developing more transparent policy in the defense sphere.

Electoral Process

1997	1998	1999	2001	2002	2003	2004	2005	2006
5.00	4.50	4.00	4.50	5.00	5.25	5.25	4.75	4.75

The Constitution and the electoral code guarantee universal suffrage, equal electoral rights, and the right to direct and secret ballot. However, electoral standards were generally low from 1990 to 2003 and thought to be declining. The irregularities registered most frequently by domestic and international observers included ballot stuffing, multiple voting, erroneous voter lists, and rigging of the ballot tabulation process by election commissions on various levels. In most regions, political parties were free to campaign and express their views. People were usually free to express their political will, though pressure was exerted on public servants and the military to support government parties. The November 2003 parliamentary elections constituted a nadir in this trend, leading to the Rose Revolution. President Shevardnadze resigned under popular pressure, and the Supreme Court of Georgia annulled the results of the party list vote owing to massive fraud (the election results from most single-mandate constituencies were not annulled).

Elections held after the Rose Revolution, namely snap presidential elections on January 4, 2004, and repeated parliamentary elections (party lists only) in March 2004, demonstrated distinct improvements. After the snap presidential elections in November 2003, the International Election Observation Mission of the Organization for Security and Cooperation in Europe and the Council of Europe noted "clear improvements, particularly in the conduct of voting, new voters' lists, the legal framework, and overall election administration." Similar conclusions were reached after the March 2004 parliamentary elections.

Both elections, however, were marked by a low level of political competition: No major political figures dared to run against Mikheil Saakashvili, who won the presidency with 96.27 percent of the vote. The bloc of the National Movement and United Democrats, which led the revolution, also carried the March 2004 parliamentary elections with 66.24 percent of the vote (later the two parties formally merged into the United National Movement [UNM]). Only one other bloc, the New Rights-Industrialists, overcame the 7 percent threshold for political parties, with 7.96 percent.

In that period, the lack of competition was attributed to postrevolutionary euphoria. However, later by-elections confirmed the trend. In by-elections on October 1, 2005, all five parliamentary seats were taken by the UNM. Neither local nor international observers reported any serious violations that would suggest an attempt to rig the ballot. However, the problem of creating an accurate voter registry persists: Many electors could not find their names on the voter list and, as a result, could not vote. It is not clear whether the problem resulted from legislation or the administration of the election.

After the Rose Revolution, an amendment to the electoral legislation was adopted that introduced the principle of voter self-registration. Its initial version included an option to register on election day, but this was later removed. This led to a situation where some people who took part in the snap elections and expected to be on the parliamentary by-election list lost their right to vote when their names were not found. Another criticism of the elections was the use of so-called administrative resources in favor of government candidates. This also implied the use of state budget resources to partially fund the campaigns of candidates.

The composition of election commissions continues to be an issue. Before 2005, Georgian election commissions were based on a balance of political party representatives, with government parties usually calling the shots. Amendments to the election code adopted in April 2005 introduced a new system of creating central and district election commissions based on neutral civil servants selected through a competitive process. According to the law, the president selects 12 candidates for the Central Election Commission (CEC) and a candidate for the chair, while the

Parliament elects 6 members and confirms the chair. Based on these parameters, a commission was created in summer 2005, but it drew protests from the opposition, which did not trust the neutrality of the new electoral administration.

The most substantive deficiency in the Georgian electoral system is the lack of strong and stable political parties competing at different levels. Most influential political parties are seen as machines for ensuring support for their individual leaders, rather than as vehicles for mobilizing citizens around competing interests and policy options. There is a tradition of dominant political parties–the Round Table from 1990 to 1991, the Citizens' Union of Georgia from 1995 to 2001, and the Union of Revival of Georgia in Achara from 1992 to 2004–that tend to merge with government structures. The Rose Revolution led to the re-creation of a single dominant party, the UNM. There are two opposition blocs in the Parliament: The New Rights-Industrialists has 17 members; the Democratic Front faction (also with 17 members) was created in fall 2005 from two party groups, the Republicans and the Conservatives, which broke away from the UNM faction, and several independent members of Parliament (MPs). The parliamentary opposition does not have any significant influence on the work of the Parliament but actively uses the parliamentary platform to publicize its views.

The 1997 Law on Citizens' Political Associations presents no significant barriers to political organization and registration. By July 2005, there were 184 political parties registered in the Ministry of Justice.[2] The only important restriction prohibits the creation of regionally based political parties. This provision was used by the Ministry of Justice to deny registration to Virk, a political party based in the ethnic Armenian-populated province of Samtskhe-Javakheti. Virk advocates creating an ethnically based Armenian autonomy in the region, which is a source of concern in Georgian society.

Although election turnout figures are usually considered unreliable owing to faulty or incomplete voter lists, a high level of participation is obvious in most critical elections, including the presidential and parliamentary elections in 2004. However, the lack of viable political parties restricts broad public participation mainly to elections or occasional protest actions.

The genuine participation of ethnic minorities is especially low (though their formal turnout in elections is relatively high). According to a 2002 census, ethnic minorities constitute more than 16 percent of the population (not counting the breakaway regions of Abkhazia and South Ossetia) and are concentrated largely in two provinces, Kvemo Kartli and Samtskhe-Javakheti. The majority do not speak Georgian, which is the country's only official language. This effectively disqualifies them from public and political life at the national level. Ethnic minorities are underrepresented in all branches of power at national and, in some regions where they reside, local levels. They are also rarely involved in political parties other than the dominant parties in power.

Civil Society

1997	1998	1999	2001	2002	2003	2004	2005	2006
4.50	4.25	3.75	4.00	4.00	4.00	3.50	3.50	3.50

The independent civic sector in Georgia is relatively large, vibrant, and influential. Its rights are for the most part protected, and the state does not impede its activities. However, the social base for NGOs is rather narrow, including mostly young urban professionals. The civic sector played an important role in the Rose Revolution of 2003 by providing authoritative monitoring of the electoral process, mobilizing support for democratic causes, and using its capacity to ensure peaceful and organized mass protests.

This increased the public visibility of the civil society sector in Georgia. According to a poll conducted by the Center for Strategic Research and Development of Georgia (CSRDG) in spring 2005,[3] 42.8 percent of those surveyed said that civil society organizations have an important or more or less important impact on current developments (in 2003, the same figure stood at 30.7 percent); 57.2 percent assessed their role as "positive" (against 45.9 percent in 2003). However, this did not translate into high participation figures: Only 7.9 percent said they had interacted with NGOs, and less than 2 percent described themselves as members of any organization.

Many experts believe that after the Rose Revolution, the impact of civil society organizations declined somewhat. This is due to several factors, which include leading activists moving to positions in government, the refocusing of donor support to reforms carried out by government, and greater differences among the leading civil society organizations on major policy issues.

There is no established format for interactions between the government and the civic sector, and contacts and cooperation are uneven yet successful in some areas. The Liberty Institute, which played a prominent role in the Rose Revolution, is now close to the new government and has influence on its policies (though it may also be critical of some of its actions). Civil society representatives are routinely included in official commissions and working groups, which define different aspects of the reform agenda, and have an impact on government decisions. The Ministries of Education and Science, Health, and Social Welfare and the Tbilisi municipality are notable for involving civil society organizations in their reform processes.

In 2005, a coalition of regional NGOs won a US$145,000 contract from the Georgian Social Investment Fund for institutional capacity building of local governance and community development. A public council, including human rights activists and public figures, is active in monitoring the penitentiary system. Their activism was important in raising awareness of the problems in prisons and led to open conflict with the minister (who was later removed). Cooperation between the Office of the Public Defender and human rights organizations on monitoring preliminary detention facilities has been successful in reducing instances of physical abuse. The Georgian Young Lawyers Association and the Ministry for Environment

Protection cooperated successfully in the process of setting up a new environment patrol force. However, the circle of organizations with which the new government is willing to cooperate is actually rather narrow. Many activists of the civic sector often express their disappointment with the new government's tendency to make important decisions without leaving enough time for broad consultations and adequate public discussion.

There were 7,581 nonprofit associations and 999 foundations registered in Georgia by April 2005.[4] Numerous organizations exist on paper only or were created for implementing just one or two projects. However, several hundred are relatively stable, and some 30 groups have permanent staff and boards. The capacity and quality of management of leading organizations are gradually increasing, and local expertise on NGO management is becoming more readily available for less developed organizations. Training and handbooks on NGO management, fundraising, and other resources are largely available. In 2004, a code of conduct for NGOs was created. However, in the last few years there has been a notable gap in capacity development: Only a relatively small group of leading organizations shows a steady trend of institutional development, while many other groups show a tendency to decline.

Georgian civil society is diverse, with the most active and visible organizations involved in democracy promotion, good governance, human rights protection, and public policy research. Many other groups are involved in environmental, social, and similar humanitarian causes. Women's and minority groups are numerous but peripheral to the mainstream. Community-based organizations have developed in some regions but require donor assistance to survive. According to the previously mentioned CSRDG poll, the wider public sees the role of NGOs as mainly defending citizens' civil and political rights, and minority rights in particular.

Civil society representatives are frequently invited by the media to comment on current political issues and policy reforms. However, only a small number of organizations and civil society personalities maintain high media visibility. In the CSRDG poll, the Liberty Institute and Georgian Young Lawyers' Association proved by far to be the most well-known civil organizations in Georgia (about 25 percent of those polled knew about these groups).

Free access to public information is guaranteed by the administrative code, but in practice there may be resistance by some state agencies to release information. Some NGOs report that after the new government came to power, accessing public information became more difficult in practice. In particular, this is true of the military and law enforcement agencies, led by former representatives of the NGO community.

According to the civil code, nonprofit organizations have the option to be registered as associations (unions) or foundations. They can also be active without registration, but in this case they cannot conduct financial operations. In practice, registration is quite easy. The Law on Grants exempts from most taxes moneys received by nonprofit organizations. The new tax code, put into effect in January 2004, instituted tax exemptions to encourage charitable giving. Businesses can now spend up to 8 percent of their gains on charitable activities to avoid taxes on that amount.

Many businesses are involved in charity, but these activities are rarely institutionalized, and only a handful of Georgian businesses have formed charitable foundations. Almost no local donations go to support civil society causes. Developed organizations usually depend on grant support from Western organizations. Only a small number use volunteer workers, and the role of income-generating activities is generally marginal. Despite some efforts to bridge the civil society and business communities, cooperation is weak. Funding from the Georgian government has increased, but its share is still small.

Georgia has a number of public associations that pursue illiberal causes. These claim mainly to protect Eastern Orthodox values from the pernicious influence of Western liberalism. In the past, some groups have been involved in violent attacks against religious minorities, civil society, the media, and the political opposition. The new government has been successful in curbing the activities of such groups, so that violence on behalf of "uncivil society" has largely stopped. These groups are free to express their opinions but do not have much political influence or seriously disrupt public order.

Georgians are free to organize and join trade unions, but so far only a few viable independent trade unions have been created, mainly in health care and education. Those trade unions that are successors to Soviet-era organizations do not play any visible role in defending employees' rights, though in 2005 their activism intensified somewhat, in particular in the course of opposing the new draft labor code, which was discussed in the Parliament. In 2005, the Tbilisi municipality issued matching grants to encourage the development of neighborhood associations; these groups were successful in organizing themselves and raising funds to provide for local needs.

During the period of independence, education standards declined, and there were numerous reports of widespread corruption. In January 2005, the Ministry of Education and Science launched an ambitious program to overhaul the university education system. A two-year-long transitional period started during which president-appointed rectors are supposed to implement reforms to bring university administration and curriculums closer to European standards. Opponents criticized the reform as compromising university autonomy. New legislation adopted in April 2005 aims at increasing the role of locally elected school boards in running public schools.

Independent Media

1997	1998	1999	2001	2002	2003	2004	2005	2006
4.50	4.25	3.75	3.50	3.75	4.00	4.00	4.25	4.25

Georgia's Constitution and laws provide considerable media freedoms that are close to the standards of developed democracies. However, in practice there are substantive problems that impede effective independence of the media and their ability to adequately inform society. Hidden or obvious tensions between the government and the media after the Rose Revolution contribute to these difficulties.

The Constitution states that "the mass media are free; censorship is impermissible" and that "citizens of the Republic of Georgia have the right to express, distribute, and defend their opinions via any media, and to receive information on questions of social and state life. Censorship of the press and other media is not permitted." In June 2004, the Parliament enacted a new bill on freedom of speech and expression, sponsored by the Liberty Institute. The law decriminalized libel, moving litigation from criminal to civil law competences. Journalists can no longer be held responsible for revealing state secrets; only relevant public servants can be charged for failing to guard them properly.

The Law on Broadcasting entrusts the licensing of outlets to the Broadcasting Commission, an independent body whose five members are appointed by the Parliament through the same procedure described for public broadcasting trustees. Licenses are issued for 10 years and extended automatically for another term unless the broadcaster violates specific requirements defined by law. In terms of legislation, there are concerns regarding the absence of special procedures for arrests and searches of media property. Currently, media organizations are required to follow the same procedures that apply to any other business, but the lengthy court procedures that tend to result from perceived violations can disrupt the functioning of the media. A widely publicized case in early 2004—when Iberia TV was searched on charges of large-scale tax fraud by its parent company, Omega—illustrates the problem.

The media market is dominated by privately owned outlets. Rustavi-2, Imedi, and Mze are the most important independent TV channels. The weekly *Kviris Palitra* and the dailies *Alia*, *Resonansi*, and *Akhali Versia* are the most popular newspapers. However, newspaper circulation is low, with most popular dailies reaching 10,000 copies at best (no precise information is available). Several successful newspapers have developed in regions outside Tbilisi over the last few years. Newspaper distribution is also mainly in private hands. There are a number of independent radio stations. Some of them (Ucnobi, Imedi, Radio Green Wave) have become forums for public debates. The ownership structure of the media is quite diverse.

Following the December 2004 Law on Broadcasting, the State TV and Radio Corporation was transformed into Georgian Public Broadcasting in summer 2005. It is supervised by a nine-member board of trustees appointed by the Parliament, with two candidates for each slot preselected by the president from a multiplicity of applicants. In December, the board issued the first guidelines for the new leadership, giving priority to the development of balanced and comprehensive information programming for 2006.

The media sector's chief concerns are insufficient professional standards, a weak economic base that makes it vulnerable to behind-the-scenes pressure and creates grounds for self-censorship, occasional episodes of violence against journalists, unfriendly attitudes of the government toward the media, difficulties accessing information, and a lack of editorial independence for journalists. Most of these concerns relate to electronic media, as it is much more influential. In early February 2004, two popular talk shows critical of draft constitutional amendments were taken off the air on the same night by Rustavi-2 and Mze. The owners of both channels insisted that this decision was motivated only by a wish to enhance programming quality.

In summer 2005, the story repeated itself with another political talk show on Mze: It was taken off the air without any explanation after Giga Bokeria, one of the leaders of the parliamentary majority, openly attacked it for alleged antigovernment bias. No political talk show reappeared afterward on the channel. However, by the end of 2005 both Rustavi-2 and Imedi (both with national coverage) had live political talk shows in which leading opposition and independent figures participated regularly and could strongly criticize the government. Two stations in the capital, 202 TV and Kavkasia, also have regular talk shows that are critical of the government. Since the Rose Revolution, there has been an obvious lack of investigative reporting. The most popular program of this kind, "60 Minutes" on Rustavi-2, was shut down in 2003. In 2005, investigative features were very rare in the Georgian media.

Although news programming is usually comprehensive, journalists and civil society organizations claim that the government is sometimes successful in blocking sensitive information from both news programming and talk shows, especially military and security issues such as the situation in South Ossetia. Government agencies restrict access to public information for those journalists who report on these topics in a critical way and provide privileged access to loyal journalists.

The advertising market in Georgia (from US$7 million to US$20 million annually) is not large enough to sustain several independent TV channels and a large number of newspapers. Media owners, including those of major TV channels, subsidize these outlets from their other businesses, and they may view these media outlets as tools to promote their interests in other areas. Media owners have been reluctant to spoil their relations with both the old and the new government, which makes them easy targets for pressure.

In 2004, the leadership in two national TV channels changed. After tax arrears brought Rustavi-2 close to bankruptcy, its owner, Erosi Kitsmarishvili, sold the company to Kimer Khalvashi, reputedly a close friend of Irakli Okruashvili, one of the top officials in the new government. David Bezhuashvili, whose brother Gela is another top official (in 2005, he was secretary of the National Security Council and later minister of foreign affairs), became co-owner of Mze. Also in 2004, two TV companies, Channel 9 and Iveria, were closed down. The first closure was the owner's decision, with no grounds to allege any government involvement. Iveria shut down its programming after its parent company, Omega, suffered huge losses resulting from tax evasion charges, which were never brought to court. Local TV companies Kutaisi and Kartli (based in Gori) were closed down, while Channel 5 in Bolnisi became government owned after the previous owner (an official of the Shevardnadze government) gave up his controlling share. Hidden government pressures are alleged in all of these cases.

The largest media scandal of 2005 involved the co-owner and main anchor of 202 TV, Shalva Ramishvili. On August 27, Ramishvili was arrested in a police sting; he was caught on tape accepting a US$30,000 bribe from Koba Bekauri, a majority MP, for squelching a feature exposing alleged corruption by Bekauri. Ramishvili was charged with extortion, and the court refused to release him on bail. However, 202 TV survived the scandal and has developed a strongly antigovernment stance.

Cases of journalists being harassed were rarer than in previous years, but there were several instances in 2005, especially outside Tbilisi. In September 2005, several Russian journalists from NTV were physically assaulted in the village of Napareuli. However, in his November 20 speech, President Saakashvili justified this attack as showing a "sense of national pride." The Russian journalists were trying to interview Georgian villagers for their opinions on the Russian pornographic movie *Julia*, which parodies Georgian president Mikheil Saakashvili and former Ukrainian prime minister Yulia Tymoshenko. There are several journalist and media associations in Georgia, but none plays an important role or defines professional and ethical standards recognized by the media community. In summer 2005, the Georgian Media Council was created with that aim.

Access to the Internet is not restricted in any way, save for economic and technical reasons. There are still no Internet providers in a number of less developed regions, and many people cannot afford to use the Internet even in larger cities where it is available. According to 2005 data from the Institute for Polling and Marketing, 17.6 percent of Georgians living in major towns used the Internet, with 9.3 percent doing this at least several times a week. Some Web sites have become vehicles for expressing and discussing diverse opinions. The government does not create impediments for the registration of new Web sites and does not try to censor or control their content.

Local Democratic Governance

1997	1998	1999	2001	2002	2003	2004	2005	2006
n/a	n/a	n/a	n/a	n/a	n/a	n/a	6.00	5.75

Georgia's political system is highly centralized, with rather weak democratic institutions on the subnational level. However, new legislation adopted in 2005 laid the foundation for a new system of local government to be created after the local elections expected in 2006. The existing system of subnational governance is regulated primarily by the 1997 Law on Local Self-Government and Government, which has been amended several times. The 1995 Constitution did not define the structure of local government, postponing this move until after the resolution of conflicts in Abkhazia and South Ossetia. Currently, there are three levels of subnational government: community (town/village), district (*raion*), and province (*mkhare*).

At the first level, heads of administrations are elected locally. At the *raion* level, there are elected councils, but heads of administrations are selected by the president from local elected representatives. There are no elected bodies at the *mkhare* level. Mayors of the two most important cities, Tbilisi and Poti, are appointed by the president. More important, competences of elected offices and councils are very restricted, with no control over reasonable budgetary resources. Local administrations depend mainly on transfers from the central government, while local taxes cover only a small fraction of the budget. Key governance functions such as police, health care, and education are formally part of both local and central government, but the national level dominates.

The Autonomous Republic of Achara has a special status, which until 2004 had not been defined by the Constitution. A clause mentioning Achara's autonomous status was added to the Constitution in 2000, but the actual distribution of powers was never defined owing to strained relations between the central government and the province. On June 20, 2004, snap elections to the Supreme Council of Achara following the forced resignation of its leadership in May brought a strong victory of 72.1 percent to the UNM, with only the Republican Party able to overcome the 7 percent threshold. The Council of Europe gave the voting a mostly positive assessment but stated that "the electoral process fell short of international standards in some regards," including accuracy of voter lists, secrecy of the ballot, and low competency of election commission staff.

On July 1, 2004, the Georgian Parliament enacted a constitutional Law on the Status of the Autonomous Republic of Achara that severely restricted Achara's autonomy. It defined the competences of the republic in the areas of education, culture, local infrastructure, and so forth, but at the same time it gave the Georgian president extensive rights. The president appoints the prime minister of Achara. The president can also dismiss Achara's Supreme Council if its activities endanger the sovereignty and territorial integrity of Georgia or if it twice consecutively fails to approve the candidacy of the Achara government's chairman.

Amendments to the Law on the Capital of Georgia, Tbilisi, creates grounds for the formation of a municipal government independent from the national authorities. The city council (*sakrebulo*) will be elected by residents of Tbilisi through a direct and secret ballot based on a mixed system (12 MPs are elected by proportional representation and 25 through multimandate constituencies based on a winner-take-all system), while the council elects the mayor.

In December 2005, the Parliament adopted the Law on Local Self-Government, which replaced the 1997 law. It introduced a one-level system of local self-government at the *raion* level. There will also be several self-governing towns. The law did not introduce any changes at the *mkhare* level. The *raion sakrebulo* will comprise representatives of each community within its territory and 10 members elected through a proportional vote. It will elect its chairperson as well as the mayor (*gamgembeli*), a public servant of local self-government who will head the *raion* administration. The draft law also provides for specific forms of citizen participation in decision making at the local level, such as citizens' assemblies, petitions, surveys, public discussions, and so forth. The resources of local governments will be audited by independent companies. The Parliament has also enacted the Law on the

Property of the Self-Governing Unit, while the draft Law on the Budget of the Self-Governing Unit is currently being discussed in parliamentary committees.

The new law introduced larger self-governing units that might be economically viable and will potentially have a greater capacity to balance the power of the national government. The *raion*, which had traditionally been the key level of sub-national government in Georgia, will for the first time come under the locally elected government. However, the law was criticized for making local self-government too distant from citizens, given that self-governance was abolished at the village and small-town levels. The government justified this change by saying that self-government at these levels could not be sustainable financially. The new legislation also reduced the financial resources for municipal governments and limited their competences to social and cultural spheres only. The new law will come into force following the next local elections, which are expected to be held in fall 2006.

Judicial Framework and Independence

1997	1998	1999	2001	2002	2003	2004	2005	2006
5.00	4.75	4.00	4.00	4.25	4.50	4.50	5.00	4.75

The Georgian Constitution guarantees all fundamental human rights and freedoms mentioned in the European Convention on Human Rights. The death penalty was abolished in November 1997. The Constitution also provides for a public defender, who is nominated by the president and elected by the Parliament for a five-year term yet not accountable to either the president or the Parliament. In 2004 and 2005, the public defender strongly criticized a variety of government actions. In practice, there have been considerable violations of human rights in Georgia. Torture in preliminary detention facilities has been a major concern, although since the Rose Revolution there have been some hopeful signs, including supportive statements from the president. In March 2005, amendments were adopted to the criminal procedures code that allow testimonies given by a defendant in pretrial detention to be used in court only if they are confirmed by the defendant in court.

In January, the Main Division for Human Rights' Protection and Monitoring was set up at the Ministry of Internal Affairs. A number of cases of physical abuse have been sent to the ministry and the general procuracy for further investigation. The office of the Public Defender has also been effective in monitoring human rights abuses but it carries out this work only in the capital. Since the Rose Revolution, 10 police officers have been convicted on charges of torture and inhuman treatment. Human rights organizations testify that there has been a significant decrease in episodes of torture, most notably in the capital. However, there are still occurrences documented by domestic and international human rights organizations. Moreover, there are repeated episodes of physical abuse during the arrest process. There are no recorded instances of torture in prisons, but extreme conditions and inadequate sanitation and medical care lead to frequent deaths of convicts.

A number of human rights problems emerged as a result of the new government's crackdown on corruption. Public officials from the previous government who were widely believed to be corrupt were imprisoned in the first months of 2004, but by 2005 very few cases were heard in court. In most instances, the suspects were quickly released, having paid hefty sums to the state budget. In February 2004, changes to the criminal code instituted a system of procedural agreements, or "plea bargains," between suspects and prosecutors to speed up the prosecution of cases. However, the new legislation does not sufficiently define the discretionary powers of the prosecution when such bargains are made, allowing room for arbitrary actions. As a result of widespread criticism from the Council of Europe and others, these procedural agreements were rarely used in 2005.

There has been significant progress regarding freedom of religion following an unpunished trend of violence in 1999-2002 against minority religions, especially Jehovah's Witnesses and the Baptist-Evangelical Church. The situation changed dramatically after the Rose Revolution. Perpetrators were arrested in spring 2004, and in January 2005 the court sentenced three of them to prison terms of one to six years. The open disruption of minority religious services has mostly stopped, though some relatively small episodes of harassment continue. In December 2005, Paata Bluashvili of Jvari, an extremist organization, was arrested for organizing an attack on Jehovah's Witnesses.

Until 2005, minority religious communities faced registration problems, including property registration. Amendments to the civil code enacted in April 2005 enable them to register as legal, nonprofit entities. Some major "traditional" churches, such as the Armenian Apostolic Church and the Roman Catholic Church, were not satisfied with this decision, as they do not want to be registered on a par with NGOs. The mainstream Georgian Orthodox Church, which since October 2002 has had a constitutional agreement with the state, continues to receive preferential treatment. Registration has already helped some religious groups to rent facilities for worship, but difficulties in securing permits to build new places of worship continue to be an important concern for religious minority organizations. In May 2005, a permanent Religions Council was established under the Office of the Public Defender. The council has become a useful resource for religious minorities to voice their concerns to the government and gain greater public legitimacy.

The Constitution provides for the independence of the judiciary, but in practice this is often compromised. The judicial system consists of common-law courts and the separate Constitutional Court. Common-law judges are appointed by the president upon nomination by the Council of Justice, a consulting body whose members are appointed or elected, in equal numbers, by the president, the Parliament, and the Supreme Court. Only candidates who pass exams organized by the Council of Justice may be nominated as judges. Reports of pressure on judges coming from the executive have become common since the Rose Revolution; this is indirectly confirmed by statistics. Courts side with prosecutors in almost all cases where arrest warrants are demanded. Courts also grant prosecutors the standard three-month preliminary detention of suspects, even in crimes that most experts consider too minor to warrant detention. Since spring 2005, however, there has been a greater and more positive trend toward releasing suspects on bail, a practice almost never used before.

Government representatives informally justified pressure by alleging that the judiciary was corrupt and could be bought by criminals. In November 2005, four Supreme Court judges who faced disciplinary charges from the Council of Justice came out publicly accusing the Georgian executive agencies of blatant pressure on courts. The government described these judges as discredited and corrupt. The Council of Justice said it would continue investigating their cases into 2006 and the Parliament suspended their right to take part in judicial activities until the investigations conclude. Some civil society organizations criticized these moves for procedural violations. In 2005, the government initiated a reform to create larger court districts: A single district court was established in the capital, and similar changes are expected in the regions. The government is striving for greater efficiency, but in the meantime judges' jobs are less stable and are more vulnerable to government pressure. On a positive note, new legislation adopted in 2005 significantly increased judges' salaries, effective January 2006.

February 2004 amendments to the Constitution included a provision stating that "Cases shall be considered by juries before the courts"–indicating that Georgia will institute the jury trial. This is intended to strengthen the genuine independence of the judiciary. However, subsequent legislation has yet to be adopted. The low rate of executed court decisions has been a traditional problem in the judicial system during the last decade. A constitutional amendment in 2004 took the Office of the Prosecutor out of the judiciary, presumably to create greater distance between it and the court.

Corruption

1997	1998	1999	2001	2002	2003	2004	2005	2006
n/a	n/a	5.00	5.25	5.50	5.75	6.00	5.75	5.50

Under the previous government, corruption was considered a major obstacle to political and economic development. The new government elected in 2004 declared the fight against corruption as its highest priority. A number of high-ranking officials from the previous government were imprisoned on corruption charges. Some appointees of the new government as well as a parliamentarian from the ruling UNM, police officers, prosecutors, and judges were also arrested on corruption charges. The February 2004 changes in the criminal code introducing plea bargains were motivated primarily by the wish to increase the effectiveness of anti-corruption efforts.

February 2004 changes to the Law on the Office of the Prosecutor and the administrative code enabled the state to confiscate the property of high-ranking state officials and their families if they fail to produce proof that the property was acquired legally. Several confiscations occurred in 2004. However, because the use of plea bargains and confiscations led to allegations of human rights abuses, they were used much less in 2005. In February 2004, the Parliament also ratified the 1990 Strasbourg Convention on Money Laundering and amended national legislation to harmonize it with this document.

The government took a major step toward preventing corruption by significantly raising the salaries of tens of thousands of public servants, military officers, and law enforcement personnel. Initially, this happened through a Development and Reforms Fund created in January 2004, but subsequently most of these salaries have been paid through the state budget. In 2004 and 2005, many public agencies went through a dramatic staff overhaul and carried out open competitions for new personnel. In 2004, offices of General Inspectorates were created in government agencies to oversee the use of public funds (a measure resisted by the previous government). The inspectorates established hotlines for the public to report government irregularities, though these have not yet proven to be effective.

The government has also established a "single-window system" to simplify relations between government agencies and citizens. In November 2004, in an effort to make the process of property registration simpler and cheaper, the Ministry of Justice created the National Agency on Public Register. The ministry also simplified procedures for getting citizen IDs and passports. In 2005, procedures were likewise simplified in tax and customs offices. Although the reform's overall principle is generally appreciated, not enough officers have been hired to carry out these new functions, and long lines have resulted, creating new incentives for corruption.

Answering the criticism that Georgia's anticorruption efforts fail to follow a comprehensive plan, the government adopted the National Anticorruption Strategy and Action Plan in June 2005. These documents focus on increased efficiency and transparency in the civil service, strengthening the offices of General Inspectorates within public agencies, setting up simpler mechanisms for issuing licenses and permits, instituting reforms in law enforcement bodies (such as creating a witness protection system), and so forth. Steps have been taken to implement some items in the Action Plan, such as creating legislation necessary for the witness protection system and proposing specific steps to simplify the issuance of licenses and permits. Critics have claimed that the National Anticorruption Strategy is not based on sufficiently thorough research of existing practices and the root causes of corruption.

There are laws requiring financial disclosure and disallowing conflicts of interest. The Information Bureau on Property and Financial Condition of Public Officials processes financial declarations. Since February 2004, public officials are required to submit proofs of legality for any acquisitions of property, but the bureau does not have the capacity to check existing information. Additionally, there is no shared assessment of the government's anticorruption measures, although there is a near consensus that corruption has decreased overall. According to the CSRDG research, in spring 2005, 46.5 percent and 46.8 percent of those polled considered the Georgian Parliament and government, respectively, to be corrupt; in 2003, these institutions were considered corrupt by 88.6 percent and 91.7 percent, respectively, of those polled. Most experts agree that institutionalized "pyramids" of corruption have been disrupted.

The 2004 replacement of traffic police with patrol police has led to a dramatically visible decrease in corruption; this is recognized even by the most radical government critics. In 2005, national exams were carried out by the Ministry of Education and Science for admission to universities. They were broadly considered an extremely successful anticorruption measure, as university admission procedures had been notably corrupt in Georgia. However, experts note the continuing (though somewhat reduced) corruption in tax and customs offices, public procurement, and road construction. Although legislation prohibits public officials and politicians from taking part in economic activities, this continues in practice. In fall 2005, such allegations against Koba Bekauri, a parliamentary majority leader, led to an *ad hoc* investigative commission in the Parliament. However, the media's weak investigative reporting reduces its role as a corruption "whistle-blower."

The government's general lack of transparent and predictable policy making is frequently cited as a major structural component in high-level corruption in Georgia. Political decisions are often made spontaneously without due consideration, and their implementation leads to violations of existing procedures. A sudden government decision in spring 2005 to distribute free diesel fuel to Georgian peasants (20 liters per family) is a case in point–the hectic process was rife with violations and widely criticized in the media. Also, nonbudgetary funds such as the Defense Fund and the Law Enforcement Fund raise grave concerns about nontransparent spending mechanisms. In 2005, in response to broad internal and international criticism, these funds were closed down and their respective expenses moved to the state budget.

Many experts note a paradox in the Georgian public's attitudes about corruption. Although people express strong criticism of official corruption, many of them resort to corrupt practices as an easy solution to their own problems. The unwillingness of many citizens to serve as court witnesses on corruption cases or cooperate with law enforcement also decreases the effectiveness of law enforcement. Many people consider cooperation with law enforcement to be an immoral act of "denunciation." The government explicitly targets these attitudes through advertising campaigns. However, most official anticorruption initiatives are generally popular, and people are rather critical of the government for not being consistent enough in this area. Georgia's position in Transparency International's Corruption Perceptions Index is low but slowly improving, from 1.8 in 2003 to 2.0 in 2004 to 2.3 in 2005. Last year, Georgia was ranked 130th out of 158 countries surveyed.

Ghia Nodia leads the Caucasus Institute for Peace, Democracy and Development (Tblisi, Georgia) and teaches politics at Tblisi Ilya Chavchavadze University. He publishes regularly on democracy theory and political development in Georgia.

[1] Imedi TV, "Georgian State Minister Accuses Opposition Leader of Undermining Army," Tbilisi. Program at 18:00 Greenwich Mean Time, April 6, 2005.

[2] Civil Society Institute, Ministry of Justice of Georgia, Mokalaketa politikuri gaertianebebis (partiebis) nusxa [The List of Citizens' Political Associations (Parties) in Georgia], Tbilisi, 2005.

[3] See www.csrdg.ge/eng/researches.php, accessed December 1, 2005.

[4] Civil Society Institute, Ministry of Justice of Georgia, Sakartvelos kavshirebis ertiani reestri (The Unified Registers of Unions in Georgia), p. 5, Tbilisi, 2005; Civil Society Institute, Ministry of Justice of Georgia, Sakartveloshi utsxo kveqnebis arasametsarmeo iuridiuli pirebis tsarmomadgenlobis reestri (The Registry of Non-Entrepreneurial Legal Entities of Foreign Countries in Georgia), p. 5, 2005.

Hungary

Capital: Budapest
Population: 10.1 million
GNI/capita: $8,370
Ethnic Groups: Hungarian (90%), Roma (4%),
German (3%), other (3%)

Nations in Transit Ratings and Averaged Scores

	1997	1998	1999	2001	2002	2003	2004	2005	2006
Electoral Process	1.25	1.25	1.25	1.25	1.25	1.25	1.25	1.25	1.25
Civil Society	1.25	1.25	1.25	1.25	1.25	1.25	1.25	1.25	1.25
Independent Media	1.50	1.50	2.00	2.25	2.25	2.25	2.25	2.50	2.50
Governance *	1.75	1.75	2.50	3.00	3.00	2.50	2.50	n/a	n/a
National Democratic Governance	n/a	n/a	n/a	n/a	n/a	n/a	n/a	2.00	2.00
Local Democratic Governance	n/a	n/a	n/a	n/a	n/a	n/a	n/a	2.25	2.25
Judicial Framework and Independence	1.75	1.75	1.75	2.00	2.00	1.75	1.75	1.75	1.75
Corruption	n/a	n/a	2.50	3.00	3.00	2.75	2.75	2.75	3.00
Democracy Score	1.50	1.50	1.88	2.13	2.13	1.96	1.96	1.96	2.00

* With the 2005 edition, Freedom House introduced seperate analysis and ratings for national democratic governance and local democratic governance to provide readers with more detailed and nuanced analysis of these two important subjects.

NOTE: The ratings reflect the consensus of Freedom House, its academic advisers, and the author of this report. The opinions expressed in this report are those of the author. The ratings are based on a scale of 1 to 7, with 1 representing the highest level of democratic progress and 7 the lowest. The Democracy Score is an average of ratings for the categories tracked in a given year.

The economic and social data on this page were taken from the following sources:
GNI/capita, Population: World Development Indicators 2006 (Washington, D.C.: World Bank, 2006).
Ethnic Groups: CIA World Factbook 2006 (Washington, D.C.: Central Intelligence Agency, 2006).

EXECUTIVE SUMMARY

Hungary's transition from Communist dictatorship to consolidated liberal democracy is one of the most successful among the former Communist-bloc countries. The free market policies characterized by aggressive privatization and fiscal and monetary discipline have followed the early institutional reforms, but human services have relied on state support. The consequent fragility of the state budget underlines the need for further reforms. The strong and stable parliamentary system has permitted consecutive governments to succeed to power smoothly. The new political elite evolved at the onset of reforms comprised former Communist-era bureaucrats and the democratic opposition of the 1980s. By the end of the 20th century, a bipolar political system had emerged with social democratic and market liberal values guiding the political Left and conservative Christian democratic values guiding the political Right, an independent business sector developing, and a colorful civil society succeeding as dynamic actors of day-to-day policy making and implementation.

Events in 2005 attest that the country has successfully passed its transition period and society is now actively engaged in policy formulation for further development. The embedding of civic participation in the political process by nongovernmental organizations (NGOs) was the prime development of the year. Responding to popular support of NGOs, in June the Parliament elected the former president of the Constitutional Court to become the head of state for five years.

Politics centered around the behavior of the two main political blocs, one led by Socialist prime minister Ferenc Gyurcsany and the other by center-right former prime minister Viktor Orban. Political life, crammed with policy reforms and successes claimed on the incumbent's side and accusations of failure, corruption, and crises from the opposition's side, demonstrated continued dynamism.

National Democratic Governance. Hungary's constitutional settings reflect the country's liberal democratic goals and democratically distribute checks and balances among the branches of government. The Parliament assumes a central role in rule making, allowing widespread public access to its work, but it has yet to comply with a number of Constitutional Court adjudications aimed at improving the democratic character of its own operation. In November, a significantly revised procedural law governing the work of public administration was entered into force, underlining the service-providing function of the administration. *Vulnerable fiscal governance and the lack of genuine political will to reconcile with the country's Communist-era past give concern to observers both internationally and domestically. Hungary's national democratic governance remains at 2.00.*

Electoral Process. The Hungarian electoral system adequately facilitates the free and fair succession of power among political parties of the Left and Right. The year brought an early start to political campaigning of parties for the national elections to be held in early 2006. While the two major parties tried to reach beyond their electorate and began competing, junior parties vied to remain parliamentary forces in the following year. The governing coalition's inability to agree on a joint presidential candidate led the candidate supported by the opposition to win and execute its four-year mandate. Parliamentary by-elections were held in Sopron to fill the empty seat of a previous individually elected parliamentarian who moved to the European Parliament. *Hungary's electoral process is stable, and its rating remains unchanged at 1.25.*

Civil Society. The legal framework governing NGOs is generally favorable, and politics does not impede the formation of nonregistered democratic citizen movements or petition campaigns. An overwhelming number of civil society organizations take an active role in providing direct social services to citizens or fellow organizations; there are several key watchdog groups closely monitoring public institutions, and there are also a handful of groups and think tanks aligned across party lines. The year 2005 marked a milestone for Hungary's civil society, reinforcing that citizens' commitment to political goals may ultimately gain a breakthrough via nonviolent means. Notably, Hungary's new president was elected by the Parliament in June following a forceful nationwide campaign by NGOs supporting former president of the Constitutional Court Laszlo Solyom as head of state. Also, the new Law on Volunteerism adopted in June – however altered from the original concept – is a result of years of NGO advocacy. *Hungary's rating for civil society stands at 1.25.*

Independent Media. Media are generally considered to be free in Hungary. The wide selection of media outlets prevents any control over freedom of the press and of access to information. Particularly in the print press, the media scene reflects Hungary's polarized political climate. Overall, although the quality of journalism in Hungary is generally adequate, the boundaries between factual information, analysis, and commentary are often opaque. Libel continues to be a criminal offense, and the high number of libel and state secrecy lawsuits that have occurred lately have raised widespread concern. The lack of proper legal regulation and financing keeps public service broadcasts at the crossroads of political and professional debate. Disputes left Hungarian Radio without a president in 2005. *Hungary's independent media rating remains at 2.50.*

Local Democratic Governance. Hungary has been a pioneer in modernizing the subnational government system in the region. Still, the system requires further reform to enable the subnational units to be financially viable. The local governmental system is highly fragmented; the financial autonomy of local governments is limited and cannot sustain the level of services mandated to them, as these units usually are not economically viable with adequate local economic activity. There is wide political consensus behind the necessary reforms of the local governments' economic system, yet in practice no steps have been taken. *Hungary's rating for local democratic governance remains at 2.25.*

Judicial Framework and Independence. The legal system, an independent judiciary, and human rights ombudspersons provide an effective framework safeguarding fundamental rights and freedoms. Hungarians have conflicting views about the impartiality of the judiciary. There is no systematic torture or ill-treatment of defendants in Hungary. Discrimination against the Roma continues to be widespread. Intolerant views exist on the margins and are not restricted from free expression, but social mechanisms respond promptly to condemn and keep such views away from the mainstream. *Hungary's rating for judicial framework and independence stands unchanged at 1.75.*

Corruption. Anticorruption legislation has been under continuous improvement in Hungary; nonetheless, implementation of these laws requires further reinforcement. Nontransparent businesses related to political parties and public officials continued to be a problem in 2005. Stories of fraudulent practices of public servants or politicians and favoritism with public procurement contracts were often in the news during the year. *Hungary's corruption rating worsens slightly from 2.75 to 3.00 owing to the disparity between efforts to stem corruption and the resulting ineffectiveness.*

Outlook for 2006. The spring general legislative elections and formation of the new government will undoubtedly prove to be the most important political event of the year. Two relatively homogeneous blocs to the left and right of the political spectrum, both under strong and enigmatic individual leadership, are expected to bring intense campaigning from the grass roots to the elite level, permeated by a number of negative defamatory elements, while society remains divided along party lines. However bitter the loss may be for any of the groupings currently running head-to-head, it is unlikely that the free and fair nature of the elections could be fundamentally questioned. In the fall, Hungarians will elect new leadership at the municipal level, and the past 15-year trend suggests that by strengthening the position of the would-be opposition, the Hungarian electorate will push the votes closer to a political equilibrium.

MAIN REPORT

National Democratic Governance

1997	1998	1999	2001	2002	2003	2004	2005	2006
n/a	n/a	n/a	n/a	n/a	n/a	n/a	2.00	2.00

Hungary's constitutional setting reflects a stable parliamentary democracy. The prime minister, elected by majority vote of the Parliament, is responsible for overall governance as head of the executive branch. The executive is controlled not only by the Parliament, where – with the exception of inquiries in the standing or temporary committees – majority parties are seldom inclined to object to governmental proposals or testimonies, but by the far-reaching authority of the Constitutional Court to review legislative acts, and the availability of judicial review of individual decisions of the executive contributes significantly to the effective checks on the administration. The Parliament assumes a profound role in appointing key independent actors of governance, including the members of the Constitutional Court, the president of the Supreme Court, and the chief prosecutor or president of the State Audit Office, often only after achieving constitutionally required broad consensus.

The Parliament's central role in rule making is unquestioned; however, the government also has the right to issue decrees as long as they do not contradict rules enacted by the Parliament. Stable resources and capacity and the adoption of close to 200 pieces of legislation and nearly 100 resolutions in 2005 testify to the Parliament's immense work.[1] Media, civil society organizations, and interested individuals all have ample access to members of Parliament (MPs) and the Parliament's work through the parliamentarians' interaction with their constituencies, the Parliament's Civil Office, simple media accreditation, and up-to-date Internet access to parliamentary records, including video broadcasts of sessions.[2] However, a plea by commercial television is pending at the Constitutional Court since August against the decision that only the Parliament's own closed-circuit broadcast service is allowed to record footage of sessions.[3]

A few anomalies are causing concern about the operation of the Parliament and contribute to a growing negative perception about its work.[4] The Parliament floor is often believed to be mere performance space for MPs, who use the space for political cabaret.[5] Furthermore, failing to comply with the Constitutional Court's rulings to meet basic constitutional requirements, MPs have accumulated a backlog of about 20 pieces of legislation.[6] Most important, the rules and procedures need to be modified in accordance with the Constitutional Court's guidance to solve issues related to the participation of nonpartisan MPs in committees, adopt new rules and procedures of the committees, and standardize the schedule of the plenary meetings.[7]

The irregularities of parliamentary committees are of great concern, since from time to time they become the centerpiece for both opposition and governing parties to hold each other accountable. Two competing investigative committees were established in 2005 to shed light on alleged wrongdoing of the two leading political competitors, Prime Minister Ferenc Gyurcsany and former prime minister Viktor Orban. Partly because of a lack of clear rules and procedures, but also in large part because of the absence of genuine political will among the MPs to explore the cases without bias and prejudice, both committees concluded their work without lucid findings and resolutions. Essentially, as analysts of the political think tank Political Capital point out, instead of searching for ultimate justice, these committees offer just another forum for parties to reinvigorate their otherwise well-known political standpoints, which behavior – instead of strengthening the parties' constituent base – further alienates undecided voters from the political process.[8]

The new Law on Administrative Procedure was adopted in December 2004 and entered into force in November 2005. The long-awaited law replaces legislation dating back to the 1950s from the country's Communist past. While the old law, especially after its overarching revision in the early 1980s, served well in its time, the new procedures were necessitated by the service-providing nature of the authorities and the evolving Internet era. The legislation is claimed to be user-friendly and more effective and is believed to increase the democratic character of the administrative process.

The adoption of this law is laudable; however, the circumstances leading up to it left a bad taste in one's mouth and is indicative of certain vulnerabilities of the legislative process. In a March interview, law professor and former Constitutional Court justice Geza Kilenyi explained his deep frustration as chief drafter of the new law: According to him, the bill fell victim to the particular interests of various ministries and in the end produced more exceptions than generally binding rules.[9] This happened in spite of the government's solemn pledge to improve the quality of the legislative process. But improvement would have to start with upgrading precisely that piece of legislation that by and large governs lawmaking, and the current act on the legal framework also dates back to the time before democratic transition began. After years of preparation, consultation, and drafting, and two years after submission of the proposal, in April the Parliament opened debate on new legislation governing lawmaking, but – in the apparent absence of the required two-thirds consenting majority – MPs immediately tabled the bill.

The Achilles' heel of Hungary's central governance lies in state finances and the ominous budget deficit. The state budget deficit in 2005 is expected to reach as high as 7 percent of the gross national product and even higher in 2006, owing primarily to the carry-on burden of expensive state-subsidized human services: health care, pension system, education, and public administration. Contributing to the lack of efficiency are the political clientism and what Tibor Navrasics, center-right political scientist and chief policy aide to Viktor Orban, describes as the "gray zone of politics and administration."[10] One prime aspect of this in Hungarian national governance is the creation of plentiful centers of power headed by a group of political appointees – state secretaries and government commissioners – filled by

Socialist MPs commonly in charge of parallel portfolios.[11] And there is little improvement in coordinating fiscal and monetary policies, largely a result of statements throughout the year by National Bank governor Zsigmond Jarai (appointed by the FIDESZ-Hungarian Civic Party). Jarai's behavior is perceived by many to be politically motivated and compromising to the credibility of monetary policy.[12]

In April, Prime Minister Gyurcsany dismissed Finance Minister Tibor Draskovics, explaining the move as a need to expedite much-needed institutional reforms; yet in August, the Economist Intelligence Unit forecasted no progress in any of the reform policies until after the 2006 parliamentary elections.[13] The capsizing fiscal equilibrium drew serious consequences in 2005 in the form of warnings received from the European Union (EU) as well as a downgrading of the state's creditworthiness by the prominent credit ratings institute Fitch Ratings. But in December, in its annual Hungary supplement, the *Financial Times* contrasted this fiscal overspending and looming financial crisis with the country's generally healthy and prosperous private economy: "Most economists forecast growth this year and next about 4 percent, compared with eurozone growth of under 2 percent."[14] Thus, while politics is in a deadlock to introduce overarching reforms in key areas of human services, owing to what the *Financial Times* characterizes as "tribal-like divisions within the society,"[15] the economy thrives thanks to the massive success of the free market.

The Hungarian secret services, military, police, and border control are overseen by the three civilian ministers. Yet the functioning of the security services continued to be in the crossfire of criticism in 2005 owing to controversies revealed and the still unresolved issue of transitional justice. Two scandals placed the secret services in the spotlight in August. First, rumors erupted around the National Security Office's activities at an obviously far-right cultural festival,[16] and later in the month, *Magyar Nemzet* uncovered an espionage incident involving ethnic Hungarians from Romania working for Romanian security services. The episode stirred political whirlwinds and resulted in a parliamentary investigation, since it involved the phone tapping of government ministers. However, the parliamentary investigation did not offer a full account of the event. Instead, the process indicated that rival political camps penetrated the services with their political motivations in the services' functioning. As the story unfolded in the fall, it became clear that the incumbents were seeking to discipline those responsible for leaking the story,[17] and at the same time the opposition had created its own self-controlled network of security informants.[18]

The first quarter of the year promised a new impetus and eventual reconciliation of some of the wrongdoings committed during the country's Communist-era past. Following Prime Minister Gyurcsany's 2004 pledge to declassify the past regime's secret service files, in January the National Security Office handed over to the Historical Archives of the Hungarian State Security the files accumulated in the Ministry of the Interior between 1944 and 1990, thereby making them available to interested researchers. Meanwhile, the parliamentary parties launched an intensive political discourse toward new legislation that would allow the files to be made accessible to the wider public. In parallel, reinforcing the need to solve the question once and for all, various lists of former collaborators naming the involvement of leading political, cultural, media, and church figures were disclosed by hvg.hu, the political think tank Political Capital, and anonymous sources.

Regrettably, the law fell victim first to the inability of crafting consensus among the opponent political blocs and, consequently, to unsettled contradictory legal objectives. Essential to complete disclosure of the files, the governing coalition could not garner the opposition's support to moderate rights protecting individual privacy vigorously guaranteed by the Constitution. In return for its backing of the bill, the opposition demanded that the law stipulate measures against revealed collaborators as well as officials of the former Communist regime, a move the governing coalition considered unrelated to the goal of the legislation. Finally, among his last acts, outgoing president Ferenc Madl referred the law adopted in May to the Constitutional Court for preventive review, and in October the Court declared that "there was no such Constitutional objective that justifies and necessitates curbing of the fundamental right [of privacy] pursuant to the full disclosure [of Communist secret services files]."[19]

Electoral Process

1997	1998	1999	2001	2002	2003	2004	2005	2006
1.25	1.25	1.25	1.25	1.25	1.25	1.25	1.25	1.25

The year 2005 brought an early start to political campaigning of parties for the national elections to be held in early 2006. While the two major parties competed with each other for greater popularity, their lesser counterparts were struggling to reach beyond the 5 percent support necessary to be elected into the Parliament in the upcoming year.

Overall, Hungarian elections have repeatedly been considered to be free and fair. An earlier insufficiency in the legal framework governing the electoral process – that is, the lack of regulation on how Hungarian citizens residing abroad on election day may cast their ballots – has been resolved permanently: The provisions required for ensuring voters' rights in line with the Constitution were formed in 2005. But the Parliament has not yet achieved formal representation of minorities, as required by the Constitution.

Presidential and national by-elections were held in Hungary in 2005. In the case of a single-seat mandate in the town of Sopron, earlier attempts failed to fill the empty seat of a previous individually elected parliamentarian from the major oppositional center-right FIDESZ-Hungarian Civic Party (FIDESZ) who moved to the European Parliament. Eventually, the new FIDESZ candidate won 72 percent of the vote against the ruling Hungarian Socialist Party (MSzP) candidate's 18 percent in May 2005.

At the beginning of June, parliamentary parties faced mutual accusations during the election of the new president, all of which revealed major tensions within the governing coalition, among oppositional parties, and between the government and the opposition. Under the Constitution, the president is elected indirectly by the Parliament by a two-thirds majority for a maximum of two five-year terms. If a qualified majority cannot be reached in either of the first two rounds, a third round with a simple majority is necessary. According to the coalition agreement, it was the right of the senior governing coalition partner, the MSzP, to nominate a presidential candidate to succeed President Ferenc Madl, whose term ended in August. The governing coalition faced tensions when its junior partner, the liberal Alliance of Free Democrats (SzDSz), considered the MSzP candidate, Katalin Szili (parliamentary Speaker and former deputy chairwoman of the MSzP), unsuitable for the post. While the governing coalition failed to agree on a mutually acceptable candidate, FIDESZ nominated Laszlo Solyom, candidate of the ecopolitical NGO "Vedegylet" (Protect the Future), who also enjoyed the formal support of more than 100 intellectuals across the political spectrum.

During and after the unsuccessful first and second rounds of voting, FIDESZ accused oppositional center-right Hungarian Democratic Forum (MDF) members of voting for the Socialist Szili in the first round. The MSzP believed FIDESZ broke voting secrecy rules during the second round by trying to record how MPs voted. Before the third round, FIDESZ alleged that the MSzP attempted to bribe opposition MPs with HUF 10 million (US$50,000) to vote for the Socialist candidate. Eventually, as the governing coalition could not agree on a mutually accepted candidate, Solyom (nominated by FIDESZ) gained 185 votes to Szili's 182 and won the ballot in the heated third round, from which most SzDSz members abstained. President Solyom is viewed by many to be able to create a new form of presidency independent from party politics, helping to bridge the political divide in Hungary. The political divide is expected to deepen, however, as the country gets closer to the national elections, which are to be held between April 1 and May 31, 2006.

This year, the political landscape is expected to be rather bleak, offering the fewest number of parties ever to represent the people in post-Communist Hungary: Only two are expected to clear the 5 percent threshold and win representation to the 386-seat unicameral National Assembly in the upcoming national elections. The SzDSz (currently with 20 seats) and the oppositional MDF (which by 2005 had lost 4 members to FIDESZ and seen 12 of its additional members become independent out of 24 seats gained) are not expected to gain enough support to be elected to the Parliament, although their status has not yet been determined. The main actors of the political scene are the MSzP with 178 seats in the current center-left coalition government and the oppositional center-right FIDESZ with 168 seats. Although for the first time since 1990, no independent candidate was elected to the National Assembly in 2002, those MDF members who left the party became independent MPs. The tendency to have fewer parties represented in the Parliament is a result of the trend toward majoritarian rule as well as the ongoing consolidation process within and among parties.

In 2005, both major parties worked on changing their images in the hopes of waging a more successful campaign. FIDESZ party leader Viktor Orban launched his "Year of National Consultation" initiative, which included the establishment of the National Consultative Committee – a focus group consisting of politicians and public figures primarily from the Right, aiming to bridge public life and the citizenry and reach supporters beyond the traditional FIDESZ base. In addition, FIDESZ looked further afield for extra-parliamentary political groups (such as the Entrepreneurs' Party) that might be integrated into its existing alliance. FIDESZ changed its national slogan from "Go Hungary, go Hungarians!" to "Change!" and returned from the Hungarian tricolor to the party's traditional orange. The new image seemed to be successful, as apart from a few weeks in the fall, the party led in the polls during the year.

A few months after the failure in the presidential elections, the MSzP began its identity campaign and aimed to build a proud left-wing party image full of energy and optimism. The party resumed its series of public finance measures (the "100 Steps" program), and by making energetic speeches in the Parliament, Prime Minister Gyurcsany dictated the political agenda. In its identity campaign, the MSzP highlighted its red color and key concepts such as "Security, Justice, and Bravery" as common values and tried to gain constituents for the party who were not particularly interested in politics. With the MSzP's campaign in the fall, FIDESZ's advance had decreased significantly by the end of the year.

With Gyurcsany incorporating liberal values in and of themselves, the liberal SzDSz may not be able to gain any seats in the Parliament in the coming year. The party struggles to show an independent and determined liberal character and continues to lose support to the MSzP. MDF party leader Ibolya David has not been able to strengthen the party. The mission of FIDESZ to unite all right-wing parties under its umbrella led to internal conflicts within the MDF and to the departure of 16 of its MPs, who looked into closer alignment with FIDESZ. Opinion polls suggest that voter support of the party is between 1 and 2 percent. It is questionable whether the reunification of the MDF with the Hungarian Democratic People's Party, which broke off nine years ago, will help the MDF to remain in the Parliament. Among several party-forming initiatives, a new political party, Live Chain for Hungary, was formed in 2005 from environmental groups such as Protect the Future, whose candidate became the president of the republic. Support for the Centrum Party and the radical far-right Hungarian Justice and Life Party was too insignificant to be measured in 2005.

Civil Society

1997	1998	1999	2001	2002	2003	2004	2005	2006
1.25	1.25	1.25	1.25	1.25	1.25	1.25	1.25	1.25

The legal framework governing NGOs aids their establishment, and operation is sound and conducive to civil society's active role in democracy. The Law on

Associations was adopted in 1989, while the rules governing the operation of foundations had already been added to the civic code in 1987. These laws and lower-level regulations provide reasonably easy requirements for forming foundations or associations, the two predominant forms of NGOs, and registration by county-level court can be denied in only a few cases. However, a 2005 study by the Environmental Management and Law Association (EMLA) tested the general interpretation of the laws when it submitted the same registration documents to 20 different courts and found that there is ample room for improvement, since each case produced a different outcome.[20]

A major development in the legal framework of NGOs is the adoption of the Law on Volunteerism in June. According to the Hungarian Central Statistical Office (KSH) statistics, in 2003 close to 400,000 individuals volunteered for public causes, contributing almost 35 million working hours, saving HUF 24 billion (US$120 million) that would otherwise have been paid in staff costs.[21] Yet a 2005 study conducted by the Nonprofit Research Association in 2004 found that almost 3.5 million Hungarian citizens were giving some form of pro bono service to their communities.[22] Since 2003, the Hungarian Volunteer Center had been conducting an erudite advocacy campaign involving a coalition of NGOs for the legal recognition of volunteer work. Hungarian NGOs, relying on the favorable attitude of media and the general public, drafted the original piece of legislation, organized a handful of public debates, and carried out consultations with the government. Despite certain criticisms that the finally approved bill does not sanction free-of-charge activities offered to the smallest NGOs, the law enables NGOs to offer modest tax-free allowances, in-kind compensation, and training opportunities to citizens working for them.[23]

Hungarian civil society can be judged as one of the most vibrant sectors of society. The U.S. Agency for International Development's NGO Sustainability Index puts Hungary's civil society in third place alongside Latvia among 29 former Soviet-bloc countries.[24] According to KSH statistics, among the nearly 75,000 registered organizations, the majority are working to provide human services, sport, and recreational opportunities to their communities.[25] Over 50 percent of them enjoy public benefit status, which has offered economic benefits to NGOs since 1997. Observers estimate that approximately half the registered groups are in fact operational. The garden variety organizations include strong Budapest-based resource centers with network institutes across the country offering training opportunities, legal counsel, technical assistance in their advocacy efforts, libraries, and Internet portals. There are also a host of politically engaged NGOs and think tanks supporting all sides of the party landscape.

Although 2005 was the first year to see a decline in overall NGO income through the 1 percent mechanism – whereby taxpayers are entitled to earmark 1 percent of their personal income tax for charities – the Nonprofit Information and Training Center (NIOK) has organized a massive nationwide awareness-raising campaign each year since the adoption of the legislation, with the active support of the media. Funding of NGOs is persistently considered problematic given min-

imal corporate support and availability of state resources, but the culture of philanthropy should gradually take root, particularly because EU institutions constantly urge businesses to conduct and report annually on their corporate social
responsibility programs.[26]

The year 2005 marked a milestone for Hungary's civil society, reinforcing that
citizens' commitment to political goals can ultimately gain breakthroughs via strategic civic mobilization. In February 2005, Protect the Future, an NGO promoting
sustainable development, garnered the support of 100 Hungarian public figures
from all sides of the political spectrum in an open letter and subsequently launched
a public campaign nominating Laszlo Solyom as the new president of the state.

The letter harshly criticized the Hungarian political culture: "Amid the scenes
of representative democracy, the political class and the client-bourgeoisie fight
their private wars by trespassing rules to attain and plunder public goods." In contrast, the initiators recalled that in the heyday of the systemic changes, as president
of the Constitutional Court, Solyom relentlessly defended the rule of law and the
spirit of the Constitution.[27]

It is true that in his former post, President Solyom was known for his active
role in developing constitutional case law and even introduced an original and
internationally emulated legal concept to interpreting liberal democratic constitutions. And his concept of the "invisible Constitution" meant that one needs to seek
the spirit or moral objective of a constitutional clause. But initially, his nomination
appeared as a bombshell to the entire political elite – not for Solyom's tenacious
reputation, but because the Hungarian Constitution does not recognize civil society's role in the presidential election process per se.

Until last February, as in previous occasions every five years since 1990, political parties were conveniently preparing to consult among themselves and their
favored candidates. But after Solyom was pitched in the public discourse and
received wide-ranging civic support, parties were forced to consider him as a
potential candidate. Solyom's active role in a 2004 campaign against the installation of NATO radar in the country, which the opposition backed to garner further
public support, also assisted in putting him forth as the opposition parties' official
candidate and in his eventual winning of the post.

Trade unions and interest groups enjoy significant autonomy in Hungary. By
far the most influential workers groups within the Hungarian government are
those in the public sector and state-owned public services, such as the various public transport companies. In addition, several organizations were established in past
years to represent farmers' interests and exhibit substantial bargaining power.[28] In
February and March 2005, farmers held a series of demonstrations and succeeded
ultimately in demanding that the government release payments mandated through
the country's pledge to the EU. While unions in the public service sector and particularly the predecessors of the former Communist unions are considered to be
closely aligned with the political Left,[29] agrarian interest groups and some larger
trade worker alliances formed around the systemic changes are frequently identified with the Right. Therefore, and because of low membership, observers consid-

er the unions to be generally weak and in need of perking up their reputations.[30]

Hungary's educational system is free from explicit political influence. The Ministry of Education bears overall responsibility in overseeing educational policy, but the altogether 1.8 million students can decide to attend public, parochial, or other private institutions.[31] Universities operate freely, particularly after the university reform introduced in 2005 was ruled unconstitutional in October by the Constitutional Court for curbing their academic independence and self-government for instating a governing board over university senates.[32]

Independent Media

1997	1998	1999	2001	2002	2003	2004	2005	2006
1.50	1.50	2.00	2.25	2.25	2.25	2.25	2.50	2.50

Media are generally considered to be free in Hungary. There is a huge selection of media outlets, and several new private television cable channels were launched in 2005. Freedom House's annual *Survey of Press Freedom* rated Hungary "Free" in 2005.

The continued high number of court cases against journalists raised concerns in 2005. Libel and secrecy laws continued to be criminal offenses, which according to many restricts press freedom. The high court annulled last year's 10-month suspended jail sentence for libel handed to editor Andras Bencsik of the weekly *Demokrata* in a case brought by an MP. The arbitrary prosecution under outdated secrecy laws of *Nepszava* journalist Rita Csik, charged in 2004 with "deliberate breach of a state secret" after she wrote a story quoting an unlawfully classified police memorandum citing criminal evidence collected on an MP, continued in 2005 with the acquittal of the journalist in the lower court (the case is to be continued in the appeals court). This was the first case since transition in which a journalist accused of breaching state secrets was brought to court.

In 2005, journalist Antonia Radai of the weekly *HVG* (*Heti Vilaggazdasag*) was also taken to court for publishing parts of a Mafia case that allegedly involved several civil servants. The indictment was classified, and one cannot know the details of what Radai is accused of under security law. According to Miklos Haraszti, the Organization for Security and Cooperation in Europe representative on freedom of the media who was allowed to attend the court trial, the provision regulating state secrets is unconstitutional on at least three or four points, all of which should be changed immediately.[33]

While acting as minister of youth and sports in 2003, Prime Minister Gyurcsany took Laszlo Torok, a journalist at the daily *Magyar Nemzet*, to court; in 2005, Torok was put on probation for libel for quoting the deputy head of the oppositional FIDESZ. According to the judicial branch's interpretation of the Hungarian criminal code, grounds for libel charges include not only statements damaging one's reputation, but publicity given to another person's derogatory statements. While politicians are under immunity, journalist quoting them are not.

In 2005, police took action against individuals who were distributing leaflets criticizing the mayor of Mako. The police explained that the activists had prepared and distributed a type of publication that should have been previously reported and thereby committed a misdemeanor against press policing. This offense used to be a tool against oppositional samizdat before the fall of Communism and is now thought to be used for political purposes.

The quality of journalism in Hungary is generally adequate, but the boundaries between factual information, analysis, and commentary are often blurred. For the first time in Hungary, *Magyar Hírlap* introduced a news ombudsman to improve journalistic standards. The main task of the ombudsman is to monitor and report on the objectivity, accuracy, and balance in news coverage of the paper.

The media landscape is dominated by market forces in Hungary, and foreign media companies are very active in both national and local newspaper markets. Only a small number of daily papers are owned locally. Local papers are particularly important and manage to keep their monopolies in the counties where they publish; their total circulation is about the same as that of the national daily papers combined. However, in the race to attract readers by print media outlets, tabloids prove to be the winners.

The 1996 Law on the Media introduced commercial broadcasting and broke up the monopoly of the state-controlled public service channels. The law established the National Television and Radio Board (ORTT), a regulatory and supervisory body whose members are delegated by political parties. The ORTT monitors the activities and programs of public and commercial broadcasting stations and grants licenses and broadcasting frequencies. Half the members of the board of trustees of the public service broadcasters' presidium are appointed by governing political parties, the other half by the opposition, leaving too much room for political interference in public service broadcasting.

The Law on the Media has been widely criticized on many grounds, and the almost decade-long wish to modify it or create a new one has approached an end. The ORTT itself prepared a new draft version, which instead of strengthening media freedom focuses on the regulation and sanctioning of TV and radio channels as well as the Internet.[34] Whether the new law will transform public service media into a modern, financially independent outlet free of political influence remains to be seen.

Attention in public service broadcasting centers around the succession of the president of Hungarian Radio. After President Katalin Kondor's mandate expired in July, the board of trustees made four unsuccessful attempts to elect a new president, thus leaving the public broadcasting station without proper legal representation. The legal status of public radio and what powers the vice presidents have in the interim before the new president is elected are unclear. It is assumed that before the national parliamentary elections there will be no consensus on the new president of Hungarian Radio, which illustrates how public interest is overruled by party politics.

Since public TV attracts only about 10 to 15 percent of viewers and has been on the edge of bankruptcy for years, the rationale for maintaining six state-sponsored stations is questionable. Nonetheless, public TV channels plan to launch three more thematic TV channels in order to compete with private channels for viewership. Owing to financial, legal, and broadcasting constraints, these plans have not yet materialized. Hungarians receive information primarily from private TV channels, most of which are foreign owned. Besides the three state-supported channels, two commercial stations – RTL Klub (affiliated with the Belgian-French RTL-UFA) and TV2 (owned by a Hungarian-American-Scandinavian consortium) – also reach the entire population. There are several commercial cable and satellite channels, such as foreign-owned radio stations and thematic TV stations.

New to the local media, Hungarian entrepreneurs such as industrialist Gabor Szeles have begun to enter the media market, which was dominated previously by multinationals. Besides buying 76 percent of the daily *Magyar Hirlap*, Szeles launched a financial and business news channel, Echo TV, in September, and a lifestyle channel, Vital TV, is to be launched soon. There are over 200 local or regional public, commercial, nonprofit, and cable radio stations, most limiting their programming to entertainment without significant original news content. According to a recent report by the Open Society Institute, "Hungarian [television] channels scarcely ever broadcast investigative reports and can hardly be labeled as watchdogs of democracy."[34]

News portals such as origo.hu and index.hu are providing readers with their own news content around the clock, and television and radio broadcasting on the Internet have become increasingly popular in Hungary. In 2005, the National Communications Authority reported a 92.5 percent increase in the number of broadband Internet subscribers,[36] yet according to GFK Hungary, market research company, only 32 percent of the adult population reported using the Internet by 2005.[37] Among the barriers to deeper Internet penetration in Hungary, experts list the still high subscription fees, low computer-equipped population, and lack of knowledge of and trust toward the Internet.[38]

Internet censorship has been limited in Hungary. To prevent state intervention, self-regulatory organizations founded by Hungarian Internet content providers such as the Hungarian Association of Content Providers have formulated a voluntary code of conduct to regulate the norms of Internet content. The planned new Law on the Media aims to regulate the Internet in order to provide legal background for the protection of personal rights and civil liberties and to apply the same liabilities and rights for both online and offline media outlets.

Local Democratic Governance

1997	1998	1999	2001	2002	2003	2004	2005	2006
n/a	n/a	n/a	n/a	n/a	n/a	n/a	2.25	2.25

Local government reform legislation took pride of place among transition laws in Hungary, and the country has been a pioneer in modernizing the subnational government system in the region. Still, the system requires further reform to enable subnational units to be financially viable and to procure and administer EU structural funds.

In Hungary, every village, town, county, and the capital has the right to freely administer local affairs autonomously. However, as a result the local governmental system is highly fragmented, with 3,158 municipal, county, and local governments and the capital, Budapest, as a separate unit. Every municipality has become a unit of local government and in each settlement provides various services, such as primary education, basic social services, health care, and public utilities. County self-governments provide public services with a regional character. There are seven countrywide local government associations, as local authorities have the right to form interest representation organizations for the protection of their common interests and promotion of their collective representation.

The process for electing local self-governments – that is, a mayor and a local representative body – every four years has generally been free and fair. Although in smaller villages it is difficult to recruit enough candidates, generally there is competition for local government mandates. In larger cities, there is a much higher partisan character of local councils than in smaller settlements. In cities with a population over 50,000, almost 9 in 10 councillors belong to a political party.[39] Mayors and local representatives along with their partners and children are required to declare their assets.

Although the legal autonomy of local governments is well protected, their financial autonomy is highly limited, and they rely heavily on state subsidies. Among the municipal governments, 91 percent represent fewer than 5,000 people, while more than half have a population under 1,000. These units often cannot sustain the level of services mandated to them, as they usually are not economically viable with adequate local economic activity.[40] Most municipalities regularly run deficits. A frequent complaint from local governments is that while providing only a fraction of the necessary financial means, the Parliament keeps assigning new public duties to municipalities. Others say that the state's sole duty is to create opportunity for local revenues.

Although municipal governments can raise their income by levying local taxes and fees, only one-third of their revenues come from local taxes. The size of the population and foreign investment creates huge differences among municipalities, favoring larger cities in their ability to raise local taxes.[41] Many municipalities have consumed most of their wealth by selling their assets to cover the expenses of new responsibilities.[42] County local governments have no right to levy taxes.

According to Tocqueville Research Center, small local governments have a greater tendency toward elitist top-down governance and are less responsive to citizens' needs than larger local governments. Because of the local governments' often opaque and unaccountable handling of finances, so goes the center's argument, the state has no trust in their capacity to handle money adequately and has silently begun a recentralization process. Social institutions that could make local leaders accountable are weak or do not exist in smaller municipalities. Fewer than one in four municipalities have media outlets independent from local government subsidies, and there are none in 58 percent of Hungarian municipalities.[43]

Citizens are particularly active at the local level in Hungary through various NGOs and local initiatives, but their participation in local public affairs through local governments is limited. Most decisions on local matters are determined by state subsidies, constraining citizens' effectiveness in influencing local matters, especially in small municipalities.[44]

Between local elections, citizens' inclusion in the decision-making process is guaranteed by a minimum of one public hearing a year, as set by the Law on Local Government. Out of the 15 local referendums held in 2005, low voter turnout invalidated the results in 5 cases.[45]

Pressured by the EU to approximate the subnational model of the EU financing system, Hungary is conducting further reforms and has identified two directions of modernization. With the creation of 168 entities at the "small region" level of administration (instead of the fragmented municipalities) and the establishment of 7 larger development regions, the reform aims to increase public service quality. The legally defined 168 small regions are meant to have three dominant functions: the performance of local governmental public services, the management of state administration tasks where local knowledge and expertise are necessary, and the operation of spatial development functions.[46]

As the reform of administrative and development units has yet to be realized, the newly introduced Law on Administrative Procedure, effective as of November 1, under the e-governance concept reaches no further than technical modernization. E-government services at the municipal level are mostly informational rather than interactive or transactional. According to a survey by GKIeNet, an Internet research and consulting company, released in May, only 3 percent of municipalities are able to receive completed online forms electronically.[47]

The 1993 Law on the Rights of National and Ethnic Minorities guarantees Hungary's 13 recognized minority groups the right to establish national and local minority self-governments. The basic tasks of these minority governments are to organize the activities of minorities, respond to their needs, and help preserve their culture and ethnic identity. Minority self-governments are financed by the state budget, and there is no central coordination of the allocation of money for them.

At the local level, 1,841 minority self-governments were elected in the fall of 2002. However, many of the elected representatives lacked any true ties with a specific minority. In 2005, the Parliament modified the Law on the Election of Minority Self-Government Representatives and introduced the registration of minority voters. The modification aims to prevent nonminorities from holding positions in minority self-governments in order to gain personal business advantages and benefits. Certain paragraphs of the law, however, have been annulled by the Constitutional Court. The original proposal would have allowed certain minority candidates to bypass local municipal elections and gain seats at the municipal level without being elected, which would have violated the direct and equal representation of local municipal elections.

Judicial Framework and Independence

1997	1998	1999	2001	2002	2003	2004	2005	2006
1.75	1.75	1.75	2.00	2.00	1.75	1.75	1.75	1.75

The Hungarian Constitution recognizes fundamental political, civil, and human rights and obliges the state to protect them. Among the legal institutions the individual's right to appeal to the ombudsman is particularly important. The four ombudsmen protect individual privacy, ethnic and national minorities, and citizens' rights generally. All four individuals are prominent legal academics and, following constitutional rules, were appointed by consensus of the parliamentary parties. The Ministry of Education employs a commissioner who protects students' rights. Prior to his election, the new president drafted a legislation to the Parliament proposing the introduction of a fifth – "future generations" – commissioner to be entrusted with care of the environment, whereas the government wishes to bring to the fore another ombudsperson to protect employee rights.

The 11-member Hungarian Constitutional Court commenced its work in 1990 and is the institution par excellence for safeguarding fundamental rights and freedoms. The Court's authoritative interpretation of the Constitution on political rights and civil liberties canceled many clauses of the legal framework and prevented a handful of newly enacted legislations from entering into force. Members' impartiality and independence are ensured through consensual election in the Parliament, but – curiously – until 2005, when the Hungarian Civil Liberties Union contested the Court in a number of instances, there was much less public scrutiny of the Court's resolutions than of the similarly elected ombudspersons.

Reaching consensus on the nominees to the Court has always been prolonged and burdensome, at times putting the Court on the verge of a standstill. The stalemate generally ends with the election of both ruling coalition and oppositional candidates. In 2005, membership decreased to the limit of eight justices, and lawmakers and the jurist community were already expecting amendments to the rules of selection to overcome the current deadlock. Finally, during the fall three new justices filled the missing seats. The former president of the Court was also reappointed, but because his term as president ended in 2005, the Court elected a new head in October. Mihaly Bihari, the new president and a former member of the Communist Party, expelled him in 1988 for his reformist views. Since then, he has become known for his bold support for the country's democratization and has molded himself as a preeminent expert of Hungary's nonviolent transition.

The Hungarian judicial branch is organized in a four-tier structure. There are magistrates at the local and county levels with jurisdiction over their districts. The highest appeals courts with larger regional jurisdiction are based in Budapest and four other large cities across the country. The Supreme Court in Budapest, charged with safeguarding the coherent interpretation of legislative acts, issues abstract judgments and develops a limited body of case law; it also serves as an extraordinary appeals forum for cases adjudicated at the highest appeals courts. At the end of

2004, there were 2,710 judges in the country, and over 60 percent of the entire judiciary had 10 or more years of court experience; however, at the local level of courts, where the majority (60 percent) of cases are concluded, this figure was only 43 percent.[48]

The judicial branch has been self-governed by the National Judicial Council since the council's formation in late 1997. The council is headed by the president of the Supreme Court, and 9 of its 15 other members are judges elected by fellow justices. The remaining members are the minister of justice, the chief prosecutor, the chairman of the Hungarian Bar Association, and two MP delegates from the judicial and financial parliamentary committees.

Hungarians have conflicting views regarding the impartiality of the judiciary. *Nepszabadsag* covered a September Median survey stating that a third of Hungarians suspect political influence behind judicial decisions.[49] *De Jure* magazine, on the other hand, in November reported on a Szonda Ipsos survey that found the judiciary to be among the most trusted institutions. Hungarians have little information about the judicial system[50] and learn of judicial proceedings only through high-publicity cases. The National Judicial Council's April resolution endorsing the code of ethics developed by the Hungarian Association of Judges is therefore particularly welcome.[51] The code of ethics sets forth unbinding rules on how justices should behave, complementing the rigorous regulations on conflict of interest in place since 1997. Judges are prohibited from holding jobs outside their duties, holding public office, or being a member of a party.

There is no systematic torture or ill-treatment of defendants in Hungary. In April, a police officer received a one-year suspended prison sentence for unlawful detention of a suspect.[52] A leaked videotape in 2005 about the extraordinary treatment of a white-collar criminal suspect contributes to Hungarians' views that law enforcement favors the rich. However, public defenders, NGOs, and their network of human rights lawyers are ready to assist disadvantaged suspects. Likewise, victims of crimes may turn to NGOs and find remedy through legal means. In November, a Council of Europe report underlined the well-known contention regarding Hungary's overburdened prison system.[53]

Intolerance against the Roma continues to be widespread. Discrimination based on race, ethnicity, and sexual behavior is particularly embedded in the society, penetrating the workplace and public services. The legal framework and practice, however, is steadily improving. In 2005, a court issued a fine of HUF 500,000 (US$2,500) against a private security company that openly discriminates against Roma. This was the first binding warrant issued under the equal opportunity legislation adopted in 2003.[54]

Illiberal views among nonstate actors are not entirely foreign, but institutions and citizens' attitudes stand firm against the pervasion of an extremist society. The Hungarian criminal code prohibits the use of totalitarian symbols, such as the Communist red star or the Nazi swastika. But free speech is amply safeguarded by the courts' decisions and rights protection watchdogs, even at the expense of the appearance of illiberal opinions in public. In October 2005, the highest appeals court of Budapest issued a warrant dissolving the allegedly cultural organization "Ver es Becsulet" (Blood and Honor), which in fact was a neo-Nazi group promoting ethnic hatred and intolerance, and was judged unconstitutional.

After the abrupt emergence of the neo-Nazi "Magyar Jovo" (Hungarian Future) group in 2004, a poll run by Marketing Centrum proved that the vast majority of Hungarians believed authoritarian views were endangering the social order.[55] But liberal democratic attitudes by far outnumber illiberal ones, and no groups can imperil social stability. Throughout the years, citizens have staged numerous antiracist and peace rallies. In May, a large antiracist demonstration was held in response to the stabbing of a Roma boy on the bus. The first ever festival held on International Human Rights Day was organized in 2005 by the Hungarian Civil Liberties Union, the Hungarian Helsinki Committee, and the Legal Defense Bureau for National and Ethnic Minorities – perhaps the three most influential human rights watchdogs in the country.[56] Also, mainstream media frequently report on illiberal views in a timely and responsible manner.

Corruption

1997	1998	1999	2001	2002	2003	2004	2005	2006
n/a	n/a	2.50	3.00	3.00	2.75	2.75	2.75	3.00

Hungary's institutional framework for preventing and curbing corruption has gone through significant improvement in past years and meets international standards. Nevertheless, the implementation of these measures requires more reinforcement and commitment not only from parties and state institutions, but from civil society as well. In 2005, nontransparent businesses closely associated with political parties and the bribing of public service employees were regularly reported in the media, suggesting continuing problems.

Hungary has a reputation for being one of the least corrupt post-Communist countries. In 2005, Transparency International ranked Hungary 40th out of 159 monitored countries worldwide.[57] Transparency International's Corruption Perceptions Index shows a slight improvement in the country's score from last year's 4.8 to 5 out of 10, where 10 indicates the lowest level of corruption. According to GfK Polling Institute's study, however, Hungarians give bribes to public service employees more frequently than the Central and Eastern European average.[58] A number of doctors use state equipment for their private profit. The practice of "gratitude money" for public health care employees, when the state-employed doctor receives money from the patient for provisions to which he or she is not entitled, is widespread.

The year 2005 was effective in revealing questionable practices: Cartels were formed (to the mutual benefit of all parties) largely from public procurement tenders involving highway construction. Parliamentary committees have been set up to investigate the family business interests of Prime Minister Gyurcsany and former prime minister Orban and have failed to come to any conclusions. By 2005, charges against more than 20 suspects had been filed in Hungary's biggest banking fraud, revealing money laundering partially involving public procurement funds at K&H Bank's brokerage arm. The scandal, in which the total sum embezzled reached HUF 23 billion (US$115 million), broke out in 2003 and allegedly has strong political ties on both the Left and the Right. Public service employees, such as public attorneys, a tax inspector, a mayor, and policemen, were caught on fraud charges, out of which many of these latter cases were successfully revealed by the Protective Service of Law Enforcement Agencies (RSzVSz). The 10-year-old RSzVSz is a monitoring agency without investigative powers in charge of fighting corruption in the law enforcement agencies.[59]

Although no independent body deals solely with corruption investigations, a number of state institutions are empowered to fight corruption. The main investigative law enforcement body is the police, while high-level corruption (involving parliamentarians, ministers, and heads of public departments) and organized crime cases fall under the jurisdiction of the Central Investigation Department of the Office of the Prosecutor. Additional institutions with enforcement authority, such as customs and tax agencies, also have separate units to combat corruption. However, cooperation among these institutions is not yet sufficient.

The State Audit Office of Hungary exercises ultimate financial control over all public and EU funds and is a completely independent agency reporting to the Parliament. The "glass pocket" law made it possible for the State Audit Office to trace the path of public funds even through private business files and widens the circle of individuals required to declare their personal assets.

However, the path of public funds is still difficult to follow. Procurement experts claim that in Hungary only about 10 percent of roughly 3,700 annual public procurement tenders are clean. Bribery, cartels, or other irregularities are likely to be present in most cases.[60] Although the "glass pocket" law, which introduced the concept of public interest, requires ministries to publish their operational costs and contracts of high value on their Web sites, little information is up to date. In addition, in 2005 the State Audit Office criticized the financial management of the Ministry of Information, where the paths of public funds distributed personally by the minister were unable to be traced. The Law on Freedom of Electronic Information adopted in July 2005 and to enter force from January 1, 2006, obliges public institutions to publish information of public interest held by them on the Internet.[61]

According to a report adopted by the Organization for Economic Cooperation and Development (OECD), Hungary needs to take further steps to combat corruption and bribery in international business transactions.[62] The report identifies the lack of well-understood laws and untrained officials as significant obstacles in fighting bribery. The OECD was concerned when one of its public official interviewees announced that bribery is "the only way to do business in certain countries" and that in such countries, "formally it is not a bribe because it takes the form of a commission." Among the report's recommendations are ensuring necessary resources for the effective functioning of the Central Investigation Department, increasing the transparency of prosecution, and enabling auditors by law to report all suspected of bribery by any employee or agent of the company to the management or to competent law enforcement authorities.

Despite the various promising initiatives the MSzP-SzDSz coalition has introduced since in government, many anticorruption policies have proved to be short-lived. The Ethics Council of the Republic, an anticorruption board aimed at facilitating the establishment of a cleaner public life, and the State Secretariat of Public Finance, established to monitor public procurement procedures and ensure transparency in the handling of public funds, ceased to exist in 2004. In 2005, however, clean public life returned to the government's agenda, and the coalition has aimed to increase openness in some areas of public life: to prevent the creation of phantom companies for tax evasion purposes, to modernize public procurement, to create a Law on Lobbying, and to modify the regulations of party financing.

Since September 2005, cartel activity resulting in the restriction of competition in public procurements has been criminalized under the changes to competition legislation. Recent modifications to the Law on Public Procurement, of which an earlier version was returned by the president to the Parliament for reconsideration, now further limits the authority of local governments to engage in contractual services without open tender.

The long planned Law on Lobbying was under discussion in the Parliament at the end of 2005. Prior to this, lobbying activity (often associated with corruption) was not regulated but was touched upon indirectly by legislation both on conflict of interest and on lawmaking and by various anticorruption regulations. The draft law aims to contribute to a cleaner public life by making public the interests behind certain legislative decisions via registering the activity of lobbyists and requiring detailed reports of their activities. However, there remains no protocol or code of ethics for political decision makers.

According to previous reports of both the Open Society Institute[63] and the Group of States Against Corruption, there is significant evidence of illegal party and campaign funding in Hungary. The operations and activities of party-based businesses lack transparency and adequate control, and there are no effective sanctioning and enforcement mechanisms in place for illicit bookkeeping of party financing. There is a discrepancy between accounting law and the legislation on parties over reporting systems, and there are loopholes in the regulation of campaign finances. The matter should have increased in urgency, as campaigning for the 2006 elections already started in 2005; however, there is insufficient political will for these changes.

Viktoria Villanyi is a program and finance officer and Roland Kovats is the deputy director of the Freedom House Europe office in Budapest.

[1] See http://www.complex.hu/kzlcim/tva05.htm and http://www.complex.hu/kzlcim/ogya05.htm.

[2] See http://www.mkogy.hu.

[3] Helyhiany miatt nem kozvetithetnek a Parlamentbol a kereskedelmi tevek (Commercial TV can't broadcast Parliamentary sessions due to lack of space) www.nol.hu/cikk/372938.

[4] A kozvelemeny a Parlamentrol-Az Orszaggyules imazsanak, a parlamenti tisztsegviselok, az orszaggyulesi kepviselok es a parlament tevekenysegenek es media-jelenletenek egyes dimenzioirol a magyar felnott lakossag koreben (Public opinion on the Parliament: About certain dimensions of the image of the Assembly, the performance and media presence of the staff and MPs amongst Hungarian adult population.) http://www.gallup.hu/Gallup/release/parlament050203.htm.

[5] Nepszorakoztato parlament-Vitanyi Ivan a politikai happeningrol (Cabaret Parliament: Ivan Vitanyi about the political shows) http://www.nol.hu/cikk/382678/.

[6] Hidegen hagyja a koaliciot az Alkotmanybirosag (The Supreme Court is ignored by the coalition) Hungarian News Agency cited on http://index.hu/politika/belhirek/?main:2005.12.13&246890.

[7] Akasztjak a hohert: A parlament alkotmanyserto mulasztasai (Executioner hung: Unconstitutional Parliament backlogs) http://www.magyarhirlap.hu/Archivum_cikk.php?cikk=95078&archiv=1&next=0.

[8] Political Capital, Jo kampanyeszkoz-e a parlamenti vizsgalobizottsag? (Are Parliamentary committees good use for campaigning?) 19 July 2005 http://www.hirszerzo.hu/cikk.php?id=999

[9] De Jure-Jogaszok Tarsasagi Magazinja (Lawyers' Social Magazine), Igy nem lehet egy orszagot kormanyozni-Kilenyi Geza a tarcak kulonutas torekveseirol es a kisiklatott reformrol (This is not the way to govern a country: Geza Kilenyi about the diverging line-ministries and the derailed reforms) 4-7 March 2005 and Jegyzo es Kozigazgatas (Notary and Administration): Uj jogintezmenyek a Ket.-ben (New institutions in the Public Administration Act) March-April 2005.

[10] Tibor Navrasics, Problemak es megoldasok 2005-A kozigazgatas valsaga (Problems and solutions:2005: The crisis of public administration) Speech delivered at Polgari Gondola conference. 1 October 2005

[11] Olcso allam hatalmas apparatussal? (Cheap state with large staff?) http://www.mno.hu/index.mno?cikk=319844.

[12] Sokat beszel-e Jarai? (Does Jarai talk much?) http://index.hu/gazdasag/magyar/jarai051220/.

[13] A valasztasokig nem lesznek reformok (No reforms until elections) Index.hu, citing Economic Intelligence Unit, 23 August 2005 http://index.hu/gazdasag/magyar/eiu050823.

[14] Financial Times Special Report-Hungary, Driver of Growth Shifts from Consumption to Exports, 12 December 2005.

[15] Financial Times Special Report-Hungary, Rivals Square Up for Election Fight 12 December 2005.

[16] Szorakozott a szeleburdi titkosszolga a Magyar Szigeten (The silly secret agent was having fun at the "Hungarian Island") http://index.hu/politika/belfold/szik0817o/.

[17] Hazugsagvizsgaloval a kemugy kiszivarogtatoi ellen? (Lie-detector against the leak of the spy story?) http://www.mno.hu/index.mno?cikk=317955.

[18] Kovernek direktben jelentenek (Kover is directly reported) http://index.hu/politika/belfold/kover1101.

[19] See 37/2005. (X. 5.) AB hat□rozat (Constitutional Court Ruling 37/2005. 5 October 2005).

[20] EMLA, Egyesuletek birosagi nyilvantartasba veteli gyakorlata-Osszehasonlito elemzes (The practice of associations' court registration: A comprehensive study) (forthcoming)

[21] HVG, Haszontalankodok (Of no use) 21 May 2005

[22] Klara Czike and Eva Kuti, Lakossagi adomanyok es onkentes tevekenysegek-Gyorsjelentes a 2004-es felmeres eredmenyeirol (Public giving and voluntary work: Flash report on the findings of the 2004 survey) (Budapest: Onkentes Kozpont Alapitvany es Nonprofit Kutatocsoport Egyesulet, 2005), 6-9.

[23] Magyar Narancs, Bekeretezve-Torveny az onkentes tevekenysegrol ("Framed": Law on volunteering) 26 July 2005 cited on www.ngo.hu/modules.php?name=News&file=article&sid=1801.

[24] USAID NGO Sustainability Index 2004, www.usaid.gov/locations/europe_eurasia/dem_gov/ngoindex/2004/index.htm.

[25] A 2003-ra vonatkozo nonprofit-adatgyujtes legfontosabb megallapitasai (Key findings of the 2003 nonprofit study) (Budapest: KSH, 2004).

[26] See http://ec.europa.eu/employment_social/soc-dial/csr/index.htm.

[27] See http://www.ke2005.hu/index.html.
[28] Vegigszantanak Budapesten a gazdak (The farmers will plough Budapest) http://index.hu/gazdasag/magyar/gazdi050216.
[29] Titkos talalkozo a Koztarsasag teren szakszervezeti vezetokkel-Uj vezeto a munkabiztonsagi fofelugyelet elen? (Secret meeting with union leaders at Republic square – New head for the workplace security supervision?) http://www.nol.hu/cikk/359109/
[30] Vedtelen tarsadalom-Thoma Laszlo a szakszervezeti valsagrol (Insecure society – Laszlo Thoma about the crisis of unions) http://www.nol.hu/cikk/382797/
[31] Statisztikai gyorstajekokztato a 2005/2006. tanev eleji adatgyujtes elozetes adatairol (Statistical flash report on the preliminary data of the 2005/06 school year) http:///www.om.hu/main.php?folderID=539&articleID=6558&ctag=articlelist&iid=1.
[32] See 41/2005. (X.27) AB Hatarozat (Constitutional Court Ruling 41/2005 27 October 2005).
[33] See Radi-ugy: hatarozatlan idore elnapolva (Radi-case: postponed to indefinite day), http://www.emasa.hu/print.php?id=870.
[34] Ibolya Jakus, "Tudomanyos Szankcionizmus (Academic 'Sanctionism')," HVG (Heti Vilaggazdasag), December 10, 2005.
[35] Television Across Europe: Regulation, Policy, and Independence (Budapest: Open Society Institute, 2005), p. 795.
[36] See National Communications Authority's website: www.nhh.hu/menu2/m2_2/2005/kozlem_051215.htm.
[37] See www.gfk.hu/sajtokoz/articles/200509081200.htm.
[38] See Internet: Evolucio vagy revolucio? (Intenet: Evolution or Revolution?), www.gfk.hu/sajtokoz/articles/200511031200.htm.
[39] Pawel Swianiewicz and Adam Mielczarek, "Parties and Political Culture in Central and Eastern European Local Governments," in: Faces of Local Democracy (Budapest: OSI/LGI, 2005), p. 25.
[40] Glen Wright, "Assessment of Progress Toward Local Democratic Systems, in: State of Local Democracy in Central Europe (Budapest: Local Government and Public Service Reform Initiative, Open Society Institute, 2002), p. 380.
[41] Zoltan Pogatsa, Europe Now: Hungary's Preparedness for the EU's Structural and Cohesion Funds (Szombathely: Savaria University Press, 2004), p. 81.
[42] Istvan Varga, Thoughts on the Financial Management Reforms of Municipalities (Gondolatok az Onkormanyzatok vagyongazdalkodasanak reformjarol), IDEA, November 13, 2003, on Web site of the Ministry of Interior.
[43] Gabor Soos, Local Government Reforms and the Capacity for Local Governance in Hungary (Budapest: Tocqueville Research Center, 2002), pp. 12-16.
[44] Daniel Pop, "Municipality Size and Citizens' Effectiveness: Hungary, Poland and Romania," in: Faces of Local Democracy (Budapest: OSI/LGI, 2005), pp. 171-199.
[45] See http://www.valasztas.hu/idokhnsz/2005nepszav.pdf.
[46] Government Decree No. 244/2003 (XII. 19.), Hungary.
[47] See "HU: Local e-government still in its infancy in Hungary, survey shows," on http://europa.eu.int/idabc/en/document/4320/586.
[48] Az Orszagos Igazsagszolgaltatasi Tanacs Elnokenek tajekoztatoja a birosagok altalanos helyzeterol es az Orszagos Igazsagszolgaltatasi Tanacs igazgatasi tevekenysegerol 2004. januar 1-2004. december 31.(Report of the President of the National Judicial Council on the general status of the courts and the work of the National Judicial Council) Birosagi Kozlony Melleklete (Supplement to the Journal of the Courts) (Budapest: hvgorac Lap- es Konyvkiado Kft, 2005).
[49] A lakossag ketharmada ketelkedik a birosagok fuggetlensegeben (Two-thirds of the populations has misgivings about judicial independence) http://www.nol.hu/cikk/377585/.
[50] De Jure-Jogaszok Tarsasagi Magazinja (Lawyers' Social Magazine), Az igazsagszolgaltatas a kozvelemenykutatasok tukreben-Merheto-e a biroi presztizs? (Public view on the judiciary – Can prestige of judges be measured?) 8-9 November 2005.
[51] See 80/2005. (IV. 12.) OIT Hatarozat (National Judicial Council decision 80/2005. 12 april 2005.); and HVG, Talar ur kerem!: Etikai kodex biraknak ("Please Mr. Robe!" – Code of ethics to judges) 2 April 2005.
[52] Felfuggesztett borton a sanyargato rendornonek (Prison on probation to the cruel police officer) Hungarian News Agency cited on http://index.hu/politika/bulvar/bilinx8975,

[53] Zsufoltsagban harmadik a magyar borton (Hungarian prisons are third in overcrowdedness) http://www.nol.hu/cikk/388894.

v "Ciganyokat nem alkalmazunk" – Felmillios birsagot kapott az orzo-vedo ceg ("We won't employ Roma" – Security company fined half a million") http://www.nol.hu/cikk/362347/

[55] A kozvelemeny gatat kivan vetni a szelsoseges eszmek terjedesenek (The public wants to curb the spread of extreme ideas) http://marketingcentrum.intronet.hu/content.php?id=332457aabe83c32f2af235edc2af0593.

[56] See http://www.tasz.hu/download/program.doc?id=14057&time=1134133119&op=cont.

[57] See http://www.transparency.org/cpi/2005/cpi2005.sources.en.html.

[58] See http://www.gfk.hu/sajtokoz/fr6.htm.

[59] Home page of Rendvedelmi Szervek Vedelmi Szolgalata (RSzVSz) (Protective Service of Law Enforcement Agencies), http://www.bm.hu/rszvsz/en/index.html.

[60] Napi Gazdasag, "A kozbeszerzesek tizede lehet tiszta," September 19, 2005; and interview on Radio Kossuth with Maria Kallai, member of the Competition Council of GVH, September 22, 2005.

[61] Act XC. of 2005 on Freedom of Electronic Information, Official Journal No. 99, July 14, 2005.

[62] Report on the Application of the Convention on Combating Bribery of Foreign Public Officials in International Business Transactions, www.oecd.org/dataoecd/39/34/34918600.pdf.

[63] Corruption and Anticorruption Policies in Hungary (New York: Open Society Institute, 2002), pp. 267-270, unpan1.un.org/intradoc/groups/public/documents/UNTC/UNPAN013152.pdf.

Kazakhstan

Capital:	Astana
Population:	15 million
GNI/capita:	$2,250
Ethnic Groups:	Kazakh (53%), Russian (30%), Ukrainian (4%), Uzbek (3%), German (2%), other (8%)

Nations in Transit Ratings and Averaged Scores

	1997	1998	1999	2001	2002	2003	2004	2005	2006
Electoral Process	5.50	5.50	6.00	6.25	6.25	6.50	6.50	6.50	6.50
Civil Society	5.25	5.00	5.00	5.00	5.50	5.50	5.50	5.50	5.75
Independent Media	5.25	5.50	5.50	6.00	6.00	6.25	6.50	6.50	6.75
Governance *	5.50	5.50	5.00	5.00	5.75	6.25	6.25	n/a	n/a
National Democratic Governance	n/a	n/a	n/a	n/a	n/a	n/a	n/a	6.50	6.75
Local Democratic Governance	n/a	n/a	n/a	n/a	n/a	n/a	n/a	6.25	6.25
Judicial Framework and Independence	5.00	5.25	5.50	5.75	6.00	6.25	6.25	6.25	6.25
Corruption	n/a	n/a	6.00	6.25	6.25	6.25	6.50	6.50	6.50
Democracy Score	5.30	5.35	5.50	5.71	5.96	6.17	6.25	6.29	6.36

* With the 2005 edition, Freedom House introduced seperate analysis and ratings for national democratic governance and local democratic governance to provide readers with more detailed and nuanced analysis of these two important subjects.

NOTE: The ratings reflect the consensus of Freedom House, its academic advisers, and the author of this report. The opinions expressed in this report are those of the author. The ratings are based on a scale of 1 to 7, with 1 representing the highest level of democratic progress and 7 the lowest. The Democracy Score is an average of ratings for the categories tracked in a given year.

The economic and social data on this page were taken from the following sources:
GNI/capita, Population: *World Development Indicators 2006* (Washington, D.C.: World Bank, 2006).
Ethnic Groups: *CIA World Factbook 2006* (Washington, D.C.: Central Intelligence Agency, 2006).

EXECUTIVE SUMMARY

President Nursultan Nazarbaev, who has held office since 1989 under Soviet rule and procured another seven-year term in 2005, has built a strong and personalized presidential regime by allowing an inner circle of close family, friends, and business associates to exert formal and informal influence over vital economic resources and political positions. A relatively vibrant phase of media freedom, civic and democratic activism begun in the early 1990s has dissipated since 1995, when Nazarbaev adopted a new Constitution giving unchecked powers to the presidency.

Since 1999, Nazarbaev has skillfully used Kazakhstan's spiraling economic growth and rising prosperity (Kazakhstan expects to be among the top five oil exporters within a decade) to further consolidate his authoritarian rule, arguing that a strong economy and social stability constitute vital preconditions for establishing democracy. He has embraced a purely formal democratization agenda by holding regular elections (none has been recognized as "free and fair" or meeting international standards) and erecting a multiparty system composed of loyal, pro-regime parties. The political system is open to the participation of prominent financial and business interests loyal to the president but closed to independent financial and political interests or social groups that propose alternative ideologies.

National Democratic Governance. The government has emphasized economic prosperity and social "stability" at the expense of developing transparent and democratically accountable institutions. Powerful financial groups and members of the presidential family fully control the Parliament and top political offices and continue to intimidate, buy off, co-opt, and even accuse as criminals their business and political opponents, critics, and independent media. While Kazakhstan has established a stable and effective governance structure, the Nazarbaev regime continues to block political participation of groups that advocate reforms and exaggerates the potential threat posed by political, ethnic, or religious extremists. The 91 percent vote obtained by Nazarbaev in the December 2005 elections – an implausible figure for an aspiring or established democracy – attests to a further strengthening of the personalistic, patronage-based system under his leadership. *Kazakhstan's rating in national democratic governance has worsened from 6.50 to 6.75 because the prospects for democratization have diminished with Nazarbaev securing another seven-year term through an implausible 91 percent vote.*

Electoral Process. Pro-regime financial interests and political parties (Otan, the Civil Party, and Asar together with nominally independent pro-regime deputies) fully control the Parliament, which does not have a single opposition or independent deputy. Of the two major opposition parties, the Democratic Choice of Kazakhstan has been banned since January 2005 and Ak Zhol has split into two factions, the dominant one adopting a more moderate stance. Though two opposition candidates were allowed to run in the elections, there was widespread use of administrative and information resources to drum up support for the incumbent. Amendments to laws on election, right to public assembly, and controlling "extremism" have imposed severe limits on the ability of nonregime candidates or parties to campaign. The December 2005 presidential election did not meet Organization for Security and Cooperation in Europe (OSCE) and other international standards for democratic elections despite improvements in election administration. *Kazakhstan's rating for electoral process remains at 6.50 despite several technical and procedural improvements in the organization and conduct of elections, the legislative base has not improved.*

Civil Society. The Nazarbaev regime has invigorated efforts to shape the civil sector through financial aid and support to nongovernmental organizations (NGOs) engaged in social and infrastructure development, as well as to those loyal to the government. The increase in financial support to NGOs is a mixed blessing, as Nazarbaev has warned that the government will "closely watch" NGOs, particularly those obtaining foreign funding. Groups engaged in advocacy campaigns, championing civil liberties, political reforms, and democratization have encountered the greatest governmental resistance and remain dependent on international funding. Though the Constitutional Court struck down the widely criticized amendments passed by the Parliament that imposed numerous restrictions on the financial and organizational capacity of NGOs, it did so only on technical grounds without raising the substantive issue of ongoing government regulation of civil society. Many other laws, such as the new Law on Extremism, amendments to the national security legislation, and new restrictions on the right to public assembly, undermine civil freedoms. *Kazakhstan's rating for civil society worsens from 5.50 to 5.75 owing to the tightening of governmental control over civil society through laws, formal and informal pressure, and increased funding by the state or agencies controlled by the state.*

Independent Media. The entire spectrum of privately owned but pro-government media worked actively to promote Nazarbaev's presidential candidacy by touting his numerous achievements. A widespread disinformation campaign against the opposition, financial harassment, confiscation of print runs, physical assaults, and criminalization of independent and pro-opposition journalists continued throughout the presidential election campaign. Opposition media were routinely penalized through court actions, specifically libel suits for violating "the honor and dignity of the president." The regime has become more sophisticated in curbing the modicum of independent media, particularly using administrative and technical tools to close down opposition Web sites or deny access to them. Amendments to the Law on Mass Media give courts far greater latitude to close down media outlets for "violating Kazakhstan's integrity," condoning "extremism," and "undermining state security." *Given the closure of almost all opposition newspapers, pervasive control over print media and the Internet, the widespread disinformation campaign against the opposition, and the frequent clampdown on the few independent newspapers, Kazakhstan's independent media rating has worsened from 6.50 to 6.75.*

Local Democratic Governance. Kazakhstan has maintained a unitary and centralized administration in which the president fully controls the appointment of *akims* (heads) of *oblasts* (regions) and *raions* (districts). These *akims*, who are nominated by the president and are accountable to him, are rotated continuously to prevent them from building an independent support base. The introduction of long-promised elections of *akims* in selected regions "on an experimental basis" in August 2005 heralds no improvement. The Central Election Commission, which exerts a top-down control, is vested with total authority to choose the districts and conduct test polls. *Despite having created a veneer of local participation, the authority granted to local and regional election commissions is extremely limited, and there is no effective legislation providing for local civic participation or spelling out powers of local councils. Therefore, the rating for local democratic governance remains at 6.25.*

Judicial Framework and Independence. Under the country's strong executive system based on presidential patronage, the judiciary – like the legislative branch – has remained loyal to the regime. It has served to protect the interests of the state and its functionaries rather than those of individuals, minorities, and the weaker strata of society. Kazakhstan has taken various steps to raise the professionalism and salaries of its judges. While the level of general public trust in the judiciary seems to have increased somewhat owing to the courts' improved performance in handling civil and criminal cases, the judiciary continues to have a very poor record in handling cases related to civil liberties, media freedom, and human rights. Though Kazakhstan has maintained a moratorium on the death penalty, it has not revoked it. The Parliament has passed a law introducing jury trials, but questions remain about ongoing government influence and the participation of presiding judges in jury hearings. *Despite notable improvement in wages and professional training for judges, the failure of the judiciary to issue a single independent verdict protecting individuals against state officials leaves Kazakhstan's rating unchanged at 6.25.*

Corruption. Since the use of public office for personal gain is particularly endemic in an oil-rich, patronage-based personalistic regime such as Kazakhstan, it is hard to document the extent of corruption in the absence of independent media and access to credible information. No independent body or inquiry into corruption exists, and top figures within the government enjoy a virtual immunity from such inquiries unless they engage in political or economic activities that challenge the president. Since the "Kazakhgate" trial has repeatedly been put off, corruption charges against Nazarbaev and his close associates remain unsubstantiated. Yet the government has invested some effort in developing civic awareness about corruption. *Improved governance and economic conditions may have helped to control corruption at lower and mid-*

dle levels of bureaucracy, but the virtual absence of an independent judiciary and media mean that it is impossible to bring to light corruption at the top echelons of the ruling elite. Therefore, Kazakhstan's corruption rating remains at 6.50.

Outlook for 2006. Capitalizing on Kazakhstan's rising prosperity and social stability, the Nazarbaev regime appears unassailable after securing another seven-year term. Having procured 91 percent of the vote in the 2005 presidential election, Nazarbaev stated that he will work to improve the conditions of those who did not vote for him and obtain their endorsement in the next election. This is an ominous message that suggests the regime will use its oil-based economic prosperity to foreclose any meaningful political debate. This creates an even more inhospitable legal and political environment for civil society groups, opposition, and ordinary citizens advocating democratization and political reforms.

It is unlikely that Kazakhstan can sufficiently strengthen its credentials to obtain the rotating OSCE chair for 2009 (to be decided in the first half of 2006), though the government will intensify international PR campaigns and seek to win influential friends abroad by extolling its dynamic economic growth. Nazarbaev has already indicated that he will run for the presidency yet again, suggesting that significant amendments to the Constitution may be in the offing to lift the two-term and age limits set for the president.

MAIN REPORT

National Democratic Governance

1997	1998	1999	2001	2002	2003	2004	2005	2006
n/a	n/a	n/a	n/a	n/a	n/a	n/a	6.50	6.75

Kazakhstan prides itself in having developed a strong and effective government, a stable society, and the most dynamic economy in the whole of Central Asia. It is the financial and banking hub of the region, with a booming market economy that has sustained annual growth of over 8 percent since 1999, mainly from increased oil exports. It registered an economic growth of 9.3 percent in 2004 (9.1 percent in 2003). Its per capita gross domestic product (GDP) of about US$3,620 is the highest, after Russia, of all members of the Commonwealth of Independent States (CIS). Kazakhstan is expected to become one of the top 10 oil exporters by the year 2012 and among the top 5 by 2020. Oil revenues constituted 57 percent of the country's budgetary revenues in 2004–2005.

Kazakhstan has carefully cultivated its image as an "oasis of stability" in the region under the leadership of President Nursultan Nazarbaev, who has held office since 1989 and secured another seven-year term in the December 4, 2005, election by obtaining 91 percent of the vote. Ethnic Kazakhs form 55 percent of the population, though their share continues to rise as the share of Slavs and other Russian-speaking groups, currently about 36 percent, declines. There is no visible tension along ethnic or religious lines, though Kazakhs enjoy numerous informal preferences and fully dominate governmental, administrative, and economic structures.

Western investments amounting to over US$25 billion, mainly in the nation's oil sector, are a testament to Kazakhstan's "stability" and growing partnership with the West. While Nazarbaev's popularity, hinging on Kazakhstan's economic success, social stability, and ethnic peace, is unquestioned, the control of his regime over the media and the use of state and administrative resources to sustain an effective PR campaign both nationally and internationally have significantly boosted the image of his indispensability and the lack of any credible alternative. Nazarbaev has offered a modicum of space for the opposition to operate but has imposed innumerable legal, administrative, organizational, and informal obstacles on it. Continuous disinformation and negative propaganda convey the message that the opposition will simply squander the nation's hard-earned socioeconomic stability and work to enrich itself instead.

The regime-sponsored political discourse hammers the point that democracy can develop only in the backdrop of economic well-being. By calling for the consolidation of the present system to achieve a vision of prosperity, the regime has excluded issues pertaining to democratization, civil liberties, and wealth redistribution. The 91 percent vote obtained by Nazarbaev in December 2005 elections – implausible in an established or aspiring democracy – attests to a further strengthening of the personalistic, patronage-based system under his leadership. This casts doubts on the potential development of democratic institutions under the present political framework and leadership.

Kazakhstan's rich resource base and speedy, nontransparent privatization of key industries in the 1990s have created powerful financial groups, interests, and "clients" of the regime, while also enriching and empowering close kin and associates of the president, who wield control over crucial economic resources and political positions. These financial interests have amassed enormous political power by creating or sponsoring political parties that control the Parliament, while capturing the country's media market and pushing out independent media channels.

The Majilis – the 67-member lower house of the Parliament – is fully controlled by pro-regime parties and independent deputies who are not formally affiliated to any political party but are loyal to the regime. The September 2004 Majilis elections failed to elect a single genuinely independent or opposition figure.

The Senate is composed of 39 deputies, 7 appointed by the president and 32 selected through indirect elections by the 14 *oblast* or regional assemblies; the capital, Astana; and the former capital, Almaty. Senators serve six-year terms, with half of the elected senators facing elections every three years. Of the 16 deputies elected in August 2005, 10 seats went to Otan and 1 each to the pro-presidential parties Aul, Asar, and the Civil Party. The remaining 3 went to candidates unaffiliated with any parties but loyal to the regime.

The president appoints the prime minister, his cabinet, and virtually all top political and administrative figures. Daniyal Akhmetov, the current premier, was appointed in June 2003. The government headed by the prime minister bears responsibility for enacting and implementing all policies but has little independent power to formulate policies or initiate legislation. No prime minister since 1998 has held the position for more than three and a half years.

Kazakhstan's military and national security services remain firmly under the control of the president, who nominates the latter's members. The country's economic success has allowed the national security services to begin developing a professional and career civil service. A new Eurasian Civil Service Training Center was established in the capital, Astana, with funding from the European Commission's TACIS program in cooperation with Kazakhstan's Agency for Civil Service Affairs. It will serve as a modern training center in Central Asia, offering courses for civil servants at various levels on key public administration topics.[1] The government has pledged to rationalize grades to compensate for regional differences, introduce a bonus system, and align public sector wages with those in the private sector. Wages for civil servants were increased by a third in May, albeit with an eye toward the presidential election and motivated by the desire to avoid any replication of the Kyrgyz events of May 2005.

Electoral Process

1997	1998	1999	2001	2002	2003	2004	2005	2006
5.50	5.50	6.00	6.25	6.25	6.50	6.50	6.50	6.50

Though Kazakhstan has cultivated several elements of a pluralistic and open political framework, such as a multiparty system, electoral competition, and diversity of privately owned media channels, these channels are composed of groups with entrenched pro-regime interests and do not engender open political participation. Political power is vested in three major pro-regime political parties – Otan (led by Nazarbaev), Asar (led by his eldest daughter, Dariga Nazarbaeva), the Civil Party (led by the industrial conglomerate Eurasia Group) – as well as clients and supporters of the regime who may or may not have a particular party affiliation. Numerous other minor parties loyal to the regime (for example, Aul, the Democratic Party of Kazakhstan, the Agrarian Party, Rukhaniyet, and the Communist People's Party of Kazakhstan) serve to create a Potemkin village-like structure of pluralism.

The major opposition parties, Democratic Choice of Kazakhstan (DCK) and Ak Zhol, have been in disarray owing to an administrative and legal clampdown on their activities and finances and a negative public image cultivated by the state-controlled media. DCK was banned in January 2005 on charges of inciting "extremism." Kazakhstan's Constitution bans the formation of parties on ethnic, racial, or religious grounds. DCK's attempt to seek registration under a new banner, Alga Kazakhstan! (Forward Kazakhstan!), was blocked because the amended Law on

Political Parties prevents a new party from acting as the legal inheritor of a banned organization. Political parties need 50,000 signatures to register with the Ministry of Justice, a tall order in a country where civic apathy is rampant and the government regulates political participation by pushing it through "authorized" (pro-regime) party channels.

The government has skillfully exploited differences and rivalries among opposition leaders and factions by urging them to play a "constructive" role. Ak Zhol has remained a target of government pressure for co-option since its inception. Its present leaders founded Ak Zhol as a more "moderate" political party by separating from the more critical DCK when its founding leaders – Mukhtar Ablyazov, ex-minister of industries, and Ghalymzhan Zhakiyanov, former *akim* of Pavlodar – were arrested in 2002 on politically motivated charges of abuse of office. Ablyazov and Zhakiyanov were sentenced to six- and seven-year prison terms, respectively, in 2003. Zhakiyanov became eligible for parole in early December, but with an eye on the presidential elections, the government delayed his release until early January 2006. Contesting the 2004 parliamentary elections as a moderate opposition party Ak Zhol won 12 percent of the vote but only one seat, which it renounced by complaining of widespread electoral fraud. Since then, Ak Zhol has intensified cooperation with the rump DCK and the Communist Party of Kazakhstan (CPK).[2]

Ak Zhol split in April 2005 when Alikhan Baimenov, one of its prominent leaders who later became a presidential candidate, advocated a "constructive dialogue" with the regime by rallying support from a majority of its members. He accused the other leaders of the party (Altynbek Sarsenbaev, Bulat Abilov, and Oraz Zhandosov) of violating party rules that bar collaboration with other political parties. The majority of Ak Zhol members remained with the Baimenov group, while the Sarsenbaev-Abilov-Zhandosov group renamed itself Naghyz Ak Zhol (the Real Ak Zhol). Two weeks after the end of the presidential election, the Supreme Court upheld an earlier refusal to register Naghyz Ak Zhol as a political party. Together with DCK, CPK, and other individual opposition members, Naghyz Ak Zhol formed a movement called Za Spravedlivyi Kazakhstan (For a Just Kazakhstan; ZSK), nominating Zharmakhan Tuyakbai, a former co-chairman of Otan and Speaker of the lower house of Parliament, as their common presidential candidate. Tuyakbai had left Otan and the government in October 2004 after criticizing the fraudulent conduct of the 2004 parliamentary election.

In contrast with the 1999 presidential election, the December 2005 election allowed opposition contenders to run. The five officially registered candidates were incumbent president Nazarbaev, Zharmakhan Tuyakbai (opposition bloc ZSK), Alikhan Baimenov (Ak Zhol), Erasyl Abilkasymov (Communist People's Party of Kazakhstan), and Mels Eleusizov (independent head of the environmental movement Tabigat).

There were some notable improvements in the organization and conduct of the 2005 elections, the implementation of existing regulation, and abidance with electoral procedures. The state TV channel Khabar broadcast a live four-round debate in which all presidential candidates except Nazarbaev participated. The efficacy of the debate was marred by the nonparticipation of Nazarbaev, purportedly owing to his prior obligations. Preliminary assessments show that the four leading TV channels devoted 49 to 77 percent of preelection coverage to the president. Tuyakbai came in second with about 12 percent.

Yet the contest for the presidency was highly unequal. As Audrey Glover, head of the long-term election-monitoring mission OSCE/Office for Democratic Institutions and Human Rights (ODIHR), pointed out, "The Kazakh authorities did not provide a level playing field for a democratic election." The entire administrative and information machinery mobilized in favor of the incumbent, while the two leading opposition candidates encountered enormous obstacles organizing public meetings and getting media coverage.

While Nazarbaev did not officially campaign, saying that his achievements speak for themselves, posters with "Nursultan Nazarbaev – Our Leader!" and portraits of Nazarbaev with the message "For Kazakhstan" were widely displayed, including on public transport, in schools and universities, and on state buildings. Railway and air passengers received tickets in envelopes with the message "Nazarbaev – Our Leader!" in yellow, red, and blue.[3] Dariga Nazarbaeva spearheaded an energetic campaign supported by all pro-presidential political parties and business interests as well as a number of government-sponsored "independent" groups and agencies. Numerous concerts, forums, and conferences were organized throughout the country praising the president's achievements and directing people toward the "right" choice. Around 80 percent of billboards and advertisements belonged to the president, with local newspapers and national media channels carrying appeals by various public organizations supporting the president.[4]

Nazarbaev won 91.01 percent of the vote. Among the remaining four candidates, Tuyakbai got 6.64 percent, Baimenov 1.65 percent, Abilkasymov 0.38 percent, and Eleusizov 0.32 percent. The preliminary statement by OSCE/ODIHR on December 5, 2005, based on monitoring by its 465 observers, noted that "despite some improvements in the election administration," the presidential election in Kazakhstan "did not meet a number of OSCE commitments and other international standards for democratic elections." None of the previous elections held by Kazakhstan has been recognized by the OSCE as consistent with international standards. These factors dampen the prospect of Kazakhstan obtaining the rotating OSCE chair for 2009 – a status that the Kazakh leadership has been angling for over the past years.

The OSCE preliminary report gave negative assessments in 27 percent of stations monitored, noting violations such as unauthorized persons interfering in polling stations, cases of multiple voting, ballot box stuffing, and tampering with result protocols. The supporters of Tuyakbai have filed more than 1,000 lawsuits alleging election violations.

The Kazakh government invited large delegations of election monitors from countries such as Russia and China, who were expected to give a positive assessment of the elections. The CIS election-monitoring group headed by Vladimir Rushailo hailed the elections as "free, open, and legitimate." The Ministry of Foreign Affairs revoked the accreditation of the CIS Election Monitoring Organization, represented by a Russian nongovernmental group separate from the official CIS monitors, when it produced a critical interim report on the elections.[5]

Kazakhstan's Law on Elections remains a major legal impediment to open and fair electoral contest. Kazakhstan has not adopted any of the substantive recommendations made by the OSCE, particularly in its final report on the 2004 parliamentary elections concerning improvements to the Law on Elections and legislative base for elections. Kazakhstan's Constitution, the Law on Elections, the code of administrative violations, and the criminal code contain various provisions on the protection of "the honor and dignity of the president" that significantly curtail public debate on vital political issues and impose limitations on election campaigns.

Amendments to the Law on Elections passed in April 2005 prohibited voters and political parties from organizing any public meetings from the end of the election campaign until the official publication of the results – a period that could take up to 12 days after voting is completed. Such a measure was designed to prevent mass demonstrations such as those that took place following the flawed elections in Georgia (2003), Ukraine (2004), and Kyrgyzstan (2005).[6]

In addition to these changes, the new Law on Extremism, amendments to the Law on Mass Media, and new legislation pertaining to national security placed restrictions on all forms of campaigning. Advertising and rallies by the opposition candidates were frequently disrupted. Campaign literature was regularly seized and destroyed, and opposition parties were repeatedly denied permission to hold events in central locations at the times requested.

Tuyakbai was personally attacked by assailants on at least three occasions during the election campaigns in eastern and south Kazakhstan. Though he avoided injury, his supporters and aide were not so lucky. Law-and-order authorities characterized these attacks as spontaneous and issued light sentences to the suspects. Opposition leaders claim to have submitted video footage that suggests both attacks were planned provocations organized by forces within the government.

Though 75 percent of the registered electorate cast their vote in the presidential election, political apathy is rampant in the country. The government is fixated on "stability" and sees any form of active ethnic discourse, civic engagement, or political mobilization of the citizenry as destabilizing and insidious. While it is true that Nazarbaev has enjoyed the consistent support of the Slavic minority, about a third of the country's population, Slavic participation in the political process has declined rapidly. The Slav share in Parliament is 19 out of 115 deputies (16.52 percent). Moreover, Slavic parliamentary deputies do not represent their ethnic constituencies. Rather, they are plugged into the patronage system controlled by the three major pro-regime parties.

A few weeks before the elections, reports were circulated in state-controlled media and government circles that the opposition was gearing up to organize large-scale protests and civic disturbances in Almaty, alluding that "foreign elements" had a vested interest in financing such uprisings. Central Election Commission chairman Onalsyn Zhumabekov, supposedly a neutral figure, accused the opposition of having prepared reports in advance that claimed spurious breaches of procedure on election day. Such reports, including rumors of imminent unrest, were part of the official strategy to disorient, intimidate, and misinform voters, who were constantly alerted to the subversive specter of revolution and warned that any change would cause destabilization.

Civil Society

1997	1998	1999	2001	2002	2003	2004	2005	2006
5.25	5.00	5.00	5.00	5.50	5.50	5.50	5.50	5.75

Kazakhstan's solid economic achievements have strengthened the state's financial and legal mechanisms of control over society and the civil sector. The government provided US$3.4 million to NGOs in 2004. Nazarbaev promised to increase state funding for NGOs to US$7.5 million per annum over the next five years. That figure may not yet match funding by key foreign donors such as the U.S. Agency for International Development (USAID) (public health and electoral reforms in particular), Counterpart Consortium (a range of social issues), and the Eurasia Foundation and the Soros Foundation (educational and civil rights issues), but it shows that the state and private businesses loyal to it are increasingly competing with foreign donors. In September 2005, Nazarbaev called for cooperation between the state and NGOs in social and infrastructure projects, warning that the government will "closely watch" NGOs. The lack of a proper legal base and judicial framework for NGOs makes an equitable partnership between the government and nonstate sector problematic and leaves the latter vulnerable to co-option by the state.

Kazakhstan's existing laws require NGOs and other nonprofit organizations to refrain from "political activities." Local courts and law-and-order officials typically determine what constitutes "political activity" in the absence of an acceptable definition. In April 2005, the Parliament passed a number of controversial amendments to the legislation pertaining to NGOs despite widespread objections by the Confederation of Nongovernmental Organizations of Kazakhstan and other domestic and international civil rights groups. Particularly controversial were two laws – officially named "On the Activities of Branches and Representative Offices of International or Foreign Noncommercial Organizations" and "On the Introduction of Amendments and Additions into Certain Legislative Acts of the Republic of Kazakhstan on Matters Related to Nonprofit Organizations" – curtailing the activities of local NGOs working on civil and political rights. These measures sought to tighten government regulation of financial interaction between local NGOs and international entities by prohibiting local NGOs from working with political parties or supporting any electoral candidates and requiring all budgets to have the tacit approval of tax authorities as well as city and provincial officials.

Nazarbaev referred the amendments to the Constitutional Court for review in

August 2005. Although the Court deemed the amendments unconstitutional[7] and rejected the bill on technical grounds, it neglected to address the larger issue of ongoing efforts to regulate NGO activities through politically motivated legislation. The scrapping of these laws resembles the abrogation of the proposed Law on Mass Media in 2004. Nazarbaev vetoed the latter, announcing the decision at the annual Eurasian Media Forum organized by his eldest daughter, Dariga Nazarbaeva, to score political points at home and abroad. Even without the draconian amendments, existing legislation already contained highly restrictive clauses on the freedom of media. Similarly, the Parliament's passage of amendments pertaining to the laws on NGOs was palpably illegal, and the restrictions were too unreasonable to be legally imposed.

There are about 4,000 registered NGOs in the country, but a vast number are either inactive, existing only on paper, or quasi-governmental, propped up to compete with independent NGOs in obtaining grants. Only about 800 are active, and fewer than 150 are able to make a positive impact. The NGO sustainability index for Eurasia published by USAID in 2004 showed a slight decline in the overall environment for NGOs in Kazakhstan with a score of 4.1 (on a scale of 1 to 10, a higher score representing lower sustainability). It noted that the increase in the number of registered NGOs has led to an overall decrease in their organizational capacity, as a large number of NGOs are quasi-governmental.

Almost half of all NGOs are concentrated in Almaty, though their number in the capital, Astana, and major towns Atyrau, Aktau, and Shymkent is increasing. Of the 300 registered NGOs in Astana, about 80 are functional and only a dozen are functioning in an effective manner. The sparsely populated rural regions in central and northeastern Kazakhstan have little NGO presence. A USAID-funded public opinion poll in October 2004 found that only 31 percent of people are aware of NGOs, and only 2.1 percent are members.[8]

Almost one-third of active NGOs are engaged in social issues, particularly those advocating for the protection, health, and welfare of children, care of the disabled, poverty alleviation, and rural infrastructure development, as well as women's support. The most active groups also receive support and funding from the government. Some well-known children's NGOs, such as Zhan, a child protection organization; Astra, promoting learning among disabled children; Bobek, promoting health and welfare; and Sad, aiding orphans and children from broken families, have cooperated with the government.

Kazakhstan Women's Information Network, consisting of eight prominent NGOs, is campaigning to enhance women's representation in the Parliament, within government, and at local levels. Currently, only 10 out of 115 parliamentary deputies (9 percent) are women. Two women candidates for the presidential election were disqualified for failing the mandatory Kazakh language test. A number of women's organizations, such as Business Women's Association, Zharia (Women's Association on Development and Adaptation), and the Feminist League, have become co-opted within the official framework after developing close partnerships with pro-regime political parties, particularly Asar. In addition, a number of groups dedicated to environmental issues, prominently the Coalition of Environmental NGOs and Network for Anti-Nuclear Campaign, have been able to function effectively.

In the first instance of private corporate financing of NGOs, Zhalgas, an NGO managing part of a USAID civil society initiative, secured a corporate partnership worth US$1 million with Kazkommertsbank, the nation's largest private commercial bank.[9] The dependence of private businesses on government patronage deters them from openly financing NGOs. Private business is often subject to informal pressure by government officials to fund groups engaged in social issues and community development programs.

Less than 10 percent of NGOs are engaged in civil liberties, human rights, and minority protection issues; these organizations are subject to the most stringent government control and are targets of considerable popular and official prejudice. This ranges from difficulties in registration and acquiring office space and technical facilities, periodic tax and financial audits, and legal and monetary constraints.

Kazakhstan's Bureau for Human Rights and Rule of Law is among the most active of the NGOs advocating for civil rights and democratization. A Human Rights Watch report states that since March, at least 33 NGOs have been investigated by officials from the Office of the Public Prosecutor and the tax police on allegations that they passed Western aid money to political opposition parties.[10] Kazakhstan's ombudsman, Bolat Baikadamov, accused the Kazakhstan Bureau for Human Rights and Rule of Law of publishing biased information and distorting the situation in Kazakhstan in its reports on human rights developments.

The 2004 parliamentary elections saw thriving civic activism among independent organizations and groups monitoring elections. Civic mobilization events in Ukraine and Kyrgyzstan have led the Kazakh government to tighten its laws and financing regulations pertaining to NGOs and civil rights groups and intensify vigilance over students and youth groups. Several youth organizations, such as the Youth Information Service of Kazakhstan, the Society of Young Professionals of Kazakhstan, and Kahar (Hero), have been subjected to raids and heightened vigilance for suspicion of attempting to enact a "Kyrgyz scenario" on the basis of foreign financing.[11] These groups were often prevented from sending independent observers to monitor the elections. A large number of government-supported "independent" observers, totaling about 16,000 nominated by various political parties supporting Nazarbaev, completely outnumbered and sidelined independent observers in the 2005 presidential election.

The Permanent National Commission on Democratization and Civil Society, appointed by Nazarbaev in June 2004 and chaired by Bulat Utemuratov (previously secretary of the National Security Committee [KNB]), holds periodic meetings with pro-regime parties and quasi-governmental NGOs, urging opposition parties and independent NGOs to engage in a "constructive cooperation" with the government and other (pro-regime) political parties. It effectively serves as a mechanism for co-opting independent civil society activists and opposition figures and delegitimizing those who refuse. While civil society groups – both domestic and international – condemned the amendments to laws on nonprofit organizations, participants in the National Commission endorsed the proposed legislation.

The Constitution bans the formation of any political party or association on ethnic, racial, or religious grounds. Citing the absence of any overt social conflict, Nazarbaev has taken pride in the prevalent ethnocultural harmony and religious tolerance in Kazakhstan. While groups such as Hizb ut-Tahrir are frequently held responsible for distributing religious propaganda materials, there is little evidence of extremist networks – whether on religious, political, or other grounds – operating within Kazakhstan or enjoying visible support. Yet Kazakhstan has passed a spate of legislation to combat "extremism" and enhance "national security" by increasing surveillance and control over outside groups and foreign sponsors as well as innumerable domestic groups.

A controversial Law on Extremism passed in February 2005, and strict antiterror legislation, containing amendments to 11 existing national security laws, was adopted in May 2005 to impose heavy penalties for "extremist and terrorist activities," including "terrorist financing." This legislation introduced restrictions on NGOs, political parties, mass media outlets, and religious organizations, though similar measures in the proposed amendments to the NGO legislation were scrapped. These laws introduce more restrictions on the activities and formal registration of religious organizations and political parties and ban financing of political parties by foreign nationals. NGOs are subject to heavy fines if they partake in any unauthorized public demonstration or if an authorized demonstration turns "disorderly" in the eyes of law-and-order officials.

A ruling by the Astana City Court banned Hizb ut-Tahrir as an extremist organization, noting that despite officially eschewing violence, it aims to establish an Islamic caliphate throughout Central Asia by calling for anticonstitutional actions. Since Hizb ut-Tahrir has no formal organization or legal status, the ban confers more legal power on the government to take action against a person or a group accused of being affiliated with it.

The education system is largely free of political propaganda or control, though social science and humanities curriculums are injected with nationalist propaganda in state-supported schools and colleges. There are several restrictions on the use of textbooks printed abroad, including those printed in Russia. While state funding for education has increased, it remains low as a percentage of GDP. An expensive private network of schools and colleges with instruction in English is growing. Under the government-supported Bolashak (Future) program, about 100 students a year are awarded scholarships to Western universities.

The law provides for the right to freely organize and form unions, but this is restricted in many ways in practice. The Federation of Trade Unions, containing vestiges of formerly state-sponsored trade unions of the Soviet era, remains the largest trade union association. Two other associations, the Confederation of Free Trade Unions of Kazakhstan and the Trade Union Center of Kazakhstan, are beyond formal state control and represent a significant number of workers.

Independent Media

1997	1998	1999	2001	2002	2003	2004	2005	2006
5.25	5.50	5.50	6.00	6.00	6.25	6.50	6.50	6.75

Kazakhstan's many privately owned media channels and newspapers are overwhelmingly tied to companies that are owned by or closely associated with government leaders or business interests loyal to the regime.

Though some degree of social and political criticism from the media is tolerated, any specific criticism targeted at the president, members of his family, and other prominent figures in the government is heavily penalized under the country's multifarious laws. Actions used against the few independent and critical media channels include denying or revoking registrations, exerting pressure on private presses to terminate existing printing contracts, suspending electricity, confiscating print runs, arson, and regular libel suits.

Freedom House's annual *Freedom of the Press* survey has rated Kazakhstan's media "Not Free" since 1993. The decline in the independent media rating since the late 1990s has coincided with the nation's economic upturn. Despite the enormous difference in economic performance and market reforms, Kazakhstan's media ratings are only marginally better than those of Uzbekistan, Turkmenistan, or Belarus.

Dariga Nazarbaeva – the president's eldest daughter, leader of the Asar party, and a media tycoon – and her husband, Rakhat Aliev, currently the first deputy foreign minister, wield virtually unrivaled control and influence over the entire informational sphere. Having bought a majority share in the privatized but state-controlled news agency Khabar, which owns the TV channel of the same name, the couple has also acquired majority shares in numerous private media outlets. Nazarbaeva, head of Khabar for a number of years and later a member of the board of directors, has now assumed a more prominent political role as a parliamentary deputy and founding leader of Asar.

Article 318 of the criminal code penalizes a person who insults "the honor and dignity of the president"; it was invoked throughout the year, particularly during the election campaigns. The crackdown on newspapers intensified in October and November during the run-up to the election. Newspapers *Soz* and *Zhuma Taims-Data Nedeli*, both sympathetic to the opposition, were frequently subjected to closure and print-run confiscations. The entire print run of *Zhuma Taims-Data Nedeli* was seized when it was determined that the paper was damaging the "honor and dignity of a presidential candidate" (Nazarbaev). Tens of thousands of copies of *Svoboda Slova* were seized after the paper reported on the business practices of Nazarbaev's youngest daughter, Alia Nazarbaeva.[12]

Meanwhile, in late November, *Egemen Kazakstan* and *Kazakhstanskaya Pravda* refused to publish materials by the opposition presidential candidate Tuyakbai in which he described the Nazarbaev regime as one based on personal power, maintaining that such characterizations "violate the honor and dignity of another presidential candidate."

The private printing company Vremya-Print unilaterally terminated its contracts with *Svoboda Slova*, *Epokha*, *Apta-kz*, *Pravda Kazakhstana*, and *Zhuma Taims* in September following pressure from authorities.[13] After editors of these papers protested with hunger strikes, the Dauir printing press, controlled by Nazarbaev's sister-in-law Svetlana Nazarbayeva, agreed to print the newspapers, thereby allowing the authorities to know the contents before the papers appeared on the stands and thus prevent their distribution whenever a critical piece was published.

A number of politically motivated government lawsuits accusing critical media of insulting officials' "honor and dignity" were filed, even in cases where the allegations referred to widely known facts or were backed up with evidence. Altynbek Sarsenbaev, a former minister of information and current co-chairman of the unregistered opposition party Naghyz Ak Zhol, was fined 5 million tenge (US$38,000) in damages on defamation charges. He stated in an October 2004 interview with *Respublika* that Khabar had monopolized the country's media market.

Soz was also asked to pay 5 million tenge (US$38,000) in damages to the KNB after the latter successfully won a libel suit against the newspaper for an article published in September 2004 that alleged the KNB was spying on leaders of the opposition Ak Zhol party.[14]

The new Law on National Security has imposed further limits on the already restricted domain of media freedom in Kazakhstan. Additional amendments to the Law on Mass Media under this legislation give courts much wider latitude to close down media outlets for "violating Kazakhstan's integrity," condoning "extremism," and "undermining state security."

A game of hide-and-seek continues between Kazakh authorities and opposition newspapers. The newspaper originally known as *Dat*, edited by Ermurat Bapi, reappeared under the name *SolDat* after being banned by authorities; it continued to publish as *Zhuma Times-Data Nedeli*, retaining the original word Dat in its various incarnations. The newspaper has been effectively banned since December 2005, as all printing presses in the country have refused to print it.

The opposition newspaper *Respublika*, which has a history of tussles with the authorities and was published previously under the name *Assandi Times* (closed in 2004 following a lawsuit that resulted in bankruptcy), was closed again in May 2005 by the Ministry of Culture, Information, and Sport. It then published under a new name, *Set' Kz*, only to have 1,000 copies seized by the authorities. Earlier in April 2005, law-and-order authorities unsuccessfully attempted to extradite from Russia *Respublika's* editor in chief, Irina Petrusheva, on charges of tax evasion. Petrusheva is a Russian citizen who fled Kazakhstan in 2002 after receiving death threats for her newspaper's critical reporting.

Prominent international organizations such as the Institute for War and Peace Reporting, Internews, and Adil Soz Freedom of Speech Defense Fund (the latter two funded in part by USAID) were subject to stricter governmental vigilance during the preelection period. As a result, independent journalists as well as staff from frequently banned opposition newspapers began publishing articles on the Internet, where they face further obstacles.

Kazakhstan has intensified control and vigilance over pro-opposition Internet Web sites. The country's leading Internet service providers, Kaztelecom, which is state owned, and Nursat, which is privately owned but regulated by the state, regularly block access to opposition Web sites and introduced technical controls such as limiting bandwidth and blocking access, even via proxy servers. Access to any material critical of Nazarbaev or members of his family is routinely blocked by the these two state-controlled Internet service providers. Furthermore, it is impossible under the current system for an independent company to provide Internet access. Though no recent reliable data are available (*CIA Factbook* estimated 250,000 Internet users in 2003), the number of Internet users may have reached about 400,000 given the rapid advance in telecommunications technology and rising standard of living in urban areas.

A new regulation introduced in September 2005 on the registration of Internet domain names requires all domains to be registered in Kazakhstan (.kz) and mentions that non-Kazakh domains can be denied registration. KazNIC, a domain-registering company, was ordered by an Almaty court to stop hosting the Navigator Web site at Navi.kz in October. Navigator registered its domain in Russia as Navikz.net but found access to its site blocked within Kazakhstan. It was forced to move its Web site out of the CIS zone when Russia's Federal Security Service visited the Web site at the request of Kazakhstani authorities who urged Russia to stop hosting the site. A court in Almaty banned the domain names Navigator and Navi in both the Cyrillic and Roman alphabets. It now publishes under the name Mizinov.net.

Reporters Without Borders has condemned these governmental controls over Internet access by complaining that "bodies that manage the country code top-level domain names (ccTLDs) are above all technical. They are not qualified to censor the contents of sites."[15] The OSCE and Human Rights Watch have also criticized the attempts to censor Internet sites.

Kazakh officials have also showed a low tolerance for humor or political satire. They shut down the popular Borat.kz Web site, created by British comedian Sacha Baron Cohen, which featured a satirical Kazakh journalist character called Borat who was styled after the sexist and racist Kazakh journalist Cohen portrays on the U.S. cable channel HBO. *Zhuma Taims-Data Nedeli* faced criminal charges by the Almaty KNB in February 2005 for insulting the "honor and dignity" of the president in a satirical article about the elections that included the sentence "Our candidate for the presidency would be Notnursultan Notabishevich Notnazarbaev."

The strange death of Zamanbek Nurkadilov, a former associate of Nazarbaev who in 2004 accused the president of misuse of power and hoarding wealth, found very little attention in the state-controlled media. Nurkadilov was found dead on November 12, 2005, with three gunshot wounds. A government inquiry pronounced the death a suicide, whereas his supporters point to evidence suggesting Nurkadilov was killed on orders given by someone in the government. Nurkadilov had informed the pro-opposition press of his intention to make "sensational revelations" pertaining to the Kazakhgate bribery case before the elections. Journalist Askhat Sharipzhanov was killed in an inexplicable road accident in July 2004 soon after a "sensational" interview with Nurkadilov, but transcripts of the interview were never found. The extent of the regime's control over media makes an independent and impartial inquiry in such matters impossible.

Local Democratic Governance

1997	1998	1999	2001	2002	2003	2004	2005	2006
n/a	n/a	n/a	n/a	n/a	n/a	n/a	6.25	6.25

Kazakhstan's centralized administrative system allows for very limited autonomy or direct public participation at the regional or local level. Its administrative subdivisions are 14 *oblasts*, 2 special administrative divisions of the capital, Astana, and the former capital, Almaty, 84 cities, 160 districts (*raions*), and 2,150 rural settlements (*auls*).

Cities have local councils (Maslihat), which are elected for five-year terms. But very little decision-making power has devolved to the councils, whose members are elected indirectly via electors, thus limiting local participation. The established procedure of electing electors, a hangover from the Soviet era, is informal and feeds on patronage. Maslihats serve primarily as rubber-stamp bodies to approve acts by local executives, though each *oblast* Maslihat, and those of Almaty and Astana, nominate two members each to the Senate. OSCE/ODIHR observers criticized the elections in 2003 as containing far greater violations than the 2004 parliamentary election.

Neither the Constitution nor the prevalent legislation provides for elections of oblast, regional, or local administrative heads (*akims*) or elaborates their powers. According to clause 4 of Article 87 of the Constitution, all *akims* are part of the unified system of executive power, are appointed by the president and the government of the republic, and may, regardless of the level they occupy, be dismissed from office by the president at his discretion. The *akims* of townships, villages, and counties report to their superior administrative heads. No mechanism exists for ensuring their accountability to the local population. A high turnover in regional leadership means that the average tenure of an *akim* is typically less than two years.

Kazakhstan revised laws pertaining to local governance in 1998, 2001, and 2004, but there is still no provision to introduce the direct election of *akims* or enhance their legal powers. The law "Local State Administration in the Republic of Kazakhstan," adopted in 2001, defines the activities and areas of competence of local Maslihats, *akims*, and administrative bodies (*akimat*). Another law, "Elections of Akims of Local Counties, Villages, and Townships," adopted in the same year, provides for introducing gradual elections of *akims* at the local level, authorizing the Central Election Commission to work out the details in coordination with the akims of the provinces involved. The Central Election Commission, and not the *oblast* or local election commissions, determines the number of electors of local *akims* in specific villages, counties, and townships. Together with the Central Election Commission and District Election Commission, the district and local *akims* play a role in ensuring that their election results are favorable to the regime.

A decree in December 2004 stated that a phased process of direct elections for *akims* at district and village levels will take place from August 2005 until the end of 2007 and that some regions will hold elections on an experimental basis. Elections for *akims* were held in four districts in August 2005 as an "experiment," which was presented to the public as a "step toward democratization." Four incumbent *akims* were "elected" in indirect elections in which deputies of the Maslihat served as electors while the real electorate was not involved. In a symbolic and propagandistic act, the Chemolgan district (the native place of Nazarbaev) in Almaty *oblast* has been the only district to hold a direct election of *akims*, which occurred in 1999.

Kazakhstan has failed to make any headway in introducing elections or establishing a proper legislative base for the rights of local and regional bodies. Holding direct local elections in the present framework does not denote a democratizing step because the incumbent *akims*, their superior heads, and members of the Central Election Commission and District Election Commission wield enormous influence in the nomination of candidates. The lack of finances available to local bodies for organizing elections is another serious limitation.

Local bodies have no budgetary powers or authority to levy taxes, as the central government determines taxation rates and budgetary regulations. Despite formal central control, some resource-rich *oblasts* have been able to enjoy de facto decentralization to a certain extent. *Akims* in the regions that have attracted the most foreign investment – particularly Aktau, Magistau, Karaganda, East Kazakhstan, and Pavlodar – have tended to exercise greater control over budgetary matters and extracted significant contributions to various "social and welfare projects" from foreign investors. Local budgets are allowed to keep all fines for environmental pollution but have to transfer other revenues to their higher authorities. *Oblasts* are not allowed to keep their surplus budget and are required to give it to the needier *oblasts*. Both donor and recipient *oblasts* have expressed dissatisfaction over this system of deduction from local budgets and subvention from the national budget.[16]

Under the present Law on Elections, political parties, public associations, and higher-level election commissions nominate candidates to serve in seven-member local election commissions, which has enhanced a top-down regulation of local election commissions, further undermining local initiative and participation.

Judicial Framework and Independence

1997	1998	1999	2001	2002	2003	2004	2005	2006
5.00	5.25	5.50	5.75	6.00	6.25	6.25	6.25	6.25

Kazakhstan's Constitution states that the judiciary is to be independent but provides no mechanisms to safeguard its independence. Under the country's strong executive system based on presidential patronage, the judiciary – like the legislative branch – has remained loyal to the regime. It has served to protect the interests of the state and its functionaries rather than those of individuals, minorities, and the weaker strata of society.

The Constitution spells out an elaborate procedure for appointing judges in which the president proposes nominees for the Supreme Court, who are then approved by the Senate. These nominees are recommended by the Supreme Judicial Council, which is composed of the chair of the Constitutional Council, the chair of the Supreme Court, the prosecutor-general, the minister of justice, senators, judges, and other people appointed by the president. The president may remove judges, except members of the Supreme Court, on the recommendation of the minister of justice.

Kazakhstan has made a significant effort to raise salaries and the level of professionalism in the judiciary. A Judicial Academy was set up with help from the OSCE/ODIHR to train judges and became fully functional in 2004 with the launch of a magistrate program. All future judges will be required to attend the Judicial Academy. The American Bar Association/Central European and Eurasian Law Initiative has been aiding judicial reforms since 1993 and has now focused attention on providing training in judicial ethics and human rights. More than three-fourths of Kazakhstan's lawyers are state employed, though the percentage of lawyers who are either self-employed or work with foreign companies is growing rapidly. The two main associations of independent lawyers are the Association of Lawyers of Kazakhstan and the Legal Development of Kazakhstan.

Supreme Court judges now receive a higher remuneration package than government ministers. The government has promised further salary improvements for low and high courts and a pension provision to make bribery "not only morally unacceptable but economically disadvantageous as well."[17]

Kairat Mami, chairman of the Supreme Court of Kazakhstan, attempted to illustrate the efficiency and "greater public trust" in the judiciary by pointing out that about 1 million civil suits and complaints were filed with the courts in 2004, almost twice as many as in 2000.[18] While the judiciary has shown increased professionalism in handling civil and criminal cases, it continues to have a checkered record in cases relating to civil liberties, political freedom, independent media, and human rights issues.

The courts have shown complete complicity in passing sentence on opponents and critics of the government without credible evidence or proper procedures. These instances include the trial in absentia of ex-premier Akezhan Kazhegeldin in 2000, opposition leaders Mukhtar Ablyazov and Ghalymzhan Zhakiyanov in 2003, and journalist Sergei Duvanov in January 2003. The politically fabricated nature of these convictions and the unjust conduct of the trials have been condemned by Amnesty International, Human Rights Watch, Freedom House, and other international organizations. Even the decision to release Zhakiyanov on parole by a local court was executed only after the completion of the presidential election to suit political priorities.[19]

Kazakhstan has maintained a moratorium on the death penalty since 2004, apparently in a bid to hold the OSCE chair in 2009. Though the judiciary has introduced life imprisonment as an alternative to the death penalty, judges are authorized to pass death sentences until the death penalty is completely abolished. Kazakhstan's justice minister, Zagipa Baliyeva, refused to provide the date when the death penalty will be abolished, stating that it depends on the development of an appropriate opinion in the society.[20]

As part of Kazakhstan's drive to "humanize its criminal prosecution system," the use of incarceration has decreased and probation and community service are being introduced as alternative forms of punishment. The number of convictions carrying prison terms decreased from 51 percent in 2000 to 45 percent in 2004. At the same time, the number of acquittals doubled. A new amnesty law will apply to some 5,000 prisoners and reduce the overall number over a two- to three-year period.[21]

In accordance with the draft state program for reforming the judicial system, approved by the Supreme Judicial Council for 2004–2006, the Majilis voted to approve a bill introducing jury trials. Kazakhstan has adopted the continental, or Franco-German, model (different from the classic, or Anglo-Saxon, model), which provides presiding judges with the opportunity to review cases along with jurors and to join them in the final decision-making process. It is believed that jury trials will help reduce graft and corruption and enhance the independence and impartiality of courts. Whether jury trials can attain this objective remains doubtful, given the low level of public trust in the judiciary and its poor track record of passing independent judgments. Also, there is a built-in potential for continued government influence and pressure on presiding judges, though ostensibly they would participate in the process "to ensure objectivity and fairness of the verdict."

The impact of these measures is reduced by a lack of reforms to the criminal code of 1998, which maintains many of the features of Soviet-era law. Amendments to the Law on Terrorism and Religion in May 2005 and the introduction of a new Law on Extremism in February 2005 heralded an increase in the power of law-and-order authorities without corresponding safeguards for civil liberties.

Corruption

1997	1998	1999	2001	2002	2003	2004	2005	2006
n/a	n/a	6.00	6.25	6.25	6.25	6.50	6.50	6.50

Corruption is endemic and at the same time difficult to demonstrate in all patronage-based personalistic regimes in which an independent media, access to credible information, and democratic accountability are absent. Kazakhstan's oil and mineral resources are under the firm control of members of the regime, including friends and associates who hold many of the formal governmental posts. This system has served to "legalize" preferential access to public office and to disguise corruption.

Under the 2001-2005 State Program on Combating Corruption, the definition of corruption has been broadened to cover gifts, property received indirectly, and an extensive list of actions pertaining to personal use of state resources. While lower- and middle-ranking officials and minor political figures have been penalized on corruption charges, top-level government officials, political actors, and regime associates and supporters remain beyond the reach of inquiry. The major political personalities who have been tried for "corruption and misuse of office" over the past years are ex-regime figures who organized opposition parties. All of them challenged the president over policy issues after having amassed considerable political power and financial influence. This proves that a direct confrontation with the president will invariably lead to accusations of corruption and financial misdealing and heavy penalties.

Though the so-called Kazakhgate corruption case made international headlines, investigations remained stalled throughout 2005. James Giffen, the main accused and a former consultant to Kazakh president Nursultan Nazarbaev, was charged in a U.S. federal court with funneling up to US$84 million in illicit payments to Nazarbaev and former prime minister Nurlan Balgimbaev in exchange for lucrative concessions to Western oil companies. Most of the charges against the indicted Giffen fall under the U.S. Foreign Corrupt Practices Act, which prohibits U.S. citizens from bribing foreign officials for business advantage.

The Giffen hearings were postponed for a third time owing to the late presentation of materials in U.S. federal court in New York, and a new trial date was set for January 2006.[22] The repeated delays have shifted international and domestic attention away from the case. The U.S. anticorruption practices law penalizes those who pay bribes but not the recipients, which all but rules out that charges will be brought against Nazarbaev or Balgimbaev. Meanwhile, Nazarbaev's latest electoral victory and sustained PR campaign to boost his image in the international media have given him an aura of legitimacy.

Kazakhstan's enormous oil and mineral resource base and lack of democratic oversight have created a fertile environment for the nontransparent accumulation of wealth by top elites. Kazakhstan established the National Oil Fund in 2001 to protect the economy from volatility in oil prices and to aid the transparent management of oil revenues. While its revenues have grown to US$5.2 billion thanks to high oil prices and growing exports, vital issues of transparency, management, and redistribution of oil fund revenues have not been addressed. The Parliament has no authority to conduct an audit of oil funds or to determine how and under what conditions the funds are to be used.

Kazakhstan joined the Extractive Industries Transparency Initiative (EITI) in October 2005. The EITI was introduced by British prime minister Tony Blair in September 2002 at the UN Sustainable Development Summit to increase transparency of payments by companies to governments and government-linked entities, as well as transparency of revenues to those host country governments. One of the memorandum's provisions requires the establishment of a National Council including interested parties such as Majilis deputies, representatives of oil and gas companies, the Ministry of Finance, and nongovernmental organizations. There are doubts about the participation of independent NGOs in this initiative. Another provision requires a mandatory disclosure of oil revenues received by the treasury from each of the 51 legal entities operating in the oil and gas industries (and any new ones that may be formed). No progress has been made on this issue thus far.

The government has continued to issue small- and medium-scale measures to combat corruption at all levels of governance and administration. A new anticorruption decree issued in April 2005 restructures disciplinary councils in all provinces, instructing them to become more public oriented, promote greater transparency, and reduce government interference in business activities. The Ministry of Interior Affairs, financial police, KNB, and Disciplinary State Service Commission are responsible for combating corruption.

Some positive efforts have been made to enhance awareness about corruption at the grassroots level. Transparency Kazakhstan, the local branch of Transparency International, together with the Interlegal Foundation for Political and Legal Research published a textbook titled *Basics of Preventing Corruption*. This publication was part of the project Combating Corruption Through Civic Education, conducted in partnership with members of Kazakhstan's Constitutional Council and Supreme Court. Though such actions denote the government's efforts to scale down corruption, it is very difficult to determine the extent of corruption and combat it without investigations by genuinely independent and impartial agencies. The problem is compounded by Kazakhstan's patronage-based judicial system, which is entirely loyal to the executive. The prosecutor-general, appointed by the president and not accountable to the government, handles inquiries into official corruption, in conjunction with the Ministries of Justice and Internal Affairs.

According to the global Corruption Perceptions Index published by Transparency International, a Berlin-based organization combating corruption worldwide, Kazakhstan showed a slightly improved rating. Its score of 2.6 was the best in Central Asia, better than the 2.2 score of oil-rich Azerbaijan. In comparison, the score for Kyrgyzstan was 2.3, Uzbekistan 2.2, Tajikistan 2.1, Turkmenistan 1.8, and Russia 2.4.[23] In 2004, Kazakhstan scored 2.2. These improvements are minimal since any score of 5.0 or below (the lower the score, the higher the corruption perception) reflects a serious corruption problem. The index defines corruption as the abuse of public office for private gain and measures the degree that corruption is perceived to exist among a country's public officials and politicians.

Bhavna Dave, a lecturer in Central Asian studies at the School of Oriental and African Studies, writes about ethnic and language politics and the construction of national identity in Kazakhstan and Kyrgyzstan. She is the author of a forthcoming book Kazakhstan: The Paradoxes of a Nationalizing State, *to be published by RoutledgeCurzon.*

[1] www.britishcouncil.org/kazakhstan-partnerships.htm.
[2] The Communist Party of Kazakhstan underwent a split in 2003 when a faction calling itself the Communist People's Party of Kazakhstan walked out to support the president.
[3] The Kazakh government appropriated yellow as the color of stability, their own retort to "rose" and "orange."
[4] Institute for War and Peace Reporting, Report on Central Asia, no. 424, part 2, December 3, 2005.
[5] www.rferl.org/featuresarticle/2005/12/f8c89ae9-4c34-4c61-9aca-ee11106dac09.html.
[6] hrw.org/english/docs/2005/10/12/kazakh11853.htm.
[7] Radio Free Europe/Radio Liberty Newsline, August 24, 2005.
[8] www.usaid.gov/locations/europe_eurasia/dem_gov/ngoindex/2004/kazakhstan.pdf. Accessed on December 16, 2005.
[9] www.cpart.kz/ss/cssi/SS%20April%202005%20Zhalgas%20KA.pdf
[10] hrw.org/english/docs/2005/10/12/kazakh11853.htm.
[11] www.kahar.name/2005-12-156.htm.
[12] Radio Free Europe/Radio Liberty Central Asia report, October 27, 2005, and Radio Free Europe/Radio Liberty Newsline, October 20, 2005.
[13] Radio Free Europe/Radio Liberty Newsline, September 29, 2005.
[14] Radio Free Europe/Radio Liberty Newsline, February 1, 2005.
[15] Radio Free Europe/Radio Liberty Newsline, December 16, 2005.
[16] Meruert Makhmutova, "Local Government in Kazakhstan," unpan1.un.org/intradoc/groups/public/documents/APCITY/UNPAN018210.pdf, accessed on December 18, 2005.
[17] Kazakhstan News Bulletin, February 18, 2005, www.kazakhstanembassy.org.uk/cgi-bin/index/180.
[18] Kazakhstan News Bulletin, February 25, 2005, www.kazakhembus.com/022505.html.
[19] www.interfax.com/3/113347/news.aspx.
[20] Gazeta.kz, November 4, 2005.
[21] Kazakhstan News Bulletin, February 25, 2005, www.kazakhembus.com/022505.html.
[22] www.eurasianet.org, August 27, 2005.
[23] ww1.transparency.org/cpi/2005/cpi2005_infocus.html.

Kyrgyzstan

Capital: Bishkek
Population: 5.1 million
GNI/capita: $400
Ethnic Groups: Kyrgyz (64.9%), Russian (12.5%),
Uzbek (13.8%), Ukrainian (1%),
other (8%)

Nations in Transit Ratings and Averaged Scores

	1997	1998	1999	2001	2002	2003	2004	2005	2006
Electoral Process	5.00	5.00	5.00	5.75	5.75	6.00	6.00	6.00	5.75
Civil Society	4.50	4.50	4.50	4.50	4.50	4.50	4.50	4.50	4.50
Independent Media	5.00	5.00	5.00	5.00	5.75	6.00	6.00	5.75	5.75
Governance *	4.25	4.50	5.00	5.25	5.50	6.00	6.00	n/a	n/a
National Democratic Governance	n/a	n/a	n/a	n/a	n/a	n/a	n/a	6.00	6.00
Local Democratic Governance	n/a	n/a	n/a	n/a	n/a	n/a	n/a	5.75	6.25
Judicial Framework and Independence	4.50	4.50	5.00	5.25	5.25	5.50	5.50	5.50	5.50
Corruption	n/a	n/a	6.00	6.00	6.00	6.00	6.00	6.00	6.00
Democracy Score	4.65	4.70	5.08	5.29	5.46	5.67	5.67	5.64	5.68

With the 2005 edition, Freedom House introduced seperate analysis and ratings for national democratic governance and local democratic governance to provide readers with more detailed and nuanced analysis of these two important subjects.

NOTE: The ratings reflect the consensus of Freedom House, its academic advisers, and the author of this report. The opinions expressed in this report are those of the author. The ratings are based on a scale of 1 to 7, with 1 representing the highest level of democratic progress and 7 the lowest. The Democracy Score is an average of ratings for the categories tracked in a given year.

The economic and social data on this page were taken from the following sources:
GNI/capita, Population: *World Development Indicators 2006* (Washington, D.C.: World Bank, 2006).
Ethnic Groups: *CIA World Factbook 2006* (Washington, D.C.: Central Intelligence Agency, 2006).

EXECUTIVE SUMMARY

There was great political upheaval in Kyrgyzstan in the first three months of 2005. Askar Akayev, the country's president since before independence, was ousted by widespread protests in the wake of the parliamentary elections. However, most of the members of Parliament, whose election sparked the social unrest, retained their mandates. The new leadership of former government officials now turned opposition leaders inherited the problems of growing poverty, corruption, the presence of "criminal elements" in the government, insecure borders, and a perceived gathering threat from Islamic fundamentalist groups. New president Kurmanbek Bakiyev promised sweeping reforms to address these concerns, but as 2005 ended, concrete actions were not much in evidence, leaving the situation in the country tenuous at best.

Since Kyrgyzstan's independence in 1991, many observers, especially in the West, have viewed the country as Central Asia's best hope for a democratic government. Western press generally portrayed the ouster of President Akayev in March 2005 as a positive step taken by a people tired of corruption and poor governance. But prior to the events of March, many of the same press outlets noted that Kyrgyzstan was, in terms of democracy, ahead of its neighbors. There were opposition parties and movements, opposition representatives were elected to the Parliament, people held demonstrations, and there was something of an independent media, though it found itself increasingly challenged. The country was poor, having little to export, but generally was peaceful.

As 2005 ended, the country remained poor, and protests and violence were rising, leading the International Crisis Group to release a report that Kyrgyzstan was becoming a "faltering state" and risked becoming "a failed state."[1]

National Democratic Governance. With the change in leadership in March, the Parliament temporarily lost its voice. Kyrgyzstan already had a presidential form of government, but the president was forced to flee on March 24, leaving behind a Parliament packed with his supporters. Kurmanbek Bakiyev, prime minister from December 2000 to May 2002, led the opposition of the Kyrgyzstan's People's Movement and became acting president after Akayev's departure. Bakiyev was officially elected president in an early poll on July 10 and kept a promise to name another opposition leader – Feliks Kulov, chairman of the Ar-Namys party – to be prime minister. Both men were soon targets of protests. Three deputies were killed, and the Parliament voted to allow its members to carry firearms for personal protection.[2] Evidence of criminal ties to officials in government emerged. The security situation in the southern part of the country deteriorated. Uzbekistan's internal problems once again spilled over into Kyrgyzstan. The new leadership promised changes, and discussion on these plans started. But the country was beset by problems after March, and even President Bakiyev said in early November that "we have to get down to the real economy, but instead we have been working like a rescue team since March." *Kyrgyzstan's rating for national democratic governance remains at 6.00, as by year's end there was much talk about reforms and accountable government but little opportunity and very little progress toward fulfilling these pledges.*

Electoral Process. Both parliamentary and presidential elections were held in Kyrgyzstan in 2005, in February-March and July, respectively. Suspicions that the parliamentary elections could be rigged appeared in January when the registration of candidates commenced. Several opposition figures were prevented from registering for residency reasons. Results showed that pro-presidential candidates (including two of President Akayev's children) won an overwhelming majority of the 75 seats in the Parliament. Protests that started before the elections against decisions to bar opposition candidates and perceived election fraud continued after the poll. On March 24, protesters stormed the president's building in the capital city of Bishkek, and President Akayev fled. Western media dubbed this the "Tulip Revolution," alluding to the 2003 "Rose Revolution" in Georgia and the 2004 "Orange Revolution" in Ukraine. Kyrgyzstan People's Movement leader Kurmanbek Bakiyev became president, though only a few people selected him initially. International and domestic monitors judged the presidential election to be generally free and fair and an improvement over previous elections. Bakiyev needed a strong mandate at the polls to legitimize his sudden rise to power, but even international monitors questioned the nearly 89 percent of the vote he received running against five other candidates. *Kyrgyzstan's rating for electoral process improves from 6.00 to 5.75 for presidential elections that international monitors agreed were an improvement over previous polls and laid solid foundations for future votes.*

Civil Society. Civic protest, including disaffected voters, paid protesters, nongovernmental organizations (NGOs), and youth movements, played an important role in the changes of 2005. A campaign against foreign NGOs was under way as the year started but vanished after the events of March. NGOs helped organize rallies, both pro- and antigovernment, as did youth groups, notably KelKel, of which there were two: one opposition and the other pro-regime. Campaigns against suspect Muslim groups followed the same pattern. Members of the banned Islamic group Hizb ut-Tahrir were detained in the first two months, but there were no reports of detentions after March. Neighboring Uzbekistan alleged that another Islamic group called Akramiya (whose existence is in some doubt) had established branches in Kyrgyzstan and set up terrorist training camps there, charges the Kyrgyz government denied. Since March, nearly all groups – NGOs, social movements and organizations, and suspect religious groups – have been unfettered in their activities. This probably reflects the number of pressing issues the new leadership was forced to confront rather than an introduction of more liberal policies. *Kyrgyzstan's rating for civil society remains unchanged at 4.50 as the country contin-*

ued to have the most vibrant civil society in Central Asia but at times seemed on the edge of anarchy.

Independent Media. The Kyrgyz independent media may be credited with sparking events that led to the ouster of President Akayev. Articles about an alleged January secret meeting between Prime Minister Nikolai Tanayev and governors and election officials to ensure that pro-Akayev candidates won seats in the Parliament helped create an atmosphere of mistrust among the electorate. Subsequent events seemed to bear out what the independent media were reporting. Harassment of independent media was evident prior to the February parliamentary elections. The independent newspaper *Moya Stolitsa Novosti*, which reported on the secret meeting, faced lawsuits from a pro-government newspaper at the start of the year. Following the change of power, the situation changed significantly. Previous pro-government media continued to be pro-government but switched to a more sympathetic view of opposition politicians, now the leaders of the country. Media that supported the previous opposition, people like Kurmanbek Bakiyev before he came to power, continued that support, thereby rendering most of the media in Kyrgyzstan effectively pro-government after March. There were no obstacles to reporting the numerous domestic and international problems that occurred after March 24. Kimmo Kiljunen, head of the Organization for Security and Cooperation in Europe/Office for Democratic Institutions and Human Rights (OSCE/ODIHR) Election Observation Mission for the presidential elections, praised the role of the media the day after elections, saying they had allowed candidates to present their views.[3] Bakiyev promised to eliminate state subsidies for the media, making all media in the country independent. By year's end, the media were starting to criticize Bakiyev and the government. If the economic situation in the country does not improve in 2006, Bakiyev and others may find themselves the targets of the same sort of disparaging press coverage that made political life difficult for their predecessors. *Kyrgyzstan's rating for independent media remains at 5.75, although Bakiyev's pledge to support independent media and actual improvements in the safety and political and legal freedoms of journalists by year's end are first steps that may indicate an improving trend in 2006.*

Local Democratic Governance. Local governance proved inept in 2005. Officials failed or refused to restrain demonstrators from holding unsanctioned protests, both before and after the events of March. The removal of the old regime left in place many local officials from that regime. There were serious breakdowns in law and order and little indication that authorities were able to cope, particularly in the southern part of the country. The degree of corruption in local governance was deep-rooted under President Akayev, and its current severity was only beginning to be understood toward the end of 2005. The government in Bishkek was beset by problems that demanded urgent action and did not have time to focus on problems of local governance or its officials. The new leadership promised to make amendments to the Constitution, including sections on local administration. But at year's end, the debate continued. President Bakiyev also appeared to waver on his pledge to implement constitutional reforms when he said in December that the amendments should be postponed for about four years.[4] *Despite stated intentions by the new government to amend laws and fight corruption, local governance was shown to be inept, sometimes unethical, and barely able to address the needs of constituencies; therefore the rating for local governance decreases from 5.75 to 6.25.*

Judicial Framework and Independence. The court system was not as active in the run-up to the 2005 parliamentary elections as it had been during the 2000 elections. The Central Election Commission (CEC) changed tactics in 2005 from charging opposition candidates to simply barring them from competing. However, CEC decisions were upheld when appealed through the courts – including the Supreme Court, which backed a decision barring former foreign minister Roza Otunbayeva and other former ambassadors from running in parliamentary elections. The court system shifted with the change of power. Some officials from the Akayev government, including the CEC chairman, were brought to trial. The courts upheld decisions, stripping President Akayev's two children of their seats in the Parliament. Neither the president nor the prime minister was seen to be influencing the decisions of the courts. *Despite an absence of evident pressure on the judiciary from the new leadership, the court system continued to render verdicts that were in line with the policies of the new authorities, so the rating for judicial framework and independence remains unchanged at 5.50.*

Corruption. Corruption became the priority issue for the post-March 24 leadership once parliamentary deputies with alleged links to organized crime became targets for assassination. President Bakiyev addressed the Parliament in late September after a second legislator was killed and told the deputies that "the fact that criminal elements have merged with law enforcement agencies is not news to anybody. You all know this perfectly well, too. Among those sitting here are people who know perfectly well about it, who know who is connected to whom and how they are connected."[5] However, even the Kyrgyz media started hinting that many of the people who came to power after the March unrest had links to criminal groups during pre-election protests. Prison riots in October drew further links between members of the government and the criminal world. Also, many former officials, including former president Akayev and members of his family, were wanted for questioning about corruption before the events of March. *Kyrgyzstan's rating for corruption remains unchanged at 6.00.*

Outlook for 2006. The outlook for Kyrgyzstan in 2006 is not encouraging. Euphoria that accompanied the change of power in March 2005 cannot last if basic social problems, such as unemployment and poverty, do not show signs of improvement. The new government has as few resources to address these problems as the previous government, though some foreign governments restructured Kyrgyzstan's debt to alleviate strain on the country's finances. The depth of corruption and links between government and criminal organizations in the country were only just starting to become clear by year's end. Governments in neighboring Central Asian states were alarmed by the March unrest in Kyrgyzstan that chased longtime president Askar Akayev from power. These states do not want instability in Kyrgyzstan but have little reason to want Bakiyev's government to succeed, given that such an outcome might similarly inspire their own populations. Though parliamentary elections sparked the turmoil that led to Akayev's ouster, most of the deputies elected in the poll remained in the Parliament; however, there was a campaign to have that Parliament dissolved. Officials such as former acting foreign minister Roza Otunbayeva did not receive positions in the new government after the presidential elections. Otunbayeva and her Ata-Jurt movement have said they will continue to be an opposition group. It was unclear at the end of 2005 just how much opposition they would provide to the new government. The problem of suspect Islamic fundamentalist groups is growing in the southern part of Kyrgyzstan, with the government of neighboring Uzbekistan saying Islamic extremists were in the Kyrgyz part of the Fergana Valley. Authorities there have done nothing to address this situation.

MAIN REPORT

National Democratic Governance

1997	1998	1999	2001	2002	2003	2004	2005	2006
n/a	n/a	n/a	n/a	n/a	n/a	n/a	6.00	6.00

Kyrgyzstan's original Constitution, written in 1993, enshrines the principles of democratic government. This is due in large part to the Kyrgyz government's willingness to accept advice from governments in the West while drafting the document. The policies of Askar Akayev, who inherited the leadership of his newly independent country, were liberal and enlightened relative to those of other governments that emerged in Central Asia during the same period.

But an ever increasing rift opened between Akayev and the Soviet-era Parliament that still remains in Kyrgyzstan. The Parliament worked to strip power from the president's office and purposely held up Akayev's reform proposals. Two days before the new Constitution came into force (May 3, 1993), the Supreme Soviet voted to transfer the powers of the head of state from the president to the prime minister.

Akayev called for, and won, a referendum on confidence in the president as head of state in January 1994, but that did not solve the problems. Deputies refused to attend sessions, saying the Parliament had become a house of intrigue. The government resigned in early September 1994, and when more than half the deputies boycotted a session of the Parliament, Akayev dissolved the body.

Referendums in October 1994, 1996, 1998, and 2003 changed more than half of the Constitution and transferred more power to the presidency. The system of checks and balances among the branches of power was drastically altered, and as a result, the Parliaments elected in 1995 and 2000 were much more compliant. The government became a clearly presidential state with a weak legislative branch and a subservient judiciary. Independent media outlets that criticized the government or government officials were brought to court on libel and slander charges, and several outlets were shut down. The right to freedom of assembly also suffered temporarily.

Demonstrations, some lasting months, were frequent in Kyrgyzstan in the last half of the 1990s. Groups demonstrated in support of opposition figures and the independent media outlets facing legal problems. But after protests during the 2000 parliamentary elections, restrictions were placed on the right to assemble and rally. Those rights were partially restored after the March 2002 protests in the southern Aksy district, when police opened fire on demonstrators supporting Senator Azimbek Beknazarov, who had been jailed in January of that year on charges of abuse of office while in a previous state post. At least five demonstrators were killed. Large protests followed against the authorities' apparent indifference and subsequent attempted cover-up, forcing out the government of then prime minister Kurmanbek Bakiyev in May 2002 and compelling the authorities to ease restrictions on the right to demonstrate.

In retrospect, those events of 2002 were a dress rehearsal for what would come in March 2005. President Akayev repeatedly pledged that he would not seek another term in the scheduled October 2005 presidential elections, which raised the stakes in the parliamentary elections for Akayev supporters in government.

Negative aspects of previous elections, such as registration obstacles for opposition candidates and pressure on voters in their workplaces and schools, reappeared at the start of 2005. Independent media reported on the "secret meeting" of Prime Minister Nikolai Tanayev with governors and election officials to plan a strategy to ensure that Akayev loyalists would win an absolute majority in the Parliament, a meeting Tanayev denied ever took place. Opposition candidates who were able to register had problems meeting with voters and finding media outlets to spread their message to voters. Independent media outlets themselves encountered legal problems.

Isolated protests, mainly in support of individual candidates barred from the elections, gradually took on an anti-Akayev character. Prior to the poll, there was evidence that protests were spreading across the country and beginning to unify. The second round of elections was held in some 40 of the 75 districts on March 13. When results started to come in, it became clear that about 90 percent of the 75 seats in the Parliament went to people considered to be Akayev loyalists. Administration buildings were burned in southern parts of the country, major highways were blocked, and on March 24 a crowd stormed the president's building. An opposition made up mostly of former government officials, including Kurmanbek Bakiyev and Feliks Kulov (chairman of the Ar-Namys [Dignity] party and former Kyrgyz vice president, who was immediately freed from jail, where he had served four years of a combined 17 year sentence on charges of embezzlement and abuse of office), took power in the country. Few noticed in the euphoria at ousting Akayev that these opposition figures, now Kyrgyzstan's leaders, played a very small role in the events that led to the change of power. In other words, the crowds wanted Akayev out of office, but they did not take to the streets to put Bakiyev in power.

Bakiyev was named president in unclear circumstances. He attempted to bring the widespread protests under opposition control, but events happened too quickly for him or any other opposition figure to give the impression of actually directing the circumstances. For the first several hours after Akayev's departure, another opposition figure, Ishenbai Kadyrbekov, was the country's new leader. A small group of opposition leaders apparently settled on Bakiyev as acting prime minister (constitutionally, Bakiyev could not be named acting president immediately). That decision was confirmed shortly thereafter by deputies in the new Parliament, many of whom at that time must have been questioning their own chances of political survival. The acting prime minister quickly, and constitutionally, filled the vacant office of the president.

The presidential poll scheduled for late October was moved forward, and Bakiyev was elected president on July 10, taking nearly 90 percent of the vote. His next closest competitor, in a field of six candidates, received less than 4 percent. The huge victory could be explained as the result of Bakiyev's pairing with Feliks Kulov. Some well-known opposition figures withdrew their candidacies, and many groups chose to throw their support behind the Bakiyev-Kulov team. Despite Bakiyev's victory, Kyrgyzstan's government was very shaky as 2005 came to an end. Most of the legislators remained the pro-Akayev candidates whose election helped spark the protests that ousted Akayev. These deputies kept a low profile in the months following the events of March, but they were reminded of their uncertain future by longtime opposition leader Topchubek Turgunaliyev, who started a campaign to collect signatures to call for a referendum on dissolving the Parliament.

It would be difficult to judge the performance of these deputies since they have not had much opportunity to look at the longer-term business of government. Protesting did not stop in Kyrgyzstan after the events of March, and Bishkek hardly saw a day of peace for the rest of the year. In June, supporters of businessman Urmat Baryktabasov, who was barred from competing in the presidential elections, tried to storm the government building. Authorities later claimed it was an attempted coup and that the organizers of the demonstration planned to kill several of the new government officials. During an inspection of a prison facility outside Bishkek in October, parliamentarian Tynychbek Akmatbayev was killed in a riot. Though evidence showed Akmatbayev was killed with a gun taken from one of his bodyguards, protesters led by Akmatbayev's brother, Ryspek, demonstrated in Bishkek. They demanded the resignation of Prime Minister Kulov, whom they held responsible for the deputy's death. A special parliamentary commission ruled in early December that Kulov was not involved.

The events surrounding Akmatbayev's death and the assassination of two other members of Parliament (in June and September) established links between parliamentarians and organized criminal groups. In late September, following the murder of Deputy Bayaman Erkinbayev, President Bakiyev addressed the Parliament and said it was clear that law enforcement agencies and organized criminal groups had "become merged." He said there were deputies present at that emergency session of the Parliament who also had links to these criminal groups.

It was therefore difficult to glean a clear picture of the government's posture toward basic rights and civil liberties. There was debate in the Parliament (October-November) about placing a temporary ban on public demonstrations. Independent media worked unfettered after the event of March, possibly owing to the authorities' focus on the urgent issues already mentioned. But some media reports linked criminal groups and members of the new government, claiming these officials were indebted to criminal organizations for helping to organize or fund protests that ousted Akayev. In late September, Bakiyev's press service released a statement reading, "Some media outlets have recently launched a new round of propaganda to discredit the new authorities, which is openly timed to coincide with the formation of a new government."[6] It continued, "The strategy of this PR campaign is not being concealed: it is aimed at accusing high-ranking officials and the president of corruption, links to the criminal world, involvement in some high-profile murders, and splitting the ranks of the revolutionaries by blaming some of them of betrayal and abandonment of the interests of the people's revolution of March." The statement concluded that Akayev loyalists were fueling this "PR campaign," but it also indicated the growing frustration of the president at the ability of Kyrgyzstan's media to report anything they wanted.

With all the problems in Bishkek, it may not have been surprising that to the south, in Kyrgyzstan's section of the Fergana Valley, there were increasing problems maintaining order. Murdered deputy Erkinbayev was involved in a "turf war" over the lucrative Kara-Suu bazaar near Kyrgyzstan's next largest city Osh. Media speculation linked Erkinbayev's assassination to that dispute. Less than three weeks before Erkinbayev's murder in September, the acting director of the Kara-Suu bazaar, Abdalim Junusov, was shot dead in his home. There were several riots at the bazaar prior to those killings.

That was not the biggest problem the new Kyrgyz leadership had in the Fergana Valley in 2005. In May, hundreds of Uzbek refugees streamed across the border to escape violence in the eastern Uzbek city of Andijan. The Uzbek government pressed hard to have all the refugees sent back, particularly as Uzbek authorities claimed that among those refugees were some of the people responsible for starting the violence in the Andijan area. Rights groups, including the office of the UN High Commissioner for Refugees (UNHCR), pressed just as hard for Kyrgyz authorities not to send the refugees back to Uzbekistan.

Later, Uzbekistan accused Kyrgyz authorities of being too tolerant toward Islamic extremists. In September, Uzbekistan's prosecutor general said the "terrorists" involved in the Andijan violence trained at secret camps in Kyrgyzstan and received weapons there.[7] When the first trials of Andijan "terrorists" were held in Uzbekistan in late September, 3 of the 15 defendants were citizens of Kyrgyzstan.

Some of their testimony, greatly questioned by international rights groups, claimed they had received training, weapons, and money in Kyrgyzstan and that their extremist group had a branch in Osh. Kyrgyz officials denied this, but some media, including Kyrgyz media, were already warning about the growing problem with radical Islamic groups in the Kyrgyz section of the Fergana Valley.

As part of the Shanghai Cooperation Organization (SCO) along with Russia, China, Kazakhstan, Tajikistan, and Uzbekistan, Kyrgyzstan was put at the center of a controversy in July. The SCO demanded that the U.S.-led coalition operating in Afghanistan set a date for withdrawing from Central Asian countries where they were using military bases. One of those bases is at Manas airport, Bishkek's international airport. Another of those bases was at Khanabad in southern Uzbekistan. After the SCO summit, the Uzbek government, smarting over U.S. criticism of the Andijan events, ordered those coalition troops off its territory. By the end of 2005, operations from the last base in Tajikistan were scaling down, leaving the Manas air base (called Ganci by coalition troops) as the only significant coalition base in Central Asia and the center of the dispute between the SCO and the U.S.-led coalition. President Bakiyev said in December that Kyrgyzstan would raise the $2 million-per-year rent for coalition use of the Manas base by 100 times.

On November 24, a two-day conference was held on constitutional reforms. The conference was organized by the Kyrgyz Office of the President, the Kyrgyz Parliament, the Venice Commission, the United Nations Development Program, and the OSCE/ODIHR. A 289-member Constitutional Conference was already at work since the events of March, but reports at year's end indicated there were at least nine versions of the amendments. President Bakiyev, who initially championed the idea of constitutional reforms, changed his stance in December, calling for putting the matter off until 2009. Bakiyev wanted to push forward with economic reforms and said, "The existing Constitution was adopted two years ago, and it is too early to say that this Constitution is bad."

Electoral Process

1997	1998	1999	2001	2002	2003	2004	2005	2006
5.00	5.00	5.00	5.75	5.75	6.00	6.00	6.00	5.75

Compared with its Central Asian neighbors, Kyrgyzstan has held the most democratic elections since all became independent after the 1991 collapse of the Soviet Union. But international observers such as the OSCE/ODIHR have never judged any of the country's elections as meeting international democratic standards. Referendums in Kyrgyzstan increased the power of the executive branch and transformed the Parliament from the unicameral Supreme Soviet to a bicameral legislature (1995 and 2000) and then back into a unicameral body again in 2005. Though a handful of opposition figures won seats in the Parliament in 1995 and 2000, they were a minority in a body that was rarely able to influence presidential decisions. The new leadership of Kyrgyzstan vowed to carry out constitutional reforms to better distribute power among the government branches and provide for free and fair elections.

As the year started, there were more than 40 registered political parties and movements in Kyrgyzstan (more than in all the rest of Central Asia), but only about one-third of these were active. In the 2005 parliamentary elections, many of the problems international rights groups complained about during previous polls were again evident. One of the first indications that the parliamentary election might not be free and fair came on January 6. Roza Otunbayeva, former foreign minister and ambassador to the United States and founder one month earlier of the opposition Ata-Jurt (Fatherland) movement, attempted to register as a candidate in a Bishkek district. Otunbayeva was registered, then just hours later her registration was revoked. The reason given was the constitutional requirement, approved in the 2003 referendum, that anyone wishing to compete in public elections must have "permanently resided in the Republic for no less than 5 years prior to the election." Otunbayeva had worked as the assistant special representative of the UN secretary-general to Georgia (in Abkhazia) in 2002-2003. Adding to suspicion over the decision was the fact that the district in which the popular Otunbayeva wished to run was the same district where Bermet Akayeva, daughter of President Akayev, was a candidate. Other former ambassadors, recently returned and also intending to compete in elections, were refused on the same grounds.

A campaign sideshow developed as the Legislative Assembly (lower house of the Parliament) debated the restriction. On January 18, an amendment to lift the residency restriction failed to pass for lack of a quorum but succeeded two days later. Yet on January 26, presidential press secretary Abdil Segizbayev said the Legislative Assembly broke procedure and that the names of several lawmakers who were not present during the vote appeared on the list of those backing the bill. The same day, the Speaker of the Legislative Assembly, Abdygany Erkebayev, said the deputies should not have voted on the bill two days after it failed to pass, citing a recently passed law stating that a bill rejected by deputies cannot be reconsidered for six months. Central Election Commission chairman Sulaiman Imanbayev echoed Erkebayev's comments two days later, also criticizing Erkebayev for allowing the second vote to take place. In the end, none of the former ambassadors were allowed to run.

On January 18, Edil Baisalov, president of the NGO For Democracy and Civil Society, complained about the selection of people for district election commissions. Baisalov said representatives of two pro-government parties – Alga Kyrgyzstan (Bermet Akayeva's party) and Adilet – dominated the leadership of district commissions.

Other opposition candidates were denied registration or had problems getting registered. On February 22, some 3,000 people in the village of Kochkor (Naryn province) protested a decision barring two opposition candidates by blocking the highway. The same day in the northeastern Issyk-Kul province, some 2,500 protesters blocked the road to protest the refusal to register two popular candidates running in separate districts (Tong and Tyup). Also that day, police in Osh closed down the local campaign headquarters of Kurmanbek Bakiyev, and about 500 protesters turned out to demonstrate. Except for a brief lifting of the blockade in Naryn province, the roads stayed blocked through the elections. The poll could not be held in one of the Issyk-Kul districts because of the protests.

The day after elections, the OSCE Election Observation Mission released its preliminary report finding that "these elections were more competitive than previous ones, but sadly this was undermined by vote buying, de-registration of candidates, interference with media, and a worryingly low confidence in judicial and electoral institutions on the part of voters and candidates."[8] That day in the southern Osh province, there were protests in the Nooken district involving some 4,000 people and another demonstration in the Aravan district involving some 5,000 people. All through March, protests spread through the country and local administration buildings were seized and occupied by protesters, but there appeared to be little, if any, coordination of these events by opposition leaders until the very end.

The unrest culminated in the events of March 24. Kurmanbek Bakiyev was named acting prime minister the next day. Ar-Namys leader Feliks Kulov, once seen as Akayev's strongest challenger and jailed on corruption charges in 2000, was freed from prison and joined the new government. At first Kulov, a longtime Interior Ministry official, worked to rein in the lawlessness that gripped parts of Bishkek in the wake of Akayev's ouster. Kulov and Bakiyev agreed not to compete with each other but instead formed a "tandem" that lasted through the year. Despite reports in the Kyrgyz media in the last months of 2005 that the two were growing apart, both Bakiyev and Kulov continued to deny there were any serious differences between them.

The events of March necessitated a new presidential election, so the already scheduled October poll was moved forward to July 10. Given the events of March, Bakiyev needed, and received, an overwhelming mandate from voters to remain head of state. Of the roughly 75 percent of voters who cast ballots, nearly 89 percent voted for Bakiyev, assuring his formal legitimacy. The OSCE preliminary assessment of that poll said it made "tangible progress." But it continued that while the poll was "for the most part free of serious problems...the quality of the process deteriorated during the vote-counting and the results-tabulation phases." Some politicians inside and outside Kyrgyzstan also questioned such a landslide victory.

Civil Society

1997	1998	1999	2001	2002	2003	2004	2005	2006
4.50	4.50	4.50	4.50	4.50	4.50	4.50	4.50	4.50

Since independence, Kyrgyzstan has exhibited the most vibrant civil society among all Central Asian states. The events of March 2005 demonstrated how active social organizations are in the country. NGOs played key roles in the events leading up to March 24 and continued to do so throughout the year. These groups represented widely divergent points of view.

As with political parties in Kyrgyzstan, there were both pro-government and opposition NGOs and social groups prior to the events of March. Kyrgyzstan's laws ban extremist or intolerant NGOs. The country is mainly Muslim but still has a sizable Eastern Orthodox population despite the emigration of many thousands of Slavic peoples since 1991. Kyrgyzstan is also home to more than 80 ethnic groups, and a strong clan system still exists.

There is evidence of a growing presence of Islamic fundamentalist groups in the southern provinces. There were incursions into southern Kyrgyzstan by militants from the Islamic Movement of Uzbekistan in the summers of 1999 and 2000, but the group's goal was the overthrow of the Uzbek government. The area around Osh, in particular, seemed to be increasingly frequented by suspect Islamic groups. The group Hizb ut-Tahrir, for example, is banned across Central Asia. Thousands of alleged members are in Uzbekistan's prisons, hundreds in Tajikistan's, and some in Kazakhstan's and Kyrgyzstan's. But the Kyrgyzstan ombudsman, Tursunbai Bakir Uulu, has called for legalizing and registering the group, a fact that explains why, allegedly, some of the group distributed Bakir Uulu campaign leaflets prior to the presidential elections.

Toward the end of the year, there was a campaign by a group called the Headquarters for the Protection of the State Language to strip Russian of its official status in Kyrgyzstan. The Kyrgyz government under Akayev had made great efforts to convince the Slavic population not to leave the country, which is one of the reasons the Russian language enjoyed such a privileged status. President Bakiyev spoke out against any change to the language's status.

It was not difficult for most opposition social groups to be registered under Akayev. NGOs and nonprofit groups are limited more by finances than by government interference. Also, as is true with Kyrgyzstan's political organizations, the sheer number of NGOs prevents any one organization from gaining much influence. Foreign NGOs obviously have a financial advantage here, but after the "colored revolutions" in Georgia and Ukraine, in which foreign NGOs were alleged to have played key roles, foreign NGOs in Kyrgyzstan were under suspicion at the start of 2005. As was equally true in Georgia and Ukraine with the so-called revolutions, in Kyrgyzstan those who came to power seemed to share that view and did nothing to obstruct the work of these outside groups.

The legal rights of such groups also seemed to be fairly well protected. The court systems have been used against opposition figures and independent media, but rarely has an NGO or nonprofit group come before the courts.

Independent Media

1997	1998	1999	2001	2002	2003	2004	2005	2006
5.00	5.00	5.00	5.00	5.75	6.00	6.00	5.75	5.75

The independent media were possibly the biggest facilitators of the events of March, publishing widely read reports on Prime Minister Tanayev's alleged secret meeting and news about the problems faced by opposition candidates. President Bakiyev campaigned on ending state subsidies to media and making all media outlets in the country independent. Modest steps toward that goal were made at the end of 2005, but there were signs that the new authorities would be no more patient toward some reporting than the previous regime.

The line between the former pro-government media and those outlets considered independent was blurred after the events of March. The pro-government media continued to produce positive stories about matters of state, except now the leadership was the former opposition, who were already supported, generally speaking, by the country's independent media.

In the first weeks after the events of March, the euphoria among the people influenced the way the country's media treated stories. For state media, that meant the rioters and unruly protesters of days before were suddenly patriots ousting an unpopular regime. Opposition media naturally trumpeted the success of the opposition in a long struggle against an unfair and corrupt government.

The new leadership has had no time to bask in its surprising success. The violence in Uzbekistan's eastern city of Andijan and the refugee problem that followed strained ties between Kyrgyzstan and Uzbekistan. International condemnation of the Uzbek government's methods of restoring order in Andijan helped earn refugee status from the UNHCR for many of those who fled Andijan. In late July, amid objections and criticism from the Uzbek government, the UNHCR oversaw the evacuation of 439 refugees to Romania. In September, Uzbek deputy prosecutor general Anvar Nabiyev accused Kyrgyz authorities of showing too much tolerance toward extremist organizations.

When three members of Parliament were murdered, allegations of criminal ties to government surfaced and were further supported by the October prison riots. Protests and demonstrations continued after the events of March, some demanding the dismissal of government officials, some calling for dismissed officials to be reinstated, some calling for access to land, and others demanding that the murders of state and local officials and businessmen be solved.

Kyrgyz media reported on all these issues, and by September the reporting of some media outlets had aggravated the new president. The president's press office released a statement saying that "some media outlets have recently launched a new round of propaganda to discredit the new authorities, which is openly timed to coincide with the formation of a new government." The statement blamed Akayev loyalists, saying that "the supporters of the previous regime can not resign themselves to the convincing victory of the new democratic forces in the presidential elections and the process of political reform nearing its logical completion, and therefore they are making another desperate attempt to destabilize the situation in the country."

In early December, some 20 people entered the independent television station Pyramida, claiming they were the new owners and had plans to switch the station's format from news and information to purely entertainment. The station had aired critical reports about Bakiyev and the Kyrgyz government. Human rights activists and parliamentary deputy Kabai Karabekov led a group of some 100 people to chase out the intruding group. Days later, Bakiyev ordered an investigation into the affair.

Kyrgyzstan's new leadership is therefore faced with the same problem Akayev's regime had – how much media criticism is too much? At what point does it so undermine confidence in government officials or hurt state policy that measures must be taken? Bakiyev wants a country with a 100 percent independent media, but recent examples of corruption in government and ties to organized crime raise suspicions about who would have the money to finance independent media outlets and how they might use such a resource to promote their own interests. The Kyrgyz leadership is aware of the Russian government's experience with businessmen such as Boris Berezovsky, Vladimir Gusinsky, and Mikhail Khodorkovsky, who the Kremlin claimed were using their media outlets to further their personal political interests.

By the end of 2005, the Kyrgyz government was in no position to relinquish all controls over the media established under Akayev. Still, Bakiyev did make an effort to start the process when he ordered the privatization of state newspapers *Kyrgyz Tusuu* and *Slovo Kyrgyzstana* and several local newspapers in December. However, the government may still be forced to start imposing Akayev-era restrictions and censorship on the media to prevent losing support and risking more civil unrest.

Use of the Internet continued to be restricted by finances and access more than by any conscious effort of authorities to curtail or monitor the medium. Large cities in Kyrgyzstan have Internet cafes, and their charges, at least in Bishkek, were reportedly dropping. It was also possible to secure Internet connections in homes, with some providers offering a monthly pass costing the equivalent of US$10 for Internet access between 6:00 p.m and 8:00 a.m. NGOs have also been providing free Internet access, especially to students.

Though the government does not monitor Internet sites, this is partly because of a lack of funds for such a special service. Internet users in Kyrgyzstan have wide access to Web sites and at the end of 2005 could, if they wished, visit pro-Akayev Web sites. However, most of the population is rurally based and does not have the money, or often the electricity, to make use of the Internet, even if they could afford a computer.

Local Democratic Governance

1997	1998	1999	2001	2002	2003	2004	2005	2006
n/a	n/a	n/a	n/a	n/a	n/a	n/a	5.75	6.25

The Kyrgyz Constitution provides only the most basic guidelines for local governance. Only two articles (76 and 77) deal with "local state administration." Local administrations are naturally bound to uphold the country's Constitution, though the heads of these administrations, whether they are governors or *akims* (mayors), are not elected but usually chosen for their loyalty to the president or because they can obey orders from the capital. Kyrgyzstan is more than 90 percent mountainous, and communications among regions, especially between north and south, are not good. Therefore, local officials not only have to be trustworthy, they must be able to react to problems quickly and independently, as help may be a long time coming.

In the run-up to parliamentary elections, it was clear that links between the capital and regions and towns had broken down. Local officials simply allowed unsanctioned protests to happen, and in cases where crowds stormed local administration buildings, officials fled the area if they could (some in the south were briefly held by demonstrators).

The slaying of Deputy Bayaman Erkinbayev in September demonstrated the links between criminal figures and some local politicians. Erkinbayev had large interests in the Kara-Suu bazaar and owned a hotel in Osh. He was a member of Parliament from the area, and would be expected to have beeen well acquainted with the local officials there. The latter clearly turned a blind eye to Erkinbayev's business dealings.

The new government has not had the opportunity to address problems with local governance; in fact, most of the officials placed by President Akayev remained at their posts during 2005 under President Bakiyev. Changes at the provincial and local levels seemed inevitable at the end of 2005, but the new government was officially sworn into office only on December 20.

Judicial Framework and Independence

1997	1998	1999	2001	2002	2003	2004	2005	2006
4.50	4.50	5.00	5.25	5.25	5.50	5.50	5.50	5.50

As 2005 drew to a close, the new leadership stated its intention to radically amend the Constitution and change the balance of power gradually from a presidential to a parliamentary form of government and hopefully embrace a truly independent judiciary. In reality, however, the country continued to operate under the legal guidelines of the previous regime. According to the Constitution, the judicial branch of government is independent. In actuality, it has almost always worked in favor of the authorities, both during Akayev's period as president and through the end of 2005 under Bakiyev and his government.

Under former president Akayev, the judicial system was the primary means of silencing government critics. Though it is constitutionally a separate branch of government, in practice its decisions seemed to support the administration. Opposition politicians, journalists, and newspapers were often fined, jailed, or shut down. The man who became prime minister after the events of March, Feliks Kulov, also seen as Akayev's leading challenger, was in jail serving a lengthy prison term for abuse of office when Akayev was chased from power. The opposition newspaper *Moya Stolitsa Novosti* was facing four lawsuits during the campaigning for parliamentary elections, one of them filed by President Akayev.[9] Former foreign minister Roza Otunbayeva was barred from competing in the February-March parliamentary election and took her appeal unsuccessfully all the way to the Supreme Court.

After the events of March, the court system switched sides. Former opposition figures, now the country's leaders, were acquitted of past convictions. An appeal by Bermet Akayeva to regain her lost seat in the Parliament was rejected. A warrant was put out for the arrest of her husband, Adil Toigonbayev, a citizen also of Kazakhstan, who was in charge of supplying the U.S.-led coalition base at Manas with fuel. Kyrgyz prosecutors alleged that he embezzled much of the money made from this deal. An investigation was launched against Aidar Akayev, son of the former president and MP, and there was a move among some former opposition politicians, notably former acting prosecutor general Azimbek Beknazarov, to lift former President Akayev's constitutional immunity from investigation or prosecution.

On December 18, Kyrgyzstan's Kabar news agency reported that the Office of the Prosecutor General had documents showing that Akayev, his family, and his friends stole some 400 million som and US$20.2 million from the state. Former prime minister Tanayev returned to Kyrgyzstan on August 22 to answer questions, was caught trying to cross the border into Kazakhstan in early September, and was placed under house arrest "at night" in Bishkek. He may also face charges despite what he claims were guarantees made ahead of his return that he would not be put on trial or imprisoned. Notably, the former chairman of the CEC, Sulaiman Imanbayev, was acquitted of charges of abuse of office in November.

Corruption

1997	1998	1999	2001	2002	2003	2004	2005	2006
n/a	n/a	6.00	6.00	6.00	6.00	6.00	6.00	6.00

Corruption has always been one of Kyrgyzstan's biggest problems, but the change in power in March brought the issue out into the open. The killing of the three parliamentary deputies with alleged ties to criminal organizations highlighted the problem. Connections between state officials and such criminal organizations became impossible to ignore or deny. Following the killing of Bayaman Erkinbayev, the second deputy murdered in 2005, President Bakiyev told a session of the Parliament there was ample evidence to suggest that many of the lawmakers were tied to criminal groups. In late November, National Security Service chief Tashtemir Aitbayev alleged Erkinbayev's murder was connected to narcotics trafficking.[10]

More disturbing were the stories appearing in the media that some in the new leadership were also tied to criminal groups. Stories emerged that the events of March were partially funded by criminal groups, or at least that some underworld figures used their local influence to start or support protests in their regions. The number of people at demonstrations – who were obviously paid protesters, at times bused in from other areas of the country both before and after the events of March – could be seen as supporting such accusations.

President Bakiyev denied having any such ties, and no stories about government-criminal relations ever mentioned Bakiyev. But the deaths of the deputies and comments like that made by Ramazan Dyryldayev from the Kyrgyz Human Rights Commission – that criminal groups in the country supported the events of March in return for Kyrgyzstan's aluminum and gold reserves – focused attention on a government that already was dealing with an overload of priority tasks.

The killing of Deputy Tynychbek Akmatbayev during a prison riot in October brought an entirely new side of systemic corruption to light. The riot at the Moldovanka prison spread to other penitentiaries, thanks to inmates having access to cell phones and e-mail. At Moldovanka, the authorities inexplicably ordered all guards and other staff to leave the facility. Interior Ministry troops and police ringed the prison for more than a day before guards returned. Not unexpectedly, prisoners took the opportunity presented by the absence of any law enforcement officials to arm themselves, and this required a forceful and deadly reentry into the prison by guards.

It then came to light that one notorious criminal incarcerated in that prison occupied 16 rooms on the top floors and that his opulent lifestyle and ability to continue his illegal dealings was little affected by being imprisoned.

The new government necessarily started to address the issue. On October 22, President Bakiyev signed a decree creating a National Agency for the Prevention of Corruption and a National Council for the Struggle Against Corruption. But the new Kyrgyz authorities were still trying to uncover the corruption of the previous regime, investigating former president Akaycv and his family and friends, while at the same time being forced to confront the fact that some of the new government officials were also involved in illegal activity.

The publicity around these events had a trickle-down effect. In early December, highway police went on strike over alleged corruption by their boss, Raimkul Kasymbek. Kasymbek responded that it was the highway police who were corrupt and merely angry at his recent introduction of a limit on how long police could stop minivans making the long runs between cities. Kasymbek said his insistence that such document checks be done quickly prevented highway police from having sufficient time to collect bribes.

Bruce Pannier has been covering events in Central Asia for Radio Free Europe/Radio Liberty since 1997. Since 1990, he has been a frequent visitor to the region.

---

[1] International Crisis Group, Kyrgyzstan: A Faltering State (Bishkek, Brussels, 16 December 2005)
[2] RFE/RL, Kyrgyz Law Makers to Carry Arms (Bishkek, 23 September 2005), Itar-Tass, Deputies of the Kyrgyz Parliament Will Now Walk With Weapons (23 September 2005)
[3] OSCE, Statement of Preliminary Findings and Conclusions (International Election Observation Mission, Presidential Election, The Kyrgyz Republic, 11 July 2005)
[4] Itar-Tass, Bakiyev Calls For Changing The Term For Conducting Constitutional Reforms in Kyrgyzstan (15 December 2005), RFE/RL, Kyrgyz President Against Hasty Reforms (15 December 2005)
[5] AKIpress, K. BakiyevOn Corruption And Criminality: It's Not Possible to Eradicate Corruption In Half A Year. (22 September 2005), Bruce Pannier, Kyrgyz Lawmaker Murdered in Apparent Mafia-Related Shooting (RFE/RL, 22 September 2005)
[6] Interfax, Supporters Of Ex-Kyrgyz Leaders Want Destabilization - President (29, September 2005)
[7] Itar-Tass, Insurrectionists in Andijan Planned To Blow Up The KAmchik Tunnel – Prosecutor General of Uzbekistan (15 September 2005) AKIpress, Prosecutor General of Uzbekistan – Weapons and Military Equipment Bought in Kyrgyzstan (15 September 2005)
[8] Itar-Tass, Associated Press, Interfax (28 February 2005)
[9] Akayev was suing Moya Stolitsa the independent paper for publishing defamatory words about property belonging to him and his family.
[10] Interfax, Agence France Press (29 November 2005)

Latvia

Capital:	Riga
Population:	2.3 million
GNI/capita:	$5,580
Ethnic Groups:	Latvian (57%), Russian (30%), Belorusian (4%), Ukrainian (3%), Polish (3%), other (3%)

Nations in Transit Ratings and Averaged Scores

	1997	1998	1999	2001	2002	2003	2004	2005	2006
Electoral Process	2.00	2.00	1.75	1.75	1.75	1.75	1.75	1.75	1.75
Civil Society	2.25	2.25	2.25	2.00	2.00	2.00	2.00	1.75	1.75
Independent Media	1.75	1.75	1.75	1.75	1.75	1.75	1.50	1.50	1.50
Governance *	2.50	2.50	2.50	2.25	2.25	2.25	2.25	n/a	n/a
National Democratic Governance	n/a	n/a	n/a	n/a	n/a	n/a	n/a	2.25	2.00
Local Democratic Governance	n/a	n/a	n/a	n/a	n/a	n/a	n/a	2.50	2.50
Judicial Framework and Independence	2.25	2.25	2.00	2.00	2.00	2.25	2.00	1.75	1.75
Corruption	n/a	n/a	3.50	3.50	3.75	3.50	3.50	3.50	3.25
Democracy Score	2.15	2.15	2.29	2.21	2.25	2.25	2.17	2.14	2.07

* With the 2005 edition, Freedom House introduced seperate analysis and ratings for national democratic governance and local democratic governance to provide readers with more detailed and nuanced analysis of these two important subjects.

NOTE: The ratings reflect the consensus of Freedom House, its academic advisers, and the author of this report. The opinions expressed in this report are those of the author. The ratings are based on a scale of 1 to 7, with 1 representing the highest level of democratic progress and 7 the lowest. The Democracy Score is an average of ratings for the categories tracked in a given year.

The economic and social data on this page were taken from the following sources:
GNI/capita, Population: *World Development Indicators 2006* (Washington, D.C.: World Bank, 2006).
Ethnic Groups: *CIA World Factbook 2006* (Washington, D.C.: Central Intelligence Agency, 2006).

EXECUTIVE SUMMARY

L atvia, slightly smaller in area than Ireland and situated on the eastern shores of the Baltic Sea, has had a complex and checkered history. After winning independence in 1920, Latvia was able to strengthen its state institutions over two decades of self-rule. Its independence was terminated abruptly during World War II, first by the Soviet occupation from 1940 to 1941, then by the Nazi occupation from 1941 to 1945. From 1945 to 1991, Latvia remained under Soviet control as 1 of 15 republics of the USSR. It was able to declare its independence following the unsuccessful putsch against Soviet president Mikhail Gorbachev on August 21, 1991.

The road to a fuller democracy, a functioning market economy, and an improved civil society has been made much easier by Latvia's historical exposure to two decades of independence, which most former Soviet states (other than Estonia and Lithuania) did not experience. After a decade of improvements, often supported by world organizations and prosperous neighboring countries, Latvia has reached a much more secure level of "normalization" reflected by greater stability and predictability in economics, politics, and civil society. Yet problems brought about by these revolutionary changes persist.

The pessimism of the immediate post-independence period in Latvia has waned, but a new polarization between the growing middle class and those who have not been able to partake in the economic upsweep has resulted in tensions and discontent. Riga and other larger urban areas have experienced a disproportional share of this new prosperity, leaving rural areas, particularly in southeast Latvia, in painful economic doldrums. The stresses and strains of an unaccustomed market economy and the burden of welfare now resting on individual shoulders have created widespread anxiety and wistful nostalgia for a past when life was less complicated. Only 60 percent of Latvia's inhabitants indicated in a fall 2005 Eurobarometer survey that they were satisfied with life, compared with an average of 80 percent for all European Union (EU) member states. In June 2004, 63 percent claimed that 15 years earlier, when Latvia was ruled by the Communist Party, their "material situation" was better. At the same time, only a tiny fraction would want to return to a Communist regime.

Great expectations for economic growth and security have been raised by Latvia's entry into the EU on May 1, 2004, and its membership in NATO in March. Latvia is slowly becoming accustomed to being part of a larger, more prosperous community and to being militarily secure. Over 50,000 people from Latvia have made use of the recently-opened borders to find work in other EU countries, and 26 percent of those polled are considering working abroad.[1]

The increasing awareness of the value of nongovernmental organizations (NGOs) as well as liberal Internet access to all types of government information have slowly built a sense of democracy and a more informed electorate. The highly competitive Latvian mass media are proving to be reliable sources of information and watchdogs against governmental abuses of power, and Latvia's political system functions well despite a perpetual series of coalition governments. The continuity and regal character of the presidency have made this position one of the pillars of political stability.

The economy continued to develop at a dynamic pace, reaching a gross national product (GNP) growth rate of 10.2 percent in 2005 and thus continuing the growth rate of previous years. Latvia's international credit ratings were raised to the "A" level for certain loan categories. By all standard economic measures, Latvia is a success story of post-Communist evolution; nevertheless, some problems persist – chiefly corruption, poverty, and relations between citizens and noncitizens over language and other issues.

National Democratic Governance. On May 1, 2004, Latvia became a member of the EU and can participate with other democratic regimes in setting common parameters and standards. The republic is receiving substantial aid from the EU, which is helping to raise the efficiency and public responsiveness of the state service. In contrast with the situation in 2004, in 2005 the four-party coalition government was relatively stable. There is a broad consensus on most areas of policy among the main governmental parties, which can best be categorized as center right. As in most parliamentary democracies, the Cabinet of Ministers initiates about 70 percent of all legislation and sets the agenda for voting. The Parliament, however, can and does modify legislation and at times has taken independent action. The public can access agendas and protocols of the meetings of the cabinet, the cabinet committees, and joint meetings of the state secretaries of ministries, who are the highest civil servants. The general public also has access to the spending details of individual ministries. The new Law on Civil Service passed in 2001 has resulted in better service and administration. *The national democratic governance rating improves from 2.25 to 2.00 owing to the government's stability.*

Electoral Process. Latvia is a parliamentary democracy, with elections to the 100-member Parliament held every four years. The most recent parliamentary elections took place in October 2002 and were considered by the Organization for Security and Cooperation in Europe (OSCE) to have achieved a "clear entrenchment of the democratic election process." In 2004, Latvia voted to elect 9 deputies to the 732-member European Parliament. Turnout was relatively low at 41.2 percent, which was somewhat better than the average of 26.4 percent for the new democracies that recently joined the EU. The elections were considered to be fair, and no irregularities were reported. Municipal elections in 530 constituencies in March 2005 went smoothly, but voter participation was down to 52.8 percent, a drop from 62 percent in 2001. *Latvia's electoral process rating remains at 1.75.*

Civil Society. The activity and visibility of NGOs in Latvia continued into 2005. In part, this has happened as a result of the growing democratic maturity of the society, but certain events and appointments have also acted as catalysts for NGO resurgence. Membership in the EU and the possibility of funding from this source has spurred many civil society groups to become more organized and cooperative with other groups and specialists. *Latvia's civil society rating remains at 1.75.*

Independent Media. Latvian mass media have remained diverse, competitive, and buoyant. The ownership of certain media, however, is still nontransparent, leading to allegations that these outlets are controlled by oligarchs. Although there are two distinct linguistic media communities, there is some overlap of audiences, especially in broadcasting. Many people also have access to television programs from other EU countries. *Latvia's independent media rating remains at 1.50.*

Local Democratic Governance. Latvia is in a quandary with respect to local governments. There are over 500 small units, but people are reluctant to amalgamate into larger, purportedly more efficient units proposed by the government and supported by many world organizations and thus lose the personal intimacy of established relationships. Local governments traditionally receive better ratings and higher trust than national structures, but there is a growing gap between the broad array of responsibilities of local governments and their limited financial and human resources. As well, there is a wide gulf between the wealthier and less endowed municipalities, leading to geographic inequity in service provision. *Latvia's local democratic governance rating remains at 2.50.*

Judicial Framework and Independence. The status, pay, and number of judges in Latvia continue to increase. In February 2004, Latvia initiated an administrative court system providing flexible oral or written adjudication of conflicts between the population and tax officials, police officers, welfare assessors, and, indeed, all government structures. This has diverted a significant number of cases from the main legal structures, thus shortening the pretrial waiting period and detention time. Other positive changes include a growing number of courtrooms, the move toward total computerization, public access to court cases, prison reforms, and the respected performance of the Constitutional Court. However, the high incidence of prolonged pretrial detention and partial access to legal aid by the poor for civil cases are ongoing problems. *Latvia's rating for judicial framework and independence remains at 1.75.*

Corruption. Latvia's Corruption Prevention and Combating Bureau has overcome most of its initial problems of leadership, funding, and cohesion, and its authority has improved noticeably in the population and among other state institutions. While allegations are relatively limited about corruption in the middle and lower levels of administration, there are unproved but continuous rumors of backroom deals made by Latvian and Russian oligarchs with top state administrators and politicians. The charges of "state capture" first formulated by the World Bank in 2000 remain unproven and unresolved. *The rating for corruption improves from 3.50* *to 3.25 owing to the Corruption Prevention and Combating Bureau's success in over-coming the initial problems of instability.*

Outlook for 2006. In 2006, Latvia will continue to consolidate its position in the EU and NATO. There is a mood in the country for governmental continuity, and the new four-party coalition ratified on December 2, 2004, could be pressured by public opinion to continue governing until the end of the current Parliament in October 2006. State institutions will continue to function with increased efficiency owing to new EU guidelines and funding. Russian-Latvian relations within the country will experience some buffeting, but there seems to be a will by both sides to lower tensions.

Rapid economic growth in the heartland will create even more discontent in the hinterlands, where stagnation will deepen. More individuals are expected to leave Latvia to work abroad. Many of these, especially Russophones, will not return to Latvia.

MAIN REPORT

National Democratic Governance

1997	1998	1999	2001	2002	2003	2004	2005	2006
n/a	n/a	n/a	n/a	n/a	n/a	n/a	2.25	2.00

The overall success of Latvia's democratic system can be gauged by its inclusion as a full member of the EU and NATO in the spring of 2004. Today, there is no disagreement that Latvia is a democracy. There is, however, disagreement on the quality and comprehensiveness of this democracy. In 2004-2005, a detailed "democratic audit" of Latvia was undertaken by social science and public policy specialists, focusing on multiple facets of democratic governance. Under the initiative of Latvia's president, Vaira Vike-Freiberga, two dozen specialists provided detailed descriptions and assessments of the achievements and weaknesses of the state system in 14 general areas with 75 separate subheadings. Each one of these subheadings was assigned scores based on the previous five years, from "very good" to "very bad."

As part of this study, in October 2004 a leading Latvian polling organization conducted a special survey, which comprised over 70 questions with answers subdivided by ethnicity, gender, age, locality, occupation, and income and was used extensively by the research specialists to arrive at their final scores. Latvia received a designation of "satisfactory" in 35 cases, "very good" in 2 areas, "good" in 18, "bad" in 16, and "very bad" in 5. The 2 worst areas concerned the ineffectiveness and irresponsibility of the civil service and corruption. The "very good" areas included high voting rates and competitive elections. The report, entitled *How Democratic Is Latvia: Audit of Democracy*, together with polling tables, is available in English at www.policy.lv.

In spite of the historical tradition of mild dictatorship between 1934 and 1940, and Soviet one-party rule, the vast majority of individuals in Latvia are strongly supportive of the present Constitution, which incorporates the basic requirements of democracy, popular elections, and citizenship and human rights. However, many people are not fully satisfied with the way actual democracy functions in Latvia. There is a significant and disturbing divergence between the Latvian and Russian populations in this regard, with other nationalities generally positioned between the two. According to the democratic audit poll, 68.4 percent of Latvians, but only 32.4 percent of Russians and 40.4 percent of others, agreed that the last parliamentary elections in October 2002 were free.[2] Similar ethnic divisions can be seen in the trust accorded by Latvians, Russians, and others to various institutions.

Expressed Trust in Latvia's Institutions in %, October 2004[3]

	Latvians	Russians	Others
President	73.1	37.1	47.2
Saeima (Parliament)	26.2	14.8	19.1
Local Government	57.6	31.1	44.9
National Government	28.9	18.2	22.5
Police	46.7	34.6	42.7
Armed Forces	63.4	39.0	55.1
Courts	40.0	27.4	36.0
Political Parties	10.6	9.4	12.4
Television	72.4	56.9	62.9
Press	66.9	46.9	59.6
Church	55.5	62.3	70.8
Commonwealth of Independent States	17.3	29.9	24.7
UN	44.9	26.4	30.3
EU	44.5	26.4	28.1
NATO	51.8	17.6	18.0

Russians and others indicated a higher level of trust in the church and the Commonwealth of Independent States, an organization of which Latvia is not a member. This divergence has many possible causes. The main source of discontent concerns the lack of citizenship for 42 percent of Russians living in Latvia.[4] The problem of citizenship is slowly moving in the right direction, however. Between 1995 and 2005, the proportion of non-citizens has decreased from 29 to 19 percent and over 105,000 people have been granted Latvian citizenship through the naturalization process.

Latvia's Parliament (Saeima) is not well structured for regularized dialogue with voters. Individual deputies are not responsible for a specific geographic area, as is the case in North America and many European states; hence people do not have a local representative office where they can air their problems and seek assistance. Indeed, this absence of parliamentary "mini-ombudsmen" is a problem in all countries entirely dependent on proportional elections. Another problem is the relatively underdeveloped lobbying structure in the country. Lobbying for one's own interests is still seen as selfish, unethical, and generally associated in the public's mind with corruption. Parliamentarians, however, are able to gauge the popular will through a very active media and through increasingly vocal professional and ethnic associations.

Moreover, new channels for participation in decision making have been created. Since June 2001, NGO representatives can officially attend meetings of the state secretaries in the Chancellery of the Cabinet, where new policy ideas, legal initiatives, and information about future proposals are discussed, vetted, and sent to respective ministries for further input. A memorandum on cooperation between NGOs and the cabinet was signed by Prime Minister Aigars Kalvitis on June 15, 2005. The objective of the memorandum as stated in its preamble is to "ensure involvement of civil society in the decision-making process at all levels and stages in public administration, thus promoting development of the basic elements of a democratic country." NGOs are provided with contact persons and telephone numbers in all departments and can ask to participate at a cabinet session to discuss a particular issue.

The Latvian government has made significant strides in providing public access to various state documents. These include Internet access to proposed legislation and to the agendas of the Parliament, the cabinet, state secretaries, cabinet committees, and parliamentary committees. Likewise, anyone can access the financial data of all ministries. Transcripts of parliamentary sessions and protocols of the cabinet and cabinet committee meetings are also available online. The Parliament has a vast support system of specialists and research librarians. Deputies can hire helpers and have access to the state-financed offices of their respective political parties.

Unfortunately, not all deputies have offices, and few of them have the ability to contact their electorate within Latvia's five broad electoral districts. Investigations can be carried out by parliamentary committees, which are empowered to call ministers and others to testify. Deputies receive a basic salary calculated on the basis of 3.2 times the average salary in state institutions. Additional pay is received for attending parliamentary committees and for housing and transportation for those living outside Riga. Attendance at parliamentary sessions is helped by the deduction of 20 percent of one's monthly salary for any nonapproved absence.[5]

Legislative initiative, however, appears to have increasingly become a prerogative of the cabinet and its ministries. In the sixth Parliament, this institution introduced 53 percent of all bills. In the seventh Parliament, the cabinet accounted for 65 percent. In the current eighth Parliament (until June 22, 2005), the cabinet introduced 73 percent of all draft legislation. This reflects a growing centralization and heightened executive power.

The judiciary is independent of direct government pressure once the Parliament confirms a judge's candidacy. However, judges are dependent on the Ministry of Justice for their wages, administrative support, offices, and instructions on new laws and procedures.

In the Latvian political system, the president functions as head of state and has the power to appoint the prime minister and veto legislation. However, vetoed legislation can be signed after a repeat majority vote in the Parliament. As for President Vike-Freiberga, her major contributions lie in her continuity, political neutrality, and high popular rating. That said, her criticisms of political and judicial matters are taken seriously.

The Latvian Constitution is a major check on governmental power, and the creation of a separate Constitutional Court in 1996 focused the best legal minds on the defense of constitutional rights. Their judgments have been wide-ranging and have garnered a high level of trust from officials and the entire population. According to polls, the Constitutional Court is considered one of the most trustworthy institutions in Latvia and, indeed, has helped diminish popular cynicism about the Latvian system of power. A new law has allowed for the suing of state organs for compensation of losses incurred by their actions or inactions. The new system of administrative courts is focused on resolving clashes between inhabitants and various state bodies.

In general, Latvia's government does not interfere in the economy except to set the broad parameters of monetary and fiscal policy. There is as yet no consensus with respect to the privatization of certain large industries in which the government holds the majority or a large proportion of shares.

The political system in 2005 was surprisingly stable, without any changes of government and minimal shifts in the cabinet. This is in contrast with the situation in 2004, when three separate governments were formed, led by Einars Repse (until March 9), Indulis Emsis (until December 2), and Aigars Kalvitis (from December on). Indeed, since independence Latvia has had 12 different governments with 10 different prime ministers. The relative calm of the current coalition in large measure reflects pressure from the population and its disgust and weariness at the perceived gamesmanship of their elected representatives.

In addition, the current prime minister, Aigars Kalvitis, has with few exceptions had a calming effect on the cabinet because of his desire to maintain a stable coalition. Kalvitis is a relatively young individual, born in 1966, who has worked in Sweden and studied in Ireland and the United States (University of Wisconsin). He has an MA degree in agricultural economics and before becoming prime minister was minister of economics and minister of agriculture. He is a member of the People's Party. Prior to December 2, 2004, the current four-party coalition worked hard to outline a common position on legislative goals and priorities, concluding with a 21-page detailed document. Indeed, all four parties are divided less by ideologies than by personalities, since all four are moderately right of center.

The civil service in Latvia has been subject to many attempts at reform. The most significant and comprehensive of these has been the Law on State Administration Structure, passed in 2001. The purpose of this law as stated in its preamble is "to secure a democratic, lawful, effective, open, and publicly accessible state administration." The law has tried to make the civil service more "people-friendly."

Although the Law on State Administration Structure is seen as a major upgrade in the role of civil servants and their duties, it does not address municipal civil servants. Likewise, the mechanisms for addressing complaints are not strongly delineated. Because of low salaries, the turnover rate in civil service positions is high, and a large number of able individuals have gone to work in more lucrative private institutions.

Electoral Process

1997	1998	1999	2001	2002	2003	2004	2005	2006
2.00	2.00	1.75	1.75	1.75	1.75	1.75	1.75	1.75

Latvia is a parliamentary democracy, and elections to the 100-member Parliament are held every four years. Deputies are elected proportionally from party lists in five large electoral districts. Only party members determine the ranking of names on the electoral lists, but voters have the right to rearrange the ranking on their chosen party list by adding a plus or minus sign next to the candidates' names. The governing cabinet is made up of individual parliamentary deputies whose seats are filled by the next candidate in line on their respective party list. The president is elected by an absolute majority of parliamentary deputies rather than by the general population.

The OSCE/Office for Democratic Institutions and Human Rights observed the elections to the eighth Parliament on October 5, 2002, and two weeks later issued its assessment and recommendations. According to the report, the election marked "a clear entrenchment of the democratic election process." It was also seen as "well administered and overall conducted in accordance with OSCE commitments and international standards for democratic elections." Voter participation rate was 72 percent of those eligible to vote, continuing a tradition of relatively high turnout observed in previous elections.

In March 2005, Latvia had 62 officially registered political parties.[6] All Latvian political parties have a weak membership base, hence their almost total dependence on expensive media advertising. Indeed, only 0.9 percent of the voting population, or 15,000 people, are party members, giving Latvia one of the lowest participation rates in Europe.[7]

During the 2002 elections, only six parties were able to exceed the 5 percent threshold for representation in the Parliament. However, the leading party, New

Era, gained only 26 out of 100 seats. For Human Rights in a United Latvia received 24 seats, People's Party 21, Latvia's First Party 10, Green and Farmers' Union Party 12, and Fatherland and Freedom 7. The parties not able to surmount the 5 percent barrier gleaned 15.9 percent of the votes. The next national elections will take place in October 2006.

Latvian presidents are chosen for a term of four years by the Parliament and require 51 votes to be elected. In the presidential elections held on June 20, 2003, only one candidate was on the ballot – incumbent president Vike-Freiberga. She was first elected by 53 Parliament deputies in June 1999 and in 2003 received 88 votes of support – 6 deputies opposed.

Latvia joined the EU on May 1, 2004, and became a participant in the third supranational level of elections to choose 9 deputies out of a total of 732 for the European Parliament. Elections were held on June 12. Voter participation was relatively low at 41.23 percent, which, however, is close to the 45.3 percent average for the 25 EU states.

On March 12, 2005, Latvian citizens were able to elect local government representatives in 530 constituencies. Turnout in these elections was 52.85 percent, much lower than the 62 percent rate in March 2001 but a comparatively high rate for local elections throughout the Western world. In many rural constituencies, there were only single slates without any competition. In Jurmala, however, 315 candidates ran to fill 15 seats, and in Riga there were 844 candidates for 60 seats.[8] The executive heads of about a fifth of the local governments were replaced as a result of the new election.

Campaign spending during these elections was monitored by the NGO Providus, which found that three parties had overspent their allowable limit. It should be noted that in all constituencies of over 5,000 people, only registered political organizations may submit candidate lists. The Corruption Prevention and Combating Bureau (KNAB) reviews political party annual reports, which contain lists of financial donors and can fine parties for illegal donations, tardy submission of reports, and improper bookkeeping. They can also initiate deregistration of parties.

In 2005, the KNAB fined 18 parties and started court proceedings against another 15 to terminate their activities as political parties. One of the key features of Latvian national elections is that all registered political parties have 20 minutes of free access to all state-operated television and radio outlets.[9]

Civil Society

1997	1998	1999	2001	2002	2003	2004	2005	2006
2.25	2.25	2.25	2.00	2.00	2.00	2.00	1.75	1.75

NGOs are protected and regulated by the Latvian Constitution, the 1992 legislation "concerning public organizations and their associations," and two new laws on public organizations passed in 2003 and 2004. The new laws required NGOs to reregister by December 31, 2005, in order to provide them with a formal status for state support and tax deductions. There are fears that many organizations will not fulfill the requirements of this new process and will lose their official recognition and accreditation.

At the fall of Communism, Latvia had no experience maintaining independent, self-sustaining organizations. Since 1996, the Danish government, the United Nations Development Program, and the Soros Fund have helped to establish and finance the NGO Center in Riga, which has become an extremely useful resource for legal support, management and leadership training, and networking. Today, the latter two organizations are considered the "owners" of the center, which publishes numerous handbooks, offers courses, and invites experts to address various aspects of group sustainability. Assistance is offered in Latvian, Russian, and English.

According to the NGO Center, which does not generally service church or sports organizations and unions, about 70 percent of civil society activists are women. About 70 percent of NGOs have no permanent staff, and over half have a membership under 30 people. Only 4 percent of groups have more than 500 members, according to the newspaper *Diena*. The NGO Center claims to interact with about 1,000 different NGOs. There are, however, new centers in other cities such as Aluksne, Talsi, and Ventspils. A new NGO center designed to service about 250 minority ethnic organizations was opened on March 26, 2004, in Riga. Another ethnic organization center was opened in Daugavpils in 2005, a project funded by the European Union's Phare program.[10]

The September 2004 polling survey for *How Democratic Is Latvia: Audit of Democracy* indicated that 61.9 percent of the population was not involved in any NGO activities. The participation rate in the various types of organizations did not differ much among ethnic groups. At a time of apparent ethnic turbulence concerning education reform in Russophone schools in 2004 and 2005, participation in ethnic minority organizations was relatively low among Russians (1.9 percent) and others (3.4 percent). Women's groups accounted for 1.5 percent of NGO members among Latvians, 1.6 percent among Russians, and no rating among others.[11] Much inspiration for women's groups has come from international sources, where women's issues are far more prominent and more actively articulated.

Nevertheless, according to *How Democratic Is Latvia*, there is a significant increase in the number and cooperation of women's groups in Latvia. The Coalition of Gender Equality was formed in 2000, and in 2003 the Women's Network of Latvia was founded by 33 groups, which increased to 40 by 2004. It is noteworthy that this coalition is a member of the European Women's Lobby, which claims a membership of over 4,000 organizations throughout the EU.[12] A reflection of the growing presence of women's NGOs can be gauged by the September 2004 adoption of the Program for Implementation of Gender Equality (2005-2006) by the government.

One of the major changes for NGOs in 2005 was the much more active and committed involvement of the Latvian government in supporting the expansion of NGO activities. In February 2005, the government proposed detailed, long-range and middle-term national programs: Basic Outlines Strengthening Civil Society 2005-2014 and Strengthening Civil Society 2005-2009. These programs of group education, motivation, inclusion in decision making, and sustainability have now become the key policy priority of the Ministry of Special Issues and Social Integration. For the first time as well, the ministry has planned to fund NGO activity in 2006. Part of the reason for this funding is the need to facilitate NGO access to EU matching funds programs and grants. The ministry has also engaged a dozen representatives of NGOs as a consultative work group to participate in its regular meetings discussing EU structural funds.

In June 2005, the Latvian government signed a memorandum of cooperation with 50 NGOs, providing the option for other groups to sign and join in this venture. Coordination of this project has been left in the hands of the State Chancellery.[13]

Group activities are becoming increasingly more visible and, with new support from the state, are also becoming more accepted by the general population. Many professions, such as education, medicine, and the police force, have mobilized their members to further their professional interests and increase their salary levels. In spite of existing problems, the depth and breadth of civil society is increasing. Indeed, Latvia has sent its NGO representatives to Georgia, Moldova, and other states of the former Soviet Union to share its experiences in successful NGO and goal attainment.

Financing of civil society activities is still the greatest problem, because private philanthropy has not yet become a tradition. Local communities such as Talsi have been able to mobilize citizens to participate in group activities. In 2005, the Talsi district recorded 181 NGOs with a membership of 2,392 and had published a catalog of all volunteer groups.[14]

Traditional Christian groups of Lutheran, Catholic, and Orthodox members are slowly beginning to conduct charitable activities, but the lack of funding and basic infrastructure and the low percentage of actual congregants (5-6 percent of the population) have limited the scope of their initiatives. In Riga, there are 13 to 15 Jewish organizations and institutions, including a school, hospital, museum, veterans' organization, social aid organization, youth center, and library. All of these are part of the larger Riga Jewish Association.

Approximately 85 nontraditional faith-based organizations have been helped by significant external financing and organizational support. Included are the Jehovah's Witnesses, Mormons, Glad Tidings, New Age, and Hare Krishnas. The activism and Western-supported charity work of these groups have attracted many new members.

In 2005, no group seriously threatened political or social stability in Latvia. However, several incidents created major polarizations in society. The Latvian Legion war veterans who had fought in the German armed forces in World War II were given permission to hold a parade on March 16. Many people, especially Russophones, saw this march as a nostalgic reinforcement of Fascism.

Greater controversy was created in July in Riga by the Gay Pride parade, which was originally allowed and then vetoed by the Riga City Council but on appeal was allowed by the courts. Gays and their supporters were frequently booed and even pelted by bystanders. Most religious leaders and many politicians expressed their opposition to this parade in the media. The Gay Pride procession assembled in the Riga Anglican Church, where a religious service was conducted by Juris Calitis, dean of the Faculty of Theology of the University of Latvia. This sparked acrimonious debates within the Latvian Lutheran Church, where homosexuality has been proclaimed a sin. Consequently, Calitis was expelled from the Latvian synod in November 2005. Some politicians reacted by beginning procedures to enshrine in the Constitution the definition of marriage as between a man and a woman and are planning to use this issue in the October 2006 elections.[15]

Civil society does not mean the absence of conflict or the resolution of all disagreements but, rather, stresses the peaceful resolution of such disagreements. There are broad differences of opinion between Latvians and Russophones. The vast majority of Latvians are opposed to Russian as a second state language (77 percent) and in favor of the educational reforms in Russian schools (76 percent). Among Russophones, 84 percent are in favor of the first item and 68 percent are opposed to the second. In spite of such diametrically opposite positions, there appears to be a certain reserve of goodwill within both groups in the almost unanimous support by Latvians (93 percent) and Russophones (97 percent) of the idea that "we must respect the national culture, religion, and traditions of all groups in Latvia even if these are very different from ours."[16] Two-thirds of Latvians were even willing to allow state support for the protection of different ethnic cultures and traditions.[17]

Independent Media

1997	1998	1999	2001	2002	2003	2004	2005	2006
1.75	1.75	1.75	1.75	1.75	1.75	1.50	1.50	1.50

The Latvian Constitution (Article 100) guarantees freedom of speech; freedom to obtain, keep, and disseminate information; and freedom to proclaim one's opinions. Censorship is forbidden. Sections 91 and 127 of the Latvian criminal code (adopted in 1999) – which carried prison time and severe fines for spreading false information about deputy candidates or defaming state representatives – were challenged successfully in the Constitutional Court in October 2003 by the newspaper *Diena*. With the concurrence of the Parliament in January 2004, criminal liability for the defamation of state officials has now been effectively removed. In June 2003, the Constitutional Court also repealed a law that required 75 percent of broadcasting to be in the Latvian language in any 24-hour period. This repeal means that the language of broadcasting will be determined solely by market considerations. New controversy was raised when legislation was introduced in the Parliament that would have given supervision rights over the media to the Ministry of Culture.

The Latvian media are free to disseminate information and views, limited only by libel considerations and the pressures of the market. Investigative journalists are free to pursue various sensitive topics, including government waste and corruption. The mass media generally enjoy editorial independence, although certain news items may be difficult to obtain from government sources. The leading newspapers readily publish a broad range of opinions from specialists and NGOs. Many newspapers are available free of charge on the Internet. According to Latvian sources from April 2005, 34 percent of the population accesses the Internet.[18] A significant development has been the virtual explosion of Internet use by young people spurred by the "friends network" (draugi.lv), which allows people to place recent photos in a "show and tell" fashion to contact old classmates and correspond with friends of friends. For a relatively taciturn culture, this program has now assembled a surprising 10 percent of the entire Latvian population, or 230,000 participants.[19]

Viewers in Latvia can choose between state-subsidized and privately owned television and radio. In television, the private Latvijas Neatkariga Televizija is the most popular station, with 21.2 percent of viewers, followed by TV3 with 16.3 percent. The state-owned LTV1 has a 11.6 percent share, and LTV7 has a 6.4 percent share. The state TV has regained its audience share after expanding its viewing hours. The viewer share of other stations is as follows: PBK 8.7 percent, TV5 Riga 3.4 percent, and other stations 32.5 percent.[20]

Radio is dominated by state ownership. Latvijas Radio, with its four different services, claimed 48 percent of the total audience in the spring of 2005. Latvijas Radio 2 holds a solid 27 percent; it broadcasts mostly Latvian music, with a sprinkling of English-language country and western. Latvijas Radio 4 broadcasts in Russian and claims 8 percent of the total audience. Software House, with a 16 percent share, is the largest private station. Next in popularity are Star FM and European Hit Radio with 5 percent each.

The most popular daily newspapers as of summer 2005 were *Diena*, *Latvijas Avize*, *Vesti Segodna* and *Chas* (both Russian), *Neatkariga Rita Avize*, and *Vakara Zinas*, according to TNS Latvia, a subsidiary of one of the world's largest market research companies. A Russophone businessman, Valeri Belokon, started a relatively upscale and technically innovative Russian-language daily, *Telegraph*, to provide a more "constructive tone in the Russian press," but the venture has not been lucrative. In 2004, its printed pages diminished from 24 to 16; and in 2005, its share of Russian readership was only 7 percent.[21]

Indeed, both major linguistic groups live in their own media space, and few read or view the other's publications and broadcast media. *Diena* did publish in both languages until 1999 but shut down its Russian-language edition because of a lack of readership. Other newspapers have experienced a similar problem. A 2005 study by the Baltic Institute of Social Sciences, *Ethnopolitical Tension in Latvia: Looking for the Conflict Solution* (available in English on the Internet), analyzed the response to educational reforms by both the Latvian- and Russian-language media. This study concluded that "press publications in Latvian and Russian offer different information, different interpretations of events, and different views. What is more, they are often tendentiously negative vis-□-vis one or the other sociolinguistic group." The study points out that the mass media serve as "organizers and disseminators of ethnopolitical discourse in society."[22] According to this study, there is not much overlap in media readership between the two linguistic groups. This is especially true with regard to newspapers. Thus, the Latvian newspaper *Diena*, which is read regularly by 35 percent of Latvians, is read by only 7 percent of Russians and 8 percent of others. The leading Russian-language newspaper, *Vesti Segodnya*, is read by 24 percent of Russians but by only 3 percent of Latvians. A somewhat less polarized pattern can be seen in broadcasting. Among Latvians, 59 percent listen to radio mostly or only in Latvian, 25 percent listen more frequently in Latvian than Russian, and 10 percent prefer the Russian stations. Among Russians, the equivalent pattern was 53 percent, 25 percent, and 10 percent. In television, there appears to be even more overlap. Among Latvians, the equivalent rates were 43 percent, 42 percent, and 13 percent, and among Russians 49 percent, 35 percent, and 13 percent.[23] In other words, over one-half of each group watches the "other's" programs.

Both local and foreign firms and individuals own a share in the Latvian mass media, but exact ownership patterns are not always transparent. The largest shareholder in *Diena* is the Bonnier Group of Sweden. The privately controlled oil corporation Ventspils Nafta owns three and possibly four of Latvia's daily newspapers. The chief representative of this corporation is Aivars Lembergs, mayor of the city of Ventspils and one of the leading oligarchs of Latvia. Yet who exactly controls *Ventspils Nafta* is publicly unknown. In the Russian media, *Vesti Segodnya* and *Komersant Baltic* are owned by Andrey Kozolv and his mother; however, their assets are mortgaged at the Parex Bank, leading to speculation as to the real influence on these papers. Another publisher of the Russian press is Aleksey Sheinin.[24]

The Bonnier Group, besides controlling *Diena*, has interests in one-third of Latvian regional newspapers as well as the only business daily in Latvian, *Dienas Bizness*, and in the Baltic News Service. It also controls one of the largest media distribution and subscription companies and large printing facilities.[25] Narvessen, a Scandinavian company, controls 60 percent of Latvia's retail publication outlets, having bought out hundreds of independent booths, whereas 80 percent of the press wholesale market is controlled by Preses Tirgus.[26] It is noteworthy that the national Broadcasting Council of Latvia has called for a law that would register the real physical owners of the media.[27]

The distribution of mass media advertising expenditures in the first half of 2005 was predominantly focused, not surprisingly, on television (38 percent) and newspapers (28 percent). The other media share was 14 percent in journals, 11 percent in radio, 6 percent in outdoor advertising, 3 percent on the Internet, and 1 percent in film. The 17 percent increase in total ads over the same period in 2004 reflects the rapid growth of the economy and consumerism. A new twist in advertising was introduced in 2005. Cigarette ads in media and sponsorship programs by tobacco companies were disallowed.[28]

Journalists and media outlets are able to form their own viable professional associations, such as the Latvian Journalists Union and the Latvian Press Publishers

Association. In Freedom House's 2005 *Freedom of the Press* survey, Latvia was ranked in the second highest group of "Free" media. The mass media still obtain the highest levels of trust of any Latvian institution. Thus, TV is trusted by 66.7 percent and newspapers by 59.9 percent of the population. Only the church and president come close, with 59 percent and 59.4 percent, respectively.[29]

Local Democratic Governance

1997	1998	1999	2001	2002	2003	2004	2005	2006
n/a	n/a	n/a	n/a	n/a	n/a	n/a	2.50	2.50

In contrast with Estonia and Lithuania, Latvia ratified a Constitution that does not include the rights and principles of local governments. Rectifying this omission has been one of the constant demands of the Union of Local and Regional Governments of Latvia. Nevertheless, Latvia has several laws that apply to municipalities, the chief being the Law on Local Governments passed on May 19, 1994, and amended over 10 times. The 530 local governments in Latvia are responsible for a broad array of functions and services. They are responsible for primary and secondary education, most social assistance (except pensions and family care benefits), health care, water supply and sewage works, county roads, solid waste collection and disposal, and about one-fifth of all housing in Latvia, to which they have legal title.

The processes of governance vary according to the size of the municipality, but all are based on fundamental democratic foundations, including open council and committee meetings and their minutes, access to deputies and the executive by local residents, procedures for review of complaints and suggestions, and public discussions and audited annual reports or reviews of budgets. Citizens also have recourse to municipal elections every four years.

Elections are free and democratic, with a turnout of 52.85 percent on March 12, 2005. In those elections, 4,179 deputies out of over 15,000 candidates were elected for 530 local governments. The majority, or 57.7 percent, were men; 41.9 percent had a higher education; 82.6 percent were Latvians, 4.3 percent Russians, and 2.2 percent of other ethnic origins, but 10.7 percent of deputies did not indicate their ethnicity.[30]

The Law on Administrative Procedure, in force since February 1, 2004, provides another element of security against arbitrary government actions. Most important, people can now dispute government actions that affect them personally by using the administrative court system for redress. Local media, mostly weeklies, serve as another system of input and reflection regarding municipal activities.

Current local governments have received a high level of approbation in many surveys. *How Democratic Is Latvia: Audit of Democracy* found that local self-governments were trusted by 48.1 percent of the people, compared with 22 percent for the Parliament and 25 percent for the national government.[31] This probably reflects the higher level of personal contact with government in small communities.

Many attempts have been made at the national level to redraw municipal boundaries, but there have been only minimal voluntary changes. The hope is that the Parliament elected in October 2006 will be able to deal with it and that reforms to decrease the numbers will be in place for the 2009 municipal elections.[32]

Financing of so many municipalities of such variable size is also a major problem. Municipalities are dependent on personal income taxes for over half their income. In 2005, municipalities were allowed to keep 73 percent of personal income tax but have been promised 75 percent in 2006. There is a provision for a certain degree of equalization between the more prosperous and poorer districts, but the richer municipalities have become increasingly opposed to subsidizing poorer municipalities. They would rather use their money for new developments and let the national budget provide the required subsidies.[33] As well, the central government provides "earmarked grants" that account for about a quarter of all municipal revenues.

Smaller municipalities have problems recruiting hardworking and honest candidates for local councils and the executive, and there have been patterns of nepotism. Controlling corruption and ensuring transparency are often difficult, especially when handing out contracts and ordering supplies. Municipalities have created an association to lobby for their interests.

A major problem faced by many municipalities is the widening economic gap between Riga and the regional areas. Riga accounts for about a third of Latvia's population but two-thirds of its GNP. The other four regions generate relatively little economic value: Kurzeme 11 percent, Vidzeme 10 percent, Zemgale 8 percent, and Latgale 4 percent. Latgale is the region with the greatest poverty and highest rates of unemployment. In Riga, unemployment is around 4 percent, but it is 25 to 30 percent in the Latgale districts. Latvians are a minority in the Latgale area.

Overall, the quality of local governments is quite variable, as is their capacity and ability to fulfill all required jurisdictional duties. However, elections appear to be fair, with a satisfactory voter turnout. In some municipalities, special deals with real estate developers, especially near the coast, have created perceptions of corruption.

Judicial Framework and Independence

1997	1998	1999	2001	2002	2003	2004	2005	2006
2.25	2.25	2.00	2.00	2.00	2.25	2.00	1.75	1.75

Latvia's Constitution provides protection for fundamental political, civil, and human rights, and on the whole these are respected by authorities and the general population. Latvians are guaranteed equality before the law, but in practice not all Latvians have equal access to justice. Over 80 percent of litigants in civil cases act without the help of lawyers. This inevitably skews the results of judgments in favor of wealthier citizens who are able to afford legal counsel. Some legal help is provided by the Latvian Human Rights Bureau. Currently, state legal aid is made available in all criminal cases but only a small proportion of civil cases. Such aid for civil cases was budgeted for 2005 to cover about 25 percent of all litigants who fell below a given poverty line.

Prosecutors are independent but have been criticized by politicians and ministers, subjecting them to pressure to investigate particular issues. The idea of jury trials has been debated, but as yet no concrete steps have been taken. After great hesitation, a new probation system was introduced in October 2003 in six districts and will eventually be extended to all of Latvia.

The 2003 Law on Court Executors (bailiffs) was expected to resolve one of the most controversial areas of the justice system. Formerly, about 70 percent of court decisions in civil cases were not implemented, and there was great potential for arbitrary actions and corruption. Now, new cadres of about 100 executors have been trained for this purpose and are subordinated directly to the courts. Nevertheless, new cases of corruption and bad judgments by leading court executors in 2005 have precipitated calls for further changes and a stricter overview of their activities.

One of the long-standing criticisms of Latvia has been the large number of prison inmates who are awaiting trial or have not yet been sentenced. In January 2005, 33 percent of the country's inmates were being held in pretrial detention, according to University of London data.[34]

Latvia has a relatively high rate of incarceration – 337 prisoners per every 100,000 persons. In January 2005, there were 7,796 prisoners in 15 institutions. Among inmates, only 5.3 percent are women and 2.9 percent juveniles under the age of 18. The 2004 incarceration rate per 100,000 persons was 339 for Estonia, 234 for Lithuania, 726 for the United States, 564 for Russia, and only 66 for Finland. Rates in Western Europe are much lower than in Latvia, averaging about 100 per 100,000 persons. Most of Latvia's prisons are about a century old and require major improvements. The Ministry of Justice has planned to rebuild and modernize all prisons between 2006 and 2014, a task that will cost 52 million lats (US$91 million USD).[35] Furthermore, the ministry plans to create a special college for prison workers to raise their qualifications. About 60 percent of inmates in the Baltic republics suffer from health problems and depression, and most inmates have trouble finding jobs after release.[36]

One of the major judicial problems in Latvia is the long waiting list for trials. Much has been done to alleviate this situation, but the problem persists. In 2003, a new Riga courthouse with 20 courtrooms was completed. Two other court buildings are being built in the city and are expected to be in service by the end of 2005 and the end of 2006, respectively. Another new building is under construction in Jurmala. On February 1, 2004, the new administrative court system began operations in Riga with 28 judges.[37] Its major responsibilities include the adjudication of disputes and conflicts between the population and national or local public servants, including police officers. Formerly, such cases were handled by regular courts. Other regional administrative courts are scheduled to open in 2006. Until then, litigants must travel to the capital city or move and engage their case by correspondence, one of the innovative advantages of this type of court system.

Other changes are also affecting court loads and improving the quality of judgments. Public notaries now have the authority to adjudicate conflicts over inheritance and wills, decreasing the number of court cases by several thousand a year. The minister of justice has also added 15 new judges to the Riga regional courts. In September 2005, there were 436 judges in Latvia; 75 percent are women.[38] The various changes in the court system have had a positive impact on the disposition rate of criminal cases. The procedure for selecting judges has become more stringent – a candidate for the bench must first pass an examination before being allowed to work as a two-year apprentice judge.

If in the past there were many vacancies, currently there is a competition for judicial appointments. The prestige of judges has risen, and so has their remuneration. The minister of justice has instituted a new schedule of gradual pay raises. The pensions of judges were also raised in 2005, allowing for the payment of 80 percent of individual average wages while on the bench, providing more peace of mind and lessening the allure of bribes.[39]

Latvian courts have often been accused of corruption, but only a few individual judges have ever been convicted or admonished about corrupt actions or perceptions. The minister of justice, Solvita Aboltina, pointed out in April 2005 that one of the key sources of such complaints was the Riga regional court, which darkened the reputation of all courts, even though no worries about dishonesty existed outside of Riga.[40] This general observation led to the resignation of the Riga court chairperson, Janis Muiznieks, and to the boycott of the annual justice conference by the court's 46 judges, who felt that they had been unjustly stigmatized. In turn, Prime Minister Kalvitis sent an official note of reprimand to the minister of justice for having made such pronouncements without any concrete proof.[41]

The whole issue was a catalyst for debate on the Web site www.politika.lv about the honesty of the courts. Almost all interviewed judges indicated that there were only a few "bad apples" and that their reputation of widespread corruption was unwarranted. In part, they blamed the media for not fully assessing all aspects of a case and noted that the tremendous caseload of the Riga court did not allow for more extensive elucidations on decisions. Mild sentences for attempted bribery, narcotics offenses, and prominent individuals feeds the popular perception of collusion and secret payments. Nevertheless, Ivars Bickovics, president of the Association of Judges and head of the Supreme Court's criminal section, pointed out that it would be impossible to bribe all three levels of judges and that no judges appear to be living beyond their means.[42]

According to the chair of the Latvian Supreme Court, Andris Gulans, there has not been any political pressure on courts. In his view, normal criticism of courts is an integral part of democracy.[43] At the same time, great political pressure was generated to replace Latvia's chief procurator, Janis Maizitis, whose term of office was to end May 15. This campaign not to reappoint him was led by the newspaper *Neatkariga Rita Avize*, purportedly controlled by Latvian oligarch Aivars Lembergs. Many people, including Latvia's president, the head of Latvia's Association of Jurists, and prominent members of the media and society came to his defense, and the Parliament voted 74 to 17 to renew his five-year mandate.[44]

The Latvian Constitutional Court is trusted more than other courts. In 2005, it made several important decisions. One concerned the financing of non-Latvian private schools. The Court concluded in September that if Latvian private schools received state financing, the principle of equality should apply to all.[45] The Court made another controversial decision in education. In May, it found the language reforms for Russophone schools to be constitutional.[46]

Corruption

1997	1998	1999	2001	2002	2003	2004	2005	2006
n/a	n/a	3.50	3.50	3.75	3.50	3.50	3.50	3.25

Although corruption in Latvia is still a major concern, there are indications that the country has moved significantly in the right direction, including increased intervention from Latvia's KNAB and pressure from international organizations and the EU. Transparency International's 2005 Corruption Perceptions Index has improved Latvia's score from 3.8 in 2003 to 4.0 in 2004 and 4.2 in 2005.

A 2002 study by the externally based World Bank-affiliated Foreign Investment Advisory Service claimed Latvian businesspeople acknowledged relatively little corruption in the middle and lower levels of public administration. In effect, the attempts to limit such corruption have been successful, but sophisticated wrongdoing such as massive tax avoidance at the highest levels is still problematic. A 2005 study of 27 countries by the World Bank and the European Bank for Reconstruction and Development has found a much more benign situation in Latvia than in most new EU states with respect to corruption, as seen by polled Latvian businesspeople (BEEPS-Business Environment and Enterprise Performance Survey). In Latvia, a smaller number indicated corruption as a problem than did those polled in most of the other states studied. More important, a comparison to a similar study in 2002 points to a significant decrease in corruption perceptions in Latvia.[47]

The KNAB, which began operations in October 2002, inspired great hope for an improvement in the fight against corruption. In June 2005, this organization employed 116 people in 15 separate sections. Its financing has also increased. In 2005, it received 2.24 million lats from the state budget and 957,582 lats (US$5.44 million) from PHARE.[48] In contrast with previous years, the KNAB has overcome internal problems of leadership, cohesion, financing, and its controversial low profile. Its increasing visibility and success at diminishing corruption has given it much greater public support. One of its most successful ventures has been monitoring political party financing and spending. The new semiannual publication on corruption, *Korupcija oC*, financed by the Soros-related organization Providus and the U.S. government, has praised the work done by the KNAB and lauded its increased authority not only in the general population, but among other state institutions.[49]

Sometimes justice takes a while, as in the case of the Latvian Green and Farmers' Union Party, which refused to surrender illegally obtained funds discovered by the KNAB in 2002. The party appealed to the administrative court of first instance, where it won its case. However, after review by several appeals courts, the party was forced to pay in 2005.[50] In June 2005, the president asked the KNAB to prepare a new draft law that would incorporate the concept of "reverse onus," requiring those state workers with suspiciously large assets to prove the origin of their acquired wealth.[51]

The mild court sentences meted out to those involved in corruption are central to the problem. One particularly surprising case was the conditional or suspended two-year sentence given to a pharmacy chain operator, Vladimirs Labaznikovs, who had attempted to bribe a KNAB worker with 50,000 lats (US$87,500 USD) in order to stop that institution from inspecting his firm's activities.[52] The refusal to accept such a large bribe reflects highly on the integrity of the organization.

Those engaged in corruption would be less likely to persist in their activities if the courts established more aggressive sentences. However, an even more significant advance worldwide would result if countries used their power to shut down or regulate all the money havens that are increasingly being used to hide ill-gotten gains.

In spite of the many sources of real and perceived corruption, moderate progress is being made. The KNAB's increased activity in limiting party finance abuses and the threat of discovery is putting many political corruption participants on the defensive. The Parliament's Anticorruption Commission has also become energized. Over 200 individual state organs and institutions have submitted their anticorruption plans to the KNAB for evaluation in line with the demands of the long-range program initiated by the government in 2004 called the National Program for Corruption Prevention and Combating 2004–2008. In similar fashion, most state ministries have drafted codes of ethics and created ethics commissions. They have also included ethical norms in their employment contracts. A new draft Law on Procurement, announced May 5, 2005, has the potential to clean up one of the most corruption-prone areas of public life.

Juris Dreifelds teaches political science at Brock University in Ontario, Canada. He is the author of chapters and articles on the Baltic area. His book Latvia in Transition *was published by Cambridge University Press in 1996.*

---

[1] Delfi, July 10, 2005.
[2] Juris Rozenvalds, ed., How Democratic Is Latvia: Audit of Democracy, Latvian University Press, 2005 (Latvian version Cik Demokratiska ir Latvija: Demokratijas Audits), p. 257.
[3] Ibid., pp. 280-98.
[4] Diena, October 13, 2005. For more detailed naturalization data in English see the web site of the Latvian Naturalization Board under "figures and facts". <www.np.gov.lv/index.php?en=>
[5] Parliamentary Web site, www.saeima.lv.

[6] Delfi, March 2, 2005.

[7] Juris Rozenvalds,ed.,How Democratic Is Latvia: Audit of Democracy, Latvian University Press, 2005, p. 91 [Latvian version].

[8] Diena, March 18, 2005; Delfi, February 1, 2005.

[9] Juris Rozenvalds, ed., How Democratic Is Latvia: Audit of Democracy, Latvian University Press, 2005, p. 83 [Latvian version].

[10] Diena, March 11, 2005.

[11] Juris Rozenvalds, ed., How Democratic is Latvia: Audit of Democracy, Latvian University Press, 2005, p. 275 [Latvian version].

[12] Juris Rozenvalds, ed., How Democratic is Latvia: Audit of Democracy, Latvian University Press, 2005, p. 155 [Latvian version].

[13] www.mk.gov.lv.

[14] Ziemelkurzemes NVO Atbalsta Centrs, [North Kurzeme NGO Support Centre], www.zkcentrs.lv.

[15] Delfi, November 8, 2005.

[16] Latvijas Avize, September 8, 2004.

[17] Ibid.

[18] Apollo, April 15, 2005, and February 16, 2005.

[19] Apollo, March 15, 2005.

[20] TNS Latvia, 2005, www.tns.lv.

[21] Baltic Institute of Social Sciences, Ethnopolitical Tension in Latvia: Looking for the Conflict Solution, Riga, 2005, p. 35. For a listing of articles in Latvian and English by this Institute see <www.bszi.lv.>

[22] Ibid., p. 16.

[23] Ibid., pp. 35-36.

[24] Ilze Nagla and Anita Kehre, "Latvia," in Media Ownership and Its Impact on Media Independence and Pluralism (Ljubljana, Slovenia: Peace Institute, Ljubljana,Slovenia; and the South East European Network for Professionalization of the Media,[SEENPM], 2004), pp. 255-58.

[25] Ibid.

[26] Diena, April 19, 2005.

[27] Ibid., September 2, 2005.

[28] Diena, June 22, 2005.

[29] Juris Rozenvalds, ed., How Democratic is Latvia: Audit of Democracy, Latvian University Press, pp. 227-28 [Latvian version].

[30] Delfi, March 24, 2005.

[31] Juris Rozenvalds, ed., How Democratic Is Latvia: Audit of Democracy, Latvian University Press, 2005, p. 229.

[32] Diena, April 18, 2005.

[33] Delfi, February 28, 2005.

[34] University of London, King's College London International Centre for Prison Studies Prison Brief, Latvia, www.kcl.ac.uk/depsta/rel/icps/worldbrief/europe_records.php?code=149.

[35] Delfi, May 17, 2005.

[36] Ibid., October 23, 2005.

[37] Diena, November 7, 2005.

[38] Ibid.

[39] Ibid., November 6, 2005.

[40] Delfi, April 27, 2005

[41] Diena, May 17, 2005.

[42] www.politika.lv.

[43] Delfi, February 25, 2005.

[44] Diena, February 18, 2005, February 10, 2005; Delfi, March 3, 2005; Apollo, February 16, 2005.

[45] Delfi, September 15, 2005.

[46] Ibid., May 13, 2005.

[47] "Latvia:BEEPS at a Glance," EBRD-World Bank Business Environment and Enterprise Performance Survey, www.ebrd.com.

[48] See the KNAB Web site, www.knab.gov.lv.

[49] This report is also available in English as Corruption oC, www.policy.lv. See comments in Delfi, August 30, 2005.
[50] Delfi, May 20, 2005, June 7, 2005.
[51] Ibid., June 27, 2005.
[52] Latvijas Avize, November 4, 2005.

Lithuania

Capital: Vilnius
Population: 3,400,000
GNI/capita: 4,500
Ethnic Groups: Lithuanian (83%), Russian (6%), Polish (7%), other (4%)

Nations in Transit Ratings and Averaged Scores

	1997	1998	1999	2001	2002	2003	2004	2005	2006
Electoral Process	2.00	1.75	1.75	1.75	1.75	1.75	1.75	1.75	1.75
Civil Society	2.25	2.00	2.00	1.75	1.50	1.50	1.50	1.50	1.50
Independent Media	1.75	1.50	1.75	1.75	1.75	1.75	1.75	1.75	1.75
Governance *	2.50	2.50	2.50	2.50	2.50	2.50	2.50	n/a	n/a
National Democratic Governance	n/a	n/a	n/a	n/a	n/a	n/a	n/a	2.50	2.50
Local Democratic Governance	n/a	n/a	n/a	n/a	n/a	n/a	n/a	2.50	2.50
Judicial Framework and Independence	2.25	2.00	2.00	1.75	2.00	1.75	1.75	1.75	1.50
Corruption	n/a	n/a	3.75	3.75	3.75	3.50	3.50	3.75	4.00
Democracy Score	2.15	1.95	2.29	2.21	2.21	2.13	2.13	2.21	2.21

With the 2005 edition, Freedom House introduced seperate analysis and ratings for national democratic governance and local democratic governance to provide readers with more detailed and nuanced analysis of these two important subjects.

NOTE: The ratings reflect the consensus of Freedom House, its academic advisers, and the author of this report. The opinions expressed in this report are those of the author. The ratings are based on a scale of 1 to 7, with 1 representing the highest level of democratic progress and 7 the lowest. The Democracy Score is an average of ratings for the categories tracked in a given year.

The economic and social data on this page were taken from the following sources:
GNI/capita, Population: *World Development Indicators 2006* (Washington, D.C.: World Bank, 2006).
Ethnic Groups: *CIA World Factbook 2006* (Washington, D.C.: Central Intelligence Agency, 2006).

EXECUTIVE SUMMARY

L
ithuania's successful transition has allowed the country to achieve a democratic system of government, political stability, and respect for the rule of law. Political rights and civil liberties are well established and protected. Power transfers have been smooth, and viable political parties function at all levels of governance. Major political forces have united the country's democratization process, market reforms, and integration with the Western community. In 2004, Lithuania joined NATO and the European Union (EU). The public strongly supported these integration processes, and aspiration for EU membership drove the country's sweeping political, economic, and administrative reforms.

The country owes much of its post-Communist success to a vibrant civil sector and free media. Since 1990, Lithuania has had 13 government administrations and has established a functioning market economy thanks to large-scale privatization, business deregulation, and liberalization of foreign trade. The country has achieved strong macro positions and remains one of the fastest-growing economies in the region. Lithuania meets all criteria (although at the end of 2005 inflation surfaced as a concern) for joining the European Monetary Union, an event that is scheduled for the beginning of 2007. Furthermore, Lithuania's judicial framework has been overhauled. Corruption, however, remains an overriding concern.

After the October 2004 national legislative elections, a left-of-center parliamentary majority and coalition government were formed. The cabinet was composed of the Lithuanian Social Democratic Party (LSDP), the New Union-Social Liberals, the Labor Party, and the Union of Peasants and New Democracy Party. The ruling coalition, led by LSDP leader Algirdas Brazauskas, was not expected to survive long. An intense rivalry for leadership was accompanied by recurrent friction and tension within the coalition. In November 2005, a conflict-of-interest scandal around the prime minister's family business provoked a cabinet crisis. The key issues on the 2005 policy agenda were the impending sale of the country's biggest industrial asset, the Mazeikiai Nafta oil refinery (after the collapse of its major shareholder, the Russian Yukos), and the long-debated tax reform.

National Democratic Governance. In 2005, parliamentary oversight was strengthened through the establishment of a new audit committee. The committee's vigorous efforts and exposure of major violations and mismanagement in the public administration sparked tension between the Parliament and the government. The National Audit Office released audit findings on 100 budgetary institutions. The auditors reported that administrative capacities were lacking and financial management and internal auditing procedures were flawed in many budgetary organizations. In 2005, the legislative work was disturbed by numerous ad hoc commissions to investigate conflict-of-interest allegations against top politicians. Law enforcement agencies became the target of increased battling for political influence, but recent top law enforcement appointments conformed to the principles of impartiality. *Lithuania's rating for national democratic governance remains at 2.50.*

Electoral Process. The new Parliament and coalition government were the center of attention in 2005. Recurrent confrontations and a series of conflict-of-interest scandals around the coalition leaders threatened the government's stability. In fall 2005, the Liberal and Center Union (LCU) underwent a split, and opponents of LCU leader and Vilnius mayor Arturas Zuokas established a separate parliamentary faction. Electoral and public campaign laws were tightened through a ban on using gifts, public entertainments, concerts, and similar events as election campaign tools. *Despite recent turmoil in Lithuania's political sphere, political mechanisms are functioning properly, and the country's rating for electoral process remains at 1.75.*

Civil Society. Lithuania's civil society sector has taken an upturn in recent years. Nongovernmental organizations (NGOs) have increasingly shown a proactive stance on public policy advocacy, and organized village communities have proliferated. The legislative framework governing NGOs has been overhauled and does not pose serious impediments to civil society groups. *However, public awareness and support of civil society remain low. Lithuania's rating for civil society remains at 1.50.*

Independent Media. In 2005, there was further ownership consolidation in Lithuania's media market. The leading print media group Respublika acquired a controlling stake in one of Lithuania's two main wire services, ELTA. The purchase caused some controversy and uncertainty over ELTA's future given the notorious reputation of Respublika's owner and publisher. Yet Lithuania's private media market continues to embrace numerous domestic and foreign interests and is subject to intense competition. Public confidence in the media stands at 50 percent, a marked drop from where it was several years ago. *The rating for independent media remains at 1.75.*

Local Democratic Governance. In 2005, political debates commenced on upcoming constitutional amendments stipulating direct mayoral elections and a new model of local government, placing the mayor as head of both the municipal council and the executive branch. Local governments were banned from spending central government subsidies designated for municipally paid social benefits on other needs. This decision followed a report by the National Audit Office concerning the misuse of one-third of social allocations from the central government. Auditors also concluded that most municipal administrations had flawed financial management and ineffective internal auditing procedures. *Lithuania's rating for local democratic governance remains at 2.50.*

Judicial Framework and Independence. Lithuania's judiciary continues to adjust to a set of new legal codes enforced from 2003 and applying EU law. In 2005, rules on the enforcement of court judgments were revised to improve the functioning of the bailiffs system, a target of severe criticism in recent years. Starting from 2005, the equal opportunities ombudsman was given a mandate to investigate not only gender discrimination complaints, but cases relating to age, sexual orientation, disability, racial or ethnic origin, religion, or beliefs. Unsatisfactory detention conditions, police abuse, and protracted property restitution are the biggest concerns, according to a recent report by the parliamentary ombudsmen. Courts continue to rank among the least trusted institutions in public opinion polls. *Lithuania's judicial framework and independence rating remains at 1.50.*

Corruption. Corruption remains a serious problem in Lithuania. Recently, focus has moved from small-scale administrative corruption to rampant political corruption. In 2005, a new chain of scandals broke as several top politicians were confronted with grave corruption and conflict-of-interest allegations. This suggests that the incidence of corruption is increasing but also that exposure has improved. Surveys show that unofficial payments in dealing with business regulations have also increased. *Lithuania's rating for corruption worsens from 3.75 to 4.00 owing to recurrent gross political scandals and entrenched regulatory corruption.*

Outlook for 2006. The outcome and consequences of the cabinet crisis will be the center of attention in 2006. If the government falls apart, the formation of a new cabinet will be likely. Local government election campaigns will commence in fall 2006, and the elections will be held in February 2007. The 2006 policy agenda will contain a range of key issues that are expected to provoke heightened political and public debates, including the adoption of constitutional amendments stipulating a new model of local government and direct mayoral elections, preparation for the introduction of the euro in 2007, and negotiations on the sale of Lithuania's prized Mazeikiai Nafta.

MAIN REPORT

National Democratic Governance

1997	1998	1999	2001	2002	2003	2004	2005	2006
n/a	n/a	n/a	n/a	n/a	n/a	n/a	2.50	2.50

Lithuania has a democratic government, with a functioning system of checks and balances. The state is a parliamentary republic in which the president nominates and, with the Parliament's endorsement, appoints the prime minister and approves the composition of the cabinet.

In 2005, parliamentary control was strengthened through the establishment of a new parliamentary audit committee after the 2004 elections. The committee was charged with overseeing enforcement of national audit findings and recommendations and enhancing efficiency and transparency of public administration. In one year, the committee exposed more than 30 major cases of law violations, mismanagement, illegitimate construction projects, protracted land restitution, and squandering of state property, prompting executive authorities to take note of national auditors' recommendations.

Initiated and led by the New Union-Social Liberals (Social Liberals), the committee caused tension between the government and the Parliament. Prime Minister and LSDP leader Algirdas Brazauskas stated that the committee exceeded its competence, interfered with the executive branch, and duplicated national auditors. Brazauskas defied the committee's findings and called for narrowing its powers. Parliamentary Speaker and Social Liberals leader Arturas Paulauskas insisted that parliamentary control become the Parliament's core focus and urged other committees to follow suit.

Admittedly, the spectrum of parliamentary oversight was never clear, so the committee's activity caused some ambiguity over the division of competence in the area of governmental and municipal oversight. In 2005, the National Audit Office made news by releasing audit findings from 100 budgetary institutions accounting for more than 80 percent of total budget spending. More than half of the audited organizations received serious remarks on mismanagement of government allocations.[1]

Lithuania's Parliament operates in an open manner, and all bills are posted on the Internet. Interest and public policy groups may take part in the political process through policy advocacy, advising, and lobbying. Yet draft legislation is not always readily available to the public. Executive authorities often propose bills or adopt new regulations without prior notice or public scrutiny, though required by law to announce policy proposals via the Internet. In 2005, the Parliament enacted 400 laws, but only 16 were entirely new or new versions of existing laws.[2] In practice, most bills, especially systemic and regulatory documents whose drafting requires administrative capacities, originate in the government. In terms of internal management, the Parliament is plagued by a disregard for rules and discipline. Parliamentarian absenteeism, unauthorized vacations, and other violations required tightening the procedures of parliamentary work.

In February 2005, the Constitutional Court resolved that a member of Parliament (MP) may lead a political party, a professional union, or an association but may not work under a labor contract or receive remuneration from said organizations. The Constitutional Court addressed ambiguities concerning the legitimacy of the parliamentary mandates of two MPs, the president of the Lithuanian Chamber of Agriculture and a professional union leader. The two MPs renounced their previous posts and retained their parliamentary seats. In 2005, a number of interim commissions set up to investigate conflict-of-interest and other allegations against top politicians and government officials upset the Parliament's work. Pollsters showed that the society was skeptical of these kinds of parliamentary commissions.[3]

The executive branch is less transparent than the legislature. The government often provides limited public access to information on regulatory proposals, arguing that the cabinet's position is not finalized in the drafting process. Cabinet sessions take place behind closed doors. To enhance transparency, government and municipal resolutions, decrees, and other legal acts will come into effect on the day of their signing after being posted on the Internet, according to legislative amendments adopted in July 2005.[4] Currently, laws are enforced upon publication in the official gazette. Also, pursuant to EU directives, information regarding official documents of all state institutions will be available on one Web site.

Key issues on the 2005 policy agenda included the future of Lithuania's most prized industrial asset, Mazeikiai Nafta,[5] tax reform, gas and energy price regulation, introduction of the euro, and the allocation of EU structural funds. The Parliament allowed the government to buy the Russian Yukos-controlled stake in Mazeikiai Nafta and to sell it with a portion of outstanding state-owned shares to a new investor. Among the contenders is Russia's largest oil company, Lukoil. The opposition fears that Kremlin-loyal Lukoil's presence would threaten national security. In June, the Parliament gave the green light to a long-debated tax reform.[6] The introduction of the euro was another much-debated issue supported practically on all sides of the political spectrum, while society is split, with slightly more leaning in favor of the euro.

The military is entirely under civilian control. The run-up and accession to NATO improved the military's administration and transparency. The main security and law enforcement services have rehabilitated after accusations of involvement in political battles in 2004. However, the government was accused of overstepping its authority in 2005 by establishing a division of law and order and governance to coordinate the work of law enforcement institutions. Political analysts noted that the ruling LSDP showed signs of discontent over the Social Liberals' "friendship with law enforcement agencies"[7] via affiliations with law enforcement chiefs. Nevertheless, recent top appointments to the Special Investigation Bureau, the National Audit Office, and the Office of the Prosecutor General conformed to the principles of impartiality. Law enforcement institutions remain largely resistant to political pressure, thanks primarily to the president's role in the appointment process.

The much-debated investigations into the status of KGB reserves continued in 2005 after suspicions surfaced that several top officials, including the foreign minister and the state security chief, were enlisted in the KGB reserves in the 1980s. The lustration commission investigating collaboration with the Soviet security service was reorganized and investigated 78 cases in 2005, as compared with 2 cases from 1999 through 2004. The Parliament is contemplating granting an additional grace period for persons willing to plead collaboration.

The civil service comprises four categories: career civil servants, political appointees, heads of institutions, and acting or temporary civil servants. The bureaucratic apparatus now accounts for 0.7 percent of the country's population and absorbs roughly 8 percent of the state and municipal budget, or 2 percent of the gross domestic product.[8] The number of civil servants rose from 18,000 in

1997 to 25,150 in 2005 and continues to grow.[9] The EU has become a popular argument to boost the bureaucratic machine, and in 2005 about 500 new positions requiring an additional LTL10 million (US$3.6 million) were opened in the government[10] to meet the growing EU membership workload.

Despite ongoing public service reform, civil servants are criticized as incompetent. Political connections, cronyism, resistance to change, inefficiency, entrenched bureaucracy, and corruption are all contributary factors to the high degree of public mistrust in the civil service. Nevertheless, professionalism and qualifications among civil servants have improved over the past decade thanks to extensive foreign assistance and the approximation of Lithuanian law with the EU *acquis communautaire*.

Electoral Process

1997	1998	1999	2001	2002	2003	2004	2005	2006
2.00	1.75	1.75	1.75	1.75	1.75	1.75	1.75	1.75

Public and political attention in 2005 focused on the coalition government and the new Parliament. After national legislative elections in October 2004, the LSDP, the Social Liberals, the Labor Party, and the Union of Peasants and New Democracy Party (UPNDP) formed a coalition government and the parliamentary majority. However, friction and fights for influence provoked a series of major confrontations, and grave conflict-of-interest scandals around coalition leaders precipitated a mounting political crisis.

Cabinet and program formation after the 2004 legislative elections was one of the slowest and most controversial in the country's postindependence history. After a long and grueling series of negotiations with left-of-center and opposition parties, the coalition of the LSDP and Social Liberals, with 31 seats in Lithuania's 141-seat Parliament, teamed with the Labor Party (39 seats) and the UPNDP (9 seats). The populist Labor Party, which boasts the country's biggest party membership and highest popularity rankings since its founding in 2003,[11] was invited to join Lithuania's 13th administration despite the antipathy of political leaders toward both the party and its chairman, Russian-born business tycoon Viktor Uspaskich. This arrangement allowed the LSDP, with only 22 seats in the Parliament, to keep Algirdas Brazauskas in office as prime minister. Arturas Paulauskas, leader of the Social Liberals, remained parliamentary Speaker. Negotiations over the division of cabinet posts focused on four key ministries administering the bulk of EU funds: transport, environment, finance, and economy.

The ruling coalition was said to constitute too many clashing interests and leaders to survive for long. From the start, the government was beset by confrontations and conflict-of-interest scandals. This distracted the Parliament and paralyzed important legislative debates, which led analysts to predict imminent political crisis. Observers widely agreed that confrontations were concerned mainly with the fight for influence between the LSDP and the Labor Party. The situation was further complicated by Labor Party chairman Viktor Uspaskich's involvement in a series of conflict-of-interest scandals. In June, Uspaskich stepped down as MP and economic minister on ethics violations, but the Labor Party remained in the coalition.

The cabinet mobilized on major policy decisions but was cast into crisis in November 2005 when Prime Minister Brazauskas was also implicated in a grave conflict-of-interest scandal. The opposition accused the prime minister of violations involving his wife and her business deals with Lukoil Baltija. It was feared that these relationships could affect the cabinet's decision on the takeover of Mazeikiai Nafta. As the opposition attempted to initiate a parliamentary investigation into these allegations, the prime minister threatened to resign and continued to defy numerous calls for greater transparency and publicity. Although talks of possible government collapse continue, cabinet fallout is unlikely, and the ruling coalition continues to display unity.

Elections in Lithuania are free and fair, and public confidence in the electoral process is secure. Viable political parties, including members of the opposition, function at all levels of government. In 2005, there were 36 registered political parties, but only 15 to 20 active players on the political scene. In 2004, the qualifying membership requirement for political parties increased from 400 to 1,000 people. This means that parties with fewer than 1,000 members will automatically be liquidated. Some argued that the tightened membership requirement was a step backward in terms of democratic freedom, while others said it discouraged "frivolous" parties from splitting up the vote.

Political parties have largely abandoned ideological rivalry and have been losing their electorate. Not incidentally, the rhetoric about the distinction between so-called traditional or established parties and nontraditional or recently founded parties disappeared after the latest elections. Furthermore, civic groups and political observers repeatedly allude to the threat of oligarchy in Lithuania. The president emphasized this in a recent annual report to the Parliament. Observers attribute these trends to the sturdy and unchanging political elite with firm ties to influential business groups over the past 15 years.

The LSDP, the foundation of the left-wing bloc, remains the most powerful and influential political party and a driving force in Lithuania's ruling coalition government. In May 2005, lacking a rival candidate, Brazauskas was reelected chairman of the LSDP by an overwhelming majority. Observers noting that the LSDP's ratings have already been affected by the scandal around Brazauskas predict serious damage in upcoming elections.

The Conservatives and the LCU are the two biggest right-of-center parties. The Conservatives' popularity ranking rose lately to the detriment of the LSDP and internal problems in the LCU.[12] After the 2004 elections, the Conservatives (with 25 seats) and the LCU (with 19 seats) formed an opposition coalition, the first coalition of this kind in the history of Lithuania's Parliament. Despite its size and fairly broad statutory powers, the opposition is considered by some observers to be the weakest of all postindependence parliamentary oppositions.

In 2005, the LCU was beset by internal squabbling and finally underwent a serious split. The party divided into two circles: One opposed party chairman and Vilnius mayor Arturas Zuokas, accused of deviating from the party's core values and autocracy; the other supported him. As a result of severe criticism of Zuokas, the chairman's opponents were evicted from the party and set up a separate, liberal faction in the Parliament. They are planning to found a new liberal party in 2006.

According to pollsters, the Parliament and political parties remain the most unpopular public institutions, supported by only 10 and 5 percent of the population, respectively.[13] A recent opinion poll from the Civil Society Institute (CSI) shows that 70 percent of society is dissatisfied with today's government, but 65 percent does not think it should be replaced, and as much as 40 percent does not see any political force able to ameliorate the present situation. According to the CSI, these results reflect society's political depression and growing alienation from the political process.[14] Passive public engagement in political life is reflected by low party membership and voter turnout; about 2.5 percent of Lithuania's citizens belong to a political party,[15] and the current Parliament was elected on a record low voter turnout of 44.3 percent.[16] Voter turnout was higher for the presidential elections.

Snap presidential elections were held in June 2004 after former president Rolandas Paksas was removed from office for gross violations of the Constitution. Ex-president Valdas Adamkus defeated UPNDP's leader, Kazimiera Prunskiene, in the second round of elections. Since the Paksas scandal, the presidency has been rehabilitated and public confidence generally restored, although society seems more attentive to the way the presidency functions. Adamkus remains the most popular political figure.[17]

In 2005, the Parliament tightened electoral and public campaign laws. In November, lawmakers banned politicians from using gifts, public events, concerts, and so forth as election campaign tools.[18] The previous year, the second round of elections was reintroduced, political donations from a single private individual were lowered,[19] political advertising was restricted, and control of donations and advertising contracts was tightened. This was meant to reduce political parties' demands for private funds and to curb the influence of campaign contributors. Yet political campaign funding contains serious flaws, and the mechanisms for ensuring compliance and transparency are inadequate.

Civil Society

1997	1998	1999	2001	2002	2003	2004	2005	2006
2.25	2.00	2.00	1.75	1.50	1.50	1.50	1.50	1.50

The Constitution guarantees the right to freely form societies and associations, and the rights of the independent civil society sector are well established and protected. Lithuania's civil society has experienced an upturn in recent years. NGOs have become increasingly engaged in policy advocacy, and local communities have proliferated. The legislative framework governing NGOs has been overhauled and does not pose serious barriers to their proper functioning. Lithuanian NGOs have significantly enhanced their organizational and managerial capacities, including in the area of constituency building. They commonly have permanent staffs but lack properly functioning boards of directors.

The past two years saw a massive proliferation of organized village communities. Their number soared from 80 in 2000 to 800 in 2003 and 1,000 in 2004. This trend was spurred largely by EU structural funds, as indicated by local communities surveyed by sociologists from Vilnius University.[20] Some communities formalized in order to apply for ongoing rural Internet projects.[21] Yet research shows that growing community awareness and joint efforts to address local community concerns gave rise to these numbers. Reportedly, many communities were mobilized to renovate crumbling school buildings and other decaying areas. As the survey indicates, village communities also aim to organize sports and cultural events, to promote leisure youth activities, and to elevate education, training, and information dissemination within the community. Village communities have reportedly good relationships with local authorities.

The Open Society Fund-Lithuania (OSFL) has established several public policy groups in the past few years. The Human Rights Monitoring Institute (HRMI) was founded in 2003 and the CSI in 2004. In early 2004, the OSFL in cooperation with 12 NGOs set up the I Can Live coalition to represent on a public policy level and to reduce social exclusion of vulnerable social groups, including drug addicts, HIV and AIDS patients, prostitutes, and convicts. The coalition is pursuing broad-based activities in Lithuania and numerous international projects. Interestingly, this coalition, and specifically the OSFL and other organizations funded by philanthropist George Soros, came under attack from the Respublika publishing group, allegedly as a counterattack for their role in a recent anti-Semitic libel case against Respublika.

Lithuanian society remains poorly organized, according to a 2005 survey from the CSI.[22] For the past six years, 17 percent of the population has belonged to NGOs or participated in civil movements. Sports and leisure groups have the biggest membership (3.2 percent), while a mere 2.6 percent belong to educational and cultural organizations, 2.2 percent to religious organizations, 2 percent to health clubs, and 1.8 percent to youth organizations. People with higher education are the most organized (29 percent). The most common reasons for nonparticipation are lack of interest and confidence in NGOs and low public outreach.

Most NGOs are registered in larger cities, but regional groups constitute the bulk of functioning organizations, with sports and active leisure groups dominating. Most foundations are devoted to youth or cultural activities. According to the Women's Information Center, there are 107 women's organizations.[23] Ethnic groups are quite active in the country's civic and cultural life. No prominent extremist groups are active in Lithuania today. Charitable activities of religious communities include care for the elderly, orphans, and disabled. Volunteerism was a rare form of NGO support until recently, mainly because Lithuania lacked a strong tradition of volunteerism and regulations discouraged the practice. Regulations were eased a few years ago but still place excessive bureaucratic constraints on some areas of volunteer work.

Legislation on nonprofits was overhauled in 2004. The previous distinction between associations and societal organizations was dropped, thus simplifying the regulation of NGOs. The change, which affected 10,000 to 11,000 of Lithuania's 15,000 nonprofits, helped establish equal legal conditions and a clearer regulatory environment for NGOs. Nonprofit associations may now generate profit, and charitable and sponsorship funds no longer have to hire paid administrators, but the use of their property and funds is regulated more strictly. Many experts continue to push for a single Law on Civil Society Groups.

Companies can donate up to 40 percent of their annual taxable profits to NGOs. Proposals to strengthen control of corporate giving and tighten reporting requirements on large donations are pending. From 2003, Lithuanian taxpayers could donate up to 2 percent of their income tax to private or public nonprofit entities. NGOs are exempt from profit tax. Most NGOs lack permanent sources of income and sufficient fund-raising capabilities. Many suffered a shortfall in funding in recent years as international donors began to withdraw from Lithuania. NGOs may also bid for government contracts, but this practice remains rather uncommon owing to a complex administrative process.

Public awareness about NGOs remains low, and most people mistrust the way they use donations.[24] Data showing the use of the 2 percent income tax deduction confirm these attitudes and perceptions. The 2 percent deduction, originally meant to boost civil society, went mostly to underfunded state-run institutions, reflecting weak public relations and fund-raising capacities of many NGOs. Some worried that voluntary giving would be discouraged if philanthropy came to be associated with compulsory taxes. Furthermore, there was room for narrow interests to abuse this provision, including fictitious organizations surfacing to absorb income tax deductions.

Citizens and noncitizen workers are free to form and join trade unions. Although unions claim a relatively small share of the workforce (about 15 percent), they are quite strong and influential.[25] A large-scale labor migration, which has intensified since Lithuania joined the EU,[26] and a sinking labor pool may further bolster their influence. Together with employers and the government, unions make recommendations on national labor policy. By law, unions sign collective agreements with employers on behalf of all employees, and the 2003 labor code requires all employers to comply.[27] Members of a union's elected governing body may not be dismissed or penalized by their employers without the union's approval. The Lithuanian Confederation of Trade Unions, the Lithuanian Labor Federation, and the Employees Union are coalitions of labor groups.

Business associations and trade unions are the most active and influential players taking part in the policy-making process through policy advocacy, advising, and lobbying; government cooperation and consultation with NGOs are not yet fully established. The media are receptive to independent public policy groups as reliable sources of information, but in general media coverage of civil activity is limited.

Observers noted that the 2005 increase of registered lobbyists[28] may be related to extensive informal representation of interest groups and legislative corruption. In current law, the concept of lobbying is applied quite broadly and includes any paid or unpaid actions of individuals or legal entities aimed at influencing legislative processes.[29] Thus, lobbying regulations can be applied to any publicly aired opinions on legislation or policy research. NGOs worry that as Lithuanian law does not regulate policy advocacy per se, and the boundaries between paid lobbying and advocacy are quite fuzzy, public policy groups actively expressing their opinions are being discredited and disrupted.

Lithuania's education system is generally free of political influence, but the government exerts pressure on school administrations through budgetary controls. The private education market has been evolving steadily over the past decade. There are 19 private secondary schools, and 6 out of the country's 21 universities are private. Yet private establishments account for a negligible 2 percent of all educational institutions.[30]

Independent Media

1997	1998	1999	2001	2002	2003	2004	2005	2006
1.75	1.50	1.75	1.75	1.75	1.75	1.75	1.75	1.75

Press freedom is well established and protected in Lithuania. Freedom House's annual *Freedom of the Press* survey has rated Lithuania "Free" since 1994. Most media outlets are privately owned, with the exception of the state-owned Lithuanian Radio and Television (LRT). The media market is subject to self-regulation. The Commission of the Ethics of Journalists and Publishers, which is composed of prominent and authoritative representatives of media associations and other public leaders, and the Office of the Inspector of Journalists' Ethics, which is appointed by the Parliament (at the recommendation of the Commission of the Ethics of Journalists and Publishers), function as independent supervisory institutions. Publications can be closed and journalists penalized only by court order. The intensely competitive private media sector includes a diverse range of print and electronic outlets at both national and local levels. One major development in 2005 was that ELTA, one of Lithuania's two main wire services, was acquired by the Respublika group.

In recent years, the degree of public confidence in the media has fallen dramatically; currently, only half of society reportedly trusts the media,[31] which played no small role in the 2003 presidential scandal and numerous other corruption affairs. Media publications and reports commissioned by political or business interests as a public relations tool have attracted heightened public attention; according to a recent opinion poll, 40 percent of the population could decipher hidden PR articles and reports–and as a result, half of this percentage lost respect for (and trust in) media outlets.[32]

The media are editorially independent and free of government interference. There are five national daily newspapers: *Lietuvos Rytas*, *Kauno Diena*, *Respublika*, *Vakaro Zinios*, and *Lietuvos Zinios*. The most popular are *Lietuvos Rytas* (with a reported circulation of 60,000), *Vakaro Zinios* (56,000), and *Respublika* (37,000). *Lietuvos Rytas* and *Respublika*, each of which owns significant interests in the print media market, are the most prominent players and old rivals, especially in their political viewpoints. Newspaper distribution was put into private ownership after the Lithuanian Post, the country's number one kiosk chain, was sold to Finland's Rautakirja.[33]

The television market comprises 4 nationwide and 27 regional operators. The only public service television, Lithuanian Television (LTV), broadcasts two national programs, LTV1 and LTV2. The leading national broadcasters are LNK, owned by Lithuania's leading private equity concern, MG Baltic; and TV3, owned by the Scandinavian Modern Times media group. These two channels captured 25 and 24 percent of viewers, respectively, according to data from October 2005, with LTV and Baltijos TV–owned by Lithuanian business giant Achema Group–following with 13 and 10 percent, respectively.[34]

Of the 47 radio stations in Lithuania, 10 commercial stations and 1 public broadcaster (with 2 stations, LR1 and LR2) operate nationwide.[35] The state-run Lithuanian Radio continues to enjoy the largest audience. Other popular radio stations are Lietus (12 percent), M-1 (10 percent), Pukas and Russkoje Radio Baltija (9 percent each), and Radiocentras (8 percent).[36] The largest commercial radio stations are owned by four major groups, three of which belong to local owners and reach the vast majority of listeners. So far, radio has been dominated by small local shareholders, but they are increasingly attracting large industrial and other capital. In 2005, a retail trade company, Senukai, bought a news-oriented radio station, Ziniu Radijas, from a U.S. owner.

Acquisitions of leading media outlets by domestic business companies in recent years heightened consolidation of media ownership among a few influential business groups and minimized foreign ownership in the Lithuanian television market. Achema Group is now the most active player on the Lithuanian media market. It owns the national daily *Lietuvos Zinios*; the fourth largest national commercial television station, Baltijos TV; popular radio stations RC2 and Radiocentras; and two publishing houses. Lithuania has no sector-specific regulation of media ownership concentration, but competition law sets a general limit at 40 percent of market share.[37]

A change in ELTA news agency's ownership was the biggest news from the media market in 2005. In July 2005, the Respublika group, publisher of Lithuania's most popular tabloids, won the auction for the state's 39.51 percent stake in ELTA. The Respublika group outbid majority owner MG Baltic, which subsequently sold off its controlling share in ELTA to the new owner. Controversy surrounded ELTA's acquisition by Respublika's owner, Vitas Tomkus, a notorious publisher and writer of anti-Semitic and homophobic articles. It is feared that Tomkus's presence can jeopardize the integrity of ELTA, which has demonstrated a solid performance on a news agency level in recent years.

According to the Lithuanian criminal code, libel or false information defaming a person can result in a fine, two years in prison, or two years of penitentiary labor. In recent years, few journalists have been convicted of such crimes. Notably, the media have obtained greater protection from the Supreme Court, which has drawn on the jurisprudence of the European Court of Human Rights, stating that criticism could be more rigorous for political figures than for private individuals.

The Radio and Television Commission regulates the activities of commercial broadcasters and participates in forming national media policy. It consists of 12 members, 1 designated by the president, 3 by the Parliament, and the rest by NGOs. The commission is financed by a percentage of broadcasters' advertising proceeds in order to secure independence from government and political groups. The government exerts some pressure on the national broadcaster, LRT, through budgetary controls. Private television operators increasingly complain that LRT, with 75 percent of its budget provided by the state, is allowed to sell advertising.

The public enjoys unhindered Internet access. Almost 22 percent of the population uses the Internet regularly.[38] In the first quarter of 2005, about 14.4 percent of Lithuanian households were connected to the Internet, up from 2 percent at the end of 2000, reports Statistics Lithuania. However, a wide gap between urban and rural indicators exists; in the first quarter of 2005, every fifth urban household had Internet access, as compared with 4 out of 100 in rural settlements.[39] The ongoing state-run rural Internet project is expected to help bridge this gap. Costly Internet services, inadequate Internet content, and a lack of home computers are the main reasons it is not used more widely.[40] Some of the most popular information portals are www.delfi.lt (targeting the Baltic States), www.google.lt, www.one.lt, www.lrytas.lt (the Web site of *Lietuvos Rytas*), and www.takas.lt (Lithuanian Telecom). There is no government agency controlling online media. According to 2003 legal regulations, online media are subject to the same self-regulation (independent supervisory institutions) as those that apply to the press, radio, and television. Proposals to write specific statutory regulation for online media have so far failed.

Local Democratic Governance

1997	1998	1999	2001	2002	2003	2004	2005	2006
n/a	n/a	n/a	n/a	n/a	n/a	n/a	2.50	2.50

Substantial power is situated at subnational levels of government. Lithuania has one level of local government, which encompasses 60 municipalities led by elected councils and 10 regional administrations governed by central appointees. Its responsibilities include municipal development, primary and secondary education, primary health care, environmental protection, social assistance, and public utilities. In certain areas such as land planning, health care, and education, both central and local authorities are involved. Ambiguities in power divisions have impeded decentralization, the distribution of fiscal allocations for municipalities, and transparent and accountable governance at the municipal level. Political parties propose abolishing regional administrations from time to time, especially before elections. However, regional governors remain influential political officials, so the removal of the regional tier of governance is unlikely.

In October 2005, the Parliament began debates on constitutional amendments stipulating direct elections of mayors and a new model of local government under which mayors would lead both municipal councils and the executive authorities. A similar system functioned in Lithuania until 2003 but was overhauled to comply with a 2002 Constitutional Court ruling that deemed unconstitutional the lack of separation of representative and executive powers in local government. From 2003, mayors remained municipal council heads, but their executive duties were delegated to the municipal council and administration. The municipal administration is led by a director appointed by the municipal council at the suggestion of the mayor. Mayors are elected by municipal councils, whose members in turn are chosen through general elections. Experts charge that the mayor has limited power to influence and control the executive branch and administration and that the existing model is prone to abuse of power and conflicts of interest.

Until recently, the idea of direct mayoral elections was supported by the political spectrum, but now it provokes disagreement within both the ruling coalition and the opposition. The ruling Social Liberals and the opposition Conservatives worry that direct mayoral elections will undermine the role and influence of political parties in municipal authorities, stimulate autocracy, and open the door for populists. It is also feared that vesting more authority in mayors would reduce the powers and role of elected councils and hence local communities. Experts also note that the new model will be at odds with the constitutional principle of the separation of powers.

Local government elections are scheduled for early 2007, but the ruling LSDP has proposed late 2006, prior to the introduction of the euro on January 1, 2007.[41] They argued that an earlier date would help avoid discussions on the euro introduction during local government election campaigns. Opponents claimed that altering the election date would be seen as an attempt to manipulate society. Nevertheless, in December the Parliament decided that the elections would be held in February 2007.

Municipal elections are universal and free. The current municipal councils were elected in December 2002, with 22 parties sharing 1,560 council seats for four years. Pursuant to a January 2005 ruling of the Constitutional Court,[42] permanent residents of Lithuania will be able to vote and run for municipal councils in upcoming municipal elections. Amendments to the Law on Political Parties allowing residents to be party members are pending before the Parliament.[43] Furthermore, the Lithuanian Association of Heads of District Neighborhoods has received calls to legitimate mixed municipal elections through proportional and single-mandate constituencies in order to enable local communities to put up their candidates to local government councils.

Legal acts by municipal councils are rarely available on the Internet; decisions are not known to the public until their enactment. Cooperation with local constituencies revolves mostly around land planning issues. Polling data cited by Transparency International's Lithuanian branch suggest that municipal officeholders dealing with routine applications receive the largest bribes from businesspeople.[44] Municipal governments generally lack funds to meet their obligations, owing mainly to mismanagement and their expanding sphere of authority. Misuse of funds is widespread. In some municipalities, administrative expenses tied to social allowances accounted for as much as 12 percent.[45] Many municipal administrations were found to have flawed financial management and inadequate or ineffective internal auditing procedures. The Parliament thus banned local government authorities from using social allocations from the central government to finance other needs and required them to return unused funds. Some worry that this restriction will bar local authorities from solving social problems independently.

The bulk of municipal revenues comes from the central government, with changes negotiated between municipalities and the central government and approved by the Parliament. Central budget subsidies accounted for 56 percent of total municipal revenues in 2005, with the remaining portion collected from personal income tax and local charges and dues.[46] Revenue volumes differ markedly across municipalities and are equalized according to specific, projected expenditure needs. Municipalities with revenue growth of more than 7 percent are required to transfer part of these funds to the state budget. Obviously, this discourages municipalities from raising more income and limits their capacities to finance independent functions. Legislative amendments proposing a revision of this provision are pending before the Parliament.

Judicial Framework and Independence

1997	1998	1999	2001	2002	2003	2004	2005	2006
2.25	2.00	2.00.	1.75	2.00	1.75	1.75	1.75	1.50

Fundamental political, civil, and human rights are well established and protected in Lithuania, and equality before the law is observed. Accession to the European Convention on Human Rights has provided an extra tier for Lithuanian nationals to appeal human rights violations.

Several state institutions merit praise for their active protection of human rights. In 2005, the parliamentary Office of the Ombudsman exposed several major violations of human rights by public officials. Unsatisfactory detention conditions, police abuse, and protracted property restitution were reported as the biggest problems.[47] The parliamentary ombudsmen investigating such complaints are acclaimed for swift and credible performance.

In 2005, the equal opportunities ombudsman was given a mandate to investigate complaints of discrimination by age, sexual orientation, disability, racial or ethnic origin, religion, or beliefs through a new Law on Equal Treatment.[48] Until now, the equal opportunities ombudsman worked only with complaints about gender discrimination. The most conspicuous discrimination case in 2005 was the Vilnius municipality's destruction of buildings in the Roma quarter in Vilnius, on the grounds of alleged drug-related crime and unlawful building activities in the quarter. The parliamentary ombudsmen found that the decision by the Vilnius authorities violated the law.

The Constitutional Court continues to serve as a powerful, independent, and reliable guardian of the country's basic laws and rights. The Constitutional Court's rulings have become central arguments in political debates, as lawmakers have increasingly tried to transfer controversial political decisions to the Constitutional Court by framing these questions as issues of constitutionality. Recent proposals suggested allowing private persons to address the Constitutional Court. This idea has met with approval by the Constitutional Court's chair, the parliamentary Speaker, and public leaders.

Lithuania's legislative and judicial framework has been overhauled in recent years. A code on civil procedure, enforced from 2003,[49] significantly eased civil legal proceedings. The new penal procedure code was tailored to secure a faster completion of procedural actions, investigations, and trials. Judges are now more involved in the pretrial stage of investigation. The new penalty execution code removed some excessive restrictions on the rights and liberties of convicts and improved the mechanism for filing and investigating their complaints. Notably, criminal penalties in Lithuania have been among the strictest and the number of prisoners among the highest in Europe. Yet as a result of loosened sanctions, the number of prisoners fell from 15,000 to 8,000 in 2005.[50]

The presumption of innocence and the right to a fair and public hearing are guaranteed by law and secured in practice. However, criminal investigations and trials are frequently protracted with lengthy court hearings. Tighter control of investigations in courts has reduced the number of protracted cases fourfold in recent years.[51] The right to a fair trial is undermined by poor court representation, yet recently a legal aid provision was finalized.[52] There are concerns over detention without trial and arbitrary arrests. The HRMI reports that illegally prolonged detention, failure to bring persons promptly before the court, and inadequate conditions for police detainees are the main problems in police work.[53] There is a critically low level of public trust in the police, reportedly less than one-fifth of the population.[54]

The president nominates, and the Parliament approves, the chair and judges to the Supreme Court and the Court of Appeals. The president appoints district court judges. The country's prosecutor general is appointed and discharged by the president upon approval of the Parliament. Most judges rule fairly and impartially, but public mistrust of judges is high. Lower-tier courts are trusted the least.[55] Corruption, protraction of trials, and a lack of respect for trial participants are the main factors undermining public confidence. Politicians and the media also distrust the judicial branch. As a result, judges work in a hostile atmosphere. Yet statistics show that a very small percentage of verdicts are appealed.

The government has no formal control over court decisions. In the lowest tier, where most cases are tried, three judges now share one assistant. Because of a high workload, high responsibility, and relatively low pay, numerous vacancies in the lower-tier courts have been reported. Judges and court chairs perform administrative functions, which not only impairs their work capacities, but raises doubts about the transparency in case assignment and judges' independence.

Public outrage peaked in 2005 concerning the inefficiency of the bailiffs system. Citizens had not been notified regarding legal restraints on their property and reported that exacted sums were significantly higher than imposed fines because of the long interval between imposition and fine payment. Several bailiffs were disciplined, and investigations were carried out by the National Audit Office. The Ministry of Justice reacted by revising the rules on enforcement of court rulings and putting a limit on the costs of recovering small amounts. It has been generally recognized that protection of creditors' interests and implementation of court judgments has improved. Yet only 6 percent of the population trusts bailiffs.[56]

Corruption

1997	1998	1999	2001	2002	2003	2004	2005	2006
n/a	n/a	3.75	3.75	3.75	3.50	3.50	3.75	4.00

Corruption is a systemic problem in Lithuania, and the public's perception and tolerance of corruption is high. Lithuania's legislative framework for combating corruption consists of nearly 10 laws on prevention and a national anticorruption campaign. However, enforcement is inadequate, and state agencies responsible for implementing the campaign have been blamed for inattention. In 2005, an interagency anticorruption commission assessed the campaign's progress and concluded that only 62 percent of the stipulated policies and measures were achieved and that coordination between law enforcement agencies, state institutions, and civil society groups was inadequate. Based on these conclusions, the government recently supplemented the campaign to strengthen control of political advertising and party donations.

Lawmakers have increasingly used legislative anticorruption impact assessment analysis as a tool to combat legislative corruption. In March 2005, proposals tasked additional law enforcement and customs agencies with corruption investigation in order to strengthen anticorruption work. The Parliament declined this proposal, suggesting it would eliminate the single institution coordinating anticorruption investigation, dissolving responsibilities, duplicating functions, and creating ambiguities in the division of competence.

The chain of scandals that broke in 2003 continued in 2005. About 10 ad hoc parliamentary commissions were established to investigate conflict-of-interest allegations against top officeholders in 2005. Former economic minister and Labor Party leader Viktor Uspaskich, LCU leader and Vilnius mayor Arturas Zuokas, and Prime Minister and LSDP leader Algirdas Brazauskas became targets of the gravest corruption and conflict-of-interest allegations, and chairman of the Chief Official Ethics Commission Algirdas Meskauskas stepped down in December on allegations of violating public procurement procedures.

Zuokas was enveloped by a number of corruption affairs during his term as mayor of Vilnius. He and several associates were sued for bribing and exerting undue influence on a Vilnius City Council member for favorable voting during the spring 2003 mayoral ballot but were cleared of all charges. The so-called subscriber affair erupted in May 2005, accusing Zuokas of receiving regular payments from Rubicon Group, a business giant engaged mostly in public utility services, in exchange for favorable decisions by the Vilnius municipality. Later, a package of documents allegedly revealed Zuokas's protection of a company linked to him in state-level project negotiations with Moscow authorities.

Uspaskich stepped down as an MP and economic minister in June 2005 after the parliamentary ethics commission found him guilty of two conflict-of-interest violations during his six months in office. The first scandal dated back to April, when the then minister was suspected of lobbying on behalf of his company during business negotiations with Moscow's government. Also, several Uspaskich-related companies received allocations of EU funds allegedly through a counterfeit business plan. To make matters still worse, Uspaskich was suspected of forging his higher education diploma. The politician claimed he had received a university-level degree from a prestigious economics institute in Moscow but was unable to provide the certificate.

Finally, in the fall of 2005 a scandal broke around Prime Minister Brazauskas. The affair involved the controversial 10-year privatization of the hotel owned by the prime minister's wife, Kristina Brazauskiene, and subsequent business deals with the hotel's former stakeholder, Lukoil Baltija. The opposition suspected these business connections could serve as a conflict of interest in deciding who should be the new strategic investor in Mazeikiai Nafta, in which Russia's largest oil company, Lukoil, was one of the bidders. The prime minister defied numerous calls to reveal the circumstances surrounding his family's business, a situation that precipitated mounting political crisis. Finally, a pretrial investigation of the hotel deal and possible abuse of official power ended with a lack of evidence of criminal offense or damage to the state.

In 2005, legal provisions on reconciling public and private interests were amended. The obligation to declare private interests was extended to chairpersons and deputy chairpersons of political parties who do not hold any official positions in state service. Instead of annual declarations, civil servants and politicians will now submit private interest declarations when they take office or assume leadership in political parties, and these declarations will be posted on the commission's Web site. Yet one out of five local politicians failed to submit declarations in time.[57]

Persons reporting cases of corruption receive general legal protections. Accepting or demanding a bribe is punishable by denying offenders the right to hold certain professional positions and by imprisonment for three to eight years. Punishment for abuse of official power includes fines, denial of the right to hold certain positions, and imprisonment for four to six years. State servants may be dismissed for abusing official power and ethics violations and can be punished by a three-year prohibition from state service.

Transparency International's 2005 Corruption Perceptions Index scored Lithuania at 4.8, a slight improvement from 4.6 in 2004.[58] In 2005, according to Transparency International's Global Corruption Barometer 2005,[59] almost one-third of Lithuanians gave bribes over the past 12 months. The majority believes the level of corruption in Lithuania has grown over the past three years. Political parties, courts, customs offices, the police, and the Parliament are seen as the most corrupt institutions. Yet according to a Transparency International survey in November 2004, most Lithu-anians consider bribes an effective tool, and two-thirds are ready to use them if needed. Paradoxically, about half the population purports never to have given bribes, but an overwhelming majority thinks that corruption is deeply entrenched.[60] Such perceptions can be explained by a wide and extensive airing of corruption allegations in the media, the main source of information on which people base their opinions about corruption. In 2005, Transparency International, the Lithuanian Free Market Institute, the CSI, and the HRMI founded the Civil Alliance Against Corruption to promote corruption prevention.

Corruption and bribery are entrenched in many areas. According to a joint Transparency International and Special Investigation Bureau survey in 2004, unofficial payments are most widespread among traffic police, health care institutions, land restitution services, and higher education establishments. Half of the encounters with traffic police involved bribes, nearly every third student made unofficial payments to schools or teachers, and one-third of patients offered under-the-table payments to doctors. A lack of accountability and responsibility in public administration, red tape, and the wide powers of civil servants are seen as the three main causes of corruption.[61] In 2005, medical workers were banned from accepting gifts from patients or their relatives during and after treatment.[62]

Corruption continues to plague land restitution and relocation procedures. Public purchase announcements must now be published on the Internet, but officials retain discretionary powers in applying public procurement criteria and assessing bids. Corruption is pervasive within Lithuania's extensive regulatory system. The state intervenes in the economy mainly through this avenue by setting quality standards, requiring numerous permits and inspections, prescribing a mandatory minimum wage, regulating energy prices, and so forth. Many see this as excessive regulation. According to a recent survey by the World Bank and Economic Bank for Reconstruction and Development, the scope of unofficial payments by firms dealing with regulatory agencies and payments to obtain government contracts has tripled since 2002.[63] Direct state participation in the economy has been minimized through large-scale privatization, including infrastructure. Privatization of the transportation and energy sectors is under way.

The Civil Alliance Against Corruption[64] has highlighted three priorities for official anticorruption work. The first is increasing transparency and communication of the public administration. The second is fighting legislative corruption, including cost and benefit analysis of public spending and other effective tools of legislative impact assessment. The third priority is ensuring effective corruption investigation by professional law enforcement institutions.

Aneta Piasecka is a senior policy analyst, and Giedrius Kadziauskas is a policy analyst at the Lithuanian Free Market Institute, a nonprofit think tank based in Vilnius.

---

[1] ELTA, "Valstybes kontrole per metus nustate 506 pazeidimo (The National Audit Office found 506 violations over the year)," July 12, 2005.

[2] Veidas, "Seimas," November 17, 2005.

[3] Veidas, "Seimo tyrimo komisijos vertinamos neigiamai, bet A. Brazausko veikla tirti reikejo (Attitudes towards parliamentary investigation commissions are negative, but A. Brazauskas' activity had to be investigated)," November 17, 2005.

[4] Seimas of the Republic of Lithuania, Astatymo ir kito teises akto skelbimo ir asigaliojimo tvarkos astatymo 1, 2, 3, 9, 11, 12, 13 straipsnio pakeitimo ir papildymo astatymas (The Law on the Revision and Supplementing of Articles 1, 2, 3, 9, 11, 12 and 13 of the Law on the Promulgation and Enforcement of Laws and Other Legal Acts), X-331, July 7, 2005.

[5] Mazeikiai Nafta accounts for approximately 10 percent of the country's gross domestic product.

[6] The reform stipulates offsetting budget shortfalls resulting from the abolition of the road tax with an interim profit tax that will be charged for the two coming years on top of Lithuania's 15 percent profit tax. Personal income tax will be gradually lowered, and a real estate tax will be imposed on private property used for commercial purposes. Critics said the boosted profit tax would seriously damage Lithuania's investment climate.

[7] Andrius Baciulis, "Valdzia imama kabinetuose (Power is taken in offices)," Veidas, September 8, 2005.

8 Eugenija Grizibauskiene, "Vis sunkejanti valdzios nasta (The burden of the government grows)," Veidas, July 7, 2005.

[9] Gintaras Sarafinas, "Jie dirba mums (They work for us)," Veidas, July 7, 2005.

[10] Eugenija Grizibauskiene, "Vis sunkejanti valdzios nasta (The burden of the government grows)," Veidas, July 7, 2005.

[11] Baltic News Service, "Darbo partijos populiarumas auga-apklausa (The popularity of the Labor Party is growing – a survey)," April 21, 2005.

[12] Lietuvos Rytas, "Populiariausi-prezidentas ir darbo partija (The President and the Labor Party the most popular)," November 19, 2005.

[13] Baltic News Service, "Lietuvos gyventojai labiausiai pasitiki Baznycia ir svietimu, maziausiai-partijomis (Lithuanians trust the Church and the educational system the most and parties, the least)," April 16, 2005; Lietuvos Rytas, "Populiariausi-prezidentas ir Darbo partija (The President and the Labor Party the most popular)," November 19, 2005.

[14] Veidas, "Politine depresija," September 29, 2005.

[15] "Lietuvos visuomene islieka menkai organizuota (The Lithuanian society remains poorly organized)," www.delfi.lt, December 14, 2005.

[16] Elections are considered valid if voter turnout is no less than 40 percent.

[17] Lietuvos Rytas, "Populiariausi-prezidentas ir darbo partija (The President and the Labor Party the most popular)," November 19, 2005.

[18] Seimas of the Republic of Lithuania Seimo rinkimu astatymo papildymo 5(1), 67(1) straipsniais ir 6, 18, 27, 30, 31, 34, 47, 48, 49, 50, 51, 56, 61, 65, 67, 68, 69, 70, 71, 72, 73, 74, 78, 79 straipsniu pakeitimo bei papildymo astatymas (The Law on the Supplement and Amendment of Articles 6, ... of the Law on Parliamentary Elections and its Supplement with Articles 5(1) and 67(1)), XP-842, November 15, 2005.

[19] To LTL 37,500 (US$13,000).

[20] Jone Kucinskaite and Aurelija Vernickaite, "Isjudino valdzios tingulys (Government's indolence

gives a push)," Veidas, August 18, 2005, pp. 30-35.

[21] Only 42.5 percent of community organizations are connected to the Internet. Ibid.

[22] "Lietuvos visuomene islieka menkai organizuota (The Lithuanian society remains poorly organized)," www.delfi.lt, December 14, 2005.

[23] Women's Information Centre, www.lygus.lt/ITC/nvo.php?v=1.

[24] Open Society Fund-Lithuania, A Survey: Philanthropy in Lithuania 2003, www.osf.lt/lt/main.htm.

[25] Lithuanian Trade Union Confederation, Trade Union Solidarumas and Lithuanian Labor Federation, Forum "Globalization and Representation of Workers After Lithuania's Accession to the EU," Vilnius, November 23, 2005.

[26] The official migration figure since Lithuania joined the EU stands at some 300,000, but the unofficial statistics are higher. Politicians admit that little could have been done to prevent such migration flows. As one remedy, a bill allowing foreign employees not to pay the income tax difference on their legal earnings when they return home is pending before the Parliament.

[27] Labor Code of the Republic of Lithuania, IX-926, June 26, 2003.

[28] Chief Official Ethics Commission, www.vtek.lt/lobizmas_info.html.

[29] Seimas of the Republic of Lithuania, Lobistines veiklos astatymas (The Law on Lobbying), IX-1385, March 20, 2003.

[30] Statistics Lithuania, www.std.lt/web/main.php?parent=294.

[31] Baltic News Service, "Lietuvos gyventojai labiausiai pasitiki svietimu ir Baznycia, maziausiai-partijomis (Lithuanians trust the Church and the educational system the most and parties, the least)," April 19, 2005; Lietuvos Rytas, "Populiariausi-prezidentas ir Darbo partija (The President and the Labor Party the most popular) ," November 19, 2005.

[32] RAIT (market research company), "Gyventojai apie uzsakomuosius straipsnius (Lithuanians about commissioned articles)," May 4, 2005.

[33] Rautakirja also controls press and video distribution companies and a chain of cinemas in Lithuania.

[34] TNS Gallup, www.tns-gallup.lt/lt/disp.php/lt_surveys/lt_surveys_29?ref=/lt/disp.php/lt_surveys.

[35] Radio and Television Commission of Lithuania, Radio and Television in Lithuania 2003/2004, 2004.

[36] TNS Gallup, www.tns-gallup.lt/lt/disp.php/lt_surveys/lt_surveys_21?ref=/lt/disp.php/lt_surveys.

[37] Seimas of the Republic of Lithuania, Law on Competition, VIII-1099, March 23, 1999.

[38] Gelme Vaisutyte, "Spartaus belaidzio interneto zonos plinta po Lietuva (Wireless Internet zones spread across Lithuania)," Veidas, October 20, 2005.

[39] Ibid.

[40] Tomas Alksnis, "Internetas namuose tampa kasdienybe (The Internet at home becomes a part of daily life)," Veidas, February 24, 2005.

[41] By law, the next local government elections must take place between December 3, 2006, and February 25, 2007.

[42] The Constitutional Court of the Republic of Lithuania, ruling on the compliance of the Republic of Lithuania Law on the Supplement and Amendment of Articles 86, 87, of the Law on Elections to Municipal Councils and its supplement with Article 88-1 with the Constitution of the Republic of Lithuania; January 19, 2005.

[43] Seimas of the Republic of Lithuania, Law on Political Parties, I-606, March 23, 2004.

[44] Transparency International Lithuanian branch, "Korupcijos zemelapis 2004 (The Map of Corruption 2004)," www.transparency.lt.

[45] National Audit Office of Lithuania; results of the financial audit of the municipalities in 2004, www.vkontrole.lt/veikla_ataskaitos.php?f.

[46] Ministry of Finance of the Republic of Lithuania, www.finmin.lt.

[47] ELTA, "Seimo kontrolieriai daugiausia sulauke skundu del policijos veiklos ir nuosavybes teisiu atk□rimo (Parliamentary ombudsmen receive the most complaints about the police and ownership restitution)," May 26, 2005.

[48] Seimas of the Republic of Lithuania, Law on Equal Treatment, IX-1826, November 18, 2003.

[49] A new civil code, aligned with EU law and international legal acts, came into effect in July 2001.

[50] Veidas, "Lietuviu nepasitikejimas sava policija didziausias visoje Europoje (Lithuanians' mistrust of their own police the highest in Europe)," June 9, 2005.

[51] Lekavicius Audrius," Nauji kodeksai stringa del klaidu ir spragu (Erros and flaws block new

codes)," Kauno Diena, May 20, 2003.

[52] Ministry of Justice of the Republic of Lithuania, www.teisinepagalba.lt/?top=en&item=en.

[53] Human Rights Monitoring Institute, Zmogaus teisiu agyvendinimas Lietuvoje: 2004 m. apzvalga (The Implementation of Human Rights in Lithuania: A 2004 Overview), www.hrmi.lt/project.php?strid=1191&id=2054.

[54] Veidas, "Labiausiai nepasitiki antstoliais (Bailiffs trusted the least)," August 25, 2005.

[55] Lekavicius Audrius, "Nauji kodeksai stringa del klaidu ir spragu (Erros and flaws block new codes)," Kauno Diena, May 20, 2003.

[56] Veidas, "Labiausiai nepasitiki antstoliais (Bailiffs trusted the least)," August 25, 2005.

[57] ELTA, "Politikai delsia deklaruoti privacius interesus (Politicians slow to declare private interests) ," May 9, 2005.

[58] Transparency International Lithuanian branch, www.transparency.org/cpi/2005/cpi2005_infocus.html#cpi.

[59] Baltic News Service, "Beveik trecdalis Lietuvos gyventoju duoda kysius (Almost a third of Lithuanians give bribes)," December 9, 2005.

[60] Transparency International Lithuanian branch, www.transparency.lt/tyrimai.php?PHPSESSID=da263936e17d2828144ac92d40dcddec.

[61] Ibid.

[62] By this decision, the Parliament revoked a 2004 provision of the civil code allowing symbolic gifts (no more than 125 litas' worth [US$65] for doctors.

[63] EBRD-World Bank, "Business Environment and Enterprise Performance Survey," 2005.

64 For more on the Civil Alliance against Corruption see Civil Society.

Macedonia

Capital:	Skopje
Population:	2 million
GNI/capita:	$2,420
Ethnic Groups:	Macedonian (64%), Albanian (25%), Turkish (4%), Roma (3%), Serb (2%), other (2%)

Nations in Transit Ratings and Averaged Scores

	1997	1998	1999	2001	2002	2003	2004	2005	2006
Electoral Process	3.50	3.50	3.50	3.75	4.50	3.50	3.50	3.00	3.25
Civil Society	3.75	3.75	3.50	3.75	4.00	3.75	3.25	3.25	3.25
Independent Media	4.00	4.00	3.75	3.75	3.75	4.00	4.25	4.25	4.25
Governance *	4.00	4.00	3.00	3.75	4.25	4.50	4.00	n/a	n/a
National Democratic Governance	n/a	n/a	n/a	n/a	n/a	n/a	n/a	4.00	3.75
Local Democratic Governance	n/a	n/a	n/a	n/a	n/a	n/a	n/a	4.00	3.75
Judicial Framework and Independence	4.25	4.50	4.25	4.25	4.75	4.50	4.00	3.75	3.75
Corruption	n/a	n/a	5.00	5.00	5.50	5.50	5.00	5.00	4.75
Democracy Score	3.90	3.95	3.83	4.04	4.46	4.29	4.00	3.89	3.82

* With the 2005 edition, Freedom House introduced seperate analysis and ratings for national democratic governance and local democratic governance to provide readers with more detailed and nuanced analysis of these two important subjects.

NOTE: The ratings reflect the consensus of Freedom House, its academic advisers, and the author of this report. The opinions expressed in this report are those of the author. The ratings are based on a scale of 1 to 7, with 1 representing the highest level of democratic progress and 7 the lowest. The Democracy Score is an average of ratings for the categories tracked in a given year.

The economic and social data on this page were taken from the following sources:
GNI/capita, Population: *World Development Indicators 2006* (Washington, D.C.: World Bank, 2006).
Ethnic Groups: *CIA World Factbook 2006* (Washington, D.C.: Central Intelligence Agency, 2006).

EXECUTIVE SUMMARY

A former constituent republic of the Socialist Federal Republic of Yugoslavia, Macedonia declared its independence on November 21, 1991. In contrast with other former Yugoslav republics, it enjoyed a peaceful and broadly uncontested transition to independence. However, full international recognition was delayed by Greek objections to the new state being called Macedonia (this being the name of a Greek province and its use, in the Greek view, implying pan-Macedonian ambitions), and admission to the United Nations was blocked until April 1993, when it took place under the interim designation "Former Yugoslav Republic of Macedonia." Although the reference to the former Yugoslav past was to be used within the UN as a result of Greek pressure, other international institutions have also used the interim reference. Besides the "name issue," during the democratization period the interethnic relations and the question of minority rights were at the forefront of the domestic political agenda. Following the warlike crisis in early and mid-2001, and the signing of the Ohrid Framework Agreement, Macedonia made a number of amendments to the 1991 Constitution that clarified the position of national minorities in the legal system, preserving territorial integrity and sovereignty.

Two major events characterized 2005: the local government elections and the granting of candidate status to Macedonia by the European Union (EU) Council of States in early December. In the local elections, the ruling coalition, led by the Social Democratic Alliance of Macedonia, won 352,089 votes, 435 elected councillors, and 37 mayors. The opposition coalition, led by the Internal Macedonian Revolutionary Organization – Democratic Party for Macedonian National Unity, won 226,295 votes, 323 elected councillors, and 21 mayors. Although the Social Democratic Alliance of Macedonia won more votes and mayors, the opposition won in the capital city, Skopje, securing the constituent municipalities of Centar, Aerodrom, Butel, Gazi Baba, and Kisela Voda. The new mayor of Skopje was an independent candidate but supported by the opposition. Among Macedonian Albanians, the ruling Democratic Union for Integration won over the opposition Democratic Party of Albanians. Although the local elections were marred by a number of irregularities, a positive recommendation was given to Macedonia by the EU Commission.

Following the 2001 conflict, the general level of security has gradually improved, and in 2005 police presence was ensured all over the country. As many police patrols are ethnically mixed, the trust of the minority communities has also improved. With the exceptions of a number of localities in the former crisis areas, where police activities require a considerable level of sensitivity, the government's authority extends over the full territory of the country. However, the question remains how to collect the illegal weapons still circulating within Macedonia.

National Democratic Governance. Macedonia's desire to become a member of the EU and NATO influences the fulfillment of democratic principles of governance. The prospect of integration has built a consensus among political groups and citizens on democracy as the basis of the country's political system, although much of the national government's work is conducted behind closed doors and the population is increasingly separated rather than integrated. The implementation of the Ohrid Agreement has stabilized the country so that citizens recognize the legitimacy of national authorities and the laws that govern them. The political system is free of such threats to stability as war or insurgencies. In 2005, the government enjoyed a year of political stability and public support for its reform agenda, yet this new stability is still very fragile. *Macedonia's rating for national democratic governance improves from 4.00 to 3.75 as a result of the normalization of the functioning of institutions and the EU-related reforms undertaken by the government.*

Electoral Process. According to the law, local elections in Macedonia are to be conducted every four years. The previous local elections took place in November 2000 in 123 municipalities. Owing to the early presidential elections (two rounds in April 2004) and the referendum on the territorial organization of local self-government units (November 7, 2004), the elections were postponed until spring 2005. The citizens elected mayors and council members of the new 84 municipalities and the city of Skopje, the voting conducted at 2,976 polling stations. In the first round, voting was regular, fair, and democratic across much of the country. But in some municipalities, a complete violation of the election process occurred. A report by the Organization for Security and Cooperation in Europe/Office for Democratic Institutions and Human Rights (OSCE/ODIHR) said the vote had "failed to meet key commitments guaranteeing universal and equal suffrage and the secrecy of the ballot." The second round of elections was much better organized, with very few irregularities observed. *Macedonia's electoral process rating worsens from 3.00 to 3.25 given the partially successful implementation of the 2005 local elections and the unfavorable assessments by the OSCE, especially concerning the conduct during the first round.*

Civil Society. Although Macedonian civil society boasts over 5,500 nongovernmental organizations (NGOs) by some estimates, the civil sector continues to lack capacities and consistent funding. In 2005, the level of quality improved in only a handful of local NGOs, while many others disappeared from the scene altogether. The main factor behind the boom in the sector is the availability of funds. Various international donors support the NGO sector in Macedonia, each with its own agenda that is often not coordinated with local needs and NGO demands. There is a top-down approach by the international community, offering funding to local organizations only if their programs and projects match the funding priorities of the donors. Few civil society groups are financially viable in the long term. Macedonian civil society has yet to attain the critical mass needed to become a serious actor at either the national or the local level. Instead of relying on funds on a project basis, local NGOs would be better served if core funding to key sectors was available from donors. *Macedonia's rating for civil society remains at 3.25.*

Independent Media. Although attacks on journalists decreased in 2005, interference with editorial policies have remained at 2004 levels. In 2005, a number of key editors and journalists from A1 Television claimed influence on their work by the owner and resigned. A few private broadcasters, such as TV Sitel or Kanal 5, are considered to be politically influenced, as the owners of these outlets are also presidents of political parties. The majority of print and electronic media are privately owned, and the German media conglomerate WAZ has owned the three biggest-selling dailies since July 2003, which could be considered an excessive concentration of media ownership. During local elections, the media generally provided diverse information to voters. The government has not yet made any attempts to amend the criminal code and the criminal character of libel. In 2005, several journalists were convicted to probationary prison sentences. Premier Vladimir Buchkovski heavily criticized unnamed media and journalists for being "manipulated and paid to write biased texts." A much-awaited Law on Access to Public Information has not been adopted. *Macedonia's rating for independent media remains at 4.25 owing to the lack of progress in decriminalizing libel and the lack of a legal framework for access to public information.*

Local Democratic Governance. Following the Ohrid Agreement, which ended the conflict between ethnic Albanian irregulars and the security forces through comprehensive reforms of the legal and the political system, Macedonia has engaged in a thorough decentralization effort, committing itself to devolve responsibilities of the central government to local government units. Devolution of powers was enacted in the spheres of urban planning and service delivery, fiscal management, and local economic development, among others. The transfer of competencies started on July 1, 2005, although many municipalities were understaffed or had low staff capacities to take over the devolved responsibilities. *Macedonia's rating for local democratic governance improves from 4.00 to 3.75 owing to the implementation of an overwhelming – and imperfect – local government reform effort.*

Judicial Framework and Independence. While the Macedonian legal framework provides for the protection of fundamental political civil and human rights and equality before the law, in 2005 the government concentrated efforts on judicial reform. One of the problems has been how to shield judges from political influence and ensure their independence. Another problem is the inefficiency of the judiciary and the enormous backlog of cases awaiting trial or execution. The main principles of reform were approved by the Parliament on May 18, 2005, by a broad majority. Draft amendments were presented by the government in June, and in August the Parliament adopted 15 draft amendments that have been debated publicly. The reform was scheduled to be completed by the end of 2005. *Macedonia's rating for judicial framework and independence remains at 3.75, the reform of the judiciary still pending.*

Corruption. According to a survey done by the domestic polling company Strategic Marketing, 73 percent of citizens believe that the government is corrupt. Given that few cases of corruption have actually been resolved, it is clear that the Macedonian public has "internalized" and "normalized" official corruption. In 2005, allegations of corruption were given wide and extensive airing in the media. Recognizing that the government has a direct impact on various spheres of the economy that have not yet been liberalized, new departments were established in the Ministry of the Interior and the Office of the Public Prosecutor to combat organized crime and corruption. The effectiveness of the State Commission for the Prevention of Corruption depends in large part on the cooperation of the state institution, the public prosecutor in particular. In May, the commission released a report complaining that the level of cooperation with the public prosecutor is very limited. *Macedonia's rating for corruption improves from 5.00 to 4.75 owing to the political will to put the issue on the national agenda.*

Outlook for 2006. Boosted by EU candidacy status, the reform process is expected to continue in 2006 and be completed in the reform of the judiciary. Further harmonizing of Macedonian legislation with EU law is expected. The national elections scheduled for the fall will be a crucial test of the speed of Macedonia's EU accession. The EU accession process is expected to further consolidate political stability. Ethnic relations might be affected by complications concerning a permanent solution to the status of Kosovo.

MAIN REPORT

National Democratic Governance

1997	1998	1999	2001	2002	2003	2004	2005	2006
n/a	n/a	n/a	n/a	n/a	n/a	n/a	4.00	3.75

Modern Macedonia came into existence in 1945 as one of the six constituent republics of the Socialist Federal Republic of Yugoslavia. When Yugoslavia disintegrated in 1991, Macedonia declared independence on November 21, 1991, and today is a democratic multiparty state. Power is divided among the three branches of government: the Parliament (Sobranie), the executive (the government with the president and premier), and the judiciary (Supreme Court, Constitutional Court, and the public prosecutor).

The unicameral Parliament (Sobranie) is composed of between 120 and 140 members elected by direct, universal suffrage. All Parliaments prior to the current one have had 120 members. According to the electoral laws adopted in June 2002 (the Law on Election of Members of Parliament of 2002, the Law on the Voter

List, and the Law on Election Districts), members of Parliament (MPs) are elected for a four-year term in six electoral districts. Each district has about 275,000 voters and elects 20 members by proportional representation subject to a 5 percent threshold. Citizens vote for an electoral list, and seats are distributed on a proportional basis, according to the D'Hondt formula. The nomination lists may be submitted by parties, coalitions of parties, or groups of at least 500 voters. At least 30 percent of the candidates on each list must be of different gender. There were 31 lists for the parliamentary elections in 2002.

The legislature has sufficient capacity to fulfill its lawmaking and investigative responsibilities. There are 18 permanent working bodies in the Parliament, 7 of which are chaired by MPs from the opposition. A Committee on EU Affairs was established in November 2003, and the government submits quarterly reports on EU integration activities to the Parliament. The assembly has also formed delegations to cooperate with the Parliaments of other nations and international organizations. The parliamentary budget is part of Macedonia's national budget and is projected by the Ministry of Finance. Since this does not necessarily reflect estimates by the parliamentary budgetary committee, there have been discussions about adopting a Law on the Parliament that would provide for a truly independent source of revenue for the assembly.[1]

Pursuant to Article 88 of the Constitution, executive power is vested in the government, which is responsible for the organization and coordination of all state administrative bodies. It initiates draft legislation, oversees the operation of state institutions, and executes laws and regulations adopted by the Parliament. In the last 15 years, the governments have been formed by a coalition of parties, typically a major Macedonian and Macedonian Albanian party and a smaller Macedonian party as a junior coalition partner. Although the president has the legal duty to nominate candidates, the Parliament appoints the premier, who is the head of government and selected by the party or coalition that gains a majority of seats in the Parliament. The current government is led by Premier Vladimir Buchkovski and includes the Social Democratic Alliance of Macedonia (SDSM), the Democratic Union for Integration (DUI), and the Liberal Democratic Party (LDP).

The Macedonian political system is semipresidential, akin to the French model. By law, the president represents Macedonia at home and abroad and is the commander in chief of the armed forces. The president may veto legislation adopted by the Parliament with a simple majority. However, this veto power is quite limited, and the Parliament can vote on the same law again within 30 days. If the law in question is approved again by a two-thirds majority, the president must sign the decree into law. Since the president is elected by direct ballot and has a term of five years, with the right to one reelection, the personality of the president has a great impact on the position's actual power. Kiro Gligorov, acting as "father of the nation" from 1991 to 1999, set the trend for strong presidents, with the late Boris Trajkovski and the current president, Branko Crvenkovski, following his example.

The Constitutional Court has a dominant role within the Macedonian judiciary. The Court oversees major acts of Parliament and the cabinet, having the power to annul legislation or decrees that are found to violate the Constitution. The Judiciary Council similarly provides oversight of the court system and judges. The Parliament appoints council members as well as Constitutional Court judges and the public prosecutor through a system of double majority voting, which requires a majority of the votes of MPs who are members of minority ethnic groups.

Although Macedonia is a parliamentary democracy, in practice the government dominates the assembly by introducing laws to be adopted or amended. Still, there are strong mitigating factors preventing the concentration of power in cases where a political party or coalition gains control (after elections) of both the legislature and the executive. First of all, the strong figure of the president works to balance the dominant tendency of the premier. Second, the Macedonian political system features an informal rule of having the government composed of a multiethnic coalition. Governing such a coalition requires advanced political skills and accommodation, which in turn necessitates much political maneuvering and compromise, making the concentration of power unfeasible.

Macedonia is a multiethnic state with a population of around 2 million. Macedonians are 64 percent of the total population, while Albanians are the biggest minority with 25 percent. As with a number of other countries in Eastern Europe, Macedonia's reforms in the last 15 years have been focused simultaneously on two issues – state building and setting up the legal base for a functioning market economy.[2] Problems consolidating Macedonia's democracy have been related to its interethnic relations. Armed conflict erupted between Albanian rebels and government forces in 2001 but was quickly ended through an EU- and U.S.-mediated agreement, signed in August of that year.

In the years after independence, Macedonian Albanians made major demands on the central government: a reform of the Constitution, greater representation of Albanians in the civil service sector, a university conducted in the Albanian language, and decentralization of state power. Gradually, reforms were enacted and improvements were made, resulting in a rise in participation of the civic sector by Macedonian Albanians in recent years. Similarly, a law was passed allowing private education in languages other than Macedonian, while a European-financed trilingual (Albanian, English, and Macedonian) university was opened in 2001. However, with a major segment of the population challenging the very foundations of the state, Macedonia could not have begun the development of a just and democratic political system before the 2001 Ohrid Framework Agreement and the subsequent adoption of amendments to the 1991 Constitution.

Since the 2001 conflict, the general level of security has gradually improved, and police presence is now ensured all over the country. Since many police patrols are ethnically mixed, the trust of minority communities has also improved. With the exception of a number of localities in the former crisis areas, where police activities require a considerable level of sensitivity, the government's authority extends over the full territory of the country. However, questions remain about how to collect illegal weapons still circulating within Macedonia.

To ensure the government fulfills its obligations from the Ohrid Framework Agreement, the EU made the further integration of Macedonia into Europe conditional on full implementation of the agreement. The EU had already signed a Stabilization and Association Agreement with Macedonia – the first signed with any government in the region – in April 2001. Macedonia's formal application for EU membership, which was submitted on March 22, 2004, was followed by a European Commission questionnaire with more than 4,000 queries. On November 9, 2005, the commission recommended that the EU council grant candidate country status to Macedonia. Moreover, the commission determined that negotiations for accession should be opened once Macedonia reaches a sufficient degree of compliance with membership criteria.

In fact, Macedonia's desire to become a member of the EU and NATO has spurred the building of a strong consensus among political groups and citizens on democracy as the basis of the country's political system. The implementation of the Ohrid Agreement has sufficiently stabilized the country so that citizens recognize the legitimacy of national authorities and the laws that govern them. And the national political system is currently free from such threats to stability as insurgency or war.

Macedonian citizens and the media have regular access to legislators and the legislative process, and parliamentary sessions are open to the public. Even so, citizen involvement in political culture is rather low. NGOs and concerned citizens have not been engaged in budget oversight, and local governance is a largely unchecked endeavor in Macedonian political life.

Macedonia has yet to adopt freedom of information legislation, which would solve many of the nation's government transparency issues, including budget monitoring. It is the last country in the region and one of only a few countries in Europe that does not have a freedom of information act. Although the Constitution says freedom of information is a fundamental human right, this has not been enough to ensure access to information. Moreover, information is not readily given to citizens, even if they ask for it explicitly. A survey by the Macedonian section of Transparency International showed that 70 percent of those citizens who requested information from state institutions had difficulties obtaining it and that 27 percent did not receive any answer from the state, while 33 percent were refused access to the needed information with no explanation.[3] Transparency International and other local NGOs have initiated a draft law that was expected to be adopted by the Parliament in 2005. Prepared and debated since 2003, this latest proposal has been given a positive verdict by the Council of Europe and Article 19 but has yet to be adopted by the Parliament.

The Law on Civil Servants enacted in 2000 regulates the status, rights, duties, responsibilities, and salaries of civil servants. As provided by law, the Civil Servants Agency was established to support the law's implementation. Since independence, however, political parties have acted as special interest groups, (mis)using power and the system's institutions to win economic benefits. Party membership is widely perceived as a significant factor when applying for jobs, and political officials appoint their followers or fellow party members rather than the most qualified candidates. Cronyism and nepotism are commonplace in both low- and high-level appointments, such as ambassadorships.

Once a political party loses power, the nonessential personnel in the ministries affiliated to it are laid off by the new minister or manager appointed by one of the main parties of the new ruling coalition, and vice versa.[4] Since middle- and senior-level civil servants are seen as political rather than technical appointments, they tend to be replaced as administrations change. Consequently, there is little policy continuity, and political maneuvering within or between parties has led to policy paralysis and held up reform. Meanwhile, the use of public sector employment as a tool of patronage has led to an overstaffed and inefficient public sector. Clearly, these practices negatively impact transparency in public procurement, the development of a market economy, and consistency in respecting the law. The close link between political power and access to economic resources exacerbates these problems.

Macedonian political parties tend to seek control of state institutions for the economic rents they provide. Elections are seen as "winner take all," with few checks and balances for the winning coalition. This system of political spoils is pervasive. Party allegiance and patronage win out over merit and policy evaluation. As a consequence, the excessively centralized Macedonian state is plagued with poor delivery of services and a lack of sufficiently skilled human resources, especially in the area of policy development and implementation. This generates bad policy making, leading to frequent amendments to legal acts.

According to the Constitution, the army and the police are under civilian control. A National Security and Defense Concept, adopted in 2003, coordinates security in cases of crisis. Under the Law on Internal Affairs, the Ministry of the Interior is responsible for the internal security of the state. The ministry has a Bureau for Public Security, which includes the Department of Police, the border police, the criminal police, and the Directorate for Security and Counterintelligence. Reforms are in progress in the Ministry of Defense and in the army, driven by the prospect of Macedonia's membership in NATO. (The country has been an active member of NATO's Partnership for Peace.)[5] This reform has already led to a reduction of military personnel. In 2005, the Ministry of Defense staff was reduced from 1,200 to 650.[6] The reform also takes into account the objectives of the Ohrid Framework Agreement in terms of achieving equitable representation of individuals from minority communities in the civil service. According to the Constitution, the commander in chief of the armed forces is the president, while a civilian minister of defense oversees all security- and defense-related activities.

Electoral Process

1997	1998	1999	2001	2002	2003	2004	2005	2006
3.50	3.50	3.50	3.75	4.50	3.50	3.50	3.00	3.25

The authority of the Macedonian government is based on universal and equal suffrage, with regular, free, and fair elections conducted by secret ballot. Moreover, the electoral system is free of significant barriers to political organization and registration, and ethnic and other minority groups have sufficient opportunities to participate in the political process. In the years since independence, the electoral system has been multiparty based, with the public engaged in the political life of the country. Power has rotated among different party coalitions representing competing interests and policy options. The field of political contenders is generally free from domination by power groups, such as the military, foreign powers, totalitarian parties, regional hierarchies, and/or economic oligarchies. Domestic and international election-monitoring organizations judged the most recent national legislative elections, conducted in the fall of 2002, to be free and fair. According to the OSCE, the most recent presidential elections held in April 2004 were free and fair, generally complied with international standards, and experienced a relatively small number of election irregularities, such as proxy voting, political violence, the presence of unauthorized personnel at polling stations, and voter intimidation.

According to the law, local elections in Macedonia are to be conducted every four years. The previous local elections took place in November 2000 in 123 municipalities and the capital city of Skopje. The next elections were to be held in 2004, but owing to the early presidential elections and the referendum on the territorial organization of local self-government units, the elections were postponed until spring 2005. Citizens elected mayors and members of councils of the new 84 municipalities and Skopje, with voting conducted at 2,976 polling stations.

On March 13 and 27, 2005, Macedonia held local elections, which were regular, free, and democratic throughout most of the country. In some municipalities, however, a complete violation of the election process occurred. Thus, after the vote on March 13, the Supreme Court ordered a repeat of first-round voting at 33 polling stations in 10 municipalities, including Skopje, and in the second-largest municipality, Tetovo. Despite just recently applying for EU membership, the multiethnic coalition government led by SDSM did not manage to keep its promise of organizing free and fair elections. A report by the OSCE/ODIHR said the vote had "failed to meet key commitments guaranteeing universal and equal suffrage and the secrecy of the ballot."[7] OSCE observers reported problems in about 10 percent of the polling stations visited, including ballot stuffing, tension in and around polling stations, and intimidation. The police were called to intervene in 20 cases, and several people were detained. Most irregularities were reported in the predominantly Albanian municipalities of Saraj and Arachinovo, near Skopje, as well as in the Roma stronghold of Shuto Orizari. Although charges were pressed against the individuals who violated the election process, the ruling coalition was to blame for failing to protect the electoral process since it had already witnessed irregularities, including fatal shootings, in previous elections in some of these same municipalities.

Many appeals and complaints were submitted to the State Electoral Commission as well as to the courts. The rejection of many of these complaints led to a boycott of the second round of the local elections by the Albanian oppositional bloc. In the second round, a Macedonian NGO, MOST, reported irregularities, including group voting and ballot stuffing, at 14 polling stations. Although Deputy Prime Minister Radmila Shekerinska maintained that less than 1 percent of the country's 2,057 polling stations were affected and Premier Buchkovski expressed "great pleasure" with the voting, saying that authorities had succeeded in blocking attempts to undermine the elections, the local elections in 2005 marred Macedonia's EU integration efforts.

In the first round of local elections, 17 mayors were elected in the 84 municipalities and Skopje. The remaining mayors were elected in the second round, which took place on March 27 and April 10.[8] SDSM in coalition with LDP and a number of other smaller parties won 352,089 votes, 435 elected councillors, and 37 mayors. The opposition coalition, led by the Internal Macedonian Revolutionary Organization–Democratic Party for Macedonian National Unity (VMRO-DPMNE), won 226,295 votes, 323 elected councillors, and 21 mayors. DUI won 113,881 votes, 213 elected councillors, and 14 mayors. VMRO-DPMNE won 117,047 votes, 136 elected councillors, and 3 mayors, while the Democratic Party of Albanians–Democratic Party for Prosperity won 110,662 votes, 131 elected councillors, and 2 mayors.[9] Although SDSM won more votes and mayors, the opposition won in Skopje, securing the municipalities of Centar, Aerodrom, Butel, Gazi Baba, and Kisela Voda. The new mayor of Skopje was an independent candidate but supported by the opposition.

Civil Society

1997	1998	1999	2001	2002	2003	2004	2005	2006
3.75	3.75	3.50	3.75	4.00	3.75	3.25	3.25	3.25

During Communist times, when Macedonia was part of the Yugoslav federation, the country's civil society was suppressed. Established institutions like the Association of Women of Macedonia or the Association of Youth of Macedonia could not in fact be characterized as nongovernmental institutions. But during the 1980s, Macedonia witnessed the rise of a plethora of civic groups, movements, and associations. The signs of emerging pluralist tendencies were especially evident on the Macedonian cultural scene. For example, in the mid-1980s, a number of young intellectuals and artists launched Makedonska Streljba, a multimedia project that was precursor to the acclaimed Slovenian movement Nue Slowenische Kunst, thus emphasizing the importance of the Macedonian language and culture in the Yugoslav context and the desire to develop new political models in Macedonia and the Socialist Federal Republic of Yugoslavia.

Following independence, opportunities for the development of civil society became real. Now, the state by law confirms the rights of the independent civic sector. In the last 15 years, the number and scope of NGOs in Macedonia have risen dramatically. Many deal with significant societal, political, and economic issues. The legal framework for the functioning of civil society is free of excessive state pressures and bureaucracy. Under the 1998 Law on Citizen Associations and Foundations, NGOs are registered as civic organizations. The law prohibits NGOs as well as trade and professional organizations, employer and employee unions, interest groups, and foundations from being involved in direct economic activities. There are, however, two significant obstacles for the civil sector that contribute to its weakness: access to information and the taxation of NGOs.

Macedonian civil society groups also lack sufficient organizational capacity to sustain their work. Most NGOs are poorly managed, lack professionalism and communication skills, and have few experienced practitioners or trainers. Key NGOs such as the Foundation for Open Society Macedonia and the Macedonian Center for International Issues have been led by the same managers/directors since their founding and dominate the activities of the civil society.

Currently, the country can boast many NGOs – over 5,500 by some estimates – but only a few groups show much in the way of capacity.[10] The main factor behind the boom in the sector is the availability of funds. Various international donors support the NGO sector in Macedonia, each with its own agenda, which is often not coordinated with local needs and NGO demands. The donors take a top-down approach, offering funding to local organizations only if their programs and projects match the priorities established by the funders in Washington or Brussels, for example. Few civil society groups are financially viable in the long term. Local philanthropy and volunteerism are almost nonexistent, while the participation of religious groups in charitable activities is minimal. A number of civic organizations represent the interests of women, physically impaired persons, and sexual and ethnic minorities, and these receive most of the attention and funding. Macedonian civil society has yet to attain the critical mass needed to become a serious actor at either the national or the local level. Instead of relying on funds on a per project basis, local NGOs would be better served if core funding in key sectors were available.

Today, Macedonian society is free of excessive influence by extremist and intolerant nongovernmental institutions and organizations. In fact, there are no visibly active organizations, private militias, or vigilante groups advocating racist or xenophobic agendas or threatening political and social stability or the country's transition to democracy. The Macedonian education system is free of political influence and propaganda.

Although the government respects the right to form and join civil society organizations, including free trade unions, it is hardly receptive to policy advocacy by interest groups, policy research centers, and other nonprofit organizations. Government officials rarely engage civil society groups by inviting them to comment on and influence pending policies or legislation. The media, on the other hand, are more receptive to civil society groups and serve as independent sources of information and commentary, thus contributing positively to the country's civic life.

Independent Media

1997	1998	1999	2001	2002	2003	2004	2005	2006
4.00	4.00	3.75	3.75	3.75	4.00	4.25	4.25	4.25

The Macedonian public enjoys a diverse selection of print and electronic sources of information at both national and local levels, representing a range of political viewpoints. The distribution of privately controlled newspapers and the media's editorial independence and news-gathering functions are free of direct government interference. In the broadcast media arena, hundreds of private outlets try to survive in market conditions that are adverse even by regional standards, making the commercial sector as overcrowded and inefficient as the public sector. The law allows Macedonian Public Television to broadcast commercials and compete for marketing revenues with private media. This is seen as the main obstacle to the financial viability of private broadcasters.

A few, such as TV Sitel and Kanal 5, are considered to be politically influenced since the owners of these outlets are also presidents of political parties. In 2005, a number of key editors and journalists from A1 Television resigned, claiming influence on their work by the owner. The majority of print and electronic media are privately owned, and since July 2003, the German media conglomerate WAZ has owned the three biggest-selling dailies, *Vest*, *Dnevnik*, and *Utrinski Vesnik*. This is considered by some to be an excessive concentration of media ownership. During the local elections, the media generally provided diverse information to voters in compliance with the election law that requires equal access to the media for all candidates and political parties during an election campaign. However, the OSCE observed a degree of bias in favor of government interests on state channels MTV1 and MTV3, though noting an improvement in MTV1's coverage of the campaign prior to the second round.

The society enjoys open access to the Internet, with a diverse range of sites and viewpoints, although penetration is remarkably low. Estimates reveal that between 6 and 10 percent of Macedonian citizens use the Internet on a daily basis, significantly lagging behind other countries in Eastern Europe.[11] Access to all sites is unrestricted, and registration of new sites is simple.[12] Still, official use of the Internet could be improved. Macedonian courts, for example, are not connected to the Internet, do not have official Web sites, and do not allow citizens to search court archives digitally. Less than 4 percent of the candidates for local elections in 2005 had Web sites. Macedonia is the last country in the region without legislation on access to public information, with a draft still in the works in 2005. With no such law on the books, citizens are often unjustifiably denied access to public information.[13]

In principle, Article 16 of the Constitution, adopted in 2004, guarantees freedom of speech and access to information. Although journalists and media outlets are able to form their own viable professional associations – the Association of Macedonian Journalists and the Macedonian Institute for Media being particularly active – the government has not yet decriminalized libel by amending various articles in the criminal code that prohibit the spread of false information and slander. While the 2005 World Press Freedom Index by Reporters Without Borders ranked Macedonia 43 – below Italy, but higher than the United States – problems with "irresponsible" journalism remain. In fact, Macedonian courts are quite efficient when it comes to trials against journalists accused of slander and defamation. In 2005, Kanal 5 TV editor Ida Protugjer was sentenced to three months' probation for allegedly miswriting that the current mayor of Skopje, Trifun Kostovski, was the owner of Eurostandard Bank. The daily *Vecer* had previously revealed this information, and even the premier pointed out that Kostovski was indeed the owner of the bank. A number of other journalists, including TV Sitel reporter Liljana Georgieva, Kanal 5 reporter Marijana Panova, *Vecer* journalist Violeta Cvetanovska, and Vest journalist Aleksandra Stojanovska, were also taken to court. The government's attitude toward journalists has not been helpful. On November 22, for example, Premier Buchkovski claimed that "some media and journalists" were "manipulated and paid to write biased texts on the tender for making new passports."[14] Furthermore, on November 28 he accused journalists of disturbing the good relations between Macedonia and Croatia, referring in particular to those journalists who reported that a Macedonian general had participated in the war in Croatia as an officer of the Yugoslav Peoples Army.[15]

The Broadcasting Council is responsible for regulating electronic media in Macedonia. The council grants licenses to media outlets and oversees compliance to regulations and established standards. A new Law on Broadcasting, adopted on November 9, was deemed by the OSCE media freedom representative as being in line with OSCE media freedom standards. The new law, which is a result of close cooperation between the Macedonian government, the OSCE, the Stability Pact for South Eastern Europe, the Council of Europe, and the European Commission, aims to ensure an effective Broadcasting Council and to establish a system for the independent functioning of the public broadcaster.

Local Democratic Governance

1997	1998	1999	2001	2002	2003	2004	2005	2006
n/a	n/a	n/a	n/a	n/a	n/a	n/a	4.00	3.75

The Macedonian Constitution defines municipalities as the basic unit of local government and establishes general principles for the organization, function, and financing of local governments, with details to be elaborated in subsequent legislation. This foundation was largely provided in the 1995 Law of Local Government, which provides for a directly elected mayor, who is responsible for administrative operations, and an elected council. Although the 1995 law identified an impressive range of local government competencies, before the 2004 reforms and for a variety of reasons, "including poor statutory drafting, apparent lack of central government resolve, and the regime of fiscal austerity to which the overall public sector has been subject since 1994, Macedonia's local governments actually exercised few of these competencies."[16]

Since the 2001 Ohrid Agreement, which ended the conflict between ethnic Albanian irregulars and the security forces through comprehensive reforms of the legal and political system, Macedonia has engaged in a thorough decentralization effort, committing itself to devolve responsibilities of the central government to local government units. The government has worked to correct the functional deficiencies of municipalities and enhance their capacity to create sustainable economic development through independently collected local revenues. Thus, decentralization also implies transferring responsibilities concerning tax collection and reallocation of funds for financing public services on the local level.

The law sets limits on the central government's authority and outlines new possibilities for free association of municipalities. With the package of laws passed in 2004, devolution of powers was designated in the areas of urban planning and service delivery, fiscal management, and local economic development, among others. To prevent the potential mismanagement of resources at the local level, a number of stringent conditions were established that have to be met before individual local authorities can assume their new responsibilities. The key challenges for decentralization reform in 2005 were the calculation of sectoral block grants – the funds that support education, health care, and social protection at the local level – and the distribution of the equalization fund. There is concern that the central government is not transferring sufficient funds to municipalities for the normal functioning of public institutions such as primary and secondary schools.

Decentralization is a strategic goal for the Macedonian government as it develops a new model of state governance. This recent distribution of power should in the long term transform the whole public administrative system, leading to a more efficient and effective government brought closer to the people. The process of decentralization is linked to three key areas: territorial division (reducing the number of municipalities from 124 to 84, including 10 within the capital, Skopje), the funding of municipalities, and the status of Skopje. The process has not been easy – local elections were postponed twice amid a dispute over the Law on Territorial Division, which has been regarded as too favorable toward ethnic Albanians, and finally took place in March 2005. The transfer of competencies started on July 1, 2005, although many municipalities lacked sufficient personnel and resources to take over the devolved responsibilities.

Municipalities are to be financed from own-revenue sources, government grants, and loans. The own-revenue sources will comprise property, inheritance, and gift taxes, sales taxes on real estate and rights, and municipal fees. Moreover, the municipalities will now be responsible for setting tax rates and municipal fees with maximum and minimum limits specified by the Laws on Property Taxes. Other local revenues will include the 3 percent share of the personal income tax paid by local residents. In addition to these revenues, the Law on Financing the Local Self-Government Units envisages a number of grants provided for municipalities from the central budget: revenues from value-added tax (general grants), block grants, earmarked grants, capital grants, and grants for delegated competencies. The law also allows municipalities to borrow additional funds in the capital markets, if approved by the Ministry of Finance.

In various surveys, Macedonian citizens express dissatisfaction with the quality of local government public services, listing poor skills, accountability, and lack of motivation as major weaknesses. Good municipal management is not easily achieved. There are considerable gaps between the human resource capacities of local self-government institutions on the one hand and the requirements implied by the devolution of competencies on the other. Even though staff was transferred from the central level to municipalities throughout 2005, establishing adequate social services at the local level will remain a challenge for several years to come.

Macedonian citizens elect municipal officials by secret ballot in direct local elections. These are held regularly and subject to independent monitoring and oversight. Multiple candidates participate in local elections and in local government bodies, which are free from dominant power groups. Democratically elected local authorities exercise their powers freely and autonomously and will have the resources and capacity needed to fulfill their responsibilities with the help of anticipated reforms. Still, a few problems remain, such as stimulating meaningful participation by citizens in local government decision making and transparency and accountability in the work of local authorities.

A 2004 survey by Transparency International revealed that 41 percent of Macedonians were not aware of their constitutional right to access public information.[17] Citizens are "reticent to react against the lack, insufficiency, or low quality of public services, the abuse of constitutional rights, and a low participation in developing and defining public policies."[18] In a few cases, municipalities, in cooperation with the international community, have encouraged citizens to get involved in policy making and legislation development, yet many Macedonians perceive government officials as "untouchable" and powerful cliques. As the debate over the country's new Law on Territorial Division demonstrated, citizens in Macedonia remain passive concerning public life and policy making until their direct interests are threatened.

On the other hand, the prevailing political culture in the country is such that the government's policy-making process is typically done behind closed doors, without the input and consultation of a wider network of stakeholders, such as citizens, civil society groups, and academic experts. A somewhat typical example was the government's decision-making process in the new territorial organization of municipalities, which was a highly secretive and reticent affair.[19]

Judicial Framework and Independence

1997	1998	1999	2001	2002	2003	2004	2005	2006
4.25	4.50	4.25	4.25	4.75	4.50	4.00	3.75	3.75

While the Macedonian legal framework protects fundamental political, civil, and human rights and equality before the law, in 2005 the government concentrated efforts on judicial reform. One pressing issue is how to shield judges from political influence. Another problem is the inefficiency of the judiciary, buried as it is under hundreds of thousands of untried cases. In 2004 alone, more than a million legal cases were processed in the Macedonian courts.[20] The courts are burdened with administrative work and are also expected to deal with a high number of misdemeanor and decided cases that require law enforcement. In March 2005, the total number of pending cases was 730,700; among these, 296,000 were "execution" cases (already ruled, needing enforcement)[21] and 227,000 were "misdemeanor" cases. The average duration of a civil proceeding is nine and a half months at first instance and over 70 days for an appeal, while in criminal cases it is nine and a half months.[22] The judiciary's insufficient infrastructure and lack of resources are also serious problems. The EU has stated that "the independence, as well as the quality, of the judiciary is further weakened by the absence of a comprehensive merit-based career system and an appropriate disciplinary system for judges."[23]

The government adopted a Strategy and an Action Plan on Judicial Reform in November 2004, outlining key changes to the country's legislation and Constitution to increase efficiency and to free the courts from political influence. The main principles were approved by the Parliament on May 18, 2005, by a broad majority. Draft amendments were presented by the government in June, and in August the Parliament adopted 15 draft amendments, which have been debated publicly.[24] Meanwhile, a new Law on Enforcement of Civil Judgments was adopted in May 2005 to abolish the separate motion for execution of judgments and to create a privatized bailiff system under the Ministry of Justice. This law will apply from 2006, subject to the adoption of secondary legislation and the necessary preparatory measures to put the new system in place. Although a new Law on Civil Procedure was adopted in September 2005 to introduce changes that should make court procedures more efficient, a new secondary legal framework will be needed to implement these changes.

Major changes have been planned regarding the composition, selection, and competencies of the Judicial Council. Throughout 2005, authorities discussed reforms to its system for electing members in order to limit political interference. An expert committee has already been hired and dismissed in that process. The Judicial Council consists of seven individuals appointed by a parliamentary commission and proposes the appointment, dismissal, and disciplinary decisions concerning judges, with such decisions then taken up by the Parliament. Since members of the Judicial Council are selected by a simple majority of votes in the Parliament, the governing coalition effectively has control over the appointment of both.

Ten constitutional amendments were passed on December 7, with the opposition VMRO-DPMNE voting against them.[25] According to Amendment 30, the competence, establishment, abolishment, organization, and operation of the Office of the Public Prosecutor are regulated by law, which is adopted with a two-thirds parliamentary majority. Amendment 38 notes that the 15-member Judicial Council is elected with a two-thirds majority. Ex officio members of the council shall be the president of the Supreme Court of the Republic of Macedonia and the minister of justice. Eight of its members must be judges. Three members of the Judicial Council shall be elected by a majority of votes from the total membership of the Parliament. Two members shall be appointed by the president, one of whom shall be a member of a community that is not of the majority.[26] According to Amendment 29, equitable and just representation of the citizens who belong to all communities shall be observed in the election of judges, lay judges, and presidents of the courts. The Parliament also passed legislation on the enforcement of the amendments specifying that by July 30, 2006, new laws on the Judicial Council, the courts, misdemeanors, the Council of Public Prosecutors, and the public prosecutor will be passed. Work on these laws and the planned reforms is expected to be completed in 2006.

Corruption

1997	1998	1999	2001	2002	2003	2004	2005	2006
n/a	n/a	5.00	5.00	5.50	5.50	5.00	5.00	4.75

Given that few cases of corruption have actually been resolved, it is clear that the Macedonian public has "internalized" and "normalized" official corruption. According to a survey by the company Strategic Marketing and Media Research Institute, 73 percent of citizens believe that the government is corrupt.[27] International reports and surveys such as Transparency International's Corruption Perceptions Index indicate that corruption in Macedonia is a serious and widespread problem that affects many aspects of social, political, and economic life despite the intensification of efforts to fight it and increased awareness of its negative impact on the country.[28] In 2005, allegations of corruption were given wide and extensive airing in the media. There was continual media coverage related to the allegedly corrupt sale of state-owned land on the main square in Skopje by former minister of transport and communication Agron Buhxaku. Other reported cases included the sale of the Sasa mine; various military barracks, apartments, and real estate; and the Electric Supply Company and alleged corruption concerning the buying of state land by greengrocer market management company Skopski Pazar. Also, much attention was focused on the failed initial tender to sell state-owned land by the National Bank of Macedonia to the Greek supermarket chain Veropulous.

According to a 2003 report by the State Audit Office released in January 2005, 18 million euros were spent by public institutions without proper documentation.[29]

A number of other irregularities were pointed out, but the government has not taken appropriate action. The minister of finance, Nikola Popovski, even objected to the report.[30] Similarly, the minister of health categorically denied wrongdoing in his sector.[31] In 2005, government agencies responsible for overseeing the liberalization of public enterprises were reluctant to review the privatization of Fershped, a company that many analysts believe was illegally privatized.[32]

A State Commission for the Prevention of Corruption was established in November 2002 and in June 2005 prepared an annex to the National Program for Prevention and Repression of Corruption on measures to prevent corruption at the local level. In 2005, new departments were established in the Ministry of the Interior and the Office of the Public Prosecutor to combat organized crime and corruption.[33] The effectiveness of the State Commission for the Prevention of Corruption depends in large part on the cooperation of state institutions, the public prosecutor in particular. In May, the commission released a report complaining that cooperation with the public prosecutor is very limited.[34] The report also stated that there "were no real effects of the fight against corruption, and the rule of law remains only a political declaration."[35] Although the report was delivered to the Parliament at the beginning of the year, it wasn't discussed until late May 2005. A recent Group of States Against Corruption report has outlined 14 recommendations to the Macedonian government in the fight against corruption.[36]

The government advertises jobs and contracts, and there are adequate laws requiring financial disclosure by public officials. However, these and laws disallowing conflict of interest are not fully implemented. Many government officials maintain other jobs while holding public office – the most obvious examples being law professors Vasil Tupurkovski (vice premier 1998-2002), Denko Maleski (foreign minister of Macedonia 1991-1993 and ambassador of Macedonia to the UN 1993-1997), and Jane Miljovski (vice premier, minister of finance, and minister of privatization 1992-1998). Moreover, the SDSM-led government has a direct impact on various spheres of the economy that have not been liberalized.

Macedonia should have achieved alignment with the EU acquis regarding electronic communications in April 2005; "all the basic starting conditions for liberalization and harmonization had to be in place by then, such as cost accounting and/or tariff transparency, [publishing an] interconnection reference offer (interconnection completely available on nondiscriminatory conditions), carrier selection and preselection, and fixed number portability."[37] The opening of this market has been frustrated by a lack of commitment at the governmental level, which has led to delays in adopting liberalization measures. Although a new Law on Telecommunications was passed in 2005, a number of bylaws need to be adopted. Passing this law without bylaws does not indicate a turning point in the government's commitment to address liberalization and transparency.

In fact, by not liberalizing markets, the government has actually helped private monopolies or duopolies in important sectors, such as telecommunications, the oil and gasoline industry, and air travel. Macedonia's market economy is further impeded by such institutional weaknesses as slow and cumbersome administrative procedures, shortcomings in the judiciary, and limited progress in land and property registration. For example, local governments are not able to sell land to interested investors without the consent of the government.

Zhidas Daskalovski is a senior analyst at the Center for Research and Policy Making and a visiting professor at the Department of Political Science at the University of Cyril and Methodius in Skopje. His newest book is Walking on the Edge: Consolidating Multiethnic Macedonia, 1989-2004, *published by Globic Press.*

---

[1] Vest, May 27, 2005, "Spikerot na Parlamentot bara finansiska samostojnost od vladata" [The head of the Parliament asks for financial autonomy from the government]; Olivera Vojnovska, "Popovski go skastri sobraniskiot budhzet za 1,5 milioni evra" [Mr. Popovski cut the parliamentary budget by 1.5 million euros], Utrinski Vesnik, October 26, 2005; and Olivera Vojnovska, "Parlamentot bara da ima svoj budzhet" [The Parliament demands its own budget], Utrinski Vesnik, September 21, 2005.

[2] Jon Elster, Claus Offe, and Ulrich K. Preuss, Institutional Design in Post-Communist Societies: Re-Building the Ship at Sea (Cambridge: Cambridge University Press, 1998).

[3] A1 Television news interview with Zoran Jachev, 17th October, 2004, "Instituciite kje Imaat Zakonska Obvrska da gi Dadat Informaciite [the Institutions Will Have a Legal Obligation to Provide Access to Information]." http://www.a1.com.mk/vesti/default.asp?VestID=38465

[4] There is huge anecdotal evidence for this behavior. A simple canvass of the Macedonian search engines Pogodok and Najdi reveals a dozen suspected cases of nepotism in 2005; the number of actual and unreported cases of nepotism may be even higher.
See www.pogodok.com.mk/search.jsp?q=nepotizam and
www.najdi.org.mk/najdi?query=%ED%E5%EF%EE%F2%E8%E7%E0%EC&metaname=naslov&sort=timestamp&reverse=on&lat2cyr=on&start=20.

[5] Macedonia joined the Partnership for Peace program on November 15, 1995.

[6] Vreme, December 29, 2005, "Uspeshni reformi vo ARM,"
www.vreme.com.mk/DesktopDefault.aspx?tabindex=8&tabid=1&EditionID=606&ArticleID=36747.

[7] See the Statement of Preliminary Findings and Conclusions by the OSCE/ODIHR Election Observation Mission on the Local Elections Held in the Former Yugoslav Republic of Macedonia on 13 March 2005 at www.osce.org/item/4376.html.

[8] According to the law, the second round of local elections is to be held 14 days after the first round is conducted. Owing to the annulment of the voting at certain polling stations in some municipalities as well as in the city of Skopje, the conduct of the second round was postponed until April 10, 2005.

[9] The election results are taken from the web page of the State Electoral Commission, www.dik.mk.

[10] See Harry Blair et al., Assessment of the Macedonian Civil Society (Arlington: USAID, 2003), p. 11.

[11] The data are from the Information Technology Committee of the Parliament, the association Internet Macedonia, and the conference "E-Society, Macedonia." See the newspaper articles at www.dnevnik.com.mk/?pBroj=2947&stID=70028; 217.16.70.236/?pBroj=2891&stID=65458; and 217.16.70.236/?pBroj=2702&stID=50449.

[12] Each new Internet site with an .mk domain is registered with MARNET (Macedonian Academic Research Network) through a simple registration form and by paying a fee of 10 euros. Each subsequent year, the fee is 5 euros. MARNET is an organizational unit within the Ss. Cyril and Methodius University and is endorsed by the Ministry of Science. More information may be obtained at dns.marnet.net.mk/index.php.

[13] See, for example, the interview with Zoran Jachev, president of Transparency International Macedonia, for A1 Television news: "Vo Makedonija teshko se doagja i do najobichna informacija"

[It is difficult to obtain even basic information in Macedonia],
www.a1.com.mk/vesti/vest.asp?VestID=48902.
¹⁴ Dnevnik, November 24, 2005, "Premierot gi obvini novinarite za potkup" [The premier accuses
the journalists for taking bribes], www.dnevnik.com.mk/?pBroj=2920&stID=67895.
¹⁵ A1 Television news, November 28, "Buchkovski povtorno gi napadna novinarite" [Buchkovski
again attacked the journalists], www.a1.com.mk/vesti/vest.asp?VestID=54836.
¹⁶ Robert W. Rafuse Jr., Why Fiscal Decentralization in Macedonia? (USAID Local Government
Reform Project: Skopje, 2001), p. 1.
http://www1.worldbank.org/wbiep/decentralization/ecalib/macedonia.pdf
¹⁷ A1 Television news interview with Zoran Jachev, "Instituciite kje imaat zakonska obvrska da gi
dadat informaciite" [The institutions will have a legal obligation to provide access to information],
from Transparency International Macedonia, October 17, 2004.
¹⁸ See Public Hearings, manual prepared by Kristina Hadzi-Vasileva (Skopje: USAID Macedonia,
Local government reform project, 2004), p. 7.
¹⁹ See further in Zhidas Daskalovski, "The New Law on Local Government Boundaries and the
Democratization of Macedonia," Review of International Affairs 55, no. 1116 (October-December
2004).
²⁰ Tamara Causidis, Sase Dimovski, and Svetlana Jovanovska, "Macedonia May Rue Hastiness,"
Balkan Investigative Reporting Network, www.birn.eu.com/index06.php.
²¹ Execution cases pertain to the Law on Enforcement. Court decisions are typically not being
enforced owing to inadequate coordination between the banks, the Central Registry, and the courts.
In practice, a company that has won a case in the courts against another firm is supposed to win
financial damages by obtaining means from the main account of the other firm. The company that
owes money leaves the main account empty, opens a new account, and continues operating.
²² See the Analytical Report for the opinion on the application from the Former Yugoslav Republic
of Macedonia for EU membership, November 9, 2005, p. 108.
²³ See the Analytical Report for the opinion on the application from the Former Yugoslav Republic
of Macedonia for EU membership, November 9, 2005, p. 21.
²⁴ A1 Television news, August 4, 2005, "Usvoeni izmenite vo pravosudniot sistem" [Reforms of the
judiciary adopted], www.a1.com.mk/vesti/vest.asp?VestID=49565.
²⁵ A1 Television news, December 7, 2005, "Sobranieto gi usvoi ustavnite amandmani" [Parliament
passes constitutional amendments], www.a1.com.mk/vesti/default.asp?VestID=55228.
²⁶ See Amendment 28 of the Constitution of the Republic of Macedonia.
²⁷ A1 Television news, January 21, 2005, "73% od gragjanite smetaat deka vladata e korumpirana"
[73% of citizens believe that the government is corrupt],
www.a1.com.mk/vesti/default.asp?VestID=41983.
²⁸ Transparency International's Corruption Perceptions Index places Macedonia 103rd in the world,
better only than Albania, which ranks 124th among the southeast European countries.
²⁹ See A1 Television news, January 24, 2005, "Vo 2003 nezakonski potrosheni 18 milioni evra" [In
2003 18 million Euros were spent illegally], www.a1.com.mk/vesti/default.asp?VestID=42080.
³⁰ A1 Television news, January 28, 2005, "Ministerot Popovski ne gi priznava naodite na drzhavniot
Zavod za Revizija" [Minister Popovski does not recognize the findings of the State Audit Office],
www.a1.com.mk/vesti/vest.asp?VestID=42250.
³¹ A1 Television news, May 20, 2005, "Sudir Megju Panovski i drzhavniot Zavod za Revizija" [A conflict between Panovski and the State Audit Office], www.a1.com.mk/vesti/vest.asp?VestID=46716.
³² One of the allegations can be found in Forum Plus, November 26, "Prvobitniot grev: sluchaj
Fershped" [The original sin: the case of Fershped]." On the reluctance of the authorities to investigate the allegations, see Kanal 5 news, May 9, 2005, "Vladini institucii protiv revizija na privatizaci-
jata na Fershped" [Government institutions against the revision of the privatization of ferhsped],
www.kanal5.com.mk/ShowNews.aspx?ItemID=5648&mid=1500&tabId=1&tabindex=0.
³³ See the Analytical Report for the opinion on the application from the Former Yugoslav Republic
of Macedonia for EU membership, November 9, 2005, p. 23.
³⁴ A1 Television news, May 15, 2005, "Godishen izveshtaj na antikorupciskata komisija" [A yearly
report of the commission], www.a1.com.mk/vesti/default.asp?VestID=46512.
³⁵ Ibid.
³⁶ Dnevnik, December 1, 2005, "14 preporaki za borba protiv korupcija" [14 recommendations for

the fight against corruption], www.dnevnik.com.mk/?pBroj=2926&stID=68415.

[37] The Stabilization and Association Agreement stipulates that the "Former Yugoslav Republic of Macedonia shall align its legislation with the telecommunications acquis, as it was in 2001 (usually referred to as the '1998 acquis'), by April 1, 2005." See the Analytical Report for the opinion on the application from the Former Yugoslav Republic of Macedonia for EU membership, November 9, 2005, p. 72. See also Dnevnik, December 10, 2005, "Usoglasuvanje na koncesiskite dogovori vo telekomunikaciite" [Concession agreements in telecommunication to be settled], www.dnevnik.com.mk/?pBroj=2934&stID=69030; and Dnevnik, December 5, 2005, "Telekomot naskoro so konkurencija?" [Competition for the Macedonian Telecom soon?], ww.dnevnik.com.mk/?pBroj=2929&stID=68588.

Moldova

Capital:	Chisinau
Population:	4.2 million
GNI/capita:	$720 (excludes data for Transnistria)
Ethnic Groups:	Moldovan/Romanian (78.2%), Ukrainian (8.4%), Russian 5.8%), Bulgarian (1.9%), Gagauz and other (5.7%)

Nations in Transit Ratings and Averaged Scores

	1997	1998	1999	2001	2002	2003	2004	2005	2006
Electoral Process	3.25	3.50	3.25	3.25	3.50	3.75	4.00	4.00	3.75
Civil Society	3.75	3.75	3.75	3.75	4.00	3.75	4.00	4.00	4.00
Independent Media	4.00	4.25	4.00	4.25	4.50	4.75	5.00	5.00	5.00
Governance *	4.25	4.50	4.50	4.50	4.75	5.25	5.50	n/a	n/a
National Democratic Governance	n/a	n/a	n/a	n/a	n/a	n/a	n/a	5.75	5.75
Local Democratic Governance	n/a	n/a	n/a	n/a	n/a	n/a	n/a	5.75	5.75
Judicial Framework and Independence	4.25	4.00	4.00	4.00	4.00	4.50	4.50	4.75	4.50
Corruption	n/a	n/a	6.00	6.00	6.25	6.25	6.25	6.25	6.00
Democracy Score	3.90	4.00	4.25	4.29	4.50	4.71	4.88	5.07	4.96

* With the 2005 edition, Freedom House introduced seperate analysis and ratings for national democratic governance and local democratic governance to provide readers with more detailed and nuanced analysis of these two important subjects.

NOTE: The ratings reflect the consensus of Freedom House, its academic advisers, and the author of this report. The opinions expressed in this report are those of the author. The ratings are based on a scale of 1 to 7, with 1 representing the highest level of democratic progress and 7 the lowest. The Democracy Score is an average of ratings for the categories tracked in a given year.

The economic and social data on this page were taken from the following sources:
GNI/capita, Population: *World Development Indicators 2006* (Washington, D.C.: World Bank, 2006).
Ethnic Groups: *CIA World Factbook 2006* (Washington, D.C.: Central Intelligence Agency, 2006).

EXECUTIVE SUMMARY

Since declaring independence in 1991, Moldova has been one of the most pluralistic post-Soviet states, even if at times it has oscillated between nonconsolidated democracy and nonconsolidated authoritarianism. The trend toward democracy has been traditionally stronger, especially throughout the 1990s, but was significantly hampered by economic problems, lack of consistent reforms, and a secessionist conflict in Transnistria. The latter has diverted Moldova's extremely limited political and economic resources from promoting reforms into efforts to reunite the country. Since the Party of Moldovan Communists (PCM) won power in 2001, Moldova's scores on democracy, electoral practices, civil society, independence of the media, and independence of the judiciary have worsened. In 2004-2005, the downward spiral stopped, and there are chances that the negative trend will be reversed in 2006. Moldova made significant progress in its effort to strengthen partnerships with the European Union (EU) and the United States. This has had a potentially positive impact on democracy efforts, but much remains to be done in the areas of media independence, reform of law enforcement agencies, and local democratic governance.

The year 2005 was marked by the March 6 elections and Moldova's efforts to come closer to the EU and NATO, as well as to obtain more EU and U.S. support for conflict resolution in Transnistria. The PCM remained in office, though with a significantly smaller majority. This has opened the way for a more balanced political system in which the opposition and civil society have a greater role to play. In fact, some of the government's centralizing tendencies are being reversed under pressure from external-internal coalitions of civil society groups, opposition parties, and Moldova's Western partners – the EU, United States, the Organization for Security and Cooperation in Europe (OSCE), and the Council of Europe.

National Democratic Governance. As a result of the March 6, 2005, elections, the PCM lost its constitutional majority; consequently, the party could reelect its leader, Vladimir Voronin, as the country's president only after an agreement with the opposition in which some potentially important democratization measures were promised and partly implemented. Moldova's efforts to come closer to the EU have generated some internal results, and the government's international credibility, particularly with the EU, has risen with the slight shift in the country's political climate. The government has been moving toward a more consensual model of interaction with the opposition and civil society groups, and a broad consensus on European integration and conflict resolution in Transnistria has been achieved. Pridnestrovskaya Moldavskaya Respublika, or Transnistria – a secessionist region in the east of Moldova — remained outside governmental control. In 2005, the prospects for democracy in Moldova once again look better, but progress will depend on the implementation of the remaining parts of the agreement between the PCM and the opposition, as well as further implementation of the EU-Moldova Action Plan. *Moldova's rating for national democratic governance remains at 5.75. The governing party has a significantly smaller majority in the Parliament, creating the basis for a more balanced political system. However, the opposition remains too weak to keep the government in check.*

Electoral Process. The Moldovan parliamentary elections were held on March 6 and were monitored closely by the international community and local observers. Only three parties or electoral blocs acceded to the Parliament owing to the high threshold, which was not revised prior to the elections. The elections were considered generally free and fair, despite the recurrence of certain irregularities. The same cannot be said of equal campaigning opportunities. The Moldovan authorities abused their position to promote their candidates to the detriment of opposition candidates. The incumbent president, Vladimir Voronin, was reelected with a large majority created with the support of certain opposition parties. In return, the ruling Communist Party promised to carry out a number of reforms that were requested by the opposition. These postelectoral reforms also include changes to the electoral code and the composition of the Central Election Commission to increase its independence from the ruling party. The 2005 parliamentary elections are a marked improvement over the 2003 local elections, despite the fact that various essential reforms were carried out only after the elections. *However, owing to the generally free and fair character of the elections and the decreasing number of violations in comparison with previous elections, Moldova's rating for electoral process reflects this progress and improves from 4.00 to 3.75.*

Civil Society. There are a number of highly skilled and potentially successful non-governmental organizations (NGOs) whose activity is constrained by lack of resources – offices, phones, computers, faxes, and so forth. Thus, the absolute priority in civil society development efforts in Moldova is to invest in capacity building and the institutional development of NGOs. The Moldovan third sector remains financially unsustainable, as it is heavily dependent on international donors. The government has been cooperating with civil society on issues concerning the European integration of Moldova and conflict resolution. As the government strives to get closer to the EU, it has been increasingly receptive to civil society advice on certain issues, but this cooperation still remains unsatisfactory. The biggest civil society activity in 2005 was related to monitoring the March 6 elections, where the Civic Coalition for Free and Fair Elections had an important role to play in putting pressure on the government to comply with international norms. *The country has a number of NGOs that are active, vibrant, and independent from government control, but there are too few. Thus, Moldova's civil society rating remains unchanged at 4.00.*

Independent Media. The state has been slowly withdrawing from controlling the media. The political agreement between the PCM and some opposition parties on the reelection of Voronin as president had a positive, albeit marginal, impact on media independence. The government renounced ownership of its two previously official national newspapers. At the end of the year, it was expected that some 30 government-owned local newspapers would cease to be financed with public money as well. However, these are minor changes in light of two unimplemented measures that have been long promised to the opposition. The first is the transformation of the public broadcasting company Teleradio Moldova into a genuinely independent media. The second is the transformation of the media watchdog Broadcasting Coordination Council, which grants licenses and oversees the media, into a genuinely independent institution. *The rating for media independence remains unchanged at 5.00, as the situation of the media has improved marginally, but not enough for an increase in the rating.*

Local Democratic Governance. Democracy at the local level remains the weakest link in Moldova's transition. Apparently, local democratic governance remains the only area where the effects of the March 6 elections and Moldova's efforts to come closer to the EU have not achieved any spillover effects. This is due to the peripheral status that local democracy enjoys in public discussions and to the low level of visibility of local developments for the international community. In fact, with the change of the mayor of Chisinau, the capital city, it is very likely that the control of local authorities will only tighten. Significant problems have occurred in Gagauzia at local level. Supported by the central government in Chisinau and the PCM, the Gagauzia leadership has been actively suppressing the opposition in the region. However, the biggest problems with democracy were in the Transnistria region, which is not under the control of the Moldovan authorities. Moldova and international organizations have been increasing pressure on Transnistria to democratize. *Democracy at the local level has not improved, nor has it worsened. Thus, the score for local democratic governance remains unchanged at 5.75.*

Judicial Framework and Independence. Moldova has put in place a very comprehensive and liberal framework to ensure fundamental human rights through the Constitution and other national and international normative acts. The problem lies in the implementation of a backlog of over 40,000 court decisions. In turn, this explains the relatively high number of cases that are brought by Moldovan citizens before the European Court of Human Rights. Other problems affect the efficiency of the Moldovan judiciary system, such as a lack of sufficient courtrooms and computer services. Moldova has been engaged throughout 2005 in an extensive reform of its judicial system. The Moldovan Parliament has revised the laws of judiciary organization to reform the system of appointments and dismissals of members of the Superior Council of Magistrates, judges of the Supreme Court of Justice, and justices of the lower courts. The main goal has been to make the judicial system more independent from political and economic influence. Steps have been taken to eradicate torture and ill-treatment and to remove the death penalty from the legal framework. Although the reform process needs to be sustained and adequate funds made available, the Moldovan government has taken encouraging steps toward reforming the judicial system. *Hence, the country's rating for judicial framework and independence improves from 4.75 to 4.50.*

Corruption. The introduction of the National Anticorruption Strategy and the corresponding Action Plan in January 2005 signaled a very promising year in the fight against corruption. Indeed, all involved public institutions and agencies, as well as the civil society, got off to a very active and convincing start in the implementation of the anticorruption Action Plan. The main efforts have been geared toward bringing anticorruption legislation in line with international norms and practices and toward outlining the competences of each of the many institutions involved to avoid duplication of activities. Concrete measures have also been undertaken to limit the spread of corruption among civil servants. Moldovan civil society and international organizations that monitor corruption are unanimous in saying that some progress has been achieved in preventing and fighting corruption. The perception, however, remains that high-profile corruption cases tend to be politically motivated and that petty corruption is punished too harshly. Despite the fact that certain public services (such as health care, education, the police, and the customs services) suffer from high levels of corruption, studies have demonstrated that public tolerance toward corruption in Moldova is decreasing. *The country's rating for corruption improves from 6.25 to 6.00 owing to the encouraging steps undertaken both by the Moldovan government and by civil society against corruption, notably through the implementation of the Action Plan; yet the awaited large-scale effects are still not felt in the Moldovan society.*

Outlook for 2006. In 2006, the prospects for democracy once again will look better. President Voronin is in his second and last term and is not pursuing further centralization. Moldova's overtures to the EU will be the main driver for the country's democratization. This will happen slowly, as the Moldovan government's commitment to democracy stems not from convictions, but from a quest for international legitimacy, mainly with the EU and the United States, whose support Moldova badly needs. The implementation of the EU-Moldova Action Plan will create some pressure on further democratization of the system. Moldova's Individual Partnership Action Plan with NATO, to be signed in 2006, will also allow some small progress on the reform of the security sector. The opposition will remain weak and divided, but the main cleavage in Moldova's political system will start emerging within the governing elite among the possible future leaders of the country.

MAIN REPORT

National Democratic Governance

1997	1998	1999	2001	2002	2003	2004	2005	2006
n/a	n/a	n/a	n/a	n/a	n/a	n/a	5.75	5.75

Since independence, Moldova has oscillated between nonconsolidated democracy and nonconsolidated authoritarianism. The Constitution generally creates the basis for a democratic system with checks and balances and significant rights for citizens to exercise control of the government. However, since the Party of Moldovan Communists (PCM) came into power in 2001, Moldovan politics have been marked by increasing centralization and a tendency toward soft authoritarianism. Despite the fact that Moldova is a parliamentary republic, the country's president, Vladimir Voronin, has been the dominant figure in politics since 2001. The government manipulates rather than violates the existing democratic framework, achieving a certain stability through co-optation of important societal, political, and economic actors rather than coercion or outright abuses of human rights. The most obvious attempts to centralize power have been traditionally reversed under pressure from the EU, United States, OSCE, and Council of Europe.

Moldova is one of some 60 countries in the world with a Law on Access to Information, adopted in 2000. A report from the Office of the OSCE Representative on Freedom of the Media stated that the law is "generally consistent with international norms and obligations...but its effectiveness has been limited by poor leadership by the government in implementing it, which has resulted in a lack of awareness by the government officials about its provisions."[1]

Virtually all political actors in Moldova publicly support democracy and EU integration as the best route to stability and prosperity. According to the Council of Europe's representative in Moldova, Vladimir Philipov, the main conflict in Moldovan politics is not the definition of strategic priorities, but the best way to achieve them. However, doubts remain about the commitment of political elites to reforms promoting democratization and EU integration.

The elections on March 6, 2005, created the basis for strengthening Moldovan democracy while maintaining governmental stability and economic growth. Despite the victory of the PCM, a new political consensus between the government and the opposition has emerged. The Communist faction in the legislature had enough votes to elect the government and the Speaker, the liberal-minded former minister for economy Marian Lupu. The parliamentary parties also launched a political partnership for European integration with a declaration that stated, "Further development of the Republic of Moldova can be ensured only through the consistent and irreversible promotion of the strategic course toward European integration, peaceful and democratic resolution of the Transnistrian problem, effective functioning of democratic institutions, and ensuring of national minorities rights."

To ensure the reelection of President Voronin, the PCM made an alliance with the three opposition parties – the Christian Democratic People's Party (CDPP), the Social-Liberal Party (SLP), and the Democratic Party (DP). As part of an agreement with the opposition, Voronin agreed to a set of 10 measures to ensure independence of the media, independence of the judiciary, decentralization of local government, greater parliamentary oversight of law enforcement agencies, reform of the electoral authorities, reform of the Communist Party, and his resignation as Communist Party chairman.

Almost all of the measures have been at least partly implemented. For example, legislative sessions are now broadcast live, and deliberations are posted verbatim on the Parliament's Web site. The government has renounced ownership of its two official newspapers (*Moldova Suverana* in Romanian and *Nezavisimaia Moldova* in Russian), even if their editorial policies remain strongly pro-governmental. The electoral process for the Superior Council of Magistrates (SCM) has been amended to make it more independent. Likewise, the Central Election Commission (CEC) has changed its appointment process so that five members are chosen by the opposition and only four by the governing party. The chairman of the CEC comes from the DP and a deputy chairman from the CDPP. The same proportional representation will be applied to the Court of Auditors, with four members appointed by the opposition and three by the governing party. The Security and Intelligence Service (SIS) has lost the right to penal investigation and preventive arrest. In addition, a parliamentary subcommission, chaired by an opposition parliamentarian, was created to oversee the SIS.

However, no visible progress has been made on three crucial reforms. There is still a need to decentralize the administration of local governments and increase their financial sustainability. Second, there has been little headway in transforming the government-controlled public TV into a genuinely independent institution and establishing an independent Broadcasting Coordination Council that would grant licenses to media. Third, there has been no progress in reforming the Office of the Prosecutor General to insulate it from political influences and presidential control.

The influence of the EU and the United States is becoming one of the most significant factors affecting Moldova's domestic political scene. There is a widespread feeling in Moldova that the country needs the support of the two actors for its internal transformation and efforts to achieve a viable settlement in Transnistria and to withstand Russian political and economic pressures. Most of the government's reforms, as well as the agreement with the opposition, were undertaken primarily to strengthen its credibility and partnership with the EU and United States.

Both the EU-Moldova agenda and a broader cooperation with Euro-Atlantic institutions have been remarkably fruitful in 2005. In February, the EU and Moldova signed an Action Plan under the EU's neighborhood policy, in which Moldova commits to significantly reform its economy and democratize its political institutions toward EU standards. In March, the EU appointed a special representative on Moldova whose main mandate is to contribute to a settlement of the secessionist conflict in Transnistria. In June, Moldova announced it would seek to sign an Individual Partnership Action Plan with NATO, and Moldovan high-level officials did not exclude the possibility that Moldova might seek to join NATO. In October, the EU's executive – the European Commission – opened an embassy in Chisinau. In December, the EU launched the Border Assistance Mission to Moldova and Ukraine with the mandate of strengthening border management between the two states and reduce smuggling around Transnistria. The EU and the United States have also become involved as observers in the effort to negotiate a solution to the Transnistria conflict.

Moldova remains divided, with its secessionist region of Transnistria maintaining its de facto independence. The Pridnestrovskaya Moldavskaya Respublika, or Transnistria, is a breakaway republic in the eastern part of Moldova, led by self-proclaimed president and Russian citizen Igor Smirnov. The European Court of Human Rights (ECHR) concluded in July 2004 that the Transnistrian republic "remained under the effective authority, or at the very least under the decisive influence, of Russia, and in any event that it survived by virtue of the military, economic, financial, and political support that Russia gave it."

Ukraine's relations with Moldova have improved significantly after Ukraine's Orange Revolution in late 2004. The Yushchenko administration in Ukraine has been less supportive of the authoritarian regime in Transnistria than was the Kuchma administration. This has had an impact on conflict resolution in Transnistria. Ukraine's president, Viktor Yushchenko, presented in May a plan to settle the conflict, urging the necessity to democratize Transnistria and negotiate the status of the region with a (more or less) democratically elected legislature from the region. As a response to the Ukrainian initiative, the Russian Federation presented its own plan in October as an attempt to keep the initiative in its hands.

Despite this, the conflict settlement efforts have been gradually moving into a EU-Moldova-Ukraine framework, in which Russia no longer plays the main role in negotiations on the status of Transnistria. Russia has also tried to support Transnistria while increasing pressure on Moldova. On various occasions, Russia stopped Moldovan exports of meat, vegetables, and wine to Russia and has announced its intention to raise gas prices in 2006. Transnistria would be excluded from these measures. In this context, President Voronin declared in an interview with the BBC in October 2005 that "Moldova can survive without exporting wine to Russia. It will be difficult but we are ready to live in cold, to freeze without Russian gas, but we will not cede. Moldova will not sacrifice its territorial integrity, sovereignty, and freedom, irrespective of the price we will have to pay."

Electoral Process

1997	1998	1999	2001	2002	2003	2004	2005	2006
3.25	3.50	3.25	3.25	3.50	3.75	4.00	4.00	3.75

Following the Orange Revolution in neighboring Ukraine, the Moldovan parliamentary elections on March 6 were watched very closely by the international community and the Moldovan civil society, including Coalition 2005, which brought together over 150 NGOs for this particular purpose.[2] Moldova is categorized as a "Partly Free" state according to Freedom House's 2005 Freedom of the World status designation.[3] However, it is often viewed by international institutions as the most successful non-Baltic post-Soviet state in ensuring generally free and fair elections since its independence in 1991, despite the persistence of several shortcomings.

Moldova has a proportional electoral system, and all candidates and parties are featured on the same ballot. Despite a Council of Europe 2001 recommendation regarding the country's high threshold for accession to the Parliament, Moldova's electoral authorities left it unchanged for the 2005 parliamentary election. The following percentages are necessary to accede to the Moldovan Parliament: 3 percent for independent candidates, 6 percent for political parties, 9 percent for a bloc of two parties, and 12 percent for a bloc of three or more parties. As a consequence, the over 15 percent of nonattributed votes were redistributed among the three parties or electoral blocs that acceded to the Parliament, leaving a large segment of the electorate without parliamentary representation.

Minor modifications were made to the electoral code by the CEC prior to the parliamentary elections, including changes to facilitate voting for students who study in a Moldovan city other than their place of residence, persons with expired passports, hospitalized persons, and detainees.[4] Numerous other changes to the code would have been necessary to ensure truly free and fair elections, including measures related to party financing and campaigning in the media. The CEC made no serious efforts to address these issues prior to the elections, thus failing to prevent an uneven playing field for candidates.

Not surprisingly, abuses by state-controlled media outlets were observed during the campaign: The ruling party was portrayed in a positive manner, as opposed to other electoral contestants. Although airtime was distributed evenly among all candidates, the day-to-day activities of the ruling party were often covered in a very favorable way, resulting in increased campaign airtime for the PCM. During the campaign, the authorities used administrative resources to harass and intimidate opposition candidates. Meetings by opposition candidates were often hindered. In the press, the main opposition parties made use of their own outlets to promote their electoral agenda. Overall, however, the ruling party had a clear advantage in terms of airtime in the media and editorial space in the press. Consequently, the Moldovan public received insufficient objective information regarding the choice of candidates and their respective programs.

Election day voting also witnessed irregularities. Polling stations were poorly equipped, often causing overcrowding. Police officers and local public officials were sometimes present at polling stations. In addition, there were cases of electoral advertising within the polling stations. Voting lists were drawn up late, with many deficiencies. Despite promises made by the CEC, insufficient polling stations were open in Transnistria for the Moldovan citizens who reside there.

In a move meant to reassure the electorate and the international community, the Moldovan authorities invited an International Election Observation Mission, including observers from the OSCE/Office for Democratic Institutions and Human Rights (ODIHR), the OSCE Parliamentary Assembly, the Council of Europe Parliamentary Assembly, and the European Parliament. The mission consisted of some 500 international observers in addition to over 2,000 domestic observers. Both international and domestic observers agreed that despite a number of irregularities during the campaign and on election day, the elections were generally in compliance with most OSCE and Council of Europe commitments and other international election standards.

The PCM, in power since 2001, obtained 45 percent of the votes, or 56 deputies out of a total 101, thereby obtaining a small majority but 5 mandates short of the 61 needed to elect the president. The Democratic Moldova electoral bloc obtained 28 percent of votes and 31 deputies, while the third political formation to accede, the CDPP, obtained 9 percent of the votes and 11 parliamentary seats.

The incumbent Communist president, Vladimir Voronin, was reelected by the Parliament on April 4 with a staggering 75 votes. He received support from the CDPP, the DP, and the SLP. The last two left the Democratic Moldova upon accession to the Parliament. These three Western-oriented parties chose to vote in favor of Voronin because he succeeded in creating a national consensus around two major policy priorities: EU integration and the resolution of the Transnistria conflict. In addition, the CDPP tied 10 conditions to its vote of approval in favor of Voronin. The majority of these 10 conditions have been met by the ruling party over the course of 2005, in particular those regarding modifications to the electoral code and the composition of the CEC.

Regarding Transnistria, elections were held to the Supreme Soviet (the Transnistrian legislative body) on December 11. These elections were not recognized either by the Moldovan authorities or by the international community and can be considered neither free nor fair owing to the quasi-totalitarian regime in place. Yevgeny Shevchuk was chosen as the new Speaker, replacing the long-standing Grigory Marakutsa, with 39 out of a total of 43 votes. Shevchuk and his Obnovlenie (Renewal) movement, which obtained 23 seats, represent the younger, more progressive segment of the Transnistrian elite. Shevchuk is closely associated with Transnistria's largest private company, Sheriff, a conglomerate owning supermarket and service station chains, a TV channel, and a football team.

Civil Society

1997	1998	1999	2001	2002	2003	2004	2005	2006
3.75	3.75	3.75	3.75	4.00	3.75	4.00	4.00	4.00

Moldovan civil society is very weak, generally lacking in institutional capacity and the barest of necessities: offices, computers, phones, faxes, and so forth. Moldova has a three-tiered civil society matrix. Tier one comprises a very limited number of NGOs that raise most of the sector's funds but are increasingly overstretched in their commitments. They have almost no competition in their respective niches. Tier two is represented by younger NGOs that interact well with international donors, possess good foreign language skills, and have international contacts but cannot develop for lack of basic equipment. They rely primarily on the enthusiasm of their members but are not sustainable in the midterm, despite their high potential. A third tier includes the bulk of NGOs, which lack equipment, offices, computers, phones, and language skills and sometimes have limited experience interacting with foreign donors, which severely limits their potential for development. One of the effects of the current situation is that there is little competition among the large, funded NGOs, resulting in an unsatisfactory level of performance. The second-tier NGOs lose their most active members to foreign companies or international organizations based in Chisinau. Third-tier NGOs are confined to a marginal status.

There are 3,424 NGOs registered in Moldova.[5] Of these, only a relatively small number are highly active and skilled civil society groups, but their number has more or less stagnated for the past four to five years. In fact, a survey on the development of NGOs conducted by CONTACT (National Assistance and Information Center for NGOs in Moldova) indicated that most Moldovan NGOs are small and inactive: 59 percent had only volunteers, while 24 percent had fewer than five employees; 35 percent had not implemented a project in the last two years, while 17 percent had conducted only one project in the same period. This suggests that roughly half of NGOs had almost no activity at all.

According to the survey, Moldovan NGOs are severely underfunded – 27 percent had no budget, and 24 percent had an annual budget of less than US$500. The number of international donors is rather limited, and most Moldovan companies prefer to give to charity rather than fund other types of NGOs. NGO cooperation with state structures is reasonably satisfactory, involving some 87 percent of NGOs; 47 percent indicate satisfaction with the level of cooperation with the state.

Civil society is free from extremist influence, and there are no militarized or vigilante groups, except in the Transnistria region. The legal and regulatory environment is not perfect, but there is no excessive state pressure on NGOs. A number of civil society leaders and activists interviewed in Chisinau said that the main problem they face is lack of support for institutional development. Periodically, the government tries to pressure civil society through reregistration rules or through attempts to establish pro-governmental NGOs or trade unions. However, these efforts generally fail because despite its overall weakness, civil society is still strong enough to oppose such measures, while the government is too weak to impose its centralizing agenda. The government acts through co-optation of civil society groups rather than coercion. The failure of government-inspired structures to replace or even seriously affect the position of established NGOs reveals a certain strength in Moldovan civil society.

In 2005, coordinated action between civil society groups and the international community prevented the government from adopting some controversial laws. The SIS proposed a draft Law on State and Official Secrets, which was approved by the government on December 2, 2004, and submitted to the Parliament for approval.

In addition, the Ministry of Informational Development elaborated a draft Law on Information. Civil society groups, Transparency International Moldova, and Access-Info actively opposed these laws on the grounds that they would limit access to information. It was claimed that accepting the law "would be a severe blow to the freedom of expression" and would have a "catastrophic impact on the people's access to public information." Nine of the most important journalist associations in Moldova claimed that the draft laws contradict European and international standards,[6] and an OSCE representative declared the draft laws to be "overly complex and poorly written." After such coordinated pressure, the Moldovan government withdrew both draft laws from parliamentary consideration.

Throughout 2005, a broad coalition of some 150 NGOs created the Civic Coalition for Free and Fair Elections. It monitored the national parliamentary elections on March 6, the local elections for Chisinau and a number of villages in July, and the rerun for mayoral elections in Chisinau in November 2005. During the elections, the coalition monitored the polling process, organized exit polls, and raised awareness about the importance of elections. Among its most useful contributions was media monitoring in which weekly reports on the lack of objectiveness of certain media outlets were publicized. With concrete data and statistical findings, the coalition put public pressure on the mainly pro-government outlets for their one-sided representation of the electoral campaign. Opposition media were not spared from criticism, either. These activities had certain, though rather limited, impact on the government.

Contact between the authorities and NGOs has been increasing. In November 2005, the Parliament presented a draft Concept on Cooperation Between the Parliament of Moldova and Civil Society, which aims at increasing cooperation between state structures and NGOs through greater involvement of civil society at the early stages of lawmaking, through more meetings, public hearings, and permanent consultations. So far, most of the interaction between the government and advocacy groups or think tanks has been confined to European integration issues and conflict resolution in Transnistria. There is a broad societal consensus on how to approach these two issues, and the government is rather receptive to advice from civil society groups.

The nongovernmental Institute for Public Policy has drafted a 650-page European Strategy for Moldova, which is likely to become the government's strategy for the European integration of Moldova. The National Commission for European Integration, comprising the highest state officials responsible for Moldova's EU integration efforts and chaired by the prime minister, includes a civil society representative. The same is true for the National Commission on the Development and Implementation of the NATO-Moldova Individual Partnership Action Plan. Although such cooperation has been positive, concerns that some NGOs are too close to the government have been expressed. Generally, civil society lacks the expertise to independently assess the government's performance on progress toward European integration and reforms. In addition, the government is still selective about the NGOs it chooses to cooperate with.

Independent Media

1997	1998	1999	2001	2002	2003	2004	2005	2006
4.00	4.25	4.00	4.25	4.50	4.75	5.00	5.00	5.00

The Moldovan Constitution guarantees freedom of expression and editorial independence and prohibits censorship in the media. Despite existing political pressure on the media, the main bottlenecks for the development of independent media in Moldova are lack of financial means and the low professionalism of journalists. Most media outlets are dependent on political or economic sponsors, and interference in editorial policy from owners is widespread. Revenues from ads and newspaper circulation are very small.

Throughout 2005, there were 28 Romanian-language newspapers and 34 Russian-language newspapers,[7] most of which are weeklies. The most widely circulated newspapers are the Russian-language *Komsomolskaya Pravda*, *Argumenty i Fakty*, *Nezavisimaia Moldova*, and *Moldavskie Vedomosti* and the Romanian-language *Flux*, *Timpul*, *Jurnal de Chisinau*, *Moldova Suverana*, *Ziarul de Garda*, and *Saptamana*. Important regional newspapers are *Cuvantul*, *Observatorul de Nord*, and *Unghiul*. The major radio stations are Radio National, Radio Antena C, and the regional Vocea Basarabiei, as well as a number of FM music stations. Radio BBC, Radio Free Europe/Radio Liberty, and Radio France International have daily news programs in Moldova rebroadcast by FM stations. Popular television networks with national coverage are Moldova 1, Pervyi Kanal v Moldove (Russian channel), and TVR 1 (Romanian channel). Important television stations that cover only parts of Moldova (mainly Chisinau) are Euro TV and PRO TV. The Russian-language independent (but pro-government) channel NIT has extended its coverage to most of the country. The distribution of print media is state controlled, but private newspapers are not discriminated against. There are no restrictions on the use of the Internet, yet access is problematic outside Chisinau, owing mainly to economic barriers. According to an International Research & Exchanges Board Media Sustainability Index 2004 estimate, some 17 percent of the population had access to the Internet.

Generally, the public enjoys broad access to various views in the print media. However, the situation is different when it comes to television. The single most important national TV broadcaster, Moldova 1, is under the control of the government. Other TV stations are either neutral and avoid political news or are overtly pro-governmental. Euro TV, owned by the Chisinau municipality, has been openly critical of the government. The urban population, especially in Chisinau, has access to TV stations that reflect different viewpoints. The situation is more difficult in the countryside, where very often the main or only source of information remains the government-controlled Moldova 1, which is one-sided in favor of the government.

The legislative framework ensuring freedom of the media is provided by the Constitution, the 1994 Law on Media, the 1995 Law on Broadcasting, and the 2002 Law on the Public National Broadcaster. In 2004, Moldova decriminalized libel and is expected to impose a ceiling on the maximum amount that may be claimed for calumny. However, despite existing legal and operational guarantees for independent media, the state of affairs regarding mass media in Moldova has been quite problematic. The situation worsened visibly after 2001, with the PCM in power. Freedom House's *Freedom of the Press* survey downgraded Moldova's rating for press freedom from "Partly Free" to "Not Free" in 2004, and the situation persisted in 2005.

However, the preconditions for greater press freedom gained a certain momentum in 2005. This was related primarily to Moldovan efforts to come closer to EU standards as well as a more balanced Parliament after the March 6 elections. Reflecting this tendency in October 2005, Reporters Without Borders ranked Moldova 74 out of 167 countries in its Worldwide Press Freedom Index, significantly better than other member countries of the Commonwealth of Independent States, with Georgia 99, Armenia 102, Ukraine 112, and Russia 138.

Despite the electoral campaign early in 2005, the reporting of scandals had a much lower profile in the media than in previous years. For instance, in 2004 two opposition media outlets (Euro TV and Radio Antena C) had their licenses suspended for three months, an investigative journalist was beaten, and most opposition journalists from the state TV Moldova 1 were fired in the summer (which led to violent clashes between journalists and the police). Nothing of that sort happened in 2005, and there were almost no high-profile scandals related to governmental pressure on the media.

The state has been slowly withdrawing from the media. The political agreement between the PCM and some opposition parties on the reelection of President Voronin in April 2005 had a positive, albeit marginal, impact on media independence. The government renounced ownership of its two previously official newspapers, *Moldova Suverana* and *Nezavisimaia Moldov*, which were financed by public money but used for government propaganda. Public financing of Infoprim, the news agency of the Chisinau mayoralty, has also ceased. Infoprim was transformed into an independent agency called Infoprim Neo. However, the two newspapers and the news agency maintain their pro-government editorial policies, despite the fact that they are no longer state owned. The government continues funding to some 30 local newspapers that it owns. In any case, these changes are somehow considerably less important than the promised transformation of the public TV Moldova 1 into a genuinely independent broadcaster and the appointment of a more independent and balanced Broadcasting Coordination Council.

The media situation that deserves the most attention is the continuing lack of independence for the allegedly public TV Moldova 1 and Radio National. In 2002, acting on a Council of Europe recommendation, Moldova adopted legislation intended to tranform the state TV into a public institution governed by an independent Council of Observers. However, the government maintains its control of the public TV by twisting the law so that the council is dominated by representatives of the government, the Communist majority in the Parliament, and a number of representatives of pro-governmental NGOs. In addition, in 2004 most of the more independent journalists from the public TV and radio were fired after a heavily biased reappointment procedure.

International organizations as well as the opposition have maintained pressure on the government to ensure greater independence for the public TV. In 2004, the OSCE and the Council of Europe in Chisinau published benchmarks for the operation of a public broadcaster in Moldova, while the EU-Moldova European Neighborhood Policy Action Plan has as a top priority the necessity to ensure respect for freedom of the media and freedom of expression.[8] Despite government promises to transform the public TV and radio into genuinely independent broadcasters, NGOs such as the Independent Journalism Center for the Association of the Electronic Press concluded on a number of occasions that Teleradio Moldova "has not registered significant progress in promoting a policy and a practice capable of persuasively exploring the values of a public service," despite some marginal progress such as new talk shows and less praise for the authorities. Despite government claims, progress on ensuring greater independence of the media in 2005 was minimal.

As for Transnistria, a March 2005 OSCE report stated, "The situation of the independent media is very difficult, with different methods of pressure applied on those few journalists who do not follow the official line," adding that in Transnistria there existed "a level of censorship rarely seen in the OSCE region," The Internet is not a viable alternative source of information – it is too expensive, and broadband access is a rarity. TV and radio channels remain under the control of the authorities, as do all but a few newspapers.

Local Democratic Governance

1997	1998	1999	2001	2002	2003	2004	2005	2006
n/a	n/a	n/a	n/a	n/a	n/a	n/a	5.75	5.75

Democracy at the local level has remained the weakest link in Moldova's transition. In fact, local governance appears to be the only area where the March 6 elections and Moldova's efforts to come closer to the EU have not achieved any spillover effects. This is due to the peripheral status of local democracy in public debate and the low visibility of local developments for the international community. Likewise, institutions of local public administration are less visible in the media, have fewer resources to promote or defend their views, and have less access to international institutions than do other actors in society.

Moldova's Constitution guarantees local autonomy and declares in Article 109 that "public administration...is based on the principles of local autonomy, of decentralization of public services, of the eligibility of local public administration authorities, and of consulting the citizenry on local problems of special interest." Thus, it sets the framework for local democratic governance, which is further developed by the Law on Local Public Administration.

Moldova is divided into 32 territorial units (*raions*). Some 170,000 people live in the Gagauz autonomy in the south of Moldova, and another 550,000 people live in Transnistria – a territory that seceded from Moldova in the aftermath of a small war in 1992. In both Gagauzia and Transnistria, local democratic conditions have been considerably worse off than in Moldova proper.

Citizens have the right to choose their local leaders based on universal, equal, and direct suffrage by secret ballot. All mayors are elected directly by citizens, while local and municipal councillors are chosen for four-year terms according to a proportional voting system. The *bashkan* (governor) of Gagauzia is elected by direct vote. Traditionally, elections have been held regularly and judged free. However, according to the Council of Europe's Congress of Local and Regional Authorities, the latest local elections of 2003 revealed considerable setbacks as central authorities appeared to abuse their capacity to influence the process.

Moldova remains a rather centralized state, and in fact, the tendency since 2001 particularly is toward greater centralization rather than vice versa. In 1998, the Law on Local Public Administration was adopted. The law created 12 administrative territorial units (*judet*), providing the basis for greater economic, financial, and political sustainability of local administration. The Communist government revoked the reform and reorganized Moldova into 32 *raions*, which are less efficient, less financially viable, and more dependant on the central government.

October 16, 2003, saw the adoption of the Law on Local Public Finances, which took away from the local authorities 50 percent of the value-added tax, a considerable source of income. Veaceslav Ionita, an expert from the Institute for the Development of Social Initiatives, claims that local taxes constitute 5 percent of the local budgets, with the rest of the incomes of mayors dependent upon *raion* councils and the *raion* chairmen (appointed by the government).[9] Interviewees from political parties as well as a number of experts claimed that mayors from opposition parties are discriminated against in the distribution of funds from the central authorities. A report on local democracy in Moldova from the European Commission and the Council of Europe has identified that "the existing legislative arrangements for calculating and distributing state grants do not seem to be objective, transparent, and clear...; the existing resource-sharing arrangements do not seem to ensure a fair distribution of resources at the level of the districts."

Serafim Urechean, mayor of Chisinau and then leader of the biggest opposition party Moldova Noastra (Our Moldova), was elected in March 2005 to the Parliament and resigned from his post. As a result, mayoral elections took place in Chisinau on July 10 and 24 and November 27, but none of them gathered enough voters to be declared valid.

In Gagauzia, the central government-supported leadership and the PCM have been actively suppressing the regional opposition. The authorities have attempted to change electoral policy in Gagauzia so that future governors would be elected by the Gagauzia Popular Assembly (the region's legislature) rather than by direct vote. In 2004, the mayor of Comrat, a leader of the regional opposition, was dismissed without a court conviction, which is against existing legal provisions. In 2005, another leading opposition figure, Mikhail Formuzal – mayor of Chadyr-Lunga and leader of the United Gagauzia movement – was accused of abuse of office and financial irregularities in managing the town and arrested on October 21. The court of appeals ordered his conditional release the same day, overturning a decision by the local court. Formuzal is considered one of the most serious contenders for the post of governor of Gagauzia in the next regional elections. On October 4, the Council of Europe issued a resolution on the functioning of democratic institutions in Moldova, which denounced the 2004 "dismissal of the former mayor of Comrat by the Popular Assembly of Gagauzia" and called on the Moldovan authorities to "investigate the reasons for the high incidence of criminal court cases against leading figures of the opposition, both nationally and in the provinces."[10]

The biggest problems with democracy were in the Transnistria region, which is controlled by Igor Smirnov, a Russian citizen. There are no viable opposition parties, very few independent NGOs, and only a few independent newspapers, which are constantly harassed. However, in April-May 2005, a significant group of deputies led by Yevgeny Shevchuk, then deputy Speaker of the Transnistrian Supreme Soviet, launched a series of initiatives to limit the powers of the Smirnov-led executive. In December, the Shevchuk-led political movement Obnovlenie won the elections to the Supreme Soviet. In late December, Shevchuk was elected Speaker of the legislature. There have been increasingly visible cleavages within the political and economic elites in the region, which can potentially form a basis for greater pluralism. The international community – EU, United States, and Ukraine-have been putting pressure on the region to democratize.

Judicial Framework and Independence

1997	1998	1999	2001	2002	2003	2004	2005	2006
4.25	4.00	4.00	4.00	4.00	4.50	4.50	4.75	4.50

Fundamental human rights (including civil and political rights) are enshrined in the Moldovan Constitution and other national legislative acts and by Moldova's adherence to universal norms and principles of international law regarding human rights. The Moldovan state thereby guarantees the right of all people to life, physical and mental integrity, and freedom of expression, conscience, and religion; the right to information; a number of political rights such as participation in public life, freedom of association, and the right to an impartial and fair trial; the right to property and private life; and the guarantee of good living conditions through the right to education and the protection of health.

The state is also bound by the Constitution and other normative acts to guarantee all political parties, organizations, and other social and political currents equal opportunities and the right to unhindered group activities. In addition, the Moldovan state also guarantees Moldovan citizens of all ethnic and linguistic groups the freedom to enjoy all their social, economic, cultural, and political rights.

Moldova ratified the European Convention on Human Rights in 1997. This year, Moldova celebrated its tenth anniversary as a member of the Council of Europe.

Notwithstanding this comprehensive and liberal framework, Moldovan citizens too often see their constitutionally guaranteed rights challenged. This explains the relatively high number of cases brought by Moldovan citizens before the European Court of Human Rights compared with those brought by citizens of other states: In 2005, 583 applications were lodged with the ECHR.[11] A crucial problem is Moldova's noncompliance with ECHR judgments. Addressing this issue, the government created in October 2005 the Department for the Implementation of Judicial Decisions within the Ministry of Justice to deal with a backlog of more than 40,000 judgments awaiting implementation. Another discrepancy is the inability of the state, owing to lack of funds, to guarantee defendants' right to legal representation.

More generally, Moldova has been engaged throughout 2005 in an extensive reform of its judicial system to ensure the protection of fundamental human rights according to European standards. Since 2004, Moldova has been implementing the National Action Plan on Human Rights. The EU-Moldova Action Plan, signed in February 2005, has largely helped to push forward this reform process.

For instance, a parliamentary committee elaborated and adopted a law for the modification of the following legislative acts: the Law on the Superior Council of Magistrates, the Law on the Supreme Court of Justice, and legislation on judiciary organization aiming to reform the system of appointments and dismissals of members of the SCM, justices of the Supreme Court, and judges of the courts. The modifications were reviewed by experts from the Council of Europe. Accordingly, candidate judges put forward by the SCM can be rejected by the president within 30 days, but only on grounds of unprofessional conduct or incompatibility. Previously, the president was not obliged to give any apparent justification for rejecting a proposed candidate, creating the impression that judges were de facto political appointments. A similar procedure is foreseen for the appointment of judges to the Supreme Court by the Parliament. Under the new law, the General Assembly of Judges elected 7 judges out of the 12 members of the SCM in November 2005. Another 2 members of the SCM are elected by the Parliament with at least a two-thirds majority. One member is put forward by the majority and the other by the opposition. The remaining 3 seats on the SCM are reserved for the president of the Supreme Court, a member of the Ministry of Justice, and the prosecutor general.

Moldova is expected to annul the probationary period of five years for judges after their appointment by the president. Instead, judges will be named for life without having to satisfy certain conditions for remaining in office, a measure designed to ensure their independence. On a practical level, the judiciary is adversely affected by the lack of sufficient courtrooms and other premises, computers and access to the Internet, and a legal database.

The Parliament has put forward a law that would modify Articles 135 and 136 of the Constitution to create jurisdictional protections for human rights and fundamental freedoms. The Constitutional Court would then become the highest court proffering final decisions. At present, this is the prerogative of the Supreme Court. The law was expected to be adopted before the end of 2005 and to serve as an alternative to the ECHR.

Indeed, Moldova has to date lost 24 cases before the ECHR out of the several hundreds that have been brought by its citizens. In February, the president proposed sanctions and fines for judges if their decisions lead to a condemnation by the ECHR. In the past few years, the increasing number of such condemnations has tarnished Moldova's image and affected its state budget. However, such an initiative runs the risk of undermining the independence of judges. Although Moldova generally complies with the decisions of the ECHR, it is unable to implement the ECHR's decision in a notable case, Ilie Ilascu and Other vs. the Republic of Moldova and Russia (2004), in which Moldova was asked to ensure the liberation of the two remaining detainees of the "Ilascu group," Tudor Petrov-Popa and Andrei Ivantoc, who have been held illegally by the Transnistrian separatist regime for over a decade.[12]

The central government in Chisinau has no authority in the Transnistria region, which has been ruled by a separatist regime since 1992. Hence, the Moldovan state is unable to uphold fundamental human, political, and civil rights there. Two stringent examples of violations by the Transnistrian authorities were exposed in 2005. First, Romanian-speaking children are discouraged or prevented from being educated in their native language.[13] Second, about 5,000 farmers are barred from accessing their farmland by the Transnistrian militia, depriving them of their source of income. Some 1,300 farmers have filed a case with the ECHR.

A new article on torture was introduced into the criminal code in June 2005 in accordance with the provisions of the Convention Against Torture and Other Cruel, Inhuman or Degrading Treatment or Punishment. A strategy on fighting violence toward the incarcerated is also under elaboration.[14] The Ministry of Justice has recognized that a lack of funds is chiefly to blame for the violation of detainee rights and the partial implementation of the 2004-2008 National Action Plan on Human Rights.[15] In addition, according to the chairman of the Association of Lawyers for Human Rights, Vitalie Nagachevski, it is necessary to review the preventive arrest practice in order to combat overpopulation in prisons. This would improve detention conditions, which presently are "inhuman and degrading."[16] Moldova has also taken steps to remove the death penalty.

Corruption

1997	1998	1999	2001	2002	2003	2004	2005	2006
n/a	n/a	6.00	6.00	6.25	6.25	6.25	6.25	6.00

The National Anticorruption Strategy and the Action Plan were adopted in December 2004 by the Moldovan Parliament and entered into force in January

2005. The National Anticorruption Strategy recognizes that corruption gravely undermines Moldova's statehood by affecting all areas of public and private life.[17] And to ensure the smooth implementation of the Action Plan, the president issued a decree authorizing the formation of the Monitoring Group, which meets on a monthly basis. The Monitoring Group includes ministries and government agencies, institutions from the judiciary, representatives from civil society (such as Transparency International), and business and local authorities. The Center for the Fight Against Economic Crime and Corruption (CFECC) is the main government agency responsible for fighting corruption and also acts as secretariat of the Monitoring Group.[18]

Throughout 2005, the Moldovan government has been very active in implementing the anticorruption Action Plan. For instance, the CFECC and the Ministry of Justice took steps in coordination with the Office for Economic Cooperation and Development and the Council of Europe to bring Moldova's anticorruption legislation in line with international norms and practices, entailing modifications to Moldova's criminal code and criminal procedure code, the elaboration of draft legislation on the financing of political parties and electoral campaigns, and modification of the legislation to combat money laundering. Also, work is in progress to outline the competences of the main institutions involved in the fight against corruption. Within the CFECC, a new division on the prognosis and prevention of corruption was established. The government adopted several decisions on preventing corruption and protectionism within public institutions, including a gradual rise in civil servant wages starting in 2005. In addition, a number of seminars and workshops were organized by government agencies and NGOs on fighting corruption.

In 2005, Moldova scored 2.9 in Transparency International's Corruption Perceptions Index (where 10 indicates a total absence of corruption). This represents a slight improvement over the 2004 score of 2.3. In light of the National Anticorruption Strategy, which the government began implementing in early 2005, such an improvement in Moldova's score comes as no surprise. Nevertheless, at a practical level, corruption continues to deeply affect everyday life in the country.

In the first half of 2005, the CFECC was alerted to 4,173 cases of corruption. During this same period, 304 criminal cases were initiated, 62 percent referring directly to corruption and 33 percent to economic and financial offenses.[19] The main criticism of the CFECC is that most "busts" involve small bribes to low-ranking civil servants, police and customs officers, doctors, teachers, and so forth. In addition, in most cases the sentences are disproportionately high, sometimes 5- to 10-year prison terms for accepting or extorting a bribe of only several hundred dollars.[20]

Transparency International Moldova's study *Diagnosis of Bribery in Business*[21] shows that the most corrupt areas in Moldova still remain health care, education, customs, and the police. The study further points out that Moldovans identify that pressure exerted by their bosses (superiors) and relatives is the main reason for corruption. An astounding 90 percent of those surveyed choose not to denounce cases of corruption. However, the study points to progress in the fight against corruption within public institutions. For instance, the total value of bribes paid by businessmen to public institutions and services decreased by almost 40 percent for the 12-month period of 2004-2005, compared with the Transparency International survey of 2002.[22]

According to the same study, Moldovan businesspeople view corruption as the second most important obstacle to developing a business, after high taxes. Around 80 percent of Moldovan businesspeople believe corruption has remained the same (43.6 percent) or worsened (36.3 percent) in 2005 compared with 2004.[23] Moldova's business environment is subject to excessive regulations and a continuously changing legislative framework that makes it prone to corruption. A new law went into effect in February 2005 that seeks to review and annul any superfluous laws and business regulations.

Public procurement is also a highly corruption-prone process. The Transparency International Moldova study further shows that only 16.2 percent of businesses participate in the public procurement process and that 66.4 percent believe a government contract can be won only through unofficial payments.[24] Conventional wisdom among businesses says there have been no serious government measures to render the process more transparent and fair.

With regard to high-profile anticorruption busts undertaken by the CFECC, there are often speculations as to the political nature of the arrests. Without putting into question the legitimacy of the arrests, it is perceived by the public that the CFECC continues to be used as a political tool targeted mainly against political and economic competitors of the ruling elite. This perception is reinforced by the extensive powers of the CFECC to make preventive arrests and conduct investigations. In addition, the CFECC is directly subordinated to the prime minister, who in turn answers to the president. A high-profile anticorruption case involved the arrest of Victor Turcanu, president of Victoriabank (one of the largest banks in Moldova), who according to his lawyer Alexandru Tanase is accused of allegedly extorting a bribe of US$15,000 in exchange for a sizable loan on privileged terms.[25] Turcanu's lawyers see this case as a setup for the elimination of their client from the Moldovan business scene.

Cases of corruption receive wide coverage in the Moldovan press and media. This has become a less hazardous activity for journalists than in the past, confirmed by the total absence of cases in 2005 of physical violence against journalists who investigate corruption. Most coverage concerns busts and investigations operated by the CFECC involving petty corruption, which does not generate a lot of controversy in the public sphere. High-profile cases, which can have political implications, are discussed in great detail in both the opposition and pro-government press and receive a great deal of political attention.

George Dura is assistant research fellow at the Centre for European Policy Studies (CEPS) in Brussels. Nicu Popescu is Open Society Institute research fellow at CEPS, editor of Eurojournal.org, and PhD candidate at the Central European University in Budapest.

[1] Office of the OSCE Representative on Freedom of the Media, Report on Moldova, September 2005.
[2] See the Coalition 2005 Web site, www.coalitia2005.md.
[3] Freedom House, Freedom in the World 2005, available at www.freedomhouse.org.
[4] Decision of 28 January 2005 of the Central Election Commission regarding the approval of the instruction with regard to certain exceptions to the voting procedure of the parliamentary elections of 6 March 2005, www.cec.md/i-ComisiaCentrala/main.aspx?dbName=Activity2.
[5] Interview by phone with an official from the Ministry of Justice, Chisinau, Moldova, 2 November 2005.
[6] See statement on Freedominfo.org, Threats to Information Access in Moldova, www.freedominfo.org/news/moldova/20050811.htm#secrets , accessed on November 8, 2005.
[7] See International Research & Exchanges Board Media Sustainability Index: The Development Sustainable Media in Europe and Eurasia, country chapter on Moldova, www.irex.org/msi.
[8] See action plan and benchmarks, www.osce.org/documents/mm/2004/03/2490_en.pdf.
[9] Interview with Veaceslav Ionita, Ziarul de Garda, October 20, 2005.
[10] Council of Europe, October 4, 2005, Resolution on Functioning of Democratic Institutions in Moldova.
[11] European Court of Human Rights, Survey of Activities 2005, www.echr.coe.int/NR/rdonlyres/4753F3E8-3AD0-42C5-B294-0F2A68507FC0/0/SurveyofActivities2005.pdf.
[12] For more information about this case and the "Ilascu group," please refer to the ECHR judgment of July 8, 2004 (application no. 48787/99), http://cmiskp.echr.coe.int.
[13] Instead, the Transnistrian authorities "encourage" Romanian-speaking pupils to attend schools that teach Romanian following the Cyrillic script and use the outdated Transnistrian education curriculum that was in use in Moldova during Soviet times. In this way, these pupils are deprived of a higher education, and their parents increasingly opt for sending them to Russian-language schools. As a result, there are claims that the Transnistrian regime is pursuing a policy of linguistic cleansing, and there are indications that the Romanian-speaking population of the Transnistrian region has decreased from 40 percent in 1989 to just 30 percent in 2005. (Source: "Militarised Transnistria Threatens Civil Society and Elections," Radio Free Europe/Radio Liberty, November 15, 2005.)
[14] Internal Report on Semestrial Evaluation of the EU-Moldova Action Plan Implementation 2005, Government of the Republic of Moldova, September 2005, p. 13.
[15] "Shortage of Funds Is Main Cause for Violations of Detainees' Rights," News Digest, OSCE Mission to Moldova, November 3, 2005.
[16] "Shortage of funds is the main cause for violation of detainees rights", Basa-Press, November 2, 2005.
[17] National Strategy for the Prevention and Fight Against Corruption-2005 Action Plan for the Implementation of the National Strategy for the Prevention and Fight Against Corruption, Transparency International Moldova, ed. (Chisinau, Moldova: Transparency International Moldova, 2005), p. 4.
[18] Other institutions in decreasing order of importance to the fight against corruption are the Ministry of Internal Affairs, the Office of the Prosecutor General and the Office of the Anticorruption Prosecutor, the Ministry of Justice, the Security and Intelligence Service, the Customs Service, and the Ministry of Foreign Affairs and European Integration. A whole series of other public institutions and agencies, including NGOs, also participate in the fight against corruption.
[19] Internal Report on Semestrial Evaluation of the EU-Moldova Action Plan Implementation 2005, Government of the Republic of Moldova, September 2005, annex.
[20] "Vames retinut pentru luare de mita" [Customs officer held on bribery charges], Flux, August 29, 2005, www.transparency.md/News/ro/20050829.htm. Other, similar cases are also available on www.transparency.md.
[21] S. Pinzari, L. Carasciuc, and I. Spinei, Diagnosis of Bribery in Business (Chisinau, Moldova: Transparency International Moldova, 2005).
[22] Ibid., p. 51.
[23] Ibid., p 38.
[24] Ibid., p 59.
[25] "Presedintele SA "Victoriabank" cercetat penal intr-un nou episod" (President of SA "Victoriabank" under investigation in a new case), Azi, January 30, 2005, www.azi.md.

Poland

Capital:	Warsaw
Population:	38.2 million
GNI/capita:	$6,100
Ethnic Groups:	Polish (96.7%), German (0.4%), Ukrainian and Belarusian (0.2%)

Nations in Transit Ratings and Averaged Scores

	1997	1998	1999	2001	2002	2003	2004	2005	2006
Electoral Process	1.50	1.25	1.25	1.25	1.25	1.50	1.50	1.75	1.75
Civil Society	1.25	1.25	1.25	1.25	1.25	1.25	1.25	1.25	1.25
Independent Media	1.50	1.50	1.50	1.50	1.50	1.75	1.75	1.50	1.75
Governance *	1.75	1.75	1.75	1.75	2.00	2.00	2.00	n/a	n/a
National Democratic Governance	n/a	n/a	n/a	n/a	n/a	n/a	n/a	2.50	2.75
Local Democratic Governance	n/a	n/a	n/a	n/a	n/a	n/a	n/a	2.00	2.00
Judicial Framework and Independence	1.50	1.50	1.50	1.50	1.50	1.50	1.50	2.00	2.25
Corruption	n/a	n/a	2.25	2.25	2.25	2.50	2.50	3.00	3.25
Democracy Score	1.50	1.45	1.58	1.58	1.63	1.75	1.75	2.00	2.14

* With the 2005 edition, Freedom House introduced seperate analysis and ratings for national democratic governance and local democratic governance to provide readers with more detailed and nuanced analysis of these two important subjects.

NOTE: The ratings reflect the consensus of Freedom House, its academic advisers, and the author of this report. The opinions expressed in this report are those of the author. The ratings are based on a scale of 1 to 7, with 1 representing the highest level of democratic progress and 7 the lowest. The Democracy Score is an average of ratings for the categories tracked in a given year.

The economic and social data on this page were taken from the following sources:
GNI/capita, Population: *World Development Indicators 2006* (Washington, D.C.: World Bank, 2006).
Ethnic Groups: *CIA World Factbook 2006* (Washington, D.C.: Central Intelligence Agency, 2006).

EXECUTIVE SUMMARY

Among the post-Communist democracies, Poland has in 16 years moved decisively toward the West, though not without paying a high price, including record unemployment and internal political compromises. Poland joined NATO in March 1999 and in May 2004 became a member of the European Union (EU), the largest among the eight former Communist newcomers. Poland's economy has been open for EU goods and partial services since 1993, but Poles started to feel the benefit of EU structural funds and agriculture subsidies only in 2005; they are still waiting for the full opening of job and service markets already enjoyed by the original 15 EU member countries. The prolonged fight over the size and division of the EU 2007-2013 budget, finally decided in December 2005, was for Poland a bitter lesson that European solidarity still means less than the interests of individual nations, especially the richer ones.

Nevertheless, 2005 may have been a breakthrough year for Poland. With a new right-wing government and a president from the same party, Law and Justice (PiS), Poland's political system has started to change. The system was created in 1989 with a peaceful, "Solidarity"-driven, negotiated break from Communism. According to PiS, the ills of the last 16 years – weak governance, political patronage in the non-nationalized part of the economy, widespread corruption in everyday life and at the highest levels of politics – have their origins in the compromises of that time. The opposition also talks about the legacy of Communism. During the elections, the new rulers pledged to radically eradicate these ills and won the support of voters. The year 2006 will show how much and by what means they will be able and willing to achieve these goals.

National Democratic Governance. Poland passed high standards of national democratic governance when it achieved EU membership in 2004, but certain holes remain in its democratic consolidation. The elections of 2005 confirmed the stability of the parliamentary democracy. The transfer of power, both in government and in the presidency, went smoothly and, especially in the latter, with a level of politeness not present before. The new prime minister was quickly established in the office, and the minority government began to create parliamentary coalitions. However, some old threats to democratic governance have not been eradicated, and a few new ones were visible. The privatization of industry, which provides thousands of politically hot positions in 1,600 treasury-owned enterprises, has been slowed by the influence of nationalist parties close to the ruling PiS. The new government tried to dismantle the civil service system, and some scandals involving the former ruling Democratic Left Alliance are still unfinished. New challenges to the rule of democracy are rising, including the illegal and traumatic hunt for Communist-era agents placed on a stolen list of 170,000 names of victims and agents; the politically biased work of parliamentary investigative commissions; and, last, the "upper hand" manner of the new government's political actions. *Poland's national democratic governance rating worsens from 2.50 to 2.75 owing to the tendency to concentrate power in the executive branch, which is dominating the political process.*

Electoral Process. The elections of 2005 – based on a well-grounded system of proportional representation and party lists in the lower chamber of Parliament and majority vote in the Senate – were generally judged to be fair and democratic. This was confirmed by the Supreme Court's decision to repeat the poll in one district (Czestochowa) owing to the lack of party affiliations marked on ballots. However, the public's strong efforts to change the electoral system into one of majority (one-mandate districts) produced no results whatsoever. The big unfulfilled promise of 2005 was the two winning parties' coalition after the elections. *Taking into account the parties' lack of attention to the proposed changes in electoral law but also recognizing the good administration of the electoral system, Poland's rating for electoral process remains at 1.75.*

Civil Society. Civil society seems to be Poland's solid ground for defending democracy. It is active and widespread, with 45,000 associations and 7,000 foundations, and composed of two main traditions: the Solidarity-led fight for political independence and the Catholic Church's inspired care for the less fortunate. It is important to note, though, that Poland's civil society is in the first stage of a civil rights movement: organizing itself to protect particular interests. There are only a few watchdog organizations aimed at protecting general civil rights: press freedom, consumers' rights (including media consumers), and voters' rights. *The weak position of trade unions and the new government's efforts to curtail civil society freedoms prevent Poland's civil society rating from improving; it therefore remains at 1.25.*

Independent Media. Polish media have a strong tradition of independence going back much further than the Communist period. The print media are almost completely privatized; among electronic media, public radio and TV maintain the strongest positions. Investigative journalists have had success in uncovering corruption and political favoritism, usually in advance of the Parliament's investigative commissions. However, journalists are poorly organized and therefore more prone to political and business pressures. The new government proved to be quick and aggressive in taking over the public media, planning "repolonization" of private media (restoration of Polish rather than foreign capital) while giving preferential treatment to an extreme Catholic media conglomerate from Torun. *Owing to threats and intimidation from the government, the rating for independent media worsens from 1.50 to 1.75.*

Local Democratic Governance. Local self-government, reinstalled quickly after the 1989 end of Communism, gave a chance to thousands of local enthusiasts to govern and improve their "local motherlands." Some of these, keen to receive funds from state- and EU-supported programs, achieved notable successes. Party politics plays a much smaller role at the lowest level of government, and independent candidates have a better chance to rally voters' support. For many young people, self-government is the school for participating in politics and governance. *Owing to the lack of significant changes, the rating for local democratic governance remains at 2.00.*

Judicial Framework and Independence. In 2005, the legal system remained the weakest area of the Polish government. The press uncovered new, startling cases of judges and prosecutors breaking the law. The court system is so lenient that most believe the judiciary is in power only to serve itself; delays in court proceedings are measured in years and negatively impact the lives of citizens. Poland is losing case after case in the European Court of Human Rights in Strasbourg. Prosecutors remain under the control of politicians, with the minister of justice also serving as prosecutor general. Prisons are overcrowded: There are 85,000 convicts, and 30,000 people have not reported to serve their sentences. The new minister of justice advocates for longer prison terms, higher prison populations, more prisons converted from military barracks, and a severe policy against those who break the law. *With general inefficiency, cases of corruption in the judiciary, and prosecutors lacking independence from politics, Poland's rating for judicial framework and independence worsens from 2.00 to 2.25.*

Corruption. Corruption seems to have a permanent place in Poland's social landscape. For years, roughly 15 percent of Poles have confirmed that they have participated in corruption. The most corrupt sector is health care. In 2005, corruption scandals were unveiled in professional soccer and the military draft. Parliamentary investigative commissions unearthed traces of corruption at the highest levels of political life, but their work was not concluded. The new government pledged to fight corruption with a new creation, the Central Anticorruption Agency, devoted solely to eradicating corruption from the top down. *Owing to the growing number of cases, new spheres affected, and lack of effective countermeasures, Poland's corruption rating worsens from 3.00 to 3.25.*

Outlook for 2006. In 2006, the new right-wing government will try to fulfill its electoral promises: fighting corruption, helping poor families willing to bear a child, better use of EU funds, new press legislation, and public media order. However, the beginning of the year looks more like "rocking the boat" than sailing it. The National Broadcasting Council was quickly reduced from nine to five members, all politicians. A new, PiS-friendly director of the Institute for National Remembrance was elected. Ruling party politicians demanded restoration of Polish capital in the media, owned largely by foreign companies ("repolonization" of them). A PiS leader accused the Constitutional Tribunal of "aiming at state institutions"; 6 out of the Tribunal's 15 judges will be nominated by the president in 2006. The justice minister announced his disbelief in prison rehabilitation and called for harsh sentences only. Faster courts for smaller criminal offenses will start operating: Prosecutors must file charges within 48 hours, and sentencing must occur within the following 24 hours, with offenders receiving up to three years in jail. At the end of the year, the new head of the Polish National Bank will be nominated by the Parliament.

MAIN REPORT

National Democratic Governance

1997	1998	1999	2001	2002	2003	2004	2005	2006
n/a	n/a	n/a	n/a	n/a	n/a	n/a	2.50	2.75

Poland is a parliamentary democracy. Its Constitution, adopted by national referendum in 1997, provides a balance among the executive, legislative, and judicial powers. Broad changes to the national law were introduced before May 1, 2004, in order to meet the requirements for EU membership; however, Poland's Constitutional Tribunal signaled that adoption of the European warrant procedure would be in formal conflict with the country's Constitution.[1]

The government is confirmed by a majority of the 460-member Sejm (lower house of Parliament). Both chambers of Parliament – the Sejm and the Senate – work on new legislation and must agree on it, then the president signs or vetoes it. The president may also send legislation to the Constitutional Tribunal (elected by the Sejm for nine-year terms), which can declare laws or parts of laws unconstitutional; its decisions are final and obligatory. The president's will may be overridden by a two-thirds majority of the Sejm. The Parliament can form investigative commissions and impeach the president.

In the latest parliamentary elections, which took place on September 25, 2005, the Law and Justice Party (PiS) won 27 percent of the popular vote, followed by Civic Platform (PO) with 24 percent. Despite long-term preelectoral promises, they could not form a coalition. PiS created a minority government with Prime Minister Kazimierz Marcinkiewicz, whose cabinet was easily approved, but it had to shop for support among other parties: the populist Self-Defense League (Samoobrona) and the right-wing League of Polish Families (LPR). PiS finally signed a parliamentary coalition, securing its minority rule, but extraordinary elections prior to 2009 are still likely.

In Poland, the most powerful political office is the prime minister, who can be recalled only by a constructive no-confidence vote. The president plays a more ceremonial role. Such was the case for Solidarity leader Lech Walesa, elected in 1990, but not for his two-term successor, former Communist youth activist Aleksander Kwasniewski, who has been in office for a decade. Kwasniewski was active in gathering support for Poland's NATO membership in 1999 and joining the EU in 2004.

In neighboring Ukraine, during the 2004 Orange Revolution, he brought two rival candidates and EU envoys to roundtable talks in order to solve the crisis over rigged presidential elections. The price for that move was a Russian "nyet" to Kwasniewski's quiet bid to succeed UN secretary general Kofi Annan. However, Russia in general seems not to have yet fully digested the independence of Poland, its nineteenth-century domain and Warsaw Pact country.

On October 23, 2005, Lech Kaczynski from PiS became Kwasniewski's successor with 54 percent of the popular vote, thus beating out Donald Tusk from PO. The expected third vote to approve the European Constitution was not held owing to the negative result of the French referendum, much to the relief of pro-European politicians; the election results might have only confirmed that the Polish-EU honeymoon is perhaps already over. In 2005, Poland's political pendulum moved significantly to the right. With an unemployment rate of 18 percent and a tsunami of political corruption scandals, PiS's calls to replace the "rotten" Third Republic compelled enough voter support for PiS to rule.

All legislation is published in the *Official Gazette* and on the Sejm, Senate, and president's Web sites, which offer much more than the obligatory *Bulletin of Public Information*. The Sejm's legislative proceedings and those of parliamentary investigative commissions are broadcast live on public TV. There is access to a significant part of government, self-government, and other public documents thanks to the Law on Freedom of Information of 2001. However, the law did not replace other acts dealing with this topic; therefore, much data, including information on recipients of EU agricultural subsidies, are still not public information.[2] Government agencies are obliged to respond to citizens' inquiries within a month but are often late.

All members of Parliament (MPs) and high-ranking government officials must declare their property annually. The media analyze these reports (posted on the Internet) with painful scrutiny, but only in one case has a well-known politician had to explain the origins of his wealth. The winning PiS declared that all public officials must formally declare the source of such property as houses, apartments, cars, savings, and so forth, which declarations will be supervised by the new Central Anticorruption Agency (CAA).

Public representatives, high-ranking government officials, and attorneys must declare if they worked for Communist-era secret police or intelligence. Those who hide this information are punished with a 10-year ban on public service after trials in lustration court initiated by the public interest prosecutor. These procedures often take years and are criticized as too lenient. To speed up the disclosure of Communist-era secret police, a list of the names of 170,000 people whose files are in the National Remembrance Institute (IPN) was copied by journalist Bronislaw Wildstein of the leading daily newspaper, *Rzeczpospolita*, and published on the Internet in January 2005. (See more in Electoral Process.) The Constitutional Tribunal's verdict allowed all citizens, not only victims of the Communist state, to inspect IPN files concerning them. PiS has plans to amend the IPN bill in such a way that the institute will replace the lustration court, the public interest prosecutor will be eliminated, and IPN files of public officials and media heads will be opened.

The Supreme Chamber of Control (NIK) audits all government institutions. Its head is nominated by the Sejm and approved by the Senate for a six-year term, which helps to keep the office somewhat immune from political influence. Since 2001, the current head of the NIK, elected by the center-right Solidarity Election Action coalition, has been auditing the two left-wing governments. If he stays in office until summer 2007, the government will have a politically friendly auditor. The chamber audits legality, efficacy, economic sense, and diligence in all levels of the central administration, Polish National Bank, state and local administration.

The early 1990s goal of creating a depoliticized, high-quality corps of civil servants working for all government agencies has not been fulfilled. Although the National School of Public Administration has been educating professional civil servants for 15 years, every government has found ways to avoid organizing contests for the ministries' general director posts. Marcinkiewicz's government has followed its predecessors' practices of nominating "acting" directors and has plans to ease the legal conditions for "transferring" people from self-government into civil service.

After 16 years of privatization, the Polish economy is now generally run by private corporations. The state still has shares in about 1,600 companies and owns close to 40 percent of the country's territory (two-thirds of which are forests and the rest arable and industrial lands).[3] With every change of government, new individuals take over management of the biggest state companies, such as the national postal service, national airports, Bank Gospodarstwa Krajowego (BGK) and Powszechna Kasa Oszczednosci (PKO) banks, national copper mines and mills, and the national oil company (Orlen).

The mysterious 2002 arrest of Orlen's CEO, Andrzej Modrzejewski, led to hearings two years later with the highest public officials in front of the parliamentary investigative commission. It was revealed that Modrzejewski's arrest in front of TV cameras was arranged by the prime minister and minister of justice and executed by the police special forces unit. Further investigations unearthed complicated connections between the J&S Company, which was an intermediary for Russian oil imports, and President Kwasniewski's circle of friends and supporters. These included industrial magnate Jan Kulczyk and a Russian spy, Vladimir Alganow, who was trying to secure Moscow's buyout of the only Polish oil port in Gdansk.

The unexpected but intended outcome of the commission's activity was a derailing of the political Left's potentially successful bid for the presidency. Wlodzimierz Cimoszewicz, candidate of Democratic Left Alliance (SLD) was called before Orlen's commission to testify about his property statement, which included owning Orlen shares. After a few weeks of bitterly fighting accusations about inaccuracies in his property statements, Cimoszewicz pulled out of the race. President Kwasniewski refused to testify in front of the commission, but his wife did. Live TV broadcasts of the proceedings helped PiS, as the most active interrogators were from this party. In this way, PiS repeated the 2004 Rywingate investigative commission success of Jan Rokita from PO.

Lew Rywin, the film producer behind the biggest bribery scandal in post-Communist Poland, was finally sentenced in the end of 2004 to two years in prison.

In 2002, Rywin had approached Adam Michnik, editor of the leading *Gazeta Wyborcza*, to arrange a US$17 million bribe for changing the law in favor of the media holding company Agora. In the spring of 2005 Rywin served six weeks and was released owing to poor health, but in the autumn, after losing an extra appeal in the Supreme Court, he was back in prison as the only conviction in the affair, which devastated Poland's political landscape. The Warsaw prosecutor looking for "the power holding group" that supposedly sent Rywin to Michnik interrogated former prime minister Leszek Miller and his closest aides. The group may face trial in the future. Rywin was also put on the list of witnesses in this case and may be pardoned if he reveals who sent him to Michnik.

The fall 2005 change of government led to a reorganization of the military intelligence services (WSI), the only part of the intelligence services not professionally verified after 1989. The WSI were accused of concealing the identities of their pre-1989 agents and post-1989 activities far beyond their mandate. The WSI is slated to be divided into intelligence and counterintelligence services, and every officer has to testify about past activities. Accusations brought by Human Rights Watch and U.S. media about alleged secret CIA prisons for torturing suspected terrorists ignited political discussions in Poland about the lack of civil control over the country's military and civil intelligence operations.

Electoral Process

1997	1998	1999	2001	2002	2003	2004	2005	2006
1.50	1.25	1.25	1.25	1.25	1.50	1.50	1.75	1.75

Poland has a multiparty parliamentary system with proportional representation introduced in 1993. The electoral thresholds are 5 percent for parties and 8 percent for coalitions. Before thresholds were introduced, there were over a dozen political parties in the Parliament and seven in the ruling coalition. Thresholds do not apply to national minorities. In practice, this means the German minority, which traditionally wins two seats in the Sejm; however, their voting power is less than .5 percent.[4] The Sejm has 460 members elected for four-year terms. The Senate has 100 members elected by majority vote on a provincial basis, also for four-year terms. The electoral system is considered free and fair; international observers have not been present even though there are no legal barriers to them. The Supreme Court electoral protest system works well. In 2005, the Court ordered the repeat of Senate elections in one district (Czestochowa), where voting cards were printed without the political affiliations of the candidates.

In fall 2005, Poland held elections for both the Parliament and the president. The third expected vote, over the European Constitution, was postponed indefinitely after the French referendum's negative result in May. The 2005 elections changed the ruling party, which has been a pattern since the first elections in 1989 ending Communist rule. The Democratic Left Alliance (SLD), the party that won 41 percent in 2001, lost badly in 2005, gaining only 11 percent and 55 seats in the Sejm. In 2001, after four years in power, the Solidarity Election Action won no mandates; however, the new parties formed from it – PO, PiS, and the League of Polish Families (LPR) – were successful in electing candidates. Only Freedom Union – the party that created the first non-Communist government in 1989 and a political partner of the Solidarity Election Action – failed to gain Sejm seats in both the 2001 and 2005 elections, seemingly ending its prospects on the political scene.

A strong signal of voter dissatisfaction was already evident in 2002 when the SLD lost local elections, winning only 24 percent of the seats. In the 2004 elections to the European Parliament, with only a 21 percent turnout, the opposition parties won easily (in 2004, 59 percent had turned out for the two-day referendum on joining the EU). The winners were PO with 24 percent, followed by the LPR (16 percent), PiS (13 percent), and Selfdefense (Samoobrona) (11 percent). The pro-European, economically liberal, and socially conservative PO was sure to take power in 2005. To its major surprise, the big winner of the September 2005 elections was PiS, getting 27 percent of the popular vote, which gave it 155 seats in the Sejm. PO received 24 percent and 133 seats. After the success of PiS presidential candidate Lech Kaczynski over PO contender Donald Tusk, the choice for prime minister was PiS's Kazimierz Marcinkiewicz from Gorzow instead of the expected winner, PO's Jan Rokita from Krakow. Therefore, the 2005 elections produced much deeper political change than anticipated.

PO's loss might have been greater if the European Constitution referendum, planned to be held together with the presidential elections, had not been suspended. In 2005, already weak Polish support for the EU waned further, despite the flow of farmers' subsidies and growing exports to the West. Three other factors also contributed to the political changes of 2005: continuing scandals involving ruling SLD politicians; fear of another wave of liberal PO reforms by a society with the highest unemployment rate in Europe; and high religious and patriotic feelings caused by the illness and death of Polish pope John Paul II.

Marek Belka's minority left-wing government, installed in May 2004 instead of earlier as promised by President Kwasniewski after the first wave of SLD scandals in 2003, did not manage to stop the downward slide of the ruling party. Success of the first Sejm investigative commission over the Rywingate affair paved the way for two others: first in mid-2004 for the dubious arrest of Orlen's CEO; and second in the beginning of 2005 for the privatization of the national insurance company Powszechny Zaklad Ubezpieczen (PZU). Both investigations continued until September 2005, focusing on the SLD's misuse of secret police and abuse of ministerial powers (the Orlen case) and the inability of different governments to privatize the national insurer (the PZU case). Part of the Orlen commission wanted to put President Kwasniewski before the State Tribunal for dubious connections with the wealthiest of Polish businesspeople.[5]

Another compromising case for the government was known as the "Starachowice affair." In 2003, the deputy minister of the interior leaked to two MP colleagues information he got from the police chief indicating that in Starachowice in south Poland, local government officials involved in an insurance embezzlement scheme would soon be arrested. The national highest-ranking police chief had to resign and now faces trial, and three politicians were sentenced to up to 3.5 years in jail. They appealed to the president for clemency; Kwasniewski reduced and suspended the sentence for one of them, Zbigniew Sobotka, causing a public uproar and protests.[6]

The January 2005 disclosure by *Rzeczpospolita* journalist Bronislaw Wildstein of a list containing some 170,000 names of Communist-era secret police agents set a harsh moral tone for the election campaign. Both PO and PiS, leading in the polls, wanted to disclose "skeletons in the closet" in order to stop "wild lustration" by Wildstein followers, who put the list online. Wildstein was fired for distributing the IPN list among fellow journalists without informing *Rzeczpospolita* about its existence (he was quickly given a job at the anti-SLD weekly *Wprost*). Several groups spoke out against the publication of the list, including left-wing parties, the influential daily *Gazeta Wyborcza*, human rights defenders, and a few bishops. These groups claimed that the list would cause suffering of innocent people, who were accused on the basis of incomplete and possibly mischievous police files and the popularity of their last names. Some of them sued Wildstein and IPN in civil cases. In this heavy atmosphere, Solidarity founder Lech Walesa was accused of being a Communist agent. Walesa was finally granted "victim" status by IPN, but only after Solidarity's 25th anniversary, which was clouded by these accusations. The death of John Paul II in April and the public mourning that followed solidified religious feelings and also helped to win positions for right-wing parties.

PO, the all-time leader in election polls, based its economic program on a promise of lowering income, value-added tax, and company taxes to 15 percent, but eliminating all tax exemptions. This would represent a slight loss for majority taxpayers, whose lowest tax break is set at 18 percent, but in reality they pay about 13 percent, due to exemptions. The socially oriented PiS bashed the "liberals" for playing to the rich and used TV commercials to threaten voters with an image of an empty refrigerator. This, plus disclosing that the grandfather of the PO presidential candidate had served shortly in the German army during the war, was enough for PiS to secure victories in both elections.

Civil Society

1997	1998	1999	2001	2002	2003	2004	2005	2006
1.25	1.25	1.25	1.25	1.25	1.25	1.25	1.25	1.25

Freedom of association is secured in Article 58 of the Polish Constitution and the Law on Associations. The only prohibitions are on those groups promoting Nazism, Fascism, and Communist ideology, racial and national hatred, secret membership, or the use of power to overthrow authorities. Freedom of assembly and demonstration is assured by Article 57; it was the most abused right in 2005.

Poland's civil society is based on the traditions of the Solidarity trade union and other anti-Communist opposition movements of the 1970s and 1980s, as well as social activity by the religiously dominant Catholic Church. Frequent changes of government in the 1990s helped to establish civil society structures: foundations, think tanks, and analytical centers in which the current opposition is maintained until the political pendulum brings its members back to the mainstream of official life. Since 2004, the Law on Public Benefit Activities and Volunteering has given nongovernmental organizations (NGOs) the option to register as "public benefit organizations," allowing tax breaks and 1 percent personal income tax donations but also stricter rules on salaries and an obligatory annual audit.

According to a 2004 survey, there are over 45,000 associations and 7,000 foundations registered as active in sports, recreation, tourism, hobbies, culture and art, education, social help, and health protection. More than 60,000 people work in the sector, which also includes 1 million volunteers. The main sources of financing are member dues, self-government donations, donations from private persons, and institutions.[7] Major donors are the Polish American Freedom Foundation and the Batory Foundation.[8]

The most well-known charity action is the annual New Year's telethon of the Great Holiday Help Orchestra. In 2005, thousands of young volunteers made over 29 million zlotys (US$9 million) from street collections and auctions, and the proceeds went to purchase medical equipment for handicapped children and the sick. Also, summer rock concerts were organized for the 14th year by TVP journalist Jerzy Owsiak.[9]

Polish Humanitarian Action, which collects money for natural disaster victims abroad, was established in the early 1990s by another charity activist, Janina Ochojska, as repayment for help that Poland received from the West during the martial law period a decade earlier.[10] The biggest charity organization in Poland is Caritas, which feeds the poor and shelters the homeless on behalf of the Catholic Church.

In the last months of 2004 and beginning of 2005, the Ukrainian Orange Revolution gave a boost to civil society activism in Poland. More than 3,000 observers of the presidential elections (out of a total 13,000) came to Ukraine from Poland thanks to the spontaneous efforts of students, political parties, and established civic organizations.[11] A symbolic tent was placed in front of Warsaw's Ukrainian embassy. For many young people, it was a repetition of their parents' participation in the Solidarity movement. By the end of 2005, similar actions were being organized, including demonstrations on the 16th of each month to support the "jeans opposition" in Belarus, where in March 2006 Aleksander Lukashenka was reelected president for a third term.

Warsaw mayor Lech Kaczynski's ban on the Equality March called by gay and lesbian rights organizations in June 2005 was a pivotal moment for the Polish civil rights movement, signaling restrictions on free expression based on the concept of "public morality." Despite the ban, a demonstration of several thousand, including left-wing politicians and foreign guests, took place on the streets of the capital;

police, under the command of the left-wing government, protected the march from gay-bashing counterdemonstrators, moving them away by force. With help from the Helsinki Foundation for Human Rights, a complaint against the ban was filed with the European Court of Human Rights (ECHR) in Strasbourg. Meanwhile, the Polish Constitutional Tribunal ruled that organizers of gatherings need only notify local authorities about them instead of asking for a permit.

In November, after the elections, another Equality March in Poznan, also banned by local authorities and therefore reduced to a few hundred people, gathered peacefully on a popular pedestrian-only street, and its participants were brutally attacked by riot police. Seventy demonstrators and some counterdemonstrators, shouting, "Gas the gays!" were detained briefly. After two months, the local court decided not to punish the demonstrators. Three counterdemonstrators were reprimanded, and other cases are pending. Other effective support has been shown by court motions from the Polish ombudsman, letters from intellectuals and the head of the Constitutional Tribunal, and demonstrations by civil rights groups in Paris, Berlin, and New York. Subsequent Democracy Revival rallies, organized in nine Polish cities, were not banned and were protected by the police.

The next group to test the freedom to demonstrate may be miners, who secured early retirement guarantees for themselves by using buttons and explosives in front of the Parliament in the summer before the elections. An organization of industry heads questioned the constitutionality of the workers' rights, and the bill may be revoked. The trade union movement has good standing in Poland, thanks to the strength of Solidarity in the 1980s (10 million people), but only a few trades are able to protect their rights as effectively as Polish miners.

The All-Poland Alliance of Trade Unions has about 1.5 million members; Solidarity has less than 1 million. The majority of these are from state-owned factories, steel mills, mines, railways, and budget-funded health care and education facilities. Private owners are trying to keep trade unions away, and supermarkets were the most effective in union bashing. However, one of them, Biedronka, acquired such a bad reputation for repressing union organizers and the permanent use of nonpaid overtime that its former employee, Bozena Lopacka, gained the nickname "another Walesa" for her fight against the company's slavish working conditions.[12]

Independent Media

1997	1998	1999	2001	2002	2003	2004	2005	2006
1.50	1.50	1.50	1.50	1.50	1.75	1.75	1.50	1.75

In Poland, the importance of free media is well understood by those whose great-grandfathers' writings were censored by czarists before 1918; whose grandfathers were publishing illegal papers under Nazi occupation; and whose fathers printed and distributed uncensored books and newspapers in the People's Poland of the 1970s and 1980s. It is no surprise, then, that according to the Polish Constitution, the state "shall ensure freedom of the press and other means of social communication."[13] However, other legal acts still contain traces of authoritarian rule, which endangers this basic freedom.

Article 133 of the Polish penal code provides up to three years' imprisonment for persons who "publicly insult the Polish nation or the state" though the statute has not been used recently. Libeling the president can carry three years in jail (Article 135§2); libeling MPs or government ministers, two years (Article 226§3); and libeling other public officials, one year (Article 226§1). The popularity of jokes about twin brothers/politicians makes the statutes on libel, particularly regarding the president, challenging for prosecutors to use. Libel suits against media professionals are common, but those found guilty are usually only fined. Over the past year, one journalist was close to serving three months in jail for libeling a local official but left prison after two days released by order of Constitutional Tribunal, which accepted the motion based on his case.[14] Other legal dangers to press freedom include court gag orders based on the "securing the motion" article in the civic procedures code, prosecutors' enforced publishing of corrections, and the authorization of interviews (the last two stipulated in the 20-year-old Law on the Press).

Despite these dangers, the Polish media landscape looks strong. Two newspapers, *Gazeta Wyborcza* (circulation 436,000 copies; owner, Polish Agora) and *Rzeczpospolita* (183,000 copies; owner, Orkla Media), are the main opinion makers. Outlets with the largest circulations are the tabloids *Fakt* (535,000 copies; owner, Axel Springer) and *Super Express* (232,000 copies; owner, Bonnier with Polish capital).

There are three major opinion weeklies: the left-wing *Polityka* (190,000 copies; owned by a journalist co-op), the center *Newsweek* Polish edition (185,000 copies; owner, Axel Springer), and the right-wing *Wprost* (168,000 copies; owner, Wprost). The 2005 newcomer *Ozon* (about 40,000 copies) is a conservative Catholic publication that has had a difficult start. In 2005, the growing influence of *Nasz Dziennik* – a conservative nationalist daily tied to Radio Maryja and Trwam TV, founded by Father Tadeusz Rydzyk, a nationalist, right-wing media evangelist with great political ambitions – led to reprimands by both the bishops of local Catholic church and the Vatican. The Catholic liberal *Tygodnik Powszech* (21,000 copies) has a strong reputation as the only independent (though censored) paper of Communist Poland. *Przekroj*, published by Edipresse (103,000 copies) enjoys a reputation as the authority in cultural matters. The private Polish weekly *Nie* (128,000 copies), run by Jerzy Urban, former spokesman for President Wojciech Jaruzelski, is anticlerical, left-wing, and often provocative.[15] Two English weeklies (*Warsaw Voice* and *Warsaw Business Journal*) and a Russian one are published in the capital.

Besides these leading titles, there are hundreds of other dailies, weeklies, and monthlies on all topics published countrywide. The local press is vibrant and produces more than 3,000 titles, but media concentration is a threat. The major media companies already dominating Warsaw-based and regional press include Axel Springer, Agora, Orkla Media, and Polskapresse (German). Poland is one of the few countries in Europe where media cross-ownership has not been regulated. Press distribution is provided evenly by the state-owned Ruch and private Kolporter companies. The Press Publishers Chamber is organizing a consortium of major publishers willing to buy Ruch when its long-awaited privatization takes place.

Polish electronic media have less freedom than their print counterparts and are controlled by the National Broadcasting Council (KRRiT), a body (formerly of nine members) elected by the Parliament and the president. In 2005, the KRRiT was composed almost completely of left-wing nominees, which caused the new government to curtail the KRRiT's membership and prerogatives before it had a chance to choose new supervising bodies of the public TVP and radio stations in 2006. The amendment to the Law on Radio and TV, reducing the KRRiT to five members (two nominated by the Sejm, one by the Senate, and two by the president, who also picks the chairperson), was shuffled through the Sejm and the Senate in the two weeks before Christmas. President Lech Kaczynski signed the amendment immediately, and five new KRRiT members were elected in the old style, all with political ties, this time to the Right. Three months later Constitutional Tribunal ruled that the president could not nominate the head of KRRiT.

TVP, the public station, has a dominant position with viewers and advertising markets with its three ground channels (TVP1, TVP2 and TVP3 together with 16 local branches), two satellite channels (TVP Polonia and TVP Kultura), and potentially more with digital webcasting. This strong position comes at the price of high commercialization and political influence on programming, formerly from the Left. Since the 2004 change of TVP leadership, programming has been more balanced but is affected by every change in the political wind. Two-thirds of TVP's income comes from advertising, the rest from broadcasting fees paid by about 50 percent of Polish households and about 5 percent of businesses. More and more commercialized, TVP looks in prime time exactly like its private competitors: movies, soap operas, and talk shows. Public service programs and award-winning documentaries are shown late at night. The privatization of public media is a political taboo. TVP's main private competitors include Polsat and TVN, the Canal+ cable channel owned by UPC, and Father Rydzyk's Trwam TV, a religious satellite channel broadcasting from Torun.[16]

Among radio stations, the public Polskie Radio – with 6 Warsaw-based channels and 17 local radio stations – has a strong position, but private competitors Radio ZET and Radio RMF FM are the leaders in audience and advertising revenues. Radio Maryja, broadcasting since 1991 and founded by Father Rydzyk, has played an important role in gathering support for right-wing political interests. During the 2005 election campaign, Rydzyk's "Sink the Platform!" rallying cry helped PiS defeat the PO.

Fifty percent of Polish households have a computer and use the Internet with its full diversity of opinions. Offensive remarks are rarely blocked, and operators claim not to be responsible for them. Child pornography is the only prosecuted Web offense. Naukowa Akademicka Siec Komputerowa (NASK), an academic institution, keeps a registry of sites, but there are no address restrictions. Almost all printing media have their own Web sites, and the number of personal Web sites and blogs has been growing rapidly.

With the strong presence of print and electronic media and the advance of online publications, there is no clear estimate of how many journalists are working in the media sector, but the minimum count would be about 20,000. There are no doubts, though, that only a few hundred of these are members of trade unions (Journalists' Syndicate and a branch of Solidarity), and only a couple of thousand journalists, mostly older professionals, are members of Polish Journalists' Association and Republic of Poland Journalists' Association. They maintain ethical codes and lobby for new press legislation and changes in the penal code, but their voice is weak and authority low. In general, journalists have no collective agreement and no wage bargaining, and publishers keep salaries secret. Strikes and other union actions – such as those enjoyed by colleagues working for the same media companies in France, Germany, or Norway – are unheard of in Poland.

Local Democratic Governance

1997	1998	1999	2001	2002	2003	2004	2005	2006
n/a	n/a	n/a	n/a	n/a	n/a	n/a	2.00	2.00

Self-government traditions are strong in Poland. This is especially true in the west and south, where more than a hundred years ago, in the absence of a Polish state, the local authorities worked with Catholic and in some cases Protestant clergy to maintain Polish schools and nurture Polish customs in choirs, folk dance, gymnastics groups, fire brigades, and credit unions. One of the first acts of the Solidarity governments after 1989 was the restoration of local self-governance by re-creating the approximately 2,500 *gminas* (Poland's basic territorial division) that had been canceled in the mid-1970s. Ninety thousand local officials were transferred from the state administration to local governments. In 1998, the number of regions (*voivods*) was reduced from 49 to 16, and 314 counties (*powiats*) and 65 cities with equal status were added.

According to the Constitution, local government is a permanent feature of the state based on the principles of subsidiarity. The powers and independence of local authorities are protected by the courts, and there is a presumption that *gmina* competences extend to all matters not reserved for other institutions of central administration. Local authorities are responsible for education, social welfare, local roads, health care, public transport, water and sewage systems, local culture, public order, and security. Municipalities are responsible for a majority of these tasks. Regional accounting chambers are responsible for auditing local authorities.

Local representatives are elected every four years. The last local elections were held in 2002, and the next are due in fall 2006. As a result of Poland's joining the EU in 2004, citizens of other EU states will be eligible to participate in the elections. Mayors of cities and towns are elected directly, as are members of local, county, and regional councils. County members elect the heads of *powiats*, and members of regional assemblies elect the heads of the *voivods*. In the 16 voivods, elected heads (marshals) must cooperate with government-nominated *voievodas*, the national authority representatives outside Warsaw. They have the legal power to control *gimna* resolutions by suspending them within 30 days if they contradict the law. Appeals to voivod decisions are filed with the regional administrative courts.

The Law on Local Government of 1990 introduced referendums as a tool of direct democracy. They are used to decide such issues as voluntary taxation for public purposes and the dismissal of the council before its term. The motion to conduct a referendum must be supported by at least 10 percent of the voters, and a referendum is valid only with a minimum of 30 percent of the voters participating. This has proved to be an empty option: In the majority of referendums, usually organized to recall local elected officials, the turnout has been too low to make them valid. In 2005, the referendum to recall the *wojt* (head) of *gmina* Konopnica in Lublin region drew only 12 percent; in four other referendums in 2004, including the recall of the mayor of Szczecin, the highest turnout was only 21 percent of voters.

Polish law limits the power of local government to levy taxes. Municipalities are allowed to collect taxes on farms, properties, forests, pet registrations, and transportation. New taxes can be organized only via a referendum, such as the 2003 referendum in *gmina* Mosina near Poznan to add a garbage collection tax. The turnout was high enough at 32 percent, but 76 percent of voters were against the new tax. Personal and corporate income taxes account for 75 percent of local government income. There is also a mechanism to redistribute taxes from richer to poorer local governments.

The central government is supposed to consult local governments on every bill that may add costs to their budgets. The Common Commission of the Government and the Territorial Self-Government is currently reviewing draft legislation on this matter; however; the time given for consultation is often extremely short, and estimations of the costs are vague. Local self-governments must consult citizens on certain decisions, such as seeking opinions from environmental organizations when granting building licenses. In Warsaw, this measure allowed environmental groups to block any serious development plans. When the environmental organization Przyjazne Miasto (Friendly Town) protested the construction of a new mall, the French investor paid it a US$700,000 "silence fee."[17] In 2004, the same group blocked another development project in Warsaw, but legal changes have made these kinds of protests less effective.

The Helsinki Foundation for Human Rights proved that the Warsaw local authorities blocked the creation of 32 associations in the last five years by demanding changes in their internal statutes. This practice was found illegal by the Warsaw court in the case of *Chomiczowka Association v. Degradation*.

In 2002, the opposition parties PiS, PO, Samoobrona, and LPR gained substantial power and were able to rule in many cities, such as Warsaw, Lodz, Bydgoszcz, Poznan, Gdansk, and Wroclaw. It is too early to say whether a similar process will happen in the 2006 local elections because left-wing parties may not have enough time to recover. In Warsaw, however, which was ruled from 2002 until end of 2005 by Lech Kaczynski, now president of Poland, it is likely that the PO, currently in opposition, will take power.

Judicial Framework and Independence

1997	1998	1999	2001	2002	2003	2004	2005	2006
1.50	1.50	1.50	1.50	1.50	1.50	1.50	2.00	2.25

As stated in the Constitution, the judiciary has full independence from the executive and legislative branches of government. The court system consists of the Supreme Court, 310 district courts, 43 regional courts, 11 appeals courts (total for the country), garrison and provincial military courts, 14 regional administrative courts, and the Main Administrative Court. The Tribunal of State is elected by the lower chamber of Parliament to determine constitutional violations by the highest officials. The Constitutional Tribunal analyzes the conformity of Polish and international laws to the Polish Constitution, adjudicates disputes of authority between central State bodies, and recognizes any temporary incapacity of the president to perform his/her office. Decisions of the Tribunal are applied directly.

Judges are appointed by the president after being nominated by the National Judicial Council, elected in majority by them. They are independent, cannot be members of political parties or trade unions, and cannot perform any public functions that might jeopardize their independence. They must be at least 29 years of age (27 for junior judges), and there is no prerequisite of performing earlier work as prosecutors or lawyers. Judges cannot be arbitrarily dismissed or removed.

The courts are considered the worst area of the Polish government, an opinion confirmed by several cases lost in the European Court of Human Rights (ECHR) in Strasbourg as well as the length of court proceedings, usually measured in years. Poland's legal system is one of the greatest deterrents to foreign investors. For Polish citizens, the system can impose years of arrest despite a "not guilty" verdict. In 2005, a Polish citizen finally received compensation in the ECHR after nine years in court with his employer. A Warsaw resident ultimately received a judgment in an eight-year property rights deliberation. Another man from Warsaw was under arrest for nine years before the court found him not guilty in 2005. Poles frequently appeal to the ECHR; in 2005, there were 6,466 Polish "inadmissible" cases, 4,571 cases "allocated to a decision body," and 4,744 "lodged" cases. In 44 verdicts, ECHR judges found Poland to be in violation of at least one count, and in only 4 cases were no violations found. It is no surprise that only 21 percent of Poles declare trust in the judicial system.

One of the worst shortcomings of Polish courts is the lack of reporting protocols. Proceedings are not recorded on tape. The court clerk rarely has a computer but, rather, generally uses pen and paper, writing down only what the judge dictates and summarizing the testimony just of witnesses, experts, or defendants. Attorneys' final speeches are not recorded at all. Extra appeals based on protocol inconsistencies are common in the Supreme Court, which is slated to be modernized with the help of EU money.

Another reason for low trust in the judicial system is the manner in which judges treat one another when breaking the law. The case of Marek Sadowski, who for 10 years escaped justice for causing an injury in a car accident, illustrates this best. When the accident occurred in 1995, Sadowski was a judge in Krakow, where he maintained immunity from the judges' disciplinary court. The case came back to light after nine years, when Sadowski became minister of justice and prosecutor general, this time protected by prosecutors' immunity. He resigned under public pressure, but his successor immediately nominated him as country prosecutor, again with immunity. The disciplinary court finally stripped him of immunity, and at the end of 2005 he was sentenced to 1.5 years' imprisonment suspended for 3 years, which means if in three years he does not commit another crime he will not serve the sentence in prison.

Sadowski's case was not the most serious. The deputy head in Suwalki district court is suspected of selling verdicts in about 100 cases with help from a local attorney. Another judge from Torun, who had been suspended with full salary from 2000 onward, in November 2005 was finally fined for false accusations he brought against his former secretary. The reason for the suspension was his friendship with a local gangster and favoritism in local court verdicts related to shootings. From 2001 to 2005, there were 58 motions in disciplinary court to release judges from immunity; all but 8 cases were denied. Judges are convinced that there have been improvements – the number of cases of judges who broke the law or code of ethics was 166 in 2002 but only 82 in 2004.[18]

Prosecutors are also held in low esteem since they are (quite rightly) considered to be part of the judiciary; in fact, however, they are under the control of the executive. According to experts, as long as the minister of justice becomes automatically appointed prosecutor general, there is no chance for autonomous, nonpolitically motivated work by prosecutors, who are under the almost military command of their superiors. Orlen's investigative commission documented how Prime Minister Leszek Miller extended pressure through the prosecutor general to the local prosecutor to arrest the head of the national petroleum company. Prosecutors themselves express different opinions: Only 12 percent say that their superiors put pressure on them.

According to the penal procedures code, prosecutors have three months to present an indictment to the court. In practice, that period is three to four times longer. Jacek Turczynski, former head of the national postal service, has been under investigation for almost three years for supposedly taking a bribe, but he was interrogated only twice, at the beginning and end of a six-month jail term. One of the wealthiest businessmen in Poland, Roman Kluska, was under investigation for 18 months, then released and refused compensation for his spectacular made-for-media arrest. Taxpayers are paying more and more for such prosecutorial mistakes: In 2000, the courts' compensations for unjust arrests for 63 people cost the treasury 700,000 zlotys (US$220,000), while in 2004 the system awarded 3.8 million zlotys (US$1.2 million) to 231 persons.[19]

Prosecutors do not have terms of office but rather may be advanced or removed at any time, which happens on a wide scale every four years. The majority have origins in Communist Poland. The left-wing government of Leszek Miller proposed a bill that would have authorized the prime minister to nominate the prosecutor general and instituted four-to-six-year terms for regional and district prosecutors, but the bill was lost in the Parliament. The current right-wing cabinet of Prime Minister Marcinkiewicz wants to keep prosecutors firmly in its hands. The result is that prosecutors are easily swayed by political winds, slowing down or accelerating work on individual cases according to their superiors' expectations.

Corruption

1997	1998	1999	2001	2002	2003	2004	2005	2006
n/a	n/a	2.25	2.25	2.25	2.50	2.50	3.00	3.25

The Corruption Barometer, an annual public opinion poll run by the Batory Foundation, shows the consistent status quo of corruption in Poland. In 2005, 15 percent of Poles confessed they had given a bribe, and the figure has hovered between 14 and 17 percent since 2000, when the poll first posed the question. Most bribes are given and taken in the health care system, and the chief bribe givers are private businesspeople.[20]

Doctors distinguish between flowers or a bottle of good alcohol handed them by a happy patient and cash given before or after treatment. The first is a "farewell gift," which doctors have accepted for decades; the second is a bribe. Very low wages in the public health care sector not only require workers to take multiple jobs, but compel them to demand money from patients for hospitalizations and surgeries.

The case of Stanislaw Ratuszny, a Szczecin shipyard worker, illustrates this point well. In 1982, Ratuszny sustained a spinal injury and was unable to work. For the next 20 years, he went through several surgeries in public hospitals, paying his doctors not only with money, but with meat products, a rarity in the 1980s, and throwing birthday parties for his doctors in the 1990s. In 2005, Ratuszny had finally had enough and went to the prosecutor. His case was supported by 18 other patients who also admitted to giving bribes to "Professor K," a well-known neurosurgeon, author of 300 scientific papers, and owner of a villa in the center of Bydgoszcz.[21] Ratuszny's case is pending. In general, there is no other solution to health care corruption than better salaries for medical personnel, but the budgetary burden is too heavy, and the introduction of at least partial payments for health care by the patient is a public opinion bombshell no politician is brave enough to play with. Private businesspeople paid for a "push" in getting EU funds: The Ministry of Culture secretary received bribes of up to 100,000 zlotys (US$31,000) from about 100 small- and medium-size business owners.

Other areas filled with corruption are the annual army draft, where getting an "unfit" health grade requires a bribe of between 2,000 and 4,000 zlotys (US$600-$1,200), and traffic offenses, where drunk driving and smaller violations may be fixed with bribes from 100 to a few thousand zlotys, paid to traffic police. In 2005, there was a bribery scheme involving Polish soccer tournaments. Longtime rumors were confirmed by Piotr Dziurowicz, head of the once strong GKS Katowice team, that multiple cases of selling matches had occurred, which included bribing soccer match referees and players. One bribe giver was caught red-handed with money in the trunk of his car. Anticorruption measures were heralded by the soccer union, but a few months later it appeared that professionals were not really interested in cleaning up the sports business.[22]

A dense atmosphere of corruption charges also clouded the outgoing left-wing government and the president. The series of corruption affairs started in 2003, with Rywingate far from over. Lew Rywin, back in jail, received an offer of clemency for disclosing details about a "power holding group." According to the investigative commission report, written by the new minister of justice, Zbigniew Ziobro, the group included former prime minister Leszek Miller. Warsaw's prosecutor started an investigation of presidential clemency for Piotr Filipczynski, aka Peter Vogel, who escaped from Poland in 1983 during a break in his sentence for murder. Vogel was caught in 1998 and pardoned a year later by President Kwasniewski on the request of the prosecutor general.[23] The frequency of such presidential pardons has led to allegations of corruption in the process. The list of over 8,000 individuals who have been pardoned is secret on the grounds of protecting privacy. President Kaczynski said he plans to change it.

According to Transparency International's Corruption Perceptions Index, Poland is the most corrupt country in the EU and the only one among newcomers where the situation appears to be worsening. In Transparency International's yearly index, Poland was ranked 70th, and among EU newcomers it is the only country where the perception of corruption has increased in the last four years. "The reasons for corruption in Poland are well-known," concludes the Transparency International report. "They include: vagueness and instability of the law, lack of transparency in government and self-government actions, volunteerism in the decision-making process, lenient attitude toward documentation and reporting, lack of personal responsibility for administrative decisions, weak system of internal control, tolerance for conflicts of interest, and lack of workable anticorruption law."[24]

Thanks to investigative reporting and NGO activity, there were some brighter spots in the anticorruption picture. For example, e-auctions in public procurement, introduced in 2004, helped in 2005 to curtail corruption in this important sphere; and in 2005, the contest procedures in self-government administration became mandatory for all professional positions. Also, in all regional police headquarters, anticorruption units were formed; their officers have a right to give "controlled bribes" as a means of provoking those who are suspected of taking bribes.

The fight against corruption was one of PiS's focus points in the elections and is on the short list of Prime Minister Marcinkiewicz's government priorities. An elite group of 500 well-paid officers will make up the CAA, led by PiS politician Mariusz Kaminski. First, the CAA will address corruption among public officials; their income and property reports will be verified professionally. The CAA will also fight corruption in public procurement, estimated at 5 to 20 percent of contracts.[25]

Critics of the CAA point out that its dependence on the government and ability to authorize and conduct secret operations – such as searches, audio- and videotaping, accumulation of sensitive personal data (on religious beliefs and sexual life) – may lead to its use as a political weapon. Additionally, it has no preventive tasks, which limits its influence on a broader scale.

Andrzej Krajewski is a freelance journalist based in Warsaw, a former TVP correspondent in Washington, D.C., and a former editor in chief of Reader's Digest *Polish edition.*

[1] Adam Gorski and Andrzej Sakowicz, "Bariery prawne integracji europejskiej w sprawach karnych" (European integration legal barriers in criminal procedures), Centrum Europejskie Natolin, Warszawa, 2005, www.wsisw.natolin.edu.pl/wsisw/wsisw.nsf/viewDOC/ AGRK-6GLNQ7/$FILE/bariery_prawne.pdf.
[2] See Poland at: www.farmsubsidy.org
[3] See 2004 State Treasury Report, www.msp.gov.pl/dokumenty/2-338.pdf.
[4] Exactly 0.29 percent. See September 25, 2005, elections results available at www.pkw.gov.pl/gallery/33/40/33402.pdf.
[5] Report from the commission last session: www.sejm.gov.pl/Biuletyn.nsf/fkskr?OpenForm&SORN.
[6] See: http://wiadomosci.wp.pl/kat,1342,wid,8124847,wiadomosc.html
[7] Polish NGOs' 2004 Report at: http://english.ngo.pl/
[8] NGOs' web sites: www.ngo.pl; PAFF: www.pafw.pl; Batory Foundation: www.batory.org.pl.
[9] See more at www.wosp.org.pl.
[10] See more at www.pah.org.pl.
[11] See more in: "Ukraina 2004-relacje obserwatorow wybor□w prezydenckich" (Ukraine 2004 - Presidential Election Observers' Reports)," Wydawnictwo Ajaks, Warszawa, 2005.
[12] Beata Pasek, "Second Walesa for Polish Employees," International Herald Tribune, February 25, 2005.
[13] Constitution of Republic of Poland, Article 14, www.sejm.gov.pl/prawo/konst/angielski/kon1.htm.
[14] See www.freepress.org.pl/old/280904_marek.html.
[15] 2004 sold copies data from Press Distribution Control Association, www.zkdp.pl/dokumenty.
[16] More on Polish TV in "Television Across Europe: Regulation, Policy, and Independence," Open Society Institute, Budapest 2005, (www.eumap.org).
[17] For more on Przyjazne Miasto (Friendly Town), see: www.batory.org.pl/korupcja/r10.htm.
[18] Agata Lukaszewicz, "Sedziowie niegodni urzedu," (Judges not worthy of their chairs), Rzeczpospolita, April 14, 2005.
[19] Ewa Siedlecka, "Nie sztuka aresztowac," (It is easy to arrest), Gazeta Wyborcza, December 6, 2005.
[20] Batory's Foundation Corruption Barometer 2005, www.batory.org.pl/english/corrupt/bar.htm.
[21] Michal Kopinski, "Szczeci?ski pacjent," (Patient from Szczecin,) Gazeta Wyborcza-Duzy Format, December 12, 2005.
[22] Pawel Wilkowicz, "Burza przed cisza," (Storm before silence,) Rzeczpospolita, December 6, 2005.
[23] Jan Pinski "Tajne konta politykow" (Politicians' secret bank accounts), WPROST, April 18, 2006. Also,"Skandal wokol bankiera,"(Scandal around bank official,) Rzeczpospolita, December 6, 2005.
[24] See www.transparency.pl/www/index.php?a=36&b=39&c=161&text=171.
[25] Interview with Mariusz Kaminski, www.radiopin.pl/goscradia.php?id=604&page=&szukaj=.

Romania

Capital: Bucharest
Population: 21.7 million
GNI/capita: $2,960
Ethnic Groups: Romanian (90%), Hungarian (7%),
Roma (3%), other

Nations in Transit Ratings and Averaged Scores

	1997	1998	1999	2001	2002	2003	2004	2005	2006
Electoral Process	3.25	3.25	2.75	3.00	3.00	2.75	2.75	2.75	2.75
Civil Society	3.75	3.75	3.00	3.00	3.00	2.75	2.50	2.25	2.25
Independent Media	4.25	4.00	3.50	3.50	3.50	3.75	3.75	4.00	4.00
Governance *	4.25	4.00	3.50	3.75	3.75	3.75	3.75	n/a	n/a
National Democratic Governance	n/a	n/a	n/a	n/a	n/a	n/a	n/a	3.50	3.50
Local Democratic Governance	n/a	n/a	n/a	n/a	n/a	n/a	n/a	3.00	3.00
Judicial Framework and Independence	4.25	4.25	4.25	4.25	4.25	4.25	4.25	4.00	4.00
Corruption	n/a	n/a	4.25	4.50	4.75	4.50	4.50	4.25	4.25
Democracy Score	3.95	3.85	3.54	3.67	3.71	3.63	3.58	3.39	3.39

* *With the 2005 edition, Freedom House introduced seperate analysis and ratings for national democratic governance and local democratic governance to provide readers with more detailed and nuanced analysis of these two important subjects.*

NOTE: The ratings reflect the consensus of Freedom House, its academic advisers, and the author of this report. The opinions expressed in this report are those of the author. The ratings are based on a scale of 1 to 7, with 1 representing the highest level of democratic progress and 7 the lowest. The Democracy Score is an average of ratings for the categories tracked in a given year.

The economic and social data on this page were taken from the following sources:
GNI/capita, Population: *World Development Indicators 2006* (Washington, D.C.: World Bank, 2006).
Ethnic Groups: *CIA World Factbook 2006* (Washington, D.C.: Central Intelligence Agency, 2006).

EXECUTIVE SUMMARY

R omania has had one of the most disputed political transitions and costliest economic transformations in Eastern Europe since the fall of Nicolae Ceausescu in 1989. Dominated by successive Communist parties during most of the time since then, the country has struggled in vain to return to 1989-1990 standards of living. This target was reached only recently, despite economic growth resuming since 2000; still, the average monthly income of Romanians remains under US$200 per capita, the lowest among former Communist countries that have joined or are candidates to join the European Union (EU). Romania's transition was far from nearing successful completion by 1997, when the European Commission formally acknowledged that the country was meeting the Copenhagen political criteria for EU accession. By 1999, when the Commission invited Romania to join the EU, Romania was struggling with structural reforms that Central European countries had already implemented in the early nineties.

The enticement of EU accession bore fruit and the country has been making reform progress, although its inflation remains the highest in the region. However, Romanian post-Communists and anti-Communists alike have been unable to solve Romania's subsistence farming problem. Romania has the highest percentage of peasants in the region (34 percent of the working population is employed in agriculture, nearly double that of Poland) who live for the most part below the poverty threshold. The existence of poor rural areas, controlled by local predatory elites who are in command of scarce resources, is the most serious problem of the Romanian democracy, as elections in such areas can be neither free nor fair. However, a self-assertive urban population has succeeded in pushing for pro-European reforms throughout a slow and painful transition. This urban populace supports the Truth and Justice Alliance (made of the National Liberal Party and Democratic Party), which began governing at the end of 2004, along with two smaller coalition partners: the Hungarian Democratic Alliance (DAHR) and the Conservative Party (CP, formerly the Romanian Humanist Party). The main opposition party is the Social Democratic Party (SDP), which governed Romania under different names for most of the country's transition period, the last time between 2000 and 2004.

In April 2005, Romania signed the Treaty of Accession to the European Union (EU), with a target date for membership in 2007. This proved that the country had succeeded to stay on track toward EU accession, even with the much-disputed elections in the winter of 2004, a subsequent change of government, and a weak parliamentary majority. Despite frequent deadlocks in the parliament through 2005, momentum toward the EU continued. The European Commission acknowledged in its yearly report published in November 2005 that Romania had made progress in justice reform and competition policy, two areas that previously had been noted as potential reasons to delay EU entry. As opposed to merely passing new legislation, in 2005 Romanian authorities placed more focus on implementation. The new government also stepped away from the policy of controlling the media through economic pressure and incentives, and released its grip on the judiciary, which is now de facto independent.

National Democratic Governance. Concerned with early elections (which were finally not held) and European accession, the new government did not improve in any substantial way the central administrative apparatus it had inherited. Policy capacity remains low and the consultation process uneven across ministries and agencies. Governing through emergency ordinances continued, as the current parliament lacks a clear majority and is frequently deadlocked. *As no significant progress occurred, Romania's national democratic governance stagnates at 3.50.*

Electoral Process. Despite the manifest political will of President Traian Basescu to organize new elections in order to give the governing coalition a larger majority, the opposition political parties prevented early elections in 2005. All parties remained well within constitutional limits during this dispute. However, the Parliament managed to block an investigation into last year's allegations of electoral fraud, and the promised improvement of electoral legislation did not occur. *Romania's electoral process score remains at 2.75 due to failure to improve electoral legislation and clear allegations of electoral fraud from the 2004 elections.*

Civil Society. Romania's civil society remained diverse and influential in 2005, leaving its imprint on various laws and policies, from the regulation of state advertising in the media to new procurement legislation. Social NGOs succeeded in raising more money from private sources in 2005, and several NGOs featured prominently in the press. *Romania's civil society rating remains at 2.25.*

Independent Media. Romania's media were relieved of considerable political pressure on editors in 2005 due to the change of government. Press coverage of politics was far more balanced than it was a year ago. Various dignitaries had to resign under public pressure, showing how influential the media have become. *Despite these positive developments, worries about corruption in the media and nontransparent ownership persisted. Romania's independent media rating remains at 4.00.*

Local Democratic Governance. Despite much discussion about decentralization, not much progress in implementing administrative reform took place in 2005. From January 2006, Romania's prefects can no longer be politically partisan; this dilemma was not solved by hiring independent prefects, however, but by having politically appointed prefects resign from their political party. *Local and county administration remains severely politicized. Romania's rating for local democratic governance therefore stagnates at 3.00.*

Judicial Framework and Independence. Despite a conservative Constitutional Court ruling to clip the wings of thorough reform, essential legislation to improve the performance of the judiciary was finally passed in June 2005. Pockets of conservative judges linked to political networks of influence do remain within the Superior Council of the Magistracy, which is now the supreme judicial body, as well as within superior courts, but the government has relinquished any leverage on the judiciary. This makes for a more independent judiciary, although not necessarily a more accountable one. *The judicial framework and independence rating remains at 4.00; however, the government's laudatory decision to reduce influence on the judiciary raises expectations for future improvement in practice.*

Corruption. New anti-corruption legislation was passed in the summer of 2005, after an independent audit criticized the 2001-2004 anticorruption strategy. In addition, the main anticorruption body, the National Anticorruption Prosecutor (NAP), was reorganized into the Anticorruption Department (NAD) within the Office of the Prosecutor General (OPG), in order to enhance its legal capability. It is too early to tell, however, if these measures are helping to tackle grand corruption, which remains Romania's number one problem. A 2005 World Bank survey shows a marked decrease since 2003 in administrative business-related corruption. *Romania's corruption rating remains at 4.25, with results anticipated from the new legislation.*

Outlook for 2006. The year 2006 will bring struggle, as Romania will try to persuade the European Council that the country is ready to join the EU on January 1st 2007, rather than prepare for another year. In a growing skeptical European environment, which still weighs the consequences of the 2004 enlargement wave, the two countries face no easy task. The European Commission will issue two monitoring reports, a spring one and an early fall one, while the European national Parliaments have to rush through by December 31 the approval of the EU accession treaties signed in 2004 for the two countries to be ready to join in 2007. The decision on the accession date, 2007 or 2008 is likely to be taken by the European Council in the fall. The target of January 2007 will prove enough to hold together, though in a perpetual state of instability, the fragile governing coalition of Romania.

MAIN REPORT

National Democratic Governance

1997	1998	1999	2001	2002	2003	2004	2005	2006
n/a	n/a	n/a	n/a	n/a	n/a	n/a	3.50	3.50

Romania's current Parliament, elected in 2004, has held a thin and tenuous majority for the government, which has been threatened by each individual absence during parliamentary sessions. As most ministers are also members of Parliament (MPs), the government summoned all at each and every important vote in 2005. It also continued to prefer government emergency ordinances as the default option for much of the legislation proposed. This was a frequent practice in previous years as well, but the urgency increased in 2004 as Romania made preparations to sign the European Union accession treaty on April 25, 2005. In the first half of 2005, 114 such emergency ordinances were passed, down from 142 the year before. Laws passed by emergency ordinance need parliamentary approval, but the Parliament can only reject, not modify, them. Like all Central European applicants, Romania had to agree to adopt the European legal acquis communautaire in full, essentially making parliamentary debate on EU accession a redundancy.

The coalition government was reshuffled on August 22, 2005, allegedly to speed up Romania's preparations for EU accession, but in fact this was a measure to compensate for the absence of early elections and an effort to purge the government of those figures unpopular with the public and the prime minister. Four ministers – all from Truth and Justice Alliance, in charge of coordinating economic activities, finance, European integration, and health – were dismissed. There were allegations in the media that the finance minister was dismissed for attempting to clean up the chronically corrupt customs service. He was replaced by a former business partner of the prime minister.

Relations and decision making within the governing coalition are regulated by a Governmental Coalition Protocol. In practice, however, political leaders within the coalition often speak without consultation, triggering a state of perpetual crisis. In 2005, the Parliament was idle for many days, debating the issue of early elections. During the fall, MPs spent weeks revising their own regulations, regardless of the significant regulations already accompanying EU accession legislation. The change of regulations was required by the ruling Truth and Justice (TJ) coalition in order to stipulate that the presidents of the two parliamentary chambers can be changed during their mandate if the majority changes. After the 2004 legislative elections, the coalition partners, the Hungarian Democratic Alliance (DAHR) and the Conservative Party (CP), had sided with the former governing Social Democratic Party (SDP), which resulted in the election of two Social Democrats as presidents of the two chambers. However, this did not prevent them from switching to the TJ government a few days later. For most of 2005, the TJ struggled to get rid of the two presidents, arguing that since the DAHR and the CP had joined the coalition, new elections should be held for the two positions. It took the government almost the entire year to amend parliamentary regulations to this effect, only to see the amendments overturned by the Constitutional Court, which ruled in November that the article pertaining to the change of presidents was unconstitutional. The Court is made up mostly of former ministers and dignitaries appointed by the SDP.

In 2005, allegations were heard from the opposition that President Traian Basescu was placing unlawful pressure on the government. Although the prime minister, not the president, runs the government, the Constitution does not explicitly forbid the president, who is directly elected, to push for a policy agenda. The president has the right to assist in government meetings and chair those he assists. In the second half of the year, it became clear that Basescu was not as influential as presumed by the opposition and that the prime minister was asserting his own will.

President Basescu also made little progress in reforming Romania's secret service, although this lies clearly within his authority. The president's draft bill to turn Romania's many information agencies into a single "community of information" was received with criticism but eventually adopted. However, the proposed package revising the current national security legislation was stopped by the Parliament. Romanian civil society also criticized the package, which was elaborated in secrecy and would have endowed agents with investigative powers that only prosecutors currently enjoy. One reason Basescu pushed for early elections was to get a majority that would pass his secret service reforms. The current majority is highly unlikely to approve either his reforms or the individuals he might nominate as heads of these agencies.

In 2005, Romania had frequent debates on voting systems and discussed introducing single-unit constituencies as a way to improve MP accountability. Currently, voting in both chambers is either secret or not registered per MP, and it is impossible for constituents to know the stands taken by their elected MPs. The TJ Alliance adopted and managed to push through one chamber a civil society-inspired law that provides for greater transparency in parliamentary voting. This law states that individual votes will be recorded whenever the vote is not secret. Still, public discontent with the lack of parliamentary accountability continues to be high.

Policy making and coordination, a chronic weak spot of the Romanian government, saw little improvement in 2005. In January, a law was amended to make it compulsory for all ministries to consult with the Ministry of Justice (and all other ministries concerned) from the beginning of the legislative process. This has resulted in better cooperation among ministries, helped by a decrease in the number of interministerial committees. Problems arise, however, from the lack of a policy planning center to generate strategies across ministries, despite the existence of such (competitive and unprofessional) units within the government.

In Romania, the quality of legislation is poor, and outside help is often brought in from consulting firms or civil society to compensate for the incompetence of professional civil servants, often previous administration hires who were tenured without merit. This outside help, however, is not always professional and makes coordination within government even more complicated. A plethora of EU advisers – each promoting the legal tradition of his or her country rather than a common European model, which is missing in many fields – makes coherence even harder to attain. Proposed legislation continues to be sent to the Parliament without a serious impact study on affordability and implementation capacity. Despite new legislative improvements, there are no notable developments in civil service reform. No serious progress was made to provide incentives for professionally motivated civil servants, and there was no attempt to create a modern human resources service to replace the current informal hiring and promotion practices with a clear system based on transparent criteria.

Civilian control over the armed forces remains a problem in Romania. There is a high suspicion that former agents of the Securitate, Nicolae Ceausescu's dreaded secret service, are infiltrating the Parliament, the government, the diplomatic body, and even the media. The agency in charge of screening the Securitate files, the Council for the Study of the Former Securitate Files (CNSAS), remains weak. Following the request of the president, the Romanian Service of Information, the Securitate's institutional heir, finally agreed to pass on the Securitate files to the CNSAS. The CNSAS was supposed to review all parliamentary candidates in 2004, but the results had not yet been released by the end of 2005, long after the elections. The kidnapping and subsequent release of three Romanian journalists in Iraq in 2005 is alleged to have helped the secret service win President Basescu's favor, although the media and civil society tend to view it negatively and would have expected a replacement of executive heads after last elections.

Romania was included in the CIA prisons scandal in Europe. The country seems to have been one of the many in Europe where secret CIA planes landed for a few hours at a time, but a European Parliament investigation found no proof that any prison or ill-treatment of prisoners took place on Romanian territory. *The Washington Post*, which alleged that President Basescu had not denied allegations when speaking with one of its journalists, later publicly admitted error and apologized.

Electoral Process

1997	1998	1999	2001	2002	2003	2004	2005	2006
3.25	3.25	2.75	3.00	3.00	2.75	2.75	2.75	2.75

In 2004, the SDP had enjoyed a near monopoly of power. By comparison, 2005 was an unstable year, dominated by the struggle surrounding the issue of early elections. The 2004 elections resulted in a seriously divided Parliament without a clear majority. Only the victory of President Basescu in the second round secured the TJ coalition government, which had a majority of only one seat and no allies. In fact, it immediately lost the presidency of the two parliamentary chambers to SDP leaders Adrian Nastase (Deputies Assembly) and Nicolae Vacaroiu (Senate) owing to a lack of support from the smallish CP. The CP had decided to divide its favors, joining the TJ-led government coalition on the one hand but voting with the opposition for the chamber presidents on the other. The four-party coalition government (TJ Alliance plus two coalition partners) passed without difficulty, and during the summer it even resisted a no-confidence vote, as the opposition feared early elections. But the resulting majority was thin and consensus over major political issues even thinner.

The newly elected president, Traian Basescu (originally from the Democratic Party, a member of the TJ Alliance) pushed unilaterally for early elections but encountered the resistance of Prime Minister Calin Popescu Tariceanu (of the National Liberal Party, the other TJ Alliance member). Polls showed early that the SDP would have fared much worse than in the 2004 elections and that the Liberals were losing popularity in favor of the Democrats, their allies, mostly because of Basescu's stand as a charismatic president. This led to a silent majority in both camps in favor of the status quo, isolating the president and the Democrats.

Relations between the president and his appointed prime minister deteriorated seriously when the latter refused to organize early elections during summer 2005. This would have been a constitutional nightmare, as no official body has the right to dissolve the Romanian Parliament. There must be two failed attempts to form a government before the president can call for new elections. Practically speaking, this would have meant that Tariceanu would have had to resign twice and then present himself twice in front of the Parliament with a new government in the hope of being rejected by his own people (because the opposition announced they would vote to keep the government). He refused, invoking the devastating floods that damaged large areas of the country during the summer. All parties remained within constitutional limits during this dispute.

Despite discussions on the 2004 election irregularities and multiple voting, the Parliament was unable to start an investigation into allegations of fraud, and the promised improvement of electoral legislation did not occur. The investigation was blocked in one of the committees, not even reaching the plenum. Police pursued isolated complaints, but no prosecutor initiated a criminal investigation, waiting for a green light from the Parliament. During the summer, the government passed as an emergency ordinance a superficially revised electoral legislation package with a view to early elections. The electoral campaign would have been reduced to two weeks had elections been organized in the fall of 2005. Not only did the move for early elections not pass, but the Parliament rejected the ordinance as well when it came time for plenum approval. The year was genuinely lost for electoral reform.

Civil Society

1997	1998	1999	2001	2002	2003	2004	2005	2006
3.75	3.75	3.00	3.00	3.00	2.75	2.50	2.25	2.25

During 2005, Romanian civil society continued a trend of positive development by playing an important role in the country's EU accession and democratization efforts. Romanian NGOs continued to act cohesively as effective advocates for various policy reforms and scored numerous successes. The more notable were in the transparency field, where NGOs brought decisive input to new legislation on procurement and to the regulation of state advertising in the media.

These positive developments were facilitated by the somewhat more cooperative approach of the new government toward civil society actors. Unlike the previous government, which made deliberate efforts to undermine active independent civil society actors, the current government improved the legislative environment governing the functioning of civil society and has started to use more NGOs as a pool of expertise for policy matters. The fact that relatively few NGO activists took government jobs, the opposite of what had happened on the previous occasion when anti-Communists had won elections (1996), also showed the increased maturity of NGOs and the clearer separation between political parties and nonpartisan civil society. By the end of 2005, only one notable civil society leader, Monica Macovei, formerly with the Romanian Helsinki Committee, continued to have a government appointment as minister of justice. Macovei did not join any political party, however, holding this position as an independent minister.

After coming to power in December 2004, the new government immediately modified two important pieces of legislation regarding civil society. First, it amended the emergency ordinance regarding the registration and functioning of NGOs, easing registration procedures by eliminating government control. The amendments also renounced the unnecessary category of "public utility" NGOs, which had been a means to gain privileged access to public funds. Second, the government passed new legislation on the sponsorship of NGOs that allows private individuals to donate 1-2 percent of their income tax to NGOs. However, these positive legal developments will not significantly improve the financial situation of NGOs; Romania introduced a 16 percent flat income tax in 2005, which at an average monthly wage of about US$200 and with fewer than 5 million economically active people makes potential contributions rather modest. However, social NGOs succeeded at a civil society "fair" to attract larger sums of corporate sponsorship funding than in the previous year.

Although the government took some visible steps in 2005 to further involve NGOs in the consultative process, these efforts were uneven across ministries and seriously hindered by the disorganization of the policy process in general. Consultations remained rather formal in most cases because of the short-term notice NGOs received; legislation and policy decisions are usually made under such time pressures that it is difficult for civil society to provide relevant or substantive input.

Although some ministries (Justice and Home Affairs) and the cabinet of the prime minister improved considerably in terms of their cooperation with civil society, others, like the Ministry of Foreign Affairs, regressed from the previous SDP era. President Basescu seldom sought the advice and cooperation of civil society, so his most important proposals in 2005 did not gain any public support and remained on paper.

Consultations with unions were the poorest from the onset, leading to avoidable strikes in 2005. Teachers and university faculty went on strike for weeks in the fall of 2004. There were also strikes of public transportation workers and civil servants. Most of these were driven by demands for wage increases, but there is some chance they could have been prevented had the unions been made a part of the policy debate. The government failed to get support for reforms in the sensitive social fields of education and health, and consultations were more actively organized only by the end of the year, when it became clear no progress could be made without forging some social consensus.

While improving its relationship with the government on the one hand, Romanian civil society also continued during 2005 to monitor governance quality. New lawsuits on the basis of the Law on Freedom of Information were filed by NGOs to push for more transparency in various ministries. NGOs also continued actively to monitor the asset statements of dignitaries and MPs. The success of civil society proposals was facilitated by a good relationship between civil society and most of the Romanian media, which look forward to the reports of different independent watchdog agencies and often use civil society figures as pundits. The relative increase of media freedom in 2005 also meant that electronic media improved their attitude toward civil society and especially toward those leaders who criticized the government (and had been virtually banned from certain TV networks before the general elections in November 2004).

Overall, Romanian civil society plays an increasingly important role in the public arena, continuing to advocate for essential reforms and to monitor government policies and actions. The government's attitude toward civil society actors has improved considerably, thus creating the opportunity for NGOs to finally play an appropriate role in the political arena as critical and competent partners rather than merely enemies of government and public institutions. Although most NGOs remain financially dependent on foreign funds, there is a trend of increasing organizational capacity and a diversification of financial sources.

Independent Media

1997	1998	1999	2001	2002	2003	2004	2005	2006
4.25	4.00	3.50	3.50	3.50	3.75	3.75	4.00	4.00

As a result of the change of government, political pressure on the Romanian media was considerably relieved in 2005. Although the media's structural problems did not vanish overnight, news coverage of parties and politicians became more balanced with the diminishment of the SDP and former prime minister Adrian Nastase. However, the situation was not reversed in favor of the new governing parties. Over the course of 2005, coverage of the opposition and the government remained balanced, according to the National Audiovisual Council (NAC), the official media watchdog.[1]

Depoliticizing the Romanian media is a challenge; most private electronic media remain openly political, with main channels owned or managed by political figures or their rather transparent intermediates. In fact, one reason the current government includes the CP, formerly an SDP ally and a notoriously unreliable partner, is the strength of TV channel Antena 1, one of the three national networks. Antena 1 belongs to the family of Dan Voiculescu, leader of the tiny CP, which is credited with 1-2 percent of the vote in opinion surveys, well below the electoral threshold of 5 percent.

The owners of other channels are hidden behind mailboxes in Switzerland or Cyprus. An appeal from President Basescu following an Open Society Institute report for more transparency in media ownership finally persuaded the NAC to ask TV networks to disclose their owners.

Besides pushing for transparency, the new government took a tougher stand on TV networks' chronic tax arrears to the state budget. The minister of finance summoned TV channels in February 2005 to start paying their long rescheduled debts, most of them to the social security budget, as media owners have tried to evade paying social security for their employees. TV network assets were frozen for the first time, which prompted PRO TV, quoted in all reports the previous year as a leading debtor, to repay most of its dues by mid-2005. The situation remains fragile, though; in the print media, the newspaper *National* closed rather than pay its debts. It transferred all assets and people, taking advantage of the weak Romanian Law on Bankruptcy, and started another daily under the name *7plus*. Numerous other outlets followed suit. Such newspapers promote the worst type of journalism, abounding in blackmail campaigns. Articles are run under false names, as most of the content is made up of rumor and defamation. Courts also have trouble distinguishing between freedom of the press and abuse of media influence for immoral or unlawful purposes.

To help clarify the media muddle, an emergency ordinance was adopted in May that amended the Law on Public Procurement by providing for more transparent and objective criteria for the acquisition of advertising space by public institutions. The ordinance requires that all contracts above US$2,500 be preceded by a public tender published on a specialized governmental Web site. A report published in 2005 found that state advertising had doubled between 2000 and 2004, as it was used increasingly to buy or reward the media.

In 2004, state advertising amounted to EUR 17 million, or 8 percent of the total advertising budget. Advertising distribution followed patterns of influence rather than audience: In 2004, the two TV channels that received the most were not at the highest audience ranking.[2] According to the same source, small channels like

National TV, with virtually no audience, received considerable sums. Monopolistic agencies – such as the national railroad, itself heavily indebted – have bought massive advertising space in the newspapers supporting the government of the time.

The government's actions in 2005 left an important segment of the media without income. Such actions were praised by the European Commission, but they were costly in terms of media support: Except for the Voiculescu media empire, the government faces either normal free press, which tends to be critical of any government, or corrupt, "captured" press, which has been decrying its serious losses. Although the trend is positive, there is still a long way to go before there is any considerable consolidation of the Romanian media landscape.

The 2004 elections brought more freedom of expression to the public media. A group of whistle-blowers from both public radio and public TV denounced political interference during the election campaign, such as the editing out of all critical analysts on public TV. The public radio, under Dragos Seuleanu, went even further, with coverage dictated verbatim by an SDP senator. A parliamentary investigation committee established in early 2005 concluded that the public media management teams had not complied with editorial and professional standards, but its task was made difficult by SDP committee members, the same individuals who had influenced public TV program content a few months earlier. This conflict of interest shows the limitations of a Parliament where the SDP is still the largest party and unable objectively to investigate its own earlier abuses of power. The public media 2003 annual activity reports were nevertheless subsequently rejected in June by majorities in both chambers, and their boards were dismissed. New heads were appointed in June following the same political algorithm, with each political party represented according to shares in the Parliament. Civil society lobbied in vain to change this system, but as it is the most widely used in Europe, an alternative failed to materialize.

In 2005, there was little advancement in the ethical and professional behavior of journalists or improvement in the self-regulatory capacity of the media community. *Evenimentul Zilei*, the most reputable newspaper in 2004, was crippled in 2005 by the dismissal of top management by its owner, Ringier, then by the mass desertion of its journalists in protest. In early June, the newspaper ran a front-page story on the minister of justice, Monica Macovei, alleging that a number of anonymous witnesses had seen her drunk at a public event. Summoned by the Romanian Press Club, the most influential media association, and facing the outcry of its own readers, *Evenimentul* promised an internal investigation. Two columnists and the editor of political news quit in protest. The internal investigation concluded that the story had been completely untruthful and that sources had been invented. Although the investigation was not followed by any sanctions on responsible parties, the newspaper has since improved its public recognition of guilt in both accuracy and credibility.

The long expected repeal of slander as a crime is still not in force, though the criminal code was adopted in June 2004. However, courts ruled mostly in favor of journalists and freedom of expression in 2005.

Local Democratic Governance

1997	1998	1999	2001	2002	2003	2004	2005	2006
n/a	n/a	n/a	n/a	n/a	n/a	n/a	3.00	3.00

Local governance did not progress significantly in Romania during 2005 as compared with the previous year, despite many months spent modifying the Law on Local Public Administration. The main reason lies in a conflict between a theoretical issue – how to endow local governments with more autonomy and accountability – and a practical problem – how to dismantle the local networks of SDP oligarchs that still control the majority of county councils even though the SDP lost the national elections in 2004.

Romania had adopted good fiscal decentralization legislation in 1988-1999, but the SDP modified it in 2001, passing most of the financial decision making to councils and council presidents. This led to the creation of so-called local barons, heads of local networks of privilege and influence. County councils are elected on the basis of party lists, so they tend to reflect the national balance of power at the time of the elections. Presidents are elected by council members on the basis of sometimes ad hoc regional alliances, which do not always mirror the national system of political alliances.

Politicization runs deep in Romanian civil service at both regional and local levels. The government found it impossible to depoliticize local administrations and even local public services (which the SDP stocked with its own people over the last four years), as most civil servants have been tenured since 1998. Prefects, whose role is largely to check on the legality of acts by local government, have traditionally been appointees of the parties in government. However, starting with 2006 they will also become civil servants. Beginning January 1, 2006, prefects appointed in 2005 have to choose between their party membership and their job. Most have resigned from the parties that nominated them in order to keep their offices.

In the wake of the inconclusive 2004 elections, the government has struggled to gain more control at the regional and local levels to compensate for the lack of control at the national legislative level. County councils, which have come to play the largest role in the distribution of local funds, are usually in the hands of local networks, which sometimes cross party lines. The government argued for new legislation that would allow council presidents to stand for reelection, even between terms, if the majority changed in the council. This would enable a shifting county majority to consolidate its gains formally (a concept that has failed at the legislative level). The opposition argued that this was an attempt to change the majority during council elections (summer 2004) by encouraging political opportunism and migration from its ranks to the government party. Indeed, the government relied on the CP, which had changed camps since summer 2004, as well as on individual defectors to cross lines and unseat some of the SDP county presidents. The European Commission expressed reservations toward this strategy: It is not clear whether the proposed plan would in fact destroy networks or merely change their political allegiance. President Basescu was also opposed to the plan, invoking his experience as an opposition mayor persecuted by a government majority on the council.

A more principled approach would have been to transfer more power from the county council directly to the municipal level, where there has been greater success in achieving accountability. The proposal was included in the draft of a new Law on Public Local Administration, but this effort became entangled in closed-door bargaining sessions. The Law on Local Public Administration was last changed in September 2004 and fails to clearly divide responsibilities and functions between local and national governments, which are instead defined (and changed) annually through the Law on the State Budget. Therefore, relationships remain blurred between mayors and prefects, between mayors and local councils, and between local councils and county councils. This leaves room for inter-institutional bargaining through informal networks based on political connections. The new Law on Public Administration, which was under debate for most of 2005, is supposed to address the main legislative loopholes regarding some of these issues. By the end of 2005, there was no conclusion on this debate.

Vertical accountability mechanisms overwhelmed the only ones that seemed to work properly at the local level, as shown by the results of the 2004 local elections, which ousted some of the most corrupt and inefficient mayors. Most SDP "local barons" were able, however, to safeguard their positions in the party. The situation was worsened by the inability of political parties to put in place their own accountability mechanisms regarding the ongoing problem of political migration. Compared with the situation in previous years, migration was very low, but after a few months the proclaimed intention of Liberals and Democrats not to accept migrants, especially not from the SDP, had started to give way. Local migration is difficult to monitor, as councillors move from one party to another in exchange for office or other perquisites.

The other important issue that stalled in 2005 was the debate on regions and regionalism. Desperate to gain a majority in 2004, the TJ coalition accepted a request of their Hungarian allies to propose a revision of the projected regional structure of Romania, which had been agreed on with the EU, to one that would secure a Hungarian-dominated region. The current structure, based on European statistical criteria (the so-called NUTS II), positions the three more populous Hungarian counties in the central region alongside Romanian counties, leading to a balanced ethnic composition. Creating an ethnically Hungarian-dominated region and granting it special administrative status on the model of South Tyrol is an old desiderate of the Hungarian elite in Romania. Sometimes divided among radicals and moderates, Hungarian politicians have always been united on this front. This proposal has not progressed, partly because of opposition from Romanian nationalists and partly because of its practical shortcomings (regardless of how territory is grouped, half of the Romanian Hungarians cannot live in the would-be special status regions, as they are too widely dispersed territorially).

In 2005, the DAHR conditioned its support for the government on the adoption of a Law on Minorities Status, which opens the door for self-government for the Hungarian community. The law deals mostly with the Hungarian community, numbering 1.5 million, and states that minorities, not individuals, are constituents of the state (Article 2). The government passed the draft, but the Senate stopped it. Even if the law passes in the Parliament, it risks being blocked by the Constitutional Court. Article 2 is clearly unconstitutional, as the Romanian Constitution defines the state as unitary, not federal, and the constituents are individual constituents, not federal units, and especially not ethnic groups. The so-called Venice Commission, a Council of Europe body that often reflects on legal minorities and rights issues, criticized the bill for bringing more confusion than clarification to the local and regional administration of Romania.

The DAHR is very committed to this legislation, however, and threatens the government that it will remove its support unless the law is passed. Besides its problematic approach to administrative reorganization, the law has chapters on minority rights that are perfectly acceptable to all Romanian politicians except the nationalist Greater Romania Party. The European Commission is also opposed to a reorganization of regions. Regions are the main tool for distributing European structural funds, and Romania is already considered to be lagging behind in its preparedness to attract such funds; therefore any change is discouraged by Brussels.

The local authorities are grouped in a Federation of Local Authorities in Romania, which was created by the central government as a mechanism for lobbying and discussing common problems. The federation has been effective in dealing with technical and practical issues, but its success in solving important problems at the national level has been limited.

Judicial Framework and Independence

1997	1998	1999	2001	2002	2003	2004	2005	2006
4.25	4.25	4.25	4.25	4.25	4.25	4.25	4.00	4.00

Judicial reform in Romania made important strides in 2005. In March, the new government adopted an ambitious revised strategy and action plan 2005-2007 to reform the justice system. Unlike previous strategies, which dealt with broader institutional aspects, these documents were aimed at the judicial process itself. These enhanced efforts to complete judicial reform came as the combined result of two key factors. First, the change in government in November 2004 produced a center-right reformist government, which included a minister of justice who had previously worked as a civil society activist and human rights lawyer for the Council of Europe. Second, the introduction of a safeguard clause regarding EU accession at the December 2004 European Council provided serious impetus, as reform of the judiciary is a top EU priority. Failure to achieve standards in this area could lead to a delay of the accession date from 2007 to 2008. The new legislation, implementation of the old, and, more generally, the whole reform process met with tremendous opposition, highlighting the main problem in Romanian transition efforts: Conservatives often outnumber reformists.

The reform package, passed in 2004, stripped the Ministry of Justice of many of its powers in order to entrust them to the Superior Council of the Magistracy (SCM). The council was elected December 2004 in a contest where heads of courts were often the only candidates to run. The result is not an accountability body, but a representative body for the top management of the judiciary, as has been the case for the last decades. The SCM was entrusted with full control over the recruitment, promotion, and management of judges.

This SCM did not delay in positioning itself as a defender of corporate interests rather than a reformer and controller of the judiciary. Members insisted on keeping their double capacity as heads of courts and controllers of the same courts. They denied the existence of corruption within the judiciary and hired most of their staff from the Ministry of Justice. Many employees of the ministry, precisely those who had been accused for years of delaying early reforms, followed the transfer of power from the ministry to the council, and considerable delays were again incurred on long-discussed reforms, such as introducing clear standards for the evaluation and promotion of judges.

Following consultation with stakeholders, a revision of the 2004 so-called three-law package on justice reform (the Law on the Superior Council of the Magistracy, Law on the Organization of the Judiciary, and Law on the Statute of Magistrates) was submitted by the government to the Parliament in June 2005 and adopted after a vote of confidence. The 2004 laws have been criticized by various organizations, including Freedom House in its 2004 report, for failing to provide accountability mechanisms for the newly empowered SCM and the Office of the Attorney General. In early July, the Constitutional Court issued a majority ruling that four important articles in the package were unconstitutional. One provided that judges must retire at the same legal age as all other employees, an effort to open the system to younger magistrates. Despite not touching on the Constitution in any way, the Constitutional Court declared the article unconstitutional as it would have also pushed into retirement the corresponding reigning generation of constitutional judges.

The Court also opposed that heads of courts, appointed by the minister of justice under the SDP, can be dismissed, followed by open competition for these offices; the Court allowed for such competitions only when the office becomes vacant. The strangest ruling was on the incompatibility of SCM membership (a permanent position) with other management positions in the judiciary. The Court ruled that this stipulation exists only for the president and the vice president of the SCM, leaving the rest of the members free to hold dual offices. The European Commission report published in fall 2005 insisted that the members not interpret this ruling restrictively and resign from one or the other of their offices. This is unlikely to occur, as the aim of the SCM is to keep control concentrated in the hands of top conservative judges.

These articles were subsequently revised, and the package was promulgated in mid-July. The package retained many positive elements, and the legal framework now offers sufficient guarantees for magistrates' personal and institutional independence, although accountability mechanisms are still frail. The package also seeks to put individual and managerial accountability and responsibility at the center of the system. It diminishes the power of the heads of courts to hand cases to selected judges, a major source of corruption and influence in the past. The revised legislation states that chief prosecutors can allocate cases to prosecutors only on the basis of clear and objective criteria, such as workload and specialization, and can no longer intervene in the activity of prosecutors subordinated to them. Competitions organized in May and August led to the recruitment of economic managers in 56 courts. They are to take over all administrative matters thus far handled by the heads of courts.

The civil and criminal procedures codes were also amended in 2005 in an attempt to simplify and speed up the lengthy and complicated judicial procedures.[3] A new ethics code for magistrates was drafted by the Ministry of Justice together with the SCM in September. This code provides for the first time in Romanian law that judges and prosecutors must not have cooperated with the former Securitate and must not currently be working for any intelligence agency.[4]

The most serious problem in the reform of the judiciary remains the conservatism of the high courts, which thanks to seniority requirements comprise primarily aged, former Communist judges. Although the Constitutional Court is supposed to be apolitical, more than half of its magistrates have openly held an SDP affiliation as ministers or advisers. SCM members have six-year appointments, while members of superior courts have life tenure. Despite efforts from the government, implementation of reforms remains a challenge. The logistics of courts and wages of judges improved in 2005, but they are still far from satisfactory, drawing repeated complaints from the main association of magistrates.

Corruption

1997	1998	1999	2001	2002	2003	2004	2005	2006
n/a	n/a	4.25	4.50	4.75	4.50	4.50	4.25	4.25

In 2005, Romania enjoyed a cleaner central government and passed more effective anticorruption plans and laws. But each concrete step was fought over fiercely between reformers and conservatives, and little progress was achieved in practice. The European Commission's regular report positively acknowledged the Freedom House audit of Romania's anticorruption strategy and the new action plans derived from it. The audit was organized at the request of the December 2004 European Council and published in March 2005. The immediate consequence of the audit – which showed the past irrelevance of the Office of the National Anticorruption Prosecutor (NAP), a special agency created to fight grand corruption that in two years had prosecuted only a political adviser and an assistant magistrate – should have been the dismissal of the NAP head (who was closely linked with the SDP).

However, his dismissal had to wait until the judicial reform package was passed by the Parliament, as the passage introduced a mechanism for holding accountable the two major prosecutors, the prosecutor general of Romania, and the NAP. Amazingly enough, the 2004 judicial reform package, although supervised by a plethora of experts, failed to create such an accountability mechanism. The SDP fought fiercely to defend the NAP, voted against the judicial reform, and used all its influence in the superior courts to halt the reform. When an NAP prosecutor finally attempted to investigate SDP transcripts found to be shielding political friends from anticorruption prosecution, the Constitutional Court expediently ruled that the NAP was not allowed to investigate MPs, although it had been created precisely to deal with top-level corruption. In a move approved by the European Commission, the NAP was then formally turned into NAD, a department within the Office of the Prosecutor General (OPG) in order to bring top politicians again under its lawful authority. However, even in the new framework it maintained its structure and separate chain of command to fulfill EU's requirement of an independent anticorruption agency. OPG is one of the least reformed structures within the judiciary, with many practices lagging behind from Communist times.

The NAP has been the beneficiary of considerable investment, and unlike ordinary prosecution offices, it has the judiciary police under its direct control. The competences of the new NAD have been narrowed to only the highest corruption cases, where the bribe is over EUR 10,000 or the material damage exceeds EUR 200,000. The NAD will also be responsible for investigating certain customs-related offenses and tax evasion where the damage exceeds EUR 1 million, as well as offenses against the EU's financial interests. A new NAD head was eventually appointed after the existing management was sacked or resigned in August. But months of corruption investigation had been lost in the contentious effort simply to empower this office to do its job. The new appointed head, a young prosecutor, Daniel Morar, has embarked on a reshuffling of the NAD's functions. He operates under very strict deadlines, as one safeguard clause that could delay Romania's accession explicitly demands convictions at the top level. Morar has complained of difficulties, as the secret service refuses to release information on those of its members who have been investigated for demanding bribes.

Between January 1 and December 31, 2005 the NAD charged 744 defendants, including a former MP, 4 magistrates, 6 lawyers, 38 employees in law enforcement agencies, 8 high-level employees in the central administration, and 17 officials and high-level employees in the county and local administrations. Others are being investigated, including Adrian Nastase, former SDP prime minister, for illegal enrichment and corruption. Nastase has always remained on the public payroll (Romanian ministers have been paid about US$600 per month throughout the transition period), owns no businesses, and has had difficulty explaining how he amassed millions of euros. The NAD also investigates members of the current

Parliament, other high-level dignitaries, magistrates, police officials, customs officials, mayors, and an entire local council accused of intervening in a public tender. Two secretaries of state of the current TJ coalition government and one deputy prime minister (from the CP) are also under investigation, proving that the impartiality of this office has increased. Courts sentenced 325 defendants on corruption grounds between January 1 and December 31, 2005, including 1 magistrate, 34 employees in law enforcement agencies, 16 custom employees, 5 officials in county or local administrations, and 6 bank directors.

Conflict of interest scandals plagued the new figures in power. During the summer debate on early elections, President Basescu charged Prime Minister Tariceanu with falling under the influence of groups linked to Romania's corrupt industrial and political networks. It was not clear what Tariceanu granted those groups; rather, the charge was that they managed to change the prime minister's position on early elections. Later in the fall, it became apparent that Tariceanu did try to give a hand to his former business partner and longtime friend, Dinu Patriciu, who was investigated by prosecutors for money laundering and other charges. Tariceanu called the prosecutor general to ask about Patriciu's file, although such disclosure is illegal under laws he himself promoted during the summer. Patriciu, a business associate of many SDP leaders, claimed he was being investigated for having attracted the enmity of President Basescu when pushing for an alliance between the Liberals and the SDP in 2004. The main source of the accusations is a former secret service officer, himself under investigation for being associated with Patriciu's business competitors in a bid to buy Romania's largest gas supply network.

While some questions can certainly be raised about Patriciu's business practices, the impartiality of the investigation against him may be in doubt. A judge dismissed most of the prosecutors' accusations, leaving only a charge of inside trading on Romania's stock exchange. Patriciu is suspected of having provided classified information that enriched many of his friends and partners, notably the prime minister himself, who owns shares in Patriciu's company. Suspicions were also prompted by the fact that the investigation is being run not by the NAD, but by the prosecutor general. The head of this office, Ilie Botos – a longtime opponent of transparency legislation and notorious for failing to investigate allegations of electoral fraud – was not replaced in 2005, as had been publicly expected. A vulnerable Botos is suspected of being keener to deliver an enemy to the president than the freshly appointed NAD head Morar. However, there is no evidence of any political pressure to pursue Patriciu.

President Basescu, the supposed anticorruption champion, also came under heavy fire in 2005. First, disclosures appeared that he conducted most of his business from a restaurant whose owners won a series of tenders for public works. He also came under criticism for his choice of administration head, a notably attractive woman with no professional background who is married to a businessman connected with SDP business networks. It became apparent that business and political networks, which are hard to separate in Romania, crossed party boundaries and managed to secure positions of top influence despite the change of regime. A negative press campaign and a public blunder revealing the administration head's professional incompetence instigated her resignation and weakened Basescu's position, though no allegations of illegal behavior were brought against the head. The issue simply highlighted the fact that a president elected on an anticorruption ticket will be watched more carefully by the media and must live up to high ethical standards.

Overall, there has been an increase in the political will to tackle corruption. The minister of justice, Monica Macovei, as well as the Office for Preventing and Combating Money Laundering and Terrorism Financing (OPCMLTF) and the National Fiscal Administration Agency, showed real commitment to fighting corruption, receiving praise from Brussels and the international media. The OPCMLTF even opened an investigation on the prime minister's bank accounts, showing that these offices are de facto independent. Public opinion supports anticorruption measures. By the end of 2005, Macovei had become the most popular minister of the Tariceanu government. Support for Basescu on this issue also remains high.

Other measures designed to fight high-level corruption entered into force in 2005 and early 2006, including the removal of immunity for former ministers in April 2005 and the adoption of new templates for wealth statements in May 2005. These statements are public and posted on government agency Web sites. A project to create a national integrity agency, which would check the validity of these statements and enforce conflict of interest regulations, is under development. In April 2005, Romania also abolished criminal immunity for public notaries and bailiffs.

The Freedom House audit criticized the lack of coordination among the many bodies fighting corruption in Romania. In one of its findings, the audit showed that control agencies such as the Financial Guard, the main state controller for businesses, and the Audit Court have sent fewer than 10 cases to the NAP for further investigation since its creation in 2003, and even those failed to lead to any prosecutions. Coordination across agencies improved in 2005, although too many competitive structures still hinder efficiency. The Ministry of Internal Affairs and Administration created a new anticorruption structure within the ministry called the Directorate General for Anticorruption, which will control the civil servants working in central and regional structures, notably the police, border police, and gendarmerie. Critics allege that the structure is based too much on the secret service staff of this ministry, and the European Commission itself expressed some skepticism.

A 2005 EBRD-World Bank survey (BEEPS) of businesses in Southeastern Europe found that Romania had made significant progress since 2002.[5] Bribery is down, and the costs of registering and operating businesses have decreased considerably. Romania is below the current Eastern-Central European average on bribes as a share of annual sales, after scoring nearly double the European average in 2002. The trend is clearly positive.

Alina Mungiu-Pippidi is the director of the Romanian Academic Society. She was assisted in the preparation of this report by Sorana Parvulescu, a researcher with the Romanian Academic Society.

[1] See the public monitoring system www.cna.ro.
[2] Manuela Preoteasa, Television Across Europe-Romania, report prepared for the EU Monitoring and Advocacy Program and Media Network Programs of the Open Society Institute, www.eumap.org/topics/media/television_europe/international/summary_report/summary_sections/cover.pdf, accessed November 11, 2004.
[3] The criminal procedures code was not passed by the Parliament by the end of 2005.
[4] Before appointing a magistrate, the SCM has the obligation to check with the CNSAS to determine whether the respective magistrate cooperated with the former Securitate. At the same time, upon appointment the magistrate has to sign a declaration stating that he is not working for any intelligence agency.
[5] See report at siteresources.worldbank.org/INTECAREGTOPANTCOR/Resources/BEEPS2005-at-a-glance-Final-Romania.pdf.

Russia

Capital:	Moscow
Population:	143.8 million
GNI/capita:	$3,400
Ethnic Groups:	Russian (79.8%), Tatar (3.8%), Ukrainian (2%), Bashkir (1.2%), Chuvash (1.1%), other or unspecified (12.1%)

Nations in Transit Ratings and Averaged Scores

	1997	1998	1999	2001	2002	2003	2004	2005	2006
Electoral Process	3.50	3.50	4.00	4.25	4.50	4.75	5.50	6.00	6.25
Civil Society	3.75	4.00	3.75	4.00	4.00	4.25	4.50	4.75	5.00
Independent Media	3.75	4.25	4.75	5.25	5.50	5.50	5.75	6.00	6.00
Governance *	4.00	4.50	4.50	5.00	5.25	5.00	5.25	n/a	n/a
National Democratic Governance	n/a	n/a	n/a	n/a	n/a	n/a	n/a	5.75	6.00
Local Democratic Governance	n/a	n/a	n/a	n/a	n/a	n/a	n/a	5.75	5.75
Judicial Framework and Independence	4.00	4.25	4.25	4.50	4.75	4.50	4.75	5.25	5.25
Corruption	n/a	n/a	6.25	6.25	6.00	5.75	5.75	5.75	6.00
Democracy Score	3.80	4.10	4.58	4.88	5.00	4.96	5.25	5.61	5.75

* With the 2005 edition, Freedom House introduced seperate analysis and ratings for national democratic governance and local democratic governance to provide readers with more detailed and nuanced analysis of these two important subjects.

NOTE: The ratings reflect the consensus of Freedom House, its academic advisers, and the author of this report. The opinions expressed in this report are those of the author. The ratings are based on a scale of 1 to 7, with 1 representing the highest level of democratic progress and 7 the lowest. The Democracy Score is an average of ratings for the categories tracked in a given year.

The economic and social data on this page were taken from the following sources:
GNI/capita, Population: *World Development Indicators 2006* (Washington, D.C.: World Bank, 2006).
Ethnic Groups: *CIA World Factbook 2006* (Washington, D.C.: Central Intelligence Agency, 2006).

EXECUTIVE SUMMARY

Russia started on the path to democracy with great hope in 1991 when the Soviet Union collapsed. While Russia's Constitution enshrines the basic principles of democracy, the current policies of the Kremlin are undermining them in practice. President Vladimir Putin's administration is effectively excluding citizen input from important governmental decisions, setting up hollow institutions like the Civic Chamber that imitate real mechanisms for social oversight. It is concentrating all power in the executive branch and minimizing the legislative and judicial branches' ability to operate independently, largely taking control of the legislature's agenda and defining policies for the country's judges.[1] Likewise, the presidential administration is undermining the ability of the regional and local governments to act as a check on other levels of government. Increasingly, groups of individuals around the president who control the levers of the state are taking over Russia's economic assets from individuals who do not have formal state power, using claims of protecting the national interest to cover up their own narrow goals.

The major theme for 2005 was the state's continuing crackdown on all aspects of political life in Russia, demonstrating that Russia is moving further from the ideals of democracy. The Kremlin continued to separate Russia from Western democracies by tightening control over the media, harassing the already weak opposition, and seeking to put greater controls on nongovernmental organizations (NGOs). At the same time, the conflict in Russia's south is spreading from Chechnya and destabilizing much of the North Caucasus. The country's inability to adopt and implement military and police reforms made clear that the state not only lacked the tools to address these problems, but was actually making the situation worse by doing nothing. Although there were some signs of a vibrant civil society on the Internet and in opposing the most restrictive Kremlin initiatives, non-state groups have not gained a broad ability to check the growing power of the bureaucracy, and the level of corruption in the country grew.

National Democratic Governance. Political power is becoming increasingly concentrated in the hands of the Russian president. Accordingly, the question of whether Vladimir Putin will actually step down when his term ends in 2008 is growing more pressing. While this top-heavy system may remain in place for the foreseeable future, it is becoming increasingly fragile, since it has less capacity to respond to public demands. At the same time, the violence of the Chechen conflict is spreading far beyond the borders of the rebellious republic. Desperate young men, suffering from police repression and a lack of jobs, are joining the extremist cause, bringing new recruits to the long-simmering conflict. *Russia's rating for national democratic governance worsens from 5.75 to 6.00. Numerous problems are accumulating that could push* *the country further away from democracy. They include a ruling elite that claims a commitment to democratic values but violates them in its behavior and extensive reliance on the use of force against segments of the population that are becoming increasingly radicalized, particularly in the North Caucasus.*

Electoral Process. During 2005, Russia adopted a package of electoral reforms that make it easier for incumbents to preserve their power. Elections are becoming more controlled and less decisive in determining the national and regional leadership. By replacing votes for individual representatives with party lists, the Kremlin helped to strengthen the bureaucracy and its political party appendage, United Russia. The latest round of amendments makes it much harder for the opposition to win representation in the State Duma, easier for the powers that be to remove candidates they do not like, and more difficult for independent observers to monitor the elections. There is little political opposition left in the country, and what remains is under constant attack by federal and regional officials. *Russia's rating for electoral process worsens from 6.00 to 6.25. The newly adopted provisions in the electoral law hand considerable power to the federal authorities and are likely to be abused in the upcoming round of national elections.*

Civil Society. With parliamentary approval for a new law on NGOs in December 2005 the presidential administration tightened its leash on Russia's growing civil society. Strong public outcry against the new legislation managed to remove its most restrictive features but could not halt the adoption of the law itself. Russian NGO activists are particularly concerned about how bureaucrats will apply the provisions of the law against groups that are critical of the government. Critics fear that the state will have broad powers to harass NGOs, thus blocking any real social oversight of the state. Groups providing alternative information about the conflict in Chechnya were a particular target. The Kremlin also sought to expand its ability to organize society by setting up the Civic Chamber, which is filled with members that toe the Kremlin line and are unlikely to provide independent oversight. At the same time, xenophobic and racially motivated crimes continued to increase in Russia with little opposition from the state. *Russia's rating for civil society worsens from 4.75 to 5.00 because of the state's efforts to curtail any unsanctioned initiatives on the part of Russian citizens. While outcry against Kremlin plans to limit social activities testified that a vibrant community of activists exists in Russia, their ability to continue functioning, particularly with restricted access to Western funding, remains in great doubt.*

Independent Media. The Putin administration continued its long-standing attack on the freedom of Russian media. Having already brought the three main national TV networks to heel, a Kremlin-friendly company this year took action against Ren-TV, a relatively minor player. The Kremlin is increasingly using its television and radio stations to spread state propaganda and replace serious political debate with entertainment programming. With dropping readership and influence, newspapers remained a secondary target, and Gazprom-Media acquired control of the prominent national daily *Izvestia*. The Internet was a bright spot for Russia, offering alternative viewpoints on difficult questions such as the conflict in Chechnya, though only to a limited audience. The appearance of new Web sites like livejournal.com is creating online communities to discuss pressing issues. This material is making its way into the traditional media, giving the Internet the potential to influence even Russians who are not online. *Russia's rating for independent media remains unchanged at 6.0. The country's political leadership spent the year fine-tuning its ability to keep alternative opinions off the airwaves, which are the main source of information for most people. At the same time, the Internet provided hope for those seeking to learn about and discuss pressing issues in a non-state-controlled format.*

Local Democratic Governance. After establishing a new set of local government institutions, the federal authorities postponed for three years the transfer of real power. Even when the reform is implemented in 2009, local governments will continue to be strongly subordinated to the regional governments and deprived of a reliable, independent tax base. Putin moved cautiously with his new power to appoint governors, avoiding putting new leaders in potentially unstable republics like Tatarstan and Kalmykia. Efforts to make the regional elite more manageable by reducing their number also moved ahead. This was exemplified in the merger of Perm oblast and the Komi-Permyak Autonomous Okrug into Perm Krai, bringing the number of regions down by 1 to 88. *Russia's rating for local governance remains unchanged at 5.75. Although few were happy with the reform of local government adopted in 2003, the decision to postpone implementation of these plans from 2006 to 2009 was another setback to establishing a local government system that can respond effectively to grassroots concerns.*

Judicial Framework and Independence. The high-profile case against Yukos leader Mikhail Khodorkovsky and the predictable guilty verdict cast a long shadow over the court system as a whole, reducing popular trust in its independence. The Kremlin clearly used the legal process, including attacks on Khodorkovsky's lawyers, to serve its political purposes. Judges unfortunately have little ability to resist pressure from the administration on key decisions. Nevertheless, the number of people appealing to the courts is increasing, and they are frequently able to win decisions against the state. The penal system is also in need of attention, as prisoners are slashing themselves with razor blades in a desperate protest against their treatment and living conditions in prisons. *Russia's rating for judicial framework and independence remains unchanged at 5.25. Russian judges need to demonstrate that they are free of executive influence. There are also warning signs that advances of the previous years, such as the use of jury trials, may be overturned.*

Corruption. Several independent research groups found that corruption increased in Russia in 2005. The basic problem is that current policies hand more power to state agencies while limiting the ability of social groups and the media to provide real oversight. This trend was most evident in the lucrative energy sector, where the Russian state secured majority ownership of the natural gas monopoly Gazprom and brought 30 percent of oil production under direct state ownership, creating numerous opportunities for corruption. Abuse of funds is also rife in Russia's policy toward the North Caucasus, adding to the troubles of this region. *Russia's rating for corruption drops to 6.0 owing to the increased role of the state in the economy, ongoing attacks on potential oversight bodies, and the failure to adopt administrative reforms that would reduce the power of bureaucrats in the country.*

Outlook for 2006. At the beginning of 2006, Russia took over the chairmanship of the G8, the exclusive club of rich democracies. Nevertheless, the thrust of the Kremlin's policies regarding democratic development cast doubt over whether the Russian system really matches the qualifications of this elite group. With Moscow insistent on imposing a solution by force, the situation in the North Caucasus will likely continue to deteriorate, bringing more unpleasant surprises as violence continues to spread in the region. With ever fewer areas for popular input into the policy process, unhappy citizens will have difficulty affecting change in ways they deem necessary. However, an influx of oil money will likely make it possible to delay necessary systemic reforms.

MAIN REPORT

National Democratic Governance

1997	1998	1999	2001	2002	2003	2004	2005	2006
n/a	n/a	n/a	n/a	n/a	n/a	n/a	5.75	6.00

The stability of Russia's political system has grown increasingly fragile thanks to the accumulation of power in the Kremlin and a spreading insurgency in the North Caucasus. With power largely in the hands of one man, succession becomes progressively more important to the system as a whole. The key question hanging over Russia's national political system is whether power will change hands in free and fair elections at the end of President Vladimir Putin's second term in 2008. Political commentators are now examining a variety of scenarios in which Putin will find a way to hold on to power by amending the Constitution or transferring power to a new center of gravity, either by making the prime minister's office more powerful or by restoring an effective one-party system under a Soviet-style United Russia in which he can rule as head of the party. Additionally, Putin could anoint a successor who would come to power in much the same way Putin himself succeeded Boris Yeltsin, benefiting from all the powers of political incumbency.

Against this backdrop of speculation, presidential adviser Andrei Illarionov, upon resigning his post on December 27, warned that after six years of Putin's leadership Russia was richer but no longer free.[2] Today there are few checks on the executive branch's power. The Federation Council's decision to release an analysis of the state's performance during the 2004 Beslan hostage incident on December 28, just as most people were preparing for the New Year and Orthodox Christmas celebrations, was only the latest example of the legislative branch's subservience. The report placed most of the blame for the botched handling of the crisis on local authorities, while exonerating the federal forces.

Russia faces further problems caused by the violent insurgency that is spreading beyond the borders of Chechnya and undermining stability in an ever widening arc across the North Caucasus. While there have been many attacks outside of Chechnya since the beginning of the war in 1994, the current level of unrest increasingly threatens the republics surrounding Chechnya. This upheaval has taken the form of numerous antigovernment military operations, including assassinations and bombings in Dagestan and Ingushetia, and a violent antigovernment attack in the once seemingly peaceful Kabardino-Balkaria. Clearly, there is plenty of blame to go around, as the crackdown by Russian authorities in Chechnya and the terrorist targeting of civilians in response have both been brutal.

The killings of officials and police officers in Dagestan have made it difficult for the government there to function properly. In the summer, Dmitrii Kozak, presidential envoy to the south, released a widely read report warning that the "uncontrolled development of events" could lead to the "collapse of the republic" and its devolution into interethnic fighting.[3] The report suggested that a significant part of the Dagestani population (7-8 percent) was ready to take up arms, capture buildings, and paralyze transportation. Moreover, many observers now see Ingushetia as a base for Chechen rebel operations.[4]

In the Kabardino-Balkaria capital of Nalchik on October 13, fighters attacked symbols of the government, such as police stations, administrative buildings, the prison, and the airport in response to the extensive crackdown on Islam in the republic. This systematic oppression occurred during the long rule of the region's former president Valerii Kokov, who resigned shortly before the attack.[5] Although the rebel Chechen leadership took responsibility for the raid, the 95 fighters killed were mainly young, local Muslims who had not taken up arms before, demonstrating that the anti-state cause is gaining active new members.[6] Young Muslims who would not have considered resorting to violence are frequently arrested and beaten, a humiliating experience that often radicalizes them, according to Ruslan Nakhushev, coordinator of the Russian Islamic Heritage organization. Nakhushev had sought to build bridges between the authorities and radicals before his disappearance in early November.[7]

Russian society has little control over the people who are supposed to protect it, and extensive distrust of the law enforcement authorities is exacerbating instability in the North Caucasus and the rest of Russia.[8] To prevent further attacks on the authorities like the one in Nalchik, military, law enforcement, and security agencies will need the cooperation of the local population. However, these enforcers of the law are often involved in crimes against the local population, such as indiscriminate sweep operations, abductions, and extortions. Following the brutal police sweep of the city of Blagoveshchensk in Bashkortostan in December 2004, there were similar sweeps in Ivanovskoe and Bezhetsk, where police arrested young people at discos and cafes. Many police officers are rotated through brutal tours of duty in the North Caucasus and return to their home regions inured to the use of violence.

Unfortunately, the quality of Russia's police is deteriorating. Interior Minister Rashid Nurgaliev complained on October 26 that half the police officers in city and rural police stations were under 30 years old and therefore lacked the necessary experience for police work. He said that the situation was "catastrophic," with the number of crimes committed by the police increasing every year. While officials admit to the problems, they have offered no plans to reform the system.

Electoral Process

1997	1998	1999	2001	2002	2003	2004	2005	2006
3.50	3.50	4.00	4.25	4.50	4.75	5.50	6.00	6.25

In 2005, the Russian authorities passed new electoral laws that make it easier to control who wins elections. These reforms reduce electoral oversight while increasing opportunities to falsify election results. Consequently, the changes do little to improve confidence in a system that already suffers from low levels of trust. Only 22 percent of respondents to a September ROMIR poll thought that elections in Russia in general were "free and fair."[9]

The electoral reforms proposed and adopted since the fall of 2004 make it harder for opposition parties to win representation in the federal legislature. With the selective application of these provisions, the authorities will be in an even stronger position. The 2005 reform continues a long-term trend in Russia in which the authorities "fine-tune" the electoral system after each voting cycle to make it more responsive to their needs.

The reforms bring a number of changes to the Russian legislature's lower house, the State Duma. All seats will now be filled through party lists, replacing a system in which half were filled by party lists and half by single-member districts. This system does not build up broad-based political parties but rather concentrates power in the hands of a few kingmakers able to determine who will become legislators. Where party list voting took place at the regional level in recent elections, local businessmen were able to buy spots on the lists and win election to regional legislatures, according to sociologist Alla Chirikova.[10] These new legislators have no real political or ideological ambitions and little interest in forming a political opposition; they are mainly concerned with pursuing their business goals, which generally means working closely with the governor. It will likely be even easier for the Kremlin to work with these people than members of previous legislatures.

Additionally, parties now need to win 7 percent of the vote to enter the Parliament and are not allowed to form electoral blocs. In the past, the electoral blocs did well against United Russia in regional legislative elections.[11] Also, there must be at least two parties in the Duma, representing not less than 50 percent of the vote. In the past, the Duma had to have a minimum of four parties. To win registration, parties must have at least 50,000 members and organizations in at least half the Russian regions, a provision that sets the bar very high in areas where political parties still have not earned widespread trust. This provision also removes the possibility for the formation of regional parties.

Under the new electoral reforms, the percentage of invalid signatures required to reject a candidate's application dropped from 25 to 5 percent of the mandatory 200,000 needed for registration.[12] As a result, the authorities can more easily remove candidates they do not want by challenging their signatures and then taking the matter to pliant courts, which likely will decide in their favor.

The reforms also allow the state budget to provide increased funding to parties crossing the 3 percent barrier in the previous parliamentary elections based on the number of votes they received. Each party will get 5 rubles (US$0.18) per vote each year, clearly favoring the biggest vote getters (113 million rubles [US$4 million] for United Russia and 38 million [US$1.4 million] for the Communist Party based on the results of the last election). In practice, though, these funds are of little importance since other sources of funding, legal and illegal, are likely to be much larger.

As a result of these reforms, the opposition will now find it harder to monitor elections. Under current legislation, only parties competing in the elections are allowed to provide election observers, and there is no provision for independent electoral observers or for journalists to watch the vote count.[13] International observers will be permitted only by invitation, a violation of the Helsinki accords, which Russia signed. The use of electronic voting machines and a ban on a manual vote count make it impossible to check the reliability of vote totals in areas where such devices are used.[14]

The political opposition disappeared almost completely after the 2003–2004 electoral cycle, which international observers declared free but not fair. Opponents of the current leadership have not been able to take advantage of the Kremlin's policy failures, such as the botched social benefit reforms at the beginning of the year.[15] Despite the weakened state of the opposition, the authorities have moved decisively against the two most open critics of Putin, former chess champion Garry Kasparov and former prime minister Mikhail Kasyanov, even though neither has much chance of replacing Putin. Kasyanov now faces criminal charges about how he acquired a summer cottage from the state; Kasparov's speaking tour across the country draws constant harassment from regional authorities following orders from above.

Civil Society

1997	1998	1999	2001	2002	2003	2004	2005	2006
3.75	4.00	3.75	4.00	4.00	4.25	4.50	4.75	5.00

During the course of 2005, the Kremlin stepped up its campaign to strictly limit the activities of independent NGOs. On July 20, at a meeting with members of the official Council for Promoting the Development of Civil Society, Putin called for restricting foreign financing of Russian NGOs' "political activities," repeating similar calls from previous years. Putin's attack was sufficiently vague to leave officials and activists in considerable doubt as to what activities he had in mind, those that focus strictly on political parties, or encompassing a broad range of environmental, social, and cultural causes. This ambiguity left the door open for abuse.

By the end of the year, the Parliament rushed through a highly controversial new law putting strict limits on Russian and foreign NGOs. Following Putin's signature, the law was set to go into effect on April 18, 2006.[16] While sharp criticism of the bill by Russian activists and Western supporters forced the Kremlin to remove the most egregious features of the legislation, the final bill was nonetheless a sharp blow to the development of Russian civil society.

The law's critics warned that it handed extensive power to the Justice Ministry's Federal Registration Service for NGOs, making it possible for the ministry to exploit vague provisions in the law to shut down organizations whose activities the government did not support. NGOs must supply information to the registration service when they receive money from foreign funders, including the purpose for the funding and how the money is actually spent. Failure to provide this information would be grounds for closing an NGO. The government agency, rather than the courts, would make the determination on the fate of the organization.

While transparency is a requirement for civil society groups in any country, many observers feared that officials would abuse the provisions of the new law for their own purposes. The Justice Ministry's Federal Registration Service reported that it had closed about 300 NGOs in 2005 and had a further 400 cases pending.[17] Provisions deleted from the bill before its final adoption would have barred foreign NGOs from operating in Russia unless they set up a Russian entity and would have required all groups operating informally to register with the authorities.

Despite clear signals that the Kremlin wanted to crack down, more than 1,300 NGOs issued a statement on November 22 charging that the legislation would limit civil society, demonstrating that not all groups were ready to toe the official line.[18] The bill was prepared hastily behind closed doors, and its drafters did not consult with NGOs. Such backroom dealing on the fate of NGOs is particularly ironic since the Kremlin was also in the process of setting up a Civic Chamber supposedly to bring together leaders of civil society to coordinate with the country's highest political authorities. The presidential administration blatantly expected to pass the law on NGOs before the chamber formally met, thus handing it a fait accompli.

The Civic Chamber was established shortly after the Beslan crisis in late 2004. Its membership was formed in the latter part of 2005, and it planned to launch operations at the beginning of 2006. The membership includes celebrities, pro-Kremlin activists, lawyers, businessmen, and many who had never held public office selected by the presidential administration. Many of the members have no obvious connection to social organizations, and only a handful are critical of the Kremlin. The body is supposed to supervise the government, Duma, media, and law enforcement. Unlikely to carry out these functions in practice, the Civic Chamber mainly represents an attempt to give the government greater influence over the NGO movement while attempting to increase government legitimacy in the civil sector.

In combination with these initiatives, the Duma has proposed handing out 500 million rubles (US$17.4 million) to NGOs in Russia and abroad as compensation for the money potentially lost from foreign funders because of the new legislation. This sum is smaller than what foreign funders are currently giving. Naturally, this money would be under the control of the presidential administration, and opposition groups would have little chance of receiving any of it. Critics complain that much of it would go to the members of the Civic Chamber.

Human rights groups are already working under difficult conditions. The administration began systematically to harass NGOs that work on issues related to Chechnya after Putin lashed out against such organizations in his State of the Nation address in 2004, according to Human Rights Watch.[19] Moscow Helsinki Group head Lyudmilla Alexeyeva charges that human rights groups are coming under increasing pressure through financial scrutiny, such as the investigation of grants, tax returns, and donations.[20] Even without official pressure, Russian human rights groups have little impact in a society that generally focuses its attention elsewhere.

While the positive forces of civil society have had difficulty establishing themselves, there has been a rise in the number of racially motivated hate crimes in Russia, according to the SOVA Center, which tracks these incidents.[21] The frequency of the attacks increased in 2005, with a record 179 incidents, though the number of murder victims dropped to 28, down from 46 in 2004. The authorities often do not prosecute these crimes, choosing to protect ethnic Russians who commit them, according to human rights activists in St. Petersburg like the Democratic Russia Party's Ruslan Linkov. Linkov cited the authorities' failure to crack down on the sale of literature that openly calls for violence against non-Russian groups.[22]

Further evidence that the authorities were turning a blind eye to intolerance came when Vladimir Yakovlev's Ministry of Regional Development prepared a draft nationalities policy that sought to form a "united multinational society under the consolidating role of the Russian people."[23] At the same time, the Kremlin is advancing nationalist youth projects, such as the group Nashi (Ours), while working with an eye toward countering the rise of youth groups such as those in Ukraine that might seek political change in Russia.[24] SOVA also notes that it has become harder to punish people convicted of racially motivated crimes.

Independent Media

1997	1998	1999	2001	2002	2003	2004	2005	2006
3.75	4.25	4.75	5.25	5.50	5.50	5.75	6.00	6.00

During the 1990s, much of the media was privatized. Since Putin came to power, there has been a reversal of this process, with the state taking over much of television and key national newspapers, especially through the instrument of Gazprom-Media.[25] The most apparent result has been the replacement of hard-hitting news reports with entertainment programming. Only the Internet provided a bright spot, with extensive discussion of current events and the establishment of new communities of online participants among the still limited numbers of people with access to the Internet.

Television news is a top priority for the political elite because Channel One, Rossiya (RTR), and NTV are the main sources of news for 79 percent of Russians, according to a September 22, 2005, ROMIR poll.[26] All programming at the three major TV networks, though varying in style, is state controlled, with weekly meetings between network executives and presidential administration officials to determine the overall shape of the news coverage.[27] The Kremlin's control over the portrayal of the events in Chechnya is particularly intense. For example, presidential staffers told electronic media representatives to replace the phrase Chechen terrorism with international terrorism and the word *jamaat*, which means local Muslim community and might be interpreted favorably, with terrorist organization or gang, according to the Web news site gazeta.ru.[28]

Moscow City's TV Tsentr is controlled by Mayor Yurii Luzhkov's government and therefore occasionally presents a different picture on national issues from that of the three main networks, demonstrating the existence of competing factions within the state. However, at the end of the year, the station fired General Director Oleg Poptsov for a show critical of Putin, Poptsov claimed.[29] Ren-TV, with relatively low ratings and less national reach than the top networks, was a bit more adventurous in its coverage than the big three, but during the summer, the Kremlin-friendly steel company Severstal and a group of German investors purchased the station from Russia's electricity monopoly, which had not required it to toe the Kremlin line. At the end of November, recently appointed Ren-TV general manager Aleksandr Ordzhonikidze removed news anchor Olga Romanova from the air in a dispute over efforts to broadcast a story about the criminal case against Defense Minister Sergei Ivanov's son. The young Ivanov had struck and killed an elderly woman with his car but was found not guilty.[30] Whatever the merits of the case against the well-connected driver, the authorities did not want extensive publicity for what appeared to be an arrogant elite who cared little about average citizens. With this attack on Ren-TV, the authorities effectively eliminated all significant alternative points of view in the broadcast media. Live broadcasts are no longer common, and shows with a range of opinions are "edited," according to Alexei Simonov of the Glasnost Defense Foundation.[31]

The state-controlled networks have replaced the feisty political talk shows of the past with straightforward entertainment, apparently seeking to distract public attention with reality shows, music, and film. To the extent that there is network coverage of political events, it is frequently biased. On the eve of the Moscow City Duma elections, Russian television stations gave much more airtime to the pro-Kremlin United Russia than any other party, according to research by *Nezavisimaya Gazeta* and the Medialogiya Research Company.[32] The data showed that during October and the first half of November, United Russia had 552 mentions, followed by the Communists and Rodina (350 each) and the Liberal Democratic Party of Russia (258). Detailed coverage and investigative reporting are left to outlets that have smaller audiences.

The national newspapers are owned mainly by media holding companies with enormous assets from the stock market, gas and oil sector, and industrial enterprises. Over the summer, Gazprom-Media bought the popular newspaper *Izvestia* from oligarch Vladimir Potanin's Prof-Media. While there has yet to be a radical shift in the newspaper's content, the state now has an effective lever to control this news outlet.

The journal *Ekspert* is one of the country's truly free publications since its staff was able to purchase the political and economic weekly from its previous oligarch owner and can survive on its income from ads and other services. The Boris Berezovsky-owned *Kommersant* is also profitable, giving it some autonomy from the state, while foreign-owned publications like *Vedomosti* work according to their own professional standards. Other alternative sources include *Novaya Gazeta*, Ekho Moskvy radio (majority owned by Gazprom-Media but operated autonomously by the journalists, who own a 30 percent stake), and 30 to 40 regional newspapers with a combined circulation of 500,000, a small fraction of Russia's 150 million population, according to the Glasnost Defense Foundation.[33]

In contrast, Russia's thousands of district newspapers, with circulations of 3,000 to 10,000, have all but lost their independence since they are heavily reliant on state subsidies. Now they retain only the right to elect their editors and receive subsidies directly from higher-level bodies, avoiding the micromanagement of district governments. The print media is continuing to lose its audience to electronic and online sources of news and therefore becoming less influential among the population.[34]

Content analysis of the media by the Glasnost Defense Foundation shows that up to 70 percent of news items are about the authorities, while reports about the opinions and initiatives of the public get much less attention and therefore are unlikely to influence policies significantly. Given the media's heavy emphasis on serving as conveyors of policy from the authorities to the population, they cannot perform their function of criticizing the authorities and gathering alternative viewpoints.

In its Worldwide Press Freedom Index issued in October 2005, Reporters Without Borders ranked Russia 138 out of 167 countries owing to controls on the media, curbs on different points of view, and biased coverage of the war in

Chechnya. The situation is likely to get worse, as state pressure on mass media is mounting, according to Pascal Bonnamour, the head of Reporters Without Borders' European Department.[35]

The Internet was the main bright spot in the area of information freedom. More than 10 million people, or 9 percent of the adult population, went online in early 2005.[36] Even more optimistic, more than 40 percent of these were under the age of 25 in 2004. Russian news sites attract wide usage during crises, such as the Beslan hostage crisis in September 2004.

The Internet provides a source of alternative information about the Chechen war, allowing the rebel fighters to address readers directly through their own Web sites. The Russian authorities have sought to suppress such access through other outlets. For example, Stanislav Dmitrievskii, head of the Nizhnii Novgorod-based Russian-Chechen Friendship Society, received a suspended two-year sentence (in February 2006) for inciting racial hatred for publishing two interviews in his newspaper in 2004 with now deceased Chechen leader Aslan Maskhadov. *Kommersant* also received a warning for publishing an interview with Maskhadov. Many politicians have suggested cracking down on the freedom of information exchange on the Internet, but the government has not taken serious steps to do so.

Blogging has also become a popular way for young Russians to learn about, and actively discuss, political and current events. The site livejournal.com, for example, is building an extensive online community and is increasingly bringing different points of view into print journals such as *Ogonek* and *Moscow News*, which mentioned the site in discussions of topics ranging from the case against Ivanov's son to the trial of a woman who murdered an attempted rapist.[37]

The authorities are also increasingly using the courts as a way to pressure journalists. In the beginning of the year, Kommersant had to pay US$1.5 million in damages for a libel suit it lost to Alfa Bank, after an appeals court reduced the initial fine from US$11.4 million. In July 2005, the tax authorities ordered the paper to pay an additional US$736,000 in back taxes for 2004, claiming that the paper had understated its profits by excluding the sum it paid to Alfa Bank.

Likewise, international observers protested the sentencing of journalist Eduard Abrosimov to seven months forced labor for an article referring to a local lawmaker's sexual preferences and an unpublished account accusing an investigator for the regional procurator of taking bribes. Reporters Without Borders particularly objected to a prison sentence for an unpublished article. In Smolensk, Nikolai Goshko received a five-year sentence for accusing the governor and two other top-ranking officials of killing his boss, the director of an independent radio station in Smolensk, without supporting evidence. Observers admitted that the journalist's work was sloppy but maintained that the sentence was far too harsh. The UN and the Office for Security and Cooperation in Europe recommend against requiring jail time for slander.

Two journalists were killed in Russia in 2005. On June 28, Magomedzagid Varisov, a journalist for *Novoe Delo* in Dagestan whose articles were often critical of the opposition, was shot in a contract killing. Pavel Makeev was apparently killed on May 21 in Rostov oblast when he tried to film illegal drag races for a TV report.[38] The Committee to Protect Journalists charges that the Russian authorities have not done enough to prosecute the killers of a dozen journalists since 2000.

Local Democratic Governance

1997	1998	1999	2001	2002	2003	2004	2005	2006
n/a	n/a	n/a	n/a	n/a	n/a	n/a	5.75	5.75

After imposing greater formal federal control over Russia's 89 regional governors during the first years of the decade, the Kremlin turned to bringing local government under the aegis of the country's vertical hierarchy. Unfortunately, rather than giving truly autonomous local officials the means to address the needs of their grassroots constituents, efforts at local reform have largely led to the imposition of greater top-down control. By making mayors more dependent on governors, the Kremlin removes one of the key checks and balances in Russia's overall political system.

Local government reform began in January 2004, doubling the number of municipalities in Russia to 24,000. "The law provided for the creation of three types of local institutions – *poseleniia* (settlements), *munitsipal'nye raiony* (municipal counties), and *gorodskie okruga* (city districts) – each with a specifically defined set of functions. This elaborate but clearly demarcated group of institutions sought to improve on the 1995 Yeltsin-era law, which allowed for numerous types of local bodies without defining their precise responsibilities," according to local government expert Tomila Lankina.[39] By the end of 2005, 84 of the 89 regions had held elections to fill these slots, with only a few North Caucasus republics failing to do so.[40] With all the new institutions and officials in place, the local government law was supposed to take effect on January 1, 2006. However, in October the federal authorities postponed implementation of the reform for three years, until the beginning of 2009.

The thrust of the 2003 Law on Local Government gives Russia's regional governments considerable authority over municipalities. Moreover, the law does not provide local government with an independent and reliable tax base to support even the modest functions assigned to it. During the process of implementation, the most politically powerful and economically self-sufficient localities have suffered the most, with cities up to 250,000 often losing their autonomous status and being demoted to urban settlements, according to the Moscow-based Urban Economics Institute.[41] Small cities now must keep extensive accounting records that further strain their meager resources. In many regions, voter interest in the new institutions has been low, with large parts of the population ignoring the municipal elections.

Even though local government advocates were not happy with the gist of the reform and the rush to elect so many new officials by the end of 2005, the last minute decision to postpone the implementation of the reform came as another blow. Now Russia has essentially established the shell of a local government system but not endowed it with any powers for the next three years. Lankina points to the rationale that presidential chief of staff Dmitry Medvedev and his deputy Vladislav Surkov provided in justifying the delay – avoiding "social instability" that might "negatively influence the results of the 2007-2008 elections"[42] – as evidence that the federal authorities hope to use the new officials as part of an effort to ensure that all goes well in the 2007-2008 electoral cycle. Allowing inexperienced local government officials to start working earlier could lead to unpredictable outcomes that would threaten the status quo.

With local government reform on hold, the Kremlin continued to tighten its control over the regions, particularly through the president's new power to appoint governors. Until the end of 2004, the population had been able to elect governors directly. In general, Putin has been cautious in his appointments, keeping in place long-serving incumbents in ethnic regions like Tatarstan and Kalmykia, where appointing a new leader might destabilize the situation. Of course, such actions cannot be stable in the medium to long term because many of the current leaders are old and change will come eventually. By canceling elections, the Kremlin now has the task of appointing regional leaders whose legitimacy depends on their ties to Moscow rather than popular approval. With the crackdowns on the media, nongovernmental groups, and the election process, the public has no outlet to vent its frustration.[43]

The Kremlin further solidified its power when the Constitutional Court ruled on December 21 that Putin's system of appointing governors is constitutional, putting an end to attempts to restore gubernatorial elections. The Union of Right Forces, one of Russia's most critical, but largely powerless political parties, had argued that annulling direct gubernatorial elections violated Russia's basic law. Kommersant argued that with this decision the Court made it possible to ignore the Constitution, effectively eliminating any need to amend it.[44] Yaroslavl governor Anatolii Lisitsyn withdrew his region's support for the case long before the decision was announced, claiming that Yaroslavl depended on federal subsidies and therefore could not afford to oppose Kremlin policies.[45]

Many mayors are no longer elected directly, as in the past.[46] Rather, they are elected by the city council from among its own members. Although cities decide for themselves how to choose their leaders, in big urban areas like Samara, the Kremlin clearly prefers the more manageable system of having the city council choose the city leader.[47] This new procedure sparked a massive protest in Samara, where 20,000 residents joined an October 25 rally to support direct elections. The city's political elite is split, with one faction banking on elections to preserve its power while its opponents seek to cancel the elections as a way of taking office. Thus, the "rules of the game" have become an object of political battle, with each side seeking to shift the rules to favor its particular interests.

Despite the Kremlin's assertions to the contrary, the November legislative elections in Chechnya had little impact on the overall situation in the republic. Real power seems to be going increasingly to First Deputy Prime Minister Ramzan

Kadyrov, the former Chechen leader Akhmad Kadyrov's son, who is widely feared for his powerful group of armed fighters. At the end of the year, the elections to the relatively powerless Moscow legislature were marred by the disqualification of an opposition party and alleged violations. In both elections, the heavy hand of the Kremlin was obvious.

Russia has also begun pushing ahead with the idea of merging regions to reduce the number of units in the federation from 89 to a more manageable figure. On December 1, the country lost one region when Perm oblast and the Komi-Permyak Autonomous Okrug officially merged into Perm Krai. The merged region will elect a single legislature in 2006, which will prepare a joint budget in 2007. In this case, as in other pending mergers, a small, poor region was integrated into a larger, richer region. In theory, the richer regions will provide subsidies to the poorer regions, taking over this burden from the federal government.[48] However, since many of the proposed projects aimed at developing the isolated Komi-Permyak make no economic sense, the financing that Okrug leaders anticipated from the merger is unlikely to appear.[49]

Judicial Framework and Independence

1997	1998	1999	2001	2002	2003	2004	2005	2006
4.00	4.25	4.25	4.50	4.75	4.50	4.75	5.25	5.25

The trial of Mikhail Khodorkovsky and his ultimate sentencing to eight years in a Siberian prison colony demonstrated that Russian justice is applied selectively and, when necessary, for political purposes. With the initial verdict in hand, the court rushed through an appeal of Khodorkovsky's sentence, rejecting the not guilty plea but reducing the term by one year, thus preventing Khodorkovsky from running in a December 2005 State Duma by-election in a Moscow district. While there may be improvements in some aspects of the judiciary's functioning, the fact that the courts remain tools of the executive branch in high-profile political cases casts a long shadow, undermining public confidence in the fairness of the judiciary.[50]

Russia has a long way to go before achieving an independent judicial system. President Putin holds frequent meetings with Russia's top judges – Constitutional Court chairman Valerii Zorkin, Supreme Court chairman Vyacheslav Lebedev, and newly appointed Supreme Arbitration Court chairman Anton Ivanov – to discuss a wide range of issues from housing to tax evasion. Indicating a desire that the judicial branch implement policies adopted by the Kremlin, at the November 9 meeting Putin said, "Hopefully our meeting will contribute to the dialogue between different branches of power in Russia, making the interaction between executive and judicial authorities more productive," according to the official ITAR-TASS news agency.[51] At their meeting, Putin and the judges also discussed reform of the judicial system and the implementation of key laws. These are substantive issues where the president can clearly influence the context in which judges make their decisions.

These meetings are problematic not because Putin is seeking to influence the judges, as any president presumably would, but because the judges see nothing wrong with it. Like other officials in Russia, the justices are susceptible to influence within a society that assumes policies are set at the top. Putin's suggestions undoubtedly trickle down through the judicial hierarchy. In lower and regional courts, chief judges have great influence over judicial salaries and which cases judges hear, thereby making it possible for them to determine the outcome of cases with a high degree of predictability.

The Federation Council confirmed Putin's appointment of Anton Ivanov, the former first deputy general director of Gazprom-Media, as chairman of the Supreme Arbitration Court on January 26. Many see the move as being connected to the fact that the courts are now considering a number of cases affecting Gazprom's interests. The previous chair had to step down because he had passed the age limit of 65.

Beyond high-level meetings, the federal authorities have a variety of ways to pressure the judges. In 2004, Federation Council Speaker Sergei Mironov suggested changing the qualifications for defining who could serve as a judge, a proposal the judges ultimately succeeded in blocking. In 2005, he suggested moving the courts to St. Petersburg. Longtime observers of Russia's courts, like Pennsylvania State University Distinguished Law Professor William Butler, claim that it often seems that whenever the Kremlin wants to exert pressure on the judges, a proposal appears that would make their lives more difficult.[52] On December 21, Zorkin publicly opposed moving the courts.

The authorities have also sought to put more pressure on lawyers involved in high-profile cases. After the Yukos trial, the procurator sought to disbar Khodorkovsky's lawyers for "drawing out" the trial. However, the Moscow Lawyers Chamber qualification commission found no reason to punish them. Yukos lawyer Svetlana Bakhmina was held in pretrial detention after her arrest in December 2004 for allegedly participating in a criminal group organized by Khodorkovsky to take over local oil companies. Robert Amsterdam, a human rights lawyer and member of Khodorkovsky's legal team, was expelled from Russia in September for alleged visa irregularities.

Despite the obvious political purposes to which the courts can be put, they have advanced in some areas. Commercial lawyers report an improvement in the arbitrazh system. New criminal and civil codes as well as criminal procedures have been adopted, and many aspects of the new legislation are implemented in practice. In contrast with the past, defendants must now be brought before a judge within 48 hours. Judges, not prosecutors, issue arrest warrants, and jury trials are now available for defendants in serious cases.[53]

More citizens are appealing to the courts, and in some important cases the courts do decide against the state's position. According to a 2003 government order, federal agencies are required to maintain Web sites informing the public about their activities. On October 18, a federal court in St. Petersburg agreed with a lawsuit brought by Yurii Vdovin of the Institute for the Development of Freedom of Information obligating seven federal agencies to open their own sites. The agencies included the Federal Guard Service, the Federal Bailiff Service, the Federal Service for Defense Orders, and the Ministry for Regional Development. Likewise, Vladimir oblast pensioner Olga Yegorova used the courts to block the authorities from opening a dump on forest land she maintained.[54]

Nevertheless, many procedural and substantive problems remain. Judges often lack the training necessary to fulfill all the new functions expected of them. The Council of Europe found that judges' salaries are not commensurate with their responsibilities, making them vulnerable to corruption and outside pressure. Conviction rates remain very high in criminal cases. Where juries are involved, about 15 percent of the cases result in acquittal, but between 25 and 50 percent of jury acquittals are overturned by higher courts, often on technicalities.[55] When the acquittal is overturned, the defendant then faces a new trial that will presumably return the "correct" decision. Jury trials are particularly unpopular with procurators and judges, who do not always believe in the presumption of innocence and must now work much harder to present and examine the evidence against the defendant. Proposals to limit the use of such trials are becoming more frequent.

Defendants still have fewer rights than in Western systems. They are often held in pretrial detention when bail or house arrest might be more appropriate. Additionally, defense lawyers are generally barred from collecting evidence during a criminal investigation, judges routinely declare defense testimony inadmissible at trial, and prosecutors can appeal acquittals or sentences they deem too lenient. In the United States, only defendants can appeal a verdict.[56] In trials such as the one against police accused of abusing citizens in the city of Blagoveshchensk, the authorities have apparently sought to intimidate witnesses.[57]

Russia is also facing growing problems with its enormous and overburdened prison system. The country had 621,148 inmates on July 1, 2005, giving it one of the highest incarceration rates in the world.[58] Russian prisons are crowded, disease-ridden, and violent. Some 250 inmates at a prison in Lgov (Kursk oblast) cut themselves with razor blades in the summer, demanding an improvement in conditions and the dismissal of the prison's administration. Subsequently, about 60 inmates at a prison colony in Smolensk oblast went on a hunger strike, and 10 slashed themselves with razor blades to protest beatings of inmates, according to the Moscow-based NGO For Human Rights. The authorities will need increased political will and financial resources to address these problems.

Putin signed a decree on July 13 transferring a number of detention centers from the Federal Security Service to the Justice Ministry's prison service. The purpose of the move is to place the investigators' handling of suspects under the supervision of the Justice Ministry, a condition Russia had to satisfy to join the Council of Europe in 1996. The council had long asked Russia to enact this reform, and although Russia's Ministry of the Interior gave up its control of prisons in 1997, the Federal Security Service managed to hold on to the centers until this year.[59] Whether the change will make any difference in practice remains to be seen.

Corruption

1997	1998	1999	2001	2002	2003	2004	2005	2006
n/a	n/a	6.25	6.25	6.00	5.75	5.75	5.75	6.00

Numerous observers of Russia independently came to the conclusion that the level of corruption in the country increased in 2005. The basic problem is that the Kremlin is handing more power to state institutions while removing societal controls over them.

An INDEM study released over the summer indicated that officials had learned to wring more money from citizens and businesses for services, which they monopolize more efficiently than in the past. While the researchers found that fewer bribes were given in 2005 than in 2001 in both business and daily life, the size of these bribes had increased. Sadly, the survey found an increased level of bribery in areas that are vital to family life: education, real estate, and armed forces draft boards.[60]

Transparency International's Corruption Perceptions Index 2005 likewise suggested that corruption is increasing in Russia, with the absolute score dropping from 2.8 to 2.4. The global average is 4.11, and the regional average is 2.67. Transparency International blamed the decline on reduced transparency in government agencies and a crackdown on independent organizations and the media. Russia ranked 126 out of 159 countries.[61] The World Bank and European Bank for Reconstruction and Development concurred, finding increasing kickbacks in awarding government contracts, with the proportion of kickbacks rising from 1.51 percent to 1.91 percent of the overall value of state contracts over the previous three years.[62]

In the face of this growing corruption, the good news is that the public is increasingly opposed to giving bribes. The INDEM survey found that there were greater efforts to avoid extortion where possible, suggesting that many in Russia had had enough and may be willing to take action against the pervasive corruption.[63] Along these lines, the Levada Center published survey data on August 9 showing that the public thought police and bureaucrats were the most criminal elements in society, with their perceived level of criminality exceeding even the level of actual mobsters.[64]

The Kremlin's policy of expanding the state's role in the energy sector, creating national champions in Gazprom and Rosneft, is likely to increase the level of corruption in the most lucrative part of the Russian economy and slow economic growth.[65] In 2005, the state increased its holdings in Gazprom to 51 percent and added the oil assets of Sibneft to the natural gas monopoly. Former Sibneft owner Roman Abramovich was the main beneficiary, apparently receiving billions of dollars for giving up his oil company. State-owned Rosneft acquired the most lucrative assets of Yukos as partial payment for a US$28 billion tax claim against the company in a shady deal following the ruling against Khodorkovsky. Controlling Yuganskneftegaz provides vast opportunities for embezzlement, according to the INDEM Foundation's Vladimir Rimsky.[66] Before 2005, private companies carried out the vast majority of Russia's oil production. Now the Russian state controls 30 percent of this sector.[67] The problem is not with state ownership per se, but with the way the Russian state operates its holdings. Growth in the sector was 9 percent a year in the last five years but has now dropped to around 3 percent.

This process is not nationalization (using Russian resources in the public interest), but a transfer of property to people with close ties to the Kremlin. The actual divisions among these different groups inside the state became apparent when Rosneft managers fought off attempts to merge their company with Gazprom into one giant state energy holding company. Kremlin chief of staff Dmitrii Medvedev chairs the board of Gazprom, while Igor Sechin, deputy chief of staff, heads the board of Rosneft. Rosneft management bitterly fought plans to merge it into Gazprom, thereby preserving control over the company's money flows. In another sector of the economy, the company that monopolizes arms exports took over Russia's largest automobile manufacturer at the end of the year.

Even in dealing with the country's poorest regions, corruption is rife. Federal transfers to the North Caucasus are the main source of criminal money in southern Russia, according to Valery Tishkov, director of the Institute of Ethnology and Anthropology at the Russian Academy of Sciences.[68] The subsidies support a clan structure that monopolizes local resources and power, creating wide public discontent. Moscow's basic policy in the region is to provide subsidies in exchange for loyalty, hoping to preserve stability even in the face of mounting evidence that the region is sliding into anarchy.

Russia is taking some steps to deal with its corruption problem, though these are likely to have little impact. In spring 2005, Prime Minister Mikhail Fradkov launched a program to double the nominal salaries of federal officials working outside of Moscow by 2008 in order to attract better talent to these jobs. Salaries for federal officials working in the regions increased by 27.6 percent in nominal terms over the first six months of 2005, but they are still lower on average than the salaries of their local counterparts, earning 8,839 rubles (US$316) per month versus 14,791 (US$530). Despite these efforts, bureaucrats' salaries are peanuts compared with their ability to make money from business; therefore, the scope for corruption remains enormous.[69]

After many years in which plans for administrative reform were successively proposed and then abandoned, on November 1 Fradkov signed the latest administrative reform blueprint and an implementation plan for the next three years. The goal is to overhaul the civil service with clear regulations and state service delivery standards. However, this plan will not be implemented anytime soon, since 2006 is devoted to the "theoretical" preparation of the reform.[70]

Similarly, Russia is working on ratifying the UN Anticorruption Convention.[71] This means reintroducing the confiscation of property into Russian law, a provision required by international standards but one that worries many rights advocates for fear it will be used by the authorities to take property arbitrarily.

Robert W. Orttung is an associate research professor at the Transnational Crime and Corruption Center of American University and a visiting scholar at the Center for Security Studies of the Swiss Federal Institute of Technology.

[1] Veronika Chursina, "Lobbitryasy," Novaya Gazeta, no. 51, July 18, 2005.

[2] Andrei Illarionov, "Drugaya strana," Kommersant, January 23, 2006.

[3] Ekaterina Deeva, "Kak budut vzryvat' Dagestan," Moskovskii Komsomolets, July 8, 2005.

[4] Mark Kramer, "Instability in the North Caucasus and the Political Implications for the Russian-Chechen War," PONARS Policy Memo No. 380, December 2005.

[5] Andrei Alekseev and Andrei Krasnov, "Terroristicheskaya kontoperatsiia," Kommersant Vlast, October 17, 2005, p. 17.

[6] Jean-Christope Peuch, "Nalchik Raids Trigger New Wave of Harassment Against Muslims," Radio Free Europe/Radio Liberty Russian Political Weekly, November 18, 2005.

[7] Ivan Sukhov, "Ruslan Nakhushev: 'Moskva daet dengi, chtoby vzryvva yt bylo,'" Vremya Novostei, September 29, 2005.

[8] "Special Services on Trust," gazeta.ru, October 21, 2005.

[9] Yekaterina Kudashkina, "No Democracy," Vedomosti, September 16, 2005.

[10] Interview with Alla Chirikova, in Maria Kravtsova, "Perezagruzka regional'nykh elit," Ekspert, October 24-30, 2005, p. 106.

[11] Nikolai Petrov, "From Managed Democracy to Sovereign Democracy," PONARS Policy Memo No. 396, December 2005.

[12] Federal Law No. 51-FZ, Rossiiskaya Gazeta, May 24, 2005.

[13] Nikolai Petrov, "A Reform to End All Elections," St. Petersburg Times, May 27, 2005.

[14] Boris Vishnevskii, "Skanner protiv demokratii," Moskovskiye Novosti, October 28, 2005.

[15] Vladimir Gel'man, "Political Opposition in Russia: A Dying Species?" Post-Soviet Affairs 21, no. 3 (2005): 242.

[16] Text of the law was published in Rossiiskaya Gazeta, January 17, 2006.

[17] Anatoly Medetsky, "Rights Group Faces Closure," Moscow Times, January 30, 2006.

[18] "Russian MPs Act to 'Curb' NGOs," BBC, November 23, 2005; and www.hro.org/ngo/about/2005/11/10-2.php.

[19] Human Rights Watch press release, "Russia: Draft Law Would Eviscerate Civil Society," November 22, 2005.

[20] Nick Wadhams, "Rights Campaigner: Sharp Increase in Attacks on Human Rights in Russia," AP, October 25, 2005.

[21] Galina Kozhevnikova, "Radikal'nyi natsionalizm v Rossii i protivodeistvie emu v 2005 godu," Sova Center, http://xeno.sova-center.ru/29481C8/6CEEC08.

[22] Vladimir Kovalev, "Human Rights Groups: Police Ignore Extremists," St. Petersburg Times, August 2, 2005.

[23] Natalya Gorodetskaya, "Narodu napisano: Vladimir Yakovlev sozdaet novuyu istoricheskuyu obshchnost'," Kommersant, October 11, 2005.

[24] Sarah E. Mendelson and Theodore P. Gerber, "Soviet Nostalgia: An Impediment to Russian Democratization," Washington Quarterly (Winter 2005-2006).

[25] Aleksei Mukhin, Media-Imperii Rossi (Moscow: Algoritm, 2005), p.5.

[26] "Television Still Main Source of Information for Vast Majority of Russians," Radio Free Europe/Radio Liberty Newsline, September 30, 2005.

[27] Alexei Simonov, "Transformations of the Fourth Estate," Nezavisimaya Gazeta, October 7, 2005.

[28] gazeta.ru, November 3, 2005 as quoted in Igor Torbakov, "War on Terrorism in the Caucasus: Russia Breeds Jihadists," Chechnya Weekly, November 10, 2005.

[29] Arina Borodina, Irina Nagornykh, and Yuliya Kulikova, "Vot i rasstalis' dva odinochestva," Kommersant, December 22, 2005.

[30] Arina Borodina, Alena Miklashevskaya, and Timur Bordyug, "Aleksandr Ordzhonikidze nastroil

Ren TV," Kommersant, November 29, 2005; and Olga Romanova, "Ya ne tvar' grozhashchaya!" Novaya gazeta, November 30-December 6, 2005.

[31] Alexei Simonov, "Transformations of the Fourth Estate," Nezavisimaya Gazeta, October 7, 2005.

[32] Sergey Varshavchik and Natalya Kostenko, "On the Eve of the Elections to the Moscow City Duma, the State Channels Are Intensively Stuffing the Viewers with Shows," Nezavisimaya Gazeta, November 19, 2005.

[33] Alexei Simonov, "Transformations of the Fourth Estate," Nezavisimaya Gazeta, October 7, 2005.

[34] "Television Still Main Source of Information for Vast Majority of Russians," Radio Free Europe/Radio Liberty Newsline, September 29 or 30, 2005.

[35] "Reporters Without Borders Official Explains Russia's Low Ranking," Radio Free Europe/Radio Liberty Newsline, October 25, 2005, citing Kommersant, October 21, 2005.

[36] D. J. Peterson, Russia and the Information Revolution (Santa Monica: Rand Corporation, 2005), p. xiv.

[37] "Sbivai nas khot' vsekh!" Ogonek, December 5-11, 2005, p. 6; and "Would-be Rape Victim Cleared of Manslaughter," Moscow News, November 30-December 6, 2005, p. 3.

[38] World Association of Newspapers, www.wan-press.org/article9048.html; Committee to Protect Journalists, www.cpj.org/cases05/europe_cases05/russia.html.

[39] Tomila Lankina, "New System Weakens Municipalities," Russian Regional Report, October 18, 2005.

[40] "Regional Polls Mark Final Phase of Russian Local Government Reform," ITAR-TASS, October 30, 2005.

[41] As cited in Tomila Lankina, "New System Weakens Municipalities," Russian Regional Report, October 18, 2005.

[42] Natalya Gorodetskaya, "Administratsiya prezidenta perenosit munitsipalnuyu reformu," Kommersant, September 19, 2005.

[43] Interview with Alla Chirikova, in Maria Kravtsova, "Perezagruzka regional'nykh elit," Ekspert, October 24-30, 2005, p. 106.

[44] Dmitrii Kamyshev and Viktor Khamraev, "Konstitutsionnaya proforma," Kommersant, December 22, 2005.

[45] No author, "Ot redaktsii: Plach Yaroslavlya," Vedomosti, October 6, 2005.

[46] Nikolai Petrov, "A Reform to End All Elections," St. Petersburg Times, May 27, 2005.

[47] Sergei Khazov, "Samara Residents Protest Cancellation of Direct Mayoral Elections," Russian Regional Report, November 23, 2005.

[48] Stephen Boykewich, "Planned Merge Worries Buryats," Moscow Times, November 15, 2005.

[49] Inna Skrypnichenko, "Permskaya oblast gotova sozdat' na svoei territorii dve osobyi ekonomich-eskie zony," Novyi Kompan'on, October 4, 2005.

[50] See Human Rights Watch briefing paper, "Managing Civil Society: Are NGOs Next?" November 22, 2005, and sources cited on p. 14.

[51] "Putin, Courts' Chairmen Discuss Reform in Judicial System," ITAR-TASS, November 9, 2005.

[52] Presentation by William Butler at American University, October 17, 2005.

[53] Neil Buckley, "Justice Is a Matter of Conviction for Russian Judges," Financial Times, October 22, 2005.

[54] Program "Vesti," "Russia" TV Channel, December 9, 2005.

[55] Peter Finn, "In Russia, Trying Times for Trial by Jury," Washington Post, October 31, 2005.

[56] Guy Chazan, "Russia's Courts Go on Trial," Wall Street Journal, May 23, 2005.

[57] Anna Politkovskaya, "Svidetelyam obeshchayut pokazat'," Novaya Gazeta, November 30-December 12, 2005, p. 4.

[58] "Ugolovno-ispolnitel'naya cicstem Rossii po sostaoyaniyu na 1 iyulya 2005 goda," Nevolya, no. 5, 2005, p. 26.

[59] "Putin Changes Authority over Prisons,"Associated Press, July 13, 2005.

[60] INDEM, "Vo skol'ko raz uvelichilas' korruptsii za 4 goda," www.indem.ru/russian.asp, survey results published July 20, 2005; United Financial Group, "Russian Corruption: Increasing, but Maturing," August 11, 2005.

[61] ww1.transparency.org/cpi/2005/cpi2005_infocus.html.

[62] Vasili Kashin and Svetlana Ivanova, "Russia's Kickback," Vedomosti, November 16, 2005.

[63] INDEM, "Vo skol'ko raz uvelichilas' korruptsii za 4 goda," www.indem.ru/russian.asp, survey

results published July 20, 2005; United Financial Group, "Russian Corruption: Increasing, but Maturing," August 11, 2005.

[64] Levada Center, "Professii: prestizhnye, dokhodnye opasnye, kriminal'nye," August 9, 2005, www.levada.ru/press/2005080901.html.

[65] Harley Balzer, "Vladimir Putin on Russian Energy Policy," National Interest, November 2005, www.inthenationalinterest.com/Articles/November2005/November2005Balzer.html.

[66] "Putin's Russia Plagued by Rising Corruption," AP, October 2, 2005.

[67] Oksana Avshina amd Petr Orekhin, "The Great Oil Nationalization," Nezavisimaya Gazeta, July 11, 2005; "Russia's Gas Giant Buys Sibneft," The Economist, September 29, 2005, www.economist.com/agenda/displaystory.cfm?story_id=4465897; and Arkady Ostrovsky, "The New Oligarchs?: Winners and Losers in the Kremlin's Grab for Oil Wealth," Financial Times, November 7, 2005.

[68] Aleksandra Samaraina, "Valery Tishkov: My poluchaem otvetnyi udar," Nezavisimaya Gazeta, November 9, 2005; and Igor Torbakov, "War on Terrorism in the Caucasus: Russia Breeds Jihadists," Chechnya Weekly, November 10, 2005.

[69] "Government Raises Bureaucrats' Salaries," Renaissance Capital, September 16, 2005, drawing on a report in Vedomosti.

[70] Konstantin Frunkin, "Government Determined to Pursue Administrative Reform," Izvestiya, November 2, 2005.

[71] www.unodc.org/unodc/crime_signatures_corruption.html.

Serbia and Montenegro

with a section on Kosovo

Capital: Belgrade
Population: 8.10 million (includes Kosovo until 1999)
GNI/capita: $2,680 (excludes Kosovo)
Ethnic Groups: Serb (63%), Albanian (17%), Montenegrin (5%), Hungarian (3%), other (13%)

Nations in Transit Ratings and Averaged Scores

	Serbia			Montenegro			Kosovo		
	2004	2005	2006	2004	2005	2006	2004	2005	2006
Electoral Process	3.50	3.25	3.25	3.50	3.25	3.50	5.25	4.75	4.75
Civil Society	2.75	2.75	2.75	2.75	2.50	3.00	4.25	4.00	4.25
Independent Media	3.50	3.25	3.25	3.25	3.25	3.25	5.50	5.50	5.50
Governance *	4.00	n/a	n/a	4.00	n/a	n/a	6.00	n/a	n/a
National Democratic Governance	n/a	4.00	4.00	n/a	4.50	4.50	n/a	5.75	5.75
Local Democratic Governance	n/a	3.75	3.75	n/a	3.50	3.50	n/a	5.50	5.50
Judicial Framework and Independence	4.25	4.25	4.25	4.25	4.25	4.25	6.00	5.75	5.75
Corruption	5.00	5.00	4.75	5.25	5.25	5.25	6.00	6.00	6.00
Democracy Score	3.83	3.75	3.71	3.83	3.79	3.89	5.50	5.32	5.36

* With the 2005 edition, Freedom House introduced seperate analysis and ratings for national democratic governance and local democratic governance to provide readers with more detailed and nuanced analysis of these two important subjects.

In *Nations in Transit 2006*, Freedom House provides separate ratings for Serbia, Montenegro, and Kosovo in order to provide a clearer picture of processes and conditions in the three different administrative areas. Doing so does not indicate a position on the part of Freedom House regarding the territorial integrity of the State Union of Serbia and Montenegro; neither does it indicate a position on Kosovo's future status. As this edition goes to print, the population of Montenegro voted in a referendum in support of independence from the State Union of Serbia and Montenegro; international authorities accepted the referendum results as legitimate and binding. Negotiations will take place over the course of 2006 for the separation of Serbia and Montenegro into independent states. The decision to keep Serbia and Montenegro together in this edition was based on country status as of the end of 2005, the year in study.

The economic and social data on this page were taken from the following sources:
GNI/capita, Population: *World Development Indicators 2006* (Washington, D.C.: World Bank, 2006).
Ethnic Groups: *CIA World Factbook 2006* (Washington, D.C.: Central Intelligence Agency, 2006).

Yugoslavia

	1997	1998	1999	2001	2002	2003
Electoral Process	n/a	5.00	5.50	4.75	3.75	3.75
Civil Society	n/a	5.00	5.25	4.00	3.00	2.75
Independent Media	n/a	4.50	5.75	4.50	3.50	3.25
Governance	n/a	5.00	5.50	5.25	4.25	4.25
Constitutional, Legislative, & Judicial Framework	n/a	5.00	5.75	5.50	4.25	4.25
Corruption	n/a	n/a	6.25	6.25	5.25	5.00

NOTE: The ratings reflect the consensus of Freedom House, its academic advisers, and the author of this report. The opinions expressed in this report are those of the author. The ratings are based on a scale of 1 to 7, with 1 representing the highest level of democratic progress and 7 the lowest. The Democracy Score is an average of ratings for the categories tracked in a given year.

Serbia

EXECUTIVE SUMMARY

Serbia's democratic transformation began much later than that of most other post-Communist countries, with the fall of the Slobodan Milosevic regime in October 2000. Democratization slowly resulted from elections won by the opposition and massive protests that forced the regime to accept the results. It was also a negotiated transition, with some members of the old regime supporting the opposition for the price of political protection. The legacy of the populist and nationalist Milosevic regime left deep ruts that continue to block transformation. The status of Kosovo, formally a province of Serbia but under international administration since 1999, allows nationalist mobilization and distracts from democratic reforms. The State Union, established by Serbia and Montenegro in 2003 under European Union (EU) mediation, succeeded the Federal Republic of Yugoslavia, which had de facto ceased to function. The State Union is also dysfunctional as a result of the different policy priorities of the two member states and strong support for independence by the Montenegrin authorities. Serbia has transformed itself dramatically since 2000, but economic interest groups formerly associated with the Milosevic regime, an insufficiently reformed security sector, and a lack of broad reforms based on political consensus continue to present obstacles to the state's democratic consolidation.

In 2005, against most expectations, the minority government of Vojislav Kostunica held on to power. While relying on the support of the Socialist Party of Serbia, still formally led by Slobodan Milosevic, the government has been able to push a series of reformist laws through the Parliament. Concessions to the Socialist Party appear mostly to protect party members from criminal prosecution. Probably the most significant development in 2005 was the "voluntary" surrender of more than a dozen indicted war criminals to the International Criminal Tribunal for the Former Yugoslavia (ICTY). These negotiated actions were problematic, as the government treated the indicted as heroes, yet they constitute great progress in bringing indicted war criminals to court. In an important step toward EU integration, the European Commission invited Serbia and Montenegro to begin negotiations for a Stabilization and Association Agreement in October 2005, following a positive feasibility study issued earlier in 2005.

National Democratic Governance. Serbia's constitutional environment remains problematic, with the dysfunctional State Union – whose charter is frequently broken by both member states and the authoritarian Serbian Constitution of 1990 – still in effect without any clear prospect for change.

Few State Union institutions work effectively. The Parliament met only for ten sessions on altogether seven days in 2005, with sessions of the Council of Ministers similarly rare and the Court of Serbia and Montenegro, operating after a two-year delay, working with administrative support out of Belgrade rather than Podgorica as originally planned. The army lacks effective parliamentary oversight. In Serbia, the government has been weak and forced to negotiate laws with the Socialist Party of Serbia. The cohabitation of President Boris Tadic of the Democratic Party and Vojislav Kostunica of the Democratic Party of Serbia has also been difficult owing to a lack of previous cohabitation experience in Serbia and burdened relations between the parties. The Radical Party remains the strongest party according to opinion polls. As the constitutional charter remains largely a legal fiction and no new Serbian Constitution has been passed, no improvement is detectable. The Radical Party, which has strong populist, nationalist, and authoritarian traits, continues to be strong and shows no substantial signs of moderating. *Thus, the rating remains at 4.00.*

Electoral Process. No major national elections were held in 2005. Elections for the State Union Parliament planned for March 2005 were postponed owing to Montenegro's opposition and will only be held in conjunction with the next parliamentary elections in either Serbia or Montenegro, if at all. The legitimacy of the government and the Parliament in Serbia has been seriously undermined by a number of members of Parliament (MPs) switching political parties. The current legislation prevents parties from expelling these MPs from the Parliament but opens the door to parties "buying" MPs or MPs blackmailing their party. *Owing to the attempts by parties to increase their number of deputies in the Parliament through potentially dubious means and the overall lack of progress to amend the constitutional charter and other framework for electoral process, Serbia's rating remains at 3.25.*

Civil Society. In 2005, the government proposed new legislation to regulate the work of nongovernmental organizations (NGOs). Although the law has some problems, it is considerably less restrictive than existing laws from the Socialist period. The introduction of the value-added tax (VAT), on the other hand, constitutes a financial burden on many NGOs, as only humanitarian aid is exempt. Relations between the government and NGOs have not improved significantly, although some ministries have been more willing to consider NGO advice. Some government members, MPs, and the head of the intelligence agency have attacked NGOs for their work and their supposed threat to national interest. Furthermore, sensationalist media and nationalist groups frequently attack NGOs. Government, media, and society remain hostile to civil society, which came under heavy attack in 2005. The initiative to amend NGO legislation constitutes a positive step. The law was not passed by year's end, but results may be seen in 2006. *Therefore, Serbia's rating for civil society remains at 2.75.*

Independent Media. After years of a chaotic media sector, the government made more serious attempts to regulate electronic media in 2005. These include initiating the privatization (to be completed by 2007) of local and national media other than the public broadcaster, preparing the licensing of statewide private TV and radio (due in 2006), and the first steps toward transforming state-run Radio Television Serbia into a public broadcaster. These measures are tentative, and criticism over the composition of the main supervisory organ, the Broadcasting Council, remains strong. Another key reform passed in 2005 was the decriminalization of slander in the new criminal code. At the same time, hate speech is not prosecuted, despite existing laws and daily occurrences in the nationalist and sensationalist media. Although many institutions continue to withhold information and do not live up to their legal obligations under the Law on Freedom of Information, requests submitted from citizens and responses from institutions about monitoring the law may mark the beginning of a phase of improved implementation. *Serbia's independent media rating remains at 3.25, because even though the law decriminalizing slander was passed, a real change in policy remains to be seen, the beginning of reforms in the electronic media sector is tentative, and the response to last year's promising Law on Freedom of Information has been slow.*

Local Democratic Governance. In 2005, the weakness of the 2002 Law on Local Government became visible with the power struggle between municipal presidents and municipal assemblies in numerous municipalities, both elected democratically in 2004. The ensuing stalemate has led to paralysis in many municipalities, referendums on recalling mayors, and new municipal elections. Furthermore, Prime Minister Kostunica has rejected any additional steps toward decentralization prior to the enactment of a new Constitution. *The lack of progress in fiscal decentralization and the deadlock in municipalities following the 2004 elections maintain Serbia's rating for local democratic governance at 3.75.*

Judicial Framework and Independence. The EU feasibility study from April 2005 called the judiciary the main weakness in Serbia's transformation. Despite some legal reforms, including the legal framework for witness protection and a new criminal code, the appointment of judges and prosecutors remains susceptible to political pressure, and corruption is ever present. However, positive steps from 2005 included the national courts' increased cooperation with the ICTY by surrendering 16 indicted war criminals and rendering guilty verdicts in war crimes cases. Furthermore, trials concerning the assassination of former Serbian president Ivan Stambolic and the attempt on the life of Vuk Draskovic, former opposition leader and current minister of foreign affairs were concluded with guilty verdicts in 2005, suggesting that special courts are generally able to try such serious crimes. Nevertheless, the ICTY repeatedly noted the need for further cooperation regarding both the arrest of Ratko Mladic (former commander of the Bosnian Serb army and wanted for war crimes during the war in Bosnia-Herzegovina), and access to information for Serbia and Montenegro to fully cooperate with the tribunal. *Serbia's* *rating for judicial framework and independence remains at 4.25. Improved cooperation with the ICTY and domestic courts' handling of serious crimes indicate positive steps taken in 2005 that may yield results in 2006. The overall framework remains politicized and prone to corruption and misuse by organized crime.*

Corruption. Corruption remains a problem in Serbia, though 2005 brought some formal improvements through legislation, criminalizing some instances of corruption in the new criminal code, and ratification of the UN Convention Against Corruption. Furthermore, the Parliament approved a strategy against corruption that will result in action plans and a new anticorruption institution. At the same time, however, the government has made no visible efforts to combat corruption. No cases from previous years have been cleared, nor have new corruption scandals resulted in high-visibility legal cases. In particular, the government continues to ignore the work and investigations of the Council for the Fight Against Corruption. *Despite the absence of substantial real-life changes, Serbia's corruption rating improves from 5.00 to 4.75 owing to improvements in the legal framework.*

Outlook for 2006. The State Union of Serbia and Montenegro is fragile and may dissolve in 2006 with Montenegro's referendum on independence, expected in May. The possible independence of Montenegro is unlikely to result in a political crisis in Serbia. However, it will involve the government and ministries in negotiating the terms of the dissolution of the State Union and the restructuring of state institutions, in particular the army and the Ministry of Foreign Affairs. The advanced human rights protection afforded by the State Union's constitutional charter would have to be replaced by adequate protection in Serbia itself.

The other main territorial issue that will dominate 2006 is the status of Kosovo. The final status will be unlikely to resemble the demands of the Serbian authorities, which offered "less than independence and more than autonomy" and categorically excluded the option of independence. Consequently, there is a serious risk of setback for reforms in Serbia. Most citizens prefer that Kosovo remain part of Serbia or the State Union, but there is widespread recognition that such an outcome might be unattainable.

Although the government lacks a minority and the governing parties have seen their popularity shrink, the opposition Serb Radical Party and the Democratic Party are unlikely to seek early elections as long as Kosovo's status remains unresolved. The status question and the question of a new Constitution, a perennial debate since 2000, are likely to overshadow other reform efforts. Significant developments can be expected in media restructuring and reform laws. Serbia (and/or Montenegro) seeks to conclude negotiations for a Stabilization and Association Agreement in 2006 to move closer toward EU integration. However, the rapid conclusion of these negotiations is partially contingent on the status of the State Union.

The growing pressure of the EU and other international organizations to arrest Ratko Mladic, together with Radovan Karadzic, the highest-ranking indicted war criminals still at large, will impact other reform efforts. In particular, continued negotiations on the Stabilization and Association Agreement are dependent on the arrest of Mladic. Domestically, the arrest is unlikely to destabilize the government or result in mass mobilization against democratic reforms.

MAIN REPORT

National Democratic Governance

2004	2005	2006
n/a	4.00	4.00

During 2005, there was little movement toward constitutional reform. The State Union of Serbia and Montenegro remained highly dysfunctional, while the outdated 1990 Serbian Constitution stayed in place. As Montenegrin authorities have shown little interest in the joint state, and Serbian authorities have made few efforts to accommodate Montenegrin interests, the State Union has not operated effectively since its establishment in 2003, and both member states have repeatedly broken the constitutional charter.

The constitutional charter, ratified in 2003, establishes weak institutions, with most competences concentrated on external relations. The State Union has a one-chamber Parliament composed of 126 deputies (91 from Serbia, 35 from Montenegro) elected indirectly by each state's Parliament. The State Union president is elected by the Parliament. The president, in turn, heads the five-member Council of Ministers, which consists of the ministers of foreign affairs, defense, and human and minority rights (all from Serbia) and the ministers of external economic relations and domestic economic relations (both from Montenegro).

The most important State Union institution, the army, remains beyond serious parliamentary control owing to the weakness of the State Union Parliament. The Ministry of Foreign Affairs has been somewhat more functional, even though ambassadors from Montenegro and Serbia have pursued diametrically opposed policies: Ambassadors from Montenegro frequently advocate the dissolution of the State Union, whereas ambassadors from Serbia have made Serbia's policy on Kosovo a priority and generally do not consider Montenegrin interests. The State Union Parliament met only 10 times in 2005, and the Serbian Parliament and its Committee for Defense and Security are not competent to oversee the work of the army. Army reforms progressed slowly in 2005, including the closure of military courts, with cases transferred to civil courts on January 1, 2005.[1]

Serbia's Constitution, adopted in 1990 under Slobodan Milosevic, establishes a semipresidential system with a directly elected president. The president is the supreme commander of the Serbian armed forces (which currently do not exist), has the right to dismiss the Parliament, enjoys various foreign policy prerogatives, and can be dismissed only by a referendum. The government is appointed by the 250-member unicameral Parliament. Because the president and the Parliament are not elected simultaneously, the odds of cohabitation are great. Although all major parties agree on the need for a new Constitution, changing it requires a two-thirds parliamentary majority and a subsequent referendum. Two draft Constitutions have been proposed by the government and president, yet neither departs fundamentally from the 1990 Constitution, and the process is currently stalled.

The Serbian government came to power following parliamentary elections in December 2003. It lacks an outright majority and relies on support from the Socialist Party of Serbia (SPS), formally (because he could not effectively govern the party from prison) headed by Slobodan Milosevic. The government is led by the conservative Democratic Party of Serbia (DSS) of Prime Minister Vojislav Kostunica and includes the small, liberal, market-oriented G17+ party of Deputy Prime Minister Miroljub Labus, the conservative Serbian Renewal Movement (SPO) of Foreign Minister Vuk Draskovic, and the conservative party New Serbia (NS). The division of the SPO into two competing groups has weakened the government, and the public approval rating for all government parties combined is less than 20 percent. Furthermore, the small Social Democratic Party (SDP), with three seats in the Parliament, left the government following its refusal to support a plan on the privatization of the state oil company in August 2005. The parliamentary majority of the government was secured by support from two Bosniak minority MPs from the Coalition for Sandzak.

The tendency of MPs to switch party allegiances has weakened the Parliament, adding to the instability of the political system. Between December 2003 and November 2005, 30 MPs left either their party or parliamentary group. Allegations suggest that bribes motivated some changes. In particular, the extra-parliamentary Movement Force of Serbia (PSS), led by the controversial tycoon Bogoljub Karic, has been accused of seeking access to the Parliament through such means.[2]

Although close governmental support enhanced the role of the Parliament and allowed MPs to have more impact on legislation, the level of parliamentary work in terms of both legislation and control of the executive has been poor. In particular, parliamentary oversight of the Security Information Agency (BIA) remains insufficient and problematic. The predecessor of BIA, the State Security (DB), was used by the Milosevic regime to control and murder political opponents and support the wars in Croatia, Bosnia, and Kosovo. Despite a name change, there is little to indicate any serious reform and agency purging. In December 2005, the BIA was accused of wiretapping MPs to identify those involved in an "Albanian lobby" supporting independence for Kosovo, an allegation the BIA denied.[3] The director of the BIA similarly stated in July 2005 that the agency is monitoring the activities of some NGOs for their links abroad, a thinly veiled threat against human rights NGOs critical of the government.[4]

Elected president of Serbia in June 2004, Boris Tadic from the Democratic Party (DS) has oscillated between confrontation and cooperation with the government. Arguably, the cohabitation between president and government has put an effective check on the executive; at the same time, it has also made decision making more complicated and resulted in a lack of clarity in some key state policy areas, especially regarding Kosovo. Tadic supported the participation of Kosovo Serbs in Kosovo elections in late 2004, whereas Kostunica opposed it – other divergent views emerged with the beginning of status talks in late 2005.

The People's Bureau, established by the president in 2004, was intended as a stopgap for an ombudsman, but the institution lacked a legal mandate and has been a key tool in promoting the president. The bureau's director, Dragan Djilas, has strong business interests in media and public relations, which makes him controversial. In September 2005, the Parliament passed the Law on the Ombudsman, formalizing the duties of this intercessory office created for citizens to turn to when all legal recourse has been exhausted.[5] As of December 2005, no ombudsman had been named in Serbia; by contrast, Montenegro, Vojvodina, and Kosovo have had ombudsmen for several years.

The Law on Freedom of Information, passed by the Parliament in November 2004, is another milestone toward increasing government transparency and accountability. The law was welcomed by key NGOs, but implementation has been slow, as many state institutions were not aware either of the law or of the information they were obliged to make available. The Youth Initiative for Human Rights tested the implementation of the law by submitting 530 requests between December 2004 and April 2005, out of which it received only 259 answers (48.86 percent).[6] In response, the Center for Free Elections and Democracy (CeSID), Transparency Serbia, and the Organization for Security and Cooperation in Europe (OSCE) have been conducting public awareness campaigns to encourage citizens and media to make use of the law.

Political and economic interests remain deeply intertwined with business tycoons, especially with respect to privatization and political parties interfering with the economy. The privatization of the state oil company and the sale of the National Savings Bank to the Greek Eurobank suggest continued influence of wealthy businessmen on political reforms.

Currently, the status of Kosovo poses a particular threat to Serbia, as the Serb Radical Party (SRS) has threatened "mayhem in the streets" and suggested that Kosovo be "occupied" if it should become independent. Additionally, small groups of skinheads and extremists have threatened violence and attacked minorities and political enemies. After a number of unresolved incidents against minorities in Vojvodina in 2004, stronger police enforcement and prosecution resulted in a sharp drop since late 2004.

Electoral Process

2004	2005	2006
3.50	3.25	3.25

Deep divisions among the reform-oriented parties and the continued strength of the extreme nationalist SRS continue to mar the Serbian party system. Currently, the state is governed by a coalition of the DSS, SPO, NS, and G17+, with strong opposition from the DS and the SRS. The DS and the governing parties share the goal of democratic reform and European integration but vary on the pace and degree. The strongest party in the Parliament and according to all opinion polls, however, remains the SRS, which is rhetorically committed to democracy but displays authoritarian traits and has subordinated European integration to extreme nationalism and social populism. The PSS similarly thrives on social populism while clearly pursuing the economic interests of its founder, business tycoon Bogoljub Karic.

In terms of support, surveys in 2005 indicate two strong parties, the DS and the SRS, each commanding a quarter to a third of voters, with the governing parties and the PSS together receiving the remaining support. This division indicates a slim majority for democratically oriented parties. Combined with repeated conflicts between Kostunica and President Tadic (although less than between the DS and the DSS earlier), these conditions make a broad coalition of democratic parties difficult to achieve and block the stabilization of the party system. In late 2005, the liberal democratic faction of the DS officially left the party and formed the Liberal Democratic Party (LDP) under the leadership of Cedomir Jovanovic, a former deputy prime minister and deputy president of the DS. The party has a strong pro-European orientation and supports a clear break with the past, but owing to its radical, reformist position, it is unlikely to enjoy broad support.

With the election of Boris Tadic in June 2004, all key offices in Serbia were filled with democratically elected officials. After a decade of massive electoral fraud, heavy-handed intervention against political opponents, and limited freedom of the media during the 1990s, elections since 2000 have been free and fair, with few (if any) irregularities. Serbia has faced frequent elections since 2000, including six ballots for the Serbian president from 2002 to 2004 alone – the first four attempts failed because of low turnout. After a string of national elections, the only polls in 2005 were municipal elections.

The key event in terms of electoral process was an election that did not take place. The mandate of indirectly elected deputies to the State Union was to expire in March 2005, two years after the creation of the State Union, paving the way for direct elections. The Montenegrin government's refusal to enact a law on electing MPs to the State Union Parliament made such elections impossible and led to negotiations between Serbia and Montenegro, mediated by the EU, on amending the constitutional charter. As a compromise, the constitutional charter was amended in June 2005 to extend the mandate of the current deputies.[7]

Another key discussion involved changing the electoral law to prevent MPs from leaving the parties on whose lists they were elected. Nearly every parliamentary group, except for the DSS and the SPS, has lost MPs since the December 2003 elections. According to a 2003 Constitutional Court decision, the mandate belongs to the MP, not to his or her party, but the matter is still being argued in the courts. These major shifts of party allegiance continue to throw the legitimacy of the current Parliament into question and raise suspicions over bribes paid to some MPs for their allegiance.[8] Considering the narrow basis of support for the minority government in the first place, this party hopping constitutes a serious threat to government stability.

Although the State Union Charter on Human and Minority Rights and Civil Liberties grants minorities the right "to a certain number of seats in the Assembly of Member States and in the Assembly of the State Union," there are no MPs from national minorities in the State Union Parliament and only a few, elected on general party lists, in the Serbian Parliament. To remedy this serious underrepresentation, the Parliament amended the election legislation in February 2004, eliminating the 5 percent threshold. Nevertheless, owing to the small size of these communities, most parties of minorities (except Hungarians and Bosniaks) will not be represented in the Parliament.

Civil Society

2004	2005	2006
2.75	2.75	2.75

The number of active NGOs in Serbia is not officially documented, but between 1991 and 2005, 8,476 legal entities and citizens' associations were registered. The Center for the Development of the Nonprofit Sector Directory of NGOs lists 2,278 NGOs in Serbia and Montenegro.[9] According to a study by the NGO Civic Initiatives, around 1,000 NGOs were active in Serbia in December 2004. Most NGOs are located in Belgrade (30 percent of all NGOs in Serbia and Montenegro). In a survey by Civic Initiatives of 516 NGOs, 23.6 percent were active in the areas of culture, education, and the environment; 17.8 percent are involved in social and humanitarian work; 15.9 percent focus on youth or the economy or are professional associations; 14.7 percent work on developing civil society; and the largest share of NGOs, 27.9 percent, deal with human rights.[10]

After years of delay, the Ministry for Public Administration and Local Self-Government presented a draft Law on Associations in November 2005. This step to improve the legal and social standing of civil society has been welcomed by international organizations and NGOs in Serbia.[11] The draft law advances the existing legal framework, and associations would no longer be required to register. Furthermore, the new law would lower the number of required founders from 10 to 3 (with only 1 required to reside in Serbia). The draft law would also regulate the registration of foreign-based associations in Serbia, which formerly required notification of the Ministry of Foreign Affairs of the State Union.[12] The Helsinki Committee for Human Rights in Serbia has criticized the draft law as being too vague and overregulating and containing problematic regulations regarding property.[13]

Currently, NGOs can be registered either at the Serbia level or by the State Union, leading to both an inadequate and confusing legal situation for NGOs. Both the Law on Civic Associations of the Socialist Federal Republic of Yugoslavia and the Law on Social and Civic Associations date from the Socialist period.

The ability of NGOs to engage in economic activity for self-support is severely restricted. The Serbian Law on Income Tax (2001) does not provide tax exemptions for individual grants to NGOs. The Serbian Law on Corporate Tax (2001) allows corporations to deduct up to 3.5 percent of income for "medical, educational, scientific, humanitarian, religious, environmental protection, and sports purposes." Corporations in Serbia may deduct 1.5 percent for cultural purposes only. Foreign donors are exempt from paying VAT on humanitarian goods, but NGOs must pay the tax except on services they might provide.[14]

NGOs, especially those active in the field of human rights and reconciliation, continue to be the target of nationalist and extremist political parties and movements. Furthermore, the government and parliamentarians have attacked NGOs. The head of the intelligence agency BIA, Rade Bulatovic, declared that the agency was monitoring the work of NGOs.[15] The conservative orientation of the government has thus cooled relations with NGOs since 2003. NGO advocacy efforts have been limited, although the adoption of the Law on Freedom of Information can be seen as one of their successes. Altogether, however, NGOs have been weak in clearly formulating policies, and think tanks remain ineffective.

Most NGOs continue to view the civil society climate in Serbia as unfavorable, although there has been an increase of contacts with both government, in particular local government, and business. According to the Civic Initiatives survey, businesses have had contact with some 61 percent of NGOs, primarily as donors. Still, most NGOs find themselves in a precarious financial situation. The average NGO budget was €56,000 (US$70,000) in 2004, but nearly half of all NGOs have a budget of less than €5,000, meaning there are a few large NGOs that financially dominate civil society.

Foreign donors continue to be the largest single source of support, accounting for 47 percent of all funds, while governments account for 14 percent and businesses 9 percent. Although this constitutes a slight upturn in domestic funding since 2002, the shift is marginal and indicates the continued importance of foreign donations.[16]

Skinhead groups and other radical organizations continue to be active in Serbia, including events denying war crimes, such as the public discussion at the Faculty of Law of the University of Belgrade in May 2005 entitled "The Truth About Srebrenica." More frequently, nationalist media and extremist groups threatened or attacked human rights NGOs and independent media. Sonja

Biserko, head of the Helsinki Committee for Human Rights in Serbia, has been accused of spying and being an enemy to the Serb people; the tabloids, which spearheaded the accusations, subsequently published her private residential mailing address.[17] The police and judicial response has been muted. In November 2005, the neo-Nazi group National Machine attacked participants at a public debate on the Fascist threat in Novi Sad. For the first time, such an incident triggered a strong state response, with police arresting members of the group and authorities publishing a list of neo-Nazi and Fascist groups, paving the way for more effective prosecution of hate speech and crimes.[18]

As in other transition countries, the role of trade unions has been weak. Only a third of all employees are members of a trade union, according to a CeSID suvey. In general, trade unions have a disproportionate number of older members and tend to have more workers from the state sector than average.[19] The two largest trade unions are the Confederation of Autonomous Trade Unions (SSSS; 850,000 members) and Nezavisnost (Independence; 180,000 members), together incorporating some 80 percent of organized labor. Nezavisnost and the smaller Association of Free and Independent Trade Unions (ASNS) split during the 1990s from the SSSS, which was controlled by the Milosevic regime. The SSSS still enjoys more support from conservative and nationalist party members, while the ASNS is more closely affiliated with reformist parties.

Both trade unions often disagree on strategy and view each other with suspicion, weakening their effectiveness. Government has played on this weakness to further strengthen the ASNS at the expense of the other unions.[20] Although the Kostunica government made a greater commitment to job protection than the Djindjic government, relations with trade unions have worsened since the government took office. The head of Nezavisnost, Branislav Canak, has accused Kostunica of breaking previous agreements.

The significance of trade unions has been decreasing owing to fragmentation and a lack of organized labor in the growing private sector. The main body of tripartite dialogue, the Social-Economic Council, established in 2001, remains dysfunctional.[21] Furthermore, trade unions continue to rely on government intervention or dialogue rather than engaging directly with companies. As a result, trade union concerns are often excessively politicized.[22]

Reforms continue in the education system, although at a slower pace than in the initial post-Milosevic years. In 2004, Ljiljana Colic, the first minister of education of the Kostunica government, was forced to resign after proposing restricted use of Darwin's theory of evolution, English as a foreign language, and computers. The new minister, Slobodan Vuksanovic, has been less erratic and resumed the reform agenda. The Law on Higher Education was adopted on August 2005, but higher education lags significantly behind European standards, according to a 2005 survey for European ministers of education concerned with the implementation of the Bologna Process.[23] Political influence remains strong, in particular in the highly politicized University of Pristina with its seat in the northern Kosovo town of Mitrovica.

Independent Media

2004	2005	2006
3.50	3.25	3.25

Serbian media are underregulated, and the number of outlets far exceeds commercial viability. In addition to numerous statewide newspapers, magazines, and TV stations, there are hundreds of local electronic and print media, often controlled by local governments. As a recent report by the Open Society Institute details, electronic outlets dominate the Serbian media scene, which has one of the lowest rates of daily newspapers sold per capita in Europe (less than 1 percent).[24] The legacy of government control and intervention remains strong, despite a decline.

Local media independence remains precarious. Controlled by local government, many media underwent purges following the local elections in October 2004. In particular, some municipal administrations controlled by the SRS removed critical journalists from their jobs in local media. Some journalists also faced threats and physical attacks. Independent media, such as the TV and radio station B92, have received bomb threats and graffiti. Local media have also been attacked for critical reporting on local politicians or their supporters. For example, in the city of Vranje, members of the municipal council have repeatedly attacked independent media.[25]

Government members also threaten and demean media. In particular, the minister for capital investments, Velimir Ilic, has repeatedly harassed B92. In one instance, he called journalists mentally ill, and his spokesperson threatened to kill the director of B92. This was not an isolated incident but rather part of a long string of abuse by Ilic toward the media. Furthermore, despite criticism from international and local NGOs and organizations, the government has either not responded or done so in a muted manner.

Sensationalist tabloids continue to dominate print media in Serbia. This style draws on nationalist resentments. Tabloids report "scandals" without serious evidence, generally to the discredit of the political system. In 2005, the largest tabloid was *Vecernje Novosti* (270,000 copies),[26] followed by *Kurir* (225,000 copies). Smaller tabloids, such as *Srpski Nacional* and *Start*, are often more radical and short-lived. More moderate tabloids include *Blic* (165,000 copies) and *Glas Javnosti* (18,000 copies). The main, quality dailies command a considerably lower print run. The largest, *Politika* (150,000 copies), which is partially owned by the German WAZ group, is followed by the liberal *Danas* (20,000 copies) and the regional daily from Vojvodina, *Dnevnik* (20,000 copies). The main weeklies include the political magazines *Vreme* (liberal) and *NIN* (conservative) and a number of more sensationalist publications, such as *Nedeljni Telegraf* or *Evropa*.

In addition to commercial interests, sensationalist media have been accused of close links to organized crime, war criminals, and the secret service. During the 2003 state of emergency, the weekly *Identitet* and daily *Nacional* (precursor to *Srpski Nacional*) were shut down – the former because of links to organized crime and the latter for breaking state of emergency regulations.

An ongoing controversy has surrounded the transformation of the state television part of Radio Television Serbia (RTS), and state radio into public broadcasting outlets and the regulation of electronic media, which have been operating without a clear legal framework. The 2002 Law on Broadcasting and its implementation are criticized by the independent media. The law establishes an agency for broadcasting, headed by an alleged politically independent Broadcasting Council. An amendment to the law, criticized by Independent Journalists' Association of Serbia (IJAS), the Association of Independent Electronic Media (ANEM), and opposition parties in the Parliament, extended the deadline for privatization of state-run media until late 2007 and introduced new terms for the members of the Broadcasting Council, already criticized for being too susceptible to political pressure. The OSCE also commented on the lack of consultation with stakeholders and the absence of a clear term of service for Broadcasting Council members.[27]

The agency is responsible for the transformation of state television into a public broadcaster, the privatization of local state-owned media, and the allocation of frequencies to private broadcasters. A draft strategy adopted by the council foresees licensing five nationwide private TV and radio broadcasters by tender in 2006.[28] It is anticipated that B92, BKTV, and Pink will be among them. These three stations are the most successful in Serbia, with B92 renowned for its opposition to the Milosevic regime. Although more commercial in recent years, it continues to advocate for a reckoning with the past and other unpopular topics. BKTV is owned by business tycoon and politician Bogoljub Karic, who aggressively promotes himself in the television news. In December 2005, Karic announced the impending sale of the station to avoid a conflict of interest. Whether such a move will result in less biased reporting remains to be seen. Pink is owned by another controversial businessman, Zeljko Mitrovic. Both Mitrovic and Karic have been close to the Milosevic regime and family and were able to establish their stations because of their ties to the regime. Pink has subsequently shifted its support to the DS and successfully expanded to Montenegro and Bosnia-Herzegovina.

The draft Law on Broadcasting introduces monthly subscription fees for all households in Serbia in order to transform the RTS into a financially independent public broadcaster. The mandatory monthly fee of 300 dinar (about US$5), which began in late 2005, has been widely criticized and has led to doubts that the RTS will become genuinely independent. The current director of the RTS, Aleksandar Tijanic, has professionalized the station but has been severely criticized by NGOs for his links to the ruling DSS, his political past (including a brief post as minister for information under Milosevic), and his verbal attacks on independent media.

The Broadcasting Council, in addition to licensing and public broadcasting, began the delayed process of privatizing state-owned media other than the public broadcaster. According to the original law, this should have been completed in 2005, but it was not. As of October 2005, the state still owned 150 media, including 14 print media, 23 mixed print and electronic media, and 100 electronic media, most of them local.[29] Although local media privatization is widely called for by international organizations, there is an already demonstrated risk that private owners will cancel noncommercially viable, minority-language programming.[30] In Vojvodina, the assembly transferred ownership of minority-language media to the minority national councils, which raises concerns about the capacity of councils to manage media and the dominance of political parties that threatens minority council independence.

Although Serbian statutes, including the 2003 Law on Public Information, prohibit hate speech, such breaches are not prosecuted. Furthermore, there have been no court rulings penalizing the media for hate speech, despite frequent occurrences. During the debates on a new draft criminal code, NGOs, international organizations, and media associations criticized plans to keep libel and defamation a criminal offense, with suspended prison sentences of up to six months and high fines. The final version of the new criminal code, passed in September 2005, decriminalized libel. Thus, by January 1, 2006, libel and emotional distress will be punishable only by financial penalties or jail sentences of up to six months. According to the Independent Journalists Association, some 300 journalists face charges for libel or emotional distress; in many cases, these journalists are associated with liberal and independent media rather than tabloids. Many cases either date back to the Milosevic era or are based on reports linking public figures to the Milosevic regime. In one case, a local journalist received a one-year suspended prison sentence for reporting about links between a businessman and the Milosevic family.[31]

The importance of the Internet is increasing steadily. By late 2005, Serbia had 1 million Internet users, reaching 13.3 percent of the population (minus Kosovo). According to a 2005 survey by Telekom Srbija and CESID, around 300,000 citizens spent at least one hour on the Internet daily.[32] The legal framework does not restrict the use of the Internet, but the new criminal code introduces cybercrime as a category. The Internet has become more accessible through new technologies (cable, ADSL) and falling prices. Formally, the monopoly of Telekom Srbija, the state-run telecommunications company, was ended in 2005, but no alternative companies have yet emerged.

Local Democratic Governance

2004	2005	2006
n/a	3.75	3.75

As a legacy of the Milosevic regime, Serbia continues to be a highly centralized state. Although the Kostunica government explicitly linked decentralization to passing a new Constitution, the current draft Constitution suggests no fundamental change in terms of decentralization.

The 2002 Law on Local Government enhanced the competences of the 165 municipalities (minus Kosovo), but in the absence of a new Constitution, the degree of local self-government remains constrained. As noted by the Council of Europe in October 2005, there have been recent measures to enhance the role of municipalities. Key questions concern the return of public land to municipal control and fiscal autonomy of municipalities regarding debts and local taxes.

In addition to municipalities, the law recognizes four cities, two of which – Belgrade and Nis – comprise different municipalities (17 for Belgrade, 5 for Nis). The 24 districts of Serbia (minus Kosovo) are administrative and do not have substantial competences or directly elected representative bodies. Vojvodina is a more significant unit of regional governance and enjoyed far-reaching autonomy before being dismantled by the Milosevic regime in the late 1980s. Some competences were returned to Vojvodina through the Law Establishing Particular Competencies of the Autonomous Province, known generally as the omnibus law, passed by the Serbian Parliament in 2002. Vojvodina thus conducts its own affairs in the areas of education and culture, which is particularly important considering the number of minorities living in the province (more than a third of the population).

Although Vojvodina has its own assembly and executive, the province cannot raise its own taxes or pass laws. Minority and regionalist parties, as well as some governing parties (including the DS), have been arguing for greater autonomy in Vojvodina, especially concerning privatization and economic policy. The existing draft Constitutions do not substantially enhance the powers of the province. The new Law on Government passed in June 2005 is problematic, as it allows the government to suspend regulations and statutes passed by the authorities of Vojvodina or municipalities. The other pro forma province in Serbia is Kosovo, whose status remains undefined pending the conclusion of status negotiations.

In 2005, problems with the implementation of the 2002 Law on Local Government became apparent. The law foresees the direct election of both the newly created post of president of the municipality and the Municipal Assembly. The Municipal Assembly elects the Municipal Council, creating two often competing executives. Consequently, many municipalities have a form of local cohabitation, with a mayor from a different party from that of the municipal majority. This has paralyzed a number of municipalities and can be resolved only through a recall referendum and election of a new mayor. Alternatively, in the case of a local assembly failing to meet for three months, it can be dissolved by the Ministry for Public Administration and Local Self-Government.

Early local elections took place in the Vojvodina town of Kula in September 2005 owing to the lack of a municipal coalition following the 2004 local elections. Although this was not a particularly significant municipality and the elections were not representative of statewide trends, all major parties campaigned heavily, including, for the first time, the LDP. The latter narrowly failed to pass the threshold. The strongest parties were the SRS (31 percent, 13 seats), the DS (19 percent, 8 seats), the PSS (6 percent, 3 seats), and G17+ (6 percent, 3 seats), while the remaining four parties each gained 1 seat.[33]

The paralysis in many Serbian municipalities highlights not only the weakness of existing laws, but also polarization at the local level. These conflicts, however, do not necessarily mirror those at the national level. The SRS, the largest party following the 2004 local elections, has managed to form local coalitions and is thus in power in 63 municipalities. These include coalitions with G17+, the DS, and other moderate and reformist parties that have excluded any possibility for coalition cooperation with SRS at the national level.[34]

The Standing Conference of Towns and Municipalities in Serbia proposed a code of ethics for local officials, which had been accepted by 142 municipalities by October 2005. The code is based on the European Code of Conduct for elected local and regional representatives of the Council of Europe.[35]

Judicial Framework and Independence

2004	2005	2006
4.25	4.25	4.25

Serbia continues to have a weak, underfunded, and poorly trained judiciary, making it susceptible to political pressure and corruption. As the European Commission noted in its *Serbia and Montenegro 2005 Progress Report*, the appointment of the judiciary remains politicized, and it has little impact on its own resources, which are determined by the Ministry of Justice. Slow work resulting in backlogs, with some court cases taking more than 10 years, continues to be a serious problem.

After several years' delay, the Court of Serbia and Montenegro – the only State Union court – began operations in 2005. The court assesses whether member state legislation is in harmony with the Constitutional Charter of the State Union of Serbia and Montenegro. Originally planned in Podgorica, the court has provisionally operated in Belgrade with funding from Serbia and without much technical support. By November 2005, the court had resolved 350 out of the more than 1,000 cases inherited from its predecessors of the Federal Republic of Yugoslavia. The European Commission notes in its *Serbia and Montenegro 2005 Progress Report* that compliance with court rulings remains in doubt owing to the contested nature of the State Union.[36]

Serbia's judicial system consists of communal, county, and commercial courts, the Serbian Supreme Court, and the Serbian Constitutional Court. In an attempt to strengthen the independence of judges and courts, the 2001 judicial reform in Serbia established the High Council of the Judiciary, which proposes judges who are later confirmed by the Parliament. A 2002 amendment to the law, however, allows the parliamentary committee for the judiciary to propose candidates in case the Parliament does not agree with the council's choices. Essentially, this strips the council of power and politicizes appointments. The council itself remains strongly influenced by the Ministry of Justice and is often logistically unable to evaluate nominations put forth by lower courts.[37] A similar problem arises from the nomination of prosecutors, who are chosen for a limited time and cannot be reelected, making their professional position vulnerable and thus susceptible to political pressure.

Furthermore, the Office of the Prosecutor is organized hierarchically, based on subordination.[38]

The ministry prepared a National Strategy for Judiciary Reform in 2004, but the Council of Europe found this strategy not to be in line with international standards. Nevertheless, the strategy has been adopted, though it was not discussed in the Parliament or publicly.[39] In March 2005, the Ministry of Justice attempted to assign the power to propose and dismiss candidates for the position of court president to the Court Administration Council, a state-controlled body, but the Supreme Court declared the move unconstitutional. Another weakness of the current judicial system is the training system. The current system has partially changed through a series of amendments passed in July 2005.

An important reform law passed in 2005 has been the adoption of a witness protection plan, key for combating organized crime. Furthermore, the Parliament passed a new criminal code in September, reformed the outdated law, and recognized previously neglected crimes, such as war crimes and money laundering. In addition, a new Law on Police, passed in November 2005, reorganized the police force and introduced more democratic principles.[40] In terms of human rights statutes, the main problems arise from either their inadequate implementation or legal shortcomings. Although Serbia and Montenegro have committed to all key human rights instruments, the State Union still lacks comprehensive antidiscrimination legislation establishing procedures and penalties.

The State Union Charter on Human and Minority Rights and Civil Liberties and the 2002 federal Law on National Minorities protect minority rights at the general level. In practice, this legal framework has not been implemented effectively through regulations and detailed legislation. Minority rights, such as the use of minority languages, remain inadequately protected in central Serbia. The National Minority Councils, a form of minority self-government, received more budgetary support in 2005 but lacks the legal competences to effectively represent minority interests. The Republican Council of National Minorities, an ad hoc body established by the prime minister in 2004, brings together the National Minority Councils and relevant resource ministries but has had limited impact on advancing minority rights.

In 2004, a series of ethnically motivated incidents against minorities took place in Vojvodina, including graffiti, damage to churches, threats, and fights. Additionally, there were attacks against Albanians, Muslims, and Ashkali (Roma from Kosovo) following anti-Serb violence in Kosovo in March 2004. Originally, police and prosecutors were mostly passive, and the Serbian government failed to take the incident seriously. Following growing international pressure, especially from Hungary, the government and police took a more proactive approach in late 2004, leading to a sharp drop in incidents in 2005. Nevertheless, criminal prosecution of these incidents remains a problem. In July 2005, a court in Nis sentenced participants in the 2004 burning of a mosque with great leniency: One person received a five-month jail sentence, seven were sentenced to three months each, and two were freed. The Muslim community and several human rights NGOs criticized the sentences.[41]

Corruption remains a potent problem within the judiciary. According to a 2005 survey among lawyers by the Center for Liberal-Democratic Study, 39 percent believe that a majority of court employees are involved in corruption. Bribes are paid to delay court cases and to secure favorable outcomes. Such bribes were used particularly by organized crime to stop investigations or secure the release of members. In a high-profile case, a Supreme Court judge and a deputy special prosecutor were arrested for taking bribes from organized crime.

There is also evidence of the continued political abuse of courts and the judiciary. A case against Marko Milosevic, the son of Slobodan Milosevic, was dropped, and the Interpol arrest warrant for Slobodan Milosevic's wife, Mira Markovic, was temporarily suspended. The suspicious circumstances in both cases led commentators and NGOs to suggest that these developments involved political support from the SPS. In September 2005, Vladan Batic, former minister of justice and prominent critic of the government, was arrested for allegedly supporting the release of a member of a criminal group in 2003 but was released 48 hours later uncharged, suggesting the arrest was politically motivated.

The trial against the individuals charged with the murder of former prime minister Zoran Djindjic in 2003 continued in 2005. Two related trials – for the murder in 2000 of former Serbian president Ivan Stambolic and the 1999 assassination attempt on Vuk Draskovic – resulted in guilty verdicts in 2005, establishing the previous regime's clear legal responsibility for seeking to kill political opponents. The main suspect in the Djindic trial, Milorad Ulemek, was sentenced to 15 and 40 years, respectively, for his role in both plots, whereas Rade Markovic, former head of the DB under Milosevic, was sentenced to 10 and 15 years. In addition, a number of other officials from the Unit for Special Operations and the DB and the former head of Yugoslav customs were sentenced to prison terms. Despite these advances, there is a general unwillingness to fully confront the legacy of the Milosevic regime, indicated by the lack of implementation of the 2003 lustration legislation.

A long-standing obstacle to ensuring the rule of law in Serbia has been the lack of cooperation with the ICTY. Kostunica repeatedly noted his opposition to the ICTY and indicated that his government would not cooperate with the tribunal. Nevertheless, the Kostunica government has made more progress in 2005 toward cooperating with the tribunal than any previous government. The Kostunica government pursued the strategy of convincing indicted war criminals to "surrender voluntarily." For this purpose, the government provided funds for the family of the surrendering indicted and generally portrayed surrender as a "patriotic duty."

As one of the first of a series of surrenders, Vladimir Lazarevic, a former general accused of war crimes in Kosovo, was met by the prime minister and the patriarch of the Serbian Orthodox Church and received a car from the mayor of Nis. Altogether, some 16 indicted persons surrendered between October 2004 and late 2005. The circumstances of some surrenders calls into question their voluntary nature, suggesting government pressure on at-large war criminals. Nonetheless, the two most important indicted war criminals, Radovan Karadzic and Ratko Mladic – the latter believed to be hiding in Serbia – remain at large and continue to frustrate the situation, as does the reluctance of Serbian authorities to openly provide the tribunal with full documentation on war crimes cases.

In July 2005, four members of a paramilitary group were sentenced to 15 to 20 years in prison for the murder of 16 Muslims from Sandzak during the Bosnian war in 1992.[42] Another key domestic war crimes trial that was concluded in December 2005 concerned the murder of Croatian civilians killed in 1991 by Serb soldiers and paramilitaries on a farm close to the city of Vukovar. Eight soldiers received maximum sentences of 20 years each, six received lower jail terms of 5 to 15 years, and two were found not guilty. Human rights organizations welcomed the verdicts as a breakthrough in the domestic prosecution of war crimes. In October 2004, the ICTY transferred the first case to the special war crimes court in Serbia. However, in July 2005 the ICTY rejected moving a case against army officers Miroslav Radic, Veselin Sljivancanin, and Mile Mrksic to either Croatia or Serbia, considering the countries unprepared for high-level war crimes cases.[43]

A turning point in the public perception of war crimes was the release of a video showing members of the Serb paramilitary unit Scorpions killing six Muslim men and boys from Srebrenica. The video, originally shown at the ICTY, was broadcast in Serbia on state television in June 2005. The brutality of the crime and the blessing by a Serb Orthodox priest as part of the video brought home the reality of war crimes and was met by broad condemnation and the rapid arrest of five unit members shown in the video (their trial began in December 2005). Although the video incident and the 10th anniversary of the mass murder in Srebrenica did not open a larger debate on facing the past, these events made it more difficult to deny war crimes committed by the Serbian side and confronted the public with the cold-blooded nature of the crimes.

Corruption

2004	2005	2006
5.00	5.00	4.75

Corruption formed an integral part of governance under Milosevic, and both the Milosevic regime and the Zoran Zivkovic government lost elections because of corruption scandals. The fight against corruption has not been a high priority of post-Milosevic governments, despite rhetorical commitments[44] and the potent power of corruption allegations in ousting governments. As a result, corruption remains deeply entrenched at all levels. According to Transparency International's 2005 Corruption Perceptions Index, Serbia's score of 2.8 is 97th among countries surveyed, constituting only a slight improvement from the 2.7 score in 2004.

Corruption reports dominate domestic media, from examples of petty corruption to bribes and corruption at the government level. One of the key corruption scandals that shaped public debate in Serbia in 2005 involved a payment to doctors at the well-respected Institute of Cardiovascular Diseases in Sremska Kamenica to reduce the waiting time for heart surgery. The case was filmed by hidden camera and broadcast on TV.[45]

The most high-level corruption scandal involved the company Mile Dragic, which allegedly overcharged the army for equipment and paid (relatively minor) bribes to army officials and the Ministry of Defense. Minster of Finance Mladjan Dinkic made the case public, resulting in the resignation of the minister of defense. The latest in a series of military corruption scandals, this case helped make the army more responsive to civilian fiscal control. In a similar case, the Ministry of Finance accused the railway company, Serbian Railways, of purchasing train cars in contravention of the Law on Public Procurement.[46] In another case, the Movement Force of Serbia was accused of offering bribes to MPs to join their party.[47] Much corruption reporting is sensationalized, lacks firm evidence, and eventually fizzles out, resulting in mutually incriminating accusations among political elites. This does little but distract from real cases of corruption and its causes.

The Kostunica government has taken some steps to improve anticorruption measures, as much of its political legitimacy rests on the fight against corruption and international pressure from the EU and Council of Europe. In past years, Serbia has undertaken serious efforts to reduce state obstacles toward private business, often creating opportunities for corruption. In a World Bank study released in October 2005, Serbia and Montenegro is listed as the country that undertook the most efforts to improve the business climate. These measures include reducing obstacles to the establishment of businesses, bankruptcy procedures, and business operations.[48]

In the past two years, the Serbian Parliament introduced key legislation to combat corruption, such as new laws on public procurement, conflict of interest, party financing, and access to information and a new criminal code. Despite these new laws, additional measures are required to complete the legal framework and implement the anticorruption strategy. In October 2005, the State Union Parliament ratified the UN Convention Against Corruption but has not ratified other international anticorruption instruments.

In contrast with the apparent commitment to introduce anticorruption legislation, the government has been unwilling to work in earnest with the Anticorruption Council, established as an advisory body to the government in 2001. The council has been raising and documenting high-level corruption cases without government support or consideration.

Following a government proposal developed with the Council of Europe, the Parliament voted in favor of a National Anticorruption Strategy in December 2005 – a step called for by NGOs and international organizations for years. The strategy is to be followed by a detailed action plan for all relevant ministries and agencies. A separate law is also planned to establish an anticorruption body to cooperate with public prosecutors. The strategy discusses goals in combating corruption in all fields, incorporates key international initiatives, and defines corruption.[49]

Following the Law on Conflict of Interest in 2004, the Committee for Resolving Conflicts of Interest began work in January 2005 after a long passive period. The law is less strict than demanded by NGOs. According to Transparency Serbia, the law does not cover all cases of conflict of interest and has a weak implementation mechanism.[50] Public officials must submit a financial report before taking office and 15 days afterward. The independent body can reprimand but not punish public officials for a conflict of interest. Between January and November 2005, the committee had 29 meetings and launched 78 complaints of conflict of interest. In about 50 percent of the cases, the officials resigned or were dismissed, and in 30 percent, officials assured the committee they would abide by its decision.[51]

Transparency International-Serbia welcomed the new criminal code for making cases of corruption a criminal offense.[52] Another key statute is the antimonopoly law passed by the Parliament in October 2005. Prohibiting monopolistic behavior and imposing high fines, the law is key to improving the business climate. At the same time, the law does not define monopolistic behavior but leaves such a decision to the government, allowing political abuse of the regulation.[53]

According to Transparency International-Serbia, the Law on Party Financing is the most problematic. It enables political parties to tap budget resources for electoral campaigns and regular operations. Each party receives an amount proportional to its parliamentary representation. The law aims to limit the influence of private donations by encouraging members to pay smaller dues rather than having a few wealthy members sponsor entire parties. Individual members can contribute up to 10 times the average monthly wage in Serbia, whereas legal entities (such as businesses) can give up to 100 times the average wage. However, the law prohibits donations from foreign countries, organizations, anonymous persons, public sector and state-owned firms, humanitarian organizations, religious communities, and a number of other legal entities.

One shortcoming, unfortunately, is its failure to regulate campaign financing in the case of referendums to recall mayors, introduced in the Law on Local Government of 2002 and used several times in 2005. Additionally, the Ministry of Finance has been unwilling to provide funds for campaign financing foreseen in the law, amounting to 0.1 percent of the national budget. Furthermore, the body established to monitor the reports by parties on income and property lacks the administrative capacity to verify the information received.

Florian Bieber is a senior nonresident research associate of the European Centre for Minority Issues, based in Belgrade, and a visiting professor at the Central European University, Budapest. He is the author of Nationalismus in Serbien vom Tode Titos zum Ende der Ara Milosevic *(Nationalism in Serbia from the Death of Tito to the End of the Milosevic Era). He was assisted in preparing the report by Dejan Stjepanovic.*

[1] B92, "Sva krivicna dela bice procesuirana," [All criminal offenses will be prosecuted], December 28, 2005

[2] Vreme, "Sta se krije iza skupstinskih kulisa," [What hides behind the parliamentary stage] December 1, 2005.

[3] Blic, "BIA prisluskivala sve poslanike," [BIA wire-tapped all deputies] December 8, 2005. The allegations in this article were denied by the BIA; see www.bia.sr.gov.yu/Ser/saopstenje08122005.html.

[4] International Helsinki Federation, "While Srebrenica's Most Wanted Are Still at Large, the Serbian Security Agency Has Human Rights NGOs in It's Focus," July 13, 2005.

[5] Danas, "Borba protiv monopolista i samovolje drzavne uprave," [Struggle against monopolies and the arbitrariness of the state administration] September 15, 2005; Blic, "Srbija dobija ombudsmana: Jos jedna brana pred nepravdom," [Serbia gets an Ombudsman: Another defense against injustice"] June 10, 2005.

[6] Danas, "Rezultati istrazivanja Inicijative mladih za ljudska prava o primeni Zakona o slobodnom pristupu informacije," [Result of the research by the Youth Initative for Human Rights on the implementation of the Law on Freedom of Information] July 27, 2005.

[7] EU Business, "EU, Serbia, and Montenegro Reach Deal to End Constitutional Crisis," April 7, 2005.

[8] Danas, "Mandati strankama ili-tajkunima," [Mandate for paries or – tycoons]December 8, 2005.

[9] See directory.crnps.org.yu/browse_place.asp.

[10] Civic Initatives, NGOs in Serbia, Belgrade, 2005.

[11] Ivana Stevanovic, "Uskoro Zakon o udruzenjima gradjana u Srbiji," [Soon Law on Civi Association in Serbia] November 8, 2005, ssla.oneworld.net/article/view/121879/1/.

[12] See www.mpalsg.sr.gov.yu/sr/novost.asp?k=83.

[13] Helsinki Committee for Human Rights in Serbia, "Comments on the Draft Law on Associations," November 18, 2005, www.helsinki.org.yu/focus_text.php?lang=en&idteks=1523.

[14] U.S. International Grantmaking, "Serbia and Montenegro," July 2005, www.usig.org/countryinfo/serbia.asp.

[15] Humanitarian Law Center, "Serbian Government Reinforces Campaign Against NGOs Dealing with the Past," press release, July 29, 2005, www.hlc.org.yu/english/Facing_The_Past/Press_Releases/index.php?file=1212.html.

[16] Civic Initiatives, NGO Sector in Serbia, Belgrade, 2005.

[17] Danas,"Sonja Biserko: Brinem za svoju bezbednost," [Sonja Biserko: I worry about my safety] September 15, 2005.

[18] B92, "Prvi zvaniean spisak neonacista," [First official list of neo-nazis] December 10, 2005.

[19] Center for Free Elections and Democracy, "Politicke podele u Srbiji u kontekstu civilnog drustva," [Political divisions in Serbia in the context of civil society], Belgrade, 2005. Available at: http://www.cesid.org/programi/istrazivanja/index.jsp.

[20] Danas, "Sindikalna moa i nemoa," [Trade union power and weakness] December 2, 2005.

[21] Danas, "Vojislav Kostunica je moje najvece razocarenje," [Vojislav Kostunica is my greatest disappointment] October 7, 2005

[22] Danas, Frank Hantke, "Slatki otrov za sindikate," [The sweet poison for trade unions] October 7, 2005.

[23] Glas Javnosti, "Ministar ne mari za visoko obrazovanje," [The minister does not care about higher education] May 27, 2005.

[24] Association of Independent Electronic Media Weekly Media Update, October 11-18, 2005.

[25] Association of Independent Electronic Media Weekly Media Update, September 13-20, 2005.

[26] There are no independent reports on print runs, but these numbers, based on the print run of one day (July 26, 27, or 28, 2005), provide an indication. The numbers were determined by the Ebert Document Center.

[27] Association of Independent Electronic Media Weekly Media Update, August 30-September 8, 2005.

[28] Blic, September 17, 2005.

[29] Politika, October 10, 2005.

[30] Vreme, November 17, 2005.

[31] Reporters Without Borders, "One-Year Suspended Prison Sentence for Journalist in Libel Case," February 2, 2005.

[32] Politika, "Milion korisnika Interneta u Srbiji," [One Million Internet Users in Serbia] December 21, 2005.

[33] B92, "Kula: Niko ima vecinu," [Kula: Nobody has a majority] September 26, 2005.

[34] Center for Free Elections and Decmocracy, "Direktorijum lokalnih samouprava u Srbiji," [Directory of local self-government in Serbia] September 2005.

[35] See www.skgo.org/code/navigate.php?Id=354.

[36] European Commission, Serbia and Montenegro 2005 Progress Report, Brussels, November 9, 2005, SEC (2005) 1428.

[37] Glas Javnosti, "Poslusnike proizvodi sistem," [Loyalty maintains the system] September 5, 2005.

[38] Danas, "Pritisci i uticaj mocnika," [Pressure and influence of the powerful] June 25-26, 2005.

[39] Institute for War and Peace Reporting Balkan Crisis Report, "Politics Sways Serbia's Judges," June 27, 2005.

[40] B92, "Skupstina usvojlia zakon o policju," [Parliament passes Law on Police] November 14, 2005.

[41] Branko Bjelajac, "Eight Sentenced for 2004 Mosque Burning," Forum 18 News Service, 28.7.2005.

[42] Deutsche Welle, "Kriegsverbrecher-Prozess in Serbien beendet," [War crimes trial in Serbia concluded] July 15, 2005.

[43] Reuters, "UN Court Will Not Send Vukovar Case to Balkans," July 1, 2005.

[44] Voice of America, "Anticorruption Fight Moves Slow in Serbia," August 5, 2005.

[45] Beta, "No Evidence, No Corruption?" November 10, 2005.

[46] Beta, "Zeleznica prekrsila Zakon o javnim nabavkama," [Railways Broke Law on Public Procurement] October 19, 2005.

[47] Danas, "Bolje da su stranke vlasnici mandata nego tajkuni," [Better that parties are owners of mandates rather than tycoons] December 8, 2005.

[48] SEE Times, "Serbia-Montenegro Tops World Bank List of Business Reformers," October 13, 2005.

[49] Government of Serbia, "Usvojena Nacionalna strategija za borbu protiv korupcije," [National strategy on the fight against corruption has been passed] December 8, 2005, www.srbija.sr.gov.yu/vesti/vest.php?id=41370.

[50] Nemanja Nenadic, Global Corruption Report 2005, Transparency International, pp. 202-05.

[51] See www.sukobinteresa.sr.gov.yu/index.php?id=10&L=3.

[52] Danas, "Transparentnost Srbija zadovoljna usvajanjem novog krivicnog zaknonika," [Transparency Serbia is satisfied with the adoption of the new criminal law] September 30, 2005.

[53] Beta, "Serbia's Competition Act," October 30, 2005.

Montenegro

EXECUTIVE SUMMARY

Montenegro's anticipated 2006 referendum on independence dominated the political debate in 2005. Despite a stable governing majority, the opposition claimed the referendum could not be free and fair under the current government, and a number of spirited local election campaigns were subject to unsubstantiated accusations of voter intimidation and bribery. Despite these distractions, the Montenegrin Parliament managed to pass some key reform legislation and began to exercise limited oversight functions. But there are additional pieces of stalled reform legislation. Political pressure on the media – especially public service television – in the run-up to the formal launch of the referendum campaign represented a step back in the establishment of an independent media. Excessive political polarization and lack of funds somewhat hindered the decentralization process, and the judiciary continued to face political interference as well as long procedural delays. Despite advancing the formalities of integration, the European Union (EU) continued to highlight deep-rooted levels of corruption as a key obstacle in Montenegro's accession process.

Overall, Montenegro continues to put in place the necessary legal framework for democratic consolidation, but slow implementation continues to be an obstacle. Problems of implementation are sometimes deliberate, but more often they result from the small-town nature of Montenegrin society, where family, connections, and friendships among a population of 670,000 have traditionally governed relationships that the law now seeks to regulate. Although the machinery of the Communist system is being dismantled, the mentality of one-party rule still influences public perceptions and interferes with the development of an open society that respects the rule of law and demands accountability from its elected leaders.

National Democratic Governance. Montenegro completed its third year of membership in the State Union of Serbia and Montenegro in 2005. An already dysfunctional state broke down further in September 2005 with a public procurement scandal in the Ministry of Defense and mutual recriminations between the two member states. However, it was the debate over the referendum on state status – whether or not the opposition would participate, whether it would be held or not, under what conditions – that dominated debate in Montenegro in 2005. In an effort to draw attention away from this issue, the EU sped up its integration process for Serbia and Montenegro. Although the governing system is stable, the inability of governing and opposition parties to enter into dialogue over a referendum without the participation of the international community does not bode well. Montenegro's Parliament adopted several important and long-awaited laws in 2005 – namely, the Law on Police, Law on the Agency for National Security, and the Law on Free Access to Information. In another positive development, the Parliament held several debates on motions of no confidence with the serious participation of the government, debated reports from the Supreme Audit Institute and the supreme state prosecutor, and held its first "confirmation" hearings for the new chiefs of the Agency for National Security and the police. These steps represented engagement of the opposition in the established institutions of the state. While the Parliament passed legislation important for depoliticizing the police and security services and for transparency in government, its implementation has hardly begun. The shocking murder of the head of the criminal police administration in August 2005 suggested that organized crime has deep roots in Montenegrin society. *For all these reasons, as well as that small advances in the behavior of the Parliament and personnel changes in the judiciary have not yet altered the dominance of the executive branch among the three branches of power, Montenegro's rating for national democratic governance remains at 4.50.*

Electoral Process. In 2005, Montenegro held four special municipal elections and one municipal vote of no confidence. The campaigns were intense battles that boiled down to mini local public opinion polls about the standing of the two opposing blocs. Each election represented a victory for the governing coalition. As in the past, each election was accompanied by unsubstantiated claims of vote buying and voter intimidation and unwillingness on the part of the losers to accept the initial outcome. Nonetheless, domestic election-monitoring groups judged the elections to be in line with international standards despite isolated problems at polling stations. *Owing to the mixing of state and political functions and an unwillingness among the ruling forces to acknowledge impropriety, Montenegro's electoral process rating worsens from 3.25 to 3.50.*

Civil Society. Despite reliance on international funding and weak volunteerism, nongovernmental organizations (NGOs) of all types proliferated in Montenegro because of an NGO law with few restrictions. There is growing awareness of the need to reform the NGO law to include tax privileges. In 2005, the most visible NGO was the Group for Changes, which increasingly styled itself as an opposition political party and declared its intention to participate in the next parliamentary elections. Its high political profile undermined the credibility of other genuine NGOs that advocate for reforms. Nonetheless, the government continued to rely on some NGOs for preparing laws, co-sponsoring education campaigns, and sharing the burden of social service provision. *Owing to a blurring of the line between NGOs and partisan political organizations pointing up the specific weaknesses of civil society, Montenegro's civil society rating worsens from 2.50 to 3.00.*

Independent Media. Montenegrins enjoy a diverse choice of print and broadcast media. Although more outlets favor independence, there is a widely read pro-union newspaper and limited pro-union broadcasters (pro-union indicating a range of views favoring some form of legal union with Serbia). In April 2005, scandal broke out over a media analysis leaked through government circles that included an assessment of media predilection to promote independence. The dismissal of the public TV program director and consequent resignation of the entire editorial team raised further fears about the independence of public service television in the run-up to the referendum. The tradition of self-censorship in the media continues, and quality investigative reporting remains limited. *Owing to the lack of substantive changes, Montenegro's independent media rating remains at 3.25.*

Local Democratic Governance. In 2005, implementation of new legislation on local self-government continued. Many municipalities increasingly reached out to include citizens in decision-making processes. Other local governments had still not enacted the basic provisions of these laws. Given the pending decision on Montenegro's state status, the goal of decentralization and depoliticization at the local level has not yet been achieved. Furthermore, individual municipalities operate with uncertain funding conditions and are burdened by bloated and politicized bureaucracies.

Because the continued political polarization blocks effective decentralization, Montenegro's local democratic governance remains at 3.50.

Judicial Framework and Independence. The independence of the judicial system remained challenged in 2005. The slow investigation of a case on the deportation of Muslims to Bosnia and Herzegovina in 1992 suggested political interference. Additionally, the hospitalization of 18 prison inmates after a police raid raised questions of brutality and resulted in a change in prison administration. The election of new presidents of the Constitutional Court and Supreme Court was met with accusations of political cronyism, but the new heads quickly started to work on improving court efficiency and accountability. One of the most significant developments was the submission of the *2004 Annual Report on the Work of the Supreme State Prosecutor*, debated publicly in the Parliament in October 2005, which represented the first step toward an effective system of governmental checks and balances. The efforts of the newly established Administrative Court represented another significant development. Accusations of political interference and complaints of lengthy judicial processes continued to plague the judicial and prosecutorial systems. By the end of 2005, no visible progress had been made toward solving either the criminal police chief's murder or any of the other gangland-style murders of the last 10 years. *Despite the report of the Office of the Supreme State Prosecutor and the effective functioning of the Administrative Court, Montenegro's judicial framework and independence rating remains at 4.25 owing to continued accusations of political influence on the judiciary.*

Corruption. In 2005, the legal framework to combat corruption was strengthened, although much of the adopted legislation and strategies have not yet been implemented. In particular, the government adopted a strategy against corruption and organized crime; new drafts of improved public procurement and conflict of interest legislation are nearly ready for adoption; the salaries for members of Parliament (MPs) and high-level officials will increase more than 50 percent in 2006; and the Law on Free Access to Information was adopted. The privatization of several large state companies was completed, continuing to reduce the state's involvement in the economy. For the first time, 1,692 public officials submitted reports on their income and property. Nonetheless, most of the political parties failed to comply with the provisions of the Law on Political Party Financing without facing any repercussions. But the most distressing event in 2005 was the assassination of Slavoljub Scekic, head of the criminal police administration in charge of investigating the 2004 murder of *Dan* editor Dusko Jovanovic and other murders from the last 10 years. *Although the preparation and adoption of the legal framework for combating corruption and, especially, the adoption of the Law on Free Access to Information would seem to warrant an improved corruption rating, the murder of the chief investigator of the most notorious crimes in Montenegro suggests that the corruption rating should remain unchanged at 5.25.*

Outlook for 2006. The referendum on Montenegro's state status is expected in May 2006, if the government and opposition can agree to compromise on referendum conditions, including the important issue of a qualified majority. The government claims that the referendum campaign will not slow progress on negotiations with the EU for a Stabilization and Association Agreement, but significant legislation adopted in 2005 has yet to be implemented. Other distractions in the implementation phase will come from local elections in 13 municipalities and regularly scheduled parliamentary elections in October. There is no doubt that the resolution of the state status issue will change the political dynamics in Montenegro, enabling it, as Prime Minister Milo Djukanovic says, to "assume responsibility for its own destiny" and hopefully proceed quickly along the road of democratic consolidation and EU integration.

MAIN REPORT

National Democratic Governance

2004	2005	2006
n/a	4.50	4.50

Montenegro adopted its governing Constitution, which defines the country as a republic within the Federal Republic of Yugoslavia, on October 12, 1992. With the adoption of the Constitutional Charter of the State Union of Serbia and Montenegro on February 4, 2003, Montenegro became one-half of the two-state union. The charter left authority for defense and foreign policy in the hands of the joint state while ceding all other responsibilities to the two member states. The Parliament of the State Union includes 35 members from parliamentary parties in Montenegro who are chosen based on their proportional strength in the Assembly (Parliament) of Montenegro. This body meets infrequently to approve international treaties and trade and loan agreements and to make State Union personnel appointments.

According to the Constitutional Charter, both member states were expected to bring their Constitutions in line with the charter within six months of adopting it – that is, by early August 2003. In Montenegro, this provision awaits implementation. Likewise, politicians in the member states have ignored a number of other provisions over the past three years – sometimes with the blessing of the international community – or implemented provisions imperfectly, undermining the legitimacy of the State Union and its institutions and contributing to its dysfunction.

As an example, the charter declares that the ministers of defense and foreign affairs cannot be from the same member state and that after two years the member state not occupying the ministerial post should assume this role. The first provision was violated in 2003 with the blessing of the international community in order to ensure the formation of a government in Serbia, and the two-year deadline for swapping positions passed almost unnoticed this year. Similarly, the Court of the State

Union was not constituted until May 2004 and barely functioned in 2005. Since Montenegro has not secured premises for the court, it currently functions out of temporary premises in Belgrade, despite efforts to have the charter specify that it would operate out of the Montenegrin capital, Podgorica.

The most apparent shortcoming in 2005 was the unobserved March 5 deadline for holding direct elections to the State Union Parliament. In 2004, the government of Montenegro insisted that implementing this provision would be a waste of time since the referendum was a year away. It also knew that it would be difficult to entice sympathetic voters to the polls given the general disdain for State Union institutions. Unable to negotiate a solution with Serbia, the mandates of the State Union MPs expired at the beginning of March, although parliamentarians met to pass a number of pressing issues on March 21 while the EU helped broker an agreement between Serbia and Montenegro. Finally, on April 7 the EU high representative for common foreign and security policy, Javier Solana, arrived in Belgrade to participate in signing amendments to the Constitutional Charter. This action postponed direct elections to the State Union Parliament until the next republic-wide election in the respective member state and requires that the member state holding the referendum "cooperate with the EU on incorporating internationally recognized standards for referendum."

These amendments – adopted by the three Parliaments in June – unleashed debates over Montenegro's independence referendum that dominated the rest of 2005. Despite EU and Council of Europe calls for dialogue within Montenegro to establish internal consensus on conditions for the referendum, the opposition refused to have a dialogue directly with the regime, claiming the referendum was not necessary and impossible to hold in an atmosphere that it deemed thoroughly undemocratic. Some members of the opposition – the Socialist People's Party (SNP) and the People's Party (NS) – expressed their willingness to discuss the referendum with Europe. Finally, in December Solana appointed a personal envoy to mediate the dialogue over referendum conditions, with the result that the SNP and NS – joined by the opposition Democratic Party of Serbs (DSS) – agreed to enter into an "indirect" dialogue with the governing parties that would continue into 2006.

For political and practical reasons, most of Montenegro's governance system is located at the republic level with a Parliament of 75 members, in which the governing Democratic Party of Socialists (DPS) and Social Democratic Party (SDP) enjoy an absolute majority and the support of the small Citizens' Party and the two ethnic Albanian parties, Democratic Union of Albanians and Democratic Alliance in Montenegro. Prime Minister and DPS president Milo Djukanovic leads a cabinet of 3 deputy prime ministers and 17 ministers, and the directly elected president of the republic, Filip Vujanovic, also hails from the ranks of the DPS.

Despite this stable governing majority – confirmed in the October 2002 elections, which the Organization for Security and Cooperation in Europe/Office for Democratic Institutions and Human Rights (OSCE/ODIHR) deemed "generally in accordance with international standards"[1] – four parliamentary opposition parties deny the legitimacy of the governing authorities, claiming they are involved in international organized crime and corruption. After a 16-month boycott in 2003 and 2004, the opposition currently participates in institutions, including the Parliament, and in 2005 referred several issues to the Administrative Court and the Constitutional Court, demonstrating that their branding of the government as illegitimate is more a political move than a destabilizing one. Fundamentally, a lack of consensus about the nature of the state exists among the competing political parties. One side believes Montenegro is a sovereign republic that agreed to share certain powers with the sovereign republic of Serbia, while the other side sees the State Union of Serbia and Montenegro as the sovereign state that has ceded certain governing powers to the republics.

The 1992 Constitution broadly defines a system of checks and balances among the branches of government in Montenegro, although the executive clearly dominates the other official bodies. This is due partly to the fact that both the legislature and the judiciary depend on the government for their budget and revenue transfers, but it also reflects a tradition in the country's governance of vesting supreme power in the executive body.

Thus, although the Parliament of Montenegro possesses defined control functions – such as the ability to initiate a vote of no confidence, the right to pose questions to ministers at the beginning of each sitting, and the opportunity to hold hearings or initiate investigations – the opposition rarely uses these tools, and when it does, the governing majority can easily block them. However, 2005 introduced some changes. The opposition succeeded in moving for a vote of no confidence in the president of the Parliament, as well as in the government as a whole and in the president.[2] The government no-confidence vote, in particular, represented a significant step forward. The prime minister and ministers attended a multiday session and demonstrated a sense of accountability by seriously answering accusations – if not to the opposition, then at least to the viewing public. Similarly, in September the president submitted to significant challenges from the opposition and defended his actions as being in the public interest.

The October parliamentary debates over reports by the Supreme Audit Institute and supreme state prosecutor also represented important milestones in the development of the Parliament's oversight functions. Both reports resulted from laws that went into force in 2004. While polemics sometimes eclipsed both debates, the mere fact that an annual report was submitted and that several MPs had read the reports and discussed them seriously was significant for establishing the principles of government accountability.

As in many Central and Eastern European countries, public access to the Parliament is by appointment only, and there is no visitors' gallery per se. Nonetheless, public television and radio stations broadcast all plenary sessions live between 11:00 a.m. and 5:00 p.m., and these are reasonably well followed by the public. In most cases, committee presidents invite the media to cover the sessions; later, journalists package them into a condensed report. Sometimes committee presidents invite outside experts to attend the sessions, and they also regularly invite the responsible ministry representative. Thus, the Parliament operates as a public institution, and citizens can follow its activities through the media or by visiting its Web site. Nonetheless, the Parliament is far from being an independent body. The governing majority rarely votes against – and the opposition rarely votes for – government-sponsored bills. Plenary debates rarely address ideological differences or varying policy directions in 2005, particularly in the highly charged atmosphere of the referendum debate and the opposition's prediction of the current regime's demise. Instead, parliamentary debate in Montenegro was used most often to score cheap points against opponents. Although such behavior can be attributed partly to the contentious nature of Montenegrin politics and complaints about the lack of alternative channels for spreading political messages, it is mostly fed by the low commitment and sparse resources given to serious legislative work.

Unfortunately, the Parliament's limited budget[3] does not provide the resources and capacity needed to fulfill its legislative and oversight functions. There are no more than 15 professional staff with legislative experience, and few speak foreign languages, use computers, or have traveled abroad. Given these deficits, the Parliament is in no position to exercise any control over the executive branch.

Parliament's Web site is used regularly by both journalists and citizens; it publishes draft legislation, adopted legislation, and minutes of plenary and committee sessions but is not updated regularly and has many gaps. Transcripts of plenary sessions are available to MPs within days of the session, and such members can share the transcripts with the public if they choose (or, more likely, if requested).

As the dominant governing body in Montenegro, the executive branch defines policy and writes and implements laws. The government as a whole maintains a Web site, and each ministry has its own page. Additionally, the rules governing the adoption of legislation provide a 15-day public comment period on most legislation, wherein the government reproduces the draft, distributes it via daily newspapers, and holds public and expert roundtables if necessary. Also, ministers make an effort to visit people and places outside of the capital city relevant to their area of responsibility.

That said, the EU in its April 2005 feasibility study directed its criticisms at the Montenegrin civil service, claiming it suffered from significant levels of corruption and lack of capacity for EU accession. The study also expressed concern over connections between organized crime and ruling bodies. Undoubtedly, the public administration – at the republic and local levels – is far too large and based significantly on patronage. Party affiliation or family connections often take precedence over professional expertise when hiring in the public sector. Dismissal of redundant civil servants is frequently avoided for fear of political ramifications. In July, the International Monetary Fund (IMF) noted that the public sector wage bill was almost 10 percent of the gross domestic product (GDP), which "is already too large as a share of the economy." Thus, it urged the government "to lower current spending and create room for capital outlays," to step up "civil service reform and reductions in public employment," and to moderate "wage increases."[4] The government did manage to reduce wage expenditures in 2005 by €5 million (US$4.1 million), but wages still totaled 32 percent of state budget expenditures.[5]

Legislation on state employees went into effect on October 1, 2004. The law required each public institution to prepare a staff structure with clear job require-ments in an effort to define a rational organization and reduce bloated bureaucracies or increase staff where needed. Many public institutions did not complete this task by the end of 2005. The government met its 2005 IMF commitments on reducing the size of public administration primarily through cuts in the army.

The fact is that out of Montenegro's 154,300 employed persons,[6] close to 60 percent are employed in the public sector. The number of people dependent on the state for their livelihood can have an impact on their freedom to make decisions independently. Thus, a growing private sector and the creation of jobs are critically important to advancing a free society in Montenegro.

After more than two years of debate between the two governing parties, draft laws on police and establishing the Agency for National Security to replace the state security service were finally passed in April 2005. The compromise that solved the long-standing dispute between the DPS and SDP allows the government to nomi-nate the heads of these institutions and for the Parliament to debate and offer a non-binding opinion on the nominations. The compromise resulted in the first confir-mation hearings (albeit closed) in the history of Montenegro's multiparty democra-cy. In September 2005, after the murder of the criminal police chief, the head of the police held a closed-door session with the Parliament's Committee for Security and Defense to brief MPs on the state of the investigation.

Implementation of the police laws should launch the depoliticization of these institutions. In a disappointing sign of failed reform in 2005, the new chief of police, Veselin Veljovic, was photographed at the local headquarters of the DPS on the day of elections in the municipality of Mojkovac. When asked to justify his actions and to state if he had arrived in Mojkovac in a state-owned vehicle, the police chief replied that he did not need to tell the opposition parliamentarian anything about his mode of transportation.[7] It is hoped that the incident was a temporary lapse in the process.

Electoral Process

2004	2005	2006
n/a	3.25	3.50

The last parliamentary election in Montenegro was held in October 2002 and was based on a proportional representation system with one republicwide constituency, a 3 percent threshold, and the use of the D'Hondt method for allocating seats. The last presidential election was in May 2003, based on a direct, simple majority vote. In both cases, the OSCE/ODIHR judged the elections generally free and fair and the election administration sound. Likewise, domestic monitoring organizations did not find any reason to question the results. However, in its last preliminary report, the ODIHR noted "deep-rooted problems in the election environment," including "lack of confidence by opposition parties in the impartiality of certain State institutions," "incomplete separation of State and party functions at all levels," and a "perception that the livelihood of public employees depends on incumbents."[8]

The March 2004 Law on Political Parties required a reregistration of political parties within 12 months. By May 2005, the former list of 64 political parties had been reduced to 24.[9] Of these, 11 are represented in the Parliament. Montenegro's political parties generally divide into two camps – pro-independence governing parties and pro-State Union opposition parties. The exceptions are the Liberal Alliance and Liberal Party, which are both opposition and pro-independence. Bosniaks, Muslims, and Albanians have their own political parties and coalitions. Nonetheless, a majority of these ethnic minority groups tend to vote for the governing DPS or SDP. Because of a special constituency of 57 polling places where a majority of the voting population is ethnic Albanian, two ethnic Albanian parties have seats in the Parliament after receiving more than 3 percent of the vote (the national threshold) in that constituency. No special provisions are made for Bosniaks and Muslims, but they are represented in the Parliament on the lists of the DPS and SDP, as are some ethnic Albanian MPs.

Party Name	Number of Seats in Parliament (out of 75)
Democratic Party of Socialists (DPS)	31
Social Democratic Party (SDP)	7
"Formal" Governing Coalition	**38**
Citizens' Party	1
Democratic Union of Albanians	1
Democratic Alliance in Montenegro	1
Government Allies	**3**
Socialist People's Party (SNP)	19
People's Party (NS)	5
Serbian People's Party (SNS)	4
Democratic Party of Serbs (DSS)	2
Pro-Union Opposition	**30**
Liberal Alliance of Montenegro	3
Liberal Party of Montenegro	1
Pro-Independence Opposition	**4**

Sources: www.skupstina.mn.yu and the National Democratic Institute.

Over the years, and owing to accusations of fraud, the legal framework for elections has undergone a number of changes with the consensus of all parties. Nonetheless, the losers in each election consistently allege voter intimidation, vote buying, voter list manipulation, and other unfair campaign practices, all of which remain unproven for the most part. Four special municipal elections and one local vote of no confidence in 2005 were no exception. While unconfirmed reports corroborate some of these accusations, reports also indicate that both sides use such techniques when possible. For example, the opposition regularly complains of bias in the public media in republic elections. Nonetheless, in the December local elections in Cetinje, where opposition parties were incumbent, the local public radio station, contrary to the Law on Radio Diffusion, was used in the interest of the incumbent administration to demonize its challengers.[10]

In each municipal election in 2005, the governing DPS-SDP coalition ousted the former local coalitions of opposition parties. In some cases, the results represented an overwhelming victory, as in Budva, where the DPS-SDP mayoral candidate received 62 percent of the vote to the SNP-SNS-NS-NSS's 38 percent (NSS is the People's Socialist Party, headed by the former Montenegrin president Momir Bulatovic). In other cases, such as Mojkovac in December, the DPS-SDP mayoral candidate won with 62 votes. Each election campaign turned into a referendum on the republic government or Montenegro's future state status. While domestic monitoring organizations noted election irregularities at some polling places and the inability of some municipal election commissions to overcome political divisions, these organizations determined that the irregularities could not have impacted election outcomes.[11]

In Montenegro, elections capture the attention of the population; many people hold political party membership cards, and political parties actively engage in door-to-door campaigning. Given the limited employment opportunities in Montenegro and the underdeveloped private sector, each election is a winner-take-all event that determines who will have jobs in the coming four years. Campaigning is vigorous, and turnout is high. Unfortunately, the appeal for votes is rarely made based on a substantive platform. Whether or not voters are intimidated, the implicit stakes in the election compel voters and campaigners to make choices on the presumption that their actions are being recorded. As such, voters – especially in more isolated areas – have retained a "big brother" mentality despite the introduction of new rules.

The dominant DPS is the primary beneficiary of this mind-set, such that competitive multiparty elections in Montenegro have never produced a rotation of power at the republic level. The overarching electoral problems highlighted by the OSCE/ODIHR in May 2003 continue to prevail and will be important factors in the upcoming referendum on Montenegro's state status.

Civil Society

2004	2005	2006
2.75	2.50	3.00

According to the Ministry of Justice's register of NGOs and political parties, there are close to 3,000 registered NGOs in Montenegro, of which perhaps 100 actually function as real nongovernmental actors. The 1999 Law on NGOs establishes the legal and regulatory framework for domestic and international organizations. At the time of its passage – when the existence of NGOs and their activities were threatened in Croatia, Serbia, and Slovakia – international experts hailed Montenegro's law as the most liberal. Unfortunately, the law has proven itself too liberal, especially without the adoption of prescribed sublaws.

Registering an NGO requires the names of five individuals and an address in Montenegro. The law doesn't define grounds for denying registration and gives very few details about revoking registration. It also places few requirements on the NGO sector in terms of financial reporting and, at the same time, provides it with few privileges. The law had anticipated the adoption of a number of sublaws to define tax and reporting obligations related to income and expenditures, but most of these have not come into force. In some cases, the laws that have come into force – for example, the Law on Economic Societies – say little about NGO obligations. Thus, NGOs have operated largely in a legal vacuum since 1999. As a result, a number of organizations on the NGO register were inactive in 2005. Furthermore, the thousands of registered NGOs include cafes, kindergartens, and other for-profit businesses that use their NGO status to avoid reporting their income and paying taxes.[12]

The NGO sector is underdeveloped and dependent primarily on international funding. Since Montenegrin tax law does not provide incentives to the private sector for philanthropy, NGOs derive very little funding from local sources. The republic and municipal governments budget annually for NGO funding. The Parliament and municipal assemblies have established multiparty committees to manage the distribution of these funds. These committees have limited criteria, and complaints arise every year about favoritism in the distribution process. In 2005, the Committee for Distributing Funds to NGOs in the Parliament received more than 350 grant applications and distributed €289,523 (US$237,409) to 157 NGOs in 14 of 21 municipalities, for grants ranging from €300 (US$246) to €8,500 (US$6,970).[13]

Given the challenging economic situation, there is a very limited tradition of volunteerism. In fact, starting an NGO and competing for funds can serve as a method of self-employment. Consequently, only a minority of registered NGOs can be considered effective in terms of research, advocacy, civic education, watchdog activities, and other social services. The government is willing to work with NGOs in most cases to prepare laws, co-sponsor education campaigns, and share the burden of providing social services. But public institutions do not respond positively to criticism from NGOs and sometimes ostracize those that are too critical. Equally, opposition political parties often refuse to cooperate with certain NGOs, as the former accuse the latter of being instruments of the government. Like so much of Montenegro, many NGOs tend to be too close to the government – or the opposition – and undermine their own claims to independence. In the run-up to the referendum, pro-independence NGOs are sometimes hard-pressed to challenge the government so as not to appear unpatriotic. Thus, the small civil society of Montenegro creates difficult conditions for effective advocacy campaigns and watchdog efforts.

In 2005, one particularly vocal NGO – Group for Changes (GzP) – undermined the credibility of the NGO sector at large. GzP models itself on the Serbian NGO G-17, which divided into an NGO and a separate political party when it entered politics as a competitor. Initially, GzP concentrated on the privatization process and general lack of transparency in government. In 2005, GzP decided that leading a change of government was the only way to oust the current political administration, which "after 15 years has not succeeded to find its own model of peaceful democratic transition and extract itself from the one-party society and command economy and to transform into a civil citizen's society with rule of law, respect for human rights and freedom with socially responsible and efficient market economy."[14] Therefore, it declared its intention to compete in the next parliamentary elections, while operating as an NGO pressure group trying to overcome the "crisis situation." In an effort to mobilize people for its cause, GzP leaders penetrated the ranks of the workers, especially those in bankrupt or privatized firms. Offering to represent the workers' interests, GzP often unrealistically radicalized their demands and escalated confrontations between workers and the government or private owners.

A case in point would be the recently privatized telephone company Telekom Crne Gore, which began negotiations with employees on a social program in the last quarter of the year. The executive director of GzP Nebojsa Medojevic convinced the workers' trade union to hire him to represent their interests in the negotiations for a percentage. Within a month, the union had cut off contact with management and was threatening to strike via the media, claiming their demands were being ignored; meanwhile, management claimed that negotiations had barely begun and that it was still open to dialogue. The trade union, however, refused discussions.[15]

The public confusion that GzP created between its NGO, political party, and business activities has damaged the credibility of the Montenegrin NGO sector. For instance, the legitimate advocacy activities conducted by the Network for Affirmation of the NGO Sector (MANS), another NGO pressure group that focuses on corruption in government, were characterized as "the opposition's attempt to instrumentalize MANS in an effort to bring down" the government. It is unfortunate that the confusing activities of a single NGO wishing to compete in elections has blurred the line between NGOs pushing for real reform and opposition parties.

Independent Media

2004	2005	2006
3.25	3.25	3.25

Montenegro has a vibrant independent media. In addition to two public TV channels, there are five private TV stations (two with republicwide coverage), one republicwide public radio station, many local public and private radio stations, several local public TV stations, four national daily newspapers, and a number of weeklies and monthly magazines.[16] Additionally, there is an independent news agency and one Internet service provider. Newspaper distribution is privately controlled, and although no legislation on media concentration exists at present, ownership of private media is generally well distributed. In 2005, the Broadcasting Agency held a successful competition for frequencies.

There are three professional journalist associations, as well as an association of broadcasters. The Montenegrin Media Institute, created with international assistance, supports the professional development of journalists and journalistic standards. Although the 2003 criminal code abolished prison sentences for insult, slander, and libel, penalties range from €5,000 (US$4,100) to €10,000 (US$8,200), which is quite high for individual journalists. Ignoring the imposed fine can result in imprisonment. Journalistic associations have long advocated for the decriminalization of libel and slander.

In terms of political viewpoints represented in the media, one of the four daily newspapers reflects the views of the opposition, while most other newspapers side with pro-independence forces – if not the government. Radio and TV news broadcasts are neutral or favorable toward the government in most cases. Even so, the opposition also receives airtime and is portrayed objectively.

In April 2005, a media analysis focusing on the favorable coverage of the independence campaign circulated through government and was leaked to the public, causing a huge scandal and opposition protests. The document suggested "directing money" to certain media and "having talks" with others. It also offended a good part of the media community in Montenegro, whose immaturity became clear in its declaration to "boycott" the minister accused of ordering and circulating the analysis. The government claimed that the document presented an interesting analysis but denied any intention of acting on its suggestions.

Despite the fact that the entire media community knew or suspected who wrote the document, not a single media outlet printed or broadcast the name, demonstrating one of the biggest weaknesses in the media: its limited curiosity and investigative capacity. The political, social, business, cultural, and local events of the day are broadcast, but with few in-depth reports on specific issues of interest and little effort to unearth hidden facts or provide a critical analysis. In part, this is due to an established culture of self-censorship in service to the forces of one's preferred state-status choice or fear of the reaction of powerful interest groups.

At the end of 2005, the dismissal of the public television program director for a minor failure to meet a legal deadline led to suspicions of government efforts to reassume control of the editorial policy prior to the referendum. The station's entire editorial board resigned, calling the dismissal politically motivated. The dismissal reportedly followed several months of behind-the-scenes pressure put on the editor in chief by the government.[17] The Friends of Public Service Broadcasting, a coalition of NGOs led by the Association of Young Journalists (AYJ), called for the resignation of the Council for Radio TV Montenegro and will closely follow developments in 2006 in an effort to prevent the nearly transformed public TV from once again becoming a tool of the authority.

Local Democratic Governance

2004	2005	2006
n/a	3.50	3.50

A major step toward decentralization began with the passage of the Law on Local Self-Government, the Law on the Election of Mayor, and the Law on Local Self-Government Financing in July 2003. Unfortunately, implementation is uneven. Some municipalities have adopted each of the nine ordinances required by the Law on Local Self-Government, while other municipalities have adopted only a few of these ordinances. Furthermore, limited financial resources, bloated bureaucracies, and lack of appropriately skilled staff hamper effective operations in a number of municipalities.

Currently, municipal government adopts its own budget and plans for development, construction, urban, capital improvement, and environmental projects. It also takes care of social and child welfare, sports and recreation facilities, libraries, communal services, and public transport.

According to law, there are several ways for citizens to get involved in the process. First, citizens elect their representatives every four years. Under the new laws, municipal mayors are elected directly, while councillors are elected according to a municipalitywide proportional representation system. As a result of the regular and special local elections held since the enactment of the local government laws, 8 of 21 municipalities now function with a directly elected mayor and an appointed city manager. In each case, these municipal elections registered high levels of participation – as much as 85 percent – as the political parties concentrated their efforts on turning them into a referendum either on Montenegro's state status or on the current government. The 13 other municipalities will hold elections under the new system in 2006.

The Law on Local Self-Government also provides for citizen initiatives, community referendums, municipal referendums, and citizen assemblies in order to provide input into local decision making. Unfortunately, in June 2005 opposition parties used the instrument of municipal referendum in an effort to dismiss the DPS mayor and provoke a new election. Thus, the intended depoliticization of the local government in the pursuit of basic public interests remains in the beginning stages and will require decreased political tensions at the republic level and an improvement in the local economic situation.

Still, a number of municipalities have begun to encourage input from the public in the decision-making process. Most municipalities have adopted the ordinance on citizen participation that generally establishes such a system over time. Several municipalities have signed cooperation agreements with local NGOs and have provided an "empty chair" to NGOs to participate in municipal assembly discussions without the right to vote. Some municipalities even open assembly discussions to interested citizens. Additionally, a number of municipalities have recently adopted a rule book with a commitment to publish data every six months on the activities of the municipal assembly and, importantly, on individual councillors. A growing number of municipalities have developed Web sites containing information useful to the public, and municipalities increasingly organize public consultations, especially over contentious issues such as urban planning.

At the end of 2005, the government established a Coordination Body for Local Government Reform, which should become operational in 2006. It will facilitate planning and decision-making processes between the central and local authorities. Additionally, in October 2005 the Parliament adopted the Law on the Capital City of Podgorica, which fulfills a long-standing promise of the DPS government to the ethnic Albanian parties that have supported the government for the past seven years. Namely, the law creates the opportunity for the predominantly ethnic Albanian town of Tuzi, situated within the Podgorica municipality, to attain the status of a "city municipality." According to news reports, Tuzi would have guaranteed access to 20 percent of Podgorica's budget.

Despite many positive developments, the two biggest continuing obstacles to effective functioning of local government and real decentralization are (1) continued politicization at the local level, producing weak administrations and political polarization; and (2) lack of sufficient and reliable funding. First, the political polarization that characterizes relations at the republic level filters down to the municipal level, where there is a winner-take-all system based on political patronage. The local government turnover from opposition parties to governing parties in four municipalities in 2005, reportedly, was not massive. Still, key leadership posts in the municipality and in local government directorates and companies did change hands. Often, especially in small municipalities, the individuals nominated based on party affiliation do not have the skills necessary to fulfill their assigned tasks. Furthermore, the proportional representation system used to elect municipal councillors results in a failure to act in the public interest. Instead, councillors serve the interests of the political parties they represent.

In the one municipality where governing parties controlled the mayor and opposition parties held the majority in the municipal assembly in 2005, the fight over patronage fully blocked the decision-making system as the opposition tried to force the mayor to act according to its will. Instead of yielding, the governing parties introduced an amendment to the Law on Local Self-Government to circumvent the municipal assembly, giving the mayor greater power.

As for funding, local governments can collect taxes, are entitled to a portion of joint taxes and fees, and receive transfers from the republic budget, but the municipalities have difficulty securing a stable source of funding for basic operating costs. One reason is that separate laws define a number of joint taxes, fees, and the way funds are divided between the government and municipalities. As an example, the Law on Tourism Organizations determined that 80 percent of fees paid to support these organizations should go to the National Tourism Organization and the municipal tourism organizations, while 20 percent should be returned to the municipalities to spend. This determination, made in 2004, was a great disappointment to tourist municipalities, which had planned to use the tourist tax as a major source of financing.

Situations like the tourist tax led municipalities to complain that the republic government provides itself with easy-to-collect revenues, leaving municipalities with the "privilege" of collecting real estate taxes. The tourist tax can easily be factored into the price of a hotel room, but there is frequent tax evasion in the case of real estate, as it is politically difficult to confiscate family homes and property.

In other cases, there are indications that the republic government makes every attempt to hold on to revenue that belongs to the municipalities by law. As an example, the Law on Local Self-Government Financing states that municipalities are entitled to 30 percent of all concession fees collected on its territory. After a multiyear battle to compel the Ministry of Agriculture to acknowledge that the law's new provisions supersede the old Law on Forestry, which gave municipalities only 10 percent of the concession fee, the ministry changed its argument, saying that forests were not a concession.

Additionally, the nonadoption of laws leaves a legal vacuum allowing the government to continue to collect and use revenue, such as in the Law on Gambling Taxes, which entered parliamentary procedure only in December 2005. Finally, opposition-controlled municipalities accuse the government of withholding or delaying money transfers. Although this accusation may have been true several years ago, the establishment of a central treasury should have eliminated the ability to withhold transfers.

Judicial Framework and Independence

2004	2005	2006
4.25	4.25	4.25

The 1992 Constitution guarantees fundamental political, civil, and human rights, including freedom of expression, religion, association, and business and property rights, which are respected by the state. The Parliament adopted a new Law on Courts in 2002; the Law on Criminal Procedure, a new criminal code, and the Law on the Supreme State Prosecutor in 2003; and the Law on Civil Procedure in 2004. As with many reforms in Montenegro's 15 years of transition, the challenge begins at the implementation stage. The *2004 Annual Report of the Ombudsman* noted that 46 percent of complaints related to the length of the judicial process and nonenforcement of court decisions, while another 38 percent related to economic, social, and cultural rights.[18] Many judicial delays related to inefficiencies in the court and prosecutorial systems, which should be addressed by full implementation of the previously mentioned laws.

In particular, the Administrative Court and the Appellate Court began work in 2005. In its first year, the Administrative Court received 842 unresolved cases from the Supreme Court and registered 1,887 new cases in 2005. By December 31, the court had issued 1,279 decisions. While many cases were minor election-related issues, more than 800 were significant decisions related to the work of public organs.[19] Significantly, for the first time the Administrative Court published all of its decisions on its Web site and in print.

Similarly, the Appellate Court will be able to interpret new laws and establish precedents that will make deciding cases easier; it also serves as a second-instance court for decisions of the commercial courts, which have the potential to control the legality of the privatization process. Thus, both the Appellate Court and the commercial courts have the ability to increase the efficiency of the judicial process, to control the work of the executive branch, and to establish a body of precedents that will expedite the judicial process.

In 2005, the judicial framework underwent personnel changes that may contribute to the depoliticization and professionalization of these institutions. The Parliament elected a new president of the Constitutional Court in June and a new president of the Supreme Court in October. Additionally, there were a number of personnel changes in the Office of the Supreme State Prosecutor. The appointment of the court presidents led to accusations of political cronyism. On the one hand, the new Constitutional Court president had been a close adviser to Svetozar Marovic, president of the State Union of Serbia and Montenegro (a Montenegrin), since 2003 and had been president of the DPS executive board in 2000 and 2001; on the other hand, the opposition accused the new president of the Supreme Court of having falsified voter rolls in 1997. Despite these charges, both appointees have actively pursued their responsibilities since their appointments. The Supreme Court president in particular immediately embarked on a tour of the Montenegrin court system, assessing the quality of the municipal courts, demanding resignations, initiating dismissals, and generally insisting on accountability from the judicial system. If sincere, these steps may bear fruit in 2006.

The process of appointing judges continues to be an obstacle to the establishment of a truly independent judiciary. According to the Law on Courts, the Judicial Council (made up of six judges, two law professors, and two well-known legal experts) nominates and dismisses judges, and the Parliament confirms the decisions. In the last two years, a number of bench vacancies went unfilled because the Parliament refused to approve certain nominations – some say because the nominee lacked the appropriate political connections, while others suggest objections to the nominee's background. The European Commission and local observers attribute the problem to "the absence of clearly defined criteria for the appointment of judges and prosecutors."[20] Meanwhile, some argue that the responsibility for nomination and dismissal should rest solely with the Judicial Council. It is unlikely that this issue will be resolved before the adoption of a new Constitution.

Another obstacle to judicial independence and its depoliticization is the lack of an independent budget for the judicial system. Like the Parliament, the judiciary depends on the government for its budget and for budget transfers, which makes long-term planning difficult. The need to negotiate with the executive and the inability to decide fully on raising salaries or infrastructure investments creates a level of political dependence that can interfere in balancing powers among the various branches of government.

In 2005, the supreme state prosecutor submitted (for the first time) to the Parliament the *2004 Annual Report on the Work of the Supreme State Prosecutor*, as required by law. The parliamentary debate on this report was lively and substantive and represented the first time that the supreme state prosecutor was called to account as a result of the 2003 Law on the State Prosecutor. In the report, the supreme state prosecutor noted that the court system has an inexplicably high number of unresolved investigations (57 percent) and unresolved indictments (69 percent), some dating back to 1987.[21] The report also noted that although the special prosecutor for organized crime had taken a number of positive steps, these developments had not yet reduced the influence of organized crime in Montenegro.[22] The mere sense of accountability created by the publication of the first annual report represents a significant step forward in creating an effective system of checks and balances in Montenegro.

In 2005, international attention was drawn to a civil suit brought against Montenegro by 27 families from Bosnia and Herzegovina whose relatives were rounded up by the police in Montenegro in May 1992 and deported back to the Foca region, where they were killed. The supreme state prosecutor opened a criminal investigation to establish responsibility for the alleged war crime and to help in deciding the civil suit. The lawyer of the relatives has accused the Office of the Supreme State Prosecutor of politically motivated sluggishness in pursuing the case. By the end of 2005, the criminal case was still under investigation.[23]

Additionally, a disturbing event at the main penitentiary in Montenegro occurred in September after the murder of the head of the criminal police administration. Police raided the prison at Spuz after midnight, and 18 inmates were hospitalized, claiming the police had beaten them. Although the police's culpability has yet to be established, the event and conditions at the prison – in particular certain privileges extended to high-security prisoners – led to a change in the prison administration. The new director of prisons has since ordered a full investigation of the police raid and prison conditions.

Corruption

2004	2005	2006
5.25	5.25	5.25

The EU's *Serbia and Montenegro 2005 Progress Report* continued to identify corruption as a "serious concern" and to assess Montenegro's anticorruption activities as "still far from sufficient."[24] While the government adopted a strategy against corruption and organized crime in August, implementation of the strategy had not begun nor was it publicly available by the end of 2005. Fundamentally, Montenegro's system of patronage penetrates deep into the public sector at the republic and local levels and is a key source of corruption for governing as well as opposition parties. As long as the Montenegrin governance system operates without a professional, competitive civil service, corruption is likely to remain a concern.

Anxiety about corruption in government increased with the August 29 gangland-style murder of Slavoljub Scekic, head of the criminal police administration. Government critics claimed the assassination proved that organized crime groups had infiltrated the government and were more powerful than the government itself.

In fact, the Scekic murder and the May 2004 murder of *Dan* news daily editor Dusko Jovanovic appeared connected. By the end of 2005, no arrests or indictments had been made in the Scekic case, and the true motive behind Jovanovic's murder had not been established. A witness protection law adopted in October 2004 has not yet been implemented because of what the EU describes as "insufficient cooperation between the judiciary and the police and inadequate financial support."[25] Although unlikely to be a panacea, the application of a witness protection law and the whistle-blower provisions of the Law on Free Access to Information (see following) may change the culture of self-imposed censorship over time in Montenegro and encourage people to speak out about corruption.

In the meantime, the government made significant progress this year in privatization, selling both the state telephone company (Telekom Crne Gore) to Hungarian Matav and the Aluminum Conglomerate (KAP) to a Russian-owned company, Salamon Enterprises, based in Cyprus. Additionally, many tourism sites on the coast were sold, such as hotels in Becici, Herceg Novi, and Ulcinj (where one hotel sale had to be annulled because of accusations of corruption). This is important given that the basis of independent Montenegro's economic survival is supposed to be tourism. The Agency for Economic Restructuring uses public tenders, auctions, increases in share capital or sales of shares, and other methods in the privatization process. Accusations of corruption in this process came from the nongovernmental sector, especially GzP, an NGO critical of the government that has already declared its intention to compete as a list of independent candidates (given the system of proportional representation) in the next election. Although no formal charges have ever been filed, there is a lack of transparency in negotiations with prospective buyers based on the claim that it protects business secrets. Consequently, rumors circulate about what privatization contracts actually entail. A major factor feeding these corruption accusations is the fact that several privatizations – such as KAP, which represents 40 percent of Montenegro's GDP and 80 percent of its exports[26] – have involved only one bidder, owing to the limited interest of foreign investors in Montenegro.

The Parliamentary Committee to Follow the Publicity and Transparency of the Privatization Processes met twice in 2005. In September, it considered and rejected the opposition-proposed resolution on "the protection of the interests of the Republic of Montenegro and its citizens in the process of the privatization of KAP"; and in November, it rejected a similar opposition-proposed resolution in the wake of the failed privatization of Niksic Ironworks.[27] In fact, in establishing the committee, the governing parties limited its mandate and effectiveness. Now, the committee meetings serve as a venue for the opposition to air its arguments about the criminality and corruption of the current government.

Montenegro continues to function under a highly criticized Law on Conflict of Interest, amended in March 2005. It prohibits members of the government, Constitutional Court judges, other judges, the supreme state prosecutor, and the deputy state prosecutor from being part of an economic entity owned by the state or a local government.[28] Unfortunately, all other public officials can continue to serve one economic entity "in exceptional circumstances." On the positive side, by the December 31 deadline, 1,692 public officials (710 republic-level officials and 982 municipal-level officials) submitted reports on income and property for 2004 as required by law. Another 66 submitted incomplete data, and 310 (16 republic and State Union MPs and 294 local government officials and councillors) still had not complied with the law.[29] In another positive development, an ad hoc parliamentary committee worked throughout 2005 on an improved version of the law, finalizing the draft in October and sending it to the Council of Europe for commentary. The new draft should enter parliamentary procedure in 2006.

In May, the Parliament passed amendments to the Law on Political Party Financing, allocating more money from the state budget to political parties and distributing funds on the basis of political party affiliation, not parliamentarian/councillor club affiliation. In essence, the amendments ensured the distribution of funds to parties with only one representative in the Parliament or in a local assembly, bypassing established privileges for party clubs that must have two or more members. Furthermore, most political parties in Montenegro failed to submit mandatory financial reports on electoral campaign spending within 30 days of the aforementioned municipal elections, and municipal election commissions and the Republic Election Commission refused to supply information to the public as mandated by law.[30]

A 2002 law governs the public procurement process in Montenegro and functions as well as can be expected. In the four years of its implementation, several provisions indicate the law's weakness. The most frequent loophole is the "shopping method," or breaking down a public procurement into segments of less than €10,000 (US$8,200) so that the easier method of three bids, rather than public tender, can be employed. Typically, in seeking three bids, the official conducting the procurement will go to "friendly" companies. In September, the Commission for

Public Procurement prepared a new draft law that if adopted would close some of the loopholes in the current law. Still, the commission president stated that in the first 10 months of 2005, the commission had received 91 complaints, twice as many as in the previous year, demonstrating an increasing level of confidence in the commission.[31] Although representing only a fraction of total procurements, 40 of the 91 complaints were accepted, 38 rejected, and 13 thrown out.[32]

After two and a half years, the government finally approved a draft Law on Free Access to Information, which the Parliament adopted in November. The law went into effect in December, at which point MANS, a Montenegrin NGO, sent 89 requests for information to 28 state institutions. By the deadline provided in the law, MANS had received 15 positive answers and no response to 31 of its requests. Similarly, the Association of Young Journalists sent 204 requests to 47 public institutions. It received 86 responses (76 positive, 10 negative). In 89 cases, the AYJ received no answer, and it failed to deliver 29 requests because it could not find any contact information for 6 public institutions. Both MANS and the AYJ report that some of the negative replies contradict the provisions of the law, such as asking organizations to explain why they need the information or claiming not to have certain information. MANS and the AYJ plan to continue to pressure the government to develop systems to comply with the law.[33]

Finally, in December the Parliament passed the Law on Salaries and Other Compensations for Members of Parliament and Officials, which will raise the salaries of high-level executive government employees, parliamentarians, prosecutors, and judges beginning in March 2006. Although salaries will remain low in comparison with those in neighboring countries,[34] the increase is an initial positive step in the elimination of corruption incentives.

Ultimately, the implementation of laws and the increasing independence of the prosecutor's office and the judiciary should enable the discovery and prosecution of corruption cases. In 2005, there were few high-level charges of corruption in the privatization process or other parts of the public service. The exception would be the initiation of an investigation of three basic court judges for abuse of office in the sale of public land in Ulcinj. Unfortunately, the failure of the Parliament to lift the judges' immunity has stalled the investigation.

Lisa McLean is senior resident director of the Montenegro office of the National Democratic Institute, where she has served for the last seven years. In addition to the institutions and individuals mentioned as sources in this report, Aleksa Ivanovic, Natasa Bulatovic, and Vladan Djuranovic provided advice and background information.

---

[1] Statement of Preliminary Findings and Conclusions, Presidential Elections, Montenegro (Podgorica, Montenegro: OSCE/ODIHR, May 12, 2003), p. 1.
[2] In May, there was a one-day no-confidence debate on the president of the Parliament and a three-and-a-half-day no-confidence debate in the government, while in September there were several days

of debate on the president's decision to sign an agreement with Croatia compensating it for damage and looting during the 1991 attack on Dubrovnik.

[3] In 2005, the Parliament's budget was €2.9 million (US$2.37 million), or 0.1 percent of total government expenditures and €38,000 (US$31,160) per MP. Law on Budget of Montenegro for 2005, December 28, 2004.

[4] International Monetary Fund Press Release No. 05/173, July 26, 2005.

[5] D.M.C., "PDV i privatizacija pune drzavnu kasu" (VAT and privatization fill the state coffers), Vijesti, February 20, 2005.

[6] Labor Force Survey (Podgorica, Montenegro: Monstat, October 2004), p. 67.

[7] D.M., "Odbor za bezbjednost odbacio opozicionu rezoluciju o zloupotrebi policije" (Board for Security threw out opposition resolution on police abuse), Vijesti, January 17, 2006.

[8] Statement of Preliminary Findings and Conclusions, Presidential Elections, Montenegro (Podgorica, Montenegro: OSCE/ODIHR, May 12, 2003), p. 1.

[9] "Ostalo samo 24 stranke" (Only 24 parties left), MINA News Agency, May 13, 2005.

[10] Stop Avoiding Your Responsibility (Podgorica, Montenegro: Center for Democratic Transition, December 7, 2005), p. 2.

[11] For examples, see among other reports Preliminary Report of the Center for Democratic Transition, Elections on March 26 (Niksic, Montenegro: Center for Democratic Transition, March 27, 2005), p. 2; Elections in Budva (Budva, Montenegro: Center for Democratic Transition, May 23, 2005), p. 2.

[12] Milena Perovic, "Oporezuj me ako mozes," Monitor, November 18, 2005.

[13] Spisak nevladinih organizacija koje su konkurisale za raspodjelu sredstava za 2005. godinu (List of nongovernmental organizations that competed for distribution of 2005 funds, September 7, 2005 (www.skupstina.mn.yu, Report from the Committee for distributing funds to NGOs); and Odluka o raspodjeli sredstava nevladinim organizacijama za 2005. godinu (Decision on distribution of 2005 funds to NGOs), Broj(number) 360, Podgorica, Montenegro, September 26, 2005 (www.skupstina.mn.yu, Report from the Committee for distributing funds to NGOs).

[14] Osnove Programa Prelazne Vlade (Podgorica, Montenegro: Grupa za Promjene, July 2004), p. 4.

[15] "Zavrsen Nacrt socijalnog programa" (Draft of the social program finished), Mina Business, October 17, 2005; "U pomoa zovu kolege," MINA Business, December 12, 2005; "Uprava: Sindikat izbjegava direktan dijalog" (Administration: Union avoids direct dialogue), MINA Business, December 19, 2005.

[16] A 2004 report of the Montenegrin Media Institute reported 108 active media in Montenegro, including 45 print publications, 43 radio stations, and 15 TV stations. Quantitative Analysis of Montenegrin Media (Podgorica, Montenegro: Montenegrin Media Institute, June 2004), p. 1.

[17] Nedjeljko Rudovic, "Montenegrins Fear Crackdown on State Broadcaster," Balkan Insight, January 21, 2006.

[18] 2004 Annual Report of the Ombudsman (Podgorica, Montenegro: Ombudsman, Protector of Human Rights and Freedom, March 2005), pp. 32 and 33.

[19] Izvjestaj o radu upravnog suda, 2005. godina (Report on the work of the Administrative Court, 2005) (Podgorica, Montenegro: Upravni Sud Republike Crne Gore Administrative Court of the Republic of Montenegro, February 2006), pp. 4 and 5.

[20] Serbia and Montenegro 2005 Progress Report, SEC (2005) 1428 (Brussels: European Commission, November 9, 2005), p. 16.

[21] Izvjestaj o radu Vrhovnog Drzavnog Tuzioca Republike Crne Gore za 2004. godinu (Report on the work of the Supreme State Prosecutor of the Republic of Montenegro for 2004 (Podgorica, Montenegro: Office of the Supreme State Prosecutor, March 2005), pp. 11-13.

[22] Izvjestaj o radu Vrhovnog Drzavnog Tuzioca Republike Crne Gore za 2004. godinu (Report on the work of the Supreme State Prosecutor of the Republic of Montenegro for 2004 (Podgorica, Montenegro: Office of the Supreme State Prosecutor, March 2005), p. 57.

[23] Montenegro Continues to Cover for Its 1992 War Crimes (Podgorica, Montenegro: Prelevic Law Firm, April 2005); Serbia and Montenegro: Compliance with Obligations and Commitments and Implementation of the Post-Accession Co-operation Programme (Strasbourg: Council of Europe, July 13, 2005), p. 14.

[24] Serbia and Montenegro 2005 Progress Report, SEC (2005) 1428 (Brussels: European Commission, November 9, 2005), pp. 17 and 25.

[25] Serbia and Montenegro 2005 Progress Report, SEC (2005) 1428 (Brussels: European

Commission, November 9, 2005), p. 16.

[26] Milka Tadic-Mijovic, "Bilans poraza," Monitor, November 25, 2005.

[27] Midland Resources, a Russian-owned company registered in Great Britain, bought a controlling stake in Niksic Ironworks for €1,000 (US$820) in June 2004. In November 2005, the Russian directors abandoned the company and its more than 2,000 workers and later asked to dissolve the contract. The preliminary audit report confirmed that Midland failed to fulfill its contractual obligations related to investments and left a debt of €2.6 million (US$2,132,000) to the state. Source: MINA Business, November 9, 2005, and February 23, 2006.

[28] The governing parties introduced the amendments after the Constitutional Court ruled that the controversial "exception" inserted at the last minute into the 2004 law could not apply to high-level functionaries who are banned by the Constitution from holding more than one state position at a time.

[29] www.konfliktinteresa.cg.yu/funkcioneri/funkcioneri.htm. The figures indicate the status of reports filed as of December 31, 2005, announced by the Commission for Determining Conflict of Interest.

[30] Report on Breaching the Law on Political Party Financing (Podgorica, Montenegro: Center for Monitoring Elections, CEMI, December 22, 2005).

[31] M. Milosevic, "Tender se namjestaju," Vijesti, October 26, 2005.

[32] Press Briefing No. 971/2005, Commission for Public Procurement, October 18, 2005.

[33] Interviews with Vanja Calovic, coordinator, Network for Affirmation of the NGO Sector, and Boris Darmanovic, executive director, Association of Young Journalists, in February 2006.

[34] For example, the prime minister's base salary went from €402 (US$330)/month to €609 (US$499)/month. Source: MINA Business, December 28, 2005.

Kosovo

EXECUTIVE SUMMARY

Governance concerns related to determining the final status of Kosovo remained high on the domestic and international agenda in 2005, with competency and political willingness being tested across the board in Kosovo's institutions.

According to the Constitution of 1974, Kosovo was one of the constitutive units of the Yugoslav Federation. Named the Socialist Autonomous Province of Kosovo, it had territory, borders, a Constitution, and government institutions similar to those of the other republics that formerly constituted the Yugoslav Federation. After the demonstrations of Albanian students in 1981, the central federal government and the Republic of Serbia undertook a series of measures toward the eventual declaration of martial law in Kosovo, which began the process of undoing the constitutional position of Kosovo in the Yugoslav Federation. The position of

Kosovo in the Yugoslav Federation was changed on March 23, 1989, when constitutional amendments were approved under the circumstances of a severe curfew in Kosovo, conducted by significant police and military forces.

These constitutional amendments began the installation of a system of apartheid, turning the majority population (the Albanians) into second-class citizens. A year later, on July 2, 1990, the Kosovo Parliament announced a constitutional declaration of independence from Serbia. Three days after, Serbia enacted a series of illegal measures, including the abolition of the Kosovo Parliament. The majority of parliamentarians were forced to leave Kosovo, while Serbia essentially began the occupation of Kosovo.

In December 1989, a new political party was established – the Democratic League of Kosovo (LDK) – which took the features of a national movement, and afterward other Albanian political parties emerged. Also at the end of 1989, the first nongovernmental organizations (NGOs), such as the Council for Defense of Human Rights and Freedoms (CDHRF), and the Mother Teresa charitable society, were established, and the organization of independent trade unions began. These very soon became trade unions of the unemployed, as within a short time the dismissal of Albanians from their jobs in dramatic numbers began. Under the leadership of the LDK and its head, Ibrahim Rugova, a peaceful protest movement was organized, and in fact, a parallel system of daily life by the majority population of Kosovo started to develop.

The parallel system was especially implemented in the areas of education and health care, while their funding was organized by the government in exile. Education was subsidized by the Kosovo Government Fund, which was created by contributions from Albanians. As the armed conflict burst out in some parts of the former Yugoslavia, in Kosovo affairs were being conducted according to a peaceful doctrine known as "rugovism." However, when Kosovo was left out of the Dayton accords, many people turned away from the LDK and Rugova and toward more militant movements.

The end of 1997 marks the public appearance of the Kosovo Liberation Army and its accelerated growth. The peaceful movement led by Rugova, although still supported by a majority of the population, had started losing its support to military forces. In 1998, battles took place in which the Serb military forces prevailed and which militarily were better prepared, better supplied, and numerically larger. Escalation of tensions and military actions continued despite international pressure and a verifying mission by the Organization for Security and Cooperation in Europe.

The end of 1998 and beginning of 1999 brought a new offensive by Serb forces. After a massacre carried out by the Serb forces in the village of Recak (January 15, 1999), the international community, and the Contact Group in particular, urgently prepared the Rambouillet Conference, whose documents were not signed by the Serb delegation. Upon that refusal, NATO forces began their military air raid against the Serb forces, while Serb forces undertook a campaign of ethnic cleansing of territories, resulting in 1 million forcibly displaced people, about 12,000 killed, and about 4,600 missing (data from 2003 collected by the CDHRF). The NATO military intervention lasted for 78 days and resulted in the signing of the Kumanovo Agreement. Serb forces left the territory of Kosovo, while on June 10, 1999, the UN Security Council promulgated Resolution 1244, whereof Kosovo was placed under the jurisdiction of the UN International Administration Mission in Kosovo (UNMIK) and NATO forces (KFOR) were introduced to provide peace and security in Kosovo and the region.

In 2000, UNMIK worked with political factions to develop the Constitutional Framework for the Provisional Institutions of Self-Government (PISG). The PISG provided substantial autonomy, delineating the powers of UNMIK and Kosovar institutions. Since 2000, Kosovar institutions have taken on more and more responsibilities – however, with mixed results. After the outbreak in ethnic-based violence in 2004, UNMIK decided to increase the pace of its handover of powers to enable domestic institutions to take on more direct responsibility for the protection of minorities as well as overall governance issues within Kosovo. The result has been mixed partially because of the larger status issues and capacity to take on enhanced capacities during a relatively short time.

In 2005, the international community began to take serious steps to finalize Kosovo's status. The process started with UN envoy Kai Eide's report to the Security Council in May that was critical of Kosovo's governing institutions. However, with the appointment of two senior diplomats, Martti Ahtisaari (former president of Finland) and his deputy Albert Rohan (Austria), to head the international delegation and Frank Wisner as U.S. representative, a timeline was set to resolve Kosovo's status. Both have made it clear that Kosovo's status will be resolved in 2006. The number one issue on the agenda is the status of the Kosovo Serb community, which has tended to work more closely with the Belgrade negotiating team than with Pristina on negotiations. Regardless, the international community holds as a key demand that the Kosovo institutions go beyond lip service and provide the Serb community with assurances that their rights will be protected. The international community has made this a crucial factor in meeting the Albanians' demands.

Ahtisaari, who brought the parties to the signing of 1999 Kumanovo Agreement (which ended NATO action against Serbia and Montenegro), started the negotiation process that will determine the final status of Kosovo. The Kosovo delegation entered the process with full independence for Kosovo as its platform, while the Serb delegation maintained a platform of less than independence and more than autonomy. Regardless of the fact that these negotiating parties stand distant from each other, the process is expected to end in 2006 and a status solution found based on the principles set down by the six-nation Contact Group on Kosovo. Those principles will include, among other things, the stipulations that Kosovo's final status must be binding but cannot be a status achieved through force.

National Democratic Governance. The transfer of power from internationals to the PISG continued with increased intensity in 2005. Elections brought the creation of a new government, and the Parliament for the first time has a real opposition, which has to some extent revived parliamentary life, although opposition parties frequently walked out of the Parliament. The political struggle of the opposition in the Parliament, although in some moments quite limited, has raised the level of political dialogue in institutions and society in general and has started to educate the public that in a democracy all subjects are open for discussion. No progress was made on the decentralization process. *Kosovo's national democratic governance rating remains at 5.75.*

Electoral Process. Since the end of the conflict in 1999, Kosovo has had two sets of local elections and two national elections, which were in general assessed as free and fair by local and international observers. Media coverage of the elections was balanced, even though there are some partisan newspapers. Political parties accepted the election results. During the first elections internationals interfered a lot to help the establishment of Kosovo government, but in the second elections internationals let locals establish government themselves, which strengthened local institutions. In 2005, electoral competences were transferred largely to the domestic Kosovo Central Election Commission Secretariat (CECS). Voter turnout has continually and rapidly decreased from the first to the last elections. Parties have difficulty communicating their distinct policies to voters – that, in concert with an election system that does not allow voters to make choices based on individual or local interests, is driving down voter turnout. *In 2005, the International Crisis Group joined the advocacy effort opposing use of the closed list system, but it appears that the 2006 local elections will take place under the existing electoral system. Kosovo's rating for electoral process remains unchanged at 4.75.*

Civil Society. In 2005, government acceptance of NGO activities decreased. The vocabulary used by people from the government to describe NGOs also changed; they described NGOs as small organizations that work for money, and chose other language that undermines or belittles NGOs' democratic role. Activists of the movement Vetvendosja were often arrested and ill-treated by police. The activities of the civil society, especially those related to anticorruption and transparency, have decreased owing to the negotiations process for the status of Kosovo, which has dampened civil society enthusiasm for criticism of the Kosovo administration. Although NGOs have continued to define their missions and started to build a profile for themselves, their public image is weak. Within the PISG, some affairs were trusted to these institutions according to the Constitutional Framework. However, the PISG had only a partial role in ownership issues, such as privatization. The civil society sector remains donor driven and depends mainly on foreign funds, as an environment conducive to local philanthropy has not been created. The number of policy- and/or advocacy-oriented NGOs increased; however, cooperation among NGOs remains low. *Kosovo's rating for civil society worsens from 4.00 to 4.25 owing to* *its stagnation and failure to provide checks and balances to the emerging government structures and its reduced public willingness to engage in critical monitoring during status talk negotiations.*

Independent Media. In general, the media are enhancing their professionalism, but there are differences between electronic and printed media. The media are still facing many difficulties. According to the Association of Professional Journalists in Kosovo, media in Kosovo experience three types of pressure: violence by the police and security personnel of governmental actors; financial constraints; and political pressure. Political pressure is used primarily against investigative journalists, while ordinary pressure is used against media by government institutions, especially in advertising matters. Printed media are more advanced, especially in the area of investigative journalism; however, circulation is very low. Electronic media have been observably more closed and cautious since the events of March 17, 2004. Meanwhile, the press is filled with articles on corruption, mismanagement of power, and other issues that the electronic media are reluctant to broach. *Kosovo's rating for media remains unchanged at 5.50.*

Local Democratic Governance. Though efforts for a serious reform of local democratic governance took a backseat to the highly politicized decentralization issue, there was a general consolidation of services. This resulted from the passage of two mandates with stable democratically elected governing structures. However, the system still lacks clear independence in running local affairs, with the special representative of the secretary-general having the ultimate power to turn over any local assembly decision on the one hand and no clear assumption of powers by the central authorities of the PISG on the other. However, there was a tendency to debate the situation openly, including at the level of local governments. *Kosovo's local democratic governance rating remains at 5.50.*

Judicial Framework and Independence. The implementation of three sets of laws makes Kosovo a unique and difficult place. Courts at all levels are overloaded with cases that remain unsolved for many years. A criminal code has been adopted by Kosovo's Parliament, but the process of implementing laws is a big concern. The Parliament has managed to adopt more laws this year, and the process of promulgating them has strengthened. *Kosovo's rating for judicial framework and independence remains unchanged at 5.75.*

Corruption. According to many reports and analyses, 2005 was marked by widespread corruption within governmental structures at both national and local levels. Though a handful of anticorruption laws were enacted, most were not implemented. Kosovars faced a year of intensive media reports on alleged corruption but saw very little in the way of legal measures to curb the abuses. A law establishing an anticorruption agency has not yet been promulgated by the Kosovo Parliament, which was itself a target of media reports on corruption. Allegations of corruption and nepotism were especially directed at the top, with the ministries, and offices of the prime minister and president leading the list. On the other hand, there was little response from high officials to improve transparency. *The rating for corruption remains unchanged at 6.00.*

Outlook for 2006. Standards and negotiations for the political status of Kosovo were the top priority for the PISG, UNMIK, and all other political structures in Kosovo during 2005. Negotiations for political status will continue to be the main if not the only issue during 2006 as well. The position of minorities, particularly the Serb minority, will determine the "future status of Kosovo." Previous experience with the Balkans crisis shows that any agreement is very fragile, and Kosovo appears to be no exception. Therefore, the settlement has to be approved by the UN Security Council. The international community will continue to be present in Kosovo after that, but it will be in a different form from the UNMIK, and the European Union will have the biggest role. Both the negotiations team and the overall process were hit hard by the death of Kosovo president Ibrahim Rugova. The LDK may split as a consequence of a possible battle among factions, and for the time being there is no leader with the authority to keep the party unified. And while everything will be led by the negotiating team modified after Rugova's death until the end of status negotiations, it is also expected that political parties will redesign their strategies, seeing Rugova's death as an opportunity to strengthen themselves. Therefore, together with the negotiations process there will be preparations for new elections, which will be required once Kosovo's status has been finalized.

MAIN REPORT

National Democratic Governance

2004	2005	2006
n/a	5.75	5.75

After June 1999, the UN took charge of creating management structures in Kosovo. Governmental power was transferred gradually to the Constitutional Framework for the Provisional Institutions of Self-Government (PISG), and dual powers in Kosovo are still present, although the process of determining the future status of Kosovo has already begun under the leadership of Martti Ahtisaari, appointed by UN secretary-general Kofi Annan. The Democratic League of Kosovo (LDK), led by President Ibrahim Rugova, won the greatest number of seats in the Parliament in the October 23, 2004 elections but could not form the government. Thus a coalition of formerly rival parties, Alliance for the Future of

Kosova (AAK), formed the government in December 2004, led by the former Kosovo Liberation Army (KLA) commander Ramush Haradinaj.

Prime Minister Haradinaj distinguished himself as a bold leader. In order to help integrate the Serb community into social developments, he managed to appoint Slavisa Petkovic, a Serb, as minister of returns and communities. Though Haradinaj gained the support of the public and the international community, the Hague Tribunal announced his indictment for war crimes on March 8, 2005. Haradinaj resigned and surrendered voluntarily to The Hague, proposing Bajram Kosumi as the new prime minister. President Rugova nominated Kosumi on March 18, 2005, and the Kosovo Parliament approved the Kosumi government on March 23, 2005. Despite worries, the government remained stable, thanks to Haradinaj's compliance with the tribunal, and focused on preparing for status negotiations.

In December 2003, the UN Interim Administration Mission in Kosovo (UNMIK) worked with the Kosovar government to approve a list of standards for measuring progress in Kosovo, which included everything from the rule of law to minority rights. Kai Eide, Kofi Annan's envoy to Kosovo, began a standards evaluation mission in June 2005; he was finished after four visits, which focused on meeting representatives of both national and local governance as well as civil society leaders. In October, Eide advised the UN Security Council in his report that status talks could no longer wait, noting that Kosovar institutions were not adequately addressing the concerns of the Serb minority. Eide also had strong criticism for Kosovo's capacity to address crime, corruption, and nepotism in the society and its institutions. The reaction to Eide's report was positive across the political spectrum.

On April 29, 2005, the special representative of the secretary-general (SRSG), Jessen Petersen, proposed the establishment of the Kosovo Political Forum to create Kosovo policy; the forum did not have the support of the Parliament Speaker (from the ruling LDK) and was disbanded after two meetings. Following pressure from the opposition and the general public, President Rugova established a status negotiations team, which included Parliament Speaker Nexhat Daci, Prime Minister Bajram Kosumi (from the coalition partner AAK), opposition leaders Hashim Thaci from the Democratic Party of Kosova (PDK) and Veton Surroi from the Citizens List Hour (ORA), and Blerim Shala (*Zeri* daily newspaper editor) as coordinator.

Kosovo's Parliament has a total of 120 seats. Hashim Thaci's PDK, established with the demilitarization of the guerrilla structure after the 1999 conflict, has 30 seats. The other small but vigorous opposition party, the ORA, run by publisher Veton Surroi, has 6 seats. Since March 2004, Serbs have boycotted the Parliament. The opposition has the force to revive parliamentary life and affect the strengthening of institutions, but shared competences between the PISG and UNMIK have proved problematic. The PDK and the ORA have frequently walked out of the Parliament in protest of Speaker Daci's authoritative behavior. Daci has blocked votes on a multitude of initiatives from the opposition, especially related to establishing mechanisms to investigate PISG misconduct.

Even so, 70 laws were approved by the Parliament in 2005, though the body is not effective in implementing legislation. The international community has noted that decentralization remains one of Kosovo's essential challenges, along with the return of the displaced and the government's exercise of power across the territory of Kosovo. For the first time after the war, direct meetings between the government ministers of Kosovo and Serbia took place in 2005. Minister of Local Governance Lutfi Haziri met his Serb counterpart, Zoran Loncar, in Vienna, and Minister of Culture Astrit Haraqija met his counterpart, Dragan Kojadinovic, in Belgrade and Bulgaria. Minister Haraqija has promised €1.5 million (US$1.89 million) more from Kosovo institutions to rebuild churches, while Haziri and Loncar discussed decentralization in Kosovo. These meetings were criticized for not being discussed and approved in advance by the Parliament.

Of Kosovo's 100,000 Serbs, one-third live in Mitrovica and the northern part of Kosovo, whereas the other two-thirds live in Serb enclaves in different parts of Kosovo. Kosovo's standard of living is low, with the average monthly salary at around €200 (US$253) and a high rate of unemployment. The privatization process of socially owned enterprises improved markedly in 2005, with another 132 privatized. The process gained momentum after the arrival of the current UNMIK Pillar Four head, Joachim Ruecker.

In May 2005, the largest opposition party formed a shadow cabinet, or so-called Good Governance Cabinet, although the activities of the body have been limited mostly to press conferences. As part of the transfer of power, on July 19 UNMIK presented the Kosovo government with drafts for establishing two new ministries (Ministry of Internal Affairs and Ministry of Justice), which were made official in December when related powers were handed over to the Kosovo government.

Although the political struggles of the opposition in the Parliament have been limited, they have helped raise the level of political dialogue in public institutions and society in general. What stability the government has achieved can be attributed to the involvement of the entire political spectrum, international influence, and a consensus in the general public of the importance of resolving Kosovo's status. Consequently, the status negotiating team is currently considered the strongest and most respected political mechanism in Kosovo governance.

Electoral Process

2004	2005	2006
5.25	4.75	4.75

Four elections have taken place in postconflict Kosovo with no observable irregularities. Elections were held at the municipal level in 2000 and 2002 and at the central level in 2001 and 2004. Domestic and international observers qualified these elections as free and fair. A record 73 percent turnout was noted in the 2000 local elections, which were the first elections after the war and showed an eagerness among the public to build domestic, democratic institutions by suffrage. However, immense discrepancies between public expectations and actual results have created a sharp sense of disappointment and have severely affected voter turnout in subsequent elections. The 2001 parliamentary elections had a 64 percent turnout, and only 51 percent of voters went to the polls in 2004. Serbian president Boris Tadic called on Kosovo Serbs to participate in the elections, directly opposing the Serbian government, the Orthodox Church, and most Kosovo Serb politicians, who had called for a boycott.

Several factors have driven down voter turnout: Political parties have a limited ability to communicate distinct policies to voters, and the election system fails to produce choices based on individual or local interests. The low level of participation shows that the public is concerned not only with the future status of Kosovo, but also with high unemployment, a failing education and health care system, and poor infrastructure.[1] However, the status issue seemed to reassert itself in 2005 with the approaching Kosovo status talks.

Since 1999, the Organization for Security and Cooperation in Europe (OSCE) Mission in Kosovo's Department of Elections has organized elections and enacted election rules. However, over the last four years the mission has transferred some of its responsibilities to the local election authorities, mainly the Central Election Commission and its Secretariat, which for the first time are expected to organize local elections in 2006.

In preparation for the last Kosovo assembly, the OSCE mission was still charged with maintaining the voter list, running the Out of Kosovo Voting[2] as well as the Count and Results Center. Though no elections were organized and maintained exclusively by the PISG, political parties have been involved in the process. Despite overall satisfaction with the electoral process in Kosovo, stakeholders were not as pleased with the election law itself.

Central and local elections have both used a proportional system with closed lists as stipulated by the electoral law. Civil society and small parties have been the loudest in calling for changes to the law that would allow for open lists in a mixed majority and proportional electoral system. Proponents claim that these changes would give the public a wider range of choices among candidates rather than political parties, as preferred by the OSCE.[3] The OSCE insists that the proportional closed-list system makes it possible to maintain the sufficient participation of women in politics and that "open lists cause confusion among the voters."

By law, 30 percent of political party candidates in all elections must be women, and the proportional representation system using "closed" party lists has indeed ensured that 28 percent of the Parliament are women, or 34 out of 120 seats. However, the system has been criticized as undemocratic because it narrows voters' choices to three or four significant political parties. REFORMA 2004, a coalition comprising 300 NGOs, launched a campaign throughout the second half of 2004 and into 2005 asking UNMIK to change the electoral law to include open lists. This advocacy effort was joined in 2005 by the International Crisis Group. However, it appears that the 2006 local elections will take place under the existing electoral system.

Electoral competences were transferred largely to the domestic Kosovo Central Election Commission Secretariat (CECS) in 2005. The OSCE states that the

CECS has proven its ability to organize elections, opening the possibility for the next elections to be run entirely from the PISG. However, this institution has yet to elect a chief executive director since the resignation last September of Adnan Merovci (the first local executive director) on accusations of bias.

The OSCE mission has thus far trained, mentored, and monitored the CECS. It continued to do so throughout 2005 by further building the capacity of the Secretariat, which operates as an apolitical multiethnic institution. Furthermore, Head of Mission Ambassador Werner Wnendt will continue to chair the commission, a body charged with election administration. The mission hopes to take a purely advisory role in the next municipal elections, which are scheduled for 2006.

Civil Society

2004	2005	2006
4.25	4.00	4.25

The postconflict development of the Kosovar NGO community can be characterized as an income opportunity rather than a civic responsibility. Along with the constitutional freedom of association, UNMIK's Regulation 1999/22 provided a legal basis for establishing and registering NGOs and created a conducive environment by organizing groups into associations and foundations. The criteria for NGO registration is simple: Three individuals must cosign the NGO act of establishment and statute, and the certificate of registration must be issued within 60 days.

The UNMIK Liaison Office was initially established in 2000, with competences for NGO registration later transferred to the Ministry of Public Services. Organizations were obliged to report to their donors, while groups enjoying public benefit status were obliged to provide an annual financial report to the NGO Registration Liaison Office. Easy registration procedures, access to donors and funding, and a lack of government interference all contributed to the establishment of a large number of NGOs, and estimates show that by the end of 2003 over 2,000 NGOs were registered.

However, this conducive environment has not produced an increase in NGO capacity, creation of internal structures, division of responsibility, financial sustainability, or an improved public image for NGOs. Until the end of 2001, most NGOs implemented projects in the areas of democracy building, minority protection, women's rights, education, and so forth, but a majority did not have a clearly defined mission. Many NGOs have registered solely to secure public benefit status, which has hurt the public image of NGOs in general. Initially, the number of policy and advocacy initiatives was very small.

After the establishment of the PISG in 2001, most donors shifted their focus from civil society to institutional building and strengthening. Some of these donors stopped funding Kosovar NGOs altogether. From 2002 to 2005, NGOs have been establishing a higher profile. The number of policy- and advocacy-oriented NGOs has increased, and they are playing a more influential role in legislative processes at the local and central levels of government. However, willingness to be critical during status talk negotiations appears to have lessened, making the organizations less of a counterweight to government powers than anticipated, at least during this time period. And despite efforts, there has been little influence by such groups on the policies of UNMIK, which has been reticent to consult civil society. UNMIK and the OSCE completely ignored the REFORMA 2004 campaign under the pretext that they had reached consensus on the election system with the major political parties.

Kosovo's NGO sector has not yet matured into a pillar of civil society. The sector suffers from a lack of openness and transparency, weak governing structures, and a poor public image. Additionally, a low level of local philanthropy means that most NGOs depend mainly on foreign funds. As an example of these shortcomings, the 2005 Trade Union of Education strike for higher teacher salaries resulted in a small increase of €7 (US$8.84) per month. It was clear from the strike that the existing organization of trade unions in fact lacks unity and is unsustainable. Without negotiation skills and public relations expertise, the union could not attract membership or followers.

However, the increasing number and strength of watchdog and advocacy organizations have led to changes in the existing government setup, language, and treatment regarding NGOs. Vetvendosja (Self-Determination), one of the largest and most controversial movements to emerge from the Kosova Action Network (KAN), is led by former student leader Albin Kurti. Responding to the upcoming final status talks, the group emblazoned its slogan, "No Negotiations – Self-Determination!" on every corner and facade in Kosovo.

Kosovo's public university has the largest number of students. Even though senior management claims the university is independent and depoliticized, the state's main political forces have not given up their influence on the institution. In 2005, the minister of education dismissed university rector Arsim Bajrami (active in the PDK) on the pretext that during his election process the legislation in force was breached. Many felt that his dismissal was a sign of change in political control of the university leadership. Legislation on the establishment and registration of private higher education institutions is quite liberal, and their number has increased. Except for the private university, American University of Kosovo, developed cooperatively by several American universities, private institutions have not had much of an impact on the education system in Kosovo.

There are no data as to whether the number of Wahhabi sect followers has increased, but they do not enjoy wide support and have no influence on the general public. The Orthodox Church is quite active and influential among the Serb population. The activities of other religious groups, such as evangelicals and Jehovah's Witnesses, are geared largely toward providing humanitarian services.

Independent Media

2004	2005	2006
5.50	5.50	5.50

In principle, all UN declarations on press freedom apply to Kosovo, since it is under UN administration. The Temporary Media Commissioner (TMC) was established by UNMIK in June 2000 to regulate the media in Kosovo[4] and affirms Articles 19 and 29 of the Universal Declaration of Human Rights as well as the five provisions on press freedom in the European Convention on Human Rights.

However, Reporters Without Borders' annual Worldwide Press Freedom Index ranks Kosovo 100 out of 167 countries researched. This makes Kosovo the worst location in Europe for press freedom and the only place in Europe where a journalist, Bardhyl Ajeti from the daily *Bota Sot*, was murdered in 2005. The data from Reporters Without Borders match the picture portrayed by the Association of Professional Journalists in Kosovo (APJK), whose end-of-year report stressed a significant increase in violence against journalists in 2005. Among over 20 cases of reported violence against journalists from police forces, municipal or central government officials, and employers, there has been only one public apology.[5]

The majority of cases involved the use of unreasonable force by members of the Kosovo Police Service (KPS). Refki Morina, spokesperson for the KPS, says this is due to a lack of proper training. "KPS officers undertake a six-month course during which there just isn't enough time to concentrate on the details of how to deal with the press, especially during protests, where both parties have a job to do," said Morina on January 13, 2005. The six-month training time for KPS officers is indeed inadequate. However, the greater issue is the lack of tradition among Kosovo police in dealing nonviolently with the public, especially the democratic press, which is viewed as "aggressive" by police officers brought up in the Communist era, when the press's job was to be far more obedient to the state apparatus.

The APJK reported three forms of pressure applied to journalists by powerful state and nonstate actors in 2005. Apart from direct use of force, mainly by state police and security staff, political and financial pressures were also brought to bear on the Kosovar media. Investigative journalists – who are labeled "opposition media" when they cover issues that portray the government in a compromising light – are frequent targets of political pressure. In most cases, state actors ban these journalists from the criticized institutions. Telephone and mobile phone text message threats are also common experiences for the majority of investigative journalists. The police response to such threats is reportedly inadequate, discouraging most journalists from reporting incidents.

The other common pressure from the government is to withdraw advertising from critical newspapers. This is an effective strategy in Kosovo's poorly developed economy and private advertising market, where state and local administration tenders and job openings make up the bulk of advertising for much of the print media. It is therefore difficult for the media's editorial and news-gathering functions to remain free of interference from the government or private owners. Yet neither political party has a complete power over newspapers or broadcast media, and the majority of the public (largely Kosovar Albanians) enjoys a relatively diverse selection, particularly in print media. However, total circulation is low: Only 20,000 copies were sold in Kosovo in 2005. Nevertheless, the print media remain the only source of investigative journalism. Since the March 17 riots in 2004,[6] broadcasting media have become even more isolated and cautious, rarely reporting on governmental transgressions. The press, on the other hand, is full of stories of corruption and misuse of public functions.

By contrast, both print and electronic sources for ethnic communities in the extremely important year to come, when final negotiations on Kosovo's status will take place, are as poor as in the immediate postwar years in Kosovo. Information programming directed to the largest minority in Kosovo, Serbs, is extreme on both ends. At one end, the minority news programming in Serbian of the public broadcaster Radio Television Kosovo (RTK),[7] is unpopular with Kosovar Serbs, who perceive it as providing politically correct, anemic, and irrelevant programming (in the Pristina media, Serb journalists are more inclined to please Albanian bosses). On the other end, the reporting from Serbia on Serbian TV stations, mostly RTS, Pink, and BK represents a view from Belgrade that is heavily politicized and detached from the everyday problems of Kosovo Serbs.

However, it is important to note that the code of journalistic conduct set by the TMC in 2000[8] to end incitements to ethnic hatred and violence in the press and broadcast media was largely respected in 2005. Although there is higher awareness than ever before that inflammatory language should not be used in ethnic contexts, this does not apply to political rival groups, where there has been a rise in public accusations, complaints, and libel lawsuits.

The majority of electronic media are privately owned, but Albanian news from the public broadcaster RTK remains the most watched and trusted news program for Kosovar Albanians. The popularity of mainstream RTK news broadcasts in Albanian does not translate to the same credibility among the Serbs. For the Serb minority, RTK's Serbian service remains the least trusted news broadcast because it is perceived as a channel for the Albanian majority. This differs from the situation in neighboring countries like Albania, Macedonia, and Serbia, where private stations have a lead on news viewership and public trustworthiness.[9]

The financial viability of private media is subject not only to market forces, but to political influences and donor commitment. Journalists and media outlets are able to form their own viable professional associations, but many consider these associations too weak and unsupportive when journalists are faced with violence, pressures from employers, or other threats. The most support offered by the more prominent associations, such as the APJK, would be a press release that is published in the Kosovar media. Newspaper distribution is part of an old state public system, Rilindja, and has functioned in the same manner for 30 years. The daily *Koha Ditore*, the most sold paper, has its own alternative distribution system for two Kosovo towns, Pristina and Prizren. There are plans to privatize the Rilindja network.

Kosovo enjoys unrestricted access to the Internet, and an Internet cafe culture flourishes throughout Kosovar towns. However, a lack of electricity directly affects the use of the Internet in many villages and homes, and it is unclear how much the Internet is used for domestic news circulation and discussion in comparison with access to news and entertainment outside of Kosovo.

Local Democratic Governance

2004	2005	2006
n/a	5.50	5.50

In 2005, local administrations continued to develop and consolidate their newly established governance structures, while some improvement in their capacities and public services was also noticed. A key highlight is the positive trend in the recruitment of minority communities: 16 of the 30 municipalities have met or exceeded targets on this point.[10] However, the overarching obstacles at the local level are connected with security concerns, the sense of uncertainty over the future status of Kosovo, and limited opportunities for civil servants in Kosovo to sustain a livelihood.

However, the prevailing issue in the debate about the future of Kosovo was the devolution of power from the central to the local level. In spite of further consolidation of local governing structures, the various plans for decentralization remained highly controversial. Initially, the question was how to return Serbs to the PISG. Belgrade-sponsored parallel administrative structures[11] continue to operate in most predominantly Kosovo-Serb municipalities. The main areas of parallel activities are courts, education, administration, and health care. A number of Kosovars rely on these administrative services, as UNMIK documents are not recognized in Serbia. The parallel health care system continues to function alongside the PISG-run health care and is financed by the Serbian Ministry of Health.

It appears that the March 2004 riots convinced the international administration to substitute its efforts to persuade Serbs to meld their parallel structures into Kosovo institutions with the decentralization of some essential functions, the most sensitive being security. Already in 2002, decentralization was promised to Kosovo Serbs in return for their participation in the elections and provisional institutions. However, according to Kai Eide, the UN envoy in Kosovo, real efforts and political will had been lacking until recently. During the summer of 2005, a desire to achieve quick results led to a less ambitious approach and insufficient consultations with those involved. Thus, the result has been "too little, too late."[12]

Implementation of the decentralization process has proved difficult. The international community had to exercise pressure on Kosovo's institutions on several occasions to advance the process. The main issue is the area and population size of the pilot municipality units. The initial proposal was changed to accommodate mainly Kosovo Serb concerns; a second, so-called plan B proposed amendments addressing those concerns and increasing the number of cadastral units within the pilot municipality units. However, Serbs boycotted the two Kosovo Serb majority pilot municipalities of Gracanica and Partesh. The boycott of these two pilot program municipalities came in the context of a general boycott of the PISG that started with the March 2004 events.

A positive step was taken on September 16 when delegations from Pristina and Belgrade met to discuss decentralization.[13] However, disagreements mounted toward the end of the year when Pristina and Belgrade appeared with their platforms for negotiations, neither of which foresaw a serious strategy for how to return Serbs to the PISG. On the other hand, the Kosovo Ministry of Local Governance began 2006 with a third new plan on decentralization, which is seen as an ad hoc solution related to the status negotiations on this issue rather than as an actual reform plan.

Specialists claim that the reform of local government has been reduced to a simple devolution of powers within the scope of decentralization.[14] Moreover, it is indisputable that the status negotiations will further hamper reform, since it is unlikely to gain the will of both Serbs and Albanians, who have opposite aims regarding Kosovo's status. Already, the actual legal framework on local self-government has shown serious deficiencies in securing the independence of municipalities to deal with local issues.[15] By the end of December 2005 the situation had not changed. Overall, there has been no change in the functioning of local administrations in line with international standards and the law, which remains under the jurisdiction of the SRSG. This is reflected in practice when the SRSG overrules the decisions of municipalities because of violations of the law.[16] The fact that it has proved virtually impossible to terminate public officials for misconduct has also raised many ethics problems.[17]

The legislation assigns public functions to the municipalities as if they are branches of the central authority,[18] thereby not taking sufficiently into account that municipalities must be political entities with a certain degree of political, administrative, and financial independence. The municipalities exercise all powers not expressly reserved to the central authority.[19] Legislation states that whatever responsibility is not reserved to the central authority remains with the municipality, but it sets no limits for the central authority to assume responsibilities by later legislation and thus does not provide safeguards to prevent marginalizing or rendering insignificant the remaining responsibilities of the municipalities.

Another important aspect of the legal framework of Kosovo is the lack of recourse for municipalities to judicial remedy against the interference of the central authority in the right to local self-government. Recourse to judicial remedy is one of the fundamental principles enshrined in the European Charter of Local Self-Government. Furthermore, financial transfers are made to municipalities by the central authority based on objective criteria, including an assessment of the financial needs and resources of each municipality and the spending priorities established by the central authority. This section bears uncertainty as to whether and to what extent the spending priorities of the central authority could prevail over the financial needs and resources of the municipalities.

Overall, the general political environment is not expected to be very reform-friendly for the upcoming status year. Thus it is unrealistic to expect any significant result on reform of local self-government before the status question is resolved.

Judicial Framework and Independence

2004	2005	2006
6.00	5.75	5.75

UN Security Council Resolution 1244 serves as a basis on which to govern Kosovo until its political status is resolved. Since then, Kosovo has been governed by three sets of laws: Yugoslav laws adopted before March 23, 1989; UNMIK regulations; and national legislation created after the establishment of the PISG.

Resolution 1244 designates the SRSG as the chief decision-making authority in Kosovo. The legislative, executive, and judicial powers are all under SRSG authority. Additionally, the SRSG is acknowledged as the final power in many issues, such as community protection, parliamentary dismissal, appointment and dismissal of local and international judges and prosecutors, decision making on certain foreign relations issues, signing laws approved by the Parliament, and other authorizations specified in Chapter 8 of the Constitutional Framework. The SRSG also has the mandate to develop provisional democratic and self-government institutions of Kosovo and to monitor the transfer of civil administration responsibilities from UNMIK to those institutions.

The SRSG is the head of UNMIK, whose structure consists of four pillars: the police and the judiciary, civil administration, democratization and democratic institutions, and reconstruction and economic development. The first two pillars are managed by the UN, the third pillar by the OSCE, and the fourth by the European Union (EU). The KFOR (NATO forces) acts outside these structures.

The governing structure in Kosovo is a complex hybrid of UN and domestic responsibilities. The UN has established a system whereby those with power (UNMIK) are not accountable to the public, while those without power (elected officials) can be held accountable by the general public. Consequently, the transfer of power to elected officials cannot be accomplished properly until the status of Kosovo is resolved; Kosovo has remained a stateless government for the past six years.

In order to fill a vacuum in legislation, UNMIK/SRSG allowed the application of Yugoslav laws approved before March 23, 1989. By contrast, in order to implement a provisional self-government framework, UNMIK/SRSG approved Regulation 2001/9, which is otherwise known as the Constitutional Framework of Kosovo. In terms of content and structure, this regulation is similar to the constitutions of countries, although there are issues that make this a legal act sui generis, representing an interlacement of local and international governance.

Chapter 2 of the Constitutional Framework fixes three main principles, which

Kosovar institutions and officials must respect. These are (1) to exercise authority in accordance with the provisions of Resolution 1244; (2) to promote and respect the rule of law, human rights, and freedoms in compliance with democratic principles; and (3) to promote and observe the principle of division of power between the legislative, executive, and judicial powers. Chapters 4 and 5 deal with human rights and the rights of communities; although the Constitutional Framework does not specify human rights separately, it accepts the international standards determined by major international acts, from the Universal Declaration of Human Rights to the Framework Convention for the Protection of National Minorities. All international documents in this field, according to Regulation 24/99 on applicable law, become a part of Kosovo law.

Chapter 5 offers guarantees for the expression and protection of ethnic, religious, linguistic, and cultural identities. The Constitutional Framework also offers constitutional guarantees for the participation of all communities in the governmental structures of the PISG. Chapter 6 of the Constitutional Framework arranges the division of responsibilities, while Chapter 7 determines the provisional institutions of Kosovo's self-government. As for responsibilities, three types are mentioned: PISG responsibilities; common responsibilities of international and PISG authorities; and reserved powers for the SRSG.

The laws approved by the Parliament of Kosovo do not enter into force unless they are officially declared valid by the SRSG. The Parliament approves laws and resolutions from its authorities within the PISG, appoints the president of Kosovo, approves or refuses the candidate for prime minister as well as the list of candidates for the government, decides on the motion for a vote of confidence in the government, and so forth. The function of the president of Kosovo is limited by the powers of the SRSG, but according to the Constitutional Framework, the president proposes the prime minister to the Parliament, represents the unity of the people, and guarantees the democratic functioning of provisional institutions, among other functions.

The last elections brought the formation of new ministries that did not exist in the previous government. Thus, the Ministry of Local Governance arose out of the Ministry of Public Services. By the end of December 2005, the frameworks for two more ministries (Ministry of Internal Affairs and Ministry of Justice) were determined. Within the Supreme Court of Kosovo, a Panel for the Issues of the Constitutional Framework was established, as Kosovo does not have a Constitutional Court. In fact, within the judicial system only the following segments function: district courts, municipal courts, a commercial court, minor offenses courts, and public prosecutors' offices.

By Regulation 28/2000, the SRSG established the institution of the ombudsperson, which is also anticipated by Chapter 10 of the Constitutional Framework. According to this regulation, the ombudsperson has vast authorities, and the only restrictions are those dealing with the peacekeeping forces (KFOR) or any misunderstanding between the international administration and its staff. In the former instance, a prior agreement between both KFOR and the ombudsperson is required. Until the end of 2005, the function of the ombudsperson in Kosovo was carried out successfully and authoritatively by Marek Antonio Nowicki, who at the end of his term suggested that he be replaced by another international.

The Parliament of Kosovo has attempted to expedite the promulgation of laws, along with cooperating with other institutions to create accompanying mechanisms for the implementation of existing legislation. Many laws have been approved, but their implementation either has not started or is not at the desired level. Lack of accompanying mechanisms, supporting legislation, and political will have been key factors in the failure to implement laws. For example, the Law on Suppression of Corruption was approved and is applicable, but an anticorruption agency has not yet been established. Although the transfer of competences to the local level has continued, there is a lack of clarity in exercising certain powers, which the internationals blame on the unskilled local level and locals blame on uncooperative internationals – in most cases, the truth lies somewhere in the middle.

Corruption

2004	2005	2006
6.00	6.00	6.00

For the past two years, the Kosovo Parliament promulgated many laws aimed at limiting and fighting corruption and ensuring the accountability of the PISG. The Law on Public Financial Management and Accountability, Law on Suppression of Corruption, and Law on Public Procurement are just a few of the corruption-related laws considered to be compatible with EU standards.

These laws envisaged fighting the kind of corruption that, unfortunately, engulfed the administration during 2005. However, some of the follow-up pieces of legislation that enforce laws on transparency and anticorruption are caught in a serious backlog in the government and Parliament. Moreover, Kosovo has a Law for Access on Official Documents that could help to increase transparency if applied. Though fully approved, the law is practically inapplicable because the government has not yet produced a list of documents that fall within its category of exempt "special interest documents."

Meanwhile, corruption and organized crime, as characterized in UN envoy Kai Eide's report, are the biggest threats to Kosovo's stability and to the sustainability of its institutions. Corruption in Kosovo is widespread at all levels,[20] but the scope of the problem is difficult to assess since no serious research has been conducted in the field. The government has not taken the necessary administrative and legislative steps to fight and prevent corruption in the provisional institutions. The Law on Suppression of Corruption is in place, but the establishment of an anticorruption agency has been delayed. Civil society has only just recently embarked on the fight against corruption, much like the political opposition. Opposition party leader Hashim Thaci's drive to make anticorruption a key political theme in early

2004 fell flat owing to widespread public perception that PDK ministers themselves were "not angels."[21]

The process is slow and lacks convincing commitment. Combating serious crime, including organized crime and corruption, has proven to be difficult for the KPS and the justice system. Over the past six years, international police, prosecutors, and intelligence officials have tried – but failed – to go beyond the surface of the corruption problem. The fight is hindered by family or clan solidarity and intimidation of witnesses, law enforcement, and judicial officials.[22] Language problems for international police and inexperienced local law enforcement institutions have contributed to this failure as well.[23]

Kosovo is not a party to the main international conventions in anticorruption (that is, the Council of Europe Criminal Law Convention on Corruption, Council of Europe Civil Law Convention on Corruption and its additional protocol, and the UN Convention Against Corruption). Although a number of these provisions have to some extent been interpreted in the domestic legislation, such as the provisional criminal code of Kosovo and the Law on Suppression of Corruption, more effort is required to launch a cohesive and forceful action against corruption.

There are frequent reports about irregularities in public tendering procedures. Recently, the Law on Public Procurement went under revision. The law reflects EU standards by defining a clear division between executive and regulatory functions, but the amendments have yet to be passed by the Parliament. It is expected that the implementation of the new law, in coordination with the external audit activities of the Office of the Auditor General, will contribute to an improvement in the situation and better use of public funds.[24]

Meanwhile, 2005 was marked by huge scandals at high levels of the Kosovo PISG. Throughout the year, newspapers were full of reports backed by facts and facsimiles in which allegations of corruption, procurement procedures violations, and receiving of gifts more than allowed by law, were made against ministers, the prime minister, and even the presidency. In June 2005, allegations of violations of the Law on Public Financial Management and Accountability by the minister of public services were published in most daily newspapers. These violations were confirmed even by representatives of the SRSG, who told the media that they would cancel the transfer over one million euros made by the ministry of public services to the presidency of Kosovo as not in accordance with law.[25] However, this assertion never became a reality. While this issue was simmering, the auditor general declared there would be an audit of the president's office, another promise that did not go beyond words.

Since 2003, a financial investigation unit staffed by Guardia di Finanza officers has conducted financial inspections of government bodies, business enterprises, and organizations receiving public funds and has also launched criminal investigations. In addition, an investigation task force – comprising representatives of the UN Office of Internal Oversight Services, the European Antifraud Office, and the Guardia di Finanza's financial investigation unit – has received a wide mandate to investigate fraud in the expenditure of public funds. The SRSG is coordinating the implementation of recommendations issued by the task force. Internal investigation services have been set up in the police and the judiciary.

However, in 2005 much of the focus was on keeping the very fragile governing coalition in existence. Most of these measures are moving slowly, while it seems the fastest operators are violators of the law, who are making the most of the lack of a code of ethics and public officials.

From an ethics point of view, the independent media in Kosovo were strictly monitored before and after the Kosovo conflict. The media in general, and especially the newspapers – which do a better job investigating stories – have developed a high sensitivity to confirmed sources. (Editors will not publish a story if it does not have two to three sources that confirm the news.) This has made it difficult for journalists to produce investigative stories because public officials do not feel duty bound to provide responses to journalists' inquiries. The Law for Access on Official Documents is not yet functional. On the other hand, before the conflict the media inherited a much more rigid code of ethics, which made it very hard for journalists to launch a serious public campaign against corruption, kickbacks, and nepotism. A general public indifference toward corruption has taken over as focus centers more around resolving the issue of Kosovo's status.

Bashkim Rrahmani is executive director of the Foundation for Democratic Initiatives. Two independent analysts, Avni Zogiani and Jeta Xharra, assisted him in preparation of this report.

---

[1] Kosovo 2004 Central Assembly Elections, National Democratic Institute, November 2004.

[2] Voting polls were open outside Kosovo for the over 200,000 Serbs who live in Serbia as refugees.

[3] "Reform Coalition Demands Democracy in Kosovo," Advocacy 2, no. 4 (April 2004), www.advocacy-center.org/Newsletters/0404special1%edition_eng.pdf.

[4] The TMC is currently preparing to become the Independent Media Commission, a fully independent agency among the PISG envisioned in Kosovo's Constitutional Framework.

[5] An UNMIK police spokesperson apologized to Visar Kryeziu, an AP photojournalist who was arrested during a street protest. Although the gesture was welcomed by members of the press, it also fueled comments that the apology came only because Kryeziu is a journalist for an international news agency; local journalists are generally viewed as far more vulnerable.

[6] OSCE and TMC reports in 2004 blamed the broadcast media for inciting violence through reports produced on days prior to and during the riots.

[7] Radio Television Kosovo (RTK) is part of the European Broadcasting Union (EBU), and according to EBU regulations, public TVs must supply minority programming which reflects the ethnic make up of a place. In this case, RTK has daily news in Serbian, Turkish, and Bosnian, and weekly news in Romani.

[8] UNMIK Regulation 2000/37 on the Conduct of the Print Media in Kosovo of June 17, 2000, and UNMIK Regulation 2000/36 on the Licensing and Regulation of the Broadcast Media in Kosovo.

[9] Media Preferences and Political Opinions in Kosova, December 2005, Index Kosova in a joint venture with Gallup International, www.indexkosova.com.

[10] Target is not a unified quota, but minority employment at central levels is estimated at 11 percent.

[11] The term parallel structures is used to define bodies that have been or still are operational in Kosovo after June 10, 1999, and that are not mandated under UN Security Council Resolution

1244. In the majority of cases, these institutions operate under the de facto authority of the Serbian government and assume jurisdiction over Kosovo from Serbia proper or operate on the territory of Kosovo.

[12] A Comprehensive Review of the Situation in Kosovo, Kai Eide, submitted to the UN Security Council on May 23, 2005.

[13] European Commission report, Brussels (COM), 9 November 2005, 561 final, europa.eu.int/comm/enlargement/report_2005/pdf/package/sec_1423_final_en_progress_report_ks. pdf.

[14] Local Governance and Administration, Leon Malazogu and Era Gjurgjeala, 2005, p. 22.

[15] The Delineation of Responsibilities Between Local and Central Authorities in Kosovo, Kosovar Institute for Policy Research and Development, January 2005.

[16] In November 2005, the SRSG declared null and void a decision of the Gjakova Municipal Assembly to discharge the executive and the mayor for allegations of misconduct.

[17] Local Governance and Administration, Leon Malazogu and Era Gjurgjeala, 2005, p. 10.

[18] Kosovo Institute for Policy Research and Development, "The Delineation of Responsibilities between Local and Central Authorities in Kosovo", January 2005, p. 12.

[19] Section 2.1. paragraph 1 of UNMIK Regulation No. 2000/45.

[20] European Commission report, Brussels (COM), 9 November 2005, 561 final.

[21] Kosovo After Haradinaj, International Crisis Group Report No. 163, May 26, 2005, p. 17.

[22] A Comprehensive Review of the Situation in Kosovo, Kai Eide, submitted to the UN Security Council on May 23, 2005, p.36.

[23] A Comprehensive Review of the Situation in Kosovo, Kai Eide, submitted to the UN Security Council on May 23, 2005, p.38.

[24] European Commission report: COM (2005) 561 final, europa.eu.int/comm/enlargement/report_2005/pdf/package/sec_1423_final_en_progress_report_ks. pdf.

[25] See www.euinkosovo.org/monitoring/2005/27062005.doc.

Slovakia

Capital:	Bratislava
Population:	5.4 million
GNI/capita:	$6,480
Ethnic Groups:	Slovak (85.8%), Hungarian (9.7%), Roma (1.7%), Ruthenian/Ukrainian (1%), other and unspecified (1.8%)

Nations in Transit Ratings and Averaged Scores

	1997	1998	1999	2001	2002	2003	2004	2005	2006
Electoral Process	3.75	3.50	2.50	2.25	1.75	1.50	1.50	1.25	1.25
Civil Society	3.25	3.00	2.25	2.00	1.75	1.50	1.25	1.25	1.25
Independent Media	4.25	4.00	2.25	2.00	2.00	2.00	2.25	2.25	2.25
Governance *	3.75	3.75	3.00	2.75	2.25	2.25	2.25	n/a	n/a
National Democratic Governance	n/a	n/a	n/a	n/a	n/a	n/a	n/a	2.00	2.00
Local Democratic Governance	n/a	n/a	n/a	n/a	n/a	n/a	n/a	2.25	2.00
Judicial Framework and Independence	4.00	4.00	2.50	2.25	2.00	2.00	2.00	2.00	2.00
Corruption	n/a	n/a	3.75	3.75	3.25	3.25	3.25	3.00	3.00
Democracy Score	3.80	3.65	2.71	2.50	2.17	2.08	2.08	2.00	1.96

* With the 2005 edition, Freedom House introduced seperate analysis and ratings for national democratic governance and local democratic governance to provide readers with more detailed and nuanced analysis of these two important subjects.

NOTE: The ratings reflect the consensus of Freedom House, its academic advisers, and the author of this report. The opinions expressed in this report are those of the author. The ratings are based on a scale of 1 to 7, with 1 representing the highest level of democratic progress and 7 the lowest. The Democracy Score is an average of ratings for the categories tracked in a given year.

The economic and social data on this page were taken from the following sources:
GNI/capita, Population: *World Development Indicators 2006* (Washington, D.C.: World Bank, 2006).
Ethnic Groups: *CIA World Factbook 2006* (Washington, D.C.: Central Intelligence Agency, 2006).

EXECUTIVE SUMMARY

Sixteen years after the collapse of the Communist regime, Slovakia is a country with a consolidated democracy and functioning market economy. The country has joined the European Union (EU) and NATO and is a member of the Organization for Economic Cooperation and Development and the World Trade Organization. Slovakia's development can be divided into three main stages. The first stage took place while Slovakia was still a part of the Czechoslovak Federation (1990–1993), as governments implemented systemic changes aimed at building the foundation of a democratic regime. The second stage lasted from 1993, when Slovakia became an independent state, to 1998. During this period, authoritarian and nationalist forces usurped political and economic power and directly caused numerous democratic deficits that subsequently thwarted the country's EU integration ambitions. The third stage began in 1998 when democratic forces returned to power; since then, they have eliminated most deformations of the previous authoritarian rule and launched vital reforms in a number of areas.

Throughout 2005, Slovakia's institutional system showed a sufficient degree of stability. The country's economic development was also stable, as gross domestic product growth neared 6 percent, unemployment declined, the annual inflation rate remained relatively low, and the favorable trend of foreign direct investment continued. Slovakia successfully seized most of the opportunities ensuing from its full-fledged EU membership, such as the use of EU funds and participation in policy debates. Although the center-right administration of Mikulas Dzurinda did not control a majority in the Parliament, it managed to put through most reform laws. Serious conflicts within the ruling coalition could not shake the government's determination to keep the reform course. In 2005, opposition parties failed to railroad through the Parliament a constitutional bill seeking to shorten the current electoral term and call early parliamentary elections.

National Democratic Governance. The system of power division in Slovakia remained sufficiently functional and stable throughout 2005. Mutual relations among particular constitutional players were generally cooperative, as no displays of power confrontation were recorded. In summer 2005, the ruling coalition's makeup saw a formal change after the Alliance of a New Citizen, one of four ruling parties, left the government; however, most members of its parliamentary caucus remained loyal to the incumbent administration. Their loyalty was made formal after the parliamentarians signed an agreement with the remaining three ruling parties – Slovak Democratic and Christian Union, Hungarian Coalition Party, and Christian Democratic Movement. The incumbent administration thus became a full-fledged successor to the original ruling coalition formed after the parliamentary elections of

2002. Subsequently, the cabinet's personnel composition saw three changes that did not jeopardize its operability and have not led to any shifts in priorities pursued in particular areas, such as culture, economy, and social affairs. The Parliament's law-making activity in 2005 may be evaluated as satisfactory, in terms of both quantity and quality. The Constitutional Court continued to act as the watchdog of constitutionality; its rulings were respected by all concerned institutions. *An amendment to the Slovak Constitution approved in 2005 further strengthened control powers of the Supreme Bureau of Supervision. Slovakia's rating for national democratic governance remains at 2.00 owing to basic trends in institutional development, operation of the system of checks and balances, civil control of military and security services, and practical execution of power.*

Electoral Process. In November 2005, Slovakia held regional elections for representatives to regional councils and governors. The elections were proclaimed free and democratic, as nothing disturbed fair electoral competition. In February 2005, the Parliament passed a new Law on Political Parties to increase the transparency of party financing as well as accountability. However, in practice political parties display a certain level of resistance to inform accurately about all aspects of spending. Based on the new law, all existing political parties were reregistered; no problems occurred during the reregistration process. *Slovakia's rating for electoral process remains at 1.25 given the functionality of electoral mechanisms and improvements in the quality of legislation on political parties.*

Civil Society. Slovakia's civil society is vibrant, and its structures are considered by experts to be among the most advanced and dynamic in Central and Eastern Europe. Nongovernmental organizations (NGOs) in 2005 did not go through major structural changes – the legislative background, financial viability, organizational capacity, and other dimensions of NGO sector development changed only slightly since 2004. However, some organizations had to limit their activities as a response to the withdrawal of foreign donors in 2005. The legal and regulatory environment for civil society is free of excessive state pressures. The NGO sector in Slovakia has a well-developed infrastructure, training, and research base. The incumbent state administration continues to have an open attitude toward NGOs. Civil society organizations have successfully created alliances against racism, and in 2005 they became leading forces in the struggle against neo-Nazi groups in Slovakia. The democratization activities of Slovak NGOs in countries with autocratic regimes became more visible in 2005. Trade unions are free in their activities, and the education system is free of political dominance. *Slovakia's rating for civil society remains unchanged at 1.25.*

Independent Media. The performance of Slovak media and journalists was free of open state interference in 2005. Politicians' direct influence on the media was further reduced after Pavol Rusko, former minister of the economy, chairman of the Alliance of a New Citizen, and founder of the largest private TV station, lost his share in the station's ownership. However, the long-term shortage of funding for public television and radio and the likelihood that both stations will see new management boards appointed in the 2006 election year suggest that political influence could soon strengthen. Also, the recently approved penal code, which outlaws the recording of private conversations with concealed devices, may harm the practice of investigative journalism. *Slovakia's rating for independent media remains unchanged at 2.25.*

Local Democratic Governance. The trend to deepen the decentralization process and strengthen local democracy in Slovakia continued in 2005. Local and regional self-governments began to perform executive powers transferred from the central government, using the funds they received as a result of the completed financial decentralization process. Self-governance organs focused on increasing their professionalism and quality of performance. Amendments to the Law on Free Access to Information and the Slovak Constitution, which strengthened the control powers of the Supreme Bureau of Supervision, enhanced the transparency and accountability of regional and local self-governance organs. In regional elections held in November 2005, new deputies of regional councils and new regional governors were elected. *Owing to the prevailing positive trend of strengthening local democracy and decentralization, Slovakia's rating for local democratic governance improves from 2.25 to 2.00.*

Judicial Framework and Independence. The process of stabilizing the country's legal system accelerated in 2005. The long-awaited recodification of criminal law was finally enacted. The new penal code introduced additional categories of criminal offenses based on the priority of protecting the lives, property, and interests of citizens. The new code of penal procedure made penal action simpler and more efficient. The judicial system remained stable and relatively effective. One problem, however, was the partially limited functionality of the Constitutional Court, which lacked the full complement of judges in 2005 because of the Parliament's inability to agree on a generally acceptable candidate. *Slovakia's judicial framework and independence rating remains at 2.00 as a result of the continuation of judicial system reform and approval of the new penal code and new code of penal procedure.*

Corruption. Corruption remained one of Slovakia's most pressing social problems in 2005. Public officials were under increasing public pressure to accept personal and political responsibility for conduct incompatible with principles of transparency. Scandals involving clientelism caused two personnel changes in the cabinet. In 2005, the Parliament passed several pieces of legislation aimed at combating corruption, most notably the constitutional amendment that strengthened control powers of the Supreme Bureau of Supervision, the amendment to the Law on Free Access to Information, and the amendment to the Law on Public Procurement. The new Law on Political Parties seeks to make party financing more transparent. Also, law enforcement organs intensified their campaign against corruption, which resulted in bribery indictments against several high-ranking officials at both central government and self-government levels. *Slovakia's corruption rating remains at 3.00, but new anticorruption legislation and the greater efficiency of the police in fighting corrupt behavior show promise of improvement in 2006.*

Outlook for 2006. The result of parliamentary elections in June 2006 will have a decisive impact on the country's future development, particularly the pace of recently launched social and economic reforms. During the period leading up to the elections, the ruling parties will likely try to convince voters about the critical importance of previously implemented reforms and the need for their continuation. The popularity of some parties in the incumbent ruling coalition makes it likely that they will participate in the new government as well, a positive sign that the current reform course will be maintained. It is likely that Slovakia's EU membership will continue to have a stabilizing effect on its social development. The country's international position and role in world politics will undoubtedly grow stronger when Slovakia becomes a temporary member of the United Nations Security Council in January 2006.

MAIN REPORT

National Democratic Governance

1997	1998	1999	2001	2002	2003	2004	2005	2006
n/a	n/a	n/a	n/a	n/a	n/a	n/a	2.00	2.00

The Slovak Republic is a stable democracy with a generally effective system of governmental checks and balances. Citizens enjoy direct participation in the political process through elections and political party activities. The Slovak Constitution guarantees the right to free retrieval, collection, and dissemination of information. In 2000, the Parliament passed the Law on Free Access to Information, which stipulated conditions for gathering information by citizens on activities of the state administration and self-governance organs. The law indicates a positive trend, though implementation has been hampered at times by bureaucratic resistance and a lack of public awareness of the constitutional right. In 2005, for instance, the Parliament approved an amendment that expands the law to include the disclosure of salaries of civil servants and other public officials. The amendment also introduced an obligation to publish information on any transfer of property of the state, self-governance bodies, or public institutions to private individuals, including information on such individuals.

More than 90 percent of Slovakia's gross domestic product is produced by the private sector. Since 1998, the government's drive toward liberalization, in policy and practice, has been the chief development trend within Slovakia's economy.

Since the collapse of the Communist regime in 1989, Slovakia has not seen any violent attempts to usurp political power, and all political players respect the fundamental rules of parliamentary democracy. However, between 1993 and 1998 a coalition of authoritarian and nationalistic parties attempted an illiberal, undemocratic concentration of political power. Yet since the return of democratic forces in 1998, the execution of power on all levels has not departed from the basic constitutional framework. Although the incumbent administration of Prime Minister Mikulas Dzurinda lost a parliamentary majority at the beginning of 2004, it has since been able to pass legislative initiatives and execute power effectively. Both attempts by opposition parties to shorten the current electoral term – calling a referendum on early elections (April 2004) and attempting to have parliament approve a constitutional law on early elections (November 2005) – failed.

For the first time since 1998, the basic principles of the governmental procedural consensus were temporarily breached in September 2005 when the opposition – with help from independent members of Parliament (MPs) – boycotted the assembly. That move meant the lack of a quorum, preventing a substitute for a recently deceased Hungarian Coalition Party (SMK) deputy from assuming his mandate. The opposition parties ended their boycott in just over a week.

Government authority and the rule of law are solid and indisputable throughout Slovakia, and domestic political development is free from displays of dominance by the military, foreign powers, or other power groups. Government stability has never been threatened by internal military conflicts or insurgencies, and currently there is no danger of such conflicts. Political party activities within the armed forces and other state institutions are forbidden, as the Slovak army and police are politically neutral.

The National Council of the Slovak Republic (Parliament) is a sovereign representative body, the sole legislative and constituent assembly, and autonomous from the executive. It has sufficient resources and capacities for the creation and enactment of bills, as well as adequate control powers. Parliamentarians frequently interpellate cabinet members and exercise oversight of state and public institutions.

Parliamentary deliberations are open to the public and media (except for closed sessions on confidential matters, such as intelligence and secret service issues). Public representatives may be present during deliberations of parliamentary committees if invited by their members. The entire legislative process (that is, verbatim wording of legislative bills, results of assembly votes, and so forth) is continuously recorded and made available to the public via the Parliament Web site. Printed shorthand records from the Parliament's plenary sessions are also available to the public. In addition, the Law on Free Access to Information has substantially improved public access to information on activities of state and public institutions.

The Constitution and relevant laws clearly demarcate the powers of the cabinet and other organs of executive power, which is subordinated to the legislative. At the beginning of its tenure, the cabinet must submit its program manifesto for parliamentary approval. The Parliament may at any time hold a vote of no confidence regarding the entire cabinet or its individual members; it may also compel the cabinet to act upon parliamentary resolutions. The loss of political support from the

Parliament may lead to the cabinet's resignation. The president is directly elected and, although relatively weak, has a number of important competences, such as a legislative veto and the right to challenge laws in the Constitutional Court.

All state agencies are subject to control by the Supreme Bureau of Supervision (NKU). The NKU regularly publishes violations of laws and bylaws by state institutions and orders the offending agencies to remedy their deficiencies. The Parliament elects the NKU chairman and NKU vice chairmen for seven-year terms. Though funded by the state budget, the NKU is free from political influence. In September 2005, the Parliament passed a constitutional amendment extending the control powers of the NKU to include all financial transfers to organs of local self-governance, legal entitites established by local governments, companies with state investment, and firms pursuing activities in the public interest.

The reform of the armed forces implemented during the past decade has introduced civilian controls that are in line with NATO, which Slovakia joined in 2004. Judicial oversight of the military and security services is sufficiently effective, and the Slovak army uses a system of martial prosecution with martial courts. The Parliament approves the military and security services budget, and spending is supervised by the parliamentary defense and security committee. Deputies, media, and the general public may access information on the activities of the military and security services, but certain types of information are considered classified and are not available to the media and public. The cabinet informs the public about its activities through special public affairs units at the Ministry of Defense, the Ministry of the Interior, and the Slovak Intelligence Service (SIS).

In 2005, representatives of some political parties voiced suspicions that information collected by the SIS was used to discredit them and that the agency was conducting unauthorized surveillance of some politicians. In November, the Parliament's Special Committee for SIS Oversight investigated these suspicions. The committee's deliberations were attended by the SIS director, who emphatically dismissed all allegations. MPs who had publicly presented statements on illegal activities of the SIS eventually failed to produce any evidence. However, during the ensuing public debate, some politicians argued that the monitoring powers of the special committee should be strengthened.

Electoral Process

1997	1998	1999	2001	2002	2003	2004	2005	2006
3.75	3.50	2.50	2.25	1.75	1.50	1.50	1.25	1.25

The authority of the Slovak government is based on freely exercised universal suffrage. Since the Communist regime's collapse in 1989, Slovakia has held five parliamentary elections (1990, 1992, 1994, 1998, and 2002), four municipal elections (1990, 1994, 1998, and 2002), two regional elections (2001 and 2005), two presidential elections (1999 and 2004), and one election to the European Parliament

(2004). International as well as independent domestic election monitors declared all of these elections free and fair.

The legislative framework provides for free and democratic competition, equal campaigning, fair voting, and the transparent scrutiny of votes. Parliamentary elections are based on a proportional system that stipulates the following thresholds to qualify: 5 percent for single running parties, 7 percent for coalitions comprising two or three parties, and 10 percent for coalitions consisting of four or more parties. Elections to the European Parliament use a proportional system. The minimum quorum to qualify for the assembly is 5 percent of the popular vote, which applies to both individual parties and party coalitions. Elections to local and regional self-governments use a modified majority electoral model. The Slovak president and regional governors are elected using a majority model with two rounds.

In February 2005, the Parliament passed a new Law on Political Parties that requires party registration by means of a petition signed by 10,000 citizens; once registered, each party may take part in parliamentary elections. The 1991 Law on Political Parties required a new party to submit only 1,000 signatures to register. However, in order to run in parliamentary elections, a party that did not have a caucus in the Parliament had to submit a petition signed by at least 10,000 of its members or regular citizens. A new Law on Elections to the National Council of the Slovak Republic passed in 2004 abolished this requirement. On the other hand, it introduced a new requirement: a deposit of Sk 500,000 (about US$16,000), which is refunded to all parties that receive at least 3 percent of the popular vote. Deposits made by parties that receive less than 3 percent of the popular vote are forfeited to the state budget. After the passage of the new law, 42 parties reregistered with the Ministry of the Interior. Although 120 political parties had been registered by the end of September 2005, 78 of them failed to submit an application for reregistration before the October deadline and were subsequently deleted from the registry.

The Supreme Court is entitled to dissolve political parties whose statutes, program, or activities violate the Constitution, constitutional laws, or international treaties. A motion to dissolve a political party must be filed by the attorney general. Since 1990, the Supreme Court has not dissolved a single political party in Slovakia. In October 2005, Slovakia's attorney general submitted a proposal to dissolve the Slovak Community–National Party, a neo-Fascist and neo-Nazi party that had been registered in June 2005. In its program (which had not been officially submitted at registration), the party advocates removing Slovakia's democratic system of government and suppressing human and minority rights and openly promulgates racial discrimination. Immediately after its registration, the party organized public rallies in several Slovak towns, apparently inciting racial hatred and religious intolerance.

Six parties are currently represented in the Parliament through their caucuses: Slovak Democratic and Christian Union (SDKU), Movement for a Democratic Slovakia (HZDS), Smer, SMK, Christian Democratic Movement (KDH), and Communist Party of Slovakia (KSS). Many other independent MPs represent a handful of nonparliamentary parties, most of which emerged after 2002 by splitting off from existing parliamentary parties.

The current government is a result of parliamentary elections that were held in September 2002 and led to a coalition of four parties – SDKU, SMK, KDH, and Alliance of a New Citizen (ANO) – which formed a cabinet with Prime Minister Mikulas Dzurinda at the head. The ruling coalition lost a majority in the Parliament in 2003 following the defection of several MPs from the ANO and SDKU caucuses. In September 2005, ANO left the ruling coalition in the aftermath of a scandal involving party chairman Pavol Rusko, who was subsequently removed from his post as minister of the economy. The ANO caucus currently includes MPs who left the ANO party following a rift within the party but remained in the ANO caucus to keep the caucus alive; it has remained unchanged. (According to law the creation of a new caucus or renaming of an existing caucus requires the whole assembly's approval, which was not possible at the time because of the government coalition's minority position.) Most ANO parliamentarians who defected from the party declared their loyalty to the administration. So the government continues to be supported in the Parliament by deputies of SDKU, SMK, KDH, ten members of the ANO caucus, and some independent deputies. All parliamentary parties have functioning structures at the national, regional, and local levels and are represented in regional and local self-governments. The representation of opposition parties in these bodies corresponds proportionally to their number of seats in the Parliament.

Although citizens are quite active in Slovakia's political life, there has been an overall decline in voter participation. Generally, the highest turnout is recorded in parliamentary elections, although this too has fluctuated over the past decade (84.4 percent in 1992, 75.6 percent in 1994, 84.2 percent in 1998, and 70.1 percent in 2002). Turnout was also relatively high in the first direct presidential elections in May 1999 (73.9 percent in the first round and 75.5 percent in the second). In 2004, the presidential elections recorded voter participation of 47.9 percent (first round) and 43.5 percent (second round).

Municipal and regional elections typically show lower voter turnouts than do national elections. Voter participation in municipal elections was 63.8 percent in 1990, 52.2 percent in 1994, 54.0 percent in 1998, and 49.5 percent in 2002. In regional elections, voter turnout was 26.0 percent and 22.6 percent (first and second round, respectively) in 2001 and 18.0 percent and 11.0 percent (first and second round, respectively) in 2005, the lowest turnout in Slovakia's modern history. Turnout of only 17 percent was recorded in the first elections to the European Parliament in 2004.

Nationwide, there is a relatively low level of public participation and membership in political parties, about 5 percent according to estimates. The party with the largest membership is the HZDS (nearly 45,000 members), followed by the KDH (20,000), the KSS (16,500), and Smer (15,000); other parliamentary parties have between 5,000 and 13,000 members.[1]

Ethnic minorities encounter no institutional obstacles to participating in political processes. About 15 percent of Slovak citizens belong to various ethnic minorities. Ethnic Hungarians form the largest ethnic minority, making up nearly 10 percent of the total population.[2] Traditionally, ethnic Hungarians have a high rate of political mobilization; as a result, this minority is represented effectively at all levels of government, mainly through the SMK. This party has been in government for seven years and has had a strong influence over the country's general social development.

In contrast, the Roma minority is not sufficiently represented owing to the ethnic group's low social status and inadequate education, a virtual absence of political leaders, and the inability of "majority" mainstream political parties to cooperate with Romany organizations. Although several Romany political parties are registered, none has gained a foothold in executive or legislative organs at the national or regional level. Representatives of Romany origin operate in local self-governance organs, especially in villages and towns with a high concentration of Romany citizens. So far, all attempts to establish an integrated political party that would represent the interests of the Romany minority have failed because of conflicting personal ambitions of individual Romany leaders.

Civil Society

1997	1998	1999	2001	2002	2003	2004	2005	2006
3.25	3.00	2.25	2.00	1.75	1.50	1.25	1.25	1.25

Mutual cooperation between government and NGOs has existed in Slovakia for years, and Slovak civil society is traditionally very dynamic and vibrant. However, in 2005 NGOs faced new challenges caused by the withdrawal of foreign funders and the need to find new ways of surviving. Some organizations limited their activities or ceased to exist. The professionalization of the civil society sector therefore became the most significant feature over the past year. EU membership, EU Structural and Cohesion funds as a source of income, and intensified cooperation with the business sector changed the "third sector" in many aspects. Many organizations, adjusting successfully to new conditions, have tended to give up activities that are focused on advocacy, raising questions about the role of NGOs in Slovak society.

Figures on Slovak NGOs are recorded in several places, including the Statistical Office of the Slovak Republic, the Ministry of the Interior, and the Ministry of Culture. At the end of December 2005, the Ministry of the Interior listed 27,100 organizations considered to be NGOs in a broad sense. Of these, 25,257 (93.2 percent) were civil associations (societies, clubs, associations, movements, trade unions, international NGOs, and various sports clubs) or their organizational units, 325 (1.2 percent) were foundations, 497 (1.8 percent) were noninvestment funds, and 1,021 (3.8 percent) were nonprofit organizations. The image of NGOs in public opinion is prevailingly positive, although some foundations have been accused of misusing donations. Those allegations accelerated after the natural disaster in the High Tatras National Park in November 2004 and prompted a serious discussion about the reliability of the third sector.

The visibility of women's organizations and initiatives – including social, political, independent, and international groups – has been increasing year by year to a total currently estimated at more than 100. Ethnic minorities, especially ethnic Hungarians, have effective cultural and civic organizations in Slovakia. However, Roma minority groups have been far less effective, with some claiming that Roma organizations are almost 20 times underrepresented in comparison with organizations connected to the majority population. Religious groups play the most significant role in charitable activities (church contributions are a deeply rooted tradition in Slovakia). All major religious groups in Slovakia – including Roman Catholic, Eastern Orthodox, Lutheran, and Calvinist congregations – are very much involved in charity activities and complement state programs, especially in social assistance services.

No openly extremist or racist organizations are registered with the Ministry of the Interior, but some do operate illegally and have increased their activities. In 2005, the police continued to systematically monitor neo-Nazi, right-wing nationalist, and extremist groups and conducted preventive actions against them. Civil society organizations operated intensively against racist groups in Slovakia, such as the neo-Nazi-oriented Slovak Community–National Party, monitoring their activities in cooperation with state institutions.

The legal and regulatory environment for civil society is free of excessive state pressures and bureaucracy and operates under norms adopted after the fall of the Communist regime. The basic legislative framework for NGOs is provided by the Constitution – which guarantees freedom of expression (Article 29), freedom of assembly (Article 28), and freedom of association (Articles 29 and 37) – as well as several related laws. Registration of NGOs is simple: Both legal entities and private citizens may establish nonprofit organizations, which are then required to serve their stated missions. The Ministry of the Interior acts not only as the NGO registry, but as the supervising institution. Taxation laws benefit NGOs, and in some fields the tax code is simpler than for the commercial sector. NGOs are also exempt from paying gift taxes and institution income taxes.

The NGO sector in Slovakia has a well-developed infrastructure, training, and research base. Unlike in previous years, no umbrella organization of elected NGO representatives currently exists to coordinate particular segments of the NGO sector – a signal of the normalization of Slovak civil society, which, especially in the mid-1990s, struggled for its autonomy. In addition to existing NGOs that provide training, Partners for Democratic Change Slovakia – together with the Open Society Foundation and the Education Center for Nonprofit Organizations – has prepared a distance learning course in many areas relevant for NGOs. An Internet portal (ChangeNet) provides information services for NGOs, and a monthly magazine, *Efekt*, published by the First Slovak Nonprofit Service Center, covers changes in laws and regulations and other relevant topics.

In 2005, the withdrawal of international donors became rather critical, especially for advocacy and watchdog NGOs that have trouble generating funds elsewhere. These organizations cannot accept money from the state because of their special role, and the business sector views their support as risky; also, their scope of activity usually precludes self-financing activities. On the other hand, NGOs working in the social area saw progress in the development of financing, with many examples of corporate support. Even though the spectrum of activity is often limited to "popular" issues (children, cancer victms, and so forth), some NGOs also received corporate donations to work in "less popular" areas, such as resocialization centers for prisoners and hospices.

NGOs continue to face problems with the administration of EU funds, since Brussels often pays grants after the completion of projects and few NGOs can afford to undertake a project without regular funding installments. Since 2005, private taxpayers in Slovakia may dedicate 2 percent (previously 1 percent) of their income tax for public beneficiary purposes, according to a 2001 amendment to the Law on Income Taxes; legal entities have been able to dedicate 2 percent of their tax liability to civil society organizations since a 2004 amendment. An increasing number of Slovak NGOs are subsidized from finances raised by their own activities and membership fees, especially groups working with youth, though most NGOs have only a small membership base.

The cooperation of NGOs and government in foreign policy development continued in 2005. Slovak NGOs became more visible by working with democratic actors in countries with autocratic regimes (Belarus, Cuba) or in transitional countries (Afghanistan, Iraq); they were particularly active during the Orange Revolution in Ukraine. Moreover, cooperation between the Ministry of Foreign Affairs and NGOs in these areas is increasingly effective, as highlighted by the ministry's Official Development Assistance program, which strengthened the country's position in democracy-building activities accross Eastern Europe.

In 2005, Slovak NGOs received substantial and predominantly positive coverage from both public and private media. The close cooperation between media and think tanks in tracking internal politics and influencing political actors and the broader public continued. Nevertheless, cooperation with journalists is still difficult for grassroots organizations, as confusion and misperceptions about the role of NGOs persist.

Slovak trade unions are free, but there are questions over whether they play an adequate role in society. The Confederation of Trade Unions (KOZ) represents fewer than 520,000 employees. The image of trade unions is predominantly negative among all segments of the population, which may be explained by KOZ's involvement in politics and the working style of trade union leaders.

The education system is fully free of political influence and propaganda, and the Ministry of Education, together with educational experts, has been attempting to diminish the dominance of Slovak majority views on history, literature, and other curricular areas. One problem that persists is the continued discussion concerning a treaty between Slovakia and the Vatican on education. A large segment of Slovak NGOs (as well as public opinion in general) views the treaty as endangering the secularized character of the Slovak educational system.

Independent Media

1997	1998	1999	2001	2002	2003	2004	2005	2006
4.25	4.00	2.25	2.00	2.00	2.00	2.25	2.25	2.25

In Slovakia, freedom of speech is protected by the Constitution and the obsolete and increasingly unsatisfactory Law on the Press from 1966. In 2005, the Ministry of Culture submitted a proposed new Law on the Press, but the draft provoked such controversial reactions that by the end of November, the ministry had not yet presented it for parliamentary deliberation. On the one hand, the bill does lay down generally accepted principles of press and media freedom – including protection of sources. It also guarantees journalists' right to information while simultaneously enshrining citizens' right to protect their privacy and reputation. On the other hand, the draft law introduces an obligation for freelance journalists to register with state organs, which the Slovak Syndicate of Journalists (SSN), the largest professional organization of Slovak journalists, has emphatically criticized.

Slovakia's legal system does not contain any provision that would allow the government to punish journalists for "irresponsible" journalism with respect to state organs. In 2002, two articles of the penal code that could be used against journalists were suspended – namely, provisions on defamation of the republic, the Parliament, the cabinet, the Constitutional Court, and the president.

In November 2005, the Parliament passed an amendment to the penal code that will take effect in 2006, whereby the recording of any confidential conversation with a concealed device will be prosecutable. The move is likely to complicate the work of investigative journalists. When discussing the new amendment, the assembly rejected a cabinet-initiated proposal to omit this provision, with some parliamentary deputies arguing that the provision would not apply to journalists. They stated that Article 28 of the penal code, which refers to the Law on the Press, guaranteed the freedom to use concealed recording devices. Declaring that neither the current Law on the Press nor the draft Law on the Press gave journalists the right to secretly record and then publish confidential conversations, the SSN said that journalists currently use these techniques only because they are not explicitly banned by the law.

Journalists and newsrooms are partially free from interference by the government or private owners. In the case of private media outlets, the greatest problem is the insufficient transparency of Slovak media ownership and, consequently, a lack of information about owners' business interests. *Media Ownership and Its Impact on Media Independence and Pluralism*,[3] an analysis of the Slovak media market, reported that ownership is "practically in several pairs of hands"; however, owing to legislative loopholes, cross-ownership of media can be suspected but not proven. Another important factor remains the lack of internal regulations, such as editorial statutes, to prevent the direct interference of media owners in editorial work.

Legislation in force since 2004 has reduced the dependence of public service broadcasters on the Parliament, which no longer elects or removes directors of public media. However, there are financial pressures owing to inadequate funding from public sources; the culprit is license fees that are set too low and legislative loopholes that allow one-third of Slovak households to avoid payment of user fees. The public media's financial vulnerability increases the risk of dependence on the decisions of political elite, who cover public media deficits from the state budget.

The scope and structure of information offered by the Slovak media are satisfactory, although the trend toward greater tabloidization continues, even at the largest dailies with the greatest impact on public opinion. Slovakia also has a broad network of regional periodicals dominated by the publisher of one of the country's two largest dailies.

The greatest risk to the independence of local broadcast media (particularly TV stations) is their interconnectedness with local self-governments. Given operation costs and the virtual impossibility of making a profit, the formation of such partnerships is understandable. As a result, however, these TV stations frequently serve as "information channels" of local governments rather than as critical media reporting on local problems.

The previously dominant position of TV Markiza was somewhat shaken in 2005 following the rise of a competitive nationwide private broadcaster (TV Joj) and the stable position of the public Slovak Television. Nevertheless, TV Markiza's news broadcasts continue to be a key source of information for many citizens. The radio market saw a fundamental change: For the first time, ratings of the public Slovak Radio were lower than those of a privately owned radio station (Radio Expres) – a result of Radio Expres's successful business strategy and the long-term stagnation of Slovak Radio. Still, public opinion polls suggest that both public service broadcasters continue to be among the most trusted institutions in the country.

TV Markiza's ownership structure saw a fundamental change in 2005 after its founder, former minister of the economy Pavol Rusko, was elbowed out. Rusko's influence over TV Markiza was the most frequent reason for criticism from the Council for Broadcasting and Retransmission, which over the past few years imposed a number of fines on the station; the last sanction dates to November 2005, when the council ordered a 10-minute shutdown of TV Markiza's main evening news broadcast. According to the council, TV Markiza's news program violated the Law on Broadcasting and Retransmission when it broadcast reportages biased in favor of the ANO party and its chairman Rusko.

Journalists and publishers, as well as private media owners, have their own professional organizations, whose influence is marginal. The largest professional association of journalists – the SSN, which comprises approximately three-quarters of all journalists in the country – has ambitions to become a strong professional organization and equal partner in collective bargaining with publishers, government organs, and other entities. Most Slovak publishers are members of the Association of Periodical Press Publishers (ZVPT), while private television and radio broadcasters are organized in the Association of Independent Radio and Television Stations.

Supervision over journalists' observance of ethical and professional rules remains poor. After a year of virtual idleness, the Press Council, established jointly by the SSN and the ZVPT as the supreme professional ethics organ, attempted to revitalize its activity in 2005 and issued several decisions. However, its esteem and acceptance in professional circles remain very low.

Access to the Internet is unrestricted in Slovakia. The number of people who work with the Internet on a daily basis increases every year. The number of regular Internet users rose from 8 percent of the population in December 2002 to almost 21 percent in July 2005, with an increase in occasional Internet users of 14 to 23 percent over the same period. Prices have been declining, and connection quality has improved over a larger portion of the country, helping to close the "digital gap" between residents of the capital and those of the rest of Slovakia. Still, a report by the Institute for Public Affairs corroborated the existence of a relatively deep gap that divides inhabitants of Slovakia by age, education, type of economic activity, household status, type of household, size of municipality, and region of residence.

Internet Penetration in Slovakia (%)

Population over 18	June 1997	April 1998	May 1999	September 1998	November 1999	May 2000	January 2001	June 2001	December 2001	December 2002	December 2003	July 2005
Use the Internet regularly	1.4	2.1	2.4	2.7	3.1	4.8	4.1	5.0	6.8	8.4	12.8	20.5 (21.5)
Use the Internet occasionally	4.1	5.7	7.1	6.0	6.3	9.4	10.4	9.8	10.0	14.5	16.5	22.6 (24.9)
Have access to the Internet but do not use it	3.9	3.7	5.2	4.4	4.4	5.3	5.2	3.3	4.7	5.1	5.4	4.8 (4.6)
Have heard/ read about or used the Internet but currently do not have access to it	60.6	63.6	62.6	67.9	70.3	68.4	68.6	70.8	68.5	64.6	59.8	48.4 (45.5)
Do not know what the Internet is	29.8	24.9	22.8	19.0	15.4	12.0	11.6	11.1	10.1	7.4	5.4	3.7 (3.4)

Note: Figures in parentheses are calculated for the entire population over 14.
Source: 1997-2003: FOCUS, 2005; Institute for Public Affairs

Local Democratic Governance

1997	1998	1999	2001	2002	2003	2004	2005	2006
n/a	n/a	n/a	n/a	n/a	n/a	n/a	2.25	2.00

The Slovak Constitution and other applicable laws provide an adequate framework for self-governance at the regional and local levels. The Slovak Republic has a dual system of public administration-state administration (organs of executive power) and self-governments (elected bodies). There are three levels of elected bodies: central (the Parliament), regional (regional assemblies), and local (municipal councils). Public administration is based on the principle of "subsidiarity," or keeping public administration functions with smaller units when no major advantage exists for transferring them to larger ones. The establishment of state and self-governance institutions is subject to laws passed by the Parliament; however, local self-governments may initiate pro bono nonstate organizations that focus on aiding local development, such as agencies, associations, funds, and so forth.

As part of public administration reform, a massive block of powers was transferred from central government organs to local and regional self-governance bodies. These bodies now address issues in education, health service, social affairs, transportation, and the environment. In order to enable local and regional self-governments to perform their delegated powers, the central government provided them with necessary funding through fiscal decentralization – in other words, the right to collect so-called local taxes. In the case of municipalities, this is the real estate tax; for regional self-governments, this is the motor vehicle tax. Municipalities and regions are autonomous in this area, although the Ministry of Finance submitted to the Parliament a specific bill that should regulate the method of setting tax rates to prevent self-governments from abusing citizens.

As part of fiscal decentralization, the cabinet at the end of 2004 issued a government order that divided income tax revenues between municipalities and higher territorial units (regions). Launching the new system of financing for local and regional self-governments was not free of problems. At the beginning of 2005, representatives of regional capitals protested that the adopted redistribution model had reduced the tax income they would otherwise have spent on city public transportation. The cabinet subsequently decided to allocate part of its financial reserve to cover the deficit in some towns, which helped alleviate this concern. Government institutions and self-governance organs cooperate in tackling local and regional problems, and in 2005 no overt conflicts occurred. In order to communicate with government institutions and present their priorities, self-governments use various associations, such as the Association of Slovak Towns and Villages, the Union of Slovak Towns, the Association of Regional Capitals K-8, and so on.

The Constitution and other relevant laws allow citizens to exercise their right to suffrage at regional and local levels. Representatives of self-governments (deputies of municipal councils and regional assemblies, mayors of villages and towns, and regional governors) are elected in direct, free, and democratic competitions. The electoral system is open to political party candidates as well as independent candidates. Elections to local and regional self-governments are held regularly (every four years) and are open to independent observers. Participating candidates and elected deputies represent a broad spectrum of opinions and political orientations.

Local and regional levels of self-governance give citizens a chance to take a much more active part in the administration of public affairs and adopt remedies when dissatisfied with local governance. Citizens' direct participation in decision-making processes is regulated by the Law on the Municipal System of Government and the Law on Self-Governance of Higher Territorial Units. Civic associations and other types of NGOs have proven to be the most effective in facilitating communication between self-governance bodies and local citizens.

Some municipalities have achieved very positive results when tackling concrete problems in cooperation with NGOs. Other self-governments remain reluctant to cooperate with NGOs and prefer bureaucratic ways of dealing with problems. In some cases, this approach has provoked citizen protests, sometimes in the form of petitions demanding removal of mayors or chairmen of local councils and calling new elections. Very important in this respect is the Law on Free Access to Information, which stipulates that self-governance bodies are obliged to provide citizens with information on their performance and activities. Generally speaking, however, self-governments have adequate funds and personnel to fulfill their duties and provide proper services to citizens.

The level of public participation in regional and local politics is similar to that in national politics; in the case of women and ethnic minorities (especially Roma), the rate of participation is higher locally than at the national level. In 2005, independent media at the central and regional levels paid closer attention to problems of local democracy, self-governance, and regional development. They frequently published articles on the performance of self-governance bodies, the activities of political players at the regional level, and a variety of local disputes and scandals. Undoubtedly, the main reason for shifting the media spotlight to these issues was the upcoming regional elections (scheduled to take place in November 2005). Additionally, ever since Slovakia became a full-fledged EU member, self-governance organs have acquired better opportunities to draw financial assistance from EU funds for local and regional development projects; naturally, this issue has attracted media attention.

Regional and local self-governments do not have the power to pass laws, which is the prerogative of the national legislative assembly. However, they do have the power to pass bylaws and regulations that apply exclusively to them. Should the need arise, self-governance bodies may turn to the courts to enforce their decisions; should the state administration unconstitutionally interfere with local matters, self-governments may appeal to the Constitutional Court. The law allows self-governments to form associations with other domestic and foreign self-governance institutions in order to assert their interests and tackle local problems. Self-governance organs, especially regions and larger municipalities, frequently cooperate with partners from abroad, particularly from neighboring countries.

One of the main objectives of the ongoing public administration reform, including fiscal decentralization, is to loosen the government's centralized grip on the country's taxation system and public expenditures. More important are the agreements among political parties represented on local decision-making bodies, which significantly impact the budgetary management of local self-governments.

Self-governments are subject to internal as well as external supervision. Internal control is entrusted to chief controllers who are appointed to local and regional self-governments for a six-year term. The NKU, which provides external control, saw its monitoring powers with respect to self-governments strengthened in 2005 after the passage of a constitutional amendment. As a result, the NKU is now entitled to control all funds expended by self-government organs in the performance of their duties. Also, the NKU will supervise the financial management of legal entities established by self-government organs.

Meetings of local and regional self-governance bodies are held regularly and are open to the public; the results of their deliberations are posted on specially designed public notice boards, via the media, and increasingly on the Internet. When gathering information on the activities and performance of self-governance bodies, journalists frequently refer to the Law on Free Access to Information. In 2005, no cases surfaced of direct pressure on journalists who report on regional and local problems. Similarly, there were no direct attempts by illegitimate groups to influence self-governance bodies. At the same time, though, the media aired stories about clientelism and nepotistic practices in public procurement and decision making over property transfers to nonstate subjects. Most of these cases had one thing in common: They involved attempts to capitalize on political and party ties to self-governance bodies.

Judicial Framework and Independence

1997	1998	1999	2001	2002	2003	2004	2005	2006
4.00	4.00	2.50	2.25	2.00	2.00	2.00	2.00	2.00

The Slovak Constitution and laws, including the Bill of Fundamental Rights and Freedoms, provide a sufficient framework for the protection of human rights. The implementation and exercise of political rights is regulated by the Law on Political Parties, the various election laws (to the Parliament, the European Parliament, and regional and local self-governments), and the Law on Presidential Elections. A number of other laws help co-create the domestic system of human rights. In 2002, the Parliament elected the first public defender of human rights (ombudsman) in the country's history. Citizens can turn to the Constitutional Court, which accepts complaints regarding violations of human rights and also issues verdicts. No cases of torture or other maltreatment of prisoners or detainees were reported in Slovakia in 2005.

The Slovak Republic, a member of the Council of Europe, is part of the European system of human rights protection and has also ratified all important international human rights documents. Citizens of Slovakia may turn to the European Court of Human Rights if they believe their rights have been violated and Slovak judicial institutions have been unable to take action or provide a remedy. In 2005, the European Court of Human Rights issued several rulings in favor of Slovak citizens in their legal disputes with the government. Most frequently, these cases involved drawn-out proceedings that violated citizens' constitutional right to a lawsuit without unnecessary delays.

The right to appeal to the Constitutional Court regarding the possible unconstitutionality of laws, government regulations, and other legal rules applied by the public administration rests with parliamentary deputies (at least 30 are required to launch an appeal), the president, the cabinet, courts of justice, and the attorney general; in certain cases, self-governments also enjoy this right. Citizens are free to turn to the Constitutional Court if they believe their constitutional rights have been violated by a state organ. In 2005, there were no attempts to mount administrative or political pressure on the Constitutional Court in order to influence its deliberations or verdicts. All concerned institutions unreservedly respected rulings issued by the Constitutional Court. The only problem complicating the Court's performance in 2005 was its incompleteness, as it was 2 judges short of the full complement of 13 justices prescribed by the Constitution. The principal reason for this state of affairs was the Parliament's inability to agree on acceptable candidates; consequently, the president was unable to appoint the 2 remaining seats. The incomplete makeup of the Constitutional Court complicated its decision making, especially the adoption of decisions by a plenum, which requires a majority of all judges (7 out of 13).

The Constitution guarantees all citizens equality before the law regardless of sex, race, skin color, language, religion, political preference, nationality or ethnicity, property status, or other categories. Some population groups encounter problems when exercising the principle of equality, such as inadequate representation of women in public posts, or are confronted with displays of racial discrimination and even racially motivated violence, as in the case of the Roma. Although the police have stepped up the campaign against various radical, nationalistic, Fascist, and neo-Nazi groups over the past two or three years – for instance, breaking up several public events attended by skinheads – law enforcement agencies have been unable to paralyze these groups, which specifically target the Roma, Jews, homosexuals, liberals, democrats, and members of so-called alternative youth groups, among others. Minister of the Interior Vladimir Palko removed two district police chiefs in Bratislava and Trnava on the grounds of ineffective prevention and investigation of such incidents and their participants.

By joining the EU in 2004, the Slovak Republic undertook all related human rights obligations, including enforcement of equal treatment principles. To comply with European Council Guideline No. 2000/43, the Parliament in May 2004 passed the Law on Equal Treatment and Protection Against Discrimination, also known as the Antidiscrimination Law. Among numerous protections, the law allowed for affirmative action with respect to certain groups (especially the Roma). In October 2005, the Constitutional Court issued a ruling in which it argued that the introduction of temporary equalization measures aimed at helping members of disadvantaged population groups, including ethnic minorities, did not comply with the principle of equality before the law that is embodied in the Slovak Constitution. Several members of the cabinet reacted by declaring that the Court's ruling would not discourage state organs from tackling problems that affect the Romany ethnic minority, whose members are confronted with low social status, poor education, poverty, and unemployment. Several years ago, the cabinet established the Office of the Government Plenipotentiary for Romany Communities, currently headed by a Romany woman. In cooperation with state institutions and NGOs, the office is implementing projects aimed at improving the situation of the Roma in education, health service, housing, job opportunities, and culture.

In May 2005, the Parliament passed a new penal code and code of penal procedure. The most serious and socially dangerous crimes are considered those against life and health, followed by crimes against freedom, human dignity, family, and youth; the third category includes property and economic crimes, while crimes against the government dropped from the top to the bottom. Punishments for verbal offenses remained – for instance, defamation of the nation, race, and political and religious opinions, including denying the Holocaust. The new code authorizes alternative punishment for less serious criminal offenses and lowers the age limit for criminal prosecution to 14 years.

Slovakia has a three-level judicial system – the Supreme Court, 8 regional courts, and 45 district courts – administered jointly by the president, the Parliament, the Ministry of Justice, the Judicial Council, and the Supreme Court. The president appoints judges acting on proposals from the Judicial Council, which is the principal organ of self-governance within the judiciary. The Ministry of Justice appoints chairmen and vice chairmen of particular courts.

International monitors have confirmed that the Slovak judiciary is independent to a satisfactory degree. However, the public's sense of legal safety continued to be impaired by the courts' inefficiency, which is exacerbated by an overwhelming and slow-moving backlog of cases. It is hoped that the new penal code will accelerate judicial proceedings – for example, by extending the scope of litigation in which a court of appeals may issue final verdicts instead of referring matters back to lower courts for repeated hearings. Public trust in the courts is also undermined by a relatively widespread belief that the judiciary is severely plagued by corruption, and several judges have been caught accepting bribes over the years.

Corruption

1997	1998	1999	2001	2002	2003	2004	2005	2006
n/a	n/a	3.75	3.75	3.25	3.25	3.25	3.00	3.00

Corruption is a frequent issue of public debate in Slovakia. Public opinion polls label corruption as one of the most pressing social problems, trailing only living standards and social security, unemployment, and health care. According to a survey conducted by the Public Opinion Research Institute at the Statistical Office of the Slovak Republic, most citizens believe that corruption exists in health care (71 percent), while others perceive it within the judiciary (34 percent), education system (31 percent), business (19 percent), the police (18 percent), district and regional authorities (16 percent), and the privatization process (14 percent).[4] According to a March 2005 survey conducted by the FOCUS agency, people believe that corruption is a greater problem in the central government than at the local self-governance level.[5]

The government's greatest challenges have been to improve the existing legislative environment (implementing administrative measures that effectively curb the space for corruption) and to mete out effective punishment for all parties involved. Adopted in November 2002, the current administration's program manifesto stressed the importance of fighting corruption; and in the following year, the government established a specialized Department of Combating Corruption. In 2003, this authority was transferred to the minister of justice. Next, the government established the Special Court of Justice and Special Prosecutor's Department, both of which focus on combating corruption.

In 2004, the Parliament approved a constitutional Law on Conflicts of Interest. This bans the president, members of the cabinet, justices of the Constitutional Court, and other top officials from pursuing any business activities, receiving pay for brokering deals between the government and private entities or corporations, or receiving income generated by either a side job or a contracted business relation that exceeds the minimum wage. Civil and public service laws precisely circumscribe the process for selecting, appointing, supervising, and remunerating civil servants. Other bills have sought to introduce the principle of zero tolerance for corruption among notaries and marshals, compulsory disclosure for customs officers, protection of whistle-blowers in the workplace and witnesses in court cases, and the post of controller in bodies of local and regional self-governance.

In 2005, the Parliament passed several other pieces of legislation aimed at combating various forms of corruption. One of the most important was an amendment to the Law on Public Procurement that introduced an obligation for all government organs to inform the Office of Public Procurement two weeks prior to concluding a procurement contract. This new requirement should make the process of public procurement more transparent. Besides making publicly available information on the salaries of civil servants and other public officials, an amendment to the Law on Free Access to Information introduced an obligation to publish information on any transfer of property of the state, a self-governance body, or a public institution to private individuals.

The new Law on Political Parties introduced stricter rules on party financial management. All political parties must now submit their complete annual financial reports to independent auditors; previously, parties were required to submit only financial statements for an audit. Another piece of legislation that is expected to have an impact on corruption is the constitutional amendment that extended the control powers of the NKU with respect to self-governance bodies, firms with some share of state ownership, and public institutions and firms pursuing activities in the public interest. The new penal code allows "agent provocateurs" to take the initiative in inciting corrupt acts among those public officials who are reasonably suspected of a proclivity to corruption.

Unfortunately, practical implementation of anticorruption measures often clashes with the passivity or even open resistance of officials at both central and local levels. Also, practical experience shows that the impact of some legislative and administrative measures has been rather limited. Although Transparency International Slovakia observed in October 2005 that the government, during its first three years in office, had fulfilled most of the tasks specified in its Anticorruption Program, some measures were not as effective as hoped. For instance, the performance of the parliamentary Committee for Conflicts of Interest has been unsatisfactory, as the committee has not once sanctioned parliamentarians who fail to observe all provisions of the Law on Conflicts of Interest regarding submission of compulsory disclosures. According to Transparency International's 2005 Corruption Perceptions Index, Slovakia's index score of 4.3 represents an improvement over the 2004 index score of 4.0, on a scale ranging between 10 (highly clean) and 0 (highly corrupt).

All institutions financed from public funds are subject to the supervisory authority of the NKU. Although top officials of the NKU are elected by the Parliament, this agency is fully independent from any political pressure when exercising its powers and performing its duties. Its findings are made public via all types of media, including the Internet, and often become the focus of vivid public debate.

Slovakia has a number of independent NGOs that are very active in fighting corruption and promoting transparency and accountability in public life, including Transparency International Slovakia, Alliance for Transparency and Corruption Combat, Alliance to Stop Conflicts of Interest, and Fair Play Alliance. There have been no attempts by the state or private individuals to hinder the activities of these groups or intimidate their activists in 2005.

The police encourage citizens possessing information on corrupt civil servants or a personal experience of corruption to participate in exposing concrete cases. The total number of corruption crimes cleared by the police in 2004 was 163. During 2005, the Anticorruption Bureau at the Presidium of the Slovak Police Force investigated 238 corruption crimes, 188 cases were finalized and submitted to prosecutors' offices for further procedure.[6] According to the Office of Prosecutor General, 67 persons were accused in corruption crimes in 2005 and 31 were sentenced.[7] Those numbers included some top officials: a member of Parliament, the chairman of the Raca District Council in Bratislava, the deputy mayor of Kosice, the mayor of Cadca, the mayor of Velky Meder, the director of an employment agency in Presov, the head of the regional land office in Trnava, the director of the land office in Galanta, and the chairman of the local council in Horna Poton. The police detained most of these public officials in the process of accepting bribes. In May 2005, a parliamentarian, Gabriel Karlin, was convicted of bribery. The party affiliations of prosecuted persons had no impact on the course of investigations or the legal actions taken against them, as the list of investigated and indicted persons includes members or nominees of ruling parties (SDKU, KDH, SMK, ANO) as well as the opposition (HZDS).

Scandals involving clientelism or corruption had a strong impact on the Slovak political scene in 2005. In September, Pavol Rusko was removed from his post as minister of the economy on the grounds of having conducted obscure financial operations incompatible with holding a public post. In October, Social Affairs Minister Ludovit Kanik resigned after coming under strong public pressure prompted by the participation of his wife's firm in a public tender to acquire financial assistance from EU funds (although it did not win the tender). Representatives of opposition parties regularly accused the minority ruling coalition of "buying" the votes of independent MPs in order to secure ad hoc majorities before crucial votes. After joining the opposition in September 2005, ANO chairman Pavol Rusko published a secretly videotaped conversation of a former parliamentarian for ANO who allegedly had been offered money for remaining loyal to the ruling coalition. While the content of the conversation failed to prove the involvement of corruption, neither did it dissipate the suspicion. The Slovak police have already launched an investigation into the matter.

Grigorij Meseznikov is president of the Institute for Public Affairs (IVO) in Bratislava. He is the author and editor of numerous publications on Slovakia's political development and party system, including IVO's annual Global Report on the State of Society in Slovakia.

Miroslav Kollar is a senior analyst at IVO and a coeditor of the Global Report on the State of Society in Slovakia. *He writes frequently about the media, culture, and the church.*

Michal Vasecka is a lecturer at the Faculty of Social and Economic Sciences of Comenius University. He is the author of numerous works on civil society and ethnic minorities.

---

[1] G. Meseznikov and O. Gyarfasova, Slovakia. Country Report based on Research and Dialogue with Political Parties. (Stockholm: International Institute for Democracy and Electoral Assistance, 2006) on www.ide.int/parties

[2] See Scitanie obyvatelov, domov a bytov 2001 (Accounting of Inhabitants, Houses and Apartments 2001), (Bratislava: Statistical Office of the SR), on
http://www.statistics.sk/webdata/slov/scitanie/namj.htm

[3] See www.seenpm.org/download.php?file=19_Ownership_Slovakia.pdf.

[4] See E. Sicakova-Beblava, Transparentnost a korupcia (Transparency and Corruption), in: Miroslav Kollar, Grigorij Meseznikov, and Martin Butora, Slovensko 2005. Suhrnna sprava o stave spolocnosti (Slovakia 2005: A Global Report on the State of Society), (Bratislava: Institute for Public Affairs, 2006), 667.

[5] See Percepcia korupcie na Slovensku. Prieskum verejnej mienky pre Transparency International Slovensko. Marec 2005 (Perception of Corruption in Slovakia. Public Opinion Poll conducted for Transparency International Slovakia, March 2005), on:
http://www.transparency.sk/prieskumy/060424_perce.pdf

[6] See Statisticke ukazovatele trestnej cinnosti v SR v roku 2005 (Statistical Parameters/Findings on

Criminal Activity in the Slovak Republic in 2005), on: http://www.minv.sk/statistiky/A-Stat.htmon
[7] See Statisticky prehlad trestnej a netrestnej cinnosti za rok 2005 (Statistical Oversight of Criminal and Non-Criminal Activity in 2005),
http://www.genpro.gov.sk/index/statistiky.php?id=604&stat_result=true&lang=skIn 2005.

Slovenia

Capital:	Ljubljana
Population:	2 million
GNI/capita:	$14,770
Ethnic Groups:	Slovene (83.1%), Serb (2%), Croat (1.8%), Bosniak (1.1%), other or unspecified (12%)

Nations in Transit Ratings and Averaged Scores

	1997	1998	1999	2001	2002	2003	2004	2005	2006
Electoral Process	2.00	2.00	2.00	1.75	1.75	1.50	1.50	1.50	1.50
Civil Society	2.00	2.00	1.75	1.75	1.50	1.50	1.50	1.75	1.75
Independent Media	1.75	1.75	1.75	1.75	1.75	1.75	1.75	1.50	1.75
Governance *	2.50	2.50	2.25	2.50	2.25	2.25	2.00	n/a	n/a
National Democratic Governance	n/a	n/a	n/a	n/a	n/a	n/a	n/a	2.00	2.00
Local Democratic Governance	n/a	n/a	n/a	n/a	n/a	n/a	n/a	1.50	1.50
Judicial Framework and Independence	1.75	1.50	1.50	1.50	1.75	1.75	1.75	1.50	1.50
Corruption	n/a	n/a	2.00	2.00	2.00	2.00	2.00	2.00	2.25
Democracy Score	2.00	1.95	1.88	1.88	1.83	1.79	1.75	1.68	1.75

* With the 2005 edition, Freedom House introduced seperate analysis and ratings for national democratic governance and local democratic governance to provide readers with more detailed and nuanced analysis of these two important subjects.

NOTE: The ratings reflect the consensus of Freedom House, its academic advisers, and the author of this report. The opinions expressed in this report are those of the author. The ratings are based on a scale of 1 to 7, with 1 representing the highest level of democratic progress and 7 the lowest. The Democracy Score is an average of ratings for the categories tracked in a given year.

The economic and social data on this page were taken from the following sources:
GNI/capita, Population: *World Development Indicators 2006* (Washington, D.C.: World Bank, 2006).
Ethnic Groups: *CIA World Factbook 2006* (Washington, D.C.: Central Intelligence Agency, 2006).

EXECUTIVE SUMMARY

Slovenia held the country's first free and democratic elections in 1990 and declared its independence from Yugoslavia in 1991. Fourteen years later, it is a democratic and economically stable country. It joined both the European Union (EU) and NATO in 2004. The country's democratic institutions are consolidated, with only minor details of institutional framework requiring additional improvement. However, the influence of the state and ruling coalitions on the economy remains substantial. The influence of political elites is especially strong in the financial sector of the economy, in infrastructure (public transport system, road management), telecommunications, and energy. Yet foreign investment in the country remains low.

The new ruling coalition and government that came to power in the October 2004 elections spent 2005 engulfed in the takeover process. The ruling coalition, comprising mostly right-wing political parties (Slovene Democratic Party, Slovene People's Party, New Slovenia–Christian People's Party, and Democratic Party of Slovene Pensioners), immediately began exercising its power over the economy by replacing numerous managers of state-owned or partially state-owned companies. Additionally, the coalition proposed a new management strategy for public broadcaster Radio Television Slovenia (RTS), the most influential media organization in the country. The new Law on Radio Television Slovenia was adopted by a slight majority in Parliament. Both the Slovene Association of Journalists and the opposition were dissatisfied with the law and demanded a referendum, which was held; however results confirmed the law and allowed it to stand.

In November 2005, trade unions organized mass demonstrations against a government-sponsored proposal for economic reform. One of the key topics of the reform package included the introduction of a flat tax. According to the trade unions, the introduction of a flat tax would seriously jeopardize the social status of workers. Furthermore, trade unions were dissatisfied with the level of dialogue between the state, employers, and trade unions. The resulting peaceful demonstrations were considered the largest mass protests in Slovenia in the last decade.

National Democratic Governance. Government power in Slovenia is divided among the three independent branches: legislative, executive, and judicial. A system of checks and balances exists but is not always effective; some Constitutional Court rulings have been incompletely enforced. The military is under efficient civilian authority. Civilian oversight of police and security services is assured by legislation, but in a case from September 2005, the Parliament failed in an attempt to inspect wiretapping procedures by the police. Despite the government's announced intention to withdraw from the economy, the mechanisms of government influence remain in place. Consequently, the government and ruling coalition's influence on the economy remains substantial. Since the formation of the ruling coalition established after the 2004 elections, the political elite's influence on the economy has become more visible. *Slovenia's national democratic governance rating remains at 2.00.*

Electoral Process. The referendum on the Law on Radio Television Slovenia was the key political event of the year, as no national elections were held in 2005. The law established new management for RTS. The referendum, with only a 30 percent turnout, confirmed the law by a slight majority. Referendums, along with national elections held in regular four-year intervals, provide a permanent forum for citizens to participate in decision-making processes. In the last decade, 10 national referendums were held on a variety of topics. As an electoral process, referendums are considered free and fair, but participation in democratic decision making is declining. *Owing to the stable and mature nature of the electoral process, including referendums, the proposed rating for electoral process remains at 1.50.*

Civil Society. The number of registered nongovernmental organizations (NGOs) in Slovenia grows every year, but some events indicate that receptiveness to civil society initiatives is declining. The recently adopted Law on Radio Television Slovenia will introduce a new way of representing civil society on the public broadcasting corporation's program council. According to the previous regulation, NGOs could autonomously appoint members to the program council. The new regulations stipulate that NGOs may only propose council members, who then must be approved by parliamentary election. Trade unions, dissatisfied with the low level of social dialogue on government-sponsored economic reforms, organized mass peaceful demonstrations. Gay and lesbian initiatives saluted the Parliament's adoption of the Law on the Registration of Same-Sex Partnership but claimed that the enacted legislation would lead to some forms of discrimination. On the other hand, the government responded positively to initiatives proposing partial segregation of pupils of Roma ethnic origin during school lessons in the region of Dolenjska. *Protests from civil society and the referendum results offset the move requiring parliamentary approval for NGO representation in media, holding Slovenia's civil society rating at 1.75, though receptiveness to civil society initiatives merits close watch.*

Independent Media. The effect of the new Law on Radio Television Slovenia will become visible in 2006, when the regulation will be enacted. However, the Slovene Association of Journalists has warned that the new regulation may increase state influence on the public broadcasting service. Currently, the media landscape in Slovenia is not exempt from the interference of powerful actors. The management board of Delo, the largest publishing company in Slovenia, replaced the chief editor of Slovenia's most influential daily newspaper, *Darijan Kosir*, claiming conflicting views on editorial policy. In the past, a clear division of responsibilities between the editorial and management boards existed to ensure that the management board did not interfere with editorial policy. Additionally, two cases came to light in 2005 of police failing to protect journalists from being victimized by powerful actors. *Slovenia's independent media rating worsens from 1.50 to 1.75 owing to indications of increasing interference by political, private owner, and powerful state or nonstate actors, in editorial independence and news-gathering functions.*

Local Democratic Governance. The principles of local democratic governance are enshrined in legislation and respected in practice. However, since nearly half of the 193 municipalities have fewer than 5,000 inhabitants, the smallest among them do not always have sufficient resources to fulfill their responsibilities efficiently. The rights of ethnic minorities are protected by the Law on Local Self-Governance of 1993, but in the case of the municipality of Grosuplje, the local Roma population's right to representation on the municipality council has not been implemented. The Slovene ombudsman for human rights warned the municipality several times to amend the statute, but his warnings have gone unheeded. *The proposed rating for local democratic governance remains at 1.50.*

Judicial Framework and Independence. The Constitution and other national legislation provide protection for fundamental political, civil, and human rights, which are respected in practice. The Constitutional Court is considered independent, highly professional, and impartial in its interpretation of the Constitution. However, a few rulings have yet to be enforced. The Constitutional Court ruling demanding that the executive restore all rights to those individuals removed from the register of permanent residents of Slovenia in 1992 has not been completely enforced. For this reason, thousands of the country's residents lack Slovene citizenship and live in a seriously compromised social situation. *Slovenia's rating for judicial framework and independence remains at 1.50.*

Corruption. The Slovene Commission for the Prevention of Corruption began work as an independent body in October 2004. Surprisingly, the opposition Slovene National Party proposed amending the Law on the Prevention of Corruption, closing the commission, and transferring its competences to the parliamentary Commission for the Prevention of Corruption. The proposal was supported by the parties of the ruling coalition, but at the end of 2005 the non-parliamentarian Youth Party of Slovenia began collecting signatures for a referendum to halt the parliamentary procedure. *Slovenia's rating for corruption worsens from 2.00 to 2.25 as transfer of the commission's competences to Parliament removes the assurance of independence.*

Outlook for 2006. Three main processes will be important in 2006. First, the future of the Commission for the Prevention of Corruption will become clearer in the beginning of the year. However, shutting down the commission and transferring its competences to the parliamentarian body would represent a significant step back in Slovenia's institutional framework. Second, the government's commitment to independent media will be tested by the parliamentary election of civil society nominees to the council of the RTS. Third, with announced economic reforms and the peaceful mass demonstrations of 2005, the government's ability to establish fruitful dialogue with trade unions will be important for further civil society development in 2006.

MAIN REPORT

National Democratic Governance

1997	1998	1999	2001	2002	2003	2004	2005	2006
n/a	n/a	n/a	n/a	n/a	n/a	n/a	2.00	2.00

Slovenia has a democratic system of government, enshrined in the Constitution and national legislation and supported by a broad popular consensus among political parties and citizens. The country's governmental system has achieved stability without coercion, violence, or other abuse of basic rights and civil liberties. Furthermore, the government's authority is extended over the full territory of the country, and the ruling coalition has a comfortable majority in the Parliament.

The government is open to public participation and citizen involvement in the decision-making process. Referendums may be demanded by citizens on specific subjects or called by the parliamentary opposition. This avenue is often used; in 2005, the opposition demanded a referendum on the new Law on Radio Television Slovenia, which will regulate public radio and television. Voters adopted the law by a slight majority in September 2005.[1]

The system of checks and balances among executive, legislative, and judicial authority is effective. Slovenia's Constitutional Court monitors the legality and constitutionality of government and Parliament decisions, and the Parliament can demand a no-confidence vote for the government. Deputies may demand explanations from government officials (cabinet members regularly answer these questions), and there has been parliamentary debate and disciplinary votes regarding the performance of certain ministers.

The Law on Access to Information of a Public Character[2] (similar to a freedom of information statute) was adopted in 2003, but implementation has been difficult. In June 2005, Jernej Pavlin, the government's press officer, sent an e-mail to all ministry spokespeople suggesting they have minimal contact with the weekly newspaper *Mladina*.[3] Had it been followed, Pavlin's suggestion would have disadvantaged *Mladina* reporters and effectively countermanded the Law on Access to Information of a Public Character. However, Pavlin's e-mail was leaked to *Mladina*, and he resigned shortly thereafter. Perhaps as a result, the media frequently invoked the law in the second half of the year with the government's cooperation.

Government influence over the economy remains substantial. The new government, formed after the October 2004 elections, appointed members to the supervisory and management boards of two state-owned financial funds, the Pension Management Fund and the Compensation Fund. Both own significant stock in nearly all large Slovene companies. Furthermore, infrastructure, telecommunications, and energy companies are mostly state owned, while the largest insurance company in Slovenia is not yet privatized and the country's largest bank is only partially privatized. As a result, the influence of the ruling coalition in the financial, energy, and telecommunications sectors, as well as other areas of the Slovene economy, is still very high. Public support for the national authorities is strong but began to decline in the second half of 2005 owing to the unpopularity of proposed economic reforms. The government's approval rating dropped from 61 percent in March to 46 percent in October 2005.[4]

According to the Constitution, the Slovene legislature is independent, and "deputies of the National Assembly are representatives of all the people and shall not be bound by any instructions."[5] In practice, however, parliamentary deputies are subject to party and coalition discipline. On only a few occasions did the parliamentary majority refuse to adopt the legislative proposals of the government. For example, the Parliament did not adopt a wine bill proposing to divide Slovenia into two wine regions. Instead, it insisted that Slovenia be divided into three wine regions to protect specific brands of wine.

Overall, the National Assembly is effective and accountable to the public. The legislative branch provides leadership and reflects social preferences by creating a forum for the peaceful and democratic resolution of differences. Parliamentary documents, including transcripts of parliamentarian debates, are available to the public online. Parliamentary sessions are open to the public, with the exception of sessions of the Commission for Supervision of the Intelligence and Security Services and some sessions of the Committee on Foreign Policy.[6] The legislative branch has autonomy from the executive. In the last decade, the parliamentarian professional apparatus has developed and strengthened the autonomous position of the Parliament. The Parliament's professional staff now effectively supports deputies during legislative processes. However, there is still insufficient staff to support effective investigative competences, and parliamentarians often fail to submit final reports related to specific investigative activities.

In 2005, the parliamentary opposition demanded a special investigation into the sale of shares in the largest Slovene company, Mercator, by the state-owned Pension Management Fund and Compensation Fund. The opposition holds that the transaction – in which 29 percent of state fund shares in Mercator were sold to two private investors – was suspicious. According to the opposition, state-owned funds would have earned much more if they had sold the shares through a public offer. The ruling coalition, however, proposed a massive investigation of all Pension Management Fund and Compensation Fund transactions in the last decade. The opposition disagreed with this move, as it would take years to review all transactions, leaving no time to investigate specifically the allegedly suspicious Mercator transaction.

The executive branch is independent and effective. It has the necessary resources to formulate and implement policies and reports extensively on the decisions of each session, publishing these reports on the government's information office Web site. Furthermore, the media generally have regular access to the executive for additional comments. In some cases, governmental officials avoid direct answers. The government administration has public relations officials, however, no officials are responsible for communicating with ordinary citizens directly. Nevertheless, public access to commentary on policy formulation and implementation is always assured.

Some details concerning the executive's role vis-a-vis other branches are not clearly defined, especially the foreign policy competences of the president, who is elected directly for a five-year term. On the one hand, the role of the president is considered ceremonial. Yet the current president, Janez Drnovsek, has decided on some foreign policy initiatives that were previously not in harmony with government policy.[7]

The young Slovene civil service functions according to democratic standards, but as of yet the sector lacks competence and professional standards. Each ruling coalition attempts to employ party loyalists inside the state apparatus. Professional diplomats especially complain that party loyalists have a better chance of obtaining ambassadorship positions.

According to legislation, defense, civil security services, and police are subject to the democratic supervision of a special parliamentary commission. In practice, however, this supervision is sometimes blocked. On September 14, 2005, for example, deputy members of the Commission for Supervision of the Intelligence and Security Services attempted to investigate the police practice of recording telephone conversations. The deputies arrived unannounced at the headquarters of the general police directorate and asked to inspect police documents, but they were not assisted. After this unsuccessful inspection, the minister of interior affairs apologized to the commission and promised that such an incident would not happen again.[8] Unannounced field inspections seem to be the legislature's only effective tool to control the practical activities of the security services. Likewise, the obstruction of field inspections indicates the security services' general attitude toward parliamentary supervision.

The military budget consists of two sections: basic development programs excluded from the general budget, such as the purchase of military equipment; and an administrative part, which is entirely transparent. Some details of basic development programs are presented only to the parliamentary Committee on Defense. Furthermore, the public does not always have accurate information concerning military and defense matters. In July 2005, Minister of Defense Karl Erjavec replaced key officials within the Ministry of Defense. The press sought a precise explanation for the replacements, as some of the officials played key roles in Slovenia's integration into NATO. The minister's cabinet answered that "replacements are in accordance with the accepted human resources plan of the government and that some ministries expressed their need for certain employee profiles."[9]

Electoral Process

1997	1998	1999	2001	2002	2003	2004	2005	2006
2.00	2.00	2.00	1.75	1.75	1.50	1.50	1.50	1.50

The government's authority is based on universal and equal suffrage and the will of the people expressed by regular, free, and fair elections conducted by secret ballot. Electoral laws are fair, and all political parties are free to campaign in electoral contests. Polling is fair, and the last election took place without any reports of ballot tabulation irregularities. Furthermore, domestic observers considered the 2004 elections to be free and fair, and no international election monitoring was deemed necessary. Foreign powers do not interfere in the electoral process, nor do power groups dominate the people's choice.

The electoral system is multiparty, and barriers to participation are insignificant: Parties with representatives in the Parliament can automatically participate in elections without hindrance, while parties without parliamentary representation must gain at least 50 signatures in each of the 8 electoral districts (there are an additional 88 subdistricts).[10] In 2004, 20 political parties and 3 independent candidates participated in the parliamentary elections. Of these, 1,395 candidates ran on party election lists, including 347 female candidates (24.9 percent), a slight increase from the 2000 elections, where the proportion of female candidates was 23.4 percent.[11] As a result, 7 political parties entered the Parliament. Among those that did not enter the Parliament are 3 active parties: Youth Party of Slovenia, Active Slovenia, and Green Party of Slovenia. Others were more or less one-man initiatives.

Table 1. National Parliament Election Results[12]

List of Candidates	Number of Votes–2004	Percentage–2004	Percentage–2000
Slovene Democratic Party	281,710	29.08	15.81
Liberal Democratic Party	220,848	22.80	36.27
United List of Social Democrats	98,527	10.17	12.08
New Slovenia–Christian People's Party	88,073	9.09	8.66
Slovene People's Party	66,032	6.82	9.54
Slovene National Party	60,750	6.27	4.39
Democratic Party of Slovene Pensioners	39,150	4.04	5.17

Source: State Electoral Commission (www.rvk.si)

The public is engaged in the political life of Slovenia, but voter turnout has declined in recent years. In 2004, 60.6 percent of voters participated in the national elections. Turnout was especially low (28.3 percent) during the European Parliament elections.

Table 2. Voter Turnout for National Parliament[13]

Year	Percent
1992	85.6
1996	73.7
2000	70.1
2004	60.6

Source: State Electoral Commission[13]

Two ethnic minorities, Italians and Hungarians, have the right to representation in the national Parliament. Their participation focuses mostly on the social, political, and economic status of minorities. Other ethnic minorities, such as the Roma, have the right to elect representatives only to local bodies of government. However, this right is not fully respected. For example, in the local community of Grosuplje, the Roma population does not have a representative on the municipal council.

Effective rotation of power among political parties representing competing interests is assured. At the end of 2004, a new government coalition was formed. The Slovene Democratic Party (SDS), the strongest oppositional party for a decade, won the elections and became the strongest member of the ruling coalition. The Liberal Democratic Party (LDS), the leader for more than a decade, became the opposition party. The LDS's inability to counter the argument that it had held power too long, especially as corruption scandals began to erode the party's image, contributed to its loss. The power rotation at the end of 2004 and the beginning of 2005 was smooth, despite a controversy surrounding the new ruling coalition's replacement of middle-ranking officials in the government administration. Furthermore, the coalition replaced a significant number of members of supervisory boards of the state-controlled Pension Management Fund and Compensation Fund, which own a substantial portion of shares in nearly all large Slovene companies.[14] However, the political power of economic elites is weak and is dominated by political elites.

Civil Society

1997	1998	1999	2001	2002	2003	2004	2005	2006
2.00	2.00	1.75	1.75	1.50	1.50	1.50	1.75	1.75

According to Slovenia's Constitution, "The right of peaceful assembly and public meeting shall be guaranteed. Everyone has the right to freedom of association with others. Legal restrictions of these rights shall be permissible where so required for national security or public safety and for protection against the spread of infectious diseases. Professional members of the defense forces and the police may not be members of political parties."[15]

Statistical data show that Slovene civil society is vibrant. According to the 2004 register of associations, some 19,246 different associations exist, and the number of registered associations increases every year.[16]

Table 3. Number of Registered Associations in Slovenia

Year	Number
1999	15,440
2000	16,194
2001	17,103
2002	17,950
2003	18,872
2004	19,246

Source: Ministry of Interior Affairs, *Statistical Yearbook 2004*

Even so, civil society was much more vibrant in the country before 1990. Initially, non-Communist political organizations appeared as farmers' trade unions in the spring of 1988 but were considered part of a network of civil society initiatives. In 1989, when the first political organizations began to appear in the form of political parties, civil society activists entered political parties. Only a few activists remained in civil society, insisting on their independent position. Hence, from 1989 the networks linking civil society initiatives disintegrated.

Currently, the majority of NGOs are more or less uninvolved in public affairs; in fact, very few associations concentrate specifically on public affairs. The majority of registered associations focus on sports (6,773), while more than 1,500 registered groups exist for volunteer firefighters, 450 for hunters, and 200 for bee breeders. Around 55 percent of the population is active in at least one civil society organization, most commonly trade unions and sports associations.[17]

The legal and regulatory environment for civil society is generally free of excessive state pressure and bureaucracy. Basic registration of associations is not complicated. According to the Legal Information Center for NGOs, registration procedures are required to take no longer than three months to complete. Currently, out of the 19,246 registered associations, more than 4,200 are headquartered in the country's three largest cities – Ljubljana, Maribor, and Celje – confirming the general trend of civil society concentration in urban areas.

Forty religious communities are registered in Slovenia, including four communities that registered as recently as 2004.[18] The Islamic community, the second largest religious community in Slovenia according to the census, appears especially underprivileged among these groups. Attempts to build an Islamic religious and cultural center in the capital, Ljubljana, have persisted for more than three decades. Despite a general agreement by the Ljubljana City Council stating that the Islamic community has the right to build a religious and cultural center in a suburb of the capital, the community has been unable to complete the necessary bureaucratic procedures and subsequently has not started building.

On the other hand, the current right-wing ruling coalition grants the Roman Catholic Church a favored position. Catholic chaplains have jobs in the Slovene army. The Law on the Police, amended in 2005, also introduced police chaplains. Owing to opposition demands, however, the Constitutional Court will make the final decision concerning the introduction of chaplains into the police force. The material status of the Roman Catholic Church changed substantially in the last few years. According to government reports from December 2005, during the decade-long process of denationalization, the Roman Catholic Church received real estate worth approximately €144 million (US$ 183 million).

The country is not free from intolerant social initiatives. In the region of Dolenjska (in northeastern Slovenia), tensions between the local Roma population and the majority have been significant. A civic initiative led by the local functionaries of the majority SDS party proposed segregating pupils of Roma ethnic origin into an elementary school in Brsljin, in Novo Mesto (80 kilometers southeast of Ljubljana). The Ministry of Education and Sport, led by Milan Zver of the SDS, deemed the initiative legitimate and has allowed "soft" segregation of pupils during lessons.[19] Yet in general, the education system is free from political influence and propaganda.

The organizational capacities of civil society groups are sufficient, but only a small portion of associations are able to employ professionals. The Legal Information Center for NGOs plays an important role in providing training and assuring information on NGO management issues in the Slovene language. However, civil society groups face the obstacle of financial viability and lack the organizational capacity to raise funds. Among all associations, those focused on humanitarian issues and the handicapped are markedly stronger in fund-raising.

Associations, religious communities, private funds, and organizations and institutes established for ecological, humanitarian, benevolent, and other nonprofit purposes do not pay taxes on income. This includes donations, membership fees, gifts, and money received from public services. On the other hand, legislation does not provide tax incentives for donations to NGOs.

Dialogue exists between civil society and the state, but NGOs are not satisfied with the current level of government receptiveness. Gay and lesbian groups were especially dissatisfied with government receptiveness during parliamentary debate on the new Law on the Registration of Same-Sex Partnership, claiming that the enacted decisions would cause discrimination. The bill was adopted by the Parliament in June 2005, but according to gay and lesbian groups, it does not assure same-sex partners the same social security, health care, pension security, and inheritance rights as heterosexual partners.[20]

The new Law on Radio Television Slovenia, regulating the management of public radio and television, created significant changes in the representation of civil society groups in the media. The previous law assured that civil society associations could appoint members to the Council of Radio Television Slovenia, which in turn appoints key managers and editors. According to the new regulation, NGOs have the right to nominate respected citizens for council positions, but the Parliament decides who will represent civil society on the council.

The argument in favor of eliminating the autonomy of civil society organizations in the appointment process was based on the belief that political parties abuse NGOs for their own ends. Cited as an example, Janez Kocijancic, president of the RTS program council, officially represented the Olympic Committee of Slovenia but from 1993 to 1997 was president of the United List of Social Democrats, a parliamentary political party. Despite sharp protests by the Slovene Association of Journalists, the ruling coalition supported the law. The parliamentary opposition, however, demanded a referendum on the subject. With a 30.7 percent referendum turnout on September 25, 2005, 50.3 percent of voters supported the law.[21]

Media are the most receptive to civil society groups as a reliable source of information and commentary. However, the voice of civil society is much weaker in media than the voice of political parties.

The state fully respects the right to form and join free trade unions. Fruitful dialogue has existed among trade unions, employers, and government in the past. In 2005, dialogue declined, and trade unions organized massive demonstrations in November against announced government-sponsored economic reforms. Trade unions declared the dialogue with government insufficient and particularly opposed the introduction of a flat tax, which according to trade unions would jeopardize the social status of workers.

Independent Media

1997	1998	1999	2001	2002	2003	2004	2005	2006
1.75	1.75	1.75	1.75	1.75	1.75	1.75	1.50	1.75

Article 39 of the Constitution protects freedom of the press. Excessive legal penalties for "irresponsible" journalism are not applied by courts in Slovenia. Yet despite solid legal protection, journalists face victimization by powerful actors. For example, in February 2001 investigative reporter Miro Petek of the daily newspaper *Vecer* was badly beaten, allegedly in connection with articles in which he described illegal business activities (in particular, money laundering at a bank) in the region of Koroska. In September 2003, five citizens were arrested and accused of carrying out the attack. The mere fact of their prosecution was considered an important step in defending the principles of media freedom, but the trial, which concluded in August 2005, was a debacle for police and prosecutors.

It came to light during the trial that police had paid a substantial amount of money to a "key" witness. According to police, Article 49A of the Law on the Police allows payment to those providing useful information. This "key" witness was also granted anonymity but revealed his identity and the fact that he had been paid for his testimony. The court decided that paid witnesses cannot be considered reliable sources. Furthermore, the additional evidence was deemed too weak, and as a result the accused were found not guilty. Thus, although the state prosecutor and police claimed for years that they had been working diligently on the case, the trial indicated otherwise.

In another case, the criminal police department in the town of Celje, without reasonable cause, gathered information on Damjana Seme, a local correspondent for the commercial POP TV[22]. When the police report with details about the reporter's contacts and sources was sent to the parliamentary Commission for Supervision of the Intelligence and Security Services in May, the activities of the police were revealed and, according to legal experts, showed that the police had no competence to collect such information.

Journalists and media can form their own professional associations. The Slovene Association of Journalists was among the most active in civil society during the referendum campaign on the Law on Radio Television Slovenia.

The media's editorial independence and news-gathering functions are not completely free from indirect interference by the government and private owners. For example, in July 2005 the managing board of the daily newspaper *Delo* announced the dismissal of its chief editor. Prior to this move, *Delo* had published articles criticizing the Competition Protection Office's decision allowing Pivovarna Lasko (Lasko Brewery) to take over Pivovarna Union (Union Brewery). Pivovarna Lasko owns 24.99 percent of shares in *Delo's* publisher (Delo). The other significant shareholders were the state-controlled Pension Management Fund and Compensation Fund. However, the managing board claimed that "the decision for the replacement comes as a consequence of differing views on editorial policy."[23] According to media practice in Slovenia, responsibilities are divided between the chief editor and the managing board. The managing board is responsible for business functions, while the chief editor is responsible for editorial policy. Thus, any interference from the managing board in editorial policy is considered illegitimate.

There are three major daily newspapers with a long history in Slovenia: *Delo*, *Dnevnik*, and *Vecer*. Other major papers are: the business daily *Finance*, the regional daily *Primorske Novice*, two sports dailies, and two daily tabloids, *Slovenske Novice* and *Direkt*. *Direkt* is new, launched in 2005. Its advertising slogan ("No mercy!") is an accurate illustration of its editorial policy. The paper is owned by the same publisher as *Dnevnik*, so its appearance did not diversify the media landscape in Slovenia. Furthermore, newspaper distribution is privately controlled, but publishing companies are not satisfied with the level of competition in this area; only one company specializes in newspaper distribution.

Two major TV organizations provide quality news programming, the RTS and the commercial POP TV, owned by Central European Media Enterprises. Competition between RTS and POP TV seems to have a positive effect. At the local level, there are more than 60 radio stations and 24 television stations.[24]

Some groups, such as the Roman Catholic Church, complain that the media landscape is unbalanced and lacks diversity. On the other hand, the Roman Catholic Church controls an influential radio station, Radio Ognjisce, and a weekly newspaper, *Druzina*. Additionally, the Roman Catholic Church owned its own TV station until 2003.

RTS is a state-owned institution, while the commercial POP TV and local radio and television stations are privately owned. Print media are also privately owned, but the state-controlled Pension Management Fund and Compensation Fund own a substantial portion of shares in some publishing companies. However, media ownership is moderately interlocked. According to some analysts, ownership interlocking may lead to excessive concentration. For example, Delo, the largest publishing company in Slovenia, owns 20 percent of the shares in Vecer, publisher of the daily newspaper by the same name; and Vecer owns 6 percent of the shares in the publishing company Dnevnik.[25]

Currently, the financial viability of private media is subject only to market forces. Yet according to the coalition contract, the government plans to establish a special fund for the "pluralization of media," stating that such a move would "assure plurality of printed and electronic media."[26] It remains unclear precisely how the fund will function. According to some, the fund would assure additional financial resources to media that are closer to the present ruling coalition but as of yet are unsuccessful in the market.

Slovene society enjoys free access to the Internet; 48 percent of households have access, and 50 percent of those between 10 and 74 years of age use the Internet regularly.[27] Recently, competition among different Internet providers has grown stronger, an improvement over the period when state-owned Telekom dictated market conditions. The government makes no attempt to control Internet content or access, and many forums provide access to the expression of diverse opinions. Even so, public debate over hate speech on the Internet began only at the end of 2005.

Local Democratic Governance

1997	1998	1999	2001	2002	2003	2004	2005	2006
n/a	n/a	n/a	n/a	n/a	n/a	n/a	1.50	1.50

The principles of local democratic governance in Slovenia are enshrined in legislation and respected in practice. Local self-government is assured by Article 138 of the Constitution. In 1993, the Law on Local Self-Governance, affecting the country's 193 municipalities, was adopted by the Parliament. It is expected, however, that the Parliament will adopt new laws, leading to the founding of new municipalities.

Government powers and responsibilities are partially decentralized. Local authorities are free to design and adopt institutions and processes of governance reflecting local needs and conditions. Central authorities consult the local government in decision-making processes that affect the local level. However, from time to time a decision accepted by the central authorities is made against the express will of the municipalities.

Local elections are free and fair and are held at regular four-year intervals. Both the mayor and members of municipal councils are elected directly. According to the Law on Local Elections (amended in 2002), foreigners with permanent resident status have the right to vote in local elections. In the last local elections in 2002, approximately 10,000 foreigners had the right to vote.

Along with political parties active on a national level, a substantial number of local initiatives participate in local elections. The number of local initiatives and independent lists of candidates in 2002 was greater than in 1998. In 2002, 17.1 percent of votes were given to independent lists or local initiatives, while in 1998 the proportion was 11.7 percent.

At the end of 2005, however, the Law on Local Self-Governance was amended.[28] These new regulations could present a substantial obstacle for independent lists and local initiatives. Specifically, nonparty initiatives will have the right to nominate a candidate for local elections only if they succeed in collecting 2 percent of voters' signatures in the municipality. In larger municipalities, the number of signatures is set at 2,500. Signatures must be verified by the local office of the state administration. Calculating, collecting, and verifying the signatures, however, involves complicated bureaucratic procedures and may jeopardize the universal right to vote and be elected. By contrast, political parties represented in the Parliament would have fewer competitors, as political parties automatically have the right to nominate a candidate.

In some local communities, local government procedures hinder minority representation. According to Article 39 of the Law on Local Self-Governance, the Roma population has the right to elect a representative to 19 municipal councils. In November 2002, however, the right to elect representatives of the Roma population was not assured in six municipalities, as municipal councils failed to bring municipal statutes in line with the rules of the Law on Local Self-Governance. In the community of Grosuplje, Roma still lack representation on the local community council. On several occasions, the Slovene ombudsman for human rights Matjaz Hanzek appealed officially to Grosuplje to amend the local community statute, but his warnings have gone unheeded.[29]

In 2002, 723 candidates ran for mayor in 193 municipalities. Overall, the participation of women in bodies of local self-government is not adequate; women constitute only 423 of the 3,231 members of municipal councils. However, the situation has improved in the last decade.

Table 4. Percent of Women in Municipal Councils

Year	Percent
1994	10.7
1998	12
2002	13

Source: *Statistical Yearbook 2003*[30]

Among 193 mayors elected in 2002, 12 were women.

Table 5. Percent of Women Elected Mayors

Year	Percent
1994	1.3
1998	4.2
2002	6.2

Source: *Statistical Yearbook 2003*[31]

Economic oligarchies do not dominate local voting, and voter turnout in local elections is high. In 2002, turnout was higher than in 1998, as presidential and local elections occurred simultaneously. A lower turnout is expected for the 2006 local elections, as public interest in local government appears to be waning.

Table 6. Voter Turnout for Local Elections

Year	Percent
1994	61.10
1998	58.29
2002	72.06

Source: Statistical Office of the Republic of Slovenia

Local governance is responsible for city planning, but citizens, businesses, and other groups are invited to participate in public debates on the issue. Individuals and civil society groups are free to submit petitions, organize demonstrations, or initiate other activities that influence local decision making. Yet despite the dialogue between local governments and civil society, the government is not very receptive to the ideas of civil society groups. Perhaps this phenomenon results from the relatively new establishment of authority within local government.

Nevertheless, the media occasionally report on the views of local civic groups, the private business sector, and other NGOs concerning local government policy. Local radio stations especially play a significant role in covering local government policy. Furthermore, according to the Law on Access to Information of a Public Character, citizens and media are guaranteed regular access to public records and information. In some cases, however, local bureaucracy avoids these obligations. Regardless, the media are free to investigate and report on local politics and government without fear of victimization.

The central authorities respect the local authorities' decision-making capabilities and independence. Local authorities are free to pass and enforce legal acts inside the framework of local government competence. They have the right to judicial remedy to protect their powers. And according to the Constitution, municipalities have the right to form associations on the regional level, but they have not yet exercised this right.

According to the Law on Local Self-Governance, municipalities should have at least 5,000 inhabitants. If economic, geographic, historical, or other reasons exist, municipalities may have fewer than 5,000 inhabitants. Among the 193 municipalities, nearly half have fewer than 5,000 inhabitants. All local governments regularly receive due resources from the central authorities, yet these resources are sufficient only for larger communities; smaller communities have problems assuring quality services to inhabitants due to the lack of financial resources. Regardless, small communities are still being founded, and it is expected that by the 2006 local elections, there will be more than 200 municipalities.

Local authorities are subject to clear and consistent standards of disclosure, oversight, and accountability. They are autonomous in setting their budgets and allocating resources. Municipalities are empowered to set staff salaries, but these are expected to remain within the overall framework of the public sector. They are also free to define staff size and staff patterns, and recruitment is based primarily on merit and experience. In general, the services provided by local government are sufficient. However, some smaller municipalities do not have sufficient resources to provide quality services.

Local authorities are free from the domination of power groups. In some cases, especially with city planning strong pressure comes from economic lobby groups, but it would be unfair to say that local governments execute the demands of power groups rather than representing the needs of citizens.

Judicial Framework and Independence

1997	1998	1999	2001	2002	2003	2004	2005	2006
1.75	1.50	1.50	1.50	1.75	1.75	1.75	1.50	1.50

The Slovene Constitution and other national legislation protect fundamental political, civil, and human rights. Freedom of expression, association, conscience, and religion, as well as business and property rights, are assured by legal acts and in practice. State and nongovernmental actors respect fundamental political, civil, and human rights. Equality before the law is assured in the Constitution and, generally speaking, in practice. In cases where equality before the law is violated, citizens have the power to appeal effectively to the Constitutional Court.

The Constitutional Court is an independent body considered to be highly professional and impartial in its interpretation of the Constitution. However, some court rulings have not been enforced, as the Parliament has not amended those statutes that are subject to the rulings.

Criminal code reform has been effective. Presumption of innocence is respected by authorities yet is sometimes misunderstood by the media. The Constitution, legislation, and practice assure access to a fair and public trial and an independent public defender and guarantee the independence of prosecutors. The Slovene judiciary uses a continental system of jury trials.

Suspects and prisoners are protected from arbitrary arrest, searches without warrants, detention without trial, torture, and abuse. However, extensive delays persist, creating a key problem within the judicial system. At the end of 2004, there were more than 566,000 unsolved cases in the Slovene courts. According to the ombudsman for human rights, approximately two-thirds of some 700 Slovene complaints lodged with the European Court of Human Rights referred to the lack of adjudication within a reasonable time frame. Thus, reducing delays is a priority of the current coalition and judicial authorities.

Judges are appointed in a fair and unbiased manner; they are nominated by the Judiciary Council and elected by the Parliament. Judicial training is intensive, and candidates are expected to pass the bar exam after two years. After passing the bar, candidates must have at least three years of experience to be elected to a judicial position. Once a candidate is elected, the office is permanent, according to the

Constitution.[32] However, the opposition Slovene National Party has proposed the reelection of judges after eight years.

Judges rule in a fair and impartial manner, and their judgments are free from political influence. However, the executive branch has some influence on the appointment of the presidents of local, district, and higher courts as well as the Supreme Court.

The legislative, executive, and other government authorities generally comply with judicial decisions, but some rulings have not been enforced effectively. For example, in 1992 the Ministry of Interior Affairs erased from the register of permanent residents of Slovenia more than 18,000 residents who did not declare Slovene citizenship. According to a Constitutional Court ruling, the status of the erased should be completely restored, but many remain without registration, leaving thousands in a seriously compromised social situation.

Corruption

1997	1998	1999	2001	2002	2003	2004	2005	2006
n/a	n/a	2.00	2.00	2.00	2.00	2.00	2.00	2.25

Corruption allegations contributed significantly to the right-wing ruling coalition's victory in the 2004 elections in Slovenia. Indeed, some unofficial networks of potential corruption were weakened following the government's recent transition. The government's most important anticorruption initiative began in October 2004 with the adoption of the Law on the Prevention of Corruption. The law requires financial disclosure and prohibits conflicts of interest, and the Commission for the Prevention of Corruption is an effective enforcer. The commission has five members: two proposed by the president, one proposed by the parliamentary Commission for Mandates and Elections, one proposed by the Judiciary Council, and one proposed by the government.

All five members of the commission have been confirmed by the Parliament. Its tasks are mostly preventive, but already nearly 5,000 functionaries of the legislative, executive, and judicial branches and local self-governments have reported their assets to the commission. In addition to monitoring the assets of functionaries, the commission ensures that functionaries do not abuse their public office for private business interests (some local self-government functionaries do not hold their public position as paid employees). The commission is also responsible for elaborating the new national anticorruption strategy but lacks investigative competences.

Surprisingly, a few months after the start of the Parliament's new term, the opposition Slovene National Party proposed amending the Law on the Prevention of Corruption. The party proposed closing the Commission for the Prevention of Corruption and transferring its competences to the parliamentary commission under the Law on the Prevention of Corruption. The initiative was supported by the parties of the ruling coalition. Some indications suggest that the bill was in fact prepared by government officials in order to remove the instrument of control. The initiative is still under parliamentary discussion, but it is likely that the commission will be closed down and its competences transferred to the parliamentary body. In this case, anticorruption policy would be executed by the Parliament without an assurance of independence.

According to a public opinion survey conducted by the Center for Public Opinion of the Faculty for Social Science of Ljubljana University, 65 percent of those who were informed about the potential closing of the commission are against the proposal and 27 percent are in favor.[33] The nonparliamentarian Youth Party of Slovenia began an initiative to call for a referendum on the closing of the commission; 40,000 signatures are required to hold the referendum sometime in early 2006.

The Slovene economy is not free from excessive state involvement. Some financial institutions and telecommunications, energy, and infrastructure companies are not yet privatized. On the other hand, the government-controlled Pension Management Fund and Compensation Fund own a substantial portion of shares in nearly all of Slovenia's major companies. In August 2005, the Pension Management Fund and Compensation Fund sold 29 percent of the stock in the biggest Slovene company, Mercator, without a public offer. According to some estimates, the shares sold for an unusually low price. An investigation into the matter by the Securities Market Agency has yet to be completed.

Participation of government officials in Slovenia's economic life is substantial. Deputy ministers and other government officials occupy positions on the supervisory boards of numerous significant companies, including the two largest Slovene banks, Telekom, Post of Slovenia, Pension Management Fund, Slovene Railways, Motorway Company and Port of Koper. On the one hand, very strict regulations prohibit the state from conducting business with companies owned by members of Parliament. On the other hand, senior state officials occupy positions on the boards of key Slovene companies. Furthermore, the government is obliged to publish tenders for all large jobs and contracts.

The public displays a high intolerance for official corruption. However, anticorruption activists do not play a significant role in public life. Journalists dealing with cases of corruption enjoy legal protection, but the unsuccessful investigation into the attack on Miro Petek has discouraged investigative reporting. Nonetheless, allegations of corruption in the media receive extensive media coverage. Still, there is a common expectation that a special group of prosecutors investigating more complex forms of crime will be established. Significantly, a Law on Witness Protection is currently undergoing parliamentary procedure.

Ali H. Zerdin is a sociologist, journalist, and deputy editor for the weekly newspaper Mladina. *He is the author of two books about* Slovenia: Generals Without Caps, *about the* Committee for Protection of Human Rights, *and* Punk Was Before, *discussing the political role of punk rock in Slovenia at the end of the 1970s.*

[1] State Electoral Commission, official results of referendum, www.rvk.si/RTVS/index3.html.
[2] Law on Access to Information of a Public Character, www2.gov.si/zak/zak_vel.nsf/zakposop/2003-01-0900?OpenDocument.
[3] Jure Trampus, "Who Is Next?" Mladina, June 6, 2005, www.mladina.si/tednik/200523/clanek/slo-tema-jure_trampus.
[4] Center for Public Opinion survey, Politbarometer, October 2005, ww.uvi.gov.si/slo/javno-mnenje/pdf/aktualno.pdf.
[5] Constitution of the Republic of Slovenia, www.us-rs.si/en/index.php?sv_path=6,17#s47.
[6] For example, hearings of future ambassadors are closed to the public.
[7] For example, President Drnovsek published his plan for Kosovo without consultation with the government. The president's plan for Kosovo is available at www.up-rs.si/up-rs/uprs-ang.nsf/dokumentiweb/AE6115581F3F6DBBC12570A5002C0DAA?OpenDocument.
[8] Joze Poglajen, "Inspection on General Police Directorate," Delo, September 22, 2005.
[9] Rok Praprotnik, "Revenge of Minister Erjavec," Delo, July 19, 2005.
[10] Article 43 of the Law on National Assembly Elections, zakonodaja.gov.si/rpsi/r05/predpis_ZAKO185.html.
[11] Slovene Press Agency, September 28, 2004.
[12] State Electoral Commission, www.rvk.si.
[13] Ibid.
[14] If we focus only on the 20 biggest Slovene companies, 10 directors were changed in 2005-among them, 1 was retired.
[15] Constitution of the Republic of Slovenia, Article 42.
[16] Ministry of Interior Affairs, Register of Associations, www.mnz.si/si/upl/urupnot/drustva_pregled_2004.doc
[17] Civicus Civil Society Index 2003/2005 in Slovenia, final report, www.pic.si/nvo/CIVICUS-osnutek_koncnega_porocila-za%20nacionlano_delavnico.pdf.
[18] Office for Religious Communities, www.gov.si/uvs/ang/frames2a.htm.
[19] Ksenja Hahonija, "Ravice, Ki Bolijo," Mladina, March 7, 2005, www.mladina.si/tednik/200510/clanek/slo-romi-ksenija_hahonina.
[20] See www2.gov.si/zak/zak_vel.nsf/zakposop/2005-01-2840?OpenDocument.
[21] State Electoral Commission, www.rvk.si.
[22] Jure Trampus. "They are following reporters," Mladina, July 25, 2005, www.mladina.si/tednik/200530/clanek/slo-tema--jure_trampus/
[23] Slovene Press Agency, "Perovic Will Propose Jani Virk for New Chief Editor of Delo," July 24, 2005,
[24] Statistical Yearbook 2004, Statistical Office of the Republic of Slovenia.
[25] Sandra Basic Hrvatin and Lenart Kucic, Monopoly, Social Game - Dealing With Media, (Ljubljana: Maska, 2005), page 207.
[26] See www.sds.si/datoteke/KP.pdf
[27] Statistical Office of the Republic of Slovenia.
[28] See www.uradni-list.si/1/objava.jsp?urlid=2005121&stevilka=5540.
[29] Annual Report of the Ombudsman for Human Rights, 2004, www.varuh-rs.si/index.php?id=940#1618; also see www.varuh-rs.si/fileadmin/user_upload/pdf/lp/vcp_lp_2004_eng.pdf.
[30] http://www.stat.si/letopis/index_vsebina.asp?poglavje=5&leto=2003&jezik=en
[31] http://www.stat.si/letopis/index_vsebina.asp?poglavje=5&leto=2003&jezik=en
[32] Article 129 of the Constitution of the Republic of Slovenia, www.us-rs.si/en/index.php?sv_path=6.
[33] Center for Public Opinion survey, Politbarometer, October 2005, www.uvi.gov.si/slo/javno-mnenje/pdf/oktober-2005.pdf.

Tajikistan

Capital: Dushanbe
Population: 6,800,000
GNI/capita: $210
Ethnic Groups: Tajik (79.9%), Uzbek (15.3%), Russian
(1.1%), Kyrgyz (1.1%), other (2.6%)

Nations in Transit Ratings and Averaged Scores

	1997	1998	1999	2001	2002	2003	2004	2005	2006
Electoral Process	6.00	5.75	5.50	5.25	5.25	5.25	5.75	6.00	6.25
Civil Society	5.50	5.25	5.25	5.00	5.00	5.00	5.00	4.75	5.00
Independent Media	6.25	6.00	5.75	5.50	5.75	5.75	5.75	6.00	6.25
Governance *	7.00	6.75	6.25	6.00	6.00	6.00	5.75	n/a	n/a
National Democratic Governance	n/a	n/a	n/a	n/a	n/a	n/a	n/a	6.00	6.25
Local Democratic Governance	n/a	n/a	n/a	n/a	n/a	n/a	n/a	5.75	5.75
Judicial Framework and Independence	6.25	6.00	5.75	5.75	5.75	5.75	5.75	5.75	5.75
Corruption	n/a	n/a	6.00	6.00	6.00	6.00	6.25	6.25	6.25
Democracy Score	6.20	5.95	5.75	5.58	5.63	5.63	5.71	5.79	5.93

With the 2005 edition, Freedom House introduced seperate analysis and ratings for national democratic governance and local democratic governance to provide readers with more detailed and nuanced analysis of these two important subjects.

NOTE: The ratings reflect the consensus of Freedom House, its academic advisers, and the author of this report. The opinions expressed in this report are those of the author. The ratings are based on a scale of 1 to 7, with 1 representing the highest level of democratic progress and 7 the lowest. The Democracy Score is an average of ratings for the categories tracked in a given year.

The economic and social data on this page were taken from the following sources:
GNI/capita, Population: *World Development Indicators 2006* (Washington, D.C.: World Bank, 2006).
Ethnic Groups: *CIA World Factbook 2006* (Washington, D.C.: Central Intelligence Agency, 2006).

EXECUTIVE SUMMARY

Ajolt was sent through Tajikistan's ruling elite in March 2005 when the once moderate and later autocratic leader of Tajikistan's northern neighbor, President Askar Akayev of Kyrgyzstan, was forced out of power shortly after the February 27, 2005, parliamentary elections, which were held concurrently with Tajikistan's parliamentary elections. This fear came despite the fact that the Tajik public appeared rather satisfied with its own political leadership, crediting President Imamali Rahmonov with having ended the civil war and instability (responsible for more than 50,000 deaths) via the 1997 peace accord with the armed Islamist-led United Tajik Opposition. Tajikistan's population loathes (if anything) political actions, such as the demonstrations that brought down Akayev's rule. Indeed, the events in Kyrgyzstan reminded many in Tajikistan of their own past, particularly the large-scale mobilizations following the country's declaration of independence in 1991 and the ensuing civil war and bloodshed. Yet despite any shortcomings of Tajikistan's present leadership and the pro-government People's Democratic Party (PDP), the public does not sufficiently trust the opposition, a series of parties with somewhat incoherent agendas and infighting. Nevertheless, in 2005 the government of President Rahmonov redoubled its efforts to suppress dissent by harassing opposition parties, closing major opposition papers, and arresting several key opposition figures (most notably the leader of the Democratic Party, Mahmadruzi Iskandarov). Not surprisingly, the Organization for Security and Cooperation in Europe (OSCE) declared that Tajikistan's February 2005 elections did not meet "international standards for democratic elections." Owing to various obstacles imposed by the government on opposition activities during the campaign, the ruling PDP gained nearly all open seats of the lower house of Parliament, with the opposition Communist Party taking 4 seats and the Islamic Renaissance Party taking 2 out of a total of 63.

Tajikistan's political woes are due partially to the ruling elite's use of "patronage and consanguineal networks" like the Kulob ethnoregional clan, which constitutes a large segment of the current regime. As such, *mahallagaroie*, or subnational regionalism, continues to pose a danger to stability in Tajikistan. Furthermore, despite impressive rates of macroeconomic growth in recent years (average 9.6 percent per year during 2001–2005), poverty and increasing income inequality threaten human and national security. The National Bank of Tajikistan (central bank) reported that the average monthly wage for the first half of 2005 was 84 somonis (US$27). Additionally, the process of privatization and moving toward a market economy has not been smooth, with privatization of agricultural lands and former Socialist collective farms, for example, being neither equitable nor transparent. The cotton sector alone faces a critical crisis of accumulated debt approaching US$300 million. Still, though the country ranks at the bottom among post-Communist states in various indicators, including per capita income (estimated at US$325 per year),[1] evidence suggests the overall rate of poverty is declining. Furthermore, two Russian conglomerates have announced their intention to invest as much as US$2 billion in the Tajik economy, mainly to build two large hydroelectricity plants and increase the capacity of aluminum production during the next six years. This will likely generate jobs and – some years hence when energy and aluminum production begins – economic benefits from the use and export of new sources of electricity.

Although in 2005 the international community contributed an estimated US$100 million to a variety of mostly socioeconomic assistance projects in Tajikistan, much of it channeled via local non-governmental organizations (NGOs), the government's new restrictions include a policy requiring international donors and organizations to report their connections and meeting agendas with Tajikistan's civil society entities. By the end of 2005, 2,500 NGOs were registered in Tajikistan, though a large majority existed only on paper and some others functioned mainly to obtain funds from Western donors. Yet in Tajikistan, as in many other Central Asian countries, societies pre-dated NGOs with the concept of the *mahalla* (neighborhood), an informal social organization active, among other places, in local teahouses, bazaars, and mosques. Some successful international NGOs, such as Oxfam-Great Britain and the Mountain Societies Development Support Program (an Aga Khan Foundation-funded agency) have successfully used the *mahalla* in their rural socioeconomic development projects in Tajikistan.

The judicial system remains highly problematic in that judges, prosecutors, and defense lawyers receive insufficient pay and are easily enticed by bribes and corruption. And despite a new law banning the death penalty, Tajikistan has not shown much progress in the area of human rights. Its treatment of prisoners does not satisfy international standards, and a 2005 UN report expresses concerns over "widespread use of ill-treatment and torture" to extract information from detained suspects.[2] Concerns include the treatment of alleged members of the Hizb ut-Tahrir (Liberation Party) arrested in the past couple of years and accused by the government of intending to topple the regime. Furthermore, child labor in various sectors of the economy, especially agriculture, violates internationally ratified laws to protect children from unfair labor practices. On the issue of corruption, an opinion poll released in 2005 indicated that 56 percent of the urban public in Tajikistan perceived the government's efforts in fighting corruption as inadequate, while Transparency International ranked Tajikistan 144 among 158 countries, a slightly worse rating compared with that of the previous year. The export commodities of cotton and aluminum have been especially susceptible to corruption by various interest groups and rent-seeking entities. In addition, drug traffic from Afghanistan continues to also serve as a source of corruption and a threat to social and political development.

National Democratic Governance. Regional affiliations, patronage, and clan networks developed during the country's brutal civil war continue to play critical and negative roles in Tajikistan, hindering steps toward genuine pluralism and democratic governance. Furthermore, events that brought down the regime in Kyrgyzstan play on the minds of Tajikistan's leadership, prompting a somewhat heavy-handed approach toward opposition parties and the media. Given such recent measures, Tajikistan increasingly resembles a form of dictatorship. Yet the public appears genuinely supportive of President Rahmonov's government, mostly because of the relative peace and stability since the signing of the 1997 Moscow peace accord. Furthermore, despite impressive macroeconomic growth, income disparity continues to worsen and the country remains the poorest among the post-Communist states. *Owing to lack of progress in bringing about genuine pluralism and distribution of power, the ongoing use of and heavy reliance on patronage networks by the ruling elite, and a heightened degree of heavy-handedness practiced against opposition groups and dissidents before and after the February 2005 parliamentary elections, Tajikistan's national democratic governance rating worsens from 6.00 to 6.25.*

Electoral Process. Despite new laws and regulations meant to significantly improve fairness and transparency in the election process, in 2005 the government continued to erect obstacles for opposition political parties and candidates. And though the OSCE described the 2005 elections as an improvement over previous years, they still failed to meet "international standards for democratic elections." Not surprisingly, the pro-government PDP won a sweeping victory of parliamentary seats. *Owing to the government's restriction on the activities of legal parties, preventing the free activity of opposition media and controlling the main media outlets in favor of its own candidates; its failure to register new political parties; harassing and detaining middle- and high-level opposition figures on likely trumped-up, exaggerated, or politically motivated charges and selective application of the law – all of which contributed to an unfair and intimidating election atmosphere – Tajikistan's rating for electoral process worsens from 6.00 to 6.25.*

Civil Society. In 2005, the authorities increased efforts to monitor and at times restrict the activities of international organizations, especially domestic civil society entities or NGOs. The government became increasingly suspicious of Western-funded NGOs' involvement in the so-called "colored revolutions", the latest series of which led to regime change in Kyrgyzstan in March 2005. Weeks later, Tajikistan's Ministry of the Interior, which is in charge of registering civil society and monitoring their activities, ordered financial audits of various domestic groups and called for all international organizations and foreign embassies to inform the ministry in advance of meetings and topics of discussion with domestic NGOs, political parties, and local journalists. Yet civil society groups continue to be productive and critical for the well-being of the country's population. *Given the new restrictions imposed by the Tajik Ministry of the Interior, especially regarding contact of international organizations with local NGOs, Tajikistan's rating for civil society deteriorates from 4.75 to 5.00.*

Independent Media. The government has been exerting increasing pressure on the media and journalists it deems critical of the state's activities. In 2005, at least four opposition papers were forced to shut down, two television stations closed temporarily, and few new licenses, if any, were issued. Furthermore, for disseminating information and stories critical of the government, two journalists were given multiyear prison sentences under the guise of theft and disorderly conduct. *Owing to an increase in government tactics of suppressing information and activities of journalists and media deemed critical of government policies and organs, Tajikistan's rating for independent media worsens from 6.00 to 6.25.*

Local Democratic Governance. Despite the fact that the *mahalla*, or neighborhood, has for centuries acted as a de facto community council and the smallest body of governance (aside from the nuclear family) in Central Asian societies, the Tajik Constitution has failed to recognize this traditional social institution. The smallest local entities of governance are the *jamoats*, or local councils, which themselves are not structured democratically and lack sufficient revenue. Qualitative and anecdotal evidence suggests that the largest segment of Tajikistan's workforce, the agricultural sector and especially those (mostly women) working on cotton farms, does not make a living wage, that the cumulated farm debt neared US$300 million by the end of 2005, and that the sector lacks any significant level of local democratic governance. *Local communities in Tajikistan are usually unable to choose their own leaders, and participation and decision making continue to be largely contingent on business and political connections, with most decisions made in a nontransparent manner. As such, Tajikistan's rating for local democratic governance remains at 5.75.*

Judicial Framework and Independence. The executive branch of the government has excessive control and influence over the legislature and judiciary. Many of the 56 constitutional amendments passed in the June 2003 plebiscite exacerbated this problem by weakening the checks and balances necessary for a democratic society. That said, the government has made some progress in the judicial system in the past few years. To placate international criticism and mimic reforms made in Russia and other member countries of the Commonwealth of Independent States (CIS), in May 2004 the Parliament passed a moratorium on the death penalty, which became law in February 2005. The government also passed a new anti-child labor law – though in practice child labor (especially in the cotton industry) continues – and an anti-human trafficking law, which allowed for the prosecution of some involved in luring women and girls into prostitution in foreign countries. Still, the judicial system remains largely unjust, corrupt, and reliant on assumption of guilt, with the state prosecutor having disproportionate power over the fate of the accused. Furthermore, torture and ill-treatment of detainees continue to be concerns, and despite some progress, the prison system remains generally decrepit, with (among other things) an estimated 16 percent of the prison population suffering from tuberculosis. There remain major shortcomings in the judicial system owing to lack of fairness of trials, disproportionate power of the prosecution, and the continuing ill-treatment of the detained. *Given only minor improvements in the law and prison conditions, Tajikistan's rating for judicial framework and independence remains unchanged at 5.75.*

Corruption. Tajikistan remains the poorest of the post-Communist states of the former Soviet Union and Eastern Europe. Despite impressive rates of macroeconomic growth, the majority of the population still lives below the poverty threshold. Furthermore, privatization, heavily encouraged by the World Bank and the International Monetary Fund, has been conducted in a mostly nontransparent fashion and primarily to the benefit of the elite. Corruption has thus been a function of both poverty and a lack of proper governance, including the government's inability to prevent financial malfeasance involving the country's major export commodities of cotton fiber and aluminum. Drug trade emanating from Afghanistan, though contributing indirectly to economic growth, has been a source of corruption and crime as well. Furthermore, the recent transfer of border guarding responsibilities from Russian-led troops to Tajik forces has proven problematic because of severe budgetary and technical shortages. *Owing to the insufficient steps taken by the government to curb corruption, a problematic privatization process, and the ongoing drug trade, Tajikistan's rating for corruption remains at 6.25.*

Outlook for 2006. The government will make a concerted effort to secure victory for President Rahmonov in the November 2006 presidential election. Given the harsh measures taken by authorities in 2005 against opposition parties and the media, and yet the public's overall approval of the president, Rahmonov's reelection (until 2013) is all but assured. That said, external factors, such as further political turmoil and instability in Uzbekistan, could lead to spillover effects in Tajikistan, thus negatively affecting Tajikistan's still fragile stability. Furthermore, the government will give in to international pressure in extending (though only partially) freedom of the press and the registration of at least one new moderate opposition party. And despite the expected and robust growth in the macroeconomy and a small but noticeable drop in the level of poverty, the gap between rich and poor will increase, a phenomenon that if not dealt with will prove destabilizing for Tajikistan in the long run. Among other things, the rural-urban divide will also widen, with cotton-growing regions enduring poverty, continued gender bias, labor exploitation, and nontransparent and corrupt land reform. Economic and political development in 2006 will depend on the government's ability to implement genuine reforms and to continue the peace-building and democratization efforts largely abandoned in the past few years.

MAIN REPORT

National Democratic Governance

1997	1998	1999	2001	2002	2003	2004	2005	2006
n/a	n/a	n/a	n/a	n/a	n/a	n/a	6.00	6.25

The 1994 Constitution provides for a directly elected executive with broad authority to appoint and dismiss officials. Amendments to the Constitution adopted in 1999 further increased the powers of the president by extending his term in office from five to seven years and creating a bicameral Parliament. In 2003, a public plebiscite overwhelmingly approved 56 additional constitutional amendments, including a formal end to state guarantees for free education and health care and a controversial amendment allowing the president to stand for election in two seven-year terms. The government interpreted the latter to mean that the standing President Imamali Rahmonov can run for reelection twice, beginning in November 2006, thus potentially remaining in power until 2020.

In March 2005, Tajikistan's leadership was shaken by the ouster of Kyrgyzstan's president, Askar Akayev, through civil demonstrations resembling the post-Communist "colored revolutions" of Georgia (2003) and Ukraine (2004). The government's recent heavy-handed treatment of the political opposition can be viewed as a measure to discourage similar activities in Tajikistan, although the regime appears to have genuine support among the public. According to a 2004 survey by the U.S.-funded International Federation of Election Systems (IFES), the majority of the population credits President Rahmonov for the country's stability and economic growth following the brutal civil war of 1992–1997. The poll showed, among other things, relatively strong support for the president, with 58 percent of those surveyed choosing Rahmonov as the most trusted figure in the country.[3] Indeed, the painful memories of the civil war, still fresh for many people, seem to have led to an antipathy toward chaos and violence and possibly an affinity toward what many would see as a benign dictatorship able to enforce law and order. Furthermore, despite widespread corruption of local officials and police and growing economic inequality, people see no alternative to Rahmonov; opposition parties lack solid platforms and agendas, are known for bickering, and appear unable to unite effectively against the rule of Rahmonov and the pro-government People's Democratic Party (PDP).

Tajikistan's major challenges stem largely from the sociocultural factors of traditional, clan-based societies, which came to the fore immediately after the country gained independence from the Soviet Union. President Rahmonov has used an informal policy of assigning important government posts to individuals from the southern Kulob region of the country, where he is from. Professor Kirill Nourzhanov of the Australian National University refers to this phenomenon as "patriarchal clan-based militias" based on "patronage and consanguineal networks." Indeed, the current government has its roots in the civil war that ensued when a coalition of warlords consolidated power shortly after Tajikistan's independence in 1992.

In addition, the 1997 Moscow peace accord introduced a new entity (with its own regional constituency from the Gharm and Pamir parts of Tajikistan): the political groups making up the United Tajik Opposition (UTO), dominated by the Islamic Renaissance Party (IRP), now the only legal Islamist political party in the Commonwealth of Independent States (CIS). The legalized opposition, along with existing government elite, have benefited from the land redistribution and privatization process, which accelerated after the peace accord. There are also allegations that the political elite has secured dominant rent-seeking positions, including involvement in drug trafficking and, to a lesser extent, benefited from international aid.[4] Despite the fact that the 1997 peace accord required the government to assign 30 percent of top government posts to opposition figures, the government has recently undone many of these appointments, reducing former opposition figures to an estimated 5 percent of posts.[5] Several regional and ethnic groups (such as the country's large Uzbek population) have been largely left out of the central government. Consequently, patronage networks,[6] ethnoregionalism, or "subnational regionalism" will continue to threaten the thin veneer of stability in Tajikistan.[7]

Poverty is a destabilizing factor as well. Given the impressive macroeconomic growth of the past dozen years, however, conditions seem to be improving. While a 1999 World Bank household survey found that 83 percent of Tajik households live below the acceptable poverty threshold, the same indicator dropped to 68 percent in 2003. Though there are no reliable figures on inequality, anecdotal evidence points to varying rates of poverty and socioeconomic development among regions and social strata in Tajikistan. Inequality has been on the rise, and prospects are precarious for hundreds of thousands of households that rely on agriculture and animal husbandry in a country where less than 7 percent of the land is arable. Nearly all state sector employees receive below subsistence wages. According to the Ministry of Economy, though the minimum monthly wage supposedly increased by 80 percent in January 2005, it still remained at only about 12 somonis (US$4) per month in early 2005. At the same time, the average monthly wage during the first half of 2005 as reported by the central bank was 84 somonis (US$27). Not surprisingly, close to 15 years after the demise of Communism, the IFES survey finds that only 36 percent of the public prefers a market-based economic system with limited state control, while 50 percent prefers an economic system where the state has full control.

Another pressing issue is the population's poor health and access to sanitary living. Conditions are worst in rural areas, where roughly only 15 percent of Tajikistan's 5.2 million rural population (out of 7 million for the country as a whole) has access to safe drinking water. The capital city, Dushanbe, also faces periodic health crises, especially during rainy seasons, when floods and landslides in the nearby Varzob valley can leave as much as half of the city's estimated 600,000 people without potable water for days. Not surprisingly, the decrepit state of the water delivery system has in the past caused epidemics of waterborne diseases such as typhoid.

Electoral Process

1997	1998	1999	2001	2002	2003	2004	2005	2006
6.00	5.75	5.50	5.25	5.25	5.25	5.75	6.00	6.25

Following independence in 1991, Imamali Rahmonov was appointed chairman by the Supreme Soviet (Parliament) of Tajikistan in November 1992. Prior to his appointment, Rahmonov was a *kolkhoz* (Soviet agricultural cooperative) leader and later chair of the executive committee of the Communist Party (CP) in the southern Kulob province. Most important, Rahmonov had been one of the organizers of the Kulobi-dominated Popular Front, a pro-regime and pro-Communist militia with a reputation for brutality and responsible for a large number of deaths mostly in the first year of the civil war in 1992. By March 1993, all opposition parties had been banned – many of their leaders and followers fleeing to Afghanistan and Iran – leaving the CP the sole legally functioning political entity. Rahmonov later managed to run for president, with two controversial victories in 1994 and 1999. In 1994, he ran against onetime prime minister (1992-1993) Abdumalik Abdullojonov (a northerner who later went into self-exile in Russia and the West) in a one-sided race that barred UTO opposition parties and was marred by irregularities.

Rahmonov strengthened his position in a September 1999 plebiscite that approved constitutional amendments extending the presidential term from five to seven years, introducing a bicameral parliamentary system (a 63-member Council of Representatives and a 33-member National Council – lower and upper houses of Parliament, respectively), and allowing the formation of political parties based on religion – this last amendment was a requirement to satisfy the terms of the 1997 peace accord. Though this plebiscite – approved by 70 percent of voters – was thought to have been generally free and somewhat fair, the ensuing November 1999 presidential election and the March 2000 and February 2005 parliamentary elections were marred by irregularities and heavily criticized by opposition parties and international observers. In the 1999 presidential election, the government made a concerted effort to exclude opposition candidates for trumped-up technical reasons, restricted political party activities, imposed curbs on the media, and essentially limited the race to the incumbent president,[8] with Rahmonov reportedly winning 96 percent of the vote. The OSCE criticized the 1999 presidential election as having had insufficient "transparency, accountability, [and] fairness," and Human Rights Watch accused the government of "extensive and egregious violations" during the campaign, referring to specific cases of fraud committed by election officials. Likewise, the 2000 parliamentary (lower house of Parliament) elections were described by the OSCE as not having met "minimum international standards." Though noting improvements in 2005, the OSCE still accused the Tajik government of failing to meet standards expected from an OSCE member state.

Based on these criticisms, the government appeared to take measures to build confidence in the February 2005 elections for the lower house of Parliament, including appointing members of opposition political parties to midlevel election commissions and amending the country's election laws in favor of a more fair and transparent election process. The OSCE described the implementation of these measures as "inadequate and arbitrary." A total of 226 candidates from the pro-government PDP, CP, IRP, Social Democratic Party (SDP), Socialist Party, and Democratic Party (DP) competed for 22 open seats – with a required election threshold for parties of 5 percent – in addition to 84 independent and nonparty candidates running for the remaining 41 seats in the February 2005 elections.

Voting took place in over 3,000 polling stations, with many providing three language options: Tajik, Uzbek, and Russian. Voters also elected representatives to local councils for provinces, districts, and towns. Constitutional amendments allowed local councils to nominate candidates to the upper house of Parliament (National Council), with each of the five regions ultimately electing five members to the national body. As predicted, the ruling PDP gained a near sweeping victory in the February 2005 elections for the lower house, taking 38 out of 41 seats. The remaining 22 seats were appointed on the basis of party slates, with the PDP, the CP, and the IRP clearing the 5 percent threshold. Based on this, the PDP took an additional 17 seats, and the CP and IRP wound up with only 4 and 2 seats, respectively. According to the country's election commission, the PDP received 74 percent of all votes, the CP 13 percent, and the IRP 8 percent. The commission also indicated that 2.9 million of the 3.1 million registered voters cast their ballots, a nearly 93 percent turnout that many have called an exaggeration.

Despite an array of six parties and self-nominated candidates, various legal actions against opposition figures in the months prior to the elections prevented some well-known politicians from running for office. Most notably, in December 2004, Russian authorities heeded a demand by the Tajik government to detain Mahmadruzi Iskandarov, leader of the Tajik opposition DP. The government claims Iskandarov's arrest was related to the alleged embezzlement of millions of dollars while he served as head of the national gas company (Tojikgaz), as well as his supposed links to organized terror groups. DP officials and Iskandarov's lawyer argue that his arrest and eventual trial allowed the government to eliminate a potential rival ahead of the February 2005 parliamentary and upcoming November 2006 presidential elections. The government also arrested a number of SDP party activists and a government newspaper, *Jumhuriyyat*, accused the SDP chair, Rahmatollo Zoirov, a onetime special adviser to President Rahmonov, of being pro-West, an agent of Uzbekistan, and a supporter of the banned Islamic Hizb ut-Tahrir (Liberation Party).

No genuine debates took place prior to the elections, and government authorities controlled political campaigning. The government closed four independent newspapers, and new papers and media outlets were prevented from registering. The state media did, however, make public service announcements about election procedures. However, the scarcity of media campaign coverage called into question voters' ability to make an informed choice. Election observers also cited widespread cases of multiple voting and noted problems at the district election commissions where protocols were filled in or illegally altered.[9] Given such measures, and given the still genuine popularity of the government, the overwhelming victory of the PDP and other pro-government candidates was not surprising.

Civil Society

1997	1998	1999	2001	2002	2003	2004	2005	2006
5.50	5.25	5.25	5.00	5.00	5.00	5.00	4.75	5.00

Prior to Tajikistan's independence, several informal "discussion groups" had already formed, such as Ru ba Ru (Face to Face) and Ehyo (Renewal), with fewer than 100 members, mostly from among the country's intelligentsia. Soon after independence, Western-style NGOs developed under the auspices of foreign donors and various socioeconomic development programs. Since then, the country has seen the creation of a variety of civil society entities in the form of registered NGOs. Though still a bureaucratic, expensive, and time-consuming process, the act of forming an NGO in Tajikistan has been simplified in the past few years. Close to 2,500 NGOs registered with Tajikistan's Ministry of Justice from 1991 to the end of 2005, though only a fraction actually function. Some of the most successful NGOs are associated with the Geneva-based Aga Khan Foundation – a modern Islamic faith-based umbrella organization that supports various socioeconomic and educational projects worldwide – and its encouragement of democratic self-rule and reliance on preexisting *mahalla* networks of governance.

The Tajik civil war created as many as 25,000 widows. According to a UN report, women continue to be victims of the economic and social woes of Tajikistan. For example, up to two-thirds of Tajik women (over 1 million) are estimated to have been victims of domestic violence and sexual abuse. There have also been reports of human trafficking for the purpose of prostitution mostly to Persian Gulf states, with anecdotal reports of trafficking to China as well. In 2003, the Parliament adopted a bill criminalizing human trafficking, with sentences of five to fifteen years' imprisonment. Still, gender disparity is especially critical in rural areas, where a patriarchal culture has been in existence for centuries and where Communism penetrated the least during the Soviet era.

An important outcome of the growing civil society in Tajikistan is the increased opportunity for women's engagement in societal change. Although women are not widely represented in the Tajik government, they have played increasingly important roles as members and leaders in civil society groups; an estimated one-third of all domestic NGOs are headed by women. During 2005, the NGO Modar (Mother) reportedly conducted workshops on how to fight human trafficking for a spectrum of government and public agencies, including law enforcement, courts, prosecutors' offices, the border guard, and tourist agencies. Other female-headed NGOs, such as Oshtii Melli (National Reconciliation), trained and provided independent election observers during the 2005 parliamentary elections and plan on a similar endeavor for the 2006 presidential election.

One criticism of Western-funded NGOs and international organizations is their impact on the domestic job market. The gap in salaries between private enterprise, the public sector, and the world of international NGOs and international organizations is so huge that, as Central Asian scholar Oliver Roy notes, a clear "internal brain drain effect" exists in Tajikistan, as in other transitional states. Consequently, many competent professionals are willing to work only for civil society entities just to maintain a decent standard of living. Western funding for civil society groups has also formed a flourishing business, where highly capable local and English-speaking technocrats have learned how to write proposals and project reports satisfying Western requirements, with local communities at times not reaping much benefit from actual projects.

Despite the success of some regional civil society groups, in recent years Central Asian governments have become increasingly suspicious of Western-funded NGO activities. Unlike NGOs in neighboring Afghanistan, which primarily promote reconstruction and economic activities, a disproportionate number of Western-funded NGO projects in Tajikistan are geared toward promoting nonmaterial concepts such as openness, pluralism, and free media, which government authorities feel threaten their authority, appear conspiratorial in nature, or open them to public criticism. Some Tajik officials believe that Western funding for civil society groups aims to form political opposition among populations of post-Communist states as the "colored revolution" phenomenon.

It is apparent that after the regime change in neighboring Kyrgyzstan and unrest and turmoil in northern Uzbekistan in 2005, the Tajik government is on guard, despite the relatively low possibility of similar events taking place in Tajikistan. As early as December 2004, when addressing a PDP congress, President Rahmonov had criticized foreign organizations, namely the Soros Foundation's Open Society Institute (OSI), which has had an office in Dushanbe for the past decade. Rahmonov accused the OSI of attempting to undermine the integrity of Tajikistan by supporting what he described as subversive media, such as the radio station Varorud and the newspapers *Odamu Olam* and *Ruzi Nav*, with the goal to "destroy" his administration. And in spring 2005, Tajik authorities ordered financial audits of many international NGOs active in Tajikistan. Furthermore, fearing political activities by local NGOs and media outlets, the Ministry of the Interior as of April 2005 required foreign embassies and international organizations to inform it of dates and topics of meetings with local NGOs, political parties, and journalists.[10] In 2005, the Tajik authorities also refused to register branch offices of two U.S.-based NGOs: Freedom House and the National Democratic Institute for International Affairs.

Independent Media

1997	1998	1999	2001	2002	2003	2004	2005	2006
6.25	6.00	5.75	5.50	5.75	5.75	5.75	6.00	6.25

The Tajik media have diminished in recent years under the pressures of poverty, relatively high taxes, emigration of cosmopolitan citizenry, and serious deterioration in the education system, producing a post-independence generation significantly less educated than those of the Soviet era. Government restrictions have thus led to a limited and often biased array of media outlets. The 1997 peace accord called for legalizing previously banned opposition party outlets (primarily newspapers), and progress was made in allowing these to function relatively freely – at least in comparison with media in surrounding states. However, the past few years have seen renewed government pressure through selective use of tax laws; arduous and costly procedures for registering new media; the occasional revocation of access to government-owned and private printing houses; and intimidation, beatings, arrests, and imprisonment of selected journalists for politically motivated reasons. In addition, Article 137 of Tajikistan's penal code stipulates a maximum five years' imprisonment for insulting or defaming the president. As such, investigative reporting on corruption and organized crime is especially risky, and harsh libel laws sustain a culture of self-censorship.[11]

Prior to the 2005 parliamentary elections, the government redoubled its suppression of independent and opposition media, using tax police and arbitrary enforcement of tax laws to shut down several newspapers. In January, the tax police accused newspapers *Nerui Sukhan* and *Ruzi Nav* and their publishing house, Kayhon, of violating the tax code and shut down their operations. *Nerui Sukhan* was allowed to publish in July but was shut down again shortly thereafter. Authorities later arrested and subsequently sentenced the paper's editor, Mukhtar Boqizoda, to two years' imprisonment and ordered 20 percent of his earnings to be paid back to the state. Boqizoda was convicted under Article 244, part 1, of theft of state property, after being found guilty of stealing roughly US$500 of electricity by connecting wires in his office to streetlights. Critics have accused the government of playing politics in this and other cases and have compared these tactics with Russia's destruction of two of its own most popular independent media outlets (NTV and TVN) a few years ago on the basis of alleged financial impropriety.[12]

In April, two television stations, Guli Bodom and Somonian (the only private TV stations in Konibodom and Dushanbe, respectively), were shut down temporarily owing to alleged noncompliance with licensing and broadcasting laws, although the airtime allocated to opposition candidates prior to the parliamentary elections is a more likely cause.[13] In mid-2005, the government allegedly ordered the Ministry of Justice to adhere to a secret ban on registering new independent media (TV, radio, newspaper, and Internet). As many as 30 applications for media registration were reportedly ignored, including that of the newspaper *Imruz*, which is affiliated with the opposition SDP. The government also arrested Jumaboi Tolibov, a well-known journalist based in the northern Soghd province. A court accused Tolibov of several violations, including "incivility," for his brazen investigation and reporting on government corruption and criticism of the regional prosecutor of the Soghd province in the newspaper *Minbari Khalq* – ironically owned by the pro-government PDP. Tolibov was later sentenced to one year of community work.[14]

Tajikistan became connected to the Internet in 1991 and by all accounts was the last country among the post-Communist states to do so. By the end of 2005, five private Internet providers existed in the country and use was slowly spreading, especially among the youth. Yet the vast majority of the population does not have the financial resources for Internet access, which for the time being is restricted to urban areas and Internet cafes at a relatively high cost by local standards of about US$1-2 per hour. The government has generally been hands-off regarding material accessed on the Internet. One of the few cases of government action with respect to the Internet happened prior to the 2003 referendum on changes to the Constitution, when authorities temporarily blocked access to a Web site run by self-exiled journalist Dodojon Atovulloev due to his critical coverage and commentaries on Tajikistan and the ruling elite.

Facing criticisms from international organizations and Western donors, the government loosened its temporary ban on some independent and opposition papers in latter part of 2005. *Ruzi Nav* was allowed to print a special edition, with a print run of 99 copies. Another paper, *Odamu Olam*, was expected to resume publication after nearly a year, and *Adolat*, an official publication of the DP, was also allowed to put out a special edition in August to honor the party's 15th anniversary.[15] Still, despite various irregularities imposed by the government, the majority of the public appears to have confidence in the country's media, with about 65 percent of those polled in an IFES survey agreeing that Tajikistan's state-run and private media provide objective coverage of social and political developments in the country.[16]

Local Democratic Governance

1997	1998	1999	2001	2002	2003	2004	2005	2006
n/a	n/a	n/a	n/a	n/a	n/a	n/a	5.75	5.75

For centuries, the *chaikhona* (teahouse), the *masjid* (mosque), and the *souk* or *bazaar* (market) have served as focal points of local dialogue on self-governance in Muslim majority societies of Central Asia. The social organization behind such dialogues has traditionally been referred to as the *mahalla* (neighborhood). In 1924, the population of Tajikistan was almost totally illiterate, leading Soviet planners and policy makers to form *likpunkty*, or centers for combating illiteracy. They also occasionally banned public expressions of religious worship and even introduced "Militant Godless Leagues." According to Shirin Akiner of the University of London, these leagues resulted in the near disappearance of Islam, save for occasional semi-Islamic practices and rituals.[17] The *mahalla*, however, never vanished, and it continues today to engage in organized activities such as *hashar* (community mobilization efforts such as repairing homes and building local facilities), *touy* (wedding assistance), and *khodaie* (remembrance of the dead). Thus, the informal social institution of *mahalla*, which during the Soviet era helped preserve a private space outside official control, continues to foster communal identity and solidarity in the post-Communist era.

The Tajik Constitution, formulated in 1994 and approved by a nationwide referendum, confirmed the existing Soviet territorial and administrative division of the country into a series of *viloyats* (provinces), *nohiyas* or *rayons* (districts), towns, settlements, and *qishloqs* (villages).[18] Today, three provinces (Khatlon, Soghd, and Badakhshan) technically uphold their own regional governments. The capital city and a series of surrounding districts are equivalent to two additional provinces or major regions. Overall, there are 62 districts and 356 *jamoats*, or local councils (similar to municipalities in Europe and North America). The Tajik Constitution defines the *jamoat* as a "system of organizing public activities...to address issues of local importance autonomously" and at the discretion of its members.[19] Ironically, the Constitution does not recognize the smallest self-organizing body, the *mahalla* – corresponding to the 3,500 villages in the country and various urban neighborhoods.

The president appoints provincial and district heads in consultation with governors and *jamoat* leaders, through the head of their respective district *hukumat* (government). Though council members can veto appointments, they seldom do. Not surprisingly, central government political organizations, such as the ruling PDP apparatus, almost always dominate province, district, and *jamoat* bodies. Local election commissions of the 2005 parliamentary elections, for example, were composed mainly of pro-government PDP members. Patronage exercised by the national government in appointing province and district administrators discourages independent decisions and policy making outside of the capital. Furthermore, owing to the central government's dominance and alleged corruption and the stagnant economy of outlying regions, most local administrative bodies in the provinces, districts, and especially *jamoats* face serious budgetary constraints.[20] Opposition parties suggest real change in Tajikistan for the better will take place only when free and fair elections occur, including at the *jamoat* level.

It is estimated that as much as 85 percent of the taxes generated at the regional level goes to the state, with a mere 15 percent remaining at the district level. To generate funds for its staff and community projects, *jamoats* spend an estimated two-thirds of their time collecting arbitrary property taxes, transportation duties, and fees from the local population. *Mahallas* and even *jamoats* continue to be devoid of any real power at the national level and remain largely outside the nation's economic and political decision-making process. Some NGOs, however, have successfully used the notion of the *mahalla* in their socioeconomic development programs via the formation of democratically elected village organizations or community-based organizations.

Close to three-quarters of the population of Tajikistan lives in rural areas, with agriculture constituting over one-quarter of the country's income and encompassing a little less than two-thirds of the national workforce. Of these, an estimated 400,000 are employed in the cotton sector, one of Tajikistan's main export commodities. Yet, despite the government's repeated declaration that cotton is a "strategic" commodity, the vast majority of cotton workers live far below the poverty threshold, while cotton farms have accumulated a debt close to US$300 million. Furthermore, many agricultural workers live under conditions described as "bonded labor" and "financial servitude." As such, local democratic governance for rural folk, who form the majority of Tajikistan's population, is in an extremely poor state.[21]

Judicial Framework and Independence

1997	1998	1999	2001	2002	2003	2004	2005	2006
6.25	6.00	5.75	5.75	5.75	5.75	5.75	5.75	5.75

The judiciary in Tajikistan – frequently co-opted as a tool to silence opposition figures – is constrained to the executive and unable to enforce the equal rights of citizens before the law. Considering Tajikistan's violent past and current brazen treatment of the opposition and ordinary citizens by ministry officials and law enforcement, the country's record on progressive governance, respect for the law, judicial independence, and human rights in the post-Soviet era has been far from exemplary. Nevertheless, there is greater freedom of expression and association compared with what exists in Tajikistan's neighboring states – notably authoritarian Uzbekistan and near totalitarian Turkmenistan. Evidence also suggests that Tajik authorities are highly sensitive about their global image and do respond to international criticism.

The right of the accused is among a list of concerns, as Tajik courts have tended to presume guilt rather than innocence when trying individuals. A 2005 UN report criticized the fact that in Tajikistan the prosecutor has a position superior to that of defense lawyers and undermines the role of the judge, thus contradicting international standards in court proceedings. Often judgments are not issued independently for fear of possible repercussions. The low pay of officials, including judges, makes the judicial system vulnerable to corruption. The UN has recommended that authorities follow through with a series of judicial reforms, including the adoption of civil and criminal procedural codes in compliance with international standards.[22]

Based on human rights reports covering conditions in 2004, allegations of torture and ill-treatment, including cases of arrest and abuse of alleged Islamists, such as supposed members of Hizb ut-Tahrir, have been made without resulting in thorough and impartial investigations in the majority of cases. The government has accused alleged followers of Hizb ut-Tahrir of planning the violent overthrow of the state and having ties to al-Qaeda. Cases of abuse by authorities are not limited to alleged Islamists, however. In June 2004, three ethnic Russian citizens suspected of murder, all members of the Awakening Baptist Church in the town of Nurek, were believed to have been ill-treated while detained by police of the local branch of the

Ministry of the Interior. Two of the suspects signed "confessions" while seemingly subjected to duress, ill-treatment, and likely torture. Both suffered concussions and were later hospitalized. The general procuracy of Khatlon province later closed their case, finding "no sign of a crime."

Prison conditions in Tajikistan are far from ideal, though in recent years improvements have taken place, notably related to the health of inmates. The judicial system remains generally unfair, and those with means bribe their way out of a prison term or trial. Overall, prisons are characterized by overcrowding, lack of food, and widespread illness. A conservative estimate puts the number of prisoners infected with tuberculosis at 1,600 out of around 10,000.[23] Evidence suggests, nevertheless, that the number of prisoner deaths due to disease has been declining in the past few years as a result of intervention and financial assistance from European donors. Still, inmate casualty figures remain critically high when compared with those of other states worldwide.

Violations of child labor laws have also occurred as a result of the persistent poverty of the majority of the population. Tajikistan is a signatory to the international Worst Forms of Child Labor Convention, which calls for measures to eliminate all forms of child slavery, forced labor, prostitution, and work that harms the health, safety, or morals of children. In an attempt to protect young workers, the government amended its labor code in May 2005, making it favorable to children's rights. However, new laws and government rhetoric have failed to prevent child labor in various sectors of the economy. The lucrative cotton industry predominantly uses female and child labor to carry out hard fieldwork. In addition, children are seen working in urban areas, selling plastic bags in bazaars and carrying groceries for shoppers, washing cars, working in restaurants, and even toiling on the flourishing construction sites in the capital city.[24]

Gender equality and the protection of women's rights are also critical issues. In 2005, the UN Human Rights Commission noted the need for training government employees as a way to prevent human rights violations by police and investigative officials. The commission also noted that the state needs to prosecute violators of human rights, provide compensation to victims, increase public awareness to protect women against domestic violence, combat human trafficking in collaboration with Tajikistan's neighbors, and take measures to ensure a higher representation of women in public life.[25] The UN promised US$100,000 to five NGOs involved in women's issues during 2006 to help implement legislation on curbing violence against women, including establishing crisis centers and shelters for victims of domestic violence. Also, in February 2005 the Tajik Parliament approved legislation on state guarantees of gender equality of rights and opportunities.[26]

Human rights organizations were surprised by the government's speedy and near unanimous ratification of amendments to the country's criminal code replacing the death penalty with life imprisonment. The abolition of the death penalty in Tajikistan results from international (mainly European) pressure and follows the line of other CIS member countries, especially Russia, which also imposed a moratorium on capital punishment. Experts agree, however, that much remains to be done to reform the country's legal system, prison network, and human rights in general. According to Amnesty International, only days before the moratorium on the death penalty in 2004, the government secretly executed at least four individuals, with the location of their graves kept secret as well per a provision in the law. The executions were carried out despite the UN Human Rights Commission's appeals, which characterized Tajikistan's actions as violating its obligations as a party to the Optional Protocol to the International Covenant on Civil and Political Rights, especially as at least two of the executed persons – Rajabmurod Zhumayev and Umed Idiyev – were convicted for crimes known to have been confessed under torture.[27]

Corruption

1997	1998	1999	2001	2002	2003	2004	2005	2006
n/a	n/a	6.00	6.00	6.00	6.00	6.25	6.25	6.25

Misappropriation of public assets, the dispensing of state benefits, influence peddling, bribes, and extortion all fall under the umbrella of abusing public office for private gain, otherwise known as corruption. According to the World Bank, "high corruption" (graft and state capture by state officials) and "petty corruption" (solicitation of bribes and extortion by civil servants) are rampant in the seven poorest CIS countries, which includes Tajikistan.[28] In recent years, the Tajik government has stated its seriousness about fighting corruption, and in 2004 it formed a special department for combating corruption in the Office of the Prosecutor General. In a televised speech in December 2004, President Rahmonov cited corruption as one of the key internal threats facing the country, along with religious extremism, organized crime, and drug trafficking. And in January 2005, the president announced cutting nearly 900 positions from the staff of the state traffic police[29] – a government organ known for its ubiquitously corrupt workforce.

Despite such measures, no hard evidence suggests that a significant dent has been made in the pervasive corruption known to exist within government and business circles. A notable case of a government figure arrested on a variety of charges, including corruption, is that of Yaqub Salimov, the former head of the Ministry of the Interior and former Tajik ambassador to Turkey, who was arrested in 2003 in Moscow and repatriated to Tajikistan, and sentenced to 15 years in prison in April 2005. Indeed, corruption remains a major impediment to proper tax collection, economic development, and foreign investment. A study by the World Bank estimates that 80 percent of small businesses pay regular bribes to tax officials.[30] And according to the most recent IFES opinion survey, the highest level of dissatisfaction (56 percent) among the Tajik public is related to inadequate anticorruption measures.[31] Transparency International's 2005 Corruption Perceptions Index assigns Tajikistan a score of 2.1 (on a scale of 1 to 10, where 1 is "most corrupt"), putting it in the same bracket as Somalia and Sudan and near the bottom of the 158 countries surveyed.[32]

Allegations of corruption especially revolve around the country's dual commodity exports of cotton and aluminum, together forming nearly four-fifths of Tajikistan's exports.[33] (During 2005, aluminum brought in revenues of over US$600 million and cotton fiber about US$160 million.) In May 2005, the government announced that TadAZ, the state-owned Tajik aluminum plant, had generated a debt of US$160 million over a 10-year period when under the directorship of Abduqodir Ermatov. Ermatov was relieved of his post as director and appointed deputy minister of economy and trade in December 2004, while the Office of the Prosecutor General instituted criminal proceedings against him and the chief accountant of the plant. Though ordered not to leave the country, Ermatov is known to have fled to the United Kingdom. The government has also hinted at bringing charges against the management of Ansol, a company headed by the Tajik oligarch Azar Nazarov (also currently in the United Kingdom) that supplied TadAZ with alumina in the 1990s, accusing it of defrauding the government of tens of millions of dollars. The prosecutor general also alleged that Ansol funded an attempted coup d'etat with the former commander of the presidential guard, Ghaffor Mirzoyev, and the former head of Tojikgaz and head of the DP, Mahmadruzi Iskandarov. Both Mirzoyev and Iskandarov are currently in government custody.[34] A London court is also hearing the case of the conglomerate Russian Aluminum, set to invest over US$1 billion in aluminum and hydroelectricity production in Tajikistan but also allegedly involved with influential Tajik business and political elite in a scheme to divert profits from TadAZ offshore.[35]

Drug trafficking has been another source of corruption in Tajikistan. Since the overthrow of the Taliban by U.S.-led forces in late 2001, there has been an upsurge in the flow of drugs from Afghanistan into Tajikistan en route to Russian and European markets. As much as three-quarters of the world's supply of illicit opiates, mostly in the form of heroin,[36] originates from Afghanistan – where in 2005 over 4,000 tons of opium were cultivated.[37] There are few reliable estimates of the amount of drugs trafficked into Tajikistan. However, in the past few years border guards and police have reportedly intercepted as much as 10 tons of drugs annually. Though the government's antinarcotics activities appear to be strengthening, the recent transfer of border responsibilities along the southern border with Afghanistan from Russian control to Tajikistan's state border protection raises concerns about the agency's severe financial shortfalls and accompanying allegations of corruption related to drug trafficking.

Border officials from both Tajikistan and Afghanistan admit that approximately 100 kilometers of the border on the Afghan side and at least 50 kilometers on the Tajik side are effectively unguarded. And minuscule wages of Tajikistan's border patrol encourages corruption and drug trafficking. In fact, wages are so low that some newly assigned Tajik border patrol troops are begging for food from local residents along the Afghan border in the mountainous Badakhshan province in southeastern Tajikistan. Though suspicions run high, few top-level officials have been charged with corruption and drug trafficking. Still, in July 2005 the government sentenced a midlevel official from the Ministry of the Interior's Drug Control

Department to 14 years in prison for attempting to sell five kilograms of heroin in Dushanbe. The government is receiving technical and foreign aid from the United States and the European Union to help guard its southern border.

In recent years, Tajikistan has experienced impressive annual economic growth rates (average 9.6 percent during 2001–2005).[38] Though most analysts consider sustained economic growth necessary for ending poverty and corruption, there is also room for caution. Increased government revenues in transition economies may well boost the confidence levels in the government and work as a disincentive for those in charge to pursue equitable and sustainable economic reforms, promote democratization, and fight corruption. Furthermore, privatization of formerly state-owned enterprises, a process heavily encouraged by international financial institutions and Western donors in Tajikistan, may have unwittingly played into the hands of local elites.[39]

Though corruption will likely be curbed if significant wage increases are made in the public sector, some of the most corrupt state structures, such as the police, require radical reform of institutional or state culture. According to Transparency International, factors such as business transparency, press freedom, and public pressure acting together can work as effective checks against corruption. Furthermore, a World Bank study on anticorruption in transition countries recommends a series of concerted actions by states to effectively curb corruption, including detailed survey data on reality and perception of corruption in the country (as a gauge to set priorities) and overall reforms in public institutions via aggressive implementation of anticorruption policies.[40]

Payam Foroughi is an independent consultant specializing in socioeconomic development and political analysis.

[1] Economist Intelligence Unit, Tajikistan Country Report (London: EIU, December 2005).

[2] UN Human Rights Committee, Human Rights Committee Concludes Eighty-fourth Session, Adopts Final Conclusions, Recommendations on Reports of Yemen, Tajikistan, Slovenia, Syria, Thailand HR/CT/669, July 29, 2005.

[3] IFES, Public Opinion in Tajikistan 2004, November 2004, www.ifes.org.

[4] Kirill Nourzhanov, "Saviours of the Nation or Robber Barons?: Warlord Politics in Tajikistan," Central Asian Survey 24, no. 2 (June 2005): 109-30.

[5] Human Rights Watch, "Human Rights Interview: Tajikistan," January 2005, www.hrw.org.

[6] Freedom House, Freedom in the World, 2005, www.freedomhouse.org.

[7] Kirill Nourzhanov, "Saviours of the Nation or Robber Barons?: Warlord Politics in Tajikistan," Central Asian Survey 24, no. 2 (June 2005): 109-30.

[8] Human Rights Watch, "Presidential Elections in Tajikistan a Farce," October 28, 1999, www.hrw.org.

[9] OSCE, Republic of Tajikistan: Parliamentary Elections, February 27 and March 13, 2005 (Warsaw: OSCE/ODIHR Election Observation Mission, May 31, 2005).

[10] Agence France-Presse, "Tajikistan Tightens Control over Contacts with Diplomats, NGOs," April 14, 2005.

[11] International Research & Exchanges Board, Media Sustainability Index 2004, www.irex.org.

[12] Bruce Pannier, "Tajikistan: Crisis of Independent Media Sparks International Criticism," Radio Free Europe/Radio Liberty, September 9, 2005, www.rferl.org.

[13] OSCE, Statement on Free Media, U.S. Mission to OSCE, September 21, 2005.

[14] Reporters Without Frontiers, "Journalist Djumaboi Tolibov Released After Seven Months in Custody," December 21, 2005, http://www.rsf.org/print.php3?id_article=16008.

[15] Radio Free Europe/Radio Liberty, "OSCE Voices Concern over Tajik Media," September 5, 2005, www.rferl.org.

[16] IFES, Public Opinion in Tajikistan 2004, November 2004, www.ifes.org.

[17] Shirin Akiner, "Between Tradition and Modernity: The Dilemma Facing Contemporary Central Asian Women," in Mary Buckley, ed., Post-Soviet Women: From the Baltic to Central Asia (Cambridge, U.K.: Cambridge University Press, 1997), pp. 161-304.

[18] Kamoliddin Abdullaev, "Current Local Government Policy Situation in Tajikistan," in Luigi de Martino, ed., Tajikistan at a Crossroad: The Politics of Decentralization (Geneva: CIMERA, 2004).

[19] Sabine Freizer, "Tajikistan Local Self-Governance: A Potential Bridge Between Government and Civil Society?" in Luigi de Martino, ed., Tajikistan as a Crossroad: The Politics of Decentralization (Geneva: CIMERA, 2004).

[20] UN Office for the Coordination of Humanitarian Affairs, "UNDP Assists in Local Government Reforms," March 18, 2004, www.IRINnews.org.

[21] P. Foroughi, 'White Gold' or Women's Grief? The Gendered Cotton of Tajikistan (Oxfam-Great Britain, September 2005).

[22] UN Commission on Human Rights, "Special Rapporteur Stresses Need to Introduce Balance of Parties in Judicial Process in Tajikistan," September 30, 2005.

[23] UN Office for the Coordination of Humanitarian Affairs, Integrated Regional Information Networks, "Poor Conditions Mean TB Still Rife in Prisons," October 5, 2005.

[24] Institute for War and Peace Reporting, Reporting Central Asia, no. 412, 2005.

[25] UN Human Rights Committee, Human Rights Committee Concludes Eighty-fourth Session, Adopts Final Conclusions, Recommendations on Reports of Yemen, Tajikistan, Slovenia, Syria, Thailand, HR/CT/669, July 29, 2005.

[26] IRIN-Asia, "Tajikistan: Gender NGOs Receive Support from UN," December 12, 2005, http://www.reliefweb.int/rw/RWB.NSF/db900SID/LSGZ-6JZCWU?OpenDocument

[27] Amnesty International, Amnesty International: Tajikistan, 2005, www.amnesty.org.

[28] Jean-Jacque Dethier, "Corruption in G-7 Countries," paper, Lucerne Conference of the CIS-7 Initiative, January 20-22, 2003.

[29] Tajik television first channel, "Tajik Leader Orders Action to Solve Country's Problems," December 24, 2004 [BBC International Reports (Central Asia), December 26, 2004].

[30] Freedom House, Nations in Transit, 2005, www.freedomhouse.org.

[31] IFES, Public Opinion in Tajikistan 2004, November 2004, www.ifes.org.

[32] Transparency International, 2005, http://www.transparency.org/publications/gcr/download_gcr/download_gcr_2005.

[33] Economist Intelligence Unit, Tajikistan Country Report (London: EIU, December 2005).

[34] Avesta (Russian), "Tajik Prosecutor-General Says Freed Opposition Boss 'Terrorist,'" BBC Mon Alert CAU, April 11, 2005.

[35] Sunday Times, "Billionaire Russian Faces UK Court Case," October 9, 2005.

[36] Vanda Felbab-Brown, "Kicking the Opium Habit?: Afghanistan's Drug Economy and Politics Since the 1980s," paper presented at the 2005 Middle East and Central Asia Politics, Economics, & Society Conference, University of Utah, September 8-10, 2005.

[37] UN Office for Drugs and Crime, Afghanistan Opium Survey 2005, November 2005.

[38] Economist Intelligence Unit, Tajikistan Country Report (London: EIU, December 2005).

[39] Philippe Le Billon, "Overcoming Corruption in the Wake of Conflict," in Global Corruption Report 2005, Transparency International, March 2005, pp. 73-82.

[40] Cheryl Gray and James Anderson, "Corruption in Transition Economies," in Global Corruption Report 2005, Transparency International, March 2005, pp. 271-74.

Turkmenistan

Capital: Ashgabat
Population: 4.8 million
GNI/capita: $1,120 (2005)
Ethnic Groups: Turkmen (85%), Uzbek (5%),
Russian (4%), other (6%)

Nations in Transit Ratings and Averaged Scores

	1997	1998	1999	2001	2002	2003	2004	2005	2006
Electoral Process	7.00	7.00	7.00	7.00	7.00	7.00	7.00	7.00	7.00
Civil Society	7.00	7.00	7.00	7.00	7.00	7.00	7.00	7.00	7.00
Independent Media	7.00	7.00	7.00	7.00	7.00	7.00	7.00	7.00	7.00
Governance *	6.75	6.75	6.75	6.75	6.75	6.75	7.00	n/a	n/a
National Democratic Governance	n/a	n/a	n/a	n/a	n/a	n/a	n/a	7.00	7.00
Local Democratic Governance	n/a	n/a	n/a	n/a	n/a	n/a	n/a	7.00	7.00
Judicial Framework and Independence	6.75	6.75	6.75	7.00	7.00	7.00	7.00	7.00	7.00
Corruption	n/a	n/a	6.00	6.25	6.25	6.25	6.25	6.50	6.75
Democracy Score	6.90	6.90	6.75	6.83	6.83	6.83	6.88	6.93	6.96

* With the 2005 edition, Freedom House introduced seperate analysis and ratings for national democratic governance and local democratic governance to provide readers with more detailed and nuanced analysis of these two important subjects.

NOTE: The ratings reflect the consensus of Freedom House, its academic advisers, and the author of this report. The opinions expressed in this report are those of the author. The ratings are based on a scale of 1 to 7, with 1 representing the highest level of democratic progress and 7 the lowest. The Democracy Score is an average of ratings for the categories tracked in a given year.

The economic and social data on this page were taken from the following sources:
GNI/capita, Population: World Development Indicators 2006 (Washington, D.C.: World Bank, 2006).
Ethnic Groups: CIA World Factbook 2006 (Washington, D.C.: Central Intelligence Agency, 2006).

EXECUTIVE SUMMARY

Containing strong elements of personal rulership, despotism, and constitutional subversion, Turkmenistan has the only remaining neo-Stalinist regime in the world, along with North Korea. Following the collapse of the USSR in 1991, the course of independent Turkmenistan's development has been determined by the arbitrary and highly authoritarian rule of the country's first and only president, Saparmurat Niyazov, who has been in power since 1985 and was granted a lifetime presidency in 1999. President Niyazov's official title is Saparmurat Turkmenbashi (Leader of the Turkmen) the Great, and he enjoys a lavish cult of personality unrivaled in the former Soviet Union and, indeed, most of the world. Niyazov has undertaken reforms aimed primarily at centralizing his own rule, allowing him to exercise power without restraint.

In 2005, the state intensified its campaign to inculcate an official ideology glorifying Turkmenistan and its leader through the promotion of the *Ruhnama* (a two-volume national code of spiritual conduct, ostensibly written by Niyazov), which is required reading in all schools. Ethnic minorities continued to be affected by discriminatory practices denying them access to most higher education and jobs in the public sector. Government authorities engaged in repression of the country's two largest religious communities: the majority Sunni Muslim and the Russian Orthodox. Communication with the outside world was further obstructed through the prohibition of the import and circulation of all foreign print media, including those produced in neighboring countries. Niyazov restructured the lucrative hydrocarbons sector to put it under his direct control, and regular purges of the upper echelons of government led to even greater job insecurity and a concomitant increase in corruption.

National Democratic Governance. Although the Constitution of Turkmenistan stipulates the formal existence of executive, legislative, and judicial branches, in practice only the executive branch exercises any real power. The presence of a fourth branch of power, the People's Council, which was granted the status of the country's supreme representative body, has displaced even the formal legislative authority of the country's Parliament. In addition to his lifetime presidency, President Niyazov acts as chairman of the People's Council with lifetime tenure. The Democratic Party of Turkmenistan, of which Niyazov is chairman, remains the only legally registered party. Turkmenistan is a police state in which the activities of its citizens are carefully monitored by hypertrophied security agencies and the president's private militia, whose members receive favorable treatment relative to the rest of the population. A major tool used to buttress the president's lavish personality cult and to create a pseudo-state ideology is the *Ruhnama* (Book of the Soul), which has been accorded the de facto status of a holy book on a par with the Koran. *Turkmenistan's rating for national democratic governance remains unchanged at 7.00.*

Electoral Process. Electoral officials in Turkmenistan engage widely in irregular procedures, such as stuffing ballot boxes and making door-to-door home visits during which voters are urged to cast their ballots. Pressure is exerted on all civil servants to vote, and failure to do so can lead to reprisals. Turkmenistan is the only country in the Commonwealth of Independent States (CIS) formally to remove limits on an incumbent president's term in office. Although he is highly unlikely to step down from power voluntarily, since 2001 President Niyazov has proposed on several occasions that an election be held before 2010, ostensibly to pass on the presidency before he reaches the age of 70. In October 2005, the People's Council, a pseudo-representative organ headed by Niyazov himself, once again rejected the president's proposal to hold presidential elections in 2009, pleading with him to remain in power until his death. While no date for a presidential election was set, the same session of the People's Council passed a resolution setting dates for elections to village, district, city and regional councils as well as to Parliament in 2006-2008. Although in theory the creation of elected councils at the district, city and regional levels (village councils have been in existence since 1992) should lead to greater local autonomy, in practice the authorities thoroughly stage-manage Turkmenistan's elections, which have little to no bearing on the democratization process. No opposition parties or movements are officially registered in the country. Unrelenting harassment by the authorities has driven the relatively small Turkmen opposition either firmly underground or into exile. *Turkmenistan's rating for electoral process remains unchanged at 7.00.*

Civil Society. Although civil society has never thrived in Turkmenistan, steady repression by government authorities since 2002 in particular has forced those independent nongovernmental organizations (NGOs) that had managed to gain a foothold in the newly independent state to either dissolve or merge with pro-government public associations. The few "NGOs" allowed to operate in Turkmenistan are generally government sponsored, such as the veterans' and youth associations, and the women's union, which is dedicated to the memory of President Niyazov's mother. Given the generally draconian restrictions on civic activism, the decriminalization of unregistered NGO activity in November 2004 has not had a significant practical impact on civil society. That same year, the government also introduced legislation facilitating the registration of minority religious communities, which allowed nine such groups to acquire official registration in 2004–2005. Despite this minimal progress, many minority religious groups remain unregistered. More importantly, registration has not brought the promised benefits, as registered and unregistered groups alike continue to be subject to police raids, detentions, fines, and other forms of harrassment. Especially outside the capital city of Ashgabat, minority religious groups have been prohibited from meeting, throwing into question the very purpose of the registration process. In 2005, in an ominous development for civil society, governmental authorities clamped down further on the country's two largest religious communities: the majority Sunni Muslim and the Russian Orthodox. Several mosques were destroyed, and Islamic religious training was effectively eliminated owing to cutbacks at the Faculty of Muslim Theology at Magtymguly Turkmen State University, which remains the only official institution for training imams. In May, Niyazov sought to further isolate the Russian Orthodox Church by attempting to subordinate it directly to the patriarchate in Moscow rather than to the Central Asian diocese in Tashkent, as is currently the case. *Turkmenistan's rating for civil society remains unchanged at 7.00.*

Independent Media. All state media in Turkmenistan are devoted primarily to extolling the activities and achievements of the president and are devoid of independent information. In 2005, the Paris-based Reporters Without Borders ranked Turkmenistan 165th out of 167 nations – immediately above Eritrea and North Korea – in its annual worldwide Press Freedom Index. Foreign journalists are rarely allowed to enter the country, and those who do gain entry are closely monitored by the State Service for the Registration of Foreigners. Currently in Ashgabat there is only one accredited foreign correspondent, who works for the Russian news agency ITAR-TASS. In 2005, another ITAR-TASS correspondent was arrested, accused of espionage, and given a 15-year prison sentence before ultimately being deported to Russia. Although satellite dishes are in widespread use in the capital city, cable television is banned throughout the country. The country's sole Internet provider, Turkmen Telecom, strictly controls all access to the Internet. The monitoring of e-mail by the state, blocked access to a growing number of Web sites critical of government policy, and high fees have successfully restricted use of the Internet to a small number of organizations and individuals. In April 2005, the government took further steps to limit freedom of information and obstruct communication with the outside world by prohibiting the import and circulation of all foreign print media, including those produced in neighboring countries. Inhabitants of Turkmenistan received no information from government media on the regime changes that occurred in 2003-2005 in Ukraine, Georgia, and Kyrgyzstan, or on the seizure of government buildings by insurgents and the subsequent shootings of unarmed civilians by government troops in the Uzbek city of Andijan in May 2005. As a result, much of the population – particularly in rural regions – has remained ignorant of the momentous changes occurring in other post-Soviet states. *Turkmenistan's rating for independent media stays the same at 7.00.*

Local Democratic Governance. Currently, local government in Turkmenistan consists of largely decorative village councils (*gengeshes*) and presidentially appointed governors that lack independence from the central government in Ashgabat. In an ostensible move to decentralize government powers and responsibilites, the People's Council amended the Constitution in October 2005 to provide for the holding of direct elections to district, city, and regional councils in 2006–2007. The new legislation transferred the right to appoint regional, district, and city governors from the president to regional, district, and city councils, respectively, which will elect leaders from among their memberships in an open ballot by a simple majority vote. Although in a less authoritarian state this transfer of power might have been hailed as a major step toward the devolution of authority from the center to local organs of government, in Niyazov's Turkmenistan all candidates for election to official posts are rigorously vetted in a preelection screening process designed to weed out any potentially disloyal deputies. Drastic cuts in the important spheres of education, social security, and health care – including the closure of regional hospitals – have further undermined local government and have had serious repercussions for the rural population in particular. Tribal identities remain strong in Turkmenistan and continue to play an important role in Turkmen society and informal local politics. *Turkmenistan's rating for local democratic governance stays the same at 7.00. The legislative changes providing for the election of regional, city, and district governors, while a positive development, will likely not in practice result in a significant devolution of power or authority to local governments.*

Judicial Framework and Independence. The Office of the Prosecutor General dominates a legal system in which judges and lawyers play a marginal role. Although formally independent, the court system has no impact on the observance of human rights but rather acts as an important instrument of repression for the regime. Convictions are based on confessions that are sometimes extracted by forcible means, including the use of torture. Turkmen authorities have refused to grant the International Committee of the Red Cross unaccompanied access to prisons, despite a visit from the vice president of that body in June 2005 for the purpose of attempting to hash out an agreement. Ethnic minorities – and Turkmenistan's ethnic Uzbek population in particular – are affected by discriminatory practices denying them access to most higher education and jobs in the public sector. In December 2005, new legislation was promulgated requiring all Turkmen citizens wanting to leave the country to acquire a foreign travel passport in addition to an identification card for use inside the country. According to the new law, the state can refuse to issue a foreign travel passport when the departure of the applicant from the country is contrary to national security interests. In November 2005, the United Nations Third Committee (Social, Humanitarian, and Cultural) approved a resolution asking the General Assembly to express to the Turkmen government "its grave concern at continuing and serious human rights violations." *Turkmenistan's rating for judicial framework and independence remains unchanged at 7.00.*

Corruption. The existence of patronage networks as the basis of power in Turkmenistan has inevitably given rise to a political culture of bribery, nepotism, and embezzlement. Niyazov regularly purges the upper echelons of his government to diminish the power bases of political elites and rid it of potential rivals. Before 2000, dismissed officials as a rule were not imprisoned or sent into exile. In recent years, however, the dizzying pace at which government officials are regularly replaced, coupled with an increased fear of arbitrary reprisal, has meant that newly appointed officials attempt to acquire perks and exploit the privileges of their offices in record time. As a consequence, corruption – particularly embezzlement and bribe taking – has been steadily on the rise. Drastic cuts in pensions, massive redundancies in government jobs, the introduction of fees for medical services, and the use of military conscripts as a source of free labor in various sectors of the economy have all indicated that the state has been having difficulty funding its huge public sector. Although President Niyazov has sought to pin the blame for budget shortfalls on his subordinates by accusing them of mass embezzlement, a more likely explanation is Niyazov's continued diversion of ever larger sums from gas, oil, and cotton revenues to a special presidential fund, a large part of which is used to finance prestige construction projects. On the pretext of eliminating corruption, Niyazov enacted legislation giving himself direct control over the country's oil and gas resources, a development that is likely to lead to an even greater siphoning off of export revenues to his special fund. *President Niyazov's assumption of direct control over the country's oil and gas resources is likely to raise corruption levels even further, with the result that Turkmenistan's rating for corruption deteriorates from 6.50 to 6.75.*

Outlook for 2006. Despite regular declarations that presidential elections should be held in 2010, President Niyazov is highly unlikely to give up power voluntarily or to allow a successor to emerge. Niyazov still appears to have sufficient coercive and administrative power to retain control of the state, although the removal of several of his most senior and longest-serving officials in recent years indicates that his concern about the possibility of a palace coup has been mounting. In view of the low level of politicization of Turkmenistan's population, a popular uprising is unlikely. Perhaps the most immediate threat to the current regime is the ill health of the president, who has suffered from cardiovascular problems since at least the early 1990s. Given the absence of an heir apparent, regime change in Turkmenistan, when it comes, could thrust the country into a conflict between disgruntled former officials and officials in the state apparatus attempting to hold on to power. Infighting among members of the latter group is likely to exacerbate political instability.

MAIN REPORT

National Democratic Governance

1997	1998	1999	2001	2002	2003	2004	2005	2006
n/a	n/a	n/a	n/a	n/a	n/a	n/a	7.00	7.00

Turkmenistan is a police state in which the activities of its citizens are carefully monitored by hypertrophied internal security agencies and the president's private militia, whose members receive favorable treatment relative to the rest of the population, such as higher salaries and privileged accommodation. The Ministry for National Security (MNB) has the responsibilities held by the Committee for State Security during the Soviet period – namely, to ensure that the regime remains in power through tight control of society and by discouraging dissent. The Ministry of Internal Affairs directs the criminal police, who work closely with the MNB on matters of national security. Both ministries have abused the rights of individuals and enforced the government's policy of repressing political opposition.

Since the coup attempt in November 2002 – when oppositionists led by Boris Shikhmuradov, a former long-serving foreign minister, sought forcibly to remove the president from power – Niyazov appears to have relied less on the MNB while devolving greater powers to his own security service, the Presidential Guard. Consisting of some 2,000 to 3,000 former security agents whose loyalty to the president has been tested over time, the Presidential Guard is not subordinated to any security service and carries out a wide range of functions on Niyazov's personal orders. Both the Presidential Guard and the MNB operate with impunity.

Although the Constitution of Turkmenistan stipulates the formal existence of executive, legislative, and judicial branches, in practice only the executive branch exercises any real power. The Parliament (Majlis) has been transformed into a presidential appendage, and presidential decree is the usual mode of legislation. All political parties must be registered with the Ministry of Justice (renamed the Ministry of Fairness in September 2003), thereby allowing the government to deny official status to groups that are critical of its policies. In December 1991, the Communist Party of Turkmenistan renamed itself the Democratic Party of Turkmenistan (DPT) and confirmed Niyazov as chairman, leaving the old Communist power structure essentially intact. Other than Niyazov's DPT and the pro-government National Revival Movement, no parties or movements are legally registered in the country. The Constitution proscribes the formation of parties with a religious or nationalist orientation (Article 28). However, since the government prevents all parties other than the DPT from registering and functioning, this ban is of little relevance. In April 2005, President Niyazov declared that a multiparty system – with a minimum of two parties in addition to Niyazov's DPT – would be in place by the time of the proposed presidential elections in 2009. However, any parties created under Niyazov's regime are highly likely to be pro-governmental "pocket" parties.

During his reorganization of political structures in 1992, President Niyazov created the People's Council (Halk Maslakhaty) to recall the Turkmen "national tradition" of holding tribal assemblies in order to solve society's most pressing problems. According to a constitutional amendment and constitutional Law on the People's Council, which were passed by that same body in August 2003, the council was elevated to the status of a "permanently functioning supreme representative body of popular authority." The 2,507-member People's Council consists of the president, the members of Parliament, the chairman of the Supreme Court, the prosecutor general, the members of the Council of Ministers, the governors (*hakims*) of the five regions (*velayats*), and the *hakim* of the city of Ashgabat;

people's representatives elected from each district; the chairpersons of officially recognized parties, the youth association, trade unions, and the women's union; the
chairpersons of public organizations; representatives of the Council of Elders; the
hakims of cities that are the administrative centers of the *velayats* and districts
(*etraps*); and the heads of the municipal councils (*archins*) of the towns and villages
that are the administrative centers of the districts.

The August 2003 law ascribed to the People's Council a number of legislative
powers, including the passing of constitutional laws, thereby officially displacing
the Parliament as the country's primary legislative body. The constitutional amendment confirmed the People's Council's hitherto de facto status as a fourth branch
of power. In reality, proposals put forward by Niyazov at sessions of the People's
Council are invariably adopted unanimously by that body, which acts to officially
validate the president's policies. At the same time that the status of the People's
Council was formally upgraded in August 2003, Niyazov was unanimously elected chairman of the People's Council, with a lifetime tenure. Since, according to the
Constitution, the president of Turkmenistan is accountable to the chairman of the
People's Council, Niyazov will remain ex officio head of state whether or not pres-
idential elections are ultimately held.[1]

Officials in Niyazov's regime are appointed based on their complete loyalty
and subservience to the president rather than on a system of merits. Niyazov, who
is also the prime minister, regularly purges the upper echelons of his government
to diminish the power base of political elites and rid it of potential rivals.[2] Since
2000, Niyazov's regular reshuffling of ministers and other high-level public sector
officials has greatly accelerated in both intensity and scope, possibly reflecting an
increasing inability to trust his officials as well as a growing sense of vulnerability.

According to the calculations of the opposition Republican Party of
Turkmenistan (in exile), as of August 2005, 58 deputy prime ministers had been
dismissed in the 14-year history of independent Turkmenistan, of whom only 5
continued to work in civil service positions. The remaining 53 were either imprisoned, in exile, unemployed, or under house arrest.[3] In the first half of 2005, in
addition to a number of ministers, deputy ministers, and regional governors, the
president dismissed two of his most senior officials, both of whom appeared to be
his possible successors. In May, Yolly Gurbanmuradov, the deputy prime minister
with responsibility for the lucrative oil and gas sector, was arrested and convicted
of embezzlement and espionage. The long-serving Rejep Saparov, a deputy prime
minister from 1992 to 2002 and head of the presidential administration until his
dismissal in July 2005, was found guilty of corruption and sentenced to 20 years
in prison.[4]

As in most personalized dictatorships, Niyazov's style of rule is marked by his
own idiosyncracies and a significant degree of interference in the private affairs of
the country's citizens. Having outlawed in 2004, inter alia, the wearing of facial
hair by young men and the use of makeup by television presenters, in August 2005
Niyazov banned recorded music and "lip synching" at weddings, funerals, and other
cultural events in order to continue "the glorious musical traditions founded by our

ancestors."[5] Perhaps the most visible component of Niyazov's authoritarian regime is a highly developed personality cult. The president's portrait is ubiquitous throughout the country, and monuments to him have been erected in all cities and densely populated areas of the country. His name, the title Turkmenbashi, and his nickname ("Serdar," meaning "Supreme Chieftain") have been given to several thousand locales and objects, including at least two cities; several districts and villages; the country's main airport; a military institute; a multitude of farms, streets, and squares; a brand of vodka; and the country's highest mountain peak. Study of Niyazov's multivolumed writings has been introduced as mandatory in all educational establishments, and his cult of personality has been extended to include his deceased parents.

A major tool used to buttress this lavish personality cult and to create a pseudo-state ideology is the *Ruhnama* (Book of the Soul), a national code of spiritual conduct ostensibly written by Niyazov. Published in two volumes, the *Ruhnama* embodies Niyazov's personal reflections on Turkmen history and traditions as well as moral directives and has been accorded the de facto status of a holy book on a par with the Koran. Imams are required to display the *Ruhnama* in mosques and to quote from it in sermons, and the country's citizens are required to study and memorize its passages. Passages from the *Ruhnama* were inscribed alongside verses from the Koran on the marble walls of Central Asia's largest mosque, which was officially inaugurated in October 2004 in Niyazov's hometown of Gipchak, outside of Ashgabat. The *Ruhnama* has been published in more than 20 languages, including Zulu, as well as in a special Braille edition.

The Parliament's first act of business in January 2005 was to declare the Year of the *Ruhnama*, indicating that the government intended to intensify even further its campaign to inculcate an official ideology glorifying Turkmenistan and its leader. Citizens must pass a written examination on the *Ruhnama* – already a fundamental part of primary and secondary school curriculums – in order to gain a place at a university or institute of higher education qualify for government employment, or even receive a driver's license. Furthermore, according to the London-based Institute for War and Peace Reporting, as of December 1, 2005, public sector employees must pass regular examinations on the country's spiritual code as a prerequisite for continued employment. The Ministry of Education in conjunction with a professional "Ruhnamist," who is present at most state institutions, carries out these tests.[6]

Electoral Process

1997	1998	1999	2001	2002	2003	2004	2005	2006
7.00	7.00	7.00	7.00	7.00	7.00	7.00	7.00	7.00

No opposition parties or movements are officially registered in Turkmenistan. Unrelenting harassment by the authorities has driven the relatively small Turkmen opposition either underground or into exile. In September 2003, following a two-day meeting in Prague, the Czech Republic, several members of Turkmenistan's opposition parties and movements issued a communiqu□ announcing their decision to form the Union of Democratic Forces of Turkmenistan (UDFT). The UDFT consists of four main groups: the Republican Party of Turkmenistan, the Vatan (Fatherland) Social Political Movement, the United Democratic Opposition of Turkmenistan, and the Revival Social Political Movement. Despite the UDFT's stated goal to work together to remove Niyazov from power, the opposition in exile remains small, weak, poor, and prone to internal division.

Independent Turkmenistan held its first direct presidential election in June 1992 under a new Constitution, although Niyazov had been popularly elected to the presidency by direct ballot only 20 months previously, in October 1990. According to official results, voter participation in 1992 was 99.8 percent, with 99 percent of all votes cast in favor of Niyazov. In January 1994, a nationwide referendum overwhelmingly prolonged Niyazov's presidential mandate until 2002, exempting him from another popular election in 1997, as required by the Constitution. Following months of speculation on the introduction of a "life presidency," the Parliament approved amendments to the Constitution at the end of December 1999 that removed the maximum two-term provision, thereby enabling Niyazov to retain his presidential post until his death. Turkmenistan therefore became the first country in the CIS to formally abandon both regularly scheduled presidential elections and popular referendums designed to extend the incumbent president's term in office.

The majority of the seats in the People's Council are distributed among parliamentary deputies and other governmental officials, with the result that the Turkmen population elects only a minority of its deputies. The most recent elections to the People's Council, as well as to local representative bodies, were held in April 2003 amid a near total absence of information about the candidates or their platforms. Electoral officials claimed a 99.8 percent voter turnout.

The first parliamentary elections in independent Turkmenistan took place in December 1994, when 49 candidates stood unopposed for the 50-member unicameral legislature (2 candidates contested the remaining seat). Parliamentary elections were again held in December 1999, with a declared participation of 98.9 percent of the country's electorate. Although 104 candidates stood for the 50 parliamentary seats, nearly all were members of Niyazov's ruling DPT and served the state in some official capacity. The Organization for Security and Cooperation in Europe (OSCE) declined to send a monitoring mission on the grounds that "the legislative framework is inadequate for even a minimally democratic election."

In line with previous elections, the country's third parliamentary elections on December 19, 2004, were widely regarded as a purely ceremonial exercise. Although 131 candidates vied for 50 seats, all had been approved by governmental authorities prior to the elections. Candidates initially were selected by district authorities and then vetted by regional authorities before being referred to the presidential administration for final approval. All candidates were members of

Turkmenistan's sole registered political party, the DPT. As in the past, the Turkmen authorities did not invite international observers – including observers from other CIS countries – to monitor the parliamentary elections, asserting that national officials were capable of monitoring the event without outside help. The elections were thus monitored by some 200 national observers and employees from Turkmenistan's National Institute of Democracy and Human Rights, which is directly subordinated to the president, together with individuals from other organizations that had nominated candidates, such as the youth association and women's union.[7]

During Turkmenistan's 14-year history of independent rule, electoral officials have declared near 100 percent voter turnout rates for all elections and referendums. To achieve such spectacularly high participation rates, electoral officials engage widely in irregular procedures, such as stuffing ballot boxes and making door-to-door home visits during which voters are urged to cast their ballots. Pressure is exerted on all civil servants to vote, and failure to do so can lead to reprisals.[8] Despite these undemocratic tactics to encourage voting, unprecedented voter apathy resulted in a record low turnout of only 76.88 percent for the December 2004 parliamentary elections. Authorities attributed the low participation rate to unusually cold weather conditions.

Although he is highly unlikely to step down from power voluntarily, President Niyazov has proposed on several occasions since 2001 that presidential elections be held before 2010, ostensibly to pass on the presidency before he reaches the age of 70 in 2010. His proposals are invariably singled out by members of the People's Council, who in publicly staged protests plead with him to stay in office until the end of his lifetime. As in previous years, delegates at the October 2005 session overwhelmingly passed a resolution in favor of removing the issue of presidential elections from the agenda, with the president casting the only dissenting vote.[9] Following Niyazov's protests that "nothing in this world is eternal" and "the fate of the nation cannot depend on one person," a compromise was reached to postpone the discussion of presidential elections until 2009.[10] Despite this decision, Niyazov is certain to continue to raise the issue of presidential elections at regular intervals, as he appears to believe that his proposals to arrange for an orderly succession win him public relations points with the international community.

Although no date was set for a presidential election, the same session of the *Halk Maslakhaty* passed a resolution setting dates for elections to village-level councils (*gengeshes*); district, city and regional-level councils (*Halk Maslakhaty*); and to the parliament (*Mejlis*). Elections to *gengeshes* are scheduled for July 2006, elections to district- and city-level *Halk Maslakhaty* will be held in December 2006, and elections to regional-level *Halk Maslakhaty* will be held in December 2007. Elections to the Parliament are scheduled for December 2008. Additionally, the elections of people's representatives to the People's Council (one from each of the country's 60 districts) will be held in December 2008.[11] Although in theory the creation of elected councils at the district, city and regional levels should lead to greater local autonomy, in practice the authorities thoroughly stage-manage Turkmenistan's elections, which have little to no bearing on the democratization process.

Civil Society

1997	1998	1999	2001	2002	2003	2004	2005	2006
7.00	7.00	7.00	7.00	7.00	7.00	7.00	7.00	7.00

Although civil society has never thrived in Turkmenistan, steady repression by government authorities since 2002 in particular has forced those independent NGOs that had managed to gain a foothold in the newly independent state to either dissolve or merge with pro-government public associations. According to Counterpart Consortium, a U.S. NGO supported by the U.S. Agency for International Development, in 2000 there were approximately 200 to 300 registered and unregistered NGOs in Turkmenistan.[12] By the beginning of 2005, that number had dwindled to 91, according to official statistics released by the Ministry of Fairness.[13] The vast majority either supported the government or received funding from the government. There are no independent trade unions, and the successor to the Soviet-era Federation of Trade Unions remains linked to the government. Other government-organized "NGOs" include the veterans' association, the youth association, the journalists union, and the Humanitarian Association of World Turkmen. The women's union, which is dedicated to the memory of President Niyazov's mother, is the only officially registered women's NGO.

Civil society in Turkmenistan was paralyzed by fallout from an attempted coup on November 25, 2002, when former foreign minister Boris Shikhmuradov and his fellow oppositionists staged an effort to forcibly remove Niyazov from power as his motorcade was traveling through Ashgabat. Turkmen authorities immediately publicized the attack as a failed assassination plot, although the opposition has declared that Shikhmuradov's aim was to capture Niyazov and force him to renounce power rather than to assassinate him.[14] Niyazov used the attempted coup to his advantage by incarcerating some of his major opponents, including Shikhmuradov, and implementing a series of new measures that curbed civil liberties even further. A new wave of repression and witch hunts was initiated in the aftermath of the armed endeavor, resulting in the arrest of at least 200 individuals with purported connections to the opposition, of whom approximately 60 were ultimately convicted for their alleged role in the coup attempt. Niyazov proposed to the People's Council that a new maximum penalty of life imprisonment with no possibility of pardon, amnesty, or parole be introduced for the crime of treason, which was very broadly defined as any crime against the state or the president. Independent civil society activists became frequent targets of detention and harassment, while Turkmenistan's government-sponsored "NGOs" were used as part of a propaganda campaign to demonstrate support for the president. Mass meetings were held and rallies staged, with participants calling for the "people's enemies" to be put to death.

Civil society activists were repressed further in November 2003 when an unprecedented presidential decree was signed into law requiring all NGOs to register or reregister with the Ministry of Fairness or face fines, corrective labor, and possible prison sentences with the confiscation of property. The law gave the authorities the right to exercise complete control over the funding and activities of NGOs, thereby effectively limiting the ability of foreign donors to provide financial aid and other assistance to civil society groups. As a result, many independent NGOs ceased to exist or began to operate under the safer label of "initiative group." In early 2004, the Dashoguz Ecological Club and the Ecological Club Catena – two of Turkmenistan's oldest operating NGOs – were stripped of their legal registration.[15]

In a move apparently designed to assuage international criticism of Turkmenistan's human rights practices, the government published new legislation in November 2004 abolishing criminal penalties for activities undertaken by unregistered NGOs, thereby reversing the November 2003 legislation. However, the decriminalization of unregistered NGO activity has not had a significant practical impact on civil society given the generally draconian restrictions on civic activism.

As with political parties and public associations, all religious congregations must register with the Ministry of Fairness to gain legal status. Before 2004, the only religions that had managed to register successfully were Sunni Islam and Russian Orthodox Christianity, although they were still subject to tight government controls. In March 2004, President Niyazov issued a decree pledging to register all religious groups regardless of creed or number. The law was amended accordingly to reduce the number of adult citizens needed to register a religious community with the Ministry of Fairness from 500 to 5. As a result of these changes, four minority religious groups managed to gain registration in 2004: Seventh-day Adventists, Baha'is, Baptists, and Hare Krishnas. In 2005, five more Protestant churches were granted registration (the Greater Grace Church, the Church of Christ, the New Apostolic Church, and the Full Gospel Pentecostal Church in Ashgabat; and the Light of the East Pentecostal Church in Dashoguz).[16]

Yet despite this minimal progress, many minority religious groups remain unregistered, such as the Catholic, Lutheran, Jehovah's Witness, Armenian Apostolic, and Jewish communities. More important, registration has not brought the promised benefits, as registered and unregistered groups alike continue to experience police raids, detentions, fines, and other forms of harrassment. Especially outside Ashgabat, minority religious groups have been prohibited from meeting, throwing into question the very purpose of the registration process.[17]

Turkmen authorities eliminated criminal penalties for members of unregistered religious groups in May 2004. (In November 2003, Turkmenistan had tightened its Law on Religion and adopted amendments to the criminal code that imposed penalties of up to one year's imprisonment for unregistered religious activity, which had hitherto been considered an administrative offense.) According to the current law, congregations that are not registered with the Ministry of Fairness are prohibited from proselytizing, gathering publicly, and disseminating religious materials, and violators are subject to penalties under the administrative code. In practice, however, state agencies have continued to treat unregistered religious activity as a criminal offense, and some believers have been given long prison sentences or sent into internal exile.[18]

In 2005, religious freedoms were further restricted in Turkmenistan despite the registration of a handful of minority religious groups and the freeing of some prisoners of conscience. In an ominous development for civil society, governmental authorities clamped down further on the country's two largest religious communities: the majority Sunni Muslim and the Russian Orthodox. Several mosques were destroyed, and Islamic religious training was effectively eliminated owing to cutbacks at the Faculty of Muslim Theology at Magtymguly Turkmen State University, which remains the only official institution for training imams.[19] In May, Niyazov attempted to further isolate the Russian Orthodox Church by seeking to subordinate it directly to the Patriarchate in Moscow rather than to the Central Asian diocese in Tashkent, as is presently the case. Such a move would have eliminated what little authority the Central Asian diocese exerts over Turkmenistan's Orthodox Church, thereby giving President Niyazov even greater control. Russian Orthodox are prohibited from bringing religious literature into the country, and requests from Russian priests wanting to serve in Turkmenistan have been routinely turned down.[20] As a 10-member coalition of NGOs based in the United States and Europe noted in a letter to the U.S. secretary of state, the government of Turkmenistan "no longer simply controls religion; it is actively trying to eliminate even state-controlled religions in order to establish a new religion based on the personality of the president."[21]

Independent Media

1997	1998	1999	2001	2002	2003	2004	2005	2006
7.00	7.00	7.00	7.00	7.00	7.00	7.00	7.00	7.00

All media in Turkmenistan are devoted primarily to extolling the activities and achievements of the president and are devoid of independent information. In 2005, the Paris-based Reporters Without Borders ranked Turkmenistan 165th out of 167 nations – immediately above Eritrea and North Korea – in its annual worldwide Press Freedom Index.[22] The president is the formal founder of the country's 23 registered newspapers and 14 registered journals and personally appoints all editors, who are answerable to him. The 4 state television channels and state radio function as mouthpieces for government propaganda.

Foreign journalists are rarely allowed to enter the country, and those who do gain entry are closely monitored by the State Service for the Registration of Foreigners. Currently in Ashgabat there is only one accredited foreign correspondent, who works for the Russian news agency ITAR-TASS. In 2005, another ITAR-TASS correspondent was arrested, accused of espionage, and given a 15-year prison sentence before ultimately being deported to Russia.[23]

Cable television – which had provided access to Russian channels and acted as the country's main source of alternative information – was banned in July 2002 after Russian television broadcast footage of poverty in Turkmenistan. During the same month, Turkmenistan's Ministry of Communications halted the import of Russian newspapers and magazines, citing high airmail delivery rates. In July 2004, Turkmen authorities suspended the transmission of Russia's Radio Mayak, which was highly popular in Turkmenistan and acted as one of the last independent media sources in the country aside from a few foreign broadcasts on shortwave radio directed at Turkmen listeners. Satellite dishes are still tolerated and in widespread use in the capital city but are prohibitively expensive for the vast majority of the population.

All access to the Internet is strictly controlled by the country's sole Internet provider, Turkmen Telecom. The monitoring of e-mail by the state, blocked access to a growing number of Web sites critical of government policy, and high fees have successfully restricted use of the Internet to a small number of organizations and individuals. According to the International Crisis Group, it was estimated that in 2004 there were only some 8,000 Internet connections in the country, although the number of users was undoubtedly higher.

A major propaganda effort to improve Turkmenistan's international image was undertaken in October 2004 when the country launched a new multilingual satellite television service. TV4 Turkmenistan, initiated by President Niyazov at an estimated cost of US$12 million, broadcasts programs in Turkmen and six foreign languages: English, Russian, Chinese, French, Arabic, and Persian. According to Niyazov, the channel's purpose is to report on various aspects of life in Turkmenistan while focusing on the country's achievements.

In April 2005, the government took further steps to limit freedom of information and obstruct communication with the outside world by prohibiting the importation and circulation of all foreign print media, including those produced in neighboring countries.[24] In the same month, Turkmenistan refused to extend the licenses of international shipping firms and express couriers, arguing that the state postal service is less costly and more reliable.[25]

Inhabitants of Turkmenistan received no information from government media on the regime changes that occurred in 2003–2005 in Ukraine, Georgia, and Kyrgyzstan or on the seizure of government buildings by insurgents and the subsequent shootings of unarmed civilians by government troops in the Uzbek city of Andijan in May 2005, with the result that much of the country's (particularly rural) population remained ignorant of the momentous changes occurring in other post-Soviet states.

Local Democratic Governance

1997	1998	1999	2001	2002	2003	2004	2005	2006
n/a	n/a	n/a	n/a	n/a	n/a	n/a	7.00	7.00

In a move purportedly intended to decentralize government powers and responsibilities, the People's Council amended the Constitution in October 2005 to provide for the holding of direct elections to district, city, and regional councils, although this seeming move toward democratization is unlikely to have a significant impact in practice. Currently, local government in Turkmenistan consists of largely decorative village councils and presidentially appointed governors that lack independence from the central government in Ashgabat. Executive power in Turkmenistan's five *velayats* and in the city of Ashgabat is vested in the *hakims*, who are appointed by the president to execute his instructions. Below the *velayat* level, the president also appoints the executive heads of the cities and districts (*shakher hakims* and *etrap hakims*, respectively), purportedly based on the recommendations of the respective *velayat*-level *hakims*. Regarding representative organs in the villages, the 1992 Constitution provided for the replacement of local soviets by councils (*gengeshes*), whose members are directly elected for five-year terms. The 528 *gengeshes* are administered by *archins*, who are elected from among their respective memberships. Some 5,500 deputies were elected to local *gengeshes* in April 2003 with little transparency and minimal media coverage and preelection campaigning.

In accordance with a resolution of the People's Council, elections to village-level *gengeshes*, district, city and regional level councils will be held in 2006–2007. District and city councils will each consist of 40 members, while regional councils will each consist of 80 members.

Perhaps more significant than the creation of new local bodies of power, the constitutional amendment transferred the right to appoint regional, district, and city *hakims* from the president to the regional, district, and city councils, respectively (the heads of the village councils – the *archins* – are already elected from among the membership of those councils), which will henceforth elect the governors from among their memberships in an open ballot by a simple majority vote. Although in a less totalitarian state this transfer of power might have been hailed as a major step toward the devolution of authority from the center to local organs of government, in Niyazov's Turkmenistan all candidates for election to official posts are carefully vetted in a preelection screening process designed to weed out any potentially disloyal deputies. Moreover, although the president no longer appoints regional governors, it is unclear whether or not he retains the right to dismiss them, since according to the new phrasing of the relevant constitutional article (Article 79), "the *hakims* are representatives of the president of Turkmenistan, the head of state, in the regions, and are accountable to him."[26] (The new local bodies of power, by contrast, are accountable to the people.) If the president does indeed retain the power to dismiss the elected governors, then the new reform of local government will be rendered virtually meaningless.

Tribal identities remain strong in Turkmenistan and continue to play an important role in Turkmen society and informal local politics. The largest tribes are the Tekke in south-central Turkmenistan (Ahal Tekke and Mary Tekke), the Ersary near the region of the Turkmenistan-Afghanistan border, the Yomud in western and northeastern Turkmenistan, and the Saryks in the southernmost corner of the country. Unlike in parts of Africa, for example, where both formal and informal tribal associations have played a significant role in political mobilization and local governance, in Turkmenistan tribalism manifests itself primarily in social practices, such as the maintenance of preferential networks, endogamy, and the persistence of dialects.

However, the exit of the Russian nomenklatura following the collapse of the USSR led to a gradual resurgence of traditionally minded regional elites vying for their economic interests, which in turn prompted Niyazov to rely more and more on a policy of divide and rule with regard to tribal and regional politics. Although a sense of national identity is being promoted at the state level, *hakims* are often, although not always, members of the tribe that is dominant in their respective regions. A disproportionate number of influential positions in central and regional government tend to go to members of Niyazov's own tribe, the Ahal Tekke.

Since approximately 2000, the government has been engaged in the systematic dismantling of key areas of the public sector, effectively undermining local government in the important spheres of education, health care, and social security, with serious repercussions for the rural population in particular. The majority of children in Turkmenistan no longer have adequate access to education. In many rural schools, it is estimated that one-half of classroom time is allocated to the study of Niyazov's quasi-spiritual guide, the *Ruhnama*, and other writings devoted to furthering his personality cult. In addition, students must demonstrate knowledge of the *Ruhnama* in order to be admitted to higher educational establishments. Over 12,000 teachers have been made redundant through a 2000 presidential decree, including those with degrees from foreign universities, which are no longer recognized.[27] Class sizes have increased and facilities have deteriorated as state funds earmarked for education have diminished.[28] The number of student places in institutes of higher education has been reduced by nearly 75 percent, and primary and secondary education has been reduced from 11 to 9 years (a circumstance that complicates the entry of Turkmen students into foreign universities). Only those who have completed two years of work experience after leaving school are allowed to go on to higher education, and the term of higher education has been reduced to just two years. All correspondence and evening courses have been liquidated. The dismantling of the education system has put in doubt the ability of the next generation of Turkmen to compete successfully in the global market.

In addition to the education sector, health care services in Turkmenistan have been systematically undermined. In March 2004, 15,000 health workers (including doctors, nurses, midwives, and medical attendants) were dismissed and replaced by untrained military conscripts. Additionally, the March "reforms" introduced user fees for specialist services that had previously been free of charge, making treatment unaffordable for many patients.[29] In a portentous development that could initiate a public health crisis, in February 2005 President Niyazov announced a plan to close all hospitals outside Ashgabat. Claiming that regional hospitals are "not needed," he said that citizens in the country's regions will have access only to medical diagnostic centers – which require payment for services – to obtain prescriptions and general advice, while those in need of hospitalization or specialist care will be required to travel to Ashgabat.[30] Hospital closures affect those in remote rural regions first and foremost, since both distance and the cost of travel will deprive many of the possibility to receive both emergency and specialist medical treatment.

Judicial Framework and Independence

1997	1998	1999	2001	2002	2003	2004	2005	2006
6.75	6.75	6.75	7.00	7.00	7.00	7.00	7.00	7.00

On May 18, 1992, Turkmenistan's Parliament adopted a new Constitution – the first Central Asian state to enact such a document after the dissolution of the USSR. The Constitution guarantees in theory the protection of basic rights and liberties, equality under the law, and the separation of religion and state. Amendments have been made to the Constitution since its original adoption, including eliminating the two-term limit for the president, prohibiting citizens from Turkmenistan from holding dual citizenship, and redefining the status and function of the People's Council. In 2005, the Constitution was amended to provide for the election of regional, city, and district governors.

Unchanged since the Soviet era, the court system in Turkmenistan consists of a Supreme Court, 6 regional courts (including 1 for the city of Ashgabat), and, at the lowest level, 61 district and city courts. In addition, the Supreme Economic Court hears all commercial disputes and cases involving conflicts between state enterprises and ministries. Because all military courts were abolished in 1997, criminal offenses committed by military personnel are tried in civilian courts under the authority of the Office of the Prosecutor General. Although formally independent, the court system has no impact on the observance of human rights but rather acts as an important instrument of repression for the regime.

The president appoints all judges for five-year terms without legislative review. The Office of the Prosecutor General dominates a legal system in which judges and lawyers play a marginal role. As in the former Soviet Union, convictions are based on confessions that are sometimes extracted by forcible means, including the use of torture and psychotropic substances.

Despite its accession to a number of international human rights agreements, which theoretically take precedence over state law, Turkmenistan has perhaps the poorest human rights record of any former Soviet republic. In December 2002, widespread concern about human rights violations prompted 10 participating states of the OSCE to invoke for the first time in 10 years the so-called Moscow Mechanism, which provides for the establishment of a fact-finding mission of rapporteurs to investigate reported violations. The OSCE report, released in March 2003, was harshly critical of human rights practices in Turkmenistan, even calling for the UN General Assembly to reexamine its 1995 recognition of Turkmenistan's status as a neutral country. In addition to the OSCE, the European Parliament, the Office of the United Nations High Commissioner for Human Rights, and the UN General Assembly have all adopted separate resolutions condemning Niyazov's regime for its human rights violations. In November 2005, for the third consecutive year, the United Nations Third Committee (Social, Humanitarian, Cultural) approved a resolution asking the General Assembly to express to the Turkmen government "its grave concern about continuing and serious human rights violations."[31]

Arbitrary arrest and detention remains a widespread practice in Turkmenistan, despite laws prohibiting it. Prison riots are a relatively common occurrence, apparently provoked by inhumane conditions. The Turkmen government has admitted to chronic overcrowding in cells, which has led to prisoners being stifled to death in extreme summer heat. Food and water remain in short supply, and prisoners are not generally provided with medical aid. Poor sanitary conditions have precipitated outbreaks of cholera, tuberculosis, and other infectious diseases. Human rights organizations have reported that inmates are routinely beaten and tortured. Turkmen authorities have refused to grant the International Committee of the Red Cross unaccompanied access to prisons, despite a visit from the vice president of that body in June 2005 for the purpose of attempting to hash out an agreement.[32] In October 2005, under an annual amnesty mandated by a 1999 law and presidential decree, the government released an estimated 8,145 inmates – two-thirds of the prison population – causing the incidence of muggings and burglaries to rise markedly in the ensuing weeks.[33] Although individuals convicted of serious crimes are theoretically ineligible for amnesty, those who can pay bribes – excluding political prisoners – are generally freed, regardless of the type of crime they were imprisoned for. Although the annual amnesties serve temporarily to relieve overcrowding, prisons quickly fill up again owing to the overall high number of arrests.

In 1999, Turkmenistan became the first CIS country to embark upon the establishment of a visa regime inside the territory of the former USSR, by withdrawing from the so-called Bishkek accord, which had established visa-free travel for citizens of the CIS. It also required its own citizens to obtain exit visas, often at considerable expense, to travel to foreign states, including neighboring CIS countries. Although the requirement for Turkmen citizens to obtain exit visas was temporarily suspended amid much publicity in January 2002, it was restored in March 2003 in the wake of the November 2002 attempted coup. However, in January 2004 the exit visa regime for citizens of Turkmenistan was again abolished, although in its stead the government implemented a number of unofficial measures to prevent free travel, such as the drawing up of an extensive "blacklist" of citizens who are prohibited from leaving the country, the arbitrary confiscation of passports, and the closure of border checkpoints. In March 2004, the president issued the Decree on the Improvement of Exit Procedures for the Citizens of Turkmenistan, after which it was reportedly somewhat easier for citizens to travel abroad. In December 2005, new legislation was promulgated requiring all Turkmen citizens wanting to leave the country to acquire a foreign travel passport in addition to an identification card for use inside the country. According to the new Law on Migration, the state can refuse to issue a foreign travel passport when the departure of the applicant from the country is deemed to go against national security interests.[34]

In line with other post-Soviet states, Turkmenistan has accorded a de facto higher status to its titular population, ethnic Turkmen, and has legitimized the adoption of policies and practices that promote their specific interests. In 2000, Turkmen was introduced as the language of instruction in all the country's schools, including in regions where ethnic Uzbeks or Kazakhs are preponderant. Higher education and jobs in the public sector have been effectively closed to non-Turkmen. Senior state officials must be able to demonstrate ethnic purity by tracing their Turkmen ancestry back several generations. Members of ethnic minorities are not allowed to apply for positions in the judicial system, in law enforcement and security agencies, or in financial and military organizations. Job applicants are required to fill out a personal information form (*maglumat*), a practice that enables employers to deny jobs to non-Turkmen as well as to those with foreign qualifications or criminal records. In addition to fluency in Turkmen, knowledge of the *Ruhnama* is a requirement for work in the public sector, which remains the main supplier of jobs.[35]

The president has attempted to eliminate the use of Russian as the main language of communication with either the outside world or among ethnic communities within the country. The Russian media are inaccessible, and Russian has been excluded from virtually all spheres of education. Although in 1991 Turkmenistan had nearly 1,500 Russian-language schools, in 2004 there was only 1, located in the Russian embassy in Ashgabat. Following the suspension of Russia's Radio Mayak in July 2004, the government mouthpiece, *Neitral'nyi Turkmenistan*, has remained the only Russian-language media source of information for the country's Russian-speaking population, which includes ethnic Armenians, Jews, and Ukrainians, among others.

These discriminatory practices have particularly affected ethnic Uzbeks. Since the end of 2002, several thousand people, primarily ethnic Uzbeks, have been forcibly relocated from the Turkmenistan-Uzbekistan border areas to desert regions in northwestern Turkmenistan. This policy presumably serves the dual purpose of reducing irredentist sentiment among Uzbeks in Turkmenistan and increasing population density in scarcely populated regions of the country. Like Russian and Kazakh schools, schools with Uzbek as the primary language of instruction have been gradually forced to switch over to Turkmen. Moreover, by the end of 2004 virtually all ethnic Uzbeks in high- and middle-level administrative positions in Dashoguz *velayat*, located on the Uzbek-Turkmen border, had been removed from their positions. Even in areas of Turkmenistan where ethnic Uzbeks constitute the majority of the population, they no longer serve as district governors, farm chairmen, or school principals.

Corruption

1997	1998	1999	2001	2002	2003	2004	2005	2006
n/a	n/a	6.00	6.25	6.25	6.25	6.25	6.50	6.75

In its Corruptions Perceptions Index for 2005, Transparency International ranked Turkmenistan as one of the most corrupt countries in the world, giving it a score of 1.8 (with 10 "highly clean" and 0 "highly corrupt"). Of the 159 countries ranked in its index, only Chad and Bangladesh were perceived as more corrupt than Turkmenistan, both of which received scores of 1.7.[36]

Rather than by the rule of law, the actual dispensation of power in Turkmenistan is determined by the vast machinery of patronage that has created local constituencies and regional alliances. Political elites have traditionally built up local power bases by allocating key posts and opportunities to their loyalists. These informal networks, which have survived the demise of the Soviet system, are frequently referred to as "clans," although they are based on patron-client relationships, often with links to extended families, rather than on actual blood ties. The existence of patronage networks as the basis of power has inevitably given rise to a political culture of bribery, nepotism, and embezzlement. Significantly, senior officials in the central government as well as regional governors have direct access to state revenues, which they use to buy the loyalty of subordinates.

Turkmenistan has continued to act as a transshipment point for illicit drugs from Afghanistan to Western Europe. It has been estimated by the international human rights group Turkmenistan Helsinki Foundation and other NGOs that Turkmenistan has the highest number of regular drug users per capita in the Central Asian region.[37] In addition to drug smugglers, the narcotics trade is an important source of income for a large number of government officials, including employees of the security agencies and the border service.[38]

Although the overall turnover rate of officials in Turkmenistan is extremely high, senior regional officials in particular tend to remain in their positions for very short periods, generally for less than a year. Given their brief tenure in office, *hakims* are inclined to give low priority to solving the problems of their respective regions, preferring instead to use their short time in power to amass personal economic benefits. Before 2000, dismissed officials as a rule were not imprisoned or sent into exile. In recent years, however, the dizzying pace at which governmental officials are regularly replaced, coupled with an increased fear of arbitrary reprisal, has meant that newly appointed officials attempt to acquire perks and exploit the privileges of their positions in record time. As a consequence, corruption, particularly embezzlement and bribe taking, has been steadily on the rise.

In recent years, drastic cuts in pensions,[39] massive redundancies in government jobs, the introduction of fees for medical services, and the use of military conscripts as a source of free labor in various sectors of the economy have all indicated that the state has been having difficulty funding its huge public sector, despite official reports of record foreign trade surpluses. Although President Niyazov has sought to pin the blame for budget shortfalls on his subordinates by accusing them of mass embezzlement, a more likely explanation is the continued diversion by Niyazov of ever larger sums from gas, oil, and cotton revenues to a special presidential fund, which is located in European and other bank accounts. This foreign exchange reserve fund, which does not form part of the state budget and is under Niyazov's control, is estimated to be worth at least 60 percent of the country's gross domestic product, with export revenues providing its main source of inflow.[40]

A significant portion of the foreign exchange reserve fund is used to subsidize prestige construction projects commissioned by the president. More than US$1 billion has been spent during Turkmenistan's independence on such projects, including a palace of congresses and arts, an independence park, two stadiums, a national museum, a series of luxury hotels, and a horse-racing center. The construction of a national theater of music and drama, a new library and exhibition center, a children's attraction park, an aquarium, a zoo, and even an ice palace and funicular railway are under way. The construction of Central Asia's largest mosque, located in Niyazov's hometown of Gipchak, is estimated to have cost US$86 million. Furthermore, Niyazov has undertaken the construction of a gigantic artificial lake in the Karakum Desert, with a planned capacity of twice that of Central Asia's entire reservoir.

In December 2005, President Niyazov undertook the restructuring of the country's lucrative hydrocarbons sector, on which Turkmenistan is dependent for the bulk of its export revenues.[41] Even before that move, the dismissal of two of his most senior oil and gas officials earlier in the year (the first in May and the second in August), followed by the removal of a number of sector leaders from September onward, had already left that key area of the economy in a state of disarray. On the pretext of eliminating corruption, Niyazov announced that he would henceforth assume direct personal control over all of the country's natural gas exports, stating that "no contract will be valid without my signature."[42] New legislation restricting the ability of the country's main oil and gas companies to sign contracts, explore for new fields, or enter into joint ventures without the president's authorization is likely to lead to a further increase in corruption by allowing for an even greater siphoning off of export revenues to Niyazov's special presidential fund.

Annette Bohr is an associate fellow of the Russian and Eurasia Programme at the Royal Institute of International Affairs in London (Chatham House). She is the author or coauthor of numerous articles and two monographs on Central Asian politics, contemporary history, and ethnic and language policies.

[1] Annette Bohr, "Turkmenistan," Eastern Europe, Russia and Central Asia 2006, Europa Regional Surveys of the World, (London: Routledge, 2005), p. 494.

[2] Annette Bohr, "Independent Turkmenistan: from post-communism to sultanism," in Sally N. Cummings, Oil, Transition and Security in Central Asia (London : RoutledgeCurzon, 2003), p. 11.

[3] Rashid Meredov Fired as Vice-Premier for "Failure to Perform Duties," Gundogar, 7 March 2005, cited in Weekly News Brief on Turkmenistan, 4-10 March 2005, Turkmenistan Project, available at www.eurasianet.org/turkmenistan.project/index.php?page=weekly&lang=eng.

[4] "Supreme Kaziyet (Court) of Turkmenistan passes sentence on Rejep Saparov," Turkmenistan.ru, 27 July 2007; Bruce Pannier, "Turkmenistan: No Job Security for Officials-Even Old Presidential Friends," Eurasianet, 28 August, 2005. www.eurasianet.org/departments/civilsociety/articles/pp082805.shtml.

[5] "Nyyazov bans recorded music at weddings and festivals," BBC Monitoring, Inside Central Asia, 28 August 2005.

[6] "Vetting Turkmen Style," Reporting Central Asia, The Institute for War and Peace Reporting, 25 November 2005, www.iwpr.net/?s=f&o=258307.

[7] Mikhail Zygar' and Elena Glumskova, "Turkmeny proguliali vybory," Kommersant' (Moscow), 20 December 2004.

[8] "Turkmen Election a Mockery," Reporting Central Asia, The Institute for War and Peace Reporting, 15 December 2004., www.iwpr.net/?s=f&o=162094.

[9] "Znamenatel'noe sobytie-den' pervyi," Gundogar website, 26 October 2005, http://gundogar.org/?0219042279.

[10] "Niyazov yields to pleas to remain in office for life," BBC Monitoring, Inside Central Asia, 30 October 2005,

[11] "Dates set for Turkmen Parliamentary Polls," Turkmen Radio 1, 15 November 2005, cited in Weekly News Brief on Turkmenistan, 11-17 November 2005, Turkmenistan Project, available at www.eurasianet.org/turkmenistan.project/index.php?page=weekly&lang=eng.

[12] The 2000 NGO Sustainability Index for Central and Eastern Europe and Eurasia, USAID, Bureau for Europe and Eurasia, www.usaid.gov/locations/europe_eurasia/dem_gov/ngoindex/2000/turk-menistan.pdf.

[13] The 2004 NGO Sustainability Index for Central and Eastern Europe and Eurasia, USAID, Bureau for Europe and Eurasia, www.usaid.gov/locations/europe_eurasia/dem_gov/ngoindex/2004/turk-menistan.pdf.

[14] Annette Bohr, "A Failed Coup After All? November 2002, Ashgabat," Central Asia-Caucasus Analyst, 18 June 2003, www.cacianalyst.org/view_article.php?articleid=1496.

[15] Erika Dailey, "New Law on NGO Activity in Turkmenistan Greeted with Caution," 30 November 2004, http://www.eurasianet.org/departments/civilsociety/articles/eav113004.shtml.

[16] Felix Corley, "Turkmenistan: Will registration end harrassment of religious communities?" Forum

[18] News Service, www.forum18.org/Archive.php?article_id=548..

[17] Felix Corley, "Turkmenistan: Religious Freedom Survey, October 2005," Forum 18 News Serivce, www.forum18.org/Archive?query=Turkmenistan%3A+Religious+Freedom+Survey%2C+October+2005.

[18] Ibid.

[19] Igor Rotar, "Turkmenistan: 'Virtual Catastrophe' for Muslim Theological Faculty," Forum 18 News Service, www.forum18.org/Archive.php?query=Turkmenistan%3A+%22Virtual+Catastrophe%22+for+Muslim+Theological+Faculty&religion=all&country=all&results=10.

[20] "Turkmenistan: Orthodox Faith Under Seige," Reporting Central Asia, The Institute for War and Peace Reporting, 18 November 2005, www.iwpr.net/?p=rca&s=f&o=257777.

[21] International Helsinki Federation for Human Rights, 29 September 2005, cited in Weekly News Brief on Turkmenistan, 23-29 September 2005, Turkmenistan Project, available at www.eurasianet.org/turkmenistan.project/index.php?page=weekly&lang=eng.

[22] Available at /www.rsf.org/rubrique.php3?id_rubrique=554.

[23] "SMI v Turkmenistane: nukakikh sobytii,"', Gundogar website, 26 October 2005, http://gundog-ar.org/?0221042186.

[24] Mehman Gafarly, "Nepechatnaia leksika," Novye izvestiia (Moscow), 19 April 2005.

[25] Nadezhda Popova, "Niyazov poobeshchal uiti v 2009 godu," Izvestiia (Moscow), 22 April 2005.

[26] "Revised Constitution of Turkmenistan to take effect on January 1," Turkmenistan.ru, 14 November 2005.

[27] "Turkmenistan wrestles with child labor issue as cotton harvest approaches," Eurasianet, 1 September 2004, www.eurasianet.org/departments/rights/articles/eav090104.shtml.

[28] Turkmenistan: The Making of a Failed State, International Helsinki Federation for Human Rights, April, 2004, www.ihf-hr.org/documents/doc_summary.php?sec_id=3&d_id=3831.

[29] Bernd Rechel and Martin McKee, Human rights and health in Turkmenistan, European Centre on Health of Societies in Transition, (London: London School of Hygiene & Tropical Medicine, 2005), pp. 24-25.

[30] Bruce Pannier, "Is Turkmen President trying to euthanize health care?", Radio Free Europe/Radio Liberty Central Asia Report, 8 March 2005.

[31] United Nations Sixtieth General Assembly GA/SHC/3842, Third Committee, 21 November 2005, www.un.org/News/Press/docs/2005/gashc3842.doc.htm.

[32] "EU Welcomes Turkmen Delegation, Reforms, 'Deplores' Some Persistent Abuses," Gundogar website, cited in Weekly News Brief on Turkmenistan, 23–29 September 2005, Turkmenistan Project, available at www.eurasianet.org/turkmenistan.project/index.php?page=weekly&lang=eng.

[33] "Crime Wave in Turkmenistan," Reporting Central Asia, The Institute for War and Peace Reporting, 17 December 2005, www.iwpr.net/?s=f&o=258741.

[34] "New Law Restricts Exit from the Country,", Turkmen Initiative for Human Rights, press release No. 186, 3 January 2006, cited in Weekly News Brief on Turkmenistan, 23 December 2005-5 January 2006, Turkmenistan Project, available at
http://www.eurasianet.org/turkmenistan.project/index.php?page=weekly&lang=eng; "New migration law comes into force," BBC Monitoring, Inside Central Asia, 1 January 2006.

[35] "Vetting Turkmen Style," Reporting Central Asia, The Institute for War and Peace Reporting, 25 November 2005, www.iwpr.net/?s=f&o=258307.

[36] Available at www.transparency.org/policy_research/surveys_indices/cpi/2005.

[37] "Narkomaniia i narkomafiia," Gundogar, 21 July 2005, http://gundogar.org/?0233042009.

[38] Annette Bohr, "Independent Turkmenistan: from post-communism to sultanism," in Sally N. Cummings, Oil, Transition and Security in Central Asia (London:RoutledgeCurzon, 2003), p. 13; "Turkmenistan: Banker claims government has own drug ring," Eurasia Daily Monitor, 9 July 2004, http://jamestown.org/publications_details.php?volume_id=401&&issue_id=3012.

[39] "Pension payments slashed and withheld," 13–19 January 2006, Weekly News Brief on Turkmenistan, Turkmenistan Project, available at
www.eurasianet.org/turkmenistan.project/index.php?page=weekly&lang=eng.

[40] "Funny Business in the Turkmen-Ukraine Gas Trade," Global Witness, April 2006, www.globalwitness.org/reports/download.php/00297.pdf

[41] "Oil, gas sector comes under president's direct control," BBC Monitoring, Inside Central Asia, 1 January 2006.

[42] Associated Press, 1 December 2005, cited in Weekly News Brief on Turkmenistan, 1–8 December 2005, Turkmenistan Project, available at
www.eurasianet.org/turkmenistan.project/index.php?page=weekly&lang=eng.

Ukraine

Capital:	Kyiv
Population:	47.5 million
GNI/capita:	$1,270
Ethnic Groups:	Ukrainian (78%), Russian (17%), other (5%)

Nations in Transit Ratings and Averaged Scores

	1997	1998	1999	2001	2002	2003	2004	2005	2006
Electoral Process	3.25	3.50	3.50	4.00	4.50	4.00	4.25	3.50	3.25
Civil Society	4.00	4.25	4.00	3.75	3.75	3.50	3.75	3.00	2.75
Independent Media	4.50	4.75	5.00	5.25	5.50	5.50	5.50	4.75	3.75
Governance *	4.50	4.75	4.75	4.75	5.00	5.00	5.25	n/a	n/a
National Democratic Governance	n/a	n/a	n/a	n/a	n/a	n/a	n/a	5.00	4.50
Local Democratic Governance	n/a	n/a	n/a	n/a	n/a	n/a	n/a	5.25	5.25
Judicial Framework and Independence	3.75	4.00	4.50	4.50	4.75	4.50	4.75	4.25	4.25
Corruption	n/a	n/a	6.00	6.00	6.00	5.75	5.75	5.75	5.75
Democracy Score	4.00	4.25	4.63	4.71	4.92	4.71	4.88	4.50	3.96

* With the 2005 edition, Freedom House introduced seperate analysis and ratings for national democratic governance and local democratic governance to provide readers with more detailed and nuanced analysis of these two
important subjects.

NOTE: The ratings reflect the consensus of Freedom House, its academic advisers, and the author of this
report. The opinions expressed in this report are those of the author. The ratings are based on a scale of 1
to 7, with 1 representing the highest level of democratic progress and 7 the lowest. The Democracy Score
is an average of ratings for the categories tracked in a given year.

The economic and social data on this page were taken from the following sources:
GNI/capita, Population: *World Development Indicators 2006* (Washington, D.C.: World Bank, 2006).
Ethnic Groups: *CIA World Factbook 2006* (Washington, D.C.: Central Intelligence Agency, 2006).

EXECUTIVE SUMMARY

T
he famous events known as the Orange Revolution changed the profile of Ukraine in late 2004–early 2005. They opened a way to positive changes in the country's political and social life, primarily in the spheres of democracy, transparency of government power, and media freedom. Since independence in 1991, Ukraine has witnessed four presidential (1991, 1994, 1999, 2004) and three parliamentary (1994, 1999, 2002) elections. Now, the third president and the fourth Parliament (until May 2006) are in power. The Constitution, adopted in 1996, introduced a presidential model of government in which the president appoints and dismisses state officials and regional governors.

Viktor Yushchenko, the third president of Ukraine, was inaugurated on January 23, 2005. The new Parliament is to be elected in March 2006 by proportional vote, which replaces the mixed 50/50 majoritarian/proportional electoral system previously used. A December 2004 constitutional reform, which was put in force in January 2006, establishes a new government model with a substantially stronger role for the Parliament and government.

Ukraine's economy is growing gradually, but the speed of gross domestic product (GDP) growth decreased from 12 percent in 2004 to 2.4 percent in 2005. Real wages are increasing more rapidly than GDP (the average monthly salary has grown from US$120 as of late 2004 to approximately US$180 as of late 2005). Media freedom has been a major benefit of the regime change: No censorship or government pressure on the media was detected in 2005. However, the Ukrainian media sector still needs strengthening, restructuring, and systemic reforms. The influence of political and economic groups in the media sphere remains strong, and public TV has not yet been introduced.

The current status of the Ukraine government can be described as "transitional." The parliamentary elections scheduled for March 26, 2006, followed by the formation of a government are either to confirm the democratic trend established by the Orange Revolution or slow down and restrict the move toward democracy. Still, a return to Kuchma-like semi-authoritarianism is unlikely in present Ukraine.

National Democratic Governance. Ukraine, on its move from a post-Soviet presidential government, is preparing to embrace a new model closer to other Central and Eastern European countries. Constitutional reforms adopted in December 2004 stipulate a substantially stronger role for the Parliament and government and limitations on the president's powers. At the same time, a new model provides risks for government stability and sustainability owing to a drastic shift of checks and balances within the political machinery and evident weaknesses in Ukraine's party system. The new regime led by President Yushchenko has proved to be substantially more transparent and democratic than the previous one. However, stable and mature institutions ensuring the rule of law and the irreversibility of democratic changes have not yet been built. The first "Orange" government (Cabinet of Ministers), chaired by Yulia Tymoshenko until September, was replaced by Yury Yechanurov's government, which is considered to be more technocratic and pragmatic in comparison with its predecessor. A governmental crisis disclosed deep personal and even ideological tensions within the Orange coalition. During 2005, the president and government never enjoyed stable parliamentary support. The military and police (Ministry of the Interior) became more transparent and accountable thanks to new leadership efforts. *Ukraine's rating for national democratic governance improves from 5.00 to 4.50 owing to evident democratization of political life after the Orange Revolution, increasing the transparency of state power to some extent.*

Electoral Process. There were no national or local elections in Ukraine in 2005. New wording of the Law on the Elections of People's Deputies, adopted in July 2005, significantly enhanced election procedures and integrated recommendations by international observers issued after the last presidential elections. These changes include the right of nongovernmental organization (NGO) observers to be present at polling stations. At the same time, this law limited freedom of the press during election campaigns by prohibiting journalists from making comments on the programs and activities of contenders. Owing to protests by the media and NGOs, these discriminatory provisions were excluded from the law in November. Elections to the Parliament, regional and local councils, and mayors of cities and villages are scheduled for March 26, 2006. For the first time, national, regional, and local elections are being held according to a proportional voting system, which replaces the mixed 50/50 majoritarian/proportional vote (for the Parliament) and majoritarian vote (for local and regional councils) previously used. The precampaign period provides hope that the government will not interfere in the process: Parties enjoy equal access to media, and no administrative barriers to political activity are detected *Ukraine's rating for electoral process improves from 3.50 to 3.25, as the beginning of the parliamentary campaign demonstrates no substantial obstacles to political activity and there is equal access to the media among various political forces.*

Civil Society. Ukraine civil society, which played a crucial role in the Orange Revolution, continues to strengthen. Unlike the government under Leonid Kuchma, the current authorities do not interfere in the third sector by levying permanent taxes and other checks, accusing NGOs of serving foreign powers, or creating additional barriers and obstacles to NGO activity. Public participation is growing on different levels: From state politics to local communities, the wave of civic activism born in revolution is still not exhausted. A number of civic councils were established by joint initiatives of the government and civic activists to promote regular links between power and society. The most active NGO participants created informal coalitions to lobby necessary changes to legislation and develop a "doctrine for the civic sector." According to a presidential decree signed on September 15, new mechanisms for cooperation between state and civil society were introduced, including annual presidential hearings (the first took place on November 28) and a president's Strategic Council. At the same time, the Parliament failed to provide essential improvements to outdated NGO legislation. *Ukraine's rating for civil society improves from 3.00 to 2.75 owing to the state's increased protection for the independence and growing vibrancy of the civil sector.*

Independent Media. Substantial progress in the area of media freedom may be considered the most evident achievement of Ukraine's Orange Revolution and regime change. Citizens currently enjoy wide-ranging pluralism in both electronic and print media. Governmental censorship, known in the past as *temniki* (government instructions designed to control the content of media broadcasts), was canceled even before the new government took power as an immediate outcome of the Orange Revolution. Nationwide TV channels in most cases provide balanced news coverage; representatives of ruling parties as well as the opposition have equal access to the media. Most nationwide media are private, and none of them was reprivatized in favor of people close to Yushchenko after the regime change, despite the fact that most still belong to the former Kuchma entourage. At the same time, the Ukrainian media sphere lacks substantial reforms and restructuring. Most media are still owned by leading financial and industrial groups, which means they can be used as a tool of political and economic "wars" within the country, especially during election campaigns. Many regional and local TV, radio, and newspapers remain in the hands of state bodies and administrations. Despite numerous declarations and promises, public TV has not yet been established. The advertising market is growing slowly, which restricts the development of an independent media sector separate from "big business." Some new independent media projects emerged as a result of growing Western investment in Ukrainian media. *Ukraine's rating for independent media improves from 4.75 to 3.75 owing to the evident progress toward genuine media pluralism and freedom.*

Local Democratic Governance. In 2005, a number of administration and territorial reforms were initiated, including local government reforms. A political consensus has been achieved on the need to decentralize government by providing more power to local and regional authorities, but the concrete shape of reform remains undecided. Local self-government councils are still limited in their real powers and financial resources. A comprehensive administration and territorial reform was presented by Vice Prime Minister Roman Bezsmertny in April 2005. This reform featured a revised division of powers between state administration and self-governance bodies, shifting powers to the lower bodies; changes in budget constitutions and spending; and redistribution of taxes according to new territorial designations. Along with the new territorial and administrative order, a new system of state governance for taxes, budgets, and municipalities is being developed. Owing to the electoral campaign, further debates on local governance reform were postponed until after the 2006 parliamentary and local elections. *Ukraine's rating for local democratic governance remains* *unchanged at 5.25, as numerous 2005 initiatives did not yet result in real improvements in this sphere and theoretical policy debate prevailed over practical actions.*

Judicial Framework and Independence. In 2005, the new leadership declared important improvements in the judiciary and began creating preconditions for their implementation, though most steps were not implemented. At the same time, the judicial system gained more independence from the executive, whose total control over the judicial decision-making process has disappeared. The principle of equality before the law, however, is still disregarded. Violations by the highest officials involved in the 2004 elections have not been prosecuted. Despite discussions about a comprehensive reform of the judiciary, criminal law, human rights protections, and related spheres, such reforms were not fully and systematically introduced in 2005. *Until commendable initial steps made in 2005 yield the planned systematic changes, Ukraine's rating for judicial framework and independence remains at 4.25.*

Corruption. The fight against corruption and the establishment of fair government power was a prominent aim of the new authorities in 2005. Former high-ranking officials accused of corruption were removed from power; however, none of these top-level corruption cases passed through the courts. There were also corruption scandals within the new team of high-ranking officials. Corruption allegations had an ambiguous impact on Ukraine's political environment. On the one hand, the scandals have demonstrated significant improvements in state transparency in Ukraine. Such a situation could not have existed in Kuchma's era of "mutual solidarity" among high officials. On the other hand, the scandals have ultimately unbalanced the emerging political system of new Ukraine. Finally, the various existing anticorruption regulations and initiatives do not take a systematic approach or articulate an overall long-term strategy but are chaotic and face strong internal resistance, thus undermining their intended effect on society. *Despite the increased prominence and airing of corruption scandals, which is commendable, Ukraine's rating for corruption remains at 5.75, as anticorruption initiatives have not yet produced systematic improvements.*

Outlook for 2006. The March 26, 2006, parliamentary elections and their outcomes pose a challenge for Ukraine. The overall campaign is considered to be mostly fair and free. The newly established parliamentary model needs to prove its sustainability and efficiency. The new constitutional system is more democratic and pluralistic than the previous presidential system, but because of the weakness of the party system and domination by oligarchic groups over most of the political spectrum, this model will not necessarily lead to a strengthening of democratic institutions and rule of law. Since no political party can form a government on its own, the core challenge is to build consensus and grow capacity within a governmental majority, whoever composes it. Serious administrative and local governance reforms are unlikely in Ukraine in 2006. It is unclear whether the new government will be ready to ensure the irreversibility of media freedom, including the establishment of public TV and broadcasting. Corruption will remain a key challenge given the lack of efficient anticorruption programs and continuing connections between business and government power.

Main Report

National Democratic Governance

1997	1998	1999	2001	2002	2003	2004	2005	2006
n/a	n/a	n/a	n/a	n/a	n/a	n/a	5.00	4.50

After Ukraine's Orange Revolution in 2004, the country has been in the process of a political transformation intended to lead Ukraine toward mature democracy. However, in some essential cases this process has lacked consistency. According to the Law on Changes and Amendments to the Constitution of Ukraine adopted on December 8, 2004, Ukraine moved toward a parliamentary model of power similar to those of other Central and Eastern European countries. This law enters into force on January 1, 2006. In practice, this measure would allow the Parliament elected in March 2006 to create a government based on a parliamentary coalition (majority). According to the new law, the president loses the authority to appoint and dismiss members of government without parliamentary approval. Furthermore, under the upgraded Constitution, the president nominates only ministers of defense and foreign affairs; other members of government are to be nominated by the prime minister. A coalition of political parties (more than 50 percent of parliamentary seats) nominates the prime minister and appoints a government, whereas the president is authorized to dissolve the Parliament if it is not able to form a coalition within 30 days. This newly created power model is more pluralistic and brings Ukraine closer toward European political traditions.

At the same time, a new model provides risks for the stability and sustainability of the government owing to the drastic shift of checks and balances within the political machinery and the evident weaknesses in Ukraine's party system. In addition, the constitutional amendments contain provisions that the Council of Europe's Venice Commission has repeatedly found incompatible with the principles of democracy and the rule of law, in particular regarding the imperative mandate of members of Parliament (MPs) and the powers of the prosecutor's office.

Ukraine still lacks legislation mentioned in the country's Constitution but not yet adopted, such as laws on the president, Cabinet of Ministers, the Parliament's temporary investigative and special commissions, pretrial inquiry bodies, and the Parliament's rules of procedure. The lack of legal provisions, for example, on the formation and function of the Cabinet of Ministers resulted in the president's continued practice of appointing deputy ministers and deputy heads of other central bodies of the executive. This raised doubts as to its compliance with the Constitution, which entitles the president to appoint only the top leadership of executive bodies. President Yushchenko has implemented a reform of the president's administration, which was a powerful "parallel government" during Kuchma's regime, giving the secretariat a more technical function. Current head of the secretariat Oleg Rybachuk expressed an ambition to develop a strong strategy-building unit within the office.

Despite certain progress, Ukraine has still not achieved European standards of economic freedom. In order to address crises in the fuel and sugar markets, Prime Minister Yulia Tymoshenko's cabinet (February-September 2005) used administrative instruments to interfere with prices by establishing maximum limits. The government tried to restrict bureaucratic procedures by introducing a "one window" principle for small-business registration, achieving partial success. Several thousand restrictive instructions for businesses were canceled. The taxation system has not yet been simplified, but related projects are under consideration in the government and the Parliament.

The Ukraine Parliament (Supreme Rada) may be considered fully independent from the executive. Unlike Kuchma, President Yushchenko has not attempted to control the Parliament through administrative pressure. Sessions of the Parliament are broadcast live on the 1st Channel of the National Radio. Yet existing freedom has another side: The lack of proper policy coordination in the Parliament-president-government triangle has led to significant dysfunction in parliamentary activity. This was clearly detected in the failure to pass all legislation necessary to join the World Trade Organization. Weakness and instability in Ukraine's party system is reflected in the Parliament. For example, more than 400 faction changes in the Parliament have been registered since the 2002 elections.

Access to public information is regulated by the Law on Information of 1991, which is considered to be relatively good but lacks proper procedures for granting access to public documents, obtaining information from state officials, and so forth. A group of NGOs (under the coordination of the local/regional NGO Kharkiv Human Rights Protection Group and the international NGO Article 19) has drafted a new wording of the Law on Information that contains detailed rules for access to information in line with European standards. The draft law has not yet been submitted to the Parliament.[1] Legislation on the "informational openness" of state bodies and officials – submitted by Serhiy Holovaty, former MP and now minister of justice – was approved in the first reading in December 2004, but the draft law contains no detailed procedures. From the moment of taking office, President Yushchenko has signed more than 40 classified decrees with the stamp "Not Subject to Publication," yet such stamps are not foreseen by any Ukraine law. This policy of nontransparency was established by former president Kuchma.

Military and security services also face reforms and transformations. As the present government is more seriously committed to achieving NATO membership (announced in 2002), current armed forces reforms by Defense Minister Anatoly Grytsenko include stronger focus on transparency and accountability in order to achieve aims fixed in the NATO-Ukraine Action Plan – namely, reforming state security structures to reflect the Euro-Atlantic Policy of Ukraine and "strengthening civil control of the Armed Forces of Ukraine and other security forces, including enhanced cooperation and oversight of the Parliament and increased participation of civilians in decision making related to security issues."[2] The security service, owing to continued restructuring (such as introducing a separate external intelligence service) and changes of leadership (Oleksandr Turchynov was replaced in September by Ihor Drizhchany), remains less subject to public control reforms. Ukraine's success in these reforms may be assessed as moderate in the military sphere and insufficient in the security services arena.

Electoral Process

1997	1998	1999	2001	2002	2003	2004	2005	2006
3.25	3.50	3.50	4.00	4.50	4.00	4.25	3.50	3.25

Ukraine's political atmosphere in 2005 was very different from that of the previous year, which significantly affected the electoral process. All political parties could enjoy freedom and media pluralism to deliver any message to society.

There were no national or local elections in Ukraine in 2005. The official campaign for the 2006 elections started on November 26; however, an informal portion of the campaign was launched immediately after President Yushchenko's inauguration on January 23. The entire political agenda in Ukraine in 2005 was determined by the forthcoming 2006 parliamentary elections, as constitutional reforms substantially increased the "price" of this election.

Prosecution of officials involved in the 2004 election falsifications served as a warning and significant deterrent to other potential transgressors. The new authorities promised that election violations would be thoroughly investigated and prosecuted. As of September 2005, the Office of the Prosecutor General had opened 1,218 criminal cases and brought 790 of them to the courts, including over 200 cases against chairmen and members of election commissions. The Ministry of the Interior had more than 700 cases opened at the end of June 2005, including over 110 cases submitted to the courts.[3] As of late 2005, more than 100 persons were found guilty.

Elections to the Parliament, regional and local councils, and mayors of cities and villages are scheduled for March 26, 2006. For the first time, national, regional, and local elections will be held according to a proportional voting system with a 3 percent threshold, which replaces the system of a mixed 50/50 majoritarian/proportional vote (for the Parliament) and a majoritarian vote (for local and regional councils). The introduction of a party-based model of election at the local level may be considered premature: The local party system remains undeveloped (party branches do not exist in many towns and districts), which has led to a large number of artificial parties and blocs pretending to be political players; local lists from large parties are stocked with names of individuals who have not previously been associated with these parties.

The new wording of the Law on the Elections of People's Deputies, adopted in July 2005, has significantly enhanced election procedures and takes into account recommendations by international observers issued after the last presidential elections.

Among the major improvements adopted in July 2005 are the following: Better rules now exist for compiling and verifying voter lists; domestic nonpartisan NGOs have the right to observe elections; the enhanced rules for election commissions provide a guaranteed number of poll workers proportional to the number of registered voters; judicial review procedures have been strengthened for complaints in all phases of the electoral process; the role of the police in the transportation of electoral material and rules for their presence at polling stations were clarified; and improved procedures have been implemented for absentee and home voting. In particular, the law provides for full inventory and de facto registration of all absentee ballot certificates and absentee voting will be possible only at a limited number of polling stations.

At the same time, this law provides limited freedom of the press during the campaign by prohibiting journalists from making comments on the programs and activities of contenders. The Central Election Commission and district election commissions were authorized to suspend, without a court order, media licenses and publications for disseminating unconstitutional materials or spreading knowingly false or slanderous statements about a party (bloc) or a candidate. Following protests by media and NGOs, these discriminatory and nondemocratic provisions were excluded from the law in November.

On August 24, 2005, in his Independence Day speech, President Yushchenko called on the Parliament to raise the election threshold. Immediately, different MPs submitted to the Parliament several draft laws proposing to set the election threshold from 4 to 7 percent. All proposals failed, however, because of the disagreement of most political parties and groups in the Parliament.

The precampaign period has indicated that the government has not interfered in the process: Parties enjoyed equal access to the media, and no administrative barriers to political activity were detected.

By the registration deadline on December 26, a total of 45 political parties and blocs had successfully submitted registration documents and were qualified to participate in the elections.

Civil Society

1997	1998	1999	2001	2002	2003	2004	2005	2006
4.00	4.25	4.00	3.75	3.75	3.50	3.75	3.00	2.75

Civil society in Ukraine played a crucial role in the Orange Revolution and continues to strengthen. Unlike the Kuchma government, current authorities do not interfere in the third sector by levying permanent taxes, accusing NGOs of serving foreign powers, or creating additional barriers and obstacles to NGO activity. At the same time, little effective policy has been implemented to support civil society and encourage NGO activity in Ukraine.

The Parliament has thus far failed to provide essential improvements to the outdated NGO legislation, especially the basic Law on Associations of Citizens, adopted in 1992. Existing legislation does not provide a clear definition of "NGO" or "nonprofit activity." All income, excluding grants and member fees, is considered business activity and subject to the same taxes levied against other business enterprises. NGOs cannot provide paid services in order to sustain their capacity. Bureaucratic regulations still require numerous and inefficient procedures, such as reregistration. All Ukrainian NGOs must submit new registration materials up to the end of 2006 to keep their legal status (this deadline has since been extended, but the reregistration requirement is still in place).

In summer 2005, a group of NGOs led by the Democratic Initiatives Foundation issued an initiative calling for the authorities to provide "Orange wings for NGOs," meaning essential improvements to legislation. The most active NGO representatives created an informal coalition to lobby changes to legislation and develop a "doctrine for the civic sector."

Public participation in civil society grew significantly during and immediately after the Orange Revolution. Though that wave of civic activism has not been exhausted, it was not as evident in 2005. In one example of NGOs widening activities on the local level, in Kyiv a number of local committees were established to protect the historic environment of downtown from uncontrolled construction activity.

A number of civic councils (collegiums) were established as joint initiatives between the government and civic activists to promote regular links between the state and society. The most active are those on foreign policy (at the Foreign Ministry), media liberty and freedom of speech, and small business and entrepreneurship. In regional centers, some administrations invited NGOs to join civic councils.

According to a presidential decree signed on September 15, new mechanisms of cooperation between the state and civil society were introduced, including annual presidential hearings (the first took place on November 28) and the president's Strategic Council. However, during preparations for the presidential hearings, the presidential secretariat failed to offer an attractive role for NGOs in designing the agenda; in response to this dominating bureaucratic approach, a number of leading NGOs refused to take part. Ivan Vasyunyk, deputy head of the secretariat and responsible for government-civil society connections, has provided selective and inconsistent policy vis-a-vis NGOs.

Growing political competition has led to an increase in politicking in NGOs. Many of them are blurring the line between government and civil society, and their independence from political and business interests is often questionable. Some parties/political organizations and business groups have established their own NGOs with goals that are different from the objectives of "natural" NGOs. Some NGOs, such as the civic campaign Pora, which was well-known during the Orange

Revolution, have been divided into "political" and "civic" branches with sometime non-friendly relations between them.

The massive explosion of civic activity has its "dark side." Some newly established radical organizations with revanchist pro-Soviet ideological backgrounds conducted actions threatening the peaceful development and even territorial integrity of Ukraine. This indicates that the civil sector remains vibrant and sensitive to the negative political trends that still appear as part of the incomplete nation-building process in Ukraine.

Ukrainian NGOs lack sustainable funding, which makes them dependent on grants from foreign foundations. However, the number of viable NGOs is growing thanks to the increasing interest of national businesses in public initiatives as a means to promote both their image and business interests.

Independent Media

1997	1998	1999	2001	2002	2003	2004	2005	2006
4.50	4.75	5.00	5.25	5.50	5.50	5.50	4.75	3.75

Substantial progress in the area of media freedom may be considered the most evident achievement of Ukraine since the change of regime. Citizens are currently enjoy wide-ranging pluralism in both electronic and print media. Governmental censorship, known in the past as *temniki* (governmental instructions designed to control the content of media broadcasts), was canceled even before the new government took power. In fact, media freedom appeared as an immediate and natural outcome of the Orange Revolution itself, rather than the product of government policy. Considering the policies of Ukraine's new leadership, not enough has been done to make these positive changes irreversible.

On March 3, 2005, the Parliament adopted a new Law on the National Council on TV and Radio Broadcasting, prepared by the parliamentary Committee on Freedom of Speech and Information. The main features of the law are reduced grounds for the dismissal of council members to guarantee their independence; abolishment of the rotating membership procedure; election of the council chairman by its members, along with curtailing the chairman's powers; and new means to impose sanctions on TV and radio outlets for noncompliance with legislation.

The new civil code, adopted in January 2003, includes a number of provisions relating to freedom of expression and information. However, some of the new rules were poorly drafted. Among the most problematic aspects of the new civil code is Article 277, section 3, which states that "negative information published about a person is considered untrue." "Negative information" is to be understood as any form of criticism or description of a person in a negative light. This provision was not in active use in the courts in 2005, but it could be applied in the future to limit media freedom.

Many regional and local TV and radio stations and newspapers remain in the hands of state bodies and administrations. Public TV, despite numerous declarations and promises, has not yet been established. Despite efforts of NGOs, a Law on Public TV and Broadcasting failed to pass in the Parliament in the second reading in November. A majority of the president's party faction, Our Ukraine, as well as smaller pro-Yushchenko factions did not vote for it. According to leading media expert Natalia Ligachova, the president does not have sufficient political will to facilitate the creation of public TV, at least before the 2006 elections, which was proved by the appointment of conservative Vitaly Dokalenko as chief of the National TV Company of Ukraine.[4] Some representatives of the new leadership continue to view media as the authorities' "resource" and advocate preservation of state control over media outlets.

Liquidation of the administration publication *Presydentsky Visnyk*, established by Kuchma, was the only example of the state leaving the media market. State ownership of media is nonetheless supported by the State Committee (a different body from the National Council mentioned earlier) on TV and Radio Broadcasting, still chaired by Kuchma appointee Ivan Chyzh.

Nationwide TV channels in most cases provide balanced news coverage, and representatives of ruling parties as well as the opposition have equal access to media. According to available monitoring data, opposition leaders are frequent guests on TV. Ratings of positive and negative information on TV detect that more criticism is addressed to the president and other officials than to opposition leaders.[5] There were no known cases of punishment or pressure on journalists for their investigative activities.

Most nationwide media are private, and none has been reprivatized in favor of people close to Yushchenko after the regime change, despite the fact that most belong to the former Kuchma entourage. At the same time, the Ukrainian media sphere still lacks substantial reforms and restructuring. Most media are owned by leading financial and industrial groups, which means those outlets can be used as a tool of political and economic "wars" within the country, especially during election campaigns. As noted in the Parliamentary Assembly of the Council of Europe report, "An implicit monopoly of the broadcast media market might jeopardize the independence and political impartiality of TV channels on the eve of the parliamentary elections."[6]

The media advertising market is growing slowly, which restricts the development of an independent media sector separate from "big business." Some new independent media projects emerged as a result of growing Western investment in Ukrainian media.

Thanks to the Internet, traditional media have lost their "privileged" role as the only promoters and purveyors of free information (such as during the Kuchma regime). The Ukrainian audience has expanded for the numerous Internet newspapers and portals. In 2005, the Ukrainian Internet audience increased by 18 percent, with a total of 7 million users (both regular and infrequent), which is about 15 percent of the population. Internet media proved to be efficient mediators between politics and society. At the same time, a number of "dirty" Internet projects were launched to operate black PR campaigns – web sites used in order to spread disinformation, false rumors and evident misperceptions about political opponents without any possibilities for their organizers to be punished – especially in the run-up to the March 2006 elections.

Local Democratic Governance

1997	1998	1999	2001	2002	2003	2004	2005	2006
n/a	n/a	n/a	n/a	n/a	n/a	n/a	5.25	5.25

In 2005, a new version of administration and territorial reform was initiated, including reforms of local government. The previous scheme for local governance featured a four-level administrative territorial hierarchy: Autonomous Republic of Crimea (ARC), *oblasts* (24), and cities with *oblast* status – Kyiv and Sevastopol; *raions* (*oblasts'* districts) and cities with *raion* status; cities; and villages and townships. Each *raion* is divided into a number of local councils (village or small-town councils).

Local governance is represented by a dual system of authorities: state administration and a self-governance council. Heads of the executive in the *oblasts* and *raions* are appointed by the president. Top executives of cities and the heads of local councils are elected by citizens. The divisions among bodies at different levels are not precise, and some administrative bodies – such as urban communities, village councils, and township councils – are not prescribed in the Constitution.

According to the dynamics of past years, there is a tendency to shift power to favor centralized local governance – that is, moving the powers and finances of self-governance gradually to executive local bodies and *oblast* and *raion* state administrations. As a result, the functions and resources of self-government bodies are almost fully occupied by state local administrations, which a priori cannot represent local community interests. Local self-government councils lack real powers and financial resources, and complicated interrelations between self-governance and state administrations block the path to transformation of the whole governance system in Ukraine.

This existing system of local governance is centralized, from the *oblast*, to the *raion*, to the local council (of the town or village). That extended chain from the state causes low efficiency and poor management at the local governance level. There are administrative imbalances among *oblasts*, leading to substantial social, economic, and territorial disproportions. These certainly comment on the inefficiency and inequality of the current administrative system.

Attempts to reform the administrative system have occurred in past years, and in April 2005 an administration and territorial reform was presented by Vice Prime Minister Roman Bezsmertny. This reform featured a revised division of powers between state administration and self-governance bodies, shifting powers to the lower bodies; changes in budget constitutions and spending; and redistribution of taxes according to new territorial designations. The reform's main principles are decentralization, distributing power and authority to lower levels, deregulation, and subsidiarity. The final stage of the reform's implementation provides a possibility for self-sufficient self-government bodies with wide powers and financial resources to address the needs of citizens.

The reform was expected to be realized through amendments to the Concept on the Administrative Reform (adopted in 1998), adoption of new laws, 4,000 subordinate acts, and constitutional amendments. Eight basic laws were drafted and debated in 2005 – the Law on Territorial Order of Ukraine, Law on Local Self-Government of Gromadas, Law on Local Self-Government of Raions, and Law on Local Self-Government of Oblasts – as well as an alteration of the Law on Local State Administrations, Budget, and Tax Regulations. Adoption of the Law on Territorial Order of Ukraine was crucial to starting the reform. It was presented in mid-April 2005 and received wide discussion throughout Ukraine.

The draft Law on Territorial Order of Ukraine stipulated the creation of a three-level administrative order: region-*raion-gromada*. The *gromada* (community) is the basic level created by uniting two or more settlements with no fewer than 5,000 inhabitants. A *raion* joins several *gromadas* with no fewer than 70,000 inhabitants. Raions can also be cities (with no fewer than 70,000 inhabitants). A region unifies standard *raions* and city-*raions*. These will include the current *oblasts*, ARC, and city-regions with no fewer than 750,000 inhabitants (Kharkiv, Odesa, Lviv, Donetsk, Dnipropetrovsk, Zaporizha, Kyiv, and Sevastopol). Altogether, there will be 33 regions. *Gromadas* will occupy the central position in the local governance system of Ukraine. According to these new authorities, the budget will also be redistributed in their favor.

Along with the new territorial and administrative order, a revised system of state governance for taxes, budgets, and municipalities is being developed. According to preliminary evaluations of state statistical bodies, the ongoing cost of reform could reach 1.3 million UAH (around US$260,000).

Major obstacles to this reform concern its implementation and timing, the latter being the more important point. Roman Bezsmertny insisted on implementing the reform before the parliamentary elections, which will take place simultaneously with local elections on March 26, 2006 – or, alternatively, to separate them and hold local elections afterward. Bezsmertny's arguments, however, were not considered by the Parliament, and the reform enactment and implementation were postponed until after the 2006 parliamentary and local elections.

Another local government reform is connected to draft Law #3207-1 on constitutional amendments. It was adopted in the first reading on December 8, 2004, and sent to the Constitutional Court for an opinion. The draft law stipulates preserving state administrations at the regional level – *oblasts*, the cities of Kyiv and Sevastopol – but abolishing them at the *raion* level and introducing executive bodies at the *raion* and *oblast* councils. Conceptually, the draft law is moving in the right direction of endowing regional administrations with additional authorities, but at the same time the proposed system could lead to an imbalance and weakening of the local governance system. Also, owing to the pressure to prepare a quick draft, the text is imperfect and poorly written. On September 13, 2005, the draft law was announced by the Constitutional Court as being in conformity with the Constitution. The law had not been adopted at the end of 2005.

On September 8, 2005, the Parliament adopted a new statute amending the Law on Status of Deputies of Local Councils to introduce immunity from criminal prosecution for local deputies. On October 6, 2005, the president signed the law but simultaneously put in a request to the Constitutional Court to review its constitutionality. If the law is not suspended by the Constitutional Court before the parliamentary elections of 2006, it could hamper the democratic character of the election campaign. First, immunity status of local officials does not meet democratic principles; second, and widely discussed in Ukraine, this will pave the way for criminal activities at the local level; third, this will substantially raise the presence of "black money" in elections.

Judicial Framework and Independence

1997	1998	1999	2001	2002	2003	2004	2005	2006
3.75	4.00	4.50	4.50	4.75	4.50	4.75	4.25	4.25

The Constitution of Ukraine, adopted in 1996, protects freedom of expression, freedom of conscience and religion, freedom of association, and business and property rights. Constitutional reforms in 2004 did not touch that basic part of the law. However, proper and sufficient implementation by state bodies, including law enforcement bodies, is obviously lacking. Law enforcement bodies and police selectively respect fundamental political, civil, and human rights, and equality before the law remains doubtful.

Since October 2005, the Constitutional Court of Ukraine has lacked a quorum and, therefore, has had no authority to consider cases. The judges' congress and the president have appointed new judges according to their quotas, but the Parliament has not; the Constitutional Court was still sidelined at the end of 2005. The Parliament's position is rooted in the fear that once the Court restores a quorum, political forces will find that the constitutional changes of December 2004 are unconstitutional. A lack of a quorum in 2005 was the reason the Court could not consider the motion on the constitutionality of the presidential decree on the extended powers of the National Council for Security and Defense, as well as the president's pleading on the immunity of local council deputies.

The principle of equality before the law is still flouted in Ukraine. The prosecution of 2004 election violations is a prominent example in this respect. Among 1,218 criminal cases opened by the Office of the Prosecutor General as of August 2005, 526 cases are considered high-profile and involve directors of large state enterprises or public officials, starting from the heads of *raion* state administrations. However, the potential violations by the highest officials involved in the elections are not being prosecuted.

Generally, the judiciary is considered one of the most corrupt bodies of the state. This is attributed to a score of legal, management, financial, and political reasons, including lack of full independence from the executive (be it financial, technical, or staffing), appointment of judges by the president, prejudiced activities of the High Judicial Council of Ukraine, and widespread bribery among judges caused by low wages. Unfortunately, not much occurred in 2005 to change this state of affairs. In May 2005, the Commission on Reform of the Judicial System, led by Petro Poroshenko, was created under the auspices of the National Council for Security and Defense. After Poroshenko's dismissal in September amid a corruption scandal, discussion of the commission's activities in 2005 was slated for the beginning of 2006 under new council head Anatoliy Kinakh.

Currently, the president of any court (except the Supreme Court and Constitutional Court) is appointed by the president of Ukraine. The possibility of indirect influence on judicial decisions by the president prompted a draft amendment to the Law on the Judicial System of Ukraine, submitted to the Parliament in January 2005. It stipulated provisions to transfer the authority to appoint/dismiss presidents of courts (and their deputies) to gatherings of judges of the court upon recommendation of the bodies of judicial self-government and following approval by the Parliament. Although the proposed draft is far from perfect, it would generally provide judges with more independence.

Ukrainian criminal law has inherited the so-called repressive Soviet system. Human rights violations are still occurring in the areas of investigation, access to the judiciary, freedom and rights of advocates, and the conditions of prisons. In 2005, NGOs active in the human rights arena as well as independent experts and legal practitioners declared the need for reforms in this sphere. Unfortunately, there were no substantial breakthroughs in reforming criminal law or criminal procedure in 2005.

Weak procedural safeguards and security before and during detention, including torture, continue to be crucial failings in the Ukrainian penitentiary system. In her June 1, 2005, intermediate report on human rights to the Parliament, Ukrainian ombudsman Nina Karpachova indicated a lack of improvement in this sphere.

The investigation of the murder of Georgy Gongadze (a journalist killed in September 2000) remained a sensitive challenge for Ukraine authorities. On March 1, 2005, President Yushchenko announced that three officers of the Ministry of the Interior who allegedly perpetrated the murder had been detained and interrogated. "I can declare here that Gongadze's murder has been solved. The murderers have been detained and are now giving evidence," Yushchenko said. As was reported later, police arrested three alleged direct suspects in the murder (Colonel Mykola Protasov, Colonel Valery Kostenko, and Oleksandr Popovych) who, according to Prosecutor General Svyatoslav Piskun, have confessed to premeditated murder. However, those who masterminded the crime have not yet been charged. Owing to the premature and as yet unfulfilled promise of President Yushchenko, as well as an inefficient prosecution, the public is gradually losing hope that justice will prevail in the Gongadze case.

Corruption

1997	1998	1999	2001	2002	2003	2004	2005	2006
n/a	n/a	6.00	6.00	6.00	5.75	5.75	5.75	5.75

Corruption has deep historical roots in Ukrainian society. The fight against corruption and the establishment of a fair government was a prominent theme in the 2004 platform of Maidan. This topic overshadowed Ukraine's political life in 2005, a year marked by corruption despite some efforts to address it.

Yulia Tymoshenko's government program Toward People, adopted by the Parliament in mid-January 2005, stipulated several provisions on fighting corruption. The program called for the dismissal of corrupt state officials, public control on budget spending, adoption of an honor code for officials, and so forth. The government also elaborated a special program on preventing corruption and bribery called Clean Hands and started to develop a new National Anticorruption Strategy and Action Plan. On April 1, the Cabinet of Ministers adopted a state program for 2005-2006 called "Contraband-Stop!". During the first months of its implementation, budget revenue from the levy of import duties had grown substantially. On November 18, the president signed a decree on high-priority measures for making the economy more transparent and fighting corruption. The plan stipulates civil monitoring of corruption in state authorities at all levels and the publication of results. Despite a substantial number of anticorruption regulations, these programs have not taken a systematic approach or articulated an overall long-term strategy but, rather, have operated in chaotic fashion with strong internal resistance.

During the so-called oil, meat, and sugar crises of spring and summer 2005, the government relied on an administrative, rather than a market, regulation of the country's economy. It imposed a price ceiling on goods, which contrary to expectations caused further price hikes and fed corruption in these spheres.

On July 1, a new Law on State Registration of Juridical Persons and Individuals came into force. With its "one window" registration plan for new businesses and individual entrepreneurs, this rather difficult process was substantially simplified and sped up. It also significantly narrowed openings for corruption among authorities involved in this procedure.

On November 18, the president signed a decree entitled On Priority Tasks on Deshadowing Economy and Fighting Corruption,[7] which among other features elaborates "corruption" as a judicial term, provides a legal definition for "conflict of interest," improves procedures of income and property declaration by state officials and their family members, limits state interference in business activities, and legalizes past income without proper taxation.

Despite certain efforts in 2005, an effective countervailing system to prevent the merger of politics and business was not introduced. On the contrary, prominent representatives of Yushchenko's entourage – Petro Poroshenko (former secretary of the National Council for Security and Defense), Oleksandr Tretjakov (former first assistant to the president), and Mykola Martynenko (head of the Our Ukraine parliamentary faction) – were accused by Oleksandr Zinchenko (former state secretary appointed by Yushchenko) of corruption and illegal lobbying of personal business interests. The accusations caused a crisis in Ukraine in September, leading to the so-called zero variant, in which President Yushchenko dismissed the government of Tymoshenko and accused persons individually.

These accusations had an ambiguous impact on Ukraine's political environment. On the one hand, the scandal demonstrated significant improvements in the transparency of power in Ukraine. Such a situation could not have existed in Kuchma's era of "mutual solidarity" among high officials. On the other hand, it has ultimately unbalanced the emerging political system of the new Ukraine and could further weaken Yushchenko's team in the 2006 parliamentary elections. This scandal substantially deepened spreading public disappointment in the new authorities, who have proved not to be a consolidated political team and are marred by the same corruption that infected the previous regime.

The process of job placement at governmental bodies still lacks transparency and public accountability. There is no clear distinction between political nominees and a professional civil service. Although many official bodies advertise job vacancies, including on their Web sites, this policy is mostly pro forma, with positions going to those candidates with personal connections to high-ranking officials rather than to applicants with the best qualifications and experience.

Law enforcement authorities, including the Office of the Prosecutor General, applied the law selectively. Accusations of corruption against officials in the inner circle of Yushchenko's entourage did not materialize into official, transparent investigations. As a result, those individuals, though dismissed from their positions, were neither officially charged nor fully cleared of suspicion.

In 2005, allegations of corruption were the frequent focus of the media. At the same time, a distinction should be made between corruption as a social phenomenon and abuse of corruption allegations by the mass media. Moreover, the mass media serve as an instrument in political battles. Cases of mass media abuses in this regard will no doubt become more frequent in the run-up to the March 2006 elections.

Although the Ukrainian public is highly intolerant of corruption among high officials or "oligarchs," they frequently consider "small" corruption as an integral part of the Ukrainian political and social culture. Petty corruption is still seen by ordinary citizens as a natural way to overcome bureaucratic procedures, which appear to be obstacles to economic and other activities. At the same time, the Orange Revolution significantly raised the public's understanding of the relationship between personal dignity, government transparency, and the pervasive and negative effects of corruption.

Oleksandr Sushko is the director and Olena Prystayko is a project director at the Center for Peace, Conversion, and Foreign Policy of Ukraine.

[1] Honoring of Obligations and Commitments by Ukraine, Parliamentary Assembly, Council of Europe, Doc. 10676, September 19, 2005.

[2] NATO-Ukraine Action Plan, NATO, November 2002, www.nato.int/docu/basictxt/b021122a.htm.

[3] Honoring of Obligations and Commitments by Ukraine, Parliamentary Assembly, Council of Europe, Doc. 10676, September 19, 2005.

[4] Nataliya Ligachova, "President Doesn't Have Political Will to Establish Public TV," Telekrirtika, October 28, 2005.

[5] Ukrainska Pravda, www.pravda.com.ua/news/2005/10/25/34891.htm.

[6] Honoring of Obligations and Commitments by Ukraine, Parliamentary Assembly, Council of Europe, Doc. 10676, September 19, 2005.

[7] President of Ukraine, www.president.gov.ua/documents/3509.html.

Uzbekistan

Capital: Tashkent
Population: 26.2 million
GNI/capita: $450
Ethnic Groups: Uzbek (80%), Russian (6%), Tajik
(5%), Kazakh (3%), other (6%)

Nations in Transit Ratings and Averaged Scores

	1997	1998	1999	2001	2002	2003	2004	2005	2006
Electoral Process	6.25	6.50	6.50	6.75	6.75	6.75	6.75	6.75	6.75
Civil Society	6.50	6.50	6.50	6.50	6.75	6.50	6.50	6.50	7.00
Independent Media	6.50	6.50	6.50	6.75	6.75	6.75	6.75	6.75	7.00
Governance *	6.00	6.25	6.25	6.00	6.00	6.25	6.25	n/a	n/a
National Democratic Governance	n/a	n/a	n/a	n/a	n/a	n/a	n/a	6.50	7.00
Local Democratic Governance	n/a	n/a	n/a	n/a	n/a	n/a	n/a	6.25	6.75
Judicial Framework and Independence	6.50	6.50	6.50	6.50	6.50	6.50	6.50	6.25	6.75
Corruption	n/a	n/a	6.00	6.00	6.00	6.00	6.00	6.00	6.50
Democracy Score	6.35	6.45	6.38	6.42	6.46	6.46	6.46	6.43	6.82

* With the 2005 edition, Freedom House introduced seperate analysis and ratings for national democratic governance and local democratic governance to provide readers with more detailed and nuanced analysis of these two important subjects.

NOTE: The ratings reflect the consensus of Freedom House, its academic advisers, and the author of this report. The opinions expressed in this report are those of the author. The ratings are based on a scale of 1 to 7, with 1 representing the highest level of democratic progress and 7 the lowest. The Democracy Score is an average of ratings for the categories tracked in a given year.

The economic and social data on this page were taken from the following sources:
GNI/capita, Population: *World Development Indicators 2006* (Washington, D.C.: World Bank, 2006).
Ethnic Groups: *CIA World Factbook 2006* (Washington, D.C.: Central Intelligence Agency, 2006).

EXECUTIVE SUMMARY

The president of Uzbekistan, Islom Karimov, began 2005 with a promise to rid the country of "alien ideologies." In a January 28 speech before the first joint session of the legislative assembly and the newly convened Senate, Karimov promised that "democracy and various so-called open society models" along with other "alien" ideas espoused by nongovernmental organizations (NGOs) would not be tolerated.[1] In the speech, Karimov linked NGOs and human rights activists to "revolutions and fundamentalism."[2] The speech was an inauspicious way to begin the year and augured the repressive actions that came later. By the end of 2005, several international NGOs had been suspended or evicted. Still others were on trial facing a similar fate. Leading journalist organizations were removed or had to suspend their activities. Worse still, by year's end several of the most prominent human rights defenders in the country were under arrest, with some being held incommunicado for a period of months. Political opposition remained banned, and the state more fully exerted its control over the media and Internet technology. The speech even revealed Karimov's foreign policy plans for the coming year by praising countries like Russia and China and omitting the United States from a list of potential allies. The speech's importance was not lost on some executive agencies as by midyear university students were tested by being required to recite it. Despite the speech's prominence in signaling the government's policy, the year 2005 will be remembered for the events at Andijan on May 13, when unknown hundreds of protesters were massacred and detained without trial by government troops.

Uzbekistan has not dealt well with the transition from Soviet republic to independent country. In economic terms, annual per capita income in Uzbekistan is US$460 and in the region exceeds only Tajikistan,[3] a country that just recently overcame a civil war. Its economic growth, however, lags far behind that of its neighbors. Where its neighbors have embarked on some modest programs of economic liberalization, Uzbekistan has responded to the challenge of independence by clamping down on border trade, escalating licensing fees, and more rigidly enforcing internal registration controls. Consequently, the World Bank ranks Uzbekistan 138th out of 155 countries for ease of doing business.[4] Uzbekistan's neighbors fare better in the survey. In addition to limiting business and enforcing registration requirements, Uzbekistan has limited freedom of expression and political dissent since independence. The administration has stridently resisted reforms that would devolve presidential power to other branches of government. Since independence, Uzbekistan has also had to confront Islamic fundamentalism. The mixture of all these elements – oppressive economic regulations, severe political repression, and the threat of Islamic fundamentalism – contributed to the events of Andijan and continue to shape Uzbekistan today.

National Democratic Governance. Although Uzbekistan's Constitution contains language that promises the separation of powers and individual rights, in both law and fact the president is able to control all branches of government and through this power is able to dominate the country. The Constitution subordinates individual rights to legislative enactments and presidential decrees and provides virtually no protection for these rights. As the president's authority is able to trump individual rights, he is also able to control the other branches of government. All judges owe their position to the president and serve for limited terms, and regional judges can be dismissed at will. Through various constitutional provisions, the president is able to control speech and decide which political groups are legal and which are not. Cumulatively, citizens have no effective recourse against state authority. In 2005, the full force of the state stifled dissent throughout the country and turned aside all demands for an investigation into one of the worst incidents of state violence in recent years. *Uzbekistan's rating for national democratic governance worsens from 6.50 to 7.00 owing to the centralization of power, the lack of public accountability, and the ability of the executive to dominate all areas of Uzbek society.*

Electoral Process. No national elections were held in 2005. Nevertheless, there has been no effort to reform any of the systemic failings that have caused every election in Uzbekistan since independence to be judged neither free nor fair. Restrictions on political speech and criminal liabilities for parties that are not registered have crushed dissent and prohibited the development of meaningful alternatives to the current regime. Owing to the onerous nature of election laws and limits on petitions, private citizens have neither the means to express dissatisfaction through elections nor the possibility to work for reform through the political process. *Uzbekistan's electoral process rating remains unchanged at 6.75.*

Civil Society. In the wake of the Andijan events, no sector of Uzbek society has faced a higher level of government harassment, intimidation, and oppression than civil society. Numerous human rights defenders have been arrested and some held incommunicado for months at a time. Human rights defenders who have not been charged with a crime have often been detained for short periods or have been placed under house arrest. Several international NGOs were suspended during 2005 or faced the threat of suspension. The government also stepped up its propaganda campaign in universities and clamped down more vigorously on civil society organizations. *Uzbekistan's civil society rating worsens from 6.50 to 7.00 owing to the severe level of repression directed against human rights defenders, NGOs, and their employees and to the intensified campaign of personality worship instigated by the authorities.*

Independent Media. Prior to 2005, local media in Uzbekistan faced severe restrictions. Throughout the course of 2005, the government of Uzbekistan launched a "smear campaign" against international media that resulted in the expulsion of the BBC, Radio Liberty, Internews, Forum 18, and other groups. Journalists were arrested and their families threatened. Moreover, the government increased its controls over the Internet, often blocking Russian- and Uzbek-language Web sites based in other countries, and restricted programming from foreign news organizations being made available in Uzbekistan. *Owing to the arrest of several journalists, the harassment and/or arrest of individuals who published statements critical of the regime, the number of criminal libel actions brought against journalists and activists, and the pervasive state control over all forms of media, Uzbekistan's rating for independent media worsens from 6.75 to 7.00.*

Local Democratic Governance. An uninterrupted line of authority consolidates the president's power and dominance over every region of Uzbekistan. Owing to the structure of local government, local governors (*khokims*) owe their position, either directly or one step removed, to the president's largesse. Consequently, citizens have little recourse to appeal abuses by the national executive when their local officials owe their position to the president. Further, local opposition is prevented from forming bona fide political parties because of the same registration requirements that hobble the development of national political parties. Finally, in the wake of Andijan, local authorities have joined the national authorities in targeting potential dissenters and members of civil society. *Because of the failure of local authorities to subject themselves to democratic reforms and because of their increased harassment of potential sources of opposition, Uzbekistan's local democratic governance rating worsens from 6.25 to 6.75.*

Judicial Framework and Independence. If a trial is power submitting itself to reason[5], the government of Uzbekistan held reason in abeyance and captured the judicial process. The authorities conducted several trials that featured large numbers of defendants–often without opening the proceedings to the public. Several defendants were held incommunicado for months at a time. Even when petitioned, judges ignored the pleas of family members and defense attorneys to visit those held in secret locations. Judges did not object to the authorities holding large numbers of citizens under the auspices of administrative or witness detentions, all the while subjecting these citizens to intense questioning without benefit of counsel or independent observation. The financial well-being of judges is dependent on the executive, as they serve for limited terms at the pleasure of the president. Judges can make few decisions in the absence of executive scrutiny. Even during civil trials, judges are observed by representatives of the Procuracy, an executive agency with the power to bring criminal charges against judges who defame the judiciary or violate the law in the course of a trial. These factors have enabled the executive to direct the judicial process. *Uzbekistan's rating for judicial framework and independence worsens from 6.25 to 6.75, given the government's refusal to provide a remedy to violations of fundamental rights against citizens by state officials, the failure of judges to protest the executive's use of their courtrooms to harass and persecute those who question the regime, and the power of the executive to appoint, dismiss, or punish judges.*

Corruption. Extensive regulations of economic activity have not only stifled economic growth, but created abundant opportunities for civil servants to augment their meager incomes. Citizens must have permission from the state to live or work in a particular location or to work in a specific field and must seek the state's permission to leave the country. Entrepreneurs must comply with a slew of regulations–many of which are not even published. Failure to be in compliance, even on trivial matters, can result in severe penalties. Consequently, the pressure on individuals to pay for the favor of civil servants is tremendous. Bribery and other offenses are serious crimes in Uzbekistan, but prosecutions tend to focus on political dissenters rather than on those who warrant punishment for their venality. Moreover, the president's family and senior members of the government continued their practice of using state power to gain financial reward. *Owing to Uzbekistan's continued failure to reform its regulatory scheme, the enactment of additional regulations through internal decrees, the failure to liberalize registration requirements on individuals, and the selective enforcement of these regulations, Uzbekistan's rating for corruption worsens from 6.00 to 6.50.*

Outlook for 2006. Civil society will continue to be in peril in 2006, as the government has not slackened its efforts to persecute any source of dissent. Indeed, the expulsion of many international NGOs from the country may increase the government's confidence in attacking civil society members because it may believe that its actions will be less scrutinized. No national elections are scheduled until 2007, when Uzbekistan will vote for its president. Karimov, currently limited to two terms, will finish his second term in 2007. Uzbekistan has not been averse to amending its Constitution, however, and may therefore waive or alter the presidential term limit provision. Accordingly, 2006 will witness either a movement to allow Karimov to stay in power beyond 2007 or the selection of a successor. Regardless of how this choice is resolved, the persecution of democratic opposition, the severe constraints on economic activity, and the state's willingness to use armed force combined with its power to dole out economic benefits to supporters reflect a system that will prevent meaningful reform from taking place in 2006.

MAIN REPORT

National Democratic Governance

1997	1998	1999	2001	2002	2003	2004	2005	2006
n/a	n/a	n/a	n/a	n/a	n/a	n/a	6.50	7.00

Uzbekistan's Constitution provides the legal framework for the executive branch to dominate the country. The individual rights enumerated in the Constitution are made subordinate to legislative enactments or executive decrees. General endorsements of international norms, such as Article 11's pledge to honor the doctrine of separation of powers, are undercut by several articles that give the president the power to rule by decree (Article 94), the power to dismiss the legislature (Article 95), the power to limit speech and assembly in accordance with security needs (Articles 29 and 33), and the ability to appoint and dismiss local and regional judges at will (Article 93[11]).[6]

Several articles are key to giving the president insuperable power to dominate the state. Article 94 of the Constitution gives the president the power to issue national decrees. The Constitution does not limit the president's power to issue decrees either in substance or in duration; consequently, the president's decrees have the full force and effect of law.

The president's decree power enables the executive to limit or curtail the individual rights set forth in the Constitution. Article 25 of the Constitution promises that individuals cannot be taken into custody "except on legal grounds." Article 28 guarantees freedom of movement "except as specified by law." Freedom of assembly and the right to petition the government can similarly be limited or denied on the basis of law. Therefore, the president's decree power combined with the administrative capacity of the executive branch can substantially circumscribe or prevent the realization of these rights.

The president is able to appoint the senior leadership for each executive agency. He is also able to direct the activities of each agency through the issuance of internal decrees. These decrees need not be made available to the public, even though the decrees control how the various executive agencies interact with the public.

These internal decrees often have a substantial impact on the governmental structure of Uzbekistan. By following various internal decrees, executive agencies have been able to detain or hold under house arrest people they deem to pose a risk of committing a crime.[7] Often these decrees create complicated licensing regimes for various activities such as prison monitoring by private citizens or forming NGOs. Since these decrees are not shared with the public, citizens have virtually no chance of meeting the licensing regulations stipulated in them. Nevertheless, individuals or organizations that conduct activities in violation of undisclosed internal decrees face possible sanctions by the authorities.

The president's unfettered power to appoint and dismiss all local and regional judges under Article 93(11) transforms the relationship between the president and the judges to that of principal and agent. Consequently, citizens even in remote courts stand not before a neutral judge, but in front of someone representing the power of the presidency. Moreover, through the agency of the Procuracy, a quasi-judicial executive ministry, the president has the power to send a representative to every court proceeding. Therefore, the executive is able to monitor any trial while maintaining the power to dismiss any judge.

Executive agencies are able to control even the routine aspects of daily life. Article 28 of the Constitution guarantees freedom of movement, but like so many other rights, it can be obviated by legislative enactment. In Uzbekistan, the law restricting freedom of movement requires every citizen to obtain permission from the state to live in a particular location. Every citizen must have a *propiska*, the document evincing this permission, or be in violation of the law. Roadblocks, frequent police checks, and the necessity of dealing with the state on a regular basis mandate that citizens have this document at the ready. The *propiska* represents the power and willingness of the state to regulate and monitor even the minute habits of its citizens. Therefore, the constitutional structure of Uzbekistan enables the president to rule without obstruction and regulate the lives of individuals whether they are engaged in mundane activities or in major political events.

The Constitution places control of the military in the president's office as well. Even following the events of Andijan, there has been no basis to assume that the president's authority is questioned by the military. Of the many controversies surrounding Andijan, there is no report, either from the Uzbek authorities or from independent observers, that anyone doubted the president's control over the military's action in the city. The lines of authority that stretch from the president to senior military leaders are not well delineated, but there is little doubt that the president is able to direct the military's actions.

Although the country is rife with rumors of possible political turmoil, little has happened since Andijan to give substance to those rumors, and little seems to threaten President Islom Karimov's hold on power. Nevertheless, there has been substantial reallocation of internal resources among some of the executive agencies. After Andijan, the Ministry of Interior had many of its personnel transferred to the National Security Service. Karimov has offered little explanation for this transfer of resources. Likewise, he has had little to say regarding the resignation of the Minister of Interior, Zokirjon Almatov, in December. Regardless, this transfer of resources and minor cabinet reshuffle have not appeared to diminish the president's power in any way.

Terrorist groups are reportedly active in Uzbekistan. The threat posed by such groups prompted the U.S. embassy to evacuate nonessential personnel during the month of June. Fortunately, no attack occurred. Although the government of Uzbekistan still blames the loss of life in Andijan on terrorist groups, its rhetoric in this regard is so extreme, such as contending that the United States is funding extremist groups, that its pronouncements in this area are not credible.

Despite Karimov's lengthy rule, he has yet to provide an adequate answer to the fundamental question of why the citizens should recognize his government. He has not won any competitive election and owes his position to his success within the Soviet bureaucracy. Perhaps realizing that the absence of an answer to this fundamental question is a cause for domestic insecurity, in 2005 Karimov sought alliances with countries that would not question the legitimacy of his domestic policies.

During a January 28, 2005, speech, Karimov announced his intention to be allied more closely with countries that have strong or even authoritarian executives rather than those that embrace democracy and limited government.[8] In his speech, Karimov pledged closer cooperation with the Commonwealth of Independent States and the Shanghai Cooperation Group–a hitherto dormant organization comprising other Central Asian countries, China, and Russia. In January, when

Karimov made the speech, the United States (which still had an active military base in Uzbekistan) called Uzbekistan a strategic partner in the war against terror. Karimov, however, made no mention of the United States as a potential ally in his January speech–a telling omission. In July, largely at Karimov's instigation, the Shanghai Cooperation Group met and issued a decree demanding that the United States set a timetable to vacate its bases in Central Asia. Shortly after the meeting of the group, Uzbekistan ordered the United States to abandon its base within 180 days. Cumulatively, not only has Karimov quelled domestic dissent, he has through his choice of allies demonstrated his intolerance toward criticism even from other states. The government's policies in 2005 prove that it continues to embrace a system in which the executive dominates the country, dissent is not tolerated, and little prospect of credible reform exists.

Spotlight on Andijan

Andijan is a city located in the Ferghana Valley, an area of eastern Uzbekistan that extends into Kyrgyzstan.[9] Trade has always been a part of the tradition of the region. In June 2004, a group of 23 independent businessmen who lived in the region were arrested for being part of a group called Akromia. Although the principles of Akromia are under dispute, there is no question that the populace of Andijan regarded the arrest of the businessmen as part of an effort to punish them for being successful and creating an independent power base in the region. The 23 businessmen were popular in Andijan in part because they reputedly paid higher wages than other employers in the region. They openly embraced Islam and reportedly conducted their business affairs in a manner that was in accordance with their religious beliefs. The government considered the group extremist and arrested them on charge of religious extremism.

The trial of the Akromia members began in February 2005 at the district courthouse in Andijan. By early May, growing protests were being held before the courthouse. On May 11 and May 12, perhaps more than 1,000 local residents were engaged in the protest outside the courtroom. Events in the early morning hours of May 13 become less clear. According to various sources, a group of armed men stormed the prison in Andijan where the Akromia defendants were held. By daybreak, large numbers of protesters had returned to areas near the courthouse to continue the protest. Witnesses report that the protesters were greeted by Uzbek military forces firing indiscriminately into the crowd. The government maintains that the military fired only at the armed men who stormed the prison.

Government troops eventually took control of central Andijan by the afternoon of May 13. The government maintains that "only" 169 people died on May 13 and no civilians were killed by the military. Witnesses to the event maintain that many hundreds died. Lists of the missing compiled by residents far exceed the figure of 169 given by the government. Numerous witnesses interviewed by Western journalists expressed concern that relatives that had disappeared were among the dead in the square. Many Western journalists reported that they were brought to sites containing freshly dug mass graves.[10]

Following the events of May 13, the international community called for an independent investigation. By the end of 2005, the government of Uzbekistan had rejected all such requests.

Soon after May 13, 2005, the government of Uzbekistan held the United States, international NGOs, the international media, and human rights activists responsible for the slaughter. Numerous articles published in official media accused NGOs of sponsoring terrorism. The government of Uzbekistan stated that the United States was trying to establish a caliphate in Central Asia by funneling support to Islamic extremists through NGOs.[11] The chief prosecutor in the first trial of those accused of crimes related to the Andijan incident repeated the government's theory in his opening statement.[12]

The arguments and conspiracy theories set forth by the government of Uzbekistan to explain the events of Andijan are plainly not credible. The administration has also rejected all calls for an investigation that would provide reliable information regarding that which transpired at Andijan. Furthermore, it has pursued a severe crackdown on civil society, NGOs, and political dissenters under the auspices of defending its sovereignty and combating "alien ideologies." By year's end, Karimov's government was even more hostile to reform than it had been when he gave his January 28 speech.

Electoral Process

1997	1998	1999	2001	2002	2003	2004	2005	2006
6.25	6.50	6.50	6.75	6.75	6.75	6.75	6.75	6.75

The most recent parliamentary elections were held in December 2004 and were judged neither free nor fair by the Organization for Security and Cooperation in Europe. The Constitution initially limited the presidency to a term of five years; however, in 2002 the Constitution was amended to lengthen the term of the president to seven years. The next scheduled election for the presidency is in 2007.

Only five political parties are registered in Uzbekistan, all expressly supportive of the president. The unregistered parties either failed one of the substantive requirements of the registration law (for example, by being affiliated with a religious belief) or failed to follow all of the various registration requirements. All unregistered parties face prosecution for carrying out their activities.

In addition to controlling the registration of parties, the executive is able to maintain strict control over political discourse in the country through its power to regulate speech. Article 29 of the Constitution gives the executive the power to prevent speech critical of the "constitutional order," and Article 67 gives the president the duty to ensure that all mass media comply with their obligation to "bear the trustworthiness of information in the prescribed manner." Consequently, the president is able to eliminate political opposition by denying registration, or (as has been Karimov's wont) the president can categorize political opposition as a threat to the constitutional order.

An example of the government's persecution of political opposition occurred during the second half of 2005. Opposition leaders formed a group called the Sunshine Coalition. They urged economic liberalization and the devolution of power from the executive to other branches of government. The group was not registered, however, and by October all of the senior leaders of the group, Sanjar Umarov, Nodira Khidoyatova, and Nigora Khidoyatova, were arrested; Umarov and Nodira Khidoyatova were still in custody at year's end.[13] The continued hostility to political opposition indicates that Uzbekistan's disdain for openly contested elections and free political campaigns is likely to continue.

With regard to the legislative branch of the government, the newly commissioned Senate of Uzbekistan, the upper chamber of the legislature, convened for the first time in 2005. The president is able to have a strong influence in the Senate as well. Of the 100 senators, 16 are appointed directly by the president, with the remainder elected.[14] The Senate has not provided a serious challenge to the president, as it is hobbled by the same speech constraints that control political discourse in Uzbekistan.

Citizens who disagree with the positions of the registered political parties have little opportunity to voice their dissent in any meaningful or legal way. The Constitution of Uzbekistan does not enable private citizens to introduce legislation into the Parliament. As an alternative to direct legislative representation, Uzbek law does provide for a referendum-type procedure enabling citizens to comment on laws that have been proposed to the legislature but not enacted. However, the referendum procedure's strict requirements make it impracticable for citizens to express their opinion to their representatives. Referendum legislation requires 5 percent of all eligible voters to sign in favor of the petition. Currently, there are approximately 14 million eligible voters in Uzbekistan. Thus, a successful petition would require the signatures of at least 700,000. Furthermore, the law requires that the signatures be drawn in a proportional manner from around the country. Given the current political situation in Uzbekistan, it is not realistic to expect citizens to gather such national support if the citizens' position is contrary to the state's.

Civil Society

1997	1998	1999	2001	2002	2003	2004	2005	2006
6.50	6.50	6.50	6.50	6.75	6.50	6.50	6.50	7.00

No sector of Uzbek society has been as severely affected by the Andijan events as civil society. Human rights defenders were arrested by the score after Andijan. Few human rights defenders escaped detention of some kind. Many were held for a period of six to eight hours and have since been subject to these short-term detentions numerous times. Many others have been subject to prolonged periods of house arrest. Even more alarming, many have been subject to criminal indictment, held without being able to contact their families, and at times tried and sentenced in secret.

One of the most egregious cases of abuse after Andijan concerns Saidjahon Zaynabitdinov, director of the organization Appealiatsia and a member of the Rapid Reaction Group of human rights activists.[15] Zaynabitdinov covered the trial of the Akromia defendants prior to May 13, 2005, witnessed the events of May 13, and reported them to international media. Shortly after May 13, Zaynabitdinov went to the neighboring Kyrgyz city of Osh to give an interview about Andijan and was arrested upon his return to Uzbekistan on May 21, 2005. As of this writing, no member of his family has been able to see him since his arrest.

The particulars of Zaynabitdinov's case typify the severity of the crackdown against human rights defenders and civil society generally. The crimes he is charged with all relate to speech and not to any action. Zaynabitdinov offered testimony to international media that directly contradicted the official Uzbek version of events. He described the context of the Akromia trial and provided physical evidence that scores of innocent people were killed in the crackdown. For these interviews and for previously published pamphlets, the state charged him with "undermining the constitutional order," slander, and disseminating information harmful to the state.

The irregularities in the case against Zaynabitdinov begin from the outset of his detention. In a pattern that has repeated itself for many human rights defenders, the authorities arrested Zaynabitdinov and did not notify his family or his attorney. Moreover, the charges against him were not clear for several months following his detention.[16] Despite numerous requests from his family, foreign diplomats, and international NGOs, none have been able to meet with Zaynabitdinov since he was initially detained. It is reported that Zaynabitdinov was not tried until January 2006, when he was sentenced to a seven-year prison term.

The arrest of another prominent Uzbek human rights defender, Mutabar Tojibaeva, reveals the government of Uzbekistan's obsession to quash dissent. Tojibaeva is the director of the Fiery Heights human rights organization. She criticized the government over the events in Andijan and publicly called for an impartial investigation of the events of May 13. In the weeks after Andijan, she was detained in several instances for short periods of time. She was also placed under house arrest for a period. During these bouts of detention, the authorities warned her to stop her criticism or face severe penalties. In late September, Tojibaeva gave an interview to Radio Liberty and voiced criticism of the government. On October 8, 2005, Tojibaeva was to fly to Dublin to attend an international human rights conference. Late in the evening of October 7, the authorities arrested her on charges related to the conduct of her private business, a fish farm. The authorities' past conduct toward Tojibaeva and the timing of the arrest reveal the charges to be nothing more than another effort to attack dissent.

In addition to these cases, perhaps as many as 100 less prominent human rights defenders have been arrested and charged with a crime.[17] Aside from the physical detentions, Freedom House has chronicled more than 30 instances of human rights defenders who have been subjected to house arrest. These house detentions can be severe. One human rights defender had a sick infant and was denied permission to obtain medical care for her child. The human rights defender then called an ambulance to treat her child. The authorities guarding her apartment refused to let the ambulance gain entry. As the infant's condition worsened, a brave neighbor was able to take the child to the hospital for treatment.

Many human rights defenders in Uzbekistan are older and suffer medical conditions. Consequently, house detentions that deny them medical care can be life threatening. The incident involving the denial of care to the infant represents the seriousness with which the authorities enforce these detentions.

The authorities' assault on civil society is not confined to human rights defenders. In 2005, the legislature amended Article 157 of the criminal code of Uzbekistan, making it a criminal offense for private citizens to give information or support to international organizations. The authorities used this article to intimidate the local staffs of several NGOs, bluntly informing staff members that if they continued to work for NGOs, they could be sent to jail. The authorities often told staff members that this crime could be obviated if they were to give regular reports to the security services on the internal activities of NGOs.

Over the course of 2005, several NGOs faced severe scrutiny from the authorities. Internews, Radio Liberty, the International Research & Exchanges Board, and Freedom House all faced the prospect of suspension. The violations often concern minor infractions of Uzbek regulations but are vigorously prosecuted nonetheless. Freedom House Uzbekistan's alleged violations included the failure to properly register its logo. After a trial in December, the court issued its decision to suspend Freedom House in January 2006.

In addition to suspending NGOs, the authorities obstructed their work by delaying the processing of visas or by increasing reporting and registration requirements. These and other intimidation tactics against international staff were common during 2005.

Religious groups also face severe constraints. All religious leaders and religious organizations must be registered with the state. Unregistered groups and religious practices that are not sanctioned by the authorities, even if hosted in a private home, are subject to criminal penalties.[18] Uzbekistan is a predominantly Muslim country, where even private religious journeys, such as the Hajj pilgrimage, are controlled by the government.[19]

In addition to controlling the activities of religious groups through the registration process, in 2005 the president issued a decree through the Department of Religion requiring all imams in the country to make a statement during Friday prayers giving thanks to Karimov for his kindness and support. The state's intrusion into the substance of religious worship seems confined so far to Islam.

As with other areas of civil society, the state's presence in education is rather blunt. All university students must take a course entitled National Ideology. During this course, students are taught items that range from the innocuous (that Uzbekistan grows the best fruit and vegetables in the world) to the hagiographic (that Karimov is the wisest person in the world). In the past year, the course has taught students that Uzbekistan's allies are Russia and China and its "greatest adversary" is the United States. The course has incorporated the government's position that the United States was responsible for funding the Islamic extremist groups that precipitated the events at Andijan.

State propaganda has also infiltrated courses that have no connection to state ideology. Students of the World Languages Institute reported that during their final exams in May and June 2005, they were asked to recite or write down in its entirety Karimov's January 28, 2005, speech condemning NGOs. The courses that had this as their final exam ranged from history to foreign language studies.

Academic freedom and scholarly inquiry are severely circumscribed in Uzbekistan. Students who took internships at international organizations such as Freedom House faced intimidation by university authorities and teachers. Several interns were called "terrorists" by their university instructors and told they had to leave the internship immediately. Many interns were summoned to discuss their affiliation with international organizations by university officers and others who identified themselves as officials from the Ministry of Education. They made the interns report on their activities with international organizations, told them that by working for international NGOs they were supporting terrorism, and threatened them with dismissal from the university if they did not either continue their reporting activities or leave the internship.

Cumulatively, these government attacks make it impossible for private citizens to find places of contemplation, solace, or intellectual growth. The traditional arenas where individuals learn, share ideas, or simply seek guidance from peers or elders have either been co-opted by the state or made illegal. Educators and religious leaders must be state actors or violate the law. Organizations that promote individual rights and transparency in government have either been suspended or so encumbered by administrative responsibilities that they have been forced into maintaining a mere presence rather than practicing constructive advocacy.

In this environment, the only groups able to voice authentic criticism of the state are those that operate clandestinely. Traditional civil society groups that celebrate life and individual dignity cannot operate by limiting their message to a few secret whispers and stay true to their mission. Those groups that can spread their message in a clandestine manner have a comparative advantage over traditional civil society organizations. Although the government surely perceives itself as the beneficiary of its policy to subordinate civil society, Islamic fundamentalists are beneficiaries of this repression as well. An analysis of why certain individuals choose to belong to fundamentalist groups is beyond the scope of this report, but in a country where NGOs, academics, religious leaders, and ordinary citizens are silenced, Islamic fundamentalists are well positioned to spread their message. Those individuals who reject both the government and the fundamentalists must therefore find solace within themselves despite the intellectual and spiritual isolation that exists when civil society is under such distress.

Independent Media

1997	1998	1999	2001	2002	2003	2004	2005	2006
6.50	6.50	6.50	6.75	6.75	6.75	6.75	6.75	7.00

In 2005, the government of Uzbekistan launched a severe campaign against journalists both international and domestic. By the end of 2005, Radio Liberty, the BBC, and Internews had to end their presence in the country either because of severe intimidation or because the authorities refused to accredit the press agencies. In October, the Committee to Protect Journalists condemned the harassment and intimidation tactics used by the Uzbek authorities against journalists. The committee called the Uzbek strategy "a smear campaign" to discredit foreign media.[20]

After Andijan, the Uzbek official media aired several television programs and ran several news articles accusing the BBC, Agence France-Presse (AFP), AP, Deutsche Welle, Radio Liberty, and others of conspiring with Islamic extremists to stage the Andijan events and topple the government of Uzbekistan.[21] The Uzbek campaign against journalists carried more impact than mere words. Some of Radio Liberty's staff members and their families were arrested and threatened.[22] BBC staff were similarly threatened, resulting in its decision to shut down its office in the country.[23] A Forum 18 reporter was detained, threatened with criminal charges, and finally deported.[24] These attacks against reporters and the hostility they evinced have made independent reporting in Uzbekistan exceptionally difficult and dangerous.

Strict enforcement of libel laws and the legal obligation of all media to follow their constitutional obligation to ensure the "trustworthiness of information in the prescribed manner"[25] have long eviscerated the independence of media based in Uzbekistan. Those who publish articles critical or skeptical of official accounts often face criminal libel charges. The charges are brought not by the state directly, but by the state-employed reporters who publish the state's version of events.[26]

It is often difficult for private Uzbek citizens to get independent accounts of events in Uzbekistan. Russian- and Uzbek-language Web sites based in neighboring countries are generally blocked by the Uzbek authorities. Web sites such as ferghana.ru, centrasia.ru, and tribune-uz.info that have posted articles critical of Uzbekistan have all at one time or another had their Web sites blocked to residents in Uzbekistan. Nevertheless, technically savvy Uzbeks have been able to access many of these articles by working through other sites that have archived them. This is one area where the government's repressive policies and leaden ways have slowed its own agents' abilities to keep critical information from reaching its people via the Internet. Perhaps aware of its own inefficiency in this sphere, the government has been particularly harsh in suppressing NGOs offering free Internet services to individuals.

The government has had comparatively more success limiting television media. All cable programming is routed through government-controlled entities. During crises, the authorities shut down cable news channels, including both the BBC and CNN. Programs about Andijan aired by foreign media, including programming aired by the Russian television network NTV, have been similarly blocked.

Local Democratic Governance

1997	1998	1999	2001	2002	2003	2004	2005	2006
n/a	n/a	n/a	n/a	n/a	n/a	n/a	6.25	6.75

The Constitution carries the president's power to the local level. Article 104 gives *khokims*, governors of regional and local areas, the power to bind all individuals and organizations under their jurisdiction to local and national rules. The president, through Articles 102 and 93(12), has the ability to nominate and dismiss all regional *khokims*. These regional *khokims* in turn have the power to appoint and dismiss local *khokims*. Consequently, the president is able to extend his control from the national level to the local level, as the position of every *khokim* is contingent on placating the president or currying favor with the regional *khokim*, who must in turn appease the president.

Prior to 2005, the interaction between local government officials and civil society representatives was minimal. After the events that took place in Andijan in May 2005, local authorities joined the national authorities in the persecution of members of civil society.

Local authorities have little possibility of asserting independence. Not only does the president's authority extend directly to the *khokims*, but all of the senior executive agencies have representation in the regions. The local offices of executive authorities must answer to senior leaders in Tashkent. The president's internal decrees that determine much of the executive agencies' conduct bind regional offices as well as the national offices. Citizens in the regions have no more recourse against violations or improper conduct of executive officials than they have in national centers.

In local elections, citizens have no greater choice than they do in national elections; they are limited to choosing candidates from one of the registered parties.

Local officials are instrumental in fulfilling labor quotas for the cotton harvest. Cotton revenue is a main source of income for the government of Uzbekistan, but the process of conducting the harvest and coercing the labor of thousands of young people is carried out almost entirely by local officials.

Local opposition groups that give precedence to local concerns over national concerns, such as groups that promise to give farmers freedom to plant crops of their choice and freedom of land tenure, are often vigorously suppressed by local *khokims* and other authorities. These opposition groups have little opportunity to effect change because of registration requirements, the difficulty of obtaining representation in the legislature, and the onerous referendum process. Consequently, groups that authentically represent local interests soon run afoul of local authorities, who are little more than agents of the national government.

Judicial Framework and Independence

1997	1998	1999	2001	2002	2003	2004	2005	2006
6.50	6.50	6.50	6.50	6.50	6.50	6.50	6.50	6.75

Owing to the constitutional structure of Uzbekistan, the judiciary is unable to maintain its independence; nor is it able to perform one of its core functions–protecting individual rights. The ability of the state to override fundamental rights–its authority to detain individuals at its own discretion, its untrammeled power to interrogate its citizens, and its determination to make it difficult for individuals to receive competent representation in court–reveals the degree to which law is unable to temper the power of the state.

The Uzbek criminal code allows investigators to detain anyone it deems a "witness" to a crime. Judges do not review these decisions. Someone detained as a witness must answer any question asked, but "witness detainees" do not have a right to counsel during the period of detention. The power of investigators and prosecutors to detain witnesses without judicial review leads to widespread abuse of this tactic. During a roundtable discussion in January 2005, a senior representative for the Procuracy boasted that the best way to solve a crime is to round up as many people as possible and question them until one of them talks. Answers obtained during the witness detention period may be used as evidence at trial. Although provisions in the Uzbek criminal code limit the length of time a person can be detained as a witness, that period may be extended at the discretion of the prosecutor without consulting a judge.

A person can also be detained in Uzbekistan even if no crime has been committed. So-called administrative detentions enable the authorities to arrest and sentence someone for up to 15 days in jail for administrative violations. People detained for administrative violations do not have a right to meet with counsel, come before a judge, or even alert family members that they have been detained. During the period of administrative detention, detainees are obligated to answer questions put to them by the authorities. People under administrative detention are particularly vulnerable to being pressured into making incriminating statements. Not surprisingly, several human rights defenders have been charged with criminal offenses during their administrative detention. The judiciary has no role in monitoring or preventing witness or administrative detentions. Even when an individual comes before a court, there is little guarantee of receiving a fair hearing. Before the accused has walked into a courtroom, it is often the case that he or she has had little meaningful legal assistance. Although the Uzbek criminal code promises every detainee the right to consult with defense counsel, the detainee him- or herself does not have the right to choice of counsel. Consequently, many so-called pocket attorneys are selected by the prosecutor (usually because of some social tie) for the defense. The state then pays the representation fee to the defense attorney thus selected.

Neither the law nor administrative practice makes it easy for the accused to hire counsel for the defense. Once in custody, the detainee has virtually no opportunity to contact family members or any outside party. Therefore, the prosecutor managing the case will assign a defense attorney even if the detainee wants a different one.

During a roundtable discussion in April 2005 in response to a suggestion from a senior Uzbek official that the law be amended to allow detainees the ability to make a phone call to family or an attorney, senior officials from the Procuracy said that the Uzbek code was already perfect and any changes would ruin it. The possibility of amending the law to allow phone calls was summarily dismissed.

The difficulty of detainees to contact independent defense attorneys and family members only increases the likelihood of abuse while the detainee awaits trial. In 2002, the UN special rapporteur on torture, Theo van Boven, found the use of torture to be "systematic" in Uzbekistan. Certainly one of the reasons for this finding is that the state can prevent a detainee from meeting with an independent party during the period of pretrial detention. Therefore, if the detainee is being abused, he or she has no opportunity to report this abuse to anyone not under the influence of the state authorities.

Once in the courtroom, parties opposing the interests of the state face a steep challenge. Criminal defendants are handicapped by defense lawyers who have at best mixed loyalties before they even enter the courtroom. Regardless, both criminal defendants and civil litigants must have their cases decided by a judge who owes his or her position to the president's office.

Judges serve only a five-year term in office. Judges not serving on the Supreme Court can be dismissed at will by the president.[27] Further, criminal charges can be brought against a judge if the prosecutor or other executive official believes the judge "violated the law while trying a case" or conducted him- or herself in a manner that "defamed the judiciary."[28]

Exacerbating a situation in which judges are both dependent on the executive for their position and under threat of criminal prosecution for conduct that "defames" the judiciary is the persistent problem of *telefonoe pravo*, or "telephone justice." This holdover from the Soviet era reflects the habit of prosecutors or other executive officials calling judges in advance of trials and telling them how to rule. The frequency of the practice is difficult to ascertain, but concerns about its prevalence are not diminished when few judges and attorneys are aware of rules limiting ex parte communications and when there are even fewer examples of such rules being enforced. Indeed, during training sessions some attorneys expressed the notion that they were reassured by communications between the judge and state officials because it delineated a way for all parties to proceed without incurring the wrath of the authorities.

Additionally, the habit of trying large numbers of defendants simultaneously seriously undermines the fairness of trials. In November, a trial of 15 defendants accused of being involved with the events in Andijan began in the district court at Toitepa. Exacerbating the problems of trying large numbers of defendants simultaneously, this trial, like numerous other Andijan-related trials, was closed to the public and to international observers.[29] Public trials are one of the few windows revealing the operation of the Uzbek criminal justice system. Not only are the Andijan trials usually closed, but the sentences convicted defendants receive are often kept from the public and family members of the accused.[30]

The few Andijan trials that have been observed reveal the paucity of fairness that prevails. In one trial of Andijan defendants, the defense attorneys opened their arguments with an apology to the people for representing the defendants. Several of the defendants themselves requested the death penalty for their actions.[31]

The Uzbek criminal justice system prevents detainees from contacting outside parties while awaiting trial, often limits them to counsel whose primary duty is to protect the interests of the state, and tries them before magistrates dependent on the state for their position and state prosecutors with the power to bring charges against the judge and the discretion to arrest anyone dear to the detainee. The law provides no mechanism for excluding evidence that may have been coerced, and trials provide no forum for detainees to contest the legitimacy of the evidence used against them. All of these factors combine to produce trials that are more a tribute to Andrei Vyshinsky, the prosecutor of the Soviet show trials of the 1930s, than to any accepted definition of the rule of law.

Corruption

1997	1998	1999	2001	2002	2003	2004	2005	2006
n/a	n/a	6.00	6.00	6.00	6.00	6.00	6.00	6.50

The extensive regulatory state, the urgent and constant need of individuals to be in compliance, a poorly paid civil service, and the rarity of bribery investigations all collude to make corruption rampant in Uzbekistan. Such corruption is most readily apparent when citizens try to acquire basic documents to live in compliance with the law. Some of the more sought-after documents are a *propiska* and an exit visa.

As noted previously, a *propiska* is a document that gives permission for an individual to live in a particular locality. Uzbekistan has carried on the Soviet policy of devoting disproportionate amounts of public resources to a few favored cities such as Tashkent. Consequently, Tashkent offers more economic opportunity than other cities in Uzbekistan and attracts workers from around the country. However, only people who have a *propiska* allowing them to live in Tashkent are legally allowed to work in that city. The rules governing the issuance of *propiskas* are opaque and the market for them robust. Civil servants often demand large sums of money to issue a *propiska* even if a person meets the legal requirements.

Those people who live and work without proper authorization and registration are subject to harassment and often are compelled to pay bribes to avoid detention. They are frequently marginalized and live in areas with similarly situated people. These areas in turn attract police scrutiny because they are a steady source of bribes.

Uzbekistan also requires citizens to have permission from the state to be able to leave the country. During the course of 2005, perhaps in response to Andijan, the authorities became more strict about issuing exit visas, and those they do issue are usually for a more limited duration. In their pursuit of official documents in Uzbekistan, individuals are often confronted by civil servants whose intransigence is an obstruction that cannot be overcome except by a bribe. Citizens have no recourse under the law to get necessary documents and so must comply with the civil servant's wishes.

In rural areas, local officials are often able to augment their income through land speculation. Prior to Andijan, one of the most persistent causes of civil unrest was the expropriation of farmland by local *khokims*. Many farmers told Freedom House and other international organizations that local *khokims* would forge land transfer documents or use their authority to redistribute land ownership to the *khokims'* own material benefit. After Andijan, the ability of citizens to protest this type of local corruption has been substantially diminished because of harsh responses from the authorities.

The intrusive regulations that control the economic activities of private citizens and enable state officials to seek bribes find their roots in a political culture of rent seeking. No one demonstrates this culture of rent seeking more than President Karimov. Karimov has used his position to enrich himself, his family, and those in his circle. Whether it is using the wealth generated by the annual cotton harvest for his own benefit or taking over successful businesses run by private citizens, Karimov has used his power to live a life of exceptional luxury.

Much of the president's lifestyle is kept from public view, as he lives in various walled compounds around Tashkent that are closed to the public. However, a better sense of the president's wealth may be gained by examining the "president's residences" that dot the country. Each significant regional city in Uzbekistan has a president's residence. These residences are usually in a walled compound operated by the local authorities–the *khokimyat*. Many of these local compounds also house hotels separate from the residences that cater to government officials and foreign travelers–thereby allowing for a glimpse into the president's lifestyle.[32] The president's residence in Namangan, a city in the Ferghana Valley, is not atypical. According to interviews conducted by the author at the facility, the president has stayed there only one night. Despite this fact, the building is adorned with luxuries. Although it is only a two-story building, it contains a German-made glass elevator so the president need not trouble himself with stairs. When the author toured the exterior of the building, workmen were installing new marble floors in the residence, because during the president's one and only night's stay, he expressed displeasure at the color of the original marble. According to workers on the site, tens of thousands of dollars were being spent to create a facility for the president that saw his presence only once since independence. This display of the state lavishing resources on its president occurs in a city that is even more impoverished than the country generally.

On a private basis, Karimov has used his position to benefit his family members. To be viable, significant business ventures in the country must often partner with one of Karimov's two daughters. Karimov's daughters' business interests include telecommunications companies such as Uzdonrobita (the country's largest mobile phone provider), soft-drink contracts, and involvement in the energy industry. The daughters also have high-profile ownership of the elite restaurants and clubs in the country. Even the entertainment industry is dominated by the Karimovs, as evidenced by the billboards that abound in the capital celebrating Lola Karimova's singing abilities.

Companies that compete with those owned by the Karimovs confront the power of state authority. Mobile phone companies that competed with Uzdonrobita had difficulty obtaining permission to build reception towers in Tashkent and found that the towers they had already built in the wealthier districts of Tashkent were in noncompliance and had to be demolished. Businesses that simply do well, such as restaurants, are often closed by the state authorities or are forced to sell to one of the Karimovs for a minimal price.

The Karimovs' wealth may be in jeopardy, however. Karimov's seven-year term is scheduled to end in 2007. Traveling the world as a private citizen will be risky for Karimov, as it is possible that he could be detained in other countries for his brutal repression of dissent and for his orders resulting in the Andijan massacre. Staying in Uzbekistan, however, may not provide any respite. Karimov has overseen the development of a system where nearly all national power resides in the presidency. He has used this power to seek and expropriate the wealth of his citizens. This system of rent seeking permeates the political establishment. Once the Karimovs are private citizens, their wealth would be a treasure that Karimov's successor, or his successor's cronies, could not ignore. The office of the presidency is the richest prize in the Uzbek political system, not only because of the power of the office, but because only that office has the power to protect the wealth of the officeholder.

In an ignoble parody of *King Lear* minus a Cordelia, Karimov has been dividing his kingdom between his two daughters. Nevertheless, he must know that once he is out of office there is no way he can protect his and his family's wealth. Although many may be positioning themselves to succeed Karimov, he too must know that in a system where promises enshrined in the Constitution can be easily violated, potential successors will have few qualms about violating any confidential promises made to him. Therefore Karimov is confronting the choice of exile to a country where prosecution for his crimes is not a possibility or an extension of his term. He will likely use 2006 to decide whether he can use a constitutional dodge to stay in power.

Robert Freedman directed Freedom House's Torture Prevention Project in Uzbekistan in 2005 and is currently an attorney in private practice.

---

[1] Esmer Islamov, "Uzbek Leaders Seek to Block Influx of 'Alien Ideologies,'" Eurasianet.org, March 2, 2005. See also Press Service of the Republic of Uzbekistan, January 28, 2005, press statement, 2004.press-service.uz/eng/rechi_eng/rechi_eng33.htm.

[2] Ibid.

[3] World Bank, Uzbekistan at a Glance, August 2005, www.worldbank.org.

[4] Economy Rankings for Ease of Doing Business 2006, www.doingbusiness.org.

[5] Paraphrasing: Robert Jackson, Opening Statement to the International Military Tribunal at Nuremberg, November, 1945.

[6] All citations for the Uzbek Constitution are drawn from the English translation made by www.umid.uz.

[7] A human rights defender gave Freedom House Uzbekistan a copy of a notice from the Ministry of the Interior citing an internal decree as its legal authority for her house detention. Copies of the document with the name of the human rights defender redacted are available upon request.

[8] Press Service of the Republic of Uzbekistan, January 28, 2005, press statement, 2004.press-service.uz/eng/rechi_eng/rechi_eng33.htm.

[9] Information on the events surrounding the Andijan protests and subsequent crackdown has been obtained from personal interviews by the author with human rights defenders in Andijan, interviews with other NGO representatives, the Report on the Andijan Uprising published by Human Rights Watch (available at www.hrw.org), and the report published by the International Crisis Group (available at www.icg.org).

[10] Radio Free Europe/Radio Liberty, "Radio Liberty Reporter Led to Mass Grave Site in Uzbekistan," press release, May 30, 2005, www.rferl.org/releases/2005/05/339-300505.asp. See also Human Rights Watch, "Burying the Truth: Uzbekistan Rewrites the History of the Andijan Massacre," September 2005, available at hrw.org/reports/2005/uzbekistan0905.

[11] Committee for Free Speech and Expression, "U.S. Delegation Ends Its Trip to Tashkent," September 28, 2005, www.freeuz.org/eng/analysis/?id1=752.
See also statement released by the Committee to Protect Journalists criticizing Uzbekistan's efforts to smear foreign media, September 26, 2005. See also Halq So'zi, "Corrupt in Conscience; Corrupt in Action," June 14, 2005, contending that a Freedom House employee was conspiring with Jack Straw to stage the Andijan events as a pretext to topple the government of Uzbekistan.

[12] Committee for Free Speech and Expression, "U.S. Delegation Ends Its Trip to Tashkent," September 28, 2005, www.freeuz.org/eng/analysis/?id1=752.

[13] BBC, "Uzbek Opposition Leader on Trial," January 30, 2006, news.bbc.co.uk/1/hi/world/asia-pacific/4660934.stm.

[14] CIA World Fact Book, available at www.cia.gov/cia/publications/factbook/geos/uz.html.

[15] The Rapid Reaction Group comprises leading human rights activists from across Uzbekistan. Freedom House regularly allows members of the group to meet at Freedom House facilities.

[16] The slander charge is particularly suspect, as it relates to articles written some time ago. In the course of a personal dispute with another human rights defender (name redacted), the other human rights defender filed a libel complaint with the local prosecutor. The complaint lay dormant prior to the Andijan events. The human rights defender who initially filed the complaint withdrew the complaint before charges were announced. The withdrawal of the complaint was rejected by the local prosecutor, and the human rights defender who filed the complaint was arrested himself for speech crimes against the state.

[17] Human Rights Watch, "Uzbekistan: Critic of Andijan Massacre Arrested," October 13, 2005, hrw.org/english/docs/2005/10/13/uzbeki11867.htm.

[18] Forum 18 News Service, Forum 18 Religious Freedom Survey for Uzbekistan, April 2005. www.forum18.org/Archive.php?article_id=546.

[19] Ibid.

[20] Sonia Winter and Adalat Najimova, Radio Free Europe/Radio Liberty, "Uzbekistan Harassment Chronology," www.rferl.org. February 27, 2006.

[21] Ibid.

[22] Ibid.

[23] BBC, "Harassed BBC Shuts Down Office," October 26, 2005, news.bbc.co.uk/1/hi/world/asia-pacific/4380166.stm.

[24] Forum 18 News Service, "Entry into the Republic of Uzbekistan Closed," August 16, 2005, www.forum18.org/Archive.php?query=uzbekistan&religion=all&country=all&results=10.

[25] Constitution of Uzbekistan, Article 67.

[26] Saidjahon Zaynabitdinov was initially arrested because he supposedly defamed state-employed reporters by questioning the veracity of their stories.

[27] Article 72 of the Uzbek Law on the Courts.

[28] Article 73 of the Uzbek Law on the Courts.

[29] Human Rights Watch, "Uzbekistan: Access to Trials Blocked," November 30, 2005, hrw.org/english/docs/2005/11/30/uzbeki12103.htm.

[30] Human Rights Watch, "Uzbekistan: Reveal Fate of Jailed Activist," January 20, 2006, hrw.org/english/docs/2006/01/20/uzbeki12481.htm.

[31] Human Rights Watch, "Uzbekistan: Andijan Show Trial Ends with Guilty Verdict," November 14, 2005, hrw.org/english/docs/2005/11/14/uzbeki12020.htm.

[32] Foreign travelers often have no choice but to stay in the khokimyat hotel because they do not have permission to stay elsewhere. Rates paid for these hotels by foreigners are well above market rates.

Freedom House Board of Trustees

About Freedom House

Freedom House is an independent private organization supporting the expansion of freedom throughout the world.

Freedom is possible only in democratic political systems in which governments are accountable to their own people, the rule of law prevails, and freedoms of expression, association and belief are guaranteed. Working directly with courageous men and women around the world to support nonviolent civic initiatives in societies where freedom is threatened, Freedom House functions as a catalyst for change through its unique mix of analysis, advocacy and action.

- **Analysis.** Freedom House's rigorous research methodology has earned the organization a reputation as the leading source of information on the state of freedom around the globe. Since 1972, Freedom House has published Freedom in the World, an annual survey of political rights and civil liberties experienced in every country of the world. The survey is complemented by an annual review of press freedom, an analysis of transitions in the post-communist world, and other publications.

- **Advocacy.** Freedom House seeks to encourage American policymakers, as well as other governments and international institutions, to adopt policies that advance human rights and democracy around the world. Freedom House has been instrumental in the founding of the worldwide Community of Democracies; has actively campaigned for a reformed Human Rights Council at the United Nations; and presses the Millennium Challenge Corporation to adhere to high standards of eligibility for recipient countries.

- **Action.** Through exchanges, grants, and technical assistance, Freedom House provides training and support to human rights defenders, civil society organizations and members of the media in order to strengthen indigenous reform efforts in countries around the globe.

Founded in 1941 by Eleanor Roosevelt, Wendell Willkie and other Americans concerned with mounting threats to peace and democracy, Freedom House has long been a vigorous proponent of democratic values and a steadfast opponent of dictatorships of the far left and the far right. The organization's diverse Board of Trustees is composed of a bipartisan mix of business and labor leaders, former senior government officials, scholars and journalists who agree that the promotion of democracy and human rights abroad is vital to America's interests abroad.